International Marketing

International Marketing

PHILIP R. CATEORA
Professor of Marketing
School of Business
University of Colorado

and

JOHN M. HESS
Professor of Marketing and
   International Business
United States International University

Revised Edition
1971

 RICHARD D. IRWIN, INC. *Homewood, Illinois 60430*
Irwin-Dorsey Limited, Georgetown, Ontario

REVISED EDITION

First Printing, June, 1971

Library of Congress Catalog Card No. 76–153168

Printed in the United States of America

To NANCY and DELPHIA

Preface

The basic premise of the revised edition of *International Marketing,* not unlike the first edition, is that in today's world of global enterprise the traditional approach of teaching the dynamic subjects of international marketing and international business from the narrow viewpoint of ocean transportation or export trade mechanics is not adequate. This edition still approaches the subject from a broad conceptual viewpoint incorporating the marketing concept into the framework of the world marketplace. It is assumed that the student or businessman using this book has an understanding of fundamental marketing concepts so no attempt is made to cover all areas of basic marketing or to explain marketing terms. Rather than teach principles of marketing using international examples, the book explores those aspects of marketing which are unique to international business. Because the differences in marketing from country to country are less conceptual than environmental, the consistent focus is on the environment and on the modifications of marketing thinking and practices occasioned by environmental differences.

The environmental approach to international marketing permits a truly worldwide orientation. This universal outlook permits consideration of marketing goods from any one country to any other country or countries. It, therefore, does not limit the reader's horizon to any specific nation or to the particular ways of doing business in that nation. Executives today are likely to be assigned to one continent today and another continent tomorrow so they must not limit their thinking to one region. Even staff executives who never get away from the home office are often responsible for decisions affecting their company's marketing programs in all corners of the earth.

The book is not geared only to the objectives, problems and challenges facing American manufacturers who would market in foreign countries. Rather, it presents a conceptual framework for marketing into and from all foreign countries and provides concrete, action-oriented benefits to marketing managers and students of marketing the world around.

Structure, continuity, and thorough coverage are the functions served by the text portion of the book. The readings and "boxes" are designed to pique the student's interest, to permit him to follow some intriguing sidelines, and to provide him with additional information in certain areas. Occasional readings make it possible to present varied viewpoints and illustrations without departing from the tight organization of the text. Also new to this edition are cases added at the end of each section. The case mix includes short cases of a specific nature, that is, a single specific problem; and longer, more integrative cases applicable to the general subject of the section. Questions and short problems at the end of each chapter remain and have been brought up to date to reflect the new material found in each chapter. It is hoped that both students and businessmen will find this approach stimulating.

Many individuals have contributed to the completion of this book. We especially want to acknowledge the helpful assistance provided by our colleagues at the University of Colorado; and Mrs. Marjorie Broward who, with genuine interest and infinite patience, provided the authors with valuable assistance in their library research. We also wish to acknowledge the support of Dean William Baughn of the School of Business, and the many students who read and criticized early drafts.

To the publishers and authors who permitted the reproduction of articles and other materials, we are also indebted.

May, 1971   PHILIP R. CATEORA
                                           JOHN M. HESS

CONTENTS

PART
II. The World Marketing Environment

4. Cultural Dynamics in Assessing World Markets   107

Introduction. Culture Defined: *Cultural Borrowing to Solve Problems. Similarities: An Illusion.* Cultural Adjustment. Cultural Knowledge. Elements of Culture: *Material Culture. Social Institutions. Man and the Universe. Aesthetics. Language. Analysis of Elements.* Cultural Dynamics.

Readings

5. Political Considerations in Assessing World Markets   145

Introduction. Governments and Political Party Systems: *Types of Governments. Political Parties. Knowledge of Party Philosophy.* The Permanency of Government Policy: *Change in Governments. Change in Political Parties. Nationalism.* Assessing Political Vulnerability. Expropriation and Other Risks of Foreign Business: *Expropriation. Other Risks Faced by Foreign Business.* Encouraging Foreign Investment: *Foreign Governments. United States Government.* Suggestions to Reduce Political Vulnerability.

Readings

6. Economic Development and World Markets   191

Introduction. Economic Development and Marketing: *Objectives of Developing Countries. Marketing's Contribution Neglected. The Role of Marketing in Economic Development.* Marketing in a Developing Country: *Level of Marketing Development. Influence of Import Orientation. Demand in a Less Developed Country. Less Developed Countries and Long-Range Potential.*

Reading

7. Geography and World Markets   217

Introduction. Climate and Topography. Population: *Rural-Urban Shifts. Opportunities in Developing Countries.* World Trade: *Differences in People. Differences in Economies. Differences in Natural Resources.* World Trade Routes.

Reading

PART
III. World Market Patterns

PART
V. International Marketing Management

Reading
Guidelines in Exporting for the Small Company, *Business Viewpoints* 805

22. International Distribution Patterns and Strategy 815

Introduction. Developing Channel Policies and Strategies: *Policy. Strategic Goals.* Adapting to Distribution Patterns: *General Patterns. Wholesale Patterns. Retail Patterns.* Building International Channels: *Tactical Decisions. Operational Challenges. Solving Distribution Problems. Motivating Middlemen.* Channel Control.

Reading
Planning for Distribution, *Marketing Insights* 849

Cases—Part V

Bibliography 903

Index 913

PART

I

An Overview

OUTLINE OF CHAPTER 1

INTERNATIONAL MARKETING DEFINED

INCREASED INTEREST IN FOREIGN MARKETS

ENTERING FOREIGN MARKETS

Alternative Strategies for Entering Foreign Markets
Exporting
Licensing
Joint Ventures
Manufacturing
Management Contracts

Categories of International Marketing Involvement
No Marketing Overseas
Infrequent Marketing Overseas
Regular Marketing Overseas
World Marketing Operations

Changes in Marketing Orientation

THE INTERNATIONAL MARKETING TASK
Marketing Controllables
Domestic Uncontrollables
Foreign Uncontrollables

ORIENTATION OF *INTERNATIONAL MARKETING*

READINGS

How Kodak Clicked Worldwide on the Marketing Plan for its Famous
Instamatic, *Business Abroad.*

Tighten Your Overseas Marketing Plan, *Marketing Insights.*

SCOPE AND CHALLENGE OF INTERNATIONAL MARKETING

"We don't merely think as an American company with extensions overseas, we think in terms of a global enterprise, a company of the world rather than any one country."[1] This statement epitomizes recent trends in international business which are having far-reaching effects upon the traditionally domestic orientation of American business. "World business," "multinational company," and "world enterprise" are all terms being used with more frequency as significantly larger number of businesses become international both in philosophy and scope of operations. For a continually growing number of firms, the entire world is considered a marketplace for their products. Rather than ask the usual question, "Where in our country should a new plant be built or a new market be developed?" more firms are asking, "Where in the *world* should a new product be made or sold?" Rather than treat foreign business as an afterthought, as was often the case among many U.S. companies prior to World War II, businesses are taking a more interested look at the potential profits which can result from active participation in markets outside the political boundaries of the United States. No more than twenty years ago, most American businesses were preoccupied with the task of meeting the pent-up demand of the domestic market. Thus, most stayed close to home, and foreign trade, if it occurred, involved the sale of temporary surpluses of production primarily intended for domestic markets. Today foreign involvement may demand more effort and resources than domestic interests. Between 1962 and 1968 exports from the United States increased almost 300 percent, to total more than $34 billion.[2] Coupled with this is approximately $51 billion of direct foreign investment which generates about $100 billion in sales.[3] Thus, sales abroad by U.S. firms both from export and direct

---

[1] "Kaiser's Global Empire," *Forbes,* April 15, 1968, p. 29.

[2] "What the U.S. Must Sell More Overseas," *Business Week,* January 4, 1969, p. 52.

[3] Based on the National Industrial Conference Board estimate that $1 in investment generates $2 in sales.

investment in 1968 was $130 billion plus, compared to only about $33 billion from the two sources just 14 years earlier. With the increased activity in international business has come a corresponding emphasis on international marketing.

INTERNATIONAL MARKETING DEFINED

International marketing is the performance of business activities that direct the flow of a company's goods and services to consumers or users in more than one nation. The striking similarity of this definition of foreign marketing and that of domestic marketing is intended. The only difference between domestic marketing and international marketing is that the activities that take place are in more than one country. While this difference may seem minor, it accounts for the complexity and diversity found in international marketing operations. The definition above is operational as marketing principles are universally applicable,[4] and the marketer's task is the same whether applied in Dimebox, Texas, or Katmandu, Nepal. If this be the case, why the study of international marketing? The answer to this question lies not with the mechanics of marketing but with the environment within which the marketing plan is implemented. The uniqueness of foreign marketing is found in the diversity of the problems and the variety of strategies necessary to cope with the different levels of uncertainty encountered in foreign marketing.

INCREASED INTEREST IN FOREIGN MARKETS

Current interest in international marketing can be explained in terms of changing competitive structures, coupled with shifts in demand characteristics in markets throughout the world. Many U.S. firms are meeting competition from all fronts, i.e., not only from other domestic firms but from foreign firms as well. Norelco (Holland), Shell Oil (Holland), Volkswagen (Germany), Honda (Japan), Necchi (Italian) are all familiar brands in the United States and, for U.S. industry, they are formidable opponents in a competitive struggle for U.S. and world markets. More firms are faced with surpluses which must be sold. The vast domestic market that has provided the U.S. marketer with an opportunity for continued growth has finally reached a point where the opportunity for continued expansion is leveling off. For many businesses new market opportunities have to be sought if profit margins are to be maintained. Companies with only domestic markets have found it increasingly difficult to sustain customary rates of growth, and many are seeking foreign markets to absorb accumulating surplus productive capacity. Companies with foreign operations have found that earnings are soaring from previously neglected overseas operations and that the return on the foreign investments is frequently higher than on those in the United States.

---

[4] The universality of marketing principles is discussed in more detail in A. Coskun Samli, "Exportability of American Marketing Knowledge," *Business Topics*, Autumn 1965, pp. 34–42.

BOX 1–1

A World of Whetted Appetites

The rising expectations of poverty-stricken millions, the new independence for colonies, and the new political orientation for some nations will result in grand transformations on every front—science, business, government, agriculture, education, standards of living, etc.

Marketing will take part in this rapid change, helping to speed economic development. In Europe it has already developed to near-U.S. efficiency; in other regions a generation may pass before changes become significant.

But no nation will be unaffected. Even the Soviet Union has made its grudging concession to marketing when it has had to resort to advertising to move heavy state inventories.

In most countries it still has a long way to go, but these next few years will see rapid improvement. International ad revenues are already climbing at a rate greater than the U.S. rate. New ad agencies are appearing daily. Auditing techniques are improving, mass distribution methods are spreading, the self-service concept is finding wide acceptance.

The "house agency" (with financial ties to an advertiser or medium) is still a major problem. But American marketers just now beginning to show up in foreign markets will have a big influence on advertising ethics.

In fact, the movement toward modern marketing will get extra propulsion from Americans going international. This will happen at all levels and in all functions of marketing, from the advertising agency to the retail store.

It took the European Economic Community to awaken the U.S. to the profit potentials the world over. Until recently, only a handful of American marketers sold abroad, and most used overseas markets as dumping grounds. They sold seconds and products that didn't come up to domestic standards; they didn't research and service needs the way they did at home.

Source: Reprinted, with special permission, from *Sales Management,* November 10, 1962, pp. 27–40.

Reviewing the figures in Exhibit 1–1, it becomes quite obvious that for some companies the profit generated on investment abroad as well as the profit from foreign sales is better than in the United States. Understandably, the opportunity for high profit margins is a very important impetus for "going international."

What occurred almost simultaneously with the economic changes in the United States was an appreciable increase in the economic well-being of many other countries which created a ready-made market for U.S.-made products. The European Common Market rapidly evolved as a market comparable in size and potential to that of the United States; in the Far East, Japan made an almost miraculous return to economic opulence. The net result is that new opportunities are available for those willing to leave the confines of their home territory. Many U.S. companies that have never ventured abroad are now seeking new markets. Companies which have had foreign experience have realized that, in order to maintain their now much-needed foreign operations and to con-

EXHIBIT 1–1

Some Big Players in the Global Game

Company	Total Sales 1967 ($000)	Number of Countries with Production Facilities	Percent Total Assets Abroad	Percent Sales Abroad	Percent Net Income Abroad
General Motors	20,026,252	24	15§	14§	7
Standard Oil (N.J.)	13,266,015	45*	56	68	52
Ford Motor	10,515,700	27*	40	36	92‖
Chrysler	6,213,383	18	31§	21†§	N.A.
Mobil Oil	5,771,776	38*	46	N.A.	45
International Business Machines	5,345,291	14	34	30†	32
Gulf Oil	4,202,121	48*	38	N.A.	29
Du Pont (E.I.) de Nemours	3,102,033	16*	12	4	N.A.
International Tel. & Tel.	2,760,572	60	47	47	50
Goodyear Tire & Rubber	2,637,710	35	22	30†	30
International Harvester	2,541,897	18*	21‡	17	10
Caterpillar Tractor	1,472,500	14	25	14	N.A.
Minnesota Mining & Mfg.	1,231,066	24	29	30	29
Singer	1,137,653	28*	58	50†	N.A.
Corn Products	1,072,940	33	47	46	49
Anaconda	1,047,815	9	44	32	57
Colgate-Palmolive	1,025,351	43*	50	55†	N.A.
National Cash Register	955,455	10	41	44	51
Massey-Ferguson	844,764	22*	84	90	N.A.
Heinz (H.J.)	690,863	15	55‡	47	57
Warner-Lambert Pharmaceutical	656,822	47	32	33	33
Pfizer (Chas.)	637,776	32	50	48	52
American Standard	599,807	21*	30	28	39
Abbott Laboratories	303,341	24	27	26	26
U.S.M. Corp.	283,528	25	50	54	57

* Includes unconsolidated affiliates and manufacturing franchises.
†Includes export sales from the U.S.
‡ Percent of net assets abroad
§ Excludes Canada
‖ Ford's profits in the U.S. were substantially reduced by the auto strike [1968].
NOTE: These twenty-five corporations, all deeply involved internationally, are among the relatively few that divulge detailed figures on foreign operations. In eight of the nineteen companies furnishing data on profits, overseas production accounted for half or more of net income. But only consolidated net income is included; if the income of *nonconsolidated subsidiaries* were taken into consideration, the totals would obviously be higher. Overseas sales accounted for 50 percent or more of the total sales of five companies (but export sales from the U.S. parent inflated this total in two cases) and were nudging the halfway mark in four others. All percentages are for the latest representative fiscal year available. "Production facilities" include manufacturing, assembly, producing, refining, and converting operations. (Italics added).
SOURCE: Sanford Rose, "The Rewarding Strategies of Multinationalism," *Fortune*, September 15, 1968, p. 105. Reprinted with permission.

tinue to grow, they have to cease running their foreign operations with their left hands. They have found that they have to spend more money and more time improving their marketing positions abroad, since the competition for these growing markets from companies around the world is becoming extremely intense. In both cases, for the firm venturing for the first time into international marketing and for the already experienced, the task is generally the same—a more thorough and complete commitment to foreign markets.

ENTERING FOREIGN MARKETS

Once a company has made the decision to "go international" it has to decide the way it will enter the foreign market and the degree of marketing involvement and commitment it is prepared to make. These decisions should reflect considerable thought and analysis of market potential and company capabilities. However, evidence tends to indicate that this is not always the process followed. Whatever the motivation, the first foreign ventures are "apt to be treated as sideshows,"[5] selecting an inadequate means of entry and failing to make the commitment necessary for strong market development. In any event, a company interested in engaging in international business has five alternatives from which to choose

Alternative Strategies for Entering Foreign Markets

There are five basic alternatives for entering a foreign market. Each has its particular advantages and shortcomings depending upon company strengths and weaknesses, the degree of commitment the company is willing or able to make, and environmental characteristics of the foreign country.

Exporting. A company may decide to enter the international arena by exporting excess productive capacity. This means of foreign market entry is the easiest and most common approach employed by companies that are taking their first international step, since the risks of financial loss can be minimized. Generally early motives are either to skim the cream off the top of the market or to gain a plus business that can absorb overhead.[6] Although the above motives are frequently the main reasons for exporting and might appear opportunistic, exporting can be a sound and permanent basis for entry into international marketing.

Licensing. A second means for getting a foothold in foreign markets without large capital outlays is licensing. Patent rights, trademark rights and the rights to use technological processes are granted in foreign licensing.[7] It is a favorite strategy for small and medium-sized companies, although by no means limited to such companies, and not many confine their foreign operations to licensing alone. It is generally viewed as a supplement to exporting or manufacturing rather than as the only means for entry into foreign markets; nevertheless, advantages of this means of entry are many. When capital is scarce, when import restrictions forbid any other means of entry, when a country is sensitive to

---

[5] Sanford Rose, "The Rewarding Strategies of Multinationalism," *Fortune,* September 15, 1968, p. 102.

[6] George Strike, "Export Business vs. Domestic Business," *International Commerce,* October 13, 1969, p. 40.

[7] For additional detail see Vincent D. Travaglini, "Licensing, Joint Ventures Aid Technology Transfer," *International Commerce,* July 28, 1969, pp. 2–6.

foreign ownership, or when it is necessary to protect patents and trademarks against cancellation for nonuse, licensing is a legitimate means of exploiting a foreign market. Although this may be the least profitable way of entering a market, the risks and headaches are less than for direct investments.

Joint Ventures. For a variety of reasons a company may decide to share management with one or more collaborating foreign firms and enter into a joint venture. Joint ventures as a means of engaging in international business have sharply accelerated during the past 10 years. As in the case of licensing, one of the strongest reasons for entering joint ventures is that "they substantially reduce, by the amount of the partner's contributions to the venture, political and economic risks."[8] Further, many countries, especially the less developed ones, prefer joint ventures as a means of foreign investment. One U.S. manufacturer with abundant experience says there are three instances where joint ventures are appropriate:

When the company lacks capital or personnel capabilities to expand its international activities otherwise,

When the company seeks to enter a market where wholly-owned activities are prohibited, and

When it may enable the company to utilize skills of a local partner.[9]

A fourth reason may be to gain access to a partner's local distribution system.

There are some objections to this means of entering other countries. The principal fear is the loss of absolute control and perhaps loss of freedom of action in production and marketing operations. Regardless of the shortcomings, joint ventures are increasing and, in many countries, may be the only means of direct investment open.

Manufacturing. A fourth and major means of foreign market entry is manufacturing within the foreign country. This strategy is employed only when the demand justifies the investment involved. A company may manufacture locally to capitalize on low-cost labor, avoid high import taxes, reduce the high costs of transportation to market, gain access to raw materials, and/or as a means of gaining entry into other markets. For example, the only way to avoid the high tariffs imposed on an outsider exporting to countries of the European Common Market may be to invest in one of the countries and thereby gain entry into the others. Recently some U.S. manufacturing firms have found, due to lower labor and manufacturing costs in their facilities outside the United States, that they can export to the United States at prices lower than they can manufacture in the United States. Thus, this too becomes a reason for investing in manufacturing facilities in foreign countries.

Management Contracts. A fifth and limited means of international market entry may be through management contracts. This approach is generally employed not by choice but as the result of external pressures

---

[8] Ibid., p. 5.
[9] Ibid., p. 6.

from the host government. After a government expropriates a foreign investment and finds a lack of national managerial capability and talent, it will sign a management contract with the deposed company: in return for a stated fee, the company continues to manage its former investment. Although not a desirable means of foreign market entry, it can be better than nothing at all.

A mistake frequently made is to look at four of these five methods of entering international business as a sequence of steps to follow as a company becomes more involved instead of as strategic alternatives to foreign market entry. Actually it is possible for a single firm to be using all five strategies at the same time in different countries throughout the world.

Besides various means for entry into a foreign market, a company may have differing degrees of marketing involvement, i.e., the extent to which it makes an investment of marketing effort.

Categories of International Marketing Involvement[10]

Regardless of the means employed to gain entry into a foreign market, a company may, from a marketing viewpoint, make little or no market investment, i.e., their marketing involvement may be limited to selling the product with little or no thought given to development of market control. On the other hand, a company may become totally involved, investing large sums of money and effort in order to capture and maintain a permanent, specific share of the market. In general, business can be placed in at least four distinct but overlapping categories with respect to foreign marketing involvement.

No Marketing Overseas. In this stage, there is no active cultivation of customers outside the national boundaries; however, sales may be made to foreign customers who come directly to the firm. Another possible entry to foreign markets for a firm in this category could be via domestic wholesalers or distributors who sell abroad on their own without any explicit encouragement or knowledge of the producer.

Infrequent Marketing Overseas. Temporary surpluses caused by variations in production levels or demand may result in infrequent marketing overseas. The surpluses are characterized by their temporary nature; therefore, sales to foreign markets are made as goods are available, with little or no intention of having continuous market representation. As demand at home increases and absorbs surpluses, foreign sales activity is withdrawn. In this stage, there is little or no change in company organization or product line.

Regular Marketing Overseas. In this stage the firm has permanent productive capacity which is devoted to the production of goods that are to be marketed on a continuing basis in foreign markets. In this case, a firm may utilize foreign or domestic overseas middlemen or it may have

---

[10] This section is based in part on two sources: "The Emerging World Enterprise" (New York: Booz, Allen and Hamilton, Incorporated, Management Consultants, 1962) and "International Enterprise" (New York: McKinsey and Company, Incorporated, Management Consultants, 1962).

BOX 1–2

From Sideshow to Main Event

The corporation is likely to economize severely on managerial resources, unloading executives who can't make the grade at home. It may seek out joint ventures to reduce risks and capital commitment. It will even accept a minority commitment, trading off some equity for the right to name, say, the vice president for finance or marketing.

The sideshow mentality found its financial expression in the gambling theory of foreign earnings, a favorite of many commentators several years back. According to this hypothesis, the firm tends to regard its foreign earnings much as a man does his winnings at a racetrack. There is a strong organizational bias toward letting the money ride: that is, to reinvest liberally in the enterprise that generated the earnings, without regard to alternative— and perhaps even more profitable—opportunities elsewhere in the international environment.

Later on, however, the company suddenly wakes up to the fact that the sideshows constitute a fair percentage of its business. It moves to set up effective central control of international operations. It turns from joint ventures since they make it difficult to exercise proper control. It starts sounding the "we are a global company" theme, albeit self-consciously. Finally the self-consciousness disappears, and it is in the multinational game for keeps.

As the process unfolds, the company faces severe organizational problems, which tend to mirror, or recapitulate, the problems earlier encountered during domestic growth. As a company expands in its national market, its small, all-purpose management gives way to a bigger organization broken down into functional specialties. There are departments for finance, marketing, production, etc. This arrangement works until the company diversifies into a number of different product lines. Then strains develop. Each product line has its own set of manufacturing and sales problems and needs its own production and marketing managers, who know that product thoroughly. The corporation-wide "functional" specialists can't fill the bill. So eventually a new organizational structure takes shape, with divisions that are profit centers built around products, a central office staff to serve them, and an executive staff in charge of strategic planning and over-all corporate administration.

Source: Sanford Rose, "The Rewarding Strategies of Multinationalism," *Fortune*, September 15, 1968, pp. 102–3. Reprinted by permission.

its own highly developed sales force or sales subsidiaries in important foreign markets. The primary basis for production remains one of production for the home markets. The foreign marketing phase is only an extension of the market for products presently being produced with, perhaps, some very minor modifications to meet foreign market needs. In this stage, substantial international investments of marketing funds and management skills are generally made.

World Marketing Operations. Companies in this category are fully committed and involved in international marketing activities. Such companies treat the world as their market and the products they sell are not surpluses from a saturated home market; they are purposely produced for world markets. This generally entails not only the marketing but the production of goods throughout the world. It is at this point that a company becomes an international or worldwide marketing firm.

Among U.S. firms there has been a very noticeable increase in activity in foreign marketing involvement on all levels, with an increasingly large number moving into categories three and four.

Changes in Marketing Orientation

Experience shows that when a company needs to rely upon foreign markets to absorb a permanent production surplus, a significant change occurs in the marketing orientation of the firm. Generally a firm moves through the four categories of international marketing involvement one at a time, although it is not too unusual for a particular company to skip one or more stages. In any event, as a firm moves from one stage to another, the complexity and sophistication of international marketing activity tend to increase. In the early stages of foreign marketing, the firm generally relies almost completely on an experienced export firm to handle its marketing tasks. As the firm gathers more experience and its involvement becomes increasingly more permanent, it may engage its own personnel in selling to specific foreign customers. In both cases, however, the marketing task is rather simple and uninvolved. Only after the firm reaches a point of dependence upon the foreign market does it begin the total marketing task and cease to shift the responsibility of marketing to a third party. Although the firm may still utilize the services of many intermediate institutions in reaching the intended market, it is done within the framework of a total marketing plan designed to achieve specific objectives. Contrast this with the firm which sells to an intermediate middleman as a final customer, with little or no concern about what happens to the product after the sale. In the latter case, the firm is involved in marketing but at a rather low level compared with the marketing-oriented firm which designs a total market plan and then assumes the responsibility for implementation of the plan to final consumer satisfaction. As competition tightens in world marketing, more and more firms are finding it necessary to become marketing oriented in their international efforts, regardless of their state of involvement. This necessarily leads to an active interest in the study of international marketing.

THE INTERNATIONAL MARKETING TASK

The task of the marketing manager is to mold the controllable elements of his decision in light of uncontrollable elements in such a manner that his marketing objectives are achieved.

In general the elements comprising the marketing environment with which the marketer must contend can be examined in terms of the degree to which their effect upon marketing activities can be controlled by the decision maker. Some of the environmental considerations can be

BOX 1–3

Green Giant Will Pull up Stakes in Italy; Cummins Engine Curtails Operations in Europe

Two U.S. companies have suffered setbacks in Europe that amount to major turnarounds. Green Giant Co., which built a $1.8-million food processing plant in Pozzaglio, Italy, in 1963, is looking for a quick buyer for the plant after four years of losses. Cummins Engine Co., which built a new truck engine plant in Britain in 1966, has abandoned its sales campaign on the Continent after getting nowhere.

Green Giant can blame France's Charles de Gaulle for its misfortune. It built the Pozzaglio plant to can corn for the British market in the expectation that Britain would soon join the Common Market. When de Gaulle rejected Britain's bid, Green Giant found **it couldn't profitably clear the tariff hurdle into Britain from Italy.** Nor could it sell canned corn on the Continent; most Europeans regard corn as animal fodder. It switched over to canning peas and beans, but **these are low-profit lines, and Green Giant couldn't get the volume to move into the black.**

Cummins, the Columbus, Ind., diesel engine manufacturer, is **keeping its beachhead in Britain, but it has closed its Brussels and London sales operations;** it will handle foreign sales from its home office in Indiana. **Cummins simply couldn't sell its engines to Europe's 40 truck makers,** most of which manufacture their own. Two-thirds of its British output is now being sold in Canada, the U.S., and Mexico. Production at its $17-million plant at Darlington is at only 60% of an annual 30,000-engine capacity. Its startup losses were $8.4-million, but the British operation moved into the black last year.

---

viewed as internal to the firm, in that greater control can be exerted over their influence upon marketing operations. Generally included are such controllable elements as the product, price, promotion, and channels of distribution. Other points can be considered as external to the firm and represent an influence which basically is beyond the decision maker's control. Included among the external or uncontrollable elements of the marketing environment are such conditions as the structure of competition, political forces, and cultural forces.[11]

The task is made more difficult in international marketing because the marketer must deal with two levels of uncontrollable uncertainty instead of just one. Uncertainty is created by the uncontrollable elements of the business environment at home that are applicable to foreign operations, plus the uncontrollable elements of the business environment found in the foreign country or countries in which he is

---

[11] For the student interested in a more complete discussion, see John A. Howard, *Marketing Management Analysis and Planning* (rev. ed.; Homewood, Ill.: Richard D. Irwin, Inc., 1963), pp. 4–9.

EXHIBIT 1–2

The International Marketing Task

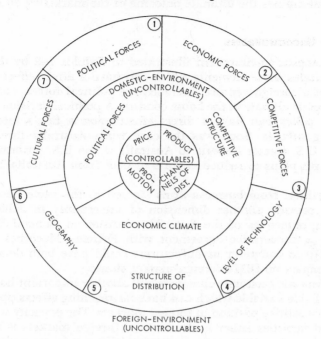

operating. An illustration of the total marketing environment is presented in Exhibit 1–2.

The inner circle depicts the controllable elements that constitute a marketer's decision area, the middle circle contains those environmental elements found at home which may have some effect upon his decision in foreign operations, and the outer circle includes the elements of the foreign environment with which the marketer must also contend.

Marketing Controllables

The successful manager constructs a marketing program that is designed for optimal adjustment to the uncertainty of the business climate. The inner circle in Exhibit 1–2 represents the area under the control of the marketing manager. Assuming the necessary overall corporate resources, the marketing manager blends price, product, promotion, and channels-of-distribution activities to capitalize on anticipated demand. These controllable elements can be altered in the long run and, usually, in the short run, to adjust to changing market conditions or corporate objectives.

Represented by the two outer circles which surround the market controllables are the two levels of uncertainty created by the domestic environment and the foreign environment. Although the marketer can blend a marketing mix from the controllable elements, the uncontrollables are just that and they must be actively adapted to, since their influence determines the ultimate outcome of the marketing effort.

Domestic Uncontrollables

The domestic environment illustrated in Exhibit 1–2 by the middle circle includes those elements which can have a direct effect upon the success of a foreign venture. Included are political forces, competition, and economic climate in the home country. A political decision involving domestic policy can have a direct effect upon a firm's international marketing success. Such was the case when Australia threatened to block all U.S. tractor imports to Australia if the U.S. government proceeded with plans to reduce imports of beef from Australia by 40 percent.

Competition from business firms located in the same base country can also provide another dimension of uncertainty in achieving the marketing objectives of the firm. The decision of General Electric to negotiate a cooperative agreement with France's Machines Bull and Italy's Olivetti computer manufacturers could have both domestic and foreign impact on IBM's foreign market share.

The domestic economic climate is still another important home-based, uncontrollable variable which can have far-reaching effects upon a company's competitive position in foreign markets. The capacity to invest in plant and facilities either in domestic or foreign markets is to a large extent a function of domestic economic vitality. It is generally true that capital will tend to flow toward optimum use; however, capital must first be generated before it can possess mobility. Furthermore, if internal economic conditions deteriorate, restriction against foreign investment and purchasing may be imposed to strengthen the domestic economy. An example of this can be seen in the recent concern of the U.S. government over the American balance of payments and the resulting restrictions imposed to reduce the flow of U.S. dollars abroad. The foregoing are only a few examples of the possible influence of the home environment upon the marketer's task. Inextricably entwined with the effects of the domestic environment are the constraints imposed by the environment of the foreign country.

Foreign Uncontrollables

Besides the domestic uncontrollable element, an even more significant source of uncertainty is presented by the uncontrollable foreign business environment depicted in Exhibit 1–2 by the outer circle. A businessman operating in his native country undoubtedly feels comfortable in forecasting the business climate and adjusting his business to these elements. The process of evaluating the uncontrollable elements in an international marketing program often involves substantial doses of cultural, political, and economic shock.

The businessman operating in a number of foreign countries might

BOX 1–4

Tips from an Expert on Operating in Brazil

Brazil has emerged again as the hottest business area in the southern hemisphere. A number of new American companies are set to enter that market, and some of them recently got tips on operating in Brazil from one of the top experts on Brazilian investment, Henry H. Patton, vice president of Deltec Securities Corp.

Patton, with more than two decades of managing the Deltec investment banking operations in Brazil, made these points in New York at an American Management Association seminar on Brazil:

"Any producer of consumer goods should get into the Brazilian market immediately. You can't afford to ignore 45-million consumers (the half of the population active in the money economy)."

"Selling stock to Brazilians can be a major public relations coup and a shrewd means of introducing a new name into the market. Of Willys' 40,000 shareholders in Brazil, there's not one who would think of buying any other car."

"But if you sell stock to Brazilians, who are financially unsophisticated about stocks, you should be prepared to offer dividends immediately."

"Taking over a local company can lead to resentment. If you do, you had better not change the name."

"It's a good policy to remit profits annually to the maximum, which is 12% before any tax disincentives come into play."

"Inflation is built into the social and economic system. One way to live with it is to keep your eye on the parallel market for currency (Brazil's 'black market'), which will give you an immediate indicator of the depreciation of the currency."

"Stay out of politics. Brazilians do not appreciate foreigners meddling in their affairs."

"Don't go in with a thin edge of your own money. You'll be undercapitalized, and you'll find yourself fighting the battle of funds rather than doing business."

"And any time you delay putting in a capital investment, it will cost you more later."

"What is 'illegal' in Brazil is not as illegal as that word is interpreted in the United States. There are literally thousands of regulations that Brazilians get around by the route of gratuities. It's the bazaar way of life, and you have to play it their way."

"Brazil is a great country in the long run, but it can be trying in the short run. If you want to enjoy life in Brazil, and it can be enjoyable, don't be obsessed with the short run."

Source: Copyrighted © 1968 by Dun & Bradstreet Publications Corp. Reprinted by special permission from the December 1968 issue of *Business Abroad*, p. 17.

find polar extremes in political stability, class structure, and economic climate as critical elements in his business decisions. The dynamic upheaval illustrated in some of the developing countries would further indicate the problems of dynamic change in the cultural, political, and economic climates in relatively short periods of time.

A listing of the more significant elements in the uncontrollable international environment is shown in the outer circle of Exhibit 1–2. These factors include (1) political forces; (2) economic forces; (3) competitive forces; (4) level of technology; (5) structure of distribution; (6) geography; and (7) cultural forces. They constitute the principal elements of uncertainty which the international marketer must cope with in designing a marketing program. Each will be discussed in some detail in subsequent chapters.

The problem of foreign uncertainty is further complicated by a frequently imposed "alien status" that increases the difficulty of properly assessing and forecasting the dynamic international business climate. The "alien status" of a business results in greater emphasis being placed on many of the uncontrollable elements than would be found with relation to these same elements in the domestic market.

The political environment offers the best example of the "alien status." The domestic marketer must always consider any political ramifications of his decisions; however, the consequences of this environmental element are generally minor. Although there is a noticeable change in government attitudes toward domestic business when political parties change as a result of national elections, this change is seldom very serious. This certainly does not hold true for a foreign company. The political environment can be extremely critical, and shifts in governments can often mean sudden changes in attitudes that can result in expropriation, expulsion, or major restrictions on operations. This section is covered in Chapter 5, which discusses the political considerations in assessing world markets. The fact is that the foreign company is *foreign* and thus always subject to the political whims of the government, to a greater degree than would be the domestic firm.

Also a problem for the marketer attuned to one environment is his frequent inability to recognize easily the potential impact of certain uncontrollable elements within another environment to which he has not been culturally assimilated. Consequently, road signs of dangers and indicators of potential in a foreign market may not always be read or interpreted correctly. The uncertainty of the different foreign business environments creates the need for a close study of the operating environment within each new country. Different solutions to fundamentally identical marketing tasks are often in order and are generally the result of changes in the environment of the market. Thus, a strategy that is successful in one country can be rendered worthless in another by changes in political climate or cultural variations, and by differences in the stages of economic development.

ORIENTATION OF *INTERNATIONAL MARKETING*

The problems of the foreign marketer result from the strangeness of the environment within which he must implement his marketing programs; and his success hinges in part upon his ability to assess and adjust properly to the impact of a strange environment. It would appear that he should possess the best qualities of the sociologist, psychologist, diplomat, lawyer, prophet, and businessman.

BOX 1–5

Amphenol Organized for Global Marketing

The sales of Amphenol products into international—or non-U.S.—markets has become increasingly important to the growth of the corporation. Just how important it's been in the past can be demonstrated easily by looking at the figures.

In 1967 (although final figures are not available), non-U.S. sales were expected to surpass $35 million. This is about 22% of projected total corporate sales. In 1957, total corporate sales were only $31 million. In other words, international sales today account for more business than the total corporation had a decade ago.

Preparing for this growth has not been haphazard. It is the result of intensive planning that began about eight years ago.

"At that time we made a basic decision that we should be a global company—not an American company with international operations. Our approach would be to serve a market in the most economical way possible.

"If we felt that the best way to serve a market was to build a plant in that market area, then we went ahead and built—or bought—a plant. If, on the other hand, we could best serve a market by exporting to it, then we decided on that approach," he added.

The figures prove the success of this planning. By 1962 Amphenol did about $5.3 million in non-U.S. business. But this was still only 6% of total corporate business. But by working away, that figure has now risen to 22%.

. . . One thing is certain: with 22% of its business coming from non-U.S. operations, international marketing is an important part of the company's strategy.

Source: From "Amphenol Organized for Global Marketing," by Richard E. Hall. *Industrial Marketing*, February, 1968, pp. 49–50. Copyright 1968 by Advertising Publications Inc., Chicago, Illinois.

In light of all the varying factors involved, with what should a text in foreign marketing be concerned? It is the opinion of the authors that a study of foreign marketing environment and its influences upon the total marketing process is of primary concern and is the most effective approach to a meaningful presentation.

Consequently, the orientation of this text can best be described as an environmental approach to international marketing. By no means is it intended to present principles of marketing but rather a presentation of some of the unique problems of international marketing. It attempts to relate the foreign environment to the marketing process and in so doing to illustrate the many ways in which the environment can influence the marketing task. Although marketing principles are universally applicable, the environment within which the marketer must implement his plans changes drastically from country to country. It is with the difficulties created by a different environment that this text is primarily concerned.

Furthermore, the text is concerned with any company marketing in or into any other country, however slight the involvement or the method of involvement may be. Hence, such terms as export trade, foreign trade, and international marketing are used interchangeably; in strictly technical terms there may be definable differences, but for the purposes of this text no distinction is recognized since these activities describe in some measure marketing from one country to another.

This first section of *International Marketing* deals with an overview of foreign marketing, including a brief discussion of the economic and historical implications. The next section deals exclusively with the uncontrollable elements of the environment and their assessment. Following are chapters dealing with world market patterns. Subsequently, the problems of organizing for marketing in international business are discussed, with a final section on international marketing management. In each chapter, an attempt is made to illustrate the impact of the environment upon the marketing process. The physical limitation of the size prohibits an encyclopedic approach to all the issues; nevertheless, the authors have tried to present sufficient detail so that the reader will appreciate the real need to make his own analysis whenever the challenge arises. It is hoped that the text provides a framework for this task.

READINGS

HOW KODAK CLICKED WORLDWIDE ON THE MARKETING PLAN FOR ITS FAMOUS INSTAMATIC*

The snap heard 'round the world by amateur shutterbugs—and international marketers—in early 1963 was Eastman Kodak Co.'s launching of its Instamatic camera simultaneously in 28 countries. Kodak remains strategically vague, but available figures indicate that overseas sales account for almost 50% of the 20-million Instamatics sold since the camera line made its debut. And even today, after four years, foreign sales of the camera and its Kodapak film cartridge are going strong—with no apparent letup in sight.

Something Simple

Kodak's international marketing theme of simplified picture-taking and ease of operation capitalizes on the overseas amateur photographer's adverse reaction to cameras featuring gadgetry. "The mass market abroad likes simplicity," said William P. Lane, assistant vice president and general manager of Kodak's international markets division. "We analyzed the typical picture-taker overseas and concluded that he wants good pictures, not photography. With the Instamatic, he is getting almost 12 out of 12 good pictures, whereas, in the past with a roll-film camera, he would have to be satisfied with nine good pictures out of the 12 taken."

The Instamatic system of photography has clicked internationally

---

beyond the wildest expectations of marketing executives at Rochester. Overseas sales of the Instamatic topped domestic sales during the first year following its global introduction, the first time in Kodak's history that one of its cameras sold more internationally than in the domestic market. After two years, almost five-million Instamatic cameras had been sold outside the United States. Four-million were sold in Europe, including about a million in Germany and 750,000 in the United Kingdom.

"Sales of Instamatic cameras abroad at the end of 1963 exceeded our original estimates fairly substantially," said Lane. "When we called in our overseas managers, their first estimates had doubled ours. Yet, that first year even exceeded their forecasts. In some overseas areas, particularly Europe, we had to cut down on our advertising until the camera supply caught up with the demand." Kodak's international sales in 1966 reached more than $600-million and accounted for almost 30% of the company's total sales. Instamatic cameras and accessories provided a substantial portion of this income.

Planning the Strategy

How did Kodak achieve this marketing coup abroad? Preparations for a worldwide market introduction began about 18 months before Instamatic finally rocketed onto the photographic horizon. Kodak officials had deliberated at length on making such a move. One point in Kodak's favor was the fact that the company had a unique saleable package (film cartridge and camera). Kodak also was ideally set up to pull off the feat. It has associate companies, including wholly-owned subsidiaries, in 46 countries. Six of the companies (United Kingdom, Canada, France, Germany, Australia, and Brazil) are major manufacturing facilities, while the other 40 provide marketing and technical services. In addition, Kodak has distributors in virtually every country and territory in the Free World.

The concept of a camera that would do everything but trip its own shutter began to evolve in the minds of engineers in Kodak's A&O (apparatus and optical) division in 1953. However, it was not until 1957 that the "easy load" project, as it was first known, left the drawing board and went into production testing.

The engineers had selected the well-established 35-mm film width because it provided good slides and enlargements. They chose the square format because it made a smaller cartridge possible. Selection of a design for the film cartridge took longer because of costing and considerations. After many tests and thousands of cartridges later, the engineers selected a molded-plastic design. Next, they turned their attention to designing a camera that would be compact, easy and fast to load and unload, and capable of taking color slides as well as black-and-white and color prints. A full line of cameras was required—one that practically everyone could afford; more advanced, intermediate-priced models; and a high-performance, fully automatic model. Company officials estimate that upwards of $6-million was spent on the development of what eventually became the Instamatic system. By 1959, the "easy load" project was starting to pick up momentum and was renamed Project 13.

After deciding to make the Instamatic a global project, Kodak organized an informal ad hoc committee to coordinate introduction of the system abroad. The 10-man group included two representatives from each of the key manufacturing companies in England, France, and Germany; a representative of Kodak's general management; a member of the international sales division; another from the international advertising division; and the amateur camera sales manager. In the early spring of 1962, the newly formed international committee, whose members had been selected as the logical, interested parties in the launching of a new product overseas, went into action. For the next six months, it was to meet in London, Paris, Stuttgart, Rochester, and other cities around the world for discussions of anticipated marketing problems. Charles Fitter, amateur products coordinator in the international markets division, and a member of the ad hoc committee, recalled some of the ticklish decisions that had to be made.

"We had to determine how much inventory was needed before the actual introduction of the Instamatic," said Fitter. "We even had to consider the needs of Kodak's photo-finishing customers. For example, they would need equipment to break open the film cartridges. Another consideration was the type and timing of the dealer presentations."

Climaxing the preparation period in the fall of 1962, Kodak's overseas managers met in Rochester for their first briefing on the Instamatic and its global debut. Until then, none knew that such a product, already nearly 10 years in development, even existed. Kodak decided then that the shipment of new cameras and film cartridges overseas would begin eight weeks in advance of the scheduled availability date in the particular country or region. This lead time schedule was set up to give the overseas dealers good stocks well in advance of the anticipated heavy consumer demand, said Fitter.

Initially, all Instamatics and Kodapak film cartridges were manufactured in Rochester. By 1964, Instamatic cameras were being manufactured in Kodak's associate companies in England, Germany and Australia, and the Canadian company was assembling the cameras. Film cartridge production began in the United Kingdom, France, and Canada in early 1965 and in Australia a year later.

Synchronizing Advertising

The advertising and publicity campaigns were closely synchronized with product distribution schedules. Sidney A. Olson of J. Walter Thompson, Kodak's ad agency, became the first outside Kodak to learn about Project 13. He was brought into the picture in early 1962 and spent the first three months on the account working with A. D. Johnson, assistant vice president and advertising director. Their first job was to select a name for the camera, and they considered hundreds of candidates before making the final choice.

"The ad message was keyed to simplicity, in keeping with the nature of the product," said Johnson. A Rochester model, Bonnie Bull, was featured in many of the early Instamatic ads overseas, but later, Kodak began to use nationals as models in foreign advertising. Utilizing overseas consumer newspapers and magazines and dealer trade publications, Instamatic ads appear worldwide in 23 language variations. A *Reader's Digest* ad, which ran in 15 dialects, was widely reproduced and later modified for use as a direct mailer. Some 5.5-million reproductions went out from Dayton, Ohio, and another 500,000 from Mexico City. Advertising materials were produced in three key centralized locations—the United States, England, and Holland. Ad materials for Latin America were turned out in Mexico City for two reasons: such materials can't be imported into Mexico, and Mexico has good quality paper stocks.

Sample press kits, which were sent out in English to all the countries eight weeks before the debut of the camera, also were translated into more than a score of languages including Arabic, Chinese, Danish, Dutch, French, German, Italian, Malay, Norwegian, Portugese, Spanish, Swahili, and Swedish.

The magnitude of the project made secrecy a mandatory watchword from the start not only because of competition, but also because an inadvertent leak to the outside could upset the overseas market. "Approximately 1,000 people in Rochester knew about the Instamatic, but the large majority of personnel at Kodak were as astounded as anyone when the story broke," said Lane. "We counted on the loyalty of those who knew the secret, and they came through for us."

To make the task of keeping the Instamatic under wraps easier, work on the project was centered around one area. "Customer-type" testing of over 2,000 production cameras and 4,000 cartridges was carried out on weekends by selected Kodak employees. Each signed a statement pledging that he would maintain security.

Despite market research, previous sales history, consumer patterns, and other market estimating tools, demand exceeded supply during the first year. "Our sales estimating department, which has been doing this sort of work for 50 years, came up with what it thought was the most realistic estimate," said Lane. "In a sense, it's kind of a guessing game. This was a unique situation, and each market has its own peculiarities that have to be handled individually. It takes a tremendous effort to launch a product worldwide from a standing start in terms of inventories."

The Instamatic system has helped change camera customs abroad. Fitter noted that more European women are using the Instamatic because of its operational ease. Historically, photography has been the domain of the European male, who prides himself in his camera ownership and in his ability to master its complexities.

Fitter also sees the Latin American mass market as having good potential, even though it is not so photographically advanced as is the European market.

The gadget-conscious Japanese market presents different problems.

"The Japanese have a tradition of buying a camera as a camera and not as a picture-taking device," said Fitter. "Cartridged film is also much higher because of import restrictions."

TIGHTEN YOUR OVERSEAS MARKETING PLAN*

American companies marketing products overseas today face the question: How can we get a bigger piece of the action abroad? For many companies, markets at home are reaching the saturation point, yet they don't seem to be able to tap into profitable markets in foreign countries as easily as they have been able to sell at home.

Companies like Singer, IBM and General Foods have found the going very profitable in Europe and other western markets. Other companies should be able to follow their lead.

What are some of the glaring sins that American marketers commit abroad? And what can they do to improve their chances in foreign markets? One man who has some ideas is Bernard Krief, president of Bernard Krief Consultants for Europe, a Paris based firm that spends much of its time giving advice to American marketing management. He is quick to point out that Americans do a great many things right, on balance, and that the mistakes we make are not all that serious.

The greatest mistake Americans make, says Mr. Krief, is in using a single marketing policy for every country in which a product is sold. This policy may be excellent for U.S. markets, but to extrapolate American strategy and research into foreign markets can be highly dangerous, he believes.

"In America, you rightfully work from the promise that the market determines the product, from every point of view. But, a product ideal for domestic needs may not fit into foreign markets—because of its name, because of the shape of its package, its marketing strategy or its advertising copy platform. This method of marketing is all right if you simply want to sell your surplus abroad, but if you really want to conquer, for example, the entire European Common Market, it could be very unsuccessful," Mr. Krief says.

Many marketing principles are as valid for Europe as they are for the U.S., but there are also many differences between the two markets. One big difference is in distribution channels.

"In Europe there are still very many mom and pop shops—very small stores run as a family enterprise. Your marketing program must recognize this reality."

In America, a marketer can build a powerful national advertising program around his product, and rely on this advertising to *pull* the product through the big chain stores. Chains cannot afford *not* to stock a heavily advertised product. In France, says Mr. Krief, chains sell only 15% to 25% of the volume of most products.

To cover the entire market, salesmen must sell the small retail shops,

---

* Reprinted from *Marketing Insights,* February 9, 1970, copyright 1970, by Crain Communications Inc., Chicago, Illinois.

almost in door-to-door fashion. "If you want to sell a soft drink, you must sell every bar separately, in addition to selling the chains. This costs a lot of money."

As a result, distribution of many products is spotty. And even if your brand is well known, retail clerks will substitute another brand when customers ask for yours.

"An American cosmetics manufacturer asks us for a market analysis," relates Mr. Krief. "We found that they were emphasizing the chain stores in their distribution and neglecting the small shops. But, in France, opinion leaders for such products are the perfumers—small, personally run shops specializing in perfumes and other cosmetics. Most cosmetics manufacturers give exclusive franchises to two or three small perfumers in each small town or shopping community.

"By selling only to the chain stores, the American company shuts itself off from valuable word-of-mouth promotion through these opinion leaders. In fact, the perfumers talked the manufacturer's products down, and substituted other brands in their place."

Mr. Krief recommended "that the company carry on with distributing to chain stores, at the same time emphasizing contacts with a maximum of 2,800 perfumers over the whole of France. To sell to more than a few shops in each town would have cheapened the image of the products."

Another problem with distribution channels is that the performance of wholesalers is uneven from country to country, says Mr. Krief. "In France, wholesalers just don't care to promote a product. They simply ask the retailer what he wants today, and they deliver it. It is very difficult to move the wholesaler. If any American company builds its strategy around the French wholesaler, it is almost bound to fail.

"In Germany, the wholesaler is very powerful, and very well organized. And you must go through the wholesaler to get at the very great number of small, family run retail stores. In Italy, the wholesalers are very aggressive, but not well organized. They sometimes lose money."

Another problem, according to Mr. Krief, is that European salesmen don't measure up to American standards. Sales training has not been developed as it has in this country. As a result, marketing plans built around personal salesmanship can fail.

And the worst of it is, these differences in distribution channels diminish the effectiveness of good advertising. In Europe, advertising aimed at the consumer doesn't always hurdle these problems. Advertising can create an image for your company and its products, but it cannot always force your products through the distribution channels. If your products are not available in retail stores, your advertising merely sells for your competitors.

Some American companies get into trouble when they decide to expand in Europe via the acquisition route. One American computer manufacturer failed to check the image of the subsidiary it acquired in France.

Too late, it found to its dismay that the French company was looked upon as a loser in its own country. Potential customers didn't want to take on the huge investment required to computerize, as long as the brand image was so poor. Now the American company has instituted an excellent sales promotion campaign, but the road ahead is difficult, to say the least.

Another common mistake is to locate European headquarters where the social life is, rather than in business centers. For example, several American companies have established Italian regional offices in Rome, rather than in Milan. This, Mr. Krief believes, is a tactical error, since Milan is the industrial capital of the country.

Mr. Krief believes many American marketing programs are under-financed when they cross the Atlantic. He cites the example of one very large company that sells only $1,200,000 per year in France, spread over 35 different products. Yet the company sticks to its domestic practice of alloting not more than 10% of sales for promoting a product. This would allow $120,000 for promoting 35 products in France, an average of about $3,400 per product. And a single one-minute spot on tv goes for $20,000. "How can they manage, under such a rule?" Mr. Krief asks.

"The European Common Market is nearly as big, and certainly as sophisticated, as the American market," says Mr. Krief. "If you are going to get in, you have to do more than get your feet wet."

What does Bernard Krief advise his clients, which have included such American giants as IBM, Gulf Oil, Ford, Philip Morris and R. J. Reynolds? "The most important point to remember is to think inter-nationally," he says. "Before you launch a product domestically, think of all the countries where you *might* sell in the future, even if your initial program is only for the domestic market. Include in your over-all program adequate research in each overseas market.

"When you design the product, when you manufacture it, when you choose the name, when you build the product image, do it in such a way that it will sell in overseas markets," says Mr. Krief.

"Try to escape 'fashion' in marketing, or at least do not slavishly follow American fashion in European markets. In America, cigarets are all packaged alike, and all are sold on the basis of giving pleasure. On the continent, we do not have the problems in cigaret marketing to the extent that you have in the U.S. We are not tied to the 'pleasure' theme. We promote the sale of cigarets there by associating with *going through* danger—such as by showing an automobile safety film."

Another fashion point: Europeans aren't as hung up on ferocious animals as Americans. Tiger paws, tigers in your tank and other zoologi-cal references often suffer in translation, Mr. Krief says.

Be true to yourself, Krief clients are told. When you set up a sophisti-cated marketing strategy in the U.S., do not try to get away with a minimum program in Europe. The days are past when Europeans will buy anything that American companies are kind enough to ship overseas.

Price realistically. It is true that European prices are rising, but not as fast as American prices these days. Products must be priced to sell the market they are intended for. One American food company tried to sell a can of soup in France for 80¢. It overlooked the fact that, in France, soup (which should be called *potage* if it is to be sold in better places) is eaten mainly as a first course. No French housewife would think of spending 80¢ for an appetizer.

Get good advice. If you plan to sell in several European countries, you should expect to research the market in each, since traditions, tastes, peculiarities, phobias and motivations vary from country to country. The German company, Bosch, asked Krief to research the effect of its name on French opinion.

The term *boche* had been applied in derision to Germans during the two world wars. Krief found that Frenchmen had no hang-ups over the name, however, and advised the company to use it on its products. Advance research such as this can prevent a lot of headaches.

Finally, says Bernard Krief, American companies should consider using sales promotion more heavily in Europe than they might in this country. His consulting firm puts quite a lot of effort into sales promotion campaigns for its clients. Why? To overcome weaknesses in the distribution system.

"If you sell to only one store out of one hundred you can spot your sales promotion events to occur within a mile radius of each store. Sales promotion creates its own media, and thus you do not waste advertising dollars in media that reach more consumers than your products reach.

"When you use sales promotion, you do not create a market for your competition. You know exactly who you want to speak to. You know your products are available before you promote." Sales promotion, Mr. Krief points out, is a collective, two-way communication between marketer and potential customer. In overseas markets, it can be especially useful.

QUESTIONS

1. Define:

    International marketing   Alien status
    Foreign uncontrollables   Licensing
    Domestic uncontrollables   Joint ventures
    Controllable elements   Management contracts

2. ". . . The marketer's task is the same whether applied in Dimebox, Texas, or Katmandu, Nepal." Discuss.

3. How can the increased interest in international marketing on the part of U.S. firms be explained?

4. Discuss the four categories of foreign business involvement.

5. Discuss the task of the marketer in the international marketplace.

6. Discuss the five alternative strategies for entering a foreign market.

7. Would there ever be a case where one firm may employ more than one of the five strategies for entering a foreign market? Explain.

Readings

1. Why was a simultaneous worldwide marketing plan necessary for the introduction of Kodak's Instamatic?

2. "The greatest mistake . . . is in using a single marketing policy for every country. . . ." Discuss.

3. Identify the main foreign uncontrollables discussed in the article, "Tighten Your Overseas Marketing Plan."

OUTLINE OF CHAPTER 2

HISTORICAL OVERVIEW

MERCANTILISM

TWENTIETH-CENTURY DEVELOPMENT
  World War I and Interwar Period
  Post-World War II Period

THE UNITED STATES AND WORLD TRADE
  From 1950 through the Sixties
    Direct Investment Challenged
    Slipping U.S. Share of World Export Markets

CONCLUSIONS

READINGS
  The United States in World Trade, *The Conference Board Record.*
  Geocentric Giants to Rule World Business, *Business Abroad.*

2

MARKETING AND WORLD BUSINESS: A HISTORICAL REVIEW

The trading of goods and services among nations of the world has been in existence for many thousands of years. Recorded history identifies in some detail the scope and importance of trade to the Egyptians, Assyrians, and Phoenicians. Archeological discovery of imported artifacts would seem to indicate that trade was widely practiced prior to the dawn of recorded history.

Why do people trade? There is no simple, definitive answer to the question. Certainly, potential economic gain would offer a strong motive. Perhaps, though, a desire for adventure, the desire to explore the unknown, is an equally strong motive. Surplus production, political motives, and humanitarian motives could also provide incentive for trading activity.

The effects of trade are usually viewed in an economic context. Measurements of the balance of payments, gross exports by product class, and debtor and creditor nation status are common measurements of trading activity. However, while the economies of world trade are important, the cultural, technological, and potential consequences of trade should not be overlooked. While the Phoenicians were trading their textiles in the Mediterranean ports, they were also trading ideas, cultural patterns, and technological progress. The practice of buying (or kidnapping) and selling slaves, inhuman as it was, contributed to the exchange of cultural patterns and values, although it should be noted that this cultural exchange did not always result in a gain to both parties involved in the trade.

The role in society of the merchant-trader has varied in the history of business. The early Greeks looked upon the businessman as a person too interested in wealth. The Romans looked on the merchant as a necessary evil for financing conquest and disposing of loot. The Islamic Arabs looked on the foreign trader as an intruder with contaminating religious and cultural ideas. The Catholic Church of the Middle Ages looked upon the merchant with a somewhat skeptical attitude in his pursuit of economic gains. Even today the world trader, especially U.S.

multinational companies, continues to be feared. This fear is perhaps best expressed by the often quoted Servan-Schreiber, writing in the *American Challenge,* that if present tendencies continue, "the third industrial power in the world, after America and Russia, could be, not Europe, but American industry in Europe."[1] Regardless of the basic attitude of society at any given time, the international businessman has played and will continue to play a vital role in shaping the economic and social progress of the nations of the world. The purpose of this chapter is to review briefly the historical development of world trade and to present an overview of the present position of U.S. international business in the world economy.

HISTORICAL OVERVIEW

In the annals of recorded history, the factors which have seemed to have some analytical value in explaining the evolving pattern of world trade are the following:

1. *Geography.* In the early development of world trade, geographical location in proximity to a market and a source of supply was important.
2. *Factor endowment.* The type and amount of factor endowment such as special skills, climate, navigable waterways, and raw materials have played a critical role in the development of international trade in some regions or countries.
3. *Political events.* The advent of wars, alliances, colonization and changing political attitudes have had corresponding impacts on the evolution of world trade.
4. *Innovation.* Progress in overcoming natural and artificial barriers to trading activity has had a significant impact on the patterns of world trade. Man-made harbors, canals, industrialization, and transportation improvements have all altered the patterns of world competition and trade.
5. *Other factors.* Factors such as social attitude toward profit, cultural emphasis on achievement, and economic cooperation and assistance have all played important continuing roles in changing patterns of world trade.

The factors noted above are all dynamic, interdependent aspects of world trade, and the importance of any individual factor changes with time. For example, oil reserves which would have been a relatively unimportant natural resource 50 years ago have given Kuwait a current annual per capita GNP of over $3,000 as compared to the less than $100 in per capita GNP prior to oil discovery.

As archeological discoveries advance our knowledge of the past, it becomes apparent that there existed well-established trade patterns three or four thousand years before the birth of Christ. The foundations

---

[1] J. J. Servan-Schreiber, *The American Challenge* (New York: Atheneum Publishers, 1967), p. viii.

of world trade were established many centuries before the mercantile period of the 16th century. As the volume of trade grew in the pre-Roman era, great trading cities developed; the towns of Asia Minor—Miletus, Rhodes, Carthage, and Corinth—were developed primarily as trading centers.

These great trading cities made a wide range of contributions to the progress of civilizations. Businessmen interested in the development of commerce took an active role in the development and administration of city affairs. The culture and administration of the trading towns produced some of the more important codes of commercial law and business practices. These codes, reflecting the merchant influence in government, formed the basis for commercial development. For example, the *disciplina etrusca* of the Etruscans (Asian Greeks) formed the basis of Roman law.

Under the expanding power of the Roman Empire, the merchants lost much of their prestige but not their importance. Their usefulness in financing military expeditions and disposing of the spoils of war was not overlooked. The Roman period brought peace and safety to the roads and sea routes used in trade, and safe travel, along with the aid of well-built Roman roads, allowed trade to develop in an orderly and efficient manner. With the gradual decay of the Roman Empire, Europe degenerated into feudalism, which discouraged trade in everything but the necessities of life which could not be locally produced.

When the Emperor Charlemagne was crowned by the Pope in 800 A.D., a new era in Church influence on society began to take shape. In the Middle Ages, the Catholic Church became the most important influence in the social, economic, and political direction of society. The monastery rose to economic and political power and at one time controlled over one third of all the land in Europe. Since the Church forbade trade with the Moslems, the early Middle Ages were a period of relative stagnation in trade.

A by-product of the Crusades, beginning in 1095 A.D., was the reopening of trade channels with the East. The Crusades whetted the appetite of Europeans for the luxuries of the East and were instrumental in the development of the Italian city-states of Venice, Genoa, Florence, and Pisa. Basically staging and supply points for the Crusades, they were also natural points of entry for returning spoils of war from the East. The widening of horizons and the subsequent intensification of rivalries between emerging European powers laid the groundwork for nationalism.

During the 15th and 16th centuries two important movements influenced commercial development in Europe. The "Renaissance," or rebirth of learning, which dictated inquiry into one's environment, and the "Reformation," which replaced the dominance of the Catholic Church with the political and economic power of local government. The breakdown of the feudal power centers allowed for the emergence of stronger national power and corresponding increases in political and economic influence. Other important events during the period included the widespread use of the compass, which allowed more freedom in exploration, and the discovery of America in 1492, which allowed for political and commercial expansion.

Several important formative influences arose from the Age of Discovery. First, the participation of ruling power in all foreign development evolved and was recognized as accepted procedure. Second (an outgrowth of the terms of royal charters granted), political and economic power exercised in the colonies was coextensive. Third, powerful national states evolved, and finally facilitating agencies for world trade were developed.

In a history of world business development, the growth of facilitating agencies carries special importance. Specialized middlemen such as export-import houses, commission agents, and other types of agents developed to handle the increasing flow of trade. Financial institutions grew to prominence by providing accumulations of entrepreneurial capital and depositories for wealth extracted in trading ventures. Risk sharing through the form of insurance and incorporation of business interests also underwent vigorous growth and development throughout this period.

From these converging forces of nationalism arose the economic and political philosophy of mercantilism.

MERCANTILISM

The philosophy of mercantilism was a key determinant of the nature and extent of political and economic legislation implemented up to the late 18th century.[2] Although it defies accurate and detailed description, the basic doctrine of mercantilism seemed to be based on the idea that the only way for a nation to grow was to amass wealth at the expense of other countries or to exploit colonial interests. The philosophy implied a static approach to the resources of the world. That is, it was assumed that there was a limited amount of wealth in the world and the country that amassed the greatest share would become most powerful. From this philosophy a number of logical developments followed: the expansion of national power as rapidly and forcefully as necessary to accumulate control over the sources of wealth, the development of powerful naval forces to protect a nation's distant wealth from encroachment, and the accumulation of a store of gold and silver. The logic of bullion hoarding was based on the belief that supplies of gold and silver were limited and constituted real "wealth." Many of the trade barriers which are in existence today were first inaugurated during this period. Subsidy and tariff, control of production, and pricing were all common methods of regulating trade during the Mercantilist Era.

With the dawning of the Industrial Revolution, new technology developed the industrial capacity of European industry to higher levels of achievement. The growth of industrialism saw the eventual disintegration of the mercantile doctrine which was replaced by a laissez-faire attitude on the part of government. The Industrial Revolution in turn

---

[2] For a complete treatment of the theory and practice of mercantilism see Eli Heckscher, *Mercantilism* 2 vol. (London: George Allan and Unwin Limited, 1936).

led to a chain of innovations that caused social and economic change unparalleled in history, perhaps until the 20th century.

The new economic liberalism of the period aided the blossoming of world trade. Total world trade increased over threefold from 1850 to 1914. The nature of trade also changed to some degree. There was a shift in emphasis by the industrialized nations to exploiting raw material sources, and in order to meet the needs of an industrialized, urbanized society, increased sources of agricultural products were also required.

TWENTIETH CENTURY DEVELOPMENT

World War I and Interwar Period

Sweeping innovations in communication, petroleum, and other energy sources continued and accelerated during the 20th century, but, gradually, commercial competition shifted to military competition and, in 1914, Europe was plunged into a war which devastated the productive capacity of central Europe as well as causing almost 40 million human casualties. After the Armistice of 1918, a period of political and economic chaos overtook the European Continent. Starvation, social disorganization, and economic chaos plagued most of the countries of Europe until the mid 1920s.

The needs of postwar reconstruction and the availability of foreign loans, especially from the United States, allowed for a good measure of economic recovery by the late 1920s. World trade began to increase and reached a peak of almost $70 billion in 1929, up from $40 billion at the peak of the pre-World War I period.

Depression struck in 1929 in the United States with far-reaching repercussions. By 1938 world trade had decreased to approximately $27 billion. Unemployment, financial instability, and economic insecurity haunted most of the industrialized countries of the world.

During the interwar period there appeared to be two general trends which influenced the development of world commerce. The first trend was toward protectionism, the principal reaction to the Depression. The economic liberalism and laissez-faire tenets of the mid and late 19th century were ignored in the scramble to promote internal economic recovery. The second trend was toward negotiation and concession among countries of the world. In 1932, in the Ottawa Agreement, the countries affiliated with Great Britain negotiated an agreement whereby each would provide preferential treatment in exporting and importing within the British Commonwealth. It is interesting to note that this agreement remains as a major stumbling block in Great Britain's acceptance into the European Common Market.

Post-World War II Period

In 1939, the world was again plunged into tragic and destructive warfare. Most of the industrial nations of the world were involved, and again the destruction in terms of industrial capacity and human misery was unparalleled in history.

Several factors emerged from World War II which have had a profound influence on the development of world trade patterns since 1945. One major factor was the almost worldwide split of communist and non-communist nations. The so-called "iron curtain" and "bamboo curtain" provided almost as effective a barrier to international trade as they did to fostering sound political cooperation. In post-World War II commerce, the types of trade, the terms of trade, and the volume of trade have all been profoundly influenced by the existence of the iron or bamboo curtains. As a result of this ideological split, traditional patterns of trade have been disrupted.

A second factor which has complicated the normal development and pattern of world commerce has been the advent of huge programs of economic assistance during the post-World War II period.

International cooperation is yet another factor which has characterized the development of international commerce since 1945. This cooperation is generally manifested in two possible forms. Countries have combined in different parts of the world to promote internal trade and mutual advantage in external trade, and voluntary associations for the exchange of ideas to facilitate the mechanics of world trade have developed. In 1947, The General Agreement on Tariffs and Trade (GATT) was negotiated in Geneva, Switzerland. In November, 1963, 58 countries had been granted full membership in the general agreement, and special arrangements had been established with 15 other countries. Basically, GATT is a complex agreement, but its essence can be stated in four fundamental principles.[3]

1. *Nondiscrimination.* Trade should be conducted on the principle of nondiscrimination. Each member country agrees that any tariff concession or trade advantage granted to one country, whether or not a member of GATT, shall be granted to all GATT member countries.
2. *Trade liberalization.* Protection shall be afforded each nation's domestic industries exclusively through the customs tariff. Thus, import quotas and licensing requirements, restrictions which nations have traditionally used to limit the volume and types of imports entering their countries, are prohibited.
3. *Consultation.* Inherent throughout the agreement is the concept of consultation, whereby member countries may meet under GATT auspices to discuss any trade problems that may arise. GATT serves as a forum for settling unprecedented disputes, as well as disputes arising from potential or actual breach of the GATT code of rules.
4. *Tariff negotiation.* That tariffs should be open to negotiation is the idea that originally inspired GATT.

GATT itself has provided the framework within which such negotiations could be held. As a result of its five major tariff conferences held

---

[3] *GATT: General Agreement on Tariffs and Trade* (Washington, D.C.: U.S. Department of Commerce, 1964), 16 pages.

between 1947 and 1963, customs duties have been reduced on tens of thousands of products traded across international frontiers. The reductions have greatly stimulated and facilitated world trade in the past two decades, as is evidenced by the doubled volume of U.S. exports (or imports) in that period.

THE UNITED STATES AND WORLD TRADE

In 1776 two major events occurred which were to shape evolving patterns of world trade far into the future. A Declaration of Independence was presented to England by her American colonies, and *Wealth of Nations,* by Adam Smith, was published. Both of these events presented demands for greater freedom to determine the destiny of commerce and socioeconomic affairs. The Declaration of Independence demanded that the colonies be free to determine their own destiny—a revolt against a basic tenet of mercantilism. The *Wealth of Nations* rejected protectionism and other forms of economic legislation and held out free trade as a positive alternative.

Under the terms of a mercantilist philosophy, the colonies were expected to provide a source of raw materials and a market for manufactured products of the mother country. The results of these restrictions did not leave the American colonies with a large industrial base when the Revolutionary War was won in 1789. However, the years 1793 to 1808 were years of prosperity for the young republic. The export sector of the economy is estimated to have increased fivefold during this period. The combination of rich natural resources, an expanding frontier, a growing internal market, and favorable export conditions led to continued prosperity.

Great Britain had led in world export trade from the early 18th century to the 1920s, when the United States passed her. With the exception of one or two years, the United States has continued to be the world leader in export trade. Further, the United States has been the top world trader (exports and imports combined) since 1940. Beginning with the decade of the fifties, however, some important changes began to occur in the pattern of world trade which would have far-reaching effects upon U.S. trade.

From 1950 through the Sixties

The rapid growth of wartorn economies and previously underdeveloped countries, coupled with large-scale economic corporation and assistance, led to new world marketing opportunities. Rising standards of living and broad-based consumer and industrial markets abroad forced the American marketer to reappraise his traditional approach to foreign markets.

Competition for foreign markets increased steadily. Foreign markets were no longer as ready to absorb the surplus production of American industry. Emerging sentiments of nationalism, coupled with heightened world competition and rapidly developing industrial capacity, removed some of the magic from the "made in U.S.A." identification. In many cases, the export manager found that not only were traditional export markets declining or disappearing, but competition for remaining world markets had evolved. Lower labor costs, less expensive raw materials, newer plant and equipment, and lower transportation costs placed severe pressure on the ability of American businessmen to compete in some important segments of the export market.

The American businessman found it necessary to focus the same marketing skills used in domestic operations to capitalize on foreign marketing opportunities. No longer was it sufficient merely to produce for export and rely on a gravity flow channel to foreign markets. The total marketing program had to be designed to match company resources with both potential foreign and domestic demand.

EXHIBIT 2–1

The Top 10 Trading Nations in 1968

	Exports f.o.b. (billions of $)	Imports c.i.f. (billions of $)	Trade Surplus (billions of $)
United States.............	$34.0	$33.0*	$1.0
Germany..................	23.8	19.8	4.0
Britain...................	15.3	18.9	−1.9†
Japan....................	12.8	13.0	−0.2
Canada..................	12.1	11.0	1.1
France...................	11.1	11.1	0
Soviet Union.............	10.5	9.4	1.1
Italy....................	9.8	10.1	--0.3
Netherlands..............	8.2	9.1	−0.9
Belgium..................	8.1	8.3	−0.2

* f.o.b.
† Calculated on balance-of-payments basis
    Data: Government agencies; National Institute of Economic & Social Research; *Business Week* estimate.

Since 1950, there has been an upward trend in U.S. exports and imports, and by 1968 (Exhibit 2–1) the United States combined exports and imports totaled more than $67 billion, leading Germany, the next closest, by $24 billion. With the increase in trading, U.S. direct foreign investment rose from about $7.3 billion in 1940 to more than $85 billion by the end of 1968. If the direct investment generated approximately $170 billion in total sales, then sales from direct investment abroad, combined with 1968 export trade figures of $34 billion, meant that the United States effectively controlled $204 billion in sales from markets abroad in 1968. When compared as a percentage of U.S. GNP for 1968, this amounts to less than 5 percent. A small figure, to be sure, but in terms of world trade, significant.

Although the United States continued to be the leading world trader in 1968, by the early 1969s she was being challenged on two major fronts: direct investment and strong competition in export markets.

Direct Investment Challenged. In the sixties there was growing animosity toward foreign investment in both industrialized and less developed countries. Latin American countries were the most hazardous, with Chile, Peru, Bolivia, Mexico and others expropriating direct U.S. investments or forcing investors to sell holdings to nationals. Just weeks before the new president of Chile, Salvadore Allende, proposed the expropriation of most of the $965 million U.S. investment in that country, the Peruvian government had announced the development of a new industrial law which provided that the government buy control of all basic industries and sell the equity to nationals.

Uncertainty about multinational investors, however, is by no means limited to Latin America or to other underdeveloped countries. In Great Britain, one industrialist, apprehensive about increased foreign investment, warned that "Britain might become a satellite where there could be manufacturing but no determination of policy."[4] While the British government has generally viewed foreign investment favorably, guidelines have been set for joint ventures between certain British and U.S. firms. In Canada, a similar concern about the size of foreign investment has led the Royal Commission on Canadian Economic Prospects to recommend that foreign-owned subsidiaries must "Canadianize," i.e., (1) appoint Canadians to companies' boards of directors, (2) staff key positions with Canadians, (3) insure that a sizable minority of equity stock be sold to Canadians, (4) purchase supplies in Canada, and (5) aggressively seek export markets.[5] And in the EEC, fear of U.S. business domination continues to smolder and is expected to flare up when the Common Market Commission makes public in 1971 a report on the strong position of U.S. investment in Common Market countries. Even Australia, one of the most open countries to foreign investment, is questioning the control of its basic industries by foreign investors.[6]

Justification for concern over the position of foreign investment in a country must be viewed from the perspective of the host country. Are foreign investors showing sufficient concern for domestic development, do they control too much of domestic basic industry and natural resources, does the volume of certain foreign imports preclude domestic competition? These questions are in the minds of government policy makers when considering the advisability of foreign investment. The answers form the challenge to future U.S. direct investment.

At the same time that U.S. firms were facing increased sensitivity to their investments, there was evidence in 1971 that, overall, the U.S. share of major world export markets for manufactured products had declined since 1962.

---

[4] "Industrialist Warns against U.S. Role in U.K. Economy," *Wall Street Journal*, January 20, 1969, p. 6.

[5] I. A. Litvak and C. J. Maule, "Guidelines for the Multinational Corporation," *Journal of World Business*, July–August 1968, p. 36.

[6] See Donald P. Brooke, "Australia as Host to the International Corporation," in Charles P. Kindleberger, *The International Corporation* (Cambridge: The M.I.T. Press, 1970), pp. 293–318.

BOX 2-1

The Multinationals

"Some of these corporations," A. A. Berle has written, "can be thought of only in somewhat the way we have heretofore thought of nations." A glance at the table shows that Professor Berle's statement is by no means just rhetoric.

GNP OF VARIOUS COUNTRIES COMPARED WITH SALES OF SELECTED CORPORATIONS
(billions of current dollars, year 1967)

Netherlands	$26.6	Ford	$10.5
General Motors	20.0	Royal Dutch/Shell	8.4
Belgium	19.7	Norway	8.3
Switzerland	15.9	General Electric	7.7
Standard Oil (N.J.)	13.3	Greece	7.1
Denmark	12.2	Chrysler	6.2
Austria	10.6	Mobil	5.7
		Unilever	5.6
		IBM	5.3
		Portugal	4.6

Source: Louis Turner, *Invisible Empires* (New York: Harcourt, 1970), pp. 135–36.
Cautionary note: corporate sales are not an equivalent of GNP's. The table vastly overstates the relative importance of corporations with respect to manpower: Portugal, for instance, has a population of 9 million, whereas GM employs less than 1 million. On the other hand, the table understates the economic strength of corporations: GM can borrow a great deal more easily than Portugal, and it controls *all* its receipts, whereas Portugal gets only the taxes from its GNP. Nonetheless, the table makes it clear that Berle's comparison was not solely a fanciful one.

All these giant corporations have one characteristic in common: they are all "multinational," meaning that they have very large manufacturing, extraction, distribution, or research facilities in countries other than the ones in which their headquarters are located. For the European firms, multinationality is not particularly new: growing up in the cramped confines of small national markets, British and Dutch and German firms have long ago expanded beyond their national borders until today Volkswagen sells 67 percent of its output outside Germany, Imperial Chemicals 50 percent outside the U.K., and Nestlé 97.5 percent of its $2 billion worth of foods and chocolates outside its native Switzerland.

What is new, however, is the rise to prominence of American firms among the multinationals. As the list above shows, of the 9 biggest multinational corporations, 7 are American. (One of these firms—IBM—is growing so rapidly that it threatens within 5 years to top General Motors and within 15 years to surpass in sales volume the gross national product of Japan.)

Source: Robert L. Heilbroner, *The Economic Problem, Newsletter*, © 1970. By permission of Prentice-Hall, Inc., Englewood Cliffs, New Jersey.

Slipping U.S. Share of World Export Markets.[7]   A study by the Bureau of International Commerce of 14 major industrial supplier nations indicated that between 1962 and 1967 exports of manufacturers from these 14 countries, excluding shipments to the United States, rose from $56 billion in 1962 to $90 billion in 1967, a gain of 60 percent. At the same time, U.S. sales of these export products, which were valued at $20.8 billion in 1967, expanded by about 25 percent. In other words, U.S. exports rose at an average annual rate of 8.7 percent, while those of all 14 supplier countries expanded at a rate of 9.9 percent per year. As a result, the U.S. share dropped from 24.4 percent in 1962 to 23.1 percent in 1967.

During this period, the U.S. share of developed markets was unchanged. The U.S. accounted for about 22 percent of all exports to developed countries in 1962, and in 1967 the percentage remained the same. However, as the first part of Exhibit 2–2 shows, even among the developed countries our progress was spotty and especially poor in EEC countries.

While exports held up among the developed countries as a group, the U.S. share of markets in developing countries slipped from 31 percent in 1962 to 29.5 percent in 1967. The second part of Exhibit 2–2 shows our greatest loss in share of market occurred in South and East Asia and the Near East.

What had happened to challenge the supremacy of American industry? Competition—from the EEC countries, Japan, and Great Britain. As one authority notes, "the American challenge is being challenged,"[8] in the EEC and other markets as well.

To most U.S. Businessmen, our world industrial leadership has been a fact of life for longer than most of us care to remember. A comforting assumption underlying much of our thinking and industrial policy making since the days of the Model T has been that U.S. industry could make, distribute, and sell more or almost anything better and more cheaply than anybody else could. For most of the past five decades this has been true . . . but . . . times have changed. In recent years significant sectors of U.S. industry have begun to feel growing competitive pressure from the rest of the world's new productive capabilities.[9]

In short, "economic power and potential have become more evenly distributed among the industrialized countries." The net result is that the United States is losing some of its former competitive edge, especially in price and technology. In fact, in comparison with Japan and Western Europe, U.S. export prices have risen steadily since 1963, placing the U.S. at a competitive disadvantage.

---

[7] This section depends heavily upon a nine-part series of *International Commerce* beginning with "Recent U.S. Trade Record: Sales Rise, but Share Slips," May 5, 1969, pp. 5–10, and concluding with "U.S. Lead in Manufacturers Trimmed by Competitors," July 7, 1969, pp. 8–10.

[8] John B. Rhodes, "The American Challenge Challenged," *Harvard Business Review*, September–October 1969, pp. 45–57.

[9] Ibid., p. 46. Reprinted with permission.

EXHIBIT 2-2

Manufactured Exports
($ in millions)

Destination	World Exports			U.S. Exports			U.S. Share		
	1962	*1967*	*Increase from '62 to '67*	*1962*	*1967*	*Increase from '62 to '67*	*1962*	*1967*	*Index (1962 = 100)*
U.S. share of manufactured exports gains in some developed areas:									
Developed areas, total...	$37,358	$62,982	69%	$8,180	$13,829	69%	21.9%	22.0%	100
Canada...................	3,817	7,237	90	2,903	5,836	101	76.1	80.6	106
EEC....................	16,127	27,079	68	2,452	3,220	31	15.2	11.9	78
Other Western Europe....	13,434	21,969	64	1,569	2,638	68	11.6	12.0	103
Japan...................	1,134	1,954	72	671	997	49	59.2	51.0	86
Australia/New Zealand/ South Africa...........	$ 2,847	$ 4,743	67%	$ 584	$ 1,138	95%	20.5%	24.0%	117
World and U.S. manufactured exports to developing markets:									
Developing areas, total......	$15,954	$21,676	36%	$4,952	$6,401	29%	31.0%	29.5%	95
19 American Republics......	5,274	6,396	21	2,589	3,198	24	49.1	50.0	102
Other Western Hemis- phere.................	695	1,026	48	224	423	89	32.2	41.2	128
South and East Asia........	4,990	7,353	47	1,378	1,748	27	27.6	23.8	86
Near East...............	1,765	2,812	59	402	578	44	22.8	20.6	90
Africa..................	$ 3,230	$ 4,089	27%	$ 360	$ 453	26%	11.1%	11.1%	100

NOTE: World exports are defined as those of Austria, Belgium-Luxembourg, Canada, Denmark, France, Federal Republic of Germany, Italy, Japan, Netherlands, Norway, Sweden, Switzerland, United Kingdom, and United States.
"Manufactured" exports cover chemicals, machinery, transport equipment, and other manufactures (principally metals, textiles, and various nondurable consumer goods) and exclude processed food, fats and oils, mineral fuel products, firearms of war, and ammunition.
SOURCE: *International Commerce*, May 9, 1969, p. 10.

BOX 2-2

Skimming the Cream

Much of U.S. business overseas developed as export business, which is never in debt: products are shipped from stateside plants and distributed to strangers with not much capital involved, and not much money invested in research or advertising. "In major markets today, you don't go far in terms of export. . . . And once you have a plant overseas, you have to go in and do a real job. A U.S. company that runs around skimming the cream off markets abroad will find his competitors going after the milk, and pretty soon the cream will be gone, too. It can't float on nothing."

Source: "How Not to Make a Killing in Europe," *Sales Management*, February 1, 1969, p. 30.

Price indices show that since 1963 American export tags have climbed 12% during the same period comparable quotes on Western European exports have risen only 3%. On Japanese goods, current exports prices remain virtually unchanged.[10]

At the same time, European and Japanese companies, which have traditionally lagged behind in engineering, manufacturing, marketing and finance expertise, are rapidly catching up. In some areas, such as steel, television, and small commercial aircraft, there is a question as to whether the United States maintains any technological lead at all.[11] Further, the Japanese have shown some interesting insights into finance and marketing,[12] which raises some question about the supremacy of the United States in these fields as well.

For the decade of the seventies and beyond, U.S. foreign businessmen will have their mettle tested on several fronts: *total competition* from German, Japanese, British, and other firms of revitalized economies; *political and economic concern* of developed and underdeveloped countries over foreign investment and trade which will be manifest in tighter restrictions; and *technology*, no longer the private domain of U.S. business. To meet these and other obstacles and be successful, perhaps even to survive, it will be necessary to make major adjustments in what may now be regarded as normal international corporate practices and behavior. Adjustments will have to be made in organizational structure to provide the control and flexibility necessary to meet new challenges. To be competitive there will be a need for greater investments in commitments to total marketing, along with a need to change attitudes vis-à-vis foreign partnerships and to heed the political and economic demands of hosts—in short, foreign investment must become multinational in orientation as well as in name.

[10] "Rising Prices: Blunting the Competitive Edge of U.S. Exports in World Markets," *Business Abroad*, November 1968, p. 12.

[11] "Why the U.S. Must Sell More Overseas," *Business Week*, January 4, 1969, pp. 40–52.

[12] For a revealing look at Japanese expertise on many fronts, see James C. Abegglen, "The Economic Growth of Japan," *Scientific American*, March 1970, pp. 31–37.

BOX 2–3

Global Business

[T]he day has passed when a major U.S. corporation can conduct business on a global scale merely with an international export department or division. Increasingly, world business operations are involving the total corporation. Increasingly, in the field of personnel, we are moving away from the international specialist and toward the realization that our capital, upward-striving businessman must have knowledge and understanding of world markets if he is to be really effective in his job.

Source: James H. Goss, General Electric Company, "Doing Business Abroad: 1965," April 29, 1965, from an address before the 1965 annual meeting of American Collegiate Schools of Business.

CONCLUSIONS

The trading of goods and services between nations is a phenomenon which has endured for thousands of years. The factors that have assumed importance in the historical development of trade patterns have varied widely from the beginning of recorded history to the present. The advent of wars, alliances, and technological improvements have constantly altered the differential advantages of the trading nations.

The attitudes of the nations toward world trade have historically vacillated between protectionism and liberalism. In the United States an examination of historical tariff policy illustrates swings from protectionism to liberalism. Typically, waves of protectionism have taken hold around the world during periods of world economic recession; similarly, liberalism tends to be more prevalent during periods of worldwide economic progress.

Rapidly changing factors will doubtless continue to shape the scope and direction of future patterns of world trade. The development of the common market concept will expand to many areas around the world and significant new trading blocks will develop. As a rapidly improving technology and communications systems further shrink the world and accelerate the level of technological diffusion, the nations of the world will become more economically interdependent. The general progress and problems of the developing countries will continue to modify old trading patterns as new markets open and new sources of competition emerge. If U.S. foreign business is to continue to grow as it has through the decade of the sixties, it must meet the challenges of the future with ingenuity.

READINGS

THE UNITED STATES IN WORLD TRADE*

JOHN HEIN

Two years ago a Conference Board study of the competitive position of the United States in world markets stated:

---

* SOURCE: *The Conference Board Record,* July, 1970, pp. 35–40. Reprinted with permission.

Competitiveness . . . will show up in the range of goods exported, in the movement of relative market shares, in relative costs and prices, and in relative delivery terms. It is also reflected in other, less tangible factors—such as servicing facilities, the effectiveness of sales efforts, technological leadership, and even style and workmanship.[1]

The study then proceeded to examine some of these manifold aspects of U.S. international competitiveness during 1955–67. While it did not arrive at any hard-and-fast conclusion, it found—not unexpectedly—that the United States had indeed lost some ground in world trade during the period under review.

In the intervening two years, the U.S. trade surplus has slumped further, and in a recent appraisal of U.S. trade through 1973 the Commerce Department sees "a probable long-term downward trend toward small surpluses or deficits."[2] It seems appropriate, therefore, to take a fresh look at some aspects of the U.S. international competitive position.

The U.S. Share in World Exports

Over the past ten years United States exports have recorded large absolute increases, almost doubling between 1960 and 1969. Yet over this same period total world exports have grown even faster—by 116% —so that the U.S. share has declined steadily (Exhibit 1). This decline, from 17.5% in 1960 to 15.4% last year, may not appear spectacular. Given the absolute magnitudes involved, however, even small changes in the relative share represent fairly large absolute amounts. Thus, a difference of only one percentage point in our 1969 share of world exports represents as much as $2.4 billion in actual exports.

EXHIBIT 1

World Exports and U.S. Exports
(billions of dollars)

Year	World	U.S.	U.S. as Percent of World
1960	112.2	19.6	17.5
1961	117.8	20.2	17.1
1962	123.9	21.0	16.9
1963	135.1	22.5	16.7
1964	151.8	25.8	17.0
1965	164.6	26.8	16.3
1966	180.4	29.5	16.4
1967	190.0	31.0	16.3
1968	212.3	34.1	16.1
1969	242.3	37.3	15.4

NOTE: Data are adjusted to exclude U.S. military-aid exports.
SOURCE: International Monetary Fund, *International Financial Statistics.*

[1] *The Competitive Position of United States Exports,* Studies in Business Economics, No. 101, National Industrial Conference Board, 1968, p. 5.
[2] U.S. Department of Commerce, *U.S. Foreign Trade—A Five-Year Outlook with Recommendations for Action,* Washington, 1969, p. 8. *Cf.* also the projections for U.S. exports and imports in 1975 and 1980 in *Economic Growth in the Seventies,* Special Report, National Industrial Conference Board, 1970, Ch. VI.

Behind this aggregate measure lies a wide range of diverse factors, of course—primarily the commodity composition of exports and the major geographic markets that absorb them. For instance, world trade in agricultural products (which still account for a relatively large share of total U.S. exports) has grown relatively slowly. The decline in the U.S. share of overall world trade therefore reflects in part the relatively greater weight of agricultural exports in our exports compared to other major countries.

For manufactured goods—which today account for over half of total world exports and for about two-thirds of U.S. export trade—the picture is even more clear-cut. The data suggest that over the 1960's as a whole the United States has lost considerable ground in terms of this country's share in the world market for manufactures (Exhibit 2). The figures also reveal that the rate of overall decline—from 24.1% in 1960 to 19.9% last year—was most pronounced in 1961, 1963, and 1965, but

EXHIBIT 2

Exports of Manufacturers by Leading Industrial Countries
(billions of dollars)

Year	Eleven Major Countries*	U.S.	U.S. as Per- cent of Total
1960	54.02	13.00	24.1
1961	56.54	12.87	22.8
1962	60.34	13.88	23.0
1963	65.21	14.47	22.2
1964	74.34	16.64	22.4
1965	83.27	17.26	20.7
1966	93.12	19.12	20.5
1967	99.76	20.77	20.8
1968	114.81	23.65	20.6
1969	134.26	26.78	19.9

* Belgium-Luxembourg, Canada, France, Germany, Italy, Japan, Netherlands, Sweden, Switzerland, United Kingdom, and United States.
SOURCE: United Nations, *Monthly Bulletin of Statistics.*

has been somewhat more moderate since then. In some years—such as 1962, 1964, and 1967—the United States even registered slight gains in its share.

It is of course important to realize that the level of, and changes in, U.S. imports—which are other countries' exports—do affect our share of the world total. Within a given world total of exports, for instance, a rise in our imports—such as has taken place in every one of the past eight years—does show up as a decline in our own export share. A more accurate measure of the U.S. position would therefore be our share of world exports of manufactures to markets other than the United States. Such an analysis, undertaken periodically by the Department of Commerce, shows that, while the U.S. share has fallen sharply from around

25% in 1960, it has remained fairly constant within the 22–23% range since 1965.[3]

One possible explanation for the decline in this country's share in world exports of manufactured goods may lie in a major change in the commodity composition of international trade. If, for example, international preferences had shifted away from those goods in which the United States originally had held a strong position and if the United States had, moreover, been unable to shift its exports sufficiently into the most rapidly growing categories, the decline in the United States' share could be more easily understood.

In order to evaluate this aspect of competitiveness, the actual 1968 share of U.S. exports of the four major groups of manufactured goods shown in international trade statistics[4] was compared with the relative share the United States *would* have had in that year, if the distribution of these four categories among total world exports of manufactures had been the same as in 1960. According to this test, the United States would have had a 19.7% ($22.62 billion) share of such trade in 1968, against the 20.6% ($23.65 billion) actually recorded.[5] Since the actual 1968 share was above the hypothetical share by about $1 billion, the United States has evidently been exporting more of those products that have become important in world trade, and it can be said that the composition of U.S. exports of manufactures has shifted slightly in favor of the United States. (If the actual U.S. share had been lower than the hypothetical one, one might assume that the U.S. was concentrating on the less dynamic sectors.)

It is particularly noteworthy that the United States has succeeded in raising substantially its exports of machinery and transport equipment —the category that has shown the greatest relative growth, on a world-wide basis, among the four major groups of manufactures. Between 1960 and 1968, the share of machinery and transport equipment in total world exports of manufactures increased from over 42% to more than 47%. At the same time, this group's importance in U.S. exports of manufactures rose from over 54% to just over 61%. But since the U.S. growth rate in this particular category lagged behind the worldwide increase, the U.S. share in the machinery and transport equipment exports of the 11 countries as a whole declined from more than 30% to about 27% over the same ten-year period.

These figures would seem to indicate that, as mentioned, the United States has been able to shift its export "mix" in the direction of those lines that have been growing rapidly, but that this shift has not been sufficient to ensure a rate of export growth corresponding to that of each

---

[3] See, *e.g., International Commerce*, June 8, 1970, p. 8. The Commerce survey covers three more countries—Austria, Denmark, and Norway—than those included in Exhibit 2, thus imparting a further downward bias to the U.S. share.

[4] Chemicals, manufactures classified by basic material input (*e.g.*, leather or wood), machinery and transport equipment, and miscellaneous manufactured articles. (Data for 1969 were not available at the time of writing.)

[5] For a description of this test, see *The Competitive Position of United States Exports, op. cit.*, p. 10, or "The United States Share in World Trade," *The Record*, August 1968, p. 28.

category as a whole. This shortfall is particularly evident for consumer goods, the major contributor to the expansion in other industrial countries' exports. Yet for the United States the share of consumer goods in nonagricultural exports has remained virtually unchanged at around 12% since 1960.

Another major factor affecting a country's share of world trade is the geographical distribution of its exports. Even if a country's export share in a given market remains unchanged, the country may register a gain or loss in its total trade, depending on the changes that have occurred in the relative importance of various markets in overall world trade.

The test applied previously to the commodity composition of U.S. exports of manufactures may also be used to determine whether U.S. export trade has been able to take advantage of differential rates of economic growth in the various areas of the world. A hypothetical share of U.S. exports in total world exports (to markets other than the United States) in 1969 was computed on the basis of the geographic distribution of such world exports in 1960 and then was compared with the actual result for 1969.[6] This test produced a hypothetical share of 15.5% for the United States in 1968 as compared with the 15.8% actually recorded for that year.[7] The difference—which amounts to about $710 million in absolute terms—might be interpreted as a reorientation (albeit a fairly small one) of U.S. exports toward those areas that have shown a relatively faster growth in imports.

The Role of Foreign Demand

The expansion of a country's imports obviously is closely related to the growth of its own economy, specifically its national income, and it is easy to see that, in different countries, different rates of growth in incomes will lead to different rates of import growth. Thus, the trend of a country's trade balance over time will depend to a large extent on the combined effects of its so-called income elasticity of demand for imports and of the income elasticity of demand of the rest of the world for that country's exports.

As a recent study has suggested, identical percentage rises in the gross national products of the United States and of other countries do not lead to equal relative increases in U.S. imports from those countries and in their imports from the United States.[8] Thus, a similar percentage increase in GNP in both the United States and the rest of the world would tend to raise U.S. imports proportionately more than it would boost total world imports from the United States.

Specifically, using trade data for 1951–66 the authors found that a

---

[6] This test is described in *Competitive Position*, p. 13, and *The Record*, August 1968, p. 29.

[7] This percentage differs slightly from that shown in Exhibit 1, since the computations on a geographical basis are based on a different set of statistics, which, moreover, do not exclude military-aid shipments.

[8] H. S. Houthakker and S. P. Magee, "Income and Price Elasticities in World Trade," *The Review of Economics and Statistics*, May 1969, pp. 111–25.

1% rise in total world GNP outside the United States would result in a 0.99% rise in world demand for U.S. exports, but that a similar increase in U.S. GNP would produce a 1.51% increase in our imports from the rest of the world. Even more striking is a comparison between the United States and 14 other major industrial countries. In this case, a 1% rise in the combined GNP of these countries tends to lead to a 1.73% increase in their imports from the United States, while a 1% rise in U.S. GNP produces a 2.23% increase in our imports from them.[9]

From these observations the authors conclude that U.S. demand is more income-elastic for the products of the developed countries alone than for the products of the world as a whole. But even more important for the U.S. position in world trade is their conclusion that, given these disparities in income elasticities of demand for imports, "the United States trade balance tends (*ceteris paribus*) to worsen over time" unless foreign countries, particularly Japan and the United Kingdom, "maintain much higher rates of growth and inflation than the United States." In other words, if the U.S. trade balance with these 14 countries as a group were not to deteriorate further, the rate of growth in these countries' combined GNP would have to exceed the U.S. growth rate by almost 30%.

On the basis of further analysis of the data for individual countries and commodity groups, the authors also find that "the share of industrial countries in United States imports and exports is likely to increase over time" and that the United States has an exceptionally high income elasticity of demand for imports of finished manufactures and hence is gradually becoming a net importer of such goods.

Prices and Costs

Most aspects of a country's international competitive position, such as market shares or the pattern of foreign demand for its exports, can ultimately be traced back to differences in price levels. In this connection it is often asserted that the United States has been "pricing itself out of world markets." Such a statement carries the implication that the growth of U.S. exports will be slowed (and that of imports speeded up) if the prices of U.S. goods tend to rise relative to those of similar goods of foreign origin.

The simplest—although, as explained below, not the most satisfactory —way of examining this proposition is to compare the price movements of internationally traded goods here and abroad. As Exhibit 3 shows, the average price (unit value) of U.S. exports of manufactures has indeed risen by much more over the past ten years than comparable prices in other major industrial countries.

There are, however, a number of reservations that attach to such a comparison, and any conclusion based on the relative movements of such standard indexes can only be considered tentative. For one thing,

---

[9] Similar relationships, based on data for the United States and ten other industrial countries for 1957–68, have also been derived by the Bank of Italy, which has published these findings in its *Bolletino* for January–February 1970.

EXHIBIT 3

Unit Value of Exports of Manufactures

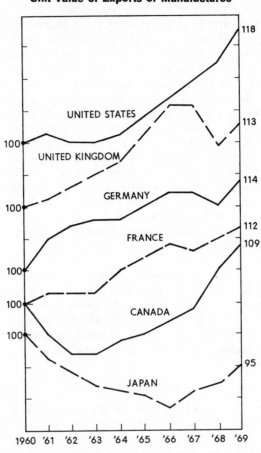

Index, 1960 = 100.
NOTES: Spaces between ticks equal 5 points of the Index.
        1969 data partly estimated.
SOURCE: United Nations.

the available export price data are values per unit of quantity within detailed export (or import) classifications. This means that the individual series of which the indexes are composed do not represent price quotations for identical commodities in successive periods, but the unit values of broader product classes. Therefore, the commodity composition of the goods comprising each class may change, as may the specification of a particular commodity; in an extreme case, a change in reported unit value may not represent a change in price at all.

Secondly, the choice of a base year greatly affects the picture of price competitiveness among different countries. Thus, although the United States has lost ground over the 1960's as a whole, export prices rose more rapidly in Canada than in the United States between 1965 and 1969. At the same time, Japan's export prices rose between 1966 and 1969, although they still were lower at the end of the decade than at the beginning.

Thirdly, even if export prices reflected actual price movements more accurately, they would still fall short of measuring international price competitiveness. This is so because the weights used in computing the indexes differ among countries, owing largely to the differing composition of exports as a whole. It is therefore impossible to conclude whether diverging price movements between two countries reflect true price differences or differences in weighting, with prices unchanged.

Finally, and perhaps most important, export price data refer only to the prices of goods that actually enter into international trade and therefore do not account for goods that a country is not exporting at all or that may have disappeared from its export lists because of severe foreign competition. Yet, the prices of domestically produced goods that are not exported may have a marked effect on competitiveness. A fall in their prices, for instance, might make them exportable or might enable them to replace foreign goods previously imported.

In view of these and related difficulties a wholesale price index is frequently used as a more meaningful barometer of how a country has fared in the area of international price competitiveness. Taking the wholesale price of manufactures as most representative of internationally traded goods, the United States performance compares quite favorably with that of other countries (Exhibit 4). Even the sharp rise in the U.S. wholesale price index since 1965 was generally matched elsewhere.

However, wholesale prices do not furnish a fully reliable key to the competitive position of different countries either. For instance, the manufacturing sector as defined by the Standard International Trade Classification (SITC), on which data for exports and export unit values are based, differs considerably from that defined under the International Standard Industrial Classification, from which wholesale price indexes are derived. Another difficulty with the use of wholesale prices in measuring export price competitiveness arises from the inclusion of prices of imported commodities. To the extent that the latter re-enter international trade, either as components or as re-exports, such inclusion is appropriate. But to the extent that they enter into domestic use, their inclusion tends to make wholesale prices less useful as indicators of external price competitiveness, particularly for countries where imports account for a large part of total domestic expenditures.

Despite these shortcomings of the traditional indicators, price inflation in the United States has generally been marked as the villain behind our unsatisfactory export performance of the past few years. However, one author recently has argued that the greater average price increase for U.S. exports might "merely be a reward for rapid improvement in the nonprice features (*e.g.*, technological content)" of many U.S. exports and that the rise in the export price index might "reflect an ability of U.S. producers to obtain a greater profit margin because of

EXHIBIT 4

Wholesale Prices of Manufactures

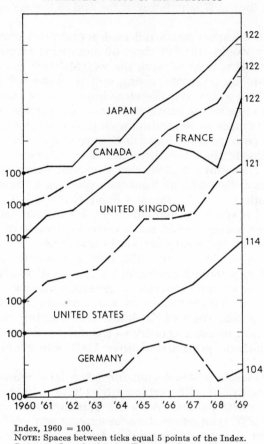

122

122

122

JAPAN

FRANCE

CANADA

121

100

100

UNITED KINGDOM

100

114

100

UNITED STATES

100

GERMANY

104

100
1960 '61   '62   '63   '64   '65   '66   '67   '68   '69

Index, 1960 = 100.
NOTE: Spaces between ticks equal 5 points of the Index.
SOURCES: Organisation for Economic Cooperation and
         Development; United Nations

superiority of products."[10] But, as he also points out, there can be little
doubt that the much sharper rise in unit labor costs in manufacturing
in the United States than abroad since the mid-1960's has affected export prices unfavorably (Exhibit 5).

U.S. Competitiveness and International Payments

The foregoing review has singled out merely three aspects of U.S.
international competitiveness, and by no means exhausts the broad
range of factors that could be considered in this context. Much could
be said, for instance, about the various forces making for a persistently
strong growth in U.S. imports, regardless of the degree of domestic in-

[10] D. L. Grove, "World Markets: The U.S. Position is Disturbing," *Columbia
Journal of World Business*, May–June 1969, p. 22.

EXHIBIT 5

Unit Labor Costs in Manufacturing

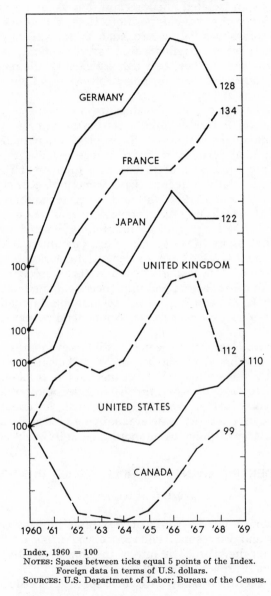

Index, 1960 = 100
NOTES: Spaces between ticks equal 5 points of the Index.
      Foreign data in terms of U.S. dollars.
SOURCES: U.S. Department of Labor; Bureau of the Census.

flation; on nontariff barriers and similar restraints abroad that tend to place U.S. goods at a disadvantage; on the role of technological innovation and structural changes abroad; and on what the Commerce Department has called "the broader production options of multinational corporations," *i.e.*, the choice of supplying foreign markets from offshore sources rather than through exports from the United States.

Beyond these and similar considerations, the U.S. trade balance and this country's international competitive position have to be seen and evaluated not as an isolated phenomenon, but as an important part of our overall balance-of-payments position. Here, a new set of questions and problems comes into the picture, such as the various links between the trade account, other current-account (service) items, and the capital account. Going even further, one can establish a distinct connection between our competitive position and the working of the international payments mechanism.

Whenever a foreign country devalues its currency—an option that is virtually closed to the dollar, due to its position at the center of the international monetary system—U.S. exports automatically lose some of their competitive edge, in terms of prices, relative to those of the devaluing country. If that process occurs a number of times, there is bound to be a cumulative effect to the detriment of U.S. goods in world markets. Since the end of 1948, the number of devaluations abroad has totaled almost 100, including the currencies of most of our major trading partners, and the average rate of devaluation (weighted by the devaluing countries' share in world trade) has amounted to almost 23%.[11] Therefore, there must have been a substantial deterioration in the competitive position of U.S. exports through these foreign devaluations alone, even if all other factors and influences remained unchanged. (By contrast, there have been only three revaluations abroad during this same period, which, *ceteris paribus*, would tend to have the opposite effect.)[12]

Thus, when an element of greater flexibility eventually is introduced into the world's exchange-rate structure,[13] it will clearly be in the United States' interest to ensure that whatever mechanism is adopted will allow exchange rates to move up when this is indicated and not just provide a one-way street for further devaluations against the dollar. Otherwise, the U.S. competitive position will gradually be eroded further and U.S. goods (and services) will be losing more ground in world markets.

GEOCENTRIC GIANTS TO RULE WORLD BUSINESS*

HOWARD PERLMUTTER

We are moving toward a world of very large multinational firms on the one hand and very small entrepreneurial firms of the "one-man show" variety on the other. The fate of the middle-sized firm is less secure. Where small firms can use all the advantages of their smallness to wage effective guerilla warfare with their speed of decision-making and

---

[11] *Cf.* M. D. de Vries, "The Magnitudes of Exchange Devaluation," *Finance and Development,* June 1968, pp. 8–12.

[12] At the time of writing, it was uncertain what would be the new parity of the Canadian dollar, which was allowed to float as of June 1.

[13] *Cf.* "Towards More Flexible Exchange Rates?" *The Record,* September 1969.

o customer needs, middle-sized firms are still too large for
and yet too small to get the human and financial resources
geographical and product scope to function as worldwide en-
stand as targets for takeovers by large firms who promise
ay to worldwide markets.

...ng to *Fortune*, there are already more than 100 U.S. firms
more than $600-million worth of sales who have overseas inter-
There are at least 70 non-U.S. firms doing a similar volume of busi-
... But when we consider the firms of the future—of 1985—it is clear
must talk about giants or supergiants. Many executives I know are
nning to double sales every seven years. By 1985 their firms will have
bled several times. This means that many *Fortune* firms by that time
be doing from $5- to $160-billion worth of sales, the latter being
ral Motors' sales of 1985!

considering that the number of employees does not grow at the
same rate, the million-man firm should not be unusual. To carry out
their current worldwide operations, General Motors already employs
740,000; Ford, 388,000; General Electric, 350,000; Unilever, 300,000;
Siemens, 257,000; Philips, 244,000; ITT, 204,000; and Royal Dutch
Shell, 174,000. Clearly, the firms of 1985 will be supergiants in size and
power.

Accounting for unforeseen technological breakthroughs and managerial attrition, I come out with the round number of 300 of these
giants in 1985. There may be 200 or 400—but I maintain they will be
distinctive because their size will place them in a separate class with
unique opportunities and problems.

*There are good reasons, both positive and negative, why such firms
will emerge.* Size is self-perpetuating—supergiants can obtain capital
more easily, and they can risk larger losses without damage. Even today,
General Electric has purportedly invested $200-million in its as yet
unprofitable venture with Machines Bull, but GE still reports profits as a
business totality. Giants will also be able to outpace the rest in research
in such advanced areas as energy, food and space technology, data
processing, aircraft, and electronics. IBM, for example, has reputedly
sunk in the neighborhood of $5-billion over four years into developing
the hardware for its 360-series computers. This takes size. Finally,
supergiants can offer medium-sized firms worldwide marketing facilities
and can afford to lure all the best people away from lesser firms.

On the negative side we may note there is nothing substantial *preventing* the formation of supergiant firms. The most likely candidate to
act as a countervailing force against the supergiants is the sovereign
state. Consumers are at best unorganized, and trade unions, I am assured by union leaders, have enough difficulty at the national level
managing and representing their constituents. On the other hand, the
weapons a sovereign state can muster seem formidable: outright nationalization, restriction of the importation of machinery and parts,
price controls, limitation of remittances to foreign parent companies,
legal guidance for labor policy, demands on the firm to export and to
conduct research within its borders.

But I submit that any given nation-state, acting alone, has limited bargaining power. When what is called the "investment climate" is considered unattractive by many firms, due to repeated threats from government, it is always possible to suggest diplomatically that other countries would seem to be better places to invest. This has had a sobering effect on the more extremist national political leaders. Nations are, after all, competing with other nations to attract human and material resources that meet worldwide standards. Even so, the supergiants which survive in 1985 will be those that will have found a partnership rather than a collision course with a large number of, if not most, host sovereign states.

Who will survive until 1985? The answer naturally preoccupies chief executives—will Royal Dutch Shell be around, will General Motors, or will Unilever?

It is very likely that the very largest of firms—like these three—will be among those who survive, though their names may be different. What of lesser corporations?

Very likely, all 1985 giants will have North American, eastern and western European, and Asiatic divisions. The North American division may have grown from U.S. firms which have been merged with non-U.S. firms to become more multinational. The western European division may include companies which were once French, Swiss, German, or British historically but which were acquired or taken over. In other words, I believe the supergiant firm will be built from different national origins which have been internationalized to the world scale.

What are the key restraining forces, inside and outside large firms, which could prevent their survival, growth, and development as world companies? One problem cited by senior executives of firms on the 300 list was the tendency for home-country interests—as, for instance, when U.S.-owned firms are asked that investment overseas be limited for U.S. balance of payments reasons. Top executives find that home-country executives frequently fail to understand the nature and dynamism of the multinational firm, and they predict trouble ahead in this area for U.S.-based firms.

The other side of this problem is that host-country political leaders also see the U.S.-based multinational firm as attuned to U.S. political and economic interests. There may be some truth in this; many executives see Europe-based multinational firms as more astute in dealing with political demands (Swiss and Anglo-Dutch firms are willing to fly the local flag where necessary or the Swiss, British, or Dutch flag where necessary).

Internally, executives most frequently bring up problems of inflexible viewpoints and national suspicions. Senior executives from both Europe- and U.S.-based firms mention resistance to letting foreigners into the power structure at headquarters, in key positions, or on the parent board. Kenneth Simmonds reported in a recent study on multinational firms that in 150 of the largest U.S. companies, only 1% of the senior executives at headquarters are non-Americans, even though the income generated overseas is about 20% of the total. There are historical reasons for this, to be sure—success in a large home market, deriving a large portion of profits in the home country, a large domestic supply of trained professional managers who know company policy and are trusted and understood more easily than "foreigners." By way of contrast, companies like Philips and Nestlé do about 90% of their business overseas, while the average of a U.S.-based international firm is about 20–30%.

This kind of ethnocentrism has its risks over the long term, however; it drives out good foreigners, raises local resistance to all ideas from headquarters, and stems the flow of information to headquarters, leading to poor planning and mistakes.

If top management seems more comfortable investing at home or seems to prefer working with home-country nationals only, or if the company's products are designed for home markets only, and resources are not assigned to adapt production to world markets, then there are strong doubts that the firm really seeks a world niche and will be around in 1985.

Ethnocentrism can be just as unfortunate a problem when it arises on the local affiliate level, too, when we can call it "polycentrism." Many country managers—particularly those in marketing—claim that "everything is different in our country." This attitude holds intrafirm communication to a minimum and generates much duplicated effort. The result of strong ethnocentric attitudes in subsidiaries is local growth at the expense of company growth. A well-organized competitor can usually beat such a firm in the worldwide marketplace. Ethnocentric and polycentric firms are unlikely to survive until 1985.

I also inquired of senior executives what, in their opinion, are the key factors driving firms forward to grow into the giants of 1985. The deciding points are human. They revolve around top management's desire to utilize human resources optimally and not let national biases waste good ideas, products, and men. The growth firm will be that which seeks to be genuinely international and builds toward this end. Such firms will plan for risk diversification through worldwide production and distribution systems and will build a worldwide information system manned by high-quality people who know local markets but are international in outlook.

What will be around in 1985 is what I call a "geocentric" firm—one with a worldwide orientation. While in our nationalistic world subsidiary ethnocentrism may have some merit, in allowing country-level management to identify more easily with local interests and ease fears about large international firms, more experienced firms find ethnocentrism too costly. An oft-repeated remark by a former chairman of the board of Unilever puts the geocentric case well: "The main problem is to Unileverize our Indian management and Indianize our Unilever management."

Many executives mistakenly equate polycentrism with geocentrism. This is evidenced in the legalistic definition of a multinational enterprise as a cluster of corporations of diverse nationality joined together by ties of common ownership. It is no accident that many senior executives in headquarters take pride in the absence of nonnationals in their subsidiaries, especially people from the head office. The implication is clearly that each subsidiary is a distinct national entity, since it is incorporated in a different sovereign state. Headquarters takes pride in the fact that few outsiders know that the firm is foreign-owned.

But the polycentric personnel policy also means that no local manager can seriously aspire to a senior position at headquarters, and lonely senior executives in the subsidiaries of polycentric companies complain that "the home office never tells us anything."

The ultimate goal of geocentrism is a worldwide approach in both headquarters and subsidiaries. The firm's subsidiaries are thus neither satellites nor independent city-states, but parts of a whole whose focus is on worldwide objectives as well as local objectives, each part making its unique contribution with its unique competence. Geocentrism is expressed by function, product, and geography. The question asked in headquarters and the subsidiaries is: "Where in the world shall we raise money, build our plant, conduct R&D, and get and launch new ideas to serve our present and future customers?"

This conception of geocentrism involves a collaborative effort between subsidiaries and headquarters to establish universal standards and permissible local variations and to make key allocational decisions on new products, new plants, new laboratories. The international management team includes the affiliate heads.

The firms which plan for geocentrism and survival in 1985 need to begin now to identify the capacities required and to develop them in the organization. Many firms are already laying out their plans for world product innovation, resource allocation, establishment of pricing levels, and so on, hard as they may be in a world of rapid change.

Fundamentally, planning for future survival involves developing a program with three- to five-year objectives aimed at improving six capacities:

1. The capacity to work with host and home country political leaders.
2. The capacity to acquire and effectively integrate small and medium-sized companies in countries other than one's home base and to energize them to function effectively as a productive part of a worldwide enterprise.
3. The capacity to develop men for international service by systematically designing challenging, attractive, and humanly possible international careers, taking account of the problems of moving men and families at different stages in life.
4. The capacity to commit to worldwide objectives personnel at headquarters, at the regional level, and in the subsidiaries, whether by product or functional responsibilities. This will require some kind of management development institution within the firm.
5. The capacity to stay in direct contact with users of company products and services everywhere in the world, and thus to know in which way each user's needs are distinctive or similar in each market.

6. The capacity to build trust and confidence among managers and experts of different nations inside the firm. It is this last capacity which is the most fundamental and also the most difficult one to achieve.

I see no other route than beginning now to build international companies, not companies based on U.S. or European domination of key positions. This means that the multinational firms of the future should include Japanese international companies as such, not as satellites of a U.S. or European firm, nor as independent affiliates, nor as joint ventures with some holding company of a truly international firm, but as one part of an integrated world partnership.

QUESTIONS

1. Define:
   Disciplina etrusca
   Mercantilism
   Industrial Revolution
   GATT
2. How may a manager of international marketing benefit from a knowledge of the history of world trade?
3. Identify the major factors underlying the historical success of trading centers. Explain the significance of each factor.
4. Trace the history of world trade and identify key dates and their significance.
5. Review the formative influences of the Age of Discovery.
6. Differentiate between the composition of world trade before and after the Industrial Revolution. What additional modern-day differences might also be identified?
7. Set forth and explain the factors characterizing post-World War II trade development.
8. Explain the role of GATT in world trade.
9. Disclose the fallacies of mercantilist thinking.
10. The pattern of distribution of U.S. exports has shifted markedly over its history. What has caused these shifts, and what further shifting might one predict?
11. Select a single product or product group and trace the historical export patterns for this group from any given country. Consider both volume and destination in attempting to explain major changes.
12. "The Industrial Revolution in turn led to a chain of innovations that caused social and economic change unparalleled in history, perhaps until the 20th century." Comment on the international marketing significance of such change.
13. During the decade of the sixties, U.S. direct investment has been challenged by host countries. What is the justification from the host countries' viewpoint?
14. What have been the main causes for the slippage in the U.S. share of world export markets?

Readings

1. According to the article "The United States in World Trade" the U.S. has lost some of its competitive advantage in world trade. Why? What does U.S. business have to do to change the trend?

2. What is a "geocentric firm"?

3. Why won't ethnocentric and polycentric firms survive until 1985?

OUTLINE OF CHAPTER 3

THE WORLD MARKETPLACE
  Market Mechanism
  Enlarging World Markets
  Alternatives to a Market System

INTERNATIONAL TRADE AND ECONOMIC WELL-BEING

THEORY OF RELATIVE ADVANTAGE
  Absolute Cost Advantage
  Comparative Cost Advantage

BALANCE OF PAYMENTS AND EXCHANGE RATES

WORLD MARKET DEVELOPMENT
  Trade and Commercial Treaties
  Multinational Market Agreements
  International Monetary Systems
  Market Development through Economic and Technical Assistance

MARKET PROTECTION
  Government-Imposed Barriers
    Tariffs
    Exchange Barriers
  Nontariff Protection
  Market Barriers

SUMMARY AND CONCLUSIONS

READINGS
  Using the Free Market to Resolve the Balance of Payments Problem, *Financial Analysts Journal.*
  Are Imports Killing Off U.S. Industries? *Business Week.*

CHAPTER 3

INTERNATIONAL TRADE CONCEPTS AND THEORY

No overview of the field of international marketing is complete without at least a review of the basic concepts underlying international trade and some consideration of international economic theory. The basis of all trade is economic and, unless they were purely politically inspired, nearly all of the debates which for centuries have surrounded the topic of international trade have been argued in economic terms. An awareness of the underlying economic theory of international business is a necessary basis for consideration of national policies and is useful to the individual corporation executive in understanding his company's position in the world economy. The fundamental concepts and theory of international economics are essentially simple. The analysis derived from these simple concepts, however, is exceedingly complex; so complex in fact that no economist has been able to develop an analytical model which adequately takes all of the variables into consideration. Instead, as so often is the case in economics, the theory of international economics is couched with myriad assumptions and accounts for only a few of the innumerable, unmeasurable, and sometimes unidentifiable variables. Despite these shortcomings, the theoretical economic constructs concerning international trade have sufficient accuracy and validity that anyone who is engaged in international marketing should have a basic familiarity with them. Jaraslav Vanek, a noted international trade theorist, asserts that "a good deal of misunderstanding and mismanagement on the part of our policy makers stems from this neglect of pure theory."

The brief exposition in this chapter provides a review of the basic ideas for individuals who have already studied this complex subject and will introduce key theoretical concepts to those who have not had a prior exposure.[1]

---

[1] The individual who has not studied international economic theory will be particularly interested in the chapter bibliography at the end of the book. See especially the simple, straightforward explanations in Part One of Walter Krause, *International Economics* (Boston, Mass.: Houghton Mifflin Company, 1963).

This chapter differs rather significantly from the typical treatise on international trade theory. While most books acknowledge that international trade theory is related to a market economy, they do not usually make this the primary focus of attention. In contrast, this chapter emphasizes the marketplace rather than production and makes a direct comparison of the world marketplace and world market economics.

Three main areas of theoretical analysis may be included in a complete work on international economic theory. The first may be called welfare economics. Here one finds discussed the concept of comparative and absolute advantage; the gains which may be achieved by nations, groups, or individuals from international trade, and the underlying basis for these gains. The second area typically has to do with monetary equilibrium and international balance of payments. The third area is closely related to the second, and it analyzes the pricing mechanism through which factor of production prices are established in the international marketplace.

This chapter places special emphasis on the economic advantages to be derived from international trading. The chronic recurrence of debate on monetary equilibrium and balance of payment adjustments requires some consideration of these subjects. However, the review in this chapter is brief because these last areas are related to world marketing only insofar as they affect the availability of money for world trading.

THE WORLD MARKETPLACE

Trading of goods has its roots in the very earliest communal living experiences of man. Primitive man had a barter system, the early Greeks had their agoras, the Romans had their forums, and today we have our shopping centers.[2] All of these are marketplaces. It is not doing injustice to the term "market" to consider the entire world today as a single marketplace. A market is a place where buyers and sellers come together to exchange their goods. Today, through intermediaries, the individual world citizen has access to the goods of the world; in return he exchanges monies which he has received for goods and services which *he* has provided.

Market Mechanism

By purchasing goods and services in the marketplace and by placing his own on the market, the citizen has, in essence, made himself subject to the market mechanism. The relevant market mechanism is that of the market in which he trades, so by trading in the world marketplace, he is partly subject to the world market mechanism. The purpose of this market mechanism is to regulate the flow and character of the goods and services which are placed on the market and to establish a rate of return

---

[2] See Vernon Mund, *Open Markets* (New York: Harper & Brothers, 1948), chaps. 1–4.

or price for those goods and services. Price serves as a primary variable in regulating supply and demand and aiding in resource allocation in a market system. If prices are too low, producers cannot afford to supply the market; if they are too high, consumers will not purchase the products. Prices regulate local, domestic, and worldwide markets, and the free market inhibits the individual who provides unwanted goods or who attempts to price his goods above the market price. Such a producer will find that he has no takers for his product. The worker who attempts to sell an obsolete skill or the manufacturer who cannot produce a product competitively will find that he must adjust his price, or his product, or his service, to meet the needs of the market condition. Manufacturers who but a few years ago were insulated both from international competition and from international markets now find the insulation of distance and time torn away. Open competition for markets, both domestic and international, is a major factor keeping industry "on its toes." One economist suggests that when this basic rule is ignored in an attempt to protect a country's domestic producers, such protection only lessens the industry's future ability to compete.[3]

Theoretically, the market is an automatic, competitive, self-regulating mechanism which provides for the maximum consumer welfare and which best regulates the use of the factors of production. The market metes out its rewards in proportion to the productivity and to the demand for the products or services of the individual, the firm, or the nation. These two factors, market demand and productivity, are the crucial determinants of the standard of living differentials throughout the world. Interestingly, economic theorist Milton Friedman suggests in a reading for this chapter that the free market mechanism itself is the most suitable one for resolving balance of payments problems.

Enlarging World Markets

If artificial barriers do not exist, the geographic size of the market for a good or service is most directly determined by the cost and speed of communications and the cost and speed of transporting individual goods or services. In recent years, each succeeding generation has found that its marketplace has grown larger, until today we live in an era of the world marketplace. Not all goods or all marketplaces participate in worldwide competition, however; for many goods, the cost of transportation is prohibitive and there is not sufficient differential production advantage to overcome these transportation costs. In theory even high-bulk, low-value products may be placed in world competition; if the domestic price of portland cement, for example, is excessively high in one country or locality, the cement can conceivably be profitably shipped into that community. As a matter of fact, cement *is* regularly shipped from North to South America.

The emergent world economy in which we live today not only brings us into a new situation of world competition but brings significant ad-

---

[3] See Lee S. Balliet, *The American Economist,* December 1962.

vantages both to marketer and consumer. The marketer now finds that new markets are open to him. He also discovers that small individual markets have grown and consolidated until they have reached an efficient market size so that he can afford to produce in them or market to them. The consumer has benefited because he now has a wider range of goods from which to choose, and unless there are artificial barriers, such as tariffs, he has the opportunity to select the lowest priced goods which can be produced anywhere in the world.

Rapid growth of both imports and exports of the United States in the two decades ending in 1970, as shown in Exhibit 3–1, indicates in itself

EXHIBIT 3–1

U.S. Exports and Imports, 1950–70

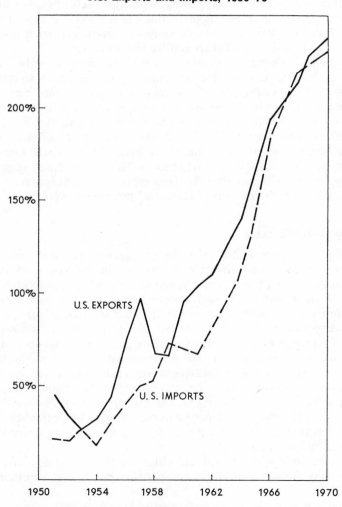

SOURCE: U.S. Department of Commerce.

that trading is beneficial, for no one buys or sells products unless he gains an advantage thereby.

Alternatives to a Market System

There are essentially only two methods of allocating goods and services and establishing prices. In their pure forms one utilizes the market system and the other is guided by central planning. Despite the problems of the market economy, extensive central planning does not appear to provide an acceptable alternative in free countries. It should be mentioned, however, that nearly every nation does engage in some central planning; and various nations distort the world's free market system when they establish tariffs and utilize other methods of trade regulation or restriction. In these instances, political expediency or the judgment of governmental officials is being substituted for the impersonal, efficient selection process of the marketplace. The reasons for such governmental intervention are discussed below.

INTERNATIONAL TRADE AND ECONOMIC WELL-BEING

Gains from international trade are derived from variation in local production advantages; these, in turn, depend on differences in capital availability, specialization of labor, natural resource advantages, and labor or management skill advantages. The benefits of regional specialization on a national basis are so widely accepted that it is surprising that so many people debate the virtue of international regional specialization. No one would seriously question the logic of shipping rice from Louisiana, where water is plentiful, to arid Nebraska, but many individuals who do not understand the operation of the international marketplace would block equally logical transfers of goods from foreign countries. Such action, however, reduces the standard of living by attempting to refute the inherent logic of international trade.

Samuelson cites Bastiat's century-old farcical letter to the French Chamber of Deputies as an example of the ultimate folly of tariffs. The same letter points up the advantages of utilizing the superior production advantage of others.

To the Chamber of Deputies:

We are subjected to the intolerable competition of a foreign rival, who enjoys such superior facilities for the production of light that he can *inundate* our *national market* at reduced price. This rival is no other than the sun. Our petition is to pass a law shutting up all windows, openings and fissures through which the light of the sun is used to penetrate our dwellings, to the prejudice of the profitable manufacture we have been enabled to bestow on the country.

Signed: Candle Stick Makers.

F. Bastiat[4]

---

[4] Paul A. Samuelson, *Economics* (5th ed.; New York: McGraw-Hill Book Company, 1961), p. 738. Samuelson's exposition of the theory of international trade is both brief and lucid. See Chapters 32 and 33.

World trading permits the fullest possible utilization of various regional advantages and, in turn, benefits both individuals and nations. The nation is benefited by using its skills and resources at the highest possible level of productivity. The individual is benefited through his ability to purchase a higher standard of living. Profit for the manager provides the specific motivation for traders, but ultimately price reduction to the consumer is the key force which underlies world trade. Such price reduction is the benefit with which trade theories are primarily concerned. When two nations can produce a greater total amount of goods by specializing than the same two nations can produce individually, then there is a specific increase in productivity and, with free trade, there is an increase in real income for the inhabitants of both nations. Besides the lower price on goods (which constitutes a greater real income if wages are constant), the people benefit through having a broader variety of goods.

Like that of nearly all nations, the U.S. policy on free trade has been one of ups and downs. In recent years the economic benefits of free trade have been acknowledged by national leaders from both parties, despite unrelenting pressures for increased trade protection. At the signing of the Trade Expansion Act of 1962, initiating the so-called Kennedy Round of tariff reductions, President Kennedy acknowledged the gains from international trade:

This act recognizes, fully and completely, that we cannot protect our economy by stagnating behind high tariff walls, but that the best protection possible is a mutual lowering of tariff barriers so that all may benefit from the free flow of goods.

In his last Economic Report to Congress in January 1969, President Johnson asserted:

While we work to reduce trade barriers, we must not drop our guard against the advocates of protectionism at home and abroad. We will never neglect the legitimate concerns of any citizens. But the only real solutions are ones that improve our economy—not ones that erect new barriers that could provoke retaliation, or insulate producers from the invigorating force of world competition.

President Nixon further affirmed our national position shortly after taking office. Responding to a February 7, 1969, press conference question about his campaign promises to seek international agreements restricting trade in some textiles, he said,

I believe that the interest of the United States and the interest of the whole world will best be served by moving toward freer trade rather than toward protectionism. I take a dim view of this tendency to move toward quotas and other methods that may become permanent, whether they are applied here or by other nations abroad.

Whereas lower price and wider variety are the benefits of international trade, the catalyst is said to be profit. The middlemen who are actively engaged in the process of trading are most likely to be in trading for the profit they can secure. From the standpoint of the nation as a

A Projected Overpass

Philadelphia Evening Bulletin

whole, the benefits of export marketing are gaining foreign exchange and maintaining a satisfactory balance of payments position in the world economy. Benefits to the consumer are perhaps best viewed through the eyes of the retailer; the businessman closest to the ultimate customer. Charles Y. Lazarus, a top retail executive and president of the American Retail Federation, states that,

To me, it seems self-evident that the consumer's interest in international trade is best served by policies which:

1. Save him money.
2. Bring him a larger selection of fashions and styles.
3. Satisfy his demands for merchandise not otherwise available from domestic suppliers; and
4. Maintain the competitive impact of imports on domestic prices, product efficiency, innovation, and fashion.

Yet he and his colleagues found in a study of some imported goods that "on some of our most in-demand imports present trade barriers are costing the consumer in sheer dollars and cents as much as 40 percent on price."[5]

Economic theories tend to assume that goods are homogeneous, but in today's marketplace quality, brand, and product differentials offer specific benefits to the consumers. A further benefit of international trade is that it provides a substitute for factor mobility; the goods rather

---

[5] *The Consumers' Stake in World Trade* (Washington, D.C.: American Retail Federation, 1969). From a speech by Charles Y. Lazarus, president, American Retail Federation, March 11, 1969.

than raw materials, laborers, or capital move from country to country or region to region.

THEORY OF RELATIVE ADVANTAGE

Three main theories of international trade have been developed in the past century and a half. They are the classical, opportunity cost, and equilibrium theories.[6] All three theories, however, have at their core the concept of relative advantage. The following sections consider relative advantage from the viewpoints of absolute and comparative advantage. The presentation follows the classical analysis which simplifies the problem by studying only two products and two nations at one time. More countries or products can be accommodated in the classical model, but adding countries or products adds little but confusion for the student. The opportunity and equilibrium models are not here considered. They add refinement, but in so doing add complications which need not concern the nonprofessional economist.

Absolute Cost Advantage

When a good can be produced more cheaply in one country than in another, the first is said to have an absolute cost advantage. The situation in which one country has an absolute advantage over another country provides a basis for easy analysis. Take, for example, the situation of wheat produced in the United States and cork produced in Spain. Both countries can produce each product, but because of climate and old native stands of cork oak, the cork will cost considerably more to produce in the United States than in Spain. Conversely, wheat costs considerably more to produce in Spain than in the United States. Therefore, assuming that the difference in efficiency (and cost) is greater than the cost of transportation, it would be advantageous for the two countries to exchange products.

It is interesting to note, incidentally, the transitory nature of a nation's advantage. Despite the fact that cork oaks do not reach maximum productivity until they are some 50 years old, California cork is now being commercially grown and harvested and has underpriced and supplanted Spanish cork in many applications.

Comparative Cost Advantage

The comparative advantage concept is more difficult to understand than that of absolute advantage. The principle of comparative advan-

---

[6] Early expositions of these theories are:

Classical. David Ricardo, *Principles of Political Economy and Taxation* (London: John Murray, 1817).

Opportunity cost. Gottfried Van Haberler, *Theory of International Trade* (New York: Macmillan Co., 1937).

Equilibrium. Bertil Ohlin, *Inter-regional and International Trade* (Cambridge: Harvard University Press, 1933).

tage applies when one country can produce both goods (assuming a two-product analysis) or all goods more cheaply than another country. International trade can beneficially take place even though one country has an absolute advantage in both or all products; in fact, much world trading is done in products in which there is a comparative rather than an absolute advantage. Each country produces and trades the goods in which it has the relative advantage. The gains come from concentrating productive effort in each country on the products that it can produce best. As the following examples show, the total output will be greater with specialization than without, so there will be more goods to share if there is specialization and trade. The same principle applies both to regions and to nations.

In its simplest form comparative advantage may be related to division of skills and labor. Consider the case of a well-known brain surgeon whose fees approach $100 per hour. The same dexterity and manual skills which make his time so valuable have given him a reputation as an outstanding cabinetmaker; he is probably a better cabinetmaker than the great majority of professionals. Still, although he makes fine cabinets as a hobby, it would be foolish of him to sell any of his time at the cabinetmaker rate of around $8 per hour. One exception: He may profitably engage in both activities if he is unable to sell all of his medical time. The factor of surplus labor is often overlooked in the application of comparative advantage.

Perhaps the concept of comparative advantage will be most easily understood through a series of examples. For the several situations which follow, imagine two rather primitive island societies in which the only goods of value which are traded are clay pots and woven sifters. Assume that maximum productivity is desired because the pots and sifters wear out rapidly or are hoarded as signs of wealth. Assume further that island Abu can produce both products more efficiently than neighboring island Bua. More specifically, the inhabitants of Abu (Abus) have natural advantages which make it possible for one man to produce either *three pots or three sifters per day*. The Buans (inhabitants of Bua) have a productivity rate of *two pots or one sifter per man day*. Each country happens to have 10 men of working age.

Illustration 1 assumes no world trade or specialization and further assumes that productive labor is allocated equally to pots and sifters. Total production is twice as high in Abu as Bua. Total production for

ILLUSTRATION 1

Production per Working Day

	Pots	Sifters	Total
Abu	15	15	30
Bua	10	5	15
Total	25	20	45

the two-island economy is 45 pots and sifters per day. The real income of the Abus is twice as high as that of the Buans.

Illustration 2 assumes that Buans attempt to specialize in their least advantageous product—sifters.

ILLUSTRATION 2

Production per Working Day

	Pots	Sifters	Total
Abu	15	15	30
Bua	0	10	10
Total	15	25	40

Because of this ill-chosen specialization, the total production of the two economies declines. The Buans are even poorer relative to the Abus than in the first illustration and the Abu:Bua standard of living ratio would be 3:1. Trade could take place if Buans wanted pots but did not want to produce them, but the real income of the Buans would still be lower than if they produced both products themselves.

Illustration 3 assumes that Bua specializes in its most advantageous product (pots) and trades with Abu for its sifters. Assume that Abu still divides its production equally between pots and sifters.

ILLUSTRATION 3

Production per Working Day

	Pots	Sifters	Total
Abu	15	15	30
Bua	20	0	20
Total	35	15	50

If there is no positive preference for one product over another, world trade need not result, but trade would be advantageous if inhabitants of Bua desired both products. It is a matter of indifference to Abus whether they make pots or sifters as they make both equally well, so prices (barter ratios, that is) would depend on the relative trading abilities of inhabitants of the two countries. If the Abus will trade on a one-for-one basis, the relative standards of living will be 3:2. Note that production at a level of 50 units per day is available for sharing, whereas it was only 45 per day without trade.

Illustration 4 shows the optimum production mix for both countries if the market *desires equal numbers* of pots and sifters. Obviously, Bua should specialize and will produce only pots. The Buans still cannot supply half of the two societies' pots. Abu will divide its production between the two products. It has the greatest relative advantage (3:1) in sifters so will emphasize sifter production; in fact, $\frac{5}{6}$ of its manpower will be devoted to sifters and $\frac{1}{6}$ to pots.

ILLUSTRATION 4

Production per Working Day

	Pots	Sifters	Total
Abu......................	5	25	30
Bua......................	20	0	20
Total	25	25	50

As in Illustration 3, one cannot determine exactly what will be the final allocation of the pots and sifters. Even in such a primitive society the division of products between the two countries will depend on "marketing" skills. Abu will never have to trade on less than a one-for-one basis, because it can produce at this level itself. At the extremes it may be possible for either country to derive the full benefits from trading: Abu could end up with 35 units of production and Bua with 15. Alternatively, Buans could gain up to 20 units. Probably the two countries would share the five units gained in comparison with the first illustration.

A few other conditions may need to be fulfilled before actual trading would take place.

1. The production gains would have to be greater than the costs of trading and shipping.
2. Products must be identical or equally acceptable in the minds of middlemen and consumers, regardless of national origin.
3. There must be a sufficiently effective market information network so that traders in both countries are aware of cost differentials.
4. The differential must be sufficient to interest an entrepreneur in trading.
5. Tariffs must not exist or must not exceed the difference in costs after transportation and profit are considered.
6. No other governmental or financial restrictions inhibit the products and trading of those products.

In summary, it is important to remember that the economic basis of international trade is no different than that of interregional trade. Goods may be shipped beneficially from one region or one country to another whenever there is a situation of comparative advantage. In other words, commodities or goods will be imported from one place to another if the imported price plus the cost of transportation and any other costs (such as tariffs) are less than the domestic price. However, trading will occur only if the costs differ by an amount which is great enough to make trading worthwhile. The last idea, essentially the element of profit, has often been neglected in the theoretical analyses of economists, but profit must be present and adequate to justify shipment of goods from one geographic location to another.

BALANCE OF PAYMENTS AND EXCHANGE RATES

As long as there are separate nations with separate monetary systems, and as long as there is trade between those nations, there will be controversy surrounding questions of balance of payments and exchange rates. This is true because the resource inequities from country to country that cause differences in standards of living are reflected by changes in payment balances and exchange rates. These devices serve as indicators of the ebb and tide of economic fortune of different nations.

A nation's balance of payments statement records all of the financial transactions between its residents and those of the rest of the world during a given period of time. Because the balance of payments record is maintained on a double-entry bookkeeping system it must always be in balance. As in an individual's own financial statement, the assets and liabilities or the credits and debits must always offset each other. But as in an individual's statement, the fact that they balance does not mean

EXHIBIT 3–2

U.S. Balance of Payments, 1969
(in billions of dollars)

		Balance of Payments Accounts		
	Transactions	*Receipts*	*Payments*	*Balance*
I.	Goods and Services......................	55.5	53.6	+2.0
	1. Merchandise trade (goods)...............	36.5	35.8	+ .7
	2. Services............................	19.0	17.8	+1.2
	a) Military........................	1.5	4.9	−3.4
	b) Investment income..................	8.8	4.5	+4.3
	c) Travel..........................	2.1	3.4	−1.3
	d) Other...........................	6.6	5.0	+1.6
II.	Private capital...........................	4.0	5.4	−1.4
	1. Long term...........................	3.9	4.7	− .8
	a) Direct investment..................	.8	3.1	−2.2
	b) Portfolio investment...............	3.1	1.5	+1.6
	c) Bank and other loans (net)..........	.0	.1	− .1
	2. Short term...........................	.1	.7	− .6
III.	Government.............................	1.3	5.4	−4.1
	1. Loans...............................	1.3	3.4	−2.1
	2. Grants and transfers...................	...	2.0	−2.0
IV.	Other...................................			
	1. Private transfers......................	...	.8	− .8
	2. Errors and omissions....................		2.9	−2.9
	3. Changes in U.S. reserve assets...........	.8	2.0	−1.2
	a) Gold (outflow is receipt)...........	...	1.0	−1.0
	b) Convertible currencies..............	.8	...	+ .8
	c) IMF gold tranche..................	...	1.0	−1.0
	4. Changes in U.S. liquid liabilities..........	9.0	.6	+8.4
	a) Foreign official holders.............	...	.5	− .5
	b) Foreign private holders.............	9.0	...	+9.0
	c) International organizations			
	other than IMF..................	.0	.1	− .1
	Total.......................	70.6	70.6	.0

NOTE: Figures may not add because of rounding.
SOURCE: U.S. balance of payments trends, 1970. *Survey of Current Business.*

BOX 3-1

US Firms Help Payments Balance: Some Figures

US companies continue to make major contributions to the US balance of payments in spite of discouraging government controls on their international activities. It is estimated that in 1968 the income from total US overseas investments reached $8.3 billion, including royalty payments and fees for parent company services. Most of this figure is profits derived from direct foreign investment by US corporations.

General Motors (GM), the world's largest industrial corporation, reports that in 1968 its contribution to the US balance of payments was $676 million, for a total of $12.3 billion since World War II. *Caterpillar Tractor,* much smaller than GM, contributed $583 million in 1968, making a total of $4.7 billion since 1954. Other companies with substantial balance-of-payments surpluses include *Clark Equipment,* $48 million in 1968, for a total of $262 million in the last seven years; *Minnesota Mining & Manufacturing,* more than $100 million in 1968 and $340 million from 1965–68; *Eastman Kodak,* $225 million in 1968, and $1.4 billion since 1963; and *Weyerhaeuser,* $129 million in 1968.

Source: Reprinted from the March 21, 1969 issue of *Business International,* with the permission of the publisher, Business International Corp. (New York).

that a nation is in particularly good or poor financial condition. A balance of payments is a record of condition, not a determinant of condition. Each of the nation's financial transactions with other countries is reflected in the balance of payments. Typically, the transactions are grouped into a few broad categories for analysis. Krause summarizes them as "(1) the current account which summarizes a country's earnings and payments during a given year; (2) the capital account which summarizes additions to, or subtractions from, a country's stock of foreign investments; (3) a gold account, which indicates monetary gold movements, and (4) the unilateral transfer account which indicates the amount and direction of grants, private and public."[7]

Exhibit 3–2 shows the balance of payments position of the United States in 1969 and identifies the major items constituting the balance. Some of the items are discussed below.

The current account is of primary interest to international marketers because it includes the international trade and service accounts. These accounts are related to another term whose mention may stir controversy—balance of trade. By definition the balance of payments must balance, but the balance of trade is not necessarily always in balance. If a country exports more goods than it imports, it is said to have a favorable balance of trade, if it imports more goods than it exports, it is said to have an unfavorable balance of trade. The differences between imports and exports are reflected in the balance of payments and constitute a major determinant of the balance of payments position. The

---

[7] Krause, op. cit., p. 62.

BOX 3–2

Gold!

The international monetary system—the agreed way of exchanging one currency for another—runs on faith. For 24 years, the bulwark of that system has been the U.S. Treasury's pledge to redeem dollars held by foreign governments for gold, at an unchanging $35 per oz. Other countries value their own money in terms of dollars, usually keep a big part of their reserves in dollars. After World War II, as other nations gradually followed the U.S. into currency convertibility and trade liberalization, those relationships helped build an enormous, dollar-based world market. Foreigners were delighted to have the mighty dollar—until fear began to erode faith in its strength.

The source of doubt lies in statistics that concern the average American little, but worry bankers, oil sheiks, speculators and most foreign governments profoundly. In 17 of the past 18 years, the U.S. has spent, lent or given away more money than it has taken in from abroad. Compared with the size of the U.S. economy (larger than all of Europe's), that balance of payments deficit seems trivial; it has averaged a 0.004% of the gross national product. But the dollars thus placed in foreign hands now total $34 billion, while the U.S. stock of gold has dwindled from a postwar peak of $24.6 billion to $10.4 billion last week, the thinnest gold line since 1936. If all the dollar holders demanded gold at once, there would be too little in Fort Knox to satisfy even a third of them. Already whetted, the speculative appetite for gold was only sharpened by the fall of the British pound last November.

The result was the greatest gold rush in history.

Source: *Time*, March 29, 1968, p. 80. Reprinted by permission from TIME, The Weekly Newsmagazine; Copyright Time Inc., 1968.

United States, for example, has in recent years had a favorable balance of trade (item I in Exhibit 3–2), but in those same years it has been in a rather unfavorable balance of payments position. This condition exists because our nontrade accounts in the balance of payments statement have reflected an outflow of funds for capital investment overseas (item II) and for military and foreign aid (item I, part 2) that was greater than the net inflow from trade. The United States has, therefore, been in the position in recent years of exporting money. Eventually, this exported money is returned with demands for payment in gold. This, in turn, has caused the gold outflows and great consternation.

It is notable that U.S. trade surplus has run from $3.5 to $6.7 billion annually in the mid-sixties; by 1968 it was only $100 million, and in 1969 it nearly balanced. Recent studies by the Department of Commerce indicate that the United States will probably be running a consistent trade deficit by 1973. The implications for the American marketer are thought-provoking.

If a country does not have gold with which to pay its foreign obligations and if it can gain no more credit, there must be some adjustments in the balance of payments through changes in exchange rates, prices, and/or incomes. In short, once the wealth of a country whose expenditures exceed its income has been exhausted, that country, like an individual, must reduce its standard of living. If its residents will not do so voluntarily, the rate of exchange of its money for foreign monies will decline, and through the medium of the foreign exchange market, purchasing power will be transferred from one country to another. For a number of years U.S. dollars have had a constant value relative to gold and have served as the basis for comparison of other money prices. Nearly every other country of the world, however, sees its currency value fluctuate from time to time, depending on the confidence in that country and its currency in the world money market. Unless the United States increases the size of the favorable balance of trade or decreases financial outflow deficit, it too may find its currency in a less stable position.

In summary then, balance of payments, balance of trade, and exchange fluctuations all relate to the basic processes of recording and adjusting international financial relationships.

WORLD MARKET DEVELOPMENT

Shrinking communication and transportation barriers throughout the world have focused attention in recent years on methods of breaking down artificial barriers which exist between otherwise natural markets. Contributing to this desire to break down market barriers has been the high level of productive capacity of the various nations of the world, particularly the industrialized nations. If a firm or a nation has adequate markets at home, it is not particularly inclined to seek markets elsewhere; but when the productive capacity outruns domestic consumption there is a natural desire to extend the borders of the marketplace. Four types of world market development activities have been significant since World War II. They are: (1) development of trade and commercial treaties; (2) development of multinational market agreements; (3) the improvement of international monetary systems; and (4) the upgrading of underdeveloped markets through economic and technical assistance.

Trade and Commercial Treaties

Prior to 1947 trade treaties were generally negotiated on a bilateral (between two nations) basis, with little attention given to relationships with other countries. Further, there was a chronic tendency to seek to raise barriers rather than to extend markets. At Geneva in 1947, the United States and 22 other countries signed the General Agreement on Tariffs and Trade (GATT).[8] Although all countries are not participants, this agreement paved the way for the first effective worldwide tariff agreement. Subsequent GATT meetings have broadened the number of participating countries so that the 90 contracting parties now account for over four fifths of the world trade. The GATT treaty and subsequent

---

[8] Gerald Curzon treats GATT in its impact at some length in *Multilateral Commercial Diplomacy* (New York: Frederick A. Praeger, Inc., 1966).

meetings have been responsible for significantly reducing tariffs on a wide range of goods. Reduced tariffs have been an important factor in the extension of world trade horizons and the development of overseas markets. Contemporary trade treaties acknowledge the fact that exports of a given country are limited by the amount which they import and therefore include the concept of reciprocal relationships. A further basis is the most-favored-nation clause, which requires that participating nations may not favor one nation over another with respect to customs, duties, or charges. In both of these basic ways the GATT treaties have underlined a basic treaty philosophy of nondiscrimination among nations.

Multinational Market Agreements

A number of multinational market groups have been developed in recent years. Most notable, of course, is the European Common Market, but it has proved to be merely a forerunner of a type of market agreement which has as its primary objective the development of broader markets through breaking down traditional market barriers. Multinational market groups are considered at length in Chapter 9.

International Monetary Systems

Inadequate monetary reserves and unstable currencies are a particularly vexing problem of world trade. So long as these conditions exist, world markets will not develop and function as effectively as they should. To overcome this particular market barrier, which had plagued international trading before World War II, the International Monetary Fund (IMF) was formed. Among its objectives was the stabilization of foreign exchange rates and the establishment of freely convertible currencies. Later, the European Payments Union was formed to facilitate multinational payments. While the International Monetary Fund has some rather severe critics, most agree that it has performed a valuable service and at least partially achieved many of its objectives.

Market Development through Economic and Technical Assistance

Although the motivation for economic and technical assistance in this cold war age is undoubtedly more political than economic, the results have been to upgrade the economies of many nations and to bring many new, small, and underdeveloped nations into the world marketplace. Many of the developing nations represent the potential growth markets of the future and should be considered in any evaluation of world markets.

MARKET PROTECTION

The theoretical and logical arguments for free trade have equal validity in all countries, yet every international businessman must face the reality that he lives in a world of tariffs, quotas, and nontariff barriers. All of the governmentally imposed barriers are imposed through the political pressures of businessmen for protection of their own markets.

Despite, or perhaps because of, the fact that the free marketplace is such an effective regulator of competition and prices, there is a tendency for individual businessmen, and nations as well, to attempt to escape the dominance of the marketplace. In international trade, nations utilize legal barriers, exchange barriers, and psychological barriers to restrain the entry of unwanted goods. Businessmen work together to establish private market barriers, and the market itself may provide formidable barriers for imported goods.

Government-Imposed Barriers

To encourage development of domestic industry and to protect existing industry, a government may establish tariffs, exchange, or psychological barriers against imported goods. Barriers are imposed not only against imports but against foreign business as well. The inspiration for such barriers may be economic or political, but they are typically encouraged by local industry. Whether the barriers are economically logical or not, the fact remains that they do exist.

Tariffs. The chief legal barriers that are utilized are tariffs, quotas, and boycotts. A *tariff*, simply defined, is a tax imposed by a government on goods entering its borders. A *quota* is a specific numerical or dollar limit applied to a particular type of goods. A good example is provided by the 1964 U.S. law which permits the Secretary of Agriculture to stop all beef imports when they are expected to exceed 10 percent of the 1959–63 average annual U.S. production. The fixed base applied to a growing market provides for a decreasing percentage of imports. A government *boycott* is an absolute restriction against the purchase and importation of certain goods from other countries. All three of these devices have essentially the same effect, and each has a variety of methods of application.

One can hardly deny that high tariffs significantly affect levels of world trade. The Hawley-Smoot Act of 1930, which established the highest tariffs in U.S. history, was quickly followed by retaliatory tariffs by nearly all trading countries. The spiderweb shown in Exhibit 3–3 graphically illustrates the results.

Customs formalities can be made excessively difficult and various forms of administrative harassment can take place at the customs door. In some cases, perishable goods have been held at customs until they have deteriorated beyond use. In other cases, goods are held up at customs for three, six, nine months or even longer, awaiting "proper documentation." Along with this type of harassment is the requirement of specific types of marks designating the country of origin of various goods.

Innumerable reasons for the maintenance of governmental restrictions on trade are espoused by protectionists, but essentially all arguments can be classified under the following headings: (1) infant industry, (2) protection of the home market, (3) keep money at home, (4) capital accumulation, (5) standard of living and real wage, (6) conservation of natural resources, (7) industrialization of low-wage nation, (8) maintain employment and reduce unemployment, (9) national defense, (10) increase business size, and (11) retaliation and bargaining. Economists in general have recognized as valid only the infant industry, the national defense, and the industrialization of underdeveloped countries arguments. Even the admission of these three pro-

EXHIBIT 3–3

The Contracting Spiral of World Trade

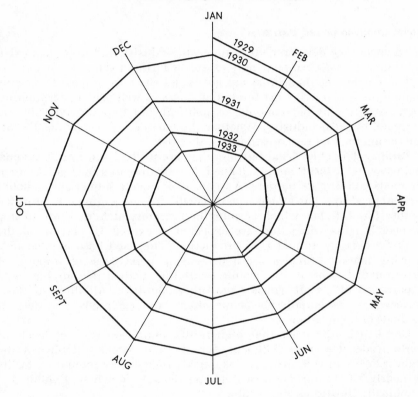

Source: Reproduced from League of Nations, *World Economic Survey, 1932–33* (Geneva, 1933), p. 8.

tectionist arguments is severely restricted and applies only in limited circumstances. Because of their acceptability, most protectionists will argue the need for tariffs on one of these three bases, whether or not they are relevant to their products. When arguing a case for protection of a particular industry, the proponents are also likely to call on the maintenance-of-employment argument because it has substantial political appeal. The ludicrous part of the situation is that these arguments are utilized when they are completely irrelevant to the product in question. Sugar, petroleum, and textiles are some good examples of protected

BOX 3–3

Protectionism Continues—Nontariff Tricks

While the first batch of Kennedy Round tariff reductions was going into effect a wide assortment of other trade barriers loomed as high as ever.

. . . Impoverished Ghana, trying to combat its balance of payments problem as well as protect fledgling native industries, has simply ruled out import licenses for 79 products ranging from suitcases to incense. Industrialized Britain departs from its otherwise liberal trade policy by banning virtually all coal imports. In Japan, which officially restricts imports as disparate as golf balls and electric generators, the government uses friendly persuasion to get importers to cut traffic in other goods that are not formally excluded.

Such protectionism persists even within Europe's supposedly cozy Common Market. Volkswagen has had lagging sales in Italy ever since that country imposed a temporary tax that craftily penalized owners of the German bug. France, challenged at home by Italy's burgeoning appliance industry, has tried everything from a deliberate customs slowdown, which piled up thousands of Italian refrigerators at the border, to a formal request, now pending before the Common Market commission, for outright import quotas. The French also forbid the import of walnuts before Sept. 25—by which time the remnants of Italy's early-ripening crop has often rotted.

. . . West Germany, whose regulations against preservatives and artificial flavorings keep out such processed foods as U. S. TV dinners, also makes it virtually impossible to import fresh Swedish whortleberries, despite the fact that it does not grow the delicacy itself. For its part, Sweden invariably excludes American apples at Christmas—and even at other times, complains one U. S. official in Stockholm, "won't allow them until they've sold their own."

. . . These are non-tariff gimmicks designed to impede the inflow of foreign goods. Wine-producing France, for example, puts a crimp on bourbon and Scotch imports by prohibiting all whisky advertising. In Italy, foreign automakers find it difficult to buy prime time on the state-owned television. Switzerland not only restricts imports of milk products but gives special help—including price supports and low-cost feed—to Swiss dairymen whose cows graze in remote areas or on mountain slopes.

Source: *Time*, January 12, 1968, p. 55. Reprinted by permission from TIME, The Weekly Newsmagazine; Copyright Time Inc., 1968.

industries in the United States for which none of the three arguments can justifiably be used in support. When arguing a case for protection, the basic economic advantages of international trade are forgotten. The fact that the consumer ultimately bears the cost of tariffs and other protective measures is conveniently overlooked.

As *Business Week* pointed out in 1969:

The American Importers Association cites a dozen reasons against tariffs and quotas stating that they: increase inflationary pressures, weaken balance of payments position, limit the consumers choice, restrict manufacturers supply sources, disrupt supply and demand, favor special interests, inject more politics and government control into the economy, require administration, proliferate, are arbitrary and discriminatory and, finally, that they hurt international relations and can start trade wars.

Free trade is easy to support in principle but nonetheless there is constant and unrelenting pressure for protection—even when it is not needed. One authority's position change in the case of Japan is indicative of real problems faced; Mrs. Elizabeth Jager, AFL-CIO foreign trade specialist recalls that for 10 years she wrote articles pleading for understanding of Japan's special need to rebuild a shattered economy. "But Japan's not a special case any more, the United States is not the only big boy on the block any more," she says. "Japan has no business having a $1-billion trade surplus with the United States when it maintains 120 illegal quotas on goods entering from the U.S. Voluntary reciprocity has failed."[9]

Exchange Barriers. A government can effectively regulate its international trade position by various forms of exchange control restrictions. A government may undertake such restrictions in order to preserve its balance of payment position or it may undertake them specifically for the advantage or encouragement of particular industries. Three main types of activity should be considered: blocked currency, differential exchange rates, and governmental approval requirements for securing foreign exchange. Blocked currency is most likely to be used as a political weapon or as a response to a difficult balance of payment situation. In effect, blockage cuts off all importing or all importing above a certain level. Blockage is accomplished by refusing to redeem national currencies on the world financial marketplace.

The differential exchange rate is a particularly ingenious method of controlling imports. It encourages the importation of goods which the government deems desirable and discourages the importation of goods which the government does not wish to have imported. The essential mechanism is that the importer is required to pay varying amounts of domestic currency for foreign exchange with which to purchase products in different categories. For example, the exchange rate for a desirable category of goods might be one unit of domestic money for one unit of a given foreign currency. For a less desirable product, the exchange rate might be two domestic currency units for one foreign unit. For an undesirable product, the exchange rate might be three domestic units for one foreign unit. Thus, in effect, an importer of an undesired product has to pay three times as much for his foreign exchange as the importer of a desired product. This device has been used by several South American countries.

One of the methods which Mexico and several other countries use in restricting imports of certain goods is to require all foreign exchange transactions to be approved by a central ministry. This central ministry will approve only transactions related to goods which the government desires to have imported. It will reject applications for foreign exchange related to purchases of products which the government does not desire to have in the country. Needless to say, these various types of currency

---

9 "Importing Woe for the Worker," *Business Week*, July 26, 1969, p. 66. Reprinted from the July 26, 1969 issue of *Business Week* by special permission. Copyrighted © 1969 by McGraw-Hill, Inc.

exchange barriers provide one of the underlying reasons for the ever-active black market in world currencies.

Nontariff Protection

The government of a country that wishes to discourage international trade (either generally or relating to a specific product) can engage in a number of psychological, legal, and administrative activities which will reduce importing. By establishing *administrative barriers,* importing can become such a complex, frustrating, and expensive process that importers will be discouraged from bringing in goods.

Sometimes importers are pressured by government or business officials to restrict their activities or level of imports of certain commodities or to limit trading activities with certain countries.

Health and labeling regulations can virtually stop transnational shipping of foodstuffs and cosmetics. Fruit content regulations vary so much from country to country that one agricultural specialist says "a jam exporter needs a computer to avoid one or another country's regulations." Plant and animal quarantine regulations serve an important function but are often used solely to keep out foreign products.

Interestingly, nonfoodstuffs are affected too, and sometimes the restrictive effect is unintentional. The U.S. auto safety law which went into effect in 1968 is a good example; rather than make the necessary changes, several European cars which did not meet the requirements were simply withdrawn from the U.S. market.

Tax penalties and subsidies play an important role in protecting markets. Several European countries have adopted a French tax scheme which, though designed to simplify tax collections, has the effect of penalizing foreign goods because it has the effect of double taxing imports. The U.S. government has repeatedly protested foreign governments' practice of giving across-the-board tax rebates on exports and imposing special border tax charges on imports. Most of these practices are against GATT regulations, but filing of complaints by the countries that are harmed is rare. Even innocent-seeming taxes may be used for control. Many countries, for example, have automobile tax structures that make it prohibitive to own large (e.g., American) cars.

A rather blatant device which fortunately has not caught on in many countries or with many goods is the "American Selling Price" law, which flatly requires that certain chemicals, dyestuffs, and footwear must be sold at prices equivalent to prices for comparable U.S. goods.

Not only imports are discriminated against in international business. Many countries make it difficult or impossible to establish foreign production subsidiaries competing with local business. For years Japan has held foreign investors at bay and virtually no important industries in that country may be 100 percent foreign owned. Many countries, of course, require substantial local participation. Strict capital and profit repatriation rules can have a nearly identical effect. European countries have bristled at foreign mergers which would mean take-over of local companies; numerous major mergers have been stopped at the last

BOX 3–4

Buy American Policy Touches off a Fuss

"It just wouldn't do for the world's largest turbine, located at a U. S. government facility, to be stamped with a hammer and sickle," said one irate lawmaker to Interior Secretary Stewart Udall. As a result of that and similar protests, Udall invoked the "Buy American" policy to shut out foreign competitors.

In justifying his use of the policy, Udall said that American manufacturers would thus be able "to demonstrate their inventive capability in the design and manufacture of these turbines and generators and [have] an opportunity to take world leadership in the hydroelectric field."

But developments are not going as expected. The Buy American policy allows as much as 49% of the money for a project to be spent on foreign components, and a large share of the outlays for Grand Coulee's new equipment appears to be going to overseas suppliers.

Source: Reprinted from the July 27, 1968 issue of *Business Week*, p. 52, by special permission. Copyrighted © 1968 by McGraw-Hill, Inc.

minute by the governments of France, Italy, and Britain within the past few years. Governments can easily exclude foreign goods from the marketplace by refusing to award public contracts for any goods that utilize foreign merchandise or to any plants or producers who have purchased foreign goods against the government's wishes.

Another type of psychological barrier is the *boycott*. This can be either formal or informal and can be government sponsored or sponsored by a given industry. It is not at all unusual for the citizens of a country to boycott goods of other countries at the urging of their government or civic groups. Sometimes a particular industry will attempt to rouse public sympathy for that industry and induce a voluntary boycott against imported competitive goods. During the past decade, for example, the U.S. steel industry has been engaged in a campaign to urge steel users to purchase domestic steel products—solely because they are domestic.

Businessmen are fully aware of the implications of nontariff protection. The complaint of a chemical executive is typical:

The major problem facing our division is the invisible barriers . . . including among other things: special taxes, unrealistic base prices on which import duties are levied, import licenses, prior deposits to obtain an import license, and unilateral trade agreements between governments. These problems have existed a long time . . . it is our feeling that they may worsen."[10]

Foreign restrictions abound but we in the United States cannot forget that in 1969 and 1970 our government was in continuing negotiations

---

[10] M. G. Duerr, J. Greene, *The Problems Facing International Management* (New York: National Industrial Conference Board, 1968).

BOX 3–5

Traps in the Jungle of Nontariff Barriers

Argentina	Importers must make interest-free deposit for six months equal to 40% of the cost-insurance-freight value of imported goods
Brazil	Imported products must pay a merchant marine improvement tax
Britain	New "loyalty rebate" by government-run steel company favors buyers who haven't used imported steels of similar type for previous six months
Canada	Canned goods may be imported only in container sizes approved by government
Finland	140% excise tax on c.i.f. duty paid value of cars, less $595, discriminates against big U.S. autos
France	Border tax on most industrial products is 20% of c.i.f. duty-paid value. Whiskey advertising prohibited
Germany	Imported pit coal and solid fuels made from coal must be consumed north of Mitteland canal
India	Commercial imports are subject to licensing, exchange controls, quotas, embargoes
Italy	Government departments apply blanket buy-Italian policies. Wine imports prohibited
Japan	Many imports controlled by complex foreign exchange allocations; Ministry of International Trade & Industry generally keeps allocations confidential
Malagasy	Prohibits imports of beer under 4% alcohol content
Malta	Bars imports of bathtubs less than 5 ft. 6 in. long
Norway	Soles of imported shoes must be made of single piece of natural leather
Soviet Union	Foreign trade handled by state agencies; trade must be bilaterally balanced; foreign suppliers have little contact with users of products
U.S.	Makers of benzenoid chemicals protected by American Selling Price system of levying high duties on imports

Source: Reprinted from the June 29, 1968, issue of *Business Week*, p. 96, by special permission. Copyrighted © 1968 by McGraw-Hill, Inc.

arranging "voluntary" agreements with the Japanese steel industry to limit sales to the United States. Similar negotiations with the governments of major textile producers have limited textile exports to the United States. The beef quotas mentioned above have never been invoked because foreign producers have been induced to stop exporting when beef shipments have reached the "peril point."

Market Barriers

The location, size, and structure of a market itself may deter international goods from entering a given marketplace. Just as large companies in the domestic market tend to ignore villages and hamlets in their marketing plans, so companies engaged in international business are likely to overlook small markets when the vastly broader potential of larger ones remains untapped. Furthermore, a country may be denied some of the possible benefits of international trading because size or remote location make it uneconomic or unprofitable as a market. Distance and aggregate purchasing power or market potential for a given product are key considerations, but they too may be modified by the extent and level of competition in a country. One market may be relatively untapped while another of similar potential cannot be considered because competition has already preempted it. Very lucrative markets may be closed to international competition through the existence of cartels or other privately imposed market barriers.

Even the habit patterns of consumers in world markets may provide market barriers. Companies are reluctant to enter markets where there is high possibility of failure because of unfamiliarity with local customs and purchasing behavior. Inadequate channels of distribution can also provide a natural market barrier to companies which wish to operate on the level of mass distribution but which find local facilities for such an undertaking unavailable.

The ultimate market barrier is competition; each year the world's nations become more productive and more efficient, with more countries and businesses achieving mass production economies. The marketing skills of the world's businessmen are also being honed and sharpened. The result is that the established trading nations are feeling additional pressures of competition, not only in the foreign markets but in their own home markets as well.

In the final analysis, natural market barriers are probably the most important deterrents to international trade. If markets appear to offer promise of great profits, most of the governmental, exchange, and psychological barriers can be surmounted by ingenious businessmen.

SUMMARY AND CONCLUSIONS

Regardless of the theoretical approach utilized in the defense of international trade, it is clear that the benefits from absolute or comparative advantage can accrue to any nation. Open markets are needed if world resources are to be developed and utilized in the most beneficial manner. It is true that there are circumstances when market protection may be needed and may be beneficial to national defense or the encouragement of infant industries in developing nations. The temptation, however, is always toward excessive market protection, or more correctly, excessive producer protection, because the consumer seldom benefits from such protection. Because free international markets can help underdeveloped countries become self-sufficient, and because open markets provide new customers, most industrialized nations have, in recent years since World War II, cooperated in working toward freer trade. Such trade will always be partially threatened by various governmental and market barriers which exist or are created for the protection of local businesses, although the general trend in the past few decades has been toward free trade.

READINGS

USING THE FREE MARKET TO RESOLVE THE BALANCE OF PAYMENTS PROBLEM*†

Discussions of U.S. policy with respect to international payments tend to be dominated by our immediate balance of payments difficulties. I should like today to approach the question from a different, and I hope more constructive, direction. Let us begin by asking ourselves not merely how we can get out of our present difficulties but instead how we can fashion our international payments system so that it will best serve our needs for the long pull; how we can solve not merely this balance of payments problem but the whole balance of payments problem.

A shocking, and indeed, disgraceful feature of the present situation is the extent to which our frantic search for expedients to stave off balance of payments pressures has led us, on the one hand, to sacrifice major national objectives; and, on the other, to give enormous power to officials of foreign governments to affect what should be purely domestic matters. Foreign payments amount to only some 5 percent of our total national income. Yet they have become a major factor in nearly every national policy.

I believe that a system of floating exchange rates would solve the balance of payments problem for the United States far more effectively than our present arrangements. Such a system would use the flexibility and efficiency of the free market to harmonize our small foreign trade sector with both the rest of our massive economy and the rest of the world; it would reduce problems of foreign payments to their proper dimensions and remove them as a major consideration in governmental policy about domestic matters and as a major preoccupation in international political negotiations; it would foster our national objectives rather than be an obstacle to their attainment.

To indicate the basis for this conclusion, let us consider the national objective with which our payments system is most directly connected: the promotion of a healthy and balanced growth of world trade, carried on, so far as possible, by private individuals and private enterprises with minimum intervention by governments. This has been a major objective of our postwar international economic policy, most recently expressed in the Trade Expansion Act of 1962. Success would knit the

---

* Milton Friedman, *Financial Analysts Journal*, March–April, 1964, pp. 21–25.

† Editor's note: The text of this paper is a statement presented by Professor Friedman on November 14, 1963, before the Joint Economic Committee on the occasion of its Hearings on Balance of Payments.

free world more closely together, and, by fostering the international division of labor, raise standards of living throughout the world, including the United States.

Suppose that we succeed in negotiating far-reaching reciprocal reductions in tariffs and other trade barriers with the common market and other countries.[1] Such reductions will expand trade in general but clearly will have different effects on different industries. The demand for the products of some will expand, for others contract. This is a phenomenon we are familiar with from our internal development. The capacity of our free enterprise system to adapt quickly and efficiently to such shifts, whether produced by changes in technology or tastes, has been a major source of our economic growth. The only additional element introduced by international trade is the fact that different currencies are involved, and this is where the payment mechanism comes in; its function is to keep this fact from being an additional source of disturbance.

An all-around lowering of tariffs would tend to increase both our expenditures and our receipts in foreign currencies. There is no way of knowing in advance which increase would tend to be the greater and hence no way of knowing whether the initial effect would be toward a surplus or deficit in our balance of payments. What is clear is that we cannot hope to succeed in the objective of expanding world trade unless we can readily adjust to either outcome.[2]

Suppose then that the initial effect is to increase our expenditures on imports more than our receipts from exports. How could we adjust to this outcome?

One method of adjustment is to draw on reserves or borrow from abroad to finance the excess increase in imports. The obvious objection to this method is that it is only a temporary device, and hence can be relied on only when the disturbance is temporary. But that is not the major objection. Even if we had very large reserves or could borrow large amounts from abroad, so that we could continue this expedient for many years, it is a most undesirable one. We can see why if we look at physical rather than financial magnitudes.

The physical counterpart to the financial deficit is a reduction of employment in industries competing with imports that is larger than the

---

[1] To simplify exposition I shall hereafter refer only to tariffs, letting these stand for the whole range of barriers to trade, including even the so-called "voluntary" limitation of exports.

[2] Many people concerned with our payments deficits hope that since we are operating farther from full capacity than Europe, we could supply a substantial increase in exports whereas they could not. Implicitly, this assumes that European countries are prepared to see their surplus turned into a deficit, thereby contributing to the reduction of the deficits we have recently been experiencing in our balance of payments. Perhaps this would be the initial effect of tariff changes. But if the achievement of such a result is to be *sine qua non* of tariff agreement, we cannot hope for any significant reduction in barriers. We could be confident that exports would expand more than imports only if the tariff changes were one-sided indeed, with our trading partners making much greater reductions in tariffs than we make. Our major means of inducing other countries to reduce tariffs is to offer corresponding reductions in our tariff. More generally, there is little hope of continued and sizable liberalization of trade if liberalization is to be viewed simply as a device for correcting balance of payments difficulties. That way lies only backing and filling.

concurrent expansion of employment in export industries. So long as the financial deficit continues, the assumed tariff reductions create employment problems. But it is no part of the aim of tariff reductions to create unemployment at home or to promote employment abroad. The aim is a balanced expansion of trade, with exports rising along with imports and thereby providing employment opportunities to offset any reduction in employment resulting from increased imports.

Hence, simply drawing on reserves or borrowing abroad is a most unsatisfactory method of adjustment.

Another method of adjustment is to lower U.S. prices relative to foreign prices, since this would stimulate exports and discourage imports. If foreign countries are accommodating enough to engage in inflation, such a change in relative prices might require merely that the United States keep prices stable or even, that it simply keep them from rising as fast as foreign prices. But there is no necessity for foreign countries to be so accommodating, and we could hardly count on their being so accommodating. The use of this technique therefore involves a willingness to produce a decline in U.S. prices by tight monetary policy or tight fiscal policy or both. Given time, this method of adjustment would work. But in the interim, it would exact a heavy toll. It would be difficult or impossible to force down prices appreciably without producing a recession and considerable unemployment. To eliminate in the long run the unemployment resulting from the tariff changes, we should in the short run be creating cyclical unemployment. The cure might for a time be far worse than the disease.

This second method is therefore also most unsatisfactory. Yet these two methods—drawing on reserves and forcing down prices—are the only two methods available under our present international payment arrangements, which involved fixed exchange rates between the U.S. dollar and other currencies. Little wonder that we have so far made such disappointing progress toward the reduction of trade barriers, that our practice has differed so much from our preaching.

There is one other way and only one other way to adjust and that is by allowing (or forcing) the price of the U.S. dollar to fall in terms of other currencies. To a foreigner, U.S. goods become cheaper in either of two ways—either because their prices in the United States fall in terms of dollars or because the foreigner has to give up fewer units of his own currency to acquire a dollar, which is to say, the price of the dollar falls. For example, suppose a particular U.S. car sells for $2,800 when a dollar costs 7 shillings, tuppence in Buritish money (i.e., roughly £1 = $2.80). The price of the car is then £1,000 in British money. It is all the same to an Englishman—or even a Scotsman—whether the price of the car falls to $2,500 while the price of a dollar remains 7 shillings, tuppence, or, alternatively, the price of the car remains $2,800, while the price of a dollar falls to 6 shillings, 5 pence (i.e., roughly £ = $3.11). In either case, the car costs the Englishman £900 rather than £1,000, which is what matters to him. Similarly, foreign goods can become more expensive to an American in either of two ways—either because the price in terms of foreign currency rises or because he has to give up more dollars to acquire a given amount of foreign currency.

Changes in exchange rates can therefore alter the relative price of U.S. and foreign goods in precisely the same way as can changes in internal prices in the United States and in foreign countries. And they can do so without requiring anything like the same internal adjustments. If the initial effect of the tariff reductions would be to create a deficit at the former exchange rate (or enlarge an existing deficit or reduce an existing surplus) and thereby increase unemployment, this effect can be entirely avoided by a change in exchange rates which will produce a balanced expansion in imports and exports without interfering with domestic employment, domestic prices, or domestic monetary and fiscal policy. The pig can be roasted without burning down the barn.

The situation is of course entirely symmetrical if the tariff changes should initially happen to expand our exports more than our imports. Under present circumstances, we would welcome such a result, and conceivably, if the matching deficit were experienced by countries currently running a surplus, they might permit it to occur without seeking to offset it. In that case, they and we would be using the first method of adjustment—changes in reserves or borrowing. But again, if we had started off from an even keel, this would be an undesirable method of adjustment. On our side, we should be sending out useful goods and receiving only foreign currencies in return. On the side of our partners, they would be using up reserves and tolerating the creation of unemployment.

The second method of adjusting to a surplus is to permit or force domestic prices to rise—which is of course what we did in part in the early postwar years when we were running large surpluses. Again, we should be forcing maladjustments on the whole economy to solve a problem arising from a small part of it—the 5 percent accounted for by foreign trade.

Again, these two methods are the only ones available under our present international payments arrangements, and neither is satisfactory.

The final method is to permit or force exchange rates to change—in this case, a rise in the price of the dollar in terms of foreign currencies. This solution is again specifically adapted to the specific problem of the balance of payments.

Changes in exchange rates can be produced in either of two general ways. One way is by a change in an official exchange rate; an official devaluation or appreciation from one fixed level which the government is committed to support to another fixed level. This is the method used by Britain in its postwar devaluation and by Germany in 1961 when the mark was appreciated. This is also the main method contemplated by the IMF which permits member nations to change their exchange rates by 10 percent without consultation and by a larger amount after consultation and approval by the Fund. But this method has serious disadvantages. It makes a change in rates a matter of major moment, and hence there is a tendency to postpone any change as long as possible. Difficulties cumulate and a larger change is finally needed than would have been required if it could have been made promptly. By the time the change is made, everyone is aware that a change is pending and is certain of change. The result is to encourage a flight from a currency, if it is going to be devalued, or to a currency, if it is going to be appreciated.

There is in any event little basis for determining precisely what the new rate should be. Speculative movements increase the difficulty of judging what the new rate should be, and introduce a systematic bias, making the change needed appear larger than it actually is. The result, particularly when devalution occurs, is generally to lead officials to "play safe" by making an even large change than the large change needed. The country is then left after the devaluation with a maladjustment precisely the opposite of that with which it started, and is thereby encouraged to follow policies it cannot sustain in the long run.

Even if all these difficulties could be avoided, this method of changing from one fixed rate to another has the disadvantage that it is necessarily discontinuous. Even if the new exchange rates are precisely correct when first established, they will not long remain correct.

A second and much better way in which changes in exchange rates can be produced is by permitting exchange rates to float, by allowing them to be determined from day to day in the market. This is the method which the United States used from 1862 to 1879, and again, in effect, from 1917 or so to about 1925, and again from 1933 to 1934. It is the method which Britain used from 1918 to 1925 and again from 1931 to 1939, and which Canada used for most of the interwar period and again from 1950 to May, 1962. Under this method, exchange rates adjust themselves continuously, and market forces determine the magnitude of each change. There is no need for any official to decide by how much the rate should rise or fall. This is the method of the free market, the method that we adopt unquestioningly in a private enterprise economy for the bulk of goods and services. It is no less available for the price of one money in terms of another.

With a floating exchange rate, it is possible for governments to intervene and try to affect the rate by buying or selling, as the British Exchange Equalization fund did rather successfully in the 1930s, or by combining buying and selling with public announcements of intentions, as Canada did so disastrously in early 1962. On the whole, it seems to me undesirable to have government intervene, because there is a strong tendency for government agencies to try to peg the rate rather than to stabilize it, because they have no special advantage over private speculators in stabilizing it, because they can make far bigger mistakes than private speculators risking their own money, and because there is a tendency for them to cover up their mistakes by changing the rules—as the Canadian case so strikingly illustrates—rather than by reversing course. But this is an issue on which there is much difference of opinion among economists who are agreed in favoring floating rates. Clearly, it is possible to have a successful floating rate along with governmental speculation.

The great objective of tearing down trade barriers, of promoting a worldwide expansion of trade, of giving citizens of all countries, and especially the underdeveloped countries, every opportunity to sell their products in open markets under equal terms and thereby every incentive to use their resources efficiently, of giving countries an alternative through free world trade to autarchy and central planning—this great objective can, I believe, be achieved best under a regime of floating rates. All countries, and not just the United States, can proceed to liberalize boldly and confidently only if they have reasonable assurance that the resulting trade expansion will be balanced and will not interfere with major domestic objectives. Floating exchange rates, and so far as I can see, only floating exchange rates, provide this assurance. They do so because they are an automatic mechanism for protecting the domestic economy from the possibility that liberalization will produce a serious imbalance in international payments.

Despite their advantages, floating exchange rates have a bad press. Why is this so?

One reason is because a consequence of our present system that I have been citing as a serious disadvantage is often regarded as an advantage, namely, the extent to which the small foreign trade sector dominates national policy. Those who regard this as an advantage refer to it as the discipline of the gold standard. I would have much sympathy for this view if we had a real gold standard, so the discipline was imposed by impersonal forces which in turn reflected the realities of resources, tastes, and technology. But in fact we have today only a pseudo gold standard and the so-called discipline is imposed by governmental officials of other countries who are determining their own internal monetary policies and are either being forced to dance to our tune or calling the tune for us, depending primarily on accidental political developments. This is a discipline we can well do without.

A possibly more important reason why floating exchange rates have a bad press, I believe, is a mistaken interpretation of experience with floating rates, arising out of a statistical fallacy that can be seen easily in a standard example. Arizona is clearly the worst place in the United States for a person with tuberculosis to go because the death rate from tuberculosis is higher in Arizona than in any other state. The fallacy in this case is obvious. It is less obvious in connection with exchange rates. Countries that have gotten into severe financial difficulties, for whatever reason, have had ultimately to change their exchange rates or let them change. No amount of exchange control and other restrictions on trade have enabled them to peg an exchange rate that was far out of line with economic realities. In consequence, floating rates have frequently been associated with financial and economic instability. It is easy to conclude, as many have, that floating exchange rates produce such instability.

This misreading of experience is reinforced by the general prejudice against speculation; which has led to the frequent assertion, typically on the basis of no evidence whatsoever, that speculation in exchange can be expected to be destabilizing and thereby to increase the instability in rates. Few who make this assertion even recognize that it is equivalent to asserting that speculators generally lose money.

Floating exchange rates need not be unstable exchange rates—any more than the prices of automobiles or of government bonds, of coffee or of meals need gyrate wildly just because they are free to change from day to day. The Canadian exchange rate was free to change during more than a decade, yet it varied within narrow limits. The ultimate objective is a world in which exchange rates, while free to vary, are in fact highly stable because basic economic policies and conditions are stable. Instability of exchange rates is a symptom of instability in the underlying economic structure. Elimination of this symptom by administrative pegging of exchange rates cures none of the underlying difficulties and only makes adjustment to them more painful.

The confusion between stable exchange rates and pegged exchange rates helps to explain the frequent comment that floating exchange rates would introduce an additional element of uncertainty into foreign trade and thereby discourage its expansion. They introduce no additional element of uncertainty. If a floating rate would, for example, decline, then a pegged rate would be subject to pressure that the authorities would have to meet by internal deflation or exchange control in some form. The uncertainty about the rate would simply be replaced by uncertainty about internal prices or about the availability of exchange; and the latter uncertainties, being subject to administrative rather than market control, are likely to be the more erratic and unpredictable. Moreover, the trader can far more readily and cheaply protect himself against the danger of changes in exchange rates, through hedging operations in a forward market, than he can against the danger of changes in internal prices or exchange availability. Floating rates are therefore far more favorable to private international trade than pegged rates.

Though I have discussed the problem of international payments in the context of trade liberalization, the discussion is directly applicable to the more general problem of adapting to any forces that make for balance of payments difficulties. Consider our present problem, of a deficit in the balance of trade plus long term capital movements. How can we adjust to it? By one of the three methods outlined: first, drawing on reserves or borrowing; second, keeping U.S. prices from rising as rapidly as foreign prices or forcing them down; third, permitting or forcing exchange rates to alter. And, this time, by one more method: by imposing additional trade barriers or their equivalent, whether in the form of higher tariffs, or smaller import quotas, or extracting from other countries tighter "voluntary" quotas on their exports, or "tieing" foreign aid, or buying higher priced domestic goods or services to meet military needs, or imposing taxes on foreign borrowing, or imposing direct controls on investments by U.S. citizens abroad, or any one of the host of other devices for interfering with the private business of private individuals that have become so familiar to us since Hjalmar Schacht perfected the modern techniques of exchange control in 1934 to strengthen the Nazis for war and to despoil a large class of his fellow citizens.

Fortunately or unfortunately, even Congress cannot repeal the laws of arithmetic. Books must balance. We must use one of these four methods. Because we have been unwilling to select the only one that is currently fully consistent with both economic and political needs—namely, floating exchange rates—we have been driven, as if by an invisible hand, to employ all the others, and even then may not escape the need for explicit changes in exchange rates.

We affirm in loud and clear voices that we will not and must not erect trade barriers—yet is there any doubt about how far we have gone down the fourth route? After the host of measures already taken, the Secretary of the Treasury has openly stated to the Senate Finance Committee that if the so-called interest equalization tax—itself a concealed exchange control and concealed devaluation—is not passed, we shall have to resort to direct controls over foreign investment.

We affirm that we cannot drain our reserves further, yet short term liabilities mount and our gold stock continues to decline.

We affirm that we cannot let balance of payments problems interfere with domestic prosperity, yet for at least some four years now we have followed a less expansive monetary policy than would have been healthy for our economy.

Even all together, these measures may only serve to postpone but not prevent open devaluation—if the experience of other countries is any guide. Whether they do, depends not on us but on others. For our best hope of escaping our present difficulties is that foreign countries will inflate.

In the meantime, we adopt one expedient after another, borrowing here, making swap arrangements there, changing the form of loans to make the "figures" look good. Entirely aside from the ineffectiveness of most of these measures, they are politically degrading and demeaning. We are a great and wealthy nation. We should be directing our own course, setting an example to the world, living up to our destiny. Instead, we send our officials hat in hand to make the rounds of foreign governments and central banks; we put foreign central banks in a position to determine whether or not we can meet our obligations and thus enable them to exert great influence on our policies; we are driven to niggling negotiations with Hong Kong and with Japan and, for all I know, Monaco to get them to limit "voluntarily" their exports. Is this a posture suitable for the leader of the Free World?

It is not the least of the virtues of floating exchange rates that we would again become masters in our own house. We could decide important issues on the proper ground. The military could concentrate on military effectiveness and not on saving foreign exchange; recipients of foreign aid could concentrate on how to get the most out of what we give them and not on how to spend it all in the United States; Congress could decide how much to spend on foreign aid on the basis of what we get for our money and what else we could use it for and not how it will affect the gold stock; the monetary authorities could concentrate on domestic prices and employment, not on how to induce foreigners to hold dollar balances in this country; the Treasury and the tax committees of Congress could devote their attention to the equity of the tax system and its effects on our efficiency, rather than on how to use tax gimmicks to discourage imports, subsidize exports, and discriminate against outflows of capital.

A system of floating exchange rates would render the problem of making outflows equal inflows unto the market where it belongs and not leave it to the clumsy and heavy hand of government. It would leave government free to concentrate on its proper functions.

In conclusion, a word about gold. Our commitment to buy and sell gold for monetary use at a fixed price of $35 an ounce is in practice the mechanism whereby we maintain fixed rates of exchange between the dollar and other currencies—or, more precisely, whereby we leave all initiative for changes in such rates to other countries. This commitment should be terminated—as the corresponding commitment for silver already has been. The price of gold, like the price of silver, should be determined in the free market, with the U.S. Government committed neither to buying gold nor to selling gold at any fixed price. This is the appropriate counterpart of a policy of floating exchange rates. With respect to our existing stock of gold, we could simply keep it fixed, neither adding to it nor reducing it; alternatively, we could sell it off gradually at the market price or add to it gradually thereby reducing or increasing our governmental stockpiles of this particular metal. Personally, I favor selling it off (which would involve removing the present gold reserve requirement for Federal Reserve liabilities) and simultaneously removing all present limitations on the ownership of gold and the trading in gold by American citizens. There is no reason why gold, like other commodities, should not be freely traded on a free market.

ARE IMPORTS KILLING OFF U.S. INDUSTRIES?*

"Where open markets attract low-wage imports that devastate a segment of our economy, an alternative must be found," declared W. L. H. Griffin, president of Brown Shoe Co., Inc., in recent House hearings on a bill to limit imports of textiles and shoes.

Griffin painted a bleak picture of the future of the U.S. shoe industry: plants closed, profits down, and "every indication" that the situation will worsen.

Other businessmen seeking quota protection for their industries complained to the Ways & Means Committee that the U.S. is not getting a fair shake in world trade. Frederick B. Dent, chairman of the international trade committee of the American Textile Manufacturers Institute, testified: "Because the U.S. is the only remaining relatively free market on earth, we are taking an inordinate share of the world's textile exports."

Representative Wilbur Mills (D-Ark.), chairman of the House committee and author of the bill, described the situation in even more dramatic terms: "It looks like somebody had tied our hands so tight that we are witnessing the elimination of one industry after another." And Commerce Secretary Maurice Stans told the committee: "We have been in many respects 'Uncle Sucker' to the rest of the world. The time has come

---

* Source: *Business Week*, July 25, 1970. Reprinted by special permission. Copyright © 1970 by McGraw-Hill, Inc.

when we must put our cards on the table and say, 'Let's play fair from now on.' "

Protectionist Push

After such testimony, the committee last week wrote a bill that not only would impose import quotas on textiles and shoes, but would pave the way for quotas on any other foreign products that win a sizable share of the U.S. market. President Nixon threatened this week to veto the bill if it passes with any trade restrictions beyond textile quotas. But the measure has strong support in Congress. If the bill becomes law, it will mark a sharp swing toward protectionism in American trade policy.

Some of the rhetoric in the House hearings suggested that large parts of U.S. industry are hanging defenselessly on the ropes, about to receive a knockout blow from cheap imports. Actually, the U.S. is doing pretty well in trade this year. The business slowdown has damped the import boom of recent years and made American producers look harder for customers abroad. As a result, the U.S. trade surplus is expected to climb to $3-billion this year, from $1-billion in 1969. And if the current busi-ness squeeze reins in the wage-price spiral, U.S. goods may recover some of the competitive edge that they lost because of inflation.

Even industries that are demanding quota protection are not doing badly against foreign competition. Textile imports still account for less than 5% of the U.S. market. Measured in millions of pairs, shoe imports have captured one-quarter of the market. In dollar volume, however, the foreign share is only 13%, because most imports are cheap shoes and plastic sandals that do not compete directly with American products. Steel imports are down as a result of a voluntary agreement by Japanese and European steelmakers to limit their sales to the U.S. In fact, American steel producers expect to ship abroad a near-record 6-million to 7-million tons this year.

Manufacturers of consumer electronics wares—radios, TV sets, phonographs, and tape recorders—oppose any restrictions on foreign products despite rising imports. Many have set up their own plants abroad or import foreign goods to round out their domestic product lines. "We have learned to compete, not stick our heads in the sand and call for protection," says Jack Wayman, staff vice-president of the Electronic Industries Assn.'s consumer products division.

Not Wide Open

Furthermore, many American industries are more than holding their own in foreign trade. Computer makers sold $700-million worth of equipment and parts abroad last year, up 230% since 1965. Chemical exports rose 40% in the same period, to $3.4-billion in 1969. Automotive exports of $3.5-billion last year were double the 1965 level, partly as a result of the U.S.–Canadian auto pact.

As it stands now, the U.S. is far from being a wide open market. More than 20% of U.S. imports, by value, are already controlled by legislative or voluntary quotas covering cotton textiles, steel, oil, wool, meat, cotton, wheat, dairy products, ceramic tiles, and other items. Average U.S. import tariffs on industrial goods are higher than Europe's.

Still, some segments of some U.S. industries are clearly being hurt by imports. In textiles, for example, the hardest hit may be the 800-odd shops that make knitted outerwear, about half of them in and around New York.

"The bulk of them are small mills—the kind where you see the owner out with a screw driver fixing the machines while his wife supervises the women workers," says George Vargish, president of Vargish Knitwear Co., Union City, N.J., and head of the National Knitted Outerwear Assn. "Imports are killing off these small mills. Last year, over 100 went out of business." Knitwear requires a lot of hard labor, and U.S. makers have a tough time competing with garments manufactured in such countries as Taiwan and South Korea, where wage rates are as low as 10¢ an hour.

Wage costs are the main problem for U.S. shoe manufacturers, too. But foreign steel has been making inroads in the U.S. partly because American mills were slow to adopt such technologies as basic oxygen furnaces while the Japanese were building the world's most advanced plants. And in consumer electronics, the Japanese pioneered in such products as transistor radios and small television sets.

Here is the situation in each of these industries:

Textiles

Cotton imports are already regulated under an international quota agreement signed in 1962. Wool imports are actually falling, because woolens are being replaced by synthetics. The real controversy is over textiles and garments manufactured with man-made fibers. Imports of man-made fiber products—mainly from Japan, Hong Kong, Taiwan, and South Korea—tripled over the past five years, though foreign products still accounted for only 3% of the domestic market in dollar terms. But in some product lines, mainly garments and apparel fabrics, the impact of foreign competition is much greater. For example, imports of men's worsted fabrics now equal 50% of U.S. production.

"Shirts have been swamped by imports," says Edward Goldberger, treasurer of M. Lowenstein & Sons, Inc., a major textile manufacturer. "White shirts have become a monopoly of these countries."

Robert P. Lynn, vice-president of Burlington Industries, Inc., points out that U.S. shirt makers turned to solid colors when they could not compete with white shirts made abroad. Then, faced with competition in solid colors, they switched to stripes. "It is a finger-in-the-dike situation," says Lynn. "You put it in here and they squirt out somewhere else."

Importers, of course, see the situation in a different light. Says Bernard Hohenberg, president of Hohenberg Co., and chairman of the textile and apparel group of the American Importers Assn.: "The manufacturers complain of foreign competition, but their mills have been operating full blast for five years. The country has absorbed their full production plus imports. If you throttle imports, you create an inflationary pressure."

Hohenberg notes that American textile makers must have long production runs to make a profit. He adds that they must "turn it out like hamburger through a meat grinder. They are totally incapable of supplying the kind of boutique trade that has developed."

Shoes

Manufacturers have mixed feelings about imports, since the big makers also operate retail outlets that sell imports. Brown Shoe and its subsidiaries operate more than 600 stores and leased departments.

Says Ronald L. Aylward, general counsel for Interco, Inc.: "There is a need for imports. The retailers and public still want to get into that segment of the market. The domestic manufacturers just want to maintain their fair share of the business."

A Presidential task force on nonrubber footwear reported last month that it found no over-all injury to the industry from imports but said that some segments may be hurt. It expects big companies, which control half the U.S. market, to increase their share, but many small concerns may go under for lack of capital and management.

Steel

The voluntary quota agreements allow foreign suppliers to ship about 15-million tons annually to the U.S. But because of a steel shortage abroad, imports this year are expected to reach only about 12-million tons.

Still, steel executives say they want legislated quotas. Says George A. Stinson, president of National Steel Corp. and chairman of the American Iron & Steel Institute: "There's a question in our minds about what will happen when overseas demand sloughs off."

Steelmakers want to keep foreign steel from expanding its share in the U.S. market by allowing imports to increase only 2% a year.

Consumer Electronics

Foreign-made radios have virtually wiped out radio manufacturing in the U.S. Some 90% of the tape recorders sold in this country bear a foreign label, and most black and white TV sets are made abroad.

Despite these inroads, most U.S. consumer electronics manufacturers are not seeking quotas. Components makers are doing a brisk export business, and many of the finished products that come into the U.S. are made abroad by American companies. Other U.S. companies market foreign-made products under their own labels.

For example, Califone-Roberts Div. of Rheem Mfg. Co. imports its Roberts tape recorders and other products from Japan. Now, though,

EXHIBIT 1

Where Imports Are Biting into U.S. Markets

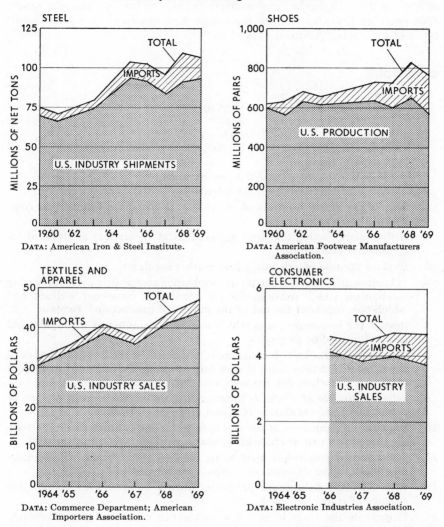

DATA: American Iron & Steel Institute.

DATA: American Footwear Manufacturers
Association.

DATA: Commerce Department; American
Importers Association.

DATA: Electronic Industries Association.

says Vice-President Charles E. Phillips, "Japanese companies are affecting us in establishing their own trade brands in the U.S. This is making it increasingly difficult for us to be competitive."

Teledyne Packard-Bell, once a large radio manufacturer, now makes only large stereo units and color TV sets in the U.S. but imports black and white sets from Japan. "We have trimmed costs and moved rapidly into advanced circuitry, but it is difficult to compete against a 12¢-an-hour wage, no matter how ingenious you are," says Kenneth R. Johnson, senior vice-president.

To offset foreign encroachments, Johnson says his company would like to export even to Japan. But he points to duties in foreign markets as high as 30%, and other export barriers such as license fees and taxes. "We need an investigation of the entire import-export problem for all types of products," Johnson says.

QUESTIONS

1. Define:

Absolute advantage	Exchange rate fluctuation
Relative advantage	Tariff
Market	IMF
Market mechanism	Psychological market protection

2. Differentiate between:
   Balance of payment and balance of trade.
   Exchange barriers and market barriers.

3. Why is the actual analysis of international economic behavior so complex?

4. Differentiate among the three main areas of theoretical analysis of international economics.

5. Explain the role of price as a free market regulator.

6. "Theoretically, the market is an automatic, competitive, self-regulating mechanism which provides for the maximum consumer welfare and which best regulates the use of the factors of production." Explain.

7. Review the economic gains which can be accomplished through world trade. Cite specific examples.

8. Interview several local businessmen to determine their attitudes toward world trade. Further, learn if they buy or sell goods produced in foreign countries. Correlate the attitudes and report on your findings.

9. What is the role of profit in international trade? Does profit replace or complement the regulatory function of pricing? Discuss.

10. Explain the economics of the situation when one country can trade with another which can produce all products more cheaply than the first.

11. What special conditions need to be fulfilled before trade will actually take place in the situation of comparative advantage?

12. Why does the balance of payments always balance even though the balance of trade does not?

13. Enumerate the ways in which a nation can overcome an unfavorable balance of trade.

14. Discuss the major types of world market development activities which have been significant in recent years.

15. Elaborate on the significance of the GATT organization to world marketers.

16. Support or refute each of the various arguments commonly used in support of tariffs.

Readings

1. "Floating rates are therefore far more favorable to private international trade than pegged rates." Comment.

2. Why does Professor Friedman advocate that ". . . there is no reason why gold, like other commodities, should not be freely traded on a free market"?

3. Defend the leather and textile industries' stand on the need for higher quotas to protect their industries.

CASES—PART I

MISSING THE TARGET IN SCANDINAVIA
A case study of competition in Nordic marketing*

We didn't go into Scandinavia cold, so to speak. Our experience there dated back quite a few years and sales volume had been built up to around $5-million annual, of which 70% was concentrated in Sweden. In a concentrated effort covering the last five years the company had gained control of 75% of the Swedish market and 65% in Norway.

(*The company, engaged in industrial marketing of raw materials going mainly into the rubber, paper and textile industries, was no newcomer to Europe. It had established a Swiss administrative operating base, operated two large manufacturing plants—in Strasbourg and Antwerp—and utilized wholly-owned distribution outlets, independent distributors and agents, and its own technical liaison offices. Annual sales totaled nearly $50-million on products with a broad variety of end-use applications, ranging from finished items such as tires and belting to foam mattresses, pillows, carpet backing, and paper coatings.*)

As we increased our manufacturing capacity and added new product lines, such as paper latex and ABS plastic resins, we decided to enter the Scandinavian market in earnest. And as we looked at Scandinavia as a market place, Sweden immediately stood out as the most important market area. As a country contributing some 45% of the Scandinavian GNP, Sweden logically represented the largest potential; we had the largest number of prospective accounts there and also the largest number of diverse end-users.

We soon learned, however, that there were certain disadvantages to concentrating industrial-product marketing efforts mainly in Sweden.

* Copyrighted © 1970 by the Reuben H. Donnelley Corporation. Reprinted by special permission from the April, 1970, issue of *Business Abroad*, pp. 29–31.

First, there was extremely severe competition. It came from U.S. suppliers operating subsidiaries there, from large European suppliers, and last but not least, from the Japanese.

Competition was so keen that industrial prices in Sweden were the lowest in Europe and, in some cases, in the world.

Little customer loyalty existed among large buyers: business was conducted mainly on price. Purchasing departments of the large users would play off one supplier against the other. Because purchasing was concentrated in certain large groups, suppliers would go after the business mainly for volume. This situation is largely unchanged today.

We soon realized that the increased competition from our European rivals called for a revision in our procedures, and we ended up revamping our pricing authority to allow for greater automony at operating levels so action on price changes could go through more quickly.

A second disadvantage was the basic reluctance of Swedish manufacturers to experiment and try out new techniques. I realize the statement sounds terribly broad, but experience proved more than once that, unlike much more adventurous Finnish and Norwegian manufacturers, Swedish prospects insisted on detailed and elaborate individual test data to be provided by the supplier, preferably based on market acceptance elsewhere, before even considering a change or something new.

Technical service charges thus can run extremely high. Coupled with low returns, these charges made Sweden a market of only marginal profit for our product line.

We developed our marketing strategy, therefore, to concentrate our efforts in Norway and Finland (Denmark did not have a particularly high demand for our products). In Sweden we cut back our technical and commercial efforts to service only very select accounts with whom we had established good technical relations.

Distribution

Scandinavia consists of four individual markets, Norway, Finland, Denmark, Sweden, notwithstanding some efforts to classify it as one. For most product lines each market requires its own distribution setup. Finding the right distributor in each market to handle your product is a major key to success.

Since these markets are small, it is particularly important to ally oneself with a distributor who has the right connections with important prospective and selected accounts. These connections can be in the form of associated lines or in certain professional and financial interests.

The business community in these relatively small markets is very closely knit, and business affairs are usually conducted through locally-established companies. Realizing these requirements, we set out to review our distributor list.

In Norway we were fortunate in having an excellent distributor who had relations with our largest customer, and he handled our full range of products. But in the three other markets it was a different story.

In Sweden our distributor was not connected with the paper industry, so we had to appoint another representative for our paper latex line. For the plastics industry, a separate distributor also was necessary.

It was a similar pattern for Finland and Denmark—different distributors for the various product lines. The policy seemed to work, however, and we were able to operate very effectively by separating the distribution of our product line in three of the four Scandinavian markets.

A requisite for marketing raw materials in Scandinavia is that you hold local stocks or that you provide very prompt delivery from a European operation or warehousing base. We started out operating from a Rotterdam storage base and then switched partially to bulk storage of latex in Rotterdam and the local market, and partially to truck and tanker delivery from our European manufacturing plants.

Two problems with delivery of bulk latex—and other bulk goods as well—are worth mentioning here: In Norway there is a limitation in the winter on road weight (we had overlooked this in one of our contracts and had based our calculations on full loads). Second, delivery by tank truck to Finland became uneconomic because we could not get enough return freight.

Marketing

Our terms of sale—based on local currency and metric quotations—were established in quite a few cases on delivery to the customer's plant. This required up-to-date information on tariffs and inland freight costs. We placed quite a few direct sales, paying the usual distributor commission (really an agent's commission) to save on costs. Terms of payment ran from 60–180 days after delivery of goods and formed an important part of our contract negotiations. We found European suppliers quite liberal with payment terms.

Preparation of documents had to receive more attention, and we changed our commercial organization to place more emphasis on this aspect. Europeans are extremely prompt and correct in their documentation, and in Scandinavia especially they are used to getting excellent service.

Technical Services

Our major problem was how to compete in technical services with the European giants. In the end it was a hurdle that contributed significantly to our eventual cutback in Sweden.

We considered it economically unfeasible to attempt to compete in Europe on an equal footing by setting up a European technical service laboratory. At the same time it would have adversely affected our image to put in a small, unimpressive facility.

So we decided on a two-pronged approach: we developed a team of highly practical, experienced application experts and installed a computerized technical information bank in North America, accessible by teletype from Europe.

This technical service policy paid off very well. In Europe we were able to recruit mature persons who were industry-trained on the practical level. Those servicing Scandinavia were a mixture of British, Norwegians, and a Dutch/American. They provided on-the-spot technical service and, in quite a few cases, solved problems for our customers in areas not even associated with our product line. This approach could be used quite effectively by other North American companies.

One should in no way underestimate the technical service the European giants provide; their service is outstanding. However, their weakness lies in a lack of seasoned and practical industry-trained people who know the entire operation and not just a limited area related to their product line. Solving an operating problem on the spot is still the best service you can provide.

Promotion

We decided not to advertise. Instead, we concentrated on sound technical literature. We found English quite adequate, and there was no need for literature in the local languages. Our promotional efforts were concentrated on individual contracts; we made elaborate entertainment provisions for technical conferences and had senior technical officers of our company present papers at local institute conferences.

We also invited selected individuals for training visits to our North American laboratory. Such trips were extremely well received and can be a significant promotional tool for other North American companies. A trip to North America is still regarded as something very special.

Financing

In a number of instances we used our own credit facilities to extend loans to customers based on our guarantee. In periods of tight money which prevailed in certain Scandinavian markets, this policy certainly made friends. In one instance our offer allowed a major customer to complete his project at the originally-forecast interest rate, and he became a very important user of our products.

We concluded contracts which included financing for bulk storage facilities at customers' plants. By financing the building of storage at plant sites we partly solved backhaul problems which developed in connection with Finland, since we moved larger quantities by sea. At the same time this approach overcame the severe winter movement problems of some areas of Scandinavia.

We also tried package deals allowing year-end discounts on the basis of total dollar turnover. Major Swedish consumers were seldom in love with this idea, feeling it limited their overall negotiating power.

Shortcomings

One part of our total Scandinavian marketing scheme which fell through, however, involved our decision to market North American-made ABS plastic resins in Scandinavia. Marketing these resins requires extensive technical service. Prime consumers include telephone companies (or companies molding telephone casings) and manufacturers of television consoles, adding machine consoles, and automobiles.

The effort required elaborate and lengthy testing—involving considerable development expenditure on the part of both the supplier and the prospective consumer. Our European group had insisted on a commitment that we would put in a manufacturing and laboratory facility in Europe prior to the commencement of any marketing. We postponed the decision on a European facility, making it contingent on our marketing performance in selling North American-made resins with existing facilities.

Strategic Retreat

This doomed our job from the start. We had no local laboratory facilities for recipe work, formulation adaptation, or color work, and we had to depend for technical support on people some 5,000 miles away who were not basically involved.

CASE I–2

WHEN IS A COMPANY MULTINATIONAL?*

Four senior executives of the world's largest firms with extensive holdings outside the home country speak:

Company A: "We are a multinational firm. We distribute our products in about 100 countries. We manufacture in over 17 countries and do research and development in three countries. We look at all new investment projects—both domestic and overseas—using exactly the same criteria."

The executive from Company A tells us that most of the key posts in Company A's subsidiaries are held by home-country nationals. Whenever replacements for these men are sought, it is the practice, if not the policy, to "look next to you at the head office" and "pick someone (usually a home-country national) you know and trust."

Company B: "We are a multinational firm. Only 1% of the personnel in our office companies are non-nationals. Most of these are U.S. executives on temporary assignments. In all major markets, the affiliate's managing director is of the local nationality."

The executive from Company B does not hide the fact that there are very few non-Americans in the key posts at headquarters. The few who are there are "so Americanized" that their foreign nationality literally has no meaning. His explanation for this paucity of non-Americans seems reasonable enough: "You can't find good foreigners who are willing to live in the United States, where our headquarters are located.

* Reprinted with permission from Howard V. Perlmutter, "The Tortuous Evolution of the Multinational Corporation," *Columbia Journal of World Business*, January–February 1969, pp. 9–10, and Pergamon Press.

American executives are more mobile. In addition, Americans have the drive and initiative we like. In fact, the European nationals would prefer to report to an American rather than to some other European."

Company C: "We are a multinational firm. Our product division executives have worldwide profit responsibility. As our organizational charts shows, the United States is just one region on a par with Europe, Latin America, Africa, etc., in each product division."

The executive from Company C goes on to explain that the worldwide product division concept is rather difficult to implement. The senior executives in charge of these divisions have little overseas experience. They have been promoted from domestic posts and tend to view foreign consumer needs "as really basically the same as ours." Also, product division executives tend to focus on the domestic market because the domestic market is larger and generates more revenue than the fragmented European markets. The rewards are for global performance, but the strategy is to focus on domestic. His colleagues say "one pays attention to what one understands—and our senior executives simply do not understand what happens overseas and really do not trust foreign executives in key positions here or overseas."

Company D (non-American): "We are a multinational firm. We have at least 18 nationalities represented at our headquarters. Most senior executives speak at least two languages. About 30% of our staff at headquarters are foreigners."

The executive from the European Company D begins by explaining that since the voting shareholders must by law come from the home country, the home country's interest must be given careful consideration. In the final analysis he insists: "We are proud of our nationality; we shouldn't be ashamed of it." He cites examples of the previous reluctance of headquarters to use home-country ideas overseas, to their detriment, especially in their U.S. subsidiary. "Our country produces good executives, who tend to stay with us a long time. It is harder to keep executives from the United States."

Questions

1. Discuss the degree of international involvement of each of the companies.
2. Which is a multinational corporation?

The World Marketing Environment

OUTLINE OF CHAPTER 4

4

CULTURAL DYNAMICS IN ASSESSING WORLD MARKETS

INTRODUCTION

Man is born a creature of need. As he matures, want is added to need. Economic needs are spontaneous and, in their crudest sense, limited. Man, like all living things, needs a minimum of nourishment; like some other living things, he is a type of shelter; and, unlike any other being, he needs essential clothing. Economic wants, however, are for nonessentials and, hence, are limitless. Unlike basic needs, wants are not spontaneous and not characteristic of the lower animals; they arise not from an inner desire for preservation of self or species but from a desire for satisfaction above the level of absolute necessity. To satisfy his material needs and wants, man consumes.[1]

The manner in which man consumes, the priority of the needs and wants he attempts to satisfy, and the manner in which he satisfies them are functions of his culture which temper, mold, and dictate his style of living. Culture is the man-made part of man's environment—the sum total of man's knowledge, beliefs, art, morals, laws, customs, and any other capabilities and habits acquired by man as a member of society.[2] It is the "distinctive way of life of a group of people, their complete design for living."[3]

Since culture deals with a group's "design for living," it is pertinent to the study of marketing, especially foreign marketing. If you consider for a moment the scope of the marketing concept—"the satisfaction of consumer needs and wants at a profit"—it becomes quite clear that the marketer must be a student of culture. What is he constantly dealing

---

[1] From *The Geography of Economic Activity* by Richard S. Thomas, p. 3. Copyright © 1962 McGraw-Hill Book Company. Used by permission of McGraw-Hill Book Company.

[2] Melville J. Herskovits, *Man and His Works* (New York: Alfred A. Knopf, Inc., 1952), p. 17.

[3] Clyde Kluckhohn, "The Study of Culture," in Daniel Lerner and Harold D. Lasswell (eds.), *The Policy Sciences* (Stanford, Cal.: Stanford University Press, 1951), p. 86.

with when he is operating as a marketer but the culture of the people (the market)? When he writes his promotional message, he must use symbols recognizable and meaningful to his market (the culture); when designing his product, the style, uses, and all the other related marketing activities, he must make them culturally acceptable, i.e., acceptable to the present society, if they are to be operative and meaningful. In fact, culture is pervasive in all marketing activities—in pricing, promotion, channels of distribution, product, packaging, and styling. The marketer is constantly in the process of adjusting his efforts to the cultural demands of his market, and although in the long run he may affect his market's culture as a result of his efforts, his most immediate activity involves reconciling his marketing program to the current culture.

It is hoped that this chapter will provide the reader with sufficient stimulation to make him sensitive to the dynamics of culture. By no means is it a treatise to which one can refer when in doubt about a particular country; rather, it is designed to emphasize the need for study of a particular country's culture and perhaps to point up some of the more relevant aspects which should be examined. The purpose of this chapter, then, is to explore briefly the concept of culture as it relates to foreign marketing, while subsequent chapters will deal with particular features of culture as they affect the marketing process.

CULTURE DEFINED

A point of departure in a study of cultural dynamics for assessing world markets would be a brief discussion of the concept of culture. To many, the term culture implies a value judgment of another person's way of life, knowledge, or social manners. A person is either "cultured" or "uncultured," the difference being that the "cultured" person has acquired a certain ability in specialized fields of knowledge, usually in art, music, or literature, plus good manners. Historians often use "culture" to mean those specific features of a civilization in which one society may have excelled, e.g., Greek culture is associated with its art and literature.[4] For the foreign marketer, these meanings of culture are much too narrow. The student of foreign marketing should approach an understanding of culture from the viewpoint of the anthropologist. Every group of people or society has culture, since culture is man's entire social heritage—"all the knowledge, beliefs, customs, and skills he acquires as a member of society."[5] Culture exists in New York, London, and Moscow just as it does among the Navahos, the South Sea Islanders or the aborigines of Australia.

Cultural Borrowing to Solve Problems

One view of culture is the accumulation of a series of the best solutions to problems faced in common by members of a given society. In

---

[4] Ralph L. Beals and Harry Hoijer, *An Introduction to Anthropology* (New York: The Macmillan Company, 1953), p. 207.

[5] Leonard Broom and Philip Selznick, *Sociology* (2d ed.; Evanston, Ill.: Row, Peterson, and Company, 1958), p. 43.

BOX 4–1

Spanish Wives Urged to Try New Foods

Madrid—Palacio Mateos, who is in charge of Spain's food education campaign, has called upon housewives to drop traditional superstitions so that their families may eat better and live healthier. His report indicates that many Spaniards are so superstitious that they refuse even to taste such products as butter, cheese, fish and even pasteurized milk. On the other hand, citizens in Cuenca Province spend half their food money on chocolate.

Source: News release January 15, 1970.

other words, culture is the means man uses in adjusting to the biological, environmental, psychological, and historical components of human existence.[6] There are a variety of ways in which man solves the problems created by his existence. Accident has provided solutions to some problems; invention has solved many other problems; and, more commonly, a society has found answers by looking to other cultures from which it can borrow, for although each society has a few truly unique situations facing it, most problems confronting all societies are similar in nature with circumstances altered for each particular environment and culture.

Cultural borrowing is almost never haphazard and not necessarily complete, but is a responsible effort to borrow those cultural ways that are seen as helpful in the quest for better solutions to a society's particular problems. What it does adopt is adapted to its needs, and once the adaptation becomes commonplace, it is passed on as cultural heritage. Thus, cultures are unique in their own right, yet are the result in part of borrowing from others. Consider, for example, American culture (United States) and the typical American citizen who

. . . begins breakfast with an orange, from the eastern Mediterranean, a cantaloupe from Persia, or perhaps a piece of African watermelon. . . . After his fruit and first coffee he goes on to waffles, cakes made by a Scandinavian technique from wheat domesticated in Asia Minor. Over these he pours maple syrup, invented by the Indians of the Eastern woodlands. As a side dish he may have the eggs of a species of bird domesticated in Indo-China, or thin strips of the flesh of an animal domesticated in Eastern Asia which have been salted and smoked by a process developed in northern Europe. . . . While smoking, he reads the news of the day, imprinted in characters invented by the ancient Semites upon a material invented in China by a process invented in Germany. As he absorbs the accounts of foreign troubles he will, if he is a good conservative citizen, thank a Hebrew deity in an Indo-European language that he is 100 percent American.[7]

Actually, in his own way, he is correct in assuming that he is 100 percent American since he has adapted each of these borrowed cultural

---

[6] Herskovits, op. cit., p. 628.

[7] R. Linton, *The Study of Man* (New York: Appleton-Century-Crofts, 1936), p. 327.

processes to fit his needs, thereby molding them into uniquely American habits, foods, and customs. And even though many phases of his culture are borrowed from others, he behaves as he does because of the dictates of his culture. Regardless of how the solution is found, once a particular path of action is deemed acceptable by society, it becomes the "approved way" and is passed on and taught as part of the group's cultural heritage. In fact, it is cultural heritage that is one of the fundamental differences between Homo sapiens and other animals. Homo sapiens pass on to succeeding generations solutions to problems, constantly building upon and expanding the culture, from which man learns a wide range of behavior. The point is, of course, that even though the basis for much of his behavior may have been borrowed from other cultures, as an American, he has put them together in a unique manner which becomes typically American and not Chinese, French, or any other culture. To the foreign marketer, this "similar but different" feature of culture has important meaning in gaining cultural empathy.

Similarities: An Illusion

For the inexperienced marketer the "similar but different" feature of culture creates an illusion of similarity which usually does not exist. Several nationalities may speak the same language or have similarities in race and heritage, but it does not follow that similarities exist in other respects, nor that a product acceptable to one would be readily acceptable to another, nor that a promotional message that succeeds in one country will succeed in another. For although they started with a common basic idea or approach, the cultural assimilation of the borrowed process developed it to meet the individual needs and translated it into something quite different.[8] A common language does not even guarantee a similar interpretation of a word or phrase. Both the Englishman and the American speak English, but their culture is sufficiently different so that a single phrase will have different meanings to the two and can even be completely misunderstood. As one international marketer points out about advertising copy:

In England, . . . to say that a wax "will not tread off" will sell more wax than the common American expression "will not wear off." Similarly, "tread marks" is more significant in England than "scuff marks" as a descriptive term.

. . . the English housewife dusts "lamp bases" instead of lamps; she purchases "tins" of a product instead of "cans"; she displays "china" or "ceramics" instead of "bric-a-brac."[9]

Among the Spanish-speaking Latin American countries, the problem becomes more difficult, since the idiom is quite unique in each country

---

[8] A concise discussion of product bias in the Central American Common Market can be found in Robert D. Schooler, "An Inquiry into Product Bias and Predilection within the Central American Common Market," *Proceedings of the Fall Conference of the American Marketing Association*, 1965, pp. 116–20.

[9] Arthur O. Fisher, "Advertising of New Products in Foreign Markets," in S. Watson Dunn, *International Handbook of Advertising* (New York: McGraw-Hill Book Company, 1964), p. 102.

and the national pride that exists within these countries tends to cause an immediate rejection of any "foreign Spanish" language. In some cases, an acceptable phrase or word in one country is not only unacceptable in another, it can very well be indecent or vulgar.

Furthermore, it should not be assumed that differences exist only between distinct national cultures. Within each culture there are many subcultures which can have marketing significance. The United States has many subcultures that even today, with mass communications and rapid travel, still defy complete homogenization. It would be folly to suggest that the South is in all respects culturally the same as the Northeastern or Midwestern parts of the United States. The general similarities of American culture are present from border to border, but regional differences exist that are of marketing importance. Subcultures are found within all cultures, and failure to recognize them can add to an illusion of sameness which usually does not exist. A single geopolitical boundary does not necessarily mean a single culture; Canada is divided culturally between its French and English heritages, although it is politically one country. A successful marketing strategy among the French Canadians may be certain failure among the remaining Canadians. The possible existence of more than one distinct culture in a country, as well as subcultures, should be explored before a marketing plan is decided upon.

These illustrations serve to emphasize that similarities should not be taken at face value. Another problem created by cultures that "are similar but different" is that, as with people, no two cultures are altogether alike. Marketers must examine each country completely in terms of their proposed products or services and not rely upon an often-used axiom that if it sells or is successful in one country, it will surely sell in any other country. As stated above, the scope of culture is very broad and covers every aspect of behavior within a country or culture. The task of the foreign marketer is to adjust his marketing strategies and plans to the needs of the culture in which he is operating.

CULTURAL ADJUSTMENT

In a domestic market, the reaction to much of the cultural impact upon a marketer's activities is almost automatic. We are frequently not aware of the various cultural influences that fill our lives. We react in a manner acceptable to our society without thought, because we are culturally responsive to our environment and have been taught acceptable behavior through various socializing agencies.[10] The task of cultural adjustment is perhaps the most challenging and important one confronting the foreign marketer; he must adjust his marketing efforts to a culture to which he is not totally attuned. In dealing with unfamiliar markets the marketer must be aware of what frames of reference he is using in making his decision or evaluating the potential of a market, since "judgments are derived from experience which is the result of the encultura-

---

[10] Herskovits, op. cit., p. 18.

BOX 4–2

Negotiating Investment in Emerging Countries

It is in the character of Americans to think of themselves as liking people, being tolerant of differences, and being the symbol of goodwill toward all. As a generalization, this image truly reflects our character. Consequently, the businessman arrives in a far-off, strange country prepared to like his hosts, wanting to be liked, but without feeling any need to study or to meet any people on an intimate basis to extend sincere respect and regard. All of this the American will agree to happily and with justifiable pride.

What he will not agree to so readily, or at all, is that he arrives with some trepidation. He is at heart quite provincial and easily disturbed when things are not similar to what they are at home—airports, restaurants, service, smells, comfort, language, action and reaction. It becomes upsetting to be in the minority. In this emotional state which characterizes him as surely as do his clothes and his idiom, the American is susceptible to errors in behavior which he should admit to but rarely does until too late. When the going gets rough, when delays and confusion get mixed up with hot weather, poor food, and upset stomach, verbal response quickly becomes uncontrolled, irritable, complaining, and damaging to attempts to establish any strong basis for negotiation.

Source: Simon Williams, "Negotiating Investment in Emerging Countries," *Harvard Business Review*, January–February 1965, p. 95. Reprinted with permission.

tive process."[11] Once frames of reference are established in a human being, "They enter as important factors to determine or modify our reactions to the situation we will face later—social and even non-social —especially if the experience is one for which precedence in accustomed behavior is lacking."[12]

Consequently, when a marketer operates in another culture, his marketing attempts may fail because he unconsciously responds to frames of reference that would be acceptable in his own culture but that are unacceptable in different surroundings. Unless special efforts are made to determine local cultural meanings, the marketer is likely to overlook the significance of certain behavior or activity and proceed with plans that result in a negative or unwanted response.

For example, a Westerner must learn that white is a symbol of mourning in parts of the Far East,[13] quite different from Western culture's white bridal gowns. Also, a time-conscious American is not prepared by his culture to understand the meaning of time to the Latin American.[14] These are cultural differences which must be purposely learned in order to avoid misunderstandings that can lead to marketing failures. This

---

[11] Herskovits, op. cit., p. 65.

[12] Herskovits, op. cit., p. 66.

[13] "Key to Asia: Respect for Differences," *Printer's Ink*, February 21, 1964, p. 46.

[14] Edward T. Hall, *The Silent Language* (New York: Doubleday and Company, Inc., 1959). See in Chapter 12 "The Silent Language in Overseas Business," a reading by Hall also covering this point.

was certainly the case in the first-named situation, which led to ineffective advertising on the part of an American firm; and the second case resulted in lost sales when a "long waiting period" in the outer office of a Latin American customer was misinterpreted by an American sales executive. To avoid such errors, the foreign marketer should be aware of the principle of *marketing relativism*, that is, that marketing strategies and judgments are based on experience, and experience is interpreted by each marketer in terms of his own culture. Thus, we take into the marketplace, whether it be at home or in some foreign country, frames of reference developed from our past experiences which determine or modify our reactions to the situations we will face. In any study of the market systems of different peoples, their political and economic structures, religions and other elements of culture, the foreign marketer must constantly guard against measuring and assessing the market against the fixed values and assumptions of his own culture.

The foreign marketer is frequently faced with the problem of not recognizing the concept of marketing relativism and thus approaching a market with a home-country frame of reference. This leads to evaluating market characteristics out of context and making decisions appropriate only for the home market. The result is all too often failure. One authority suggests that "the unconscious reference to one's own cultural values [is] the root cause of most international business problems overseas."[15] He refers to the unconscious reference as the natural "self-reference criterion" or SRC, i.e., it is automatic to refer to one's home country frame of reference. In order to avoid errors in business decisions, the SRC must be isolated and recognized so that its biasing effect is minimized if not eliminated. To avoid the SRC one needs to make a cross-cultural analysis isolating the SRC influences. The following steps are suggested as a framework for such an analysis.

Step 1. Define the business problem or goal in terms of the home country cultural traits, habits, or norms.

Step 2. Define the business problem or goal in terms of the foreign cultural traits, habits, or norms. Make no value judgments.

Step 3. Isolate the SRC influence in the problem and examine it carefully to see how it complicates the problem.

Step 4. Redefine the problem without the SRC influence and solve for the optimum business goal situation.[16]

Obviously this approach demands a knowledge of the culture of the foreign market as well as knowledge of one's own culture. Surprisingly enough, understanding one's own culture may also require additional study, since much of the cultural influence on market behavior remains at an unconscious level and is not clearly defined.

CULTURAL KNOWLEDGE

There are two classifications of knowledge regarding cultures which the marketer should possess in order to cope with the problems of a

---

[15] James A. Lee, "Cultural Analysis in Overseas Operations" *Harvard Business Review*, March–April 1966, p. 106.

[16] Ibid., p. 111. Reprinted with permission.

BOX 4–3

Colors Communicate

Hong Kong is a city inclined towards red; in Thailand the color is yellow; India tends toward reds and oranges. These are not political colors, but colors that connote a fusion of religious beliefs.

To the Chinese, red is very lucky, but a Thai prefers yellow as a lucky color. The combination of blue, black and white is, to the Chinese, suggestive of a funeral. The whole idea of color to an Asian is coupled with beliefs. And the social strata does not necessarily indicate color preference, but more forcefully the religious belief and the local beliefs of the population.

Far too many Western businessmen believe that most Asians have become Westernized in their outlook. This is true in part. But Westernization and education do not usually completely replace the culture and beliefs of an Asian's forefathers. They do tend merely to make a more intricate alliance between his culture and religious bonds. The approach required to sell an Asian any commodity must retain the basic formula of catering to national pride, acknowledging equality and understanding the Asian's beliefs.

Color is a touchy thing. Advertisers are advised to take into consideration the religious and superstitious beliefs connected with color before using them. The color combinations of green and purple are acceptable throughout Asia. These colors are supposedly attributed to the time when religious leaders wore these colors.

A prominent international manufacturer of water-recreation products learned an expensive lesson recently in Malaysia. Its home office received heated requests from its Malaysian distributors to stop shipments on all products colored green. The distributors reported that numerous customers associated the firm's colors of green with the jungle and illness. As many illiterate customers purchase strictly by color appeal in this area of the world, it was obvious that the eye—and not the advertising—was the key to expanding product sales.

Source: *Printer's Ink*, February 21, 1964, p. 53.

different culture. One is a need for factual knowledge about a culture that is usually obvious and must be learned. The different meanings of color, different tastes, and other traits indigenous to a culture are facts which a marketer can anticipate, study, and learn. The other is a need for interpretive knowledge, an ability to understand and to appreciate fully the nuances of different cultural traits and patterns. The meaning of time, attitudes toward other people and certain objects, the understanding of one's role in society, and meanings of "life" illustrate the areas of interest in a culture which can differ considerably from one culture to another and which require more than factual knowledge to be appreciated fully. Interpretive knowledge requires a degree of insight which may best be described as a "feeling." You must be able to project yourself into the situation. It is that kind of knowledge which is most frequently dependent upon past experience for interpretation and is most prone to misinterpretation if one's home-country frame of reference is used. Ideally, the foreign marketer should possess both kinds of knowledge about his market. Generally, most of the facts about a particular culture can be learned by researching published material dealing with that culture. This effort can also transmit a small degree of empathy, but to appreciate the culture fully, it is necessary to live with the people for some time. Since this ideal solution is not generally practical for a foreign businessman, other solutions must be sought. Consultation and cooperation with bilingual nationals with marketing backgrounds would be the most obvious answer to the problem. This would have the further advantage of helping the marketer acquire an increasing degree of empathy through association with people who understand the culture best—natives.

The successful foreign marketer must become culturally sensitive, that is, significantly attuned to the nuances of culture so that he can objectively see, evaluate, and appreciate another culture. In other words, he must possess a certain degree of cultural empathy. Perhaps the most important steps in achieving cultural empathy and objectivity are to recognize the need for empathy and to acquire knowledge of a culture. Further, he may find it necessary to reinvestigate the assumptions on which he bases his judgments, especially if these frames of reference are strictly from his own culture.

It is imperative for the foreign marketer to learn the intricacies of cultures different from his own if he is not to be at a disadvantage in a foreign market. A place to begin is a careful study of the elements of culture.

ELEMENTS OF CULTURE

The anthropologist studying cultures as a science must investigate every possible side of a culture if he is to obtain an accurate, total picture. To meet this purpose, there has evolved a "cultural scheme" which embodies all the various parts of culture. It is with the same thoroughness that a marketer should view culture, if he is accurately to assess the marketing consequences of the cultural differences that may exist within a foreign market.

Culture includes all parts of life. The scope of the term "culture" to the anthropologist is illustrated by the elements he includes within the meaning of the term. They are as follows:

1. Material Culture
    Technology
    Economics
2. Social Institutions
    Social organization
    Education
    Political structures
3. Man and the Universe
    Belief systems

4. Aesthetics
   Graphic and plastic arts
   Folklore
   Music, drama, and the dance
5. Language[17]

In the study of man's way of life, the anthropologist finds these five dimensions of culture useful because they encompass all the activities of man's social heritage which constitutes his culture. They serve as a framework or pattern for the study and analysis of man's different cultures. Similarly, the foreign marketer may find such a "cultural scheme" useful as a meaningful framework to use in evaluating his marketing plan or in studying the potential of a foreign market; each element is instrumental to some extent in the success or failure of a marketing effort, since they constitute the environment within which the marketer operates. Furthermore, many of these factors are those which we react to automatically in our native culture and so must purposely learn in another. Finally, these are the factors with which marketing interacts and which are basic in the understanding of the character of the marketing system of any society. Since each of these dimensions of culture has some influence upon the marketing process, it is necessary to study the implications of all the differences of these dimensions in an analysis of a specific foreign market. A brief examination of each of these elements will help to illustrate the variety of ways that marketing and culture are interwoven.

Material Culture

Material culture is divided into two parts, technology and economics. Technology includes the techniques used in the creation of material goods; it is the technical know-how possessed by the people of a society. Economics is the manner in which people employ their capabilities and the resulting benefits. Included in the subject of economics are the production of goods and services, their distribution, consumption, means of exchange, and the income derived from the creation of utilities. Material culture affects the level of demand, the quality and types of products demanded, and their functional features, as well as the means of production of these goods and their distribution. The marketing implications of the material culture of a country are obviously many. Electrical appliances will sell in England or France but find few buyers in countries where less than 1 percent of the homes have electricity. Even where electricity is available, economic characteristics, such as the level and distribution of income, may limit the desirability of types of products. Electric toothbrushes and electric carving knives are totally acceptable in the United States, but, in countries of less affluence, not only are they unattainable and possibly unwanted, but they may be considered a spectacular waste, since disposable income could be spent more meaningfully on better houses, clothing, or food.

---

[17] Herskovits, op. cit., p. 634.

Social Institutions

Social institutions also affect marketing in a multitude of ways. Social organization, education, and political structures are concerned with the ways in which man relates to his fellow man, organizes his activities in order to live in harmony with one another, teaches acceptable behavior to succeeding generations, and governs himself. The positions of men and women in society, the family, social classes, group behavior, and age groups are interpreted differently within every culture. Each institution has an effect upon marketing because each influences behavior, values, and the overall patterns of life. In cultures where the social organizations result in close-knit family units, for example, it is more effective to aim a promotional campaign at the family unit than at an individual family member. Travel advertising in culturally divided Canada pictures a wife alone for the English audience but a man and wife together for the French segments of the population, since the French are traditionally more closely bound by family ties.

The social institution of education affects literacy which in turn affects marketing promotion. In countries where literacy rates are extremely low, conventional forms of printed promotion cannot be used successfully; therefore, more radio and movie advertising is employed in promotional strategy. Certain types of political institutions hinder the development of marketing organizations, as well as the marketing of politically vulnerable products.[18] In some European countries cartels are permissible, but within the political boundaries of the United States, they are strictly forbidden.

Man and the Universe

Man and the universe is a relationship that generally results in a form of religious belief and a related power structure. The impact of religion upon the value systems of a society and the effect of value systems upon marketing must not be underestimated. Religion has much to do with people's habits, their outlook on life, the products they buy, the way they buy them, even the newspapers they read. In Belgium and the Netherlands, for example, the population is divided between Roman Catholics and Protestants, each group having its own newspapers. Logically enough, "Advertising decision (particularly choice of media) . . . may be taken on the basis of the politics and religion of the target prospects."[19] In Latin America the church's involvement may extend well beyond the family into the community as well. As one writer warns,

. . . the life of the family and of the individual is greatly and continuously involved with the Church. One must not exaggerate the implications of this relationship of the individual, the family, and the community to the Church. But one should also be careful not to underestimate it. It gives the

---

[18] See Chapter 5, p. 154 for a discussion of this point.

[19] Albert Stridesberg, "The Benelux Countries," in *International Handbook of Advertising,* op. cit., p. 416.

life a certain quality and adds something to the meaning of daily activities which is lacking in the United States.[20]

While food, clothing, and behavior are frequently affected by religion, the most subtle influences of religion can extend to the acceptance of a promotional message.

In Puritanical cultures it is customary to think of cleanliness as being next to godliness. The body and its functions are covered up as much as possible.

But in Catholic and Latin countries, to fool too much with one's body, to overindulge in bathing or toiletries, has the opposite meaning. It is that type of behavior which is considered immoral and improper. Accordingly, an advertising approach based on Puritanical principles, threatening Frenchmen that if they didn't brush their teeth regularly, they would develop cavities or would not find a lover, failed to impress.

To fit the accepted concept of morality, the French advertising agency changed this approach to a permissive one.[21]

The more permissive advertising stressed the fact that frequent brushing was modern, and chic, although not absolutely necessary.

Aesthetics

Closely interwoven with the effect of man and the universe are a culture's aesthetics, i.e., the arts, folklore, music, drama, and the dance. The aesthetics are of particular interest to the marketer because of their role in interpreting the symbolic meanings of the various methods of artistic expression, color, and standards of beauty in a particular culture. Without the culturally correct interpretation of a society's aesthetic values, product styling is seldom successful. Insensitivity to aesthetic values not only leads to ineffective advertising and package design, but it may also lead to offending the proposed customer or creating a negative impression. Closely interrelated to folklore and religion, symbolism is paramount in nonverbal communication. The uniqueness of a culture can be quickly spotted in its symbols, with their distinct meanings. The Japanese, for example, revere the crane as being very lucky, for it is said to "live a thousand years," whereas the use of the number 4 should be avoided completely since the word for 4, "shi," is also the word for death in Japanese.[22]

Language

Language also has meaningful impact upon marketing strategy. The importance of understanding the language of a country goes almost without saying. The successful marketer, however, must achieve expert communications, which requires thorough understanding of the lan-

---

[20] Frank Tannenbaum, *Ten Keys to Latin America* (New York: Alfred A. Knopf, Inc., 1962), p. 65.

[21] Ernest Dichter, "The World Customer," *Harvard Business Review*, July–August, 1962, p. 116.

[22] "Key to Asia: Respect for Difference," *Printer's Ink*, February 21, 1964, pp. 47–48.

BOX 4–4

Marketing in India

The first day of the new moon in India is considered a very bad day for conducting business. Many otherwise Westernized well-educated Indians simply will not become involved in nor associated with business affairs at this time, as they feel it is bad luck.

It would be considered very poor planning to advertise a product in a birthday or wedding setting with the models wearing black dresses or suits. It is simply not considered auspicious to display black at such pleasant occasions.

As to seasons of the year, the Hindu New Year, Divali, is considered an excellent time to do business and the Hindu makes it a specific point to transact a piece of business on that particular day for good luck, to open the way for good tie-in promotions and a receptiveness to forceful promotions at that time.

While English is widely used throughout India, for vernacular authenticity it is best to tailor the approach. For example, an advertiser could generally use Tamil dialect in South India, Hindu in North India, and Gujarati around Bombay.

The cow is a sacred animal to the Hindu in India. It would be extremely unwise for a food-product manufacturer to extol the joys of a beef sandwich. Similarly, Muslim beliefs preclude promotion in settings where ham or bacon are shown.

It would be a mistake to show a Hindu god in any kind of deodorant promotion. This would be the equivalent of running an ad in Western media for boot polish with the trade name of Jesus.

Source: *Printer's Ink*, February 21, 1964, p. 47.

guage as well as the ability to speak it. Those responsible for an advertising campaign, for example, must appreciate that "it is not just the obvious differences between tongues but that of idiomatic nuances"[23] that should concern him.

A dictionary translation is not the same as an idiomatic interpretation, and seldom will the dictionary translation suffice. Two familiar statements to most Americans are "Body by Fisher" and "Let Hertz put you in the driver's seat." Translated, they not only lose their intended meaning, but they become meaningless translations to "Corpse by Fisher" and "Let Hertz make you a chauffeur."[24] Of all the cultural elements which the marketer should study in order to gain some degree of empathy, language may be one of the most difficult stumbling blocks to overcome. Many believe that to appreciate fully the true meaning of a language, it is necessary to live with the language for years. Whether or not this is the case, the foreign marketer should never take for granted that he is effectively communicating in another language. If a

---

[23] Norton B. Leon, "Creative Strategy for International Advertising," in *International Handbook of Advertising*, op. cit., p. 183.

[24] "Translations Can Be Tricky," *Sales Management*, October 2, 1964, p. 40.

BOX 4–5

Coca-Cola Company Products at Home in 138 Countries

Coca-Cola in Amharic	Coca-Cola in Bengali	Sprite in Thai
Fanta in Amharic	Fanta in Bengali	Coca-Cola in Turkish
Sprite in Amharic	Coca-Cola in Chinese	Fanta in Japanese
Coca-Cola in Arabic	Fanta in Chinese	Sprite in Japanese
Coca-Cola in Cyrillic	Coca-Cola in Japanese	Coca-Cola in Thai
Coca-Cola in Greek	Coke in Japanese	Fanta in Thai
Coca-Cola in Hebrew	Coca-Cola in South Korean	

marketer himself cannot master the vernacular, he should enlist the aid of someone within the foreign country, even though the problem of effectively communicating with him may still exist. Should a qualified national not be available, the marketer should seek out an immigrant from the foreign country to assist in translations and other communication problems. The more recent the immigration, the better, since the translator can lose the illusive idiomatic touch of his mother tongue after being away from it for too many years.

Analysis of Elements

In an analysis of a potential market, it is advisable to consider these elements of culture and evaluate each on the basis of how it could possibly affect a proposed marketing program. Although some may not have a direct impact, others may be totally involved. As a broad generalization, it could be said that the more complete the marketing involvement or the more unique the product, the more opportunity or need there is for a thorough study of each cultural element. If a company is simply marketing an existing product in an already developed market, the need for the study of the total culture is certainly less than for the marketer who is involved in total marketing, from product development, through the actual promotion, to the final selling.

The foregoing discussions have pointed out the unique and different sides of culture and the process of cultural assimilation of borrowing ideas and practices—in other words, how cultures grow and change over time. This dynamic character of culture is significant in assessing new markets, even though the changes generally occur in the face of resistance. In fact, any change in the currently accepted way of life meets with more resistance than acceptance. Since the marketer is usually trying to introduce something completely new or something improving what is already in use, this resistance to cultural growth should be thoroughly understood.

CULTURAL DYNAMICS

A characteristic of human culture is that change does occur. That people's habits, tastes, styles, behavior, and values are not constant but are continually changing can be verified by reading 10-year-old magazines. This gradual cultural growth, however, does not occur without some resistance. New methods, ideas, and products are held to be suspect before they are accepted, if ever, as the "right way or thing." Whether innovations are developed internally through invention, experimentation, or by accident, or introduced from outside through a process of borrowing, cultural dynamics always seem "to take on a positive and at the same time a negative aspect."[25]

The degree of resistance to a new pattern tends to vary; in some situations new elements are accepted completely and rapidly, and in others, resistance is so strong that acceptance is never forthcoming or, at least, is very slow. Studies show that the most important point in determining what kind and how much of an innovation will be accepted depends upon the degree of interest in the particular subject, as well as how drastically the new will change the old. From observations, those innovations most readily accepted are those that hold the greatest interest within the society.[26] For example, the rapid industrialization in parts of Europe has changed many long-honored attitudes involving time and working wives which would have been previously unacceptable. Today there is interest in ways to save time and to make life more productive. The leisurely, continental life is rapidly going by the board. With this time-consciousness has come the very rapid acceptance of many innovations which would have been resisted by most just a few years ago. The point is probably best made by this short vignette of Rijke Van Dorp, Amsterdam secretary, who

. . . rushes home to her honeymoon flat, turns up the thermostat to warm the rooms quickly, and empties a packet of Knorr "instant stamppot" into a pan of boiling water.

---

[25] Herskovits, op. cit., p. 635.

[26] Ibid., p. 36.

BOX 4–6

Baby Food Battle Shaping in Argentina

A battle of baby foods is shaping up in Argentina.

Until early in 1970 prepared baby foods were rare in this predominantly middle-class country. Then with a great splash of advertising, an Argentine subsidiary of the British-based Rickett-Colman group has begun selling 20 varieties of "Fortris" in greater Buenos Aires markets.

The company, called Brassovora, has thus jumped the gun on the U.S.-based Heinz company, which has been conducting a test market for its baby food since last May in Cordoba, the third largest city. There are rumors that another U.S. giant, Gerber, will plunge into the fray.

Up to now the Argentine mother has had to cook meat and vegetables from scratch, strain them and then coax junior into eating the stuff. A marketing study showed it was taking about four hours out of the Argentine mother's day to do all this. The study found a sizable pool of prospective baby food consumers. There are about 1½ million children under the age of 2 in the population of 23 million.

Heinz has pegged its prices at a level about 40 per cent above the average cost in the United States or Europe, Woddis says, and so has Brassovora.

Source: News release, March 20, 1970.

To anyone who knew the Dutch of just a few years ago, this would seem to paint a totally inaccurate picture. How could there be an instant stamppot? The words are almost contradictory. Preparing this traditional Dutch dinner stew was always a day-long job. It took hours of dicing and mashing vegetables, cutting pieces of meat, adding spices and seasoning into a simmering stew.

The fact that the Dutch now accept instant stamppot is more than just a sign of change in their culinary habits. It is a reflection of a new pace and a new attitude.[27]

Although a variety of innovations are completely and quickly accepted, others, which might even be similar, meet with firm resistance.

It has been the American experience that, with more and more wives working, convenience in purchasing is more and more acceptable. Instant foods, self-service, and electrical equipment to extend the effectiveness and productivity of fewer hours are sought and wholeheartedly accepted, as well as being economically feasible as a result of the extra income the working wife adds.

In Japan there is a similar revolution occurring in the acceptance of Western ways, e.g., the world's most advanced electronically controlled commuter trains, 4½-inch television receivers, and Western dress, to mention a few; but there is still resistance to the reform of the archaic script. Japan's "simplified" alphabet has 2,304 symbols making the

---

[27] "New Horizons for the Consumer," *Sales Management*, February 16, 1962, p. 44.

BOX 4-7

Suffering Chileans Win Back Siesta

SANTIAGO, CHILE—Reformist President Eduardo Frei's "Revolution in Liberty" yielded to a counterrevolution of popular discontent Saturday and brought the siesta back to the capitol's shops and stores.

Last year the government successfully implanted the straight shift in government offices and in factories to increase production and efficiency, and to eliminate the midday transportation crush.

The commercial sector was never content with the straight shift which eliminated the three-hour lunch break. Haggling between the clerks' organization and retail owners' associations over what the government-decreed eight-hour shift should be caused several experimental changes of schedule.

The public in general never adopted the habit of midday shopping, another evidence of disapproval.

The 39 mayors of Santiago province, under stiff pressure from commerce, voted 38–1 Friday night to discard the straight shift from 10:30 A.M. to 6:45 P.M.

The government announced acceptance Saturday of their proposal for a return to a split shift of 9 A.M. to 1 P.M. and 3:45 to 7 P.M. with an extra evening hour Fridays and a half-day on Saturdays.

Source: News release August 23, 1969.

typewriter so complex that few Japanese reporters have ever mastered it; their stories are usually filed in longhand.[28] Yet suggestions for reform meet with resistance. In fact, an influential Japanese magazine recently published two articles denouncing any proposed change and further demanded that the Chinese characters which children must memorize as part of their education be increased from 1,850 to 3,000.[29] Such reaction to changes that affect our cultural character is found in every society; those changes that will alter that character most radically are usually those that meet the strongest resistance.

The French are undergoing many changes in our rapidly moving world, but they are trying to preserve one last stronghold in their *haute cuisine*. France, the land of fine foods delicately prepared and served in the leisure of the two-hour lunch, is seeing the fast expansion of *le snack* and *le self*, two "Frenchified" English words meaning the lunch counter and the cafeteria. The resistance is strong and can be summed up by one Frenchman who commented, "Anybody who eats there deserves it. . . . Le snack and le self are two more steps in the progressive vulgarization of the French way of life."[30] Despite the attempts to maintain the status quo of French food and food service, the timesaving

---

[28] "Nearly Everybody Reads Asahi," *Business Week,* July 6, 1968, p. 105.

[29] Arthur Koestler, "For Better or Worse: Her Course Is Set," *Life,* September 11, 1964, p. 68.

[30] "Hot Dog Hits Low Note in Paris High Cookery," *New York Times,* April 21, 1963, p. 42.

innovations are gaining acceptance. This process of growth and the reactions to it are relevant to the marketer, whether he is operating in his own culture or in a foreign one, for surely his marketing efforts are more often than not cultural innovations. As one anthropologist points out, "the market survey is but one attempt to study this problem of acceptance or rejection of an internal change . . . [and] In every attempt to introduce, in a foreign society, a new idea, a new technique, a new kind of goods, the question [of acceptance or rejection] must be faced."[31]

This ethnocentricism, which can be defined as the feeling within a culture that it is superior and any others are, in varying degrees, inferior, barbaric, or at best peculiar, complicates the process of cultural assimilation from other cultures.[32] Ethnocentricism is an intense identification with the known and familiar and a devaluation of the foreign and the unknown.[33]

There are innumerable instances, however, where the foreign is not rejected but is actually preferred. The status-valued imported product is a commonly found illustration of this inconsistency. The acceptance of a foreign product may be the result of fashion, a weathervane of wealth, or, as Dichter observes, the result of inferiority feelings about local products. Dichter cites the example of a subsidiary foreign tobacco firm in Venezuela which had difficulty selling its brand of cigarettes manufactured in Venezuela; the people preferred the same cigarettes imported. Dichter notes that "while the Venezuelans bought the imported brand, they would not buy the same brand made locally because they saw the words *hecho in Venezuela* on the package.[34]

India has also had problems with the feeling of inferiority about domestically produced items. Local manufacturers with modernized production facilities found that they could not compete with the foreign-made products nor with locally handmade items. The modernized plants with higher investments and better materials required higher prices than those charged for crude handmade goods, but less than imported goods; yet the consumers were "unwilling to pay them a higher price, believing that the quality of all Indian brands is equally bad. On the other hand, in competition with large scientific manufacturers they are handicapped because people are not prepared to purchase their brands, believing that invariably the foreign brands are superior.[35]

This phenomenon occurs principally among the developing countries, which are especially prone to have doubts about their capabilities. For the foreign marketer, who wants to manufacture a product within a country where there may be a similar reaction, it would mean not only

---

[31] Herskovits, op. cit., p. 559.

[32] For an interesting account of product bias caused by regional fears, jealousies, and animosities, see Robert D. Schooler, "Product Bias in the Central American Common Market," *Journal of Marketing Research,* November 1965, pp. 394–97.

[33] Leonard Broom and Philip Selznick, op. cit., p. 43.

[34] Dichter, op. cit., p. 115.

[35] Ralph Westfall and Harper W. Boyd, Jr., "Marketing in India," *Journal of Marketing,* October 1960, p. 17.

gaining general product acceptance but additional effort in building local self-confidence. As Dichter points out, the solution in Venezuela would be in "raising Venezuelan self-assurance to make them genuinely quality-conscious—in the sense of having faith in their ability to recognize quality, instead of accepting it blindly in a foreign product while doubting it in a Venezuelan product."[36] One must hasten to add that the foregoing are only examples for particular kinds of products, and that an overwhelming preference for foreign-made goods over domestic goods is not a common pattern of behavior. To the contrary, for most products, the "best" is almost always made at home by the "best" craftsmen.

Resistance to change adds long-term product introduction to the problems of marketing. Plans for product introduction would have to include extended introduction periods if product acceptance required any changes in behavioral patterns that would meet resistance within the culture. This problem is not confined to foreign marketing. The U.S. market for prepared cake mixes (an American product) experienced a long time lag before they were fully accepted. The same held true for some permanent waves, automatic dishwashers, and other laborsaving devices. Although the likelihood of resistance exists with any product, whether in the domestic or foreign market, the likelihood is greater in a foreign market, and certainly this resistance to change is one of the important characteristics of cultural dynamics in assessing the potential of world markets.

SUMMARY AND CONCLUSIONS

A complete and thorough appreciation of the dimensions of culture may well be the single most important gain to a foreign marketer in the preparation of marketing plans and strategies. The marketer can control the product he offers in a market—its promotion, price and eventual distribution methods. He cannot control the cultural environment within which these plans must be implemented, however. Since he cannot control all the influences upon his marketing plan, he must attempt to anticipate the eventual effect of the uncontrollable elements and plan in such a manner that these elements do not preclude the achievement of marketing objectives. Planning marketing strategy in terms of the uncontrollable elements of a market is necessary in a domestic market as well; but when a company is operating internationally, the task is more complicated because the new environment is influenced by elements unfamiliar and sometimes unrecognizable to the marketer. For these reasons, special effort and study are needed to achieve enough understanding of the foreign culture to cope with the uncontrollable features. Perhaps it is safe to generalize that of all the tools the foreign marketer must have, those which help him acquire empathy for the ways of another people are the most valuable.

---

[36] Dichter, op. cit., p. 115.

READINGS

HOW DIFFERENT IS THE FRENCH-CANADIAN MARKET?*

BRUCE MALLEN

A marketer operating in any given market does so within a framework of constraints. These constraints must be adapted to by the marketer and his strategy, if he is to survive and profit. The word "adapt" must be emphasized, as few if any individual marketers (firms) can change few if any of these constraints. The marketer, not the constraints, must adjust. To adjust the marketer must have a thorough understanding of the entire framework of constraints on his marketing system. These constraints have been referred to in such differing contexts as: exogenous factors, external factors, frames of reference, and the environment. The latter term seems best suited to the purposes of this article.

One can denote several environmental factors within which the marketer must operate. These include the political-legal-governmental environment, the physical-geographical-climatic environment, the demographic-economic-financial environment, and the ethical-sociological-philosophical environment. It is this last environmental dimension with which this article is concerned. This ethical-sociological-philosophical environment will be termed, for purposes of brevity, the cultural environment—a term denoting the "way-of-life" of a market. Certainly, the "way-of-life" of one's market is a key environmental factor to which the marketer must adjust and through which he must appeal to his market.

It is the purpose of this article to describe the cultural environment of the Canadian consumer market, emphasizing how it differs from other similar markets. The article will first discuss the English-speaking cultural aspects of the country. Because of our strong bicultural character, a subsequent section must be devoted to the French-Canadian cultural environment. A final section discusses some of the implications of these cultural settings for the marketer.

The English-Canadian Cultural Environment

Demographic and economic statistics and profiles certainly contribute to an understanding of the needs and structure of a market. However, in order to get at the "flavour" of a market, one must understand its cultural environment. This added dimension will aid the marketer in obtaining a greater depth of understanding than he would if he were simply to rely on the bare statistics of the situation.

Unfortunately, the definitive work on the Canadian society has yet to be written. The literature still does not provide a scholarly research which describes the Canadian "way-of-life" in all, or at least in most of its ramifications. There have been a number of works, however, which

* *The Business Quarterly*, Autumn 1967, pp. 59–66.

attack small sections of the problem. One can obtain a "feel" for the Canadian cultural environment by generalizing about these many sociological studies. It must be noted, though, that the most the reader can expect from such an approach is an impressionistic view. It is the purpose of this section to provide the reader with a "feel" for the environment, rather than a clear-cut description. The approach, then, is to isolate those key concepts which the literature on the subject seems to provide.

Canada, of course, lies in the mainstream of Western Civilization and Culture. It has been, and is, a blend of British, American, and French values. The values of these three cultures themselves are relatively similar. For example, all three are basically Christian and democratic cultures, and spring from the Judeo-Christian-Greco-Roman tradition. All three place a high value on the individual, are "this-worldly," and are to a more or less degree materialistic, i.e., place a relatively great emphasis on increasing the standard of living. Thus, describing the Canadian culture as a distinct entity has proved perennially difficult. It has been particularly difficult to distinguish the Canadian character from the American one. Indeed, it may be added that this constant attempt to distinguish our culture from the U.S. culture, or for that matter, from any other culture, is itself a national trait which I will later refer to as "negative nationalism."

During the past decade, events of paramount importance have taken place in Canada. These events have been altering Canada's social structure and have placed this country in a state of social flux. The prolonged parliamentary debates on obtaining a distinctly Canadian flag, the antagonisms between French-Canadians and English-Canadians, and Canadian fears of American economic domination and cultural absorption are expressions of the economic and cultural flux in Canada. There is a rising feeling of nationalism among English-Canadians vis-à-vis the United States, and among French-Canadians vis-à-vis English Canada. It appears that English-speaking Canadians are starting to feel more like Canadians and French-Canadians more like French-Canadians. There is social unrest within these groups. French-Canadians are demanding a larger role in the economic and business affairs of Canada.

This section will deal with the Canadian culture in general, emphasizing the English-speaking aspect of it. However, the following section will deal with French-Canadian culture. It is important to do so because the marketer, in evolving a marketing strategy in Canada, must realize that French- and English-Canadians often have, for a given product offer, different buying motives and habits. The reason for these differences may often be found in the differing cultural environments. And further, it is important to remember that the French-Canadian accounts for 30% of the total Canadian market.

This description of the Canadian cultural environment will concentrate on the differences, particularly the differences from the American environment. It must be remembered throughout that the similarities are much more prevalent. But to mention these similarities is beyond the scope of this article and would really serve no useful purpose. Most of these similarities are recognized, consciously or unconsciously, by the marketer. There are, however, as we shall see, some important differences beyond simply such superficial ones as spelling and the meaning of certain words.

Cultural Traits

Four key concepts, or traits, appear to distinguish the Canadian cultural environment:

Negative nationalism.

Conservatism.

Mosaic diversity.

Biculturalism.

Canadians, living so close to the most powerful nation on earth and constantly being bombarded with American ideas through their own media, or just as likely American media, are concerned with the possibility of cultural absorption. In order to meet this threat there is a strong tendency to point out, consciously or unconsciously, how the Canadian culture differs from the U.S. It is as if the Canadian culture has created a defense mechanism against cultural oblivion.

Canadians enjoy what may be called a "negative nationalism." Whereas other nationals talk about what they are, Canadians pride themselves on what they are not. And then, of course, there is a great difference between precept and practice.[1]

Most studies on Canadian cultural society have noted the pervasive, conservative attitude. This conservatism has both positive and negative dimensions and portrays itself in many ways.

Canadians are said to be more stable, orderly, and to have more respect for authority. For example, the "West" was never quite as unruly in Canada as it was in the United States. This was probably due to the strength of the Northwest Mounted Police. One sees less violence and strife on the labour scene, on the political scene, and on the social scene. These traits have led one authority to label Canada as a "sophisticated democracy."[2] Another authority sees this trait as one derived from the tradition of the English model which stands for stable political forms, for public dignity, and for social orderliness.[3]

---

[1] Richard Laskin, "Canada as a Society: Some Observations," in Richard Laskin (editor), *Social Problems: A Canadian Profile*, (Toronto: McGraw-Hill Company of Canada, Limited, 1964), p. 20.

[2] Scott Symons, "The Meaning of English Canada," *Executive*, Vol. 6 (July, 1964), p. 31.

[3] Kaspar D. Naegele, "Canadian Society: Further Reflections," in Bernard R. Blishen, Frank E. Jones and Kaspar D. Naegele (editors), *Canadian Society* (Toronto: Macmillan Company of Canada Limited, 1964), p. 502. See also J. Bartlet Brebner, *Canada: A Modern History* (Ann Arbor: The University of Michigan Press, 1960), p. 522; Bruce Hutchinson, "The Canadian Personality," in Malcolm Ross (editor), *Our Sense of Identity* (Toronto: The Ryerson Press, 1954), pp. 42–43; Claude T. Bissell, "The Image of America in Canada," address delivered at the Canadian Studies Seminar, University of Rochester, March 16, 1962.

It is also said as part of this conservatism that Canadians tend to be more realistic, practical and prudent. However, this often means they are less optimistic of the future and so less willing to take the required risks for development. They tend to be quieter, to be less emotional and impulsive and to possess a greater degree of humility. The latter traits often label them as a duller and a drabber people, less sociable, overly reserved and less expressive.

A third cultural differentiating trait is the one of mosaic diversity.[4] This third trait is very closely associated with the final one of biculturalism. However, I will hold the discussion on the fourth trait for the section on the French-Canadian culture.

By the mosaic diversity or, to use another term, cultural pluralism, I am referring to the slower rate of cultural assimilation of Canada's different ethnic groups. Whereas in the United States the ideal for the ethnic minorities is to assimilate as quickly as possible, there is not this kind of pressure on the New Canadian. Indeed, the very term "New Canadian" will suggest the existence of this trait. One seldom hears of a New American. Canada is a mosaic, not a melting-pot.

Certainly one very important contributing factor to this is the importance and numerical strength of the French-Canadian minority. Their culture was assured a separate existence through the British North America Act which ostensibly provided for the respect of their separate language, religion, political rights and institutions. This has probably led to a similar type of respect for the minor ethnic groups. Perhaps another determinant of this mosaic trait is the absence of strong, overt patriotism. Canadians, unlike the Americans, are not flag-wavers (and only finally designed one after 98 years of existence). One does not hear of a Royal Commission into un-Canadian activities. Or for that matter, one does not hear talk of the "Canadian way of life."

The French-Canadian Cultural Environment

The following section will not present a statistical profile of the French-Canadian market. The reader should refer to Quebec statistics, which though comprising both English-Canadians on the one hand, and excluding French-Canadians outside of the Province of Quebec on the other hand, still comprises the vast majority of the French-Canadian market. The rest of the French-Canadian market is to be found in extreme eastern Ontario, northern New Brunswick, as well as a scattering of outposts in the rest of Canada. It is of interest to note that the U.S.–Canada border itself is not a culture-proof one. There is quite a large French-Canadian market in the New England States. An excellent, statistical oriented study of the French-Canadian market is one prepared

---

[4] Many authors have made comments on this trait. A sample of these comments can be read in the following: Dennis Wrong, "Background for Understanding," same as footnote 1 at p. 28; same as footnote 3 (Brebner) at p. 526; Malcolm Ross, *Our Sense of Identity* (Toronto: The Ryerson Press, 1954), p. IX; Vincent Massey, *Speaking of Canada* (Toronto: Macmillan Company of Canada Limited, 1959), pp. 33–35.

by Pierre Lefrancois.[5] An analysis of the statistical profile will show variations from the Canadian average in the distribution of income, age, education, population, expenditure, family size and other demographic and financial factors.

Historical Perspective

It is impossible to comprehend the cultural environment in French Canada without at least some minimum knowledge of the political and social events of Quebec since 1959. These events are frequently grouped under the label "Quiet Revolution."[6]

The Quiet Revolution can be expressed as a nationalistic renaissance into the world of 20th Century materialism. The French-Canadian has had a long history of nationalistic movements. But the Quiet Revolution is a French-Canadian nationalistic movement, with a big difference. It is an outward-looking, rather than an inward-looking movement. It is a movement towards the acceptance of the materialistic way of life of the American and English-Canadian cultures, rather than a movement away from these ideals. This is reflected in a shift in slogans from *Je Me Souviens* (I remember) to *Maitres Chez Nous* (masters in our own house).

The French-Canadian culture has always been fearful of assimilation in a sea of English-Canadian and American culture. Like the negative nationalism discussed in the previous section, French-Canadian history is a struggle to prevent cultural oblivion. However, the French-Canadian has taken a much more positive defense to this problem than has the English-Canadian. He has been able to define himself in terms of what he is, rather than in terms of what he is not.

The French-Canadian culture has shaped itself into a homogeneous society with far less variations on the basic themes than one finds in the English-Canadian culture. This, too, can be interpreted as a defense mechanism against cultural oblivion. The mores and folkways of French-Canadian society regarding assimilating forces have been more rigid. For example, while the English-Canadian is quite ready to accept one of his culture who is Catholic, it has been quite difficult for a French-Canadian to recognize another French-Canadian, but of the Protestant faith, as truly a part of his society.

The reader will see, however, that much of this is changing. I mention now what will be worth repeating again; that the sociology of French-Canada is a sociology of change. This change is affecting the culture's philosophical and psychological outlook, its power structure, its educational forms, its internal relationships and its social stratifications.

The urbanizing and industrializing forces which have affected all of

---

[5] Pierre C. Lefrancois and Gilles Chatel, "The French-Canadian Consumer: Fact and Fancy" (Chicago: American Marketing Association, June, 1966, Annual Conference Proceedings, published in Fall, 1966).

[6] See, for example: Hugh B. Myers, *The Quebec Revolution* (Montreal: Harvest House Limited, 1964).

the North American continent since the war have, and are having, a profound effect on the French-Canadian culture. These two forces are prime determinants in the growing shift and movement towards the English-Canadian ideology. Paradoxically, however, it must be remembered that the growing acceptance of the English ideology is being accomplished through a nationalistic bent. That is, the French-Canadian culture is as determined, if not more determined than ever, to maintain its cultural identity.

These forces of urbanization and industrialization built up for a generation enormous pressures which were held in check by the reactionary Duplessis regime. The Duplessis regime made use of several futile nationalistic moves in order to provide a safety valve for these increasing pressures. However, these "safety valves" were rather superficial. The dam burst with the death of Maurice Duplessis in September, 1959. The final vestiges of the retaining wall were washed away with the provincial Liberal election of 1960 and the ascendency of Premier Jean Lesage. The Chief was gone, the Roi Negre was no longer on the scene.[7] The renaissance men, the intellectuals, now seized the power and initiative. The age of patronage seemed to be at an end. In June, 1966, the Lesage government lost its majority in the Legislature to the National Union. However, at this writing it does not appear that the latter party desires to or can return to its reactionary policies of the Duplessis era.

Quebec's Quiet Revolution has initiated changes on many fronts. Probably the two most important and far-reaching fronts are the educational and industrial. The provincial Liberal government nationalized the Shawinigan Power Corporation in order to provide a basis for wide industrial development. They attracted several large industries to Quebec and endeavoured to spread the benefits of industrialization to areas other than Montreal (though hopefully, not at the expense of Montreal). The educational reformation has been no less progressive. The recommendations of the Parent Commission and the implications of the Bill 60 legislation and establishment of the Department of Education will have profound effects on the French-Canadian culture. It will be better able to participate in the highly industrial and urban society of this era.

Cultural Traits

The following will discuss some of the cultural characteristics of French Canada. Again, it must be kept in mind that it is most difficult to describe in the static terms available to us a society which is undergoing such rapid change. Many French-Canadians are caught in a tension between the older traditional ways and what may be termed the

---

[7] The Roi Negre was a theory that English Canada, though abhorring the internal political manoeuvres of Duplessis, nevertheless collaborated with him and allowed him to do pretty much what he wanted within Quebec, so long as he didn't directly restrict the freedoms of the English-speaking Canadians. This idea is based on the pattern of British colonialism in Africa by which the British controlled the external policies of a Negro leader, but allowed him to behave as he wanted with his own people.

newer, urban and industrial emancipated way of life. This has shown itself, for example, in some loosening of the traditional strong family bonds and a move towards the North American equalitarian and democratic family type, rather than the maintenance of the authoritarian form. French-Canadian culture, as any culture in a period of rapid change, is experiencing a fuzzy collective self-image. French-Canadians can no longer identify with the traditional stable image generated by their former religious, educational, kinship, stratification, and philosophical characteristics, and yet they certainly cannot identify with the English-Canadian culture. They have moved from one but have not (and may not and probably do not want to) reached the other.

One must also bear in mind, in discussing the cultural characteristics of French Canada, that though having many differences, this culture is still very much a part of (though less so than English Canada) the North American culture. Again, I will concentrate on the differences, but as with English Canada, the similarities are much more prevalent. In addition, the following point must be considered:

> Income and education being two important determinants of the social class, we may conclude that on the average French-Canadians belong to a lower social class than English-Canadians.
>
> . . . it is our opinion that much of the difference in attitudes that market researchers have detected between French- and English-Canadians can be accounted by differences in social status.[8]

Thus it may very well be that as the income and educational gaps are closed French-Canadian consumer behaviour may become identical with English-Canadian behaviour. However, this hypothesis has yet to be tested.

The French-Canadian culture has certain distinguishing characteristics. Obviously, one of them is the language itself. It will not do to simply translate promotional material from English into French. Certain English expressions are nonsensical when translated into French, and vice versa. For example:[9]

> "To murder the King's English" should be translated as: "To speak French like a Spanish cow."

Of course, it is not the language differences that are of fundamental importance. It is the more basic cultural differences which I will now discuss. Biculturalism is the real issue, not bilingualism.

The French-Canadian philosophical and psychological outlook tends to be more introspective, more humanistic, more historical-oriented, more emotionally based, and less materialistic and pragmatic (though as I have mentioned, this is changing rapidly).[10]

---

[8] Same as footnote 5.

[9] Maurice Brisebois, "Industrial Advertising and Marketing in Quebec," *The Marketer*, Vol. 2 (Spring–Summer, 1966), p. 10.

[10] For a short discussion on these points, see Jean Falardeau's *Roots and Values of Canadian Life* (Toronto: University of Toronto Press, 1960); and Mason Wade, *Canadian Dualism* (Toronto: University of Toronto Press, 1960), p. 415.

A distinguishing characteristic of the French-Canadian culture is the strong sense of religious authority.[11] Again, this sense appears to be diminishing. However, it is probably nevertheless still true that the religious institution is still a powerful (though certainly not all-powerful) factor in French Canada.

The basic idea of this paper about the emerging shape of the new society is that the traditional elites [clergy] are still the commanding ones in French-Canadian society . . . . The decisive importance of the clergy and its ascendency over the French-Canadian political and commercial spheres have not decreased in the transition from the rural to the industrial society. Quite the contrary—the clergy's importance has been strengthened.[12]

Thus the parish is still one of the fundamental social units in the French-Canadian culture. The other fundamental social unit, the family, though also undergoing change, is still of primary importance. The French-Canadian culture assigns a major role to the family. Family ties are close and wide. Indeed, one can say in general that French-Canadians are used to a social relationship which is of a highly personal and emotional character. This is sometimes in conflict with the English relationship and the economic world where "efficiency" is what matters. Nepotism is not considered the evil that the English culture often assigns to it. The family relationship is so strong that only ten years ago one author maintained that there was no trend towards transformation of the present French-Canadian urban, kinship system to the more restricted system reported for the United States or English Canada.[13] At the beginning of this decade another authority, Mason Wade, was still of this general opinion:

The French-Canadian family will probably always remain a stronger social unit because of powerful cultural traditions. Early marriage, with the prompt formation of new families, will probably always remain more typical of French Canada than of English Canada. And it is doubtful whether la creature will become, or want to become, as emancipated from domestic concerns as the English-speaking career woman.[14]

The greatest sociological change that appears to be taking place in the French-Canadian culture lies in the area of social class and stratification. The Quiet Revolution, together with the basic trends to urbanism and industrialization and "vocational" education (engineering, economics, business), is leading to a shift in prestige amongst the various

---

[11] F. C. A. Jeanneret, in Douglas Grant (editor), *Quebec Today* (Toronto: University of Toronto Press, 1960), p. 308; Rauol Blanchard, *Le Canada Francais* (Montreal: Librarie Artheme Fayard, 1960), p. 296, quoted in Thomas Sloan, *Quebec, the Not-so-Quiet Revolution* (Toronto: The Ryerson Press, 1965), p. 30.

[12] Hubert Guindon, "The Social Revolution of Quebec Reconsidered," *Canadian Journal of Economics and Political Science*, Vol. 26 (November, 1960), p. 546. Again, however, note that this was written at the very beginning of the decade.

[13] Philippe Garigue, "French-Canadian Kinship and Urban Life," in Marcel Rioux and Yves Martin (editors), *French-Canadian Society* (Toronto: McClelland and Stewart Limited, 1965), pp. 358–372.

[14] Same as footnote 10 (Wade) at p. 416.

occupations. No longer can the traditional professions of clergy, law and medicine continue to preempt the elite positions in the social hierarchy. The growing new middle class, which is less traditional oriented, wealthier, more attuned to youth and big business, is moving into the limelight occupations and professions associated with economic power.[15]

Today almost everything is changing, and there is general agreement that it should change. Quebec is in the midst of a social revolution, all the more explosive for having been long repressed. But one thing has not changed: French Canada's preoccupation with survival, with preserving its own identity, with remaining stronger than ever, despite the vastly increased pressure of outside forces upon Quebec in the post-war period.[16]

Conclusions for the Marketer

There are a number of marketing implications which one can derive from the above differentiating traits in both the English and French markets. Knowledge and understanding of these traits are particularly important in the promotional segment of the marketing mix. One must not fall into the trap that a disregard for these traits would certainly bring. There are some obvious taboos associated with such traits. For example, many U.S. appeals which emphasize traits opposite to the ones discussed above could boomerang. Thus the appeal to patriotism, the loud, gaudy appeal, the selling of completely new concepts, the disregard of ethnic minorities and their cultural requirements, are only samples of things that can go wrong if one does not incorporate into his marketing strategy appeals which match the needs of a cultural environment similar and yet not the same as that of the United States, the United Kingdom, or France.

Marketers must particularly understand that French Canada is different and must adapt their marketing strategy to meet the needs of this difference. Language obviously is an important factor to consider. For example, the U.S. media overflow into Canada has relatively minor effect on French Canada, and thus cannot be depended upon, as it often is in English Canada, to support U.S. subsidiaries' advertising campaigns. And of course, as mentioned above, promotional material and appeals cannot, without considerable danger, be translated directly from the English. Marketers must consider the element of humanistic and Latin outlook on the part of the French-Canadian. The cold rational appeal may be the wrong answer. The strongly religious and family overtones of the French culture must be integrated into the marketer's plans. There are obviously religious and kinship taboos which the

---

[15] For a discussion of the new middle class, see Jacques Brazeau, "Quebec's Emerging Middle Class" in Isaiah A. Litvak and Bruce Mallen (editors), *Marketing: Canada* (Toronto: McGraw-Hill Company of Canada Limited, 1964).

[16] Mason Wade, *The French-Canadian Outlook* (Toronto: McClelland and Stewart Limited, 1964), Preface to the Carlton Library Edition.

marketer must not inadvertently break. A "family" appeal may have greater strength in this market than in the English-Canadian market. Particularly when one defines "family" in a very broad sense. Above all, the marketer must be completely aware of the flux this society is in, and must keep himself informed of the changes and trends that are and will come about.

French-Canadians do show some interesting differences in their buying behaviour. They tend to have low home, bonds, stock, car, camera and electrical ownership, while having high gasoline, car accessories, liquor, food and clothing consumption. Perhaps because of their strong traditionalism they tend to shop less in chain stores, but however are more loyal once they do shift.[17]

> There is a better acceptance in Quebec of premium-priced products.
> In Quebec, 60% of food sales are made by independent grocers; in Ontario, only 38%.
> Home-made soup is served in 80% of all French-Canadian homes, but only 40% in English-Canadian homes.
> Margarine has not caught on in Quebec.
> The French consumer has a greater affinity for perfume.
> French Canada's consumption of beer is divided 90% ale, 5% lager. Ontario's is 55% ale, 45% lager. 95% of Geneva Gin sold in Canada is consumed in Quebec, where it is properly known as Gros Gin.
> Premiums and coupons are much more popular in Quebec.
> Quebec housewives have a particular fetish for bonuses in this form.
> Quebec leads all other provinces in per capita sales of soft drinks, corn syrup, maple syrup, molasses and several other sweets and delicacies. In other words, Quebec has a sweet tooth.
> In Quebec homes, a full meal is served both at noon and in the evening.
> Quebec people are inclined to spend much more time with their radio sets in use and in watching television than are people in other parts of Canada.
> Decafinated coffees are more popular in Quebec than elsewhere.
> In a sample of 31 food store commodities, 14 are above Canadian average consumption level, and 15 are below.

At the same time, one must recognize that many of the differences between French and English preferences, taste, and purchasing behavior can be attributed to external facts. They do not necessarily represent the symptoms of deep-lying ethnic-based assimilarity. For example, French-Canadians have sometimes been cited for slowness in taking to new products. This could be due to inadequate media exposure.[18]

---

[17] Same footnote as 9 at p. 11.

[18] Verne Atrill, "Don't Dig Too Deep for French Disparity," *Marketing*, Vol. 69 (November 20, 1964), pp. 36–37.

THE EUROPEAN MARKETPLACE: SOCIAL CHANGE AND CONSUMER'S CHOICE*

DR. ERNEST ZAHN

Before many years are out it will be commonplace for marketing men to look on the free countries of Europe as one huge area of potential customers. The Common Market challenges them to plan their strategy on a scale to match the bounds of the Continent. What will this entail? Town life and home life, patterns of consumption and labour conditions, the structure of the distributive trades and the impact of mass media— we shall need to study all this and much else if we want to keep ahead of developments and take the right decisions to meet them. The executive's grasp of the future will depend on how sensitive he is to all that is going on around him. So the basic question comes out. Just how far do we really understand the processes in which we find ourselves involved?

Take the rising standard of living. This is not one single, simple process. It may be true, as has been argued, that all European countries are traveling the same road towards what has been called "salvation through industrialization" and it may be possible, therefore, to forecast some of the probable changes in living habits as the process continues. Even so, there are still great differences between one place and another, between one nation and another, and in the rates at which they change. These differences reveal themselves in a great diversity of what people will buy. Economic development is certainly affecting culture and customs, habits and attitudes, traditions and mentality; but these, in turn, are reacting on what is going on in the economy—in production, consumption and distribution. You may detect the general trend; but look around Western Europe and you will discover all sorts of subtle variations in the speed and character of the change. Here the emancipation of women may be moving more slowly. There peasant and aristocratic attitudes may persist. The Netherlands and Sweden had their industrial revolutions late. In consequence, their cities, unlike some others elsewhere, do not have to struggle against the inheritance of the coal and steam age. In Belgium, by contrast, the antagonism between the Walloon and the Flemish parts has been largely explained by the differences between older and newer industrial settings. In the Flemish part the rise of the new, affluent middle classes took place under much more favourable conditions. All this colours domestic habits and the attitudes of people towards products.

Can we identify these subtle distinctions to a point where we can use our understanding of them to forecast social change? Market research, to be sure, does reveal social and cultural change. Consumer goods give evidence, in the jargon of the business, of "innovation-mindedness," "achievement-orientedness" or "cultural lags." Some marketing companies collect an impressive bundle of facts about some characteristics of modern society. There is a growing volume of empirical findings

* Reprinted, with special permission, from *Progress*, the Unilever quarterly, No. 274, Vol. 49.

about people's behaviour as consumers. To generalize from these facts, however, is not so easy. It requires a well-organized, systematic effort before the social scientist can contribute to long-term policy.

One question indicates the complexity of the problem. Why are people more ready to change their habitual behaviour in one direction than in another?

It seems to be easier, for instance, for people to become familiar with refrigerators, washing machines, vacuum cleaners, television sets and other technical novelties than it is for them to change their pattern of food habits or the style of their furniture and houses. Forecasts have been made of how many families will buy and own various household appliances by 1970, but who is going to forecast the qualitative changes in the delicate fields of food and domestic taste?

Let us look a little closer at food habits. Food is—just as clothing—an intriguing subject in cultural anthropology; there is a good deal of literature about the meaning of all sorts of goods and services in society. Some food products are so rooted in traditions and so intimately involved in people's ways of life, that we cannot think of them without being reminded of the countries whose favourites they are. Italian spaghetti, Hungarian paprika, French wines, and, of course, the Dutch herring are almost national symbols. The Russians nicknamed the Germans "sausage eaters."

What are the reasons for these preferences and dislikes? Before we may expect to find an answer to such a delicate problem, we must ask the right sort of question. The question, for instance, why Italians eat spaghetti or why Hungarians eat paprika should not be asked with the intention of getting a simple explanation. We can only accept such facts and try to understand them within the whole cultural pattern. This is a genuine field of study. It can be analysed by adequate scientific methods.

The more the adoption of a new product means changing a strong behavioural pattern, the less likely is a rapid increase in sales. Marketing, under these circumstances, becomes a problem of long-term introduction, and the product manager becomes what the Americans call a change agent. We are told that the sale of milk products in Italy is affected by the fact that 85 percent of all Italian infants are nursed by their mother during the first three months of their life, compared with only 45 percent in Switzerland. This, of course, is not merely a problem of "dietary change."

The evolution of food consumption patterns cannot simply be explained by pointing at the changing composition of household expenditures and the per capita consumption of specific items (such as bread, sugar, fat). The rate and scope of social change is not wholly revealed by economic statistics. There is no fixed causal relation between expenditure patterns and habits. A higher living standard may result in a better and more expensive quality of food but not necessarily in a substantial change of taste and preference. Bread consumption figures, for instance, show an increase in the share of more nutritive and more fancy types of bread in total bread consumption (in France this share rose from 50 percent to 85 percent between 1950 and 1959), and the total per capita consumption of bread declines in parallel to the increasing consumption of foodstuffs with a higher content of protein and fat. The circumstances, however, under which bread is eaten, the preference of having bread in a particular form during meals: this did not change markedly in the various countries.

Many new products are only accepted to the extent to which they fit into the existing habits of cooking. Some so-called "ready-to-serve products" have become a new element in the traditional *préparations culinaires*. Dehydrated soups, for instance, are served on their own in some countries or only with additions of spices; but in other countries, they are added to homemade soup as stock thickeners or used as a basis for individual preparations. There is evolution rather than revolution, continuity rather than sudden changes in diets. A good many national dishes survive and are being further developed and refined. We still have a great diversity of taste in Europe, and as far as taste and habits change slowly, a rapid establishment of a standardized European pattern is very unlikely. The new prestige demand for more exotic food and the delicatessen boom in the affluent countries mean an addition rather than a revolution. Thus, Italian restaurants in London still have to make concessions to the English taste.

There is, however, another most interesting aspect of all this. Cooking is becoming more and more a hobby and an ambitious pleasure among the better educated middle class families, and this also applies in the U.S. The aesthetic appeal of the mechanized kitchen and of stylish design in household machinery has had a favourable impact on this development. The modern housewife, sensitive as she is about anything to do with cooking, can derive a great satisfaction from the pleasure, power and prospects of providing meals. Cooking can be a challenge to creativeness and imagination—contrary to cleaning, which can become frustrating. There is reason to believe that the "closed" patterns of food consumption will develop more and more into "open" patterns, into experiments of an art of unlimited proportions.

Delicate factors behind demand—demand for prestige, for recognition and for reassurance about one's role and place in society—have acted as an immense stimulus to the psychological refinement of products. Knowledge about human relations, group dynamics, patterns of culture and personality structure is being applied in order to identify the new "necessities" on the higher level of want satisfaction. Market research is leaving behind its original character of pure commercial fact finding. In advertising, there is a shift of emphasis from the technical characteristics of the product to social and psychological meanings. There is supply and demand on the subtle and sensitive psychological level of symbols and images. Marketing research has got a new branch: motivational research.

The approach of the Common Market emphasizes the importance of this. For product images vary from country to country. The same product may be a prestige item in one area and quite common in another. In England, beer is a common thing but wine is a luxury; in Portugal it is sometimes the other way round. In France where people eat nine or ten times as much soup as in England (in Scotland people eat four times as much) soup is an integral part of the daily meal, whereas, in England, it is one of several pre-main course alternatives. Products have also been classified according to the extent to which buying decisions are determined by social conventions and "reference group influence." Not all consumer goods are equally well suited to play a significant role in interpersonal relations. This explains, to some extent, their varying prestige or fashion value in conspicuous and competitive consumption. Market research people have had to find out how "sociable" different products are and how their social roles and aesthetic values can be improved. Kitchen utensils, rather prosaic necessities in every household, become attractive by a contemporary industrial design so that even husbands are struck by the new shelf appeal.

Then again, some products are more cosmopolitan in their appeal than others. In the Netherlands, cigarettes can only be sold in English packages which give the illusion that they come from England or the United States. The word cigarette is never printed in the Dutch spelling. Tests have revealed that some people associate the look of the Dutch word *sigaret* unconsciously with the lower class, or "the poor." The contrary is true in the case of cigars. These are upper-class symbols, appealing to the Dutch national consciousness and bearing names of figures of Dutch history (Willem II, Karel I). In France, the cigarette has a French image (Gauloises, Gitanes) and so typical that its prestige value is felt in Switzerland and Belgium, where one can buy cigarettes with the French appeal.

Comparisons of product images and product functions in the various countries can reveal essential differences between the countries. Assume for a moment that we could get an inventory of characteristics in all important markets for consumer goods; we should be able, then, to exemplify the differences between various patterns of life. By looking simultaneously at the varying functions of many heterogeneous products, we might even find evidence for determining the rate and scope of social change. It is, for instance, a common thing to say that English people are conservative. I hesitate to repeat any such generalization as we know that they very often spring from mere surface impressions. On the other hand, we must admit that there are certain general characteristics in national ways of life which reveal themselves in global comparisons. Comparisons of market research findings, can, to some extent, justify such expressions as conservatism or progressiveness, applied to specific countries or groups of people.

Britain has a relatively low replacement rate for domestic furniture and cars, and it has been said that there were "no sweeping changes in style and fashion during the past twenty years." We are told that the "middle class conservatism of suburbia is still solidly in favour of reproduction furniture" and *The Times Review of British Industry* has called car designs "conventional, and to some extent unimaginative." *Retail Business* tells us that one of the weaknesses of the shirt market in Britain has been a lack of collar styles and sleeve lengths. Some new markets in household appliances seem to confirm rather than to contradict the general picture of conservatism. The success of electric blankets is said to be due to the lack of central heating. Still another token of conservatism in consumer attitudes may be a high brand loyalty in some daily spending—in, for instance, the fact (again according to *Retail Business*) that only one out of twenty smokers in Britain is a "floating smoker" and that Players and Senior Service account for 70 percent of all plain and medium priced cigarettes. Are we allowed to generalize from such data? We must certainly be very cautious, but the more data we can get, say, for an international or cross-cultural comparison, the more sense it will make to use such expressions as conservatism or progressiveness—as long as we do not build theories on national character.

Contrary to the underdeveloped countries, the Western world is blessed by a mental climate which provokes and stimulates an ever-growing expansion. Much has been written about the competitive element in consumer behaviour. Mass consumption has been described as a revolution by which the old pattern of bourgeois society has been reversed. Consumer investment items (cars, household machinery, television sets) are said to be informative symbols of success in an achievement-oriented middle class society. They are star-products of prosperity and progress, new necessities on a higher level of want satisfaction, and people who cannot afford them are suffering from what now is called "secondary poverty": a state of the mind rather than a state of the stomach. *Non paupertas sed cupiditas fecit dolorem.*

Consumer durables or consumer investment items are a matter of "outlays of choice" rather than of routine buying. The growing importance of outlays of choice or "discretionary spending" in total consumer expenditures increases the role of psychological imponderables in the economy. In "higher income group" countries such as Switzerland, where people spend about 28 percent of their money on food (including a wide choice of luxury items), there is plenty left for discretionary spending on other goods and services, but in countries such as Greece (58 percent of income spent on food) the customer's influence is proportionately lessened. In other words: In an affluent society consumers have more chance to influence the economy through their decisions. "The richer a community, i.e., the larger the number of families who are in a position to make many genuine decisions, the more probable it is that 'subjective' factors will influence economic developments," is the way George Katona puts it in *Psychological Analysis of Economic Behaviour*.

The attention of consumer research is, therefore, particularly focused on decision making. What factors contribute to specific buying decisions in the household and what do we know about the processes of decision making? Rising young families are more likely to be "innovation leaders"; they have visions of a rising standard of living and problems posed by the need to care for young children. Where a major improvement is needed in the housework's productivity because of the demands made upon the housewife, investment in labour-saving equipment is more likely. Households are expanding firms and family growth is, just like a growing business corporation, a challenge to long-term planning. It is important to realize that what is sometimes somewhat naïvely called "status symbolism" or "keeping up with the Jonses" has, in fact, a deeper and more complicated meaning. The desire to possess goods, to get ahead, to be free from drudgery and to increase social prestige reveals a new need for social security. It is a social security which must be obtained and maintained by adjustment to a constantly changing environment.

Consumer goods are the contemporary type of personal property. That has been the case since the ancient types of property such as land, factories and other sorts of production goods were transferred from the well-to-do families to corporations or the state. A great many social functions and privileges involved in the ownership of these old types of personal property (including the employment of servants) have been replaced by the variety of consumer goods. Market research people are studying the roles and meanings of goods within the contemporary patterns of family careers and suburban life, and it looks as if these roles, meanings and symbolic values will become more and more the essential content of supply and demand.

Thus what we call "consumer behaviour" is much more than an economic occurrence. It stands for contemporary attitudes and expectations, for aspirations and ambitions, for "the climate of expansion." People are not mechanical users of goods and services but choosers of ways of living in a changing world. That has its consequences for business and it implies new responsibilities.

QUESTIONS

1. Define:

Cultural empathy	Marketing relativism
Culture	"Cultured"
"Culture scheme"	"Similar but different"
Ethnocentrism	Material
"Design for Living"	Aesthetics
SRC	Frame of reference

2. "Culture is pervasive in all marketing activities." Discuss.

3. What is the importance of cultural empathy to the foreign marketer? How does he acquire cultural empathy?

4. Why should a foreign marketer concern himself with the study of culture?

5. What is the popular definition of culture? What is the viewpoint of cultural anthropologists? What is the importance of the difference?

6. It is stated that members of a society borrow from other cultures to solve problems which they face in common. What does this mean? What is the significance to marketing?

7. "For the inexperienced marketer the 'similar but different' feature of culture creates an illusion of similarity which usually does not exist." Discuss and give examples.

8. Outline the elements of culture as seen by an anthropologist. How can a marketer use this "cultural scheme"?

9. What is material culture? What are its implications for marketing? Give examples.

10. Social institutions affect marketing in a variety of ways. Discuss, give examples.

11. What are some particularly troublesome problems caused by language in foreign marketing? Discuss.

12. Suppose you were requested to prepare a cultural analysis for a potential market, what would you do? Outline the steps and comment briefly on each.

13. Cultures are dynamic. How do they change? Are there ever any resistances to change? Are there cases where changes are not resisted but actually preferred? Explain. What is the relevance to marketing?

14. How can resistance to cultural change influence product introduction? Are there any similarities in domestic marketing? Explain, giving examples.

15. Prepare a cultural analysis for a specific country and product.

Readings

1. What does "negative nationalism" mean in the article, "How Different Is the French-Canadian Market"?

2. What are the most important marketing implications of the differences which exist in the Canadian market?

3. Discuss the major points in "The European Marketplace: Social Change and Consumers Choice."

OUTLINE OF CHAPTER 5

INTRODUCTION

GOVERNMENTS AND POLITICAL PARTY SYSTEMS

  Types of Governments

  Political Parties

  Knowledge of Party Philosophy

THE PERMANENCY OF GOVERNMENT POLICY

  Change in Governments

  Change in Political Parties

  Nationalism

ASSESSING POLITICAL VULNERABILITY

EXPROPRIATION AND OTHER RISKS OF FOREIGN BUSINESS

  Expropriation

  Other Risks Faced by Foreign Business

    Exchange Controls

    Import Restrictions

    Tax Controls

    Price Controls

    Labor Problems

ENCOURAGING FOREIGN INVESTMENT

  Foreign Governments

  United States Government

SUGGESTIONS TO REDUCE POLITICAL VULNERABILITY

SUMMARY AND CONCLUSIONS

READINGS

  How to Analyze Foreign Investment Climates, *Harvard Business Review.*

  The Expropriation Experience of American Companies, *Business Horizons.*

CHAPTER 5

POLITICAL CONSIDERATIONS IN ASSESSING WORLD MARKETS

INTRODUCTION

"Junta Confiscates Last Remaining Holdings of Jersey Standard," "Go Mexican or Else," "The U.S. and Canada: How Nationalism Clouds Marketing," "Sears Warehouse Burned in Venezuela," "Leftists Gain in Italy," "Mayor of Palmero Physically Seizes Raytheon Plant," "Brazil: Financial Crisis Waits on Politics" are all recent headlines descriptive of the complex and dynamic political environment facing the international marketer today.

An undeniable and critical fact when doing business in a foreign country is that permission to conduct business is controlled by the government of the host country.[1] A fundamental point in assessing the political climate toward business in another country is that each independent state has the recognized right to either grant or withhold permission to do business within its political boundaries. The host government can and does control and restrict a foreign company's activities by encouraging and offering support or by discouraging and banning its activities, depending upon the pleasure of the host. A foreign business operates only as a guest and at the convenience of its host.

National environments differ widely: Some countries are economically developed, while others are underdeveloped; some countries have an abundance of resources, while others have few or none; some countries are content with the status quo, while others seek drastic changes to improve their relative positions in the world's community. Of primary importance is that a government reacts to its environment by initiating and pursuing those policies deemed necessary to solve the problems created by its particular environment.[2] Reflected in its policies and atti-

---

[1] An exception to this, of course, may be the communist-bloc countries, where a government other than the host country may be involved. A somewhat similar situation also exists in "free world" nations, as under the Battle Act of the United States so far as trade with communist nations is concerned.

[2] Walter Krause, *The International Economy* (New York: Houghton Mifflin Company, 1954), p. 403.

tudes toward foreign business are a government's ideas of how best to promote the national interest in light of its own resources and political philosophy. The government is an integral part of every foreign business activity—a silent partner who has nearly "total" control. Therefore, the host country will judge every foreign business venture by standards as variable as there are nations, political philosophies, degrees of economic development, and environmental factors affecting human needs and wants.

Before a company commits itself to operating within a country, it should spend considerable effort in assessing the dominant political climate. Such an assessment should cover at least the following: (1) the current form of government, (2) the current political party systems, (3) the stability and permanency of government policy, and (4) the risks or encouragements to foreign business resulting from political activity. In all situations the fundamental policies and attitudes toward foreign business may differ drastically as a result of the different directions taken to achieve national goals. Frequently, errors are made by foreign marketers in not appraising correctly, if at all, the significance of the role of government in the success of their business ventures. The purpose of this chapter is to explore some of the more salient political considerations in assessing world markets.

GOVERNMENTS AND POLITICAL PARTY SYSTEMS

For a realistic appraisal of the political climate, a marketer should begin his assessment with a thorough study of the broad, basic factors of the more formal structures of government. What type of government does the country have? Is it primarily a democracy, dictatorship, monarchy, socialistic or communistic state, or does it have tendencies in the direction of any one of these forms of government? With knowledge of the form of government, the observer may gain some insight into the impending business-political environment.

Types of Governments

The type of government is determined by the "procedure through which the citizens form and express their will and the extent to which their will controls the composition and policy of government."[3]

Most states can be classified as having either parliamentary or absolutist governments. Parliamentary governments can be further subdivided into either republics or constitutional monarchies, and absolutist governments include as variations absolute monarchies, dictatorships, and "people's republics."[4]

Under parliamentary government the people are consulted from time to time to ascertain the majority will, and, therefore, policies of the

---

[3] W. S. Woytinsky and E. S. Woytinsky, *World Commerce and Government* (New York: The Twentieth Century Fund, 1955), p. 580.

[4] Ibid., p. 582.

government theoretically reflect the majority opinion of the population. Under absolutist government, the ruling regime dictates government policy without specifically consulting the needs and wants of the people; popular voting is only a window dressing since the outcome of the election is preplanned, with the results reflecting the will of the ruling regime rather than that of the electorate.

In an absolute monarchy or dictatorship, there may or may not be the sham of an election; a "people's republic," however, is characterized as a parliamentary system although in name only—elections are held; voting is mandatory; yet no more than one effective choice of candidate is offered. Public elections are conducted solely for purposes of propaganda. A frequent test to determine the difference between a parliamentary and an absolutist government is whether or not popular elections are important in forming the policy of the government. If this test were applied to a "people's republic," it would most certainly be classified as an absolutist government.

Vital to the foreign businessman is the makeup of the current government and the predominant philosophy toward business in general and foreign business in particular. Is the government conservative, middle-of-the-road, or leftist? Does the existing business climate include support of the free enterprise system or does state ownership of industry prevail? Answers to these questions can be determined in part by examining the philosophy of the political party in power.

Political Parties

Under parliamentary government, where public opinion is influential in forming policy, political parties have as one of their tasks the crystallizing of public opinion around definite legislative and administrative measures. The marketer must be concerned with political parties because of their influence on the prevailing attitudes of the government toward business, and, more specifically, because they are instrumental in determining the role foreign business must play within the economy.

Political party systems within a government can be divided into four distinct types of organizations: two-party system, multiparty system, single-party system, and dominated one-party system. The two-party system consists of two strong parties that typically succeed each other in control of the government. The governments of the United States and England are good examples of this type of political party arrangement. Usually within this system the two parties have different philosophies, and when they succeed one another, the impact upon business and government relations can be more drastic on foreign firms than on domestic.

In an interview with a spokesman for the Labour Party in England, for example, some fundamental differences in attitudes on foreign business between the Labour and Conservative parties of Great Britain were pointed up. The discussion involved how the spokesman for the Labour Party proposed to handle any problems of the balance of payments getting out of hand when his party was in power and he was the prime minister. He stated that he would not hesitate to place temporary limitations on imports of manufactured goods and that he would also extend exchange controls if necessary. This approach was in direct contrast to the philosophy of the then ruling Conservative Party, which had been gradually liberalizing the controls on foreign business for several years. Later when the Labour Party was put into power, there were indeed some significant changes made; among other controls, a 15 percent surcharge on imports was instituted.

A variation of the two-party system is found in Colombia. In 1958, after some years of an oppressive dictatorship and partisan violence which nearly resulted in civil war, the Conservative and Liberal parties agreed on a 16-year accord in which the presidency would be rotated every four years. The accord ends in 1974. To date the "national front" arrangement has led to a semblance of stability, but many political and economic observers feel that this accord has hampered any long-range plans for economic development, since the government inevitably changes every four years.[5]

In the multiparty system, no single party is strong enough to gain control of the government, and the government is formed through coalitions of various parties. In contrast to the two-party system, the multiparty system has frequent and continuous changes of coalition parties, since the longevity of each coalition is dependent upon the cooperation of each one of its partners, all of whom are typically at philosophical odds. The multiparty system with all its problems is best typified by Italy. Other modern governments with multiparty systems are Germany, France, Belgium, and the Netherlands.

At the other extreme from the multiparty system is the single-party system, which has one political party dominating to such an extent that no other parties have any real chance of gaining control in an election. Situations of this nature generally exist in young countries early in the development of a parliamentary system. As they advance, significant changes occur and a multiparty system generally develops. Mexico is a good example of a single-party system: the PRI Party (revolutionary party) is virtually guaranteed election in every national vote.[6] Open elections are held, but the opposing parties' slates of candidates seldom pull more than a nominal vote, since the PRI has the popular support of the vast majority of the electorate. For a young country in the throes of economic development, a sound one-party system may provide a degree of stability and continuity of development that is necessary or at least helpful for rapid growth.

The fourth political party system is a different version of the dominated one-party political system. In this type, the dominant party actively quells any true opposition and inhibits the growth and normal operations of other parties. Instead of the dominant party's having the support of the majority in open and free competition, all competition is

[5] "Colombia Creeps Back from the Brink," *Business Week,* April 26, 1969, p. 128.

[6] For an interesting account of political parties in Latin America, see Frank Tannenbaum, *Ten Keys to Latin America* (New York: Alfred A. Knopf, Inc., 1962), chap. 8.

severely restricted, and the controlling party gets support because no effective opposition is permitted. Instead of the dominated one-party system developing into a two-party or multiparty system, it will gradually be transformed into a dictatorship or "people's republic."

Knowledge of Party Philosophy

Particularly important to the marketer is the current attitude of the government toward foreign business. Equally important, however, are all the basic philosophies of the parties represented within the country, since it is probable that any one of the other parties might come into power, thereby altering the prevailing attitudes. In addition, it is important to study the entire political system of a country because each party's philosophy can have significant effect on the general direction of the political policies of the government. It is not unusual for a winning party in an election to consider the policies advocated by the other party or parties.

In a multiparty system this is usually more the case than the exception, since a coalition is required in order to form a government. In Italy, which has a multiparty system, the Socialist Party, although not in control of the government, has been able to exert sufficient influence upon the dominant Christian Democratic Party to persuade the premier to nationalize Italy's electric power industry. Most Italian businessmen regarded this move as a partial payment by the Christian Democrats for the political support received from the Socialists on other issues.

Even in a single-party system, as in Mexico where the PRI Party is always in power, attitudes and philosophies of the other parties remain important. This is especially true since the electoral reform law of 1963 provides that any party receiving at least two and one-half percent of the total Mexican national vote will receive no less than 5 seats in the Chamber of Deputies and can receive up to 20 seats.[7]

In summary, a firm assessing the political climate of a foreign government should consider existing governmental philosophy as well as the long-range direction of its political development whenever possible. The latter requires a knowledge of the various political parties and their attitudes toward business and government, and more important, their attitudes toward foreign business and government.[8]

THE PERMANENCY OF GOVERNMENT POLICY

The foreign businessman finds the stability or instability in the continuity of a government's policies in the country within which he operates

---

[7] Julio A. Fernandez, *Political Administration in Mexico* (Boulder, Col.: Bureau of Governmental Research and Services, University of Colorado, 1969), p. 27.

[8] For an interesting example of the government's marketing role in one South American country, see Peter D. Bennett, "The Role of the Government in the Promotion of Efficiency in the Retail Marketing of Food Products in Greater Santiago, Chile," *Proceedings of the Fall Conference of the American Marketing Association,* 1965, pp. 105–9.

to be of prime importance, since the degree of stability directly affects the permanency of the policies applicable to his operations. Government policy is always in a state of gradual change; business, however, must be primarily concerned with radical change in policy, a situation which creates a climate of uncertainty. Such radical change may be defined as instability.

Although government policy may alter the potential of some markets, foreign investment can be profitable under any type of government so long as there is some long-run predictability of government policy. It is the unpredictable and drastic shifts in government tactics that deter investments because the ensuing risks of uncertainty are too great. As one authority points out, "What seems to worsen the investment climate and to deter new investment is not the hostility of local business or governmental corruption but the coming to power of a radical reform government."[9]

Instability usually results from one of at least three causes: (1) a change in form of government, (2) a shift in political parties at the head of the government, and/or (3) a rise in feelings of nationalism. Inherent in these three shifts are changes in philosophy which can result in drastic readjustments of policy toward foreign business.

Change in Governments

The most drastic changes in government-business relations can occur when one type of government is replaced by another. In many instances retaliation against exploiting foreign business becomes the political battle cry of the reform government. Thus, foreign business becomes a scapegoat "against which to spend the pent-up fury of both social discontent and national frustration."[10] Once in power, the reform government can create a public image of success and spectacular accomplishment by instituting reprisals against foreign "exploiters." The change to the Cuban government of Fidel Castro illustrates what can happen to foreign investment when a reform government comes to power. Prior to Castro's revolution, there was a dictatorship that welcomed foreign business; but the current "people's republic," after confiscating foreign business investment, has followed a policy of no foreign investment.

Some of the most chronically unstable governments are in Latin America; a special report on Latin America, even though dated, illustrates the situation clearly:

A few years ago, Latin America appeared to have entered a new era of democratic government when such dictators as Argentina's Juan Peron and Venezuela's Marcos Perez Jimenez were thrown out and replaced by civilian regimes. When the charter of the Alliance for Progress was signed in August last year (1962), only three old-style dictatorships remained—in Paraguay, Haiti, and Nicaragua.

The ink on the charter was hardly dry, however, when the resignation of

[9] R. D. Robinson, *International Business Policy* (New York: Holt, Rinehart and Winston, Inc., 1964), p. 127.

[10] Ibid., p. 128.

BOX 5–1

Argentina Needs Bolivian Gas

When a speeding auto or a faltering Bolivian revolution, starts to skid, you step on the gas to accelerate it and regain control.

That is what Gen. Alfredo Ovando Candia did in Bolivia in October when he authorized the seizure of the 150-million-dollar Bolivian Gulf Oil Co.

His three-week-old revolutionary government had failed to capture the imagination and support of the masses of Bolivia's 4.5 million people. Some bold gesture, some drastic action, was urgently needed. And Bolivian Gulf, the biggest oil company in the country, was a convenient whipping-boy.

But, while the seizure was painted in patriotic colors, as a defense of national sovereignty, it stopped work on a 325-mile pipeline that was to carry 150 million cubic feet daily of natural gas to neighboring Argentina.

The pipeline was to have been financed, in part, with money obtained from the World Bank and Bolivian Gulf itself was one of the guarantors of the loan. With the company taken over by the government, which is impoverished and whose credit is no good, the international bank hesitated to disburse the funds.

Bolivia thereupon began to seek other financing for the project and reportedly dickered even with the Soviet Union and Romania. Neither Moscow nor Bucharest showed much interest in the idea.

But, with the arrival of a mission from Hungary, other Latin American countries became convinced that the Bolivians really were willing to throw themselves into the communist embrace to get the foreign funds they need.

It was at that juncture that the Argentine government took a hand in the game. Buenos Aires let it be known that Argentina needs Bolivian gas and would be willing to co-sign the loan from the World Bank for the pipeline.

As seen by observers in Brazil, which also keeps careful watch of events in Bolivia, Argentine supervision of the Bolivian project will mean some "denationalization" of the Bolivian Gulf properties.

Source: *The News*, Mexico City, January 15, 1970.

Brazilian President Janio Quardros and a threatened military clash there threw Latin America's biggest country into a political crisis from which it hasn't yet recovered. Since then the armed forces have toppled presidents in Ecuador, Argentina, and Peru, while only direct U.S. intervention prevented a military coup in the Dominican Republic. Venezuela has had two bloody revolts this year, involving both communist and marine garrisons.[11]

In view of such political turmoil, is it any wonder that one of the main points made by the special report was that direct annual U.S. private investment in Latin America tumbled from a peak of $1.2 billion in 1957 to $140 *million* in 1962? While the situation has improved somewhat since 1962, conditions are still far from stable. In 1964, Brazil and Bolivia fell under military rule, Argentina followed in 1966,

---

[11] "Special Report: Latin America," *Business Week*, September 22, 1962, p. 178. Reprinted from the September 22, 1962, issue of *Business Week* by special permission. Copyrighted © 1962 by McGraw-Hill, Inc.

and the most recent military coup was in Peru in 1968.[12] However, from an economic view these ruling military "juntas" do not necessarily mean economic chaos. For example, the military regime in Brazil has managed to cut inflation from a 90 percent annual rate in 1964 to a 20-year low of 25 percent in 1969.[13] Attitudes toward foreign investment have ranged from encouragement for those investments that fit the government's economic plan to expropriation.

Although frequent and radical changes in government generally develop sufficient uncertainty to deter investment, the comments of one executive of an international company present a somewhat different viewpoint. He points out that his company has had successful operations in one notoriously unstable Latin American country without any fundamental shifts in government policy toward his firm. The difference appeared to be that changes in the government did not mean shifts of administration, but changes in the legislative group only. The administration had remained constant. In fact, he pointed out that the top administration with whom his company dealt had been in office much longer than similar top administrators in the American government. Thus, the policy relationship between his company and the government was stable, despite constant changes in the formal government.[14] As a result of his experience, he suggested that an appraisal of prospective countries for investment should include even those countries that have reputations of instability, with additional investigation into the administrative portion with which the investing company would be dealing. It is possible that the administrative part of the government would be stable even though there had been a history of several government overthrows. Although the above may be an exceptional case, it does point up the fact that countries with the most unstable governments can offer favorable business opportunities.

Change in Political Parties

Changes in the political parties at the head of a government can also result in unstable conditions, although not so severe as an overthrow of the government. Generally, changes in policy are made so that the operation of foreign businesses is more in line with the philosophy of the new party. In some instances, a new political party at the helm might result in action as severe as nationalization or expropriation of an industry. The usual results, however, are tightening or lessening of various government controls. When the Liberal Party gained power in Canada in 1963, the immediate reactions were proposals for tougher bargaining on tariffs with the United States and suggestions for stepped-up pressures from the new Canadian government against foreign-owned businesses to increase exports of Canadian-made products and decrease

---

[12] "New Breed of Generals," *Business Week*, October 12, 1968, pp. 36–38.

[13] "Peru Turns Tougher," *Business Week*, February 15, 1969, pp. 32–33.

[14] Rowland Burnston, "Over-All Criteria for Selecting a Particular Company, Planning Overseas Operations," International Management Series No. 1, 1962, p. 15.

BOX 5-2

Social Reform in Peru

On August 9, 1970 the Peruvian government announced the development of a new industrial law which provides that the government buy control of all basic industries and sell the equity to nationals. Preliminary reports indicate that the government intends to buy at least two-thirds control of most companies in basic industries over a ten-year period. Foreign owners of companies in other industries will have to sell 51% control to Peruvians within a fairly short period, and eventually divest themselves of all but 25% ownership. Further, each company will be required to re-invest 15% of its net profits annually in company shares for the account of its employees until the employees own 51% of the concern.

On August 14, the regime took another step against foreign investment, specifying which of the 13 auto assembly plants would be allowed to remain. Only five made it. The two biggest, Ford and General Motors, will be out of business by the end of 1970, although Ford will continue to import and sell tractors. Chrysler won rights to make two types of cars and three trucks. Now, only about 10% of each auto is locally made, but that figure must reach 35% by next April. Chrysler must also sell 51% of its shares—about $5 million—to local investors.

Augusto Zimmerman, spokesman for President Juan Valasco Alvarado of Peru, argues: "We have had massive foreign investment for decades, but Peru has not achieved development. Foreign capital will now have to meet government social goals."

Source: Reprinted from the August 29, 1970, issue of *Business Week*, p. 26, by special permission. Copyright © 1970 by McGraw-Hill, Inc.

imports into the country. The automobile industry was the immediate target, with pressures exerted to produce more component parts and accessories in Canada. Should the industry, almost totally owned by American manufacturers, fail to comply, a spokesman for the Liberal Party suggested that legislation forcing it to comply would be demanded in order to bring it into line with the new policy.

Nationalism

An intensive feeling of national pride and unity, nationalism, may accompany a change in government or political philosophy, or it may simply be an awakening of a nation's people to pride in their country. Nationalism may be present in the most stable government, but intense national pride is probably more frequently associated with the newly developing nations. Manifest in their feelings are "national political unity and a desire for national economic betterment and self reliance."[15]

A growth in socialism is often accompanied by an intensification of nationalism, although feelings of nationalism may be just as strong

---

[15] Laurence W. Towle, *International Trade and Commercial Policy* (2d ed.; New York: Harper and Brothers, 1956), pp. 13–14.

under a free enterprise system. While generally considered a phenomenon of the less developed economies, "Buy American" policies are evidence that the most mature nations have some feelings of nationalism which color trade relations with other countries.

A trend toward greater feelings of nationalism can bring about expropriation; however, more often than not, public opinion tends to become "anti-foreign business" and many minor harassments and controls of foreign investment are supported, if not applauded. Even though few countries are exempt from a touch of nationalism, the more mature countries are, the more realistic are the effects of nationalism upon their commercial policies.

Ambitious nations struggling along the road of economic development quite naturally have a strong sense of national, social, cultural, and economic unity and pride. The unfortunate result is that often these feelings of nationalism are channeled in directions which cause a country to formulate policies that are deterrents to sound and rapid economic growth. Commonly, the net result is that a foreign company actually making sound contributions to the economic growth of the host nation falls prey to well-intended, but nonetheless unsound, changes in policy.

Changes in governments, shifts in power of political parties, and strong feelings of nationalism all lead, at times, to conditions which create unstable relations between governments and foreign businesses, thereby creating risks for the foreign investor. The following discussion deals with how political climate affects a product's acceptability.

ASSESSING POLITICAL VULNERABILITY

Some products appear to be more politically vulnerable than others, i.e., because of particular circumstances they receive special governmental attention which can be either favorable or unfavorable, depending upon the product. Favorable political attention can result in protection, reduced tax rates, exemption from quotas, control of competition, and other types of concessions. This can be illustrated by India's attempts to encourage investments in high-priority industries by reducing corporate taxes, ending price controls, and even exempting foreign technicians from income taxes.

Political vulnerability, however, also can lead to labor agitation, public regulations, price fixing, allocation quotas, expropriation, regulation and control, or other forms of government harassment if the product is considered to be nonessential or undesirable. For example, a leading Brazilian industrialist successfully blocked a proposed competing plant facility to be built by American Can Company by subsidizing a communist protest, complete with student demonstrations. In Colombia, a tobacco monopoly, with government sanction, managed to keep machinery for a new British-American tobacco company plant on the docks for nearly two years, effectively killing the project.

Attitudes toward politically vulnerable products can change from unfavorable to favorable overnight, depending on the intent of the government. Roadblocks designed by Indian bureaucrats had been so formidable that three American firms backed out of a $40 million fertilizer plant. Yet, a year later, the change in political climate was such that another firm was able to come to terms with the government and secure the necessary permits in a day and a half. The reversal in the attitude of the Indian government came with the realization that foreign investment was necessary in support of the industry for agriculture. Prior to the change, there was the belief that the opportunities for this kind of industrial investment should be left to nationals.

There are at least as many reasons for a product's political vulnerability as there are political philosophies, economic variations, and cultural differences. Unfortunately, there are no set rules for a marketer to follow to determine definitely whether or not a product will be subject to political attention. By answering the following questions, however, a marketer may detect clues to a product's vulnerability.

1. Is the availability of supply of the product ever subject to important political debates? (sugar, salt, gasoline, public utilities, medicines, foodstuffs)
2. Do other industries depend upon the production of the product? (cement, power, machine tools, construction machinery, steel)
3. Is the product considered socially or economically essential? (key drugs, laboratory equipment, medicines)
4. Is the product essential to agricultural industries? (farm tools and machinery, crops, fertilizers, seed)
5. Does the product affect national defense capabilities? (transportation industry, communications)
6. Does the product include important components that would be available from local sources and that otherwise would not be used as effectively? (labor, skills, materials)
7. Is there local competition or potential local competition from manufacturers in the near future? (small, low investment manufacturing)
8. Does the product relate to channels of mass communication media? (newsprint, radio equipment)
9. Is the product primarily a service?
10. Does the use of the product, or its design, rest upon some legal requirements?
11. Is the product potentially dangerous to the user? (explosives, drugs)
12. Does the product induce a net drain on scarce foreign exchange?[16]

If answers to each of these questions are scored from 1 to 10, from a strong "yes" to a strong "no," the lowest scoring products would be subject to the most intense political pressures. They would receive favorable political attention if they contributed to the achievement of national goals or unfavorable attention if they were nonessential in view of current national needs. For those products with unfavorable vulnerability scores, the risks would be great, whereas for those with favorable scores, encouragement and special considerations would be generally available.

---

[16] Richard D. Robinson, "The Challenge of the Underdeveloped National Market," *The Journal of Marketing*, October 1961, pp. 24–25. Reprinted from *The Journal of Marketing*, published by the American Marketing Association.

BOX 5-3

Mexico Says It Again: "Mexicanize"

The Mexican government is putting stronger pressure on U.S. subsidiaries to "Mexicanize."

The government is not attempting anything along the lines of its forced nationalization of oil companies in the 1930s or the 1960 purchase of foreign-owned power companies. Instead, Mexico is using a careful carrot-and-stick persuasion to increase local participation in foreign subsidiaries.

Latest American subsidiary to fall into line is International Telephone & Telegraph's Standard Electrica de Mexico, which plans to offer 40% of its stock to Mexican investors this fall. The ITT decision comes on the heels of the sale by General Electric de Mexico of 10% of its shares and the purchase by Mexican industrialist Bruno Pagliai of a 50% interest in Scripto de Mexico.

Mexican law decrees that companies operating in some industries must be partly Mexicanized and suggests that foreign capital be limited in other industries if local money is available. These laws have been used in the past to force Mexicanization by such companies as American Smelting & Refining Co. and American Metal Climax, Inc.

The GE and ITT moves weren't required by law. Mexico now puts the squeeze on foreign companies in more subtle ways.

When a company applies for an import permit, for example, government officials are likely to ask the company to present a plan for Mexicanization.

As more and more companies yield, the pressure is bound to mount for such companies as Ford, General Motors, and Anaconda, which still insist on full ownership of their Mexican subsidiaries.

Source: Reprinted from the August 24, 1968, issue of *Business Week*, p. 78, by special permission. Copyrighted © 1968 by McGraw-Hill, Inc.

For the marketer doing business in a foreign country, a necessary part of any market analysis is an assessment of the probable political consequences of his marketing plans—some marketing activities are more susceptible to political considerations than others. Basically, it boils down to the evaluation of the essential nature of his immediate activity. The following section explores some of the more salient types of risks that face a business whose products and activities are politically vulnerable.

EXPROPRIATION AND OTHER RISKS OF FOREIGN BUSINESS

The kinds of risks resulting from the political implications of a company's activities can range from expropriation, the most severe, to many lesser but still important government activities such as exchange controls, import restrictions, price controls, and labor policy. Each of these politically and/or economically inspired sanctions against foreign business is sufficiently important and occurs with enough frequency to require the special consideration of the foreign marketer; in most foreign business ventures, one or all of these risks are incurred to some degree and must be accepted as political realities of the environment when a marketer is doing business overseas.

Expropriation

The most extreme consequence of a hostile political environment faced by a foreign investor is confiscation of his property by the host country. Expropriation of foreign business, with or without reimbursement, is probably the most critical politically induced risk of foreign business. Modern economic history is replete with cases of expropriation; some better known examples are Mexico's take-over of the foreign-owned railway system in 1937 and the oil industry in 1938; Guatemala's take-over of foreign-owned banana plantations in 1953; Iran's attempted nationalization of British-owned oil interests in 1952,[17] the Cuban expropriation of all industry; Brazil's take-over of U.S.-owned electrical power plants; and the 1969 expropriation of Standard Oil's holdings by the government of Peru.

The motivation of a country that expropriates foreign investment is frequently couched in deep sentiments of nationalism. Why does a nation feel that it must seize foreign investment? Many reasons are given, but basically such action stems from the belief (whether or not correct is immaterial) that the country's national goals and self-interest can best be served by government ownership rather than by foreign control of a particular industry.

Expropriation is typically justified on the grounds that the industry is critical to national defense, national sovereignty, national wealth and/or national economic growth, and thus the nation's interests require that the industry not be controlled by a foreigner. Consequently, certain industries are more susceptible to expropriation than others. Public utilities are a frequent target, since it is universally held that they are critical to economic growth as well as being instrumental in defense capabilities. Mining, oil, and other natural resources are also especially vulnerable, since the nation's wealth is at stake. Other types of industries can be as defenseless as those mentioned above if the industry is the primary basis for the country's economy. Another justification for expropriation is the strong feeling held by many that foreign businesses have typically exploited the national wealth of the host country, taking everything from the country and giving nothing in return.

Expropriation does not always mean total loss for the foreign investor. In some cases, the investment is nationalized and the government reimburses the investor for the value of his losses; the reimbursement is seldom felt to be "equitable" by the foreign owner, but there is less stigma attached to such government action if some payment is made. Confiscation is especially alluring to the underdeveloped country; as one observer noted, confiscation ". . . is easy and all it requires is a

---

[17] Krause, op. cit., p. 266.

BOX 5–4

Latin Reformers Seek More from Business

"It looks as if Dow has got too damn much money here," said a petrochemical executive in Santiago, Chile, this week. He was referring to Dow Chemical Co.'s $21-million investment in a petrochemical complex scheduled to come on stream this month. But he could have been talking about any of the U.S. companies, from copper producers to bankers and hotel keepers, that have a $965-million investment stake in Chile. Practically all of it is earmarked for expropriation by Salvador Allende, Chile's Marxist president.

We want to recover for Chile the resources that now go to the Capitalists," said Allende, wearing a workingman's leather windbreaker and open shirt at his shabby downtown headquarters following the election. "We have much against American capitalism which has infiltrated our country. We are going to finish with foreign influence."

"We were invited to come here, which I keep reminding them," says Budd Venable, executive vice-president of Petrodow. He notes that the government decree permitting Dow's investment provided guarantees for the company. "But we will have Allende as president," he says, "and if you want to know what's going to happen, read his program."

Allende's program pledges nationalization of petrochemicals along with mining, banking, trade, communications, and other industries. Allende says he will pay foreign companies for expropriated property, but he has never explained how. As a result, businessmen are pessimistic about chances for getting adequate compensation. Says a wary American businessman in Santiago: "With 30% inflation, he could issue generous face value bonds that would soon be so much wallpaper."

Governments in other Latin countries have also been putting the squeeze on American companies:

The Bolivian military junta seized Gulf Oil Co.'s fields last year. Gulf is still dickering on terms of compensation under a deal that would turn over operation of the fields to Spain's industrial holding company.

The Venezuelan government is tightening restrictions on foreign banks and has decided to grant no more oil concessions. Oil companies, mostly American, will have to work for the government petroleum agency under contract in drilling new acreage.

Colombia gave the nod to France's Renault over Detroit's Big Three and other auto makers in bidding on a new assembly plant in Medellin. To get the permit, Renault had to agree to buy and market abroad an amount of Colombian products equal in value to the auto components that it imports.

Source: Reprinted from the September 12, 1970, issue of *Business Week*, pp. 104–5, by special permission. Copyright © 1970 by McGraw-Hill, Inc.

decree. It is dirt cheap, for it costs nothing at all, and it seems to transfer national wealth and property from foreign hands to their own."[18]

Some authorities believe that the risks of expropriation will be less in the future for three important reasons. One is that countries are coming

---

[18] Tannenbaum, op. cit., p. 234.

to realize that foreign investment is necessary to the achievement of desired growth potential and that expropriation, whatever the reason, typically dries up much needed investment capital. Furthermore, past experience has shown that government ownership does not always yield the desired results. In fact, in some cases, experience has shown that after expropriation of an industry, the industry has faltered and its contribution to the national economy has decreased. A second fact which may alter future attempts at expropriation is the more stringent economic pressure being levied against the offending nation by the country of the exploited firm when equitable reimbursement is not made. The third reason is derived from the activities that investing firms are undertaking to make themselves indispensable and less vulnerable in a host country. Such activities include encouraging nationals to invest in the business venture, employing nationals in important management positions, and generally attempting to erase the constant suspicion that the foreign firm is somehow exploiting the host country.

Although the threat of expropriation may be abating, it still persists and is of prime significance as a political risk in doing business abroad. More common and frequent risks come from the multitude of minor but nonetheless costly harassments often encountered when a marketer is doing business in another country.

Other Risks Faced by Foreign Business

Expropriation of a foreign business with or without restitution is an extreme course for any government. Instead of expropriation, most businessmen abroad are faced with less drastic but nevertheless troublesome risks of politically condoned or inspired controls and pressures exerted against foreign operators. Political objectives under the banner of national security and/or the protection of infant industry are demanded despite the cold economic facts involved.

Exchange Controls. Exchange controls stem from shortages of foreign exchange held by a country. A recurrent problem of the foreign investor is that of getting his profits and investments into the currency of his home country. When a nation faces shortages of foreign exchange, controls may be leveled over all movements of capital or, selectively, against the most politically vulnerable companies in order to conserve the supply of foreign exchange for the most essential uses.

Exchange controls are also extended to products by applying a system of multiple exchange rates to regulate trade in specific commodities classified as necessities or luxuries. Necessary products are placed in the most favorable (low) exchange categories, while luxuries are heavily penalized with high foreign exchange rates.

In countries with an especially difficult balance of payments problem, earnings as well as principal have been frozen for considerable periods of time.[19] Such extreme measures are infrequent, as are those cases of

---

[19] Krause, op. cit., p. 267.

some countries limiting profit remittance to a small, fixed percentage of net assets.[20]

Currency convertibility is becoming less of a problem than it has been, but most countries maintain regulations for control of currency. In the event that an economy should suffer a setback or foreign exchange reserves suffer severely, the controls on convertibility can be imposed rapidly.[21]

Import Restrictions. Selective restrictions on the imports of raw materials, machines, and spare parts are a fairly common strategy to induce foreign industry to purchase more of its supplies within the host country and thereby create markets for local industry.[22] Although this is done in an attempt to support the development of domestic industry, the net result is often to hamstring and sometimes to interrupt the operations of established industries. The problem then becomes critical when there are no adequately developed sources of supply within the country.

Tax Controls. Taxes must be classified as a political risk when they are used as a means of controlling foreign investments. In such cases they are often raised without warning and in violation of formal agreements. A squeeze on profits is affected by raising taxes significantly as a business becomes established; oil companies have found this a frequent problem. There are cases where initial agreements have called for specific tax rates, only to be increased considerably after some degree of success. Venezuela boosted the taxes on U.S. oil companies to 65 percent of net income and, in addition, placed a ceiling on the prices of the company's oil. In those underdeveloped countries where the economy is constantly threatened with shortages of funds, unreasonable taxation of successful foreign investments frequently appears to be the handiest and quickest means of finding operating funds.

Price Controls. Essential products that command considerable public interest, such as drugs and medicines, gasoline, and tires, are often subjected to price controls. These controls are generally applied during inflationary periods, and when inflation is particularly rampant, the consequences of price ceilings can be extremely costly. The problems of a company faced with price ceilings during the two years that the value of the cruzeiro in Brazil decreased by as much as two thirds were almost insurmountable. Since periods of inflation are not restricted to only a few countries, this type of risk must be considered for most areas. Rampant inflation itself can be very costly under any circumstances, but when coupled with stringent price controls, the result is often disastrous.

Labor Problems. In many countries labor unions have strong government support that they use effectively in getting special concessions from business. Layoffs may be forbidden; profits may have to be shared;

---

[20] Harold H. Whitman, "Financial Problems and Risks Operating Abroad," *International Management Series No. 1,* p. 30.

[21] Alexander O. Stanley, *Handbook of International Marketing* (New York: McGraw-Hill Book Company, 1963), p. 139.

[22] Whitman, op. cit., p. 29.

and an extraordinary number of services may have to be provided. In fact, in many countries foreign firms are considered to be fair game for the demands of the domestic labor supply.

In France, the belief in full employment is almost religious in fervor; layoffs of any size, especially by foreign-owned companies, are looked upon as national crises. When, as a result of cutbacks in demand, both General Motors and Remington Rand attempted to lay off workers in their French plants, the French Minister of Industry reprimanded them and stated that he would not allow "certain isolated enterprises to practice an irresponsible policy that does not respect the social contract linking a financially powerful enterprise to the labor it employs." Although both General Motors and Remington Rand were privately assured that the minister's remarks were only for public consumption, the reaction is indicative of the role between government and labor in many countries. An interesting sidelight is that the same conditions that forced General Motors and Remington Rand to lay off workers were affecting domestic French industry as well so that it too was laying off personnel; but apparently this situation went unnoticed by the government. In Mexico, not only is the freedom to fire restricted, but recent amendments to the constitution legally obligate companies to share profits with their employees. A "national committee" has been set up to determine the amount of a firm's profits and the extent to which they must be shared with labor. The committee is composed of representatives of government, management, and labor, each with equal representation. It is felt that the representation is not balanced fairly, since labor unions are regarded as, in effect, arms of the Mexican government. As a consequence, many believe that management will be outnumbered 2 to 1.

Another labor problem is the restriction sometimes placed upon the entry into a country of key technicians. In order to force the hiring of nationals, some countries will not provide work permits to technically trained personnel, regardless of whether or not men with similar talents are available within the country.

While no one of these risks is sufficiently detrimental to ruin a venture, they can separately or collectively cause trouble and seriously affect the profitability of a firm's operation. Obviously, it takes more than risks of this nature to deter foreign investment. This is expressly borne out by the increased investments that continue to pour into so-called "risky" countries. One reason that foreign capital can still be found, despite the risks involved, is that the U.S. government encourages American investment abroad by offering protection against certain political risks.

ENCOURAGING FOREIGN INVESTMENT

Many countries encourage foreign investment. In fact, within the same country, although some foreign businesses fall prey to politically induced harassments, others may be placed under a government umbrella of protection and preferential treatment. The difference lies in the evaluation of a company's contribution to the nation's self-interest.

Foreign Governments

The most important reason for the encouragement of foreign investment is that it affords the most rapid means of providing necessary goods and services. Actually, foreign investment can often be instrumental in accelerating the development of an economy. In fact, many countries are coming to realize that foreign investment, properly controlled, need never be discouraged because the benefits outweigh most of the disadvantages involved.[23]

One underdeveloped country has openly invited investors to literally take over the industrialization of that country. The many inducements include tax exemptions, protection against competing imports, unimpeded movement of capital and profits, plus a multitude of other concessions. Naturally, direct contribution to the economy is a necessary prerequisite for such special treatment. Colombia's most recent ten-year development plan allows for special considerations to foreign investors, including income tax exemptions of up to 100 percent, providing the company's "sole business is the development of a basic industry necessary for Colombia's development."

Coupled with direct encouragement from the host country is the assistance an American company can receive from the U.S. government. The intent is to encourage investment by helping to minimize and shift some of the risks evolving from foreign political considerations.

United States Government

The U.S. government is motivated for economic as well as political reasons to encourage American firms to seek business opportunities in other countries. This has resulted in a variety of services and inducements intended to prompt the American firm to go overseas. The kinds of assistance can be divided into two distinct areas: those activities designed to create favorable climates for foreign investment, and those activities designed to assist day-to-day operations. An official of the Bureau of Foreign Commerce summed up the role the United States hopes to take in encouraging foreign business investment when he remarked:

In the broadest possible sense, our entire foreign policy and our domestic economic policy may be said to aid the management of foreign operations. They both have among their purposes the development of the sort of peaceful, stable, prosperous world in which free enterprise, including American free enterprise, can operate. . . . In a somewhat narrower but still broad perspective, our foreign economic policy has among its purposes the creation of a climate conducive to successful business operations by traders and investors.[24]

---

[23] An excellent source of information on foreign investment in Venezuela is Thomas T. Murphy, "Venezuela as a Foreign Investment Target," *Business Topics,* Autumn 1964, pp. 23–29.

[24] Clarence I. Blau, "U.S. Government Resources in the Management of Foreign Operations," International Management Series No. 1, p. 59.

Part of the government's efforts to create favorable climates for overseas investment are the various activities designed to help minimize some of the more troublesome politically motivated risks of doing business abroad. The government provides assistance against the risks resulting from the deliberate activities of foreign governments, such as losses arising from expropriation, revolutions, confiscation, war, and the inability to transfer profits and capital because of exchange restrictions.

Government support in minimizing political risks comes in at least two ways. One way is through various agencies which offer guarantees against specific types of risks. In essence, the government provides the means whereby a foreign investor can purchase insurance against particular risks. Another means of help covers the most severe political risk, expropriation; limitations have been placed upon the granting of U.S. aid to those countries which have expropriated American-controlled property without equitable restitution.

The Export-Import Bank (Eximbank) is a U.S. government agency whose prime purpose is to underwrite financially international trade and investment activities of American firms. It also provides for guarantees against certain kinds of political risks. For a cost of one half of 1 percent per year of the guarantee coverage, a foreign investor can get coverage of up to 95 percent of loss because of political risks. Those insurable risks include inconvertibility, war, confiscation, civil disturbances, and the cancellation or restriction of export or import licenses.[25]

The Agency for International Development (AID), in conjunction with its aid to underdeveloped countries, has provisions for limited protection in support of "essential" projects in approved countries and for approved products. The costs of coverage are similar to those of the Eximbank and coverage extends to the basic "political risks" of convertibility, expropriation, and war.[26]

Besides the guarantees offered by the various insurance programs, the Hickenlooper amendment to the Foreign Assistance Act of 1962 also provides assistance in case of expropriation through direct economic action against an offending country. One of the major deterrents to foreign investment is the threat of confiscation by the government. The Hickenlooper amendment to the Foreign Assistance Act was designed to retaliate against expropriation. The major provision of this amendment is that all foreign aid will be cut off to any country that expropriates American investments without adequate compensation within a reasonable time.

The legislation has had some effect, as evidenced by the recent behavior of Brazil, a particularly risky country for expropriation. In 1962, Brazil began a series of costly (to American investors) expropriations: an ITT (International Telephone and Telegraph) subsidiary was taken over, as well as a subsidiary of American and Foreign Power Company. In both cases, there was little or no compensation, and it appeared that

---

[25] Stanley, op. cit., p. 391.
[26] Ibid., p. 523.

BOX 5–5

Bolivia Will Pay Gulf No Interest

Gulf Oil Corp. decided last week to accept compensation on unfavorable terms for its expropriated Bolivian fields. The company will get $78.6-million from Bolivia as compensation for a net investment calculated at $101-million by an independent French auditor retained by the La Paz government. Gulf will get the money over a period of 20 years at no interest.

Compensation will be paid out of 25% of the income from Gulf's former fields in eastern Bolivia. Payments will end after 20 years even if the agreed sum has not been reached, and before then if the oil reserves run out.

The deal still hinges on getting financing from the World Bank [See Box 5–1] and other sources for construction of a $46.5-million gas pipeline to Argentina. The Bolivian government has the choice of starting payments to Gulf on Jan. 1, 1973, or three months after the first export of natural gas to Argentina.

For a while at least, Gulf is expected to buy crude oil from its former fields. Gulf and other companies that buy Bolivian oil and gas will make payments to a trust administered by New York's Morgan Guaranty Trust Co. The bank will pay 75% of this income to Bolivia's government oil company and 25% to Gulf—less a special tax imposed by La Paz.

Source: Reprinted from the September 19, 1970, issue of *Business Week*, p. 79, by special permission. Copyrighted © 1970 by McGraw-Hill, Inc.

restitution would come only after years of pleading the companies' cases in Brazilian courts. The Brazilian government, however, suddenly worked out an equitable arrangement which provided for partial payment in U.S. dollars and the balance in cruzeiros to be invested in Brazil. The apparent reason for this about-face was the fear of losing recent pledges of much needed foreign aid from the United States.[27] For the most part, it has been those countries that need foreign aid that have been most susceptible to the lure of expropriation. It appears that the Hickenlooper amendment may be a most effective means of discouraging a foreign government from resorting to such extreme measures as the confiscation of a foreign business without proper restitution.

SUGGESTIONS TO REDUCE POLITICAL VULNERABILITY

Even though a company cannot directly control or alter the political environment of the country within which it operates, there are measures to be taken that can lessen the degree of susceptibility of a specific business venture to politically induced risks.

Foreign investors are frequently accused of exploiting a country's wealth at the expense of the national population and for the sole benefit of foreign investors. Although these charges are not wholly unsupported

---

[27] "Brazil Patches up ITT Expropriation on Eve of Pleas for Renewed Aid from U.S.," *Business Week*, February 2, 1963, p. 86.

by past experiences, today's enlightened investor is seeking only a reasonable return on his investments commensurate with the risk involved. Yet, to achieve these goals, hostile and generally unfounded fears must be overcome.

Countries, especially the less developed, fear foreign investment for such reasons as the following:

1.   A suspicion that the larger and more experienced United States companies will eventually absorb domestic industry.
2.   A strong suspicion that American companies are exploiting the economy of the host country for the benefit of foreign investors and at the expense of the local populace.
3.   That the rate of economic and social progress may be slowed or altogether stifled as a result of the foreign corporation's political influence in demanding a preservation of the *status quo*.
4.   A fear that foreign business methods, especially those of the United States, are too high pressure and result in the vulgarization of popular taste and the "Americanization" of traditional culture.
5.   Resentment and criticism toward American personnel for remaining aloof and not attempting to understand their host culture and thus failing to assimilate into the foreign community.[28]

As long as fears of this nature persist, the political climate for a foreign investor will continue to be hostile. Are there ways of abating the fears expressed above? One source suggests that the following are the necessary procedures to heed in attempting to improve the public image of a company and lessen the political vulnerability of its activities. A company is advised to remember that:

1.   It is a guest in the country and should act accordingly.
2.   The profits of an enterprise are not solely the company's, but that local "national" employees and the economy of the country should also benefit.
3.   It isn't wise to try to win over new customers by completely "Americanizing" them.
4.   Although English is an "accepted" language overseas, a fluency in the language of the international customer goes further in making sales and cementing good public relations.
5.   It should try to contribute to the country's economy and culture with worthwhile public projects.
6.   It should train its executives, and their wives too, to act appropriately overseas.
7.   It is best not to conduct business from the United States but to staff foreign offices with competent nationals and supervise the operation from home.[29]

The U.S. Kaiser Corporation's investment in Brazil offers an excellent illustration of minimizing political vulnerability. In a country noted for

---

[28] Charles E. Allen, "Public Opinion: Achilles Heel of U.S. Business Overseas," an address before the Business Council for International Understanding, June 1960, as reported by Robert Theobald, *Profit Potential in the Developing Countries* (AMA Research Study No. 53, 1962), pp. 87–88.

[29] "Making Friends and Customers in Foreign Lands," *Printer's Ink*, June 3, 1960, p. 59.

BOX 5-6

Canada's Guiding Principles of Good Corporate Behavior as They Relate to Objectionable Corporate Practices of Subsidiaries

Good Corporate Behavior	*Related Objectionable Practices*
1. Full realization of the company's growth and operating potential.	1. Multinational corporate planners abroad institute expansion and cutback plans without regard for host country plans and aspirations.
2. Make Canadian subsidiary self-contained, vertically-integrated entity with total responsibility for at least one productive function.	2. Keeping subsidiary primarily an assembler of imported parts or distributor of goods produced elsewhere so that operations can more readily be shut down or transferred.
3. Maximum development of export markets.	3. Filling export orders to third country markets from headquarters country stocks, earning credits for headquarters country's balance of payments rather than host country's.
4. Extend processing of host country raw materials through maximum number of stages.	4. Create as few materials-processing stages as possible in materials-sources country to minimize political leverage.
5. Equitable pricing policies for international and intracompany sales.	5. Negotiated or spurious prices designed to maximize taxable income in low-tax-rate jurisdictions.
6. Develop sources of supply in Canada.	6. Preference for headquarters country or third country sources for purposes of corporate convenience or political leverage.
7. Inclusion of R&D and product development activities in Canada.	7. Concentration of R&D and product design activities in headquarters country, so that host country never develops these capabilities.
8. Retain substantial earnings for growth reinvestment.	8. Use of profits earned in host country to finance expansion in headquarters or third country.

Source: Exhibit B of "Canada's Guiding Principles: Magna Carta or Strait Jacket," a paper presented to the Annual Meeting of the Association for Education in International Business, Chicago, December 1968. Reprinted with permission.

its harassment of foreign business and threats of expropriation (some of which have been carried out) "Willys-Overland do Brazil" has gone unmolested. The reasons are probably found in the following facts about their Brazilian operation. Whereas other U.S. industries are wholly owned subsidiaries, Willys-Overland is only 49 percent owned by the U.S. Kaiser Corporation; the remaining 51 percent is owned by 48,000 Brazilians. Most American-owned companies close their top executive positions to Brazilians, but Willys' managing director answers to an operating committee of five Brazilians and four Americans. Furthermore, instead of parts to assemble, Brazil's Willys produces an automobile that is "Brazilian from taillights to engine block—the first car to be completely designed, tooled, engineered and manufactured in Brazil." One observer noted, "the government wouldn't dare attack Willys. It would have 48,000 angry people to answer to."[30] Kaiser operates successfully in a number of other "risky" countries as well.[31]

Although many of those interested in doing business overseas may not feel that they can go as far as Kaiser, there is certainly much to be said for attempting to become more closely identified with the ideals and desires of the host country. To do so might render a marketer's activities and products less politically vulnerable, and although it would not necessarily eliminate all the risks of the political environment, it might reduce the likelihood and frequency of some of the politically motivated risks of doing business abroad.

SUMMARY AND CONCLUSIONS

Vital to every marketer's assessment of a foreign market is an appreciation for the political environment in the country within which he plans to operate. Government involvement in business activities, especially foreign-controlled business, is generally much greater than the businessman is accustomed to in the United States. The foreign marketer must strive to make his activities politically acceptable, or he may find that he is subjected to a variety of politically condoned harassments. In addition to the harassments which can be imposed by a government, the foreign marketer frequently must face the problem of uncertainty of continuity in government policy. As governments change political philosophies, a marketer who is accepted under one administration may find that his activities are completely undesirable under another. The U.S. government may aid American business in its foreign operations, and for those companies which a country considers vital in achieving national economic goals, the host country often provides an umbrella of protection not extended to others. An unfamiliar or hostile political environment does not necessarily preclude success for a foreign marketer if the marketer is aware of the limitations imposed by the environment and plans accordingly.

---

[30] "World Business," *Time*, September 28, 1962, p. 53.

[31] For an interesting report on Kaiser's international activities see "The Jeep Still Going Strong," *Forbes*, April 15, 1965, p. 47.

READINGS

HOW TO ANALYZE FOREIGN INVESTMENT CLIMATES*

ROBERT B. STOBAUGH, JR.

In the home office of a U.S.-based multinational enterprise, the international vice president and his staff are reviewing their foreign operating results for the last few years; profits have been down, and some subsidiaries are showing losses. They know that in many cases the deteriorating profit position is caused primarily by environmental factors in the foreign countries. They wonder, "When we make new investments, how should we take into account the various economic and political conditions encountered in different countries?"

This scene is being repeated numerous times this year. Profits from foreign operations of U.S.-based companies have been falling, and some subsidiaries have even been reporting significant losses.[1] Clearly, there is a need for U.S.-based managers to do a better job of analyzing the different economic and political conditions when making foreign investments. In this article I shall discuss the various methods used by 40 U.S.-based multinational enterprises in a variety of industries and recommend those methods which I think should be used.

Although most of the executives interviewed in this research study shared a common belief about the importance of the foreign investment climate, there are great differences in the practices they used to consider the environmental risks and uncertainties. While some companies made thorough studies of various elements of investment climates, many others did little analysis. Instead, the latter often based their investment decisions on stated policies such as: "We do not want to lose our share of the market" or "We are in the country to stay and are investing for the long run."

For the purpose of discussing what companies actually do in analyzing foreign investment climates, as well as what they *ought to* do, I have divided the companies' approaches into four basic types: (1) *go–no go;* (2) *premium for risk;* (3) *range of estimates;* and (4) *risk analysis.* Most companies at present take one of the first two approaches, but the latter two are more sophisticated and indicative of the direction in which many companies are moving.

First, a cautionary note: as the reader will realize, any grouping of a large number of behavioral patterns into a few categories does an injustice to the variety existing in the real world. Thus there are some companies that use a mixture of various parts of the approaches discussed here. Furthermore, analyses are used by various individuals in the company in different ways to further their own goals; and so, sometimes within one company, different managers use different techniques

* Source: *Harvard Business Review,* September–October 1969, pp. 100–108. © 1969 by the President and Fellows of Harvard College; all rights reserved.

[1] See U.S. Department of Commerce, *Overseas Business Reports* (Washington, November 1967), p. 13; see also "Celanese Reports $77 Million Loss for All Last Year," *The Wall Street Journal,* February 20, 1969.

depending on the task at hand. With these reservations in mind I shall proceed to discuss the four approaches.

Go–No Go

In this approach the manager either accepts or rejects a particular country based on an examination of one or two characteristics. Often, no further serious study is given to investment climate. Typical of such an attitude is this statement by an international division planning manager of a large U.S. chemical company:

> We have not considered investing in Brazil because of the rapid devaluation of currency. We have experienced foreign exchange losses in the devaluation of foreign currencies and these upset our board of directors. Therefore, we made the decision not to consider investing in Brazil.

Without a study of the company's assets and opportunities for investing abroad, it is impossible to say whether this was the best decision for the company to make. However, some of this chemical company's major U.S. rivals are investing heavily in Brazil.

Although the *go–no go* approach has an advantage in reducing the amount of investigation to be done in looking for foreign investment opportunities, it has a major disadvantage in that some very good investment opportunities are passed over because a country was rejected on the initial screening.

Premium for Risk

This more advanced method is sometimes used in conjunction with the *go–no go* approach. The company using *premium for risk* demands a higher return on investment (ROI) from proposed projects in countries with "poor" investment climates than from comparable projects in countries with "good" investment climates. For example, some companies use a 10% after-tax ROI as a minimum in highly developed countries. Their basic assumption is that less risk is involved in the former than in the latter.

Other companies use specific cutoff points for different countries. For example, one company has a cutoff point of 13% for Country A and one of 15% for Country B, which has a comparatively poorer investment climate in the judgment of the international division planning manager.

Various levels of sophistication exist in using this *premium for risk* method. Some companies use the consensus of several of their executives in deciding on the size of the premium to place on various countries. A few other companies, about 20% of those interviewed, have some type of scale for rating countries by their investment climates. An example of one U.S.-based multinational company's rating scale is shown in Exhibit 1. This has the benefit of formalizing judgment; but remember that such formalization does not necessarily make it correct. For example, as discussed later, inflation is not necessarily "bad."

EXHIBIT 1

Corporate Rating Scale for Determining a Country's Investment Climate

Item	Individual Subcategory	Range for Category
Capital repatriation:		0–12
No restrictions	12	
Restrictions based only on time	8	
Restrictions on capital	6	
Restrictions on capital and income	4	
Heavy restrictions	2	
No repatriation possible	0	
Foreign ownership allowed:		0–12
100% allowed and welcomed	12	
100% allowed, not welcomed	10	
Majority allowed	8	
50% maximum	6	
Minority only	4	
Less than 30%	2	
No foreign ownership allowed	0	
Discrimination and controls, foreign versus domestic businesses:		0–12
Foreign treated same as local	12	
Minor restrictions on foreigners, no controls	10	
No restrictions on foreigners, some controls	8	
Restrictions and controls on foreigners	6	
Some restrictions and heavy controls on foreigners	4	
Severe restrictions and controls on foreigners	2	
Foreigners not allowed to invest	0	
Currency stability:		4–20
Freely convertible	20	
Less than 10% open/black market differential	18	
10% to 40% open/black market differential	14	
40% to 100% open/black market differential	8	
Over 100% open/black market differential	4	
Political stability:		0–12
Stable long term	12	
Stable, but dependent on key person	10	
Internal factions, but government in control	8	
Strong external and/or internal pressures that affect policies	4	
Possibility of coup (external and internal) or other radical change	2	
Instability, real possibility of coup or change	0	
Willingness to grant tariff protection:		2–8
Extensive protection granted	8	
Considerable protection granted, especially to new major industries	6	
Some protection granted, mainly to new industries	4	
Little or no protection granted	2	
Availability of local capital:		0–10
Developed capital market; open stock exchange	10	
Some local capital available; speculative stock market	8	
Limited capital market; some outside funds (IBRD, AID) available	6	
Capital scarce, short term	4	
Rigid controls over capital	2	
Active capital flight unchecked	0	
Annual inflation for last 5 years:		2–14
Less than 1%	14	
1%–3%	12	
3%–7%	10	
7%–10%	8	
10%–15%	6	
15%–35%	4	
Over 35%	2	
Total		8–100

FUNDAMENTAL FLAWS.   While a rating scale might be useful as one of several variables in screening many countries as part of a search process,[2] its use in the *premium for risk* approcah presents at least two types of problems:

First, the various elements of the investment climate often have different effects for different projects. For example, the profitability of a plant built to serve the domestic market would more likely depend on the granting and continuation of tariff protection than would the profitability of another plant erected to serve the export market.

Second, as is always the case with rating scales, it is difficult to assign proper weights for each category of investment climate.

Regardless of whether a rating scale is used, the *premium for risk* approach as normally used contains a serious flaw in that the assignment of a risk premium for a country assumes that the degree of risk is uniform over the life of the project. This typically is not the case because the risks differ for various years of a project's life. An undesirable event occurring in Year One of the project has a much more serious effect on the net present value or rate of return of the project than does an undesirable event occurring in Year Three. Thus it is difficult to take this difference into account by assigning a single premium that will apply for the life of the project.

In theory, this last-mentioned problem might be overcome by using a discounted cash flow technique in which a different discount factor is used for each year of the project's life. Also, in theory, different weights on a rating scale could be assigned for different projects in the same country depending on the importance of various environmental elements to project profitability. However, in practice such corrections become so complicated and arbitrary that they mainly serve to highlight the difficulties in assigning proper weights and in selecting a proper risk premium.

In spite of these flaws, the *premium for risk* technique is used by 80% of the U.S.-based managers interviewed, primarily because of its simplicity and because of their own intuitive feelings that it is difficult to make accurate estimates about the future in foreign countries.

However, in the belief that explicit estimates should be made of the possible effect of various factors on an individual project, I shall now discuss the two more sophisticated approaches. These have a major advantage over the first two techniques in that they give the executive a better idea of the range within which the profitability will likely be. Thus the executive has a better idea of the degree of risk involved in selecting a project with a high expected value compared with one with a low expected value. Also, with two projects that have the same ex-

---

[2] See my article, "Where in the World Should We Put That Plant?" *Harvard Business Review,* January–February 1969, p. 129, wherein I found that after correcting for other relevant factors a country with a "good" investment climate begins production of individual petrochemicals about 10 years before a country with a "poor" investment climate.

pected value, the executive can select the one with the lesser degree of risk.

The simplest of the more sophisticated approaches is the *range of estimates*. It can be used quite readily with hand calculations. Its disadvantage is that while it gives a "likely" range of outcomes, it does not give explicit probability estimates of the various possible outcomes and it gives no estimates for outcomes outside the likely range. The *risk analysis* approach, on the other hand, does give explicit probability estimates over the whole range of possible outcomes, but it has the disadvantage of requiring an electronic computer to perform extensive calculations.

Range of Estimates

In using this technique, the company manager makes his best estimate of what the values will be for the various factors that will affect the project's profitability. To do this, he identifies the crucial variables, estimates as best he can what these variables will be at different times in the future, and obtains a resultant estimate of cash flow (and other target variables, such as reported net profit). He then varies his estimates of these crucial factors in order to determine the sensitivity of the cash flow to changes in each factor. He then selects those factors having the greatest effect on project profitability and varies his estimates of them and different combinations of them within a reasonable range; this enables him to estimate a likely range within which the resulting cash flow will be.

STABLE FACTORS. It is sometimes possible to make very accurate estimates of a number of variables that enter into the profitability analysis. Many of the variables may have been stable for some time and can thus be expected to remain so. Recognizing that the relative stability of these items is not constant from country to country, here are typical examples:

Income tax rates.
Depreciation allowance rates.
Availability of loans in terms of quantity and cost.
Tariff rates.
Presence of exchange controls.

LESS STABLE FACTORS. Other variables which might be more difficult to predict than the typical examples just cited are changes in currency value and political and economic stability. To estimate possible changes in currency value, the manager will wish to review closely the balance of payments of the country and to estimate future developments. He thus will study a number of items and their relationships to one another. For example:

Number of exchange rate changes in recent years (e.g., last 5 to 10 years).
Level of currency reserves.

Direction of change in level of reserves.
Amount of variability in level of reserves.
Trend in exports and imports.
Variation in annual exports and imports.

There is no pat formula by which a manager can estimate changes in currency exchange rates. The difficulty of making such a prediction is illustrated in Exhibit 2, which shows an estimate made by a multi-

EXHIBIT 2

Estimates of Currency Strengths for Selected Countries

Country	Change in Exchange Rate between July 1966 and December 1968
Estimated in July 1966 to have a strong currency:	
Portugal	NC*
Sweden	NC*
Thailand	NC
Australia	NC
Denmark	−8%
Peru	−31%
Estimated in July 1966 to have a weaker currency than those above:	
Turkey	NC
India	NC
Pakistan	NC
South Korea	−4%
New Zealand	−19%
Finland	−23%
Brazil	−42%
Chile	−46%

* NC = Less than a 1% change.
Source: *International Financial Statistics*, March 1969.

national enterprise in July 1966. Two of the six currencies with a "strong" rating have been devalued since July 1966, with an average devaluation of 20%. Five of the eight currencies with a "weak" rating have been devalued since July 1966, with an average devaluation of 27%. Thus one can conclude that although accurate estimates are difficult to make, it is possible to discriminate to some extent between "strong" and "weak" currencies.

In actual practice, only 15% of the surveyed companies made a systematic analysis of currency strengths and weaknesses, and these typically were large companies with sizable staffs in central or regional offices. The remaining companies relied primarily on the advice of banks, with the smaller enterprises tending to rely on U.S. banks and the larger ones on both U.S. and foreign banks. The danger of such reliance can be seen in this comment by the manager of a U.S. branch bank in London: "It is not a bank's job to advise companies about the long-term outlook for a foreign currency. Our job is to provide quotations for current exchange rates and the cost of cover."

Certain factors which can be measured quantitatively, such as past inflation and expected future inflation, can be used by the manager in estimating economic stability. A number of qualitative factors, such as the existence of various power groups in the country, must be used in estimating political stability; this presents a difficult estimating task, but research provides insights which will be helpful in making this estimate.[3]

ANALYTICAL APPLICATION.   Let us take one factor that is frequently on the minds of U.S.-based managers investing abroad—the possibility of currency devaluation—and let us assume that we are interested in cash flows available for repatriation to the parent company or for reinvestment in the subsidiary. Because of the misunderstandings which this factor has caused, I shall present a rather detailed example.

For an investment analysis of the project, we first identify the risk of currency devaluation by the foreign country. We do this by a study of the country's currency reserve position and its expectations on exports, imports, and other balance of payments items.

Let us further assume that as a best estimate we predict a devaluation of 20% at the end of Year Two of plant operation. We then estimate the effect of such a devaluation on each item in the operating statement and balance sheet. For example, assume:

> The plant is selling to both the domestic and the export markets.
> The plant uses both domestic and imported raw materials.
> The foreign currency is devalued 20%. (In this case the peso is the monetary unit.)
> The unit costs of domestic raw materials and labor will rise 10%.
> The company raises domestic and export prices by 10% in terms of local currency.
> The export sales will increase because the 10% rise in export prices in terms of local currency will result in a lower priced product in terms of dollars after the devaluation. (Since the export price in dollars was $1.00 or 1 peso before devaluation, afterwards it is $0.88 or 1.10 pesos.)

After taking these factors into account, we estimate that our cash flow is increased from 700,000 pesos to 865,000 pesos, a decrease in dollar equivalent from $700,000 to $692,000. If devaluation takes place at the end of Year Two, then the cash flows for Year Two and Year Three would be as shown in Exhibit 3. Accordingly, as a result of the devaluation, there is a reduction of $8,000—the difference between $700,000 and $692,000—in the amount we have for reinvestment in the country or for returning to the United States (assuming no restrictions on remittances).

---

[3] See Gabriel A. Almond and James S. Coleman, editors, *The Politics of the Developing Areas* (Princeton, New Jersey: Princeton University Press, 1960).

EXHIBIT 3

Effects of Currency Devaluation on Cash Flow

Item	Units (in millions)	Unit Price (in pesos)	Expenditures (in millions)	Total
A. Before devaluation (exchange rate: 1 peso = $1.00):				
Export sales...................	1.00	1.00	1,000,000	
Domestic sales.................	2.00	1.00	2,000,000	
Total income..................				3,000,000
Imported raw materials........	0.20	1.00	200,000	
Local raw materials............	1.00	1.00	1,000,000	
Local labor (man-hours)........	0.50	1.00	500,000	
Fixed cash charges, excluding depreciation:				
In dollars...................			300,000	
In pesos....................			300,000	
Total expenditures............				2,300,000
Cash flow.....................				700,000
Dollar equivalent..............				$700,000
B. After 20% devaluation (exchange rate: 1 peso = $0.80):				
Export sales...................	1.30	1.10	1,430,000	
Domestic sales.................	2.00	1.10	2,200,000	
Total income..................				3,630,000
Imported raw materials.........	0.22	1.25	275,000	
Local raw materials............	1.10	1.10	1,210,000	
Local labor (man-hours)........	0.55	1.10	605,000	
Fixed cash charges, excluding depreciation:				
In dollars...................			375,000	
In pesos....................			300,000	
Total expenditures............				2,765,000
Cash flow.....................				865,000
Dollar equivalent.............				$692,000

An analysis of the balance sheet must be made in order to determine whether additional capital is needed to finance the company. In this case, we estimate that because of additional sales, we must invest an extra 100,000 pesos or $80,000 to provide required working capital. Therefore, in the investment analysis these resulting estimates of differences in cash flows of $8,000 yearly for each year after Year Two and for an $80,000 lump sum at the end of Year Two must be considered in determining the present value of internal rate of return of the project.

Calculating the effects of devaluation this way is not consistent with the book value method used by accountants. Although several variations exist, the commonly accepted practice is to show the long-term assets and liabilities as unchanged in dollar value, while the changes in dollar value of short-term assets and liabilities are assumed equivalent to the change in currency value.

Therefore, the "loss" shown on the parent company's books is equal to the change in dollar value of the net current assets. Almost surely this loss would not be the same loss identified in our cash flow analysis (i.e., $80,000 lump sum plus $8,000 yearly). For example, we might have a book loss of $120,000 as shown in Exhibit 4. There are various methods of calculating the book or unrealized exchange loss; and other factors, such as domestic taxes, affect the decision. However, my point remains that we should be guided primarily by estimated changes in cash flow and not by estimated changes in book value.

EXHIBIT 4

Example of Devaluation Loss on Basis of Book Value

	Expressed as Pesos	Applicable Exchange Rate (dollar per peso)	Equivalent Dollars
Before devaluation:			
Current assets..............	1,000,000	1.00	$1,000,000
Current liabilities...........	(400,000)	1.00	(400,000)
Net current assets..........	600,000	1.00	600,000
Fixed assets................	2,000,000	1.00	2,000,000
Long-term debt.............	(1,000,000)	1.00	(1,000,000)
Equity....................	1,600,000		$1,600,000
After devaluation:			
Current assets..............	1,000,000	.80	$ 800,000
Current liabilities...........	(400,000)	.80	(320,000)
Net current assets..........	600,000	.80	480,000
Fixed assets................	2,000,000	1.00	2,000,000
Long-term debt.............	(1,000,000)	1.00	(1,000,000)
Equity....................	1,600,000		$1,480,000

Note: Devaluation "loss" equals "equity after devaluation" minus "equity before devaluation" equals $120,000.

In actual practice many U.S.-based multinational managers adhere rigidly to the book value method in order to determine the effects of devaluation. I suspect that this strict adherence has probably caused as many headaches and misunderstandings as any other single factor in the international business field.

For example, in some cases subsidiaries' profits have increased in dollar terms with inflation but managers are held responsible for book value losses. Furthermore, the surveyed executives were unanimous in their agreement that devaluation and inflation are "bad" elements in a foreign investment climate. This belief, of course, is not valid for all investments. A good example of this is a U.S.-based multinational company that purchases raw material from a certain host government on a long-term fixed-price contract in local currency. Whenever the local currency is inflated, the company increases its product prices right in step, thereby increasing its profits at a faster rate than the inflationary rise.

In the example shown in Exhibit 3 and Exhibit 4, only a "best estimate" is used. However, the use of a single "best estimate" does not give a range within which the company can be "pretty sure" of what the outcome will be. Therefore, as indicated previously, managers should compensate for this shortcoming by (a) doing a sensitivity analysis to determine the effect of some reasonable variation in those variables believed to be most critical, (b) picking the variables or combination of variables that are most important in terms of their effect on cash flow, and (c) using "optimistic" and "pessimistic" estimates in order to calculate probable "highs" and "lows." Such a procedure might result in an optimistic estimate of a devaluation of 20% in Year Seven and a pessimistic estimate of a devaluation at the beginning of Year One (compared with our best estimate of a devaluation at the end of Year Two).

Similarly, optimistic and pessimistic estimates are made for other important factors, such as the amount of export sales or the rise in local wages.

POTENTIAL OBSTACLES. There are two possible pitfalls in using the *range of estimates* approach: (1) the manager must be on the lookout for variables that change in the opposite direction and thereby tend to offset one another; (2) he must avoid the indiscriminate use of all the pessimistic estimates of variables in any one case. Otherwise, his estimated outcome will be much more pessimistic than the actual outcome is likely to be. Despite these dangers, because of its thoroughness as well as the fact that it gives some idea of a range within which the actual result will be, this approach with the optimistic and pessimistic outcomes generally is superior to the *premium for risk* approach discussed earlier.

However, there are still other analytical techniques available that permit a fourth—and even more sophisticated—analysis of foreign investment projects.

Risk Analysis

Inasmuch as its potential for high payoff has been proved on domestic projects, the use of *risk analysis* is now being extended to foreign projects. In this approach, which is actually a sophisticated application of probability theory, an estimate is made of the probable outcomes of various events. For example, in the case of devaluation, we would assess the probability of devaluation in each time period (e.g., each year) and the probability of the amount of devaluation in each of those time periods. Thus in Year One, we might estimate a .100 probability of devaluation. Of this .100, we might estimate a .025 probability for a 15% devaluation, a .050 probability for a 20% devaluation, and a .025 probability for a 25% devaluation.

Similarly, we would estimate probabilities for the other important variables, and then use a simulation model to obtain a distribution of the probable profits, as shown in Exhibit 5. For comparison, this figure also shows the single-point "best estimate." It is clear that *risk analysis-* gives us a better picture on which to base a decision.[4]

Another example of the use of explicit estimates is shown in Exhibit 6 for the question of nationalization. Corporate executives often worry about changes in foreign governments. As an aid in clarifying what the possible results might be, a diagram showing possible outcomes should be made. For Year One, the exhibit shows a .500 probability that the government will be overthrown, but a .810 probability that the plant will not be nationalized. Such an estimate might lead to a different managerial decision than a vague guess by a manager.

EXHIBIT 5

Estimated Rates of Return on Investment

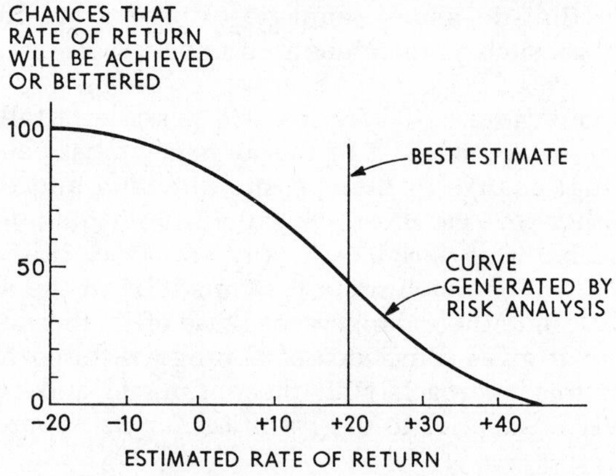

CHANCES THAT
RATE OF RETURN
WILL BE ACHIEVED
OR BETTERED

ESTIMATED RATE OF RETURN

Note: In reading the graph, the "best estimate" is a 20% return on investment; the "Risk Analysis" curve shows an 80% probability of at least a 0% return on investment, a 50% probability of at least a 19% return on investment, and a 20% probability of at least a 30% return on investment.

Further estimates would also have to be made for subsequent years and added to this diagram. The outcomes should then be used in a probability analysis as previously discussed. As the estimated outcomes in later years are dependent on events in earlier years, there are some difficulties encountered because of the complexity involved; however, methods are available for handling these problems.[5]

I shall mention one other refinement in the direction in which project analysis will move. To aid in making the decision when the downside risk is more crucial to the company than the upside potential, a method should be used to determine the risk preference as an aid in selecting

---

[4] For the use of this technique in domestic projects, see David B. Hertz, "Risk Analysis in Capital Investment," *Harvard Business Review*, January–February 1964, p. 95.

[5] See Robert Schlaifer, *Analysis of Decisions under Uncertainty* (New York: McGraw-Hill Book Company, Inc., 1969), Chapter 9.

projects.[6] One of the problems of investment analysis is that individual managers often have a different risk preference from that decreed by company policy. As an illustration, some company managers interviewed said that it was their company's policy to use the same cutoff rate abroad as in the United States. Yet 50% of these managers deliberately did not follow this policy; instead, they would not pass foreign projects on to a

EXHIBIT 6

Probability Analysis—Year One: Government Overthrow

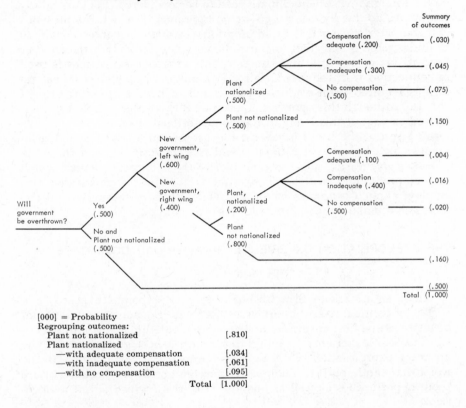

[000] = Probability
Regrouping outcomes:

Plant not nationalized	[.810]
Plant nationalized	
—with adequate compensation	[.034]
—with inadequate compensation	[.061]
—with no compensation	[.095]
Total	[1.000]

superior unless the project had a higher return than the U.S. cutoff return on investment.

INTERMEDIATE STEP. Rather than jump directly from the *go—no go* or the *premium for risk* approach to the use of *risk analysis,* many companies will likely find it easier to start initially with the *range of estimates* technique. After becoming familiar with its powers and limitations, the manager can then move in the direction of the more sophisticated *risk analysis.*

As the reader realizes, numbers can reflect some judgment but not all.

6 John S. Hammond, III, "Better Decisions with Preference Theory," *Harvard Business Review,* November–December 1967, p. 123.

Thus, even though the analysis suggested above will provide the executive with superior insight into the probable results of an investment, he obviously will not expect that a single number or even a range of numbers will obviate the need for additional executive judgment in making an investment decision.

In Summary

When considering foreign investments, the various elements making up the foreign investment climate need to be considered explicitly. Many companies do this by using a *go–no go* approach in which the presence of a characteristic, such as rapid inflation, considered by the company to be undesirable is sufficient to cause the company to scratch the country from its list of potential investments. This approach sometimes is used in connection with the *premium for risk* method in which a higher return is required from countries considered to have a poor investment climate. Although this approach is used by 80% of the companies interviewed as part of this study, it has some serious flaws.

As a result, the trend is toward the use of more sophisticated techniques, such as *range of estimates* and *risk analysis*. Both of these approaches give the executive a better idea of the likely range within which project profitability will be. The latter is the most sophisticated and employs explicit estimates of the probable effects of the individual elements that make up a country's investment climate.

THE EXPROPRIATION EXPERIENCE OF AMERICAN COMPANIES*

FRANKLIN R. ROOT

When an American firm invests abroad, it becomes exposed to a variety of political risks that are associated with the actual and potential behavior of the host government. The most severe breakdown an American firm can experience in its relations with a host government is the arbitrary expropriation of its business properties.[1] Such action is the worst that can happen to a company's foreign operations because future profit opportunities as well as business assets are wiped out at a single stroke.

Quite understandably, American executives are very sensitive to the threat of expropriation in a foreign country. Indeed, an expropriating government may not only poison the investment climate of its own country but also that of neighboring countries. After Castro's seizure of American business properties in Cuba, the flow of U.S. direct investment to the rest of Latin America fell off abruptly. In 1959 American companies invested $338 million of new capital in Latin America, an amount about equal to the average yearly U.S. investment for the 1950–60 dec-

---

* Reprinted with permission from *Business Horizons*, April 1968, pp. 69–74.

[1] This article uses a broad interpretation of *expropriation* that includes any seizure of American property by a foreign government whether or not compensation is offered and paid.

ade. In 1960 (the year when major expropriations took place in Cuba) new investment tumbled to $95 million; in 1962 business investors withdrew a net amount of $32 million from Latin America. In brief, the Cuban expropriations probably cost the rest of Latin America at least $500 million worth of new U.S. business investment during the years 1960–62.

Although expropriation may darken the investment climate of an entire region and deter new foreign operations for several years, we know very little about the experience and policies of American companies in this critical area. In order to remedy this situation in some measure, we asked international executives several questions about the expropriation experience of their companies. Answers were obtained through both a mail survey and personal interviews conducted during the first quarter of 1966.[2] Survey replies came from international executives in 106 companies (a 32 percent rate of response), and personal interviews were held with executives of another 18 companies. All except 2 of these companies are among the 500 largest industrial corporations listed in the *Fortune Directory*. Our sample, therefore, is made up of big companies with extensive international experience that collectively account for a sizable share of U.S. private investment abroad.

Before looking at the experiences of the companies included in this study, some brief remarks about the expropriation of U.S. business properties by foreign governments are in order.

A Short History of Expropriation

American business has been hit by six major expropriations of foreign business properties since World War I (see Exhibit 1). The first significant one was the direct outcome of the successful Communist Revolution in what is now the Soviet Union. Ideologically opposed to private enterprise, the new Soviet government seized all business property belonging to foreigners and nonforeigners alike, and proclaimed its right to expropriate without payment of compensation. Since U.S. investment was only about 5 percent of total foreign investment in the Soviet Union ($3.5 billion), American losses were modest compared with the French ($1.2 billion), the British ($536 billion), and the German ($426 billion). In the 1930's, negotiations between the United States and the Soviet Union to obtain compensation for American properties were largely fruitless. The massive Soviet expropriation of foreign business property signaled a new era in relations between Western business and foreign governments. It provided a blueprint for later communist seizures in Eastern Europe, Mainland China, and Cuba and helped pave the way for nationalist take-overs in Latin America, the Middle East, Africa, and Asia.

The first noncommunist nationalist expropriation of foreign business property on a significant scale occurred in Mexico in 1938 when the

---

[2] The writer wishes to thank the following graduate students for their help in this phase of the research: Thomas F. Egge, John T. Franz, Charles A. Graves, Paul D. Haring, Joseph A. Sarnowski, and Anthony J. Walton.

government took over the properties of international petroleum companies.[3] The initial offer of compensation was rejected by the companies, but negotiations led to a final settlement of American claims in the 1940's. Unlike the Soviet expropriation, which was universal, the Mexican one was selective, involving foreign petroleum properties only. Since 1938, such selective measures have been taken against U.S. investments in Argentina, Guatemala, Chile, Colombia, Brazil, Syria, Ceylon, and other developing countries. For the most part selective expropriation has focused on the petroleum and public utility industries, and in some instances on only one company.

Expropriations in Eastern Europe and Mainland China after World War II were universal in accordance with communist ideology. Eastern European governments, however, have been somewhat less inflexible on compensation than the Soviet government. Yugoslavia has made full payment for the American properties it expropriated in 1946, and the U.S. government has concluded agreements for partial compensation with Poland, Romania, and Bulgaria. No compensation has been offered by Communist China.

EXHIBIT 1

Major Expropriations of U.S. Business Property by Foreign Governments

Country	Date	Estimated Amount of U.S. Assets Expropriated (millions of dollars)
Soviet Union	1917–20	175
Mexico	1938	120
Eastern Europe*	1945–48	240
Cuba	1959–60	1,400
Argentina	1963	237
Indonesia	1965	160

* Czechoslovakia, Hungary, Romania, Poland, Bulgaria, Yugoslavia, and Austria (Soviet occupied area).

Undoubtedly the most traumatic expropriation experience of U.S. business took place in Cuba in 1960. For over half a century American companies operating in Cuba were able to ignore political risks with impunity. Not a single company bothered to obtain investment guaranty insurance from the U.S. government to protect its Cuban investments. Disaster struck in 1960 when scores of American firms were taken over by the Castro government. No compensation was received for the seized properties because it was tied to American purchases of Cuban sugar, which were soon halted by the U.S. government. In any event, since compensation was offered in 50-year Cuban government bonds at 2 percent interest, it failed to meet the "international standard" of prompt, adequate, and effective compensation.

---

[3] Between 1927 and 1938 the Mexican government also seized American-owned ranches valued at $10 million.

Although there is no comprehensive list of American companies whose properties have been seized by foreign governments, we are able to identify 187 U.S. companies that have experienced expropriation since the end of World War I. These companies were involved in 240 separate acts of expropriation, 171 in communist countries and 69 in noncommunist countries. The measures taken in Cuba alone accounted for 137 seizures of American business property. All of the communist expropriations were universal, while all of the noncommunist actions were selective, with the single exception of Indonesia.[4]

Expropriation Experience

Executives in 38 of the 124 companies in this study reported one or more seizures of foreign business properties. Altogether these companies have undergone sixty-six separate acts of expropriation, of which forty-six occurred in communist countries. The experience of these companies is a microcosm of the expropriation experience of American companies in general. They have encountered such action in all regions of the world and in every period since World War I. Six-tenths of the companies have suffered expropriation *only* in communist countries, half of them in Cuba alone.

The remaining fifteen companies have met with selective expropriations in noncommunist countries and in several instances with universal communist expropriation as well. Half of the selective actions (ten out of twenty) involved petroleum companies (in one case a petroleum tank car company), and three of them involved in the same public utility company. Other selective expropriations occurred in the packaged food, office machinery, and pharmaceutical industries; in addition, one rubber plantation was seized. Except in the case of the public utility company, the properties of other foreign companies in the same industry were also taken over by the host government.

THE EXPROPRIATION SEQUENCE

The expropriation experience of an American company may be conceived of as a sequence of choices, actions, and other behavior on the part of the business enterprise, the host government, and the U.S. government.

1. The first phase is made up of a variety of events over a short or lengthy period of time that collectively *warns* management that expropriation is imminent or probable within the foreseeable future.

2. The next phase is the response pattern of management to this warning: management may try to *prevent* expropriation and/or try to *minimize* prospective losses by following one or more courses of action.

---

[4] In 1965 the Sukarno government took control of thirty-two American-owned companies operating in Indonesia. No compensation was offered on the ground that property rights still belonged to the companies. The victory of noncommunist forces at the end of 1965 brightened prospects for the return of the seized properties to the companies.

3. The third phase is marked by the *seizure* of the company's properties by the host government so that management no longer controls the enterprise.

4. The fourth phase is the *offer* (or nonoffer) of compensation for the seized properties by the host government.

5. The fifth stage is the response pattern of parent company management to this offer. Management may *accept* or *reject* the initial offer, enter into *negotiations* with the host government, take *legal action* in the host country, and/or turn to the U.S. government for *diplomatic support.*

6. The sixth and last stage is the settlement of the company's claim through the payment of compensation by the host government, possibly including the reversal of expropriation and the return of the properties to the company.

This sequence—warning, management response, seizure, compensation offer, management response, and settlement—offers a framework for the analysis of individual cases of expropriation. In some instances certain phases may not occur. For example, management may have no warning and therefore show no response to a warning. Most commonly, final settlement does not occur, and the sequence remains open-ended We shall now look at actual experiences in terms of this sequence.

American management usually has some warning of an impending expropriation of its foreign properties. Only one-fifth of the executives interviewed declared that their companies had *no* warning of a particular expropriation. Remarks such as these are typical: "The company had been aware of antagonistic feelings in Brazil for about one and one-half years prior to Goulart's overthrow." "There were recurring threats." For a big majority of companies, then, expropriation did not come as a bolt out of a friendly blue sky. It was presaged by black clouds and the sound of thunder.

Could your company have prevented this expropriation by following different policies? None of the executives in the study thought so, and only one executive was uncertain. Here are some representative comments:

Expropriation was the consequence of political developments leading to a complete Communist take-over. Cuban national businesses were expropriated along with foreign interests.

Action was carried out in line with a campaign promise [Argentina].

About the only action the company was able to take in an effort to prevent the expropriation was to tell the story of how much benefit its investment had been and was to the Brazilian economy. We told our story to anyone who would listen and especially tried to contact influential government associates.

In each incident there was nothing that could be done about the impending seizures but wait [Ceylon, China, Egypt].

These expropriations occurred because of political events which were completely outside the control of the United States [Soviet Union, East Europe, China, Indonesia, and Cuba].

Although unable to *prevent* expropriation, executives in more than half of the companies reported taking steps to *minimize* prospective losses. The most common steps were a cutback in inventories and a complete cessation of new investment in the foreign enterprise. Other steps included a cutback in receivables, a cessation of shipments to the host country, the payment of all commercial debts owed to U.S. suppliers, the reduction or elimination of the parent company's guarantee on local borrowing, a cutback in cash holdings, heavy local borrowing, an increase in remittances to the United States, shipment to the subsidiary on letter of credit terms only, and a cutback in production. All of these measures were intended to reduce the real and net financial assets owned by the parent company in the host country; some of them were not always feasible. One executive said his company was unable to withdraw funds from the host country because of exchange restrictions imposed well in advance of expropriation.

We had a foreign partner who doubted the plant would be expropriated [Cuba].

The people in Cuba convinced management that nothing was going to happen—so the plants were left open. This meeting was on a Wednesday and on the following Friday the plants were taken over.

Only one-fifth of the executives declared that its companies took *no* action to limit prospective losses. (Another fifth said it did not know.) Some of the executives said nothing could be done. (One answered this question with the single word "Pray!") And two executives put the blame on local subsidiary management.

At the time of expropriation did the host government offer any compensation? Three-quarters of the executives answered no to this question. The others said there was a compensation offer, but almost all indicated that this offer did not include prompt payment, was not adequate, and was not made in dollars.[5]

As we have noted, executives considered the compensation offer by the host government as either nonexistent or unsatisfactory in one or more respects. The possible courses of action open to management under these circumstances are negotiation, legal action in the host country, and/or a request for diplomatic support by the U.S. government. Less than one-third of the companies that underwent expropriation entered into negotiations with the host government regarding the terms of compensation. Although we do not know why the majority of companies did not try negotiation, a plausible explanation is that management did not believe negotiation to be an effective course of action, given the circumstances and attitude of the host government.

What role (if any) did the U.S. government play in this entire situation? In personal interviews, executives in four companies that had encountered expropriation *only* in Cuba all agreed that the U.S. government played no significant role because it was powerless to offer any assistance. Executives in two other companies (the properties of one company were seized in Syria in 1960, and it was threatened with expropriation in Brazil in 1964; the other company was expropriated in

---

[5] Only two executives interpreted the statement on compensation made by the Cuban government in 1960 as a genuine offer.

Egypt and Cuba in 1960) also said the U.S. government was not a factor in the situation.

On the other hand, executives in four companies declared that the U.S. government had played a positive role in their own expropriation experience. One mentioned the effectiveness of the Hickenlooper Amendment in Ceylon as well as American negotiations with the Ceylonese government.[6] Two executives were grateful for U.S. diplomatic support in Indonesia, and one of them also thought the U.S. government did everything it could in Cuba, short of sending in the Marines. An executive of a company that has gone through several expropriations in Latin America cited the value of the Hickenlooper Amendment, diplomatic pressure, and excellent cooperation from the U.S. State Department.

Did your company ever receive compensation for its expropriated properties? Executives in twenty-seven companies (out of thirty-six responding to this question) declared that there had never been any compensation. Twenty-five of these companies met with expropriation *only* in communist countries, eighteen in Cuba alone. Executives also stated no compensation was received in Mexico (1938), Germany (1939), Argentina (1948 and 1963), Syria (1960), and Algeria (1965).

Eight companies (about one-fifth of the respondents) reported receiving compensation in the Soviet Union:[7] Hungary, Mexico, Ceylon, Egypt, Indonesia, Brazil, Colombia, and Argentina. In the case of Hungary, the American company had no manufacturing facilities, and the inventory of its local branch was purchased with local currency in 1948 by a national organization. Except for Hungary, all the compensation was in dollars or in dollar bonds. Only half of these companies were satisfied with the amount of compensation.

Policy Changes Resulting from Expropriation Experience

As a result of its expropriation experience, did your company make any changes in its policies and operations in other countries? In personal interviews with executives in ten companies that had undergone expropriation, half said there were no changes. Three executives, however, cited these changes:

Greater degree of caution in investment policy. We are fighting a strong rearguard action, but are prepared for the worst in countries where we are under threat of expropriation. We have developed public relations programs to show the value of foreign investment.

We seek more control over our subsidiaries and try to set up wholly-owned subsidiaries.

We now keep copies of all foreign records in the United States because we

---

[6] The Hickenlooper Amendment to the Foreign Assistance Act of 1961 requires a suspension of U.S. foreign aid to any country that expropriates American property without offering prompt, adequate, and effective compensation. This provision was applied (for the first and so far only time) to Ceylon in 1963.

[7] In November, 1933, the United States and the Soviet Union set up the Litvinov assignment fund as a preliminary settlement of American expropriation claims. Further negotiations were unsuccessful, but later some American claims were paid from these funds by the Foreign Claims Settlement Commission.

lost them in Cuba. Our experience may have caused a holdup of marginal type investments or may have caused some investments to become marginal, for example, in Brazil.

It is evident that the risk of expropriation should not be ignored by the management of international companies. As observed earlier, at least 187 American companies have experienced one or more expropriations by foreign governments since the end of World War I. The experiences of our sample companies are bitter from start to finish with only modest exceptions. Only a minority of companies received any compensation for asset losses, and no company was compensated for the loss of future income. In the light of this experience, international executives are well advised to appraise the risk of expropriation (as well as other political risks) in an explicit, systematic fashion before committing resources to a foreign country. This approach to the problem would not only lessen future losses but also prevent the forfeiture of new investment opportunities because of indiscriminate fears of expropriation.

QUESTIONS

1. Define:

Parliamentary government	Confiscation
"Peoples" republics	Currency convertibility
Absolutist government	Hickenlooper amendment
Single-party system	Political vulnerability
Expropriation	

2. "An undeniable and critical fact when doing business in a foreign country is that permission to conduct business is controlled by the government of the host country." Comment.

3. What are the main factors to consider in assessing the dominant political climate within a country?

4. What are the different ways governments can be classified? Briefly illustrate with an example of a particular country.

5. Political party systems within a government can be divided into four distinct types of organization. List and define each.

6. Why is a working knowledge of party philosophy so important in a political assessment of a market? Discuss.

7. What are the most common causes of instability in governments? Discuss.

8. Discuss how governmental instability can affect marketing.

9. What are the most frequently encountered political risks in foreign business? Discuss.

10. Expropriation is considered a major risk of foreign business. Discuss ways in which this particular type of risk has been minimized somewhat as a result of company activities. Explain how these risks have been minimized by the activities of the U.S. government.

11. How do exchange controls impede foreign business? Discuss.

12. How do foreign governments encourage foreign investment? Discuss.

13. How does the U.S. government encourage foreign investment? Spell out the implications in foreign marketing.

14. What is the Hickenlooper amendment? What role does it play in foreign marketing?

15. Discuss some measures a company might take to lessen its political vulnerability.

16. Why do lesser developed countries fear foreign investment? Is there any evidence that these attitudes are changing? Are there steps a company can take to lessen these fears? Discuss.

17. The Kaiser Corporation has been particularly successful operating in countries with governments unfriendly to most foreign investment. Why? What are the lessons that might be learned from Kaiser's experience?

18. Select a country and analyze it politically from a marketing viewpoint.

Readings

1. Discuss briefly the four approaches (go-no go, premium for risk, range of estimates, and risk analysis) used to assess the investment climate of a foreign country.

2. Why is there a trend toward the more sophisticated techniques such as range of estimates and risk analysis in accessing investment climate in a foreign country?

3. Professor Root suggests a sequence of six events which occur in a country's expropriation of a foreign investment. Discuss what a company might do in each of these stages to forestall or avoid the final outcome.

OUTLINE OF CHAPTER 6

INTRODUCTION

ECONOMIC DEVELOPMENT AND MARKETING
    Objectives of Developing Countries
    Marketing's Contribution Neglected
    The Role of Marketing in Economic Development

MARKETING IN A DEVELOPING COUNTRY
    Level of Marketing Development
    Influence of Import Orientation
    Demand in a Less Developed Country
    Less Developed Countries and Long-Range Potential

SUMMARY AND CONCLUSIONS

READING
    Vick in India, *Sales Management.*

6

ECONOMIC DEVELOPMENT AND WORLD MARKETS

INTRODUCTION

Few nations are content with an economic status quo; instead, the battle cry of most of the world is *economic growth,* a demand which reflects a universal impatience with low standards of living, poverty, and the general lack of opportunity that plagues most of the world's people. Countries with mature economies are concerned with maintaining their rate of economic growth, and countries at the other extreme of the economic spectrum are preoccupied with the problems of establishing economies that can mature and offer some of the rewards of economic advancement.

After hundreds of years, in some cases a thousand or more years, of little change in their way of life, populations are stirring and are protesting the prevailing conditions. As a result, poverty and stagnations over much of the world are giving way to progress . . . and in many cases the entire economic, social, and political fabric is being replaced.[1]

Prime opportunities of the seventies and eighties for the international marketer are the less developed countries of the world where three quarters of mankind lives. It would be an error of the greatest magnitude for a marketer contemplating entry into a foreign market to ignore the universal vision of "industrialization" held by most countries. It would be an error because the skills of marketing will "prove critical in the generation ahead to the development of countries and regions which contain a clear majority of the world's population." It would be an error because in a growth economy "marketing is the major opportunity."[2]

Furthermore, it would be an error because the desire for economic growth may be the single most important environmental element to

---

[1] John P. Young, *The International Economy* (4th ed.; New York: The Ronald Press Company, 1963), p. 473.

[2] Walt W. Rostow, "The Concept of a National Market and Its Economic Growth Implications," in Peter D. Bennett (ed.), *Marketing and Economic Development* (American Marketing Association Proceedings, Fall 1965), p. 11.

which the foreign marketer must adjust his marketing task. The economic growth stage of a country affects its outlook toward foreign business activity, the demand for goods, the distribution systems found within a country and, indeed, the entire marketing process. It is growth which forces successful marketing to achieve the zenith of the marketing concept. In static economies, consumption patterns become rigid and marketing is typically nothing more than a "supply effort."[3] In a dynamic economy, consumption patterns frequently change quite rapidly, and marketing is constantly faced with the challenge of detecting and providing for new levels of consumption and of matching marketing effort with ever-changing market needs and wants. Certainly a nation's economy and its dynamic nature must be paramount in the evaluation of any potential market, domestic or foreign.

As part of the world marketing environment to which the marketer must become attuned, economic development presents a two-sided challenge. First, a study of the general aspects of economic development is necessary to gain some empathy for the economic climate which exists within developing countries. A country's economic development aspirations, marketing's assigned role in such expectations, and marketing's actual role should all be examined in order to gain some appreciation for the environment which faces a foreign marketer in a developing country.

Second, the state of economic development should be studied with respect to market potential, including the present level of economic achievement attained by the country and the economy's growth potential. The level of economic development dictates the kind and degree of market potential that exist, while a knowledge of the dynamism of the economy allows the marketer to prepare for dramatic economic shifts. To begin, a definition of economic development is in order.

Economic development is generally understood to mean an increase in national production that results in an increase in the average per capita gross national product (GNP). An increase in average per capita GNP alone, however, is not sufficient to denote the implied or expected meaning of economic development. Besides an increase in average per capita GNP, most interpretations of the concepts imply a widespread distribution of the increased income as well. Consider, for example, the problems encountered in using per capita GNP as a sole measure of economic development for a country such as Kuwait where the per capita GNP, the highest in the world, is over $3,000. In spite of this figure, it cannot be considered an example of an economically developed country for a variety of reasons, including a limited distribution of wealth. Economic development, as commonly defined today, also tends to mean *rapid growth*—improvements achieved "in decades rather than centuries."

Perhaps the most widely recognized model used for classifying countries by stage of economic development is that presented by Rostow. He identifies five stages of development—growth is the movement from one

---

[3] John Fayerweather, *International Marketing*, "Foundations of Marketing Series" (Englewood Cliffs, N.J.: Prentice-Hall, Inc., 1965), p. 24.

stage to another and all countries in the first three stages are considered to be underdeveloped.[4] Briefly, Rostow's stages of development are as follows:

Stage 1 *The Traditional Society.* Countries in this stage lack the capability of significantly increasing the level of productivity. There is a marked absence of the systematic application of the methods of modern science and technology. Literacy is also low as well as other types of social overhead.

Stage 2 *The Preconditions for Take-Off.* This second stage includes those societies which are in the process of transition to the take-off stage. During this period, the advances of modern science are beginning to be applied in agriculture and production. The development of transportation, communications, power, education, health and other public undertakings are begun in a small but important way.

Stage 3 *The Take-Off.* At this stage countries achieve a growth pattern which becomes a normal condition. Human resources and social overhead have been developed to sustain steady development. Agricultural and industrial modernization lead to rapid expansion in these areas.

Stage 4 *The Drive to Maturity.* After take-off, sustained progress is maintained and the economy seeks to extend modern technology to all fronts of economic activity. The economy takes on international involvement. (This is the stage in which an economy demonstrates that it has the technological and entrepreneurial skills to produce not everything, but anything it chooses to produce.)[5]

Stage 5 *The Age of High Mass Consumption.* The age of high mass consumption leads to shifts in the leading economic sectors towards durable consumers' goods and services. Real income per capita rises to the point where a very large number of people have significant amounts of discretionary income.[6]

For purposes of this chapter, the terms *lesser developed, underdeveloped,* etc., will refer to those countries whose economies would fall in one of Rostow's first three categories. In order to quantify this degree of development, it is frequently the practice arbitrarily to place all those economies with less than $300 to $500 annual per capita income in the underdeveloped category. A range of this sort does classify most of the nations of Africa, Asia, Latin America, and Southern and Eastern Europe as underdeveloped.[7] Under the preceding conditions, a "developing country" will refer to those underdeveloped countries that are taking steps to move from a lower stage to a higher one with some degree of success. The authors realize, of course, that such an approach in identifying underdeveloped countries is not without its faults, but nevertheless, it will serve in the ensuing discussion.

---

[4] Young, op. cit., p. 475.

[5] Walt W. Rostow, *The Stages of Economic Growth* (London: Cambridge University Press, 1960), p. 10.

[6] Ibid., pp. 4–11. Reprinted with permission.

[7] See the following for viewpoints on what constitutes an underdeveloped nation on a per capita national income basis: Leon V. Hirsch, *Marketing in an Underdeveloped Economy: The North Indian Sugar Industry* (Englewood Cliffs, N.J. Prentice-Hall, Inc., 1961), p. 4, and Benjamin Higgins, *Economic Development* (New York: W. W. Norton and Company, 1959), p. 6.

ECONOMIC DEVELOPMENT AND MARKETING

For a thorough assessment of economic development and marketing, a marketer should begin his appraisal with a brief view of the basic facts and objectives of economic development. If an international marketer is to be capable of adjusting to a foreign economic environment, he must be able to answer such questions as: (1) What are the objectives of the developing nations? (2) What role is marketing assigned, if any, in economic growth plans? (3) What contribution must marketing make, whether overtly planned or not, in order for a country to grow successfully? (4) What attitudes prevail which may hamper marketing strategies, development, and growth? and (5) How can the market potential, present and future, be assessed?

Objectives of Developing Countries

Industrialization is the fundamental objective of most developing countries, although for an appreciation of its impact upon a nation's people, economic growth must be viewed as a means to an end rather than as the end itself. Certainly, most countries see in "economic growth" the achivement of social as well as economic goals. Satisfaction of non-material as well as material needs must be achieved in order to fulfill the desires and aspirations of most underdeveloped nations. This would include better education for all, better and more effective government, and the elimination of social inequities as well as improvements in moral and ethical responsibilities of both the public and private sectors of the economy.[8] As one author has noted, the principal objectives of developing countries are:

1. To be free to determine their own future economically, politically, and culturally.
2. To raise the standard of living as quickly and as far as possible.
3. To create a society that equitably distributes its products and services.
4. To develop a government that will mobilize the people into a dynamic force for development.
5. To participate actively in cooperative organizations made up of other developing nations.[9]

A knowledge of these objectives can help explain the attitude and behavior toward marketing which often exist within an underdeveloped country in the growth stage. The fact that most countries wish to be free to determine their economic, political, and cultural future goes far in explaining the potential vulnerability of a foreign marketer in these countries. Because foreign marketers are outsiders, it is often assumed that their presence is limiting the achievement of these objectives. Frequently, this feeling results in political and governmental harassment and, sometimes, consumer boycott of goods.[10] The widespread fear and

---

[8] Young, op. cit., p. 475.

[9] Howard D. Lowe, "Doing Business in the Developing Countries," *Business Horizons,* Fall 1965, p. 26.

[10] See Chapter 5 above.

resentment of foreign control of the economy commonly leads to the adoption of policies and actions which at times retard rather than facilitate economic progress.[11] Foreign enterprise and marketing, however, can play a significant role in helping countries achieve their growth objectives, even though marketing's crucial role is often not appreciated.

Marketing's Contribution Neglected

How important is marketing to the achievement of the goals mentioned above? Unfortunately, to those who are responsible for planning, marketing, or distribution, often does not hold a meaningful position. Emphasis is placed upon the development of techniques for increasing production and production efficiency, i.e., "they [economic planners] are production—rather than marketing—oriented."[12] Distribution tends

. . . to be ignored or regarded, somehow, as an inferior kind of economic activity, and thus, it is difficult to get development economists and policy makers to accord problems of efficiency in distribution the same attention they give automatically to problems of production, investment and finance.[13]

There is a strongly held opinion that an economic system must first have the capacity to produce before the level of consumption and distribution becomes a problem. With this opinion in mind, the Peruvian government invested $19 million in a fertilizer plant in Cachimayo without making provision for sale and distribution of the product.

A few weeks after the commencement of production, the plant had accumulated what was described as a year's inventory and had to be closed. Farmers who could have increased their productivity substantially were not provided with needed educational programs and technical assistance in the use of commercial fertilizer. Also, the fertilizer was initially priced about three times the price of guano, and purchasers had to pick up their fertilizer from the plant and transport it to their farms. While the plant at Cachimayo had an overwhelming inventory and was not producing, there was a severe shortage of fertilizer in the Camana Valley, a nearby area.[14]

The lack of concern for distribution and economic planning extends to the technical assistance offered by developed countries as well. The United States, for example, virtually has ignored many of the problems of distribution or marketing in its technical assistance programs designed for underdeveloped countries.[15] There are several reasons which

[11] Young, op. cit., p. 476.

[12] E. Jerome McCarthy, "Effective Marketing Institutions for Economic Development," in Stephen A. Greyser (ed.), *Toward Scientific Marketing* (American Marketing Association Proceedings, 1963), p. 393.

[13] Walt W. Rostow, "The Concept of a National Market and Its Economics Growth Implications," op. cit., p. 19.

[14] William P. Glade and Jon G. Udell, "The Marketing Concept and Economic Development: Peru," *Journal of Inter-American Studies*, October 1968, p. 542. Reprinted with permission of the publisher, the University of Miami Press, Coral Gables, Florida.

[15] Leon V. Hirsch, "The Contribution of Marketing to Economic Development— A Generally Neglected Area," in William D. Stevens (ed.), *The Social Responsibilities of Marketing* (American Marketing Association Proceedings, December 1961), p. 414.

might explain such orientation. First, it seems logical to be more concerned with production than consumption in an underdeveloped country. In a country where the vast majority of the population live at or below subsistence level, the distribution of more goods and services would appear to present a minor and even welcome problem. Second, in many cultures, marketing is considered to be a wasteful activity.[16] Anyone engaged in marketing is considered to be a parasite on society; even in the more mature economies, the middleman is suspect. In the United States, for example, a constant stream of inquiry is directed at the role and efficiency of the middleman. The utility of advertising, product planning, and innovation is constantly questioned in even the most mature economic systems. Third, the cultural or traditional rigidity found in the distribution structure of many countries has caused neglect of the distribution problem. The resistance of the small merchants to the advent of the supermarket in Europe is an example of a traditional and, in some respects, cultural rigidity.

Another complication which leads to general neglect is that marketing is intangible and difficult to quantify compared to production, where "accurate quantitative information is important for planning purposes."[17] Furthermore, of all the skills, marketing skills may be the most difficult to transfer from one economy to another. Machines can be built in the United States and used in Egypt, but a marketing plan or system adequate for the American market will more often than not be unusable in another culture. One American noted that "while technical or production know-how is about 100% transferable to Mexico from the U.S., marketing know-how is only about 20% transferable."[18]

Finally, the low evaluation of marketing found in many underdeveloped economies can be explained by the fact that effective marketing, unlike production, cannot develop without the use of money. The widespread use of money is a relatively new and unusual practice for many economic groups; therefore an aura of mystery and sometimes distrust surrounds its use. Further, the small segment of the population accustomed to the use of money in these underdeveloped economies is frequently of an ethnic background different from that of the majority of the population, a situation which does not alleviate the uneasy attitude about money and the distribution system on which it thrives.[19] With such a negative reputation, the obvious question is whether marketing actually makes a contribution to the economic development of a country and, if so, how it does.

---

[16] Ralph Westfall and Harper W. Boyd, Jr., "Marketing in India," *Journal of Marketing,* October 1960, pp. 11–17.

[17] Reed Moyer, "The Structure of Markets in Developing Economies," *MSU Business Topics,* Fall 1964, p. 43.

[18] E. R. Barlow, *Management of Foreign Manufacturing Subsidiaries* (Cambridge: Division of Research, Graduate School of Business Administration, Harvard University, 1953), p. 26, as quoted in Hirsch, *Marketing in an Undeveloped Economy,* p. 22.

[19] Hirsch, *Marketing in an Underdeveloped Economy,* op. cit., p. 21.

The Role of Marketing in Economic Development

Marketing *is* critical in economic development; furthermore, marketing can be a central force in the continued development of both Western and communist nations. Rostow notes,

If I am correct that men must, in the generation ahead, diffuse the process of modernization out over long neglected rural regions, creating new efficient networks of distribution, we shall see not merely new and challenging tasks for those who command the skills of distribution but a new theoretical respect and appreciation for the art of that widening of the market which, for so long, was taken for granted.[20]

Marketing is an economy's arbiter between productive capacity and consumer demand. As the level of production rises, changes must occur in the marketing structure if a balance is to be maintained between higher production and higher consumption. Thus, the marketing process is a critical element in effectively utilizing the production resulting from economic growth to provide a higher standard of living. Effective marketing, then, not only helps to improve the life-style and well-being of the people in a specific economy, but it has more far-reaching effects by upgrading world markets. After all, a developed country's best customer is another developed country.

Although marketing may be suspected by many as being a somewhat passive function which makes little contribution to development, it is, in fact, instrumental in laying the groundwork requirements necessary for rapid development. Essential to the growth of any economy is a developed marketing system that provides effective distribution for whatever a country produces. What generally exists in an underdeveloped country is an inefficient, "outrageously" high-cost market structure where most of those engaged in marketing are barely managing to survive. Poor physical distribution, failure to match market needs with productive potential, and ineffective demand all result in waste which "has to be seen to be believed."[21] What is needed, as one economist points out, is a marketing system to replace the traditional "trader and merchant" system which generally exists. By providing "a physical distribution system, adequate financing of the distribution of goods and the matching of production capacity and resources with consumer needs, wants, and purchasing power,"[22] marketing can help to eliminate some of the inefficiencies which sap the economies of underdeveloped countries. In fact, "marketing might by itself go far toward changing the entire economic tone of the existing system—without any change in methods of production, distribution of population or of income."[23]

Marketing also helps to increase the size of existing markets. Although

---

[20] Rostow, "The Concept of a National Market," op. cit., p. 20.

[21] Peter F. Drucker, "Marketing and Economic Development," *The Journal of Marketing,* January 1958, p. 255.

[22] Ibid., pp. 255–56.

[23] Ibid., p. 255.

marketing cannot create purchasing power, it can uncover and direct that which already exists and thereby increase the level of economic activity. Increased economic activity leads to enlarged markets which set the stage for economies of scale in distribution and production that may not have existed before.[24] In effect, a beneficial circle frequently develops—effective and efficient marketing leads to increasing market size which leads to further improvements in marketing and production efficiency, and so on.

Another important contribution of marketing to very underdeveloped economies is the growth or spreading of a money economy. Many underdeveloped economies have significant nonmonetized economic segments. In India, for example, as late as 1960, it was estimated that at least one third of India's agricultural production and about one fourth of its gross national product was nonmonetized.[25] Until an economy has established monetary systems, growth is stunted at a very low level. Since marketing requires a money system in order to flourish effectively, it helps to spread the "money habit" throughout the economy. With money instead of barter as a medium of trade, a society can develop a wider choice in consumption opportunity; marketing also works to provide this wider choice. Since the range of available products generally increases as marketing grows, people are exposed to a greater variety of goods. The possibility of acquiring these goods can have a stimulating effect upon the self-discipline and motivation of the people.[26]

When people are exposed to more goods, their wants increase, with the result that people are often moved to higher levels of production, longer hours, and greater dependability in order to acquire the financial resources that purchase the new trappings of the "good life." Instead of labor meaning only subsistence living, as in many backward economies, it can become the means of attaining a more satisfying list of wants.[27]

The growth and stimulation which result from increased desire for material possessions frequently lead to the development of much needed managers and entrepreneurs. For accelerated economic growth, a country must have a ready supply of entrepreneurs who "can see and seize the opportunities for joining the available capital with the available resources in new combinations."[28] Even with ample capital and opportunity, unless there are enough indigenous "Schumpeterian entrepreneurs" of vision who will run the purposeful risk of taking the action necessary for development, rapid growth can be thwarted.[29]

Effective marketing leads to the higher levels of economic opportunity which can spawn local entrepreneurs by creating the opportunities for

---

[24] Hirsch, "The Contribution of Marketing to Economic Development," op. cit., p. 414.

[25] Hirsch, *Marketing in an Underdeveloped Economy*, op. cit., p. 26.

[26] Hirsch, "The Contribution of Marketing to Economic Development," op. cit., p. 415.

[27] Hirsch, *Marketing in an Underdeveloped Economy*, op. cit., pp. 26–27.

[28] Higgins, op. cit., p. 709.

[29] Ibid., p. 709.

BOX 6–1

Marketing in India

Indians buy household utensils by the pound instead of by the unit. If they did not, they suspect the manufacturer would pound the metal thinner than the buyer believed it to be. Sugar is sold only in extremely coarse crystals—partly because it is more difficult to adulterate in that form. Almost all consumers buy grain and grind it themselves. Flour can easily be adulterated with chalk dust. Even grain must be sorted, virtually kernel by kernel, or sand and other foreign matter will be slipped in to add to the weight. There is a flourishing market for empty containers for cosmetics, toilet goods, and medicines. Unless the labels are destroyed when the contents are used, the jars, bottles, and cans will be refilled with sub-standard products and sold as the original. In 1957, health authorities in Delhi estimated that 25% of all the food bought in that city was adulterated. Sawdust, husks, colored earth, and ground seeds were found in various foodstuffs, accounting for 10 to 50% of the total weight of the products.

Source: Ralph Westfall and Harper W. Boyd, Jr., "Marketing in India," *Journal of Marketing,* October 1960, p. 16. Reprinted from the *Journal of Marketing,* published by the American Marketing Association.

small business and the stimulus for development of professional management.[30]

Finally, marketing contributes to the development of standards for economic behavior, integrity, and product and service reliability.[31] In many underdeveloped countries, there is a painful lack of standards of morality in business and personal relationships.[32] If most of the population is living on a subsistence level, the struggle for survival tends to overshadow the importance of private ownership of personal property; with such an attitude, the pattern for honesty set in all parts of the society bears little relationship to the level of honesty accepted as normal in the United States.[33] Business needs standards of integrity, honesty, workmanship, and quality if it is to expand. Thus, as business develops in scope and size, it fosters the development of these characteristics. As Drucker points out, the activity of Sears in Latin America resulted in making customers more cognizant of value, in forcing consumer credit, in changing attitudes toward the customer, store clerks, suppliers, and merchandise. Sears's growth has spawned the creation of new local businesses with higher standards of workmanship, quality, and delivery to supply Sears with goods. The net result is that in a very few years, the science of management has been advanced at least a generation in these countries.[34]

---

[30] Drucker, op. cit., p. 256.

[31] Ibid., p. 259.

[32] Simon Williams, "Negotiating Investment in Emerging Countries," *Harvard Business Review,* January–February 1965, p. 89.

[33] Lowe, op. cit., p. 30.

[34] Drucker, op. cit., p. 257.

The consequence of marketing's contribution to economic development is not only humanitarian in purpose, but also "it is good and profitable business with extraordinary growth potential."[35]

Regardless of the level of the economy, economic growth creates opportunities for the astute marketer. Marketing can and does make numerous contributions to the development of an economy. It promotes efficiency of distribution, it increases the size of markets, it helps to foster the monetary economy, it creates the opportunity for and develops entrepreneurs, and finally, it promotes higher levels of economic and social integrity, dependability, and industriousness.

In appraising the environment within which a marketing plan has to be implemented, the foreign marketer must be aware of the economic growth objectives and the potential of the country in question, of the role he will be expected to assume, and of the probable result of his efforts upon the development aspirations of the host country. The marketer still must concern himself with the marketing task of adjusting his service to the foreign economic conditions. He must be aware of how the various stages of economic development affect marketing.[36]

MARKETING IN A DEVELOPING COUNTRY

In making a market appraisal, the level of economic development achieved by a country must be reviewed in order to anticipate the limitations which may exist in the marketplace and which must be accounted for and adjusted to in marketing plans and strategies.

A marketer should be alerted against superimposing a sophisticated marketing program, i.e., one designed for the United States, upon an underdeveloped economy. Marketing effort must be keyed to each situation: It is a job of "custom tailoring" for each set of circumstances. A promotional program in a country where 90 percent of the population is illiterate is vastly different from such a program in a country where 90 percent of the population is literate. Pricing in a subsistence market poses different problems from pricing in the "affluent society." The distribution structure should provide an efficient method of matching productive capacity with available demand. An efficient marketing program is one which provides for optimum utility at a single point in time, given a specific set of circumstances. Thus, the marketer must match his efforts with the requirements of the particular level of economic development. In evaluating the potential in a developing country, the marketer must make an assessment of the existing level of marketing development within the country.

Level of Marketing Development

As an economy grows, marketing skills develop to fulfill the needs of the economy and the development of marketing institutions and meth-

---

35 Ibid., p. 258.

36 For a discussion of marketing and economic development in Mexico, see Douglas Felix Lamont, "A Theory of Marketing Development: Mexico," in Peter D. Bennett (ed.), *Marketing and Economic Development* (Proceedings of the Conference of the American Marketing Association, Fall 1965), pp. 44–45.

odology roughly parallels the stages of economic development. Exhibit 6–1 illustrates the various stages in the marketing process as they develop in a growing economy. The table is subject to all the limitations of the static model and represents in some respects an idealized type of evolutionary process. Economic cooperation and assistance, technological change, political, social, and cultural factors could, and usually do, cause significant deviations in the evolutionary process. However, the table should serve to focus on the logic and interdependence of marketing and economic development.

A brief study of Exhibit 6–1 will reveal roughly the state of marketing at each stage of economic development. As a generalization, as a nation develops and industry grows, marketing institutions evolve to fulfill the distribution needs created at each new level. The more developed an economy, the greater the variety of marketing functions demanded, and the more sophisticated and specialized the institutions become to perform marketing functions.

Perhaps the most strikingly obvious illustration of the relationship between marketing development and the stage of economic development of a country can be found in the evolution of the channel structure. One study found that,

1. The more developed countries have more levels of distribution, more specialty stores and supermarkets, more department stores, and more stores in the rural areas.
2. The influence of the foreign import agent declines with economic development.
3. Manufacturer-wholesaler-retailer functions become separated with economic development.
4. Wholesaler functions approximate those in North America with increasing economic development.
5. The financing function of wholesalers declines and wholesale markups increase with increasing development.
6. The number of small stores declines and the size of the average store increases with increasing development.
7. The role of the peddler and itinerant trader, and the importance of the open-garden fair, declines with increasing development, and
8. Retail margins improve with increasing economic development.[37]

Also developed are the myriad facilitating agencies required to support a growing economy. Advertising agencies, facilities for marketing research, repair services, specialized consumer financing agencies, and storage and warehousing facilities are created to serve the particular needs of expanded markets and economies. It is important to remember that these institutions do not automatically come about, nor does the necessary marketing institution simply appear. As one marketing authority noted,

---

[37] George Wadinambiaratchi, "Channels of Distribution in Developing Economies," *The Business Quarterly*, Winter 1965, pp. 74–82. Reprints of this article in its entirety, at a cost of $1 each, may be obtained from *The Business Quarterly*, School of Business Administration, The University of Western Ontario, London 72, Canada.

EXHIBIT 6-1

Evolution of the Marketing Process

Stage	Substage	Examples	Marketing Functions	Marketing Institutions	Channel Control	Primary Orientation	Resources Employed	Comments
Agricultural and raw materials (Mk.(f) = Prod.)[1]	Self-sufficient	Nomadic or hunting tribes	None	None	Traditional authority	Subsistence	Labor Land	Labor intensive No organized markets
	Surplus commodity producer	Agricultural economy— i.e., coffee, bananas	Exchange	Small-scale merchants, traders, fairs, export-import	Traditional authority	Entrepreneurial Commercial	Labor Land	Labor and land intensive Product specialization Local markets Import oriented
Manufacturing (Mk.(f) = Prod.)	Small scale	Cottage industry	Exchange Physical distribution	Merchants, wholesalers, export-import	Middlemen	Entrepreneurial Financial	Labor Land Technology Transportation	Labor intensive Product standardization and grading Regional and export markets Import oriented
	Mass production	U.S. economy from 1885–1914	Demand creation Physical distribution	Merchants, wholesalers, traders, and specialized institutions	Producer	Production and finance	Labor Land Technology Transportation Capital	Capital intensive Product differentiation National, regional and export markets
Marketing (Prod.(f) = Mk.)	Commercial— Transition	U.S. economy from 1915–29	Demand creation Physical distribution Market information	Large-scale and chain retailers Increase in specialized middlemen	Producer	Entrepreneurial Commercial	Labor Land Technology Transportation Capital Communication	Capital intensive Changes in structure of distribution National, regional and export markets
	Mass distribution	U.S. economy from 1950 to present	Demand creation Physical distribution Market and product planning, development	Integrated channels of distribution Increase in specialized middlemen	Producer Retailer	Marketing	Labor Land Technology Transportation Capital Communication	Capital and land intensive Rapid product innovation National, regional, and export markets

[1] Mk.(f) = Prod.: Marketing is a function of production.

In marketing, as in other areas of social and economic activity, institutions and methodology do not arise simply through chance. Rather, they are a reflection of the particular environment in which they are found. The institutions which are engaged in marketing, and the methods used to market output, reflect the environmental factors which are lumped together and called the market.[38]

Part of the marketer's task, and the reason he studies the economy, is to determine what there is about the strange environment which will be useful to his purposes and how much adjustment will be necessary to carry out his stated objectives.

In some less developed countries, it may be up to the marketer to institute the very foundations of a modern marketing system. As discussed in subsequent chapters, adequate research agencies are not available in many countries, and advertising media may be inadequate.

The limitations which may affect the usefulness of Exhibit 6–1 in the evaluation of the market system of a particular country stem from the fact that the marketing system is dynamic and open rather than closed and static. To expect neat, precise progression through each successive growth stage, as one might find in the geological sciences, is to oversimplify the complex nature of marketing development.

One important and significant factor in evaluating a developing market is the influence of borrowed technology on the acceleration of market development. Examples can be found where countries or parts of countries have been propelled from the 18th century to the 20th century in the span of two decades. In such cases, a country might spend a relatively short time in any given stage, bypass stages completely, or telescope several stages into one.

Influence of Import Orientation

The source of manufactured goods consumed can condition and influence the characteristics and development of a country's market system. If there is a strong dependence upon imported manufactured goods, the structure of the market and general business practices reflect this dependency. Developing countries which rely heavily on importing a large percentage of manufactured goods often show a distinct set of characteristics in their marketing systems.

Some of the differences between a foreign-based market system and a domestic-based system result from two factors. First, the foreign-based market system creates a "seller's market"; and second, the source of supply is limited and controlled by a few importers. The entire marketing system develops around the philosophy of selling a limited supply of goods at high prices to a relatively small number of affluent consumers. There is no desire for market penetration, nor is there much need to develop a system of mass distribution, since demand exceeds supply and, in most cases, the customer seeks the supply. This, of course, is in con-

---

[38] Leo G. Erickson, "Analyzing Brazilian Consumer Markets," *MSU Business Topics*, Summer 1963, p. 11.

trast to the mass consumption–distribution philosophy of a domestic-based system such as prevails in industrialized nations like the United States: In such cases it is generally a "buyer's market," and supply can be increased or decreased within a given range. This creates a need to penetrate the market and push the goods out to the consumer, resulting in a highly developed system of intermediaries. One authority notes that an import-oriented market system usually works backwards:

> Consumers, retailers, and other intermediaries are always seeking goods. This results from the tendency of importers to throttle the flow of goods, and from this sporadic and uneven flow of imports, inventory hoarding as a means of checking the market can be achieved at relatively low cost, and is obviously justified because of its lucrative and speculative yields.[39]

This import-oriented philosophy is manifest in much of the activity and behavior in marketing. For example, in an import-oriented market, an upper ceiling on prices is set by imports, and once prices are set they become rigid.[40] An interesting anecdote told by an authority on Brazil concerned a bank which had ordered some piggy banks for a local promotion. The promotion went better than expected and the banker placed a reorder of an amount three times the original. The local manufacturer immediately increased the price, and despite arguments that pointed out reduced production costs and other supply-cost factors involved, he could not be dissuaded from this move since to him the demand was up so the price must also go up. This "one deal" mentality of pricing at the retail and wholesale levels exists because in an import-oriented market, goods come in at "a landed price and pricing from there on (is) simply an assessment of demand."[41] Thus, variations in manufacturing costs are of little concern; each shipment is a deal, and when that is gone the merchant simply waits for another good deal basing the price of each deal on the landed cost and the assessment of demand at that point in time.[42]

The import-oriented philosophy also affects the development of intermediaries and the functions which they perform. Since the customer is expected to seek out the supply, most of the distribution systems are local in nature and rarely do they exceed regional coverage. To the importer, national distribution is of little importance; his primary concern is limited to those highly populated areas that can afford high-priced merchandise. The concept of national distribution is contrary to his import-oriented philosophy and the relationship between the importer and any middleman which exists in the marketplace is considerably

---

[39] A. A. Sherbini, "Import-Oriented Marketing Mechanisms," *MSU Business Topics*, Spring 1968, p. 71. Reprinted by permission of the publisher, the Bureau of Business and Economic Research, Division of Research, Graduate School of Business Administration, Michigan State University.

[40] A. A. Sherbini, "Marketing in the Industrialization of Underdeveloped Countries," *Journal of Marketing*, January 1965, pp. 28–32.

[41] Donald A. Taylor, "Marketing in Brazil," in Peter D. Bennett (ed.), *Marketing and Economic Development*, (Proceedings of the American Marketing Association, Fall 1965), pp. 110–15.

[42] Ibid., p. 114.

different from that found in domestic based manufacturing or mass marketing systems. The idea of a channel as a chain of intermediaries performing specific activities and each selling to a smaller unit beneath it until it finally reaches the ultimate consumer is relatively unknown. In an import-oriented economy, an intermediary may not sell to a specific link in the channel but to a range of other intermediaries. Some simultaneously assume all the different functions—importing, wholesaling, semiwholesaling, and retailing—while other middlemen are so specialized that a high degree of division of labor is created. Such tasks as financing, storage, trucking, shipping, packaging, breaking bulk, etc., may each have to be performed by separate agencies, thereby creating an extremely high cost distribution.

Besides different operating procedures, an import-oriented market dominated by an importer-wholesaler system may present some special public relations problems that can obstruct the goals of the marketer who attempts either to substitute locally manufactured products for imported ones or to make a total market commitment in the country.[43]

One student of international marketing warns that serious conflicts can develop between the manufacturer or marketer of import-substituting products and the existing intermediaries in the market system of the host country. The major point of contention is the threat posed by the foreign marketer who, with his mass marketing philosophy, attempts to control the distribution process to the point where consumption causes shifts in the location and control of many marketing activities and functions.

In an import-oriented marketing system, the locus (of market activities and functions) lies near the consumer end of the marketing channel. Many marketing functions such as sorting and assorting, selling, storage and warehousing, advertising and promotion, and financing are performed by wholesale and retail intermediaries.

But the establishment of domestic manufacturing of the import substitution type (or mass-marketers) invariably shifts the locus of marketing functions to the production end of the channel. This is particularly true of advertising and promotion, standardization and grading, and storage and warehousing.[44]

This shift, in the eyes of the local importer-wholesaler, invariably alters his position from a dominant one in the marketplace to a secondary one. Since it threatens his very existence he spares "no effort in resisting changes in the locus of marketing functions."[45] Resistance may be in the form of outright warfare, bargaining, or eventual government intervention on the behalf of the domestic importer-wholesaler.

---

[43] The assumption here and throughout the book is that the foreign marketer enters a market with the intent of making a full commitment, i.e., establishing market objectives and maintaining a continuous market representation, with broad distribution and market penetration. This approach is taken regardless of whether the products marketed are manufactured within the political boundaries of the country or are imported.

[44] A. A. Sherbini, "Import-Oriented Marketing Mechanisms," op. cit., p. 72. Reprinted with permission.

[45] Ibid., p. 72.

In addition to the problems resulting from a country having an import-oriented market system, developing nations seldom have a very large or significant middle-income class—the market consists mainly of the very wealthy and the very poor. This creates some interesting demand characteristics which must be considered in the planning and estimating of market potential.

Demand in a Less Developed Country

In estimating market potential in less developed countries the international marketer is confronted with myriad problems. Perhaps the basis for most of the difficulty stems from the economic dualism which exists, i.e., the coexistence of modern and traditional sectors within the economy. The modern sector is similar in many ways to a more developed country: It is centered in the capital city, has jet airports, international hotels, new factories, and a small Westernized middle class. But as one authority notes,

> Only miles but often centuries away is a traditional sector consisting of the remainder of the country's population, producing and consuming at the levels and by the methods of the past. This dualism has obvious effects on the size of the market and hints of the nature and organization of economic activity.[46]

In estimating potential under these economic conditions, the marketer is confronted with two markets, one in the modern sector and the other in the traditional sector. They are substantially different and require different approaches for marketing success: The difference is such that they cannot be combined into a single market estimate. The modern sector demands products and services similar to those found in any industrialized Western country, while the traditional sector demands items that are more indigenous and more basic to subsistence.

If an economy is import-oriented, the modern sector may not be much of a market, either in size or kind of products demanded. A result of import orientation is the development of a highly segmented, thin market. The importer tends to specialize in the unique needs of a relatively narrow range of customers.

> Thus the aggregate demand for a "given product" often consists of many thin and heterogeneous demand schedules that are not necessarily additive.
> The demand for even a simple product such as imported sardines sometimes reflects a high degree of consumer attachment to certain product attributes; for example, shape and type of tin, sauce packed or oil packed, flavor, and price. Foreign exporters who sell in world-wide markets generally find it economically feasible to cater to thin domestic market segments in the developing countries.[47]

For a company desirous of developing a long-term market commitment within a country, it may be economically impossible to serve all the thin

---

[46] Dole A. Anderson, "Developing National Markets: The Thailand Case," *MSU Business Topics*, Spring 1969, p. 31.

[47] Sherbini, "Import-Oriented Marketing Mechanisms," op. cit., p. 72. Reprinted with permission.

BOX 6–2

Multi-Cultural Market

An outstanding characteristic of South Africa is the awesome fragmentation of consumer markets. The apartheid policy has drawn world attention to the many ethnic strata of the society. . . . Each major racial group is, in turn, split into sub-groups. Several of the most important Bantu tribes apparently do not lose much love over each other. Among the whites, the 60% Afrikaans-speaking majority embraces a style of life which tends to differ from the English-speaking minority in details. This may be of importance in some markets (for example, Afrikaners often prefer to entertain at home, while many English-speaking South Africans would rather take their guests to a restaurant or club).

Other differences among consumer groups, too, appear to stand out starker here than in the United States or Western Europe. The contrast between urban and rural seems especially strong. Indeed, it is tempting to speak of several economies within the country, the extremes of which are a highly advanced one focused on the urban white population and a highly underdeveloped one experienced by the rural Bantu (who are nevertheless better off economically than the average rural Negro anywhere else in Africa). . . .

Clearly, the fragmentation of consumer markets offers marketing management an unusual challenge, that is, whether in a given case to go in for a strategy of homogenization (overcoming the barriers between segments) or one of heterogenization (capitalizing on the very existence of the many small niches).

Source: Hans B. Thorelli, "South Africa: Its Multi-Cultural Marketing System," *Journal of Marketing,* April 1968, pp. 40–41. Reprinted from *Journal of Marketing,* published by the American Marketing Association.

market segments, and a single segment may be too small to warrant any substantial market investment.

The traditional sector may offer the greatest potential if, as one scholar suggests, a company is willing to change from a production orientation, i.e., trying to sell exactly what it now produces, to

. . . a "marketing concept" approach to business management. While the concept is complex in its ramifications, it may be summarized as a shift in approach from the policy of attempting to market that which is produced to a policy of gearing investment, production, and distribution to an intimate knowledge of the needs of the market.[48]

This can mean substantial changes in marketing strategies and tactics: penetration pricing as a means to market cultivation, new distribution practices devised to afford economical means of placing products now found only in the modern sector throughout the economy, redesigning products so that they are more fitting to the various conditions of life

---

[48] Glade and Udell, "The Marketing Concept and Economic Development: Peru," op. cit., p. 541.

found in the traditional sector, and/or changes in promotional objectives. Products which are accepted, adequate, and necessary for industrialized Western markets may be unknown and for the most part unusable in the traditional sectors of a developing nation. Since product design must be geared to the basic, simple wants of the population, promotion must have as one of its purposes the creation of primary demand, acquainting the market with the attributes of a "new" product. Besides changes in market strategies, this market orientation approach could necessitate a longer investment period before profitability occurs than would be customary in the modern sector.

Less Developed Countries and Long-Range Potential

The growth of tomorrow's markets will include expansion in industrialized countries and the development of the traditional side of the less developed nations, as well as continued expansion of the modern sectors of such countries. In fact, the greatest long-range potential is to be found in growth in the traditional sector, realizing, however, that a profit may require not only a change in orientation but a willingness to invest time and effort for a longer period of time. The development of demand in a traditional market sector means higher marketing costs initially, compromises in marketing methods, and even the redesigning of products; in other words, market investment today is necessary in order to achieve future profits.

In some of the less developed countries, it may well be up to the marketer to institute the very foundations of modern marketing systems, thereby gaining a foothold in an economy that will some day be highly profitable. The price paid for entering in the early stages of development may be lower initial returns on investment, but the price paid for waiting until the market becomes profitable may be a blocked market with no opportunity for entry. Once a country gains some momentum in development, feelings of nationalism begin running high and, if foreign companies are allowed to operate, there is a tendency to give preferential treatment to those that have helped in its development, closing all doors to others. The political price a company must be willing to pay for entry into a market in a less developed country is entering when most of the benefits of the company's activities will be enjoyed by the host country. When profitability is assured, a country can pick and choose from among many who will want to get into the market.

Some companies are currently developing products specifically for the needs of the traditional sectors of less developed countries. A well-known U.S. soap company has introduced a new hand-operated washing machine which resembles an old-fashioned butter churn more than a modern-day washer.[49] The idea is that it can be sold for $10 to $12 and can be operated by a simple pumping action. The price and the degree of

---

49 "Inventing Backwards—Some Firms Simplify Products for Markets in Poorer Countries," *Wall Street Journal*, May 27, 1969, p. 1.

mechanization make this product practical for large segments of the traditional sector of many less developed countries. The company believes that the washer will be a boon to women who have always had to scrub clothes in streams or tubs. Other companies are following suit. New Jersey Standard, for example, has introduced a kerosene stove which sells for about $2 in Latin America and the Far East. The stove is designed for consumers who would normally use open fires. It admittedly is not a profitable venture; in fact, the company claims it isn't intended to be profitable. It is basically a promotional device to sell kerosene as well as a means for gaining market penetration into the many underdeveloped countries around the world where there is a need for a more efficient cooking system than open fires. National Cash Register is another company which is pursuing a strategy of the future. With their Japanese subsidiary, they have developed a crank-operated cash register which they have successfully sold in the Philippines, Latin America, the Orient, and Spain. With only half the parts of more advanced registers, the machine sells for about half the price of the cheapest models available in the United States. There is a demand for these low-cost machines, and the director is quoted as saying that the hope is that as the countries progress, their customers will advance to more automatic machines, giving National Cash Register a foot in the door of a growth market.

SUMMARY AND CONCLUSIONS

Economists have noted that the standard of living has progressed more in the past 50 years than in the previous 2,000 years. Unfortunately, not all parts of the world have shared equally in the progress of mankind during the past half century. While the residents of some economically affluent countries are enjoying a long, healthy, and prosperous existence, residents in other regions live in semiprimitive, disease-ridden areas, working from dawn until dusk to scrape together the means of survival.

Since World War II, the scope and level of technical and economic assistance and economic cooperation programs have significantly increased. In the short span of two decades, these programs and other factors have enabled some nations of the world to advance their standards of living by two centuries.

As a nation develops, its capacity to produce develops pressures, typically in the distribution structure. To date, primary emphasis has been placed upon establishing production rather than distribution systems. The stages of growth in the marketing process evolve to meet the needs of an expanding economy.

Doubtless, growth rates around the world will continue to progress at an uneven rate. An acceleration of the transfer of technology, new common markets, and continued economic cooperation and assistance will result in a generally increased standard of living for the free world and a challenge to all astute world marketers.

READING

VICK IN INDIA*

SM Interviews Gurcharan Das

U.S. marketers looking toward India soon find cause for doubt. A market of 500 million people (the world's second largest country, more populated than Latin America and Africa combined), India is also 300 languages, six distinct social classes, hundreds of castes, 11 major religions, and an economy chained to the past. For these reasons only a few outsiders—one of them Vick—ever venture there. Annual sales of its VapoRub are only $2 million—the biggest VapoRub market outside the U.S.—but what India is teaching Vick about how to survive in underdeveloped nations is worth far more than that. Here, SM [Sales Management] talks with Gurcharan Das, a Vick product manager, about those lessons.

SM: What's the biggest problem for marketers new to India?

DAS: Creating a market. Unlike in the U.S., where the emphasis is on getting a larger market share, foreign companies in India find they must create a market. They often forget this and spend only at a level to maintain their leadership instead of going out to increase the size of the market.

SM: That means turning to media. How's that done in India?

DAS: There's a lack of media there. No TV. India has very good radio, but, except on a single station, there are no commercials. Until recently you didn't have store audits. There are few reliable audience figures for media and no specialized promotion houses. Moreover, the literacy rate is only 27%, which limits the number of people you can reach through the press. So a marketing man has to be a generalist, doing the work of many people. And an innovator.

SM: What sort of innovation?

DAS: In media, for one thing. Vick is a pioneer of the large-scale, organized use of cinema for advertising. Lever Brothers is another one. India, one of the largest producers of movies in the world, has over 5,000 cinemas. We convinced theater owners that one-minute advertising shorts used before the feature meant additional revenue for them. Today, almost all these cinemas show our commercials. When we introduce a product, the purchaser of a movie ticket gets a free sample and, of course, sees our commercial.

SM: What about people who can't be reached by film?

DAS: You innovate further. The cinema reaches about 120 million Indians. That leaves about 75% of the population uncovered. To overcome this, we conceived a two-pronged distribution-cum-promotion program for rural areas. Basically, it involved sending two men to rural marketing centers on bazaar days to distribute samples. Incentives let us

---

* Reprinted from *Sales Management,* October 1, 1969, pp. 44–48.

create a nucleus of consumers who spread word of our products through word of mouth and handbills. Sampling is very important to us.

SM: Were these methods applied for VapoRub?

DAS: Yes, coupled with the cinemas and using small units at a low price. VapoRub momentum really picked up after we introduced a 5-gram tin, which cost the customer 7¢. That's one-quarter of the quantity in the U.S. jar. Also, we sold VapoRub specifically for colds. In India, there's a habit of using a balm for all kinds of pains, and it was tempting to sell VapoRub as such a balm. But we didn't.

SM: What's another successful foreign product in India?

DAS: Dalda, a vegetable oil made by Lever Brothers. It's like Crisco. Dalda is the largest selling branded product there, worth about $60 million a year. They've done fantastic pioneering work. Today, if you ask for vegetable oil, you ask for Dalda, which has become a generic household word.

SM: What other products are suited to the Indian market?

DAS: Food products, definitely. Particularly in the nutrition supplement field.

SM: Are Indians apprehensive of U.S. or other foreign products?

DAS: Not at all. If it's American, it's considered quality. Many Indians are crazy about anything foreign. This is because imports are banned, except for essential goods, to help India to its economic feet. Consider this example of how Indians revere foreign products: we make VapoRub in India under a trademark owned by the American company. It's the same formula as in the U.S. But occasionally Indians smuggle the "made in U.S.A." jar into the country just because it has a foreign label. And pay twice the price for it.

SM: What should we know about the Indian consumer?

DAS: A popular misconception here is that the average Indian consumer is too poor to buy things. But the per capita income comparison is misleading. Even if only half the Indian population is considered economically active—and I think that is a valid assumption—you have a population in excess of the U.S.'s. Assuming that you are not selling refrigerators but low-cost mass products, you have a pretty large market. Indians have demonstrated that they, too, want the fruits of industrial society: cars, transistors, etc. And this demand isn't limited to urban centers alone. Over 50% of the national income is found in rural areas.

SM: India is, can we say, notorious for its regional differences?

DAS: Yes, and they are considerable. Northern and southern India are like two different countries. Each of the 17 Indian states has a different kind of people with different languages, culture, and traditions, ranging from the 15th century to the 20th century. A marketing man really has to know all the people.

SM: But isn't marketing activity mainly confined to urban areas?

DAS: That's true, but the urban market is over 100 million people— and that's the population of Germany, Sweden, and Spain combined.

SM: What about distribution?

DAS: That's a problem. Towns are far apart, and although India has the largest railway network in the world, transport is nowhere near as developed as in the U.S. You can't say, "By Friday I want 20 cases in such and such a place." It'll most likely be the Friday two months hence. So, ensuring that every town has stock is a real challenge. We have resorted to a system of "town stockists" in over 500 towns who have a contractural obligation to keep two months' stock.

SM: How often do your salesmen service them?

DAS: About once a month, according to the town's importance.

SM: How do your salesmen travel?

DAS: By train. They don't have cars.

SM: Do they also service retail accounts when visiting a stockist?

DAS: Yes. Our stockists are rarely as aggressive as rack-jobbers or big wholesalers in this country, so we can't depend on calling "key accounts" alone. Besides, there are no retail chains in India. Thus, a man has to call on all the retail outlets in a town.

SM: What about salesmanship itself?

DAS: Commercial relationships are more personal in India. A salesman who has been on a beat for a long time establishes a personal relationship with his clients, who would not hesitate to help him out in a clutch. The backslapping salesman doesn't go far in India.

SM: What makes a salesman tick? Money?

DAS: Money, yes, but it isn't everything. The treatment of people is very important. In India, when the boss gets angry, the man takes it very personally.

SM: How much does a salesman earn?

DAS: If you add his incentives, approximately $800 a year. With this, he can lead the life of a middle-class citizen.

SM: What about selling costs?

DAS: The selling operation is more expensive internationally than in the U.S. Although labor is cheap, you need more salesmen, and freight is an expensive item in distribution costs. Selling costs outside the U.S. are almost twice as high.

SM: Describe pricing policies.

DAS: The usual attitude is that income is low, so companies tend to underprice their products. Vick almost underpriced Clearasil when it considered selling it at 39¢. I went to drug stores and discovered that cosmetics were selling at much higher prices. Eventually, we sold Clearasil at 60¢, and it has done very well.

SM: How strong is brand loyalty?

DAS: Very strong. If a customer is satisfied with a product, he doesn't necessarily change over to a new one just because it is new.

SM: What about the availability of raw and packaging materials?

DAS: They're much scarcer in India, and, therefore, the purchase function in a company is very important. Sometimes more important than marketing. In the U.S., you're used to dictating to the factory what to produce, depending on consumer demand. In India, it's often the reverse—you sell what the factory produces.

SM: What help do the advertising agencies provide?

DAS: The major international agencies are represented, and a number of Indian agencies, such as A.S.P., are doing excellent work. My impression, however, is that Indian agencies aren't as thorough in their work and don't work and don't take responsibility as easily as do the agencies here.

SM: What other media besides cinema does Vick use?

DAS: Newspapers follow cinema in importance. Radio is now opening up for commercials. We have to advertise in a number of languages, and no periodical gives us a circulation of more than 300,000. That means signing up a large number of papers to get an adequate circulation, and that tends to be expensive. We are now adopting a regional copy approach—writing original copy and treating each region as if it were a separate market. Results are good.

SM: Can one get along on English only?

DAS: A number of consumer companies in India reply only on the English press, and they certainly have achieved a respectable sales volume in the big cities. But if you want to penetrate to the masses, you have to reach them in their own language.

SM: What's involved in market testing?

DAS: Concept testing is very useful. By that I mean finding out how people will react to a product even before it goes into test market. For example, our Vicks Formula 44 is a big success in the U.S. The commercial shows a man coughing and an EKG line on the brain called the "cough control center." It worked well here. In India, it didn't, because when people saw the line in the brain move, they thought something was wrong with the man's brain, and they got frightened. Now we use an EKG line without the brain. It works.

SM: How is Vick organized internationally?

DAS: It is basically decentralized, and the Indian operation is run entirely by Indians. The Latin America and Far East areas make up a separate division handled by one office in New York. Africa and Europe make up another division in Paris.

SM: India is now at a particularly awkward stage in her development. Could this mean serious trouble politically and economically?

DAS: India's problem is economic and not political. India is the largest democracy in the world, a stable democracy. There has been a responsible exercise of power since independence. There have been no revolutions, and, most likely, there won't be any. Communism doesn't stand a chance, despite small pockets, because India is a country with traditions of private property and freedom deeply ingrained.

QUESTIONS

1. It is possible for an economy to experience economic growth as measured by total GNP without a commensurate rise of the standard of living. Discuss fully.

2. Why do technical assistance programs of more affluent nations typically ignore the distribution problem or relegate it to a minor role in development planning? Explain.

3. Discuss each of the stages of evolution of the marketing process. Illustrate each stage with a particular country.

4. As a country progresses from one economic stage to another, what in general are the marketing effects?

5. Locate a country in the agricultural and raw material stage of economic development and discuss what changes will occur in marketing when it passes to a manufacturing stage.

6. What are the consequences of each stage of marketing development on the potential for industrial goods within a country? For consumer goods?

7. Discuss the significance of economic development to international marketing. Why is the knowledge of economic development of importance in assessing the world marketing environment? Discuss.

8. Select one country in each of the five stages of economic development. For each country outline the basic existing marketing institutions and show how their stages of development differ. Explain why.

9. Select one country each in Asia, Western Europe, North America, and Latin America in the manufacturing stage of development. See Exhibit 6–1. Explain the differences in similarities among the countries in market potential for consumer goods.

10. Why should economic development be studied by a foreign marketer? Discuss.

11. "It would be an error of the greatest magnitude for a marketer contemplating entry into a foreign market to ignore the universal vision of 'industrialization' held by most countries." Comment.

12. Discuss Rostow's five stages of economic development. Give examples of countries in each stage.

13. What are the objectives of economically developing countries? How do these objectives relate to marketing? Comment.

14. What is marketing's role in economic development? Discuss marketing's contributions to economic development.

15. Define the following terms:
    Underdeveloped
    Economic development

Reading

1. List some guidelines for Vick or any other company selling a consumer product to follow when marketing in India.

OUTLINE OF CHAPTER 7

INTRODUCTION

CLIMATE AND TOPOGRAPHY

POPULATION
  Rural-Urban Shifts
  Opportunities in Developing Countries

WORLD TRADE
  Differences in People
  Differences in Economies
  Differences in Natural Resources

WORLD TRADE ROUTES

SUMMARY AND CONCLUSIONS

READING
  Commodity Flows in a Developing Economy, *Economic and Business Bulletin*

GEOGRAPHY AND WORLD MARKETS

INTRODUCTION

Geography, the study of the earth's surface, climate, continents, countries, peoples, industries, and products, is an element of the environment which confronts the marketer but which generally receives little of his attention. There is a tendency to study the manifestations of the effect of climate, topography, and available resources rather than to study these geographical factors as important causal agents in the marketing environment. The physical character of a nation is perhaps the principal and broadest determinant of both the characteristics of a society and the means by which that society undertakes to supply its needs.[1] Thus, the study of geography is important for the student of foreign marketing when evaluating marketing and its environment.

It is beyond the scope of this chapter to discuss the physical characteristics of every nation. To do so would serve little purpose and, in fact, would be contrary to the book's orientation. The peculiarities of each nation should be examined during the dynamic market assessment.[2] Furthermore, to spend time viewing each nation in depth might cause a loss of perspective of the world, the relationship of one country to another, and the ensuing marketing consequences.

It is more effective to examine the world as a whole in order to acquaint the reader with the broad scope of world markets and the effect of the diversity of geography upon the profile of the various markets. For this reason, the orientation of the chapter is to look at some of the more important geographic characteristics of the world which may affect markets and which should be taken into consideration when examining the environmental aspects of marketing.

This chapter will discuss some of the characteristics of world markets

---

[1] Robert Bartels (ed.), *Comparative Marketing: Wholesaling in Fifteen Countries* (Homewood, Ill.: Richard D. Irwin, Inc., 1963), p. 3.

[2] See Chapter 17 below for a discussion of market assessment.

that must be weighed in order to effectively establish marketing plans. A secondary purpose is to provide the student of international marketing with a greater awareness of the world, its complexities, and its diversities, an awareness which can well mean the difference between success and failure in marketing ventures.

Climate, topography, and population will be examined as some of the broader and more important elements of geography. In addition, a brief look at traditional world trade routes will complete the presentation of a broad view of geography and world markets.

CLIMATE AND TOPOGRAPHY

As elements of geography, the physical terrain and climate of a country are important environmental considerations when appraising a market. The effect of these geographical features upon marketing can range from the rather obvious influences upon product adaptation to the more profound influences upon the development of the marketing systems within a country.

Altitude, humidity, and temperature extremes are all climatic features which may affect the use and functionality of products and equipment. Products that perform well in temperate zones may deteriorate rapidly or require special cooling or lubrication to function adequately in tropical zones. Manufacturers have found that construction equipment used in the United States required extensive modifications in order to cope with the intense heat and dust found in the Sahara Desert region. Within even a single national market, climate can be sufficiently diverse to require major adjustments. In Ghana a product adaptable to the entire market must be able to operate effectively in one climatic extreme of desert heat and dehydration to the other extreme of tropical rain forest and consistently high humidity.

By affecting the character of a nation's economy and its economic and social development, geography has an even more direct influence upon marketing. South America represents an extreme but well-defined example of the importance of geography in marketing considerations. The economic and social systems that exist there today can be explained in part in terms of the geographical characteristics of the area.

South America is a continent 4,500 miles long and 3,000 miles wide at its broadest point, two thirds of it comparable to Africa in its climate, with 48 percent of its total area being made up of forest and jungle and only 5 percent arable.

Mountain ranges cover the west coast for 4,500 miles with an average height of 13,000 feet and a width of 300 to 400 miles. This is a natural, formidable barrier which has prevented the establishment of commercial routes between the Pacific and the Atlantic coasts.

Once the Andes are surmounted, the Amazon basin of 2,000,000 square miles lies ahead. It is the world's greatest rain forest, almost uninhabitable and impenetrable. Through it runs the Amazon, the world's second largest river which with its tributaries has almost 40,000 miles of navigable water. On the east coast is another mountain range covering almost the entire coast of Brazil with an average height of 4,000 feet.

South America presents a geographic picture of natural barriers that inhibit national growth, trade, and communication. It shows a vast land area with a population concentration on the outer periphery and the interior isolated and almost uninhabited. The major cities of the South American countries are within 200 miles of the coast, but even the cities are often separated from each other by lack of communication and frequently a lack of roads. Thus, national unity and an equal degree of economic development are nearly impossible. Many citizens of South American countries are so isolated that they do not recognize themselves as part of the nation in which they live. Geography has divided South America into secluded communities.

Another characteristic of Latin American countries is the population concentration in major cities. In almost every case, a high percentage of the total population of each country lives in a few isolated metropolitan centers. Here are located most of the wealth, education, and power, while the surrounding rural areas remain almost unchanged from one generation to the next, usually at subsistence level. In many areas, even the language of the rural people is not the same as that of metropolitan residents.[3]

Under circumstances like those in this South American example a market is rarely homogeneous. In Colombia there are four major population centers separated from one another by high mountains. As a result of this physical isolation, each center has a different climate, dialect, style of living, and population characteristics. Thus, from a marketing view, the four centers really constitute four distinctly different markets.

Although the geography of Latin America may seem extreme, a further study of geography will reveal that many areas in the world have topographic and climatic variations of equal extremes. Consider, for example, the physical and/or climatic variations that exist within such countries as Canada, Russia, and India.

Imagine the formidable problems of appraising market potential or devising a marketing mix that would successfully reconcile the diversities in such situations. Although the hurdles are not insurmountable, geography cannot be ignored because of its direct effect upon marketing in such activities as communications and distribution. Furthermore, there may be indirect effects through its geographical ramifications on the society and culture of the country, all of which ultimately must be reflected in marketing activity. Many of the peculiarities of a country (i.e., peculiar to the foreigner) would be better understood and anticipated if its geography were studied more closely.

The effect of natural barriers upon market development also must be considered. Because of the ease of distribution, coastal cities or cities situated upon navigable waterways are more likely to be trading centers than are landlocked cities. Cities not near natural physical transporta-

---

[3] This discussion is based in part on a monograph by Herbert V. Prochnow, president of the First National Bank of Chicago, "Economic, Political, and Social Trends in Latin America" (Chicago: The First National Bank of Chicago, n.d.).

tion routes generally are isolated from one another even within the same country. Consequently, when planning distribution systems, it would be unwise to assume that one distribution point could serve a wide territory. In discussing the problem of distribution to Africa, one marketer pointed out that,

A shipment from Mombasa on the Kenya east coast to Freetown on the bulge of West Africa could well take longer than the faster and more frequent freight service operating directly from New York and London. Even within the country more than one distribution center may be necessary; a Nairobi (Kenya) site, for example, would find it almost impossible to service adequately the Mwanza region on the Tanganyika side of Lake Victoria, only a few hundred miles away, although both are in British East Africa.[4]

As countries develop, natural barriers are adapted to rather than overcome. The task of surmounting natural barriers is left to more affluent generations. Thus, geography, or at least topography and climate, may be of great importance in underdeveloped countries where man has not had the time or economic capability to overcome such obstacles. In Ecuador, for example, the road conditions are such that it is hardly possible to drive a car from the port of Guayaquil to the capital of Quito only 200 miles away.[5] Contrast this to the accomplishments of more economically advanced countries, where formidable mountain barriers are frequently overcome. A case in point is the recently completed 7.2 mile tunnel which cuts through the base of Mont Blanc in the Alps. This highway tunnel brings Rome and Paris 125 miles closer and provides a year-around route between Geneva and Turin of only 170 miles; it was previously a trip of nearly 500 miles when snow closed the highway over the Alps.[6]

In summary, the marketer should consider the effects of climate, altitude, humidity, temperature, and such upon his product; but he should also examine the more complex effect of geography upon general market characteristics, distribution systems, and the state of the economy.

POPULATION

Although not the only determinant, sheer numbers of people are significant in appraising potential consumer demand. Factors such as rates of growth, age levels, and distribution of people in rural and urban areas are all closely related to the demand for various categories of goods.

Exhibit 7–1 illustrates the increase in population by continents over the past 167 years. Although the early figures are only rough estimates, the tremendous increases in population are very evident.

Recent estimates indicate that there are over three billion people in

[4] Edward Marcus, "Selling the Tropical African Market," *The Journal of Marketing*, July 1961, p. 31.

[5] Henry Deschampsneufs, *Selling Overseas* (London: Business Publications Limited, 1960), p. 48.

[6] "Opening of $47-Million Tunnel under Mont Blanc Will Give Boost to French-Italian Trade," *Business Week*, July 17, 1965, p. 142.

EXHIBIT 7–1

Estimated Population by Continent

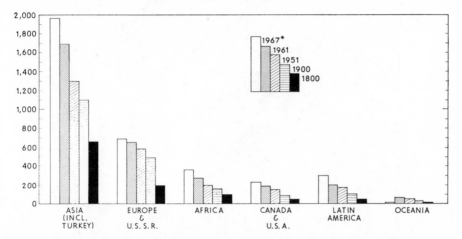

SOURCE: *The Shorter Oxford Economic Atlas of the World* (3d. ed.; London: Oxford University Press, 1965), p. 10. 1967 data from *Statistical Yearbook of the UN, 1968* (New York: United Nations, 1969).

the world. At current rates of growth, there will be between six billion and seven billion by the year 2000.

Exhibit 7–2 shows the distribution of the growth of the world population per square mile: the most remarkable feature is how sparsely settled most of the world really is. In only a few areas is the density over 125 persons per square mile: China, Japan, India, and Western Europe.

When the world is drawn in proportion to population size instead of land masses, as it is in Exhibit 7–3, a striking picture of population density appears. Notice how much larger Great Britain is when the map is drawn on a population scale (Exhibit 7–3) than when land mass is the scale (Exhibit 7–2).

Rural-Urban Shifts

In addition to the population increase, there has been a significant shift of population from rural to urban areas all over the world. Many ramifications of this trend are of direct importance to marketing.

Shifts of population from rural to urban areas are of recent significance. In the early 1800s, less than 3.5 percent of the world's people were living in cities of 20,000 or more and less than 2 percent in cities of 100,000 or more. The real beginning of worldwide urbanization, starting in Europe, came with the Industrial Revolution and by the 1950s, over one fifth of the people of the world lived in cities of 20,000 or more.

Present-day urbanization is still concentrated in Europe, although the shifting from rural to urban in Asian areas has shown a slight increased rate of growth over that in Europe. The free countries of Europe have a

EXHIBIT 7-2

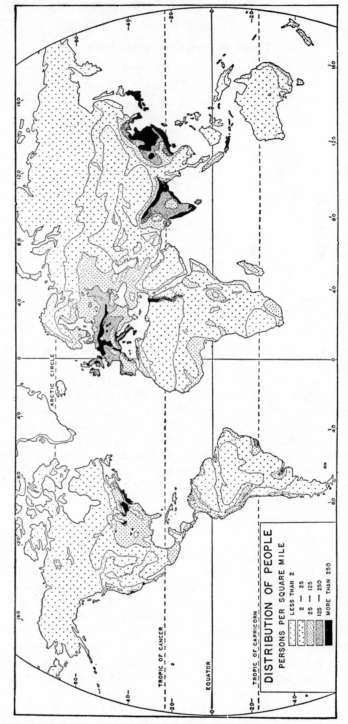

DISTRIBUTION OF PEOPLE

PERSONS PER SQUARE MILE

LESS THAN 2
2 — 25
25 — 125
125 — 250
MORE THAN 250

SOURCE: Reprinted with permission of The Macmillan Company from *Economic Geography* by Clarence T. Jones and Gordon G. Darkenwald (New York: The Macmillan Company, 1954), p. 11. Copyright 1954 by The Macmillan Company.

EXHIBIT 7-3

Key Map: Continents and Selected Countries on the Scale of Their Population, around 1950

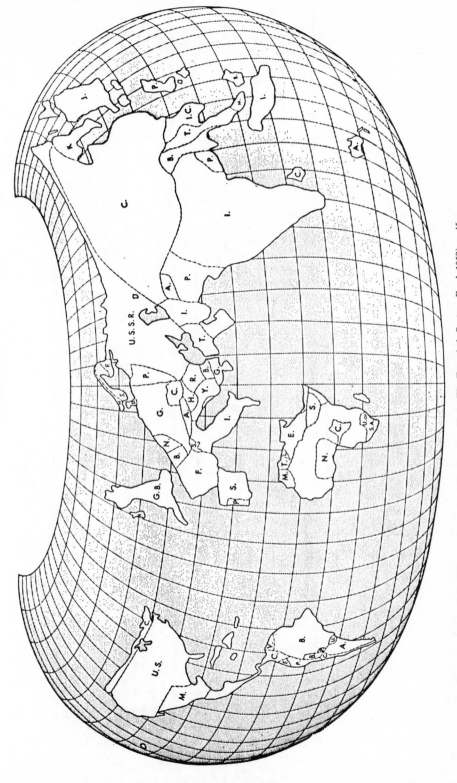

SOURCE: W. S. and E. S. Woytinsky, *World Population and Production* (New York: The Twentieth Century Fund, 1953), p. 45.

EXHIBIT 7-4

A Comparison of Twenty Countries*

	Australia	Canada	New Zealand	U.S.A.	Belgium	West Germany	Netherlands	U.K.	France	Italy
Total population (thousands)	11,751	20,441	2,726	199,118	9,581	59,876	12,597	55,068	49,890	52,334
Percentage employed in Agriculture, Forestry and Fishing (% of working population)	11.1%	8.8%	14.4%	4.9%	7.4%	13.5%	......	4.3%	19.9%	24.8%
Percentage employed in Mining and Manufacturing (% of working population)	43.5%	35.1%	41.7%	35.4%	47.0%	44.6%	......	48.8%	48.5%	40.9%
Gross national product per head ($U.S.)	2,260	2,805	2,001	4,037	2,039	2,021	1,804	1,977	2,324	1,279
Expectation of life (years) Male	67.9	68.35	68.4	66.7	67.7	67.6	71.1	68.1	67.8	67.2
Female	74.2	74.17	73.7	73.8	73.5	73.4	75.9	74.2	75.0	72.3

	Japan	Norway	South Africa	Sweden	Brazil	Phillippines	Turkey	Ceylon	Egypt	India
Total population (thousands)	99,920	3,784	1,143	7,869	85,655	54,656	32,710	11,741	30,907	511,115
Percentage employed in Agriculture, Forestry and Fishing (% of working population)	24.2%	19.4%	10.1%	18.4%	52.5%	57.1%	......	47.7%	53.5%	72.9%
Percentage employed in Mining and Manufacturing (% of working population)	34.5%	44.9%†	33.1%	43.3%	19.0%†	17.9%	......	21.4%	19.2%	15.9%
Gross national product per head ($U.S.)	1,158	2,199	618	3,041		278	353	153	......	......
Expectation of life (years) Male	67.7	71.0	......	71.6	39.3	48.8	52.7	61.9	51.6	41.9
Female	72.9	76.0	......	75.7	45.5	53.3	52.7	61.4	53.8	40.5

* Figures are deduced from statistics of varying reliability and should be treated with reserve.
† Including construction.
SOURCES: U.N. Demographic Yearbook, 1967 (New York: United Nations, 1967), pp. 473–74, and Statistical Yearbook, 1968 (New York: United Nations, 1969), pp. 591–98.

population of roughly 310 million. More than a quarter of the population in both England and France lives in the greater London and Paris areas, and about 20 percent of West Germany's population is settled in urban areas of the Ruhr district.

Current trends in urban, rural, and total population are illustrated for selected countries in Exhibit 7–5. Regardless of the state of their economic development, the rise in urban population in all the countries

EXHIBIT 7–5

Trends in Urban-Rural Population, 1800–1962
(plotted on a semilogarithmic scale)

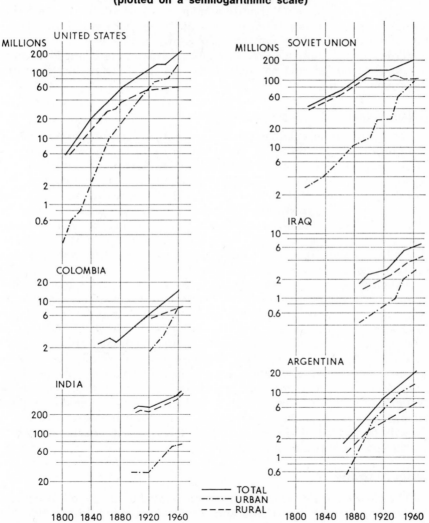

SOURCE: Richard S. Thoman, *The Geography of Economic Activity* (2d ed., New York: McGraw-Hill Book Company, 1968), p. 27.

is extraordinary. Note, for example, that in the United States and Argentina, urban population now exceeds rural population.

It was reported in a study of world urbanization that all countries now usually classified as underdeveloped have more people living in rural areas than do all countries usually classified as technically advanced.[7]

The move from farms to cities in search of a higher standard of living is not always fruitful; nonetheless, urbanization does form the nucleus of a mass consumer market. Such a mass market is generated because the urbanites are less self-sufficient than people living in rural areas. Urbanites must depend upon others to produce most of their basic needs for survival, whereas those living in rural areas generally produce most of what they consume. Without doubt, massive population centers that do not have the economic means of satisfying needs and wants above the subsistence level do not make lucrative markets; yet the growing underdeveloped countries are reacting to far-reaching changes in international, economic, and political affairs and they are rapidly changing their economic basis.

Opportunities in Developing Countries

People in former colonial empires, primitive tribes, and more settled communities that have existed in relative isolation and that represent more than a billion of other than Caucasian peoples are determined to improve their living conditions and share in the opportunities of the world. In a matter of decades, these peoples are seeking and achieving rates of economic growth which have taken other countries centuries to achieve. Population centers that for all practical purposes were markets for only the barest necessities of life at the end of World War II are today relatively lucrative markets for industrial goods as well as an increasing variety of consumer goods.

Although absolute numbers of people may not constitute a market, coupled with rapid economic growth they can produce amazing results. What is occurring in Africa today gives an insight into the future possibilities of such a situation. Nowhere is industry less developed than in Africa; yet a recent United Nations's survey "estimates that industrial production in Arab, black, and white Africa will double in the next twenty years."[8] Although the industrial base is small and founded primarily on the conversion of agricultural raw materials, the United Nations's report noted that Africa was beginning to develop or expand its own metals, machines, chemicals, and textile industries. It is this growth in industrial production that develops the means on which market potential is based.

WORLD TRADE

The basis of world trade can be simply stated as the result of equalizing an imbalance in the needs and wants of a society on one side and

[7] Richard S. Thoman, *The Geography of Economic Activity* (New York: McGraw-Hill Book Company, 1962), p. 27.

[8] "Africa Doubling in a Decade," *Time*, December 14, 1962, p. 63.

supply and demand of goods on the other. Countries and societies have demands·for many goods which may or may not be available within their own boundaries. Those who have an excess of goods of one kind or another trade for commodities that are in demand but are not economically available or are in short supply at home. In short, trade is the result of differences among countries. There are at least three reasons countries differ in what they trade for and produce:

1. Differences in culture and skills.
2. Differences in the stage of economic development.
3. Differences in the availability of natural resources.

Differences in People

Different cultural development has provided the people of some countries with skills and talents which are difficult to duplicate and are in demand the world over. The Swiss excel in the manufacture of watch movements and other precision instruments, products which they can export in exchange for products in short demand in their country. Parisians have a cultural heritage of producing high-fashion women's clothing which has set the style for much of the world. Differences of this nature often result in world trade.

Differences in Economies

The various economies of the world are all in different stages of development, with diverse needs and wants. At one end of the scale are Colombia and other Latin American countries and many of the nations of Africa, which are eager for industrialization. They have little or no industry and no means to produce the necessary products to meet the industrial needs of their aspirations. The products of highly developed industrial economies are necessary; therefore, they trade with France, the United States, and other industrialized countries for the equipment necessary to create their own industrial base. At the other end of development are nations with mature economies and sizable populations which can afford the luxuries of an affluent society and whose wants in part have long been satisfied with products from around the world. Many of these products come from the lesser developed countries; thus, trade is created.

Differences in Natural Resources

Some countries are better endowed than others with natural resources. Most of the tin in the world is found in the tropics, and coffee, which requires a special climate, is grown in only a few countries; yet these products are consumed in some degree by most of the world. All countries have wants and needs which they cannot gratify domestically; hence, world trade must satisfy these desires. The different bases of world trade are vividly pointed up in Exhibit 7–6.

EXHIBIT 7–6

Trade of Leading Fifteen World Trading Countries, 1967*
(in millions of currency)

	Imports		
Country	U.S. $ Value of Total Imports	Dollar Value— Principal Import	Dollar Value Sales by Leading Supplier
United States.........	$26,813	$2,762.4 Petroleum, crude & partly refined	$7,099.0 Canada
West Germany.........	$17,351	$1,164.0 Petroleum, crude & partly refined	$2,138.4 U.S.
United Kingdom.......	$17,186	$1,407.8 Machinery, other than electric	$2,217.9 U.S.
France...............	$12,381	$1,586.3 Machinery, other than electric	$2,495.4 West Germany
Japan.................	$11,664	$1,457.2 Petroleum, crude & partly refined	$3,212.8 U.S.
Canada...............	$10,057	$2,140.5 Transport equipment	$7,425.9 U.S.
Italy.................	$ 9,697	$1,328.1 Petroleum, crude & partly refined	$1,689.9 West Germany
U.S.S.R..............	$ 8,537	$ 636.3 Clothing	$1,411.3 East Germany
Netherlands...........	$ 8,338	$ 802.9 Machinery, other than electric	$2,116.9 West Germany
Belgium..............	$ 7,176	$ 735.6 Machinery, other than electric	$1,518.9 West Germany
Sweden...............	$ 4,699	$ 605.9 Machinery, other than electric	$ 891.9 West Germany
Switzerland...........	$ 4,129	$ 408.1 Machinery, other than electric	$1,171.9 West Germany
Australia.............	$ 3,453	$ 627.4 Machinery, other than electric	$ 875.3 U.S.
East Germany.........	$ 2,972	219,593* Tires for motor vehicles	$1,429.0 U.S.S.R.
Denmark..............	$ 3,147	$ 344.9 Machinery, other than electric	$ 587.7 West Germany

EXHIBIT 7–6 (continued)

	Exports		
Country	U.S. $ Value of Total Exports	Dollar Value— Principal Export	Dollar Value Sales to Leading Customer
United States..........	$31,243	$5,950.9 Machinery, other than electric	$7,143.0 Canada
West Germany.........	$21,736	$4,952.2 Machinery, other than electric	$2,511.9 France
United Kingdom.......	$13,869	$2,848.2 Machinery, other than electric	$1,684.4 U.S.
France................	$11,380	$1,407.7 Machinery, other than electric	$1,971.1 West Germany
Japan.................	$10,442	$1,733.6 Transport equipment	$3,048.8 U.S.
Canada...............	$10,553	$1,739.8 Transport equipment	$6,788.8 U.S.
Italy..................	$ 8,702	$1,516.5 Machinery, other than electric	$1,535.9 West Germany
U.S.S.R...............	$ 9,649	$ 720.0 Equipment for complete industrial plants	$1,414.5 East Germany
Netherlands...........	$ 7,288	$ 662.6 Electrical machinery	$1,900.4 West Germany
Belgium...............	$ 7,032	$1,161.9 Iron and steel	$1,509.0 Netherlands
Sweden...............	$ 4,525	$ 775.6 Machinery, other than electric	$ 593.9 United Kingdom
Switzerland...........	$ 3,496	$ 499.4 Watches, clocks and parts	$ 453.9 West Germany
Australia..............	$ 3,362	$ 846.5 Wool and other animal hair	$ 656.8 Japan
East Germany.........	$ 3,159	170,076† Electric motors	$1,419.0 U.S.S.R.
Denmark..............	$ 2,532	$ 318.7 Machinery, other than electric	$ 558.5 United Kingdom

* Order determined by total value of imports and exports.
† Number, not monetary value.
SOURCE: *Yearbook of International Trade Statistics* (New York: United Nations Publishing Service, 1969).

Of all the countries of the world, the United States is the largest world trader. The 1967 figures of dollar value of exports and imports (Exhibit 7–6) show that the value of foreign trade in the United States was $58 billion.[9]

Exhibit 7–7 shows the composition of foreign trade for the United States. Notice that the exports are those products in which the United

EXHIBIT 7–7

Composition of U.S. Foreign Trade

SOURCE: W. S and E. S. Woytinsky, *World Population and Production* (New York: The Twentieth Century Fund, 1953), p. 183.

States excels either in talent or abundance and that the imports are typically raw materials in short supply but vital to the economy and manufactured goods that can be produced more economically elsewhere. Most countries engage in some form of trade, some more than others, as their needs differ. Exhibit 7–8 is a distorted world map showing continents and countries drawn on the scale of their exports.

---

[9] *Yearbook of International Trade Statistics* (New York: United Nations, 1969), pp. 12–19.

EXHIBIT 7-6

Six Regions of World Trade (after Folke Hilgerdt):

Distorted World Map Showing Continents and Countries on the Scale of Their Exports, 1952

The six regions shown in this chart are as follows: A. Tropics; B. United States; C. Regions of Recent Settlement; D. Continental Europe; E. Noncontinental Europe; F. Rest of the World.

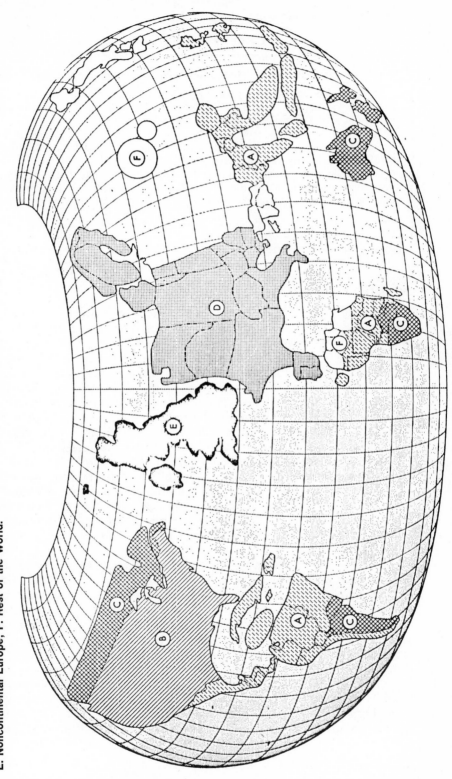

SOURCE: W. S. and E. S. Woytinsky, *World Population and Production* (New York: The Twentieth Century Fund, 1953), p. 45.

BOX 7–1

Only Five Gas Stations on 473-Mile Moscow-Minsk Highway in Soviet Union

The Russian motoring from Moscow to Minsk, say, would be well advised to take heed should he see a "last-chance-to-fill-up" sign. The next gas station may be a long time in coming.

The road between Moscow and Minsk is 437 miles long. It is one of the Soviet Union's major east-west highways and along its entire length there are just five gas stations and one garage.

Projecting this paucity of automotive way stations into national terms supports indications that about one-fifth of the estimated one million automobiles in the Soviet Union is normally laid up waiting for the attentions of a mechanic.

Source: *The Washington Post*, 1969.

WORLD TRADE ROUTES

The major world trade routes have developed between the two most industrialized continents—North America and Europe. It might be said that world trade routes bind the world together, minimizing the differences of the lack of physical proximity, natural barriers, abundance of resources, and the fundamental differences between peoples and economies. Early trade routes were, of course, overland; later came sea routes and finally, in present times, air routes to connect countries. Regardless of the means of transportation, the main trade routes present a vivid picture of the world's countries attempting to overcome economic and social imbalances created in part by the influences of geography.

The leading sea lanes illustrated in Exhibit 7–9 and world trade figures in Exhibit 7–6 can be compared to show the relationship of the volume of import-export trade and trade route importance. Exhibit 7–9 includes rail as well as sea routes of countries involved in world trade. The most obvious feature is the relationship of industrialization and the degree of economic development and the available means of surface communications.

To discuss trade routes and not pay particular attention to air communications would indeed be an oversight. Exhibit 7–10 illustrates the rather complete system of air routes for the world. Although airfreight may not be extremely important as a percentage of total transportation of foreign trade, it is expanding in importance with larger and faster aircraft. For particular commodities (i.e., items of high perishability and/or high unit value), it is one of the major means of transport. The world's airlines reported 570 million ton-kilometers in international airfreight in 1956 and 1,260 million in 1961, excluding the shipment of mail.[10] Thus, the volume of airfreight more than doubled in five years, and the services offered have expanded as rapidly. A leading airline advertises that it has regularly scheduled cargo flights taking off or

---

[10] *Statistical Yearbook of the United Nations* (1962), p. 384.

landing every 2¼ minutes around the clock and around the globe. The top 10 commodities shipped by air are as follows:

1. Newspapers, magazines, periodicals, books, and catalogues.
2. Industrial and agricultural machinery.
3. Personal effects.
4. Electrical equipment and appliances.
5. Surface vehicles and parts.
6. Printed matter.
7. Chemicals, drugs, and pharmaceuticals.
8. Clothing.
9. Cloth and textiles.
10. Baby poultry.[11]

An interesting comparison between surface communications (Exhibit 7–9) and air routes (Exhibit 7–10) is the air service to the world's less industrialized countries. Although air routes are the heaviest between points in the major industrial centers, they are also quite heavy to points in less developed countries. The obvious reason is that those areas not located on navigable waters and those places where the investment in railroads and effective highways is not feasible often can be adequately served only by air. Air communications have had the effect of making otherwise isolated parts of the world reasonably accessible.

SUMMARY AND CONCLUSIONS

One British authority admonishes foreign marketers to study the world until "the mere mention of a town, country, or river enables it to be picked out immediately on the map."[12] Although it may not be necessary for the student of foreign marketing to memorize the world map, a prospective international marketer should be reasonably familiar with the world and its climatic and topographic differences. Since geography is an important environmental element, however, the need for geographical knowledge is greater than that of being able to discuss the world. For the marketer whose career has been restricted to one country, many of the important marketing characteristics of geography may be completely unknown and thus overlooked when marketing in another country. For someone, for example, who has never been in a tropical rain forest where annual rainfall is at least 60 inches and sometimes exceeds 200 inches, it is difficult to anticipate the need for protection against high humidity, or for someone who has never been in the constant 100° plus heat of parts of the Sahara region, the effects of dehydration can be a particularly difficult problem to foresee.

Aside from the simpler and more obvious ramifications of climate and topography are the more complex geographical influences upon the development of the general economy and society of a country. In this case, the need for studying geography is more to provide the marketer with an understanding of why a country has developed as it has rather than only a guide to adapting marketing plans. In summary, geography is one of the environments of foreign marketing which should be understood and

---

[11] Ibid., p. 11.
[12] Deschampsneufs, op. cit., p. 46.

EXHIBIT 7–9

Surface Communications

SOURCE: *Oxford Economic Atlas of the World*, 3d ed. Reprinted with permission.

Surface Communications

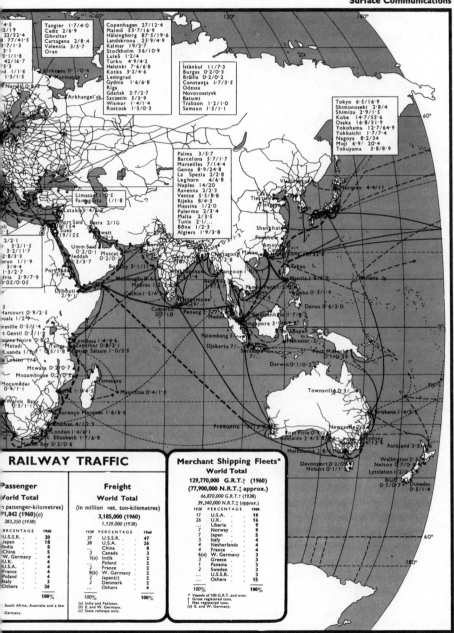

Tangier 1·7/4·0
Cadiz 2/6·9
Gibraltar
Cartagena 2/8·4
Valencia 3/5·7
Oran

Copenhagen 27/12·4
Malmö 33·7/16·9
Hälsingborg 87·5/19·6
Landskrona 25·9/4·9
Kalmar 19/2·7
Stockholm 36/10·9
Luleå 1·2/4
Turku 4·9/4·2
Helsinki 7·6/6·8
Kotka 3·2/4·6
Leningrad
Gdynia 1·6/6·8
Riga
Gdańsk 2·7/2·7
Szczecin 5/3·9
Wismar 1·4/1·4
Rostock 1·3/0·3

İstanbul 11/7·3
Burgas 0·2/0·3
Brăila 0·2/0·2
Constanţa 1·7/3·5
Odessa
Novorossiysk
Batumi
Trabzon 1·2/1·0
Samsun 1·5/1·1

Tokyo 6·5/16·9
Shimonoseki 2/8·4
Shimizu 2·9/1·5
Kobe 14·7/55·6
Osaka 16·8/31·9
Yokohama 12·7/64·9
Yokkaichi 1·7/7·4
Nagoya 8·2/34
Moji 6·9/ 20·4
Tokuyama 3·8/8·9

Palma 3/5·7
Barcelona 5·7/1·7
Marseilles 7/14·4
Genoa 8·9/24·6
La Spezia 2/2·8
Leghorn 4/6·8
Naples 14/20
Ravenna 2/2·3
Venice 5·5/8·8
Rijeka 8/4·3
Messina 1/2·0
Palermo 2/3·4
Malta 2/3·5
Tunis 2·1/...
Bône 1/2·3
Algiers 1·9/3·8

Limassol 1/2·5
Famagusta 1/1·8

Latakia 1·4/2·2

Port Said 1 Basra 2/1G

Suez 19/1 55

Umm Said 0·2/0·1 Muscat
Jeddah 0·3/3·7   0·2/0·

Bombay 3·1/11·8

Port Sudan

Djibouti
2/9·1

Colombo
28/10   Penang 2

Mombasa 1·4/4·6
Zanzibar 0·8/2·1
Dar es Salaam 1·0/3·5

Mtwara 0·2/0·7

Mozambique 0·2/0·

RAILWAY TRAFFIC

Passenger		Freight	
World Total		**World Total**	
(in passenger-kilometres)		(in million net. ton-kilometres)	
?1,842 (1960)(a)		3,185,000 (1960)	
383,350 (1938)		1,129,000 (1938)	
1938 PERCENTAGE	1960	1938 PERCENTAGE	1960
U.S.S.R. .	20	37 U.S.S.R. .	47
Japan .	18	38 U.S.A. .	26
India .	8	... China	8
China .	5	3 Canada .	2
W. Germany .	4	3(a) India .	2
U.K. .	4	... Poland .	2
U.S.A. .	4	2 France .	2
France .	4	8(b) W. Germany .	2
Poland .	4	2 Japan(c) .	2
Italy .	3	2 Denmark .	2
Others .	26	... Others .	4
	100%		**100%**

South Africa, Australia and a few
Germany.

(a) India and Pakistan.
(b) E. and W. Germany.
(c) State railways only.

Merchant Shipping Fleets*
World Total

129,770,000 G.R.T.† (1960)
(77,900,000 N.R.T.‡ approx.)
66,870,000 G.R.T.† (1938)
39,340,000 N.R.T.‡ (approx.)

1938	PERCENTAGE	1960
17	U.S.A. .	19
26	U.K. .	16
...	Liberia .	9
7	Norway .	9
7	Japan .	5
5	Italy .	5
4	Netherlands .	4
4	France .	4
6(a)	W. Germany .	3
3	Greece .	3
1	Panama .	3
2	Sweden .	3
...	U.S.S.R. .	3
	Others .	15
100%		100%

* Vessels of 100 G.R.T. and over.
† Gross registered tons.
‡ Net registered tons.
(a) E. and W. Germany.

EXHIBIT 7–10

Air Communications

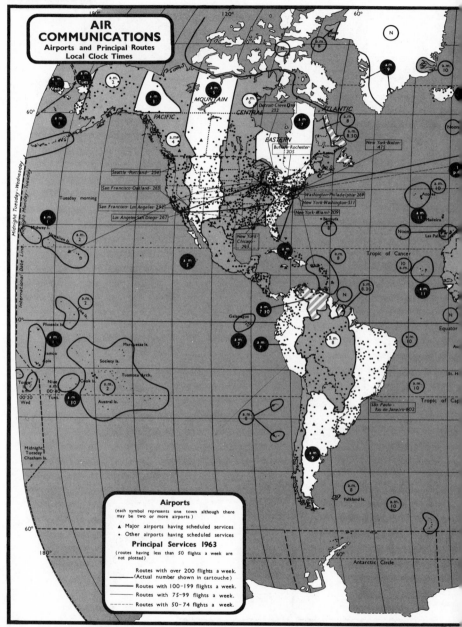

Air Communications

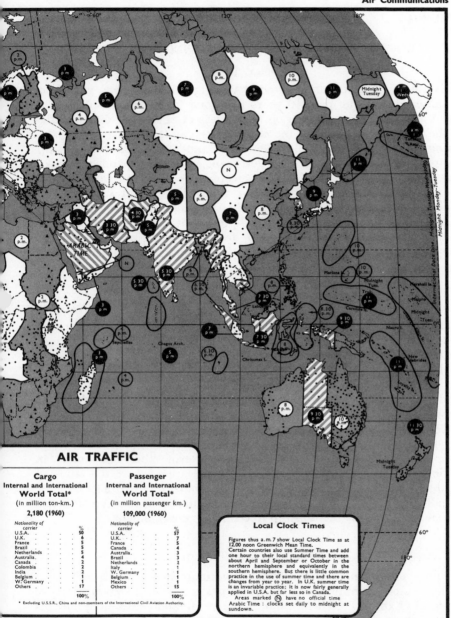

AIR TRAFFIC

Cargo Internal and International World Total* (in million ton-km.) **2,180 (1960)**		Passenger Internal and International World Total* (in million passenger km.) **109,000 (1960)**	
Nationality of carrier	%	*Nationality of carrier*	%
U.S.A.	50	U.S.A.	57
U.K.	6	U.K.	7
France	5	France	5
Brazil	5	Canada	4
Netherlands	5	Australia	3
Australia	4	Brazil	3
Canada	2	Netherlands	2
Colombia	2	Italy	1
India	2	W. Germany	1
Belgium	1	Belgium	1
W. Germany	1	Mexico	1
Others	17	Others	15
	100%		**100%**

* Excluding U.S.S.R., China and non-members of the International Civil Aviation Authority.

Local Clock Times

Figures thus a.m. 7 show Local Clock Time as at 12.00 noon Greenwich Mean Time.
Certain countries also use Summer Time and add one hour to their local standard times between about April and September or October in the northern hemisphere and equivalently in the southern hemisphere. But there is little common practice in the use of summer time and there are changes from year to year. In U.K. summer time is an invariable practice; it is now fairly generally applied in U.S.A. but far less so in Canada.
Areas marked Ⓝ have no official time.
Arabic Time : clocks set daily to midnight at sundown.

which must be included in foreign marketing plans to a degree commensurate with its influence upon marketing effort.

READING

COMMODITY FLOWS IN A DEVELOPING ECONOMY*

JAMES G. HAUK

Everett E. Hagen[1] has asserted: "Although the economic growth of Colombia during the past 40 years has gone largely unnoticed by the world at large, one can count on the fingers of one hand, the countries of the world whose rate of increase in per capita income during this period has been greater." Between 1938 and 1960 total freight shipments increased 700 percent, truck transportation expanded thirteen times, and air freight increased nineteen times. Unfortunately, little is known about this transformation, or about the current status of the marketing system, despite the fact that Colombia is in the beginning stages of a marketing revolution. The present article summarizes recent additions in marketing knowledge by focusing on the physical distribution network, a vital sector in Colombia's economic development.

The Basic Model

Every country can be regarded as an input-output system in a physical distribution sense. Goods move in from other countries in the form of imports and goods move out in the form of exports. These components are connected to an internal dimension which has to do with the flow of products between regions within the country. Environmental forces are the determinants affecting the source and destination of goods, the kinds of transportation used, the mobility of the process, and other such elements.

This model will be used as a general guide. We will present the physical flow pattern and also make an attempt to explain the way in which environment has determined this pattern. While not much can be done within a few pages, at least a basic approach to the study of comparative marketing can be illustrated. Something can also be done to indicate the importance of geographic environment to physical distribution as well as its relationship to economic development.

The Movement Pattern

Three major ranges of the Andes mountains stretch north and south in the western third of Colombia, some peaks reaching 18,000 ft. above sea level (Exhibit 1). These mountains have not only presented barriers to the flow of goods, but they have also influenced the present pattern

* Reprinted with permission from *Economic and Business Bulletin*, Temple University, School of Business Administration, Spring 1968, pp. 37–42.

[1] Everett E. Hagen, *On the Theory of Social Change*, Washington, D.C., The Brookings Institution, 1964, p. 40.

EXHIBIT 1

Location of the Andes Mountains in Colombia

of physical distribution. The broad features of commodity flows are shown in Exhibits 2 and 3. Exhibit 2 indicates the inflow of goods from foreign countries. The pattern is explained, at least superficially, by a governmental policy which restricts imports largely to industrial goods. In addition, Colombian industry has a high degree of concentration.

In fact, 98 percent of the 18,000,000 people reside in the western half of the country or in an area smaller than Texas. Industry is even more concentrated. About 70 percent of total factory output takes place in a triangle whose apexes are formed by the three largest cities of Bogotá, Medellín and Cali. This triangle contains only 5 percent of the land area and 20 percent of the population, but it receives 65 percent of total imports.[2] It is also the major source of the country's coffee crop, which accounts for 70 percent of dollar exports.

[2] Population data derived from XII *Censo Nacional de Población*, Bogotá, DANE, 1965; Factory output derived from *Informe Congreso Nacional*, Bogotá, DANE, 1965.

EXHIBIT 2

Inflow of Goods to Colombia from Foreign Countries

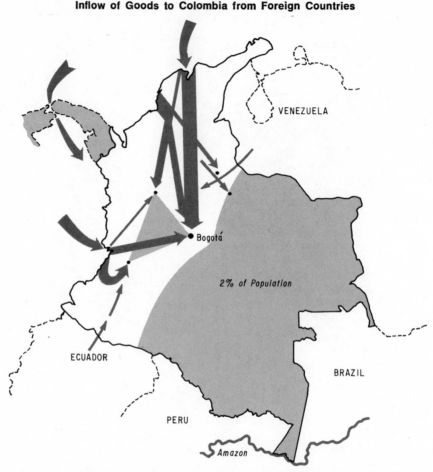

Source: Data derived from *Anuario de Comercio Exterior* (Bogota: DANE, 1964) and from *Estudio del Transporte Nacional* (Bogotá: Ministerio de Obras Públicas, 1962).

While it is not possible to explain market structure entirely by geography, it is clear that a combination of tropical location and mountainous terrain has had an effect. When the Spaniards first landed on the north coast in the early 1500's they were attracted to the interior mountains in their search for gold. They found gold but they also found a number of other conditions conducive to settlement, one of which was the climate. The city of Medellín, for example, has an average temperature of 70.1 degrees with an extremely low inter-seasonal variation. High altitudes contain climatic conditions differing greatly from the low areas along the coast and in the eastern half of the country. Consequently mountains have attracted both population and industry, in contrast with the United States where they generally have had a re-

EXHIBIT 3

Air Cargo between City Pairs
(tons in 1965)

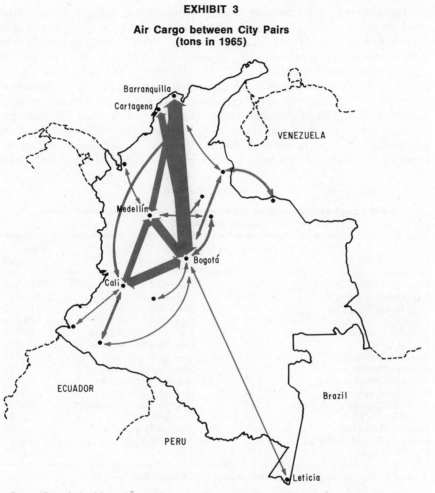

Source: Data derived from *Boletín Mensual de Estadística* (Bogotá: DANE, April 1966), pp. 112–14.

pelling effect. They have also helped to create ideal conditions for the production of coffee.

NORTH-SOUTH DIRECTION. The movement of goods in Colombia is generally north and south following the direction of the Andes, similar to the early years in our own country when goods moved along the Atlantic seaboard and in the direction of the Appalachian mountains. The pattern also reflects the location of the Magdalena River, the major transportation artery during the early development of Colombia.

Data on air cargo between city pairs are an indication of the north-south direction (Exhibits 3 and 4). One can argue that they do not depict the total movement of goods with a high degree of accuracy since they are biased toward long distance shipments as well as those made to areas relatively inaccessible by land. Moreover, only about 1 percent of the ton-miles of cargo transportation is done by air, despite the fact that most physical distribution takes place in mountainous terrain and that Colombia has a highly developed air system. Nonetheless, air routes bear a close resemblance to the road and rail structure, both of which have a clear north-south direction.

THE OUTFLOW OF GOODS. Two features of the outflow process should be emphasized: Exports are concentrated in a few extractive products and there is a high degree of product specialization by port. Considering the six products which account for 90 percent of dollar exports and 96 percent of ton exports, we find that each has a "favorite" port. All of the crude petroleum is channeled through the Covenas-Mamonal area,

EXHIBIT 4

Air Cargo and Passenger Transportation on High Volume Routes;
Colombia, S.A., 1965

Route	Tons of Cargo	Route	Number of Passengers
Bogotá to Barranquilla	10,706	Bogotá-Cali	135,617
Barranquilla-Bogotá	8,369	Cali-Bogotá	135,932
Bogotá-Cali	7,246	Medellín-Bogotá	126,257
Bogotá-Medellín	6,898	Bogotá-Medellín	121,514
Medellín-Bogotá	4,383	Barranquilla-Bogotá	75,548
Cali-Bogotá	4,248	Bogotá-Barranquilla	74,403
Bogotá-Cartagena	3,138	Bogotá-Cucuta	53,531
Bogotá-Cucuta	2,156	Bucaramanga-Bogotá	42,968
Medellín-Barranquilla	2,127	Bogotá-Cartagena	42,651
Cartagena-Bogotá	2,123	Cartagena-Bogotá	42,496
Bogotá-Bucaramanga	1,966	Bogotá-Bucaramanga	42,364
Medellín-Cali	1,651	Cali-Medellín	42,171
Barranquilla-Cali	1,461	Pereira-Bogotá	41,900
Barranquilla-Medellín	1,409	Medellín-Cali	41,442
Pereira-Bogotá	1,326		

SOURCE: *Boletín Mensual de Estadística* (Bogotá: DANE, April 1966), pp. 112–14.

nearly all of the bananas through Santa Marta, 71 percent of the wood through Turbo, 80 percent of the coffee through Buenaventura, 89 percent of the cement through Barranquilla, and all of the fuel oil through Cartagena.[3] Not only does each major export tend to go through a single port, but each port concentrates most of its outflow efforts on one product. This contrasts sharply with the inflow task where efforts are spread among hundreds of different industrial goods.

Several other features associated with the general movement of goods can be summarized as follows:

1.   Physical distribution is concentrated in the western half of the country.
2.   There is very little commodity flow directly to bordering countries.

---

[3] Data derived from *Anuario de Comercio Exterior*, Bogotá, DANE, 1964.

Even today there are no road nor rail facilities enabling direct contact with three of the five bordering countries.

3. Trucking is the major form of transportation. Excluding pipelines it is estimated that trucking accounts for over 50 percent of the ton-miles of cargo transported each year. Another study in the Antioquia region showed that manufacturers, in particular, used trucks for over 90 percent of total dollar shipments.

4. As compared with the United States, physical distribution lacks mechanization. Horseback still dominates in the outlying areas and in the cities it is common to see individuals pulling carts of merchandise for several miles. Milk is still delivered to the home by horsedrawn cart.

5. Colombia now assembles products from 65 countries and disperses goods to 70 countries located on every major continent. Coffee alone is sold to 33 countries, including Japan, Sweden, the Union of South Africa, Australia, and Paraguay. In total, international marketing (imports plus exports) accounts for about 20 percent of national income, a ratio far higher than in the United States.

Historical Isolation

Until the 1920's, the Colombian people were relatively isolated from other countries and from one another as well. Several segmented regions existed, each with its own cultural and economic base. Trade, limited for centuries between regional groups, has recently increased internally. Nevertheless, isolation persists, partly because the western third of the country contains the most diversified land conditions of any comparable area in Latin America.[4] This diversity not only made transportation difficult but it also made self-sufficiency in narrow geographic zones reasonably feasible. In the distant past, Indian tribes at the high altitudes could produce wheat and potatoes, trading them for the tropical products produced by other tribes a few miles away at the low altitudes.[5] Later, with the growth of cities, the same conditions permitted survival without much marketing between major regions.

Transportation problems entail bridging mountain ranges in order to develop relationships with remote areas and constructing transportation networks almost entirely in the mountains. Only 350 miles of roads existed in the country as late as 1928 and a large part of these were impassable during various times in the year. The principal route from the north coast to the capital city of Bogotá was the Magdalena River which was unnavigable much of the time. Goods moving by this route (about 450 air miles) had to be loaded and unloaded six or seven times and passengers could make the trip by a combination of water and rail in seven and a half days under the best of conditions.[6]

---

[4] Preston James, *Latin America*, New York, The Odyssey Press, 1959, p. 100.

[5] Gilbert J. Butlund, *Latin America: A Regional Geography*, London, Spottiswoode Ballantyne & Co., Ltd., 1961, p. 178.

[6] Clarence F. Jones, *Commerce of South America*, Boston, Ginn and Co., 1928, p. 284.

These conditions have changed greatly in the last three decades, Colombia being cited as one of the two recent examples of the "big push" in the transportation area.[7] Between 1928 and 1960, the number of road miles was increased from 350 to 35,000, or approximately 100 times. In 1942, a road was completed between the two major population centers of Medellín and Cali. And in 1961 the capital city of Bogotá was connected by rail with the north coast part of Barranquilla.

PRESENT MOBILITY.   How mobile is the physical distribution system at present? Using Wilfred Owens' measure, constructed by reference to the number of rail miles per 10,000 square miles, the number of road miles per person, etc., Colombia has a freight mobility index of only 11.3. This is well below Japan, Chile, Argentina, Canada, and a majority of other countries in the world.[8] In addition, it should be noted that road and rail wind and climb through the mountains which lengthens distance and reduces speed. Also the absence of direct land transportation with three of the five bordering countries negatively affects mobility in international logistics.

On the positive side, however, the index excludes air and water and for this reason it underestimates the capacity to move goods. Colombia has a well developed air system, a long coastline and several major rivers. Some of the latter are contributing very little to trade at present but their potential in this respect is good. Also, road and rail facilities have been constructed in the part of the country where nearly all of the people reside. This provides a kind of mobility which Owens' index does not take into account.

Regardless of the exact degree, it is clear that the physical distribution of Colombia has improved in the past 30 years. The most authoritative study yet conducted on transportation in the country concludes that nearly all of the people now have reasonable access to roads leading to the major cities.[9] Thus within a relatively short period of time one of the basic conditions for market unification has occurred.

A New Era

Colombia is now entering a new era. Relatively modern factories have risen in the major cities, many of which are beginning to export. No longer does the geographical environment have the strong constraining effect which it had several decades ago. While physical distribution is a major problem, other aspects of marketing are gaining in relative significance. For the first time many firms are able to consider seriously the development of distant markets and as they do so the problems of market research, advertising, distribution channels and other elements in exchange are coming to the forefront.

Nonetheless the effect of geography is clear: it has fostered a market structure by influencing the geographical distribution of population. It also helps to explain the present north-south direction of the transporta-

[7] Wilfred Owens, *Strategy for Mobility*, Washington, D. C., The Brookings Institution, 1964, p. 37.

[8] Ibid., p. 14.

[9] *Estudio de Transporte Nacional*, Bogotá, Ministerios de Obras Públicas, 1962.

tion system, the emphasis on trucking as a means of physical distribution, and the fact that air transportation is highly developed. Colombia had the first commercial airline to operate on a continuous basis in the Western Hemisphere, established in 1920. Today there are about 450 airports throughout the country, many enabling access to regions otherwise inaccessible.

Major problems still exist in international logistics, some of which are caused by inadequate transportation facilities connecting Colombia with bordering countries. While members of the Latin American Free Trade Association are presently trying to improve ocean shipping very little is being done to improve land transportation. In this respect, consider the implications of a rail system from Colombia to Brazil and Argentina. This route is considerably shorter than the present ocean routes and it might also stimulate development at interior points that are presently contributing very little to economic development. Certainly air is an alternative, but there is a question as to whether it is better than rail.

It is not only transportation which needs attention. There is also a lack of other facilities which are necessary for effective mobility. Recently Colombian cattlemen found a good market for their product in Peru, but Peruvian port facilities quickly presented a bottleneck. Inadequate handling equipment, lack of refrigeration facilities, and poor capacity in general were more serious limitations than transportation itself. There is also a need to diversify exports and to develop an effective marketing system within Colombia which will connect the major cities with the outlying areas where most of the people reside.

Finally the need for relaxation in governmental controls should be emphasized. This is particularly evident with respect to controls over imports, which have hindered production planning by greatly complicating the logistics of physical supply. Importing an industrial good requires a myriad of steps arranged in a time sequence from need recognition to receipt of the good. They include completing a questionnaire for governmental use, securing income tax clearance, depositing from 10 to 120 percent of the dollar value of the proposed import with the central bank, making application for an import license, presenting a customs declaration in quadruplicate, and scores of others associated with the shipment of goods and their nationalization at the port of entry.

Conclusion

Each country is unique with respect to the macro-flow of goods. The patterns and the problems reflect a number of environmental forces including geography, the stage of economic development, and governmental regulation. A great deal could be learned by studying the process in a number of different countries. Since comparative marketing is indeed "one of the great frontiers of marketing thought,"[10] this approach deserves recognition.

---

[10] Reavis Cox, "The Search for Universals in Comparative Studies of Domestic Marketing Systems," *Marketing and Economic Development,* Chicago, American Marketing Association, 1965, p. 162.

QUESTIONS

1. Why study geography in international marketing? Discuss.
2. Pick a country and show how employment and topography affect marketing within the country.
3. Discuss the bases of world trade. Give examples illustrating the different bases.
4. The marketer "should also examine the more complex effect of geography upon general market characteristics, distribution systems, and the state of the economy." Comment.
5. The world population pattern trend is shifting from rural to urban areas. Discuss the marketing ramifications.
6. Select a country with a stable population and one with a rapidly growing population. Contrast the marketing implications of these two situations.
7. "The basis of world trade can be simply stated as the result of equalizing an imbalance in the needs and wants of society on one side and the supply and demand of goods on the other." Explain.
8. How do differences in people constitute a basis for trade?
9. ". . . world trade routes bind the world together. . . ." Discuss.
10. Why are air routes so important in less developed countries? Illustrate your answer with examples.

Reading

1. Geographic environment affects the development of physical distribution networks. Discuss.
2. Discuss the effects geography has had on Colombia's economic development.

OUTLINE OF CHAPTER 8

INTRODUCTION

BASES FOR LEGAL SYSTEMS

JURISDICTION IN INTERNATIONAL LEGAL DISPUTES
  International Commercial Law
  Jurisdiction of U.S. Laws

LEGAL RECOURSE IN RESOLVING INTERNATIONAL DISPUTES
  Problems with Litigation
  Arbitration

    Tribunals for Arbitration
    International Chamber of Commerce
    Arbitration Clauses

Enforcement of Arbitration Clauses

COMMERCIAL LAW WITHIN COUNTRIES

PROTECTION OF INDUSTRIAL PROPERTY RIGHTS—
    A SPECIAL PROBLEM
  Inadequate Protection
  Prior Use versus Registration
  International Conventions

SUMMARY AND CONCLUSIONS

READINGS
  The Language Barrier, *Columbia Journal of World Business*
  Modern Piracy: Chinese "Brigands" Steal Brand Names in Hong
    Kong, *Advertising Age*

CHAPTER 8

THE INTERNATIONAL LEGAL ENVIRONMENT

INTRODUCTION

Among the many components of the marketer's operating environment are the laws which govern his business activities. The legal environment of the foreign marketer takes on an added dimension of importance since there is no single uniform international commercial law which governs foreign business transactions. Laws are different from country to country, and instead of the marketer having to concern himself with only one set of laws, he is confronted with as many different legal environments as countries within which he operates. Furthermore, in transactions between different countries, the marketer is faced with the recurring problem of determining which country's legal system has jurisdiction over his activities.

The legal systems of the world's countries are so varied and complex that it is beyond the scope of this text to explore the laws of each country individually. There are, however, some legal problems that are common to most international marketing transactions which should be given special attention when operating abroad.

A summary of these potential problems is found in a checklist by *Business International;* it was compiled as a help in developing awareness in the legal problems of foreign marketing. The list includes those elements related to marketing that are most prone to legal difficulty:

1. Rules of competition on (*a*) collusion, (*b*) discrimination against certain buyers, (*c*) promotional methods, (*d*) variable pricing, (*e*) exclusive territory agreement.
2. Retail price maintenance laws.
3. Cancellation of distributor or wholesaler agreements.
4. Product quality laws and controls.
5. Packaging laws.
6. Warranty and after-sales exposure.
7. Price controls, limitations on markups or markdowns.
8. Patents, trademarks, and copyright laws and practices.[1]

---

[1] "48 Management Checklists for Foreign Operations," *Business International,* January, 1964, p. 8. Reprinted with permission.

The list is not meant to be a complete compilation of all the possible legal problems; it deals only with those problems peculiar to marketing. The marketer must also concern himself with the laws that apply to business in general. The purpose of this chapter is to provide the reader with a broad view of the international legal environment, leaving to the marketer and his legal counsel the detail necessary in the evaluation of a particular country's legal system. In so doing, it is hoped that the reader will have a better appreciation for the need of knowledge of legal systems and the very important necessity of securing expert legal advice when doing business in a foreign country.

BASES FOR LEGAL SYSTEMS

The legal systems of the countries of the world stem from one of two common heritages—the "common law," derived from English law and found in England, the United States, Canada, and most other countries which have at one time been under English influence; and "civil" or "code" law, which is derived from Roman law and found in the majority of the countries of the world. To the marketer or anyone having to conduct business abroad, the difference between these two systems may be of more than theoretical importance, since the due process of law may vary considerably between code law and common law countries.

The basis for common law is tradition, past practices, and legal precedent set by the courts through interpretations of statutes, legal legislation, and past rulings. Common law seeks "interpretation through the past decisions of higher courts which interpret the same statutes or apply established and customary principles of law to a similar set of facts."[2]

Code law is based upon an all-inclusive system of written rules (codes) of law. Under code law, the legal system is generally divided into three separate codes: commercial, civil, and criminal. While common law is recognized as not being all-inclusive, code law is considered complete as a result of "catchall" provisions found in most code law systems. For example, under the commercial code in a code law country, the law governing contracts is made inclusive with the statement that "a person performing a contract shall do so in conformity with good faith as determined by custom and good morals."[3] Even though code law is considered inclusive, it is apparent from the foregoing statement that there might be some broad interpretation necessary in order to include everything under the existing code.

Commercial law can vary in meaning between common law and code law countries. Under common law, commercial disputes are subject to laws which may be applied to either civil or commercial disputes; there is no specific recognition of commercial problems as such. Code law differs in that there is a separate code specifically designed for business. The commercial code has precedent over other codes when matters of

---

[2] Leslie Llewellyn Lewis (ed.), *The Dartnell International Trade Handbook* (1st ed.; Chicago: The Dartnell Corporation, 1963), p. 513.

[3] Ibid., p. 513.

business are under jurisdiction. This provision results from historical recognition that legal problems of merchants are often unique and thus should have special status under the law.

Steps are being taken in common law countries to codify commercial law, even though the primary basis of commercial law is found in precedents set by court decisions. An example of uniformity and a measure of codification is the acceptance of the Uniform Commercial Code by more than forty-nine states in the United States. Similar strides toward a unified commercial code have been made in England.

As shall be discussed later (in the section on Protection of Industrial Property Rights), laws governing industrial property rights offer the most striking differences between common and code law systems. Under common law, ownership is established by use; whereas under code law, ownership is determined by registration.

In some code law countries, certain agreements may not be enforceable unless properly notarized or registered; whereas in a common law country, the same agreement may be binding so long as proof of the agreement can be established.

There are sufficient differences between common and code law systems with regard to contracts, sales agreements, and other legal problems that it is necesary for an international marketer familiar with only one system to enlist the aid of legal counsel, even with the most basic legal questions.

An illustration of where fundamental differences in the two systems can cause significant difficulty is in the performance of a contract. Under common law in the United States, it is fairly clear that impossibility of performance does not necessarily excuse compliance with the provisions of a contract unless it is impossible to comply for reasons of an "act of God," i.e., some extraordinary happening of nature which could not reasonably be expected or anticipated by either party of a contract. Hence, floods, lightning, earthquakes, and similar occurrences are generally considered acts of God. Under code law, acts of God are not limited solely to acts of nature but are extended to include "unavoidable interferences with performance, whether resulting from the elements, forces of nature, or unforeseeable human acts,"[4] including such things as labor strikes and riots.

For example, consider these two situations: A contract was entered into to deliver a specific quantity of cloth. In one case, before delivery could be made by the seller, an earthquake caused the destruction of the cloth, and compliance was then impossible. In a second case, pipes in the sprinkler system of a warehouse where the material was stored froze and broke, spilling water on the cloth and destroying it. In both cases loss of the merchandise was sustained and delivery could not be made. The question is whether the parties in these cases were absolved of their obligations under the contract because of the impossibility of delivery. The answer depends upon the systems of law invoked.

In the first situation and under both common and code law, the earth-

---

[4] Lewis, op. cit., p. 533.

BOX 8-1

Contract—A Piece of Paper

This leads to the next point, which is the Japanese view of the contract. The Western view of the contract is that a legal contract between two parties whose validity is upheld by the courts is binding upon the parties. The Japanese view is that a contract is a piece of paper and that people are human beings. Should there be an obligation of one person to another person, then society expects the obligation to be honorably discharged. The penalty for failure to discharge the obligation is dishonor of oneself, one's name, and one's family, perhaps for generations to come. . . .

At the same time, since all contracts refer to obligations which must be discharged in the future and the Japanese feel extremely uncertain about the future, the Japanese side prefers that contractural obligations be left as vague as possible, in order to provide for maximum flexibility. . . . The question arises as to the role of the courts. One must say that they play a very minor role and that if legal proceedings are involved in adjudicating a contract then the parties will probably never do business again. Faith and good will have been destroyed. The limited number of Japanese lawyers and judges per capita is illustrative of the minor role played by the legal process. . . .

The discussion of the contract can not be left here, because there is yet to be described the Japanese view of the Western emphasis on the contract. As might be expected, the Japanese, for whom the written contract plays such a small role, are more than curious about the foreign businessman and emphasis on the written contract. . . .

To a Japanese businessman, the whole scene arouses dire suspicions on his part. He is puzzled at the foreigner's concern with words and phrasing and the foreigner's delight on the signing; in fact, the signing ceremony usually involves a visit from abroad of some vice-president or even board chairman. The Japanese, more often than not, does not dismiss this as some strange Western ceremonial right. He assumes (often incorrectly) that he has been taken in some way, and that that is the reason for the glee on the Western side.

Source: Herbert Glazer, *The International Businessman in Japan: The Japanese Image* (Tokyo, Japan: Charles E. Tuttle Company, Inc., 1968), pp. 59–62. Reprinted with permission of the publisher.

quake would be considered an act of God and impossibility of performance would excuse compliance under the contract. In the second situation, the courts in common law countries would probably rule that the bursting of the water pipes did not constitute an act of God if it happened in a climate where freezing was expected. Therefore, impossibility of delivery would not necessarily excuse compliance with the provisions of the contract. In code law countries where the scope of impossibility of performance is extended considerably, the destruction might very well be ruled as an act of God, and thus release from compliance with the contract could be obtained.[5] The foreign marketer must be especially concerned with the differences between common and code law systems

[5] Lewis, op. cit., p. 534.

when operating between countries using the two different systems, since the rights of the principals of a contract or some other legal document under one law may be significantly different from their rights under the other. It should be kept in mind that there are also real differences between the laws of two countries using common law as well as differences between two countries using code law. Thus, the problem of the marketer is not only one of appreciating the significance of the basis for the law in a particular country, i.e., whether or not it is a common or code law country, but also one of anticipating the different laws which regulate his business regardless of the basis for the legal system of the country.

JURISDICTION IN INTERNATIONAL LEGAL DISPUTES

One of the problems of international marketing is determining what legal system will have jurisdiction when disputes arise. A frequent error is to assume that commercial disputes between citizens of different nations are adjudicated under some supranational system of laws. Unfortunately, there is no judicial body to deal with legal commercial problems arising between citizens of different countries.

International Commercial Law

In the everyday discussions of foreign business, it is often erroneously implied that there exists a body of international law to which all foreign trade activities are subject. The confusion probably stems from the existence of international courts, such as the World Court at The Hague and the International Court of Justice, the principal judicial organ of the United Nations. These courts are operative in international disputes between sovereign nations of the world but not between private citizens. Unless a commercial dispute involves a national issue between states, it would not be handled by the International Court of Justice or any similar world court.

Since there is no body of rules which is concerned solely with commercial transactions, thereby constituting an "international commercial law," the foreign marketer must look to the legal systems of all the countries involved—the laws of his own country, and/or the laws of the countries within which he is conducting business. This, then, is the added dimension of the legal environment which becomes significant in foreign marketing. Every country has its own legal system to which the foreign marketer must tailor his operations.

Since there is no international commercial law, when international commercial disputes arise the problems must be settled under the laws of one of the countries concerned. The paramount question in a dispute is whose law governs. Although this may appear to be an easy question to solve, it is not. Jurisdiction over private, international legal disputes is generally determined in one of three ways: (1) on the basis of jurisdictional clauses included in contracts, (2) on the basis of where a contract was entered into, or (3) on the basis of where the provisions of the contract were performed.

The most clear-cut decision can be made when the contracts or legal documents supporting a business transaction state very clearly whose law is to predominate. In fact, it is advisable to include a jurisdictional clause in all contracts in order to avoid the problem of determining jurisdiction after a dispute arises. A clause similar to the following one will, in most cases, establish jurisdiction in the event of any future disagreements:

That the parties hereby agree that the agreement is made in Colorado, USA, and that any question regarding this agreement shall be governed by the law of the state of Colorado, USA.

In the illustration above, it is agreed that should a dispute arise the laws of the state of Colorado would be invoked. If the complaint were brought in the court of another country, it is probable that the same Colorado law would govern the decision. Cooperation and a definite desire to be judicious in foreign legal problems has led to the not uncommon practice of foreign courts judging disputes on the basis of the law of another country or state whenever applicable. Thus, if an injured party from Colorado brings suit in the courts of Mexico against a Mexican over a contract which included the clause above, it would not be unusual for the Mexican courts to decide on the basis of Colorado law. This is assuming, of course, that it was recognized that Colorado law prevailed in this dispute, either as a result of a prior agreement by the parties or on some other basis.

A jurisdictional clause does not always solve the legal problem of what laws should be invoked. Even with a specific clause establishing jurisdiction, if the contractual events are not, in effect, entered into or executed within the state indicated, courts have been known to disregard the jurisdictional clause and apply different rules in determining what law governs. In cases where there is no jurisdictional clause, or where such a clause is not effective, decisions are sometimes arrived at on the basis of where the contract was entered into. In such disputes, the laws of the country or state where the contract was created predominate. Other legal disagreements are sometimes settled on the basis of where the provisions of the contract were performed. The laws of the country where the business transaction was actually carried out are invoked in judging a dispute. In all cases where there is no jurisdictional clause, the governing legal system is determined by one of the two methods above. Since there is no clear-cut procedure concerning who has jurisdiction, and since the laws of one country may typically be more favorable than another, it is probably wise to include in all agreements a clause stipulating whose laws are to govern. In most cases, courts will uphold these clauses, provided substantial acceptance or performance of the agreement has actually occurred within the designated state.

Jurisdiction of U.S. Laws

Another point of the international legal environment to consider is that when leaving the legal boundaries of his country, a businessman is not necessarily exempt from the laws of his country. For example, regardless of the nation within which he is doing business, a U.S. citizen is still subject to the internal revenue laws of the United States.[6] In addition, there are other laws of the country that follow wherever businessmen go, "so that at any given time, a United States citizen in a foreign country must look to the laws of that country, but he must also keep in mind that he is still a U.S. citizen and simultaneously subject to the rules of his own sovereign."[7]

The question of jurisdiction of United States laws over acts committed outside the territorial limits of the country has been settled by the courts through the application of a long-established principle of international law, the "objective theory of jurisdiction." "This concept holds that 'even if an act is committed abroad, that is, outside the territorial jurisdiction of the U.S. courts, those courts can nevertheless have jurisdiction over it, if this act produces consequences or effects within the U.S.' "[8]

There are exceptions to the statement above, the most important being that a U.S. citizen would not be punished for violating a U.S. law if the violation resulted from the observance of local foreign law. Also, only those violations of U.S. laws that "affect our foreign or domestic trade"[9] are considered subject to the U.S. legal system *when* operations are outside the legal jurisdiction of U.S. courts. Although most foreign marketing activities by U.S. firms would have no effect upon U.S. foreign or domestic trade, there is a growing concern on the part of the international marketer about the effects of U.S. antitrust legislation. Outright purchases, mergers, licensing, and joint ventures with foreign firms have been on the increase in recent years, sparking considerable interest by the Antitrust Division of the Department of Justice.

The question of jurisdiction and how U.S. antitrust laws apply is frequently asked, but only vaguely answered. Whether or not U.S. laws are applicable may be determined by analyzing the few court cases pertaining to conduct in foreign countries and court actions in the domestic market. Either way "the inferences are of uncertain value."[10] The few foreign cases stem from flagrant, collusive activities and fail to shed much light on the legality of "such activities abroad as exclusive dealing, joint sales, patent licensing, or participation in mergers or joint ventures."[11] Domestic cases are of less help, since what is lawful in the United States may not be clearly so in a foreign country if U.S. commerce is not clearly affected. The basis for determination ultimately rests with the interpretation of paragraph one of the Sherman Act, which states that "every contract, combination . . . or conspiracy in

---

[6] For an interesting note on U. S. income tax laws, see "IRS Keeps Its Hand in When You Work Abroad," *Business Week*, April 13, 1968, pp. 106–7.

[7] Andrew W. Brainerd, "An Enlightened Legal Perspective on Foreign Business Operations," *Export Trade*, June 5, 1961, p. 29.

[8] Andre Simons, "Foreign Trade and Antitrust Laws," *Business Topics*, Summer 1962, p. 27.

[9] Ibid., p. 38.

[10] Corwin D. Edwards, "The World of Anti-trust," *Columbia Journal of World Business*, July–August 1969, p. 14.

[11] Ibid., p. 14.

restraint of trade or commerce among the several states or with foreign nations is hereby declared to be illegal . . ." Obviously, any unauthorized private, concerted restraint of commerce, any monopolization or any attempt to monopolize, or any act or practices that will reduce competition is illegal under the Sherman Act: The difficulty occurs in the interpretation of when an act will or does fit such restrictions, thereby becoming illegal. Take for example the following case:

The Justice Department in a February, 1968, suit against the Gillette Company is seeking an injunction against the acquisition of the shares of Braun A.G., of Germany. Does Gillette's acquisition of Braun restrict competition in shaving devices in the United States, given the fact that Braun makes electric razors, and that Braun had previously relinquished its rights to a third company to sell in the U. S. until 1976?[12]

According to the Justice Department, which ordered Gillette to divest itself of Braun, the answer to the question posed above is "Yes!" This and similar moves in the antitrust area,

. . . demonstrate once more the need for new criteria to determine what is and what is not legal in today's widened business world . . . (and) really point up the dangers and absurdities inherent in the practice of trying to apply national laws to international business situations.[13]

Adding to the confusion is the fact that many European countries are adopting laws similar to the U.S. antitrust laws. These are being used not only to regulate antitrust activities within the home country but, in some instances, quite openly to reduce the effect of U.S. competition.[14]

Thus, the foreign marketer is faced with the unique problem of having to consider at least two different legal systems in his planning. If the scope of his operations includes more than one foreign country, the number of legal systems to be considered increases.

LEGAL RECOURSE IN RESOLVING INTERNATIONAL DISPUTES

When it becomes apparent that the settlement of a dispute cannot be resolved on a private basis, the foreign marketer must resort to more resolute action. Many international businessmen prefer to attempt a settlement through arbitration than to sue a foreign industry.

Problems with Litigation

Lawsuits in public courts are generally avoided for numerous reasons. One nationally known attorney commented on his observations of lawsuits between citizens of different countries that although almost all of them ended in spurious victories, "the cost, frustrating delays, and extended aggravation which these cases involved were certainly more

---

[12] Raymond Vernon, "Anti-trust and International Business," *Harvard Business Review*, September–October, 1968, p. 86. Reprinted with permission.

[13] Walter Guzzardi, Jr., "Business Around the Globe—Report from Bonn," *Fortune*, August 1968, p. 47.

[14] "E.E.C. Anti-trust Policy: Gearing to Buck American Competition?" *Business Abroad*, November 28, 1966, pp. 13–15.

BOX 8–2

Gillette versus Sherman Anti-Trust

Last December the Gillette Company bought for fifty million dollars all the common stocks of Braun A. G., a German manufacturer of appliances whose most successful product is an electric shaver. With this acquisition, Gillette gained entry into the electric shaver market in Europe and other parts of the world where Braun shavers are sold. It also picked up Braun's considerable capacities as an industrial designer of quality and style. On their side, Braun's owners, Erwin and Arthur Braun, got a good price for their company. Besides the obvious reason of personal gain, the Braun brothers were moved to sell to Gillette because they believed that Gillette's financial strength offered their companies new opportunities for world wide expansion. **A Threat to Future Competition?** To this happy marriage, however, the Justice Department saw several impediments. Braun does not sell electric shavers in the United States, where it has cross patent and license arrangements with Ronson Corporation. Gillette does not manufacture or sell electric shavers anywhere. But the Justice Department contends that all "shaving instruments," electric shavers as well as safety razors, are competing for the same market. And Justice believes that some day, perhaps after the exploration of the Braun-Ronson agreement, Braun might enter the U.S. market with its own electric shaver. Therefore, the merger between Gillette and Braun, if allowed to stand, would rule out potential competition in the future between Braun shavers and Gillette razors and blades.

In Justice's view, Gillette's strong position in wet shaving in the U.S., where it has well over half the market, adds to the undesirability of the merger. Further, Department of Justice lawyers have pointed out that with the merger Gillette takes over Braun's rights to certain Ronson patents and processes, and that competition between Gillette and Ronson might be lessened, too. So the government has filed suit to compel Gillette to divest itself abroad. Gillette is fighting the case.

Source: Walter Guzzardi, Jr., "Business around the Globe—Report from Bonn," *Fortune,* August 1968, p. 47. Reprinted from *Fortune* magazine by special permission.

oppressive by far than any matter of comparable size" that he had seen in the United States. His advice was to seek a settlement if at all possible.[15]

Other reasons which are frequently considered as deterrents to litigation are:

1. Fear of creating a poor image and damaging public relations.
2. Fear of unfair treatment in a foreign court. (Although not intentional, there is a justifiable fear that a lawsuit will result in unfair treatment. What occurs is that a suit in a court may result in the decision being made by either a jury or judge who isn't well versed in trade problems and the complex intricacies of an international business transaction.)

---

[15] Andrew W. Brainerd, "An Enlightened Legal Perspective on Foreign Business Operations, Part 2," *Export Trade,* June 12, 1961, p. 32.

3. Difficulty in collecting a judgement which may otherwise have been collected in a mutually agreed settlement through arbitration.
4. The relatively high cost and time required when bringing legal action.[16]

One authority suggests that the settlement of every dispute should follow three steps: first, try to "placate" the injured party; if this does not work, "arbitrate"; and finally, "litigate."[17] The final step is typically taken only when all other methods fail. Actually, this advice is probably wise whether one is involved in an international dispute or in a domestic one.

Arbitration

For the foregoing reasons, the majority of international commercial disputes are resolved by arbitration rather than litigation. The basic principle of arbitration is for the parties involved in the dispute to select a disinterested and informed party or parties to referee and finally determine the merits of the case and make a judgment that both parties agree to honor. In actual practice, however, formal rules and procedures are established for entering into an arbitration agreement.

Tribunals for Arbitration.   Although an informal method of arbitration as outlined above is workable, most arbitration is conducted under the auspices of one of the more formal domestic and international arbitration groups organized specifically to facilitate the mediation of commercial disputes. These groups have available experienced arbitrators and formal rules for the process of arbitration and, in most countries, the decisions reached in formal mediation are enforceable under the law.

Among the formal arbitration organizations are:

1. The Inter-American Commercial Arbitration Commission, which conducts arbitration in disputes between the businessmen of 21 American republics, including the United States.
2. The Canadian-American Commercial Arbitration Commission, which functions in disputes between Canadian and U.S. businessmen.
3. The London Court of Arbitration, which is restricted to those cases that can be legally arbitrated in England. Decisions by the London Court of Arbitration are enforceable under English law and English courts.
4. The American Arbitration Association, which was one of the early arbitration tribunals organized in the United States and was originally concerned only with disputes within the United States. Later, however, its activities were expanded to worldwide scope.
5. The International Chamber of Commerce, which is an affiliation of Chambers of Commerce of many of the world's nations. With its

---

[16] Brainerd, op. cit., June 5, 1961 and June 12, 1961.
[17] Philip MacDonald, *Practical Exporting and Importing* (2d ed.; New York: The Ronald Press Company, 1959), p. 152.

worldwide scope, it has established a Court of Arbitration whose rules are used in conducting arbitration.

International Chamber of Commerce. Regardless of which formal arbitration organization is used, the procedures are basically similar. Arbitration under the rules of the International Chamber of Commerce affords an excellent example of how most organizations operate.[18] When an initial request for arbitration is received, the Chamber first attempts a conciliation between the disputants. If this fails, the next step is to start the process of arbitration. The plaintiff and the defendant select from among acceptable arbitrators one man each to defend their case, and the ICC Court of Arbitration appoints a third member, generally chosen from a list of distinguished lawyers, jurists, and/or professors.

The arbitrators arrange for a meeting that includes both parties and after hearing each side present its case, the ICC members make a decision and an award. The history of ICC effectiveness in arbitration has been spectacular; of two hundred decisions recorded, approximately twenty have been rejected by the litigants. Of the twenty decisions rejected, all but one have had the arbitration decision upheld in the courts when further litigation was pursued.

An actual case of arbitration by the ICC follows:

In Paris recently an English businessman came before a group of International Chamber of Commerce officials with the complaint "a few weeks ago I signed a contract with a Japanese firm to buy 100,000 plastic dolls for $.80 each. On the strength of the contract I presold the entire lot in London at $1.40 per doll. Now the Japanese manufacturer informs me that a strike has increased his costs so that he cannot afford to deliver the dolls at less than $1.50 each. Since I'm already committed to delivery of these at $1.40, I maintain the Japanese firm is committed to make delivery at $.80. I'd like to have the matter arbitrated."

.　.　.　.　.

To settle the complaint of the English doll importer, . . . ICC's conciliation and arbitration service . . . appointed a single arbitrator: a former Scandinavian Supreme Court Justice. The two parties met in Stockholm before their arbitrator, who brought to the case great experience and an unbiased view. His decision was that the Japanese firm must hold to the original agreed-upon terms. Thus, the inviolability of an international contract was asserted.[19]

The case was settled to the satisfaction of both parties. This case is also an excellent illustration of the kinds of problems that can arise in contractual obligations between parties in code and common law countries. Under Japanese law the strike probably would be considered an act of God, and, thus, compliance with the provisions of the original contract would be excused. The Englishman, however, under his law, would not accept the Japanese's reason for not being willing to comply, since the strike would not be considered an act of God under English common law.

---

[18] Oscar Schesgall, "Settled Out of Court," *Reader's Digest*, May 1964, pp. 25–28.
[19] Ibid., pp. 25–26.

This case is an illustration of successful arbitration. It must be emphasized, however, that the success of arbitration depends upon the willingness of both parties to accept the arbitrator's rulings.

Arbitration Clauses Most authorities recommend that contracts and other legal documents include clauses specifying the use of arbitration in case of dispute. As one authority points out,

> . . . arbitration is most successfully employed when provision for this method of dispute settlement is incorporated in the contract executed by the seller and buyer. Attempts to refer a dispute to some arbitration group after the disagreement arises many times fail, since one party or the other is unwilling to agree on the form of arbitration, the place of arbitration, or the like.[20]

The following is an example of an arbitration clause suggested by the American Arbitration Association for inclusion in all legal documents where arbitration may be necessary.

> Any controversy or claim arising out of or relating to this contract, or the breach thereof, shall be settled by arbitration in the United States, in accordance with the Rules of the American Arbitration Association and judgment upon the award rendered by the Arbitrator(s) may be entered in any court having jurisdiction thereof.[21]

Even though it is suggested that arbitration clauses be included in a contract to avert later problems, there is some question of the legality of enforcing arbitration agreements which have been made prior to a dispute.

Enforcement of Arbitration Clauses

Arbitration clauses generally require agreement on two counts: (1) The parties agree to arbitrate in case of dispute according to the rules and procedures of some arbitration tribunal. (2) They also agree to abide by the awards resulting from the arbitration. Difficulty arises when the parties to a contract fail to live up to the agreements. Companies may refuse to name arbitrators, refuse to arbitrate, or after arbitration awards are made, they may refuse to honor the award. In most countries, arbitration clauses are recognized by the courts and are enforceable by law within those countries. There is a U.S. federal arbitration law which recognizes the legality of arbitration clauses and establishes the necessary legal procedures to enforce such clauses. Some foreign countries have similar laws which may also include provisions that allow for the enforcement in local courts of awards made in courts of another country.

Not all countries, however, have the necessary statutes to enforce arbitration clauses. The courts of many Latin American and European

---

[20] MacDonald, op. cit., p. 153.

[21] Morgan Guaranty Trust Company, *Export & Import Procedures* (New York, September, 1965), p. 73.

countries do not recognize the enforceability of these clauses. In spite of this, an arbitration clause is probably wise because it establishes the original intent of the parties. This may be sufficient to convince the parties to arbitrate, even though the clause actually may be unenforceable.

Experience to date suggests, however, that foreign arbitration awards or judgments confirming arbitration clauses are generally enforceable in foreign courts, even in the absence of binding national laws on the matter. Presumably, this international cooperation is due to the voluntary nature of arbitration as opposed to the coercive nature of adjudication, which sometimes arouses nationalistic feelings.[22]

Since the laws and procedures vary from country to country, arbitration can be used as a sort of "legal esperanto" to bridge the gap between the differing legal systems.[23]

COMMERCIAL LAW WITHIN COUNTRIES

The marketer should always be aware that, when doing business in more than one country, he must deal with different legal systems. This problem can be especially troublesome when the marketer desires to formulate a common marketing plan to implement in several countries. Although he may be able to negate the differences in language and customs, he may still be hampered by the legal differences between countries.

Obviously, each country has laws which regulate activities in promotion, product development, pricing, and channels of distribution. These laws can be very complicated, with the result that even the widely accepted practice of using premiums in a promotional effort can cause problems.

In discussing this problem, one marketer remarked that "there's no one way to promote a product with premiums throughout Europe."[24] His reference was to the diverse and often difficult restrictions found in Europe regarding the use of premiums. Consider, for example, the different restrictions that exist in the following countries.

In Austria premium offers to consumers come under the discount law which prohibits any cash reductions that would give preferential treatment to different groups of customers. Since it is considered that most premium offers would result in discriminatory treatment to buyers, they are not normally allowed.

Premium offers in Finland are allowed with considerable scope as long as the word "free" is not used and consumers are not coerced into

22 "International Arbitration," *World Business*, quarterly publication by the Economic Research Division of the Chase Manhattan Bank, New York, January, 1969, p. 10. Reprinted with permission.

23 Ibid., p. 10.

24 "Sales Promotion in Europe . . . It's Tough," *Sales Management*, January 3, 1964, p. 24.

BOX 8–3

Comparative Ads—Legal?

Comparison is universal and certainly quite a natural and often an effective form of expression, but it is definitely "verboten" in German advertising copy.

When American advertisers first discovered this situation, their reaction was one of complete amazement and disbelief. I would be most reluctant to hazard a guess as how many man hours of highly creative thought Americans have devoted to finding some way around this inescapable German advertising handicap.

Actually, there is no formal law which makes comparative advertising extra-legal. However, under the law against unfair competition—which is more than 50 years old—advertisers are prohibited from acting contrary to "moral standards." And "moral standards," as established by precedent in years of legal rulings, prohibit comparative advertising.

For example, if a German meat processor advertises one of his products as being "better than knockwurst or even knockwurst with a digestive additive," his competitors who sell knockwurst would surely initiate a temporary injunction to force him to stop such advertising until the matter could be decided by a court. Without a doubt, any court in Germany would rule such an advertising slogan contrary to "moral standards," and the meat producer would undoubtedly be forced to pay heavy damages to the competitors. . . .

Legal action against comparative comparisons in business can and has extended beyond media advertising. Recently, during a meeting of the customers of a German grocery chain which is organized as a cooperative society, one of the company officials demonstrated to the meeting the efficiency of the chain by comparing his firm's prices to those of the competitors. On the average, his prices were 9.5% lower than those of the other local retailers and subsequently, a legal suit was filed against the cooperative by its local competitors. The judge ruled against the co-op, imposing a stiff fine ordering the co-op's officials to refrain from making such competitive comparisons in the future.

Source: W. Harry Wilkens, "Complex Laws Cloud German Ad Picture," *Printer's Ink*, November 23, 1962. Reprinted with permission.

buying products. France also regulates premium offers which are for all practical purposes illegal, since it is illegal to sell for less than cost price or to offer a customer a gift or premium conditional upon the purchase of another product. Furthermore, a manufacturer or retailer cannot offer products different from the kind in which he deals (for example, a detergent manufacturer could not offer clothing, or kitchen utensils; the typical cereal premiums would be completely illegal under this law).

In West Germany the laws covering promotion in general are about as stringent as can be found in any country. In fact, the laws are so "voluminous and complicated that any advertiser contemplating a promotional campaign should consult a lawyer."[25] Most kinds of promotion are allowed but with severe restrictions.

Although the examples above cover only the national statutes regarding the use of premiums in promotion, they illustrate the diversity in the laws often found between countries. These differences are apparent not only in advertising but in pricing, sales agreements, and other commercial activities as well. A frequent marketing approach to Europe is to consider the continent as if it were a unified market. Earlier chapters have illustrated the fallacy of this approach. The problems created by differences in laws between countries are no less pronounced than the difficulties arising from the differences found in social custom, taste, and economies existing between foreign nations.

There is some hope, especially among the Common Market countries, of eventually having a common commercial code. But this has not yet been achieved and some of those U.S. companies that have operated under the erroneous belief that the Common Market is truly common in all respects have had spectacular failures. Although the EEC is a beautiful picture of economic cooperation, for the marketer it is still a matter of dealing with six different countries, cultures, and languages, as well as six different legal systems.

Progress toward unification of the commercial code is being made in the European Common Market, as evidenced by the steps taken toward a unified patent law. Should such attempts at unification materialize, one patent could be filed with a single patent office and be binding in all six countries instead of the current method of filing patents in each of the different countries. This step could lead to a unified commercial legal system for all EEC countries and eventually for a majority of the trading nations of the world. In fact, the Scandinavian countries now have virtually identical laws and present plans call for the eventual adoption of a "Nordic" patent system, under which an applicant can acquire patent protection in each of the countries by filing a single application in any one of them.[26]

Until this time, however, a businessman who decides to invest in a country abroad will have to deal with the multiple legal ramifications of his moves as well as the purely business considerations. For example, a decision to construct a manufacturing plant in a European country should include an analysis of the different legal systems found among the alternate countries. Such facts as "their corporate laws, the effective tax burden in each, tax and financial incentives . . . and a broad range of legal questions should be included in any evaluation of potential building sites since these legal points may differ drastically between countries."[27] The same careful investigation of the legal environment is equally important for planning marketing activities.

---

[25] Ibid., p. 25.

[26] Joseph P. Lightman, "Patent Laws Summarized in 125 Nations Worldwide," *International Commerce*, August 11, 1969, p. 6.

[27] Walter W. Brudno, "Overseas Operations: A Legal Checklist for Management," *Management Review*, March 1962, p. 55.

PROTECTION OF INDUSTRIAL PROPERTY RIGHTS— A SPECIAL PROBLEM[28]

Companies spend thousands of dollars establishing brand names or trademarks for their products which will symbolize quality and a host of other product features designed to entice customers to buy their brands to the exclusion of all others. Millions of dollars are spent on research to develop industrial properties such as products, processes, designs, and formulas, in order to provide a company with an advantage over competitors. Such industrial properties are among the more valuable assets a company may possess. Names like "Kodak," "Coca-Cola," or rights to processes like Xerography, the production of nylon, and cellophane, are invaluable. Normally these properties can be legally protected to prevent other companies from pirating or infringing upon such assets.

Inadequate Protection

The failure to adequately protect industrial property rights abroad can lead to the loss of these rights in potentially profitable markets. Because patents, processes, trademarks, and copyrights are valuable in all countries, some companies have found that their assets have been appropriated and profitably exploited in foreign countries without license or reimbursement. Furthermore, they often learn not only that another firm is producing and selling their product or using their trademark, but that the pirating company is the rightful owner in the country where they are operating.

There have been frequent cases where companies have lost the rights to trademarks and have had to buy back these rights or pay royalties for their use. One of the most unusual cases involved a U.S. citizen residing in Mexico who proceeded to register in Mexico, a code law country, the brand names and trademarks of some 40 companies. Included among the 40 were such well-known names as "Carter's Little Liver Pills" and "Bromo Seltzer."[29] Although most of the companies were able to regain control of their brand names, the procedure required lengthy litigation and considerable help from the U.S. government. If the culprit had not been so blatant in pirating 40 such well-known brands, he probably would have been completely successful. Others have had singular success in pirating processes and demanding significant payment from their original owners. For example:

A manufacturer of a special kind of material used extensively in the pharmaceutical industry licensed a well-known company to make his particular quality [of product] in return for a royalty. He made no attempt to retain control or supervision of the market. The licensor received his royalties during the first year of the arrangements, but no further payments thereafter. On

---

[28] For a comprehensive coverage see, Lawrence J. Eckstrom, *Licensing in Foreign and Domestic Operations* (3rd ed.; Essex, Conn.: Foreign Operations Service, Inc., 1964).

[29] Ibid.

inquiry, the licensee told him that his particular process was no longer being used. He found that the material was indeed somewhat altered, yet the licensee was able to produce this new material only by using the licensor's process. A more carefully drawn agreement could have avoided and minimized these consequences.[30]

Problems like these are the result of inadequate protective measures taken by the owners of valuable assets. Company oversight in properly protecting itself stems from many causes. One of the more frequent ones is the error in assuming that since the company has established its rights in the United States, it will be protected in all the countries of the world or at least be able to establish rightful ownership should the need arise. This error is made because the businessman fails to understand that most countries of the world do not follow the common law principle that ownership is established by prior use.

Prior Use versus Registration

In the United States, a common law country, ownership of industrial property rights is established by prior use, i.e., whoever can establish first use is typically considered the rightful owner. In fact, before trademarks and brand names can be registered, they must actually be in use. In many code law countries, however, ownership is established by registration rather than by prior use, i.e., the first to register a trademark or other property right is considered the rightful owner. Therefore, a company which believes that it can always establish ownership in another country by proving that it had used the trademark or brand name first is laboring under a false impression that may lead to the loss of these assets. However, prior registration may be subject to challenge under certain laws by a person "who claims and can prove that he was the first publicly to use the market. Upon such proof, he may be able to have the registration cancelled."[31] Avoiding the possible loss of industrial property rights which may be profitable either for the company to sell directly or to license others to produce and sell in foreign markets is generally a matter of properly registering them within these countries. This task may be facilitated by the existence of several international conventions which provide for simultaneous registration in member countries.

International Conventions

Many countries participate in international conventions designed for the mutual recognition and protection of industrial property rights. There are three major international conventions; the United States is a member of two. The three are as follows:

---

[30] Charles Henry Lee, "How to Reach the Overseas Market by Licensing," *Harvard Business Review*, January–February 1958, p. 78. Reprinted with permission.

[31] Joseph P. Lightman, "How Countries of the World Treat Trade-Mark Rights," *International Commerce*, May 23, 1966, p. 2.

1. The Paris Convention for the Protection of Industrial Property, commonly referred to as the "Paris Union," includes a group of 50 nations, including the United States, which have agreed to recognize the rights of all members in the protection of trademarks, patents, and other property rights. Registration in one of the member countries insures the same protection afforded by the home country in all the other member countries.

2. The Inter-American Convention includes most of the Latin American nations and the United States. It provides protection similar to that afforded by the "Paris Union."

3. A third important convention is the Madrid Convention, which established the Bureau for International Registration of Trademarks. There are some 22 member countries in Europe which have agreed to automatic trademark protection for all members. Even though the United States is not a participant of the Madrid Convention, if a subsidiary of a U.S. company is located in one of the member nations, the subsidiary could file through the membership of its host country and thereby provide protection in all the 22 countries for the U.S. company.

Once a trademark, patent, or some other industrial property right is registered, most countries require that these rights be worked and properly policed. The United States is one of the few countries where a patent can be held by an individual throughout the duration of the patent period without being manufactured and sold. In other countries, it is felt that in exchange for the monopoly provided by a patent, the holder must share his product with the citizens of the country. Hence, if patents are not produced within a specified period, usually from one to five years (the average is three years), the patent reverts to public domain. This is also true for trademarks; products bearing the registered mark must be sold within the country, or the company may forfeit its right to a particular trademark.

Companies are also expected actively to police their industrial property in bringing to court any violators. Policing can be a difficult task, with success depending in large measure on the cooperation of the country within which the infringement or piracy takes place. For an interesting report on piracy and the difficulty of policing industrial property rights internationally, see the accompanying reading on piracy in Hong Kong ("Modern Piracy: Chinese 'Brigands' Steal Brand Names in Hong Kong").

SUMMARY AND CONCLUSIONS

The foreign marketer faces a multitude of problems in his efforts to develop a successful marketing program. There are difficulties created by the political climate, by cultural differences, by the geography of a country, by strange business customs, and by the stage of economic development of the country in question. A primary marketing task is to develop a plan that will be enhanced or at least not be adversely affected by these and other environmental elements. Entwined among the problems are legal issues that not only hamper a successful operation but also, in some cases, create insurmountable legal roadblocks.

The myriad questions created by different judicial systems, different laws, and different legal systems indicate that the most prudent path to follow at all stages of foreign marketing operations is one which leads to competent counsel well versed in the intricacies of the international legal environment.

READINGS

THE LANGUAGE BARRIER*

HENRY P. DE VRIES

To the international business executive and his legal adviser the language barrier poses a constant and elusive problem. At critical points in the management decision process, the area of uncertainty resulting from language differences remains an effective circuit breaker in the transmission of ideas. In formation of contracts, in preparation of corporate documents, in negotiation and settlement of disputes by arbitration or court proceedings, in any reference to foreign laws or concepts, the language factor is ever present.

The international business community has found various ways of assisting the meeting of minds. An example that readily comes to mind is the increasing use of standardized international instruments containing their own definitions in various languages or referring to uniform definitions of terms. Perhaps the most universal solution in our contemporary world is found in the tremendously expanded development of English as the international language of commerce, diplomacy and science.

In this century English has become the most widely spoken language on earth. It is only fifty years since English was first accepted as the authentic language counterpart of French in the Treaty of Versailles. Today, it is the language medium of exchange used in trade agreements between Peking and members of the Soviet bloc and in cultural agreements between Egypt and Indonesia. Nearly one in ten of the world's people use English as their primary language and nearly one in four understand it to some degree. The American abroad may be forgiven for assuming that the language problem is simply one of spreading even more the use of a language already so widely accepted as a means of communication.

Conveying Legal Ideas

In practice, the chief problem today is in the area of transference of legal ideas. To the businessman a contract or a corporate document is

---

* Reprinted with permission from the July–August 1969 issue of *The Columbia Journal of World Business.* Copyright © 1969 by the Trustees of Columbia University.

essentially a set of operating rules to be followed as a matter of mechanics in arranging details of delivery, payment, place and date of meetings and similar details. The lawyer views the same instrument from the moment of its creation through the lens of a judge's or arbitrator's eyes. When foreign legal elements are involved, the lens will have to be at least bi-focal. For operations, the contract must be understandable in the language of the personnel who must be guided by it. For settlement of disputes, the same contract or written communication must be presented not only in the formal language of the deciding body, but must be so translated as to carry a maximum burden of persuasion. In counselling on the meaning of a contract, in contrast to the advocacy necessary for litigation, the lawyer will rely on the least favorable translation for his legal opinion in order to minimize the scope of the calculated risk.

Translation Problems

To mention the language barrier is to refer to translation as the channel of communication. The importance of understanding the purpose of a particular translation is evident. A routine translation, merely to have a preliminary notion of the contents of the foreign letter, may be completely justified, while reliance on an "official translation" of a foreign law or governmental document may be a major blunder.

The businessman is often unaware of the special problems raised by translation of legal instruments. To translate is always to interpret, that is, to embody an opinion as to the legal meaning of the contents. Disputes as to the meaning of words invariably arise in marginal situations when more than one meaning is possible. Translating from legal English is usually more difficult than to express oneself directly in the foreign language. Though English may have become an international language, legal English is the product of a unique set of historical circumstances. As Professor Keeton, a leading English historian, has remarked, "Even today the language of the law is so completely permeated by Norman-French terms that it is impossible to imagine the legal system without them."

To the normally complex problem of ascertaining meaning in a single language, the addition of the foreign language factor multiplies the variables of selection and expands the area of uncertainty. Translation of legal language in contrast to scientific information is not a mechanical matching of words. With the aid of computers, over a million words a month are being translated into English from Russian technical works. In contrast to words which embody physical descriptions, most legal concepts leave room for value judgments. As stated by Professor Philippe Kahn, in fairly extravagant terms, "In translating from the foreign language into that of the court, there is a transfer of concepts, expressing the intellectual life of two peoples, the assimilation of a civilization."

In litigation, a point to be noted results from differences in court procedure. In U.S. courts and arbitration tribunals, generally speaking, the emphasis is on presenting the facts to the judge or jury through the oral testimony of the parties or witnesses in open court. Foreign language documents or laws are normally presented through the oral testimony of experts retained by the parties. In noncriminal cases abroad, parties are generally barred from testifying and translations are most often admitted only when made by "official translators," with knowledge of English as well as their own language tested by the simplest of public examinations.

Use Court's Language

The vital point to bear in mind is that the process of translation to be properly controlled must be effected during the period of drafting of the instrument. From the point of view of potential litigation, legal instruments should be written in the language of the decisional body which will settle the disputes arising in connection with the instrument. The legal language of that body will govern, regardless of the law chosen by the parties or the language actually used in the instrument.

The German Supreme Court has held that a translator is not the agent of the party who employed him at the time of preparation of the original contract but merely a conduit. If he commits an error so that the contract as signed does not correspond to the real intention of the party who signed it, the latter can rescind the contract. The Supreme Court of France has held that a French judge can disregard the translation of a court-appointed expert translator. The instrument involved was a licensing agreement in the English language, calling for royalties calculated on the basis of a percentage of "gross income." This was translated by the expert as "revenus bruts" and by the lower court as "revenus de toute nature" and "montant brut du chiffre d'affaires." The French Supreme Court held that the lower court's own translation, even if erroneous, could not be reviewed. "The translation of a contract written in a foreign language involves an exercise of the lower court's sovereign power to interpret written instruments."

Bilingual or multilingual instruments in various counterparts normally contain a choice of language clause, indicating which text is to prevail in case of divergence. Such a clause is truly effective only if the controlling language chosen is that of the decisional body. In the French case just mentioned, only a French language contract would have been binding on the court as evidence of the intention of the parties as to the meaning to be given to the term "gross income." This conclusion is not limited to foreign courts. When the 1819 Treaty with Spain was first applied by the Supreme Court of the United States in litigation involving the status of private land grants after acquisition of Florida by the United States, the Court faced the problem of translating the Spanish "las concesiones quedarán ratificadas y reconocidas." The authentic English text of the Treaty read: "The grants shall be ratified and confirmed." As so read, the Treaty would have left in doubt the ownership of substantial tracts of land. Disregarding the authentic English version, the Supreme Court applied its own translation to find the meaning to be "the grants shall remain ratified and confirmed."

The Translator

Arguably, a critically important translation of a foreign legal text should not be the work of a single person. Julian Green, the American author who wrote in French, has been quoted as saying "I am more and more inclined to believe that it is almost an impossibility to be absolutely bilingual." A leading research manual insists that "one can translate faithfully only from a language one knows like a native into a language one knows like a practiced writer." In truly critical and decisive issues of translation and interpretation, the process should be bilateral, from one language by the lawyer familiar with that language and that country's law into the language of the law of the decisional body by a lawyer trained in that legal system.

Finally, it should be observed that just as no contract can be drawn to foresee every contingency, so no translation can eliminate all future disputes as to meaning. Particularly in international business relations, where most disagreements tend to be channelled into the language area to avoid implications of improper motives for non-performance, the translation should be carefully analyzed. There is no simple solution to the language barrier. The need is to examine both sides to determine when a language other than English should be the language of the parties and to be aware of the means of controlling language transference.

MODERN PIRACY: CHINESE "BRIGANDS" STEAL BRAND NAMES IN HONG KONG*

DON BENSON

When Milton Caniff created "Terry and the Pirates" a generation ago, the slanty-eyed villains of his comic strip were experts in murder, extortion and kidnaping—pirates, in short, of the old school.

Today, those traditional Chinese pirates are fast disappearing from the high seas, but as far as international marketers are concerned, they have been replaced by more evil brigands. These new Chinese pirates—most of them landbased and headquartered here in Hong Kong—filch brand names, trademarks and copyrights.

When a consumer walks into an Asian dispensary, for instance, to buy a tube of toothpaste, his brand preference may well have been influenced by the hundreds of thousands of dollars which Colgate-Palmolive invests in Asia to build consumer recognition for its distinctive red-and-white toothpaste box and tube. Most stores stock the familiar Colgate box in quantity.

* Reprinted with permission from the October 22, 1962, issue of *Advertising Age*. Copyright 1962 by Advertising Publications Inc.

Pirate and Victim—*Imitating package and label, brand pirate in Far East sells at lower price than Vicks VapoRub. In several Asian markets, Vicks has resorted to package in gold foil, which is generally prohibitively expensive to imitate.*

But on the shelves alongside are dozens of imitation Colgates—all identical in size, shape and coloring—bearing spurious names such as "Goldcat," "Goldbee," "Coalgate," "Goldent," "Goalgate," "Goldkey" and "Goldgate"—all in the same type face used by the real Colgate. Even alert, English-speaking Westerners are occasionally fooled, and an Asian consumer who buys solely by the color and the general shape of the letters on the box hasn't a chance.

Very often, the retailer himself doesn't know he's been taken. Few read or speak English and when the pirate brand is foisted on him, he thinks he's getting genuine Colgate at a low, bargain price.

Dozens of small manufacturing operations in Hong Kong make a livelihood out of producing phony brand-name products. They manufacture counterfeit Arrow shirts, bogus Terylene fabrics, sham Zenith batteries, synthetic Brylcream, imitation Parker pens, fake Ronson lighters, false Vick's VapoRub and a spurious Quink Ink. They sell Pang's (Pond's) cold cream, Yalf (Yale) locks, Del Mundo (Del Monte) catsup and Sehning (Schering) drugs.

Very often international advertisers are unaware that their brand is being counterfeited until they get complaints from tourists and other indignant purchasers as far afield as Africa and South America who have found the imitation product unsatisfactory.

By the time advertiser can bring legal action against the counterfeiter, he often finds that large shipments of the phony brand have been exported to dozens of his overseas markets in every corner of the world. He's surrounded by a rising chorus of complaints. Even if he closes up the offender's assembly line, the counterfeiter merely pays his minor fine to the Hong Kong government, selects another brand to imitate, moves to a new plant and gets to work.

A chief watchdog representing international manufacturers (who want their brand names protected) in this area of the world is Francis W. Kendall, head of Fidelity Inspection Service, one of the few companies of its kind anywhere.

An old China hand, Mr. Kendall has been in Asia for more than 30 years and was an airline executive up until nine years ago when Sanfor-

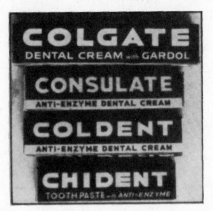

Copycats—*In the Far East, even English-speaking Westerners have been fooled by counterfeit toothpastes passed off as Colgate with similar names and red-and-white packages.*

ized came to him for help in finding out who was producing phony labels sewn into non-shrinkproof shirts. Mr. Kendall had the police conduct a series of raids and in a short order racked up 27 convictions. Fidelity Inspection Service was born shortly thereafter and now grosses about $20,000 annually, representing among several hundred clients, Eveready Batteries, Ray-O-Vac, Terylene and the Swiss watch manufacturers.

"We operate on a monthly retainer basis, making regular market surveys on behalf of our regular clients," Mr. Kendall said, "and then take on special assignments for other manufacturers. We usually press the offender for an agreement to cease and desist, or aid the advertiser in pressing criminal charges, if the violation is flagrant. Bangkok is fast catching up to Hong Kong as a home of phony brand names, and Taiwan —which does not recognize international copyright—has long been an offender."

Taiwan figured recently in a complex case involving pirated versions of the *Encyclopaedia Britannica*. Complete imitations of the encyclopedia—except for the section on China which is dropped to avoid offending Chiang Kai-shek—were being shipped from Taiwan at $60 a set, well under the price which this Chicago publisher charges for the genuine product.

Britannica sent emissaries to Taipei who were promised that the shipments would stop, but sets continued to be exported. Finally Britannica got other book publishers on its side and lobbied so effectively in Washington that it was rumored Chiang was told that U.S. ICA funds would be choked off unless the bogus encyclopedias stopped flooding the world market.

Today, Chinese presses still turn out the $60 Britannicas. But you allegedly can't get a set unless you pick it up in Taiwan. Never underestimate the cleverness of the Chinese pirates, though; sets leak out somehow.

Printing piracy is old stuff for Asia. The Taiwanese regularly turn out a Chinese translation of *Reader's Digest,* and a bogus Japanese edition

Cutex and Imitator—*Asian brand cheat (left) imitates Cutex polish remover (right). When brand comes in distinctive jar, brand pirates pay urchins to search garbage dumps for empties.*

as well, although they have no permission from *Digest* headquarters in Pleasantville, N.Y.

Recently the trade in bogus books from Hong Kong, at 50% to 80% below U.S. costs, became so hot that U.S. Customs now holds up all shipments from the Crown Colony for a copyright check.

"Interestingly enough," Mr. Kendall said, "the Chinese Communists are quite fair about brand names. They flooded the market with bogus Parker pens a few years ago but when we told their Hong Kong lawyers of the violations, they apologized quickly and stopped the manufacture."

Brand piracy becomes more than a matter of politics or dollars-and-cents when antibiotics are involved. Often spurious drugs get on the Asia market. Most are authentic chemically, but the pirates frequently dilute the dosage to make the supply fill more capsules and provide a larger margin of profit. The unknowing patient gets less than the prescribed dosage, and his recovery may be affected accordingly. Pfizer and Parke-Davis have both experienced piracy in Asia.

Advising international advertisers on how to avoid piracy, Mr. Kendall said: "Advertisers should register all their patents, trademarks and brand names in every one of their international markets. It costs a small fee to do so, of course, but it gives the advertiser a legal base on which to move against pirates. Advertisers should also register the complete designs of their marketing containers including the colors used. This prevents the 'Goldcats' and 'Goldbees' from infringing on the genuine item by merely changing a couple of letters.

"I don't think we'll ever completely lick the problem of brand name infringements in Asia," he continued. "When you have 2,000,000 hungry refugees in a town like Hong Kong, for instance, all eager to work and highly skilled, it's only natural that some of them turn to putting out imitations of products they know will sell.

"Some times the intent is highly flattering and completely innocent, rather than criminal. After all, how much does an ex-business man, a refugee from deep in the interior of China, know about brand names and international copyright anyway?"

QUESTIONS

1. Differentiate between common law and code law. Show how the differences may affect marketing activities.

2. How does the international marketer determine what legal system will have jurisdiction when legal disputes arise?

3. Discuss the state of international commercial law.

4. Discuss the limitations of jurisdictional clauses in contracts.

5. What is the "objective theory of jurisdiction"? How does it apply to a firm doing business within a foreign country?

6. Discuss some of the reasons why it is probably best to seek an out-of-court settlement in international commercial legal disputes rather than to sue.

7. Illustrate the procedure generally followed in international commercial disputes when settled under the auspices of a formal arbitration tribunal.

8. What are industrial property rights? Why should a company in international marketing take special steps to protect them?

9. In many code law countries ownership of industrial property rights is established by registration rather than prior use. Comment.

10. Discuss the advantages to the international marketer arising from the existence of the various international conventions on trademarks, patents, and copyrights.

11. "The legal environment of the foreign marketer takes on an added dimension of importance since there is no single uniform international commercial law which governs foreign business transactions." Comment.

Readings

1. Brand name infringements are especially prevalent in Asia. Give some examples and suggest ways in which infringements can be stopped.

2. Discuss how the "self-reference criterion" may apply in the translation of legal documents.

CASES—PART II

CASE II-1

PROBLEMS IN OPENING A RETAIL STORE IN SPAIN*

With all its know-how, Sears Roebuck and Company, a major retailer in the United States and with over 20 years of successful marketing in Latin America, finds their vast experience didn't prevent some major pitfalls in opening a new store in Barcelona, Spain.

"Sears tiene do todo" (Sears has everything) says the bouncy jingle that saturates local airwaves. All over Barcelona, 108 billboards blare the news that Sears soon will be the city's favorite store. Not long ago Sears paid the bill for a big party to which it invited 200 important Spaniards. And 20,000 members of the country club set recently found Sears credit cards that they hadn't applied for in their mailboxes.

"Sears Who? Sears What?"

Sears' executives learned a hard lesson in humility when they showed up in Spain four years ago to organize their Spanish subsidiary, Sears, Roebuck de Espana S.A. Hardly anybody had ever heard of Sears.

"We'd go in to see a manufacturer," recalls Robert Herzfelder, general merchandise manager of Sears de Espana, "and he'd say, 'Sears who? Sears what?' " Spanish manufacturers that Sears wanted to place orders with would smile tolerantly on learning that a store was still in the planning stage and tell executives to come back if it ever got beyond that.

It's way too early, of course, to tell how Sears' $13.2 million investment in its Spanish subsidiary will fare. But Sears figures it has the success formula down pat, and it believes it has mastered its problems abroad better than many American firms could hope to.

For one thing, Sears' planners picked their market carefully. A retail

---
* Facts and detail from *Wall Street Journal*, March 27, 1967, pp. 1–10. Used with permission of the *Wall Street Journal*.

275

power in Latin America since 1942 (it now operates 98 stores there), Sears has accumulated considerable know-how in Hispanic affairs. Rather than tackling Europe by rushing into one of its developed and hotly competitive economies, Sears chose the poor sister that only in the past few years has begun to thrive. Sears hopes to identify itself and its goods with the increasingly affluent Spanish middle class, just as it has in Latin America.

Made Mainly in Spain

Sears found out years ago in Latin America that it couldn't expect to stock its foreign stores mainly with goods made in the United States. Latin Americans drove the point home when they closed their borders to imports and forced Sears men to help establish local producers.

Here is Spain, Sears' executives say that perhaps their most acute problem has been finding adequate suppliers of goods. Not that there aren't plenty of Spanish producers; it is their very proliferation and individuality that has made it hard for Sears to manage. An industrial guide to Spain lists 11,000 makers of furniture, for example.

Gerard Meyer, a Sears' supervisor, turned up 3,000 sweater makers; Iqualda, a town of 60,000 persons 40 miles north of Barcelona, has 400 all by itself. Many switch their production into other items with disconcerting frequency. "An industrial guide may show one company making shirts," Mr. Meyer says, "a personal visit may reveal it is making trousers, and next year it will be making jackets."

Sears values the opening stock in its Barcelona store at $5 million, $4 million of which represents products of Spain. About 80% of the 55,000 items on hand were manufactured by 1,500 Spanish suppliers selected from 7,000 that Sears dealt with at one time or another. The biggest Spanish supplier accounts for only $300,000 in goods—television sets.

Felipe Palou and his wife, both about 75 years old, are typical Sears suppliers here. They make ceramic horses with whistles in the bases (Sears doesn't know the reason for the whistles, but executives say the horses have been popular tourist purchases). The Palou's factory is their kitchen oven.

When the Palous finished making up their first Sears order recently, "We got a letter that said the horses were ready and a friend of a friend would bring them in," says Jose Blanch, a buying supervisor. Sears paid for the $16 order in cash; the Palous never had seen a check.

Labeling-to-order is almost unknown in Spain, and producers have a fierce pride in their brand names. Mr. Meyer never could induce one shirt supplier to change his label to Sears. "It carried his own name," Mr. Meyers says, "and you'd think we were trying to steal his baby." Sears refused to budge, and the shirt maker refused to do business.

After two years of argument, Sears' buyers thought they had finally got another supplier, a maker of babies' goods, to ship in plastic bags labeled "Sears." But the merchandise arrived in bags marked with the maker's usual label. "He said he just forgot," says a Sears' buyer.

Sizing Up

Equally vexing was the problem of getting manufacturers to standardize sizes in women's clothing (men's sizes usually are comparable from item to item in Spain). Women's sweaters of approximately the same size may be marked 35, 36, 37, 1, 2, 3, A, B, or C. "If a woman likes my brand," one sweater maker told Sears, "she knows what size she is." Sears found that dresses marked size 10 varied by as much as 1½ inches around the hips.

About 60% of women's clothing in stock consists of suits, compared with a typical proportion of 20% in an American store. "The Spanish woman is more conservative than either the United States or South American women, in her colors, in her make-up, in her dress," says Rudy Greer, president of Sears de Espana.

Spanish customs are changing, though, and in many ways Sears is helping to change them. Gonzalo Sanchis, a 32-year-old former automobile mechanic, says: "Before, I was artisan. (Before Sears, that is.) Now, I am industrial."

Mr. Sanchis runs a small boat-trailer factory outside Barcelona. Sears' order of 30 trailers encouraged him to display a few at a boat show, which brought in orders for 70 more. Mr. Sanchis used to buy supplies and parts only as needed, like other small Spanish producers. But now he says, "Everywhere I have material stocked for the future."

Shirt Shakeout?

A shirt company president says that Sears' presence will force Spanish stores to stock shirts with measured sleeves. Now, men's shirts are made only to neck sizes with sleeves of "average" length. Standardization is expected to hasten a decline in men's shirt brands (now numbering about 600) because retailers won't have the space to stock every size of all brands.

But easily the most revolutionary innovation Sears is bringing is retail credit, considered almost sinful by some conservative Spaniards. Big-ticket appliances commonly are sold on installment terms, but ordinary charge accounts are seldom employed. "Credit is still looked on as a shameful act," says Mr. Greer. "It shows inability to pay. We're trying to change a sociological concept."

Sears calls its Spanish credit department the "department of personal accounts." Ads stress the convenience of credit cards, not the slower-pay aspects, and don't even use the word "credit."

Some Spanish bankers wonder how the credit system will mesh with the Spaniards' sense of "el picaresco"—light-hearted, mischief-making —and suspect it may become popular for the wrong reasons. "But the credit system has worked in Latin America," Mr. Greer says. "I don't think Spaniards will react more negatively than Peruvians or Mexicans."

While Sears' buyers were working to develop their sources of Spanish merchandise, construction workers were putting up the Barcelona store. It is stunning to many townsfolk. It has no windows, a novelty in a place where inside electric lighting is minimal. Curious onlookers have been puzzled by the big glass display cases carried into the store. Spanish retailers generally show goods in plain wooden bins.

Questions

1. Identify the aspects of Spanish culture which created problems for Sears. Contrast each aspect of the Spanish culture with what occurs in the United States and discuss the differences and their effect upon Sears operations.

2. In what special ways did Sears try to overcome the problems they faced in Spain? What didn't they do that they should have done?

3. Identify any evidence of an "indigenous frame of reference" in Sears' activities in Spain.

4. Explain why Sears' 25 years of experience in Latin America didn't help them avoid the pitfalls they encountered in Spain. Can you see any instances where their Latin American experience might have actually led to difficulty, e.g., one Spanish-speaking country is like all others?

5. Identify problems which Sears must overcome that may lead to a higher cost of operation than found in the United States.

6. Outline the fundamental basis for operations of a U.S. Sears store (e.g., family brands, standardization of products) and discuss whether or not these practices can be made operational in Spain. What specific market-action must be taken to make these practices operational? If so, at what cost? If not, what probable effect will this have on their success?

CASE II–2

POLITICAL CONFLICT IN THAILAND*
Cigars or Cigarets?

In December, 1968, the Thailand government gave U.S. Tobacco (Asia) Ltd., 30 days to close its company's cigar making operations which the Thai government claimed were in conflict with the government's monopoly on all cigaret manufacturing. U.S. Tobacco insisted that they had been making "little cigars" rather than cigarets since their production began in May, 1967, when they were granted licenses and permits to produce "little cigars" similar to those made in the United States. "Little cigars" are the same length and thickness as cigarets, but the similarity ends there, as they contain the same tobacco used in regular cigars and are wrapped in dark brown paper or tobacco leaf. Cigar tobaccos are more alkaline than those used in cigarets and thus are much stronger than in cigarets.

The government informed U.S. Tobacco that they could continue in Thailand only if they switched their entire production to "regular size" cigars because a law had been passed redefining "little cigars" as ciga-

---

* Based in part on an article, "Thailand Tells Lorillard to Turn Out Cigars There, Not Cigarettes," in the December 13, 1968, issue of the *Wall Street Journal*, p. 22. Used with permission of the *Wall Street Journal*.

rets, thereby putting U.S. Tobacco in direct competition with the Thai government. This all happened after the May, 1967, licensing and after U.S. Tobacco's investment in plant and equipment. U.S. Tobacco was advised that the new law was most probably enforceable since they were in competition with a government monopoly and, if they didn't cease production of "little cigars" by the end of the year, they should be prepared to face the consequences.

What motivated the Thais to change the law? The complete answer lies with the Thai lawmakers but some contributing factors can be surmised. Certainly fear of competition between U.S. Tobacco's "little cigars" and the government's cigarets was part of the decision. Perhaps also a factor was the attempt to clear away any confusion about the definition of a regular cigar, "little cigar," and cigaret. In other countries recently, some companies have been rolling their cigarets in tobacco leaves and calling them "little cigars" as an obvious attempt to avoid advertising restrictions imposed against cigarets but not cigars. Additionally, due to these increased restrictions on cigaret advertising and due to the general health concern among the smoking population, some tobacco companies have begun to use the lighter, milder cigaret tobaccos in "little cigars" in an apparent attempt to attract cigaret smokers. Some industry sources believe that "little cigars" made with cigaret tobacco blends do compete with cigarets to some extent. Perhaps this is in part an explanation for the Thai government's move against U.S. Tobacco although all U.S. Tobacco's "little cigars" produced in Thailand to date were made with cigar tobacco and not with cigaret blends.

This course of government action is not in line with the expressed general attitude toward foreign investment. In fact, the following information on the economy, on government policy and on government objectives seems to show that such behavior is out of character.

The Government of Thailand

Thailand is a constitutional monarchy with a centralized government which controls all important agencies of power and policy.

His Majesty, King Bhumiphol Adulyadej, is the ninth reigning monarch of the House of Chakri. In constitutional terms, the King is the Head of State and Chief of the Armed Forces. However, he does not exercise the sovereign power directly, but through the three branches of government: the executive, the legislative and the judicial. His public actions must be countersigned by a responsible minister. In other words, public action is taken by officials who countersign the royal acts.

Thailand's form of government has been rather stable and has helped to foster a sound economy.

The Economy of Thailand

Thailand covers an area of about 514,000 square kilometers and has a population of about 33 millions. The density of population thus approximates

64 persons per square kilometer. But of the total land area only about 20% can at present be cultivated.

The gross national product in 1966 amounted to about 87 billion Baht, or 4.2 billion U. S. dollars (20.8 Baht = 1 U. S. dollar). The level of income per head, about 2,600 Baht or nearly 130 U. S. dollars per year, compares favorably with most other countries in South East Asia.

The economy of Thailand is based primarily on agriculture, including forestry and fisheries. Rice and rubber are the most important among major crops, followed by maize, jute and kenaf, in agricultural production. If the number of people employed in agriculturally-based industries such as rice-milling, sawmilling, jute-processing, oil extraction and marketing of farm products are taken into account, almost 90% of the total work force are dependent directly or indirectly on agriculture for their livelihood.

While tobacco is not considered a major agricultural product, it is of importance. Below are some pertinent data on tobacco crops and the manufacturing of tobacco products.

1. Number of cigaret rolling factories in 1965: 87.
2. Production of manufactured tobacco products (metric tons).

1961	1962	1963	1964	1965	1966
9,739	10,525	10,148	10,409	10,057	11,123

3. Production of tobacco leaf (metric tons).

1961	1962	1963	1964	1965	1966
48,000	47,000	63,000	63,000	62,000	n.a.

4. Export of tobacco leaf (metric tons).

1963	1964	1965	1966
3,782	6,147	6,046	7,702

5. Imports of tobacco leaf (metric tons).

1963	1964	1965	1966
3,673	4,957	5,619	8,833

Foreign trade plays an important role in the promotion of economic growth and stability in Thailand. The market growth of the Thai economy in the postwar years owes much to the increased exports of primary products such as rice, crude rubber, teak, tin and, more recently, maize, jute and kenaf, and cassava. Rice and rubber account for 35% and 15%, respectively, of the total value of exports. Agricultural products in total, including jute and kenaf, cassava, and teak, in addition to rice and rubber, constitute about 90% of the value of exports. Among nonagricultural products, tin is the only appreciable item of export.

More than 50% of the total imports are manufactured goods, half of which are machinery, equipment and other capital goods. Although some trade deficits have been experienced by Thailand, these have been more than offset by invisible receipts, foreign grants and loans. The national foreign exchange reserves are thereby steadily augmented, providing a strong base for the maintenance of external financial stability of the country.

Foreign trade also plays a significant part in Thailand's national development plans.

National Development Plans

Thailand's first National Economic Development Plan covered the six-year period, 1961–1966. It was principally designed to coordinate the development

expenditures of the public sector. The Government is now embarking on a second five-year plan, 1967–1971. The new plan is significantly more comprehensive than the first and calls for an accelerated rate of growth of national income. Its coverage has been expanded to include:
1. Emphasis on social development and the distribution of the benefits of economic growth.
2. Manpower development planning to relate the educational program to the requirements for trained manpower.
3. Explicit attention to the private sector and special studies of manufacturing industry, trade and services.
4. Regional planning to ensure the allocation of resources to accelerate development of the remote areas of the country.

Furthermore, the new plan is based on more thorough analysis of financial implications and of projections of the macro-structure of the economy as a whole.

The basic objective of the Second Plan is to raise the income and living standards of the people by making the fullest use of the resources of the country. Particular emphasis is placed on the achievement of more equitable income distribution and assistance to rural areas, the development of the private sector, the strengthening of national security, and maintaining financial stability in order to inspire domestic and international confidence.

The Department of Technical and Economic Cooperation describes the economic system of Thailand as "one of free enterprise." A department publication states:

The fact that planning has recently been adopted as an instrument for accelerating the rate of economic growth does not in the least make the economy less worthy of this description. While public investments are planned and programmed, private enterprises are left to operate freely. Little discrimination is made between domestic and foreign investors; both enjoy the same rights and privileges under the Industrial Investment Promotion Act.

Given political and economic stability, Thailand should be able to accumulate domestic capital and attract foreign investment for industrialization and diversification of its economy, and hence be able to fulfill its long-term national aspirations.

The U.S. Tobacco Company must certainly have a different opinion. As one officer remarked, "We believe the type of action taken against U.S. Tobacco Ltd., could cause great concern about future American investment in Thailand."

Questions

1. How can the apparent contradiction between what the government says it is doing, i.e., fostering an economy of "free enterprise," and what it has done to U.S. Tobacco be explained?
2. Should the Thai action "cause great concern about future American investment in Thailand"? For all types of industry? Why?
3. How can the Thai government legally do what it has done?
4. Why do you suppose they passed the law redefining "little cigars" as

cigarets so soon after awarding U.S. Tobacco a license to produce "little cigars"?

5. Would you rate U.S. Tobacco's investment in Thailand as having high political vulnerability or low vulnerability? If high vulnerability, what steps can they take to lower their vulnerability?
6. What legal or other recourse does U.S. Tobacco have?
7. How could the U.S. Tobacco Company have avoided the problem?
8. What action should U.S. Tobacco take now?

CASE II–3

IMPLEMENTING THE NATIONAL MARKET CONCEPT*

Note: The purpose of this informal memorandum is to suggest how, concretely, actions by CIAP might set in motion operations designed to reduce urban-rural market barriers. An action program addressed to this objective must embrace four elements:

1. Spreading the concept.
2. National and international research to provide a long-run basis for national integration programs.
3. Operations within nations (or between nations) which can be undertaken promptly in the public and private sectors, or by way of regional experiments.
4. External action and support for national integration programs.

What follows sets out an action program under these four headings.

1. Spreading the Concept

a) CIAP could call upon the Chairman to distribute widely an appropriately re-edited version of the Secretariat paper. The paper could go to governments and private groups with whom we have connection; and we could request these groups to make it available to a wider public.

b) Although the Alliance for Progress Committees in the various nations in the Hemisphere may play a more substantial role in executing the project (see below, paragraph 3), we could request them to organize one-day seminars designed to examine the concept, on the basis of the revised Secretariat paper, in the light of the problems of their own countries, as they see them.

2. Research

Although national market projects can be set in motion immediately (and, indeed, are going forward in some countries), it is evident that problems of distribution have been neglected in the postwar generation; and we shall need, with the passage of time, much more systematic

---

* Reprinted with permission of the Pan American Union, General Secretariat of the Organization of American States.

research. The Chairman could, for example, request the governments
to set in motion such research on a national basis; and we might request
ECLA to engage some of its research resources in examining systematically distribution problems in specific fields. From contacts with Mr.
Santa Cruz of CIDA, I gather he would be sympathetic to increased emphasis on marketing problems in the field of Latin American agriculture.

Specifically, what is required is systematic evidence on:

a) The gap between prices paid to producers and prices paid by consumers in such fields as meat, milk, fish, fruit and vegetables, and export commodities, with an exact analysis of the factors that determine
this margin;

b) A comparison of prices paid in urban and rural areas for manufactures of interest to lower income groups in such fields as: basic agricultural equipment, textiles, shoes, household utensils, durable consumers goods, with an analysis of factors determining this gap; and

c) The potentialities of regional development, within nations, designed to produce integrated agricultural-industrial complexes.

3. Immediate Courses of Action

The Chairman could:

a) Request the governments of the Hemisphere to include within
their current development plans and programs measures to improve
urban-rural interchange and to lower the market barrier; and

b) Request the Committee of Nine to take account of such programs
in evaluating national plans.

What is involved, of course, is the working out between the public
and private sectors of a set of specific collaborative actions in which the
government acts, for example, directly to enlarge warehouse facilities,
improve public slaughterhouse operations, build refrigeration units,
license more common carrier units, and provide credit for improved
marketing operations, while giving special priority, in credit operations,
to private firms willing to engage in the more economical distribution
of lower income manufactured goods, as well as to cooperatives and
super-markets prepared to organize the more economic marketing of
foodstuffs into the cities. Domestic development banks could play a
peculiarly important role in this context.

In addition, the governments might encourage the creation of joint
government-private planning units to explore in specific regions the
potentialities of integrated agricultural-industrial development. There is
little doubt that a movement of industry away from the great Latin
American cities will be central to development strategy in the next decade. Such developments ought to be planned on an integrated agricultural-industrial basis.

From knowledge already available to us, we know that certain types
of operations in this field can be (and are) profitable in Latin America;
for example, chicken production and marketing in Mexico and Colombia; certain modern milk production and distribution operations; the
soft drink and Singer Sewing machine operations in the villages; the

emergence of super-markets and discount houses and cooperatives in certain Latin American cities, etc. There is no reason why governments and private groups cannot accelerate this trend even before research is completed on a national and regional basis.

What is needed to begin are two things: acceptance of the reality and critical importance of the problems; and initiatives, if possible collaborative initiatives, on the side of both the public and the private sector.

It is obvious that a large part of actual national market operations should be conducted by the private sector. In fact, the concept is a direct challenge to the private sectors in Latin American nations to perform that function which, in the end, is the ultimate justification for private enterprise; namely, efficient production and distribution of modern manufactured goods and agricultural produce to the mass of the population. Thus far, the sophisticated private sector in Latin America has had a creative impact on only a small proportion of the population. The implementation of the national market concept is, in fact, a central task we should assign the private sector within the Alliance for Progress.

It is, therefore, natural for us to consider how the national Alliance for Progress Committees, which embrace the private sector, can work to implement the concept. These Committees evidently differ in the quality of their composition and in their capacity to take responsibility for organizing the private sector role in the national market enterprise. Leaving a certain flexibility, we should, nevertheless, suggest that the heads of these Committees consider whether they contain the private sector leaders capable of working with the governments and initiating a private sector program; or whether they could set up, from either existing or expanded membership, special subcommittees charged with the task. Where it is possible, there would be great advantage in using the Alliance for Progress Committees in this way, since it would give to them a major function beyond their present information assignments; and it would help dramatize the Alliance for Progress effort to provide to the peoples of Latin America, via private enterprise, better and cheaper food and better and cheaper manufactured goods.

4. International Action and Support

Aside from requesting the Committee of Nine to put emphasis on improved measures to integrate national markets within national development plans, CIAP could empower the Chairman:

a) To work with the Inter-American Bank, IBRD, and the United States AID authorities in providing advisory services, technical assistance, and capital to carry forward specific national market projects; and

b) To urge foreign enterprise engaged in Latin America to play a role of cooperation, if not leadership, in assisting with national market projects in the countries where they are engaged. There is no aspect of foreign private enterprise where full collaboration with local public and private authorities is more required than in the marketing field; but it is also true that there is no activity where technical know-how developed in the United States, Western Europe, and Japan is more needed in

Latin America, for the time being, than in the skills of modern marketing.

CASE II–4

WHEN INTERNATIONAL BUYERS AND SELLERS DISAGREE*

No matter what line of business you're in, you can't escape sex. That may have been one conclusion drawn by an American exporter of meat products after a dispute with a West German customer over a shipment of pork livers. Here's how the disagreement came about:

The American exporter was contracted to ship "30,000 lbs. of freshly frozen U.S. pork livers, customary merchantable quality, first rate brands." As the shipment that was prepared met the exacting standards of the American market, the exporter expected the transaction to be completed without any problem.

But when the livers arrived in West Germany, the purchaser raised an objection: "We ordered pork livers of customary merchantable quality—what you sent us consisted of 40% sow livers."

"Who cares about the sex of the pig the liver came from?" the exporter asked.

"We do," the German replied. "Here in Germany we don't pass off spongy sow livers as the firmer livers of male pigs. This shipment wasn't merchantable at the price we expected to charge. The only way we were able to dispose of the meat without a total loss was to reduce the price. You owe us a price allowance of $1,000."

The American refused to reduce his price. His determined resistance may have been partly in reaction to the implied insult to the taste of the American consumer. "If pork livers, whatever the sex of the animal, are palatable to Americans, they ought to be good enough for anyone," he thought.

It looked as if the buyer and seller could never agree on eating habits.

---

* Copyright © 1968 by Dun & Bradstreet Publications Corp. Reprinted by special permission from the November 1968 issue of *Business Abroad*.

PART
III
World Market Patterns

OUTLINE OF CHAPTER 9

INTRODUCTION

HISTORY OF MULTINATIONAL ECONOMIC ORGANIZATIONS
  Predecessors of the European Common Market
  European Cooperation after World War II

LA RAISON D'ETRE
  Economic Factors
  Political Factors
  Geographic Proximity
  Social Factors

PATTERNS OF MULTINATIONAL COOPERATION
  Regional Cooperation Groups
  Free-Trade Area
  Full Customs Union
  Common Market
  Political Union
    The Commonwealth of Nations
    Enforced Political Union

MULTINATIONAL MARKETS TODAY
  Europe
  Middle East
  Africa
  Asia
  The Americas

STRATEGIC IMPLICATIONS FOR MARKETING
  Opportunities
  Problems
  Requirements

SUMMARY AND CONCLUSIONS

READINGS
  Europe: "Then Will It Live . . . ," *Time.*
  World Benefits from EFTA, *EFTA Reporter.*

CHAPTER 9

MULTINATIONAL MARKET GROUP

INTRODUCTION

Economic cooperation has become an international byword since the conclusion of World War II. Encouraged in part by the success of the European Common Market, numerous other countries have banded together into various kinds of multinational economic groups in the hope that such organizational forms will help them to perform economic miracles.

Essentially, a multinational market is created when a number of individual countries agree to take positive steps to reduce trade and tariff barriers among the participating countries. Organizational form varies widely among different market groups, but the universal orientation of such multinational cooperation is economic benefit for the participants. Sometimes political and social benefits accrue, but the dominant initial motive for affiliation remains economic.

Economic integration through customs unions relates directly to the marketing function of business. Such cooperation comes about to facilitate the marketing of one country's goods in another country and, conversely, to facilitate the acquisition of lower priced goods produced elsewhere. Development of multinational markets is partly a function of the stage of economic development of the participating countries; as nations expand their productive capacities, they also need to expand the boundaries of their markets. Without mass marketing facilities and mass markets, the modern mass production capacity (or the surplus productive capacity of relatively inefficient nations) cannot be successfully employed.

The inner six and the outer seven (the European Common Market and the European Free Trade Association) are the foremost and best publicized examples of economic cooperation. A number of others do exist; some of them are Central American Common Market, British Commonwealth of Nations, Council for Mutual Economic Assistance, Afro-Asian Organization for Economic Cooperation, and the Latin American Free Trade Association.

Multinational market groups form large markets which provide potentially significant opportunities for the international businessmen. The combined population size of the European Common Market, for example, is similar to that of the United States. Although it may not be feasible to attempt marketing into each of a number of separate nations, economic union of those same nations may offer a logical market because of the increased size of the markets within a tariff boundary. The student should be alert to the marketing implications of multinational market developments reviewed in this chapter; the present and future impact of such market groupings in world business is greater than ever anticipated in the early days of the markets in question.

The history of economic unions and the characteristics contributing to their success or failure will be discussed in this chapter. Primary attention will be focused on the European Common Market (ECM), not only because of its successes, but also because it represents the most highly developed type of multinational market group in existence.

The reader should not interpret limited coverage given to other markets as indicative of their lack of importance or of the author's lack of interest in these markets. To cover even one market adequately would require a full book (at least 15 have been written solely on the Common Market), so in the single chapter available for this entire subject, it seems preferable to concentrate on one market. Organizational alternatives will be considered, as will the marketing implications of economic unity.

HISTORY OF MULTINATIONAL ECONOMIC ORGANIZATIONS

Recent success and publicity about the European Common Market make many people believe that economic union is a new concept. Contemporary economic unions have deep roots and are at least partly based on other already existing political and economic unions. Although both political and economic cooperation are required, economic motivations have been stronger than political motivations in the formation of many countries. History reveals that it has not been unusual for a king to arrange the marriage of his daughter or son in such a way that his kingdom and economic power would be extended. The United States of America and, more recently, the Union of Soviet Socialist Republics are both aggregations of individual sovereign states which have joined forces not only for political reasons but for economic benefit as well. Imagine the difficulties if each state in the United States had the power to levy tariffs at its borders; among other detriments, confusion, increased prices, and retarded trade would follow.

Predecessors of the European Common Market

In sharp contrast to Britain, which was politically and economically unified as early as 1603, European efforts at meaningful unions defied all serious attempts for many years. There were hopes for a unified or at least partially unified Europe after the War of 1812, but the Peace Congress of Vienna failed at consolidation. Germany, for example, consisted of some 39 confederated states with hundreds of customs frontiers retarding economic progress. Prussia finally took the lead toward German unification in the 1830s and formed a Zollverein in which some 18 states accepted the Prussian rates of duty and custom procedures. The authority of the Zollverein was not limited to tariffs, however, but included the monetary system, weights and measures, internal taxes, and other economic measures. After some three decades of operation, Bismarck's reign replaced the Zollverein, but the economic benefits of the union were highly evident. In his excellent analysis of the Common Market in German history, E. Strauss writes that "the 30 odd years of the Zollverein were a time of quick economic growth for Germany, which was transformed from a technically backward and mainly agricultural society into one of the leading industrial states on the continent."[1] Despite its successes, the Zollverein was a weak instrument, and political unification was required if the new Germany was to benefit from its partial economic unification. Germany's subsequent economic and political success caused economic scholars of the time to advocate and seek economic union. An influential advocate of the common market concept was Friedrich Naumann who, in his 1919 book *Mitteleuropa,* advocated immediate economic union between Germany and Austria-Hungary. He saw the Mitteleuropa as a nucleus of the European market, including virtually all continental Europe west of Russia. Unlike the military establishment, he did not visualize military conquests but saw instead leadership for Germany. Germany's defeat in World War I did not end thoughts of the unified Europe under German leadership. In 1931 Austria and Germany announced that they had formed a new customs union, but the international court of justice struck it down as being contrary to the peace treaty. Perhaps the sustained German dream of economic unification of Europe is nearing reality in the European Common Market. In any case, it is evident from this history of past attempts at union that the development of the EEC is a result of trial and error and gradual political and economic development.[2]

European Cooperation after World War II

It is perhaps an odd twist of history that the United States has played such a dominant role in assisting Europe to the most successful economic cooperation it has ever known. Before World War II had ended, the United States took the initiative in the Bretton-Woods conference, at which 50 nations met to seek ways to establish lower trade barriers, long-term development loans, and liquid short-term funds, all of which would permit world trade to grow. From this conference came General Agreement on Tariffs and Trade (GATT), International Monetary Fund (IMF), and the International Bank for Reconstruction and Development (IBRD) to perform those functions. After the war, America's

---

[1] E. Strauss, *Common Sense about the Common Market* (London: George Allen and Unwin, Ltd., 1958), p. 27.

[2] See A. E. Walsh & John Paxton, *The Structure and Development of the Common Market* (New York: Taplinger Publishing Co., Inc., 1969).

With permission of *The Denver Post* and Conrad.

". . . COMMON MARKET, HELL! . . .
THAT'S A SUPERMARKET . . ."

Marshall Plan led to the development of the Organization for European Economic Cooperation (OEEC) in 1948. Through the OEEC, the United States channeled 12½ billion dollars to give tangible demonstration to the benefits of economic cooperation. In the decade of the OEEC's existence, the European Payments Union was also formed to facilitate international credit within the European countries. The European Coal and Steel Community, formed in April 1951, is perhaps the most direct forerunner of the European Common Market. It has provided, at least in part, the pattern for the further development of the European Common Market. All groups mentioned above led eventually to the formation of the European Common Market and the European Free Trade Association. The OEEC was replaced in 1961 by the Organization for Economic Cooperation and Development (OECD) as the vehicle of North American participation in European economic affairs.[3] The OECD is essentially a vehicle for communication and cooperative action.

LA RAISON D'ÊTRE

Successful economic union requires that a number of factors be favorable to such economic cooperation. The various economic, political, social, and geographic factors provide the basis for success or failure in cooperative efforts. Major defects in any one factor can destroy the union

---

[3] The scope of the OECD has been expanded to include some non-European nations such as Japan.

BOX 9-1

France's Complex Game over Britain and EEC

France is doing its best to create the impression that it is hammering out a deal with its five Common Market partners to get talks started with Britain on the long-delayed question of British membership in the community.

The French moves may be only window-dressing. France doesn't want to be stuck again with the onus of blocking British entry. The whole question of British membership was frozen by Charles de Gaulle's veto in January, 1963.

On the surface, the basic issue appears to be whether Germany, Italy, Holland, Belgium, and Luxembourg can agree by the end of the year on a farm price support program satisfactory to France. If they can, France says it is willing to lift its veto on discussing British membership.

The farm issue is not a specious one. France's farmers are heavily subsidized by the Common Market agricultural fund. In turn, they grow so much grain that France has a sizable surplus for export. Germany, in particular, resents having to subsidize French farm exports.

French sources say the farm issue is close to solution—that Bonn is now willing to accept a farm subsidy formula linked to a promise that the Common Market will reexamine its farm production goals.

But France has left itself a convenient "out." Even if it agrees to lift its veto on discussing British entry, it wants no date for opening of the membership talks announced at The Hague meeting.

That leaves France a clear chance to press its demand that a detailed agenda be drawn up in advance of negotiations with Britain. This would set forth all the questions to be dealt with in the negotiations—farm prices and subsidies, non-tariff barriers, and so on.

Source: Reprinted from the November 15, 1969, issue of *Business Week*, p. 46, by special permission. Copyright © 1969 by McGraw-Hill, Inc.

unless the others provide sufficient strength to overcome the weaknesses. In general, the advantages of economic union must be rather clear-cut and significant, and the benefits must greatly outweigh the disadvantages before nations will forgo their sovereignty. Often a strong threat to the economic or political security of a nation is needed to provide the impetus for cooperation.

Economic Factors

Regardless of their other characteristics, nearly every type of economic union shares the development and enlargement of market opportunities as a basic orientation. Usually, markets are enlarged through preferential tariff treatment for participating members or common tariff barriers against outsiders. Enlarged, protected markets stimulate internal economic development by providing assured outlets and preferential treatment for goods produced within the customs union. Consumers are likely to benefit from the lower internal tariff barriers which exist among the participating countries. In many cases, as in the European Common Market, external as well as internal barriers are reduced because of the greater economic security afforded for domestic producers by the enlarged market.

Nations with complementary economic bases are least likely to encounter frictions in the development and operation of a common market unit. The European Common Market includes countries which have diverse agricultural bases, different kinds of industry, and different natural resources. It is significant that most of the problems which the European Common Market has encountered are concerned with products in which several countries have significant productive capability and for which the national producers desire protection. Similar productive capabilities are likely to be one of the major stumbling blocks in the success of such nearly homogeneous markets as the Central American Common Market (CACM) countries. One advantage which these Latin countries do have, however, is that the economic base is not highly developed. A major orientation of CACM so far has been to encourage the different member countries to follow different industrial lines. Protecting markets from exploitation by foreign companies was a major factor in the development of the CACM and has become an increasingly important element in common market developments.

Political Factors

Political amenability among countries is a basic requisite for the development of a supranational market arrangement. Participating countries must have comparable aspirations and general compatibility if they are to give up any part of their national sovereignty. State sovereignty is likely to be one of the most cherished possessions of any nation and will be given up only if there is promise of significant improvement of the national position through cooperation. The exclusion of Britain from the European Common Market probably best typifies the political problems of forming a union. Early in 1963 it appeared that the only barrier to Britain's entry in the Common Market might be the unwillingness of that country to enter. This reservation proved to be illusory, however, and Britain enthusiastically sought membership, only to have it vetoed by France's President De Gaulle. The cause was truly political, and even French economists agreed that Britain's entry was logical and beneficial for the market as a whole. The leadership in this instance was not amenable, and, according to political analysts, President De Gaulle was apparently primarily concerned that Britain's entry might lessen the power, prestige, and effectiveness of France in the Common Market. At this writing, Britain is again evidencing strong interest in joining the EEC, and it is not too impractical to predict the possible future merger of the EEC and the EFTA. Such a goal, in fact, already is actively discussed and sought by many EFTA leaders.

Economic considerations provide the basic catalyst facilitating the formation of a customs union group, but political elements may also be important. The uniting of the European Common Market countries was partially a response to the outside threat of Russia's great political and economic power; the countries of Western Europe were willing to settle their family squabbles to present a unified front to the Russian bear. The united front is also quite evident from time to time in negotiations between the EEC and USA. The United States had its finger in the political pie, too, for it was concerned about developing an economic and political union which would provide a lasting countervailing power in Europe. A basic premise of the European Common Market is that it will gradually develop into a political as well as economic union. As one historian comments, a customs union can seldom be regarded as a permanent arrangement. Its members must sooner or later decide if they are to go forward or backward.[4]

Geographic Proximity

Although it is not absolutely imperative that cooperating members of the customs union has geographical proximity, such closeness may facilitate the functioning of the common market. Transportation systems, basic to any marketing system, are likely to be interrelated and well developed when countries are close together. Countries which are widely separated geographically have a major barrier to overcome in attempting economic fusion.

Social Factors

Cultural similarity can ease the shock of economic cooperation with other countries. The more similar the cultures, the more likely a market is to succeed because members will be able to comprehend the outlook and viewpoints of their colleagues. Although there is great cultural diversity in the European Common Market, the member countries do share a long-established Christian heritage. Another element of homogeneity is that they are all aware of being "European."

Language is a part of culture that does not work such a barrier in the Common Market countries as one would expect. Although there are four major languages (all official documents are published in French, German, Italian, and Dutch), such linguistic diversity does not impede trade because European businessmen have historically been multilingual. Nearly every educated European can converse and do business in at least two or three languages; thus, in every relationship, there is likely to be a linguistic common ground. The Europeans have conducted business in one another's language for years. In Europe, vacations as well as business trips in other countries are the rule rather than the exception.

Summarizing, it would appear that the major features of a successful economic union are that the countries have complementary economies and be able to combine to provide a large-sized market. They should have politically amenable leaders who are willing to give up sovereignty.

---

[4] W. O. Henderson, *The Zollverein* (first U.S. ed.; Chicago: Quadrangle Books, 1959), p. 343.

Geographical and cultural proximity further facilitate the functioning of such unions.

PATTERNS OF MULTINATIONAL COOPERATION

Multinational market groups may take several forms which vary significantly in the degree of cooperation, dependence, and interrelationship among the participating nations. In a sense, the United States may be thought of as a fully operative, integrated, economic group of states. The Constitution requires that there be no tariff barriers between the regions or states.[5] The United States provides a common external trade barrier for all states and there is free flow of labor and capital from one state or region to another. These U.S. characteristics also represent the principal characteristics of a fully economically integrated union. The United States is both politically and economically integrated, but there are some economic unions which are not politically integrated and there are political unions which are not completely integrated economically. In some nations various regions or "states" have the power to limit the entry of products from other states through tariffs. There is, for example, a small amount of product exclusion in the United States, as in the case of milk and some agricultural products; but internal tariffs are not tolerated by the Constitution. In this section we shall examine five possible types of arrangements for regional economic integration: Regional cooperation for development (RCD) plans, free-trade area arrangements, customs union programs, common market arrangements, and semipolitical unions.[6]

Regional Cooperation Groups

A new variety of multinational market group developed in recent years is called Regional Cooperation for Development (RCD). In the RCD arrangement, several countries agree to participate jointly with business in developing certain basic industries which will be beneficial to the economy. Each country makes an advance commitment to participate in the financing of new joint-venture projects and to purchase a specified share of the output of production facilities that are developed.

In one RCD, Turkey, Pakistan, and Iran are cooperating with private industry in some 12 to 15 different projects. One, for example, established the Iranian Aluminum Company in cooperation with Reynolds Metal Company, which will provide technical assistance and has a contract to permit it to manage the operation for 10 years. Reynolds has a 25 percent equity; Pakistan, 10 percent; and Iran, 65 percent. The group will build a 50,000-metric-ton production facility. Pakistan has agreed to buy 10,000 tons annually for five years at world market prices.

---

[5] This not to say, however, that there are no trade barriers within the United States. Tariffs are unconstitutional, but health, safety, and other kinds of regulations may be used to exclude out-of-state products. For example, try to buy Florida oranges in California.

[6] This section is patterned in part on the exposition of Bela Balassa, *The Theory of Economic Integration* (Homewood, Ill.: Richard D. Irwin, Inc., 1961).

Regional cooperation groups are not like common markets in that there is normally not an elimination or lowering of tariffs or a structuring of external tariffs. In a sense, they are simply joint ventures in which various governments cooperate with private business in developing new facilities. Such cooperation, however, is likely to presage fuller multinational developments.

Free-Trade Area

The European Free Trade Association (EFTA) and the Latin American Free Trade Association (LAFTA) are examples of the weakest form of regional economic integration.

The key function of a free-trade association is to provide a mass market eliminating the barriers which impede the flow of goods and services among participating member countries. The EFTA was a rather natural outgrowth of the work done by the Organization for European Economic Cooperation (OEEC) and partly a response to the European Economic Community (EEC—the European Common Market).[7]

The Latin American Free Trade Association was established at the urging of the United Nations Economic Commission for Latin America, which found that the potentialities of inter-American trade were extremely promising.[8]

Although a free-trade association does not establish common external barriers and does not provide for a free flow of labor and capital within countries, such a cooperative venture has important nontariff benefits. In general, the very act of association leads to increased communication and cooperation on economic matters. The centralized agency acts as a clearinghouse when the countries can upgrade the entire area.

Full Customs Union

The customs union represents the next logical stage in the development of cooperation. The customs union has the free-trade areas attribute of reduced or eliminated internal tariffs; in addition, it establishes a common external tariff on products imported from countries that are not members of the customs union. The customs union is a logical stage of development in the transition from free-trade area to a common market. The Benelux nations, for example (Belgium, Luxembourg, and the Netherlands), have been participants in a customs union dating back to 1921.

Some other customs unions are those which exist between France and Monaco, Italy and San Marino, and Switzerland and Leichtenstein. In 1965, the United Kingdom and Ireland developed a customs union which is expected to evolve into a full free-trade area.

---

[7] See Graduate Institute of International Studies (Geneva), *The EFTA and the Crisis of European Integration* (London: M. Joseph Ltd., 1968) and *EFTA, European Free Trade Association: The Stockholm Convention and Freer World Trade* (Geneva: EFTA, 1959).

[8] See Attiat A. Fanay, "The Latin American Free Trade Area," *Inter-American Economic Affairs,* Summer, 1963.

BOX 9-2

Progress Toward Creating a Common Market

GOALS

The European Economic Community (EEC) was established by the Rome Treaty of 1958. The Treaty and subsequent EEC decisions called for a common market and unification of certain national economic policies.

Establishing a Common Market

Abolition of internal customs duties and creation of a common external tariff applied to nonmember imports by the end of the transition period (December 31, 1969).

Elimination of quantitative restrictions and other nontariff barriers to trade within the Community by the end of the transition period.

Adoption of a common commercial policy involving harmonizing national export assistance programs and establishing common trade agreements with third countries.

Creation of a common agricultural policy providing for free trade within the Community and unified marketing and pricing for farm goods, both internally and in external trade, by end-1969.

Harmonization of indirect taxation in order to eliminate export subsidies and border taxes on imports by December 31, 1969.

ACHIEVEMENTS

Some of the goals of the Rome Treaty were to be met on December 31, 1969, at the end of a twelve-year transition period, while deadlines for other objectives were not definitely set. The table below describes the progress made toward achieving the main objectives of the EEC.

All customs duties on trade in industrial goods within the Community were abolished on July 1, 1968, and the tariffs on goods imported from nonmembers were fully harmonized on the same date.

All quantitative restrictions on trade in industrial goods among the Six were removed on July 1, 1968. Other nontariff barriers still remain, but are scheduled for elimination by end-1972.

Little progress has been made on standardizing national policies of export assistance; member countries still maintain bilateral trade agreements with third countries.

Common policies have been established for most products, but the Six must still agree on final agricultural financing arrangements. Also, recent currency moves by France and Germany have interfered with common price arrangements, at least temporarily.

Four of the members, excluding Italy and Belgium, will have adopted the value-added tax system by year-end; unification of rates has not begun.

Unifying the Economies of the Six

Abolition of restrictions on the movement of workers and on the right to establish a business anywhere in the Community, by the end of the transition period.

Elimination of restrictions on capital movements "so far as may be necessary to ensure the proper functioning of the Common Market."

Adoption by end-1969 of common policies for transportation services, which will eliminate discrimination in rates and harmonize conditions of competition.

Establishment of common rules preventing practices which distort or restrain competition, whether by private businesses or member governments.

Coordination of economic and monetary policies through consultations and collaboration of member governments.

Adoption of measures to harmonize national energy policies with regard to sources of supply and pricing, and coordination of science and technology policies.

Creation of a common industrial policy, including elimination of obstacles to cross-frontier mergers and adoption of a uniform company law.

Free movement of workers is close to achievement, and EEC nationals can establish businesses in many sectors without legal restrictions, but some national health and safety regulations discriminate against foreign companies.

Considerable liberalization has been achieved for direct investment among member states, and although other types of capital movements are still controlled, members are working on such matters as harmonizing taxes on security issues.

The Community has harmonized some technical regulations, but the Six must still solve many problems. Therefore, it has been decided that the common policy will be completed in three stages ending sometime after 1973.

The definition of unfair business practices has been clarified in a body of case law, but further work is needed to eliminate discrimination arising from national public procurement policies and national aid programs.

The Six have established a number of consultative committees but policy making is still a national prerogative. However, members are working on a plan to improve coordination before end-1969.

The Community is currently working on a long-term program to establish common policies for energy, but this might prove difficult because differences in natural resources lead to divergent national policies. Science and technology are still under study.

The Six have agreed to work for a common patent convention, but otherwise progress has been slow because of the wide variety of issues involved and because of opposition to the idea of a single EEC company law.

Source: "The European Common Market: Progress Report," *World Business*, October 1969, p. 7. Reprinted with permission of the publisher, Chase Manhattan Bank.

BOX 9–3

EFTA–EEC Unity?

Despite the present impediments to an EFTA–EEC link, a strong feeling persists that Europe will not indefinitely be split in two. From an economic point of view, the formation of both EFTA and EEC cut across historical trade flows, and created artificial boundaries. Political motivations are at least as important. Although some of the EFTA nations have a tradition of non-involvement in European affairs, others—notably Great Britain—desire to participate in decisions that will shape the continent's political future. This reluctance to remain isolated, although changeable and hard to define, nevertheless remains a force working for eventual European unity.

Source: From a pamphlet, "The European Free Trade Association," issued by the First National City Bank of New York.

Common Market

The common market builds on the reduction or elimination of internal tariffs and the development of a common external tariff structure which is characteristic of the preceding class of economic integration. It adds the further element of a free flow of capital and labor from country to country. Thus, a common market is a common marketplace, not only for goods, but also for services (including labor), and for capital. It is in every sense a unified economy and lacks only political unity to become a nation. The common market may establish further objectives and additional devices to assure effective economic integration. Some idea of the scope of these activities may be gained by reviewing the provisions of the Treaty of Rome which established the European Common Market—an outstanding example of regional market integration.[9]

1. Tariffs, quotas and other barriers to trade are to be gradually eliminated over a transition period of 12–15 years, so that the effects of tariff reduction will not be too severe (the actual rate of tariff reduction has been considerably faster than originally anticipated).
2. During the period of transition on internal tariffs, a universal uniform schedule will be created to apply to imports from nonmember countries.
3. Restrictions on the movement of services, labor, and capital and business enterprise among the Common Market countries are to be abolished.
4. Cartels and other similar devices restrictive to trade are prohibited (unless they contribute to improvements in production and distribution or to technical and economic progress).
5. Monetary and fiscal policies are to be coordinated and payments are to be freed.

---

[9] More detailed information about the European Common Market will be found elsewhere in this chapter and in the readings for this chapter.

BOX 9–4

Europe Tries to Keep Its Boom in Balance

Consumers and businessmen revel in wave of prosperity sweeping the Common Market. Growth rates soar. But governments are moving to check inflationary dangers

Lobsters were available in only the most exclusive food shops in West Germany a year ago. Today, in German supermarkets, they are selling like bratwurst, at $4 frozen, $25 live.

Hausfraus tucking such delicacies into chock-full grocery carts have their counterparts all over Europe—from the Dutch charwoman who just packed husband and children into a new car and camping trailer for a vacation in sunny Spain, to the French policeman joining a six-month waiting list to buy Ford's jaunty Capri coupe.

Happy days. With new signs of prosperity popping out faster than the blossoms of a late spring, Europe is in the midst of a business upturn so vigorous that only the wariest observers refuse to call it a boom. Not since the early years of the Common Market, when trade barriers were falling fast and companies were eagerly grabbing for new markets, has business been so good in so many countries.

West Germany, its "economic miracle" restored after a crushing recession, still is riding a wave of prosperity that scored a growth rate of 7% in real terms last year.

In France, consumers have all but ignored government attempts to dampen spending in the aftermath of the franc crisis last fall. Estimates of real economic growth for this year have just been revised upward to 5.8%.

Italy's consumers are stepping out, too, and the economy is responding: Industrial production in January and February was 6.4% ahead of last year.

Reacting to the ebullience of Europe's biggest industrial powers, other countries—including Belgium, Holland, Switzerland, and Sweden—are racing ahead as well. And businessmen in every corner of Europe are making the most of some golden opportunities.

Roaring ahead. "Business is great—in capital letters," says a Ford of Germany spokesman who reflects the euphoria that permeates some of Europe's biggest companies. In the first quarter of 1969, Ford sold 56% more cars in the Common Market than in the same period last year.

Other companies are just as happy. Worldwide sales of Hoechst, the German chemical giant, were up 21% in the first quarter of this year compared with 1968. Domestic sales rose 17%. "We're already operating at full capacity," says Hoechst chief executive Karl Winnacker. "But we are determined to expand our capacity as rapidly as we can."

Source: Reprinted from the May 10, 1969, issue of *Business Week,* by special permission. Copyright © 1969 by McGraw-Hill, Inc.

6. Common agricultural policies are to be established.
7. Two investment funds are to be established: one to operate in Europe; the other, in the associated territories. These funds are intended to channel capital from the more advanced and industrial-

ized areas to the less developed regions of the community and its dependencies.

8. The principle of equal pay for equal work for women and men will be applied and methods of computing overtime will be standardized.

9. A social fund is created to help relieve economic injuries to workers resulting from the formation of the common market.

It seems indeed obvious that the founders of the European Common Market intended it to be a truly common market; so much so that economic integration must obviously be supplemented by political integration in order to accomplish these objectives completely. In such an arrangement the members of the Common Market will become truly interdependent members of a supranational community.[10]

Several nations of Central America have banded together into the Central American Common Market (CACM), which provides a most successful example of cooperation in normally individualistic Latin America. A somewhat unique feature of CACM is that the group formally allocates production authority for certain manufactured products to individual member countries. In this way the group hopes to encourage development by essentially granting the whole market to a producer.

The Andean Common Market, formed in 1967, has somewhat similar goals and has stressed full economic integration.

Political Union

Political union of economic affairs may be voluntary or enforced; but regardless of the motivation, such union must ultimately depend on economic logic for success.

The Commonwealth of Nations. *Time* magazine has commented that:

. . . the Commonwealth of Nations is clearly impossible. Except for the colonial past, its 18 member nations—five white, nine black, four brown— have nothing, not even wealth in common. They are divided by almost every possible denominator; color, geography, education, culture, nationalism and economic interests. And so, before each meeting of the Commonwealth Prime Ministers in London, logical men quite logically predict its collapse. They are always wrong. The Commonwealth not only staggers through but it keeps growing.[11]

Indeed, it is somewhat unbelievable that the British Commonwealth survives at all. Its completely voluntary organization provides for the loosest possible relationship which could be classified as economic integration. Still, its membership covers one-fourth of the earth's land mass, contains one-fourth of the world's people, and carries on within its confines one-third of the world's trade.[12] Despite its size, the bonds which hold together the Commonwealth are hard to visualize. One Whitehall official has commented that "I am not sure that all this scrutinizing is a good thing. The Commonwealth is something that may dis-

---

[10] See Stephen Holt, *The Common Market* (London: Hamish Hamilton, 1967).

[11] "How to Keep Alive," *Time*, July 24, 1964, p. 32.

[12] Calvin B. Hoover, *Economic Systems of the Commonwealth* (Durham, North Carolina: Duke University Press, 1962).

appear if you stare at it too hard."[13] Although it is technically neither a legal nor a political conglomeration, the Commonwealth can best be classified as a political union based on economic history and the sense of tradition. One authority comments that the real binding forces are the English language and parliamentary democracy.[14] The Commonwealth does not even share the common internal tariff structure which characterizes even the weakest of the other forms of economic integration. The Commonwealth trade preferences (about which there was so much debate when Britain was considering entering the Common Market) are based solely on a series of bilateral treaties between Britain and the other individual members of the Commonwealth. There is no standardized trade advantage among the countries, and each country makes its own (and different) arrangements concerning the preferences of Britain.

Despite its loose bonds and its informal relationship, the Commonwealth still exists as an example of one form of politically based economic integration and cooperation.

Enforced Political Union. Reacting to the popularity and exceptional success of the Marshall Plan, Joseph Stalin in 1949 established the Council for Mutual Economic Assistance (COMECON). Although it is centrally controlled and more tightly organized than the Commonwealth, COMECON has not approached any of the other methods of economic integration in effectiveness. In its early years COMECON was at least partly an agency for the exploitation of its member countries, the Eastern European satellites. COMECON then followed Stalin's orders to the letter, but because of the satellites' defensiveness, it was not an effective union. In 1956 the controlling council dictated that its new emphasis would be on the development of an international division of labor among council members. This idea, too, has failed to rouse any enthusiasm in the participating members, partly because of poor central planning and partly because of residual national sovereignties. Except for the political pressures involved, COMECON can be said to have failed as an agency for economic integration because its member countries do not meet the basic requisites for effective union and because it has failed to establish agencies which might permit some gains (such as a currency clearinghouse to assure convertibility). East European's economies are not complementary; language and cultural barriers exist; and the satellite countries are unwilling to give up what sovereignty they do possess. It is no wonder that the COMECON has had negligible positive impact on the economic development of its member nations.

MULTINATIONAL MARKETS TODAY

Even though the emphasis in this chapter has been on the European Common Market, many other of the world's multinational market arrangements have been mentioned, and several others deserve mention. The following pages summarize only basic information about the world's

---

[13] "Can the Commonwealth Survive?" *Business Week*, January 18, 1964, p. 81.

[14] Gordon Patrick Walker, *The Commonwealth* (London: Secker and Warburg, 1962), p. 202.

major market groups. The very number of groups attests to the vitality of the multinational market group movement, which seems to be the dominant theme of international trade in the last half of the 20th century.

Europe

In a little over a decade, Europe has been transformed from a group of some 30 small segmented and weak markets into a number of strong, coherent multinational market groups. The Economic Commission for Europe for the United Nations has more than accomplished the goals which it originally set out to accomplish when it was formed immediately after World War II. Nearly every type of multinational market grouping is found in Europe, and all have functioned with relatively high degrees of success. The EEC and EFTA both have reached the point of completely eliminating internal tariff barriers on manufactured goods, and important progress is being made in eliminating agricultural barriers as well. Population, wealth, and the general economic well-being of Western Europe have benefited greatly from the establishment of the various markets.

Many of the world's multinational market arrangements have been mentioned thus far, and several others also deserve mention. Exhibits 9–1 through 9–4 summarize the basic information about the world's market groups.

Middle East

Less developed than Europe to begin with, the Middle East has been slower to catch on in the formation of successfully functioning multinational market groups. Even there, some progress is now being made toward the development of freer trade. Countries belonging to the Arab Common Market have set a goal of free internal trade by 1974 and are planning to homogenize external tariffs at some later date. A new variety of economic cooperation group has been pioneered through the Regional Cooperation for Development, developed jointly by Pakistan, Iran, and Turkey, which has already made some impressive strides in encouraging basic industrial production in those countries. So far, the RCD's have not made provisions for lowering or eliminating tariffs or building a common external tariff wall, but the degree of cooperation is encouraging.

Africa

Africa's multinational market development activities seem to be characterized by a great deal of activity but very little progress. This is perhaps understandable considering the political instability which has characterized Africa in the last decades and considering the unstable economic base on which Africa is required to build. The United Nations Economic Commission for Africa has held numerous conferences but

EXHIBIT 9–1

European Market Groups

Name of Association	Countries Involved*	Population in Millions	GNP per Capita in $ U.S.
1. European Economic Community (EEC) or the Common Market. Established by Treaty of Rome, 1957. Also known as European Common Market or "Inner Six."	Full members:*		
	Belgium	10.6	2,040
	France	50.0	2,325
	Italy	53.0	1,280
	Netherlands	13.0	1,805
	Luxembourg	.3	2,155
	West Germany	60.0	2,025
	Associate members: Burundi, Cameroun, Central African Republic, Chad, Congo (Brazzaville), Congo (Kinchasa), Dahomey, Gabon, Ivory Coast, Malagasy, Mali, Mauritania, Niger, Rwanda, Somalia, Senegal, Togo, Upper Volta.		
2. European Free Trade Association (EFTA). Formed in 1959 at Stockholm. Also known as the "Outer Seven."	Full members:		
	Austria	7.5	1,455
	Denmark	5.0	2,485
	Iceland	.2	2,805
	Norway	4.0	2,200
	Portugal	9.5	490
	Sweden	8.0	3,045
	Switzerland	6.2	2,640
	United Kingdom	56.0	2,015
	Associate member:		
	Finland	4.8	1,525
3. British Commonwealth of Nations (Commonwealth). Established at Ottawa in 1932.	Full members:		
	Australia	12.0	2,245
	Canada	20.5	2,806
	Ceylon	12.0	155
	Cyprus	.6	765
	Ghana	8.2	215
	India	515.0	315
	Malaysia	10.2	2,057
	New Zealand	2.8	120
	Nigeria	45.0	85
	Pakistan	122.0	115
	United Kingdom	56.0	2,015
	Associates, colonies, and protectorates: Barbados, Botswana, Gambia, Guyana, Kenya, Lesotho, Malta, Malawi, Mauritius, Sierra Leone, Singapore, Swaziland, Tanzania, Tobago, Trinidad, Uganda, and Zambia.		

EXHIBIT 9–1 *(Continued)*

Name of Association	Countries Involved*	Population in Millions	GNP per Capita in $ U.S.
4. Council for Mutual Economic Assistance (CEMA), established 1949. Also called COMECON.	Full members:		
	Albania	2.0	998
	Czechoslovakia	14.4	1,711
	East Germany	17.1	1,640
	Hungary	10.2	865
	Outer Mongolia	1.2	416
	Poland	31.9	783
	Rumania	19.5	930
	Soviet Union	237.8	1,950
5. Belgium-Luxembourg Economic Union, established 1921.†	Belgium Luxembourg }	see 1. above	
6. Benelux Economic Union‡	Belgium Luxembourg Netherlands }	see 1. above	
7. United Kingdom and Ireland Free Trade Area, December, 1965.	United Kingdom	see 1. above	
	Ireland	2.9	1,025
8. Italy and San Marino Customs Union	Italy	see 1. above	
	San Marino	.018	n.a.
9. Switzerland and Liechtenstein Customs Union	Liechtenstein	.02	n.a.
	Switzerland	see 2. above	

* The United Kingdom, Norway and Denmark have applied for full membership.
† Establishes joint trade policies, free movement of capital, persons, and goods.
‡ A common market as regards movement of capital, persons, and goods.

EXHIBIT 9–2

Middle East Market Groups

Name of Association	Countries Involved	Population in Millions	GNP per Capita in $ U.S.
1. Arab Common Market	Iraq	8.7	265
	Kuwait	.5	3,565
	Jordan	2.0	290
	Syria	5.8	200
	U.A.R.	30.6	190
2. Regional Cooperative for Development	Pakistan	115.0	1,222
	Iran	26.5	286
	Turkey	33.0	325

EXHIBIT 9–3

African Market Groups

Name of Association	Countries Involved	Population in Millions	GNP per Capita in $ U.S.
1. Afro-Malagasy Economic Union (L'Organization Afro-Malgache de Co-Operation Economique)	Cameroun..................	5.6	143
	Central African Republic......	1.5	131
	Chad......................	3.5	79
	Congo (Brazzaville)..........	1.0	176
	Dahomey...................	2.6	70
	Gabon.....................	5.6	143
	Ivory Coast................	4.2	268
	Malagasy..................	6.5	115
	Mauritania................	1.2	150
	Niger.....................	3.6	90
	Rwanda...................	3.4	40
	Senegal...................	3.8	215
	Togo.....................	1.8	120
	Upper Volta...............	3.6	90
2. Council of the Entente	Dahomey...................	2.6	70
	Ivory Coast................	4.2	268
	Niger.....................	3.6	90
	Upper Volta...............	3.6	90
3. East African Common Market	Kenya.....................	10.0	120
	Tanzania..................	12.3	75
	Uganda...................	8.0	95
4. Equatorial Customs Union	Cameroun..................	5.6	143
	Central African Republic......	1.5	131
	Chad......................	3.5	79
	Congo (Brazzaville)..........	1.0	176
	Gabon....................	5.6	143
5. Maghreb Economic Community, Libya	Algeria....................	12.5	242
	Libya.....................	1.8	910
	Morocco..................	14.2	189
	Tunisia...................	4.7	210
6. Organization of African Unity	All independent African countries except Rhodesia and South Africa		
7. West Africa Customs Union	Dahomey...................	2.6	70
	Ivory Coast................	4.2	268
	Mali......................	4.9	70
	Mauritania................	11.2	150
	Niger.....................	3.6	90
	Senegal...................	3.8	215
	Upper Volta...............	3.6	90
8. East Africa Customs Union (1967)	Ethiopia...................		
	Kenya.....................	10.0	120
	Rhodesia..................	4.7	240
	Sudan....................	14.5	112
	Tanzania..................	12.3	75
	Uganda...................	8.0	95
	Zambia...................	4.0	300

EXHIBIT 9–4

Latin American Market Groups

Name of Association	Countries Involved	Population in Millions	GNP per Capita in $ U.S.
1. Central American Common Market (CACM), established in 1961 by General Treaty on Central American Economic Integration (Mercado Comun Centroamericano (MCC), sometimes called Central Free Trade Association.	Full members; Guatemala	5.0	290
	El Salvador	3.2	290
	Honduras	2.5	240
	Costa Rica	7.0	425
	Nicaragua	2.0	363
2. Latin American Free Trade Association (LAFTA), formed 1960 at Montevideo, Uruguay.	Argentina	24.0	650
	Brazil	86.0	350
	Colombia	19.5	290
	Paraguay	2.3	225
	Uruguay	3.0	535
	Chile	9.0	605
	Ecuador	5.5	250
	Mexico	46.0	530
	Peru	12.5	325
	Venezuela	24.5	947
3. Transatlantic Free Trade Area	Proposed alliance with EFTA Canada	20.8	4,350
	U.S.	202.0	3,190
4. Andean Common Market, 1967.	Bolivia	3.8	179
	Chile Colombia Ecuador Peru	see 2. above	
5. Caribbean Free Trade Association (CARIFTA), 1965. Effective 1968.	Antigua and dependencies	.062	N.A.
	Barbados	.253	385
	Dominica	.072	217
	Grenada and dependencies	.103	212
	Guyana	.710	310
	Jamaica	1.913	491
	Montserrat	.015	272
	St. Kitts-Nevis-Anguila	.056	238
	St. Lucia	.108	251
	St. Vincent and dependencies	.093	185
	Trinidad and Tobago	1.030	822

has been hampered by governmental inexperience, undeveloped resources, manpower problems, and chronic product shortages. It has, however, managed to sponsor an African Development Bank, which began making loans against this $250 million capital in 1967. ECA is also working to induce African members to develop modern customs services

BOX 9–5

Economic Cooperation in Africa

Under conditions existing in Africa a project of economic cooperation designed to encourage relatively free circulation of trade among the member countries is of no value whatever. Such a project could not lead to greater cooperation among the productive facilities because in most cases there are few such facilities. At the same time, free competition of existing productive entities would aggravate the present inequalities among the member countries. More advanced countries that have natural advantages would progress more rapidly while their less advanced neighbors would probably realize a declining rate of development when exposed to the impact of competitive forces.

This means that from the static point of view, African economies have very little to gain from economic cooperation. Their gains are focused on the dynamic aspects of integration, and stem from the economic integration and structural change. It appears, therefore, that economic integration, economic development, and change in the social and economic structure are actually three different aspects of economic progress. . . .

African leaders will have to convince themselves that part of the political independence that they only recently won from the colonial powers will have to be surrendered to some supernatural African institutions in order to speed up development of their continent.

On purely economic grounds, integration of Africa will have to succeed in the long run simply because it is inevitable if Africa wants to progress. There are numerous compelling technical, financial, and marketing reasons that will push African nations toward establishing closer economic ties. The requirements of large-scale technology, need for larger markets, and huge amounts of investment capital will force Africa to cooperate and to integrate. It is almost certain that without this cooperation and integration, the chances for significant economic and social progress in the foreseeable future are very small indeed.

Source: André Simmons, "Economic Integration of Africa," *MSU Business Topics*, Winter 1969, pp. 73–79. Reprinted by permission of the publisher, the Bureau of Business and Economic Research, Division of Research, Graduate School of Business Administration, Michigan State University.

and to adopt the Brussels tariff nomenclature which is pretty much standard in the Western world.

Political sovereignty is a new enough phenomenon to most African nations that they are not about to give it up without specific and tangible benefits in return. As André Simmons has pointed out in his study of economic integration of Africa,

A national economy with two million inhabitants who, on the average, have an income of a hundred dollars per year has an aggregate purchasing power equal to that of an average American community of about fifty thousand people. No one in this country would seriously suggest that a town with fifty thousand people could exist as an independent, political and economic unit.[15]

---

[15] André Simmons, "Economic Integration of Africa," *MSU Business Topics,* Winter 1969, p. 72.

Still another problem in African common market development is that only one tenth of all African trade is intraregional, so there is virtually no history of intercontinental trading on a large scale.

Two basic approaches to the integration of Africa are being employed. The first attempts to bring together a few (three or four) nations into close economic relationships which would emphasize economic growth in the industrial sector. The second approach involves more grandiose schemes grouping a large number of nations (perhaps 12 to 15) and is designed to bring about cooperation in nearly all areas of economic activity, including transportation, education, manpower, natural resources, and agriculture, as well as industrial development.

It is difficult to specify the extent of progress among the various organizations listed in Exhibit 9–3. The goals and stability of each vary greatly.

In 1958, the Pan-African Freedom Movement for East and Central Africa (PAFMECA) was formed. Its goal is to prevent economic fragmentation of Africa. The Casablanca Group, including Egypt, Ghana, Guinea, Mali, and Morocco, was started in 1961. It agreed on measures of political and economic cooperation, including the creation of a common market, an African payments union, an economic development bank, and a joint air and shipping line. The group planned to eliminate trade ceilings and customs duties among its members within five years.

The Monrovia Group (Inter-African and Malagasy States Organization), organized in 1961, consists of the Afro-Malagasy Group plus Ethiopia, Liberia, Libya, Nigeria, Sierra Leone, Somalia, Togo, and Tunisia. It produced a plan similar to that of the Casablanca Group, including a common market and development bank.

Asia

About one third of the world's population (even excluding mainland China) lives in Asia and the Far East, but this massive population produces less than 2 percent of the world's industrial output. The United Nations Economic Commission for Asia and Far East (ECAFE) has worked diligently to strengthen the Asian market through the development of multinational market groups. It has also created the Asian Industrial Development Council, dedicated to the development of trade and commercial arrangements and multicountry joint ventures which will speed the industrialization of Asia. It has also created the Asian Development Bank, which has been in full operation since 1966 and has an authorized capital of $1 billion (a third of which is subscribed to by European and North American countries). Despite the low volume of trade in the area, Asia does have a heritage of international trading, and one third of its international trade has been on an interregional basis. This, coupled with the fact that many of the Asian nations are members of the Commonwealth and already have established working relationships, makes the future of multinational economic organizations promising.

The rapid economic progress of Japan in the past decade provides

BOX 9–6

CACM Weathers Another Storm

The Central American Common Market (CACM), most successful of the integration movements in the LDCS, is wrestling with another crisis. Companies in CACM find themselves caught in the temporary but distressing difficulties that result when kinks in the integration machinery bring the entire mechanism to a brief but sudden halt.

The latest crisis was provoked by Nicaragua's temperamental President Anastasio Somoza, who was responsible for a similar flurry last year. . . .

This time, President Somoza issued a decree late last week, unilaterally imposing a tax on all imports into Nicaragua from the other four CACM countries. The first result was, once again, trucks with startled and confused drivers piling up on both sides of the Nicaraguan borders. Next, El Salvador, quickest to react to such goads, banned all Nicaraguan imports, causing further traffic jams on the never-too-smooth CACM highways.

While the trucks were piling up and company executives tearing their hair, the Ministers of Economy met in Guatemala to see how they could get the fat out of the fire this time. They came up with an ingenious expedient, i.e., for the four other CACM countries to impose countervailing taxes on Nicaraguan goods, with the money, however, held in escrow for refunding when the crisis passed. With this device, trade is again moving in CACM.

While the Somoza tactics are unfortunate, Nicaragua does have cause for complaint. It is the only one of the CACM countries to promptly ratify and deposit all integration treaties and protocols as they are drawn up. Guatemala and Costa Rica follow after varying periods, but Honduras and El Salvador have been irritating General Somoza. They have been extremely slow in both the executive and legislative levels in meeting their integration obligations. . . .

Underlying this integration horse-trading, however, is a more fundamental problem. Nicaragua has, in the past three years, piled up a mounting trade deficit in intra-CACM trade. Nicaragua is CACM's largest producer of agricultural crops for domestic consumption, and, while industrial integration has been achieved to a large extent in CACM, agricultural integration has not. As a result, Nicaragua finds itself buying CACM industrial goods while the other CACM countries do not necessarily buy its agricultural goods.

Source: Reprinted from the March 7, 1969, issue of *Business International,* p. 80, with the permission of the publisher, Business International Corporation, New York.

an example of the potential accomplishments of industrialization and serves as an important stimulus to market development. As a major supplier nation to the Far East, Japan has been most active in helping in the formation of Asian common markets.

The Americas

The United States of America and the Economic Commission for Latin America have both played major roles in the development of the various market groups in Latin America. Progress has been somewhat slow because of political instability of the Latin American nations, but there has been the Central American Common Market, which in only eight years has seen internal trade among its member nations rise from $37 million to $260 million and which has achieved internal free trade for 98 percent of the products on its common customs classification code and a common outer tariff for some 95 percent.

The Latin American Free Trade Association has made less progress but nonetheless there is talk of developing a Latin American Common Market; CACM group has already committed itself to participate in such a movement. The newly established Andean Common Market has made some notable strides in the first years of its existence and is aiming at common external tariffs by 1980 and full economic integration by 1985. There have even been various proposals for a transatlantic free-trade association and a U.S.–Canadian customs union, but so far these have been the subject of only informal talks.

STRATEGIC IMPLICATIONS FOR MARKETING

Coalition among nations into multinational market groups provides certain unique situations to the international marketer. Specific areas of marketing action are discussed throughout the bulk of the book, but several items that are particularly related to multinational markets are here reviewed.

Opportunities

Large mass markets are the chief benefits created for the marketer through economic integration. Many national markets that are too small to bother with individually take on new dimension and significance when they amalgamate with markets from cooperating countries. The European Common Market is nearly equivalent to the United States in population and has an internal trade volume of some $25 billion plus an import volume of over $30 billion. The Commonwealth has nearly four times as much population and a similar import volume. The European Free Trade Association comprises a substantial market of some 90 million people, with an import volume of nearly $45 billion. Large markets are particularly important to the American businessman who is accustomed to mass production and mass distribution. Not only are the markets large in numbers, but they are also rapidly improving in purchasing power. Although not so spectacularly successful, the other markets are also improving continually and provide significant marketing opportunities.

An additional benefit to the marketer is that market group countries are improving their marketing institutions. Improvement in channels of distribution, advertising, and transportation facilities provide opportunities for an aggressive foreign marketer to utilize his technical skills and abilities.

Increased market size and a developing infrastructure have worked very much to the advantage of the American marketer who has experience and skills in utilizing mass marketing techniques. Because of former market limitations, foreign competitors have lacked the experience needed to operate successfully in mass market economies that have been developed in multinational markets.

Problems

Any phase of international marketing presents large numbers of problems. Some, however, seem to be uniquely related to multinational markets.

Major problems are related to market dissimilarity, intensified competition, nationalism, emphasis on intramarket trading, overproduction, power politics, and inflation. Common markets are not so common in fact as they are in name. The heterogeneous nature of cooperating countries requires that individual attention be given to the component parts of the multinational groups.

Extremely strong competition is likely to confront the marketer who is participating in a common market. The marketer who may have things pretty much his own way domestically is likely to find that his strongest counterparts in other countries share his interest in common markets and are also permitted to make a strong entry into such markets. One American businessman in Europe comments that "national psychologies are often still at the heart of the trade problem" and notes that despite the progress of the common market, national loyalties are not changing much. To date, the common markets have not gotten far in eliminating language barriers, cultural barriers, advertising media problems, or even completely eliminating tariff and nontariff barriers between countries within a given market group. Life continues to be complicated for the international marketer.

Supranational politics may be employed to shut out foreign-based firms and protect home markets. Besides affecting exporters, such political action may also damage the business of foreign-owned firms which have production and marketing facilities within a common market area. More importantly, the size and economic health of the markets has actually created competition and strengthened foreign competitors who now are more able than formerly to obtain the benefits of large-scale production and mass distribution. Thus the marketer has more competitors and stronger competition than ever before. The existence of a full-scale common market may completely change the rules of the game. Clark Equipment Company, which manufactures forklift trucks and construction equipment, years ago established 12 plants in Europe and Britain. The company's European vice-president says, "Only the biggest and most competitive fork-lift companies can now survive,"[16] so the company is involved in the question of whether to eliminate a number of its production facilities and concentrate all manufacturing in one country. The manager estimates that the market in Europe is now so competitive that well over half of the 40 or so European competitors

---

[16] "E.E.C. Reaches a Momentous Goal," *Business Week*, June 29, 1968, p. 94.

are not operating profitably and most will either be absorbed by other companies or disappear. Companies in every European Common Market country have been faced with a series of intense and difficult competitive questions as tariffs have been successively reduced.

Although partially excluded in the European Common Market, cartels may still be formed. Such cartels are fairly likely to exclude foreign-based firms.

Multinational market groups tend to increase the trade among the member nations and decrease their trade with nonmember nations. U.S. exports to the European Common Market have been reduced as much as $650 million per year since the formation of the Common Market. Politics aside, the major factor holding Britain out of the European Common Market has been the intense competition which British agricultural products would introduce into the European market—one already excessively competitive and characterized by strong national market barriers. The European Free Trade Association's situation is similar.

Overproduction with resultant price cutting and profit deterioration may be a common phenomenon in some of the multinational market areas. In their eagerness to become established in these areas, some manufacturers will construct production facilities or capacities beyond the short-run market potential. In 1969, total exports and imports of EFTA countries grew about 2 percent, whereas intraarea trade rose by nearly 10 percent.

Several such facilities working toward long-term markets can create chaotic market conditions in the short run. In some countries the cost of entering the market will be too great, considering the slow payoff rate. Many manufacturers, therefore, will have to decide between entering an unprofitable market or being excluded from it permanently.

Political power struggles are likely to take place among the various members of the multinational market organizations. Such power struggles can be particularly disruptive to the market; foreign companies may find themselves in a scapegoat position. The European Common Market is well established and functioning smoothly; yet one sees and will continue to see headlines like this: "Is EEC Splitting at the Seams?: Franco-German Rivalry Virtually Has Killed the Old Concept of 'Community.' "

Inflation is another threat to which common markets seem particularly susceptible. Rapid changes in the production base, large influx of capital, and generally stimulated economic activity almost inevitably lead to inflation. Yet these are the dynamic factors which contribute to the success of multinational market groups. The marketer who does not include allowances for inflation in his plans may find his profit picture considerably altered.

Europe has experienced two full cycles of overproduction and price cutting since the foundation of the European Common Market. These came about in a period in which essentially there was world economic growth and stability. Fortunately, nations are now more sophisticated fiscally and working hard to prevent problems of inflation and excessive problems of currency fluctuation.

BOX 9-7

The Common Markets

The issue of narrow economic nationalism vs. the international company is drawn even sharper in the case of economic integration movements—whether common markets as in the case of the European Economic Community and the Central American Common Market, or free trade associations as in the case of EFTA and LAFTA. These movements represent partial acknowledgement by the governments concerned that hot-house industries, existing within their own borders by the grace of restrictions against foreign goods and investments, are not in the public interest, that such industries represent a misuse of resources, and that the welfare of their populations is better served by companies producing in quantity for a larger-than-national market. Yet these same governments fail to recognize that the most productive units of all, and thus the most beneficial to their citizens, are those that have the freedom to compete on sheer economic grounds for the entire world market unhindered by tariffs and other artificial barriers. Worse yet, some of them hold the view that their country should be the situs of all or most of the plants that are expected to spring up or expand to serve the common market or free trade region of which their country is a part. This is, of course, the very antithesis of the whole economic integration idea. Governments that suffer this form of economic myopia often find ways of throwing up administrative and other barriers to the entry of goods and capital from their common market partners as the more formal tariff and quota hurdles against them are dismantled.

As much of a headache as this is to international corporations, an even worse migraine is the reluctance of some economic integration officials to see such firms entering their region and giving effect to the integration effort by setting up large, regional plants. The tragedy here is that the international corporation is uniquely equipped through its human and financial resources, its experience in mass production, and its very concepts, to put flesh on the legal bones of common market and free trade treaties.

Source: "1985—Corporate Planning for Tomorrow's Market," *Business International,* 1967.

Requirements

Because they are dynamic and because they have great growth possibilities, the multinational markets are likely to be especially rough and tumble for the external businessman. These markets may be more difficult to profit from than some of the apparently less desirable single national markets. The requirements for profitable entry are essentially the requirements of a competitive marketplace anywhere—a high degree of marketing ability, total commitment to the competitive effort, versatility, and (perhaps especially at this point) fast action. The secretary of a German manufacturers' association said, "We tell our members to get busy now. We tell them 'Get in there, set up your outlets, hire your agents, prospect for customers—or you will be dead ducks.' "[17] Besides

---

[17] Ernest O. Hauser, "The Common Market—Europeans Love It!" *Rotarian,* July 1964, p. 14.

these requirements, the foreign businessman must also deal with the multinational market problems and complications related to trade restrictions, exchange and financial arrangements, marketing barriers and limitations, as well as the general problems of communications and acculturation in a single but nonhomogeneous market.

SUMMARY AND CONCLUSIONS

The experience of the multinational market groups developed since World War II points up both the possible successes and the hazards which such groups encounter. The various attempts at economic cooperation represent various degrees of success and failure, but, almost without regard to their degree of success, the economic market groups have created great excitement among marketers.

Economic benefits possible through cooperation relate to more efficient marketing and production: marketing efficiency is effected through the development of mass markets, encouragement of competition, the improvement of personal income, and various psychological market factors. Production efficiency derives from specialization, mass production for mass markets, and the free movement of the factors of production. Economic integration also tends to foster political harmony among the countries involved; such harmony leads to stability, which is beneficial to the marketer.

The marketing implications of multinational market groups may be studied from the standpoint of firms located inside the market or of firms located outside which wish to sell into the markets. For each viewpoint the problems and opportunities are somewhat different; but regardless of the location of the marketer, multinational market groups do provide great opportunity for the creative marketer who wishes to expand his volume. Market groupings make it economically feasible to enter new markets and to employ new marketing strategies which could not be applied to the smaller markets represented by individual countries.

The success of the European Common Market and the European Free Trade Association and the relative success of some of the other multinational market groups indicate that there will be continued development in this field. Such development will continue to challenge the international marketer by providing continually growing market opportunities.

READINGS

Although the figures in this reading are somewhat dated, it remains probably the finest piece of reporting on the concept and dream of the Common Market and provides the kind of historical perspective necessary to understand the entire multinational market movement which has caught up most of the nations of the world.

EUROPE: "THEN WILL IT LIVE . . ."*

There lives today near Paris an ascetic, unobtrusive Frenchman who may ultimately succeed where others, from Charlemagne to Napoleon, ultimately failed. He commands no armies or popular following, but his work is worth uncounted divisions to the West. He has neither title nor portfolio, but he has privileged access to every chancellery of Western Europe. He has no formal higher education, but the world's most brilliant economists regard him as their peer. He has never joined a political party, but parliamentarians across Europe flock to his summons. His name is Jean Monnet, and he is the practical apostle of European unity whose new, growing organizations—notably the Common Market—are remaking the scarred old face of Europe and changing the balance of power throughout the world.

Scarcely a decade after a war-ravaged Europe seemed hopelessly dependent on U.S. dole, a revitalized Continent is going through the greatest boom in its history, excelling Soviet progress, matching and even competing with U.S. economic power. At a time when the U.N. is in disarray and U.S. policy makers are looking to other institutions and communities for strength, such institutions and such a community are developing in Europe. At a time when so much heed is paid to the "new" nations, with all their bursting little new nationalisms, it is Europe's old nations, relaxing nationalist feuds, which are forming a fresh center of strength for Western civilization.

Revolutionary Cooperation

In Brussels last week, the Common Market's Council of Ministers took another huge step forward when it accepted Britain's bid for membership and set the first negotiating sessions for next week. At the risk of jettisoning deep-rooted ties with the Commonwealth, Britain had finally decided that her own and the West's future lay in European unity, by Prime Minister Harold Macmillan's ponderous admission: "The plain fact is that the formation and development of the Community has created, economically and politically, a situation to which we are compelled to react."

What attracts the British, almost irresistibly, can be seen all over Europe. Everywhere, the quarrelsome Continent is caught up in a quiet revolution of cooperation. On a busy Turin street corner, a pretty Dutch policewoman expertly directs traffic. In Florence, work is in progress on the University of Europe, financed by six nations and scheduled to open its doors in 1962. A Bonn delicatessen owner makes his twice-weekly trip to Belgium to buy vegetables for his newly finicky customers and grumbles: "They won't buy German vegetables any more, even when they're cheaper." Looking toward outer space, Britain, France and West Germany are establishing a $200 million project to build a European rocket. Deep beneath the Alps, workmen are blasting an auto tunnel

---

* Courtesy *Time,* the Weekly Newsmagazine; Copyright Time, Inc., 1961.

under Mont Blanc; when it is completed next year, Paris and Rome will be 124 miles closer by car.

Meanwhile, back from a summer of skimming with passportless ease all over the Common Market countries were bikini-bronzed girls and tousle-haired boys, members of the new, low-budget international set that motor-scoots and camps with blithe disregard of frontiers—which are often posted with neat new signs proclaiming, "Another Border But Still Europe." And some 1,150 school children from a dozen nations were enrolled in Brussels' Common Market European high school— multilingual, intercultural, stocked with history texts that are no longer patriotic tracts but tell both sides of such old, bitter feuds as the Franco-Prussian War.

Uncommon Development

Europe today is a tangled skein of alliances and associations, knitting the nations together for everything from the defense of the free world (NATO) to the telecasting of the Scots Guards into the homes of Athenians and Ankarans (EUROVISION), and the exchange of trade (EFTA), aid (OECD), and commemorative postage stamps (CEPT). Some of these organizations are not radically different from the old familiar alliances that the European nations have always found it convenient to form in times of relative peace. The drastic new departure that galvanizes all the others is the six-nation Common Market, comprising France, West Germany, Italy, Belgium, Luxembourg and The Netherlands.

Conceived by Jean Monnet and in force for 3½ years, the Common Market aims to eliminate trade barriers among the six countries—and ultimately to integrate their economies. In basic economic theory, it is as old as Adam Smith, as familiar as the United States—the world's largest common market. It aims at free trade within the largest possible area, enabling industries to cut costs, labor to specialize, capital to move freely where needed in a mass market—to the economic benefit of producer, worker and consumer. But set against Europe's age-old rivalries and stubborn economic nationalism, in which trade barriers used to be as fanatically guarded as national borders, the Common Market is an astonishingly uncommon development.

Dream of Order

Like many revolutionary ideas, united Europe is not a new notion but an old one revived. The dream of order and unity once embodied in the Rome of the Caesars lived on through the Middle Ages, not only in the Roman Catholic Church but in that embattled but strangely viable anachronism, the Holy Roman Empire. Even after it disintegrated, and the last remnants of feudal internationalism gave way to popular nationalism, the European idea remained; and even if Europeans themselves at times forgot it, the rest of the world could not. For most of 2,000 years the culture, commerce and conquests of the peoples of

Western Europe shaped the world's destinies. European traders and explorers knit the world, European armies subdued it, European adventurers settled it, European lawgivers pacified it, European artists and philosophers remade its esthetic norms. European artisans launched the Industrial Revolution, and European capital carried it to the ends of the earth.

But as Europe's influence grew, so did the scale of its conflicts, and at the end of the second World War, Europe lay prostrate between the new giants in world affairs, the U.S. and Soviet Russia. Precisely because the old Europe seemed irrevocably dead, a great hope arose that a truly new Europe might be possible at last. In the immediate postwar years, Churchill launched his movement for a United Europe, Count Richard Coudenhove-Kalergi, a tireless Pan-Europist from the 1920s, summoned a group of European parliamentarians to discuss political unity, the European Union of Federalists urged Europe to "federate now," and in 1949 most of these groups came together to establish the Council of Europe. Skeptics refused to believe that anything practical would ever come of these idealistic and largely futile efforts. And yet the power of the ideal itself would not fade. Spanish Philosopher Salvador de Madariaga expressed it better than anyone else.

"Above all, we must love Europe," he wrote, "this Europe to whom La Gioconda forever smiles, where Hamlet seeks in thought the mystery of his inaction, where Faust seeks in action comfort for the void of his thought, where Don Juan seeks in women met the woman never found, and Don Quixote, spear in hand, gallops to force reality to rise above itself. This Europe must be born. And she will, when Spaniards will say 'our Chartres,' Englishmen 'our Cracow,' Italians 'our Copenhagen'; when Germans say 'our Bruges,' and step back horror-stricken at the idea of laying murderous hands on it. Then will Europe live, for then it will be that the spirit that leads history will have uttered the creative words: *'Fiat Europa!'* "

The Common Cause

One force that, more than any other, put reality behind this poetic vision proved to be Europe's great offspring, the U.S. Americans, seeing Europe from a distance and therefore as a unit, had often been better Europeans than many Europeans. Thus, when the U.S. offered the Marshall Plan in 1947, it shrewdly insisted that the European nations cooperate in estimating their needs and in spending the funds. OEEC, the multi-nation agency through which Marshall Aid was pumped into Europe, was a crucial example of cooperation. Followed by the NATO alliance, it prepared the way for Jean Monnet's boldly planned Coal and Steel Community, direct forerunner of the Common Market.

By 1950, Europe was well on the recovery road, except for West Germany. Question was, how to rebuild Germany into NATO in a fashion acceptable to France, thrice attacked by German armies in the last hundred years? It was Jean Monnet, then directing France's postwar economic recovery, who found the answer: to pool the coal and steel resources of France and Germany—the Ruhr, the Saar, Lorraine, over which so many Franco-German conflicts had erupted—under a supranational authority.

With few exceptions, the European Coal and Steel Community has proved a huge success. In eight years, steel production in its six member countries (France, Germany, Italy, Benelux) has jumped 100%, to 73 million tons in 1960—nearly equal the U.S. output. The organization has largely eliminated the national taxes on coal and steel production, applied international through rates on coal and steel shipments. It has developed the most advanced social and job-security system in the world for its 1,500,000 workers, who have free movement to jobs anywhere within the six countries, full salary unemployment benefits up to a year. Above all, it has made supranationalism stick; it has independent authority to levy taxes, and the decisions of its nine-man international High Authority are binding on member governments.

Thus from Europe's grimiest coalfields and bloodiest battlefields grew the great experiment in unity. For, argued Monnet in 1955, why not expand the Coal and Steel Community to embrace the total economic life of the six members and create a European Economic Community, including a Common Market and an atomic energy pool, Euratom. France had doubts but was swept along by the other members. In 1957 the Common Market was ratified in the Treaty of Rome—and no one missed the memories of past unity which the name of that city still evoked in Europe. A year later, France was in serious economic straits, and De Gaulle had come to power with scornful views on supranational ventures. Economists predicted gloomily that France would have to delay the first, crucial 10% tariff cut. But France met its commitments on time, and, under De Gaulle, continued as an enthusiastic Common Market partner.

Cleaned Out

In a protectionist Europe, where everybody from parsnip growers to pavingstone makers was sheltered by tariffs, businessmen almost to a man fought the Common Market right up to the moment it became fact, fearful that it would put their protected industries out of business. Monnet's answer was to bring the Market into existence gradually, reducing tariffs at easy stages to allow industries time to adjust to the new competition. It has worked surprisingly well. In Belgium, some inefficient coal mines have shut down. In France, whose industry was the most highly protected of the Six, perhaps 20% of the marginal electrical firms and 30% of the small textile shops (up to 20 employees) have shut down; most had been teetering on the edge of bankruptcy for years. But France has also had pleasant surprises. While French industry always feared that it could not compete with the Germans, particularly in the electrical field, the French have found that they cannot only compete in price and quality, but often beat the Germans at their own game.

Jean Monnet's creation is also working a revolution in the taste and preferences of the West European consumer. Paris' Galeries Lafayette, biggest department store in France, in 1957 imported only 1% of its goods. Today its counters sag with Italian clothes, furniture and glassware, German linen, leather goods and housewares, Dutch clothing and pottery—and some 8% of its sales are imported goods. Thanks to reduced tariffs, Dutch blouses that in 1958 sold for $10 now sell for $2.50, are one of the best selling items in the store. A 1958 French refrigerator sold for $187. Today the same French company, under pressure from German competition, sells a larger and better refrigerator for only $120. "Before 1958, no French firm would dream of putting out a cheap, well-designed, ready-to-wear range of women's clothes," says Galeries Lafayette Chief Buyer Jean d'Allens. "Now several are selling women's skirts for as little as $10, and selling them all over the Common Market."

A Bonn wineshop now sells Hennessy cognac at $3.75 a bottle while the best German *Weinbrand* at the same price gathers dust.* From tiny Fiats to elegant Ferraris, some 400,000 imported cars have been sold in West Germany. In a posh Düsseldorf shoe salon last week, a matron, eyeing the latest square-toed model, snapped: "Is it Italian?" Replied the salesgirl: "Madam, we sell only Italian shoes." German sausage and French *pâté* are pouring into Belgium at twice the pre-1958 rate. One of Brussels' largest stores laid on a Common Market exhibition earlier this year called "Europe on Your Plate." Supplies were cleaned out.

"I don't know what to do about this European craze," complains a West German adman. "Once, all you had to do to sell a product was to say, 'Made in Germany.' Now take cigarettes, for example: to make our German brands competitive, we have to imply that people are smoking them all over Europe. It's the same with everything from soup to schnapps—you have to show people using it in Paris, in Brussels, in Rome."

Largest Importer

In less than four years since it began operating, the Common Market has become one of the fastest-growing economic units on earth. Industrial production soared an astonishing 12% last year alone. Gross national product zoomed some 7% v. the U.S.'s 4½% in 1960. Russia claims a somewhat larger G.N.P. than the Common Market, but taken together, the U.S., the Common Market, and (if the merger is completed) the United Kingdom form a potential economic force that could overwhelm the Russians.

The Common Market is now the world's largest importer of all kinds of goods ($30 billion worth last year), the second largest exporter of manufactured goods. Its monetary reserves have swollen to more than $16 billion, nearly equal the U.S. reserves of $18 billion. In its internal drive toward economic integration, the Common Market has performed

---

* Recalling Goethe's lines:

> *Ein echter deutscher Mann mag keinen Franzen leiden,*
> *Doch ihre Weine trinkt er gern.*
> (*A real German cannot abide a Frenchman,*
> *Yet he likes to drink his wines.*)

even more spectacularly. Trade among the Six has increased 45% in three years, this year is averaging $1 billion per month. As a result, the Six have reduced tariffs among themselves by 30% on almost every commodity except agriculture and petroleum products, are speeding up their timetable for more cuts. What was initially to be a twelve-year transition to an integrated economy is now scheduled to take place in eight years or less.

Merger Bender

European industry has not only learned to cut costs and compete, but to cooperate. Some 250 private trade and merchandising associations have mushroomed, ranging from the huge Common Market Association of Chemical Industries to the European Bed Union, from the Common Market Association of Beer Wholesalers to the European Brush Manufacturers. Acronyms abound: Euromalt (malt makers), Euromaisers (corn producers), Unecolait (dairymen) and Unipede (the European Committee for the Producers and Distributors of Electrical Energy).

Common Market businesses have gone on a merger bender. Germany's Messerschmitt and France's Fouga are jointly making aircraft. Italy's Innocenti and Germany's Hans Glas are making cars together, Luxembourg's Dostert and Germany's Wilhelm Siebel truck trailers. Agfa and France's Vedette are collaborating on cameras. Eurista is a new French-German coalition making electrical resistors. Gasoline is now distributed in France and Germany by Desmarais. The Société Française PIC and Krupp recently signed an agreement to build a petroleum plant. "Within a few more years," says a West German industrialist wonderingly, "no government will be able to pull out of the Community. The businessmen won't let them." This is precisely what Jean Monnet is counting on.

The New Civil Servant

The shape of a United Europe is already evident in the institutions of the Common Market. The cerebral cortex is housed in a new concrete-and-steel nine-story building on Brussel's appropriately named Avenue de la Joyeuse Entrée. Here the European Commission, a nine-man executive, plots the grand strategy and supervises the daily details of the Common Market's operation.

The only national check on the commission's decisions reposes in the Common Market's Council of Ministers—one from each of the Six. But it is a limited check at best. The council cannot initiate proposals to the commission, only pass on the commission's proposals to it—and it can modify them only by a unanimous vote. The commission usually prevails. In addition, the Six have also established a seven-man Court of Justice, which arbitrates technical disputes. The Six have set up a 142-member Parliament that meets periodically in Strasbourg, consists of parliamentarians elected by and from the members' national legislatures. But the Treaty of Rome stipulates that in time the representatives are to be elected by direct vote of the Community's populations. Though their work is often highly technical, the men who run the Common Market seldom forget its ultimate purpose: "Make no mistake about it," says the European Commission's president, German Economist Walter Hallstein, "we are not in business, we are in politics. We are building the United States of Europe."

In the process, the Common Market has developed a new prototype of the European civil servant. The members of the Common Market executive and their staff drive cars marked with special European license plates, send their children to the European high school, and, except for accents, have lost many of their national traits or concerns. Of all these new civil servants, still the most tireless at 72 is Jean Omer Marie Gabriel Monnet, the most dedicated internationalist of them all—although at the same time he remains as thoroughly French as Cognac, the town of his birth.

Primitive Pooling

Monnet's tough peasant heritage is stamped in his broad face and his short, stocky, muscular body. His paternal grandfather, a farmer-mayor of Cognac, lived to the age of 102. Jean Monnet's mother lived to be 87, his father, Jean Gabriel, to 83. A staunch conservative, Jean Gabriel used to warn young Jean that "every new idea is bound to be a bad idea." There is no evidence that Jean paid any attention.

Jean Gabriel Monnet founded the brandy firm of J. G. Monnet & Co., groomed Jean and his brother Gaston to be his international salesmen. There was to be no nonsense of a university education for his sons. And in the local Cognac high school, Jean showed little intellectual promise anyway: he had, and still has, a poor memory, and floundered in the rote system of French instruction. At 18, Jean was sent off to Canada to peddle brandy in the raw Canadian boom towns of 1906 such as Calgary, Moose Jaw and Medicine Hat. He was pleasantly surprised by the absence of class barriers and the ingrained suspicions that so characterized the European mentality. One day in Calgary, while looking for a horse and buggy to rent, he came across a stranger hitching up his horse. When Monnet asked him the whereabouts of a livery stable, the man countered: "Can you ride?" Monnet said yes. "All right," said the man, "take my horse. When you're through, just hitch it up here." Monnet remembers it as his first lesson in pooling resources.

Matches and Railroads

When World War I started, Monnet was rejected for the French army because of a kidney ailment (nephritis), entered the French Ministry of Commerce as a junior official. At the time, France and Britain were bidding against each other for badly needed raw materials, despite the fact they were allies, and no one seemed to know what to do—except Monnet, who proposed an Anglo-French high commission to coordinate procurement and supplies. By war's end, Monnet had made such a brilliant impression in Paris and London that, though only 31, he was appointed Deputy Secretary-General of the League of Nations.

In 1923 Monnet left the League to come home and save the family brandy business, devastated by the war. In two short years he had it bubbling money again, then went wandering as an international banker and economic troubleshooter. He spent a year (1933–34) in Peking as financial adviser to the Chinese government, raised money to repair China's vast, decrepit railroad system. He opened a Wall Street brokerage house, made a fortune and lost it in the 1929 crash. The Polish government called him in to plan a currency reform it never carried out. The Swedish government appointed Monnet one of the liquidators of the complex, bankrupt Kreuger match empire.

Meanwhile, Monnet's personal life took an international turn. At a Paris dinner party in 1928, he met darkly handsome Silvia de Bondini, a painter and wife of an Italian diplomat. Silvia soon left her husband; after five years of trying to obtain an Italian divorce, she was whisked to Moscow by Monnet, for a quick Moscow divorce and wedding. The gay Gallic bachelor became a devoted family man (the Monnets have two grown daughters). At their home at Houjarray, some 20 miles west of Paris, he often talks through his notions with Silvia while she paints.

Worth the Gamble

As World War II started, France and Britain pressed Monnet back into his old World War I job of organizing their joint production and rearmament to meet the Nazi challenge. In London, during the big German offensive of June 1940, it was evident to Monnet that the French government would soon surrender, and in a desperate attempt to keep France in the war, he suggested one of the few impractical schemes of his career: the immediate unification of France and Great Britain. Monnet put it to De Gaulle, who agreed it was worth the gamble. Both men went to Churchill, and the result was Churchill's historic but futile "declaration of Franco-British Union." Monnet then flew to Bordeaux in a big Sunderland Flying-boat to try to evacuate the whole French Cabinet. The Cabinet refused to budge, for fear of being labeled cowardly *émigrés*. A disappointed Monnet returned to London with the flying-boat full of refugee families.

Winston Churchill thereupon endorsed Monnet's French passport personally, sent him to Washington to help coordinate Anglo-American war-supply planning. It was Monnet who conceived the idea of Lend-Lease. And it was Monnet who coined President Roosevelt's famous fireside-chat slogan: "We must be the great arsenal of democracy."

Long before the war ended, Monnet was planning ahead. In 1943 he went to Algiers to coordinate U.S. aid to Free French forces in North Africa. There, De Gaulle was orating almost daily about *"la grandeur française."* Monnet told him bluntly: "If you are not very careful, there will be no *grandeur*. We are a small country, we have been plundered, and our economic base has been largely destroyed. France may become a backwater of Europe." Grumbled De Gaulle: "Well, what do you propose?" In an incisive, seven-page memorandum, Monnet suggested rebuilding France's economy under the guidance of a central committee made up of representatives of labor and management and every French political party. The plan was put into effect in 1947, with Monnet as its chief until 1952; it has since grown into a permanent agency that still supervises the French economy as part of the Common Market.

Unfinished Business

For all their success, Monnet's institutions still have a long way to go toward his goal.

Despite Europe's growing international sentiment, old animosities remain, from the South Tyrol to Flanders, and might flare up again in time of stress. Economically, the biggest stumbling block so far to a fully integrated European economy is agriculture. Like the U.S., the Common Market nations together are nearly self-sufficient; they produce 90% of the wheat they consume, 70% of the feed grain, 92% of the sugar and 95% of the meat. They actually overproduce pork, potatoes and vegetables. And, as in the U.S., agriculture is everywhere highly protected with state subsidies and price supports.

Another bit of unfinished business consists of cracking down on Europe's notorious net of cartels. For the moment Europe's continuing boom, providing enough trade for everybody, has put the problem of the competition-restraining cartels far down on the priority list. Also, free movement of labor within the Market area is still more theoretical than real. The Community has provided migrant workers with comprehensive social security, but the age-old reluctance of workers to move persists, though Italian workers now provide more than 60% of the Belgian mining industry's labor force. The fact is, unemployment is so low all over the Community that few workers need to migrate. The Market's boom has even reduced chronically underemployed Italy's jobless total to a bare 800,000.

U.S. industry recognized the Market's potential from the start. U.S. corporations have been pouring capital into Europe at a record clip ($844 million in 1960 alone). And though the Common Market was expected to import fewer goods from the U.S., American exports to the six-nation area last year actually soared 42% (to $3.4 billion) over the 1959 level. In time, Common Market manufacturers, including U.S. subsidiaries, will undoubtedly supply a far higher proportion of the consumer goods, from plastic ice buckets to portable TV sets, that now come largely from the U.S. But the loss will be more than canceled out by rising sales of U.S.-made capital goods—sophisticated electronic control systems and specialized heavy machinery.

Six Plus What?

While the U.S. cooperated enthusiastically, Britain hesitated. But with last week's British move to join, the Common Market faces perhaps its greatest opportunity. Negotiations are likely to be long and difficult.

But if Britain comes in, much of the rest of Western Europe outside the Six is likely to follow. The result could be not only a true United States of Europe, but the creation of a mighty economic powerhouse dwarfing Russia in the world's industrial hierarchy.

As early as 1952, Monnet urged the British to join the Coal and Steel Community. Motivated by its historic aloofness from the Continent, as well as respect for its Commonwealth ties, Britain said no. The answer was the same when the Common Market was born in 1957. "We crushed Napoleon and his idea of European unity," snorted a Cabinet minister, "and we can do the same again." Britain's response to the Common Market was to assemble a rival-bloc European Free Trade Association— but with little enthusiasm, since Britain was convinced that the Common Market would never work. Its runaway success caused a painful about-face. While the Six's growth rate swelled, Britain's per capita output rise stayed at a stagnating 2%. As the Six traded more and more with one another, Britain's vital exports to the Continent declined. The vaunted Commonwealth relationship proved less and less profitable: trade between Britain and the Commonwealth nations has actually declined in the last five years.

Coming late with hat in hand, Britain is in poor position to do much bargaining with the Common Market. But it must try to get safeguards both for British farmers—more highly protected than even the Six's— and for its Commonwealth trading partners, whose agricultural products would be forced into competition with Europe's own. One after another, speakers at a Commonwealth Parliamentary Conference in London last week warned that British membership may even spell the end of the Commonwealth. Warned Laborite Emanuel Shinwell, one-time Minister of Defense: "We shall suffer disillusionment before many years are passed. We shall discover we have made a tragic mistake."

Within the Common Market, the main opposition to British membership comes from France, whose own colonies produce many of the same raw materials that are exported by the Commonwealth. There is suspicion also that Britain intends to reap the economic advantages of membership but resist political integration with the Continent. In fact, by overruling France's delaying tactics and welcoming Britain's application last week, the other Common Market countries recognized the wisdom of Jean Monnet's prophecy: "Once a Common Market interest has been created, then political union will come naturally."

Preaching Mission

Monnet continues with almost Pauline dedication to this gospel. Recently, one of the cutters at Monnet's London tailor, Lesley & Roberts, stopped while measuring him for a suit and said: "I hear you're connected with the Common Market idea. Can you explain what it's all about?" Monnet sat down and preached to the tailor for an hour.

More and more, preaching is his mission. Since 1955 he has been working full time as the apostle of European unity, at the head of his own private lobby called the Action Committee for a United States of

Europe—one of the most potent political pressure groups ever assembled. It is premised on Monnet's conviction, "In a democracy, the people who matter are the political parties and the trade unions," and the committee's membership reads like a *Who's Who* in European politics and labor. Thus when Monnet proposes an idea, the governments of the Six know it already has the backing of an impressive group of politicians and labor leaders. His most recent proposal: a plan for a European monetary reserve fund, leading eventually to a common, single European currency.

Ahead is an even greater dream—an Atlantic Community in which the U.S. and Europe will be full partners. No one realizes better than Monnet the meaning of such an Atlantic union for the fractious, fragmenting world, chaos-riven as it is from the East River to Elisabethville, from Berlin to Namone. "Union is not an end in itself," says Monnet. "It is the beginning on the road to the more orderly world we must have in order to escape destruction. The partnership of Europe and the United States should create a new force for peace."

WORLD BENEFITS FROM EFTA*

It can be demonstrated that a great deal of the increased trade and prosperity in the Atlantic area has been due directly to liberal trade policies in Western Europe and in the United States. In this country, you have been accustomed for centuries to a single large market and your production and service industries have from the beginning been built on that basis. During all that period Western Europe consisted of many fragmented markets, for the most part confined to the populations living within national borders. Speaking in concrete terms, you have to remember that even ten years ago the countries which now make up the Common Market and the European Free Trade Area were split into 14 separate national markets. Now these have been reduced to two, the first with a population of 180 million and the second with 100 million people. This means that ten years ago, to give one example, the Norwegian manufacturer had a home market of a little more than 3 million people; now his home market is 100 million, a totally different proposition. In creating these large markets, of course, we are paying the U.S. the compliment of copying your example.

The biggest gains our member countries have made from free trade have naturally been inside the new market. The EFTA countries' trade with each other is now almost three times what it was ten years ago. Whereas in 1959 that trade was $3½ billion in each direction, this year it will be about $10 billion in each direction. In the ten years before EFTA was created, trade between the countries concerned grow at just over 3% a year. Since EFTA began, trade amongst them has increased by more than 11% a year.

In the face of this real life experience of the benefits of free trade it

---

* Excerpts from Sir John Coulson's speech to the American Importer's Association in New York on December 5, 1969. *EFTA Reporter,* December 10, 1969, p. 3.

is really a little difficult to listen seriously to protectionist arguments. Ten years ago there was considerable anxiety among industrialists in the various EFTA countries. They feared the destruction of whole industries and even whole regions. Accustomed to protection, they insisted that the EFTA Treaty should contain an escape clause so that governments could reimpose trade restrictions to save hard-hit industries from catastrophe. Nothing of the kind has happened. The escape clause has never been used. Even the most vulnerable industries in EFTA have found that they can stand up to open competition by specializing in the production of those goods for which they have the right combination of advantages.

Perhaps the best testimony that free trade helps without hurting was provided by an investigation which we carried out in EFTA more than a year ago. At the request of the trades unions, a close investigation was made to see if the labor force had been adversely affected by the dismantling of trade barriers in EFTA. The report from every country was the same, that no industries could be found where labor had lost jobs or earnings as a result of increased imports from other members of the Area. Indeed, real earnings in EFTA have risen fairly steadily through the whole period of the dismantling of barriers to trade.

Your country has been one of the main indirect beneficiaries of free trade in EFTA. Our imports from the United States were valued at $4.1 billion last year, a rise of almost 120% on the 1959 figure. In fact, surprisingly enough, the EFTA countries have increased their imports from you more than from their neighbors in the Common Market. You have improved your share of our markets from 9% to 10½% over the past decade. You have also improved your balance of trade with us, because EFTA exports to the United States have risen 95% compared to the 120% rise of your exports to us.

The larger EFTA market has been of particular interest to certain groups of American exporters. For example, U.S. machinery and transport equipment has increased its sales in the EFTA countries four-and-a-half times since 1959; as a result EFTA is now a net importer of that equipment from the United States, whereas in 1959 it was a net exporter. The sales of the U.S. chemical industry to EFTA have grown two-and-a-half times and sales of miscellaneous manufactures have quadrupled.

But the benefits of EFTA to the United States are not limited to these large increases in trade. It is ironical that American corporations were quicker to take advantage of the new dimensions than their European counterparts. Being already organized to operate on a continental scale, it was natural for U.S. industries to move into the big markets of Western Europe by establishing production subsidiaries. In 1960 U.S. direct investment in Western Europe was less than $7 billion. By 1968 it was almost $20 billion—and that figure does not include another $5 billion of portfolio investment.

In other words, in the past decade hundreds of U.S. corporations have established production and sales networks in both the Common Market and EFTA. Whereas U.S. trade with Europe has doubled since 1960,

U.S. investment has trebled and the European production of U.S. corporations now exceeds their exports to Europe by a considerable margin.

QUESTIONS

1. Elaborate on the problems and benefits for international marketers from multinational market groups.
2. Explain the political role of multinational market groups. Identify the factors on which one may judge the potential success or failure of a multinational market group.
3. Explain the marketing implications of the factors contributing to the successful development of a multinational market group.
4. Imagine that the United States was composed of many separate countries with individual trade barriers. What marketing effects might one visualize?
5. Discuss the possible types of arrangements for regional economic integration.
6. Differentiate between a free-trade area and a common market. Explain the marketing implication of the differences.
7. It seems indeed obvious that the founders of the European Common Market intended it to be a truly common market; so much so that economic integration must obviously be supplemented by political integration in order to accomplish these (Common Market) objectives completely. Discuss.
8. Select any three countries which might have some logical basis for establishing a multinational market organization (such as Canada, U.S. and Mexico). Identify the various problems which would be encountered in forming multinational market groups of such countries.
9. U.S. exports to the European Common Market are expected to decline in future years. What marketing actions may a company take to counteract such changes?
10. "Because they are dynamic and because they have great growth possibilities, the multinational markets are likely to be especially rough and tumble for the external businessman." Discuss.
11. Differentiate between a full customs union and a political union.
12. Define:
    OECD
    Zollverein
    Commonwealth

Readings

1. "Europe: 'Then Will It Live . . .'" was written when the European Common Market was still somewhat of a dream. How has this dream fared in the intervening years?
2. Discuss Jean Monnet's role in establishing ECM. Could it be said to be the work of one man?
3. Monnet once prophesied, "Once a common market has been created then political union will come naturally." Comment.

OUTLINE OF CHAPTER 10

WORLD MARKETS FOR CONSUMER GOODS

INTRODUCTION

Dynamic changes are being brought about in world markets as a result of rapid growth in productive ability. Industrialization, urbanization, rising productivity, higher incomes, mass production, and technological progress in Japan, Western Europe, Mexico and many other countries of the world are creating an atmosphere that is described by some as a world consumer revolution. For an increasing number of people of the world, more and more purchasing decisions are prompted by a desire for the "good life" rather than simple need. The net result is that markets around the world not only are different from a marketer's domestic experience but are in such a state of dynamic change that old "truths" are no longer valid. Instant tortilla meal is consumed in Guatemala, hotdogs and hamburgers in France; supermarkets are displacing the specialty store and market vendor in some countries; and Japanese products are being praised for craftsmanship, quality, and originality.

Intended for American firms, the statement below from a *Japan Times'* promotional brochure illustrates what is occurring in some world consumer markets.

The Japanese way of living is now undergoing a great change—a change resulting from the high economic growth rate and the subsequent rise in the standard of living.

The change is taking place everywhere in Japan, even in the remotest part of the country. The phenomenon may be described as a process of transformation of the Japanese way of living into the Western Way.

Mt. Fuji, geisha, and samurai symbolized Japan of over a century ago. Foreign visitors nowadays will see TV aerials wherever they go in Japan. If they look into Japanese homes, they will see an electric washing machine, electric toaster, electric fan, electric or gas heaters, cameras and other such modern products in almost every home. And the kimono is worn only for special occasions, such as holidays and parties.[1]

---

[1] "Survey on Imported Goods," *The Japan Times*, Report #4, January, 1964 (No. 1, 1-chrome, Uchisaiwaicho, Chiyoda-ku, Tokyo, Japan.)

While the above statement may suffer from the customary puffery of advertising, great strides in consumer goods ownership have occurred in Japan. For example, ownership of washing machines increased from 63.3 percent of the households to 85 percent. Electric refrigerator owners jumped from 45 percent to 84 percent and television ownership from 90.9 percent to 96.7 percent.[2] Further, by 1970, Japan was the third largest economy in the world, and, if present trends continue, predictions are that it will be "the world's most affluent nation by the end of the century."[3]

Old stereotypes, traditions, and habits are being cast aside entirely or tempered, and new patterns of consumer behavior are emerging. Indeed, the international marketer operating without benefit of recent market research and relying upon stereotypes or stale knowledge of market traits is faced with the uncertain task of sorting fact from fiction about the market characteristics in other countries.

Continual and rapid changes are so much the rule in today's consumer markets that it is essential for change to be recognized and viewed in its proper perspective. An important fact about the transformation of consumer behavior is that it is not occurring at a uniform rate throughout the world, nor is the character of the change necessarily the same. The foreign marketer is faced typically with at least two common problems: one, the foreign market will differ from the home market; and, two, the market generally will be in a dynamic flux, with changes occurring much more rapidly than is typical for the U.S. market. All markets are constantly changing, but the change that is experienced in many foreign countries can be more drastic and erratic than will usually be found in the United States or any other mature economy. For example, in just over 10 years, automobile ownership in EEC countries has risen from 1 in 10 people owning a car to 1 in 6.[4]

Consumer life styles are frequently altered as a country's economy moves from one level of economic development to another, and the resultant impact upon market characteristics is often sudden, causing rapid change in degree and/or kind. In many instances markets for a product seem to develop overnight and grow with the rapidity often associated with fads. Failure to heed these differences and their implications can end in costly disappointment. Business annals have recorded many marketing failures which can be attributed to the lack of understanding of differences in market characteristics both at home and abroad.

Just as it is necessary to know as much as possible about the needs of customers at home and how best to satisfy them, so also is this knowledge essential for foreign markets. Precise information about foreign markets is of particular importance because there are frequent

---

[2] Mitsuru Inuta, "Japan Consumer Market Ever Changing and Growing," *Industrial Japan,* October 1969, p. 125.

[3] James C. Abegglen, "The Economic Growth of Japan," *Scientific American,* March 1970, p. 31.

[4] "A Common Market Eleven Years After: Still Promises?" *Sales Management,* February 1, 1969, p. 37.

differences in one or more essential market parts and because the marketer's personal knowledge is less reliable. Nevertheless, if the marketer is fully aware of the peculiarities of a particular market, selling abroad need not involve any greater risk than selling at home. Unfortunately, despite all the evidence in support of thorough market analyses when entering a foreign market, one of the seemingly easier methods resorted to is to rely upon stereotypes of consumer market behavior or to assume that each new market is the same as the marketer's country; i.e., if the product sells in Dallas, it will sell in Tokyo or Berlin.

There are universal similarities in wants; as income increases, practically everyone desires the good life, as characterized by consumer goods. At the same time, it must be recognized by the marketer that when crossing from one culture to another, separate characteristics of nationality and stages of economic and industrial development determine consumer behavior to a great extent. Therefore, even though everyone seeks the good life, each group's interpretation of the good life as reflected in consumer behavior is anchored heavily in cultural heritage. This is why consumer behavior in France is different in many respects from consumer behavior in Canada, even when personal incomes and purchasing power are similar. In many countries, the ultimate in affluence is achieved when a family has reached the standard of living experienced in the United States.

It is with such economies as those of Japan, West Germany, France, and Mexico, which have rapidly increasing standards of living, that this chapter will be concerned. The primary objective is to explore the world customer and the market he creates. A discussion of rising incomes, which are the basis for much of the dynamic change and increasing market potential, will be followed by product strategy and development methods. Some common pitfalls facing the international marketer will be discussed, along with significant trends in the consumer behavior of the affluent people of the world.

MARKET GROWTH AND POTENTIAL

In recent years more and more people in foreign countries have received greater income that is being used to satisfy an ever-increasing list of wants and needs. Markets are people with needs and wants and the means to satisfy these wants. Increased wealth in some countries has created new markets and sparked trends in behavior parallel to the U.S. experience. These new markets and behavior trends are changing the socioeconomic structure of these countries to such an extent that they will never again be the same.

Growth in Different Economies

Increases in world opulence are spotty; not every country has a better than subsistence income, nor are all countries gaining at the same rate. Mexico, a rapidly developing but still relatively underdeveloped economy, offers different market opportunities than the more

EXHIBIT 10-1

Economic Growth in Selected Countries, 1963-68

Country	National Income						Private Consumption	
	Total 1968 ($ billions)	% Change (in current prices) 1963-68	Per Capita 1968 ($)	% Change (in current prices) 1963-68	GNP 1968 ($ billions)	% Change (in constant prices) 1962-67	1968 ($ billions)	% Change (in constant prices) 1963-68
Belgium-Luxembourg	16.48†	49.3	1,655†	39.3	21.7	23.7†	14.0	43.0†
France	86.36	58.3	1,730	36.1	126.6	27.1	77.1	49.4
Germany	109.84	39.6	1,826	40.6	132.2	19.2	74.3	37.6
Italy	60.61	56.8	1,149	64.6	74.8	25.8	47.6	54.2
Netherlands	20.55	73.7	1,612	63.7	25.2	27.6	14.2	62.6
Greece	5.70¶	54.5§	645¶	55.0	7.6	44.9	5.2	44.4
Turkey	10.63	61.9	317	60.1	11.6	38.1	7.9	44.7§
Austria	8.46	43.1	1,151	41.1	11.4	22.0	6.8	40.2
Denmark*	9.52	65.7	1,955	54.1	12.4	22.2	7.8	64.8
Norway	6.90	59.5	1,807	53.1	9.0	27.6	4.9	47.0
Portugal	4.33	68.2	456	72.7	5.0	35.2	3.7	59.5
Sweden	22.32	59.4	2,821	56.1	25.6	36.9	14.1	47.9
Switzerland	14.35	45.9	2,412	51.7	17.2	20.2	9.9	41.7
U.K.*	79.44	34.0	1,437	10.9	102.1	17.4	64.8	33.7
Finland*	5.58	42.8	1,190	15.6	8.0	19.2	4.5	56.0
Iceland*	0.35¶	67.4§	n.a.	n.a.	0.4¶	24.7	0.3¶	75.3§
Ireland*	2.35	49.3	809	21.8	3.0	17.3	20.4	41.7
Spain*	21.68	84.1	669	94.4	25.2	103.2	17.8	85.5

*Currency devalued in last five years.
† Belgium only.
§ 4-year increase.
¶ 1967.
Source: *Business Europe*, January 2, 1970, pp. 4–5.

stable and more mature economies of Western Europe, or the highly volatile economy of the world's newest industrial nation, Japan. Each of these areas is experiencing a disparate rate of economic growth and offers unique market potentials and varied degrees of market saturation. Nevertheless, as economies grow, purchasing power and demands for a variety of consumer goods increase, creating marketing opportunities for the astute marketer.

Western Europe. Countries in Western Europe offer an example of what happens to demand for consumer goods when personal incomes rise. Exhibit 10–1 shows that during the period between 1963 and 1968 per capita income in most European countries increased considerably; many experienced more than a 50 percent increase in this five-year period. Since incomes rose at a faster rate than retail prices, there was a net increase in purchasing power; the result was a substantial rise in demand for consumer goods previously considered luxuries. For example, between 1958 and 1968 ownership of automobiles in Germany increased from 5 out of 100 people to 18 out of 100, and television ownership rose from 4 out of 100 people to 24 out of 100.[5] Exhibit 10–2

EXHIBIT 10–2

German Standard of Living, 1958–68

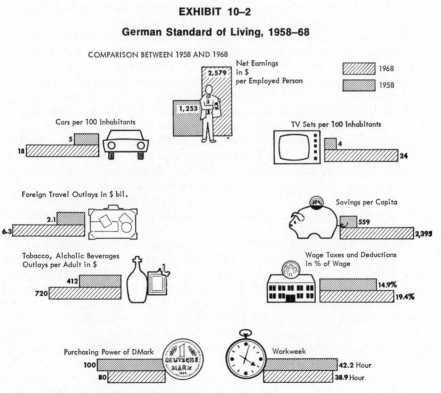

Source: *German American Trade News,* April, 1969, p. 10.

[5] Heinz Pentzlin, "German Economic Perspectives, Fact and Fiction," *German American News,* April 1969, p. 10.

BOX 10–1

Mass Market for Mexico?

For Juan Davila Castillo, a thirty-three year old Mexican machinist, life is good these days. He earns only forty-eight dollars a week at the new Volkswagen factory near Puebla, but he often works enough overtime (up to thirty-six hours) to take home eighty dollars. He and his family recently moved into a modest house in a new development; he owns a refrigerator, a T.V., a stereo console—and there is space inside his gate for a new car.

Davila is doing better than most Mexicans his age, but he is representative of a new prosperity that has brought business in Mexico to the take-off point. Production has climbed steadily through this decade. Now the payoff is coming: mass purchasing power in a country that until recently was considered underdeveloped.

Source: "A Jumping Market below the Border," *Business Week,* July 12, 1969, p. 120. Reprinted from July 12, 1969 issue of *Business Week* by special permission. Copyrighted 1969 by McGraw-Hill, Inc.

shows some other interesting facts on how the German standard of living changed in the 10 years between 1958 and 1968.

While the decade of the sixties in Western Europe was good, the outlook for the seventies is even more impressive. Gross national product is expected to grow at a 4 percent rate, which means that by 1978, Europe's GNP will be close to one trillion dollars, a market the size of the United States in 1970.[6] Further, disposable income of private households is expected to grow at an annual rate of 7 percent, amounting to $3,700 per head in 1985, compared to $1,110 in 1965.[7]

Steadily rising incomes provide the purchasing power that enables consumers to acquire goods in increasing numbers. Thus, as consumers become wealthier, sales of durable goods and services will profit most. For the more advanced countries, key manifestations of today's consumer affluence are automobiles and household consumer durables; their possession means comfort, entertainment, and a new way of life for those who can afford them.

Mexico.   Contrasted with Western Europe, Mexico presents an entirely different economic picture. Though the economy has grown at an average annual rate of better than 6 percent since 1960, annual per capita incomes remained only $479 in 1968.[8] In 1969, it was estimated that 47 percent of Mexican families had a monthly income of $89, compared with 33 percent in 1963;[9] there is an increasing number of families sharing the wealth. Even though the income is low when compared to countries of Europe, the impact of this increased wealth is

---

[6] *Business Europe,* January 16, 1970, p. 19.

[7] Ibid., p. 18.

[8] *Indicators of Market Size for 135 Countries,* (reprinted; New York: Business International Corporation, 1969).

[9] "A Jumping Market below the Border," *Business Week,* July 12, 1969, p. 121.

nevertheless impressive. A recent study found that "13% of Mexican families own a car, 20% have a washing machine, 25% a refrigerator, 43% a blender, and 67% a radio."[10] In fact, a 12 percent to 16 percent annual rate of increase has been common for many of these products. One study showed that between 1960 and 1968 annual auto sales rose from 28,000 to more than 100,000. During the same time span, the production of TV sets nearly quadrupled to 375,000, and refrigerator output more than tripled to 160,000.[11] Listed below is the annual rate of growth experienced for a selected group of durables and nondurables during the late 1960s.[12]

Durables		*Nondurables*	
Automobiles	18%	Cosmetics	11%
TV sets	40	Soft drinks	7
Refrigerators	11½	Shoes	4½
Gas stoves	11½	Evaporated milk	11½

As in Europe, the outlook for the 1970's will be impressive, with forecasters predicting a per capita income of $1,000 by 1980. While income is low by U.S. or European standards, Mexico's continued economic growth will mean increased purchasing power and an ever larger consumer goods market.

Japan. As a market Japan presents yet a different set of opportunities. As Exhibit 10–3 shows, the rate of growth of the Japanese economy has been considerably better than that of West Germany, France, Britain, or Italy, and the forecast for growth through 1975 is even more encouraging. The rising incomes and improved standard of living have produced a consumption-oriented middle class with changing habits of diet, dress, use of leisure time, and consumption of luxuries. In 1968, Japanese consumers spent $69 billion, a 14 percent increase over 1967; and increases were projected to be near 14 percent in 1969. The net result is a tremendous demand for almost all kinds of consumer items, from leisure goods to Western style clothes and readymade apparel. A recent report indicated that the diffusion rate of durable consumer goods (see Exhibit 10–4) has been rapid and many items are reaching the level of ownership found in the United States. The demand for consumer goods is so high that all but 10 to 12 percent of Japan's total industrial output is consumed by the Japanese. In fact, contrary to the popularly held opinion that Japan's economic growth is the result of exports,

Japan exports less of its production than most industrialized countries: 10 to 12% of its total output, about half as much as West Germany and Britain. Indeed, the success of Japanese companies in the export market grows out of high domestic demand. In manufacturers from umbrella frames to motorcycles the initial growth has taken place to supply a rapidly expand-

---

[10] Ibid., p. 120.

[11] Ibid., p. 120.

[12] "Selling Opportunities in Mexico's Emerging National Markets," *Business Abroad,* February 1969, p. 29.

EXHIBIT 10–3

Gross National Product, Japan and Selected Countries, 1958–75

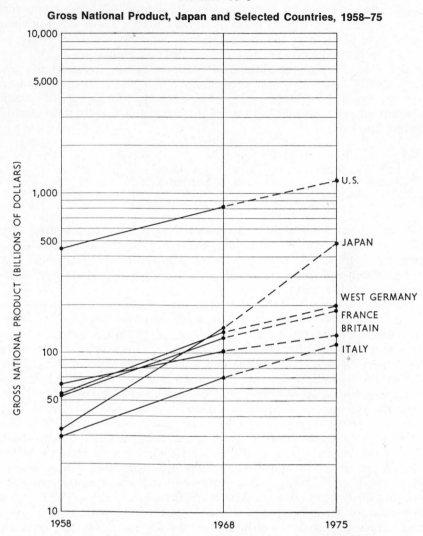

Source: "The Economic Growth of Japan," *Scientific American*, March 1970, p. 34.

ing domestic market, with the export thrust following three to five years later.[13]

The average Japanese urban family has an estimated disposable income of $2,387, which, although a relatively low dollar amount, permits a living standard equal to many in Western Europe.[14] For, in addition to rising income, Japanese employers often provide their em-

---

[13] Abegglen, op. cit., p. 31. Copyright © 1970 by Scientific American, Inc. All rights reserved.

[14] Inuta, op. cit., p. 129.

EXHIBIT 10–4

Ownership of Consumer Durable Goods, Japanese Families, 1964 and 1968

	Households Possessing		% Change 1964–68
	February 1964	February 1968	
Television sets...................	90.9	96.7	6.3
Electric washing machines.........	66.3	85.0	28.2
Electric refrigerators..............	45.2	84.0	85.8
Electric fans.....................	58.7	80.1	36.5
Oil stoves.......................	33.0	66.7	102.1
Electric cleaners.................	32.8	59.8	82.3
Carpets..........................	....	35.3	....
Stainless sinks...................	11.1	33.5	201.8
Motor cars......................	2.8	14.0	400.0
Color T.V. sets..................	...	3.9	....
Air conditioners.................	0.4	2.2	450.0
Sewing machines.................	80.0	83.6	4.5
Cameras........................	53.1	66.2	24.7
Tape recorders..................	9.4	26.0	176.6
Pianos..........................	3.3	6.4	93.9

Source: "Japan Consumer Market Ever Changing and Growing," *Industrial Japan*, October 1969, p. 125.

EXHIBIT 10–5

Market Growth in Selected Countries (1968)

Country	Telephones in Use Jan. 1967 (000)	TV Sets in Use		Passenger Cars in Use	
		1967 (000)	5-Year Increase (%)	Jan. 1 1968 (000)	5-Year Increase (%)
U.S...............	98,446	74,800	29	84,400	29
France...........	6,554	7,998	133	10,465	59
Germany.........	9,532	13,404	86	11,293	69
Italy.............	6,468	7,509	117	7,370	145
Netherlands.......	2,513	2,517	97	1,800	140
U.K.............	11,376	14,776	21	10,555	61
India............	961	7*	1,650	442	38
Japan............	16,012	19,625	56	3,836	380
Argentina........	1,527	1,705	101	1,152	106
Brazil...........	1,432	3,000	110	1,359	84
Mexico...........	931	1,860	100	891	65
Venezuela........	309	650	18	476	53
Ghana...........	36	1	100†	33	39
Kenya...........	57	14	536	82	11‡
Nigeria..........	75	52	420	76	52
Zambia..........	38	10	33	46	15§

* 1,000 in schools and village centers.
† 2-year increase.
‡ 4-year increase.
§ 3-year increase.
Source: *Indicators of Market Size for 135 Countries* (reprint ed., New York: Business International Corporation, 1969.)

ployees with many fringe benefits, including such fringes as free or partially subsidized housing, transportation, lunches, medical assistance, recreation facilities, and even family vacation resorts; furthermore, company-owned stores sell goods at discount prices to employees. These factors help boost the average amount of discretionary income to levels higher than the dollar amount reflects. Signs of prosperity are everywhere.

Even though household goods purchases have grown steadily with rising income for the last decade for all three of these markets, market saturation[15] of key consumer goods is far from being reached. If U.S. standards of ownership are used for comparison, it is evident that even Europe's market for many durables has barely been touched. Although the examples presented were selected from rapidly industrializing countries, similar patterns of consumer behavior can be found in other countries that are experiencing rising incomes and increasing affluence.

Measuring Consumer Purchasing Power

Most of the free world is experiencing some degree of economic growth, although personal incomes are not increasing in all countries at the same spectacular rates found in Japan and Western Europe. Income growth is not uniform in all countries nor have most countries approached the levels found in the United States, but the impact of steadily increasing income does have appreciable effect on market potential. With income increases, however slight, come significant changes in purchasing patterns. In fact, consumption-income relationships appear to follow Engel's laws on consumption. Engel's laws as interpreted for modern economies state:

1. As a family's income increases, the percentage spent on food will decrease.
2. As a family's income increases, the percentage spent on housing and household operations will be roughly constant (with the exception of fuel, light and refrigeration, which will decrease).
3. As a family's income increases, the percentage spent on all other categories and the amount saved will increase (with the exception of medical care and personal care items, which are fairly constant).

Support for the applicability of Engel's law can be found in both European behavior and in lesser developed areas. After extensive study of South African consumers, one noted authority stated that the "native buying patterns did follow Engel's law and that as income increased

---

[15] If it is assumed that each consumer or consuming unit, e.g., a household within a market has a need for a product, then market saturation is that point where 100 percent of the consumers or households own the product. At this point, market growth would be dependent solely upon the replacement or the acquiring of two or more of the product and the normal growth that would result from population increases and/or new family formations.

above a certain level, the African consumer spent relatively less on staples and relatively more on luxuries, such as gaudy clothing, radios, flashlights, and beer."[16]

Even with increasing incomes, the majority of people in the world are quite poor; however, this does not mean that no profitable markets exist in those areas where per capita income is very low. Thus, using only national per capita wealth as a gauge of market potential can result in disregarding otherwise profitable markets for some consumer goods. Gross national product is perhaps the most frequently used measure of potential because it is often the only measure of wealth available. It must, however, be employed with caution as a measure of market potential, since the method of calculation can often lead to inaccurate impressions when widely diverse economies are being examined.

Private Production. One point that should be included in evaluating GNP figures is the private production of goods for family consumption; i.e., family gardens and other food production which are not generally incorporated in GNP calculations. Thus, a low per capita income may be representative of a higher purchasing power since less income is spent for such items as food and clothing. As one authority points out about South African consumers:

> Average income of native workers is very low, ranging from $250 to $300 or even $1,500 a year, which is considered a very good income. This is better than it sounds, because nature is so bountiful that the native can live off the land with little trouble and little cash.[17]

The Family as a Purchasing Unit. It must also be kept in mind that the purchasing unit is the family rather than the individual; thus, income per family unit may be more revealing as a gauge of market potential than per capita figures. In Latin America, conservative estimates indicate that the average family unit is composed of five persons, so the relatively low per capita GNP of $402 in 1961 is, in terms of family purchasing units, over $2,000 per year.

Stage of Economic Development. In earlier discussions concerning stages of economic development, it was shown that some types of consumer goods were in great demand in the poorest underindustrialized countries because the need for certain products existed, but there were either no production facilities or very limited ones within the country. All these local elements should be evaluated along with GNP before a market is ruled out as unimportant.

Unevenly Developed World Markets. In economies which undergo rapid growth, it is not unusual for the economic development to be uneven; whereas in a comparable economy that has a slower growth rate, the development would be more uniform. Ownership of consumer goods and life styles associated with a particular degree of economic development may in fact not be found in those economies that have attained their affluency rapidly. In such instances the usual standard of living

---

[16] "South African Consumer Is Like U.S. Counterpart, Professor Reports," *Advertising Age,* October 21, 1963, p. 129.

[17] Ibid.

BOX 10-2

Factory Workers Worktime Cost of Selected Consumer Goods

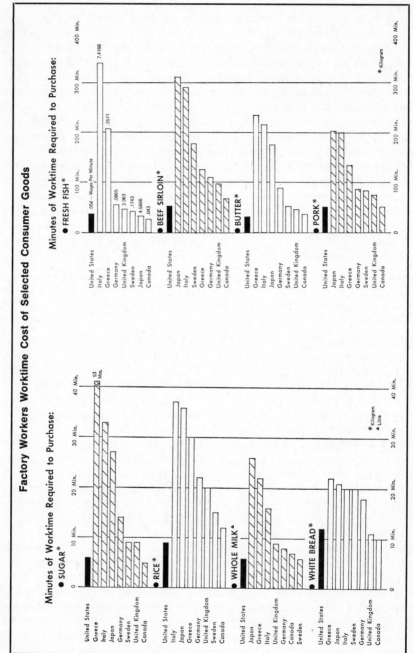

Source: National Industrial Conference Board, Inc., Road Maps of Industry No. 1645.

measures may be completely inoperative. For example, in France per 100 households there are only 15 bathrooms with a bathtub or shower. If this percentage is used as a measure of the living standards in France, it would have to be presumed that France is a very backward country; yet, if automobile ownership is used as the criterion, France emerges as one of the most developed countries in the world.[18] The deviations from the expected that result from uneven growth are many. In a country where television ownership approaches the point of saturation, one might assume that ownership of a necessary appliance like a refrigerator would be equally as high. Yet in England, where 80 percent of the households had a television set in 1961, only 28 percent had a refrigerator. Since inconsistencies of this nature are numerous in the ever-expanding world markets, it is imperative that a marketer be certain that his measures of development and methods for forecasting potential be re-examined in light of the circumstances present in the anticipated market area.

PRODUCT DEVELOPMENT FOR INTERNATIONAL MARKETING

As countries become more affluent, demand develops for more and different kinds of products, thereby creating opportunities for the world marketer. For most firms, product development consists simply of adapting already domestically successful products to the needs of a foreign consumer. Unfortunately, adaptation frequently means selling what is produced for the domestic market in the same manner it is sold at home, disregarding all but the most obvious differences in market requirements. Journals are replete with the sad histories of companies which have followed this rather naïve policy. The marketer's self-reference criterion (SRC) is perhaps the most difficult obstacle to overcome in product development. If a product is successful in the domestic market, then why shouldn't it also be successful in another? Most of the effort expended and the time required to achieve domestic market acceptance is ignored when a company goes into a foreign market.

A product that has done well in the U.S. for twenty-five years goes to Europe and flops. A dismayed management wonders why, forgetting that those twenty-five years of developing and adapting the product, gaining public confidence, and building a name all took place on U.S. soil, not in Europe. Why should Europeans tumble overnight? Although, those twenty-five growing years may safely be telescoped to five when a product goes to Europe, they can't be skipped entirely.[19]

Small firms as well as giant corporations can be guilty of such costly oversights. Indeed, the most spectacular failures are often found among the giants.

One example of this is an undisputed American leader in cake mixes

---

[18] "Business around the Globe," *Fortune*, November 1962, p. 82.

[19] "How Not to Make a Killing in Europe," *Sales Management*, February 1, 1969, p. 30. Reprinted by permission from *Sales Management, The Marketing Magazine.* Copyright, 1969, Sales Management, Inc.

BOX 10–3

Marketing with an English Accent

You can score a smashing success in the United Kingdom while marketing one product with U.S. techniques and fall on your face with the next, according to Peter B. Warner, the new international marketing director of Quaker Oats Company. "We have language in common with the English, but that doesn't mean selling methods and products can be transferred as easily across the Atlantic as across state borders," says Warner, a tall, spare, graying man in his middle years. "Some things don't go over for reasons that seem mysterious at first." He cites two Quaker Oats examples. "Instant Quaker Oats was successful from the start, just as it was here," he says. "The English housewife responded beautifully to its taste as well as to our advertising and merchandising. She didn't, however, take at all to Captain Crunch, a breakfast cereal that's a winner here. One reason, probably, is child appeal. We sell the youngster on demanding Captain Crunch. English consumers are not nearly as child oriented. Kids don't make the buying decisions, Mama does."

Source: Reprinted by permission from *Sales Management, The Marketing Magazine,* February 1, 1969, p. 39. Copyright, 1969, Sales Management, Inc.

which tacitly admitted failure in the English market by closing down operations after five unsuccessful years. Taking its most successful mixes in the U.S. market, the company introduced them into the British market. A considerable amount of time, money, and effort was expended to introduce its variety of cake mixes to this new market. With benefit of hindsight several probable causes can be seen for the company's failure. Traditionalism was certainly among the most important. The British eat most of their cake with tea instead of dinner and have always preferred dry sponge cake, which is easy to handle; the fancy iced cakes favored in the United States were the type introduced. Fancy, iced cakes are accepted in Britain, but they are generally considered extra special and purchased from a bakery or made with much effort and care at home. The company introduced what they thought to be an "easy" cake mix. The "easy" cake mix was considered a slight to housewifely duties. Housewives felt guilty about not even cracking an egg, and there was suspicion that dried eggs and milk were just not as good as fresh ones. Therefore, when the occasion called for a fancy cake, an "easy" cake mix was simply not good enough. Ironically, this same company had faced almost identical problems, which they eventually overcame, when introducing "new" easy cake mixes on the U.S. market about 15 years earlier. There was initial concern about the quality of mixes and the resulting effect on the housewife's reputation as a baker. Even today there remains the feeling that "scratch" cakes are of special quality and significance and should be made for those extra-important occasions. This, in spite of the fact that the uniform quality of results from almost all mixes and the wide variety of flavors far exceeds the baking ability of a majority of housewives.

BOX 10–4

Avoiding Brand-Name Bloopers Overseas

ARA, ARAS, ARAT. A Latin verb conjugation? Not on your life! These are three of the computer non-words that Esso Chemical Company has collected for the arduous task of selecting brand names for new products distributed around the world. . . . It's far from easy to pick a product brand name, for the appropriate word in one language could prove scandalous in another one. . . . For example, Esso can market its fertilizer Engro any place in the world except French-speaking countries, for a possible association with the words en gros (in effect—I can get some "cheap") forced a modification. In French speaking countries, the name Engro becomes Enagros.

A Southern leather preservatives manufacturer had a similar problem when he planned to market his line in the Common Market countries under the name Drek. The manufacturer, who had selected the name because it "sounded virile," changed his mind, however, when he discovered that in German it means "dirt."

Customs foreign to U.S. businessmen can cause other complications, which make the task of selecting an overseas brand name or advertising slogan a tedious and often risky task. After portraying his product on a lady-lovely with a statue of Buddha in the background, a ladies' footwear manufacturer/exporter found that in Southeast Asia, where feet are regarded as most indelicate parts of the human body, to show one's soles while sitting is considered grossly discourteous. The indelicate advertising was considered a religious affront, and the blooper brought bushels of anti-American propaganda.

In India, however, where fourteen official languages can complicate almost any communication, Esso solves a brand marketing problem by emphasis on a trade mark instead of a name. The company uses an elephant along with the familiar Esso oval to identify its kerosene—but the company had to be very careful to depict an elephant of obvious Indian ancestry rather than an African species.

Source: Reprinted by special permission from the July 24, 1967, issue of *Business Abroad*, p. 17. Copyrighted © 1967 by The Reuben H. Donnelley Corporation.

The problems of adapting a product to sell abroad are similar to the ones associated with the introduction of a new product at home. Standard or regular items in a domestic market are sometimes entirely new in a foreign market. Products are not measured solely in terms of their physical specifications; the nature of the new is in what it does to and for the customer—"to his habits, his tastes, and his patterns of life."[20]

What significance, outside of the intended use, might a product have in a different culture? When product acceptance requires changes in patterns of life, habits, tastes, the understanding of new ideas, the acceptance of the difficult to believe, or the acquisition of completely new tastes or habits, special emphasis must be used to overcome natural resistance to change.

---

[20] Chester Wason, "What Is New about a New Product?" *Journal of Marketing*, July 1960, pp. 52–56.

A foreign marketer cannot take the steps necessary to assure the success of his operation unless he fully appreciates the "newness" of a product to a foreign consumer, i.e., how people react to newness and whether or not a product is new to the market. There are different degrees of newness, and an important first step in adapting a product to a foreign market is to determine the degree of newness perceived by the intended market; a second factor of importance is the characteristics of an innovation and how these characteristics affect acceptance. Each helps to explain how the consumer reacts to a new product and the time it takes to accept different, new products. It is with this understanding that better product strategies can be developed for international markets.

Old Products as Innovations

Many products which are successful in the United States and have reached the maturity or even decline stage in their life cycle may be perceived as new in another country or culture and thus must be treated as innovations. From a sociological viewpoint any idea perceived as new by a group of people is an innovation. Whether or not a group accepts an innovation and the time it takes for the adoption of an innovation depend upon its characteristics. Products new to a social system are innovations and knowledge about the diffusion (i.e., the process by which innovation spreads) of innovations is helpful in developing a successful product strategy.

Successful new product diffusion is dependent upon the communication of relevant product information and the matching of new product attributes, the social system, and individual consumer attributes. Marketing strategies can guide and control to a considerable extent the rate and extent of the new product diffusion.[21]

A critical factor in the newness of a product is its effect upon established patterns of consumption and behavior. In the cake mix example above, the fancy iced cake mix was a product that required acceptance of the "difficult to believe," i.e., dried eggs and milk are as good in cake as the fresh products; and of the "acquisition of new ideas," i.e., easy-to-bake fancy cakes are not a slight to one's housewifely integrity. In this case, two important aspects of consumer behavior were directly affected by the product and the product innovation met with sufficient resistance to convince the company to leave the market. Had the company studied their target market before introducing their product, perhaps they could have avoided the failure. Another U.S. cake mix company did enter the British market but carefully eliminated most of the newness of their product. Instead of introducing the most popular American cake mixes, the company asked 500 British housewives to bake their favorite cake. Since the majority baked a simple, very popular

[21] Thomas S. Robertson, "The New Product Diffusion Process," in Bernard A. Marvin, (ed.), *American Marketing Association Proceedings* (Chicago: American Marketing Association, June 1969), p. 86.

BOX 10–5

Ford's Maverick Makes Its Debut

CUAUTITLAN, State of México—Ford Motor Co. has officially presented the Mexican version of its Maverick.

About 130 new units rolled out of the plant here Saturday and headed for various cities in the country where the company has dealers.

The new cars, of which 1,800 units were produced this year, are called Falcon Mavericks here and are similar to the U.S.-made Maverick. They will substitute the Falcon here with almost the same characteristics on the inside.

The car sells for 42,390 pesos* fully equipped. Without optional equipment, the car costs about 39,000 pesos.

A company official said the Maverick, produced here for the first time, will cost 3,627 pesos less than the Falcon when it was on sale in Mexico.

The cars that left the plant Saturday will be on exhibit at the 115 Ford sales centers in Mexico.

The engine is a V-8 289 with 195 horsepower. Other characteristics include manually-operated stick shift, collapsible steering wheel (in case of accident) and hydraulic brakes. It is a two-door sedan.

However, an official said a four-door Maverick may be produced here next year. Increased production of units is also expected, the official added.

The Falcon Maverick is the first family sports car produced here, the official said.

* Approximately $3,391 U.S. Currency.

Source: *The News*, Mexico D. F., July 26, 1970, p. 25.

dry sponge cake, the company brought to the market a similar "easy" mix and gained 30 to 35 percent of the British cake mix market.

The second cake mix represented more familiar tastes and habits that could be translated into a convenience item, and it did not infringe upon the emotional aspects of preparing a fancy product for special occasions. Consequently, after a short period of time the second company's product gained acceptance, while the others did not.

Degrees of Innovativeness

As perceived by the market, there are varied degrees of newness which categorize all new products. To each category, there are myriad reactions, requiring different strategies to overcome resistance. In giving a name to these categories one might think in terms of (1) congruent innovations, (2) continuous innovations, (3) dynamically continuous innovations, and (4) discontinuous innovations.

1. A *congruent* innovation is actually no innovation at all because it causes absolutely no disruption of established consumption patterns. Some products do fit this category; the best example would be an exact duplicate of an already existing product—exact in the sense that the market perceives no newness, e.g., marketing cane sugar vs. beet sugar.

2. A *continuous* innovation has the least disruptive influence on established consumption patterns. Alteration of a product is almost always involved, rather than the creation of a new product. Examples include: fluoride toothpaste, menthol cigarettes, and annual new model automobile changeovers.

3. A *dynamically continuous* innovation has more disrupting effects than a continuous innovation, although it still does not generally involve new consumption patterns. It may mean the creation of a new product or considerable alteration of an existing one. Examples include: electric toothbrushes, electric hair curlers, and the Mustang automobile.

4. A *discontinuous* innovation involves the establishment of new consumption patterns and the creation of previously unknown products. Examples include: television, the computer, and the automobile.[22]

Most innovation in the U.S. economy is of a continuous nature. However, a product that could be described as a continuous innovation in the U.S. market would be a dynamically continuous innovation, if not a discontinuous innovation, in many industrialized nations of the world. For example, when the cake mix was first introduced into the American economy, it was a dynamically continuous innovation. However, over the years it overcame resistances, consumption and behavior patterns changed, and it was accepted in the U.S. market. Indeed, there are many continuous innovations involving the cake mix itself, such as the introduction of new flavors, changes in package size, elimination of dried eggs in favor of fresh eggs, et cetera. That same cake mix, now a part of the U.S. eating habits, is a congruent innovation when a new brand is offered on the U.S. market. If it is offered in a new, unique flavor, it is a continuous innovation; if it is introduced at the same time into a market unfamiliar with cake mixes, it is a dynamically continuous innovation. That same product also could be classified as a discontinuous innovation in a market which had no previous knowledge of cakes. In all cases, we are dealing basically with a cake mix, but in terms of acceptance and marketing success we are dealing with people, their feelings, and their perception of the product.

Continuing to refer to the previous example, the second U.S. cake mix company which entered the British market with a sponge cake had, in fact, changed the product innovation from being a dynamically continuous innovation to one of a continuous innovation by simply altering the cake in the mix from a fancy cake to a rather simple and already accepted dry sponge cake. Thus, one advantage of analyzing a product in terms of its degree of innovativeness is to be able to determine what may be done to alter the degree of newness in order to gain quicker acceptance. Even a tractor must be modified to meet local needs and uses if it is to be accepted in place of the ox-drawn plow.

The time the diffusion process takes, i.e., the time it takes for an innovation to be adopted by a majority in the marketplace, is of prime importance to a marketer. Generally speaking, the more disruptive the innovation the longer the diffusion process takes. As has been noted,

---

[22] See Robertson, op. cit., p. 81.

"In spite of America's generally favorable attitude towards science and technology, a considerable time lag is required before an innovation reaches wide acceptance."[23] The extent of a product's diffusion and its rate of diffusion are mainly a function of the particular product attributes. "The emphasis given particular attributes and the overall brand image created are critical marketing decision areas."[24]

Characteristics of Innovations

One study of the diffusion of innovations proposes a set of five characteristics which are relevant in accounting for differential diffusion rates. These characteristics are (1) relative advantage, (2) compatibility, (3) complexity, (4) divisibility, and (5) communicability.[25]

(1) *Relative advantage.* Relative advantage is the degree to which an innovation is better than the product it replaces or with which it competes, i.e., an innovation with relative advantage has additional value as perceived by the consumer. The more relative advantage perceived by the consumer, the quicker the adoption process, and conversely, the less relative advantage perceived, the slower the adoption process.

(2) *Compatibility.* Compatibility is concerned with how consistent a product is with existing value and behavior patterns. For a product that is not compatible with past behavior requires restructuring of thinking, or necessitates engaging in different modes of behavior, the diffusion process will take longer.

(3) *Complexity.* Complexity refers to how difficult it is to understand and use the new product. The more complex the product, the longer the rate of diffusion, and conversely, the less complex, the quicker the adoption process.

(4) *Divisibility.* Divisibility is the degree to which a product may be tried, on a limited basis, without complete commitment to the product. If the product is a take-it-or-leave-it proposition with limited ability to sample or purchase in a limited quantity, the greater the risk involved in adopting the innovation and the slower the adoption process will be.

(5) *Communicability.* Communicability refers to the ease with which the results of an innovation may be communicated to others. Some innovations or product results are easily observed while others are difficult to describe. An integral part of the adoption process of an innovation is the ability for others to be aware of the advantages of accepting the new product. The easier it is to communicate the advantages of the innovation through print media, by word of mouth, or by observation, the more rapid the diffusion rate will be.

In general, it can be postulated that the rate of diffusion is positively related to relative advantage, compatibility, divisibility, and communica-

---

[23] Everett M. Rogers, *Diffusion of Innovations* (New York: The Free Press öf Glencoe, 1962), p. 2.

[24] Robertson, op. cit., p. 84.

[25] Rogers, op. cit.; p. 124.

bility, but negatively related to complexity.[26] Thus, an innovation which would take the longest time for diffusion through a market would be a product with low perceived relative advantage, noncompatibility, extreme complexity, indivisibility, and difficult communicability; whereas an innovation taking the least amount of time for diffusion would be a product where the consumer could perceive maximum advantage, extreme compatibility, no complexity, high divisibility, and easy communicability, no complexity, high divisibility, and easy communicability. Such characteristics of innovations provide a product profile which can be extremely useful to the marketer.

These characteristics of innovations provide a useful model for planning product strategy, since an international marketer can affect the rate of adoption of an innovation by changing its characteristics through physical modifications, advertising, and/or sales promotion efforts. A product can frequently be modified physically to improve its relative advantage over competing products, enhance its compatibility with cultural values, and even minimize its complexity. Its relative advantage and compatibility can also be enhanced and some degree of complexity lessened through a company's advertising efforts. Small sizes, samples, packaging, and product demonstrations are all sales promotion efforts which can be used to alter the characteristics of an innovation and accelerate its rate of adoption. The marketer must not only recognize the degree of innovativeness which his product possesses in relation to each culture, but his efforts must reflect an understanding of its importance to product acceptance and adoption.

MYTHS AND STEREOTYPES

Because many parts of the world are undergoing a consumer revolution, the marketer contemplating entrance into a foreign market can avoid some of the pitfalls if they are understood in advance. Some of these pitfalls are myths, which may or may not have been founded in fact and others are stereotypes which are no longer valid because of improved standards of living and other social changes. In order to implement a successful marketing plan, all parts of the actual cultural and economic characteristics for each selected market must be thoroughly analyzed to expose any myths or stereotypes which may exist.

Unfortunately, myths are frequently based upon some evidence of truth, are generally logical, and thus can become substitutes for proven fact. To entrust marketing success to half-truths or unfounded "known fact" or "obvious traits" in today's rapidly evolving world market is indeed foolhardy. Market characteristics are changing so rapidly in some nations that it is risky to base decisions on facts that were true last year, much less to substitute obvious facts for sound research.

For example, if asked the question, "Who eats the most spaghetti, the German, Italian, or Frenchman?" the obvious answer, the Italian, would

---

[26] Robertson, op. cit., p. 85.

be incorrect,[27] since the German and Frenchman eat spaghetti more often than the Italian. The Italians eat spaghetti, but the majority main staple is not pasta but a cornmeal mush in which, incidentally, Quaker Oats found a winning product in precooked two-minute *palenta*. If this comes as a surprise, so might the following:

French and Italian housewives are not as interested in the culinary arts as housewives in Luxembourg and Belgium.
The Dutch never touch vodka.
The German male uses more cosmetics and beauty aids than does the Frenchman.[28]
Ernest Dichter noted,

We all "know" that Frenchwomen are very fashion conscious. Yet a study recently showed that this was exactly one of those glib stereotypes that have little if any basis in reality. The purchase of a dress or coat is as much or more of an investment for the Frenchwoman than for the American woman. . . . It is not enough, therefore, to tell a Frenchwoman that a garment is fashionable. She also wants to know, in a way, the "trade-in-value" of the dress or blouse. How long will the fabric last? How many years will she be able to wear it?[29]

The Japanese, their country and their economy, are a favorite target of myths; some are based in part on truth, but the rapidly growing Japanese economy turns yesterday's half-truths into today's fiction. For example, how frequently does one read about Japan's teeming millions and inexhaustible supply of cheap labor? The truth is that Japan is experiencing a labor shortage. "An estimated 1 million jobs are now unfilled in Japan and the shortage is intensifying steadily."[30] Another myth of recent origin is that Japan's economic growth is a result of exports, when in fact Japan "exports less of its production than most industrialized countries: 10 to 12% of its total output, about half as much as West Germany and Britain."[31] Indeed, the success of Japanese companies in the export market is attributed to high domestic demands, a fact those who believe in the above-mentioned myths may find difficult to accept. These are all examples of truths known about particular markets that have been laid to rest with effective research. However, as soon as one myth is proved wrong, another comes along to replace it.

A myth of more recent origin is the belief that the European Common Market is in reality a homogeneous market. Since these six countries have grouped together in an economic coalition, there have been some spectacular economic changes; but in many respects the countries

---

[27] "How to Define A European," *International Management*, August 1963, pp. 19–23.

[28] Based on materials in *The European Common Market and Britain* (Pleasantville, N.Y.: Reader's Digest Association, Inc., 1963).

[29] Ernest Dichter, "The World Customer," *Harvard Business Review*, July–August, 1962, p. 114.

[30] "A Shortage of Workers Changes Japan," *Business Week*, January 31, 1970, p. 70.

[31] "The Economic Growth of Japan," *Scientific American*, March 1970, p. 31.

Box 10–6

New Myths in the Making?

Europe Survey Unearths Array of Market Facts

New York, *Nov. 10*—In Ireland, home of the potato, 55% of the households use instant potatoes.

Sweden is the leader of the 16 countries of western Europe in the use of frozen fish and meat, with 54% of that sea-faring nation consumers of these frozen products.

Britain, where afternoon tea is an age-old tradition, has the largest number of instant coffee homes (86%).

Denmark, rather than Germany, has the largest percentage of beer drinkers, with 85% of adult Danes qualifying as regular beer drinkers.

These are some of the surprising findings in *Reader's Digest's* 212-page marketing study, "A Survey of Europe Today.". . . The survey found that 69% of all European adults drink wine; France leads the league, with 86% of its families indulging. Beer, however, replaces wine as the most popular drink in Austria, Belgium, Britain, Germany, Ireland, the Netherlands and Scandinavia. Although Denmark has the largest number of regular beer quaffers, the Germans are unsurpassed in the amounts consumed, with the annual per-capita rate hitting 131 quarts annually. Surprisingly, Ireland has the highest proportion of non-drinkers among the countries surveyed.

Britons are, by far, Europe's leading pet food buyers, spending more than $240,000,000 a year on such products, the study showed. In cosmetics, Britain and Sweden are the pacemakers, with girls starting to buy beauty products (usually beginning with nail polish) at the age of 12. British women also use more face powder, while French women, who have a vast reputation for their elegance, show only moderate beauty consciousness. . . .

Although Europe is generally regarded as the style-setting center of the western world, eight out of 10 European women reported, "I wear what suits me, whether it's fashionable or not."

In Italy, 69% of the families have television, but only 51% have bathrooms. Three-quarters of the households in Europe now own a TV set. Sweden leads the pack, with 88% of its families owning a TV set, while only 29% of Portuguese families own a set.

Advertising as a phase of marketing is better regarded here in the States than in any of the 16 European countries.

---

remain uncommon as a market. The German remains a German in thought; indeed, he does not react as a Frenchman or Italian would or even as a "European common man," and he probably will not for generations to come. Consequently, marketers who have been successful with a product in one European country are frequently surprised to find the same product unacceptable in a neighboring Common Market country.

The differences among the countries in the Common Market are still a very real fact. Such things as different languages, legal systems, climate, terrain, and economic conditions may raise havoc with any single marketing plan designed for the entire economic community. In addition, behavioral differences exist that create effective barriers to the successful marketing of many products. Such products as cars, detergents, cigarettes, and some appliances may be truly international in appeal in that their acceptance is not affected significantly by cultural differences. Others, however, more sensitive to variations in taste, custom, and habit, meet real barriers to acceptance.

A comprehensive study emphasizes the diversity among the six countries in tastes and preferences for numerous products. Throughout the study striking differences were found among the countries in everything from attitudes about cooking to opinions about the quality of workmanship found in each other's products. Use of canned vegetables, for example, was found in only 4 percent of the Italian households, while 41 percent of the French and 56 percent of the Dutch homes used them. Similar differences were found in the use of various kinds of oils for cooking; the French preferred butter; the West Germans favored margarine; the Italians relied on olive oil; and the English were prime users of lard.

Such diversity should dispel any ideas that the EEC is a common consumer market. Although not everyone succumbs to this myth, it is natural to assume that since the EEC is a successful economic integration, there has also been a successful integration of tastes, habits, and behavior. But,

There is nothing in common between the disciplined factory worker of the Ruhr and the barely educated and impoverished farm worker of Southern Italy. These national differences of language and culture are matched by regional distinctions that can be equally marked.[32]

Some similarities do exist and, as time passes and there is more interaction among the countries, there will surely be more; economic interaction, however, does not automatically produce a blending of cultural and consumer characteristics.

No one familiar with U.S. marketing history should expect the EEC countries to drop their national heritages rapidly. Even after being united for over a century and a half, the United States has not developed a national market with national instead of regional tastes. Similarly, even in an era of rapid, mass communications and close political ties, it is unrealistic to anticipate in the near future common consumer tastes among people who have maintained national cultures and rivalries for centuries.

TRENDS IN WORLD CONSUMER MARKETS

A result of the various social and economic changes which are occurring in many countries of the world are numerous trends in market characteristics which, if continued, will result in significant changes in world markets. Among the more pronounced trends are the development

---

[32] "The Common Market Eleven Years After: Still Promises?" *Sales Management*, February 1, 1969, p. 39.

of mass merchandising, the changing role of women in the economy and society, and a willingness to use installment credit.

A rapid transition in "traditional retailing" is occurring in some countries mainly because of the development and wholehearted acceptance of mass merchandising, including self-service, checkout counters, prepackaged and frozen foods, adequate parking, and big stores which stock as many as 20,000 different products. These innovations represent a significant departure from shops catering to a daily pattern of shipping for food at as many as six specialty shops. This is not to say that "traditional retailing" has disappeared, but only that in many countries significant changes are taking place.

Less than 10 years ago there were fewer than 11,000 self-service stores operating in all of Western Europe; by 1964 their number had increased to 93,000, and by 1968 there were 140,000 stores featuring self-service merchandising.[33]

More spectacular is the growth in the last decade of full-fledged supermarkets in Europe.

In Germany, where almost half the stores are self-service, 72.3% of all food sales are chalked up by supermarkets. In Holland, the 32% segment of supermarkets or self-service stores do a big 62% of all business, comparable to Sweden's 28% doing 69% of the business. . . . Even in conservative France, the small 3.9% self-service segment of her 318,000 shops does almost 20% of all grocery trade.[34]

The trend in self-service supermarkets is not limited to developing Western Europe. Supermarkets now account for about 30 percent of food and similar products sold in major cities of Mexico, an increase from 15 percent only five years ago.[35] Similar growth in mass merchandising is underway in Japan, along with the widespread use of trading stamps. It appears that there exists among the Japanese the same consumer zeal for trading stamps that is found in the United States, even though they were introduced into the Japanese market only in 1963.[36]

Retailing changes are not limited to the growth of supermarkets and discount houses. Automatic vending has developed to help solve such problems as personnel shortages, higher pay, profit squeeze, and restrictions on business hours which are found in Europe and elsewhere.

Another important fact in the consumer boom experienced in Europe and other parts of the world is the working wife who not only provides additional family income to purchase the ever-increasing list of consumer products, but who also helps fill a dire labor shortage. Currently in Europe about one third of all married women are employed, three million of whom are mothers, and the number of working wives increases annually. To the marketer this means an ever-increasing de-

[33] "Europe's New Shopping Centers," *Business Abroad*, October 1968, p. 22.

[34] Ibid., p. 22.

[35] "Selling Opportunities in Mexico's Emerging National Markets," *Business Abroad*, February, 1969, p. 30.

[36] A. J. Alton and George O. Totten. "Trading Stamps in Japan—Boom in the Making?" *Journal of Marketing*, April 1965, p. 12.

BOX 10–7

Co-ops Play Major Role

The Scandinavian cooperative organizations have a profound influence on sales of all types of consumer goods. Their activities bear watching by would-be entrants to the markets where they are active.

For example, Kooperative Förbundet, the big Swedish coop, tops the list of the first ten industrial and commercial organizations in Sweden in sales and claims to be number one in Scandinavia. With a major stake in consumer retailing, its 1967 sales rose 10% to 4.6 billion krowns (1 dollar = 5.7 kr.), including 2.05 billion kr. of its own manufacturers and some 414 million of exports.

The 275 societies affiliated with K. F. account for memberships covering 1.4 million homes, about 25% of the nation's total. K. F. accounts for 17% of all retail sales, including 24% of food sales. Its sales outlets are diminishing in number but increasing in size. By the mid 1970's it forecasts the number of retail outlets in the movement will have fallen to 920 (compared with 3900 in 1965) but it is anticipated that of these 920 stores, about 180 will be department stores, 190 supermarkets, and 550 food shops.

Some 30 companies are affiliated with K. F., producing a wide range of goods from detergents to cosmetics. And as these have developed, its factories have had to look outside their own organization for other markets, including export. In 1967 K. F. exported goods valued at 414 million kr. and its overall policy is to expand in this sector.

K. F. recently added two discount houses in the Stockholm suburbs. With comparatively low land prices and a high rate of turnover, their prices average about 11% lower than in city stores.

The new outlets are geared to the motorized public. If, as forecast, every third person in Sweden owns an automobile by 1970, the discount house idea could well spread rapidly, a factor of no small importance to American exporters.

---

mand for laborsaving devices, convenience foods, and other means of extending the time at home after work.

A trend of considerable significance that generally develops as incomes grow and the trappings of the good life are sought is the extension of individual purchasing power with the use of installment credit. Based on U.S. development, installment credit is in its infancy in the rest of the world, but there are substantial growth factors in this area. The total credit outstanding in EEC countries and the United Kingdom in 1968 was $25 billion (compared to about $113 billion in the United States), while prior to World War II credit was almost unknown to the average European. The continued and increased use of credit is seen as important in increasing Europe's effective demand for household appliances and automobiles during the near future.

To the retailer, installment sales in culturally different markets pose some distinct problems. In northern Nigeria, merchants were blocked in repossessing television sets from purchasers who had defaulted when the sets were placed in the "harems"—an area of a household which is strictly off limits to outsiders.[37] In most countries installment sales are handled in the same manner as those in the United States, although repossessions in case of default may be more difficult in certain situations.

It is interesting to note the parallel between the growth of these trends in many of the world's markets and the economic development of the respective countries. Perhaps a valid generalization would be that as a country experiences higher personal incomes, rising productivity, urbanization, and all the other trappings of industrialization, a "consumer revolution" could be anticipated which would include the development and acceptance of such innovations as mass merchandising, increased employment of women and the increased use of installment credit. The development of these trends in parts of Europe and Japan as well as many other countries of the world can be compared to similar development in the United States after World War II.

SUMMARY AND CONCLUSIONS

Although rising incomes, increased economic security, economies of mass production, and changing social patterns have not advanced to the same degree in all countries, where they have developed considerable adjustment in market characteristics has occurred. The impact of these social and economic trends will continue to be felt in many countries during the next decade, causing significant changes in distribution systems, personal shopping habits, and consumer demand. The continued growth of these trends requires that the foreign marketer constantly evaluate the dynamic aspects of his market, since it is likely that many of today's market facts will be tomorrow's myths.

READINGS

HOW NESTLÉ ADAPTS PRODUCTS TO ITS MARKETS*

NORRIS WILLATT

All the world over, what is easier, simpler, more straightforward than a cup of instant coffee? You remove the lid from the jar, measure a spoonful of powder into the cup, add hot water, and presto, a refreshing and invigorating drink.

That's the way it seems to everyone—except the manufacturer. Thus, to Nestlé Alimentana S.A., of Vevey, Switzerland, which invented the product in the 1930's and is the biggest seller of it today, a cup of instant

---

[37] "Television Becomes Popular in Africa, Problems Unique," Associated Press, Lagos, Nigeria, November 20, 1964.

* Reprinted by special permission from the June 1970 issue of *Business Abroad*, pp. 31–33. Copyrighted © 1970 by The Reuben H. Donnelley Corporation.

coffee is a multiplicity of different beverages. It represents not one but many markets, to each of which the company must cater.

Nestlé produces one type of instant coffee for Americans, who like theirs light and bland: a totally different variety is made for Italians, who prefer it dark, and so thick that the spoon almost stands up in it. The varieties offered on the French and British markets are somewhere between the two extremes, again to cater to local taste.

Age also makes a difference. In Sweden, for example, Nestlé's target is every age group. In Britain the company tends to aim its promotion at the younger generation, which, as part of a general revolt against tradition, increasingly has switched to coffee from the national beverage, tea. In the United States, though the reverse is by no means true, the older people remain the most confirmed coffee drinkers, while many youngsters like to experiment with other beverages.

In Brazil and other coffee-producing countries of Latin America, a major function of marketing is to overcome local prejudice against instant coffee—to counteract the theory that instant is an inferior substitute for the ground variety which plays so important a part in the national economy. In Central Africa, the company had to create a market from scratch, after establishing an instant coffee facility at Abidjan, capital of the Ivory Coast, as a contribution to local industrialization.

While coffee is perhaps the outstanding example, considerable flexibility also is necessary in marketing most of the company's main products, which include canned and powdered milk, chocolate, soups, preserves and similar culinary items, cheese, frozen foods, and even mineral water. As a result, the product itself, and the way it is merchandized, may vary greatly from one market to another, or even in different areas of the same market.

Some few years ago, Nestlé was motivated to develop a special variety of its instant tea product, Nestea, to cater to a fast-growing market for iced tea in the U.S. South and Middle West.

Similarly, in West Germany the company gets its best results with thick, creamed soups, which traditionally have appealed to the local palate. But these get a poor response in Latin America where the preference always has been for the lighter varieties of bouillon.

To meet these consumer needs, marketing at Nestlé is both largely decentralized and destandardized. The Swiss firm is a truly multinational enterprise, far more so—its executives say—than most of international competitors in food processing.

Although Nestlé has three important factories in Switzerland, and its brightly-packaged products crowd the shelves of virtually every grocery store in this country of 6-million, the rather incredible fact is that over 97% of its business (and 206 additional factories) is outside the home country. In all but a few countries around the globe, Nestlé is the leading producer of food products.

Again in contrast with typical competition, Nestlé does not operate abroad exclusively or mainly through subsidiaries or controlled affiliates. Instead, it forms a variety of different ties with "allied" companies, a term chosen to cover such different relationships as outright ownership, joint venture, trademark licensing, technical assistance—a broad spectrum.

Against such a background, management long ago accepted that it was impossible to make the key marketing decisions at Vevey. These had to be left to the people on the spot, a decision reinforced by the philosophy that "the closer the man is to the battlefront, the better his decision is likely to be."

Where, and most crucially, the company does exercise firm, centralized, standardized control is over the decision-making process. This is uniform throughout the whole global marketing territory. In all areas, product and marketing managers approach their task in precisely the same way.

Their two chief weapons are a general fact book and a product fact book. The general fact book establishes such data for the market as total population, the rate at which it is increasing, and breakdowns by age group, income level, and so on. The product book comprises everything that can be established about the product: How much is consumed, in what form, at what price, by what percentage and among which groups of the population: also, how much of the market belongs to the company, and what are the estimated shares of competitors.

In a highly sophisticated market, such as the United States, this procedure is routine, and the necessary data are more easily procured. But in many of Nestlé's markets, for example, in some parts of Latin America, Africa, Asia, even the basic statistics don't exist. In such situations, the company has to organize its own basic data through market research.

It often hires students, in teams of as many as 200 at a time, to interview housewives in the home. In some countries, natives can easily be trained to ask simple sample questions "Do you have the product? May I see it? How often do you use it?" at the door. The policy of using local people inspires confidence, whereas foreigners might only arouse suspicion or antagonism.

Each marketing area headquarters must provide annual marketing plans for every product within its jurisdiction; these cover both the short and long term. In addition to detailing the next 12 months, the product plan includes a forecast of sales, profits, market shares, expenditures and other related parameters, in more general form, for the next seven years.

The individual product plans usually are drawn up by product managers, who, in a smaller territory, also may be the marketing managers. Product managers are, typically, bright and energetic young men, mostly recruited locally, and usually in their early 30's. Plans are carefully analyzed and scrutinized by the marketing manager.

The area marketing plan is the sum total of the various product plans, and this is submitted for approval or review by top management, with the help of a central advisory group. In practice, these plans are approved about 95% of the time, according to the company. Even if differences of opinion arise between marketing managers and the advisors, the views of the man in the field are likely to prevail.

To the extent possible, the company does standardize and is always aiming at more ways to do so. Thus, baby food formulas, a staple item, are uniform everywhere, on the grounds that "the mother from Hamburg who goes on holiday to Venice or Malaga wants to be sure that her baby suffers no change in diet."

On the other hand, Nestlé offers not just one but several different formulas to meet the preferences of pediatricians, including, for example, humanized milk (the nearest to the natural milk of the mother), sweetened milk, and acidified milk to aid the digestion of fats.

Confectionery, which used to be more standardized—witness the famed Nestlé slab, rival of the Hershey bar—now has become a faster changing business. It is more and more characterized by so-called creative involvement, which implies greater specialization both in the product and in the merchandizing of it in specific markets.

Then, as already noted, the key to the successful marketing of instant coffee is flexibility in adapting to local taste. Americans and the Italians probably will never agree on what is a "good cup of coffee." However, in these and all markets, Nestlé pursues a standard policy to upgrade the product in the eyes of the customer.

This involves a three-stage strategy. In any new market, the first stage is to sell instant coffee as a convenience item, saving time and trouble: "We do the percolating for you." The next stage is to establish it as "real coffee." The third and final stage is to convince the consumer that it is comparable in every way to ground coffee. With the recent evolution of freeze-dried coffee, which is said better to retain aroma and "body," Nestlé believes it has reached Stage 3.

To some degree, labels, packaging and sizes can be standardized internationally. But flexibility still is necessary. For example, a giant-size pack of coffee is ideal for U.S. supermarkets, where the housewife normally does her heavy shopping only once a week. But it is entirely inappropriate for the store in an African township, where the local women tend to shop daily, or even more than once a day. They need much smaller, four- and even two-ounce packs.

Moreover, the latter packs may have to be more durable than those suitable for industrialized countries, since the product may lie around exposed in dusty, leaky, humid village stores for days or even weeks at a time. Preservation of quality standards under such conditions puts a premium on secure packaging.

The advent of television as a universal means of communicating with the shack as well as the mansion permits the standardization to an increasing extent of advertising and promotion. Nestlé uses the medium extensively wherever it can. Where it still can't, the company relies on newspapers (mostly the news columns), color magazines, billboards and other outdoor displays.

Among illiterate populations, which still are to be found in many countries where the company is in business, the most effective promotional message can be a poster depicting a pitcher of milk alongside a healthy-looking local child. Consumers dictate the policy.

Throughout Latin America Nestlé markets its powdered milk under the brand name of Nido, Spanish for "Nest." But to illiterate Indians, it is known as *La Leche de los pajaritos*, "the milk of the birds," which identifies with the company logo of parent birds feeding their young in the nest.

In less developed countries, the best form of promoting baby food formulas may well be the clinics which the company sponsors, at which nurses and doctors in its employ offer child-care guidance service. One fruitful by-product of this operation is that at christening and birthday parties Nestlé products often are given as presents.

A striking example of Nestlé versatility in adapting tactics to local conditions occurred in Hong Kong. Nestlé organized the Lactogen Diaper Derby, a race for babies who had to crawl unaided over a measured distance. Parents could (and did) encourage the contestants by calls, shaking rattles, and so on, but were forbidden to give any physical help.

Winners of preliminary area elimination and final meetings moved on to the Grand Final at a leading Hong Kong hotel. Winners and runners up received cash and consolation prizes in the elimination contests, while the champions were awarded a silver trophy and medals. The public reaction was highly favorable, and coverage by local news media was reinforced by advertising, featuring contest winners. The Derby was subsequently revived in four more successive years.

In many other countries, including even some of the highly industrialized ones, the retailing of food, as with most merchandise, is a highly decentralized, not to say fragmented operation, involving doing business with a multitude of small traders. In these circumstances, marketing involves close attention to personal attitudes and even idiosyncracies.

In the less developed countries, effective distribution may call for unusual, imaginative techniques. Thus, in Bangkok, the capital of Thailand and a community of canals, the Nestlé shop goes to the customer, not the other way about. The shopkeeper cruises the waterways in a boat laden with Nestlé products and displaying Nestlé advertising material. In some African communities, the channel of distribution is peddlers, young women who tote the products around on trays on their heads.

In such circumstances, it's clear that only the people on the spot can assess the market potential and develop the marketing strategies necessary to exploit it.

THE DIMENSIONS OF CONSUMER MARKETS ABROAD*

DAVID BAUER

Most forecasts point to a slackening of economic activity in the major industrial countries during the current year.[1] In some of these, expan-

---

* Reprinted by permission from *The Conference Board Record,* June 1970, pp. 42–46.

[1] *Cf.* "The World Economy in 1970," *The Record,* March 1970.

sion may be limited by labor shortages, but in others—notably the United States and the United Kingdom—the most important constraint remains the continuation of restrictive monetary and fiscal policies. The primary aim of these policies is to curb inflationary pressures by holding down overall spending, particularly by consumers, and some indication of the expected impact is given in Exhibit 1.

In the United States, as well as in Canada, France, and Germany, growth in this year's consumer expenditures (in real terms) is expected to lag behind the gains posted in both 1969 and—excepting Germany's figures—1968. While the increase projected for the United Kingdom is large compared to last year's, it is generally in line with the moderate growth rate of 2½–3% recorded throughout the 1960's. For Japan,

EXHIBIT 1

Actual and Projected Changes in Real Consumption, Selected Countries, 1968–70

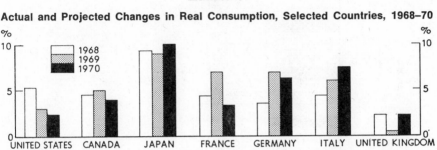

Sources: Organisation for Economic Cooperation and Development; The Conference Board.

where consumer spending has been growing at an annual rate of over 8% in recent years, a similar gain is expected in 1970.

The Record of the 1960's

This year's outlook for the major countries corresponds fairly closely to their actual experience during the 1960's. The growth of consumer expenditures in the United States in 1960–69 was slightly ahead of that recorded by Western Europe as a whole. However, Europe's relatively poorer performance can be attributed largely to only moderate increases in consumer outlays in the United Kingdom and several of the smaller countries on the Continent. In the Common Market, on the other hand, the growth in consumer expenditures outpaced the United States figure (Exhibit 2).

The largest gains over that ten-year period occurred in France, Italy, and the Netherlands. Even in 1969, when widespread strikes in Italy cut into industrial production, retailers were able to maintain sales by trimming their inventories, while those workers who suffered a loss of wages were frequently able and willing to draw on their savings. Outside Europe, the growth in consumer spending in Canada and Japan also has exceeded the U.S. record, and in Japan the margin has been substantial.

EXHIBIT 2

Changes in Consumer Spending and Prices, Selected Countries, 1960–68

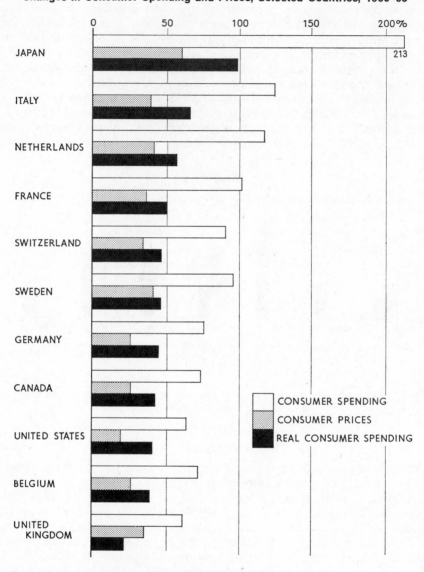

Sources: International Monetary Fund; The Conference Board.

This general pattern prevails whether the comparison relates to consumer expenditures in current prices or in real terms.

Price rises in the United States have usually run well below those in other countries, although the margin has narrowed in recent years as U.S. prices climbed sharply, reflecting capacity shortages associated with the material and manpower requirements of the Vietnam conflict. During the first half of the 1960's, prices in the U.S. rose approximately 6% as against 20% in Europe.

Differences in Expenditure Levels

Measuring the growth rate of consumer spending is a far easier task than comparing the absolute levels of expenditures. Exchange rates are generally used to convert different countries' consumer sales (as well as other aggregates, such as gross national product or national income) into a common currency. For example, the Organisation for Economic Cooperation and Development (OECD) estimates that the 1967 gross national product of the major industrial nations was $1,600 billion, of which $900 billion was accounted for by consumer expenditures. These estimates were made by converting output and spending as measured in yen, marks, francs, etc., into dollars at 1967 exchange rates. The most serious shortcoming of this technique, as the OECD is quick to point out, is that official exchange rates usually are not reliable guides to the relative purchasing powers of different currencies. A 1966 study by the OECD compares the level of real per capita consumer spending in a number of countries in 1960 by using data on both the actual purchasing power of each country's currency, and on consumption of items —such as steel, meat, automobiles, etc.—as a proxy for total real consumption. The results of this study, updated to a more recent year, are given in Exhibit 3, along with estimates of per capita consumption calculated on the basis of exchange rates.

The estimates show that while per capita consumption in most countries is substantially below the U.S. level, the gap often is not as wide as comparisons based on exchange rates alone seem to indicate. In the United Kingdom in 1969, for instance, total consumer expenditures were £29 billion and total population was 55.5 million; the per capita consumption figure of £523 when converted to U.S. dollars (at the rate of £1 = $2.40) is $1,255, or 43% of the U.S. per capita figure. In contrast, estimates of consumption based on adjustments to reflect the purchasing power of the pound *in the United Kingdom* (comparisons based on exchange rates reflect, in effect, the purchasing power of the pound *in the United States*) show that real consumption in the U.K. was equal to roughly 55% of the U.S. average.

The estimates in Exhibit 3 must be interpreted with caution, however, since relatively little information is available concerning the level of real consumption in countries outside the U.S. In general, the estimates indicate that consumption in Canada and Sweden comes closest to the U.S. level. In spite of the rapid gains in real consumption achieved in Italy and Japan, the *level* of consumption in these countries is still substantially below the U.S. average.

The gap in consumption between the U.S. and other countries stems primarily from the gap in incomes; depending upon the method used to convert national figures to a comparable base, incomes in Europe, Canada and Japan range up to 75% below the U.S. level. Additionally, however, the allocation of after-tax income also makes for lower consumption expenditures abroad. Again, estimates are tentative, but United Nations national-accounts data indicate that savings account for a larger portion of disposable incomes abroad than in the U.S., while consumption accounts for less. Though purchases of goods and services accounted for approximately 94% of disposable income in the U.S. between 1960 and 1967, the figure was below 90% in many European countries.

The ratio is probably lowest in Japan, where a number of factors have combined to produce a relatively high level of savings. Japanese consumption habits traditionally have been frugal in comparison to Western standards; additionally, many Japanese workers receive large wage

EXHIBIT 3

**Estimated per Capita Consumption Expenditures,
Selected Countries and Years
(United States = 100)**

	Estimated Consumption Based on Differences in Purchasing Power	Estimated Consumption Based on Exchange Rates
United States (1969)	100	100
Sweden (1967)	79	69
Canada (1969)	76	72
Switzerland (1967)	59	63
Germany (1969)	59	43
France (1968)	57	57
United Kingdom (1969)	55	43
Netherlands (1967)	49	42
Japan (1966)	41	25
Italy (1968)	34	32

Note: Estimates are based on partial data and indicate general rather than precise rankings.

Sources: Organisation for Economic Cooperation and Development; The Conference Board.

bonuses once or twice a year, and competition among savings institutions for these (as well as for regular wage and salary payments) is intense. A third factor, evident also in many parts of Europe, is the large number of farmers and small shopkeepers who save a high proportion of their incomes in order to smooth out irregular fluctuations in earnings and also to provide funds for their businesses. The self-employed in the United States also tend to save a relatively large share of their incomes, but they constitute a much smaller percentage of this country's work force.[2]

---

[2] Cf. *Factors Moderating Unemployment Abroad*, Studies in Business Economics No. 113, National Industrial Conference Board, 1970, pp. 25–26.

Patterns of Spending

As might be expected, there also are marked variations between the major countries in the shares of consumer expenditures allotted to various categories, such as food, clothing, etc. (Exhibit 4). These variations reflect significant but largely unquantifiable differences in culture and tastes, as well as more readily measurable influences, such as average family size, age distribution, and relative income levels. The relationship between each of these variables and the pattern of consumer demand cannot be easily isolated. Demographic characteristics, for instance, play a major role in explaining variations in the demand for consumer goods—spending for household goods and services is largely dependent upon population growth and the rate of new household formations—but low income levels may, in turn, limit this demand.

In Italy, for example, the average size of households headed by a wage or salary worker is roughly 4.0 as compared to 3.5 in Germany;[3] Italians, however, spend a substantially smaller portion of their earnings on furniture and household operations, partly because incomes are low and a relatively large portion of these incomes must be spent for food. It should be noted that the relatively low levels of income in Italy (and the pattern of consumer spending which results from these levels) are partly related to demographic characteristics. In Italy, only about 13% of the wives of male wage and salary workers are employed, whereas the pertinent figure in Germany is around 21%.

Income, population characteristics, and similar variables are important factors in explaining the demand for consumer products, but spending habits also are influenced by the supply of goods and services. In both the U.S. and Europe, housing shortages causing the "doubling-up" of many families and individuals are partly responsible for holding expenditures for rent[4] and furnishings to a level that is not indicative of potential outlays if additional housing units were to become available. Increased spending on housing would of course curb the funds available for other less essential items.

Because housing is a commodity for which there is no close substitute, the rent paid for dwelling units is little affected by the prices of other goods. For many other consumer products, however, the amount purchased will depend partly upon the price of competing products. In the United States, prices of many types of personal services are high—and the demand for these services is consequently lowered—partly because most services are labor-intensive and the cost of labor in this country

---

[3] A recent Department of Commerce study listed the results of surveys conducted in 1962–64 which showed that *within* most countries, low-income households tend to have fewer members than households in high-income brackets. Nevertheless, the 3.6 person average in German *high-income* households (households in the 89–92 percentile) was less than the 3.8 average in Italian *low-income* (7–16 percentile) households. Cf. "Consumer Expenditures and Levels of Consumption," *Labor Developments Abroad,* July, August, and September 1969.

[4] Figures on expenditures for housing do not include the purchase of a home; this transaction is considered a capital transaction (comparable to the purchase of a capital good by a manufacturer) and is thus excluded from consumer expenditures.

EXHIBIT 4

Consumer Expenditures by Major Categories, 1967
(in percent)

	Food	Beverages	Tobacco	Clothing	Rent	Furniture	Household Operations	Personal Care and Health	Transportation & Communication	Recreation
United States	19.0	2.9†	1.9	9.2	14.2	7.3	7.4	8.6	14.6	5.4
Canada	20.0	5.2	2.6	8.0	15.8	4.3	6.9	8.8	14.0	5.2
Germany	33.0			11.4	10.9	21.0‖	...	4.0	8.2	7.7
Italy	37.3	5.0	3.1	10.1	9.3	3.0	7.6	7.5	9.9	8.2
Netherlands	27.1	3.6	3.6	13.9‡	8.1	10.0	9.3	7.6	5.0	6.0
Sweden	24.6	6.6	3.3	10.3	10.2	7.0	5.6	3.9	15.2	9.3
Switzerland	24.2	10.1		7.9	12.1	6.1	7.3	6.3	10.6	12.3§
United Kingdom	24.8	6.3†	6.0	9.9	11.8	6.2	7.3	2.3	12.4	7.6
Japan	37.0			11.7	8.6	8.2	7.3	31.9§		

* Includes fuel and light.
† Alcoholic beverages only
‡ Includes household textiles
§ Includes miscellaneous services
‖ Radios, record players and television sets included under "recreation."
Note: Categories not shown include miscellaneous services and purchases made abroad.
Source: United Nations, *Yearbook of National Accounts Statistics,* 1968

is high; on the other hand, goods which can be produced using a minimum amount of labor are relatively inexpensive.

In many European countries, however, the reverse is often true, and the price of services relative to commodities helps explain variations in consumer spending patterns. For example, the price of domestic help in Europe is low relative to the price of household durables. Since maid service is a partial substitute for appliances, households in Europe may spend a higher proportion of their disposable incomes for domestic help (and a lower proportion for appliances) than is the case in the U.S.

Factors Influencing Prices

The price structure of consumer products is shaped by a host of factors. In addition to the relative supplies of capital and labor, prices reflect the availability of raw materials, climatic conditions, transportation costs, and the incidence of taxes (including import duties). Taxes may influence both the composition and level of spending.

Increased reliance on value-added taxes (VAT) in Europe in recent years may have checked spending for consumption, particularly of non-essential items, because a relatively large share of these taxes is borne by the consumer rather than the manufacturer or distributor. Imposition of the VAT in Germany boosted prices by at least 1% in 1968, according to OECD estimates; a similar increase occurred in France when the tax on commodities was extended to services. In both France and the Netherlands, the VAT may have provided manufacturers with an opportunity to increase selling prices by an amount larger than the tax levy; at any rate, Dutch officials found it necessary to impose price controls shortly after the VAT were introduced.

In addition to the *structure* of consumer prices, consumer spending may also be affected by the rates at which prices and incomes are increasing. If prices are rising much more rapidly than incomes, consumers may spend more of their incomes on goods in order to escape paying higher prices for the same goods at a later date. Even if prices *and* incomes are increasing at the same rate, consumers may still spend more. Although equal increases in prices and incomes presumably would have no effect on real living standards, consumers may pay more attention to the higher earnings than to the jump in prices. Feeling more affluent, consumers may then decide to purchase goods which, in the past, they considered beyond their reach.

QUESTIONS

1. Terms: Define and show the significance to international marketing:

Market saturation	"Traditional retailing"
Engel's law	Innovation
Unevenly developed markets	Relative advantage
Myths and stereotypes	Divisibility
Palenta	Dynamically continuous innovation
"European common man"	

2. Old products (i.e., old in the U.S. market) may be innovations in a foreign market. Discuss fully.

3. Explain the importance of rapidly growing economies of Japan and Western Europe to international marketing.

4. In measuring consumer income and market potential, what are some of the factors one must consider?

5. Discuss the main pitfalls of world markets for consumer goods which face the foreign marketer.

6. How do myths and stereotypes cloud the international marketing picture? Discuss.

7. Is the common market a homogeneous market? Discuss. Will it eventually become a true common market?

8. Discuss the consumer-oriented trend in world markets.

9. What is the affluence/consumption lag? How might knowledge of this help to prevent market failures?

10. Discuss how the dynamic changes in the world affect markets for consumer goods. Is there apt to be a sudden change in this situation? If yes, what will cause it and what will occur to consumer demand?

11. ". . . If the product sells in Dallas, it will sell in Tokyo or Berlin." Comment.

12. How can a country with a per capita GNP of $100 be a potential market for consumer goods? What kinds of goods would probably be in demand? Discuss.

13. Discuss some of the problems in estimating market demand which result from unevenly developed markets. Give examples.

14. What effect has the employment of women in Europe had on market demand for consumer goods? Illustrate.

15. Discuss the four types of innovations. Give examples of a product which would be considered by the U.S. market as one type of innovation but a different type in another market. Support your choice.

16. Discuss the characteristics of an innovation which can account for differential diffusion rates.

17. Give an example of how a foreign marketer can use knowledge of the characteristics of innovations in product adaptation decisions.

Readings

1. According to the reading, "How Nestlé Adopts Products in Its Markets," the company follows a policy of decentralization and destandardization in order to meet consumer needs. Considering the types of products Nestlé markets, explain why this policy is necessary but may not work if they had a different product mix.

2. As incomes have increased in many markets abroad, there are "market variations between the major countries in the shares of consumer expenditures allotted to various categories. . . ." Why is this true? Would you expect expenditure patterns in these countries to become more similar as time passes? Discuss.

OUTLINE OF CHAPTER 11

INTRODUCTION

THE INDUSTRIAL PRODUCT

  Stage of Economic Development

  Political and National Implications

  Product Design

  Concept of Quality

  Variations in Product Features

  Service, Replacement Parts, and Standards

  Universal Standards

CHANNEL STRATEGY FOR INDUSTRIAL PRODUCTS

PROMOTIONAL PROBLEMS ABROAD

  Industrial Trade Fairs and Trade Centers

  Proper Emphasis in Promotional Mix

PRICING AND COMPETITION

  Price-Quality Relationship

  Leasing in International Markets

SUMMARY AND CONCLUSIONS

READINGS

  Is There an Industrial Market for You in Mexico? *Industrial Marketing*

  International Leasing: Filling Equipment Needs of Capital-Short Customers around the World, *Business Abroad*

MARKETING INDUSTRIAL PRODUCTS INTERNATIONALLY

INTRODUCTION

Many texts on principles of marketing contain a discussion of industrial markets and their significant differences from markets for consumer goods. The differences are basic and generally considered the result of two fundamental factors: (1) the inherent characteristics in the nature of the products, i.e., industrial products are those goods and services used in the process of creating other goods and services, while consumer goods are in their final form and are consumed by individuals; and (2) the motive or intent of the user, i.e., industrial consumers are generally seeking a profit, while the ultimate consumer is seeking self-satisfaction. These differences are manifest in buying patterns, demand characteristics, and selling techniques.

The committee on definitions of the National Association of Marketing Teachers in its statement on the fundamental differences between industrial and consumer marketing reported that four important differences exist between these two markets, resulting in major diversity in marketing practices. The differences are as follows:

1. Differences owing to the nature of the market or the buyer.
2. Differences arising from organization or operational setup.
3. Differences arising from the characteristics of the product.
4. Miscellaneous differences which include such points as the need for a highly skilled sales force and speed and dependability of delivery.

In the marketing of both kinds of goods, the fundamental marketing concepts and principles are the same; however, there is considerable diversity in the tactics used to implement the marketing programs and in the degree of emphasis applied to the various components of the marketing mix for the two different kinds of goods. The tactics are sufficiently unique to warrant special emphasis.

Whether a company is marketing at home or abroad, the differences between industrial and consumer markets remain; in both cases, programs and tactics are further affected by the uniqueness of the environment of the particular country. As has been discussed in earlier chapters, a marketing program which is successful in one country may require considerable adjustment to be successful in another, simply because of the different environment within which the marketing program is implemented.

Foreign marketing requires that a clear distinction between the two kinds of goods be maintained because of the basic differences in marketing activity between industrial and consumer goods and because of the additional and oftentimes unique emphasis demanded by the changing environments inherent in marketing from one country to another. For example, a fundamental characteristic of industrial marketing which is true the world over is that goods are purchased on a performance basis. In those countries, however, where the culture of a prospective user has not equipped him with the basic rudiments of technical skills often considered given in other cultures, extraordinary steps have to be taken to insure that such simple tasks as adequate maintenance are properly fulfilled. Otherwise, the company runs the risk of having the reputation of its products injured through no fault of the product but because of improper use or poor maintenance. As one authority states:

> Lack of maintenance, overloading or misuse of machinery are very common in some overseas markets, and much work has to be done by an exporter to prevent his particular machinery from getting a bad name, not because of any inherent defect in it, but because it has been misused. After all, there are still many millions of people in the world who could see the point of putting petrol in a motor car to make it go, but who would not bother about filling up with oil; just as it is still exceedingly common practice to run a machine until it breaks down and then think about repairing it: maintenance is, it is so often held, unnecessary or a waste of time and money.[1]

Aside from the problems created by environmental differences between countries, there are two significant trends which should also be considered in the marketing of industrial goods abroad: (1) a rapidly growing demand and (2) sharply increasing competition from both revitalized and reconstructed former industrial giants like West Germany and new industrial opponents such as Japan. To remain competitive in today's foreign market requires for many a reevaluation of their marketing programs in light of these trends. The successful manufacturer of industrial goods for foreign trade cannot expect to be sought out to have his goods *bought;* he must effectively compete with the many eager and relatively new competitors who are actively *selling* to increasingly more demanding customers.

Growth is occurring not only in the sale of tangible industrial goods but in the sale of intangibles or services as well. Rapid economic growth, active competition, and the lack in many developing countries of a ready pool of highly skilled technicians and experts have created a steadily growing international market for services ranging in purpose from marketing research to engineering assistance.

---

[1] Henry Deschampsneufs, *Selling Overseas* (London: Business Publications Limited, 1960), p. 104.

The objective of this chapter is to discuss the special problems in marketing industrial goods internationally, the increased competition and demand for industrial goods, and their implications for the foreign marketer.

THE INDUSTRIAL PRODUCT

Since an industrial product is purchased for business use and thus sought, not as an entity in itself, but as part of a total process, the buyer naturally places stress on such features as dependability, performance, and costs. In foreign markets these features are complicated for the marketer by the differences that exist between countries. Such variations place different emphasis upon dependability, performance, and costs. One such complicating factor is the degree of industrial development achieved by different countries.

Stage of Economic Development

Perhaps the most significant environmental factor affecting the market for industrial products is the degree of industrialization. Although generalizing about countries is a dangerous practice, the stage of economic development of a country can be used as a rough gauge of market characteristics for industrial goods. Regardless of the stage, demand for industrial products exists, but different levels of development typically result in changes in the demand and the kinds of quality of industrial goods sought.

Since industrial goods are products for industry, it is only logical that there is a relationship between the degree of economic development and the character of demand for industrial goods found within the country. One authority suggests that nations can be classified in one of five different stages of development. This classification is essentially a production-oriented approach to economic development in contrast to the marketing-oriented approach used in Chapter 6.[2] Although the development of productive facilities parallels the evolution of the marketing process, the emphasis in this section is upon the development of manufacturing as a basis for the demand for industrial products rather than the development of the marketing process. A production-orientation is helpful since at each stage some broad generalizations can be made about the level of development and the industrial market within the country.

The first phase of development is really a preindustrial or commercial stage where there is little or no manufacturing and the economy is almost wholly based upon the exploitation of raw materials and agricultural products. The demand for industrial products is confined to a rather limited range of goods used in the simple production of the country's resources, i.e., the industrial machinery, equipment, and goods

---

[2] See Chapter 6 for a more complete discussion of marketing and economic development.

required in the production of these resources. During this stage a transportation system develops which creates a market for highly specialized and expensive construction equipment that must be imported.

The second stage reflects the development of primary manufacturing concerned with the partial processing of raw materials and resources which in stage one were shipped in raw form. At this level there is a demand for the machinery and other industrial goods necessary for the processing of the raw materials prior to exportation. For example, in Kenya, a trade mission reports the need for empty jute bags, sulphur in lumps, bleaching powder and alum for a sugar factory, and fertilizers for a plantation.

The third stage of development is characterized by the growth of manufacturing facilities for nondurable and semidurable consumer goods. Generally, the industries consist of small local manufacturers of consumer goods having relative mass appeal. In such cases, the demand for industrial products extends to entire factories and the supplies necessary to support manufacturing. Liberia is a country at this stage of development, and the Liberian Development Corporation has been focusing attention on the possibility of developing small- and medium-size industries, such as shoe factories and battery and nail manufacturing. Such a degree of industrialization requires machinery and equipment to build and equip the factories and the supplies to keep them operating. Liberia's chief imports from the United States are construction and mining equipment, motor vehicles and parts, metal structures and parts, and manufactured rubber goods.[3]

A country at stage four is really a fairly well-industrialized economy. This stage reflects the production of capital goods as well as consumer goods, including such products as automobiles, refrigerators, and machinery. Even though there is production of industrial goods within the country, there is still a need for the importation of industrial goods; however, the demand is for the more specialized and heavy capital equipment not yet produced in the country but necessary to supply domestic industry. Exhibit 11–1 illustrates this phenomenon in the Scandinavian market. This stage is often accompanied by a rapid growth of consumer demand which in turn creates an increase in demand for industrial goods. In Italy, for example, a U.S. Department of Commerce study revealed that, as a result of a fairly rapid increase in auto ownership in Italy, there is a sizable increase in the need for diagnostic and testing apparatus. There are presently about 2,000 shops that have this equipment but there is a need for approximately 23,000 repair shops with such modern equipment as wheel alignment indicators and motor analyzers. It is this kind of equipment which will be produced within the country as it moves from the fourth to the fifth stage of development, complete industrialization.

A country in stage five has reached a point of complete industrialization which generally denotes world leadership in the production of a large variety of goods. Countries that have achieved this level typically

---

[3] "Liberia," *International Commerce*, July 14, 1969, p. 61.

compete the world over for markets for both their consumer and industrial goods. Even though a country might be completely industrialized, a demand still exists within it for industrial goods from other countries. Characteristic of a high degree of industrialization is a tendency to specialize in the production of certain goods which by no means would include everything such an industrialized nation would need. Such specialization creates intense competition with domestic industries as well as with foreign industries. Japan has achieved or is on the threshold of achieving the fifth stage of industrial development. Although it is an industrialized economy, there is still the need to import such products as automated industrial equipment, electronic computers, bookkeeping

EXHIBIT 11–1

The Scandinavian Market for Industrial Goods, 1964–67

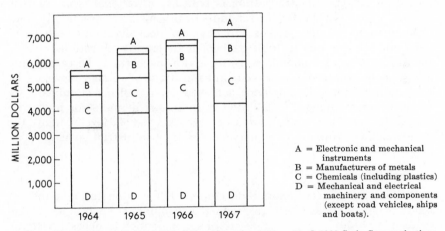

A = Electronic and mechanical instruments
B = Manufacturers of metals
C = Chemicals (including plastics)
D = Mechanical and electrical machinery and components (except road vehicles, ships and boats).

Source: Reprinted from *Industrial Marketing*, November 1969, p. 66. © 1966 Crain Communications, Inc., Chicago, Ill., U.S.A.

and accounting machines, and scientific controlling and measuring equipment. Just a few years ago, a widely held impression of trade with Japan was that the market consisted mainly of raw materials. Although there is a vast market for raw materials in resource-poor Japan, there is also a vast market for industrial goods. In fact, the leading U.S. exports to Japan is machinery, which increased to $510 million in 1969.[4] The mushrooming industrial growth in the various countries is not a threat to demand, but a widening market for more advanced and highly engineered products.[5]

Although each stage of industrial development appears to be very clear-cut, most countries are actually in a state of economic and indus-

---

[4] "Japan," *International Commerce*, July 14, 1969, p. 38.

[5] The basis for the various stages of economic development was taken in part from William Copulsky, "Forecasting Sales in Underdeveloped Countries," *Journal of Marketing*, July 1959, pp. 36–40.

trial flux striving for greater and more rapid economic growth. As one observer noted: "Don't expect to sell an automation feature in places where people till their fields by hand. On the other hand, don't underestimate the newly awakening nations. The term 'underdeveloped' can be very deceiving. Ghana owns and operates a *research reactor.*"[6]

Not all segments of a nation's economy will be at the same stage of development. An economy may operate at several levels of industrial development at once, but one degree of development will be more prominent than any other.

Political and National Implications

Additional points to keep in mind when studying industrial markets are the political and national implications affecting the demand for industrial goods. Industrialization is typically a national issue, and industrial goods are the fodder for industrial growth. Consequently, purchasing motives and patterns can have political overtones both internally and internationally. Industrial goods frequently are counted among the implements of economic warfare, and a market may be turned into a battlefield of international political aspirations of foreign powers. The stage of economic development achieved often reflects significant internal political changes in addition to increased demand for industrial goods. In fact, in some cases at certain stages of development, the government is in reality the customer for most industrial goods.[7]

Product Design

Besides the effect economic development has upon the demand for kinds of goods, it also affects product development. Each stage of advancement requires a greater degree of sophistication in necessary equipment since the general technological proficiency of a country is tied closely to its economic development. For example, a country in the third stage of industrialization does not have an adequate pool of trained technicians, nor has the general level of technical abilities reached a very significant degree of achievement. Therefore, the adequacy of a product must be considered in relation to the general environment within which it will be operated rather than solely on the basis of technical efficiency. Equipment that requires a high degree of technical skill to operate, maintain, or repair can be completely inadequate in a country that lacks a pool of technically skilled labor.

United States manufacturers have often been guilty of violating the concepts of good design of products for foreign markets to such an extent that they are accused of having little or no concern for customers outside the United States. Generally cited as evidence of this is the United States's rather reluctant role in helping set up world standards

---

[6] Louis H. Aricson, "Some Facts and Fallacies in Planning International Sales," *Export Trade,* July 1, 1963, pp. 10–12.

[7] For further detail on the political sides of marketing it is suggested that the reader refer to Chapter 5 on political environment.

for industrial equipment. The American Standards Association has reported that U.S. industry has not even taken the trouble—or spent the money—to have its 1,700 national standards translated for use in foreign countries. The reason usually given for this lack of interest is that markets are too small to justify design change; thus, American manufacturers often have failed to capitalize on a potential that could be created by product design. In light of the competition that exists today, a company must consider the nature of its market along with the possibility of designs adapted to such markets if it is to remain competitive. More and more American companies are reaching the conclusion that to compete effectively internationally they will have to put aside American designs that have been resisted by foreign buyers and develop new ones aimed at the special needs of the overseas market. Success in foreign markets "depends on giving those markets the kind of products they need and want, products which are not necessarily those designed for U.S. markets."[8]

Concept of Quality. Industrial marketers frequently misinterpret the concepts of quality. Good quality as interpreted by a highly industrialized market may be completely inadequate when interpreted by the less developed emerging nations. For example, an African government had been buying hand-operated dusters for use in distributing pesticides in the cotton fields. The dusters were loaned to individual Negro farmers. The duster supplied by the corporation was a finely machined device requiring regular oiling and good care. But the fact that this duster turned more easily than any other duster on the market was relatively unimportant to the native farmers. Furthermore, the requirement for careful oiling and care simply meant that in a relatively short time the machines froze up and broke. The result? The local government went back to an older type French duster which was heavy, turned with difficulty, and gave a poorer distribution of dust, but which lasted longer in that it required less care and lubrication.[9] In this particular situation and at this specific time, the French machine possessed the more relevant quality features and therefore in marketing terms possessed the highest quality.

It must be remembered that the concept of quality is not an absolute measure but one relative to use patterns and/or predetermined standards. Best quality is best in the sense that the product adheres exactly to specified standards which have been determined by expected use of the product. Since use patterns are frequently different from one economy to another, standards will vary with the result that superior quality in one country falls far short of superior quality as determined by needs in another country.

Variations in Product Features. The design and quality of a product should be viewed from many points. The extreme variations in climatic conditions create problems in designing equipment that is universally

---

[8] "Designs on Foreign Markets," *U.S. News and World Report,* April 12, 1965, p. 117.

[9] Richard D. Robinson, *International Business Policy* (New York: Holt, Rinehart & Winston, 1964), pp. 178–79.

operable. Products that function effectively in the United States may require major design changes in order to operate as well in the hot, dry Sahara region or the humid, tropical rain forests found in parts of Latin America. Trucks designed to travel the superhighways of the United States may experience operational difficulties in the mountainous regions of Latin America on roads that more closely resemble Jeep trails than superhighways. There are many variations found among nations which must be considered if a manufacturer desires to make a product that is functional for its markets. One authority suggests the following as being important considerations in designing a product for a particular country.[10] On the left are various features that may affect design, and on the right are the areas of design affected.

Level of technical skills	Product simplification
Level of labor cost	Automation or manualization of product
Level of literacy	Remarking and simplification of product
Level of income	Quality and price change
Level of maintenance	Change in product tolerances
Climatic differences	Product adaptation
Isolation	Product simplification and reliability improvement
Differences in standards or number systems	Recalibration of products and resizing
Availability of other products	Greater or lesser product integration
Power availability	Resizing product
Special conditions	Product redesign or invention

In each case, the change required may be adjustments in functional features rather than fundamental design revisions. Nevertheless, the more adaptable the product is to the particular needs of a market, the more competitive the company is likely to be.

Service, Replacement Parts, and Standards

Effective competition abroad requires prompt deliveries and the ability to furnish spare and replacement parts without delay, as well as proper product design. In the highly competitive Common Market, for example, it is mandatory to be in a position to give the same kind of service a domestic company or a Common Market company can give. One U.S. export management firm warned that U.S. business may be too apathetic about Europe, treating it as a subsidiary market not worthy of "spending time to develop." He cites the case "of an American firm with a 3 million dollar potential sale in Europe which did not even give engineering support to its representative when the same sale in the States would have brought out all the troops."[11]

---

[10] Robert Theobald, "Profit Potential in the Developing Countries," American Management Association Research Study No. 53 (1962), p. 61.

[11] "U.S. Apathy in Europe?" *Business Abroad*, February 1969, p. 1.

A recent study of international users of heavy construction equipment revealed that, next to the manufacturer's reputation, quick delivery of replacement parts was of major importance in purchasing construction equipment. Furthermore, 70 percent of those questioned indicated that they bought parts not made by the original manufacturer of the equipment because of the difficulty of getting original parts. Neglect of proper sales service because orders are small is often the excuse given; yet one can only speculate on orders lost to competitors because one small order was not properly handled.

Time and again, we learn that a definite order has been placed by a Nicaraguan importer in good standing, who thereafter either does not receive a response from the American exporter or a much delayed response. . . . Oftentimes, orders for replacement parts are virtually ignored by the American exporter. No one need stress the importance of the timely availability of spare parts to retain a market.[12]

Besides the competitive disadvantage of not providing adequate parts service, the foreign marketer may also be foregoing the opportunity of participating in a very lucrative after-market. Since some kinds of machine tools use up five times their original value in replacement parts during an average lifetime and thus represent an even greater market, one international machine tool company has capitalized on the need for direct service and available parts by changing its distribution system from the "normal" to one of stressing rapid service and readily available parts. Instead of selling through independent distributors as most machine tool manufacturers in foreign markets do, this company has established a series of company stores and service centers similar to those found in the United States. As a result of the change, the company stands ready to render service through its system of local stores, while most competitors dispatch servicemen from their home-based factories. Servicemen are kept on tap for rapid service calls in each of its network of local stores, and each store keeps a large stock of standard parts available for immediate delivery. The net results of meeting industrial needs quickly are keeping the company among the top suppliers in foreign sales of machine tools.

Universal Standards

A lack of universal standards is another problem faced by manufacturers of industrial products for foreign trade. A former U.S. Secretary of Commerce stressed the need for common standards if the United States was to compete effectively in foreign markets. In a speech he stated: "Only if there are common standards among nations sharing common economic interests will our products have equal competitive footing; . . . new international standards, I'm convinced, can increase American exports, can increase world trade."[13]

---

[12] "Each Sales Neglect Aids U.S. Competitors in Central America," *International Commerce*, October 27, 1969, p. 3.

[13] "Hodges Sees Global Standards Key to U.S. Survival in World Markets," *Export Trade*, March 11, 1963, pp. 5–6.

BOX 11-1

Superior U.S. Service

The solution does not lie only or principally in further effort by the U.S. government. U.S. business could do more to help itself. The reputation U.S. business has gained in this African nation over several years for failing to answer correspondence, for frustrating referrals to inefficient European associates, for service on maintenance and parts, failure to provide catalogues and data in metric terms, and a "take it or leave it" attitude on terms is depressing. It is particularly so when one discovers that many of the criticisms are fully justified.

Source: "U.S. Methods Seen Detrimental to North African Sales," *International Commerce*, October 27, 1969, pp. 2-3.

In the United States there are two major areas of concern to the industrial exporter. One is a lack of common standards for highly specialized equipment manufacturing, such as machine tools, and the other problem area is in the use of the inch-pound[14] or English system of measurement. Domestically, the use of the inch-pound and the lack of a universal manufacturing standard are not much of a problem, but it causes many serious consequences when affected products are scheduled for export. Conflicting standards are encountered in test methods for materials and equipment, quality control systems, and machine specifications. Most countries except England and its former colonies use the metric system, and the difficulty and complexity of change or adjustment from the inch-pound system to the metric system and vice versa creates many costly problems. There are some major steps being taken to help alleviate the problem.

Efforts are being made through international organizations which have as their purpose the creation of international standards; for example, the I.E.C. (International Electrotechnical Commission) is concerned with such things as standard specifications for electrical equipment of machine tools.[15] Another international organization interested in the development of world standards is the I.S.O. (International Organization to Standardization). In the United States there is some evidence of a gradual change to the metric system; however, the process will be a slow one since equipment and machine tool manufacturers are reluctant to shift while there is still a need for interchangeability of parts calibrated on the present inch-pound system. For this reason, the time and cost that would be required to successfully shift completely from one system to another is difficult to justify in the eyes of many. It has been pointed out that "General Electric, for example, estimates that its own conversion to the metric system would cost in the area of 200 million dollars and Ford Motor Company fears the switch might

---

[14] Also referred to as the "foot" or "yard-pound" system.
[15] Deschampsheufs, op. cit., p. 100.

BOX 11–2

Make Everything Interchangeable

Caterpillar now is organized so that both its people and its products are interchangeable on a worldwide basis. We have a freedom of transfer of people between plants, subsidiaries, and countries, and our products have a complete dimensional interchangeability which is vital to both the international contractors and to the military. Interchangeability of product and components is the major criterion for operating outside the U.S. We design the basic product in the U.S. and adapt it overseas to local conditions for complete functional, dimensional, and endurance interchangeability. This means we can begin production of a tractor in Aurora, Illinois, make its pistons in Japan, its crankshaft in France, and the final drive in Australia, on metric or linear scale, and run the machine to our satisfaction in any of these locations. We can use several different languages and two measuring systems on a drawing and still turn out a workable piece of machinery. This approach gives Caterpillar a tremendous logistics advantage. It means the international contractor and the military can get delivery on parts, components, and product from several sources and can buy for different currencies.

Source: "The Multinational Diet That Helps 'Cat' Thrive," *Business Week,* August 13, 1966, pp. 70–77. Reprinted by permission.

take up to 25% of its capital investment."[16] Possibly, as American industry's sales are more and more accounted for by foreign customers, the need will be justified. And, it appears that evidence of that need is already emerging.

From 1960 to 1966 U.S. exports to metric countries dropped 16%, while exports to non-metric countries rose during the same period by 11%. That's the reason the Commerce Department's National Bureau of Standards has undertaken an exhaustive study of what a massive change-over to the metric system would do to the U.S. economy.[17]

In the meantime, steps have been taken to ease the problem: most products destined for overseas shipment have both weights and dimensions in the dual systems; the pharmaceutical industry has changed to the metric system entirely; and the chemical industry has also begun to convert. In the latter two cases, however, the problems faced in conversion were much simpler than those faced by equipment manufacturers. Another point of interest is the decision by the British governmen t to convert to the metric system by 1975. Since England and the United States are the major users of the foot-pound system, perhaps England's decision will be instrumental in effecting a change in the United States. When Britain does convert, the United States will be alone with a

---

[16] *Sales Management,* February 1, 1969, p. 29.

[17] Reprinted by permission from *Sales Management, The Marketing Magazine,* February 1, 1969, p. 29. Copyright, 1969, Sales Management, Inc.

complicated, outdated system of weights and measures that will have tremendous competitive consequences.

The marketing of industrial goods in the domestic market requires service, available replacement parts, and uniform standards in order to be successful in competitive marketing. When a company goes overseas, however, these problems are magnified because of distribution problems, inadequate service facilities, and differing standards that lead to incompatibility of machinery and equipment. These problems cannot be ignored but must receive extra emphasis if the company intends to assign itself to a long-range "complete" commitment in foreign markets. Product is only one of the decision areas affected by the environment of the overseas nation facing the industrial marketer operating in foreign countries; channels of distribution and their availability are others.

CHANNEL STRATEGY FOR INDUSTRIAL PRODUCTS

There are available to the foreign marketer of industrial goods a multitude of channel alternatives to effect the distribution of goods. American firms distribute in three distinct ways:[18] through American-based export middlemen; through foreign-based middlemen; and through company-managed and organized sales forces. Companies can use any combination of these three means of distribution or only one, depending upon the extent of their involvement in foreign marketing, their organization, production facilities, and financial status. In each category, several different kinds of institutions are available for use, or several kinds of company-owned sales organizations are utilized.

The type of distribution employed depends upon several factors. The use of domestic-based exporters is probably adequate for small companies without extensive acumen in foreign operations or for a firm that prefers a minimum of involvement in foreign sales. Those companies, however, that intend to become truly international in scope and are totally committed to foreign marketing need the more direct methods available. The decision to deal with an agent or distributor or to set up an independent sales organization is influenced by a multitude of factors —availability of adequate middlemen, finances, desired control of sales, character of the product. The successful use of entirely different methods of distribution by two large companies serves as a good illustration. A leading manufacturer of machine tools has established its own sales distribution points throughout Europe. The decision was based on the need to provide rapid service for its equipment in order to remain competitive and on a desire to participate in the lucrative parts market associated with the use of its products. It was found that this method of distribution was the most suitable for the company's circumstances. On the other hand, a leading manufacturer of farm and earth-moving equipment has recently changed from direct distribution through company-owned sales subsidiaries to the use of independent local distributors. It was decided that independent local distributors would provide this company with a stronger organization that was more economical

---

[18] For a complete discussion see Chapter 20.

BOX 11–3

Rivals Are Nipping at IBM's Heels

When Paris Metro executives decided to buy twenty small computers to take tickets on a new subway line, they got taken instead. Possibly out of Pan-European chauvinism, they bypassed the U.S.'s Honeywell in favor of Holland's Phillips, which promptly bought the computers from Honeywell, labeled them Phillips, and boosted their price 30%. If Honeywell made computers in France, the run around might have been avoided—and partly because of snafoos like this, American computer makers have caught the IBM itch to manufacture overseas.

The incentive is Europe's burgeoning data-processing market, which is expected to surpass 2 billion dollars this year and is growing at twice the U.S. rate. IBM started assembling computers overseas in the 1950's and now dominates 60% of the continental market. Five years ago, General Electric bought up French and Italian computer makers in a costly effort to block IBM that has yet to pay off. Now, Honeywell, National Cash Register, Univac, and Burroughs are rushing to open new European plants, mostly to make office-sized data-processing equipment.

Making computers in Europe is more expensive than in the U.S., but quicker delivery and easier understanding of clients' needs outweigh the higher costs. Above all manufacturing in Europe is good politics, especially since government clients are the biggest computer users.

Source: *Business Week,* January 17, 1970, pp. 48–49. Reprinted by permission.

and far more stable since its products are sensitive to economic shifts. Particularly in smaller markets a distributor would be better able to weather economic ups and downs by carrying complementary products. Furthermore, the manufacturer felt that a local distributor would be more effective than its own sales organization because the former would have better market knowledge and would eliminate the normal break-in period required by company-owned operations. A final point—through the use of local distributors, the company could exploit markets that were too small to support a company sales organization but needed the services available from locally based distribution points. In today's buyer's market, unless a company can provide after-sales service, including prompt delivery, repair, and adequate supplies of replacement parts, a direct sales force may not be effective. As one marketer noted about selling industrial goods in Latin America:

> It is more evident than ever that fine social contracts no longer are enough to sell U.S. industrial equipment in South America. The representative or agent who handles many lines from a small office is slowly losing ground to the engineering firm which can prepare technical bids . . . [and] stock spare parts.[19]

The evolving market pattern indicates that the company which plans a long-range program abroad and wishes to remain competitive will have

---

[19] Stephan W. Kann, "Changing Marketing Patterns in South America," *Industrial Marketing,* March, 1959, p. 45.

to select full service distributors or organize its own sales unit to include a complete stock of parts and full service facilities. Since agents do not normally provide much in the way of extra services, a company which utilizes agents in its distribution system must arrange for the additional services through other means.

International trade fairs and trade centers found throughout the major market areas of the world may also be considered methods of distribution. Although these fairs do provide a means for the introduction of new products or an introduction into new markets, thereby helping to establish trade relations, they are primarily classified as promotional activities and will be discussed in the following section on promotion.

PROMOTIONAL PROBLEMS ABROAD

The promotional problems encountered by the foreign industrial marketer are little different from the problems faced by domestic marketers. A major exception is the availability of specialized media in some countries. The paucity of ad media, however, is of greater concern in selling consumer goods since industrial markets are easily reached through catalogs, direct mail, and trade fairs, which are important promotional media in international marketing.

Industrial Trade Fairs and Trade Centers

Trade fairs date back in history to the time when most trade was centered at markets or fairs. Today's international fairs are generally government-sponsored attempts to facilitate foreign trade. Governments, among them the U.S. government, often sponsor international trade fairs within their own countries which are open to domestic and foreign exhibitors. They also sponsor fairs and trade centers in other countries to facilitate foreign trade for their domestic industries in these countries.

Fairs provide the facilities for a manufacturer to exhibit and demonstrate his products to potential users. They are an opportunity to create sales and establish relationships with agents and distributors which can lead to more permanent distribution channels in foreign markets. Thirty-nine American firms participated in a seven-day electronics production equipment exhibition in Osaka, Japan, and came home with $1.6 million in confirmed orders and estimates for the coming year of $10.1 million. Five of the companies were seeking Far Eastern agent/distributors through the show and each was able to sign a representative before the show closed.[20] Trade fairs are scheduled periodically and any interested manufacturer can reserve space to exhibit his goods.

The American government has also established permanent trade centers where products from various American industries are exhibited for specific time periods. In 1970, there were seven permanent U.S. trade centers in London, Frankfurt, Milan, Bangkok, Stockholm, Tokyo, and

---

[20] "Japanese Show Ends with Ten Million Dollars in Projected Orders," *International Commerce*, November 10, 1969, p. 21.

Rome.[21] The trade center functions in the same manner as a trade fair except that the former is permanent and operates the year around. It has an average of eight to ten shows a year.

An interesting variation of the trade fair is a trade ship. The Japanese outfitted the *SS Sakura Maru* with the exhibits of several hundred Japanese firms, and in four months of visiting foreign ports, it generated sales of over $15 million for the Japanese companies represented. It was such a success that the U.S. government followed suit with the *SS Trade Fair* which houses several hundred exhibitors and calls on some 30 ports around the world in areas not typically served by international trade fairs or trade centers.

Proper Emphasis in Promotional Mix

Although international trade fairs are generally successful means of promotion, they should not be expected to serve as a primary means of promotion, since they do not provide the range of promotional coverage necessary for industrial goods. Rather, a combination of promotional devices is required in an adequate promotional mix. A recent survey in England indicated that the entire promotional mix in at least one industry may need some overhauling. The survey included both the buyers and sellers of machine tools. The sellers were asked to give the percentage of their promotional dollar spent on various media, and the buyers were asked to list in order of importance the channels of information they regarded as important in hearing about industrial goods. The results of this particular study indicated that the media emphasis being employed was incorrect. Suppliers revealed that their promotional funds were spent in the following manner:

Display advertising	34%
Exhibitions	27%
Leaflets, brochures, and catalogs	26%
Direct mail	4%
House organs	4%
Miscellaneous	5%

Buyers, however, indicated the following sources (shown in descending order of importance) as means of gathering data on industrial goods:

Technical journal ads
Manufacturer's catalogs
Leaflets and brochures
Technical journal editorial items
Exhibitions
House organs

As this study disclosed, the machine tool manufacturers are placing emphasis on exhibition as a major selling technique, whereas 84 percent of the buyers surveyed indicated that, although they encouraged their technical staffs to attend trade fairs, they considered them to be an

---

[21] *Business Abroad,* January 1970, p. 12.

inadequate means of disseminating industrial product information.[22]

It should be kept in mind that this survey was limited to a particular industry and country and therefore would not be generally applicable; however, the apparently improper emphasis brought to light by the study does suggest that other promotional mixes may be as out of phase as the English machine tool manufacturers in question. A foreign marketer who is unsure of his promotional mix and who has no substantial evidence of what the proper mix should be would be well advised to conduct research on market and industry characteristics before obligating promotional funds to any "obvious or normal" promotional pattern.

PRICING AND COMPETITION

One of the outgrowths of the rapidly growing world markets for industrial goods is the considerable price competition among those vying for this expanding market. The problem is compounded by aggressive competition from suppliers and by the political involvement of the governments of some manufacturers. As was mentioned earlier, industrial goods are often the cannon fodder of an economic war being waged to win the political allegiance of the underdeveloped countries. As a result, foreign marketers may often be confronted with impossible price competition when prices are shaded by a foreign government for political rather than economic reasons. Today, India, Brazil or any of the other underdeveloped and industrializing nations can buy Russian-made machinery and equipment at prices at least 50 percent lower than those charged by American manufacturers for similar goods. Such political price competition cannot be surmounted by private industry.

American manufacturers are facing other kinds of price problems abroad, too. It has been charged that they are pricing themselves out of the market and that they possess a too conservative policy with regard to price and credit. Reports from India indicate that while there is a booming market in that country for machine tools, selling American products is difficult if not impossible because of the manufacturer's insistence on payment in dollars. The Soviet bloc nations and our West European competitors are not making this mistake.

Although European concerns offer liberal credit terms and payment in almost any of the world's currency, U.S. manufacturers are hesitant about granting credit and usually demand payment in dollars. One authority on international marketing asks,

As a practical matter, how important are prices in making purchasing decisions? Of course, if there are substantial differences as between two sources of supply price can become dominant. Nevertheless, in world as in domestic markets, unless the differential is great, there may be other more important factors.[23]

---

[22] "Industrial Marketing in Great Britain," *Industrial Marketing,* January 1964, pp. 21–22.

[23] "Is the U.S. Being Priced Out of World Markets?", Laurence P. Dowd, in *Marketing Concepts in Changing Times,* by Richard Hill, ed. Proceedings of the 1960 Winter AMA Conference, 1960, p. 185.

BOX 11-4

Credit Lack "Cuts U.S. Export Muscle"

The Commerce Department is determined to bring about improvements in U.S. export financing and aims to reconcile "varying views within Government as to the methods and priorities," a Department official told businessmen recently.

Speaking to the 43rd annual meeting of the Propeller Club of the United States at Savannah, Ga., Harold B. Scott, Director of the Bureau of International Commerce, said that lack of competitive export financing "is cutting into the muscle of our export expansion effort."

He reviewed the current situation in this field:

"As matters now stand, most of our major competitors are able to extend lower-cost, more flexible export financing.

"Export credit competition takes place in the international marketplace. Accordingly, our competing nations—but not the United States—have insulated export financing from domestic monetary conditions and policies, usually by central bank discounting of export paper.

"The United States, without comparable facilities, suffers a disadvantage when U.S. domestic interest rates are high, as they now are. We fight a difficult battle when we try to compete with foreign export financing that is based on rates pegged below foreign domestic money costs.

"Preferential rates for medium-term export financing are approximately as follows for five leading nations: United Kingdom, 5½%; France, 4½ to 5.8%; West Germany, 7.5%; Italy, 5.9%; and Japan, 4 to 7%.

"By contrast, interest charges on U.S. commercial bank financing for export financing today range from 9 to 11%.

"In addition to the problem of U.S. export interest rates, to reach our annual export goal of $50 billion by 1973, forecasts indicate we will need up to $10 billion additional export financing—an amount exceeding combined commercial bank capabilities under present monetary conditions and of Ex-Imbank potential under present federal budget priorities.

"Last month, the National Export Expansion Council recommended substantially increased resources and exemption from budgetary limitations for the Ex-Imbank, as well as immediate exemption of export paper from the Federal Reserve Voluntary Credit Restraint Program. And to solve interest cost and liquidity problems and to insulate export credit from the vicissitudes of domestic monetary conditions, the Council recommended an effective facility to rediscount short-, medium- and long-term export paper that would be fast and automatic and could provide competitive interest rates to exporters, banks and foreign buyers."

Source: *International Commerce*, October 27, 1969, p. 10.

Price alone is not generally the sole determinant of purchase. In fact, there are reports that Venezuelan firms have indicated a willingness to pay 30 to 40 percent more for U.S. industrial products than for European if they could have adequate credit: presumably this is because of the better quality image of U.S. products. However, U.S. industrial goods are now being challenged on this front also, by other competitors.

It's not so much a case of deterioration of American quality, but rather the improvement of overseas offerings. Some of the German and Japanese machine tools match our own. And industrial buyers also point out that traditional quality advantages of U.S. products are narrowing along with the increasing variety and sophistication of foreign made goods.[24]

Equally important in industrial sales are the "other" factors, such as dependability, service, and parts replacement.

Price-Quality Relationship

The price-quality relationship also plagues the United States manufacturer. Standard requirements for quality of industrial products sold in the American market that require commensurately higher prices may be completely out of line for the needs of many of the underdeveloped growth markets of the world. Rather than question if American manufacturers are pricing themselves out of the world markets, it may be more appropriate to ask whether or not they are advancing themselves out of some world markets with products of extremely high quality. When you pay your bank 7½ percent a year or less and your labor $4.50 per hour or more, laborsaving features of a product make sense, but not when the going rate of pay is *$1.50 per day* and you have to pay 2 percent per month for money as in Mexico.[25] The laborsaving features of a product just do not mean much when time is not really worth much. Equally fallacious are arguments on the ability of machinery to hold close tolerances "where people are not quality control conscious, where production runs in the American volume sense do not exist, and where very skilful workmen cost so little that you can afford to let them take their time to do what amounts to selective fits in assembling and repairing work."[26] This does not mean that there is no interest in quality or costs in countries like Mexico, but that the achievement of low costs and good quality in these countries is not "through high-production, high-precision equipment and minimum labor cost but through the use of skilful labor under close supervision with the minimum of the most versatile low-cost equipment adequate for the job."[27] Hence, for the company that wishes to market its industrial goods in some countries abroad, it may be necessary to design products for the export market with fewer functional features in order to lower the price and thereby compete effectively on price.

Leasing in International Markets

An increasingly important selling technique that is helping to alleviate high prices and capital shortages for capital equipment is the leasing

---

[24] "Rising Prices: Blunting the Competitive Edge of U.S. Exports in World Markets," *Business Abroad*, November 1968, p. 14. Copyrighted © 1968 by The Reuben H. Donnelley Corporation. Reprinted by special permission from the November 1969 issue of *Business Abroad*.

[25] Willard M. Fox, "Is There an Industrial Market for You in Mexico," *Industrial Marketing*, October 1960, p. 88. See reading at end of this chapter.

[26] Ibid., p. 89.

[27] Ibid., p. 120.

BOX 11–5

Japan's Remarkable Machine

Japanese auto industry was created in its present form virtually by government decree—with, of course, the ascent of business. It all began in 1956 when the government enacted the Machinery Industry Promotion Law, pointedly aimed at shifting Japan's economic base from textiles and toys to heavy industry, with the emphasis on steel and automobiles. The auto makers pumped a staggering 4.7 billion dollars into new factories and equipment in the 60's. In 1969 alone, they put in 900 million dollars. Investments like this have helped them put up some of the world's most highly automated plants. In 1970, in huge, modern factories, Japanese car makers will turn out 5.6 million cars, trucks, and buses, second only to Detroit's projected 11 million vehicles. Now the Japanese are reaching for an even bigger prize—they are trying to become an international power in computers. They have a long way to go. True, Japan is already in second place to the U.S. in the number of computers installed world-wide. But the figures are 5600 machines to the U.S.'s 52,500. The Japanese started the revolution in consumer electronics by putting transistors in practically everything. Now, the government business establishment is determined to create a powerful computer industry. The Ministry of International Trade and Industry regards this as its next major project.

"The success of Japanese policy in autos has created a kind of psychosis in the Ministry," says one electronics executive. "They think they can do the same with any industry."

"We expect the Japanese to be a factor in the mini-computer market in the U.S. within a few years," says the Director of Industry Research for International Data Corporation. "Japanese computer companies are starting to set up sales and service organizations in Korea and are eyeing Taiwan. After a look around the Far East, a British expert predicts: 'The Asian market is soon going to be saturated by Japan.' U.S. trading superiority in technologically advanced products is being challenged on many fronts."

Source: "Japan's Remarkable Industrial Machine," *Business Week,* March 7, 1970, pp. 59–74. Reprinted by permission.

system.[28] The concept of equipment leasing has been slowly becoming important as a means of selling capital equipment in overseas markets.

The system of leasing as used by industrial exporters is not unlike typical lease contracts used in the United States. The terms of the leases generally run from one to five years, with payment made monthly or annually; included in the rental fee is covered for servicing, repairs, and spare parts. Just as the contracts for domestic and overseas leasing arrangements are similar, so are the basic motivations for leasing and the shortcomings. For example:

1. Leasing opens the door for a large segment of nominally financed foreign firms which can be sold on a lease but might be unable to buy for cash.

---

[28] "What's News?" *Business Abroad,* October 1969, p. 2.

2. Leasing can also ease the problems of selling new experimental equipment, since less risk is involved for the users.
3. Leasing helps guarantee better maintenance and service on overseas equipment.
4. Equipment leased and in use helps to sell other companies in that country.
5. Lease revenue tends to be more stable over a period of time than direct sales would be.

The disadvantages or shortcomings, however, take on a more international flavor. Besides the inherent disadvantages of leasing, there are some problems compounded by international relationships. In a country beset with inflation, lease contracts that include maintenance and supply parts, as most do, can lead to heavy losses toward the end of the contract period. Further, countries where leasing is most attractive are also those where spiraling inflation is most likely to occur. The added problems of currency devaluation, expropriation or other political risks are operative longer than if the sale for the same equipment is made outright. In the light of the aforementioned perils, there may exist greater risk in leasing than outright sale; however, there is definitely a trend toward increased use of this method of selling internationally.[29]

SUMMARY AND CONCLUSIONS

Adaptability is the key to the industrial markets of the world. Industrial users must buy on a profit basis; therefore, products which fulfill their needs exactly, not more nor less than they need, are the products which will be in demand. Companies which adapt their products to the variety of differing needs are the ones that should be the most effective in the marketplace. Industrial markets are lucrative and continue to grow as more countries strive for at least a semblance of industrial self-sufficiency.

Furthermore, although a particular country's state of economic and industrial development may not provide the industrial marketer with profitable demands for his products at a particular point in time, the future potential should be examined thoroughly with the thought of gaining market position. It must be remembered that the economic development of a country can pass through several stages in a short period of time. A company which establishes itself in a market and assists in this growth before it is profitable may find itself in an unparalleled competitive position once the market does develop.

As the market grows, however, so does competition from the world's industrial nations. Success will most probably be enjoyed by those companies which are user-oriented and produce for the specific needs of their industrial customers.

---

[29] "How Clark Sees the Leasing Market in Europe," *Business Abroad,* May 13, 1968, p. 15.

READINGS

IS THERE AN INDUSTRIAL MARKET FOR YOU IN MEXICO?*

WILLARD M. FOX

Selling industrial products in Mexico can be rough—if you try to use the methods that work in the United States and Canada.

True, if you are tactful, you speak French to your prospects in Montreal—but, the French-Canadian lives under the common law and understands the Anglo-American ways of looking at things and of doing business. When you cross the Rio Bravo (Rio Grande to you), you step into a different industrial world.

Mere translation of your catalogs and sales literature and advertisements into Mexican Spanish is not enough. While many Mexican business men know English well and often have degrees from American universities or engineering schools, their attitudes and their problems are different. They have no natural bent in favor of the United States, and there is no historical reason why they should. On the contrary, real or fancied slights from Americans, memory that the United States took half of Mexico, or just a generally antipathy toward "Sajones" frequently produce an anti-Gringo bias.

When you get down to brass tacks, there is no reason why a Mexican should prefer an American industrial product (all else being equal) to that of a German, British, Japanese, or other competitor. And, if he can also buy "Hecho en México" at the same price, quality considered, the foreign exchange saving gives him reason to do so.

Nevertheless, many American industrial marketers are making money in Mexico and will have a lot more as Mexico's industrialization goes on. They do so by realistic practices, fitted to Mexican—not American—industrial facts of life.

"Time Isn't Money"

"Time is money" is an American cliché; but, in Mexico, money is money and time isn't worth much. The just recently increased minimum wage in Mexico City is the equivalent of $1.12 a day and it is less elsewhere.

In the "Republic," i.e., outside the Federal District, a "maestro" (master mechanic, master painter, master carpenter, etc.) will work from daylight to dusk for $2 by the day and be glad to get it. He will do an excellent job with the crudest of tools, and not gripe about making do with practically nothing. Factory hands consider $1.25 to $1.75 princely wages, in the outlying states.

A typical "Help Wanted" advertisement in a leading Mexico City newspaper of Feb. 4, 1960, translates to read: "Typist and switchboard operator wanted in an important firm; the typist must be very respon-

---

* Reprinted, with special permission, from *Industrial Marketing*, October, 1960.

sible, beginning salary $52 a month, and for the switchboard operator $28. Apply, etc." Since no mention is made of an "English week," these salaries are for a five-and-a-half-day week from, probably 8 A.M. to 6 P.M. or from 9 A.M. to 8 P.M. which would mean a lunch hour from 2 to 4 P.M.

On the other hand, if you have $1,400 you want to lend on good security, that $1,400 will bring you $28 a month. If you are the conservative type, you can get 15 per cent a year on a real estate mortgage or you can buy a mortgage bond of the telephone company that will give you a current yield of more than 10 per cent and a yield to maturity of better than 12.5 per cent! This relationship between what people are worth and what pesos are worth takes a little mental adjustment on the part of Americans used to high wages and low bond yields.

Also, in the first nine months of 1959, Mexico mined 410,367.9 metric tons of iron ore, an amount that the Great Lakes ore fleets could probably handle in one sailing with half the boats tied up. New Jersey, not usually thought of as much of an iron ore state, mined more than this tonnage in 1955. While Mexico is a steel importing country, its consumption annually is just about what the U.S. steel industry can knock out in nine or ten shifts.

This combination of $2 a day labor, 2% a month money, and an effective market of small size explains why the Mexican business man wants 50 to 100% a year profit on his invested capital and goes about getting it by taking all the profit the market will bear on the volume he can sell easily.

"Labor Saving" No Argument

Industrial marketing men in the United States spend a lot of time and ingenuity on developing entirely valid proofs that a given piece of equipment replacing another given piece of older equipment will pay for itself out of labor savings (increased production per man hour) in "X" months. Smart industrial salesmen make a lot of sales (in the United States and Canada) through written proposals based on cost-saving studies in their prospects' plants. Industrial publications are full of advertisements based on case histories, attested to by the customers themselves, of proved savings that paid for the equipment in a few months.

Such arguments leave a Mexican business man cold. They just don't fit his situation. What is good business when you pay your bank 6% a year or less and your labor $3 an hour or more, makes no sense at all when you pay men $1.50 a day and the bank or the bondholders 1% a month.

Also, arguments based on the ability to hold close tolerances do not mean too much in a country where people are not quality control conscious, where production runs in the American volume sense do not exist, and where very skillful workmen cost so little that you can afford to let them take their time to do what amounts to selective fits in assembling and repairing work.

This is not to say that Mexican business men have no regard for quality or for costs. They are very cost conscious and becoming increasingly quality conscious. Rather, the road to low costs and good quality in Mexico is not through high-production, high-precision equipment and minimum labor cost but through the use of skilful labor under close supervision with the minimum of the most versatile low-cost equipment adequate for the job. The same formulae you use to establish lowest total net cost of a piece or a lot are valid in both countries; but the difference in the figures you put into the equations produces very different answers.

In its present stage of development and for years to come, the best job in Mexico can be done with a combination of 1960 American management methods and 1910 or 1920 or 1930 job shop or pilot plant equipment. This equipment, of course, can be styled and streamlined for efficiency and eye appeal and operator safety, but it does not need elaborate instrumentation and delicate controls.

Industrial Growth

The 1960 census of population is expected to show that Mexico has around 33 million people, of whom about 34% are estimated as "economically active." Of these 11 million economically active people, a high proportion are misemployed or disemployed—really unemployed in any productive sense. These unfortunates include the *peones* who scratch out the barest kind of living on poor land with poor tools and poor seed; the ubiquitous bookblacks, lottery ticket sellers, and hawkers of baskets, rebozos, pottery and other wares; the pitiful "retailers" who try to make a living by selling fruits and vegetables from two-by-four stands on the streets; and the hordes of domestic servants who earn five or six cents an hour.

The Mexican government—extremely interventionist in its philosophy—is striving hard to wipe out illiteracy and to promote industrialization. About two-thirds of its annual budget goes into "investment" in the infra-structure of roads, schools, etc., and into state-owned or state-participation business.

The government monopolizes the oil industry through Pemex, owns the railroads, and is deeply involved in such other basic industries as steel and cement. Through Nacional Financiera (the government development bank) it controls the largest Mexican steel corporation—Altos Hornos—which has recently acquired control of the third largest steel company, La Consolidada, which was formerly owned by U.S. interests.

Manufacturing has been growing at a rate of 6% per annum; electric power consumption, 11%; and steel in 1960 is expected to resume its historic growth rate of 14% a year. Altos Hornos plans to increase its capacity from 600,000 to 1 million tons, and Krupp is reported to be studying the building of a 500,000 ton mill in Michoacán to take advantage of the large iron ore reserves there.

The government has two compelling reasons for forcing industrialization as rapidly as possible and doing all it can to boost the high growth rates even higher.

1. The first is that it is faced with a population growth of 3% a year; a young population, so that the potential labor force is growing faster than population itself; and a desperate need to raise the standard of living of a population with a per capita income around $250 a year, compared to more than $2,000 in the United States and Canada.

2. The second is that it sees industrialization as the only way to decrease Mexico's vulnerability to the effects of world price declines in its export products—cotton; gold, silver, and base non-ferrous metals; coffee, sugar, and other tropical agricultural products. The current administration is working heroically to avoid another devaluation, and its efforts appear to be succeeding. By industrializing, it saves foreign exchange and strengthens its balance-of-payments position, thereby protecting the international value of the peso. An emerging middle class aspires to a standard of living comparable to what it sees north of the border, and will not take denial calmly.

Realists, but

While opposition parties are permitted and do exist, Mexico is a one-party country. The ruling party (PRI—Party of Revolutionary Institutions) is the heir of the Mexican Revolution of 1910–1917. Not Marxist, it was a leftist movement and had strong socialist and egalitarian-agrarian roots.

Consequently, Mexico is both a welfare state and a mixed economy with the government playing a larger role in business than the U.S. federal government does in American economic affairs. Every elected Mexican official must give at least lip service to the revolutionary ideals, and some men in government genuinely lean strongly toward socialism and many really believe in a mixed economy.

However, they are fully aware of the population trend and of the low standard of living of the majority of Mexicans, and are determined within the limits of their philosophy to do what they can to improve the situation. As a practical matter, they can do nothing to check the birth rate, and they know it.

They know that the salvation of Mexico depends upon the creation of productive jobs, and that it takes capital investment to create jobs. They also know that Mexico cannot generate the capital it needs anywhere nearly as fast as it needs that capital.

They are well aware, too, that political instability (though now happily a thing of the past) and recurring devaluations have made the majority of Mexicans fearful of any investment except real estate, with the result that the money Mexico needs for industrial investment is put into land. Consequently, they see to it that the door is open to foreign capital on the same terms as Mexican capital, except in certain basic industries that are reserved for the government or for Mexican investors.

They have gotten the yen for expropriation of foreign holdings pretty well out of their systems anyhow; but the antics of Castro in Cuba and the terrific come-backs of West Germany and Japan have forcefully reminded them that when you need the foreign money, kicking the foreigner who has it is a bad thing.

Gringos are not loved by Mexicans, but their business ethics and products are respected. The importance of U.S. investment (in 1959, some $80 million of new money) is recognized, and American companies can count on fair treatment in their courts. They have to have foreign money. They know it. They accept the fact.

U.S. Marketing Edge

While European and Japanese products have acceptance—and metric screw threads—a common border and a great deal of border trade give American products an edge. The United States is taking a little over half of Mexico's tangible product exports, and tourist expenditures, border trade (mostly American) and bracero (Mexican peon labor in U.S. agriculture) earnings are almost as large as total merchandise exports. That is, of every dollar that Mexico earns from exports of goods and services combined, the U.S. provides about 78 cents. Of Mexico's total imports, the United States sells about 76%. In the first nine months of 1959, Mexico had an excess of exports over imports and a favorable dollar balance. But apart from this very important ability to pay, other factors work for American businesses, too.

Mexicans do not particularly like Americans. They envy them and resent them. Nevertheless, they respect American business integrity and willingness to live up to a contract. They also have found out that American equipment usually works the way it is supposed to work, and that replacement parts fit, and quality is very uniform. In other words, they have learned that Americans pay attention to quality control and standardization. This is very un-Mexican, and they love it.

Psychologically, Americans have a great many advantages. Americans expect competition and regard it as inevitable. We, therefore, expect to work to get an order and to take care of it properly. If something does go wrong, we try to make it right. We look to repeat business for our profit, knowing that it often costs more to sell the first order than we can possibly recover from it. We try for volume enough to sell our plant capacity, and we price to make volume operation possible.

Those are not usual Mexican habits. By just doing what comes naturally to us, we give the kind of service and delivery and follow-up that few Mexican firms habitually give, and being closer to Mexico than our European and Japanese competitors we have communications and transportation time advantages going for us. In Mexico, as a matter of fact, "super" has acquired a meaning of "American," and, therefore, "good." There are supermotels, superhardwares, super parts dealers, etc., meaning American service or American stocks, and possibly the ability to speak English.

Selling in Mexico

There are five basic ways that you as an American firm can sell in Mexico:

1. You can export to Mexico, from your U.S. or foreign plants, using a Mexican broker or distributor, *provided* Mexico cannot or does not produce the product or produce it in sufficient quantity to supply local demand. This is the hardest way, as you may need to arrange many import permits and will have to work with customs brokers, banks and probably lawyers.

2. You *may* be able to work out either a licensing deal or a subcontracting deal with a Mexican firm that can make your products, exporting parts not available in Mexico, with fees for engineering and technical service that you render.

3. You can operate an assembly or finishing plant, using Mexican labor and some Mexican components if they are available, but importing parts and materials from the United States or from other foreign plants you own

4. You can manufacture in Mexico, using as much Mexican material as is available that meets your quality standards. This, like method 3, involves setting up a wholly-owned Mexican subsidiary corporation.

5. You can follow method 4, but take in a Mexican partner. In a few industries, you may *have* to take 51% Mexican capital into partnership, and in some others you may be smart to do so.

Your particular situation will determine which is best. A common sequence is 1–3–4, as a business grows; but other sequences have been used.

Ideally, Mexican officials would like step 5, but they will settle for a lot less. If you can qualify yourself as a "new and necessary" industry, i.e., if you make something not made in Mexico that will save foreign exchange and produce some jobs and some markets for Mexican raw materials, you can get red carpet treatment.

This *may* include: exemption from some federal taxes (and state taxes, if you stay outside Mexico City when you locate your plant); tariff protection; possibly imposition of quotas to make life tougher for your competitors who do not manufacture in Mexico; and, almost certainly, a preferred position as a vendor to government departments and government-owned or government participation businesses who can use your products.

If you make, in Mexico, something that saves dollars that the government buys, it will often pay a higher price in pesos than it has to pay in dollars simply to save exchange and help the balance-of-payments.

Mexican Partners

American companies often take a dim view of taking in foreign partners. However, there can be some advantages, particularly if the partner is a banking or financial group that has no interest in getting involved with production and distribution.

Such a group can smooth your way in the many dealings you will have with government. It can make it easier to get the licenses you need and to arrange to bring in management and technical personnel you need. It can help with credit lines and credit problems, besides providing cash that cuts your own commitment. It may be able to provide useful contacts with vendors and customers, and through its legal and statistical departments, to give you aid in making contracts, locating plants and defining markets.

Get Ready

Obviously, if you decide to come into Mexico, you are going to need expert advice. In Mexico City you will find American advertising agencies, accounting firms, customs brokers, financial institutions, management engineering firms and marketing counsellors, who know Mexican problems and American methods and points of view. Very likely, you will find quite a number of your U.S. vendors and customers already established and doing a profitable business in Mexico, so that to a degree you will be among friends.

One thing is sure. Industrially, Mexico is moving ahead and moving faster percentagewise than the United States. True, the market today is small by American standards, but it is growing. Mexico is the natural bridge between English-speaking North America and the Spanish (and Portuguese) speaking republics of Central and South America. Should a really close-knit Latin American common market evolve, as it may in the coming years, a strong Mexican operation can be a tremendous competitive asset.

INTERNATIONAL LEASING: FILLING EQUIPMENT NEEDS OF CAPITAL-SHORT CUSTOMERS AROUND THE WORLD*

Equipment leasing—a multibillion dollar business in the United States and mushrooming fast in Europe and Japan—also is accelerating into the developing nations of Africa, Latin America, and the Far East.

Prudential Insurance Co. helped give the concept an overseas push last month when it put up $7-million of the $10.8-million in equity and long-term financing needed to get a new company, TAW International Leasing, underway with continent-wide operations in Africa. Thomas A. Wood, president of TAW, said he already had scouted out at least $14-million worth of potential business in 11 countries and expects to lease nearly $9-million worth of equipment in Africa over the next year.

Already planning eventual expansion into Latin America and Asia, Wood thus joins a growing list of international leasing firms who are taking aim on a multimillion dollar market in the developing world. The customers there include not only local firms but governments and subsidiaries of foreign corporations hemmed in by scarcity of local capital.

·   ·   ·   ·   ·

TAW—launched with the blessing of the U.S. Agency for International Development—will be the first American leasing firm in Africa

---

* Reprinted by permission from the May 1970 issue of *Business Abroad,* pp. 11–24. Copyrighted © 1970 by The Reuben H. Donnelley Corporation.

and one of the few companies in the world leasing in a big way on the continent. Consumer hire-purchase is familiar to African enterprise, said TAW president Wood, "but equipment leasing as we think of it in the United States is hardly offered at all."

Wood sees developing countries as "practically made for leasing—they have abundant manpower for growth but lack capital and the equipment it can provide." Through leasing, he said, that capital can be provided "more cheaply and more conventionally than by any other means."

Prudential, which has taken a leading role in U.S. job opportunity programs for minority groups, sees TAW International Leasing as a vehicle to help satisfy social needs in other parts of the world. Frank J. Hoenemeyer, executive vice president of Prudential, said the insurance company "believes as does TAW, that leasing techniques, which have proved so fruitful here at home, can provide a substantial portion of the capital, equipment, and facilities necessary to promote the economic and social welfare of these developing nations."

Industrial equipment leasing—in 1952 barely a $10-million business and now nearing a $20-billion annual volume in the United States—also remains a growing glamor business in industrial Europe and Japan.

Although major U.S. leasing outfits have been in the world market for years, concentrating mainly in Europe, equipment leasing is still attracting newcomers and expansions, with a growing list of potential customers.

First National of Boston's decision to go into Japan on a major scale with Japanese partners underscores the rapid expansion of these techniques for capital equipment expansion needs in the Far East.

In Southeast Asia, Hertz—a name automatically associated with car rental services in more than 100 countries—has moved into heavy equipment leasing (heavy construction, logging, and mining machinery). . . .

.   .   .   .   .

According to Ned Mundell, president of U.S. Leasing Corp., leasing in Germany has grown 50% a year over the past five years; in France it has grown 40% yearly; and in Japan the growth has been 40–50%.

A Stanford Research Institute study indicates outstanding lease contracts in Europe totaled $1.3-billion at the end of 1968. By the end of 1980, SRI estimates this figure will reach $15-billion. In Japan Bank of Boston's leasing venture is off to a strong start with $10-million already on the books, and John Allen, vice president of its Boston Overseas Financial Corp., adds: "Our business there should double or triple in the next couple of years."

.   .   .   .   .

Overseas leasing receives much of its impetus from the tightness of the money market, combined (for U.S. firms, at least) with the direct investment curbs of the OFDI. In developing countries the need is accentuated because a long-term money market may not exist, even though OFDI regulations may not apply so stringently. The scarcity of medium- and long-term credit may force local authorities to place limitations on any financing beyond three years. Local institutional investors in such countries may be prohibited from investing in manufacturing enterprises. Often, the upshot is that local officials can be empowered to countersign a $10,000 lease payment but lack authority to authorize a $1-million investment.

Manufacturers hoping to cash in on the advantages of leasing over borrowing will find many of the options available in the States, and a few extras besides, in overseas deals.

Overseas leasing can save companies foreign exchange in establishing a new plant abroad besides offsetting restrictive investment regulations. The lessee invests in the new plant only partially with his own funds, and leases the rest in local currency. "The technique can result in a substantial reduction in foreign currency exposure," according to Allen.

Multi-currency leasing overseas is also gaining favor, reports U.S. Leasing's Mundell. This is particularly common in container leasing. A lessor in the U.K., for example, may own equipment in Denmark, and the currency of payments may be marks or lire. A manufacturer who is leasing containers around the world may be making payments in dozens of local currencies at each container depot.

Not all leasing techniques used in the United States are always found outside the United States. Captive leasing, where a manufacturer sets up a leasing firm to lease its own products, is one gambit that is still not common overseas, due in part to the less liberal provisions for amortizing property elsewhere.

Though leasing warehouse space and other real estate has become more widely used abroad in recent years, some countries specify that the user of real estate rather than its owner has the right to amortize property. In such a case it makes no sense for a leasing company to buy up real property for leasing.

Purchase options—where a lessee may take over ownership of leased property at the expiration of the lease by applying his lease payments against the market value of the equipment—will not be found in countries (like Venezuela) which recognize such agreements as conditional sales arrangements and tax them as such.

Generally, however, purchase options are popular in developing countries. Wood says, "In Africa most customers demand purchase options on the equipment they lease. So leasing there becomes a full-payout means of financing eventual ownership."

Full-payment leasing, where the total value of the equipment is returned in lease payments during the lease period, is hardly competitive in the U.S. with the more usual residual lease, in which payments cover only a certain percentage, say 80%, of the equipment value during the initial lease period. Overseas, full payout lease is still encountered, especially in developing areas.

One of the special values to leasing overseas is as a hedge against both obsolescence and inflation. In highly technological production, it is advantageous for many manufacturers to avoid tying themselves to equipment which, quickly outdated, leaves them trying to get their mileage out of expensive but behind-the-times capital goods.

In allowing a leasing company to take the obsolescence risk, a manufacturer who leases his equipment is only tied into it for the life of the lease, typically five years. During this time the lessee (the equipment user) can expense his lease payments for tax relief in most countries, making up what he may have lost by depreciating owned equipment.

And even though leasing is admittedly a higher-cost way of obtaining equipment than by straight borrowing, First Boston Financial Corp. vice president Earle Mace says a cash flow comparison often shows that "in the longer run leasing is cheaper than either financing or outright investment."

He and others familiar with leasing explain that a lessee can expense all his lease payments. Had the lessee invested or borrowed, he could have depreciated the owned equipment over its useful life for tax benefits (though the Treasury Dept. is reported to be considering "cost-recovery period" depreciation which would allow firms to depreciate at more favorable individual rates), but he could have expensed the lease payments in a much shorter time for a greater tax shield during those years.

If the lessee had used an accelerated depreciation schedule in countries where this is offered, depreciation allowances in later years would offer little or no tax shield, compared to the continued lease payments in the same years on non-owned equipment.

Companies which use leasing as an inflation hedge know that most leasing contracts spell out a specific payment schedule over the lease period. Such a set schedule benefits the lessee, whose payments decline in real value over time with inflation. Borrowing does not always offer the same hedge against rising prices because prime borrowing rates may go up and contracts have their interest rescheduled, or escalation clauses may be written into the loan repayment. Some leasing companies are reported to be taking a second look at repayment scheduling, but as yet leasing still protects the lessee in such countries as Brazil and Argentina.

And though much of the impetus behind overseas leasing today must come from the current monetary squeeze, lessors do not look for companies to trade their leases for loans even when interest rates come back down again: "We do not look for any decline," says Mace. When lower interest rates come, lessors will feel the relief in their own equipment financing and be able to pass this on to customers in lower lease payments.

Some of the local techniques companies use abroad in leasing can help them get around other investment restrictions. In Mexico banks may hold only a certain share of their investments in real property. One Mexican bank was engaged in a vigorous expansion program which entailed buying out a number of local banks; as it gained control of their physical facilities as well the bank soon ran up against the real property restrictions. It got round this by selling the buildings to a leasing company and then leasing them back.

For a number of years U.S. firms have employed such sale and lease-back arrangements to raise working capital for domestic inventory expansion. The firm sells owned property to a leasing company to gain liquidity and then leases the equipment back from the leasing company. In other countries sale and leaseback often has the more indirect benefits of the Mexican case above. Allen explains why it is popular in such countries as Argentina, Brazil, and Venezuela:

"In inflationary economies, assets often have a book value in local currency far below their true market value. By disposing of these assets through a sale-and-leaseback arrangement, companies can realize the higher market value yet still retain use of the assets."

In another case in South America, a foreign firm wanted to buy a local TV station, but local officials were determined to block the attempt. The foreign firm instead bought the TV station's building and tried the ploy of leasing the building to the TV station. Lease payments were geared to equal 50% of the station's profits after taxes, and termination of the lease would make the station liable to the foreign firm for an amount equaling 50% of the current market value of the station's shares. In effect, the lease represented a 50% investment in the TV station. In this case, the local authorities saw through the arrangement and disallowed it, but the attempt is illustrative of what bypasses can be tried via lease techniques.

There is practically no limit to the array of lease goods abroad now. Besides the usual transport equipment and machinery, Mundell tells of bottle leasing in Japan and tire leasing in Canada. One company even discussed leasing a yacht for exploration in the Mediterranean.

Transport equipment has always been a big lease item because of the need to fit local requirements and meet short-term demand changes. A good example is railroad cars, due to differing rail gauges in various parts of the world. GATX has made much of its fortune in this business. Leasing aircraft ground equipment as a means of gaining short-term use of facilities for peak periods is another. This is the backbone of companies like Hudson Leasing Co.

In Latin America, in addition to vehicle fleets, earth-moving equipment is in heavy demand as a lease item. In Japan Bank of Boston expects most of its business in $100,000–250,000 items like production equipment and rolling stock. "Computers are not often leased in Japan now, but we see no reason why this could not also become a big item there," adds Allen.

In West Africa fishing is a widespread industry, and TAW plans to be ready with boats and equipment.

Leasing energy systems would seem to offer vast potential overseas. Many U.S. firms lease the heating and electrical system in their building rather than owning it, and shopping centers here often lease their whole power supply independently. Energy-system leasing might as easily become a means for new towns and industrial parks in developing countries to provide their power supply. An added attraction to this lies in the fact that maintenance of the system generally falls under the contracted responsibilities of the leasing firm.

TAW will at first arrange maintenance of its equipment by the manufacturer, but increasingly Wood hopes to establish local servicing through TAW-trained personnel. Wood says TAW has already received an inquiry from Ethiopia concerning energy leasing, and he expects TAW could do a great deal of business in this line.

Along these lines leasing companies look for the advent of nuclear power to open up the whole new area of leasing reactor cores. The initial investment required for a nuclear power station and the power core to fuel it can lie beyond the means of most municipalities; leasing can offer them an out.

In investigating a lease arrangement overseas, Allen says the thing to look for is "first of all reliability. Be sure the lessor is one who can offer you reliable equipment at a reasonable price." Allen favors bank-connected leasing companies like First Boston's and others because he believes they are more likely to lay out alternative means of financing industrial needs. "Bank-connected firms will hold no special brief for leasing," he says, "because they can refer you to another department for other means of financing without losing the business."

QUESTIONS

1. Define the following terms and show the significance to international marketing:

   Inch-pound system   Trade ships
   Trade centers   Universal standards
   Trade fairs   I.S.O.
   Price-quality relationship

2. What are the differences between consumer and industrial goods and what are the implications to international marketing? Discuss.

3. Discuss how the various stages of economic development affect the demand for industrial goods.

4. "Industrialization is typically a national issue, and industrial goods are the fodder for industrial growth." Comment.

5. ". . . the adequacy of a product must be considered in relation to the general environment within which it will be operated rather than solely on the basis of technical efficiency." Discuss the implications of this statement.

6. Why hasn't the U.S. been more helpful in setting universal standards for industrial equipment? Do you feel that the argument is economically sound? Discuss.

7. What role do service, replacement parts, and standards play in competition in foreign marketing? Illustrate.

8. Discuss the part industrial trade fairs and trade centers play in international marketing of industrial goods. What is the difference between industrial trade fairs and trade centers?

9. Discuss some of the more pertinent problems in pricing industrial goods.

10. What is the price-quality relationship? How does this affect a U.S. firm's comparative position in world markets?

11. Discuss leasing of industrial goods in foreign markets. Why is leasing used by the seller? By the buyer?

12. Select several countries each at a different stage of economic development and illustrate how the stage affects demand for industrial goods.

13. England has recently indicated it will shift from the inch-pound system to the metric system. What effect do you think this will have on the traditional U.S. reluctance to such a change? Discuss the economic implications of such a move.

Readings

1. What makes Mexico a good market for U.S. industrial products? Show how Mexico's desire for industrialization affects market demand for industrial products.

2. "Selling industrial products in Mexico can be rough—if you try to use the methods that work in the United States and Canada." Comment and give examples.

OUTLINE OF CHAPTER 12

INTRODUCTION

REQUIRED ADAPTATION

THE COMPLEXITY OF THE PROBLEM
Relationship between Culture and Business Customs
Areas of Diversity
Problems of Change

BUSINESS STRUCTURE
Size
Ownership
Various Business Publics
Sources and Level of Authority
Top-Management Decision Making
Decentralized Decision Making
Committee Decision Making

MANAGEMENT ATTITUDES AND BEHAVIOR
Personal Background
Business Status
Objectives and Aspirations
Security and Mobility
Personal Life
Social Acceptance
Advancement
Power

PATTERNS OF COMPETITION

MODE OF DOING BUSINESS
Level of Contact
Communications Emphasis
Formality and Tempo
Business Ethics
Negotiation Emphasis

SUMMARY AND CONCLUSIONS

READINGS
The Silent Language in Overseas Business, *Harvard Business Review*
A Report on Bribery and Corruption, *The Director*
Must You Tell a Funny Story?, *Columbia Journal of World Business*

12

BUSINESS CUSTOMS AND PRACTICES IN WORLD MARKETING

INTRODUCTION

Lack of knowledge of overseas business practices is a serious deterrent to foreign trading. An even more serious threat to successful international marketing occurs when one does not realize that he lacks knowledge and stumbles ahead assuming that other business cultures are similar to his own milieu. Lack of comprehension of the market environment can preclude a business from successful operations in a foreign country. Even a company successfully doing business overseas may find that it is paying a stiff penalty for its inadequate information base. Only the most naïve and unsophisticated businessman would attempt to sell a consumer product abroad today without trying to understand the ways of foreign customers. Nonetheless, a businessman is still sometimes prone to assume that his *business* counterparts in other countries share his interests and motivations. Nothing can be further from the truth. The tragedy of this misconception is that the marketer is more likely to deal with businessmen than with consumers in international trade. Since industrial products constitute a large proportion of the goods sold in foreign markets, the majority of the sales contacts are with businessmen. Even when selling consumer goods, the exporting firm is most likely to deal with businessmen in arranging distribution or production. In such cases, the foreign firm will be in direct contact with the public.

Innumerable barriers lie in the way of the international marketer who attempts to sell his products or services to foreign markets. Knowledge of the business culture, management attitudes, and the methods of doing business can remove many of these barriers. One authority on doing business in Japan comments that "without flexibility in his own attitudes in accepting or at least tolerating differences in such matters as ways of bathing, flavors of food, modes of dress, and basic patterns

405

of thinking the visiting businessman will seldom be able to negotiate a satisfactory conclusion." Barriers take many forms, but it is not unusual to have a circumstance in which one negotiator's business proposition is accepted rather than another's because "he understands us."

Besides removing barriers which may obstruct business transactions, a comprehension of business customs and practices of customer countries can be an important factor in lowering the cost of doing business. Development of overseas executives is in itself an expensive activity; one firm estimates that it costs $30,000 and takes 24 months to prepare a man for a top management position in Japan. The cost of inefficiency, the cost of lost contracts, and the direct extra expenses that are incurred through lack of understanding cannot be ignored and can change a potentially profitable relationship into a marginal or losing one.

Although the dominant role of the general culture in the development of the business culture should be recognized, this chapter nonetheless will focus on matters more specifically related to business environment. Further introduction to the cultural side of international marketing can be found in the preceding chapter. Besides an analysis of the need for adaptation the present chapter explores the complex problems of marketing in various business cultures and reviews the structure of international business processes. Structural elements, attitudes, and behavior are examined, along with patterns of competition and the modes of doing business.

REQUIRED ADAPTATION

Adaptation is one of the key concepts in international marketing, and willingness to adapt is a crucial attitude. Adaptation, or at least adaptability, is required on small items as well as large. In fact, very often the small, seemingly insignificant situations are the most crucial. On writer comments that more than a toleration of an alien culture is required, that there is a need for affirmative acceptance as different but equal. Through such an affirmative acceptance, adaptation becomes easier, for it is almost natural when there is an appreciation of the outlook of those with whom one is dealing. Every trading country throughout history has learned that it must adapt. For instance, even in ancient Greece Solon the lawgiver (c. 639–559 B.C.) persuaded fellow Armenians to adopt the Euboic system of weights and measures to facilitate commerce with Asia Minor. It has taken American business a long time to learn in international trade that it must adapt not only personal relationships but also products and promotional materials to the needs of the customer country. One frequently encounters instances where Latin American countries have purchased goods from Italy or Germany rather than from the United States because U.S. businessmen insisted on providing English instructions and using nonmetric methods of weights and measures. Fortunately for the U.S. balance of payments, the American businessman is learning to adapt.

Indeed, the one trait that distinguishes the American businessman abroad from his forebears is that he has become the Great Adapter.

In the Orient he has learned to make points without winning arguments—lest his adversary lose "face." In Italy he has learned to argue, so that the Italians will take him seriously. In Switzerland he has learned to be precise, because the Swiss take things literally. In Britain he uses "soft sell"; in Germany, "hard sell." In Mexico he emphasizes price; in Venezuela, quality.[1]

The same article that contains the optimistic quote above continues, however, in a vein that aptly illustrates the problem of adaptation. For example, one U.S. executive located in Italy is quoted as saying that American executives feel lonely in that milieu: "I'm convinced a company here should be run by an Italian, . . . Selling capital goods to a few customers involves delicate personal relationships. It's an area where I don't feel competent."[2]

The focus on adaptability is reiterated in several different ways in an article which lists "ten basic criteria that all those who wish to deal with individuals, firms, or authorities in foreign countries should be able to meet." The ten are (1) tolerance, (2) flexibility, (3) humility, (4) justice and fairness, (5) adjustability to varying tempos, (6) curiosity and interest, (7) knowledge of the country, (8) liking for others, (9) ability to command respect, and (10) ability to integrate (oneself into the environment). In short, add the quality of adaptability to the qualities of a good executive for a composite of the abilities needed. The requirement for adaptability and adaptation does not mean that the business executive or representative must give up his native ways or must change in every respect to conform with local customs. It is impossible as well as undesirable for a businessman, particularly one in the country for a short time, to conform so completely. An Englishman does not expect a German to act, speak, and live like an Englishman; but this does not eliminate the need for the German to understand the Englishman's motivations. It would be foolish for an American to give up the ways which have contributed so notably to American success. Rather, it is necessary that he give up the ways which are offensive to his customers and business associates. What is needed is a separation between cultural imperative, cultural adiaphora and cultural exclusives. The first refers to the business customs and expectations which must be conformed to and met. Cultural adiaphora relates to areas of behavior or to customs to which cultural aliens may, but need not, conform or participate. It is not particularly important, but it is perfectly permissible, to follow the custom in question. Executives should also recognize certain cultural exclusives; that is, customs or behavior from which the foreigner is excluded. It is not appropriate that a Christian attempt to act like a Muslim. Such an attempt would be repugnant to a follower of Mohammed. Therefore, the businessman must have the adaptability and perception to know when he is dealing with an imperative, when he is dealing with adiaphora, and when he is dealing with exclusives.

---

[1] "Yankees Who Don't Go Home," *Business Week,* July 24, 1965, p. 48.
[2] Ibid., p. 51.

THE COMPLEXITY OF THE PROBLEM

In this age of shrinking distances between world markets and of rapid change, confusion seems to be the predominant feeling in the mind of a businessman who is contemplating overseas business relationships. It is difficult to cope with so many different problems and an environment that is so rapidly changing. Even the international marketing expert who specializes in a single foreign country finds that today he must be especially alert and perceptive to be in step with the spirit of the time. The complexity of the situation seems to be based on three points. First, business customs are derived from the basic culture in which the businessman operates. Such cultures may be and usually are complex in themselves. Second, there is great behavioral diversity not only among nations but also within a nation's own subcultures. Third, all cultures, and particularly the business segments of these cultures, are in a state of change today.

Relationship between Culture and Business Customs

The behavior of businessmen and the culture of a nation are inextricably intertwined. Although the culture is modified by the presence of foreign business, we generally think of this interrelationship in terms of business customs and practices being influenced by the culture of a nation or region in which the foreign business operates. Certainly this is the appropriate place for emphasis, but we should also bear in mind that in today's business-oriented world economy, the cultures themselves are being significantly affected by business activities and business practices. Cultural anthropologists know that the intermarriage of traders from foreign tribes and foreign lands have significantly affected the private as well as the business customs of the adopted group. Indeed, nations such as Germany have been formed to facilitate interregional and intergroup trading relationships.[3] The European Common Market today provides an example of a potential future supernation which has its roots in what is essentially a trading alliance. Most languages, both historical and modern, contain examples of the intercultural effect of international marketing relationships; the words Caterpillar, Coca-Cola, and Ford are accepted parts of the local idiom in large parts of the world. Although the effect of business intercourse on the basic culture is acknowledged, this in no way detracts from the fact that the more common cultural relationship is that of business accommodating itself to the native culture. Because individual orientation and cultural patterns change slowly, the domination of a culture in a business situation is inescapable. Every businessman is at least partially a captive of his cultural heritage; he cannot escape his religious background, his language heritage, or his political and family ties. His business and daily habits and customs are more likely to be those of his own people than the habits and customs of other businessmen from other countries. James Lee characterizes this tendency as the self-reference criterion and suggests that this

---

[3] See E. R. A. Seligman, *The Economic Interpretation of History* (New York: Columbia University Press, 1902).

BOX 12–1

Business in Japan

One of the surprises met by the foreign businessman who wants to conduct "business" in Japan is to be submitted to a series of questions which establish his various relationships with wife, children, and the management of the firm concerned. Is the man we Japanese are dealing with "related" to the world of things and persons? In other words, are we dealing with another living organism whose truth and strength is verified by the multiplicity of ties which a strong living being necessarily contracts? This time-consuming process of questioning is not precisely verification of information, but rather getting to know the man as he *is*. Who can say that he knows somebody just by looking at his name card? Besides, the whole group must get to know the new element, and to the great bewilderment of the foreigner, his interlocutors change practically with every meeting. The Japanese are not impenetrable—they can be inter-pollinated.

The whole structure of Japan can thus be considered as a gigantic living organism in which each part is playing a role, but where there is no place for an outsider. . . . It appears from the above that one cannot singularize one individual or one thing in Japan, because nothing has value by itself, but only in its relation to other things. It is also impossible to analyze a concept in the perspective of Japanese culture because of the risk of losing at least half of the content.

Source: From Maurice Bairy, "Japanese Ways," in R. J. Ballon (ed.), *Doing Business in Japan* (Tokyo: Sophia University, 1967), pp. 5–6. Reproduced by permission.

ethnocentricism causes problems when (1) communicating with the company headquarters, (2) adapting to local cultures, or (3) keeping up with political and economic change.[4]

The businessman must be aware that his foreign counterpart judges his own standard of living by his peers, who also provide his motivational frame of reference. Although the internationally minded businessman might take on the trappings and appearances of business behavior from other countries, his basic frame of reference will still be his own culture. In fact, the culture tends to dominate not only the domestic businessman but also his foreign visitor. One writer comments that

though Japan has successfully added Western methods to its own vigorous business enterprise, its ancient culture remains triumphant. And the U.S. manager of his company's Japanese affiliate—perhaps himself an alien "minority of one" in his own plant, soon discovers that the fascinating differences between East and West are more than skin deep.[5]

Prolonged military occupations have historically been characterized by the phenomenon of the invading troops being partially assimilated into the local cultures as they adopt the foreign ways which add convenience or pleasure to their lives. Perhaps such an assimilation of

---

[4] James A. Lee, "Cultural Analysis in Overseas Operations," *Harvard Business Review*, March–April 1966, p. 106.

[5] "The U.S. Executive in Japan," *Business Week*, June 13, 1954, p. 143.

visiting business executives is inevitable as well as desirable. The process is not all one way, of course, and the culture also inevitably is changed by the military or business "invaders" as well.

Areas of Diversity

Predominance of local cultures in international business customs implies that there will be nearly as great a diversity in business as in personal customs. Such diversity takes place not only among countries but *within* countries as well. There is a tendency to want to regard countries as simple organisms made up of a group of similar components, but this is seldom the case. One particularly interesting reaction came from an American-trained Japanese responding to an article about Japan in the *Harvard Business Review.* Jiro Tokayama comments that the article was most interesting to him and very well written, but "we must admit that it is truly difficult to generalize about any society. Japan is particularly resistant to classification." Perhaps one should not classify and generalize about businessmen and business groups. For example, if you were given the job of describing the U.S. businessman, what would you come up with? Obviously, you would not try to generalize that this man was extremely aggressive, tall, handsome, affable, and financially successful, nor would you indicate that he lives in the suburbs, is Roman Catholic, and follows conservative economic and political positions. Certainly, one would not attempt to describe a "typical" businessman; yet the same individual who would not attempt such generalizations in his own nation is often tempted to generalize about countries about which he knows even less.

We may find diversity not only among countries, but also among different types of businesses and among businessmen of different ages. The outlook of management at different levels of business will certainly vary. *Fortune* writer Gilbert Burck captured the essence of the diversity within business when he reported that "Every bad European management practice could be found in the U.S. and every good American practice could be found in Europe."[6]

The areas of diversity must be explored country by country as the businessman encounters them. Because every side of business activity shows diversity, the student of the foreign business culture must constantly analyze, classify, and generalize if he is to understand foreign business and its environment. It is particularly important, however, in actually dealing with foreign businessmen to be certain that the classifications do not blind the international marketer to the specific variations and diversity which are so crucial to his success.

Problems of Change

As if the problems of cultural derivation and diversity were not enough, the businessmen must also deal with a constantly changing

---

[6] Gilbert Burck, "The Transformation of European Business," *Fortune,* November 1957, p. 147.

situation. The commercial frontier today is a composite montage of the old and new ways. Young men tend to do business one way; the older men, another. It seems that within a country even the businessmen themselves are in a quandary over the culture to which they should adhere. The *Fortune* article cited above comments about this change in the European businessman. "To keep pace with this (European) market, business also finds itself broadening and democratising, so to speak, its management functions. This is the real Americanization of Europe. . . . Even as it expands it is decentralizing, shedding its authoritarianism, humanizing itself and becoming market-minded." Businessmen of the world collect good ideas regardless of their source; such idea collecting often results in business customs that blend Oriental, European, and American business behavior. This type of eclectic borrowing has resulted in a certain amount of confusion and chaos in the face of progress. A report on Spain characterizes the "caught in the middle" situation in which the emerging countries seem to find their business practices. "Advertising in Spain and Portugal is in the transitional stage between being a vigorous free-for-all in which anything goes and a para-profession in which nearly everything is governed by laws, regulations, and codes of procedure."[8]

If possible, the problem of dealing with changing conditions is even more complex and difficult than that of dealing with the cultural diversity of business. The tempo and scope of change in the international business scene can best be observed at a distance. The description of European businessmen in 1954 contrasts markedly with contemporary descriptions of the European businessman and his behavior.[9] Numerous significant changes take place within even a single decade which rather completely differentiate the businessman of the two periods. Reliance on earlier information is, in many cases, irrelevant and in some cases can be downright misleading and detrimental. In England, for example, the leadership of business has shifted gradually in recent years from family to professional management. Further, description characterizing Italian business as slow moving may have been accurate in 1955, but is completely misleading in the seventies. Marketers can be easily led astray if they rely on old information and fail to allow for changes.

BUSINESS STRUCTURE

The same patterns of diversity and change that characterize business customs and habits also pervade the structure of business firms. It is difficult, if not impossible, to evaluate and describe fully the structural patterns in different countries. The world marketer must determine for himself the impact of the particular circumstances in which he deals.

---

[7] Burck, op. cit., pp. 146 and 150.

[8] *Iberian Opportunity* (London: London Press Exchange, 1964), p. 2.

[9] See, for example, Frederick W. Harbison and Eugene W. Burgess, "Modern Management in Western Europe," *The American Journal of Sociology*, July 1954, pp. 15–23.

The chief significance of structural forms is that it will affect decision making and authority patterns among customers. Chief elements which should be evaluated are size, ownership, authority patterns, and the relationship of the business to its various publics.

Size

Size is significant in business structure analysis, for it has several interesting ramifications. One method of analyzing business behavior patterns compares businesses of a similar size in different countries. Pursuing this approach briefly, we might simply classify businesses into large-, medium-, and small-scale firms, neglecting the more esoteric and academic discussions of what constitutes a large, medium, or small business. Let us simply say that a large business is one with large numbers of employees and functionalized management. A medium-sized business is one with functional organization, but one in which management personnel are likely to be in direct contact with the workers and/or customers. A small business, defined for our purpose, is one where the management is directly responsible for the supervision of employees and comes into direct contact with the customers on a routine basis. At a given size level, the managerial outlook from country to country might be fairly similar in some respects. The large organizations are probably most homogeneous from country to country as a result of professionalized management and, quite often, because of the adaptation of American business methods by large businesses. Businessmen in medium-size and small firms are less likely to have felt the impact of management practices from other countries. Management in the smaller firms is likely to be more closely tied to the customs and attitudes of the country than to the attitudes of the counterpart businessmen in other countries.

The composition of business firms classified by size varies greatly from country to country. Nearly every industrial country has some extremely large business firms, and every nation has large numbers of small and very small businessmen. It should be noted, however, that actual size is hard to measure in situations of interlocking directorates, financial leverage, or other tying arrangements that combine nominally separate firms into a de facto unity. Consider some of the industrial-financial-commercial combines of Japan, for example. Mitsui & Co. is a trading company with sales of some $6 billion. It it affiliated with industrial and financial firms and has direct (and mostly exclusive) trading rights for over 1,000 other Japanese companies.

The significant question is not that of the range between the large and small but the composition of the business community. *Fortune* magazine regularly compiles a list of America's 500 and the world's 200 largest industrial firms. The United States has almost twice as many firms as the rest of the free world in the over $500,000,000 sales and about the same ratio in the over $250,000,000 sales bracket. Exhibit 12–1 provides some relative size comparisons on the large business sector of the world economy. Similar data are not readily available or

BOX 12–2

The European Countries with the Largest Sellers
(in $ millions)

Country	Number of Companies with Annual Sales Exceeding				
	$2,000	$1,000	$500	$250	$125
UK..................	7	13	43	92	175
Germany.............	3	14	31	51	75
France...............	—	8	19	37	49
Sweden..............	—	—	3	12	17
Italy................	2	3	7	11	16
The Netherlands.......	3	3	5	8	15
Switzerland..........	—	1	6	9	11
Belgium*.............	—	1	2	5	10
Norway..............	—	—	—	—	2
Finland..............	—	—	—	—	2
Austria..............	—	—	—	—	1
Luxembourg..........	—	—	—	1	1
Denmark.............	—	—	—	—	1
Total..........	15	43	116	226	375

* Includes Agfa-Gevaert.

Source: *Business Europe*, December 19, 1969 p. 403.

comparable for other sectors of the economy, but it is axiomatic that business firms in the United States generally are larger in size than they are in other parts of the world. Advertising expenditures provide a few interesting comparisons. The United States has 100 advertisers who spend over $6½ million a year on advertising. All the rest of the world has only 15 advertisers who exceed this volume of expenditure. Total advertising expenditures in only 10 nations exceeded the amount spent by Procter and Gamble Company in the United States.

Management behavior and customs—or more specifically, management skills, orientation, and operational patterns—will vary greatly in organizations of different sizes. Awareness of the industry structure for a given country can provide significant clues to management behavior.

Business size will affect the volume of sales to an individual firm, the type of representation that is required, the number of outlets needed for market coverage, and the number of sales representatives needed to cover a given industry segment, and will have numerous other marketing implications.

Ownership

Foreign business ownership patterns vary significantly from the ownership patterns of American business. In the United States, businesses tend to be privately owned by first- or second-generation business-

EXHIBIT 12–1

Big Business around the World

Foreign Rank of Company	U.S. Rank of Company	Sales Volume ($000)	Name of Company	Location
	1	$22,755,403	General Motors	Detroit, Mich.
1		9,215,772	Royal Dutch/Shell Group	Netherlands-Britain
	4	8,381,633	General Electric	New York
10		2,281,728	Hitachi	Japan
	34	2,251,562	Continental Oil	New York
20		1,731,250	Farbenfabriken Bayer	Germany
	45	1,738,364	Grace (W.R.)	New York
30		1,394,920	BASF (Badische Anilin-& Soda-Fabrik)	Germany
	63	1,399,523	Republic Steel	Cleveland, Ohio
40		1,193,781	Nippon Kokan	Japan
	77	1,185,809	Coca-Cola	New York
50		989,403	Gutenhoffnungshutte	Germany
	105	974,883	Borg-Warner	Chicago
60		908,435	Ugine Kuhlmann	France
	108	897,591	Mead	Dayton, Ohio
70		791,564	Charbonnages de France	France
	126	793,190	Youngstown Sheet and Tube	Youngstown, Ohio
80		730,327	Canada Packers	Canada
	133	734,365	Heinz (H.J.)	Pittsburgh
90		665,500	Imperial Tobacco Group	Britain
	152	664,891	Combustion Engineering	New York
100		600,310	De Beers Consolidated Mines	South Africa
	163	602,263	U.S. Industries	New York
110		538,500	Degussa	Germany
	184	535,972	Dana	Toledo, Ohio
120		512,640	Bowater Paper	Britain
	191	514,832	Diamond Shamrock	Cleveland, Ohio
130		459,442	British Aircraft	Britain
	212	453,004	Seagram (Joseph E.) & Sons	New York
140		422,600	Klockner-Werke	Germany
	228	423,361	Rohm & Haas	Philadelphia
150		398,165	Toa Nenryo Kogyo	Japan
	237	397,192	Polaroid	Cambridge, Mass.
160		376,069	Buderus'sche Eisenwerke	Germany
	242	377,014	Admiral	Chicago
170		352,068	Snow Brand Milk Products	Japan
	258	351,693	I.P.L.	Chicago
180		327,930	Associated Portland Cement Manuf.	Britain
	276	329,039	Tecumseh Products	Tecumseh, Mich.
190		303,054	Bunge y Born	Argentina
	290	301,014	Richardson-Merrell	New York
200		284,799	Hiram Walker-Gooderham & Worts	Canada
	298	285,099	Dan River Mills	Danville, Va.

Source: "The Forture Directory" *Fortune*, July–August 1969.

men or they are owned by private investors who have purchased stock and vested management in professional managers. Public ownership of major companies throughout the world is becoming more common. Capital demands of rapid growth, increased availability of investor funds, and merger activities have all emphasized the shift from family to public ownership.

Ownership variations are wide from country to country; but at least three additional key patterns that are of minimal importance in the United States may be identified. They are: government ownership, family (clan) ownership, and cooperative ownership. Government plays a large and perhaps a dominant role in business ownership in many free countries. There are few if any countries which have so little government investment in business as the United States (for example, some 40 percent of the capital in Brazilian business is government owned; in Norway, the government's investment approaches some 70 percent of productive enterprise). In some nations complete industries have been nationalized and are owned directly by the government. Italy's ENI (Enté Nazionale Idrocarburi) petroleum monopoly is an example of this type of operation.

The family business dynasty is a second ownership pattern which prevails in many countries. In some countries three or four families dominate the entire business and financial scene, and it is essential that the international marketer be in a favorable position with these families to succeed in business. Such family holdings are in some cases the residuals from a feudal age where land wealth was concentrated in the hands of the very few. In other cases, family fortunes are based on generations of expansion from humble industrial or financial enterprises. In many instances, an entire industry will be virtually in the complete control of a single family group. In Germany, for example, the name Krupp is practically synonomous with the word steel; the Indian family Ghanshyam-das Birla controls some 350 Indian business concerns. One of the world's great family-owned concerns is the European empire of the Rothschilds; in Japan Mitsubishi Iwasaki, Mitsui, Sumitomo and other families loom large on the industrial scene. It is interesting to note that, as developing nations become more industrialized, there are greater opportunities for an ever-growing number of industrial and commercial leaders. Rapid industrialization permitted the United States to bypass quickly the period when the Morgans, Du Ponts, and Carnegies were individually preeminent in American industry. Every industrialized nation boasts a large number of post World War II success stories where individuals with no family ties have managed to establish their own miniature industrial empires. The American example and greater amounts of wealth in the hands of ordinary citizens have also contributed to a growing ownership of stocks among the general public, thus further diversifying the ownership base.

A third form, the cooperative enterprise, particularly the consumer cooperative, has made little headway on the American business scene. Quite the reverse is true in Europe, where many of the larger businesses are owned cooperatively. Such general ownership is likely to contribute to development of the utilization of professional managers. An outstanding example of this type of organization is the Migros cooperative in Switzerland; Migros accounts for a majority of the retail food sales in Switzerland and has significant market shares in other countries and other product areas.

Various Business Publics

Another point affecting the policies and behavior of businessmen is the degree of responsibility to the various business publics; that is, the government, consumers, labor, and the stockholders. Assessment and generalization about business responsibility are subject to the same hazards of diversity and change that plague any cultural evaluation. The social relationships of business are in a particularly active period of ferment and change in today's age of industrial awakening, growth, and world consciousness. The predominant direction of change has been from narrow self-seeking or owner-serving to a viewpoint of responsibility to the public at large. American business seems generally to be characterized by a basic loyalty to stockholders, with considerable emphasis on the consumer; the marketplace is a key regulator of action. In other countries labor occupies a particularly warm place in the hearts of business managers and owners. Many Latin American countries have strongly militant labor groups which are in a position to demand their rights. With the diversity found in every phase of business, we find that the European employer may be indifferent to the rights of his workers or may be extremely paternalistic. One writer comments that

the socially conscious employer is a benevolent industrial lord who takes care of the people in his domain, partly because of humanitarian motives and partly because of fear of uprising masses. At the other extreme are the owners and employers who recognize no responsibility to workers, to the community, or to the society as a whole—who live according to the doctrine of *sauve qui peut* (roughly, anything goes). They look upon labor as an economic commodity while they live in constant fear of political agitation for basic changes in ownership and management.[10]

It is interesting to note that the varying national attitudes toward responsibility to labor were stumbling blocks in the early formation of the European Common Market. Countries like France, Italy, and Belgium were traditionally more welfare-oriented than were Germany and the Netherlands. Guaranteed lifetime employment is common in many welfare-oriented economies where the governments avidly protect workers' rights.

In most countries it appears that the consumer is the only business public without a preferential position in the eyes of business. It is only when the consumer exerts force through the marketplace that he receives full consideration. The relationship of business to its various publics significantly affects the attitudes and behavior of foreign businessmen and should be understood by the overseas marketer.

---

[10] Frederick W. Harbison and Eugene W. Burgess, "Modern Management in Western Europe," *The American Journal of Sociology*, July 1954, p. 19.

BOX 12–3

European Stockholders Learn to Talk Back

In Milan last weekend, irate stockholders of chemical giant Montecatini Edison bombarded the board of directors with coins and copies of the company's annual report. In Neckarsulm, West Germany, shareholders in auto maker NSU Motorenwerke hissed and hooted down a banker trying to cajole them into supporting a takeover by Volkswagen.

Before the long and vitriolic sessions broke up, rebellious Montedison shareholders had forced directors to postpone consideration of a proposal that would give government agencies veto power over the company's operations. And their German counterparts won a bigger slice of the royalties VW stands to earn on licensing NSU's revolutionary rotary piston Wankel engine.

. . . . .

Montedison shareholders got their backs up over an attempt by two government companies to grab control by quietly buying shares. IRI, the giant state industrial holding company, and ENI, the state oil company, started picking up stock in Montedison more than a year ago, and together now have 5% to 10% of the total outstanding. Montedison's profits had been lagging, and the government move was called an effort to rescue Montedison from hard times. But many shareholders—including Leopoldo Pirelli, chairman of the giant tire company of that name and a Montedison director—saw it as an attempt to nationalize Italy's largest corporation. But Pirelli found little support among fellow board members for his stand.

Up in arms. That left it to the small shareholders to keep their company out of government hands. For the first time in Italy, stockholders organized, and Milan was plastered with posters calling on stockholders to unite.

Against this background, the annual meeting opened last Saturday in an atmosphere of near-violence. Police lined up across the street from the Montedison building on Milan's Foro Buonaparte, while inside speaker after speaker derided and cursed the government's actions.

The dissidents, sporting red, white, and green flags in their lapels, surprised company insiders by coming up with 72-million votes, nearly 10% of the outstanding shares. In a showdown, the state companies and their allies still would have carried the day. So the rebels started a filibuster.

"I am willing to stay here until Thursday or Friday or Saturday," shouted one dissident, "until public opinion forces the government to intervene and throw out the scoundrels who bought into this company."

Source: Reprinted from the May 3, 1969 issue of *Business Week* by special permission. Copyrighted 1969 by McGraw-Hill, Inc., p. 34.

Sources and Level of Authority

Business size, ownership, and public accountability combine to influence the authority structure of business. The diversity which characterizes each of the elements naturally creates a diversity in authority structure. Knowledge of authority patterns is crucial to the international marketer. He must be perceptive and discerning if he is successfully to consummate negotiations in international trade. Each company, indeed each decision, relates to a somewhat different authority structure, but it may be useful to examine three authority patterns. The three are top-level management decisions, decentralized decisions, and committee decisions.

Top-Management Decision Making.   The prerogative in decision making tends to be retained in top management in situations where family or close ownership gives absolute control to the managers and where business size is small enough to make such decision centralization possible. Management in most industrially developing countries prefers to make its own decisions, wherever possible. Historically this also appears to have been the dominant pattern in American business until approximately the time of World War I. Writers commenting on European business agree that European management has limited decision-making authority and that such authority is guarded jealously by top managers. Although the results of the 1954 study are obsolete in some respects, we can agree with Harbison and Burgess that "in the European firm the number of persons in management is relatively small, decision making is highly centralized, and the burden of routine administrative duties borne by individual executives is extremely heavy." These authorities also comment that personalities rather than objectives seem to be the primary organizational foci. Another commentator suggests that European companies "tend to put up restrictive barriers between departments" to force decisions up to the top level. A recent study by a group of organizational theorists indicates that managers in most countries have a basic conviction that subordinates are generally inadequate people. Viewing subordinates as inadequate naturally tends to lessen the amount of authority that will be delegated. The researchers went further to state that "in all countries there universally is far more belief in shared objectives participation and in individual control than there is for belief in the capacity of others for initiative, individual action, and leadership." They found that managers in European countries have particular scorn for the abilities of subordinates and, therefore, favor centralized decision making.

Brazil and other countries that have a semifeudal land-equals-power heritage tend to exclude decision-making participation by middle management and deemphasize upward mobility. In this kind of situation, management decisions are made by the family members who dominate the various businesses.

Decentralized Decision Making.   When executives at various levels of the business hierarchy are given rather complete decision-making authority over their own function, the decision pattern may be characterized as decentralized. England's colonial and civil service heritage seems to have placed considerable emphasis on decentralized decision making. The large scale of business and the highly developed management systems of American business also are conducive to decentralized decision making. Attitudes favoring decentralized management decisions are bound to permeate other cultures as businesses grow and professional management ranks develop.

Committee Decision Making.   Management by group decision or by consensus may be called committee decision making. Committees may

A Place for Everyone

Protectionism is deeply rooted in the Japanese way of doing business. In Japanese industry, every person and every business has a place, which is guarded by elaborate rituals. Businesses reach decisions by an exquisitely deliberate process of consensus seeking. In most companies, reports TIME Correspondent Frank Iwama, this process is symbolized by the long row of printed boxes running down the side of policy papers. Every executive involved must put his "chop" (mark) in a box, signifying his agreement, before any decision can be moved along. The next step is to present the decision to one of the "day clubs" of supposed competitors that meet regularly to shape policy for groups of companies. Consensus reached in one of these clubs must then be presented to the government, which supplies an average of 80% of the capital on which Japanese firms operate. It is also legal for industry associations to make the kind of decisions that U.S. competitors could never get away with. For example, they can determine how much each company in an industry should cut production during a recession.

This cozy system is capable of enormous dynamism. Once a decision has been reached, everyone who participated works single-mindedly to carry it out. But foreign companies are kept out of Japan largely because they might not abide by decisions of the day clubs, and those that are allowed in are prevented from becoming too pushy.

Source: "Japan's Struggle to Cope with Plenty," *Time,* August, 1969, p. 69B. Reprinted by permission from TIME, the Weekly Newsmagazine; Copyright Time Inc. 1969.

operate on a centralized or decentralized basis, but the concept of committee management by a group implies something quite different than the individualized functioning of the top management and decentralized decision-making arrangements mentioned above. Because Far Eastern cultures and religions tend to emphasize harmony and the perfectability of man, it is not surprising that group decision making predominates. Despite the emphasis on rank and hierarchy in Japanese social structure, business places great emphasis on group participation, group harmony, and group decision making—but on a top management level. Stanley Miller comments that a management group will not take action without almost unanimous endorsement for the action and that such group decision making tends toward "management by clique."[11] In studying Java, one researcher learned that group harmony is stressed above all things and that the native workers do not want authority over others for fear of discord. Such societies naturally tend to prefer group decision making.[12]

The demands of these three types of authority systems on a marketing man's ingenuity and adaptability are quite evident. In the case of the authoritative and delegated societies, the chief problem may be to deter-

[11] Stanley S. Miller, "Management by OMIKOSHI," *Management International,* Vol. 3, No. 1 (1963), p. 59.

[12] Ann Ruth Willner, "A Case Study of a Javanese Factory," *Human Organization,* Summer 1963, p. 133.

mine the individual with the authority. In the committee decision setup, there is obviously a requirement that every committee member be convinced of the merit of the proposition or product in question. The marketing approach to these different situations will obviously be quite varied.

MANAGEMENT ATTITUDES AND BEHAVIOR

The training and background, i.e., cultural environment, of management significantly affect their personal and, therefore, their business outlook. Society as a whole establishes the social rank or status of management, and the cultural background partially dictates the pattern of aspiration and objectives among businessmen. All these influences relate to the sympathy of managers toward innovation, new products, and doing business with foreigners. The results of such management attitudes and objectives are directly reflected in the development of the man, his business, and his nation. No one can question the different effects of the frontier ethic of hard work, saving, and prudence, and the contrasting free-wheeling, easy-living, hedonism of the ancient Greek.

Personal Background

The successful foreign marketer is constantly alert to the fact that all business executives are subject to their own cultures and religions. He also knows that his foreign customers' objectives and aspirations are further tempered by their training and broadening cultural horizons. The outlook of the wealthy inheritor of a going business will vary considerably from that of the struggling entrepreneur. Some managers learn their skill on the job and limit themselves to the industry where those skills best apply; others are trained in management and are less restricted by type of industry in the application of those skills. In most parts of the world, an official goes to work for a company rather expecting to spend his entire life there. He may emerge through the ranks of apprenticeship or work up through the business hierarchy. How different will be the outlook of such a company-oriented businessman from that of the professional managers who are now beginning to be developed in business schools throughout the world!

Business Status

The role of the businessmen has been questioned in nearly every society, and social status has often been denied to this group. In recent years, however, businessmen throughout the world seem to be expressing greater concern about their status. Because businessmen in different countries and in different cultures have different outlooks on status, the experienced international marketer adapts his approach to these differing viewpoints. In Japan, status seeking means to seek to learn the status of others so that one can pay them suitable respect. In some countries, individuals prefer lower status. It is not unusual to find that individuals would rather work at lower wages and under more difficult conditions than be foremen, because if they are foremen, they will be out of the class of their friends and will be required to give up a secure (if low) status position. In other countries, the businessman is actively striving to overcome this barrier.

European marketers have traditionally been suspect in the eyes of their customers and fellow businessmen, but in recent years this image has changed. The current European economic boom, which owes so much to efficient international marketing, has been so successful that the image of European businessmen is changing in society. The image of the businessman in America has also moved upward in the past few decades. In India, with its highly structured caste system, businessmen and young people are likely to aspire to higher classes. One source comments about members of the Marwari caste (in India), indicating that "many Marwaris respected only for their business shrewdness now long for the social standing that Burla (a business leader) has earned for himself."

Objectives and Aspirations   C-3

The objectives and aspirations of individual managers are likely to be reflected in the goals of the business organization and in the practices which prevail within the company. In dealing with foreign businessmen, the marketer must be particularly aware of the varying objectives and aspirations of management. In the United States, we tend to emphasize profit or high wages. In other countries, managers are more likely to emphasize security, good personal life, acceptance, status, advancement, or power. Individual goals, of course, are highly personal in the United States or any other country, so that one cannot generalize to the extent of saying that managers in any one country will hold a specific orientation. Managers are not homogeneous. Nevertheless, it is still useful to identify the patterns which may prevail within a given country.[13] Besides the differences based on national heritage, an individual's goals also depend partly on his possessions (what he already has), his age, his position in management, and the structure of the business which employs him. In general, middle management personnel are not highly concerned about the profit position of the company because they have no direct responsibility or control over it.

Security and Mobility. Personal security and job mobility relate directly to basic human motivation and therefore have widespread economic and social implications. The word "security" is somewhat ambiguous and this very ambiguity provides some clues to managerial variation. To some, security means good wages and the training and ability required for moving from company to company of the business hierarchy; for others, it means the security of a position for life with their company; to still others, it means an adequate retirement plan and other welfare benefits. In European companies, particularly in the countries which

---

[13] For some interesting generalizations relative to comparative achievement patterns in different patterns in different nations, see David McClelland, *The Achieving Society* (Princeton, N.J.: D. Van Nostrand Co., Inc., 1958). See also his *Motivating Economic Achievement*, New York: The Free Press, 1969).

were late in industrializing, such as France and Italy, there is a strongly paternalistic orientation and it is assumed that an individual will work for one company for the majority of his life. The culture of Japan and other Eastern countries also incorporates such paternalistic notions, and the employer feels full responsibility for guaranteeing employment security to his personnel. Company and individual attitudes regarding employment security are changing rapidly, particularly in countries like West Germany, where peace and prosperity have lessened the memories of the insecurities of the world wars and where labor shortages have encouraged middle management to shift from company to company, thus relieving, at least partially, the parent company of its paternalistic role.

The implication of this security orientation for the marketer is that the prospective middle management customer is less likely to take a chance or accept innovation. He in no way wants to put himself in a position where he can possibly alienate the company. He has little to gain by such risk and much to lose.

Personal Life.   To many individuals, a good personal life precedes profit, security, or any other goal. In his worldwide study of individual aspirations, David McClelland discovered that the culture of some countries stressed the virtue of a good personal life as being far more important than profit or achievement. The hedonistic outlook of ancient Greece explicitly included work as an undesirable thing which got in the way of one's search for pleasure or a good personal life. Perhaps at least part of the standard of living which we enjoy in the United States today can be attributed to the hard-working Protestant Ethic from which we derive much of our business heritage.

The family ownership pattern prevalent in most countries around the world would imply that the objectives of the firm are most likely to be the objectives of the owners. As one author comments, the business "exists by and for the family, and the honor, the reputation and wealth of one (the business) are the honor, wealth, and reputation of the other." The unimportance of wealth as compared to a good personal life in some of the developing countries is provided in a commentary by an African student from Kenya. He says, "Among Africans, there is not such a thing as keeping up with the people next door. Each individual is satisfied with what he has, and if he can get more, well and good; if not, he keeps up with what he has. We do not see things in terms of wealth as being that important."

Social Acceptance.   In some countries, acceptance by one's neighbors and fellow workers appears to be a predominant goal within business. The Oriental outlook is reflected in the group decision making that is so important in Japan and the Japanese place high importance on fitting in with their group. Similarly in Java, the emphasis is on group harmony. As mentioned earlier, it has been found that in this country native supervisors don't want authority over others lest it reduce their acceptance by their colleagues.

Advancement.   In younger businesses, executives are changing the old business standards in many nations by seeking more rapid advance-

BOX 12–5

SALARIES AND BENEFITS: The Golden Fringe

Company limousines roll through the British countryside carrying executives' children from their boarding schools to holidays at home. France's nationalized coal companies provide their engineers with rent-free homes. Swedish businessmen hunt elk in company-owned forests. Officials of Rio de Janeiro's Mesbla department store enjoy free vacations at their company's summer resort. All these—and many more—are the fringe benefits that are taken for granted by executives abroad, and account for the fact that they can often live high on salaries that usually run much lower than those in the U.S.

Such fringes are most generous in West Germany, where companies lavish benefits on the lowliest employees as well as on the highest executives. A manufacturer passes out free opera tickets. Brewery hands carry home two to four liters of beer every day; . . . .

Such largesse is nominal compared with what a middle-ranking executive gets. His rent is often subsidized, and he also has the use of a company car and chauffeur. In many cases, the company hires a gardener for him, stocks his wine cellar and pays his utility bills. On weekends, the executive can relax at one of the firm's winter or summer retreats. Once a year he may choose to recuperate at Baden-Baden or some other spa, imbibing mineral waters and immersing himself in medicinal mud at company expense. Other Germany executives annually are given blank airline tickets for themselves and their wives. They may fill out the tickets for "business" trips to any place they care to visit.

Instead of paternalistic emoluments, Italian executives often collect under-the-table cash bonuses, which the company camouflages on its books as "miscellaneous expenses." Payments to top managers run as high as $20,000 a year. Small private firms rely on generous automobile allowances.

By comparison, British executives lead a constrained existence. Since 1965, entertaining has been disallowed as a tax-deductible expense for British companies. Tax officials have plugged most other benefit loopholes as well, and corporate perquisites are miserly, especially at London headquarters. In the provinces, some fringes survive. Company mechanics repair the cars of board members; doctors are on call for executives and their families.

Life for French executives, too, is growing a bit less opulent because of recent tax reforms. As long-standing masters of tax evasion, many French businessmen still manage to support their families largely at company expense. But there is now an extra tax on company-owned cars, and it is becoming increasingly difficult for a top executive to prove that, merely for business entertaining, he really needs a company-paid mansion staffed with cook, butler, chauffeur and gardener. He might get away with writing off a hunt as a business expense, and at least a few executives still enjoy a time-honored French fringe benefit: charging off to company advertising expenses the rent and bills of their mistresses.

Source: Reprinted by permission from TIME, The Weekly Newsmagazine; Copyright Time Inc. 1969.

BOX 12–6

Thailand: Behind Every Successful Woman

"A man is the foreleg of the elephant and the woman the hind leg," according to an old Thai saying. If that is so, the hind legs are doing more than their share of the walking in present-day Thailand. In increasing numbers, the women of Thailand are abandoning the sheltered life of the home to pursue careers in business. For all their delicate femininity—their diminutive, porcelain prettiness, their singsong voices and their flowering silk robes—they have proved to be tough businesswomen whose impact on their country has already been extensive.

. . . . .

Behind the surge of feminine enterprise are some powerful new social and economic forces. Most of the Thai businesswomen started with at least some inherited wealth but, like women the world over, were encouraged by education to escape the housewife's role and test themselves in man's arena. Furthermore, as living costs have risen so has the women's desire to help their husbands earn a larger share of the good life. Thai husbands, who have a strong preference for dignified but low-paying careers in civil service and law, left a vacuum in the business community that the women have rushed to fill. Consequently, their roles cut across the entire spectrum of Thailand's commerce and industry. Women own about 90% of Bangkok's real estate and have heavy interests in transportation companies, construction firms and restaurants.

. . . . .

As the businesswomen make ever deeper inroads into Thailand's commerce, they exercise great tact and diplomacy in dealing with their men. They take the position, in fact, that behind every successful businesswoman is a loving helpmate.

Source: *Time*, December 17, 1965, pp. 91 and 92. Reprinted by permission from TIME, The Weekly Newsmagazine; Copyright Time Inc. 1969.

ment than has been traditionally acceptable. Such audacity derives, at least partly, from the expanded promotional opportunities which are developing throughout the world. As in the United States, an increasing amount of attention throughout the world seems to be given to aggressive young businessmen who feel that they should be compensated or promoted on the basis of merit rather than on the paternalistic, family hierarchy system of the past.

Power. Although there is some power seeking by business managers throughout the world, power seems to be an important motivating force, particularly in the South American countries. In these countries the business leaders are not primarily profit-oriented but use their business positions to make them social and political leaders.

PATTERNS OF COMPETITION

In nearly all the world except the United States, the 20th-century orientation toward competition has been to avoid it whenever possible.

The prevailing idea has been to share markets rather than to expand them, but since World War II this viewpoint has gradually been giving way to a more aggressive international and national competition. Cartels are private business agreements, usually among firms in different countries, to share markets, control production, and set prices. Cartels were a highly developed part of European business before World War I. Between the two world wars, the cartelization of European industry was intensified and it is now flourishing again.[14]

The participation in worldwide markets and particularly the development of the European Common Market have been major influences in the development of a free-trade orientation in Europe. One commentator says,

European business confronted with new opportunities and enjoying constantly better public relations is becoming expansion-minded and even receptive to the idea of competition. Lately it has been prodded by anti-trust and anti-cartel legislation; and although this legislation is still less likely to achieve its literal objectives than U.S. anti-trust legislation does, it should eventually have profound effects on business ideals and attitudes, even as U.S. anti-trust legislation has.[15]

Japan also has participated in the philosophy of sharing markets rather than expanding them and has a tendency to prefer to share markets and control prices rather than to indulge in what the Japanese call "wasteful competition." In the past the government has protected domestic manufacturers but now is opening up to freer competition.[16] The Japanese are, of course, aggressive competitors on the world marketplace but, like most businessmen, compete only if they have no other good alternative.

Government action is significant in shaping the patterns of competition within a country. Common Market countries have a clause in the charter which prohibits agreements, mergers, and other concerted practices tending to restrict free trade. The United States has its antitrust legislation, and other countries have similar laws implementing competition, but in many countries the government also acts as a deterrent to competition. The Norwegian government, for example, establishes appropriate gross margins for retailing and wholesaling operations and is actively involved in price setting in the manufacturing sector of the economy. Japan's MITI (Ministry of International Trade and Industry) has a very direct role in regulating international commercial enterprises in Japan. Nearly every South American country has an agency to regulate foreign competition within its borders.

Personal friendships and national sympathies can significantly affect competitive relationships in the international marketplace. Interestingly, Europeans tend to be more suspicious of each other than of outsiders. When a French company looks for a partner, it usually prefers an American to a European or even to another French company.

---

[14] See Chapter 18 for greater detail on cartels.

[15] Burck, op. cit., p. 149.

[16] Louis Banks, "Japan: The Open Door with a Catch," *Fortune*, July 1963, p. 136.

Friendships, of course, always play a part in the business relationship; but in many foreign countries, personal friendship for a vendor or a feeling of allegiance to a vendor's country may be of major importance in a business situation—even when other things are not equal. Such relationships and trust often precede price and quality. Highly developed reciprocal relationships are a fairly logical extension of the concept of friendship, and eventually even commercial bribery may enter the picture. In many foreign countries, bribery is considered to be a routine business function and, if not generally condoned, the practice is at least generally ignored.

MODE OF DOING BUSINESS

As one would anticipate from the diverse structures, management attitudes, and behavior encountered in international business, there is considerable variation in the methods employed in doing business. No matter how thoroughly prepared one may be when approaching foreign markets, there is still a certain amount of cultural shock when the un-initiated trader encounters the actual business situation. In conducting business negotiations, the international marketer will soon become aware that there are differences in his contact level, communications emphasis, and in the tempo and formality of foreign businesses. Ethical standards are likely to differ, as will the negotiation emphasis. In most countries the foreign trader is likely to encounter a fairly high degree of government involvement.

Level of Contact

Business customs in a given country seem to emphasize one particular kind of contact: top-level, middle-management, or group contact. In most countries, including European, executives are reluctant to relinquish their authority, so business contacts are made at a relatively high level of management. The situation is somewhat modified in the United States, where there is a considerable amount of delegation of authority. The trader in the United States is likely to find that he is dealing with someone in middle management. In Central and South America, middle or lower management or government employees tend to seek to aggrandize their positions by attempting to participate, or appear to participate, in decisions over which they have no jurisdiction. In the Far Eastern cultures that stress cooperation and group decision making, a trader will deal with a group rather than an individual.

The title or position takes precedence over the individual holding the job. Many firms allow no correspondence to go out with a person's name that is legible to the recipient. Replies are made to a certain file number or to a specific title because communications are between companies, not between individuals working for companies. In some companies a functionary called a "disponent" oversees the handling of all correspondence. Direct mail will not get through unless sent to the correct title or carrying a proper code number.

Communications Emphasis

Language is the basic communication tool of businessmen attempting to trade in foreign lands; yet businessmen, particularly U.S. businessmen, all too often fail to develop even a basic understanding of a language, much less mastery over the linguistic nuances that reveal unspoken attitudes and information. One writer comments that "even a good interpreter doesn't solve the language problem. By nature and structure, English and Japanese inter-translate badly, and there are conceptual differences between them. Business terms in English and Japanese often have separate meanings."[17] The lesser known languages pose particular problems because it is difficult to find business representatives who can handle any but the three or four major languages. Educated Britains tend to be at least bilingual; yet one prominent English businessman scores his colleagues by quoting, "One Italian buyer, an Anglophile of long standing, summed up the attitude of all too many British firms by attributing to them the saying: 'Speak English or be damned!' "[18]

Probably no language is readily translatable into another, and the concept of the meaning of words differs widely in different languages. It is interesting to note that the Japanese do not like to have their contracts written in the Japanese language because, among other things, it has a tendency to be too vague and nonspecific. The Japanese instead prefer to make English-language contracts where words have more specific meaning.

It is not enough to master the basic language of a country; the astute businessman must also gain a complete mastery over the language of business as well as the silent languages of nuance and implication. Edward T. Hall's reading at the end of this chapter, "The Silent Language in Overseas Business," reviews the languages of time, space, material possessions, friendship patterns, and agreements. Communication mastery, then, is not only the mastery of a language but a mastery of customs as well. Such mastery can be developed only through long association.

Formality and Tempo

Breezy informality and haste seem to characterize the American business relationship, but these behavior patterns seem to be an American exclusive which businessmen from other countries not only fail to share but also fail to appreciate. The apparent informality does not indicate a lack of commitment to the job. Comparing British and American businessmen, one English executive commented:

This emphasis on one compelling interest makes the American businessman a most formidable force. At a cocktail party or a dinner he is still "on duty." If he is impressed by a young guest's command of his subject or facility

---

[17] "The U.S. Executive in Japan" *Business Week,* June 13, 1964, p. 144.

[18] George Worledge, "Italy as a Market for British Goods" *Sales Director* (Alfred Pemberton, Ltd., Reprint), April 1964.

in selling an idea, the American is quite likely to mark the young man down as a potential recruit, and act on that assumption.

The English businessman, with his more diffuse interests and his readiness to separate social occasions from business requirements, is much less likely to seek out talent at non-commercial gatherings. Indeed, the average English businessman is just less concerned with spotting talent. . . .

Lack of enthusiasm is the biggest curse in British industry. It is contagious. It affects every department in an organization. It can lead to promising inventions being abandoned, able individuals being neglected, and workers losing pride in the job.

Northern Europeans seem to have picked up some of the American attitudes in recent years, but in most other countries the historical pattern continues to prevail. Businessmen who expect maximum success must be prepared to deal with foreign businessmen in a way that is acceptable to them. The South American businessman depends greatly on friendships in his business relationship but will establish these friendships only in the South American way: slowly, over a considerable period of time. A typical South American is highly formal until a genuine relationship of respect and friendship is established. Even after such a relationship has been established, the South American is slow to get down to business and will not be pushed. In keeping with his culture, *mañana* is good enough for him. One side of a South American formality is that there is no involvement of business in personal life.

The Japanese is more likely to intermix his business and personal life; but he is also unharried in his business relationships, so unharried, in fact, that the American or European businessman is likely to lose his patience and composure in dealing with the Japanese. The Japanese executive is exceedingly courteous but may, in fact, use his courtesy and lavish treatment of guests as a future competitive weapon. The patient attitude is derived from his indifference to the future. Professor Inatomi contends that:

The Japanese do not have any notion of time because they do not have any notion of self. Indeed, time exists only by reference to a term, or definite extent. But, according to the Japanese conception, there is no term, there is only a continuous flow. There is no past, no future: time is what measures an action, or rather time is marked by the change of action. It seems that time is an immense reservoir from which you can help yourself. Time belongs to nobody, it is at the disposal of everybody. Everybody can dip and the supply is inexhaustible. Time is what marks life, chiefly the psychological life, which is run, as it has been surmised, by all the others. To appropriate time would be to make it "mine." To direct time supposes a self. Time is simply the dimension in which the Japanese live; they do not own it. This is one explanation for not keeping appointments, set with so much eagerness and seriousness. Time possesses them, not the contrary![19]

Speed of adaptation is critical to success in international business. One writer comments, "U.S. companies in Europe probably have made more mistakes and corrected them in the last eight years than European

---

[19] Maurice Bairy, "Japanese Ways," in R. J. Ballon (ed.), *Doing Business in Japan* (Tokyo: Sophia University, 1967), p. 15. Reproduced by permission.

JAPAN: School for Spies

Filching trade secrets to keep up with the competition is a device as old as buying and selling, and just as international. Nowhere does it flourish more than in Japan. An estimated 10,000 commercial spies honeycomb Japanese industry; in Tokyo alone there are 380 detective agencies that specialize in stealing corporate secrets. Last week industrial espionage achieved a new pinnacle of respectability in Japan with the opening of the Institute for Industrial Protection, a school avowedly established to train spies and counterspies for Japanese corporations.

Legal Theft. Japanese industrialists complain that they lose millions of dollars yearly because spies pass the plans for their secret new products to competitors. But there is no law in Japan against stealing trade secrets so long as no patents are violated, and products still in development are naturally not patented. "The only way to operate," says one Japanese industrialist grimly, "is to tighten security and then spy right back on those who are spying on you."

The new school is intended to help companies do just that. Its president is cagey Tadashi Kurihara, 70, who learned the ins and outs of espionage as a career diplomat and onetime Ambassador to Turkey. On his nine-man staff are seasoned operatives from Japan's wartime intelligence services, including Yuzuru Fukamachi, 65, a onetime navy code specialist, and Tatsuo Furuya, 55, Japan's intelligence chief in wartime Shanghai. President Kurihara and his men claim to be down to earth about their job. Says Kurihara: "We wear trench coats for warmth, not atmosphere."

Measures & Countermeasures. The students—there are 50 in the first batch—are mostly bright young executives in their late 20s. Their companies selected them to attend the institute, and also pay their tuition ($112 per student).

During the four-month course, the students will learn how to use dozens of complex espionage devices. They will be taught how to tap a telephone from a distance by beaming a ray from an infra-red listening device into the receiver, and how to coat documents with a colorless dye that will penetrate even through leather gloves to blacken the fingers of anyone touching the document. "Naturally," purrs Old Shanghai Hand Furuya, "we have a counter-formula which will nullify the dye's effect, and only our students will know about it."

After graduation the students, since they all come from different companies, are likely to end up using the institute's measures and countermeasures on one another. Shrugs President Kurihara: "At least, all our students will have an equal chance. They will make worthy adversaries for each other."

companies have in the last 60. The American turn-around time is barely a millisecond compared to the ponderous, phlegmatic response of the average European company."[20]

Business Ethics *E-4.*

The moral question of what is right and appropriate poses many dilemmas for the domestic marketer. Even within a country, ethical standards are not defined, and there is no common frame of reference among businessmen. The problem of business ethics is infinitely more complex in the international marketplace because opinions of what is right are spread even more widely because of basic cultural diversity. What is commonly accepted as right in one country may be completely unacceptable in another. Giving business gifts of high value, for example, is generally condemned in the United States, but in most other countries of the world, gifts are not only accepted and condoned but expected. The question of international business standards of morality is one which cannot be adequately dealt with until there is a major degree of cultural homogenization through business, political, and social intercourse among different countries.[21]

Negotiation Emphasis *E-5.*

Basic elements of negotiation are no different in any country: they relate to the product, its price and terms, services related to the product, and, finally, friendship between the vendor and his customers. The differences between businessmen of various nations relate not to different negotiation elements but rather to the hierarchy of values and to varying emphasis among the elements.

The government is virtually a third party to all international business agreements because it is almost a force in negotiations in foreign countries. The government may be directly represented or it may be indirectly represented through the businessman's awareness of governmental policy, position, or attitude. Currency availability, admission of goods, physical properties and packaging, advertising, employment conditions, reparation of profits, and many other factors are likely to be closely regulated in dealings with foreign countries by the government.

SUMMARY AND CONCLUSIONS

Business customs and practices in different world markets vary so much that it is difficult to make valid generalizations about them; it is even difficult to classify the different kinds of business behavior that are encountered from nation to nation. The only safe generalizations are that the businessman who is working in a country other than his own

---

[20] "U.S. Business in the New Europe," *Business Week,* May 7, 1966, p. 96.

[21] See Howe Martin, "Bribery and Corruption in International Business," in *Essays in International Business,* Fall 1969, pp. 18–25.

must be sensitive to his business environment and must be willing to adapt when such adaptation is necessary. Unfortunately, it is seldom easy to know when such adaptation is necessary, because in certain instances adaptation is optional and in others it is actually undesirable.

Business behavior is derived in large part from the basic cultural environment in which the business operates, and as such, is subject to the extreme diversity which is encountered among various cultures and subcultures. Environmental considerations significantly affect the attitudes, behavior, and outlook of foreign businessmen. Motivational patterns of such businessmen depend in part on their personal backgrounds, their business positions, sources of authority, and their own personalities.

Varying motivational patterns inevitably affect methods of doing business in different countries. Businessmen in some countries thrive on competition, while in others they do all possible to eliminate it. The authoritarian, centralized decision-making orientation in some nations contrasts sharply with democratic decentralization in others. International variation characterizes contact level, ethical orientation, negotiation outlook, and nearly every other part of doing business. The foreign businessman can take no phase of business behavior for granted.

The new breed of international businessman that has emerged in recent years appears to have a heightened sensitivity to cultural variations. Sensitivity, however, is not enough; the international trader must be constantly alert and prepared to adapt when necessary. He must always realize that, no matter how long he has been in a country, he is not a native and in many countries he will always be treated as an outsider. Finally, he must avoid the critical mistake of assuming that his knowledge of one culture will make him acceptable in another.

READINGS

THE SILENT LANGUAGE IN OVERSEAS BUSINESS*

EDWARD T. HALL

With few exceptions, Americans are relative newcomers on the international business scene. Today, as in Mark Twain's time, we are all too often "innocents abroad," in an era when naiveté and blundering in foreign business dealings may have serious political repercussions.

When the American executive travels abroad to do business, he is frequently shocked to discover to what extent the many variables of foreign behavior and custom complicate his efforts. Although the American has recognized, certainly, that even the man next door has many minor traits which make him somewhat peculiar, for some reason he has failed to appreciate how different foreign businessmen and their practices will seem to him.

---

* Reprinted, with special permission, from *Harvard Business Review*, May–June, 1960, pp. 87–96. © 1960 by the President and Fellows of Harvard College; all rights reserved.

He should understand that the various peoples around the world have worked out and integrated into their subconscious literally thousands of behavior patterns that they take for granted in each other.[1] Then, when the stranger enters, and behaves differently from the local norm, he often quite unintentionally insults, annoys, or amuses the native with whom he is attempting to do business. For example:

In the United States, a corporation executive knows what is meant when a client lets a month go by before replying to a business proposal. On the other hand, he senses an eagerness to do business if he is immediately ushered into the client's office. In both instances, he is reacting to subtle cues in the timing of interaction, cues which he depends on to chart his course of action.

Abroad, however, all this changes. The American executive learns that the Latin Americans are casual about time and that if he waits an hour in the outer office before seeing the Deputy Minister of Finance, it does not necessarily mean he is not getting anywhere. There people are so important that nobody can bear to tear himself away; because of the resultant interruptions and conversational detours, everybody is constantly getting behind. What the American does not know is the point at which the waiting becomes significant.

In another instance, after traveling 7,000 miles an American walks into the office of a highly recommended Arab businessman on whom he will have to depend completely. What he sees does not breed confidence. The office is reached by walking through a suspicious-looking coffee-house in an old, dilapidated building situated in a crowded non-European section of town. The elevator, rising from dark, smelly corridors, is rickety and equally foul. When he gets to the office itself, he is shocked to find it small, crowded, and confused. Papers are stacked all over the desk and table tops—even scattered on the floor in irregular piles.

The Arab merchant he has come to see had met him at the airport the night before and sent his driver to the hotel this morning to pick him up. But now, after the American's rush, the Arab is tied up with something else. Even when they finally start talking business, there are constant interruptions. If the American is at all sensitive to his environment, everything around him signals, "What am I getting into?"

Before leaving home he was told that things would be different, but how different? The hotel is modern enough. The shops in the new part of town have many more American and European trade goods than he had anticipated. His first impression was that doing business in the Middle East would not present any new problems. Now he is beginning to have doubts. One minute everything looks familiar and he is on firm ground; the next, familiar landmarks are gone. His greatest problem is that so much assails his senses all at once that he does not know where to start looking for something that will tell him where he stands. He needs a frame of reference—a way of sorting out what is significant and relevant.

---

[1] For details, see my book, *The Silent Language* (New York: Doubleday & Company, Inc., 1959).

That is why it is so important for American businessmen to have a real understanding of the various social, cultural, and economic differences they will face when they attempt to do business in foreign countries. To help give some frame of reference, this article will map out a few areas of human activity that have largely been unstudied.

The topics I will discuss are certainly not presented as the last word on the subject, but they have proved to be highly reliable points at which to begin to gain an understanding of foreign cultures. While additional research will undoubtedly turn up other items just as relevant, at present I think the businessman can do well to begin by appreciating cultural differences in matters concerning the language of time, of space, of material possessions, of friendship patterns, and of agreements.

Language of Time

Everywhere in the world people use time to communicate with each other. There are different languages of time just as there are different spoken languages. The unspoken languages are informal; yet the rules governing their interpretation are surprisingly *ironbound*.

In the United States, a delay in answering a communication can result from a large volume of business causing the request to be postponed until the backlog is cleared away, from poor organization, or possibly from technical complexity requiring deep analysis. But if the person awaiting the answer or decision rules out these reasons, then the delay means to him that the matter has low priority on the part of the other person—lack of interest. On the other hand, a similar delay in a foreign country may mean something altogether different. Thus:

In Ethiopia, the time required for a decision is directly proportional to its importance. This is so much the case that low-level bureaucrats there have a way of trying to elevate the prestige of their work by taking a long time to make up their minds. (Americans in that part of the world are innocently prone to downgrade their work in the local people's eyes by trying to speed things up.)

In the Arab East, time does not generally include schedules as Americans know and use them. The time required to get something accomplished depends on the relationship. More important people get fast service from less important people, and conversely. Close relatives take absolute priority; nonrelatives are kept waiting.

In the United States, giving a person a deadline is a way of indicating the degree of urgency or relative importance of the work. But in the Middle East, the American runs into a cultural trap the minute he opens his mouth. "Mr. Aziz will have to make up his mind in a hurry because my board meets next week and I have to have an answer by then," is taken as indicating the American is overly demanding and is exerting undue pressure. "I am going to Damascus tomorrow morning and will have to have my car tonight," is a sure way to get the mechanic to stop work, because to give another person a deadline in this part of the world is to be rude, pushy, and demanding.

An Arab's evasiveness as to when something is going to happen does not mean he does not want to do business; it only means he is avoiding unpleasantness and is side-stepping possible commitments which he takes more seriously than we do. For example:

The Arabs themselves at times find it impossible to communicate even to each other that some processes cannot be hurried, and are controlled by built-in schedules. This is obvious enough to the Westerner but not to the Arab. A highly placed official in Baghdad precipitated a bitter family dispute because his nephew, a biochemist, could not speed up the complete analysis of the uncle's blood. He accused the nephew of putting other less important people before him and of not caring. Nothing could sway the uncle, who could not grasp the fact that there is such a thing as an *inherent* schedule.

With us the more important an event is, the further ahead we schedule it, which is why we find it insulting to be asked to a party at the last minute. In planning future events with Arabs, it pays to hold the lead time to a week or less because other factors may intervene or take precedence.

Again, time spent waiting in an American's outer office is a sure indicator of what one person thinks of another or how important he feels the other's business to be. This is so much the case that most Americans cannot help getting angry after waiting 30 minutes; one may even feel such a delay is an insult, and will walk out. In Latin America, on the other hand, one learns that it does not mean anything to wait in an outer office. An American businessman with years of experience in Mexico once told me, "You know, I have spent two hours cooling my heels in an executive's outer office. It took me a long time to learn to keep my blood pressure down. Even now, I find it hard to convince myself they are still interested when they keep me waiting."

The Japanese handle time in ways which are almost inexplicable to the Western European and particularly the American. A delay of years with them does not mean that they have lost interest. It only means that they are building up to something. They have learned that Americans are vulnerable to long waits. One of them expressed it, "You Americans have one terrible weakness. If we make you wait long enough, you will agree to anything."

Indians of South Asia have an elastic view of time as compared to our own. Delays do not, therefore, have the same meaning to them. Nor does indefiniteness in pinpointing appointments mean that they are evasive. Two Americans meeting will say, "We should get together sometime," thereby setting a low priority on the meeting. The Indian who says, "Come over and see me, see me anytime," means just that.

Americans make a place at the table which may or may not mean a place made in the heart. But when the Indian makes a place in his time, it is yours to fill in every sense of the word if you realize that by so doing you have crossed a boundary and are now friends with him. The point of all this is that time communicates just as surely as do words and that the vocabulary of time is different around the world.

The principle to be remembered is that time has different meanings in each country.

Language of Space

Like time, the language of space is different whenever one goes. The American businessman, familiar with the pattern of American corporate life, has no difficulty in appraising the relative importance of someone else, simply by noting the size of his office in relation to other offices around him:

Our pattern calls for the president or the chairman of the board to have the biggest office. The executive vice president will have the next largest, and so on down the line until you end up in the "bull pen." More important offices are usually located at the corners of buildings and on the upper floors. Executive suites will be on the top floor. The relative rank of vice presidents will be reflected in where they are placed along "Executive Row."

The French, on the other hand, are much more likely to lay out space as a network of connecting points of influence, activity, or interest. The French supervisor will ordinarily be found in the middle of his subordinates where he can control them.

Americans who are crowded will often feel that their status in the organization is suffering. As one would expect in the Arab world, the location of an office and its size constitute a poor index of the importance of the man who occupies it. What we experience as crowded, the Arab will often regard as spacious. The same is true in Spanish cultures. A Latin American official illustrated the Spanish view of this point while showing me around a plant. Opening the door to an 18-by-20-foot office in which seventeen clerks and their desks were placed, he said, "See, we have nice spacious offices. Lots of space for everyone."

The American will look at a Japanese room and remark how bare it is. Similarly, the Japanese look at our rooms and comment, "How bare!" Furniture in the American home tends to be placed along the walls (around the edge). Japanese have their charcoal pit where the family gathers in the *middle* of the room. The top floor of Japanese department stores is not reserved for the chief executive—it is the bargain roof!

In the Middle East and Latin America, the businessman is likely to feel left out in time and overcrowded in space. People get too close to him, lay their hands on him, and generally crowd his physical being. In Scandinavia and Germany, he feels more at home, but at the same time the people are a little cold and distant. It is space itself that conveys this feeling.

In the United States, because of our tendency to zone activities, nearness carries rights of familiarity so that the neighbor can borrow material possessions and invade time. This is not true in England. Propinquity entitles you to nothing. American Air Force personnel stationed there complain because they have to make an appointment for their children to play with the neighbor's child next door.

Conversation distance between two people is learned early in life by copying elders. Its controlling patterns operate almost totally unconsciously. In the United States, in contrast to many foreign countries, men avoid excessive touching. Regular business is conducted at distances such as 5 feet to 8 feet; highly personal business, 18 inches to 3 feet—not 2 or 3 inches.

In the United States, it is perfectly possible for an experienced executive to schedule the steps of negotiation in time and space so that most people feel comfortable about what is happening. Business transactions progress in stages from across the desk to beside the desk, to the coffee table, then on to the conference table, the luncheon table, or the golf course, or even into the home—all according to a complex set of hidden rules which we obey instinctively.

Even in the United States, however, an executive may slip when he moves into new and unfamiliar realms, when dealing with a new group, doing business with a new company, or moving to a new place in the industrial hierarchy. In a new country the danger is magnified. For example, in India it is considered improper to discuss business in the home on social occasions. One never invites a business acquaintance to the home for the purpose of furthering business aims. That would be a violation of sacred hospitality rules.

Language of Things

Americans are often contrasted with the rest of the world in terms of material possessions. We are accused of being materialistic, gadget-crazy. And, as a matter of fact, we have developed material things for some very interesting reasons. Lacking a fixed class system and having an extremely mobile population, Americans have become highly sensitive to how others make use of material possessions. We use everything from clothes to houses as a highly evolved and complex means of ascertaining each other's status. Ours is a rapidly shifting system in which both styles and people move up or down. For example:

The Cadillac ad men feel that not only is it natural but quite insightful of them to show a picture of a Cadillac and a well-turned out gentleman in his early fifties opening the door. The caption underneath reads, "You already know a great deal about this man."

Following this same pattern, the head of a big union spends an excess of $100,000 furnishing his office so that the president of United States Steel cannot look down on him. Good materials, large space, and the proper surroundings signifiy that the people who occupy the premises are solid citizens, that they are dependable and successful.

The French, the English, and the Germans have entirely different ways of using their material possessions. What stands for the height of dependability and respectability with the English would be old-fashioned and backward to us. The Japanese take pride in often inexpensive but tasteful arrangements that are used to produce the proper emotional setting.

Middle East businessmen look for something else—family, connections, friendship. They do not use the furnishings of their office as part of their status system; nor do they expect to impress a client by these means or to fool a banker into lending more money that he should. They like good things, too, but feel that they, as persons, should be known and not judged solely by what the public sees.

One of the most common criticisms of American relations abroad, both commercial and governmental, is that we usually think in terms of material things. "Money talks," says the American, who goes on talking the language of money abroad, in the belief that money talks the *same* language all over the world. A common practice in the United States is to try to buy loyalty with high salaries. In foreign countries, this maneuver almost never works, for money and material possessions stand for something different there than they do in America.

Language of Friendship

The American finds his friends next door and among those with whom he works. It has been noted that we take people up quickly and drop them just as quickly. Occasionally a friendship formed during schooldays will persist, but this is rare. For us there are few well-defined rules governing the obligations of friendship. It is difficult to say at which point our friendship gives way to business opportunism or pressure from above. In this we differ from many other people in the world. As a general rule in foreign countries friendships are not formed as quickly as in the United States but go much deeper, last longer, and involve real obligations. For example:

It is important to stress that in the Middle East and Latin America your "friends" will not let you down. The fact that they personally are feeling the pinch is never an excuse for failing their friends. They are supposed to look out for your interests.

Friends and family around the world represent a sort of social insurance that would be difficult to find in the United States. We do not use our friends to help us out in disaster as much as we do as a means of getting ahead—or, at least, of getting the job done. The United States systems work by means of a series of closely tabulated favors and obligations carefully doled out where they will do the most good. And the least that we expect in exchange for a favor is gratitude.

The opposite is the case in India, where the friend's role is to "sense" a person's need and do something about it. The idea of reciprocity as we know it is unheard of. An American in India will have difficulty if he attempts to follow American friendship patterns. He gains nothing by extending himself in behalf of others, least of all gratitude, because the Indian assumes that what he does for others he does for the good of his own psyche. He will find it impossible to make friends quickly and is unlikely to allow sufficient time for friendships to ripen. He will also note that as he gets to know people better, they may become more critical of him, a fact that he finds hard to take. What he does not know is that one sign of friendship in India is speaking one's mind.

Language of Agreements

While it is important for American businessmen abroad to understand the symbolic meanings of friendship rules, time, space, and material possessions, it is just as important for executives to know the
rules for negotiating agreements in various countries. Even if they cannot be expected to know the details of each nation's commercial legal
practices, just the awareness of and the expectation of the existence of
differences will eliminate much complication.

Actually, no society can exist on a high commercial level without a
highly developed working base on which agreements can rest. This base
may be one or a combination of three types:

1. Rules that are spelled out technically as law or regulation.
2. Moral practices mutually agreed on and taught to the young as a
   set of principles.
3. Informal customs to which everyone conforms without being able
   to state the exact rules.

Some societies favor one, some another. Ours, particularly in the business world, lays heavy emphasis on the first variety. Few Americans will
conduct any business nowadays without some written agreement or contract.

Varying from culture to culture will be the circumstances under
which such rules apply. Americans consider that negotiations have more
or less ceased when the contract is signed. With the Greeks, on the other
hand, the contract is seen as a sort of way station on the route to negotiation that will cease only when the work is completed. The contract is
nothing more than a charter for serious negotiations. In the Arab world,
once a man's word is given in a particular kind of way, it is just as binding, if not more so, than most of our written contracts. The written contract, therefore, violates the Moslem's sensitivities and reflects on his
honor. Unfortunately, the situation is now so hopelessly confused that
neither system can be counted on to prevail consistently.

Informal patterns and unstated agreements often lead to untold difficulty in the cross-cultural situation. Take the case of the before-and-
after patterns where there is a wide discrepancy between the American's
expectations and those of the Arab:

In the United States, when you engage a specialist such as a lawyer
or a doctor, require any standard service, or even take a taxi, you make
several assumptions: (a) the charge will be fair; (b) it will be in proportion to the services rendered; and (c) it will bear a close relationship
to the "going rate."

You wait until after the services are performed before asking what
the tab will be. If the charge is too high in the light of the above assumptions, you feel you have been cheated. You can complain, or can say
nothing, pay up, and take your business elsewhere the next time.

As one would expect in the Middle East, basic differences emerge
which lead to difficulty if not understood. For instance, when taking a
cab in Beirut it is well to know the going rate as a point around which

to bargain and for settling the charge, which must be fixed before engaging the cab.

If you have not fixed the rate *in advance*, there is a complete change and an entirely different set of rules will apply. According to these rules, the going rate plays no part whatsoever. The whole relationship is altered. The sky is the limit, and the customer has no kick coming. I have seen taxi drivers shouting at the top of their lungs, waving their arms, following a redfaced American with his head pulled down between his shoulders, demanding for a two-pound ride ten Lebanese pounds which the American eventually had to pay.

It is difficult for the American to accommodate his frame of reference to the fact that what constitutes one thing to him, namely, a taxi ride, is to the Arab two very different operations involving two different sets of relationships and two sets of rules. The crucial factor is whether the bargaining is done at the beginning or end of the ride! As a matter of fact, you cannot bargain at the end. What the driver asks for he is entitled to!

One of the greatest difficulties Americans have abroad stems from the fact that we often think we have a commitment when we do not. The second complication on this same topic is the other side of the coin, i.e., when others think we have agreed to things that we have not. Our own failure to recognize binding obligations, plus our custom of setting organizational goals ahead of everything else, has put us in hot water far too often.

People sometimes do not keep agreements with us because we do not keep agreements with them. As a general rule, the American treats the agreement as something he may eventually have to break. Here are two examples:

Once while I was visiting an American post in Latin America, the Ambassador sent the Spanish version of a trade treaty down to his language officer with instructions to write in some "weasel words." To his dismay, he was told, "There are no weasel words in Spanish."

A personnel officer of a large corporation in Iran made an agreement with local employees that American employees would not receive preferential treatment. When the first American employee arrived, it was learned quickly that in the United States he had been covered by a variety of health plans that were not available to Iranians. And this led to immediate protests from the Iranians which were never satisfied. The personnel officer never really grasped the fact that he had violated an iron-bound contract.

Certainly, this is the most important generalization to be drawn by American businessmen from this discussion of agreements: there are many times when we are vulnerable *even when judged by our own standards*. Many instances of actual sharp practices by American companies are well known abroad and are giving American business a bad name. The cure for such questionable behavior is simple. The companies concerned usually have it within their power to discharge offenders and to foster within their organization an atmosphere in which only honesty and fairness can thrive.

But the cure for ignorance of the social and legal rules which underlie business agreements is not so easy. This is because:

The subject is complex.

Little research has been conducted to determine the culturally different concepts of what is an agreement.

The people of each country think that their own code is the only one, and that everything else is dishonest.

Each code is different from our own; and the farther away one is traveling from Western Europe, the greater the difference is.

But the little that has already been learned about this subject indicates that as a problem it is not insoluble and will yield to research. Since it is probably one of the more relevant and immediately applicable areas of interest to modern business, it would certainly be advisable for companies with large foreign operations to sponsor some serious research in this vital field.

A Case in Point

Thus far, I have been concerned with developing the five checkpoints around which a real understanding of foreign cultures can begin. But the problems that arise from a faulty understanding of the silent language of foreign custom are human problems and perhaps can best be dramatized by an actual case.

A Latin American republic had decided to modernize one of its communication networks to the tune of several million dollars. Because of its reputation for quality and price, the inside track was quickly taken by American company "Y."

The company, having been sounded out informally, considered the size of the order and decided to bypass its regular Latin American representative and send instead its sales manager. The following describes what took place.

The sales manager arrived and checked in at the leading hotel. He immediately had some difficulty pinning down just who it was he had to see about his business. After several days without results, he called at the American Embassy where he found that the commercial attaché had the up-to-the-minute information he needed. The commercial attaché listened to his story. Realizing that the sales manager had already made a number of mistakes, but figuring that the Latins were used to American blundering, the attaché reasoned that all was not lost. He informed the sales manager that the Minister of Communications was the key man and that whoever got the nod from him would get the contract. He also briefed the sales manager on methods of conducting business in Latin America and offered some pointers about dealing with the minister.

The attaché's advice ran somewhat as follows:

1. You don't do business here the way you do in the States; it is necessary to spend much more time. You have to get to know your man and vice versa.

2. You must meet with him *several times* before you talk business. I will tell you at what point you can bring up the subject. Take your cues from me. [Our American sales manager at this point made a few observations to himself about "cookie pushers" and wondered how many payrolls had been met by the commercial attaché.]

3. Take that price list and put it in your pocket. Don't get it out until I tell you to. Down here price is only one of the many things taken into account before closing a deal. In the United States, your past experience will prompt you to act according to a certain set of principles, but many of these principles will *not* work here. Every time you feel the urge to act or to say something, look at me. Suppress the urge and take your cues from me. This is very important.

4. Down here people like to do business with men who *are* somebody. In order to be somebody, it is well to have written a book, to have lectured at a university, or to have developed your intellect in some way. The man you are going to see is a poet. He has published several volumes of poetry. Like many Latin Americans, he prizes poetry highly. You will find that he will spend a good deal of business time quoting his poetry to you, and he will take great pleasure in this.

5. You will also note that the people here are very proud of their past and of their Spanish blood, but they are also exceedingly proud of their liberation from Spain and their independence. The fact that they are a democracy, that they are free, and also that they are no longer a colony is very, very important to them. They are warm and friendly and enthusiastic if they like you. If they don't, they are cold and withdrawn.

6. And another thing, time down here means something different. It works in a different way. You know how it is back in the States when a certain type blurts out whatever is on his mind without waiting to see if the situation is right. He is considered an impatient bore and somewhat egocentric. Well, down here, you have to wait much, much longer, and I really mean *much, much* longer, before you can begin to talk about the reason for your visit.

7. There is another point I want to caution you about. At home, the man who sells takes the initiative. Here, *they* tell you when they are ready to do business. But, most of all, don't discuss price until you are asked and don't rush things.

The Pitch

The next day the commercial attaché introduced the sales manager to the Minister of Communications. First, there was a long wait in the outer office while people kept coming in and out. The sales manager looked at his watch, fidgeted, and finally asked whether the minister was really expecting him. The reply he received was scarcely reassuring, "Oh yes, he is expecting you but several things have come up that require his attention. Besides, one gets used to waiting down here." The sales manager irritably replied, "But doesn't he know I flew all the way down here from the United States to see him, and I have spent over a week already of my valuable time trying to find him?" "Yes, I know," was the answer, "but things just move much more slowly here."

At the end of about 30 minutes, the minister emerged from the office, greeted the commercial attaché with a *doble abrazo,* throwing his arms around him and patting him on the back as though they were long-lost brothers. Now, turning and smiling, the minister extended his hand to the sales manager, who, by this time, was feeling rather miffed he had been kept in the outer office so long.

After what seemed to be an all too short chat, the minister rose, suggesting a well-known café where they might meet for dinner the next evening. The sales manager expected, of course, that, considering the nature of their business and the size of the order, he might be taken to the minister's home, not realizing that the Latin home is reserved for family and very close friends.

Until now, nothing at all had been said about the reason for the sales manager's visit, a fact which bothered him somewhat. The whole setup seemed wrong; neither did he like the idea of wasting another day in town. He told the home office before he left that he would be gone for a week or ten days at most, and made a mental note that he would clean this order up in three days and enjoy a few days in Acapulco or Mexico City. Now the week had already gone and he would be lucky if he made it home in ten days.

Voicing his misgivings to the commercial attaché, he wanted to know if the minister really meant business, and, if he did, why could they not get together and talk about it? The commercial attaché by now was beginning to show the strain of constantly having to reassure the sales manager. Nevertheless, he tried again:

What you don't realize is that part of the time we were waiting, the minister was rearranging a very tight schedule so that he could spend tomorrow night with you. You see, down here they don't delegate responsibility the way we do in the States. They exercise much tighter control than we do. As a consequence, this man spends up to 15 hours a day at his desk. It may not look like it to you, but I assure you he really means business. He wants to give your company the order; if you play your cards right, you will get it.

The next evening provided more of the same. Much conversation about food and music, about many people the sales manager had never heard of. They went to a night club, where the sales manager brightened up and began to think that perhaps he and the minister might have something in common after all. It bothered him, however, that the principal reason for his visit was not even alluded to tangentially. But every time he started to talk about electronics, the commercial attaché would nudge him and proceed to change the subject.

The next meeting was for morning coffee at a café. By now the sales manager was having difficulty hiding his impatience. To make matters worse, the minister had a mannerism which he did not like. When they talked, he was likely to put his hand on him; he would take hold of his arm and get so close that he almost "spat" in his face. As a consequence, the sales manager was kept busy trying to dodge and back up.

Following coffee, there was a walk in a nearby park. The minister expounded on the shrubs, the birds, and the beauties of nature, and at one spot he stopped to point at a statue and said: "There is a statue of the world's greatest hero, the liberator of mankind!" At this point, the worst happened, for the sales manager asked who the statue was of and, being given the name of a famous Latin American patriot, said, "I never heard of him," and walked on.

The Failure

It is quite clear from this that the sales manager did not get the order, which went to a Swedish concern. The American, moreover, was never able to see the minister again. Why did the minister feel the way he did? His reasoning went somewhat as follows:

I like the American's equipment and it makes sense to deal with North Americans who are near us and whose price is right. But I could never be friends with this man. He is not my kind of human being and we have nothing in common. He is not *simpatico*. If I can't be friends and he is not *simpatico*, I can't depend on him to treat me right. I tried everything, every conceivable situation, and only once did we seem to understand each other. If we could be friends, he would feel obligated to me and this obligation would give me some control. Without control, how do I know he will deliver what he says he will at the price he quotes?

Of course, what the minister did not know was that the price was quite firm, and the quality control was a matter of company policy. He did not realize that the sales manager was a member of an organization, and that the man is always subordinate to the organization in the United States. Next year maybe the sales manager would not even be representing the company, but would be replaced. Further, if he wanted someone to depend on, his best bet would be to hire a good American lawyer to represent him and write a binding contract.

In this instance, both sides suffered. The American felt he was being slighted and put off, and did not see how there could possibly be any connection between poetry and doing business or why it should all take so long. He interpreted the delay as a form of polite brush-off. Even if things had gone differently and there had been a contract, it is doubtful that the minister would have trusted the contract as much as he would a man whom he considered his friend. Throughout Latin America, the law is made livable and contracts workable by having friends and relatives operating from the inside. Lacking a friend, someone who would look out for his interests, the minister did not want to take a chance. He stated this simply and directly.

Conclusion

The case just described has of necessity been oversimplified. The danger is that the reader will say, "Oh, I see. All you really have to do is be friends." At which point the expert will step in and reply:

Yes, of course, but what you don't realize is that in Latin America being a friend involves much more than it does in the United States and is an entirely different proposition. A friendship implies obligations. You go about it differently. It involves much more than being nice, visiting, and playing golf. You would not want to enter into friendship lightly.

The point is simply this. It takes years and years to develop a sound foundation for doing business in a given country. Much that is done seems silly or strange to the home office. Indeed, the most common error made by home offices, once they have found representatives who can get results, is failure to take their advice and allow sufficient time for representatives to develop the proper contacts.

The second most common error, if that is what it can be called, is ignorance of the secret and hidden language of foreign cultures. In this article I have tried to show how five key topics—time, space, material possessions, friendship patterns, and business agreements—offer a starting point from which companies can begin to acquire the understanding necessary to do business in foreign countries.

Our present knowledge is meager, and much more research is needed before the businessman of the future can go abroad fully equipped for his work. Not only will he need to be well versed in the economics, law, and politics of the area, but he will have to understand, if not speak, the silent languages of other cultures.

A REPORT ON BRIBERY AND CORRUPTION*

A Dutch businessman living in North Africa told a journalist: "I had a talk only recently with a high-ranking minister. He ordered a refrigerator from me. Naturally, the next day I sent him the most expensive model we sell. A fortnight later I discovered that one of my clerks had sent a bill with it. That was a very stupid thing to do. I immediately rang the minister to apologise and to say that, of course, we would be very happy if he would accept it as a little token of our esteem. He thanked me nicely and the matter was closed. But it was a near thing. . . . If you start thinking on European lines of behaviour here, you might as well move out."

Throughout northern Europe, at least, it is often assumed that standards of business behaviour start slipping East of Suez. The extent to which this calls for compromise from the European businessman is a matter of opinion. And opinions vary widely not so much about the principle of compromise—"if we don't, our competitors will. . . ."—but about where to draw the line. A Dutch exporter admitted cheerfully that in the 'younger' countries *some* bribery was an absolute necessity. Several companies paid a regular retainer to fairly highly placed men in the governments of various developing countries. "But so do all our European and American competitors. Orders may depend on whether your British or French or American competitor has bought the assistance of a better man than yours." And there's no shame about gifts for prospective customers. "They expect that. Sometimes they also expect an invitation to come and see our works in Holland. We are usually glad

---

* Reprinted, with special permission, from *The Director*, London, June, 1963, pp. 465–467.

to comply. It's not very expensive, really, if you're out to get an important order; and it creates an atmosphere of trust and friendliness." The Dutch, at any rate, claim that if their exporters "aren't always angels" their own government stands aloof from the marketplace. Perhaps too aloof for some Dutch directors: the authorities are very strict in adhering to the Berne Agreement in settling terms for export credit financing and insurance, and The Hague refuses to budge an inch, despite occasional business pressure.

In Western Germany queries about business ethics more immediately prompt political reflections. Take East-West trade. But for the Government's restraining hand, West Germany could and would do far more trade with the Communists. Since the Berlin Wall was thrown up, however, the Bonn authorities have tried, for example, to discourage firms from taking stands at the Leipzig Fair. Many of the larger companies have stopped going to Leipzig—although smaller firms with more to lose have not followed suit, and several big companies do the same business behind scenes, arguing plausibly that by not having a stand at least they do not give propaganda ammunition to the Communists. The well-worn charge that the Germans give a hidden subsidy to exporters by remitting the turnover tax on internal trade seems also largely unfounded, the Germans pleading that this remission is no more than the equivalent to British remission of purchase tax.

But private industry energetically going after foreign orders can cut a less edifying figure. According to one experienced British visitor to West Germany: "They spend considerable sums bribing the right people or in providing entertainment that amounts to the same thing . . . just recently, for instance, members of an East European delegation went home complaining that they had been paid only DM50,000 each (well over £4,000) and that the French had proved far more generous." So the Germans are really no worse than others, after all—including (the Germans say) the British?

There is the story that, in a quandary as to how to meet an Arab ruler's wish for female company, the Foreign Office in London decided the right department to deal with it was the Home Office. In West Germany, certainly, 'entertainment' seems occasionally to veer into shady twilight activities. There are the firms which pay girls—£100 a night was one figure suggested—to look after the 'requirements' of visiting executives. At the top of the customer list, according to one German businessman, are visitors from the Middle East—"but the Far East and South America are not far behind . . . and Europe is by no means innocent."

And at this stage, it is alleged, the authorities are involved. "Recognising that this kind of thing goes on and costs a lot, they discreetly allow selected firms to register for tax purposes appreciably less than their true exports." But this—says one German man of the world to another—is common practice in other countries. The Japanese, comes the afterthought, are far worse.

Are they? The sagging standards sometimes encountered in Europe are often attributed to the need to make the non-European feel quite at home. In Japan courtesy seems an apter word than corruption: the foreign visitor—when it comes to 'entertainment'—gets what he wants, even if it is to the distaste of his host. A journalist long resident in Tokyo comments that "when it comes to business ethics, this country is like the little girl with a curl . . . when she's good she's very very good, and when she's bad she's horrid."

Japan, in this as in other contexts, is the land of paradox. "Its businessmen can display almost incredible loyalty to foreign associates or can deal blithely with several rival firms at once. They can stick to the most rigid ethical standards or be guilty of pirating designs, dumping and worse. They can be men who keep their word so faithfully that a written contract is never demanded or necessary—or men so devious that a contract is worse than useless."

The key—for the visitor anxious to deal with companies of integrity— is to go through the 'correct channels.' Far more than in Britain or the United States, "a Japanese firm's reliability can be gauged accurately from its reputation and standing. Reputable Japanese businessmen have to be immensely jealous of their good name, precisely because there are many rotten apples in the barrel. But the reliable Japanese businessman is very cautious and conscientious indeed, often as worried about the 'devious foreigner' as he may be about them."

Japan—along with formerly British-ruled territories—holds a high reputation in the broad and generally uncharted regions of the Far East. The practice of 'kumshaw' (literally, *thank you*) abounds throughout parts of Asia, although the newly arrived British businessman is usually advised by his bank or trustworthy contact that the kumshaw, or tip, is no longer the considerable transaction it used to be and that if he is asked for it, he should think again about the deal. In China, comments an observer in Hong Kong, the Communist Government has done away with most of the basis on which corruption can be practised. "Even in the three difficult years just ended, when there were stories of incipient corruption among officials in many parts of China, the instances where this affected big international transactions were very few indeed." But in Taiwan and South East Asia, tales of greedy middlemen and officials with reluctant pen-fingers but large and empty pockets are still related. When *initiating* business, the new entrant may have it put to him that he ought to make it worthwhile to the person who can introduce him to the man he wants or the official he needs. If he goes to experienced compatriots for advice, he'll be told often as not to use his common sense— but to avoid anything blatant or inflated. And after all where the counterpart of a Board of Trade official whose approval is needed for a deal or a shipment is receiving a monthly salary equivalent to say, 30s., then the temptations are built in. Trade strains to find a way, even at the expense of ethics, when politics intervenes. The Malayan Government, for example, has banned trade with South Africa, but Union businessmen say that they still send in the same amount of goods, through Chinese traders, who manage "to swap enough labels and change enough invoices, and grease enough palms to get away with it."

Do stories of corruption provide the exceptions that prove the rule:

that the world over, business is generally honest? The average American businessman concedes that he is still something of a Puritan in his overseas dealings, that he lacks the experience of the British; but all the same, he claims, "in most areas of the world there is need for little but clean, hard dealing." However, just as Europeans start making qualifications about Africa and the Middle East, the Americans hesitate when they come to discuss Latin America. One company official (in machine manufacture) recalls: "We had landed a government contract—well, we thought we'd landed it. At the last minute, a government official said he had discovered a vital defect in our machines. If it was not corrected, the machinery would be dangerous. . . . We didn't believe him, but we offered to check the machines and correct the flaw. But the official said there wasn't time. The machines would be adjusted locally, and we would pay the bill. With a cheque to him. I saw one of the machines later, and if anything had been done, I couldn't discover what. . . ."

This was apparently a sophisticated piece of bribe-taking. Simpler cases are illustrated by the cynical comment from an American trader: "On the docks, where the heat is often so intense it really is difficult to move, the Latin workers can set records for slowness. It's sometimes surprising how fast they can move after the dock boss has been properly taken care of . . . ." Graft of course is an American word, traditionally applied to government. But for years any American businessman asked whether diplomatic pressure had been applied to squeeze out a contract for him would have laughed; it was a joke in Latin America that if the U.S. businessman wanted down-to-earth advice he should go to the German Embassy. With payments troubles providing the spur, American diplomacy lately has become far more commercially-minded. But, says an American businessman, "we are generally unlikely to ask for diplomatic pressures except in cases where assets are nationalised or some other cataclysmic event occurs. . . ."

And the British? Travellers' tales abound, of course: usually to the discredit of other nationalities. The other day, the managing director of a British company came back from a former Colony with the account of the minister who returned from Scandinavia with a blonde mistress and a business deal signed: the two being largely cause and effect. The British abroad maintain a high reputation, but perhaps are not renowned for compromise for nothing. Last month, Sir Richard Powell asked a meeting of one of the Institute's branches: "Is there anyone in this room who can honestly say that he does not from time to time come across examples of business behaviour which cause him to have misgivings? If so, I think he can count himself a fortunate man."

What should the British businessman do when abroad he sees competitors gaining an advantage over him by dishonesty? The Board of Trade will take up complaints concerning, say, export subsidies; but there is no official department able to investigate and act on charges of corruption. As a first step, however, the exporter should report anything suspicious to the British consulate or embassy in the area concerned. Action may be impossible but in a world of trade rivalry, ammunition is always useful.

Bribery and corruption are among the hazards of business life, internationally and locally. Whether one country is worse than another is a matter for debate: it takes two to make a bargain, bribes are given as well as received. The more honest a country's businessmen, too, the more readily they may admit that their own standards are not always what they should be.

MUST YOU TELL A "FUNNY STORY"?*

WILLIAM F. WHYTE

The international dinner had gone very well until a U.S. businessman got up to speak. Within a period of five minutes, he made the following errors:

1.   He decided to tell a "funny story."
2.   The story turned out not to be very funny to his listeners.
3.   While the businessman told the story in English, in the process he used two words in the language of his host and badly mispronounced them.
4.   The point of the story cast aspersions on the moral standards of the women in his host's country.
5.   To compound the insult, the story teller added a supplementary point, making an unfavorable comparison of the women of his host's country with those of a traditional rival.

Five errors in five minutes! Was this a new world's record on the international banquet circuit? Was the businessman stupid? Did he lack experience in international gatherings? The answer was no to both questions. He had been highly successful in building a business that took a great deal of intelligence and imagination. He had been going to international meetings for years. Before the speech making, he had participated actively and intelligently in the conversation, showing himself to be well informed and sympathetic to the international interests of other people.

Why did he perform the way he did? The answer is both simple and basic. The businessman was acting out a behavior pattern which was appropriate in business circles in his own culture and was not appropriate abroad.

All the other errors depended upon the initial decision to tell the "funny story." Some years ago, a perceptive foreigner, with much international experience, made this comment: "I have noticed a peculiar thing about your American businessmen in international gatherings. Whenever they speak, they must always begin by telling a 'funny story' —even though the story always makes everybody else uncomfortable. Why do you think they do that?"

* Reprinted with permission from the July–August 1968 issue of the *Columbia Journal of World Business*. Copyright © 1968 by the Trustees of Columbia University in the City of New York.

In following this aspect of American business culture, the business-man blunders into a behavioral area where the culture may be unique. North Americans see no incongruity between humor and serious communication. Latin Americans, Continental Europeans, and no doubt other people do see such an incongruity. To them, if a man is serious about what he is doing he talks seriously; when he is being frivolous, he tells jokes. A witty remark, if directly relevant to the point in question, will be appreciated, but a "funny story" is something else again. It communicates to the listeners that the speaker is not really serious about what he is doing and saying.

The foreigner who has had some experience in dealing with American businessmen learns to make allowances for their peculiar behavior. He says to himself, "The man sounds like a fool to me, but I must recognize that he is not really a fool; he just gives that impression." Such allowances are hardly flattering.

Did the other four errors have some cultural logic to them or did they just reflect the personality of the speaker? It can be argued that the other errors were culturally determined, given the initial decision to tell the "funny story."

In an international gathering, the story that was a big hit at home is likely to fall embarrassingly flat. Is this because other nationalities have no sense of humor? No. It is because the nature of humor varies widely from culture to culture. A joke that is surefire in the United States is more than likely to fall flat abroad. While even a successful joke will seem out of place in a serious meeting abroad, the unsuccessful joke compounds the crime.

It Is Not Funny

Why should the funny story turn out to be insulting? While the U.S. businessman allows himself latitude in determining what it is in the present situation that is going to remind him of the story he is determined to tell, he does feel better when he is able to establish a reasonably logical connection between situation and story. Therefore, when he finds himself in an international situation, he is likely to reach out for an international-type joke. The jokes he will know from home experience are very likely to deal in national stereotypes: the stuffy formality of the Englishman, the authoritarian rigidity of the German, the prevalence of mistresses and lovers in French society, and so on. When such national stereotypes are presented in an impersonal dramatic presentation—as, for example, in the movie, "Those Daring Young Men and Their Flying Machines"—a good time may be had by all, but when a person is confronted with national stereotypes in the story directed at him, he must make an effort to suppress his feelings of annoyance and embarrassment.

In telling his story, this U.S. businessman touched a sensitive nerve in the feelings of his hosts regarding their own language. When a person makes an effort to speak the language of the country he is visiting, his hosts will put up with clumsiness in expression, at least giving the man credit for making the effort to learn their language and thus showing a serious interest in understanding them better. But when he speaks entirely in his own language and then throws in two simple foreign words which he badly mispronounces, the effect of his foreign language usage is quite different. His hosts then say to themselves, "This man does not think enough of us and our language even to say two simple words reasonably correctly."

Why dwell at such length on this one problem of inter-cultural communication? It is not to say that this sort of behavior presents a major obstacle to international understanding, but it is a minor irritant. It seems useful to examine the case for what it tells us generally about the intercultural problems of the U.S. businessman abroad.

What Is the Moral?

When he goes abroad to do business he recognizes that he needs advice in a number of specialized fields: business law, labor law, the practices of financial institutions, and so on. Without hesitation, he obtains the services of consultants on such matters.

If he cannot speak the language of the country and the people with whom he wants to deal cannot speak his language, he recognizes that he must work through an interpreter, but at least in Europe and in Latin America most of the people with whom he might want to deal are multilingual. Therefore, it is not easy for him to see why he should have any problem communicating with them. If the businessman of the host country dressed in exotic clothing, he would recognize at once that they were quite different from him in important ways and that he would need advice on managing his relations with them. But in Europe, Latin America, and many other parts of the world, the businesmen with whom he comes into contact will be wearing business suits much like his own and will not behave in any way that makes the cultural differences immediately obvious to him.

The U.S. businessman who speaks for his company abroad is probably a successful individual at home. He is likely to have great confidence in his ability to handle inter-personal relations. He is accustomed to structuring his inter-personal relations himself, and he is not accustomed to asking other people how he should behave. When he finds himself abroad and communicating in his own language with people who seem to look and act much like himself, it does not occur to him that the behavior which is effective at home may be ineffective abroad. While he readily recognizes the need of a legal consultant, an economic consultant, and perhaps other specialists, it never occurs to him that he needs a cultural consultant. But until the businessman abroad recognizes the need for such cultural consultation, he is likely to act "like a bull in a china shop." Unfortunately his hosts will be so polite to him that the bull never discovers how much china he has broken, as he pushes ahead in the good old American way.

QUESTIONS

1. "More than a toleration of an alien culture is required, . . . there is a need for 'affirmative acceptance as different but equal.'" Elaborate.

2. "We should also bear in mind that in today's business-oriented world economy, the cultures themselves are being significantly affected by business activities and business practices." Comment.

3. "In dealing with foreign businessmen, the marketer must be particularly aware of the varying objectives and aspirations of management." Explain.

4. Suggest ways in which a businessman might prepare himself to handle unique business customs he may encounter in a trip abroad.

5. Business customs and national customs are closely interrelated. In what ways would one expect the two areas to coincide and in what ways would they show differences? How could such areas of similarity and difference be identified?

6. Formulate a set of rules or standards to follow when doing business in any foreign country.

7. Identify both local and foreign examples of cultural imperatives, adiaphora and exclusives. Be prepared to explain why each example fits into the category you have selected.

8. Contrast the authority roles of top management in different societies. How will the differing views of authority affect marketing activities?

9. Do the same for aspirational patterns.

10. What effects on business customs might be anticipated from the recent rapid increases in the level of international business activity?

11. Cite instances of legislation regulating business behavior which might be related directly to customary business behavior.

12. Interview some foreign students to determine the types of cultural shock they encountered when they first came to your country.

13. Differentiate between:
    Private ownership and family ownership
    Decentralized and committee decision making

14. Define:

Cultural imperative	"Fortune Directory"
Cultural adiaphora	Cartel
Cultural exclusive	Silent language
Eclectic borrowing	

15. Review the international sections of back issues of a number of business and news magazines for evidence of business customs affecting business behavior. Write up at least three such instances.

16. Brief a text dealing with the economic life of a nation and identify differences between the business behavior evidenced in rural and urban areas and between large and small businesses.

17. By exploring UN and foreign government sources attempt to develop a table or chart identifying business size patterns in one foreign country.

18. In what ways will the size of a customer's business affect his business behavior?

19. Identify and explain five main patterns of business ownership.

20. Compare three kinds of decision-making authority patterns in international business.

21. Explore the various ways in which business customs can affect the structure of competition.

22. Why is it important that the businessman be alert to the significance of business customs?

Readings

1. Explain Hall's concept of "the language of time."

2. How can a marketer prepare himself to deal with the "silent languages" of world business?

3. Prepare a statement which would adequately brief an Egyptian businessman for marketing contact work in the United States. Use Hall's languages of time, space, things, friendship, and agreements for your format.

4. "Bribery and corruption are among the hazards of business life, internationally and locally." Discuss.

5. It is unrealistic to apply the moral standard learned in one country to business dealings in another. Defend this position.

CASES—PART III

PROPOSED JOINT VENTURE: LEGAL OR ILLEGAL?*

Put yourself into the shoes of the General Council of a hypothetical U.S. automotive company. Detroit Motor Corporation, considering a possible joint venture with a French firm, Automobiles S.A., in Ecuador, Detroit and Autosa have been exporting their competing lines to Ecuador but have been told that import restrictions to take effect May 1, 1968, will make further exporting impossible.

The government has offered both companies a ten-year tax benefit and free importation of components, however, if they will manufacture locally.

Since the economic situation is uncertain, the market small, and local managerial skills unavailable, both firms decide that the only way to continue to sell cars there is to build a single factory—each to provide fifty per cent of the capital, including patents and technology.

Questions

1. Is the proposed venture legal under the U.S. antitrust laws?
2. The above case is fairly simple. Suppose Ecuador didn't clap a complete ban on car imports, but its tariffs were so high that exporting automobiles there was unprofitable. Would this justify creation of a local joint venture with the French competitor under U.S. laws?
3. So far, as counsel for the Detroit Motor Corporation, you have wrestled only with the antitrust implications of establishing the joint venture. Now consider the problems of operating. Suppose Autosa, seeing only a small market in Ecuador, required Detroit to stop exporting cars from the United States to Peru and Bolivia as well. Would this be in violation of U.S. antitrust laws?

---

* Leo M. Drachsler, "Risky Joint Ventures: How the Long Arm of U.S. Anti-Trust Laws Can Reach Overseas," *Business Abroad*, October 30, 1967, pp. 30–35. Reprinted by permission.

4. Suppose there was an agreement to export to Peru only at a price no lower than that of the joint venture. And another agreement to keep the joint venturers' cars out of Argentina, where Autosa has a wholly owned subsidiary. Would these two activities be in violation of the U.S. antitrust laws?

5. Discuss in detail the answers to the above questions.

CASE III–2

ARBEITSGEMEINSCHAFT DEUTSCHE TIEFKÜHLKETTE, E.V. (A)*

In the fall of 1957, Mr. E. Rudolphi, Director of the Arbeitsgemeinschaft Deutsche Tiefkühlkette, E.V. (German Frozen Food Assoc.) was wondering how best to promote the sale of all types of frozen foods to the German public. In an effort to find an answer to this question he had recently invited eight German advertising agencies to submit suggestions concerning the approach that should be used. The presentations of these eight agencies were scheduled to be held during the coming two weeks. Because of his vital interest in the overall problem of promoting frozen foods, Mr. Rudolphi was eagerly looking forward to the agencies' presentations. It was his intention to retain, on a permanent basis, that agency which he felt offered the soundest and most logical promotional program.

The Arbeitsgemeinschaft Deutsche Tiefkühlkette, E.V. was an association which had been formed earlier in 1957 for the purpose of promoting the sale of all types of frozen foods to the German public. The association was composed of members from all segments of the German frozen food industry. These included manufacturers and processors of frozen food, major wholesale organizations selling frozen food, manufacturers of freezers, refrigerators, and transportation equipment, and various transporters of frozen foods and makers of packaging materials.

Upon its formation, the association had engaged Mr. Rudolphi, a man with several years experience in the frozen food industry, to act as its full-time director. Mr. Rudolphi maintained an office in Bremerhaven from which he directed and coordinated the overall efforts of the association.

Background on the German Frozen Food Industry

The roots of the German frozen food industry went back over 30 years to 1936. Beginning in that year experiments were made with the freezing of fish. Shortly afterwards freezing experiments were also begun with fruits and vegetables. In spite of these experiments, however, little widespread use was made of this new form of food processing during the late '30's or the war years that followed. In 1948, just before the German currency reform, a small scale attempt was made by several manufacturers and processors to expand the frozen food industry. This

---

* Copyright 1970 by l'Institut pour l'Etude des methodes de Direction de l'Entreprise (IMEDE), Lausanne, Switzerland. Reprinted by permission.

attempt turned out to be premature, however, and was largely unsuccessful.

Not until 1955 did the industry start to grow in any systematic way. At the beginning of 1955 ten fish-processing companies were producing frozen fish for export and eight companies were processing fruit and vegetables. Subsequently this number grew very rapidly until, by the fall of 1957 there were a total of 42 German companies manufacturing or processing frozen foods.

During this same period, German consumption of all types of frozen foods went from about 2,500 tons in 1955, to an annual rate of about 12,000 tons as of the fall of 1957.[1]

In spite of this growth, annual *per capita* consumption of frozen foods was still only about 0.22 kg for the year of 1957. As a basis for comparison, it might be pointed out that in the United States and in Sweden, the two countries with the most advanced frozen foods industries, the 1957 rates of consumption were about 25 kg/capita and 2.5 kg/capita respectively.

The "Tiefkühlkette"

Frozen foods cannot be traded without freezers. Thus one of the biggest initial problems confronting the German frozen food industry was that of building a "Tiefkühlkette" or frozen food chain. In order to be preserved properly, frozen foods must first be frozen at a temperature of $-40°$ centigrade, and stored at a temperature no higher than $-18°$ centigrade. The term "Tiefkühlkette" referred to the various steps in the distributive chain at which it was necessary to have refrigeration equipment. Ideally, for the chain to be complete, it would be necessary for manufacturers, wholesalers, retailers and housewives all to have freezer facilities available. Moreover, refrigerated cars and trucks would also have to be available for transporting frozen foods to wholesalers and retailers.

In 1957 almost all of the manufacturers and major wholesalers of frozen foods were beginning to get adequate freezer capacity to meet their present needs. The number of freezers in retail stores, however, was still very small. Whereas there had been about 5,000 freezers in retail stores in 1956, in 1957 this number, while doubled to 10,000, still represented freezers in less than 6% of Germany's 170,000 retail outlets. The cost of purchasing a 300–400 liter retail freezer was approximately 2,500 Deutsche marks. As a rule of thumb it was commonly felt that in order for a retailer to break even on his freezer operation he must realize a monthly turnover of one mark per liter of freezer capacity.

---

[1] The 12,000 tons for 1957 was broken down among food products approximately as follows:

Vegetables & Fruits	5,000 tons
Poultry	4,000 "
Fish	1,500 "
Prepared Dinners	500 "
Ice Cream	1,000 "

At the consumer level, about 2,000,000 families, or 13% of all German households[2] had refrigerators as of 1957. In almost all cases, however, these refrigerators were quite small and had either inadequate freezer compartments for storing frozen foods or no freezer compartments at all. This meant that, in almost all cases, housewives who bought frozen foods had to use them the same day. The cost of a household refrigerator varied from 500 D. marks for small refrigerators with no freezer storage space to 1,700 D. marks for a large, American-type refrigerator with a large freezer compartment, total capacity of about 300 liters. Generally speaking a small refrigerator with a little freezer compartment cost about 60 D. marks more than one without freezer space.

The Arbeitsgemeinschaft Deutsche Tiefkühlkette, E.V.

Though the number of frozen food processors grew rapidly during the period from 1955 to 1957, none of these processors was large enough to finance a program to educate the public on the proper use of frozen foods or to undertake a large-scale advertising and marketing program for its own brand. Yet in all segments of the industry, the feeling existed that if frozen foods were ever to realize their full potential in Germany, someone would have to first undertake to educate the public as to their use. Only in this way could a strong demand be developed for this relatively new class of foods.

Realizing that no single firm would probably ever be large enough to undertake the job of stimulating primary demand, the various companies comprising the industry decided to combine their efforts. Thus, in 1957, they created the "Arbeitsgemeinschaft Deutsche Tiefkühlkette," which literally translated means "Work Cooperation of the German Frozen Food Chain." In all, 60 firms became members of the new association. Of these, 40 were food processing firms.[3] The remaining membership was made up of large food wholesalers and buying groups, a few makers of freezers, refrigerators, packaging materials, and transportation equipment, and finally, some transporters of frozen foods.

The primary purpose of the association was to work for a better understanding of frozen foods among consumers and to attempt to stimulate a strong public demand for all types of frozen food products. A second job which the association hoped to be able to accomplish was that of providing better education for the wholesale and retail trades on the care, handling and promotion of frozen foods. Finally, the association hoped to be able to study various technological questions connected with maintaining and improving quality standards at all levels of the frozen food chain.

The association was to have both a president, elected from among the

---

[2] Total German households in 1957 = approximately 18,000,000.
  Total German population in 1957 = approximately 50,000,000.
  Total German population in 1959 = approximately 55,000,000.

[3] These 40 represented 95% of the 42 German firms engaged in the processing of frozen foods.

members, and a full-time director. The president was to act primarily in an exofficio capacity. The director, on the other hand, was to be responsible for coordinating the association's overall activities. To fill the director's position the association engaged Mr. Rudolphi. Prior to taking over the leadership of the association, Mr. Rudolphi had for several years been general manager of one of Germany's leading frozen food processing companies.

Funds to finance the activities of the association came from three sources: regular dues paid by members, special assessments also paid by members, and proceeds from the sale of promotional materials. Regular dues for each member varied from 100 D. marks per month to 250 D. marks per month, depending on that member's ability to pay. In the budget for the coming year regular dues were expected to provide about 100,000 D. marks of income. The second source of funds was special assessments. These were to be made in the event that the association wished to undertake any special promotional projects. Mr. Rudolphi estimated that during the coming year he could count on obtaining a maximum of about 130,000 D. marks through these special assessments. The sale of promotional materials to wholesalers and retailers was expected to provide the third source of funds. The sale of these promotional materials was not expected to be a profit making activity, however. Rather it was anticipated that the funds obtained in this way would merely be a contribution to help cover the expense of producing these materials.

Thus, in attempting to plan the association's overall activities for the coming year, Mr. Rudolphi felt he could count on a budget of approximately 230,000 D. marks, plus any funds he might be able to get from the sale of promotional materials to the trade. Mr. Rudolphi felt that the size of this budget would be an important factor to bear in mind when he assessed the presentations of the advertising agencies which were scheduled to be held in the next couple of weeks.

How Mr. Rudolphi Viewed the Job of the Association

Since his appointment as director of the association, Mr. Rudolphi had done a good deal of thinking about the overall task ahead. As a result of this thinking, he had reached several preliminary conclusions concerning the approach which the association should use to accomplish its aims. He expressed his views as follows:

Few items of daily use are as bound by traditions as are foods. In the mind of the average housewife, frozen food is something very new. While the actual contents of the package are familiar, the presentation of these contents, as well as their method of preparation, is so radically different as to make frozen food seem like an entirely new product. Initially, therefore, the housewife has a natural resistance to frozen food. Before she can begin using frozen foods, she must overcome a certain shyness toward them. Thus, one of our primary jobs must be to convince the housewife of the familiarity of the contents of a package of frozen foods and then teach her the advantages which this new food processing technique offers.

The advantages of frozen foods are fairly obvious. They always taste fresh. They have high nutritional value because the vitamins are preserved almost completely in the freezing process and because only high quality foods are used. They are simple and quick for the housewife to prepare. And, finally, they can be bought and used independent of the season of the year.

The only disadvantages of frozen foods are that they are still slightly more expensive[4] than fresh or canned foods and they must be consumed the same day that they are bought if the housewife does not have a freezer compartment.

Still we feel that the advantages far outweigh the disadvantages. Our biggest problem is to decide how best to get this message across to the housewife. One can get an idea of the magnitude of our task by taking a brief look at the results of a study which was made for us not too long ago by a market research firm. In this study a representative sample of 2,007 housewives from all over Western Germany and West Berlin were asked how much they knew about frozen foods. The results of the study were as follows:

Detailed knowledge	7%
Sketchy knowledge	22
Rather vague knowledge	31
No knowledge	2
False ideas	4
Never heard about it	34
	100%

From these sketchy figures one can begin to appreciate the fact that we've got a big job on our hands, particularly with our limited budget. I would estimate that, even if we were to get a lot of free publicity, it would cost 800,000 to 1,000,000 D. marks for a successful country-wide campaign to introduce frozen foods to the buying public. As it is, our budget for the coming year is only about 230,000 D. marks. Under these circumstances, I think that all we can hope to do is to start the ball rolling.

As I see it the advertising and promotion function of the association will only be temporary in nature. Of necessity any activity which we do along this line will have to be completely impartial with respect to brands and different classes of frozen foods. This type of cooperative industry-wide advertising can work only so long as the market is sufficiently undeveloped as to offer sufficient possibilities for expansion to all participants. Consequently, once we succeed in creating a public awareness for frozen foods as a whole, it will probably be time for the association to fade out of the advertising picture and for individual firms to take over. These firms can then try to build selective demand for their particular brands.

This doesn't mean that there will no longer be a need for the association once frozen foods are successfully launched on the German market. On the contrary, it is quite conceivable that the association will always perform important functions for the industry. One of these functions might relate to the job of establishing and maintaining quality standards. At present, quality is still somewhat of a problem in the industry. This is a result of several factors. In some instances the quality of the foods used in the freezing process itself has been inferior. In other cases the freezing process itself has been faulty. Finally, it has often been the case that an imperfection has existed in the "frozen food chain" which has caused thawing and then refreezing before the merchandise has reached the hands of the consumer. Whatever the

---

[4] Frozen foods were an average of 30% more expensive than fresh or canned foods in 1957.

reason, the problem of quality has occasionally tended to give frozen foods a black eye. Because of this, I feel, and most of the members of the association seem to agree, that there is a need to think about the possibility of establishing an industry-wide code of quality standards and providing a continuing means of insuring adherence to these standards. It will probably be the association that will be in the best position to administer an industry-wide program for quality control. Thus in the long run, the association might well find itself involved in the setting up of a permanent testing laboratory, the establishment of an "Association Seal of Approval," the periodic checking of members' facilities, or any one of a number of other steps. However, all of these things are probably still a long way off.

Right now I am much more concerned about what I considered to be the association's first task: that of educating the public and stimulating a strong primary demand for frozen foods of all kinds. That's why I am anxious to see what these advertising agencies are going to come up with in their presentations during the next two weeks. I certainly hope they will have some good ideas.

CASE III–3

BREAKING IN A U.S. SALESMAN IN LATIN AMERICA: TO BRIBE OR NOT TO BRIBE

The Starnes-Brenner Machine Tool Company of Iowa City, Iowa, has a small, one-man sales office headed by Frank Rothe in Latino, a major Latin American country. Frank has been in Latino for about ten years and is retiring this year (1970); his replacement is Bill Hunsaker, one of Starnes-Brenner's top salesmen. Both will be in Latino for about eight months during which time Frank will show Bill the ropes, introduce him to their principal customers and, in general, prepare him to take over.

Frank has been very successful as a foreign representative in spite of his unique style and, at times, complete refusal to follow company policy that doesn't suit him. The company hasn't really done much about his method of operation although from time to time he has angered some of the top company men. As President McCaughey, who retired a couple of years ago, once remarked to a vice president who was complaining about Frank, "If he's making money—and he is (more than any of the other foreign offices), then leave the guy alone." When McCaughey retired and the new chief took over, he immediately instituted organizational changes that gave more emphasis to the overseas operations. He moved the company toward a truly world-wide operation into which a "loner" like Frank would probably not fit. In fact, one of the key reasons for selecting Bill as Frank's replacement, besides Bill's being a topflight salesman, is Bill's capacity as an "organization" man. He understands the need for coordination among operations and will cooperate with the home office so that the Latino office can be expanded and brought into the "mainstream."

The company knows that there is much to be learned from Frank, and Bill's job is to learn everything possible. Some of Frank's practices the company certainly doesn't want to continue, but much of his knowledge is vital for continued, smooth operation. Today, Starnes-Brenner's foreign sales account for about 15 per cent of the company's total profits, compared with about three per cent only ten years ago.

The company is actually changing character from being principally an exporter without any real concern for continuous foreign market representation to world-wide operation where the foreign divisions are part of the total effort rather than "stepson" operations. In fact, Latino is one of the last operational divisions to be assimilated into the "new" organization. Rather than try to change Frank, the company has been waiting for him to retire before making any significant adjustments in their Latino operations.

Bill Hunsaker is 36 years old with a wife and three children; he is a very good salesman and administrator although he has had no foreign experience. He has the reputation of being fair, honest, and a "straight shooter." Some, back at the home office, see his assignment as part of a grooming job for a top position, perhaps eventually the presidency. The Hunsakers are now settled in their new home after having been in Latino for about two weeks. Today is Bill's first day on the job.

When Bill arrived at the office, Frank was on his way to a local factory to inspect some Starnes-Brenner machines that had to have some adjustments made before being acceptable to the Latino government agency which was buying them. Bill joined Frank for the plant visit. Later, after the visit, we join the two at lunch.

Bill, tasting some chili, remarks, "Boy! this certainly isn't like the chili we have in America." "No, it isn't, and there's another difference too . . . the Latinos are Americans and nothing angers a Latino more than to have a 'Gringo' refer to the United States as America as if to say that Latino isn't part of America too. The Latinos rightly consider their country as part of America (take a look at a map) and people from the United States are North Americans at best. So, for future reference, refer to home either as the United States, States, or North America, but for gosh sakes not just America. Not to change the subject, Bill, but could you see that any change had been made in those S–27s from the standard model?" "No, they looked like the standard. Was there something out of whack when they arrived?" "No, I couldn't see any problem —I suspect this is the best piece of sophisticated bribe taking I've come across yet. Most of the time the Latinos are more 'honest' about their '*mordidas*' than this." "What's a *mordida*?" Bill asks. "You know, '*Kumshaw*,' '*Dash*,' '*Bustarella*,' '*Mordida*'; they are all the same: a little grease to expedite the action. '*Mordida*' is the local word for a slight offering or, if you prefer, bribe," says Frank.

Bill quizically responds, "How much bribery does it take to make successful sales anyway?" "Oh, it depends on the situation but it's certainly something you have to be prepared to deal with." Boy, what a greenhorn, Frank thinks to himself, as he continues, "Here's the story. When the S–27s arrived last January, we began uncrating them and right away the 'Jeffe' engineer, 'Jeffe,' that's the head man in charge, began extra careful examination and declared there was a vital defect in the machines; he claimed the machinery would be dangerous and thus unacceptable if it wasn't corrected. I looked it over but couldn't see anything wrong so I agreed to have our staff engineer check all the machines and correct any flaws that might exist. Well, the 'Jeffe' said there wasn't enough time to wait for an engineer to come from the States, that the machines could be adjusted locally, and we could pay the bill with a check made out to him. So, what the hell do you do? No adjustment his way and there would be an order cancelled; and, maybe there was something out of line, those things have been known to happen. But for the life of me I can't see that anything had been done since the machines were supposedly fixed. So, let's face it, we just paid a bribe and a pretty darn big bribe at that—what makes it so aggravating is that that's the second one I've had to pay on this shipment."

"The second?" asks Bill. "Yeah, at the border when we were transferring the machines to Latino trucks, it was hot and they were moving slow as blazes. It took them over an hour to transfer one machine to a Latino truck and we had ten others to go. It seemed that every time I spoke to the dock boss about speeding things up they just got slower. Finally, out of desperation, I slipped him a fistful of pesos and, sure enough, in the next three hours they had the whole thing loaded. Just one of the 'local customs' of doing business. Generally though, it comes at the lower level where wages don't cover living expenses too well."

There is a pause and Bill asks, "What does that do to your profits?" "Runs them down, of course, but I look at it as just one of the many costs of doing business—I do my best not to pay but when I have to, I do." Hesitantly Bill replies, "I don't like it, Frank, we've got good products, they're priced right, we give good service, and keep plenty of spare parts in the country, so why should we have to pay bribes to the buyer? It's just no way to do business. Hell, you've already had to pay two bribes on one shipment; if you keep it up, the word's going to get around and you'll be paying at every level. Then all the profit goes out the window —you know, once you start, where do you stop? I'd say that the best policy is to never start; you might lose a few sales but let it be known that there are no bribes; we sell the best, service the best at fair prices and that's it."

Oh boy!! Frank thinks to himself as he replies, "Granted we give good service but we've only been doing it for the last year or so. Before that I never knew when I was going to have equipment to sell. In fact, we only had products when there were surpluses stateside. I had to pay bribes to get sales and, besides that, you're not back in the States any longer. Things are just done differently here. You follow that policy and I guarantee that you'll have fewer sales and a heck of a lot more headaches. Look, Bill, everybody does it here; it's a way of life and the costs are generally reflected in the mark-up and overhead. There is even a code of behavior involved. We're not actually encouraging it to spread, just perpetuating an accepted way of doing business."

Patiently and slightly condescendingly, Bill replies, "I know, Frank, but wrong is wrong and we want to operate differently now. We hope to set up an operation here on a continuous basis; we plan to operate in Latino just like we do in the United States. Really expand our operation and make a long-range marketing commitment, grow with the country!! And, one of the first things we must avoid are unethical. . . ."

Frank interrupts, "But really, is it unethical? Everybody does it, the Latinos even pay *mordidas* to other Latinos; it's a fact of life—is it really unethical? I think that the circumstances that exist in a country justify and dictate the behavior. Remember man, 'When in Rome, do as the Romans do.' " Almost shouting, Bill blurts out, "I can't buy that. We know that our management practices and techniques are our strongest point. Really all we have to differentiate us from the rest of our competition, Latino and others, is that we are better managed and as far as I'm concerned graft and other unethical behavior has got to be cut out to create a healthy industry. In the long run, it should strengthen our position. We can't build our future on unethical practices."

Frank angrily replies, "Hell, it's done in the States all the time. What about the big dinners, drinks, and all the other hanky panky that goes on? What is that, if it isn't '*mordida*' the North American way? The only difference is that instead of cash we pay in merchandise." "That's really not the same and you know it. Besides, we certainly get a lot of business transacted during those dinners even if we are paying the bill." "Bull, the only difference is that here bribes go on in the open; they don't hide it or dress it in foolish ritual that fools no one. It goes on in the United States and everyone denies the existence of it. That's all the difference—in the United States we're just more hypocritical about it all."

"Look dammit," Frank continues almost shouting, "we are getting off on the wrong foot and we've got eight months to work together. Just keep your eyes and mind open and let's talk about it again in a couple of months when you've seen how the whole country operates; perhaps then you won't be so quick to judge it absolutely wrong."

Frank, lowering his voice, says thoughtfully, "I know it's hard to take; probably the most disturbing aspect of dealing with business problems in underdeveloped countries is the matter of graft. And, frankly, we don't do much advance preparation so we can deal firmly with it. It bothered the hell out of me at first; but, then, I figured it makes its economic contribution, too, since the payoff is as much a part of the economic process as a payroll. What's our real economic role anyway, besides making a profit, of course? Are we developers of wealth, helping to push the country on to greater economic growth, or are we missionaries? Or should we be both? I don't really know, but I don't think we can be both simultaneously and my feeling is that as the country prospers, as higher salaries are paid and better standards of living are reached, we'll see better ethics. Until then, we've got to operate or leave and, if you are going to win the opposition over, you'd better join them and change them from within, not fight them."

Before Bill could reply, a Latino friend of Frank's joined them and they changed the topic of conversation. . . .

Questions

1. Is what Frank did ethical? Whose ethics? Latino's or the United States'?
2. Frank's attitude seems to imply that a foreigner must comply with all

local customs, but some would say that one of the contributions made by U.S. firms is to change local ways of doing business. Who is right?

3. Should Frank's behavior have been any different had this not been a government contract?

4. If Frank shouldn't have paid the bribe, what should he have done, and what might have been the consequences?

5. What are the company interests in this problem?

6. Explain how this may be a good example of an indigenous frame of reference at work.

7. Do you think Bill will make the grade in Latino? Why? What will it take?

8. How can an overseas manager be prepared to face this problem?

CASE III–4

MILLER LABORATORIES, INCORPORATED*
Parrinian Ethics Case[1]

Miller Laboratories, Incorporated is a large ethical drug firm with headquarters in Los Angeles, California. The firm manufactures for both *human* and *veterinary* markets, and concentrates mainly on biologicals (such things as: serums, vaccines, intravenous solutions, plasma, and blood fractions) and pharmaceutical specialties. It does business in fifty-eight countries in addition to the United States. In eight of these countries Miller has no representatives; the company merely accepts and fills whatever unsolicited orders it receives from these markets. In the other fifty countries, appointed representatives actively promote sales. To help finance its rapid expansion abroad, Miller has incorporated its foreign sales subsidiary, Miller International Laboratories Corporation, in Panama to take advantage of that country's tax laws. All Miller's sales abroad are made by MILC, which buys from the parent company at very low prices so that the profits on the foreign sales accrue to MILC in Panama rather than to the parent company in the United States. Panama does not tax these profits, whereas the U.S. corporate profits tax of 52% would, of course, apply if the profits were earned by or remitted back to the parent company.

Because of the nature of its products and a number of other factors involved in its business, Miller has always used distributors to handle sales in foreign countries. Matters of volume, capital investment, etc. have thus far made it unwise for the firm to establish its own branches abroad, although it does have a few jointly owned or wholly owned affiliated companies.

Drug distribution required a double sales effort. The usual sales force is required to service the wholesale drug houses and the retailers. In addition, another group of salesmen, called a "detail" force, is required

---

* Reprinted by permission of Richard H. Holton, University of California, Berkeley.

[1] The facts in this case are reported substantially as they occurred. The name of the firm has been changed.

to contact the doctors, who must be introduced to the products and convinced of their value before they will prescribe their use. In foreign countries some drug distributors perform both of these functions. Others rely on their principals to do the detailing while they restrict their own activities to the servicing of wholesalers and retailers.

Miller usually has better sales results when doing the detailing job itself. But because of capital and administrative limitations imposed by rapid expansion, it presently prefers to select a distributor who handles both sales and detailing. However, in some cases it has taken over detailing when there was no suitable alternative. It uses one or more distributors per country, depending upon the size and the geographic dispersion of the market, and it performs partial or complete manufacturing operations within certain countries because of legal or economic considerations.

Recently, Miller has found some advantages in establishing affiliated companies in foreign countries. In these cases, it has tried outright ownership, majority control, equal participation with nationals, minority participation, and licensing, depending on the specifics of the situation.

In late 1960, Miller established a subsidiary company in Parrina, a South American nation. This subsidiary was jointly owned by Miller and the president of the subsidiary, who was a Parrinian national and the former distributor of Miller products in Parrina. All of the employeys were Parrinian citizens, although a majority of the board of directors were Miller home office executives, and Miller owned a majority interest in the company.

On the first item that the subsidiary company began to manufacture Miller encountered certain ethical problems which it had never encountered in the United States.

There is no international treaty covering the use of trade marks or trade names as there is covering patents. Most countries have, however, as a part of their domestic laws, regulations which protect a foreigner's trade mark or trade name if his products have been regularly sold in other countries. Some countries have no such regulations. These are mostly countries which have not signed the international patent agreement, notably Cuba, Costa Rica, Argentina, Italy, Japan, and Parrina.

For a number of months preceding the establishment of the Parrinian subsidiary, Miller had been developing a new "wonder drug" under the name "Stermed." The name had been duly registered in the United States. "Stermed" was expected to be especially effective in treating infections of the epazutic. Since this was the first time any drug had been deemed capable of benefiting the epazutic, several articles had appeared in medical journals mentioning and explaining this development and calling it by the Miller trade name.

When the first of these articles appeared, Mr. Louis Rera, a Parrinian citizen, registered the name "Stermed" with the Parrinian government and received the exclusive right to use it in Parrinian commerce. Mr. Rera had no way of knowing whether or not the new drug would ever be fully developed or, if it were, whether it would prove effective, gain general acceptance, and be made available in Parrina. But, he was certain that *some* new drugs would eventually be sold in Parrina, and he made his living by registering all the new names he could find and sitting back to await developments. It was small concern to him actually whether any particular one paid off, because it was his experience that enough of them did to permit him to live very well simply by subscribing to foreign journals and trade publications, reading them, and registering new names that appeared therein.

"Stermed" did prove to be remarkably effective and quickly achieved world-wide acceptance. In due course Miller decided that it would be the first of its products to be entirely manufactured in Parrina. Of course, when Miller executives attempted to register the name they were informed by the Parrinian officials of Mr. Rera's rights. Actually, they expected this because the president had had dealings with Mr. Rera on one or two other occasions. Mr. Rera had been first to the post because Miller does developmental work on many products which never reach the market, and it does not find it profitable to register every potential name in every potential market. By the time it had considered "Stermed" promising enough to register in all markets, Mr. Rera had already acted. Actually, he had only beaten Miller by a few days, but Miller ignored him until it was ready to enter the Parrinian market.

When subsidiary executives approached Mr. Rera, he was pleasant enough but very businesslike; he asked five thousand dollars for his rights in the name.

Miller wanted to use the same name it was using in the rest of the world, so by dint of considerable bluffing and bargaining, the firm paid Mr. Rera four thousand dollars and began production and distribution of "Stermed."

The Miller development staff provided the Parrinian subsidiary with complete manufacturing instructions, test procedures, and quality control standards. These instructions were followed to the letter in the Los Angeles plant, and any lots which did not measure up were destroyed. Miller management assumed that the same would be true in the subsidiary, but they were mistaken.

The Parrinian attitude toward drug standards was somewhat more liberal, a fact which the home office quality control inspector discovered when he visited Parrina on his first routine inspection trip. The Parrinians clearly understood all the requirements, but they did not enforce them rigorously. Their attitude seemed to be best put into words by the local quality control supervisor. He said that if someone died, it couldn't be proved that the medicine was at fault, and it was too expensive to be overly careful about quality. He said that the president had just the past week cautioned him about helping to hold down expenses, and it was certainly expensive to flush a whole batch of "Stermed" down the drain. By checking the records, the inspector found that two borderline lots, which should have been dumped, had been packaged and were awaiting shipment in the local warehouse.

The inspector wired all the details to the home office executives who immediately phoned the president of the Parrinian subsidiary and had him order the destruction of the suspected lots. They then requested that he and his quality control inspector spend a few days in Los Angeles. There, they carefully instructed them on the need for rigid enforcement and urged them to hold meetings with all employees as soon as possible to instill a proper regard for quality standards.

Such prompt action was only possible because Miller held a majority interest in the subsidiary company so that there was no disputing its decisions. In fact, such quality requirements were a principal reason for Miller's holding majority control in all joint ventures.

The Parrinian officials had no sooner left than the Miller home office received the following letter from one of their competitors, another international drug firm.

Dear Sirs:

On October 10th Mr. Juan Alvarez, one of your representatives in Parrina, called on Dr. A. P. Reginio. During the course of his visit he told Dr. Reginio that it was common knowledge in the drug industry that our product, Medico, was ineffective and might possibly be injurious in its recommended applications.

As you are well aware, we have more than adequate proof of the effectiveness of Medico and there is no evidence whatever that it is in the least injurious when used as recommended.

We urgently request that you write to Dr. Reginio retracting the statement made by Mr. Alvarez, and that you inform Mr. Alvarez of his error.

> Yours very truly,
> XXXXXXXXXX XXXXXXXX

This was not the first such letter Miller had received from its competitors, and Miller had been forced on several occasions to send just such a letter to them.

The ethics of drug detailing in the United States forbid disparaging another firm's products. These products are made with professional care, and every firm uses the utmost caution in preparing them. If disparagement became common, doctors would soon have no confidence in what the detail men told them, and the courts would soon be full of lawsuits.

However, in South America disparagement of competitors' products is one of the most generally accepted sales techniques. Everyone concerned knows this, and, for the most part, the doctors take such comments with a grain of salt. Only rarely do complaints crop up.

Miller home office officials forwarded the letter to Parrina with instructions to take care of the matter and to continue with the education program which had been started earlier in an attempt to get Miller detail men to cease employing such tactics in their interviews with doctors.

Questions

1. In the bargaining with Mr. Rera, the company must have in mind some maximum amount it would be willing to pay. How should the company determine this figure?

2. Was the Miller decision to have the questionable stocks of Stermed in Parrina destroyed an economic one or a moral one? By what logic would the decision have been economically justifiable?

3. Is Miller's policy of requiring its Parrinian detail men not to make derogatory comments about the competitors' products economically justifiable, or must it be defended only on ethical grounds?

IV
Organizing for Marketing in International Business

OUTLINE OF CHAPTER 13

INTRODUCTION

PLANNING INTERNATIONAL OPERATIONS
  Complicating Parameters
  Company Objectives, Resources, and Outlook
  The Marketing Plan

ORGANIZATIONAL STRATEGY
  Structural Basis
  Locus of Decision
  Maintaining Flexibility

HEADQUARTERS ORGANIZATIONAL ALTERNATIVES
  Centralization, Regionalization, and Decentralization
  A Word on Autonomy
  Managerial Arrangements
    Domestic Top Executive
    Export Division Head
    Extension of Functional Divisions
    Product Managers
    Export Committees

OWNED INTERNATIONAL AFFILIATES
  Branches and Subsidiaries
  Joint Ventures
    Marketing Motives
    Financial and Manpower Advantages
  Consortia

EXTERNAL ARRANGEMENTS
  International Licensing
  Franchising
  Management Contract
  Open Distribution

SUMMARY AND CONCLUSIONS

READING
  The Tortuous Evolution of the Multinational Corporation, *Columbia Journal of World Business*

DYNAMICS OF INTERNATIONAL PLANNING AND ORGANIZATION

INTRODUCTION

Reorganizing, reforming, restructuring, and regrouping seem to be characteristics of the international business organization. The requirements of operating in different markets and meeting various market conditions constitute prime causes for the organizational fluctuations which seem to be omnipresent in international marketing. At the same time, marketing problems are intensified by structuring organizations in an inflexible manner so that they cannot grow with the market opportunities.

The dichotomy generally drawn between export marketing and overseas marketing is partly fictional; from a marketing standpoint, they are but alternative methods of capitalizing on foreign market opportunities. Although the two do have some different types of problems and have long been considered to be separate approaches to selling internationally, they need not be completely differentiated as alternatives. As typically viewed, export operations involve goods produced in one country and marketed in another, whereas overseas operations relate to international business with production facilities overseas. Studying organizational patterns from this viewpoint is misleading because in many instances the organizational structure for international marketing will be identical in both instances. The difficulty of relating the two seems to stem, in part, from the organizational planner's habit of structuring an organizational framework around the location of production. This chapter will show that the structure of markets, competition, and the parent company's marketing organization are much more relevant to international marketing operations than production location.

In establishing plans, and in organizing for their implementation, companies around the world are increasingly focusing attention on profits and marketing as key variables. In country after country, the traditional production orientation is shifting to marketing.

Ownership and control of marketing operations are key determinants

BOX 13–1

Global Growth Prompts General Electric Revamping

The General Electric Co. of the US has reversed the major organizational restructuring of 1967 that broke up its international division and created ten worldwide product groups. GE has now announced that it is reshaping its regional and export division into an international group. Headed by a newly appointed vice-president and group executive, the new international group will be on a lateral line with the ten product groups, directly under top management, but in a key spot, since the company chairman will have primary cognizance of it. It will comprise three area divisions, Europe, the Far East, and Latin America, as well as the International General Electric export division. During the past two years all the above divisions reported to various product groups.

Although GE has not yet clarified its specific intent in recreating the international group, it seems clear that it was spurred both by the rising volume of overseas business, its potential growth, and the complications that ensued from trying to operate in international markets through an organization of strictly product pattern. Among the problems incurred by this form (especially on the scale necessitated by GE's diverse product businesses) are duplication of know-how on many organizational levels, absence of a single corporate structure (and image) in a particular country, reporting lines in operations that cross divisional lines, and coordination of regional policy and planning across divisional lines.

In the future GE may opt for the type of structure that resembles a "grid," in which product and area divisions have overlapping responsibilities for all areas and product lines. Committed as it is to the concept of worldwide product business, it seems unlikely that GE would return to a pure international-division pattern.

Source: Reprinted from April 25, 1969, issue of *Business International*, p. 134, with the permission of the publisher, Business International Corporation (N.Y.).

of international marketing organization. Location or domicile of the legal corporate home office has too often been a major factor determining organizational structure. New corporations increasingly are selecting their domicile country on the basis of market and tax factors.

This chapter reviews the planning requirements for international marketing, and isolates and identifies some of the elements contributing to the complexity of international organization. Further, the basic elements relevant to international marketing organization and the alternative organizational relationships are presented in a simple, straightforward, almost skeletal form. The reader should not assume from this that the problem of organizing for international marketing is a simple one. Indeed, the organizational requirements of worldwide markets are such that a single company may use half a dozen or more different arrangements for marketing abroad. Furthermore, each of these varied organizational arrangements may also have alternative suborganizational structural patterns. International organization is not always complex, but many international situations have inherent factors which tend to complicate organizational matters.

There is some overlap between this chapter and the chapters pertaining to distribution channels, international management, and export procedure. There is, however, a basic difference in scope: the international marketing organization materials pertain specifically to the *internal* and overall corporate organizational arrangement used to facilitate decision making. Channels of distribution, sales, and export considerations relate to specific alternatives used to implement the organizational plan at the level of the middlemen and sales personnel used to negotiate sales and to move goods.

Many of the considerations reviewed in this chapter may also pertain as much to the organization of international business in general as to international marketing as such. The general focus, however, is on the role of marketing in international organization and the chapter stresses planning and organization for effective marketing internationally. Specific discussion of controlling the international marketing organization appears in Chapter 16.

PLANNING INTERNATIONAL OPERATIONS

Planning the organization of an international operation is difficult at best. The organizational plan must allow for rapid growth of the international function, changing markets, ever-varying challenges, and differing marketing arrangements in different markets. The plan must take into account the changing parameters of the external environment and blend them with corporate objectives and abilities in order to develop a sound, workable marketing program. The complicating parameters and the hazards in establishing an international organization are so great that adequate planning is a mandatory prerequisite to successful market entry. Planning is an inherent part of all managerial functions, but nowhere are the risks as great as in organizational planning. The entire foreign operation can be jeopardized by poor planning or improper organization.

Planning relates to the formulation of goals and methods of accomplishing them. As such, planning is both a process and a philosophical or conceptual device. Structurally, it may be conveniently viewed on the levels of corporate planning, strategic planning, and tactical planning. International planning at the corporate level is essentially long-term planning incorporating generalized goals for the enterprise as a whole. Steiner indicates that strategic planning is also conducted at the highest levels of management and deals with long- and short-term goals of the company. Tactical planning is "concerned with the organization of resources to execute strategic plans."[1]

Tactical planning is short term, and detailed and is delegated to large numbers of people working within a given organizational subunit.

---

[1] George A. Steiner and Warren M. Cannon, *Multinational Corporate Planning* (New York: The Macmillan Company, 1966), pp. 11 to 13.

Organizational and operational planning must take place at all three levels if international marketing systems are to function effectively.

Exhibit 13–1 diagrams the steps in the planning cycle of a highly developed corporate planning concept and process system.

Complicating Parameters

Regardless of the approach to organizing for international business, corporate planners must consider the various elements which complicate the task of organizing for international marketing. The domestic marketing situation is likely to have enough areas of conflict and variation to tax the skill of an able executive; international marketing poses the further challenges of even more problem areas and more variation within them. Each of the parameters surrounding the marketer's international environment offers special circumstances which contribute to the complexity of organizational patterns. Some of the problems reviewed below are duplicated domestically, but others are not.

Company growth and the dynamic nature of the market itself are likely to cause recurring organizational restructuring. World market conditions are changing more rapidly on the whole than are domestic markets in any industrialized nation, and, as the market situation changes, modifications are often required in a company's organization. A company may find that it has to use several different types of marketing organizations as it enters different countries differing in marketing problems and requirements. International business is growing rapidly and great changes in magnitude often call for corresponding changes in the international organization.

Market opportunities and increasing commitment to worldwide business have caused firms which only a few years ago considered themselves to be purely national to shift on a large scale into the arena of multinational business. In less than a decade some companies have moved from the national to the transnational level of operation. As scale of business changes, company philosophy and organization must keep pace.[2]

Geographical distance may cause a company to organize its business so as to minimize the time and expense of executive travel. Cultural and economic differences from country to country not only require special attention, but they limit the flexibility of the organization in shifting management from one area to another. There is little problem in moving a man from New York City to Chicago, but it may be nearly impossible to move an equally adaptable man from Paris to Berlin (a considerably shorter distance).

Nearly every country has governmental regulations which affect marketing organization as it pertains to that country: Some nations have local ownership requirements; some require that a certain per-

---

[2] Charles P. Kindleberger, "American Business Abroad" (New Haven: Yale University Press, 1969), p. 179 ff. See also W. W. Cain, "International Planning: Mission Impossible?" *Columbia Journal of World Business*, July–August 1970, pp. 53–60.

EXHIBIT 13–1

Diagram of Steps in the Planning Cycle

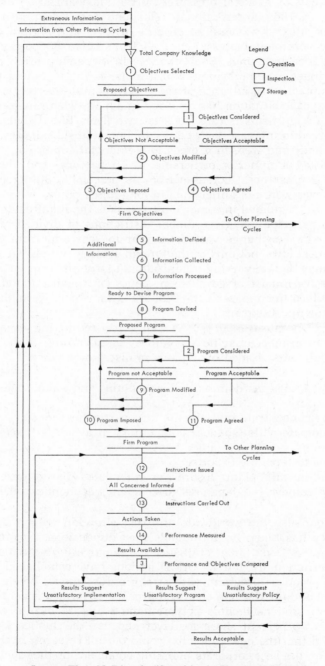

SOURCE: W. A. M. Edwards, "Organizing for Planning in Imperial Chemical Industries Limited," in George A. Steiner and Warren M. Cannon, *Multinational Corporate Planning* (New York: The Macmillan Company, 1966), p. 65.

centage of indigenous personnel be employed; others require production to be undertaken locally. Mexico provides some interesting examples of the effects of national pressures on the Mexicanization of U.S. subsidiaries. In 1969, International Telephone and Telegraph's Standard Electra de Mexico, General Electric de Mexico, and Scripto de Mexico all felt governmental pressure to sell from 10 to 50 percent of their equity to local nationals. Such changes in ownership often require de facto changes in organization, and in none of the instances were such offerings planned in advance of the governmental intervention.

The opposite situation has occurred in Japan, where majority ownership by foreign firms is rare. At least two firms found themselves virtually forced to increase their equity in Japanese subsidiaries that were losing money and were in a precarious financial condition. Unilever in 1969 shifted a minority ownership to 70 percent, and Heinz under similar circumstances increased from 49 percent to 80 percent equity. These moves were not anticipated in long-range plans.

Pricing is regulated in some countries, as is the requirement for local financial participation. Government restrictions of divided repatriation and monetary exchange vary from year to year and from country to country. Tax laws, not only of the foreign country but also of the parent nation, may dictate varying organizational structures for each country. The massive impact of government policy on organizational structure is exemplified in changes in the U.S. tax laws, which overnight changed tax havens into tax traps.

Change in government policy can force rethinking organizational strategy overnight; imagine the impact on planning of the following "commandments" issued by Japan's ministry of finance.

1. Avoid industries dominated by medium- and small-scale Japanese producers.
2. Don't concentrate investments in a particular industry.
3. Participate with Japanese competitors in avoiding "excessive competition."
4. Promote Japanese exports.
5. Avoid lay-offs, plant closures, or other labor disruptions.
6. Help achieve the Japanese government's economic policies.

Consider also the worldwide antitrust situation, which in the past few years has taken on formidable new dimensions. Not only is the United States Department of Justice more active in enforcing antitrust laws internationally, but 21 OECD nations have established a new restrictive practices program, with strong enforcement. When Monsanto Chemical and the German chemical firm Bayer formed a joint company, Mobay, to produce flexible polyurethane foam, Monsanto was forced to sell its 50 percent share to Bayer because the Justice Department contended that the new company would curtail research in the product area. Even the best corporate planning could not predict such unprecedented actions.

From the few areas mentioned in this section, it is obvious that the elements complicating international marketing organization planning are neither static nor homogeneous.

Company Objectives, Resources, and Outlook

Evaluation of a company's objectives and resources is crucial in all stages of planning for international operations. Each new market entered may require a complete evaluation relative to the parent company's objectives and resources. It is true that many companies have been successful in international operations without an explicit formal appraisal of objectives or even a written plan. Nevertheless, such operations are not completely devoid of implicit consideration of both long- and short-term objectives and requirements. As markets grow increasingly competitive, as companies find themselves faced with more alternatives, and as the cost of entering foreign markets increases, companies need such planning.

The international planning task is, in many ways, similar to domestic planning, but there are a few market differences. All planning should start at the level of defining objectives. One of the more recent results of the increased emphasis on international trading has been to force organizational replanning and hence more acurate development of objectives. Definition of objectives harmonizes the orientation of the domestic and international divisions, thus permitting consistent policies pertaining to all countries. Lack of explicit objectives has allowed companies to rush into promising foreign markets, only to find that activities there conflict with, or detract from, the companies' primary objectives.

Foreign market opportunities may not parallel corporate objectives and may call for changing the objectives or abandoning or changing the scale of international plans. One market may offer immediate profit but have a poor long-run outlook. Another may offer the reverse situation. One organizational arrangement may couple high returns and high investment, whereas another may permit cheaper entry but not provide market strength. Only if the corporate objectives are clear can such differences be reconciled effectively.

A National Association of Manufacturers study of selected members with foreign subsidiaries attempted to identify the companies' objectives in establishing foreign subsidiaries. The responses are recorded in Exhibit 13–2. Firms which have not entered the market or have not entered it by the subsidiary route might have rather different objectives.

After a company's objectives have been harmonized, management must determine whether it is prepared to make the level of commitment required for successful international operations—commitment in terms of dollars to be invested, commitment in terms of personnel for managing the international organization, and commitment to stay in the market long enough to recognize a considerable return on these investments. Some companies apparently have the idea that they can dabble in international business and pull out if it doesn't look profitable, but such an approach is generally inefficient and wasteful.

Occasionally such casual entry is successful. In the early 1950s, for

EXHIBIT 13–2

Specific Objectives in Establishing Foreign Subsidiaries

Reason	*Firms*
Maintenance and expansion of overseas markets...........	36
Foreign restrictions and requirements for U.S. companies...	18
Tax advantages; tax deferral...........................	15
Exchange restrictions; financing requirements..............	12
Insulation of parent company from foreign lawsuits and taxation...	12
Obtaining business not available on an export basis........	9
Meeting competition in local areas.......................	9
Serving foreign markets more effectively.................	5
Providing or ensuring a source of raw materials............	5
Other reasons..	10

SOURCE: National Association of Manufacturers.

example, Charles Pfizer Co. tentatively moved into international markets by putting a few salesmen in Cuba, Canada, Mexico, and Britain. Working out of hotel rooms, the salesmen tapped a pent-up demand for drugs and soon had built a $10,000,000-a-year export volume "without even trying." By 1970 overseas operations accounted for over 50 percent of the company's total sales volume. Such success stories are not rare in virgin foreign markets; but, more often than not, market success requires a long-run orientation.

If the company does not commit adequate resources, it may find that it runs out of working capital before the anticipated advantages have had an opportunity to emerge. The degree of commitment to an international marketing cause can also considerably affect the extent of the company's involvement. If a company is uncertain of its prospects, it is likely to enter a market half-heartedly or place great emphasis and reliance upon overseas partners or middlemen. Lack of commitment may cause a company to use inefficient marketing methods, channels, or organizational forms and may cause the failure of a venture which could have succeeded with full commitment and support by the parent company.

Without adequate planning, companies entering well-developed markets, such as those of Western Europe and the United States, may not find easy going.

The Marketing Plan

The international marketing plan is designed to optimize the benefits anticipated when resources are committed to the attainment of objectives. The marketing organizational plan must account for the type of organizational arrangements to be used, the mode and timing of entry, and the scope and location of responsibility. The localization of decision-making authority and the degree of autonomy at various levels of such decision-making authority are crucial areas for decisions in the planning stage. Responsibility for every one of the marketing functions must be clearly planned in advance of market entry. If such functional responsibility is not clearly designated, the company may lose flexibility and decisiveness in its crucial early months in foreign markets. If lines of authority are clearly defined, then the equally important lines of communication will usually function properly.

Accurate and thorough programming of the international operation must consider what actions will optimize the time of entry into international markets. Poor timing can cause a company to enter a foreign market at a disadvantage; some such companies have been forced to withdraw from overseas markets and in the process have been soured on the entire idea of doing business internationally.

Timing in the current context refers not only to the proper moment of entry but to short- and long-term implications as well. Even the form of organization used is subject to timing. What may be an appropriate organization at one time in one market may be completely inappropriate at another time.

Enough flexibility must be planned into an organization to account for the contingencies which will inevitably arise. Many companies have established a type of organizational structure which at its inception was logical and economical but which proved to be unsatisfactory in a later market situation. A company should not be in the position of becoming locked into one kind of marketing structure, nor should it be in a position in which it will have to take great losses in order to modify its position. Companies in international partnerships have sometimes found that their partners did not have the capital or the ability to cope with growing market potential; the companies have then been forced to buy out their unsatisfactory partners at exorbitant prices or get along with an unsatisfactory operation. Because of the dynamic nature of international business, some executives tend to think in rather short-run terms, even though long-range planning is crucial to continuing successful operations. In a period as short as five years, a business situation may change completely or a business relationship may undergo a complete transformation. Andrew Brainerd, a Chicago attorney, speaking on international licensing, comments that in some situations

the business increases and finally blossoms, the original term of the license agreement expires, and unless the *American licensor has made provisions earlier* for an automatic extension without further negotiation, or has purchased shares of the licensee in an attempt to assure a continuation of the agreement, the whole technology has been passed abroad, but the obligation to pay has expired.[3]

Since planning is typically related to market factors, it is logical to approach the entire subject of international organizations from the standpoint of marketing requirements. Long-run benefits often can be planned for; witness the emergence of a great market in the European

---

[3] Andrew W. Brainerd, "License or Equity," *International Trade Review* (Reprint), September 1962, p. 4

Economic Community. Many companies establish what are essentially uneconomical operations in order to be in a position to capitalize on market developments.

Short-run planning and annual forecasting are also integral parts of the marketing plan. Companies use various methods of planning, but nearly all include a country-by-country plan and many include a product-by-product plan as well. Minnesota Mining and Manufacturing Company (3M), for example, has a "sales potential evaluation technique system" which it applies to some 100 different countries. It divides the countries into categories by general magnitude of size potential and, using market and economic data, establishes sales potential figures on both a product and country basis through the use of indexes for each product line in each country. All figures are related to the parent company's U.S. sales potential figures. This system has been well received by managers in a majority of the countries and is used for setting target sales levels, allocating manpower and capital, and evaluating continuing performance.

ORGANIZATIONAL STRATEGY

Contemporary thought and writings in the field of organizing for international business seem to have fallen behind the requirements of international marketing. An American Management Association research study on international organization included case studies of the organization of some 30 international business firms. At least half of the case studies included a comment to the effect that the organization was in a state of transition or that the company's international organization had recently been changed. Organizational changes are not limited to firms in any one country; a Marketing Science Institute survey of European marketing revealed that over one half of the companies studied had recently changed their international marketing organizational structure.

One cannot ignore the dynamic nature of international business in assessing such frequent changes. Stagnant thinking in the field of international organization, however, may be at least partly responsible for the frequent reappraisals accorded international organization by companies in this field. Perhaps part of the problem is that the traditional organizational orientation is obsolete. Location of the production facility has often been used as the primary basis of organization; yet, in today's market-oriented world economy, the location of production may no longer be crucial to organizational matters.

Innumerable considerations must be reviewed when establishing an organization for doing international business. There are, however, five areas which should be given prime consideration: production, ownership (financial), control, legal, and marketing. Admittedly, production costs and legal requirements forcing local production in foreign countries must be conformed to; but, when a company is concentrating on capitalizing on market opportunities, the question of where a product should be produced is relatively unimportant. The issue of full ownership by the parent company versus joint ventures and other partnership arrangements is also somewhat irrelevant from the viewpoint of market opportunity. Legal requirements and tax considerations cannot be ignored, but because they are statutory and represent given and known parameters, they provide little basis for policy arguments.

Even the country in which the corporation is domiciled is basically irrelevant to the marketing process, except that it may be logical to locate a parent company or distributing company in a tax-shelter country to minimize the costs of doing business. Tax-shelter countries such as Lichtenstein offer a bewildering assortment of corporate arrangements to the international firm. One lawyer in Valdouse, Lichtenstein, who specializes in handling international corporate headquarters, has identified some 30 different corporate forms in use in that country.

Perhaps the ultimate organizational questions relate to the ability of an international marketer to compete effectively in various markets and to the ability of the company to control and profit from such competition. Profit generation depends on the ability of a firm to market its product successfully, regardless of the product's country of origin. It is especially logical, therefore, that companies doing business overseas organize their international operations to meet marketing requirements.

Structural Basis

International business organizations are usually structured around considerations having to do with a product, a function, or the geographical location of activities; sometimes all three are considered and combined in one organizational form. The product oriented organization places responsibility for worldwide distribution on the product manager, who is in charge of all distribution anywhere in the world, including the parent company. Under the functional arrangement, each functional manager is responsible for the performance of his function, wherever it may take place. Thus the advertising manager may be responsible for advertising throughout the world, the product development manager is responsible for all product development within the company or its subsidiaries, and management of the sales function is the responsibility of the international sales executive. Following the geographical setup, a manager is responsible for all products and all functions within a given geographical area which has been designated as his jurisdiction; within his area, he virtually runs the company, because he is responsible for all aspects of its operation.

Typically, organizations combine these various approaches depending on geographic, market, and manpower factors. For one product they may use a geographic arrangement, for another, a product arrangement. Some functions may be handled centrally for all countries, and others may be decentralized. For a large firm, the combined approach is likely to be virtually mandatory, because world conditions vary so widely.

Locus of Decision

Discounting, for a moment, questions of centralization of management, considerations of where decisions will be made, by whom, and by what method constitute a major element of organizational strategy. Management policy must be explicit about which decisions are to be made at corporate headquarters, which at international headquarters, which at regional levels, and which at national or even local levels. Most companies not only indicate the types of decisions to be made at these different levels but also provide limits on the amount of money that can be spent at each level without review by the next higher level. Determination of policy strategy, a tactical decision level, becomes a prime determination in choosing the level of decision. Tactical decisions normally should be made at the lowest possible level where such decisions can be made without country-by-country duplication. If a tactical decision applies to several countries, it should probably be made at the regional level, but if it applies to only one country, it should be made at the national level.

Once the decision has been made about the level of decision and has been promulgated by policy directive, there is still a question of who will be responsible for making the decision. Some companies with widespread operations have taken great pains to internationalize their board of directors so the board policies will be more acceptable in operating countries. When U.S. expatriate managers and foreign national managers are working together either in a training or working capacity, it is especially important to delineate carefully the areas of decision making responsibility for each party. Sometimes the American expatriate is so involved in adapting to a new country that he is essentially ineffective as a decision maker for an initial period of some weeks or months; since this acclimatization period differs among persons, management must deal with each manager on an individual basis. Care must be exercised and a decision maker must be specified when companies have merged and two or more persons share a common job assignment at the headquarters level. Predetermination of the final decision making authority among product managers, functional managers, and line managers also can lessen the possibility of conflict.

When determining the locus of decision, management should also consider the method of decision making to be employed. Europeans tend in the direction of having one fairly highly placed executive make decisions autonomously. Americans are more likely to delegate decision making to a lower level of management and use various committee arrangements. Japanese are noted for their committee type of decision making calling for "consensus."

Maintaining Flexibility

In developing its organizational strategy, management must maintain as much flexibility as possible to permit for future reorganizations, mergers and dissolutions. Sometimes an organizational arrangement can be modified only with governmental consent. It took Saint-Gobain, Europe's largest glassmaker, two years of concerted effort and negotiations with the government to transform a branch operation into a subsidiary. Countries often have vested interests in a given type of

BOX 13–2

Ringi System

Organizational problems are best exemplified in a typically Japanese management practice called the *ringi* system. The Japanese term is composed of two ideograms; the first one, *rin,* means in the context that subordinates submit a proposal to their superiors, and the second one, *gi,* means discussion. Since in the traditional Japanese business organization formal authority for making decisions is concentrated in the hands of the chief executive, the president of the company, those in charge of a specific task cannot make independent decisions regarding their own job. They are expected to write a description of the matter in the form of a proposal which is then coordinated with related departments, and finally submitted for decision to the president. Only then may the proposal be acted upon. This process of decision-making involves in fact a large number of people. The original written document, *ringisho,* is passed around to all concerned; each affixes his seal on the document as evidence that he has seen it and passes it on to the next department. A head of department or section who disagrees usually adds his own opinion besides stamping his seal. This procedure in itself is probably not peculiar to Japanese management as a method of communication and decision in a centralized organization. It is, however, characteristically Japanese in its intimate relation to group decision-making.

Source: Quoted, with permission, from *Doing Business in Japan,* p. 171, edited by Robert J. Ballon and published by Sophia University, Tokyo, 1967, in cooperation with the Charles E. Tuttle Co., Inc.

organization, particularly if production facilities or extensive distribution facilities are included. Raytheon, a U.S. electronics components manufacturer, found itself in luck when it had to liquidate its Palermo, Sicily, firm, Raytheon Elsi; because this was a separate subsidiary organization rather than a branch of the parent company, Raytheon has been able to disavow some $12 million worth of debts.

Initial corporate form can significantly affect the types of relationships developed in any kind of merger negotiations. Most of the developed countries of the world have been engulfed in a merger wave in recent years. The presence of large-scale American operations has caused other businesses to reappraise their own scale and seek growth through various types of conglomerates, holding companies, and mergers. Many of these mergers are cross-national and thereby complicate organizational arrangements even further. One of the conclusions of a business strategy conference sponsored by France's National Association of Doctors of Economics was that American companies are open-minded and likely to shape their organizations to fit the markets in which they are dealing, whereas European companies tend to be locked into national molds. Such rigidity limits the effectiveness of many foreign companies.

To the student or businessman who is new to international operations, the organizational task is indeed complicated. A thorough understanding of the alternative arrangements and their advantages and disadvantages makes the task easier, however. The organizational process is further facilitated by careful analysis of the functions to be performed, the control desired, the corporate and market situations, and the available alternatives. Organizational patterns are dynamic not static; they must grow and change with the situation. So the object, at a given time, is not to develop the perfect organization but to develop the one best suited to the moment and offering maximum flexibility for future modification.

HEADQUARTERS ORGANIZATIONAL ALTERNATIVES

Organizational arrangements employed in international marketing are difficult to categorize. Nearly every company has its own peculiar modification of a standard organizational pattern, and many employ different patterns for different markets. Some firms profess to have one kind of organization, but analysis of their operations reveals an altogether different organizational setup. In such a situation, it is important to consider basic factors relating to marketing organization.

Some important questions relative to organization are as follows:

1. At what level will policy decisions be made?
2. How long can the command chain be?
3. What staff support will be given?
4. Will corporate or external resources be utilized?
5. How much control is desired over the distribution organization?
6. Will decision making be centralized or decentralized?
7. What type or level of sales representation is needed?

The answers to these and other questions will provide the general orientation for marketing organization.

International marketing organization often can be analyzed in terms of geography, function, and product. A company may be organized by product lines but have geographical subdivisions under the product

EXHIBIT 13–3
Schematic Marketing Organization Plan Combining
Product, Geographic, and Functional Approaches

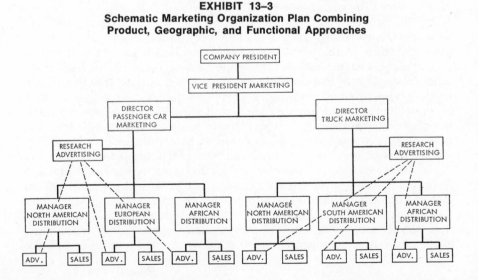

categories. Both may be supplemented by functional staff support. Exhibit 13–3 shows such a combination. Modifications of this basic combination arrangement are used by a majority of large companies doing business internationally.

Regardless of the approach to organization, someone in the parent company must be responsible for the international function. Even when foreign operations are almost completely autonomous, they retain their autonomy only because the parent chooses to permit it. Exhibit 13–4 shows some of the more basic relationships that are possible. The top grouping shows various types of arrangements which may be used at the parent company level. The group on the left shows alternate ways of handling foreign business through a company-owned marketing organization. The group on the right includes alternate ways of handling foreign business through nonowned or external organizations. Each group will be discussed below or in Chapter 20, but it is well to bear in mind that corporate organizational arrangements may include *several* of the variations identified in the chart. A company may, for example, have a subsidiary in one country, a sales force in another and a licensee in yet another market. Such a conglomerate organization may best serve

EXHIBIT 13–4
Alternative Organizational Patterns

CORPORATE MANAGEMENT OF INTERNATIONAL MARKETING

a company's objectives at a given point in time. For analytical purposes, however, the various subelements are considered separately in this and subsequent chapters.

Centralization, Regionalization, and Decentralization

An infinite number of organizational patterns for *headquarters activities* of multinational firms could be identified, but most can be fitted into one of three main categories: centralized, regionalized, and decentralized organizations. The fact that all types of systems are used indicates that each has certain advantages and disadvantages. The chief advantages of centralization are the availability of experts at one location, the ability to exercise a high degree of control on both the planning and implementation phases, and the centralization of all records and information. Libby, McNeil and Libby provides a good example of a company which just a few years ago eliminated regional autonomy and centralized all administration of overseas activities in their company headquarters in the United States. To Libby, the key advantage is that it requires only one level of management between the company headquarters and national organizations, thus eliminating several layers of managerial middlemen. The company has gained significant personnel economies through the action and is able to delegate more operating authority than previously because the caliber of personnel is higher. The company now is organized along straightforward functional lines, with the marketing division responsible for marketing research, advertising, product management, sales, and distribution.

Companies which do not do a large volume of international business may prefer to work on a basis of extreme decentralization by selecting competent men and giving them full responsibility for national or regional operations. The chief advantage is that these men are in direct day-to-day contact with the market for which they are responsible; the chief disadvantage is the partial loss of control and lack of a broad company view. Massey Ferguson is a good example; the company had decentralized to the extent of having nine major market subsidiaries, each of which operates quasi-independently. In every case the subsidiaries are run by nationals; the nine divisions are supported by an "export" subsidiary in Toronto which provides staff support and maintains contact with all of the regional subsidiaries.

For most large companies, the trend seems to be toward regionalized management systems which attempt to combine the control and expertise advantages of central organization with the close contact of decentralized organization. Many companies have at least a European subsidiary and some four or five regional headquarters. Union Carbide, for example, has subsidiaries in Europe, the Middle East, the Far East, Latin America, and Africa. This company, with sales outside the United States of nearly $800 million, departed from a centralized organization because the operation was too large and growing too rapidly to be handled effectively from the central headquarters. The roster of companies using the regional approach sounds like a listing of America's blue-chip industries and includes Caterpillar, Chrysler, Colgate-Palmolive, Dow Chemical, Esso, Hewlett-Packard, IBM, and dozens of others. It appears that the regional organizational arrangement has proved itself for businesses doing a large volume overseas.[4]

A Word on Autonomy

For its international activities, American business has historically favored corporate-owned organizational arrangements giving wide lati-

---

[4] See Kenneth Simmonds, "Multi-National Question Mark, Well Not Quite," *Columbia Journal of World Business,* Fall 1966, pp. 115–22, and National Industrial Conference Board, *Organization Structures of International Companies* (New York, 1965). This book provides organization charts for some forty-two companies operating multinationally and provides information on the rationale for each chart.

tude and relative autonomy to foreign management. As suggested above, there is a growing trend toward centralization of authority for higher level decisions and for closer control. Nevertheless, probably a majority of companies engaged in world trade today utilize some form of autonomously managed organization. In this organizational arrangement, the parent company has a department, or owns a subsidiary, in which the chief executive runs the company autonomously, almost, in fact, as if it were his own company. If the department or subsidiary is primarily involved in exporting, the manager will usually be located in the country of the parent company. If he is managing foreign sales operations, he usually works out of the foreign office. Usually, the manager's prime responsibility is to return a reasonable profit to his parent company. How he accomplishes this goal is largely his concern. By fixing the responsibility for profit contribution directly on a division or subsidiary manager, such an organizational arrangement—as long as it is successful—frees home office corporate officers from worrying about international affairs. The field manager of the autonomous organization is particularly flexible in his ability to meet emergencies and challenging situations.

In an organizational chart, an independent export division or department is directly under the president; despite his organizational location, the manager of the *autonomous* international division or department has the authority to act almost independently of the parent company. Essentially the same considerations apply to autonomous foreign subsidiaries, except that in such an organization legally separate companies are employed. Autonomous geographic territory managers operate in the same way as department or subsidiary managers, except that the territorial manager typically reports to an international division manager and is responsible only for a limited geographic territory. He still, however, operates his regional department or subsidiary as though it were his own company, with profit responsibility only.

The primary disadvantage of autonomous operation is that it places great power and responsibility in the hands of a man or group of men who may not be in close communication with the parent company and who may be forced to act without the benefit of company advice, discussions with other corporate officers, or help from functional area specialists. One commentator correctly observes that "international business now is too brisk and important to be treated in such a fashion." Because an autonomous operation may depart from company goals, objectives, and operating procedures, many international firms prefer to subordinate the owned entity to the corporate hierarchy. Such arrangements facilitate integration of foreign and domestic marketing operations and permit better utilization of parent company staff support capabilities.

Managerial Arrangements

Someone in every company with international operations must be responsible for the success or failure of the international activity. Such direction may seem almost nonexistent or it may be quite apparent, but it is always there. At least five alternative managerial arrangements are commonly utilized in headquarters organizations, as follows:

1. Domestic top executive.
2. Export division head.
3. Extension of functional divisions.
4. Product managers.
5. Export committees.

Domestic Top Executive. The foreign operations of some companies, like Colgate-Palmolive and Ford Motor Co., are closely integrated with overall company operations and dominated by a domestic company president or marketing vice president. One writer comments that "the idea under the strong executive approach is to break down the sharp separation of domestic and foreign operations at higher management levels. A separate international division remains, but its job is only to coordinate day-by-day operations. It is not concerned with broad policy questions."

Export Division Head. The export division head arrangement for international marketing may be controlled by a domestically located export division head or by the president of a subsidiary foreign trading company. Such organization is common because it permits delegation of authority but still permits close liaison between the foreign and domestic operations.

Extension of Functional Divisions. In some companies, functional area control management is undertaken by individuals who are responsible for functional areas in the parent company. In this case the parent company advertising manager is also responsible for the advertising activities in the foreign operations. International sales activities for Hewlett-Packard Company, for example, are managed directly by the vice president of sales.

Functional organization requires segmentation of the marketing task into its various elements. Such a breakdown makes it possible to gain flexibility and control of functional components. Some activities may be controlled by the home office; some may be controlled by the foreign branch office; and others may be controlled directly by a product manager. Such a breakdown might identify the following functional areas: (1) managerial functions (pricing, product development, and overall marketing strategy), (2) sales functions, (3) advertising functions, (4) marketing research functions, (5) physical handling, and (6) customer services.

Product Managers. Product specialization, direct responsibility, and fast action characterize organizations utilizing product managers or product line managers. In this sort of arrangement, the domestic product manager may be responsible for foreign sales of his product. The job of the product manager is so broad, however, that often he cannot handle both domestic and international operations. Product specialization is still made possible by assigning the international marketing of each product, line, or group of lines, to one individual. Thus, as in domestic marketing arrangements using this type of organization, each kind of product may be marketed using the most suitable methods.

The Celanese Corporation of America has organized its diverse product lines into three main groups: chemicals, plastics, and synthetic fibers. Products in each of these three groups are marketed quite differently from products in the other two groups. Procter & Gamble has a similar market orientation for its diverse products. The manager of each product line is primarily responsible for the marketing of his product in overseas location.

Export Committees. Group management is a fairly popular device in companies that are new to international business. Export marketing committees typically include representation of marketing, advertising, production, and finance. The export committee approach allegedly offers the advantage of balanced home office supervision of international activities, but such an administrative arrangement is most likely to work satisfactorily in a company that does not highly prize aggressive international marketing.

OWNED INTERNATIONAL AFFILIATES

A company may be active in the market through its own organization by establishing a sales force, a branch, or a subsidiary, or by participating in a joint venture or a consortium. Management of the international sales force is reviewed in Chapter 15; the other arrangements are considered below.

Branches and Subsidiaries

Like their domestic counterparts, branches are an integral part of the company. Organizationally, the branch in São Paulo may differ little from the branch in Salt Lake City. Operationally, of course, the branches may be quite dissimilar; the São Paulo branch may be more autonomous, but not necessarily. Even within a country branches may differ widely in the nature of their assignment, function, and operation. The branch is simply an outpost or detachment of the company placed in a given location to accomplish designated goals on a local level. Often a branch is responsible only for the selling function; in such a case the branch manager is essentially a sales manager whose prime responsibility is supervising salesmen, handling orders, and solving local problems. Branches may have broader responsibilities, however, including full management of the marketing function for the assigned areas. Some branches operate as quasi-independent companies and may have production and other operational responsibilities.

Subsidiaries differ from branches chiefly in that they are separate companies which have been organized to perform functions assigned or delegated by the parent company. By definition, a subsidiary is controlled by the parent; often, but not always, it is wholly owned by the parent. Ownership may be shared for financial reasons, to satisfy foreign governmental requirements, to permit management equity participation, or for other reasons related to the parent company's goals. Many subsidiaries are full-scale companies covering major regions (perhaps, as with IBM World Trade Corp., all of the world outside the parent country), undertaking full-scale operations, and having dollar sales volumes in tens of millions. On the other hand, subsidiaries may be small local operations organized to perform narrow functions in a limited market. The range of operating methods is nearly as wide; subsidiaries may be completely autonomous, independently financed enterprises or may be totally dependent upon the parent in nearly all respects. In either case, the pattern of operation is entirely subjective and not likely to show up on organization charts.

Joint Ventures

Just as merger fever swept across the United States during the decade ending in 1970, joint venture fever has been sweeping the world. Probably some 90 percent of the U.S. companies that are highly active in world trade participate in at least one joint venture somewhere in the world. Many companies number their joint ventures in the dozens.

Numerous varieties of international partnerships exist between participating companies in different parts of the world. If the parent firm has adequate representation in the relationship, it will be able to exert significant control on the marketing of its product. There are numerous legal methods of joining companies which desire such an arrangement, but the joint venture form is essentially a merger or a partnership of two or more participating companies which have joined forces. Joint ventures are usually formed for marketing, financial, and/or managerial reasons.

Marketing Motives. The chief marketing reason for joint ventures is probably to gain access to markets. Nearly all of the developing countries, and many developed countries, require at least some degree of local participation of firms operating in their country. Automobile makers, for example, have been completely closed out of Japan, but, after many attempts, Chrysler Corporation has finally worked out a joint venture arrangement with Mitsubishi involving "collaboration in research and development related to automotive products and joint distribution arrangements in world markets." Chrysler has a minority interest in the company (35 percent) but the move is considered a major breakthrough. Interestingly enough, Chrysler also entered Britain, Spain, and France with volume minority ownership but escalated its ownership to a majority in each country. Market access is a tremendously compelling force; as the director of Unilever commented about firms' operations, "In India there was pressure on us to make our shares available locally when we expanded our business there a few years ago. We did not need the money, but we sold the shares. Things are not always done for purely economic reasons."[5]

Mergers with distributor companies or companies which already have well-established local distribution may provide rapid market access and distribution to foreign companies entering a country. When American

---
[5] "Nationalism Sets Boundaries for Multi-National Giants," *Business Week,* June 14, 1969, p. 98.

BOX 13–3

Ten Ways to Control a 50–50 Joint Venture Abroad

1. Issue two kinds of stock—voting and non-voting—that will divide the profits evenly but give a majority vote to the US side.

2. Arrange the deal 49–49 with 2% in the hands of a third party friendly to the US side.

3. Provide in the by-laws that the US side will have a majority of directors.

4. Have the by-laws stipulate that the US directors (even though equal in number with the partner's directors) will appoint the management.

5. Have the by-laws provide that in the case of a tie vote, the position of the US side will prevail.

6. Arrange a 50–50 deal, but with a management contract awarded to the US investor.

7. Arrange a contract for the entire output of the jointly owned producing facility to be sold to a US controlled marketing company. The marketing company should get what it wants from the producing company.

8. A modification of number 7: give 51% of the producing company to the local partner in exchange for 51% of the selling company.

9. Satisfy the pressure for 50% local ownership by putting the local 50% in the hands of a local insurance company that has no interest in management.

10. Better yet, spread the local 50% over a multitude of shareholders. Union Carbide in India and Kaiser in Brazil have thousands of local shareholders.

Source: Reprinted from "75 Management Checklists for Foreign Operations" (1966), pp. 31–32, with the permission of the publisher, Business International Corporation (N.Y.).

companies first entered Europe after World War II, they found in many cases that distribution facilities were inadequate and that there was insufficient local capital to expand them. In such instances the American firms formed partnerships and provided needed funds to strengthen the local middlemen.

Sometimes companies join forces in order to broaden the line of merchandise that they have available, thereby gaining marketing efficiency and a better public image. European companies have been merging at a rapid rate to bring their scale of operations up to a level where they can compete efficiently with large American companies which have entered Europe. Another market reason for joint ventures is that local firms possess market information and marketing know-how which would take years for a foreign company to acquire. Such participation minimizes the risk of market failure and speeds the marketing effort.

Financial and Manpower Advantages. Financially, it is sometimes desirable to merge with foreign companies because the merger provides access to local capital markets and combines the resources and fundraising capabilities of the companies. As a low-cost method of keeping up with the growing requirements of their international clients, advertising agencies have employed the partnership method of expansion extensively in the last decade. Most agencies seek a foreign agency with which they can work compatibly and attempt to make some kind of arrangement suitable to both parties. In some cases, part interest in the foreign agencies is actually purchased; in others, no money changes hands, and a stock exchange or other working relationship is established.

Sometimes international partnership arrangements provide tax advantages, but in most cases the purpose of the joint venture is to gain access to a market without committing major amounts of funds or personnel. Most companies seek a foreign firm with which they can work compatibly in an attempt to make an arrangement suitable to both parties. In some cases part interest in the foreign companies is actually purchased; in others no money changes hands but a stock exchange or other working relationship is established.

The worldwide shortage of capable management manpower has been another cause of mergers. Numerous joint ventures have been worked out so that nationals with managerial ability could be acquired. In some countries it is almost impossible to gain effective distribution without joining forces with firms which have already developed large sales forces.

Joint ventures may be characterized by the nature of the parties involved, some of which include manufacturers' distributors, governmental agencies, management groups, and investors. One typical arrangement is for a manufacturer is one country to perform a venture with a distributor in another country. This may be arranged by acquiring partial ownership of the distributor or by setting up a third company in which both parties have a share. A common arrangement in less developed countries is for an American manufacturing firm to provide part of the capital and all of the management for a group of foreign investors who put up money as their share of the joint venture. Another common arrangement is for manufacturers from two different countries to join forces to produce and distribute complementary lines through one another, or to distribute the combined lines in a third country.

Ultimately the success of any joint venture depends on the ability of the partners to operate synergistically rather than destructively. Usually one participant dominates the operation, but there are some examples of firms which have operated successfully on a purely 50–50 basis. Many times even a minority ownership is sufficient to assure a company of control over a joint venture if it is careful to establish appropriate management contracts or to take other steps to assure control in advance of the formation of the joint venture.

Consortia

The consortium or syndicate is similar to the joint venture in many ways and could be classified as a type of joint venture. It is worth separate consideration, however, because it has two unique characteristics. One is that it typically involves a rather large number of participants, and the other is that it frequently operates in a country or market in which none of the participants is currently active. Consortia are developed for pooling resources, both financial and managerial, and to lessen risks. Often huge construction projects are built under a consortium arrangement in which major contractors with different specialties form a separate company specifically to negotiate for and produce one job. Koppers Company and Blaw-Knox joined forces to build the Eregli steel mill in Turkey, for example. One firm usually acts as the lead firm, although the newly formed corporation may exist quite independently.

EXTERNAL ARRANGEMENTS

A company may turn over the task of international marketing to an external group or organization in which it has no ownership. Because it lacks equity, the producer company can seldom exert extensive control over the external organization.

In some instances, the external group may represent little more than an element in the channel of distribution; in others, it substitutes for the parent company's own international organization when dealing with some external organizations. It is often difficult to determine when corporate organization ends and the channel of distribution begins.

Beside the channel middlemen (who are considered in another chapter) the chief types of external arrangements are: (1) international licensing, (2) franchising, (3) management contracts, and (4) open distribution.

International Licensing

Licensing in international business may take several forms; licenses may be granted for production processes, for the use of a trade name, or for the distribution of imported products. In some circumstances, licensing provides an ideal entree into foreign countries that might otherwise block nondomestic enterprises. Licenses may be closely controlled or may be virtually autonomous. Licenses may make it possible to expand the world trading horizon without great capital or personnel commitments on the part of the parent company. As in any other international marketing arrangement involving outside companies, the parent must be careful that his licensees have the requisite capabilities for a successful business operation.[6]

The parent company, too, must have certain strengths if it is to succeed in licensing around the world. Specifically, it must have adequate capital for basic investment requirements, and competent personnel to handle contracts with and supervision of licensees. It must also have a competent domestic organization and be in a potentially healthy market situation. Some companies have had unsuccessful experiences in licensing. One commentator says that "some companies which originally embraced this proposal voluntarily have found that the burden of supervising and inspiring licensees to greater productive activity . . . . is a

---

[6] See *Organizing for Maximum Income from Foreign Licensing Agreements* (New York: Business International Corporation, 1965). This monograph provides considerable detail on the strategy and methods of licensing.

EXHIBIT 13–5
Licensing

ADVANTAGES

1. Higher return per invested asset.
2. Often the fastest way to get into a market.
3. No danger of nationalization.
4. A riskless entree—if coupled with option to buy.
5. Fewer currency exchange difficulties.
6. Cross-licensing benefits.
7. No staffing problems.
8. Access to a captured market.
9. Entry to market too small for investment.
10. Licensee's experience, sales organization, relations with local government.
11. Technical assistance contracts offset pre-royalty losses.
12. Capital equipment can be leased to licensee.
13. Management contracts can control licensee and defray initial licensing costs.
14. Useful in industries controlled by local government (radio, TV, military, transportation, oil, public utilities).
15. Entry into non-capitalist markets (Egypt, Yugoslavia).
16. Control of market by licensing a manufacturer and setting up own sales, services company.
17. Avoids joint-venture arguments over financial policy, accounting procedures, partner's tax practices.
18. No IRS trouble re intercorporate pricing.
19. No anti-trust trouble.
20. No problems with public stock issues.

DISADVANTAGES

1. Sets up potential competitor.
2. Renewals become more difficult, especially if no continuous flow of know-how.
3. Foreign government may be unwilling to accept US components for critical products.
4. Foreign government may disapprove "oath of secrecy" by licensee re know-how.
5. Quality control, management and production techniques difficult, especially for new product.
6. Difficulty with licensee's sales and servicing.
7. Licensee gets spare parts business, also may switch component business to foreign competitors.
8. Licensees may seek third market concessions.
9. Some licensees sell inferior goods in third market under licensor's trademark.
10. Difficult liaison between manufacturing licensee and sales subsidiaries.
11. Difficult to persuade licensee to install new equipment.
12. Licensee may refuse to pay for equipment already written off in US.
13. Inflexibility: licensee cannot be coordinated for worldwide profit peaking.

SOURCE: Reprinted from "75 Management Checklists for Foreign Operations" (1966), p. 20, with the permission of the publisher, Business International Corporation (N.Y.).

task far less remunerative and far more uncertain than a few good wholly owned operations in the more predictable countries."[7]

Licensing, however, does provide the basis for many success stories in various kinds of businesses. For example, a Brooklyn office equipment and supply company, The Old Town Corporation, derives about one half of its net profit from foreign licensing operations that account for less than one tenth of the company's sales volume. Exhibit 13–5 highlights some of the advantages and disadvantages of licensing as a method of doing business in foreign countries.

Large and small companies can expand intensively through licensing, and some companies have as many as several hundred international licensees. Pepsi-Cola is a notably successful international licensor. Pepsi-

---

[7] Brainerd, op. cit., p. 4.

Cola franchise holders own their bottling plants, employ national personnel, and control advertising and sales promotion. Pepsi-Cola International sells the foreign bottlers Pepsi-Cola concentrate and provides promotional support and advice on operations.

Franchising

Franchising is a form of licensing sufficiently important to warrant separate consideration because it is one of the fast-growing phases of international marketing. A franchise is essentially a marketing device in which the franchiser provides a standard package of products, systems, and management services, and the franchisee provides market knowledge, capital, and his own personal involvement in management. The combination of skills permits flexibility to deal with local market conditions and yet provides the parent firm with a reasonable degree of control over operations. The franchise system permits the franchiser to follow through on the marketing of his products all the way to the point of the final sale and is an important form of vertical market integration. Originally developed in the United States and popularly applied to quick-consumption consumer goods, the concept of franchising actually includes durable goods, services, and industrial products. One manufacturer of prefabricated steel building systems, Strandsteel Corporation of Houston, Texas, established franchised builders and distributors in over 30 countries in fewer than five years. Potentially, the franchise system provides an effective blending of skill centralization and operational decentralization. It appears that the franchising variety of licensing will be an increasingly important form of international marketing.

Management Contract

Quite a different kind of arrangement for doing business with companies overseas is the management contract. The name of the arrangement designates the function performed. The contracting company enters into an agreement to manage all or some functions of another company's operations. In return the management firm receives management fees, a share of the profits, and sometimes an option to purchase stock in the company at a given price. The management contract may be used to assure control in joint ventures or consortia in which the company has only a minority interest. It may also be used when the company has a majority interest but wishes to gain an immediate return for services directly rendered by the company personnel. In some instances companies that have been expropriated or "purchased" by local governments are able to maintain a profitable position by consenting to operate the enterprise through a management contract. The management contract may be used in any type of organizational or contractual arrangement. It often permits participation in a foreign venture without capital risk or investment and is a major tool for maintaining managerial control in situations where governments require nationals to own a majority of stock interest. The Willys-Overland venture of Kaiser Industries in Brazil is a good example; the U.S. firm has only about one third of the voting stock but operates and maintains full control through a management contract. It receives fees from the contract plus revenue patent and trademark agreements. The other two thirds of the stock is distributed among some 28,000 stockholders; Willys feels this arrangement will protect it from the excessive nationalism often exhibited by the Brazilian government.

Open Distribution

The final type of external arrangement for marketing goods in foreign countries to be considered, open distribution, is an explicit policy which may be chosen as a course of least resistance. Open distribution means simply that the company is willing to sell products to overseas or domestic customers or middlemen for overseas consumption. No commitments or tying arrangements are made concerning the goods or their marketing. Open distribution requires virtually no effort; it gives the company no control and often results in no sales. In a sense, one could say it is an absence of an organization rather than an organizational method. As the term is here considered, the great majority of companies do ignore international markets and distribute their goods internationally only when the initiative is taken by the customer or some middleman. In such operations, goods may be sold to foreign importers or to export commission houses. (The latter in general work for the customer and receive a buying commission for finding merchandise and making shipping arrangements.) Sometimes purchases are handled through a commissionaire (or resident buyer) who represents foreign customers through a domestic office. The commissionaire handles all financing and shipping obligations; to the vendor then, such sales are virtually identical to domestic transactions. Finally, the company may sell to another domestic middleman, such as the export merchant or export jobber. The former purchases goods on his own account and sells them into foreign markets; he acts in his own interest and derives his compensation and profit from the margin between his buying cost and selling price. The export jobber (sometimes called a cable merchant) is also a merchant middleman buying and selling on his own account, but he deals on a job lot basis and is less likely to have continuing relationships with either customers or suppliers.

SUMMARY AND CONCLUSIONS

Market-oriented firms build their organizations around company objectives, the structure of the market, and the competitive-environmental situation in which they must work. Because of varying objectives or needs, the organization that suits one company in a given market situation will not be satisfactory for another. Similarly, the company organization which meets corporate objectives may be suitable for one market but not another. Organizing for marketing may be complicated even for one country; but when a company is doing business internationally, the problems are multiplied. Company objectives may vary from market to market and from time to time; the structure of international markets also changes periodically and from country to country, and the competitive, governmental, and economic parameters affecting organization are in a constant state of flux. These variations require the international marketing executive to be especially flexible and creative in his orientation to organization for international marketing.

Although channels of distribution relate to marketing organization and are employed in the organization for the distribution of goods, they should not be considered basic determinants of organizational structure. Level, type, and extent of control are far more relevant organizational determinants and, as such, are given prime consideration in the marketing approach to international organization. This chapter considers international organization first from the viewpoint of the parent company arrangements which are used in directing the world marketing operation. Second, it considers the various arrangements which may be used in the actual operations of the worldwide marketing activity. These arrangements are reviewed as either owned or external and include a variety of alternatives. Either owned or external organizations may be subject to tight or loose control, depending on the wishes of management; but usually the external organizations are less easily or adequately controlled by the parent company. Many international marketers utilize several different organizational structures; as such, they may be classed as having a conglomerate organizational pattern.

Long-range forecasting, coupled with effective planning, can minimize the problems associated with organizing for international marketing. The necessity for change, adaptation, and restructuring cannot be completely overcome, however, in growing companies that are operating in constantly changing markets. Because world markets are so dynamic, organization for international marketing should be built around the dynamic elements. A static organization, such as one built around the more stable production base, seldom is in tune with the dynamics of the market. The corporate planner is doing well if he can minimize the disruptive effects of constant change. He is most likely to succeed if he orients his thinking around the marketing aspects of organization and develops a dynamic organizational structure for operating in the marketplace.

READING

THE TORTUOUS EVOLUTION OF THE MULTINATIONAL CORPORATION*
A Rose by Any Other Name . . .

HOWARD V. PERLMUTTER

Two hypotheses seem to be forming in the minds of executives from international firms that make the extent of their firm's multinationality

* Reprinted with permission from the January–February 1969 issue of the *Columbia Journal of World Business*. Copyright © 1969 by the Trustees of Columbia University in the City of New York.

of real interest. The first hypothesis is that the degree of multinationality of an enterprise is positively related to the firm's long-term viability. The "multinational" category makes sense for executives if it means a quality of decision making which leads to survival, growth and profitability in our evolving world economy.

The second hypothesis stems from the proposition that the multinational corporation is a new kind of institution—a new type of industrial social architecture particularly suitable for the latter third of the twentieth century. This type of institution could make a valuable contribution to world order and conceivably exercise a constructive impact on the nation-state. Some executives want to understand how to create an institution whose presence is considered legitimate and valuable in each nation-state. They want to prove that the greater the degree of multinationality of a firm, the greater its total constructive impact will be on host and home nation-states as well as other institutions. Since multinational firms may produce a significant proportion of the world's GNP, both hypotheses justify a more precise analysis of the varieties and degrees of multinationality. However, the confirming evidence is limited.

State of Mind

Part of the difficulty in defining the degree of multinationality comes from the variety of parameters along which a firm doing business overseas can be described. The examples from the four companies argue that (1) no single criterion of multinationality such as ownership or the number of nationals overseas is sufficient, and that (2) external and quantifiable measures such as the percentage of investment overseas or the distribution of equity by nationality are useful but not enough. The more one penetrates into the living reality of an international firm, the more one finds it is necessary to give serious weight to the way executives think about doing business around the world. The orientation toward "foreign people, ideas, resources," in headquarters and subsidiaries, and in host and home environments, becomes crucial in estimating the multinationality of a firm. To be sure, such external indices as the proportion of nationals in different countries holding equity and the number of foreign nationals who have reached top positions, including president, are good indices of multinationality. But one can still behave with a home-country orientation despite foreign shareholders, and one can have a few home-country nationals overseas but still pick those local executives who are home-country oriented or who are provincial and chauvinistic. The attitudes men hold are clearly more relevant than their passports.

Three primary attitudes among international executives toward building a multinational enterprise are identifiable. These attitudes can be inferred from the assumptions upon which key product, functional and geographical decisions were made.

These states of mind or attitudes may be described as ethnocentric (or home-country oriented), polycentric (or host-country oriented) and geocentric (or world-oriented). While they never appear in pure form, they are clearly distinguishable. There is some degree of ethnocentricity, polycentricity or geocentricity in all firms, but management's analysis does not usually correlate with public pronouncements about the firm's multinationality.

Home Country Attitudes

The ethnocentric attitude can be found in companies of any nationality with extensive overseas holdings. The attitude, revealed in executive actions and experienced by foreign subsidiary managers, is: "We, the home nationals of X company, are superior to, more trustworthy and more reliable than any foreigners in headquarters or subsidiaries. We will be willing to build facilities in your country if you acknowledge our inherent superiority and accept our methods and conditions for doing the job."

Of course, such attitudes are never so crudely expressed, but they often determine how a certain type of "multinational" firm is designed. Exhibit 1 illustrates how ethnocentric attitudes are expressed in determining the managerial process at home and overseas. For example, the ethnocentric executive is more apt to say: "Let us manufacture the simple products overseas. Those foreign nationals are not yet ready or reliable. We should manufacture the complex products in our country and keep the secrets among our trusted home-country nationals."

In a firm where ethnocentric attitudes prevailed, the performance criteria for men and products are "home-made." "We have found that a salesman should make 12 calls per day in Hoboken, New Jersey (the headquarters location) and therefore we apply these criteria everywhere in the world. The salesman in Brazzaville is naturally lazy, unmotivated. He shows little drive because he makes only two calls per day (despite the Congolese salesman's explanation that it takes time to reach customers by boat)."

Ethnocentric attitudes are revealed in the communication process where "advice," "counsel," and directives flow from headquarters to the subsidiary in a steady stream, bearing this message: "This works at home; therefore, it must work in your country."

Executives in both headquarters and affiliates express the national identity of the firm by associating the company with the nationality of the headquarters: this is "a Swedish company," "a Swiss company," "an American company," depending on the location of headquarters. "You have to accept the fact that the only way to reach a senior post in our firm," an English executive in a U.S. firm said, "is to take out an American passport."

Crucial to the ethnocentric concept is the current policy that men of the home nationality are recruited and trained for key positions everywhere in the world. Foreigners feel like "second-class" citizens.

There is no international firm today whose executives will say that ethnocentrism is absent in their company. In the firms whose multinational investment began a decade ago, one is more likely to hear, "We

EXHIBIT 1

Three Types of Headquarters Orientation toward Subsidiaries in an International Enterprise

Organization Design	Ethnocentric	Polycentric	Geocentric
Complexity of organization	Complex in home country, simple in subsidiaries	Varied and independent	Increasingly complex and interdependent
Authority; decision making	High in headquarters	Relatively low in headquarters	Aim for a collaborative approach between headquarters and subsidiaries
Evaluation and control	Home standards applied for persons and performance	Determined locally	Find standards which are universal and local
Rewards and punishments; incentives	High in headquarters, low in subsidiaries	Wide variation; can be high or low rewards for subsidiary performance	International and local executives rewarded for reaching local and worldwide objectives
Communication; information flow	High volume to subsidiaries orders, commands, advice	Little to and from headquarters; little between subsidiaries	Both ways and between subsidiaries. Heads of subsidiaries part of management team
Identification	Nationality of owner	Nationality of host country	Truly international company but identifying with national interests
Perpetuation (recruiting, staffing, development)	Recruit and develop people of home country for key positions everywhere in the world	Develop people of local nationality for key positions in their own country	Develop best men everywhere in the world for key positions everywhere in the world

are still in a transitional stage from our ethnocentric era. The traces are still around! But we are making progress."

Host-Country Orientation

Polycentric firms are those which, by experience or by the inclination of a top executive (usually one of the founders), begin with the assumption that host-country cultures are different and that foreigners are difficult to understand. Local people know what is best for them, and the part of the firm which is located in the host country should be as "local in identity" as possible. The senior executives at headquarters believe that their multinational enterprise can be held together by good financial controls. A polycentric firm, literally, is a loosely connected group with quasi-independent subsidiaries as centers—more akin to a confederation.

European multinational firms tend to follow this pattern, using a top local executive who is strong and trustworthy, of the "right" family and who has an intimate understanding of the workings of the host government. This policy seems to have worked until the advent of the Common Market.

Executives in the headquarters of such a company are apt to say: "Let the Romans do it their way. We really don't understand what is going on there, but we have to have confidence in them. As long as they earn a profit, we want to remain in the background." They assume that since people are different in each country, standards for performance, incentives and training methods must be different. Local environmental factors are given greater weight (see Exhibit 1).

Many executives mistakenly equate polycentrism with multinationalism. This is evidenced in the legalistic definition of a multinational enterprise as a cluster of corporations of diverse nationality joined together by ties of common ownership. It is no accident that many senior executives in headquarters take pride in the absence of non-nationals in their subsidiaries, especially people from the head office. The implication is clearly that each subsidiary is a distinct national entity, since it is incorporated in a different sovereign state. Lonely senior executives in the subsidiaries of polycentric companies complain that: "The home office never tells us anything."

Polycentrism is not the ultimate form of multinationalism. It is a landmark on a highway. Polycentrism is encouraged by local marketing managers who contend that: "Headquarters will never understand us, our people, our consumer needs, our laws, our distribution, etc. . . ."

Headquarters takes pride in the fact that few outsiders know that the firm is foreign-owned. "We want to be a good local company. How many Americans know that Shell and Lever Brothers are foreign-owned?"

But the polycentric personnel policy is also revealed in the fact that no local manager can seriously aspire to a senior position at headquarters. "You know the French are so provincial; it is better to keep them in France. Uproot them and you are in trouble," a senior executive says to justify the paucity of non-Americans at headquarters.

One consequence (and perhaps cause) of polycentrism is a virulent ethnocentrism among the country managers.

A World-Oriented Concept

The third attitude which is beginning to emerge at an accelerating rate is geocentrism. Senior executives with this orientation do not equate superiority with nationality. Within legal and political limits, they seek the best men, regardless of nationality, to solve the company's problems anywhere in the world. The senior executives attempt to build an organization in which the subsidiary is not only a good citizen of the host nation but is a leading exporter from this nation in the international community and contributes such benefits as (1) an increasing supply of hard currency, (2) new skills and (3) a knowledge of advanced technology. Geocentrism is summed up in a Unilever board chairman's statement of objectives: "We want to Unileverize our Indians and Indianize our Unileverans."

The ultimate goal of geocentrism is a worldwide approach in both headquarters and subsidiaries. The firm's subsidiaries are thus neither satellites nor independent city states, but parts of a whole whose focus is on worldwide objectives as well as local objectives, each part making its unique contribution with its unique competence. Geocentrism is expressed by function, product and geography. The question asked in headquarters and the subsidiaries is: "Where in the world shall we raise money, build our plant, conduct R&D, get and launch new ideas to serve our present and future customers?"

This conception of geocentrism involves a collaborative effort between subsidiaries and headquarters to establish universal standards and permissible local variations, to make key allocational decisions on new products, new plants, new laboratories. The international management team includes the affiliate heads.

Subsidiary managers must ask: "Where in the world can I get the help to serve my customers best in this country?" "Where in the world can I export products developed in this country—products which meet worldwide standards as opposed to purely local standards?"

Geocentrism, furthermore, requires a reward system for subsidiary managers which motivates them to work for worldwide objectives, not just to defend country objectives. In firms where geocentrism prevails, it is not uncommon to hear a subsidiary manager say, "While I am paid to defend our interests in this country and to get the best resources for this affiliate, I must still ask myself the question 'Where in the world (instead of where in my country) should we build this plant?' " This approach is still rare today.

In contrast to the ethnocentric and polycentric patterns, communication is encouraged among subsidiaries in geocentric-oriented firms. "It is your duty to help us solve problems anywhere in the world," one chief executive continually reminds the heads of his company's affiliates. (See Exhibit 1.)

The geocentric firm identifies with local company needs. "We aim to be not just a good local company but the best local company in terms of the quality of management and the worldwide (not local) standards we establish in domestic and export production." "If we were only as good as local companies, we would deserve to be nationalized."

The geocentric personnel policy is based on the belief that we should bring in the best man in the world regardless of his nationality. His passport should not be the criterion for promotion.

The EPG Profile

Executives can draw their firm's profile in ethnocentric (E), polycentric (P) and geocentric (G) dimensions. They are called EPG profiles. The degree of ethnocentrism, polycentrism and geocentrism by product, function and geography can be established. Typically R&D often turns out to be more geocentric (truth is universal, perhaps) and less ethnocentric than finance. Financial managers are likely to see their decisions as ethnocentric. The marketing function is more polycentric, particularly in the advanced economies and in the larger affiliate markets.

The tendency toward ethnocentrism in relations with subsidiaries in the developing countries is marked. Polycentric attitudes develop in consumer goods divisions, and ethnocentrism appears to be greater in industrial product divisions. The agreement is almost unanimous in both U.S.- and European-based international firms that their companies are at various stages on a route toward geocentrism but none has reached this state of affairs. Their executives would agree, however, that:

1. A description of their firms as multinational obscures more than it illuminates the state of affairs.
2. The EPG mix, once defined, is a more precise way to describe the point they have reached.
3. The present profile is not static but a landmark along a difficult road to genuine geocentrism.
4. There are forces both to change and to maintain the present attitudinal "mix," some of which are under their control.

Forces toward and against

What are the forces that determine the EPG mix of a firm? "You must think of the struggle toward functioning as a worldwide firm as just a beginning—a few steps forward and a step backward," a chief executive put it. "It is a painful process, and every firm is different."

Executives of some of the world's largest multinational firms have been able to identify a series of external and internal factors that contribute to or hinder the growth of geocentric attitudes and decision. Exhibit 2 summarizes the factors most frequently mentioned by over 500 executives from at least 17 countries and 20 firms.

From the external environmental side, the growing world markets, the increase in availability of managerial and technological know-how in different countries, global competition and international customers, advances in telecommunications, regional, political, and economic communities are positive factors, as is the host country's desire to increase its balance-of-payments surplus through the location of export-oriented subsidiaries of international firms within its borders.

In different firms, senior executives see in various degrees these positive factors toward geocentrism: top management's increasing desire to use human and material resources optimally, the observed lowering of morale after decades of ethnocentric practices, the evidence of waste and duplication under polycentric thinking, the increased awareness and respect for good men of other than the home nationality, and, most importantly, top management's own commitment to building a geocentric firm as evidenced in policies, practices and procedures.

The obstacles toward geocentrism from the environment stem largely from the rising political and economic nationalism in the world today, the suspicions of political leaders of the aims and increasing power of the multinational firm. On the internal side, the obstacles cited most frequently in U.S.-based multinational firms were management's inexperience in overseas markets, mutual distrust between home-country people and foreign executives, the resistance to participation by foreigners in the power structure at headquarters, the increasing difficulty of getting good men overseas to move, nationalistic tendencies in staff, and the linguistic and other communication difficulties of a cultural nature.

Any given firm is seen as moving toward geocentrism at a rate determined by its capacities to build on the positive internal factors over which it has control and to change the negative internal factors which are controllable. In some firms the geocentric goal is openly discussed among executives of different nationalities and from different subsidiaries as well as headquarters. There is a consequent improvement in the climate of trust and acceptance of each other's views.

Programs are instituted to assure greater experience in foreign markets, task forces of executives are upgraded, international careers for executives of all nationalities are being designed.

But the seriousness of the obstacles cannot be underestimated. A world of rising nationalism is hardly a pre-condition for geocentrism; and overcoming distrust of foreigners even within one's own firm is not accomplished in a short span of time. The route to pervasive geocentric thinking is long and tortuous.

Costs, Risks, Payoffs

What conclusions will executives from multinational firms draw from the balance sheet of advantages and disadvantages of maintaining one's present state of ethnocentrism, polycentrism or geocentrism? Not too surprisingly, the costs and risks of ethnocentrism are seen to outbalance the payoffs in the long run. The costs of ethnocentrism are ineffective planning because of a lack of good feed-back, the departure of the best men in the subsidiaries, fewer innovations, and an inability to build a high calibre local organization. The risks are political and social repercussions and a less flexible response to local changes.

The payoffs of ethnocentrism are real enough in the short term, they

EXHIBIT 2

International Exeutives' View of Forces and Obstacles toward Geocentrism in Their Firms

Forces toward Geocentrism		Obstacles toward Geocentrism	
Environmental	*Intra-Organizational*	*Environmental*	*Intra-Organizational*
1. Technological and managerial know-how increasing in availability in different countries	1. Desire to use human vs. material resources optimally	1. Economic nationalism in host and home countries	1. Management inexperience in overseas markets
2. International customers	2. Observed lowering of morale in affiliates of an ethnocentric company	2. Political nationalism in host & home countries	2. Nation-centered reward and punishment structure
3. Local customers demand for best product at fair price	3. Evidence of waste and duplication in polycentrism	3. Military secrecy associated with research in home country	3. Mutual distrust between home country people and foreign executives
4. Host country's desire to increase balance of payments	4. Increasing awareness and respect for good men of other than home nationality	4. Distrust of big international firms by host country political leaders	4. Resistance to letting foreigners into the power structure
5. Growing world markets	5. Risk diversification in having a worldwide production & distribution system	5. Lack of international monetary system	5. Anticipated costs and risks of geocentrism
6. Global competition among international firms for scarce human and material resources	6. Need for recruitment of good men on a worldwide basis	6. Growing differences between the rich and poor countries	6. Nationalistic tendencies in staff
7. Major advances in integration of international transport & telecommunications	7. Need for worldwide information system	7. Host country belief that home countries get disproportionate benefits of international firm's profits	7. Increasing immobility of staff
8. Regional supranational economic & political communities	8. Worldwide appeal of products	8. Home country political leaders' attempts to control firm's policy	8. Linguistic problems & different cultural backgrounds
	9. Senior management's long term commitment to geocentrism as related to survival and growth		9. Centralization tendencies in headquarters

say. Organization is simpler. There is a higher rate of communication of know-how from headquarters to new markets. There is more control over appointments to senior posts in subsidiaries.

Polycentrism's costs are waste due to duplication, to decisions to make products for local use but which could be universal, and to inefficient use of home-country experience. The risks include an excessive regard for local traditions and local growth at the expense of global growth. The main advantages are an intensive exploitation of local markets, better sales since local management is often better informed, more local initiative for new products, more host-government support, and good local managers with high morale.

Geocentrism's costs are largely related to communication and travel expenses, educational costs at all levels, time spent in decision-making because consensus seeking among more people is required, and an international headquarters bureaucracy. Risks include those due to too wide a distribution of power, personnel problems and those of re-entry of international executives. The payoffs are a more powerful total company throughout, a better quality of products and service, worldwide utilization of best resources, improvement of local company management, a greater sense of commitment to worldwide objectives, and last, but not least, more profit.

Jacques Maisonrouge, the French-born president of IBM World Trade, understands the geocentric concept and its benefits. He wrote recently:

> The first step to a geocentric organization is when a corporation, faced with the choice of whether to grow and expand or decline, realizes the need to mobilize its resources on a world scale. It will sooner or later have to face the issue that the home country does not have a monopoly of either men or ideas. . . .
>
> I strongly believe that the future belongs to geocentric companies. . . . What is of fundamental importance is the attitude of the company's top management. If it is dedicated to "geocentrism," good international management will be possible. If not, the best men of different nations will soon understand that they do not belong to the "race des seigneurs" and will leave the business.[1]

Geocentrism is not inevitable in any given firm. Some companies have experienced a "regression" to ethnocentrism after trying a long period of polycentrism, of letting subsidiaries do it "their way." The local directors built little empires and did not train successors from their own country. Headquarters had to send home-country nationals to take over. A period of home-country thinking took over.

There appears to be evidence of a need for evolutionary movement from ethnocentrism to polycentrism to geocentrism. The polycentric stage is likened to an adolescent protest period during which subsidiary managers gain their confidence as equals by fighting headquarters and proving "their manhood," after a long period of being under headquarters' ethnocentric thumb.

"It is hard to move from a period of headquarters domination to a

---

[1] Jacques Maisonrouge, "The Education of International Managers," *The Quarterly Journal of AIESEC International,* February 1967.

worldwide management team quickly. A period of letting affiliates make mistakes may be necessary," said one executive.

Window Dressing

In the rush toward appearing geocentric, many U.S. firms have found it necessary to emphasize progress by appointing one or two non-nationals to senior posts—even on occasion to headquarters. The foreigner is often effectively counteracted by the number of nationals around him, and his influence is really small. Tokenism does have some positive effects, but it does not mean geocentrism has arrived.

Window dressing is also a temptation. Here an attempt is made to demonstrate influence by appointing a number of incompetent "foreigners" to key positions. The results are not impressive for either the individuals or the company.

Too often what is called "the multinational view" is really a screen for ethnocentrism. Foreign affiliate managers must, in order to succeed, take on the traits and behavior of the ruling nationality. In short, in a U.S.-owned firm the foreigner must "Americanize"—not only in attitude but in dress and speech—in order to be accepted.

Tokenism and window dressing are transitional episodes where aspirations toward multinationalism outstrip present attitudes and resources. The fault does not lie only with the enterprise. The human demands of ethocentrism are great.

A Geocentric Man—?

The geocentric enterprise depends on having an adequate supply of men who are geocentrically oriented. It would be a mistake to underestimate the human stresses which a geocentric career creates. Moving where the company needs an executive involves major adjustments for families, wives and children. The sacrifices are often great and, for some families, outweigh the rewards forthcoming—at least in personal terms. Many executives find it difficult to learn new languages and overcome their cultural superiority complexes, national pride and discomfort with foreigners. Furthermore, international careers can be hazardous when ethnocentrism prevails at headquarters. "It is easy to get lost in the world of the subsidiaries and to be 'out of sight, out of mind' when promotions come up at headquarters," as one executive expressed it following a visit to headquarters after five years overseas. To his disappointment, he knew few senior executives. And fewer knew him!

The economic rewards, the challenge of new countries, the personal and professional development that comes from working in a variety of countries and cultures are surely incentives, but companies have not solved by any means the human costs of international mobility to executives and their families.

A firm's multinationality may be judged by the pervasiveness with which executives think geocentrically—by function, marketing, finance, production, R&D, etc., by product division and by country. The takeoff to geocentrism may begin with executives in one function, say marketing, seeking to find a truly world-wide product line. Only when this worldwide attitude extends throughout the firm, in headquarters and subsidiaries, can executives feel that it is becoming genuinely geocentric.

But no single yardstick, such as the number of foreign nationals in key positions, is sufficient to establish a firm's multinationality. The multinational firm's route to geocentrism is still long because political and economic nationalism is on the rise, and, more importantly, since within the firm ethnocentrism and polycentrism are not easy to overcome. Building trust between persons of different nationality is a central obstacle. Indeed, if we are to judge men, as Paul Weiss put it, "by the kind of world they are trying to build," the senior executives engaged in building the geocentric enterprise could well be the most important social architects of the last third of the twentieth century. For the institution they are trying to erect promises a greater universal sharing of wealth and a consequent control of the explosive centrifugal tendencies of our evolving world community.

The geocentric enterprise offers an institutional and supra-national framework which could conceivably make war less likely, on the assumption that bombing customers, suppliers and employees is in nobody's interest. The difficulty of the task is thus matched by its worthwhileness. A clearer image of the features of genuine geocentricity is thus indispensable both as a guideline and as an inviting prospect.

QUESTIONS

1. Define:

Product manager	Managing agent
Autonomous-owned organization	Complementary exporter
Joint venture	Open distribution

2. Elaborate on the reasons for frequent changes in international organizational structures.

3. How can international organization for marketing best be stabilized?

4. "The dichotomy typically drawn between export marketing and overseas marketing is partly fictional; from a marketing standpoint, they are but alternative methods of capitalizing on foreign market opportunities." Discuss.

5. Explain the relationships that exist among organizational structure, channels of distribution, and the international sales force.

6. Review the parameters complicating international marketing organization.

7. Differentiate between international and domestic planning.

8. How will entry into a developed foreign market differ from entry into a relatively untapped market?

9. Explain the importance of timing in marketing planning.

10. What is the value of the marketing approach to international organization?

11. Explain the "Schematic Marketing Organization Plan Combining Product, Geographic, and Functional Approaches."

12. Explain the five headquarters-level managerial arrangements. Cite an instance when each might be used.
13. Illustrate the alternative positions where a CEM might fit on an organization chart.
14. How do governments influence the organizational pattern of companies in international business?
15. Formulate a general rule for deciding where international business decisions should be made.
16. Explain the popularity of joint ventures.

Reading

1. Explain the term "collegial management" and tell how it operates.
2. How effective would the typical American executive be in a collegial situation? How does it differ from the committee management system so common to the United States?
3. Identify the problems associated with collegial management and tell how they could be overcome.

OUTLINE OF CHAPTER 14

INTRODUCTION

FINANCIAL PLANNING FOR MARKETING

General Approach

Policy Questions

Profit Planning

MONEY AND MONEY SUPPLY

National Monetary Goals

Monetary Aims of International Companies

FINANCIAL REQUIREMENTS FOR INTERNATIONAL MARKETING

Working Capital

Overhead

Inventory

Channel and Consumer Credit

Capital Investment

Market Penetration Investment

CREDIT: A COMPETITIVE WEAPON

Channel Credit

Consumer Credit

International Credit Management

Credit Policies

Credit Information

RISK MANAGEMENT

PAYOUT PLANNING AND STRATEGY

**SOURCES OF FUNDS FOR INTERNATIONAL MARKETING OPERA-
TIONS**

Private Sources

Equity Holders

Edge Act Banks

Investment Companies and Trusts

Commercial Finance and Factoring Companies

Overseas Development Banks

Noninstitutional Lenders

Commercial Banks

Government Sources

International Governmental Sources

National Government Funds

State and Local Funds

SUMMARY AND CONCLUSIONS

FINANCING INTERNATIONAL MARKETING

INTRODUCTION

International marketing must be financed for any type of international activity in which a company may be engaged. Financial requirements and policy may dictate in part the kind of marketing arrangements to be utilized. Inability to find foreign middlemen with adequate financial resources may force a company to establish its own overseas marketing operations, or a company may be compelled to establish an overseas partnership in order to meet local financial ownership requirements or to provide a vehicle for financing foreign distribution.

Marketers have an interest in the financial function because money is a basic tool facilitating marketing activities. Effective financial arrangements significantly strengthen competitive marketing positions. In addition to being concerned with the purely marketing aspects of financing, the marketer must also be aware of his company's financial objectives. He must know about the level of profits required from his operation, the expected balance between long- and short-term profits, and whether corporate policy calls for monies to be repatriated or further invested in the customer countries.

This chapter emphasizes the financial requirements of international marketing; it considers sources of funds, international credit and payment arrangements and mechanics. Considerable attention is paid to methods of minimizing financial risks, but the entire treatment is concerned less with the mechanics of international finance than with th
strategic marketing implications related to financing.

FINANCIAL PLANNING FOR MARKETING

General Approach

Financial planning for international business intertwines inextricably with overall corporate planning, and the decision framework is similar.

Operational questions pertaining to financial requirements and sources are considered later in this chapter; other questions deserving review here pertain to basic policy and to the ultimate question of profits.

Policy Questions   *long T- or short T-?*

Policy questions can never be resolved satisfactorily without consideration of the basic objectives of the firm—more specifically the marketing objectives of the firm. Only when basic objectives are defined is it possible to make decisions relative to ownership, control, timing, and profit. In all instances, financial planning must be developed within the context of host- and parent-country laws and politics. The financial demands of marketing on the parent company depend on the extent to which foreign participation is employed—participation of both financial and operational character. It is obvious that if a foreign partner provides investment, the parent will need to supply less money; less obvious but of greater potential impact are the financial implications of marketing decisions (such as an exclusive distribution agreement with a foreign middleman) which either obligate or relieve the parent company of the extensive costs associated with marketing and distribution.[1]

The locus of financial decision making markedly affects operations, financial requirements, and profit possibilities. Fayerweather suggests that the basic alternatives are a fragmented (decentralized) or a unified (centralized) approach to financial fund flow manipulation. He suggests that,

The fragmentation approach argues for decisions which treat the foreign units as self-contained enterprises dealing with the parent company essentially as independent companies. The unification approach treats them in much the same manner as integrated segments of a domestic company with the financial decisions dominated by overall corporate considerations.[2]

Taxation and host nations typically favor fragmentation, whereas corporate control considerations usually favor unification. Reality, however, demands that financial arrangements blend the two elements so most companies' operations are partially fragmented and partly unified.

Long- versus short-run profit and financial goals also direct the methods of financing marketing operations and, typically, dictate the nature of the marketing program to be utilized. Short-term return of investment suggests minimizing investment, even though doing so might mean higher costs of operations. As examples, consider the exporter versus the international marketer, the situation where facilities are rented rather than owned, the setting of prices to skim the cream and get out rather than penetrate, the use of middlemen rather than the development of a company sales organization. The list can be lengthened ex-

---

[1] See Chapter 13 for information on organizational alternatives and Chapter 22 for perspective on distribution strategy.

[2] John Fayerweather, *International Business Management* (New York: McGraw-Hill Book Co., 1969), p. 152.

tensively, but the implication of short- versus long-run commitment on marketing decisions is obvious.

Political factors may slightly or severely limit the alternatives available for financing international marketing operations. The requirements for foreign ownership have been discussed in the preceding chapter. Governments, both foreign and home country, simultaneously enhance and inhibit policy choices. The U.S. government, for example, has shifted position on encouragement of foreign capital investment several times in recent years.[3] Late in the Johnson administration, U.S. companies were slapped with rather stringent limits on foreign investment and required to repatriate increasing amounts of their foreign profits. The rules were relaxed only a year later under the Nixon administration. Foreign governments may offer loans, free land, tax advantages, or preferential market treatment to induce desirable companies to locate in their country, but on the other hand they may discourage or directly prohibit foreign companies. For example, to gain concessions, the French government long delayed action on a Phillips Petroleum Co. application to build a polyethylene plant. To the later chagrin of the French, the company built in Belgium instead.

Profit Planning

Since profitability typically constitutes the primary measure of success of most business enterprises, profit planning is a vital element of management. International operations afford relatively great opportunities for profit management because of the alternatives related to differing tax rates, levels of operation, investment return, and opportunities for monetary manipulation. The number of alternatives exists proportionally (probably geometrically) to the number of countries, products, and companies (or subsidiaries) involved. Marketing decisions are directly affected by decisions regarding availability of funds for marketing, choice of profit center, cost of money, required rates of return, profit shifting, and opportunity cost factors.

The multinational firm has numerous alternative levels and locations for profit centers. In international operations a profit center is considered to be the location where profits are finally declared in financial statements. Within limits, companies with various subsidiaries operating in different countries have the ability to locate profits wherever they wish by manipulation of costs, prices on intracompany transfers, accounting methods, sale location, inventory levels, and other cost or revenue items. Within the bounds of the law, propriety, and stockholder preference, the ideal profit center is located in such a way that profits are maximized where tax rates are low, exchange convertibility high, and risk minimal.

National policies significantly affect profit management alternatives. Various governments encourage their corporate residents to let profits emerge in their countries by offering various inducements. Liechten-

---

[3] See Jack N. Behrman, "Foreign Investment Muddle: The Perils of Ad Hoccery," *Columbia Journal of World Business*, Fall 1965, pp. 51–59.

BOX 14–1

Five Clubs for Moneymen

The money managers of the non-Communist world meet regularly through a network of five important clublike organizations. The organizations:

The International Monetary Fund is a specialized agency of the United Nations that has 102 member countries, acts as a sort of central bank of the national central banks. The IMF oversees the world's supply and flow of gold and currencies, recommends ways to promote financial stability and serves as a meeting ground for both the prosperous and the developing nations. Armed with $16 billion in gold and currency pledged by its members, the IMF stands ready to grant loans to nations in financial crisis, be it from inflation or balance-of-payments deficits. Its meetings: once a year.

The Paris Club—also known as the Group of Ten—is a blue-ribbon panel of finance ministers and governors of central banks from the IMF's ten leading industrial powers: Belgium, Britain, Canada, France, Germany, Italy, Japan, The Netherlands, Sweden and the U.S. The Ten quietly take on study assignments for the IMF (current study: proposals for a new type of international reserve currency) and, when necessary, supplement IMF loans with their own hard currencies. In the latter case, they contribute quotas under an agreement called the General Arrangements to Borrow, which is known as GAB. Meetings: whenever necessary, usually several times a year.

The Basel Club is a gathering of the central-bank governors from the same ten nations, plus Austria and Switzerland. The club grew out of the regular meetings in Basel of the semigovernment Bank for International Settlements (BIS), which arranges short-term credits for central banks. The central bankers make a three-day weekend of it, gathering two days ahead of the BIS meeting for a round of closed-door talks to inform and advise each other on monetary problems and plans. IMF Managing Director Pierre-Paul Schweitzer calls the exclusive group the "best club in the world." Meetings: once a month in Basel.

Working Party III is a special and highly influential subcommittee of the 21-nation Organization for Economic Cooperation and Development (OECD), an offspring of Western Europe's Marshall Plan cooperation. It is composed of both government officials and central bankers from Europe and the U.S. The subcommittee passes on the credit-worthiness of governments and, in cooperation with the BIS, runs a continual "surveillance" of the international monetary system. Its great power comes from the fact that its decisions are usually accepted by the money-lending nations. Meetings: once every six weeks in Paris.

The Club of Six is a committee of central bankers from the nations belonging to the European Common Market. The Six usually huddles after Basel Club meetings to mesh Common Market banking policies, also joins quarterly with Common Market finance ministers to meet as the Monetary Committee of the Common Market.

Source: Reprinted by permission from TIME, The Weekly Newsmagazine; Copyright Time, Inc., May 14, 1965.

stein, Switzerland, the Bahamas and Panama encourage corporate formation and profit taking by offering low income-tax rates, which encourage location of holding companies or trading subsidiaries in these countries. (Such subsidiaries facilitate control of international operations of the trading of goods among subsidiaries.) Puerto Rico has made great economic strides by offering complete tax freedom for a number of years to new firms. Brazil has a program to encourage economic development in its northeastern sector by permitting companies to reduce their tax bill by 50 percent by investing amounts equal to 50 percent of their tax liability in that area.

Maximum profit opportunities are constantly shifting from country to country and product line to product line. Since return on investment must be planned on the basis of the alternative investment opportunities that are available, the opportunity cost of money is a major consideration. In the decade of the 1950s, for example, returns for European investments were noticeably higher than for U.S. firms; by the mid 1960s Europe had become more competitive, and returns on investment in Europe were about equal to those in the United States. To attain high return rates, marketers are shifting their efforts to the less developed countries.

Market conditions, competition, and other market factors are so often direct determinants of profitability that much of the responsibility for selection of the best profit opportunities depends on the marketer's judgment. Nearly every company that is deeply involved in multinational marketing has a listing of market opportunities arranged in a hierarchy of profitability and based on a series of factors including risk and size of investment. Obviously, major investment decisions will be made at the levels of top management, and officers representing all major functions will be involved. International investment, marketing, and market potentials must always be given highest priority in such a study, but numerous international failures attest to the frequency with which market factors are ignored. In one instance, a huge processing plant was built in an underdeveloped African country to take advantage of cheap labor and good local supplies. The several-million-dollar plant was closed within a year because local markets could not absorb the output and competitors from other countries blocked the products from entering Europe, where the company had expected to market the bulk of its output. International marketing decisions are complex because the unpredictable must be predicted and noncomparables compared.[4]

MONEY AND MONEY SUPPLY

Convertibility, inflation, deflation, exchange restrictions, purchasing power, gold standard, black market, Eurodollars—all these pertain to one of the basic tools of the international marketer, money. One generally thinks of monetary consideration as the primary domain of the

---

[4] Jack Zwick suggests a useful scheme for aiding management in making the investment decision in "Models for Multicountry Investment," *Business Horizons,* Winter 1967, pp. 69–74.

finance man, but any international marketer can attest to the fact that the finance man's concerns are those of the marketer also. Money plays a dominant role not only in terms of the development and living standard of a nation but also in terms of the success or failure of an individual company's marketing efforts. A brief review of some of the basic monetary considerations particularly relevant to the marketer may lend perspective to the entire question of the strategies related to financing international marketing.

National Monetary Goals

Every nation is concerned about the relationship of the value of its money to that of the monies of other countries in the world, and every nation is concerned about the size and growth of its monetary fund. Arthur Burns, former chairman of the President's Council of Economic Advisors, says, "A potentially serious threat to economic stability and freedom comes from international monetary disorders and their attendant repercussions. . . . Without a stable monetary system the problems of maintaining political and economic freedoms are compounded." He continues, "Historically, policies and actions that impede and reduce freedom have received their greatest stimulus as a result either of war or of monetary disorder."[5]

Nations consciously manipulate their monetary relationships to aid in the achievement of national goals. The basic alternatives that interact are the stability of purchasing power of a given money within a country and stable international exchange rates. Typically, these two goals are not consonant but competitive; stable exchange rates may, therefore, be antithetical to stable purchasing power, so a choice often must be made between internal and external goals. The amount of attention given to money in recent years would make one feel that nothing is quite so important as monetary relationships, but as one writer puts it,

In judging the economic progress of nations over long periods, the importance of money should be neither underestimated nor exaggerated. As contrasted with the initiative, inventiveness, and the productivity of the population, money is essentially a passive instrument to facilitate transactions. Over short periods of time, increases or decreases in the quantity of money can profoundly influence the level of output or prices, but over the long run more fundamental forces of productivity and thrift predominate. The monetary system is one of many things that people take for granted while it is working well, but give extraordinary attention to when it malfunctions.[6]

Monetary Aims of International Companies

Generally the monetary objectives of international companies relate to financing of their activities at the lowest possible cost, minimizing risk on international investment, exchanging foreign currencies, main-

---

[5] *Monograph on International Payments and Exchange Rates,* Chamber of Commerce of the United States, p. 1.

[6] Ibid., p. 3.

taining a maximum amount of flexibility in handling their money (including shifting it from country to country freely without exchange losses), and finally, maximizing the competitive marketing benefits to be gained through use of monies.

Not too many years ago, the world money market was heavily dominated by the United States; U.S. citizens and companies provided large amounts of the moneys which were available in the world market and U.S. companies were the dominant borrowers. Increasingly, however, world money markets have become truly international. More sources of funds within both developed and developing countries are available to businessmen, and businessmen from more companies are actively borrowing in international money markets. Japan, for example, is becoming an increasingly active borrower in foreign markets, whereas Germany has become a major supplier of money.

In recent years a new form of highly mobile money has been developed—the Eurodollar. Eurodollars are U.S. dollars on deposit in overseas banks, including foreign branches of U.S. banks. The largest deposits are in London, but there are market centers throughout Europe and also in such out-of-the-way places as Nassau. Banks lend Eurodollars for short periods to finance world trade. To offset tight money, U.S. banks borrow Eurodollars from their foreign branches. Because of U.S. controls on the export of dollars, borrowers, especially the offshoots of American companies, also float long-term Eurodollar bond issues (called Eurobonds) in Europe. As indicated in Exhibit 14–1, the cost of money does differ in varying markets, and international firms have the choice of operating in many money markets.

Such differences present significant challenges to international financial officers, and management of international funds is a major activity for international firms. Some of the factors pertaining to minimizing risk and exchange convertibility are discussed elsewhere in this chapter, but the use of liquid corporate funds is one other factor which should be mentioned. Many companies actually make more profit through skillful manipulation of their uncommitted funds than they do through international operations. These profits come directly from foreign investments, short-term investments, future trading, and revaluation. Because these are not marketing activities, they will not be considered further here, but the marketing benefits to be gained through effective money management should be briefly reviewed.

Simply by having adequate monetary resources at his disposal, the marketing manager can effect greater profits by lowering his costs or by increasing sales volume. Adequate inventories can be maintained if funds are available—a critical variable in international business where restocking might take months. The business with plentiful purchasing power can usually buy merchandise more cheaply by buying directly or in quantity, or have a wider range of sources by being able to pay in cash. Plentiful money can permit a marketer to build the marketing channels which will be most effective for his firm—regardless of cost. Furthermore, advertising can be treated as a capital expenditure only if adequate funds are available. Ability to finance customer purchases is

EXHIBIT 14–1

National Interest Rates and International Differentials
(end of 1960–end of June 1969)

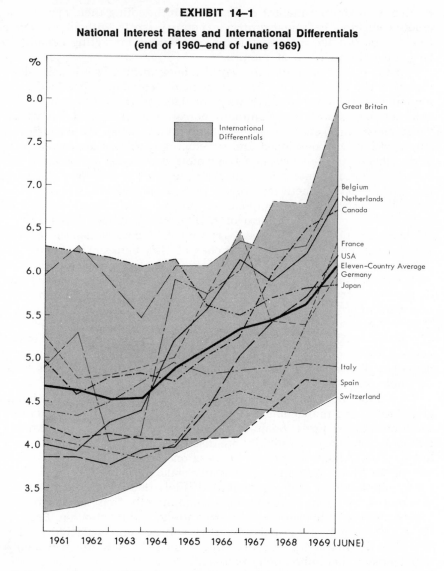

another business-building competitive activity often denied to under-financed companies. Many other marketing arguments for having adequate money can be advanced, but the above should suffice for illustrative purposes.

FINANCIAL REQUIREMENTS FOR INTERNATIONAL MARKETING

Working Capital

Distance and time lags are the chief elements differentiating the problems of financing international marketing activities from those re-

BOX 14–2

The World's Money: Some Representative Exchange Rates per U.S. Dollar

Dollar		*Peso*	
Australia	1.1198	Argentina	.0029
Bahamas	.9823	Bolivia	.085
Canada	.9245	Colombia	.0620
Ethiopia	.40	Mexico	.0801
Hong Kong	.1755	Philippines	.2570
Singapore	.3300		

Deutsche Mark		*Pound*	
Germany (West)	.2518	Egypt	2.31
		Israel	.34
		Jamaica	2.8045
		Nigeria	2.8155
Franc		Turkey	.1111
Belgium	.02015	United Kingdom	2.7995
France	.2030		
Guinea	.0041		
Malagasy	.0041		
Senegal	.0041	*Rupee*	
Switzerland	.2317	India	.1334
Tahiti	.0113		

Krone		*Shilling*	
Denmark	.1448	Kenya	.1402

Lira		*Yen*	
Italy	.00161	Japan	.002765

Source: Bank quotations, 1970.

lated to domestic marketing. Government involvement, through tariffs, taxes, financial participation requirements, exchange restrictions, and fluctuating monetary values, further complicates the financial picture.

Effective management of the financial functions of marketing can be a strategic factor not only affecting profit but possibly having great impact on the company's ability to develop marketing channels. Furthermore, marketing credit can help to expand primary demand by putting products within the financial reach of ever-greater portions of the population.

The time lags caused by distance and crossing international borders add cost elements to international marketing. Time lags may develop from many causes but are especially evident in export operations. Even in a relatively simple transaction, money may be tied up for months while goods are being shipped from one part of the world to another; then customs clearance may add days, weeks, or months; payment then may be held up while the international payment documents are being transferred from one nation to another; and breakage, commercial dispute, or governmental restrictions may add still further delay.

Cash flow planning becomes especially important in international marketing because of the kinds of delays encountered. Companies entering international business without adequate cash flow planning may find their business profitable but learn that the profit is all on the books and that the slower cash flow of the international operation demands significant injections of funds to maintain cash position. Communications difficulties also emphasize the need for effective cash planning.

In domestic markets, progress (incremental) payments may be received for a product which is in the process of custom development or for which there is a long production process. Such terms may be available in international contracts, but rather typically the manufacturer or developer of such goods for foreign customers must wait until the products are actually produced and delivered before he can receive even partial payment. Nearly every international transaction encounters some kind of time lag during which the marketing financing must be provided. Even when a company is dealing with its own subsidiaries or branches in overseas operations, financial time lags exist.

International marketing activities require financing for (1) working capital, (2) inventory, (3) accounts receivable for local channels of distribution, (4) consumer credit, (5) development of production facilities, and (6) accommodation of merchandise adjustments which may be required.

Overhead.   Because of time lags, shipping costs, duties, and other expenses, foreign operations typically require larger amounts of working capital than domestic activities operating at the same volume levels. Overhead costs for expansion into a foreign market are likely to be considerably greater than for expansion into an additional domestic market. Travel costs alone rapidly consume working capital funds. In one instance, a U.S. firm discovered that it was spending more on travel than on salaries. According to Lurie estimated per diem expense (not including transportation) may be expected to run about $30 in Central America and most of Western Europe: $35 in most of South America, Australia, Scandinavia, the Far East, the Caribbean, Mexico, and the Middle East; $45 in Africa; and $50 in Venezuela and France.[7]

The time lags mentioned above tie up great amounts of working capital so that the turnover of working capital and the cash flow rate are generally considerably slower than in domestic operations. Even the costs of communicating and maintaining a control system are higher in international operations. Marketing overhead costs can be kept under control through careful and creative management. One company, for example, was using a U.S. advertising agency for its extensive European publicity activities. By shifting to a French agency it was able to save thousands of dollars in travel, telephone, wages, and other overhead costs associated with this function. Marketers can effect savings on overhead activities in all marketing functions through alert cost management.

Start-up costs provide the additional working capital requirement for

---

[7] Richard Lurie, *Passports and Profits* (New York: Doubleday 1964).

the company that is entering new international markets. Such costs may come as a surprise to the firm accustomed to operating in a familiar domestic market, the company must pay for information which might be assumed or acquired without cost in the home country. Start-up costs also include the legal and incorporation costs, establishment of an office, purchase of licenses and so forth. Sometimes start-up costs also include payments to governments or government officials for the opportunity to do business in a country. Marketing research may loom as a major expense, particularly when a company has to research three or four countries before embarking on a business enterprise in any one of them. Start-up costs are generally not recoverable even if the business does not succeed; they are lost even if the business is not started, so they must be viewed as sunk costs.

Inventory. Adequate servicing of overseas markets may require goods to be inventoried in several locations. The marketer's effectiveness in managing inventories can have considerable effect on the financial requirements of this function. One company which handles all U.S. distributors from two factory warehouses found that it needed six foreign distribution points to maintain a reasonable delivery schedule. The six warehouses together handled less merchandise than either of the U.S. outlets. Slow transportation forces maintenance of relatively larger inventories than in domestic situations where fast transportation can rapidly replenish local inventories. Even political factors may influence inventory levels. Some countries have such severe currency controls that it is almost impossible to maintain adequate inventory levels or reasonable supplies of spare parts. In quite another instance a pesticide manufacturer laid in a two-year inventory of one of its products because the Mexican government had notified it that the border would be closed to the product after three months' notice. Several years elapsed with no notice, but the company, to stay in the market as long as possible, was compelled to invest several hundred thousand dollars in surplus inventory.

Channel and Consumer Credit. Later in this chapter, credit will be discussed as a competitive weapon, but it should be mentioned here also in the context of working capital requirements. Both channel credit and consumer credit may make extreme demands on company resources. In many countries, no institutional sources are available for handling consumer credit, so the manufacturer or the distributing firm must provide the credit. Such credit extensions become hazardous in markets with rapid inflation because customers tend to delay payment of debts as long as possible so as to pay them off in deflated currencies. In some countries long credit terms are customary, so the manufacturer may find himself in the position of handling relatively long-term loans and may face a normal 45- to 60-day turnaround on consumer credit. Similar or more extended requirements exist for industrial products.

Channel credit requirements have surprised many American firms. Most of the world's middlemen are dreadfully underfinanced, and if they are to buy goods in economical quantities, interim credit must be provided by the producers. A recent study by the National Industrial

Conference Board quotes some international businessmen. The vice president and general manager of a drug company's international division says,

Increased sales volume by our foreign production units will require fresh capital in proportion to their sales increases. By fresh capital we mean short- and long-term bank loans, overseas debenture issues to some extent, and internally generated funds (i.e., retained earnings). To date, our prime source of fresh capital has been retained earnings; however, because of the U.S. balance-of-payments requirements requiring us to remit a greater proportion of our earnings than heretofore, we will undoubtedly rely more and more on outside capital.[8]

In the same study, the international finance director of a machinery and equipment company says he expects increasing foreign sales volume to require additional working capital to "support from 50% to 75% of the sales increase," with "most of the funds to be supplied by the commercial banking systems of the host countries." The general manager of an apparel firm's international division notes that "Very substantial amounts of fresh capital (particularly medium-term working capital) will be required to support our international growth over the next three years."[9]

Capital Investment

In some instances markets are closed to foreign businesses unless they produce the goods locally. The French government, for example, has given notice to Ford that if it expects to keep its large volume of sales in France, it should be producing there. Ford has prudently agreed to build its next European plant there. In such cases the production facility itself is a crucial element to market entry. In such circumstances the production facility itself may be considered part of the marketing system because market requirements alone dictated the expenditure of funds for the product's facility. Without market restrictions, the production could be accomplished in existing facilities without added production facility investment. In considering financial implications, therefore, the cost of the production facility may logically be related to marketing as a cost of market entry. Often a more extensive production facility may be required in a foreign country than is required in the United States because of a lack of suitable subcontractors and suppliers of component parts. The firm may be required to produce goods abroad that it would normally purchase.

Capital investment requirements for marketing facilities per se are rather obvious; warehouses, shipping docks, retail stores, sales offices, and the like all require significant capital investment in physical facilities. A capital investment commitment may also be necessary for investment in middlemen or establishment of a company sales force. These

---

[8] *Outlook for Overseas Production* (New York: National Industrial Conference Board, 1969), p. 23.

[9] Ibid.

perhaps can be most appropriately considered, however, as market penetration investments.

Market Penetration Investment

It is difficult to classify market penetration investment, since it can be thought of as a capital investment or a current expenditure. In accounting terms, most marketing penetration investment is considered current expenditure; from a planning standpoint, investments in promotion, building of channels, and manpower actually represent a long-term investment of a sunk-cost nature. Companies which do not maintain any production or inventory facilities overseas may still have a very large investment in attempting market penetration.

The costs associated with promotion and advertising are rather obvious and basically parallel the kind of expenditures necessary to open new markets in the United States. One difference, however, is that the cost of promotion may be greater in foreign markets, relative to anticipated sales. Markets are smaller, media may be more expensive, multiple media may be required, and other similar factors push the investment up.

It is never inexpensive to establish a channel of distribution, but here again the problems of international distribution may require extra-large channel investments. Foreign middlemen are seldom adequately financed and may require extensive long-term credit if they are to carry adequate inventories and offer their customers adequate credit. The American firm may find its competitive position is weaker in world markets than in domestic markets because so many more competitors are vying for customers in certain product lines. One U.S. company which marketed insecticides in Spain through seven local distributors found that within a period of less than three years, six of these distributors had been purchased, or partially purchased, by competitive firms, thus completely blocking the initial supplier's distribution. The firms were German, Italian, French, Belgian, and American. In some markets, such as Spain, the same company finds that it must compete both with companies which have their own distribution subsidiaries and with firms which have interest in other agricultural chemical distributors. The company found similar situations in Latin America, South Africa, Australia, and southern Europe. To maintain a competitive position the company in question was virtually forced to make major investments in buying various distributors throughout the world; many of these ventures are profitable but, nonetheless, huge amounts of funds have been required to maintain market position.

One company operating in Nicaragua was squeezed out of the market entirely within a two-year period because competitive firms had purchased all of the outlets. In that instance the company cooperated with some other noncompetitive suppliers and organized a distribution company which was foreign owned but financed largely by the supplier companies. In this case the company invested only $50,000 and has been rewarded by annual sales generating approximately $40,000 per year net return on investment. Some companies utilizing similar arrangements have discovered that they cannot always buy partial control and expect to dominate the channel; companies have purchased 10, 15, 20 percent equity in a distribution company and still found it to be handling competing products.

Manufacturers of durable goods have found that they often must provide funds for service facilities before their products will be accepted. Japanese automakers met with little success in the United States until they learned this fact and provided funds for adequate service facilities and expanded inventories.

Cost of training, relocation, and downtime add considerably to the manpower investment necessary to open new markets. If foreign personnel are to be used, a company incurs large financial obligations for recruitment, selection, training, and development of the foreign field force. Exhibit 14–2 shows how long it may take to bring foreign man-

EXHIBIT 14–2

The Cost of Developing a Foreign Sales Force

| Year | Sales* (in MM/$U.S.) | Number of Personnel with Expenses Paid By | | | | % Paid from Local Markup |
		New York	Commis-sion	Local Markup	Total	
1963	.04	1½	9	0	1½	0
1964	.7	2	0	0	2	0
1965	1.5	3	2	2	7	28
1966	6.6	4	7	5	16	32
1967	9.6	6	12	10	28	36
1968	15.3	10	20	25	55	45
1969	17.0	15	25	43	83	52
1970 (est.)	19.0	13	27	57	97	60

* Actual data—company name confidential.

power to the point where its cost is no longer a drain on the company. In this instance the company is growing, sales are growing, the number of men required is growing, but note that in eight years of operation the company is still subsidizing some 15 percent of its manpower directly from the New York office and that commissions are not adequate to cover manpower costs.

In some instances companies have contributed directly to the cost of road facilities and distribution centers, invested in radio and television stations to be assured of high-quality coverage, and made other such investments designed to upgrade the very basic marketing infrastructure of the countries in which they are doing business. As foreign distribution systems grow, the financing of a nation's marketing infrastructure is less likely to fall on individual companies.

CREDIT: A COMPETITIVE WEAPON

Credit and payment terms have become major weapons of international competition in the global marketplace. U.S. business historically has been reluctant to offer advantageous credit terms in foreign markets, but strong domestic markets and product preference internationally permitted U.S. businessmen to thrive despite the lack of credit. That such conditions no longer prevail is expressed often in the U.S. Department of Commerce's overseas business reports. For example,

Extended credit terms are an important factor in selling to [in this case] Iran. Moderate-size foreign exchange reserve and the willingness of West German, British, and Japanese firms to offer favorable credit terms will increasingly put U.S. businesses at a disadvantage in the market unless they can make available comparable terms of payment.

Despite such statements, one cannot charge that American business has been blind to the requirements of credit. Consider the following statements:

Credit is becoming as important to making an export sale as the price of a product. . . . In the last three years our exports accounts receivable have risen 21 percent faster than the growth in total foreign sales.

We carry our own paper on export sales, and I think this is true of most big companies these days.

Until a year ago we were selling open account overseas only to our own distributors; now we're selling nearly half our export volume that way, and it's working out well.

We now sell on open account in Scandinavia, Germany, France, and Israel; and we're lengthening the terms in other countries. For instance, we're giving up to 120 days in Italy now compared with payment on delivery a few years ago.

From the base of the world's richest nation, American businessmen should be able to outstrip all competitors on the availability of credit—once they decide it is necessary.

Channel Credit

Accounts receivable financing may impose great strains on international working capital. Both middlemen and industrial customers have learned that they are in a position to pressure manufacturers into continuously longer and longer credit extension because credit terms are becoming an increasingly important marketing weapon in the battle for competitive position in international markets. American suppliers are discovering that their marketing and product advantages are being offset by more advantageous financial terms from competing foreign suppliers. To get goods into the channel of distribution, marketers may have to compensate for the middlemen's lack of capital by providing consignment merchandise, floor-plan financing, or long-term credit. Without such financial assistance, most foreign middlemen can't handle

BOX 14–3

Market Entry via Credit

Ingersoll Rand, whose sales of heavy drilling rigs suffered for several years from Swedish competition of so-called light equipment, mounted a special attack that has given excellent results. When the Brokke tunnel (one of Norway's biggest, in the upper part of Setesdalen and ending at Kristiansand in southern Norway) was to be built, the U.S. company persuaded one of the contractors to try out an Ingersoll drilling rig. To convince the rather sceptical contractor, Betongbygg A/S of Kristiansand, Ingersoll worked out a favorable lease-installment-purchase package that was hard to resist.

Betongbygg started the rig, and found that it worked faster than any equipment previously used for drilling in the country (as an added bonus, explosives could be used more economically, leaving the tunnel face cleaner).

After the Brokke trial, several other Norwegian contractors in quick succession purchased the Ingersoll rigs, and Betongbygg (now the country's largest contracting firm) put the machine to use at one of Europe's biggest power projects, the Sira-Kvina plant. Vested with the prestige of successful use in Norway, the Brokke trial has had repercussion on Ingersoll's sales as far away as India.

Source: Reprinted with permission from *Business Europe,* Geneva, July 5, 1967, p. 211.

adequate inventories. In some instances, adequate channels do not even exist, and it may be necessary to help the middleman finance his own operation before market segments can be tapped. Industrial marketers often find that they are called upon to extend medium- to long-term credit in situations where they would not have offered credit at all a few years earlier. Sophisticated marketers often find themselves arranging five- to seven-year payout programs for foreign customers of capital equipment.

Consumer Credit

The world's consumers have learned since World War II that credit helps them bridge the gap between their consumption aspirations and their income. By the early 1960s many American businesmen realized that they had to offer credit to *middlemen* if they were to be successful in competing with foreign countries. By the end of the decade, the companies had begun to learn that they had to go further and offer consumer credit as well. Such credit extension is risky and ties up much capital, but it is not necessarily without profit. In Latin America consumer credit may carry interest rates of 2 or even 3 percent per month. In countries with fairly stable economies, such rates provide significant profit opportunities. In countries like Brazil, however, the chronically high rate of inflation may wipe out credit profits completely.

Whenever possible, manufacturers should probably avoid consumer credit extensions as part of their basic merchandising program. If consumer credit looms as a profitable field it should be appraised as such and handled through an entirely separate company formed specifically for such a purpose.

International Credit Management

The credit policies of individual firms doing business in foreign markets have direct relevance to the success of foreign marketing operations. Even if the credit assistance offered by the government is inadequate, the marketer can capitalize on credit as a competitive weapon by creatively managing that function of marketing. It is hard to imagine that marketers whose expenditures are supported by capital-rich countries such as the United States cannot manage their resources in a manner which will strengthen the marketing effort. Customer credit is, in the final analysis, subject to the policies established by individual companies. The foreign marketer's role in setting and managing credit policies and credit operations should not be minimized.

Credit Policies

Probably no country in the world has as highly developed a credit system as the United States; yet U.S. businessmen reverse their orientation entirely in dealing in the international market. Certainly no businessman wants to give away his profit through unpaid bills, uncollectible instruments, or exchange-rate losses; nevertheless, businessmen in many trading countries, such as Britain, have long ago learned that the principles of international credit are basically no different from those of domestic credit.

Doing business internationally requires an acquaintance with a larger variety of documents and imposes some problems in seeking credit information, but the well-informed businessman finds that he needs take only a little extra care in his international transactions. Credit policies certainly must be flexible enough to accommodate the widely varying situations encountered in international trade. Effective marketing credit management, for example, might dictate that when profit margins and gross margins are particularly narrow, vendors cannot extend credit as liberally as when they have wide margins. As a matter of policy, every international businessman should expect to rely on either internal or external experts who specialize in international credit and payment arrangements.

Credit Information

Credit information for international accounts becomes increasingly better and more available each year. Credit information is available from a number of basic sources. Some of these are as follows: (1) World Trade Directory Reports, a service of the U.S. Department of Commerce, are reports based on information gathered by foreign service officers.

BOX 14–4

Italy: Butterflies in the Boom

Italy's sensational consumer economy has soared to new heights—but Italian bankers and economists worry that it has risen on the wings of butterflies. "Butterflies" is the Italian nickname for *cambiali,* the instant-credit promissory notes that flit from one holder to another through Italy's credit-happy economy. No one knows for sure the exact value of the *cambiali* now in circulation in Italy, but knowledgeable bankers estimate that their worth may equal the total value of Italy's currency.

The *cambiali* look like ordinary U.S. bank checks—but the resemblance ends there. In Italy's consumer boom, the buyer of a refrigerator or bedroom set signs a promissory note for each monthly installment. He thus may sign as many as 48 *cambiali* for one TV set or refrigerator. The merchant who sells him the goods uses the *cambiali* to pay his own bills, just as if they were currency, and his supplier or landlord in turn uses them to pay off his debts. The notes may pass through 20 or more hands before they finally roost in a bank for collection. If the bank—which makes its profit on *cambiali* by discounting them by 2% to 12%—has trouble collecting from the original signer, it applies a dreaded remedy. Unless the delinquent pays up, the bank publishes his name in the Bollettino dei Protesti, a kind of debtors' *Who's Who,* and also begins court proceedings to recover the loss.

What bothers the Italian financial community is that so many of the *cambiali* end up in the collector's hánds. By signing the *cambiali* with abandon to finance everything from furs to apartments, thousands upon thousands of Italians have run up staggering debts. Nearly every day the Italian press discovers another case of someone obligated to pay out more monthly on *cambiali* than he actually earns.

Source: Courtesy *Time;* Copyright Time Inc., 1963.

Credit check reports on one foreign firm are provided to businesses for a nominal fee. (2) The international division of Dun and Bradstreet, Inc., is rapidly becoming a major source of information on customers abroad. Most major industrial countries have credit information companies similar to Dun and Bradstreet which can be consulted; but most firms find it more convenient to work with the more familiar local company. (3) The Foreign Credit Interchange Bureau is an arm of the National Association of Credit Men and provides credit information based on the credit experiences of other members. (4) Some American banks maintain credit files on overseas firms as part of their total financial service.

Few American firms run credit checks on international customers when the transactions are arranged on a cash basis, but such a practice is justifiable. The difficulty of agreeing on disputed goods or the problem of returning unaccepted goods shows the wisdom of checking on the general reliability of the overseas customer; a credit check provides such information.

RISK MANAGEMENT

The same types of business or commercial risks encountered in domestic business are also encountered internationally, and all can be reduced by an effective risk-management program. Problems of insolvency, protracted default, or refusal to pay bills are familiar. Less familiar, however, are those related primarily to international business, such as the political risk, exchange-rate fluctuation risk, and exchange availability risk.

International and domestic risks share many similarities. As with other kinds of risks, international risk can either be avoided or assumed or shifted to third parties. Various techniques are available for accomplishing each of those goals.

Until the institution of the Foreign Credit Insurance Association (FCIA) under Eximbank in 1962, American businessmen operated at a disadvantage regarding international credit insurance. Nearly every trading nation except the United States had a well-established export credit system. Some of the features of the various systems are shown in Exhibit 14–3, which covers only a few of the countries. Prior to the development of the FCIA program, U.S. companies fairly often diverted business to Canadian or European operations, where they could work under credit insurance terms. Many times when this was not possible American firms were faced with the problem of losing business or taking on excessive risk. Now that the United States has a workable credit insurance system, other trading countries have been active in revising their rates and coverage to provide even more advantageous terms for their own exporters.

Although the Agency for International Development (AID) program has a credit insurance feature, the bulk of the insured international business undertaken by U.S. firms is covered by the program of the Foreign Credit Insurance Association. This is a group of over 75 American marine, casualty, and property insurance companies which cooperate with the Export-Import Bank in providing protection for both commercial and political risks. The commercial risks covered are essentially those normal credit risks encountered in day-to-day business. The political risk provisions relate to the problems of war or revolution, currency inconvertibility, and cancellation or restriction of import licenses. These and other similar political actions are beyond the control of both the buyer and the seller.

Another type of risk encountered by the international marketer is related to the problems of financial adjustments. Such risk is encountered when there is controversy about the quality of goods which have been delivered (but not accepted), or a dispute over contract terms, or some other type of disagreement over which payment is withheld. One company, for example, shipped several hundred tons of dehydrated potatoes to a distributor in Germany. The distributor tested the shipment and declared it to be below acceptable taste and texture standards (which had not been explicitly established). The exporter was faced with the alternatives of reducing the price, reselling the potatoes, or shipping them home again. Each alternative involved considerable cost.

EXHIBIT 14–3

Representative Export Credit Insurance Systems

		Belgium	Canada
ADMINISTERED BY	1.	Office National Du Ducroire (O.N.D.), an autonomous government owned corporation.	Export Credits Insurance Corp. (ECIC), an autonomous government owned corporation.
	2.	Cie. Belge D'Assurance Credit, a private organization owned by banks and insurance companies. Covers only Western Europe—commercial risks for own account; political risks, as agents for (1); and separate policies.	
ELIGIBILITY CRITERIA	1.	Who Eligible: Any enterprise with main office or operations in Belgium. Exporter may transfer policy to his financing institution. What Eligible: All goods and services, including contract work abroad, consulting and advisory services, consignment stocks.	Who Eligible: Resident persons or corporations carrying on business in Canada. Local sales by foreign subsidiaries of Canadian companies, when goods exported from Canada by policyholder, may be covered against risk of non-payment by buyers in the country where subsidiary operates. What Eligible: Consumer and capital goods (including consignments for exhibits), technical, etc., services, exported from Canada and wholly or predominantly Canadian origin.
	2.	Who Eligible: Any Belgian firm; also any foreign firm not domiciled in country of another export credit insurer. What Eligible: All types of exports, except diamonds and furs.	
MAIN TYPES OF POLICIES	1.	Specific—political risks only on (a) individual contracts, or (b) all short-term sales to individual country. Global, or "overall arrangement"—combined commercial and political risk cover when all or approved portion of credit sales offered. No cover for commercial risks alone.	Contracts policy covers from receipt of order; shipments policy from shipment date. Whole turnover policy covers all short-term credits to insurable markets (U.S. excluded, as private cover available). Exceptionally, other reasonable exclusions permitted. Specific policy covers medium term (capital goods) credits, and services.
	2.	Global—all or approved portion of credit sales, short term. Specific, medium term. Cover provided for commercial risks only, or combined commercial and political risk—latter under separate policy as agent for (1).	
PRINCIPAL RISKS COVERED	1.	Before Shipment: a) Private debtors: insolvency, not simple default; political occurrences or measures in buyer's country. b) Public debtors: non-fulfillment, plus political occurrences in buyer's country. After Shipment: a) Private debtors: comprehensive commercial and political as above. This comprehensive cover available only under "global" or "overall arrangement" policy. b) Public Debtors: protracted default due to buyer's delinquency or due to political measures abroad.	Before and/or after shipment—combined commercial and political risk covers: Insolvency, protracted default, exchange blockage or transfer delay; war, revolution, etc.; cancellation of import license; imposition of new restrictions; added handling, etc., charges due to interruption or diversion of voyage outside Canada and continental U.S. and which are due by buyer but impracticable to recover; any other cause of loss beyond control of both exporter and buyer and not otherwise insurable.
	2.	Pre- and Post-Shipment: For own account—insolvency, protracted default. As agent for (1), political risks as above under separate policy.	
PERCENT OF COVERAGE	1.	Generally 75% on commercial risks, private debtors. To 80% on delayed payment and transfer risks, public debtors. To 85% political risks, private debtors. To 90% political risks under global (whole turnover) policy.	To 85% of loss—insurance to exporters. To 80% of contract price (or 100% of financed portion)—direct guarantees to banks financing capital goods exports of minimum unit value approximately $250,000 and minimum payment term 2 years. Guarantees are unconditional and cover financed portion (maximum 80%) of total contract price. Effective only after delivery, the exporter normally being covered under his own policy during pre-delivery period.
	2.	Normally to 80% on commercial risks, (to 85% in Benelux countries); same as (1) above for political risks.	
PREMIUM RATES	1.	According to risk. Rates for c.a.d. transactions, after shipment are: Political risks alone 0.2 to 1%. Commercial and political—private debtor 0.3 to 1.3%. Longer terms to 5%.	According to risk. No published schedule. Average on all business (mostly short-term) since inception is approximately 1%.
	2.	According to risk—no published schedule.	

Source: R. Gerald Fox, "The Business of Financing Exports," *Bankers Monthly, National Magazine of Banking & Investments*, June 15, 1963, pp. 14–15. Reprinted by permission.

EXHIBIT 14–3 (continued)

	West Germany	*Japan*
ADMINISTERED BY	A syndicate consisting of Hermes Kreditversicherungs, A.G. and Deutsche Revisions—und—Treuhand A.G., private insurance companies, as agents for the government. Only Hermes has contact with the public. Treuhand advises on transactions involving governments, etc. Power to make decisions is vested in an Interministerial committee assisted by an advisory board.	Export Insurance Section, International Trade Bureau, Ministry of International Trade & Industry (MITI). Section of a government department.
ELIGIBILITY CRITERIA	Who Eligible: Exporters domiciled in Federal Republic of Germany. What Eligible: Sales and consignments of all types of goods and services of German origin, also including goods of foreign origin sold to third countries by traders domiciled in Germany.	Who Eligible: Any resident exporter. What Eligible: Goods or services produced, processed or assembled in Japan.
MAIN TYPES OF POLICIES	Individual policies are available for: (a) single transactions, (b) transactions with the same buyer, and (c) with several buyers in one or more countries. Global policies are available for all credit sales to all or to approved group of buyers. Special policies, for transfer and conversion risks only, may cover single or recurring transactions. Both short-term and medium-term credits are insured.	1. General export (specific), covering political, catastrophe and other non-commercial risks from fifth day after insurance contract date. 2. General export (global), covering same risks as (1) above, from insurance contract date. 3. Export proceeds (specific), covering same risks as (1) above, from shipment date on medium term credits for capital goods and services. 4. Export bill (specific), covering direct unconditional guarantees to banks negotiating related documentary bills.
PRINCIPAL RISKS COVERED	Before, and/or after shipment: Private debtors: Insolvency, but not simple default; transfer delay, suspension of payments, and other non-commercial risks. Public debtors: Same except protracted default is then also covered as a "political risk." Pre-shipment risk on made-to-order capital goods; also services, construction and consignment contracts, etc., are covered for both private and public debtors.	Insolvency, protracted default; war, revolution, civil war; exchange transfer delay; new import-export restrictions; any other cause of loss beyond control of exporter or importer occurring outside Japan.
PERCENT OF COVERAGE	To 70% of invoice value for commercial risks. To 80% for conversion, transfer and other non-commercial risks. To 80% of production cost (or, for export merchants, of purchase price) on pre-shipment risks.	Respectively, as to 4 types of policy (see above): 1. To 90%. 2. Consumer goods, 90% of loss, with maximum liability 30% of contract price; capital goods, 90% of loss—maximum liability 80% of contract price. 3. To 90%. 4. To 80% of bill amount.
PREMIUM RATES	Pre-shipment risk, 1% of amount guaranteed. Commercial risk, private buyers c.o.d. terms—0.75%. Deferred payment terms, basic rate 1.5% plus 0.1% of credit outstanding for each month beyond 6 months. Public Buyers: Basic rate graduated according to face value of policy, ranging from 1% to 0.5%, plus 0.05% per month on credit actually outstanding for terms to 2 years.	1. 0.472% for 8 months; 0.062% for each added 4 months. 2. Consumer goods—0.0665% for 12 months; capital goods 0.0665% for 18 months. 3. Standard rate—0.294% for first 3 months, 0.07% for each added 3 months. 4. Approximate average 0.56%.

	United Kingdom	*United States*
ADMINISTERED BY	Export Credits Guarantee Dept. (ECGD), a government department directly responsible to the President of the Board of Trade. An Advisory Council represents commercial insurance, banking and industry. Consultative body which advises on commercial risks involving large amounts, unusual accounts, etc.	1. Export-Import Bank of Washington, a government-owned, lending and guarantee institution. 2. Foreign Credit Insurance Association (FCIA), an unincorporated association of commercial insurance companies, insuring 50% of commercial credit risks for own account and administering insurance of remaining 50% of commercial risks and 100% of political risks for account of EximBank.

EXHIBIT 14–3 (concluded)

	United Kingdom	*United States*
ELIGIBILITY CRITERIA	Who Eligible: Exporters resident in U.K. and in some cases, their overseas subsidiaries and others; banks, etc. financing exports. What Eligible: All exportable goods and services, including merchanting transactions overseas, processing operations abroad, stocks held overseas, trade fair participation, market penetration costs and the like.	Who Eligible: 1. Banks and others financing medium-term credits without recourse to exporters. 1 and 2 Exporter: Any U.S. exporter. What Eligible: 1. Goods and services of U.S. origin and manufacture, not destined for military use. 2. Legally exportable goods produced or manufactured in the U.S. shipped to approved buyers in friendly foreign countries.
MAIN TYPES OF POLICIES	Comprehensive policy covers all or approved portion of credit sales—short-term, or may include medium-term for certain products to regular buyers on terms to 5 years. Specific policy covers capital goods not open to whole turnover cover, overseas plant installation work, and services. All policies cover combined commercial and political risks, either from contract or shipment date.	1. Medium-term only; single or repetitive sales to specific buyers: (*a*) Direct guarantees to banks and others financing without recourse to exporter—political risk only for earlier maturities; combined political and commercial risk for later maturities. (*b*) Direct guarantee to exporter when exporter unable to arrange private non-recourse financing —combined commercial and political risk cover. 2. (*a*) Short-term (to 180 days, exceptionally to 1 year): To exporter declaring all sales to eligible markets, with option to exclude Canada and irrevocable Letter of Credit sales; combined commercial and political risk cover or political risk only. (*b*) Medium-term (181 days to 5 years—capital goods) single transaction or repetitive sales to same buyer—case by case—comprehensive or political risks only.
PRINCIPAL RISKS COVERED	Combined commercial and political risk cover. After Shipment: Insolvency; protracted default; buyer's failure or refusal to accept goods; exchange transfer, war, revolution, cancellation of import permit, and other non-commercial risks beyond control of exporter or buyer: Confiscation of or prohibition to re-export consignment stocks abroad. Any other cause of loss, occurring outside U.K., beyond control of exporter or buyer, and not normally insurable with commercial insurers. Before Shipment: All above risks, also cancellation or non-renewal of U.K. export license, or imposition of new export licensing restrictions.	Before Delivery: 1. Guarantees to non-recourse financing institutions. 2. To Exporters: Combined commercial and political cover from date of shipment or of sales contract. After Shipment: 2. To Exporters: Combined commercial and political cover from shipment date. After Acceptance: 1. Guarantees to banks and others: Political risks only for early maturities; combined commercial and political cover for all later instalments; to exporters—combined commercial and political cover for all instalments. Note: (1) and (2) include, as political risks, loss due to: Inability to legally convert to dollars and transfer to U.S., law preventing importation, cancellation of an import permit, revolution, expropriation or confiscation, added costs incurred through interruption or diversion of voyage due to political causes. Commercial risks include insolvency and protracted default.
PERCENT OF COVERAGE	To 85% against insolvency, protracted default, etc. (commercial). 90% to 95% against exchange transfer and other causes. To banks, on medium-term credits £100,-000 and over—90% of defaulted payment, exporter bearing 10% of risk. Financing guarantees for long-term foreign projects—full guarantee to lender, with exporter carrying "initial payment" and "completion payment" portions of contract.	1. Medium-term guarantees (buyer required to pay, in cash, minimum 10%, in some countries 20%, of invoice value by delivery date) exporter must retain at own risk minimum 15% of remaining credit portion: (*a*) to banks and others —85% of credit portion (i.e., to 100% of amount financed); (*b*) to exporters—to 85% of credit portion. 2. Short-term: commercial risks 85%, political risks 95%. Medium-term 85% of all risks.
PREMIUM RATES	Short-term: Average just over 0.3%; Small Exporter policy, flat 0.75%. Medium-term: Correspondingly higher; may run between 3% and 10% of contract price for a 5 year instalment credit. When direct bank guarantee added to exporter's policy, flat charge of approximately 0.75% added.	Variable, according to market and to duration and type of payment terms. Rate schedules not published.

BOX 14–5

Buying the Good Life on Easy Terms

New Tool. Credit always has been important to Mexico's myriad small retailers, down to the peddlers—called aboneros—who sell watches and radios to rural Mexicans, then tramp the countryside each month to collect installment payments.

But it remained for Sears, Roebuck & Co. to introduce to Mexico—in 1947—the concept of credit as a mass merchandising tool. "People warned us that this wasn't wise," says Norvell E. Surbaugh, president of Sears, Roebuck de Mexico, "but our collection experience here has been just as good as it is in Chicago."

Now most of the major department stores issue their own credit cards, and independent distributors of hard-goods stress easy terms.

Says Neil J. Morrow, marketing director of Singer Mexicana: "Some 80% of our business is credit. We have to give credit terms of two years or more to generate the volume we require." Around 60% of Sears' Mexican sales are on credit—"about the same as in the States," says an executive—while at Palacio de Hierro, an upper-crusty department store that launched its own card in 1958, credit accounts for 65% of sales.

With credit getting so important so fast, smaller retailers have been quick to get in on the card schemes just introduced by Mexico's two biggest banks. Banco Nacional, which claims 90,000 card holders after a year of trial operations, says its card is accepted by 10,500 businesses in 212 Mexican cities and towns. Archrival Banco de Comercio, which brought out its own card last month with a claim of 100,000 holders, says 2,000 merchants have signed up.

Fast Check. The rapid rise of credit creates problems in a country where many consumers are just getting used to handling cash. Although the big retailers and banks claim Mexicans pay up as readily as borrowers anywhere, they go over new loan applications very carefully.

Although there is less risk of great loss in the adjustment situation, it is possible that the selling company can have large sums of money tied up for relatively long periods of time until the client accepts the controversial goods. In some cases, goods have to be returned or remanufactured, and in other instances contracts may be modified in order to alleviate the controversies. All these problems are uninsurable and costly.

Exchange-rate fluctuations inevitably cause some problems for the international marketer, but most firms are sufficiently aware of these fluctuations that they can take protective action to minimize their unfavorable effects. Devaluations pose some problems but seldom take the international businessman unaware; he is able to lessen the risk of loss through devaluation by minimizing his holdings of currency that he thinks is to be devalued and by hedging against the currencies in question. Hedging in money is essentially no different from any other kind of hedging in the marketplace. Basically it consists of forward sale for dollars of a currency in danger of devaluation. Capital hedging will neutralize effects of devaluation so that no loss will be incurred.[10]

PAYOUT PLANNING AND STRATEGY

The international marketing executive is plagued with a problem which does not concern his domestic counterpart; he must not only sell the goods but must also find ways to repatriate payment for the goods and profits from his operations to the parent country. In so doing, he is concerned with handling the profit, managing payout, and accomplishing repatriation of funds.

The multinational marketer has the option of allocating the profit from his activities to a variety of locations. Profit may be taken in a country in which the goods are sold, in a country in which they are produced, in the headquarters country, or perhaps in still another country. Profits may be allocated in such a way as to provide the maximum profit for the subsidiary or for the corporation as a whole. By taking profits in a country with low tax rates, for example, the net profit after taxes can be optimized. The marketer may want to take his profits in countries that have sound currencies, or he may want to take his profits in countries where the funds are needed to finance further operations.

Profit can be allocated through manipulation of prices charged for goods exchanged internationally or through allocation of expenses; the marketing manager's salary, for example, may be charged off to the operation of any of the countries mentioned above. Sometimes to bring profits to the home company the parent may charge its subsidiary licensing fees, or franchise fees, or it may allocate increasing portions of home-office expenses to the subunit. Generally such decisions are not made by the marketing manager of the foreign operation but are determined at the corporate level; the international marketing man works within the goals dictated by the corporation. Such corporate direction, it should be noted, often creates friction because the manager of a foreign operation wants to be able to show that his operation is profitable and is seldom to let all the profits be drained off into another country. Even though the operation contributes the same amount of profit either way, he does not feel as comfortable when profits are not apparent.

Payout of profits is not only a question of location but may also be considered from the standpoint of time. Sometimes it is sensible to postpone profits from one tax-paying year to another or to stockpile profits to provide the basis for further expansion; such activities are especially important in these days of widespread investment control. U.S. capital controls, for example, are virtually forcing American firms with overseas subsidiaries to retain profits abroad so that they can be used for expansion of overseas operations.

Both capital repatriation and repatriation of funds from the sale of

---

[10] Craig Henderson, "The Treatment of Risk in Capital Investment Projects," *European Business,* January 1968.

goods are important to the marketer. If he can sell the goods but cannot return the funds, he soon finds that he is in a position of having no more goods to sell. Solutions include bartering (in which goods from a customer country are traded directly between countries) and third-country (or three-way) trading without the use of financial exchange. Sometimes only part of the selling price of goods can be repatriated directly, and a portion, perhaps 20 to 30 percent of the total price of goods, may be bartered. One English company sold airplanes worth $5 million to Brazil but had to take its entire payment in Brazilian coffee. Obviously, vendors may find themselves in businesses they don't particularly enjoy, but specialized barter brokers are relieving this problem to some extent.

A somewhat different technique using some of the same concepts is called switch trading. In switch trading, three or more parties are generally involved, one party from each of the countries that have bilateral payment agreements with one or more of the other countries involved. Essentially the goods are sold twice in this kind of trading. When funds are blocked—that is, when they cannot be exchanged for the home-country currency in question—the money may be repatriated through the exports of goods from the foreign country to the parent country. Many countries maintain a list of goods on a deblockage list, and if these goods are exported, the funds need not be repatriated. Obviously there are other financial alternatives to repatriation. The company that is having trouble repatriating funds may choose to reinvest them in other local enterprises or to extend its operations in that country. Sometimes if a company has stockholders in the foreign country, it simply pays out dividends directly from the foreign subsidiary rather than from the parent country. For this reason, some large multinational companies are encouraging the sale of their securities in foreign markets in which they operate. Such an action taken when foreign capital may be sent to the parent country could lessen foreign exchange problems at some later date.

SOURCES OF FUNDS FOR INTERNATIONAL MARKETING OPERATIONS

Working capital for international marketing operations usually is derived from the assets of the company engaging in international trade or exporting. Private external sources, however, may be utilized for financing inventory, accounts receivable, construction of physical facilities, and other financing needs. Public sources of funds are likely to play a more important role in financing marketing operations internationally than they do domestically. A number of supranational agencies are engaged in financing international development and marketing activities, and the foreign marketer may also turn to foreign, national, state, and local governments for various kinds of financial assistance. This section will review briefly the major private and public sources of financing international business operations. Unfortunately, data on the extent of usage and volume of financing private business through each source are not available.

It is very evident, however, that in recent years the development of foreign capital markets has been significant. Because of their excellent credit rating, American firms are often the beneficiaries—in most of the world, investments in American companies are looked upon with great favor. The company financing international marketing operations must diligently explore each of the sources to determine which offers the best alternative.

Even companies that have the ability to finance their entire international operation need to be concerned with foreign sources. More local capital may be required than the international company is willing to put into a given country, for political reasons. Specifically, numerous countries in recent years have placed strict controls on the amount of capital which can be invested overseas. In the United States, for example, permission must be obtained from the U.S. Office of Foreign Direct Investments any time more than $1 million is going to be invested overseas. Local financial participation laws may require that at least part of the ownership of foreign operations be national, so that companies may find themselves in the position of helping local participants to find capital sources in the foreign markets. Middlemen, importers, and franchisees also often rely on vendor companies for assistance in securing financing.

The magnitude of international investment by U.S. firms is indeed staggering. In 1969 the total book value of U.S. direct investments abroad was over $55 billion and had been rising at the rate of nearly 10 percent per year for the preceding decade. That $55 billion investment has been generating an annual sales volume of some $45 billion, plus over $5 billion each year in dividends and royalties remitted to the United States. American multinational corporations in recent years have financed nearly 40 percent of the overseas operation from cash flow generated from abroad, over one third from external sources abroad, and about one fourth through capital transfers from the United States. Starting in 1965, voluntary restrictions on capital transfers from the United States were urged by the U.S. government: a few years later, restrictions became mandatory because of balance of payments shortages. These restrictions have caused American firms to seek other sources of financing abroad, with the result that by 1968 American firms were borrowing about $2 billion a year through Eurobond issues (compared to about $295 million in 1965). In addition to this, American firms raised about $100 million on the Swiss capital market alone in 1968. Eurodollars (essentially U.S. dollars which are held in Europe) constitute a major source of short- and medium-term funds for American business abroad.

Private Sources

In international business, companies often cooperate both to share the risk and to provide a greater capital and credit base. Sometimes, as is so frequently the case in international oil consortia, the cooperation is between companies in the same country which join in joint ventures for operating in other countries. In other instances, companies from different countries join forces to do business in one of the countries in question. The Iraq Petroleum Company, for example, is jointly owned by British Petroleum, Royal Dutch/Shell, Compagnie Française des Petroles, Jersey Standard, and Socony Mobil. Joint or single ventures doing exporting or operating overseas may be financed directly from existing company sources or by utilizing the company's credit in the financial marketplace. Equity and debt funds may be secured from the private sector of the world economy in any of the ways mentioned below.

Equity Holders.   England, Japan, the United States, and a few other countries have highly developed stock markets. But increasingly, private funding is becoming an important factor in international business. Marketers still cannot look to widespread public equity sources in most countries. But as nations become more affluent, increasing amounts of surplus capital are making their way into American business firms operating abroad. Germany has been a heavy investor in American business. Swiss fund sources have always been useful. Increasingly, large family fortunes are being invested in diversified international firms. Despite these sources, the dominant source of private financing undoubtedly will continue to be association with individual local partners who provide equity financing.

Debt financing has also become a major factor in recent years, with what is commonly called the Eurobond providing millions of dollars of investments for American firms operating abroad. Eurobond is simply a bond of debenture which is issued and sold in Europe using the collateral of the American company as security. Eurobond has the advantage that it does not dilute equity; for the investor the bond is beneficial because it guarantees a fixed rate of return and a definite repayment date.

Edge Act Banks.   Two classes of institutions are permitted under the Edge Law (Section 25a) of the Federal Reserve Act of 1919 (commercial banks and investment banking houses). One class handles only investments and does not provide commercial financing; the other is of interest to corporations engaged in international operations. The latter class of Edge Act corporation provides long- and medium-term financing in cooperation with other financial partners. Edge Act banks are less likely to provide the capital needed for marketing operations than for industrial developments.

Most Edge Act banks are subsidiaries of large U.S. banks; for example, Bamercial International Financial Corporation is a subsidiary of the Bank of America NT&SA, and the Chase International Investment Corporation is owned by the Chase Manhattan Bank.

Investment Companies and Trusts.   Nearly every nation has a number of its own investment companies which have been formed to exploit business opportunities through financial participation both in their own and foreign countries. One outstanding example in the United States is the IBEC (International Basic Economy Corporation). A Rockefeller family investment, IBEC has assets of $700 million (U.S.) invested in a wide variety of projects and subsidiary operations. A cooperative international investment group called ADELA Investment Company was

EXHIBIT 14–4

International Bond Issues by U.S. Firms, January–February 1969

Parent Company	Issuing Company	Currency	U.S.$ (mil.)	Term (yrs.)	Coupon (% p.a.)	Issue Price	Yield (% p.a.)	Conversion Premium (%)
Philip Morris Inc.	Philip Morris Int. Finance Corp, Del.	$	40	20	4.75	100	4.75	15.8
Murphy Oil Corp.	Murphy Oil International Finance Corp. Del.	$	25	20	5.0	100	5.0	16.5
Commonwealth United Corp.	Commonwealth Overseas NV, Neth. Antilles	$	30	15	5.75	100	5.75	12.0
Walter Kidde Corp.	Walter Kidde Overseas NV, Neth. Antilles	$	30	20	5.0	100	5.0	12–15
Leasco Data Processing Equipment Co.	Leasco International NV, Neth. Antilles	$	20	5	7.0	99.5	7.03	straight
Equity Funding Corp.	Equity Funding Capital Corporation NV, Neth. Antilles	$	25	20	5.25	100	5.25	13.7
Chrysler Co.	Chrysler Overseas Capital Corp. Del.	$	25	15	7.0	97	7.22	straight
Denny's Restaurants Inc.	Denny's International, NV Neth. Antilles	$	15	20	5.5	100	5.5	18.4
Tyco Laboratories Inc.	Tyco International Finance NV, Neth. Antilles	$	25	15	5.0	100	5.0	n.a.
Gulf Oil	Transocean Gulf Oil Co. Del.	$	30	12	7.0	97	7.22	straight
Giffen Industries Inc.	Giffen International NV, Neth. Antilles	$	20	15	5.75	99.5	5.78	11.0
Occidental Petroleum Corp.	Occidental Overseas Capital Corp. Del.	$	20	15	7.5	98	7.65	straight
SCM	SCM Overseas Capital Corp. Del.	$	15	20	5.25	100	5.25	14.4
International Harvester Corp.	International Harvester Overseas Cap. Corp. Del.	Sfr.	13.75	15	5.5	99.5	5.53	straight
Sears Roebuck	Sears Intern. Finance Co. Del.	Sfr.	13.75	15	5.5	100	5.5	straight

Source: Reprinted from the March 14, 1969, issue of *Business International*, p. 86 with the permission of the publisher, Business International Corporation, New York.

formed in 1964 with the object of combining economic development and profit-seeking motives. Financed by blue-chip companies from the United States (Ford Motor Co., First National City Bank of New York, Standard Oil–New Jersey, and IBM World Trade Corp.) and some major European companies (Sybetra, Italy's Fiat, Instituto Mobiliare Italiano, Belgium's Petrofina, and the Swiss Bank Corp.) ADELA focuses its attentions on joint ventures in Latin America. In general, investment companies' motives range from outright altruism to hard-nosed profit seeking and follow equally diverse organizational patterns. Asia has not been neglected in terms of international banking, either. Private Investment Company for Asia (PICA) with authorized capital of $40 million is being sponsored by Japanese, North American, European, and Australian investors. PICA will provide equity financing and medium- and long-term loans. Some of the U.S. shareholders are: Bank of America, Caltex, Caterpillar, Chase-Manhattan, General Motors, ITNI, Standard Oil–New Jersey, National Cash Register, and United Foods.

Commercial Finance and Factoring Companies. Most major industrial countries have fairly well-developed finance companies which operate outside the commercial bank system. Such companies factor receivables, installment contracts, or accept other kinds of security. They also directly handle overseas installment credit through international offices located throughout the world. Examples of companies operating in this field are the Commercial Credit Company, operating in Europe through a series of companies tied to the American parent by operating agreements, and the Beneficial Finance Company, which has its own branch offices in various countries.

Overseas Development Banks.[11] In many countries commercial banking syndicates provide funds for local development activities. Although they operate on a private basis, these companies often secure their funds either from national or international governments. Although overseas development banks are not available. Examples of development banks are Industrial Credit and Investment Corporation of Bombay, India, a private corporation which will invest on an equity or a loan basis, as will the privately owned Industrial Development Bank in Istanbul, Turkey. Examples of banks with mixed ownership are the Industrial Credit Company in Ireland and the Agricultural, Industrial and Real Estate Credit Bank in Lebanon.

Noninstitutional Lenders. In many countries of the world, large sums of capital are held by individuals who prefer not to institutionalize their wealth. Without an organized capital market, it is difficult to tap these sources; but an international marketer with a sound proposition and good contacts can often find these sources of local capital. He may be able to finance his operations with a single silent partner or through a joint venture with one family.

Commercial Banks. Domestic or foreign commercial banks are of prime importance not only in facilitating but also in financing international business activities. Many banks maintain branches, subsidi-

---

[11] Lewis C. Stanley, *Handbook of International Marketing* (New York: McGraw-Hill Book Company, 1964), p. 421.

EXHIBIT 14–5

Source: *Eurodollar Financing*, Chase Manhattan Bank, 1970.

BOX 14–6

Kraftco Decides to Spread Its Ownership Worldwide

Kraftco Corp. has recently listed its common stock on the stock exchanges of London, Toronto, and Montreal, and has applied for listing in Brussels, Zurich, Antwerp, Geneva, Lausanne, Berne, and Basel. Hitherto, the stock was traded only on the New York and Australian exchanges.

Kraftco, one of the world's largest manufacturers of processed packaged foods, has manufacturing facilities in 17 countries and distributes to over 100 countries. Stock ownership is now primarily in U.S. hands, but the corporation believes that listing the stock on overseas exchanges will facilitate the internationalization of share ownership.

The London stock exchange permits U.S. firms that have already satisfied the requirements of the U.S. Securities and Exchange Commission to be listed in the U.K. without undergoing the normal investigatory procedure required of corporations applying for listing. However, U.K. residents who purchase stock in U.S. firms with sterling must pay the investment Dollar Premium, which is currently 55%. Other recent new listings of U.S. firms on the U.K. exchange include Kaiser Aluminum & Chemical, Occidental Petroleum, and Leasco Data Processing.

Source: Reprinted from the May 30, 1969, issue of *Business International*, p. 170, with the permission of the publisher, Business International Corporation, New York.

aries, or agencies in foreign countries. International banking services may be provided through nearly any bank through a correspondent bank relationship. As a major source of secured and unsecured short-term financing, commercial banks often make loans against outstanding letters of credit or may discount export bills of exchange and time drafts.

Domestic and foreign banks have been increasingly active in providing financing for international businessmen. Often special bank subsidiaries are developed by a group of foreign banks for handling international funding. One such group, initiated by Bankers Trust Company of the United States and including 14 European banks, is called the International Company for Medium Term Credit. Another is the European Bank for Medium Term Credit, sponsored by three European banks. The Bank of America has a French bank to form a holding company with $2½ million in capital, which is specifically used for funding international companies.

Government Sources

The great majority of public sources of funds for international business is oriented to industrial development activities. Some agencies, however, interpret industrial development quite broadly and make funds available for a wide range of business activities. Public funds for private businesses may be secured from four different governmental levels—the international government, the national government, state governments, and local governments. The national, state, and local govern-

EXHIBIT 14–6

Agencies Which Help Finance Foreign Trade and Investment

	Eximbank	Agency for International Development (AID)	World Bank Group		
			International Bank for Reconstruction and Development (IBRD)	International Development Association (IDA)	International Finance Corporation (IFC)
Function	Aid in financing U.S. exports through the extension of credits or assisting others to provide financing on conventional terms to purchasers of exports from U.S. entities or non-U.S. entities doing business in the U.S.	Administer the U.S. foreign economic assistance program, including the extension of loans to less-developed countries on concessionary terms.	Promote the economic development of member countries primarily by extending loans on conventional terms for specific high-priority projects.	Promote the economic development of less-developed member countries by making credits on concessionary terms, thereby lessening the burden on the recipient countries' respective balance of payments positions.	Encourage the growth of productive private enterprise in developing countries by extending loans and non-controlling equity capital, providing underwriting and standby commitments, and attracting outside financing.
Criteria and limitations	Availability of funds from private sources; extent of participation of other sources of credit; effects on the U.S. economy; existence of "reasonable assurance of repayment" or "sufficient likelihood of repayment"; total foreign indebtedness of recipient country; and the recipient country's total obligations to the Bank. Eximbank may not back sales of military equipment to a less-developed country; support export sales in a country at war with U.S. or aiding such a country; or assist exports to Communist countries except sales declared by the President to be in the national interest.	For Project loan: Project must give reasonable promise of contributing to the economic development of the country concerned; be consistent with other development projects in the country; have a satisfactory prospect of paying out; and be non-competitive with domestic U.S. enterprises. Program and sector loans: Prospective recipient country must demonstrate a need based on balance of payments considerations.	Government guarantee required when borrower is a private entity; borrowing country must be creditworthy; borrower must be unable to obtain funds from other sources on reasonable terms; loan decisions are made only on the basis of economic development considerations; loans must be for specific projects; funds may be spent only for purposes for which a loan was granted; project must have high economic priority; and recipient enterprise must have productive potential.	Government guarantee required when borrower is a private entity; borrowing country must be creditworthy; borrower must be unable to obtain funds from other sources on reasonable terms; credit decisions are made only on the basis of economic considerations; credits must be only for specific projects; funds may be spent only for purposes for which loan was granted; project must have high economic priority; and recipient enterprise must have productive potential. Per capita income level of borrowing country should be below $250.	The Corporation considers the degree of economic development of borrowing country; availability of sufficient capital from private sources on reasonable terms; prospects of profitability; evidence of sound planning; sponsorship from companies with proven industrial experience; extent of sponsor's share capital in enterprise; provision for local investor participation; and project's economic priority for the country. It will not lend where primary object is refunding, direct financing of trade, or land development.
Eligible borrowers	U.S. entities operating in other countries, and non-U.S. entities, public or private.	Project loan: foreign governments, U.S. and foreign public and private entities. Program and sector loans: foreign governments.	Member governments, their political subdivisions, and any public or private entities in their territories.	Member governments, their political subdivisions, any public or private entities in their territories, and any public international or regional unit.	Private firms in developing member countries.
Lending volume (FY 1969)	$835 million commercial credits; $225 million for purchase of military items.	Project loans—$200 million; program loans—$465 million; sector loans—$40 million.	$1.4 billion.	$385 million.	Total commitments of about $93 million.
Number and size of loans (FY 1969)	More than 100 loans—$70 million to $600 thousand, with $5 million median.	46 Project loans—$300,000 to $30 million; 10 program loans—$1.2 million to $194 million; 4 sector loans—$5 million to $15 million.	84 loans—$2 million to $82 million, with $11 million median.	38 loans—$800,000 to $125 million, with $5 million median.	27 commitments — from $6,000 equity investment to $22 million combined loan and equity investment, with $1 million median.
Current interest rates and fees	6% interest; ½% commitment fee on undisbursed balance.	2% interest during grace period, 3% thereafter. Re-lending by foreign governments may be at prevailing domestic rates.	7% interest, commitment charge of ¾%, accruing from a date 60 days after date of loan agreement.	No interest. Service charge of ¾% per annum to cover IDA administrative costs.	9%· interest per annum; commitment fee equals 1% per year on undisbursed portion of the loan.
Loan maturities	1 to 15 years, not including grace periods. Most are for 7 to 10 years.	Generally 40-year terms with 10-year grace period to foreign governments; re-lending by foreign governments may be for shorter periods.	15 to 30 years, including grace periods which run until projects are operational. Most are on 20 to 25 year terms.	50 years, including 10-year grace period, following which 1% per annum of principal is repayable over next 10 years and 3% per year over next 30 years.	Usually 7 to 12 years. Amortization is generally on a semiannual basis after a grace period.
Currency of repayment	U.S. dollars.	U.S. dollars.	Currency lent.	Currency lent or another convertible currency.	Generally currencies lent or invested, most commonly dollars.
Resources	Capital of $1 billion, $1.2 billion reserves, and borrowing rights from the Treasury. Additional assets may be acquired through sale of securities on private capital markets.	Annual appropriations by U.S. Congress. FY 1970—$1.4 billion for economic assistance, including $555 million for development loans.	$23 billion subscribed capital, including $2.3 billion paid-in and available for lending. Major sources of funds are sales of bonds on world capital markets and loan repayments.	About $3.2 billion in funds available for lending, of which about 70% is already committed.	More than $400 million, including paid-in share capital of $106.6 million and a $200 million line of credit from the IBRD. The Bank may lend about $200 million more.

Source: Reprinted with permission from *International Commerce,* May 18, 1970.

EXHIBIT 14–6 (continued)

| Inter-American Development Bank (IDB) | | ADELA | Asian Development Bank (ADB) | |
Ordinary Capital Resources	Fund for Special Operations		Ordinary Capital Resources	Special Funds Resources
Contribute to the acceleration of the process of development of its member countries individually and collectively by providing loans on conventional terms.	Contribute to the acceleration of the process of development of its member countries individually and collectively by providing loans on concessionary terms.	Foster the economic development of Latin America by strengthening private enterprise through provision of capital and entrepreneurial and technical services.	Finance loans on conventional terms and technical assistance for projects and programs to foster economic development in and among the developing countries of Asia and the Far East.	Provide loans on concessional terms for high priority development projects in developing member countries.
The Bank must take into account the creditworthiness of the borrower, may finance only specific projects, must consider the ability of the borrower to get financing from private sources on reasonable terms, and may not finance a project on a member country's territory if the member objects.	The Bank must take into account the creditworthiness of the borrower, may finance only specific projects, must consider the ability of the borrower to get financing from private sources on reasonable terms, and may not finance a project on a member country's territory if the member objects.	Criteria fall into two major categories—(a) return on investment, including reputation and contribution of local investors, availability of competent management and technical knowledge or proposals for obtaining them, evidence of adequate market demand for products, feasibility of engineering and production aspects of the project, and earning and growth potential of the enterprise; (b) contribution of the project to the host country's development. ADELA also looks at the investment climate in the host country.	Loans to be made in less-developed country members of ADB.	Loans to be made in less-developed member countries of ADB.
Member governments, private local firms or joint venture enterprises with local participation, and public or private relending agencies.	Member governments, private local firms or joint venture enterprises with local participation, and public or private relending agencies.	Private entities in Latin America.	Any member government or any agency, instrumentality or political subdivision thereof, or any entity or enterprise operating in the territory of a member.	Governments of developing country members.
$209 million.	$413 million.	$65.5 million.	$76 million.	$22 million.
19 loans—$33.5 million to $1 million, with $10 million median.	46 loans—$30.8 million to $0.3 million, with $10 million median.	24 long-term commitments, $3.5 million to $50 thousand, with $370 thousand median.	14 loans ranging from $1 million to $10 million.	6 loans, $1 million to $7.7 million.
8% annual interest, including 1% commission alloted to special reserve; 1¼% commitment fee on undisbursed balance.	2¼-3¼% interest per annum; service charge of ¾%.	Negotiated in each case taking into account borrower's needs and cost of funds to ADELA.	6⅞% interest per annum including 1% commission plus commitment charge of ¾ of 1% per annum on unused balances of loan.	Interest rates have ranged from 1½ to 3% per annum, including ¾ of 1% service charge.
7 to 25 years, including grace period. Most are for 15 to 20 years.	15 to 30 years, including grace periods generally not exceeding 5 years. Most are for 20 to 25 years.	Normally 6 months to 5 years; when loans are combined with equity capital, repayment period may exceed 5 years.	10 to 25 years with grace periods from 2 to 5 years. Most are for 12-15 years.	From 16 to 40 years, including grace periods from 5 to 10 years; average maturity, 27 years.
Currency lent.	Mexico and Venezuela repay in currency lent; others may pay in their own currencies. Service charge payable in dollars.	Currency lent.	Currency lent.	Currency lent.
$2.74 billion subscribed capital, of which $388 million paid-in. Major source of funds is sales of bond issues on world capital markets.	$2.33 billion in member contributions.	$187.3 million, including available borrowing facilities totaling $130.5 million and $50 million from paid-in capital shares.	Subscribed capital, $1,004 million: of which subscribed paid-in capital, $502 million and callable capital, $502 million; borrowings, equivalent $21 million.	$72.7 million available for lending, including $14.6 million set-aside from Ordinary Capital plus $58.1 million from contributions.

ments often will finance business activities of all sorts that are likely to bring greater prosperity within their bailiwick.

International Governmental Sources. The list below includes only the agencies which, as presently constituted, provide funds for private business activities. As shown in Exhibit 14–6, a number of other international development agencies do exist, but most have little direct interest for the marketer except as they provide funds which are likely to be expended for equipment and supplies utilized in their development programs.

The World Bank (IBRD). Formally known as the International Bank for Reconstruction and Development, the IBRD has some 60 member nations and has made development loans emphasizing development of power, communication, and transportation, with some attention also being given to agriculture and private projects. Private firms can borrow money from the World Bank when the government of the country in which they are to operate will approve or guarantee the project.

International Finance Corporation (IFC). Although it is affiliated with the World Bank, the IFC places considerably greater interest on financing business investment which will foster international economic development. The IFC operates only with private enterprise and provides up to 50 percent of the capital of the enterprise. It participates only when sufficient private capital is not available from other sources. IFC operates as an investing partner.

International Development Associations (IDA). Like the IFC, IDA is an offshoot of the World Bank. It makes both public and private loans to countries that are members of the IBRD.

Inter-American Development Bank (IADB). Limited to nations that are members of the Organization of American States, the IADB both invests and makes loans to private business and to governments, with emphasis on engineering and feasibility studies and on projects in which IADB funds can be coupled with private capital for the provision of capital assets.

The European Investment Bank (EIB). Organized as an arm of the European Common Market, the European Investment Bank provides long-term funds to complement private sources when adequate money is not available.

National Government Funds. The United States has set up several organizations as part of its mutual security program which are designed to speed the development of certain countries. In addition, nearly every country has its own national organization to facilitate development within the country. For example, France has its Caisse Nationale Des Marches De l'Etat which finances firms working on government contract. The Nacional Financiera of Mexico is a government development bank which finances private enterprise when it contributes to the development of the nation. Germany has a program designed to make direct capital loans to businesses operating in underdeveloped areas of Germany.

Some countries, such as Belgium, are especially eager to encourage foreign investment and are participating directly in the equity financing of foreign companies. One example is the Societe Nationale d'Investissement (SNI) for which the Belgian government provided 75 percent of the funds. The company was developed to take minority shares in manufacturing ventures. It recently purchased a 34 percent equity in a several-million-dollar fiberglass project of Clark Schwedel in the United States.

Export-Import Bank. Eximbank is the primary U.S. government agency in the business of providing funds for international trade and investment. Besides its many private financing functions, Eximbank also plays a key role in the U.S. export credit insurance program. This agency makes medium- and long-term loans to foreign countries, the proceeds of which must be expended on goods purchased in the United States. It also provides medium-term export credit for U.S. exporters. Besides these activities, Eximbank is also the primary administrator for the foreign currencies abroad which are generated by the sale of U.S. surplus farm commodities. Cooley funds, as they are called, are available to American businesses operating abroad.

Agency for International Development (AID). Functioning as an activity of the Department of State, AID has a major commitment to economic development working through private enterprise. Like Eximbank, AID also operates in Cooley funds, but it also has its own appropriation of U.S. dollars.

The Inter-American Social Progress Trust Fund. This trust fund is a source of capital for private borrowers as well as governments and other groups in the Americas.

State and Local Funds. In many foreign countries, funds are available from governments on levels comparable to our states or municipalities. In Germany, for example, the *laender* (states) may provide direct capital or free land or plant facilities. Massey-Ferguson GMBH, for example, was induced to build a plant in Eschwege when the company received cheap credits from the state. A subsidiary of the U.S.'s Clevite Corporation received assistance from the city of Freiburg in the form of funds with which to build a plant.

SUMMARY AND CONCLUSIONS

Although financing of international operations is not the formal domain of the marketing executive, he should be acquainted with the particular requirements, sources, problems, and opportunities associated with financing of international marketing operations. The financial needs of international marketing differ considerably from those of the domestic market. Most specifically, the international marketer must be prepared to invest larger than normal amounts of working capital in inventories, receivables, channel financing, and consumer credit. It is possible that market entry may even require financing of production facilities for purely marketing reasons. The international marketer needs to be willing to undertake the additional financial burdens if he is to operate successfully in foreign countries. Indeed, adequate financing may spell the difference between success and failure in foreign operations. The willingness of the marketer to carry adequate inventories in strategic locations or to provide consumer or channel credit which he would not be likely to furnish in his home country may be key elements in market development.

Financial risks associated with international marketing are greater than those encountered domestically, but such risk taking is necessary for effective operations. Many companies have been so conservative in their credit and payment terms that they have succeeded in alienating foreign customers. Consumer credit may be particularly perilous, but often no one but the marketer is willing to provide such credit; so if the consumer is dependent on credit for his purchases, the marketer must take this risk. Larger inventories threaten possible financial loss through obsolescence or deterioration, and the totally larger financial involvement of international marketing may significantly alter the risk-return relationship. Nonetheless, these risks, as well as those of exchange availability or fluctuation and the various political risks, can be accommodated in an effective marketing plan.

The high cost of credit in foreign countries and the relative lack of capital available for financing operations may mean that the American marketer is in an especially good position to capitalize on opportunities, because of his superior capital position. The marketer needs to be well acquainted with the financial side of marketing if he is to capitalize on these opportunities.

QUESTIONS

1. Define:

IBRD	AID
IFC	FCIA
Eximbank	Bill of exchange
Cooley funds	Revocable letter of credit

2. Explain why marketing men should be concerned with the financial considerations associated with international business.

3. Identify the financial requirements for marketing internationally which are most likely to concern the domestic marketer.

4. Discuss the differences between financial requirements for export marketers and for overseas marketing operations.

5. Review some of the ways by which financial requirements can be reduced by variations in marketing policies or strategies.

6. "Whenever possible, manufacturers should probably avoid consumer credit extensions as part of their basic merchandising program." Discuss.

7. What significance do government sources of funds have for marketers?

8. Discuss the importance of Eximbank and its services which facilitate international marketing activities.

9. "The principles of international credit are basically no different from those of domestic credit." Elaborate.

10. Identify the major sources of international credit information.

11. Compare the advantages and disadvantages of bills of exchange and letters of credit.

12. Review the types of financial risk involved in international operations and discuss how each may be reduced.

OUTLINE OF CHAPTER 15

INTRODUCTION

MANPOWER NEEDS

    Home-Office Personnel

    Temporary Personnel

    Marketing Managers Abroad

    Foreign Sales Forces

STRATEGIC MANPOWER DEPLOYMENT

    Strategic Factors

    Organizational Relationships for Sales

    Market Location and Country of Origin

        Home-Office Management

        Foreign-Managed Sales Operations

    Organization Patterns

REQUISITE CAPABILITIES FOR MARKETERS

    Personal Characteristics

    Job Skills

    Personal Orientation

SOURCES OF MARKETING MANPOWER

    Expatriates

    Third-Country Manpower

    Foreign Nationals

DEVELOPING INTERNATIONAL MANPOWER

    Recruitment and Selection

    Training

    Compensating

    Motivating

SUMMARY AND CONCLUSIONS

READING

    Not So Multinational After All, *Interplay of European American Affairs.*

INTERNATIONAL MARKETING MANPOWER MANAGEMENT

INTRODUCTION

Unless firms doing business in foreign countries rely entirely on exporting or on middlemen, sooner or later they are confronted with the problem of managing manpower (perhaps including a force of salesmen) in overseas markets. As international business becomes increasingly competitive, large numbers of companies find that unless they take direct responsibility for the management of marketing manpower in foreign markets, they cannot accomplish marketing objectives or achieve the desired level of sales activity. The relationship of sales activity to the overall marketing organization should be noted. In terms of the organizational structures discussed in Chapter 13, the overseas sales force would be classified as an "owned" element of the international marketing organization.

What kinds of marketing personnel are involved? Obviously, all who have direct and continuing responsibility for international marketing activities, including those in the home-office organization. This chapter, however, concerns itself primarily with those who have direct field assignments, most specifically with the men who constitute the international sales force and its managers. This group constitutes the numerical bulk of men employed in foreign positions, and it is this group that deals most directly with the middlemen and the public in foreign markets.

When one thinks of an international sales force, he may assume that it will be composed of salesmen who are recruited from the parent country and managed by the parent company. Such a view does not adequately answer the question, "What is an international sales force?" Such a force may indeed be composed of men from the parent company and be managed by the parent company; the sales force however may be made up of foreign nationals directed by a foreign sales manager or by a domestic sales manager operating abroad. Finally, of course, some sales organizations are composed of men from *both* the parent country and the country in which business is being sought. To think in terms of an international sales force doing business in one particular foreign country is also misleading. In many instances, an international salesman will do business in a number of different countries.

International organization, international distribution channels, and international manpower management are three interrelated aspects of international distribution arrangements, yet each is distinctly separate. International organization relates to the *corporate organization* that is employed for doing business internationally; international channels of distribution pertain to the *outside middlemen* who may be employed in distributing goods internationally; and international manpower operations include activities of salesmen and sales management personnel who are *directly employed* by the company and who seek business for the company in international markets.

Although the conceptual orientation to marketing manpower management is similar in both domestic and foreign operations, international sales force management is confronted with a variety of unique problems. These problems are given primary consideration in this chapter.

The manpower-needs requirements and organizational structure of the international marketing function present some interesting variations. The task of building, training, compensating, and motivating the international force confronts businessmen with unique problems at every stage of its development and management. The materials in this chapter illustrates some of the alternatives and problems that confront the firm attempting to manage its own foreign sales operation.

MANPOWER NEEDS

Study after study of the problems of international businessmen focuses specifically on the need for qualified manpower and the continuing shortage of it. One participant in a National Industrial Conference Board study put it squarely:

I don't think it's wrong to say that virtually any type of international problem, in the final analysis, is either created by people or must be solved by people; hence, having the right people in the right place at the right time emerges as the key to a company's international growth. If we can solve that problem, I am confident we can cope with all the others.[1]

The shortage of competent manpower is no more evident than in marketing. As one scholar puts it,

Any company can get into a new market and sell products for a limited amount of time, but if a company really wishes to stay in that market, it must build a whole organization around its product or service.[2]

The NICB chart reproduced as Exhibit 15–1 illustrates this, as do the two following quotations:

---

[1] Michael G. Duerr and James Greene, *Managing International Business; The Problems Facing International Management* (New York: National Industrial Conference Board, (1968), pp. 14–15.

[2] Dmitris N. Chorafas, "Developing the International Executive," AMA Research Study 83, 1968, p. 69.

EXHIBIT 15–1

Shortage of Local Management Talent, by Function and Region
(total number of citations and percent distribution)

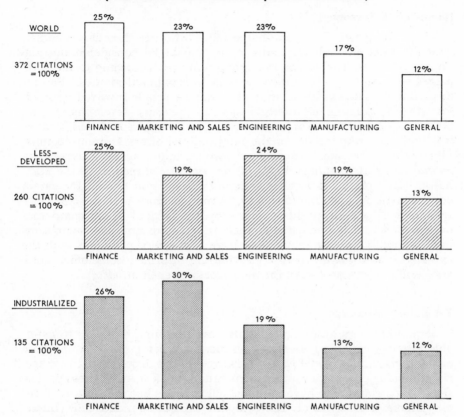

Source: Michael G. Duerr and James Greene, *Foreign Nationals in International Management* (New York: National Industrial Conference Board, 1968), p. 11. Reprinted with permission.

Marketing is definitely the most difficult function to fill overseas. This shortage is not peculiar to any particular country, but the skill itself seems to be lacking in most countries.

I find that it is extremely difficult for our distributors to get proper sales personnel. In fact, in all of these countries, with the exception of Brazil and Argentina, it is very difficult to find good middle management talent, good sales managers, and good salesmen.[3]

As markets develop in size and wealth and as they attract increasing number of competitors, there is likely to be a continuing shortage of qualified marketing manpower.

Four main categories of manpower requirements can be identified in connection with the international marketing effort: (1) home-office

---

[3] Michael G. Duerr and James Greene op. cit.

personnel, (2) temporary personnel, (3) marketing managers abroad, and (4) foreign sales forces.

Home-Office Personnel

All of the personnel at the home office who are directly concerned with the international marketing effort should be considered international personnel. The size of this group will vary according to the company's level and type of involvement in international markets. Besides those directly responsible, it may also include people involved with advertising, packaging, distribution systems, product development, and other functional areas. Top management may even be included because it is indirectly responsible for the international effort. In many companies a virtual prerequisite to promotion to top management is experience in international positions. About 80 percent of the men at Chase Manhattan Bank placed in foreign assignments are sent abroad for career development. As one executive says, "A man is smart to have some overseas time if he really wants to move up the ladder." Many companies have been seriously hampered in their efforts to extend their operations internationally because they do not have home-office personnel with the experience and qualification to provide the informed home-office guidance and support necessary for the success of such an effort.

Temporary Personnel

Troubleshooters and start-up teams are personnel who are transferable to any location where new operations are being initiated or where existing operations have lost key personnel or are experiencing managerial difficulties. General Motors Corporation has a team of these professional expatriates who have no home-office duties but are shuttled from assignment to assignment. The company calls these men HOSP (home-office-status personnel) because they are assigned to the home office and are compensated as though they were based in New York. The director of personnel says, "They are members of a mobile international cadre who may be deployed to any part of the world where we have operations." GM's operations provide an interesting perspective on the manpower needs of a large international operation. The company has more than 165,000 employees engaged in business outside the United States; of this number, about 2,000 are assigned to the overseas division but located in the United States, about 300 HOSP's are located abroad but assigned to the United States, and the remaining 162,000 plus personnel have overseas assignments; nearly all of these are nationals of the countries where they are involved.

Marketing Managers Abroad

A third category of manpower international operations includes the foreign marketing management personnel who are actually assigned in the foreign countries. Here again the number of personnel involved

BOX 15-1

Europe Needs Pros

How to increase U.S. exports can be summed up briefly: Send abroad salesmen (regardless of titles) who speak the market language, have studied and know the market, have experience, are mature enough to command respect and be compensated in a way that reflects the top-management attitude toward selling. So far they have been nice, clean-cut, sheep-skin-bearing kids, who may be good enough covering Sunken Arches, Neb., but not a hard, highly competitive market in Europe. This market takes real senior-level pros who know the language, product, and market.

J. HOWARD
Pully (VD), Switzerland

Source: Letter to the editor, *Sales Management,* February 15, 1969. Reprinted with permission.

varies according to the operation, but, generally, it is not large. For a given country, it may include only one man who is the marketing manager for that country, or if it is a large operation, it may include a marketing manager, an advertising manager, a sales manager, and a man in charge of middleman relationships. Such men may be either foreign nationals or expatriates, but recently a great effort has been made on the part of most companies to utilize foreign nationals in as many management positions as possible.

Foreign Sales Forces

The sales force itself constitutes by far the largest manpower requirement abroad for most companies. Obviously, some companies will not have any salesmen abroad when they use other types of middleman arrangements. Companies that do have their own sales force typically average 10 to 12 salesmen in the field for each person who is assigned at the managerial level.

Three types of salesmen should be identified: (1) The *expatriate* salesman, a man who is working in a country other than his own; (2) the *foreign* salesman, a man who is working in his own country when that country is not that of the parent company; and (3) the *cosmopolitan* salesman, a special sort of expatriate salesman who works in various countries. The cosmopolitan salesman is expatriate by definition and may operate out of the parent company's country or out of another nation. These types are identified for analytical purposes and refer to individuals. It should be remembered, however, that a given company may use all three types of salesmen and may even employ all three types in a single foreign operation.

A special need is filled by *missionary* salesmen, who operate in foreign countries supporting or supplementing normal channels of distribution. In most instances, they work on a temporary basis in attempting to seek goodwill in the marketplace, to establish new products, to stimulate sales, or to achieve other special purposes. Missionary salesmen may be expatriates or may be foreign nationals hired for such activity.

In many world markets it is nearly impossible to secure aggressive sales promotion effort through middlemen; yet in the same market, it may be completely infeasible for a manufacturer to establish his own selling organization or to make any kind of controllable distribution arrangement. In such instances, a manufacturer might well consider the use of missionary sales, as did the Green Giant Company when it test-marketed Niblets and Mexicorn in the United Kingdom. The company not only used a food broker firm but also hired missionary salesmen to supplement the broker's work in contacting retailers and jobbers. Apparently this system worked well, because the following year when the company introduced its products in the London market, it hired a 75-man "blitz crew" to promote the product in retail outlets. Still later the company hired eight "Green Giant Girls" for continuous merchandising support at the retail and jobber levels. The specific task of a missionary sales force varies from situation to situation, but in every instance the objective of using such sales personnel is to supplement the promotional effort of the regular sales force or middlemen.

STRATEGIC MANPOWER DEPLOYMENT

Acute shortages of marketing manpower in world markets, coupled with the high cost of maintaining personnel in international positions, absolutely require effective organization for the strategic use of the manpower that is available. The speed and simplicity of international travel (at least to major market areas) have added flexibility to international organization by making it virtually possible for a man to be in two places at once. According to studies by the Port of New York Authority, nearly one-half million trips to Europe were made by American executives in one year. Ease of travel has facilitated the use of organizational arrangements employing foreign nationals because home-office personnel can be rapidly deployed when foreign units need advice or support. Nevertheless it is critical that the available manpower be carefully organized so as to utilize its capabilities most fully.

The international sales force represents the front line of the marketing function and should be organized so that it can capitalize on sales opportunities wherever they occur; therefore, it may be necessary to have a different type of organizational arrangement for each different market. In any case, the organizational pattern will depend on the strategic factors discussed in this section and will have as a prime characteristic the kind of personnel employed and the location of their sales management.

Strategic Factors

Regardless of the type of company or its market locations, certain strategic factors affect the organizational approach to the overseas selling and sales management task. One primary determinant is the structure of the international corporate organization. Location of production and other managerial functions, subsidiary pattern, and pattern of ownership will affect the selling organization. If the company, for example, has foreign operating subsidiaries, it is likely that the selling function will be located under such subsidiaries.

The objectives which the sales force is to accomplish will significantly affect the organizational arrangement which will be used. Market domination will require more and better sales and sales management personnel and more staff support than mere market participation. A company that attempts to cover all segments of a market will operate quite differently from one that attempts only to deal with large accounts. The implications of these and other differences in objectives are relatively obvious, but still some companies attempt to build a sales organization without an explicit statement of what the company is trying to accomplish.

Perhaps even more important is the stage of development of the market or markets in which the sales force will work. The size of the sales contact task, coupled with the volume of sales, will indicate the number of salesmen who will be involved and will provide some information about the continuity of their task. If salesmen are located in a single market for a long period of time and if there is substantial volume, a permanently established sales force of foreign nationals normally would be developed. On the other hand, if sales volume is not great, or if purchases are infrequent, it may be that the markets can best be served through special trips by expatriate salesmen. Geographic proximity of the markets will also partly dictate the type of sales and sales management arrangement. If markets are close to one another, field sales supervision is more likely to be feasible. If the active markets are far from one another, the company may wish to manage its scattered salesmen from the home office. Another market development factor relates to the level of competition. If competition is not too keen and if competitive companies are not particularly well represented, it may be that a company may not sell and service a market as intensively as if it were more competitive. Such a practice may not reflect sound long-run marketing strategy but may be an effective short-run expedient. If a market is entered when it is in a relatively noncompetitive state, it may be serviced by salesmen making infrequent calls. As competition becomes more intense, however, the company may have to establish a permanent sales force in order to secure its share of the business.

To some extent, the exigencies of the manpower situation will dictate the approach to overseas sales organization. Sometimes adequately trained foreign personnel are not available; expatriate personnel must then be used in a given market. In other circumstances, it might be desirable to utilize expatriate personnel, but none are available or willing to enter the market. Foreign nationals may have to be employed, even though they cannot, in that case, give the same caliber of sales representation. The same problems exist at the sales management level; even though it might be desirable to manage a group of foreign nationals with a foreign national, no such person may be available. A company, therefore, may have to use an expatriate sales manager until such time as a replacement can be developed.

Governmental restrictions and regulations may dictate that a company's sales representation be constituted of individuals who are native to that country. Sometimes nations with such regulations permit direct supervision from other countries; in other instances, it may be necessary to form a foreign sales subsidiary which not only employs foreign salesmen but also is partially owned by nationals. Sometimes government regulations indirectly favor the use of expatriate salesmen. For example, some South American countries (notably Argentina) have such severe regulations pertaining to the discharging or firing of nationals that companies would rather send their own salesmen than be saddled with a staff of incompetent or noncooperative nationals who cannot be discharged without a legal struggle. In still other cases, where the law or tax structure is such that expatriate salesmen are at a distinct disadvantage, the use of nationals is encouraged.

All these strategic factors must be taken into consideration before a company develops its overseas selling organization.

Organizational Relationships for Sales

Since the international selling function may be organized in many ways, the international planner must take various elements into consideration. Some of the factors to be considered may not even appear on the organization chart—one pertains to whether the sales management personnel are located in the parent country; a second depends on whether foreign or expatriate sales personnel are employed. Organizational structures also vary depending on the existence, nature, and location of the staff support functions serving the sales organization. Geographic responsibility and product sales responsibility must also be considered; these factors are normally reflected in the sales organization chart.

Market Location and Country of Origin

Sales management personnel may operate in either the home country or in the market location. Regardless of where they work, such managers may supervise either expatriate or foreign sales personnel. Some of the problems and advantages arising from the use of each of the various combinations of these two factors are considered here.

Home-Office Management. Three different situations involve a sales force that is managed from an office in the parent country. They are (1) domestic salesmen working from the parent country, (2) expatriate salesmen, and (3) foreign salesmen. In the first situation, the salesmen serving the foreign markets are members of the domestic sales force who are dispatched periodically for sales forays into foreign countries. The domestic force may be employed for foreign representation when the foreign countries are close at hand, when they represent a relatively small or noncontinuous sales volume, or when a high degree of technical assistance or liaison with the parent company is required. Small or technically oriented companies may depend entirely upon the domestic force for their foreign sales representation; but even in large companies, the domestic sales personnel are likely to participate in occasional international transactions.

The use of expatriate salesmen who are managed from the parent company location constitutes a second arrangement. In this arrangement, salesmen from the home country of the parent company are transferred to foreign markets on a relatively permanent basis but are still managed from the home office. In most situations, such a sales force is recruited from the regular domestic sales force of the company and virtually constitutes an extension of the domestic sales network. This alternative might be used when sales representatives are so widely scattered across the globe that there are too few in any one location for field supervision.

Communications and cultural differences may make close supervision nearly impossible in the third situation, wherein foreign personnel are managed from the home country. Nevertheless, foreign salesmen might be employed in a variety of instances calling for home-office management.

Foreign-Managed Sales Operations. When a foreign sales force is managed locally, the local manager may depend on the parent company for direction or he may operate in a fairly independent or autonomous manner. Under the first alternative, field sales management is at the foreign level with general policy direction and staff support from the home office. The salesmen and the field sales managers may be expatriate or foreign personnel. Such detached management is called for whenever there is a relatively large field sales force or when foreign markets are a great distance from the home-company operation.

The second alternate approach to foreign-managed sales activity calls for a virtually autonomous foreign sales operation with little or no direction or staff support from the parent company. This type of autonomous arrangement may actually represent a different organizational form if foreign sales subsidiaries are utilized. When the foreign subsidiary is not called for, corporate goals can be accomplished by the use of an autonomous foreign manager who manages his functions as a separate subsidiary, even though his organization does not have that legal status. Sometimes even a single salesman operates autonomously with virtually complete control over all market and selling activities in his territory. He may receive virtually no support from the home office, which in turn may see his orders as its primary form of communication. In general, the autonomous foreign management arrangement is utilized when no particular staff assistance is required for the foreign operation or when companies are large enough to have a fully developed foreign selling function.

Organizational Patterns

A number of schematic sales organization charts reflecting the information above are shown in this section. They depict only three of the many possible ways of organizing the international selling function. The three basic forms shown, however, do describe the arrangements used in a majority of international operations. The charts represent only the organization of the selling function. They do not show the entire international business organization nor even the entire international marketing organization that might be used.

EXHIBIT 15–2

Simple Line Sales Organization

CORPORATION PRESIDENT

VICE PRESIDENT MARKETING

SALES MANAGER

SALESMEN IN ALL COUNTRIES

EXHIBIT 15–3

Geographically Decentralized International Sales Organization with Centralized Staff Functions

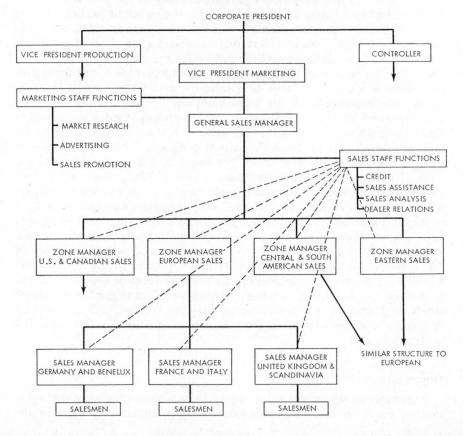

In reviewing these organization charts, remember that they identify basic relationships and do not necessarily identify the national origin of the salesmen or sales management personnel. Nor do they show, in all cases, whether the sales management function will be located in the parent country or the customer country.

Exhibit 15–2 depicts a simple line sales organization in which either foreign or expatriate salesmen working in all countries report directly to the home-office sales manager, who is responsible for all domestic and international selling activities.

Exhibit 15–3 shows how a geographically decentralized sales staff may be serviced with centralized staff functions. The general sales manager in this example is likely to operate in the parent country of the company. The zone managers may be located in the country of the parent company but are more likely to be centrally located in their zones. The zone manager for European sales, for example, might be located in Paris, where he could maintain communications with his three subordinate national sales managers. In this example, sales staff functions would probably be undertaken in the parent country, and the staff personnel would communicate both with the zone managers and with the national sales managers.

The structure envisioned in Exhibit 15–4 would probably be used only

EXHIBIT 15–4

**Geographically Decentralized International Sales Organization
with Decentralized Staff Functions**

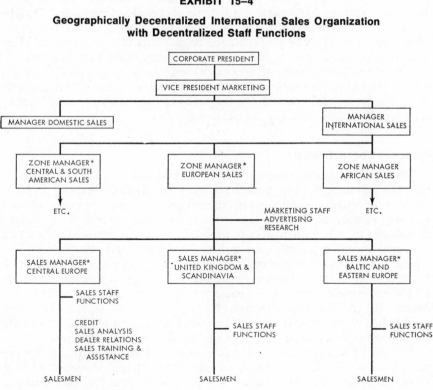

* May be sales subsidiaries.

by a company with rather highly developed international sales activities and a large volume of sales. The manager of international sales may be located in the parent company's home country or may be located abroad in some convenient city. It is most likely that the zone managers would be centrally located in the territories for which they are responsible. Decentralized staff functions could be undertaken under the zone managers, but in this case they are even more thoroughly decentralized and are the responsibility of the regional or national sales managers. In such a situation, both the manager of international sales and the zone managers act primarily in a line management and coordination capacity; each of the national or regional managers provides his own staff support. Note that some of the zone or regional sales offices may be organized as sales subsidiaries, but they still retain their subordinate position in the organizational hierarchy.

REQUISITE CAPABILITIES FOR MARKETERS

A previous section identified several classes of international manpower, ranging from the foreign salesman operating in his own country to the expatriate manager or the transnational specialist. Obviously, the requirements for different positions will vary considerably. A foreign salesman operating in his own country needs only the attributes of an effective salesman, whereas the transnational manager may require skills and attitudes comparable to those of a foreign diplomat. Despite the range of difference, it is worth considering some of the basic requisites leading to effective performance on the part of a manager or salesman who is called upon to function in a country other than his own. All effective executives and all successful salesmen, regardless of where they are operating, share certain characteristics, but international operation calls for special attention in the areas of the man's personal characteristics, his skills, and his orientations.

Personal Characteristics

Maturity is a prime requisite for expatriate and cosmopolitan personnel. Managers and sales personnel working abroad typically need to work more independently than their domestic counterparts; all are serving as company representatives in countries where the company reputation may be still in the process of formation. Personnel working overseas are often called upon to make decisions and offer services for which the domestic counterpart might be able to seek staff support. If the company lacks confidence in the ability of its men to make decisions and commitments without constant recourse to the home office, they cannot be individually effective. Even when there is a rather well-established overseas sales force, the men may not be able to receive the same level of assistance that is available to domestic salesmen.

Exhibit 15–5 shows that there is a good deal of difference in the perceived personal characteristics of executives from societies with as close cultural ties as the United States, Britain, and Canada. Imagine the variation if executives from extremely dissimilar cultures were evaluated.

International personnel require a kind of emotional stability not demanded in domestic positions. Regardless of their location, they are always living in cultures dissimilar to their own, to some extent always under scrutiny, and always aware that they are official representatives of the company abroad. They need to be sensitive to behavioral variations in different countries but not be so hypersensitive that their own behavior is affected adversely. Finally, managers or salesmen operating

EXHIBIT 15–5

Semantic Differential Pictures

Source: Reprinted with permission from Joe Kelly, *Organizational Behaviour* (Homewood, Ill.: Richard D. Irwin, Inc., 1969), p. 471.

in foreign countries require considerable breadth; they need knowledge about many subjects, both on and off the job, and probably should be able to handle several different languages.

Job Skills

In addition to all the intangible skills the international marketer must have in handling interpersonal relationships, he must also be an effective salesman. It would seem self-evident that every marketing person in a foreign position is directly involved in the selling effort and must possess a "sales sense" that permits him to cut through personal, cultural, and language differences and deal effectively with the selling

BOX 15-2

Decisions by Intuition

Latin Americans are not so interested in results as are Anglo-Americans. Action is important to a Latin American but not from a results point of view. The utility of results is relatively unimportant. Since he is a man of passion, action becomes more important than results because it allows the free expression of inner feelings. This is the important element—spontaneous expression. In fact, passion opposes logic. Logical action requires that expression can be subordinated to the will; logical action reflects a deliberate speed and a predetermined direction. Passion reflects spontaneity of action at whatever speed and direction the emotion of the moment generates.

The Latin American relies heavily upon intuition, the passion of the intellect, to point out the solutions to problems. Thought proceeds in a series of direct revelations or perceptions of "truths" concerning the object being contemplated. These perceptions are independent of any demonstrated reasoning process and, therefore, neither verifiable nor repeatable. The tendency is toward action which appears improvised. This characteristic frequently leads Latin Americans to act without planning, at least without conscious planning.

Source: E. C. McCann, "An Aspect of Management Philosophy in the United States and Latin America," *Academy of Management Journal*, June 1964, p. 65. Reprinted with permission.

situation. Exhibit 15–6 offers some pointers in selling to the British, but careful analysis will disclose that most of the points pertain to selling in any country.

Many international salesmen feel that the sales process is similar regardless of the country. One thing that is not similar is the language. The salesman who is going to operate on a continuing basis in a foreign market should be master of the language of a country in which he is working. The ability to handle a language is one prerequisite to the understanding of a foreign culture. Learning the language, however, is only the first step. As one individual has said, "I thought my biggest problem over here (in Paris) would be learning the language, but it's nothing compared with getting the hang of how these people go about their business." Any long-run assignment to a foreign country requires language ability; but many companies have found that if they provide adequate interpreter assistance, they can accomplish much by sending a top-notch salesman from the home country on limited selling tours into many countries. In selling technical products, the man's scientific and engineering skills may be more important than his communication ability.

Personal Orientation

The marketer who expects to be effective in the international marketplace needs to have a favorable outlook on his international assignment.

EXHIBIT 15–6

Seven Tips on Selling to the British

1. The "soft sell," is more effective by far than a blatant, aggressive pitch for business.
2. Cultivate a sense of humor that is whimsical rather than funny. Learn to laugh at yourself. Then you can laugh at us—and you will be home.
3. Don't rush into Christian (first) names, or you may rush out of them fast. The British make friends slowly; but when you are in, you stay in. Customer loyalty is still very strong in Britain, so let it develop at a British pace, and it will be yours for keeps.
4. Learn to like the ways and habits of the British, and don't tell us how quaint it is to drive on the left-hand side of the road; or how peculiar our money is; or that no one knows how to mix a dry martini. We are quite different from you in many ways, but we are not always stupid.
5. Don't imagine we are as slow as we seem. We don't discuss decisions unless we have something to say, but we do make major decisions more quickly than you do. Allow us to make up our own minds—you'll be surprised how quickly we can do this.
6. Aim to be introduced by someone acceptable locally. We British set great store by a person's connections as well as his qualifications. One word from the right person will open doors otherwise permanently closed, even those of the busiest executive.
7. Don't try to beat us—join us. As any firm knows, one good local representative is worth twenty visits.

Source: "How to Sell the British—A Britisher Talks Back," *Sales Management*, February 29, 1965, p. 98.

People who do not genuinely like what they are doing and where they are doing it stand little chance of success. One executive commented about the danger of overmotivating people to accept overseas assignments: "Failures have usually been the result of overselling or talking him into something, showing him the bright side of the picture, and not warning him about the bleak side." A member of the management board of Nestlé says success in international assignment requires individuals who are interested in adventure and who, therefore, will actively enjoy the challenges of working abroad.

An international salesman must have a high level of adaptability whether he is working in a foreign country or in his own. If he is an expatriate working in a foreign country, he will have to be particularly sensitive to the habits of his market; if he is working in his own country for a foreign company, he must be able to adapt to the requirements and the ways of doing business of the parent company. A study of international managers revealed that inability to adapt to the foreign environment was a primary reason for failure in overseas positions. Note in Exhibit 15–7 that the two leading reasons given for overseas failure of management men relate to inability to adapt, and these reasons account for nearly half the reported failures. Doubtless the same things cause problems for salesmen and sales management personnel.

The problems of adapting to business customs were reviewed in some detail in Chapter 12, but one additional example of the type of international diplomacy required of a salesman may be enlightening. In telling of his work in India, one reporter commented as follows:

EXHIBIT 15–7

Reasons Given for Failure at International Managerial Positions

Reason	Number of Companies
Inability to adapt (either family or man) to foreign environment	25
Cultural shock	9
Personality or emotional immaturity	8
Overestimated managerial capacity	8
Not willing to work the long hours	7
Character and integrity	4
Inability to deal effectively with foreign subordinates	3
Failure to adapt to local business conditions	2
Couldn't get along with local boss	1
Inability to handle expanded job functions	1
Lack of specific skills	1
Total answers	69

Source: Lawrence L. Steinmetz, "The Staffing of Foreign Divisions and Branches: A Descriptive Study of Methods and Techniques Employed by Companies in the United States in Recruiting and Selecting United States Nationals to Manage Foreign Operations" (Ph.D. dissertation, University of Michigan, 1964), p. 96.

One of the hazards of the meeting was the danger of being plied with a continuous round of Coca-Colas. It was impossible to convince the merchants that there was no positive correlation between American citizenship and a preference to this soft drink. On those occasions when I was able to persuade my hosts that I did not want a coke, they gave me an Indian soft drink which must have contained half of India's sugar production. An anthropologist later told me how he survived the soft drink hazard. He told the Indians that it was against his religion to drink carbonated beverages—a statement which they found immediately acceptable.[4]

Successful adaptation in international affairs is based on a combination of attitude and effort. An individual's best intentions may lead him astray if he is not careful to study the customs of the country in which he is working. Such a study should be initiated before he arrives in the country, and the man must then continue to study and learn from his activities in the field. One useful approach is to listen to the advice of other businessmen operating in foreign countries and to the advice of foreign businessmen themselves. The director of a large industrial firm acknowledges the need for adaptability but adds an element which might be called cultural empathy as a prerequisite for foreign success. Such cultural empathy is clearly part of a man's basic orientation because if he is antagonistic to his environment, he is hardly likely to be effective. Dmitris Chorafas has noted:

The ability to respect a country's customs and ethics is the second most important asset right after flexibility. Each country has something interesting

---

[4] Leon V. Hirsch, *Marketing in an Underdeveloped Economy: The North Indian Sugar Industry* (Englewood Cliffs, N.J.: Prentice-Hall, Inc., 1961), p. 10.

BOX 15–3

Tomorrow's International Executive

Let me tell you about the kind of men I think we shall need to man our overseas operations in the future.

This man will not just be a specialist in finance, marketing, engineering, or manufacturing. He must be well-rounded and able to operate with little or no staff in all areas of the business.

One of the prime requisites will be his ability to teach as well as to learn. This becomes of paramount importance in situations where we are trying to staff and man overseas operations with as many nationals as possible. The ability to pass along the plans and requirements of the parent company in a way that foreign business partners can understand and accommodate, is going to have a telling effect on the success of the enterprise.

If he is going to teach, the businessman will have to know something that he can teach. This means a thorough schooling in one or more of the basic business disciplines and at least a workable knowledge of the others.

Some qualifications may sound forbidding in the light of the romance and glamour that is sometimes associated with work in the international arena. Let me say a word about that. There really is not much romance in overseas assignments. They all have their pluses and minuses. Some are almost hardship assignments when the total family is considered. They require some of the staunch qualities of the pioneer.

Source: James H. Goss, vice president and group executive, International Group, General Electric Company, in *Doing Business Abroad,* April 29, 1965.

for the cultured man. His ability to adjust to local culture makes his assignment a challenge. Besides, making a good adjustment is practically synonomous with making right decisions. A man who thinks the same way whether he is in Japan, Chile, Belgium, Italy or the United States will never be a successful executive.[5]

Speaking of Japan, Professor Yoshino suggests that

adjusting to the more visible aspects of the culture is difficult enough but adjustment to the day to day working environment as well as to the manner in which the business is carried out in Japan is considered to be even more difficult. The latter kind of cultural shock is very subtle but nevertheless is just as real as the former type.[6]

The personal characteristics, skills, and orientation which identify the potentially effective man have been identified and labeled in many different ways, and each person studying the field has his own preferred list of characteristics. Yet rising above all the characteristics there is an intangible something which some people have referred to as factor X or a sixth sense, implying that regardless of the individual attributes, there is a certain blend of personal characteristics, skills, and orientation

---

[5] D. Chorafas, op. cit., p. 70.
[6] M. Y. Yoshino, "Administrative Attitudes and Relationships in a Foreign Culture," *MSU Business Topics,* Winter 1968, p. 63.

EXHIBIT 15–8

Ethiopian and American Views of the Ideal Manager

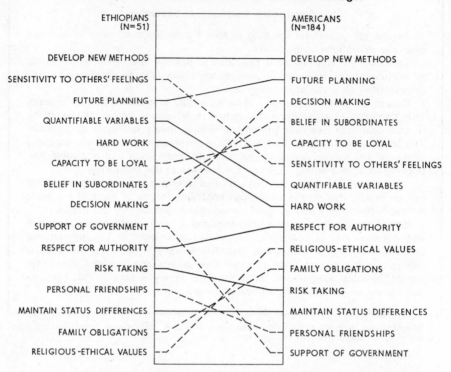

ETHIOPIANS
(N=51)

AMERICANS
(N=184)

ETHIOPIANS	AMERICANS
DEVELOP NEW METHODS	DEVELOP NEW METHODS
SENSITIVITY TO OTHERS' FEELINGS	FUTURE PLANNING
FUTURE PLANNING	DECISION MAKING
QUANTIFIABLE VARIABLES	BELIEF IN SUBORDINATES
HARD WORK	CAPACITY TO BE LOYAL
CAPACITY TO BE LOYAL	SENSITIVITY TO OTHERS' FEELINGS
BELIEF IN SUBORDINATES	QUANTIFIABLE VARIABLES
DECISION MAKING	HARD WORK
SUPPORT OF GOVERNMENT	RESPECT FOR AUTHORITY
RESPECT FOR AUTHORITY	RELIGIOUS-ETHICAL VALUES
RISK TAKING	FAMILY OBLIGATIONS
PERSONAL FRIENDSHIPS	RISK TAKING
MAINTAIN STATUS DIFFERENCES	MAINTAIN STATUS DIFFERENCES
FAMILY OBLIGATIONS	PERSONAL FRIENDSHIPS
RELIGIOUS-ETHICAL VALUES	SUPPORT OF GOVERNMENT

Note: Dashed line denotes pair of ranking distributions found to be significantly different.
Source: James A. Lee, "Developing Managers in Developing Countries," *Harvard Business Review*, November–December 1968, p. 61.

which is hard to pinpoint and which may differ from individual to individual but which produces the most effective overseas personnel. Exhibit 15–8 highlights the differing views of people from different cultures on the importance of various attributes of the ideal manager.

SOURCES OF MARKETING MANPOWER

Logically speaking, any level of marketing manpower may be derived from one of three sources: (1) the home country of the hiring firm, (2) the country in which the firm is doing business, and (3) a third country. As we have said, personnel in the first category are called expatriates; those in the second, foreign nationals; and those in the third, third-country personnel. Actual employment practices place heavy reliance on expatriates for top- and middle-management positions. At present, for example, it is estimated that some 40,000 Americans have the primary responsibility for managing foreign operations of U.S. companies. This pattern is changing rapidly to place additional emphasis on foreign nationals' management, but the ease and familiarity of using

BOX 15-4

Differing Philosophies

Thus, American managers seem to feel that human relations in Europe have an authoritarian and paternalistic flavor, and consider the social distance between individuals a remnant from feudal times. Europeans, in turn, believe America to be guilty of promoting excessive egalitarianism and status stripping which, in their eyes, is not only naïve and unrealistic, but must inevitably destroy management effectiveness in the long run.

Source: Otto Nowotny, "American versus European Management Philosophy," *Harvard Business Review*, March–April 1964.

expatriates is appealing to international companies, regardless of their headquarters' location. Americans prefer to have their operations managed by Americans, Germans by Germans, Japanese by Japanese, and so forth. At the operative level, business long ago learned that it must depend heavily on foreign nationals. When international business was functioning at the level of one salesman per foreign country or per several foreign countries, expatriate salesmen made a certain sense, but now with hundreds of salesmen in some markets it is not only impractical but virtually impossible to field an expatriate sales force. Even if such a force could be constructed, the cost would be prohibitive and the effectiveness low.

Expatriates

An expatriate is one who is working in a country or countries other than his own. Relatively speaking, expatriate salesmen are declining in importance as the volume of world trade increases and as more companies find that they are able to secure foreign nationals who can fill marketing positions.

Expatriates may be committed to a foreign assignment for varying lengths of time, ranging from a few weeks or months to a lifetime. Some expatriates have one-time assignments (which may last for years), after which they are returned to the parent company, whereas others are essentially professional expatriates who work abroad in country after country. Still another type of expatriate assignment involves a career-long assignment to a given country or region, one which is likely to lead to assimilation of the expatriate into the foreign culture so that he may more closely resemble a foreign national than an expatriate. Marketing personnel on expatriate status are likely to cost the company a great deal more than foreign nationals, so the company should be certain that their effectiveness is commensurate with the added expense. In most contemporary situations, companies attempt to establish the foreign operation using expatriate personnel, then phase them out at the earliest possible time in favor of foreign nationals. Nevertheless, the expatriate salesman may have a number of advantages over the foreign national. For example, he may have more adequate technical training and a better knowledge of the company and its product line. Often he is selected from the company's domestic sales force so that the company has adequate knowledge not only of his technical ability but of his personal dependability and effectiveness as well. The expatriate salesman often will be more effective than the foreign salesman in communicating with the parent company; by having worked with it, he knows better what is expected and what special assistance he can receive in accomplishing his sales job. Because they are not natives, expatriate salesmen may sometimes add to the prestige of the line in the eyes of foreign customers.

Despite his advantages, the expatriate salesman does encounter the handicaps which go along with doing business in an unfamiliar culture. In some instances, a company will be forced to use foreign salesmen because of legal barriers against expatriates. The company may also find itself up against some real cost differentials when it attempts to keep a salesman in the field and maintain his standard on a domestic level. Expatriate salesmen often judge their compensation by a dual standard which includes both the foreign standard of living and comparison of pay levels of domestic salesmen. Pay may be irrelevant in some of the world marketplaces with less desirable living conditions because it may be nearly impossible to find salesmen other than foreign nationals who are willing to live in undesirable countries.

In general, it makes most sense to use expatriate salesmen when products are highly technical or when selling requires engineering or other technical services calling for an extensive backlog of information which may not be easily imparted to a foreign salesman. Furthermore, since many national markets will not support full-time salesmen, these markets must be serviced through other types of middlemen or by cosmopolitan sales personnel who go from country to country or who allocate only part of their time to foreign markets away from their home office. When it first began engaging in international exporting, the Hewlett-Packard Company, for example, serviced foreign markets by sending the sales manager or a salesman directly from its U.S. offices on short business trips abroad.

If an expatriate sales force is being developed, will personnel from the company's regular sales force be recruited or will new men be sought for the expatriate positions? When salesmen are taken from the regular sales force, the exact nature and location of their new assignment should be made very clear or disillusionment may set in. The attitude of the family to living abroad for extended periods should certainly be considered, for dependents' attitudes have proved to be a stumbling block for many individuals who themselves may be perfectly willing to work overseas.

Many companies hire young people right out of college, run them through a training program, and then ship them off to foreign markets. Companies using this approach must be on the lookout for the individual with the free-trip-to-Europe mentality who has no intention of staying with a company any longer than the novelty of working abroad appeals to him or who is unwilling to take anything but a choice overseas

BOX 15–5

Foreign Manager's Batting Average

Nevertheless, although expatriates often exaggerate the problem, study of the plants and the operating results indicated that there were in fact many evidences of weaknesses in foreign national managers judged by U.S. standards. Low productivity, amateurish or paternalistic industrial relations, nonexistent production control, the "executive complex," failure to follow through, the lack of a sense of the importance of time—all these reported features were found to have a significant basis in fact. There were some notable exceptions—men who were praised and well accepted by the American managers. These men were apt to be at the top of organizations, very westernized in their general appearance and manner. But they were relatively few and far between.

Of course weaknesses of management abroad should come as no great surprise. Lack of experience, cultural differences in values and business emphasis, a dearth of schools of management, an absence of a tradition of business leadership and efficiency all contribute to management weaknesses. Management is a new concept in many countries. Knowing this, it is curious that American businessmen overseas were regularly shocked, surprised, irritated, and disappointed over the performance and behavior of foreign national managers.

Source: W. Skinner, *American Industry in Developing Economies* (New York: John Wiley & Sons, Inc., 1968), pp. 201–2. Reprinted with permission.

assignment. To be successful, the recruit must know exactly what he is getting into and be prepared to put in long years in foreign positions. Not too many years ago, direct hiring was fashionable and it appeared that this would be a standard entry for foreign operations. In recent years, however, it has become apparent that many companies have become disillusioned with this approach because they have found that they were in the position of sending out young men who knew little about the company or its products. Many companies decided that if about the company or its products. Many companies decided that it they had to use expatriate salesmen they would prefer to have someone who knew a considerable amount either about the foreign market or about the company. They found it preferable to train individuals in one rather than in two important areas.

Third-Country Manpower

With the growing internationalization of business, it is not unusual to encounter a special type of expatriate who may be called a "third person" because he is from country A working for a company headquartered in country B, in country C, or in countries C, D, E, etc. Such third-country arrangements are most likely to be found in management levels but are infrequent in the sales force. Development of third-country executives reflects not only a growing internationalization of business

BOX 15–6

Culture and Skills

Experience has shown us that some skills just develop better in particular places, and these skills normally have little to do with the national origin of the person concerned. Those of you who know South America know how the Argentinian enjoys being sad. This is true whether he is of German or Italian or Japanese origin. Just across the border the Brazilian really enjoys being happy and this is true whether he is of German or Italian or Japanese origin.

If you want to look for skill in dress designing, you go to France; you would not go to Germany. If you want skill in brewing, you go to Germany; you don't go to Brazil. If you want skill in far-out architecture, you go to Brazil, not Japan. If you want skill in ship building, you go to Japan, not the United States. If you want skill in large-scale industrial organization, you go to the United States.

Source: J. R. Ritchie, remarks, Transnational Personnel Session of 53d National Foreign Trade Convention, November 18, 1968, p. 89.

but acknowledges that manpower skills and motivations are not the exclusive property of one nation. Furthermore, such personnel reflect the "growing up" of international business. Burroughs Corporation provides an example of third-country crossbreeding. At one time their Italian company was run by a Frenchman, their Swiss company by a Dane, their German company by an Englishman, their French company by a Swiss, their Venezuelan company by an Argentinian, and their Danish company by a Dutchman. It is hard to pin an "ugly American" label on such a company. Unfortunately, such third-country arrangements are rare below top management, but there is a growing trend toward the use of third-country personnel.

The handling of third-country marketing personnel differs little from that of any other expatriates, who share the same general type of adjustments, the same compensation problems, the same cultural shock, and the same requirement for adaptation, regardless of the home country.

Foreign Nationals

The historical preference for using expatriate managers from the home-office country is gradually giving way to a preference for foreign nationals. The vice president of IBM World Trade Company summarizes the case which historically has been made for using Americans abroad.

In the past, most American companies doing business abroad, including IBM World Trade, have depended primarily on Americans to fill the international jobs and to provide the communications links between the subsidiaries and the home office. And in many cases, Americans have been assigned to manage local subsidiaries directly.

There have been good reasons for this. For one thing, it is more convenient. The American is there and he's easy to identify. He speaks the language of the home office and he thinks that way too. And in the American tradition, he is mobile, ready to pick up his family and furniture to move to just about any spot on the globe.

On the other hand, most of us have believed that foreigners are not very mobile; that their ties to home and country are stronger than their ambitions. Therefore, they are really not candidates for the top jobs in international operations.

Furthermore, a lot of us believed that a foreigner running a local subsidiary of an American company would rather report to an American boss because he is neutral, less prejudiced and because he has better contacts back at the home office.

And I think most of us have had a natural bias toward American managers. We believe they are more aggressive businessmen, more flexible, and are exposed to better management training.[7]

Studies made for IBM, however, have changed some of the notions mentioned above. In one survey the company discovered that over half of its European managers have an interest in pursuing a management career outside their home country and that most of the European managers would prefer reporting to the best man available, regardless of his nationality. An ironic twist to the whole story is that Americans are becoming increasingly attuned to using the foreign managers, but the foreign personnel who previously had strong preferences for working for American firms are finding new opportunities in their home countries or in third countries. Foreign nationals cite a number of reasons for preferring foreign companies, but one of the chief problems is that the foreign national seldom feels that he is treated as equal to the American expatriates. At the same time, however, there is a clear indication that the number of foreign nationals who are qualified for marketing management positions is growing rapidly—despite the international shortage of marketing managers.

At the level of the salesman, the picture is clearly biased in favor of the foreign national. Most companies with sales forces abroad are using foreign nationals because such men transcend both cultural and legal barriers. Furthermore, the companies often find that more foreign manpower is available and that the salary and selling expenses are lower for foreign salesmen than for expatriates. National Cash Register Company, which pioneered the development of foreign sales forces, has developed its in-training process to the point that it is almost as efficient at training in foreign markets as it is domestically. Selection and training do remain as problems, however, for companies that do not have such long experience. Sometimes companies actually find that the foreign salesmen are so close to the culture in which they are working that they are not able to provide effective representation. Such problems are rare but might arise when radical innovations are involved.

Foreign salesmen are most likely to be effective in situations which do not call for extensive or continuing technical training. Foreign salesmen generally should be used whenever the market is large enough to support a number of salesmen and when continued representation is called for. Field supervision may be through either a foreign or expatriate sales

---

[7] E. S. Groo, remarks, Transnational Personnel Session, 53rd National Foreign Trade Convention, November 18, 1968, pp. 79–80.

manager, but in the conditions described above, most companies find it advisable to utilize foreign sales management whenever possible.

DEVELOPING INTERNATIONAL MANPOWER

Several types of manpower are needed to undertake the international marketing function on a large scale: (1) managerial personnel, (2) staff functionaries, and (3) field salesmen. Each requires a somewhat different type of handling, but for all groups it is necessary that the men be recruited, selected, trained, compensated, and motivated. When all these tasks have been accomplished an international marketing force has been initiated, but it needs continuing supervision and control. Cost factors alone dictate effective performance in international manpower management; regardless of the organizational arrangements which are utilized, it is costly to maintain an international marketing operation. Even if it is composed of only one man operating out of the home office, costs will be considerably higher than maintaining that same man in a domestic market. If a large field force is used, costs mount even more rapidly: travel, living expenses, interpreters, and less effective use of time all contribute to the cost of overseas selling. The cost of maintaining a sales manager in foreign operations is also higher than in domestic markets. One company, operating out of the United States, estimates that it cost some $30,000 just to replace a foreign sales manager. The cost of establishing a foreign sales force is estimated to be about three times higher than the cost of establishing a domestic force; furthermore, the turnover rate in international operations is considerably higher. Both recruiting and the continuing costs of salaries and maintenance vary widely for different types of salesmen.

Although the stages in the development of overseas manpower are the same as those in domestic marketing situations, one should not be deceived into overlooking the vast differences in the approaches utilized and the problems encountered in accomplishing these steps in the world market. The manpower sources delineated in the preceding section (e.g. expatriate, third country, and foreign national) further complicate the problems associated with developing international marketing manpower because each of the groups must be handled somewhat differently when being recruited, trained, and compensated. Motivation is especially complicated because the firm is dealing with different levels, different sources, different nationalities—and always dealing with individuals. To simplify analysis, marketing men are divided into managers and salesmen. This section can hardly provide a handbook for performing personnel functions but offers insight into the complexities associated with developing an international marketing force.

Recruitment and Selection

To recruit and select men effectively for international positions, management must know exactly what it expects of its personnel. A formal job description can aid management in expressing its desires, but those responsible for preparing such a description must make certain that they are concerned not only with the immediate problem but also with the long-run needs of the company. In addition to descriptions prepared for each type of marketing position, the criteria should also include special requirements indigenous to various countries. With the continuing shortage of marketing manpower at both the management and the sales levels, it is imperative that companies develop intensive and extensive recruiting procedures. Virtually all of the techniques used in domestic personnel recruiting are effective in world markets, but some additional avenues need to be explored as well.

Many U.S. companies recruit foreign students while they are on American campuses and some have taken campus recruiting techniques from the United States and applied them to foreign markets, where such recruiting is fairly rare. Some companies, such as Procter & Gamble, have had considerable success in hiring foreign students in American universities for assignment in their native countries. Such students combine a knowledge of both cultures and so need only be trained in the company aspects of their job.

Raiding other companies for executive personnel continues to be a major source, one in which American companies have had the distinct advantages for the past 20 years because in most countries it has been prestigious and lucrative to work for an American company. In recent years the trend has been reversed, however, and many managers who have been trained in American companies have found that this type of experience provides them with the credentials most wanted by foreign companies; an exodus of foreign executives from American companies has begun. One surprising source of personnel is foreign nationals who are not living in their home country. One company advertised throughout Europe for Irish expatriates who wanted to return home and very quickly filled its personnel quotas.

If a foreign selling force is to be recruited, whole new sets of problems confront the company. Generally, a foreign sales force will be drawn from the country in which it is to work, but sometimes personnel from other nearby countries are included. A chief problem in recruiting a foreign sales force is that there is generally no well-established pool of experienced personnel who are ready to bring experience and developed ability to the job. Acquisition of foreign companies and development of joint ventures with existing foreign companies have been important methods of acquiring manpower for some companies. These arrangements are especially important when the goal is to build a large field force in a relatively short period of time.

Recruitment of expatriate personnel from within a company is a delicate subject. One must be careful not to oversell the foreign positions; yet the advantages of foreign assignments should not be overlooked. In most companies there are many people interested in overseas assignments to prime (North European) locations but fewer takers for the less desirable assignments in Africa, the Middle East, or the poorer Latin American countries. Exhibit 15–9 summarizes some of the advantages and disadvantages of foreign assignments as seen by expatriates themselves.

Manpower selection criteria need to harmonize the requirements of

EXHIBIT 15–9

Advantages and Disadvantages of Expatriate Assignments

	Percent of Expatriates Citing Factor
Advantages:	
Higher pay	17%
Broader experience and responsibility	16
Learn about people and customs	15
More rapid advancement	14
Self-pleasure and accomplishment	11
Travel abroad	9
Higher living and prestige	6
Avenue for top-executive jobs	3
Tax benefits	3
Education for self and children	3
Domestic help	3
Disadvantages:	
Lack of modern way of life	36%
Being away from home	25
Schooling	17
Less chance for advancement in U.S.	9
Language and customs difficulty	7
Lack of adequate medical care	6
Lack of housing	4
Uncertainty due to unstable local government	3
Forgotten by home office	3

Source: Richard F. Gonzalez and Anant R. Negandhi, *The United States Overseas Executive: His Orientations and Career Patterns* (East Lansing: Division of Research, Graduate School of Administration, Michigan State University, 1967), p. 109. Reprinted by permission of the publisher.

the positions with the requisite skills, attitudes, and personal character-istics discussed earlier in this chapter.[8] Tests, interviews, recommenda-tions and all the other familiar personnel selection devices of domestic business are employed overseas. One caution, however: When Ameri-cans interview foreign personnel they tend to place excessive emphasis on the prospective employee's degree of "Americanization." They are likely to be so impressed by the person's handling of the English language and by his educational credentials that other attributes which may be more important to the foreign position may be overlooked. In general, it can be said that the standard techniques of recruiting and manpower selection are applicable internationally.

In most instances, however, experienced personnel are not available, so the selection job becomes particularly difficult. Sometimes job criteria may be set at several different levels so that a company which finds that it is encountering difficulty in hiring individuals to meet the maximum established criteria can move down through successively lower sets of standards until it is able to find personnel who are at least minimally

---

[8] See F. A. Teague, "International Management Selection and Development," *California Management Review*, Spring 1970, pp. 1–6.

acceptable. Obviously such a situation creates severe complications and places a great burden on the training and management functions.

Training

The nature of the training program will depend largely on whether the objective is to prepare expatriate or foreign personnel for the overseas positions. Emphasis in training expatriate personnel will probably be focused on the customs and special foreign sales problems that will be encountered. Foreign national personnel are not likely to need such training but will need more emphasis on the company, its products, technical information, and the selling methods which are to be utilized. In training both types of personnel, the sales training activity will be freighted with problems because the trainer will be dealing with long-established behavior and attitudes. In working with foreign nationals, one encounters habits which are continually reinforced by local culture. Even the personnel's attitude toward learning can detract from the success of the training program. Expatriates have essentially the same problem because they, too, are captives of their habits and patterns. Americans, particularly, may think that there is not too much to be learned from the foreign culture or from the way things are done in a foreign country. Before any training can be effective, open-minded attitudes must be established. Training can take place either in the country of the parent firm or in the country in which the salesman will work. Whichever alternative is chosen, the sales manager can be certain that translators, travel, and other cost elements will make training personnel for foreign locations more costly than training domestic personnel. At the management level, it is most likely that foreign personnel will be brought to the United States periodically (sometimes for extended periods) for experience, exposure, and training in the home-office and home-country situation. At the level of the sales force, most of the training is undertaken by foreign management personnel, with their activities supplemented by American executives abroad or visits from home-office personnel.

Continuation training may be more important in foreign markets than in domestic ones because there is less routine contact with the parent company and its marketing personnel. Like initial training, continuation training will cost more in overseas than in domestic markets, but it is probably even more vital in the foreign situation because routine company contact is less frequent. On-the-job training is a continuing form of training not only for field personnel but for management as well. In many instances, expatriate personnel are not directly responsible for the management process but are on hand primarily to perform a training function for local management. A Peace Corps volunteer in Peru has written a commentary on his training function which might serve as a model for businessmen.

The slums around Chimbote stretch for miles and miles, staggering the imagination.

My job is to get these people, my neighbors, organized, to make them

BOX 15–7

European versus American Outlook

The most striking difference between the outlooks of Europeans and Americans lies in their orientation toward time. It is as if they were standing back to back, with the European inclined to look to the past and present, and the American seeing the present and the future. The European's attachment to the past accounts for his respect for such characteristics as wisdom, stability, convention, necessity, quality, and diversity. The American's more futuristic outlook leads him to respect vitality, mobility, informality, abundance, quantity, and organization.

Source: Otto Nowotny, "American versus European Management Philosophy," *Harvard Business Review,* March–April 1964.

better able to compete in the city for their rights, and to try and get them to raise their standard of living back to the human race.

I teach in the local school during the days and I teach carpentry to adults at night. Both are important jobs, but I consider them only a front. Teaching kids, while fun for me and hilarious for the rough housing students, is only an excuse for being in the *barriada.*

For example, our school has no roof. It would be a ten dollar project and about one day's labor for two or three Peace Corpsmen to build that roof. Yet we don't do it. If we gave my school a roof, it would always be that, a gift, the *gringo's* roof. When it needed fixing, no one would fix it.

If it takes me a year to talk my neighbors into putting on that roof, it will be worth it. Because it will then be their roof on their school. It would be a small start, but in the right direction. Maybe then we'll take on a little harder project, and step by step build up a powerful organization that is interested in progress and strong enough to do something about it.

It has to be an organization that doesn't need me, however; otherwise it would collapse when I leave.[9]

One type of training is frequently overlooked; home office personnel dealing with the international marketing operations should have training directly oriented to making them responsive to the needs of their foreign operations. In most companies there is no such training and the requisite sensitivities are expected to be developed (perhaps through osmosis) in the process of dealing with foreign affairs. A few companies not only have indoctrination programs but send home-office personnel abroad periodically to increase their awareness of the problems of the foreign operations.

Compensating

Developing an equitable and functional compensation plan which will combine balance and motivation consistency and flexibility is ex-

---

[9] Tom Carter, "If You Think It Will Be Picturesque, Forget It!" *The Peace Corps Reader* (Washington, D.C.: Peace Corps, 1969), p. 7. Reprinted with permission.

BOX 15–8

The High Cost of Good Living

City	Apartment	Evening Out	Hotel Room	Car Rental	Liquor	Parking	Tuition
Boston.............	$425	$120	$43	$140	$15	$3.50	$2,200
Brussels...........	300	200	28	129	11	1.50	1,200
Chicago...........	400	160	42	125	14	2.50	1,600
Hong Kong........	500	90	30	72	9	2,40	650
Houston...........	200	123	24	156	13	2.00	900
Los Angeles.......	400	200	34	130	16	2.50	1,340
London...........	450	100	45	80	13	2.00	800
Milan.............	325	180	30	130	10	2.50	800
New York.........	650	190	32	140	15	7.00	2,000
Paris.............	400	124	36	110	11	3.25	1,500
San Francisco......	360	120	30	130	17	3.00	1,100
São Paulo.........	400	150	25	145	19	1.50	1,000
Tokyo.............	850	400	22	82	30	4.50	900

Apartment. Monthly rent for two-bedroom, western-style, fully equipped, in first-class area near central city.

Evening out. Tab for four people for three-course meal in first-class restaurant, two drinks before dinner, bottle of good vintage wine, brandy or cordial; theatre tickets [orchestra]; visit to nightclub or cabaret with two drinks or bottle of champagne; taxi ride of about 5 miles.

Hotel room. Nightly rate for standard double room in first-class hotel.

Car rental. Weekly rate, including gasoline, for medium-sized car driven 500 mi.

Liquor. One qt. well-known Scotch whisky; one qt. good quality gin.

Parking. Average all-day rate in central city.

Tuition. Cost per year in first-class private school, elementary grades.

Source: *Business Week*, March 21, 1970, p. 65. Reprinted with permission.

tremely challenging in international operations. This is especially true when a company operates in a number of countries, when it has individuals who work in a number of countries, or when the force is composed partly of expatriate personnel and partly of foreign personnel. The simple situation of a foreign salesman working in his own country is not much more complicated than a domestic compensation problem, except the widely fluctuating cost-of-living patterns prevailing in many parts of the world may add a more dynamic element than is normally found in the United States.

Fringe benefits play a great role in many countries. Salesmen in a high fringe-benefit country have a proportionately lower level of take-home pay than in other countries. Sometimes men working in high-tax countries prefer liberal expense accounts and fringe benefits, which are nontaxable, to direct income subject to high taxes. Fringe-benefit costs are high in Europe. In Belgium fringe benefits add about 35 percent to salary costs; in Germany, 40 percent; and in France, nearly 60 percent.

Pay may be a significant factor in making it difficult for a man to be repatriated. Often, the man will find that he is making considerably

EXHIBIT 15–10

**Executive Salary Comparison by Function and Country
(direct salary U.S. dollars)**

Country	Marketing	Manufacturing	Industrial Relations and Personnel	Finance	Research
Belgium...............	$15–25,000	$14–24,000	$10–14,000	$14–21,000	$13–20,000
France................	17–29,000	18–28,000	11–19,000	15–26,000	16–22,000
Germany..............	16–28,000	15–23,000	12–20,000	14–21,000	13–23,000
Italy..................	16–24,000	17–25,000	10–16,000	13–19,000	15–21,000
Luxembourg...........	13–22,000	12–21,500	9–12,000	12–18,000	12–17,000
Netherlands...........	16–26,000	14–22,000	11–19,000	14–22,000	13–18,000
United Kingdom........	14–22,000	10–18,000	9–12,000	12–18,000	11–18,000
United States.........	27–38,000	24–33,000	13–22,000	26–35,000	18–27,000

(The column group header "Executive Function" spans Marketing, Manufacturing, Industrial Relations and Personnel, Finance, and Research.)

Source: Towers, Perrin, Forster & Crosby, Consultants, 1968.

more money and has a lower cost of living in an overseas market, and he cannot afford to return to the parent country without a cut in pay or in his standard of living. Such a situation is indeed frustrating for the man, but it may cause serious equity, assignment, and relocation problems for the company.

Conglomerate operations, which include both domestic and foreign personnel, cause the greatest problems in compensation planning. Expatriates tend to compare their compensation with that which they would have received at the home office; at the same time, foreign personnel and expatriate personnel are likely to compare notes on salary. Even though there may be differences in compensation level which are easily and logically explained, the group receiving the lower amount will almost always feel aggrieved and mistreated.

Short-term assignments for expatriates complicate the compensation issue, particularly when the short-term assignment extends for a longer period of time than anticipated. In general, short-term assignments involve payment of overseas premiums (sometimes called separation allowances if the family does not accompany the man), all excess expenses, and allowances for tax differentials. Longer assignments include home-leave benefits or travel allowances for the wife to visit the employee. Many companies estimate that these expenses will approximately equal the base compensation of the man. Every company has its own approach to the solution of the compensation problem. Unfortunately, in most cases compensation policy has grown in a piecemeal manner patterned on the U.S. compensation system. Since such an approach is often inadequate, most companies are rethinking their remuneration plans and attempting to harmonize their international programs. Ideally an effective compensation system is equitable, competitive, consistent, and flexible; it also reflects the fact that remuneration includes both monetary and nonmonetary rewards, direct pay, and intangibles. Keeping these goals in mind will make it possible to implement workable compensation plans which will help attract, retain, and motivate high-quality personnel.[10]

Motivating

Marketing is a business function requiring high motivation, regardless of the location of the practitioner. Marketing managers and sales managers typically work hard, travel extensively, and have day-to-day challenges and measures of performance. Selling is hard, competitive work wherever undertaken, and a constant flow of inspiration is needed to keep personnel on their toes. Consideration of national differences must always be borne in mind in motivating the marketing force. Foreign salesmen and managers can have quite different motives from those of expatriate salesmen and expatriate managers. Each group may require different motivational approaches. One company found that its salesmen were losing respect and had low motivation because they did not have girls in the Japanese branch offices to pour tea for customers. The company learned that when the male personnel served tea they lost face; so tea girls have been authorized for all branches.

Nearly all the devices and techniques used to motivate a domestic sales force may be successfully employed in a foreign situation when they have been modified to meet the outlook and orientation of the personnel involved. All men work basically for remuneration, so the compensation program can be an effective motivator. When National Cash Register of Japan (which has some 5,000 employees in Japan) established a commission plan for salesmen, other businessmen were scandalized; commission sales are an alien practice. The salesmen, however, have responded favorably to the increased earnings realized through the commission system. Goodyear's experience in Japan was exactly the opposite; its employees opted for annual pay raises rather than merit increases and thought all salesmen hired in a given year should maintain comparable base pay throughout their tenure with the company. To motivate the men, Goodyear uses individual bonuses as rewards for exceeding quotas and to encourage competition among its various branches.

Communications are also important in maintaining high levels of motivation; foreign managers need to know that the home office is interested in their operations and want to be in on what is happening in the parent country. Everyone performs better when well informed. Some companies use the "college football" approach in "controlling the emotional swings of salesmen from peak to depth and back to peak again." Salesmen around the world seem to respond to the typical American "rah rah" sales meeting; one U.S. executive in Japan mixes drive and praise in his pep sessions and finds that "the staff hits peak

10 John Vivian and Carlos Michelsen-Terry, "International Remuneration," *World*, May 1969, pp. 51–57.

BOX 15–9

Britannica Rues a Wave of Zeal

Few U.S. companies in Japan have done more to blend deftly into the local landscape than has Encyclopedia Britannica (Japan), Ltd., in the past seven years. It has a Japanese partner, employs Japanese in key executive positions, emphasizes fluency in Japanese for its American employees, and motivates its 2,000-man sales force with Britannica songs and banzai cheers every morning.

But this past week, Britannica was sticking out like a sore thumb. The Japan Consumers Union charged the wholly owned subsidiary with fraudulent salesmanship, the first time a foreign firm has been attacked on these grounds. In complaints filed with the Tokyo district prosecutor's office and the Fair Trade Commission, Britannica was charged with misleading families into buying 24-volume sets of erudition with purportedly vague promises that it would help their children learn English. The complaint states that salesmen would first quote a price of $1,275, and then cajole potential buyers with "bargain rates" that cut the tab back to $598—which is what Britannica executives say the package should cost.

Further, unhappy buyers could not get their yen back. And, claims Tomokazu Iwata, the consumer group's leader, Britannica salesmen duped the gullible by talking them into signing "questionnaires" that turned out to be sales contracts. When buyers tried to break the contracts, claims Iwata, salesmen cautioned that "American business is not easy to back out on, and we have to go through with the deal."

The Heavies. No one is militating against the product. Crown Prince Akihito and even one Consumers Union official are among the 120,000 satisfied customers. Britannica's energetic salesmen are the heavies. Some of them,

---

performance shortly thereafter, then they fall off sharply until he calls them into the locker room again three weeks later."

Promotion and the opportunity to get ahead and improve status are important motivators, so the company needs to make clear the opportunities for growth within the firm. Expatriate managers express one of their greatest fears is that they will be forgotten by the home office, but such fears can easily be allayed.

All the cultural differences reviewed in Chapters 4 and 12 affect the motivational patterns of salesmen, so a manager must be extremely sensitive to the personal behavior patterns of his men. Imagine the sales manager's problem if he expects Orientals to deal with customers on a single-contact basis or if he tries to have Mexican salesmen do business at lunch. Blending company sales objectives and personal objectives of the salesmen and other employees is a task worthy of the most skilled manager, but it must be undertaken if personnel are to be highly motivated and effective in their work.

the complaint charges, promoted the encyclopedia as easy to read by show-ing only illustrations or portions edited specifically for children. In return for their zeal, salesmen were awarded with costly sales promotion prizes (trips to Hawaii, cars, and color TV sets) that are illegal in Japan.

Britannica Japan's president John Stegmaier quickly bought newspaper space to say that the company was "profoundly shocked" by the charges, and so sorry to have caused any customer inconvenience. "When you have as many people as we do all over the country," Stegmaier argues, "it's al-most unavoidable to have a few who are going to misrepresent or exagger-ate. When it happens, we fire them fast."

To help that pink-slipping, the company was installing special telephone lines and a complaint department last week. "If we're violating any Japanese laws," says Britannica's General Counsel Thomas Curtis in Chicago, "we'll get the matter corrected. I know there have been some problems there, be-cause consumerism is growing in Japan, just as it is here."

Some of Britannica's troubles may stem from the relative novelty of its door-to-door salesmanship in Japan. Japanese housewives may have been accustomed to periodic visits from salesmen (herb medicines, bank accounts, even cars are solicited on doorsteps), but not Britannica's brand. It paid off last year with Japan producing fully half of the parent company's foreign sales—$19.4-million. But that quota, say the consumer advocates, came at considerable cost to Japanese eardrums.

A Britannica salesman, once he got through the customer's door, would pitch the package for as long as four hours, and, says one Japanese ruefully, "it is very hard for us to say no."

Source: *Business Week*, November 21, 1970, pp. 34–35. Reprinted with permission.

SUMMARY AND CONCLUSIONS

An effective international manpower force may constitute one of the world marketer's greatest concerns. The company sales force represents one of the major alternate methods of organizing a company for foreign distribution and, as such, is on the front line of a marketing organiza-tion.

The role of marketers in both domestic and foreign markets is rapidly changing, along with the composition of international sales forces. Such forces have many unique requirements which can be filled by expatri-ates, foreign nationals, third-country personnel, or a combination of the three. In recent years the pattern of development has been to place emphasis on the foreign personnel operating in their own land.

The overseas selling force is likely to be organized in such a way that it may be managed from the home office or from a foreign sales office, but regardless of which of the several alternate organizational arrange-ments is utilized, the problems of developing an overseas sales force remain frustratingly real. It is likely that in future years we shall see considerable growth in the number and importance of international sales forces as large, well-financed companies learn that they must shift from dependence on external middlemen to dependence on an inside sales force which can be more completely managed and which gives a company a better chance for success in increasingly competitive markets.

READING

NOT SO MULTINATIONAL, AFTER ALL*

JOHN THACKRAY

In the past couple of years, the notion of the multinational corporation has been fashionably popular among big business executives; though they use the term "multinational" with some vagueness and imprecision as to its meaning, or as to what it should mean. To some executives in big business it is a present reality; to others it is not yet in existence, but only at the development stage; to some it is measured by the degree of foreign profit a company has; to others it is measured by the number of foreign manufacturing plants a company has; to still others a company is or is not multinational depending on "an attitude of mind on the part of management."

Regardless of the exact meaning attributed to the term, it is universally liked. Multinational is a word with, for businessmen, a pleasantly expansionist ring to it; with intimation of new, widening horizons, greater and greater conquests ahead. Perhaps it also invokes a suggestion of imperial, corporate majesty.

Interviews with a number of international big businessmen also suggest that for them the idea of the multinational company connotes what might lightly be called the "United Nations syndrome"—the hopeful notion that the international industrial corporation is going out to embrace the peoples of the world, to bring them together in its ample bosom and thus work against the spirits of nationalism that disturb the peace of our world. In their wilder moments such businessmen dream of a world corporate order which is harmonious, technologically brilliant and beneficent.

Some of this optimism may be slightly misplaced. While multinational companies will doubtless continue to reach out for greater expansion in those countries where they operate, and to march into new territories, it is by no means certain that they will evolve into institutions that are truly internationalist in spirit, in fact and, especially, in *management,* which almost none of them is at present.

There are two broad classes of managers in the large international company. One is the national of the parent company, working either

---

* *Interplay of European/American Affairs,* November, 1968, pp. 23–25.

somewhere in the domestic operations, abroad or at headquarters. The second is the indigenous executive manning the foreign outpost.

The existence of these two unequal classes is seldom mentioned by the persons involved; and when admitted, it is softly, softly. Corporate ideology declares that all men have equal opportunities for advancement and success—every toiling executive has the president's slide rule or the president's nameplate somewhere in the drawers of his desk.

There are good and sufficient reasons as to why there should be these two classes of executives. But their existence presents a serious impediment to the creation of a managerial structure and an executive corps in multinational companies that can be, in the fullest sense, internationalist—where the significance of a man's nationality might be no more than the color of his tie or the style of his shoes. Because of these two classes, we may never see what would be the acid test of managerial multinationalism: an Italian president of an American-owned multinational, for example, or a Latin American running a Dutch-owned multinational.

Capital has its own nationality. As things stand at present, it is unlikely that shareholders in multinational companies—tame as they are —would accept a foreigner as the chief executive officer and caretaker of their investments. Equally, politicians, statesmen and government civil servants would probably object to a foreigner holding billions of dollars worth of industrial power.

Of course, the nationality of a company's capital could be broken up, at least partially, by selling a piece of the ownership in the foreign subsidiary to local residents. This has been done on a number of occasions. There is, however, reason to believe that in most cases this is not an attractive course of action for most multinational companies, which achieve their maximum profit through a worldwide integration of production and distribution. To take one piece of a multinational combine and make it an autonomous profit-making instrument, with a responsibility to local shareholders for earning an adequate profit in its sector, both inhibits headquarter's freedom of action and eliminates some of the economic benefits of global integration. The oil companies, for instance, do not lend themselves to being divided into sectional, geographic units. The same is true of most large-scale and technologically sophisticated manufacturing operations.

Then, to state the obvious, another barrier to corporate internationalism lies in the fact that men's lives are rooted in national customs, habits and values which they have accepted from childhood. Within the multinational corporation this means that most executives are conservatively wedded to their own little national turf. Consequently we find that there are few transfers across national frontiers. To be sure, we see more than a handful of foreigners in the lobbies, elevators and offices of the headquarters of most multinationals. These people are usually there only for temporary training, indoctrination or consultation. Sooner or later, most will be returned home.

Where there's an experienced senior executive who is a national of the subsidiary's country of operations, he will rarely be transferred abroad; not because he is discriminated against—though there is some of that—but, just as often, because he doesn't want to move. Many a European executive for an American multinational has declined an invitation to step up the ladder of promotion and join the staff at head-quarters in New York, Akron, Detroit or Columbus. As one executive at Singer put it: "Take a senior manager of ours in the British subsidiary. He has a whole style of life over there—the old school tie and all that—and he accepts so-called promotion to New York. His first few days here, someone who is almost a complete stranger walks into his office in his shirtsleeves and calls him Joe. Why should he like that?"

There are some exceptions, however. There is one small class of executives that apparently accept frequent cultural dislocation as the price of ambition. These are what might be called the "internationalist executives"—a small group of men in any company who, either by accident or design, spend a large part of their careers hopping from country to country as required by headquarters. Such executives, in the words of one of them, "must remain mobile, must be able to live in different societies and adjust quickly—if you don't adjust you're finished —must be willing to be transferred to Hong Kong tomorrow if necessary . . . must commit themselves to mobility."

Every large international company has its group of internationalist executives. It is always small: usually less than five percent of the whole international staff. Their main function is to handle the periodic crises and emergencies in the outlands of the corporate empire.

In Indonesia, Royal Dutch Shell used to be represented by Dutch executives who ran a company which was financially owned by Shell's Dutch chain of interlocking subsidiaries. When Sukarno threatened to nationalize all Dutch business in Indonesia, Shell quickly transferred the ownership of the Indonesian company to one of its Canadian subsidiaries and, in the incredibly short space of one month, with no disruption of production, moved all its Dutchmen out of the country and replaced them with British, Canadian and American workers. When IBM urgently needed a marketing manager in India, to give another example, it sent out a member of its internationalist executive group, who found a replacement, trained him, then returned to New York.

The number of multinational companies that get their best executives to join this internationalist group is probably quite small. Certainly, in most of the American-owned multinationals, an executive's safest route to the top is never to leave the head office court. Some years ago a high man in du Pont was sent to Europe on a tour of duty. He received the news glumly. Fearing that he would lose his place in the pecking order at Wilmington, he arranged that nobody would occupy his office during his absence and that his name would remain flying reassuringly on the door.

What this man feared, others happily embrace. There are executives who sacrifice some ambition for the perks and fringe benefits of foreign service. They leave their own and their company's mother country because of the attractions of foreign service premiums, extra bonuses, cost of living allowances and hardship allowances. "You go to this cocktail party in Sao Paulo, and meet this couple. She's from South Carolina. And she tells you she has a cook, a maid and a gardener who cost next to nothing a week. And the company provides him with a chauffeured limousine for his private use. You can feel it in your bones that they are never going to leave," says a British businessman. These are, of course, very familiar colonial types. Maybe, though, they are a diminishing group. According to a study prepared by McKinsey & Co., the management consultants, the largest numbers of colonial executives are in countries with underdeveloped economies, where local talent is hard to find. Based on a survey of 700 American-owned companies operating in 18 countries, McKinsey found that "on the average, 70 percent of the surveyed European managing directors were local nationals, contrasted with 30 percent in Latin America. Within Latin America the proportion of local national managing directors ranged from a low of 14 percent in Venezuela to a high of 37 percent in Argentina."

In many ways the multinational's network of foreign subsidiaries is not very different from the domestic subsidiary structure. Both have to execute centrally-formulated company policy. As can be imagined, this can and does lead to conflict and disagreement. But the tensions tend to be much worse in the foreign subsidiary, and for a simple reason. An order given from New York to a subsidiary in Illinois has a very different character to the recipient than the same order from New York to a subsidiary in Scandinavia or Japan. The men in New York and Illinois have, in many respects, a common identity which is not shared by Japanese and Americans. This writer personally witnessed the founding of the London branch of Arthur Andersen & Co., one of the largest chartered accounting firms in the world. Because of the many dictates laid down from Chicago, some of them very trivial, some of them entirely inappropriate to local conditions, British accountants who had joined the firm were formally "re-educated" in a way that was professionally humiliating.

No doubt such mistakes and such arrogance are found less and less often these days. The foreign investments of the new multinationals have grown to the point where they can no longer be treated as casual "dumping grounds" for surplus investment funds and surplus technology. Yet there are almost no multinationals where the foreign subsidiaries participate in formulating companywide policy. (H. J. Heinz, incidentally, provides an interesting illustration of a company that does.) In the majority of companies, however, the flow of information between headquarters and the foreign subsidiaries occurs at middle management levels. The impact of this process can be considerable. Volkswagen's American subsidiary, staffed mostly by non-Germans, has made some important contributions to company-wide public relations and advertising. Still, there are no non-Germans among the senior management group at Wolfsburg, and perhaps some Americans in the company feel the lack, or will in the future. Even IBM, where foreign operations produce about a third of all revenues and profit, the president of the international company, a Frenchman, is the only non-American out of 38 IBM officers.

The difference between the two classes of executives is most concretely expressed in the disparity of remuneration—a difference that is particularly large in U.S.-owned multinational companies. "When I am in England," says a U.S. executive, "I am always hearing from our people over there that they'd be making three times as much as they make now, if they worked over here in the States."

There is little that a multinational can do about this, even supposing it wanted to. Each nation has a distinctive pay scale, end product prices and national productivity. "There is a market for personnel, and we try and get the best value we can in the marketplace," said an oil executive. "Does that mean we discriminate with our salaries? Yes, it does—when the market discriminates."

It is often maintained that business management is pretty much the same the world over. "Our problems in Manila are not so different from our problems in Cincinnati," declared a Volkswagen man. If the whole world spoke Esperanto and had the same laws and customs, then business problems could be solved on a global scale.

But international business language, though fairly standard everywhere, is limited by the differences in men's mother tongues. Misunderstandings and confusions are quite frequent. A few years ago, for instance, the manager of one of the Shell refineries in Latin America wrote a performance review, or job appraisal, on one of his subordinates, a Dutchman. This report was very flattering. According to its author, it would guarantee the man further promotion. The performance review was shown to the subordinate, who immediately became wretchedly unhappy. With tears in his eyes, he declared that on no account could this document be forwarded to headquarters in Europe. Why? Because the writer had described him as "ambitious." The manager explained that the word ambitious meant nothing but good. The longer he explained, the more miserable the subordinate became. Eventually the muddle was ironed out. Shell's refinery management at The Hague is mostly composed of Dutchmen. To these men the word ambitious is opprobrious, signifying that, as the manager later explained, "he was a guy wearing cleated shoes and ready to run up the backs of the next men up the line."

The problems of language have an effect on the entire process of management, putting those who don't speak the company tongue at a distinct disadvantage. "Not only is it difficult to learn to speak another language, but the second thing, for a manager, is that to be effective in the business field he must be able to *win arguments*. That's the big problem," says a German at IBM.

All of which suggests that despite the commonality of executive experience and the relative simplicity of business methodology there are powerful influences that divide and separate men in the multinational corporation. The multinational corporation may indeed be "one world" unto itself. But it is a world that contains many frontiers, many inequalities of power, status and money which will probably never be entirely eliminated.

QUESTIONS

1. Define:
   Expatriate
   Third-country personnel
   Line and staff organization
2. Why may it be difficult to adhere to set job criteria in selecting foreign personnel? What compensating actions might be necessary?
3. Why does the conglomerate sales force cause special compensation problems? Suggest some alternative solutions.
4. Under what circumstances should expatriate salesmen be utilized?
5. Discuss the problems which might be encountered in having an expatriate sales manager supervising foreign salesmen.
6. "To some extent, the exigencies of the manpower situation will dictate the approach to overseas sales organization." Discuss.
7. How do legal factors affect international sales management?
8. Explain why a company might use a sales organization like that shown in Exhibit 15–4 rather than that shown in Exhibit 15–3.
9. How does the sales force relate to company organization? To channels of distribution?
10. "It is costly to maintain an international sales force." Comment.
11. Adaptability and maturity are traits needed by all salesmen. Why should they be singled out as especially important for international salesmen?
12. Interview a local company that has a foreign sales operation. Draw an organization chart for the sales function and explain why that particular structure was used by that company.
13. Evaluate the three major sources of multinational manpower.
14. What factors complicate the task of motivating the foreign sales force?

Reading

1. Review the barriers to "corporate internationalism."
2. Discuss the implications of Thackray's two classes of executives.

OUTLINE OF CHAPTER 16

INTRODUCTION

CONTROL AS A MANAGEMENT TOOL

CENTRALIZATION OF CONTROL

GENERAL CONTROL CONCEPTS

IMPACT OF ORGANIZATONAL STRUCTURE ON CONTROL

AREAS OF CONTROL
  Volume Control
  Price Control
  Product Control
  Promotional Control
  Channel Control
  Marketing Manpower Control
  Profit Control

CONTROL SEQUENCE
  Establish Objectives
  Select Control Method
  Set Standards
  Locate Responsibility
  Establish Communication System
    Periodic Inquiry
    Automatic Systems
    Company Records
    Field Audits
    Communication Breakthroughs
  Evaluate Results and Make Corrections

SUMMARY AND CONCLUSIONS

READING

  Foreign Operation: A Guide for Top Management, *Harvard Business Review.*

COORDINATING AND CONTROLLING WORLD MARKETING OPERATIONS

INTRODUCTION

Few business firms control all their domestic functions or activities as thoroughly as they should; still fewer firms adequately control their international activities. To be sure, many understandable reasons exist for not exercising adequate control; nonetheless, continuous coordination and effective managerial control are prime requisites for successful marketing operations. Time lags, cultural lags, communication lags, and varying objectives contribute to the difficulty of establishing and managing an effective system of control for international marketing operations.

The complexities of the international business situation should alert managers to the *special* importance of exercising close control over the international marketing operation. The need for control over international activities has been recognized since the days of traders operating in the far-flung outposts of the Roman Empire, the expanses of the New World, and the European colonies spread over the entire globe. Imagine the control problems of the Hudson Bay Company or the East India Company.

Ironically, even today international business activities frequently receive inadequate coordination or control from top management. Such neglect comes about partly because of the markedly different orientation to these functions in domestic and foreign marketing operations. Many domestic firms lack a well-established communications system but depend on the "feel of the market." Such "feeling" may be possible in the domestic market where there is intimate contact, but it certainly cannot be depended on for controlling far-flung international operations.

Another cause of neglect is that companies may have no real interest in foreign market development. Goods are often exported to foreign markets with little thought of follow-up. Many times overseas business is turned over to an export manager who runs an almost autonomous operation with no coordinating or controlling strings attached. Some companies offer the necessity for flexibility and fast action as an excuse for lax control. Control systems, however, can be established which will not restrict managerial prerogatives in such a way as to impede aggressive marketing.

Parent companies may be content with less than optimal overseas profits because they are not sufficiently committed to their international operations to exert effective control. Unbelievable as it may seem, the sales manager of one firm receiving 26 percent of its sales for international operations recently commented to one of the authors that because foreign sales showed steady growth he didn't really know or care what was going on in the foreign markets. No one else had any responsibility for international marketing in that company; yet the sales manager was willing to depend on fate for the continued growth of the firm's international marketing operation.

To perform consistently at an optimum profit level, all forms of international organization, centralized or decentralized, require a functioning coordination and control system for *every* functional area. Pricing policy and levels, manpower utilization, channel and physical distribution arrangements, advertising, market evaluation selling arrangements, and even the products themselves benefit from well-implemented coordination and control systems.

Establishment of such a comprehensive system is no easy task; a system which adequately controls the operations of one company may overcontrol the activities of a second or undercontrol those of yet another. Furthermore, even within a given company a variety of control systems may be needed, if the company operates in divergent market situations. As a comptroller for Mobil Oil Company puts it, "The major challenge is to create sufficient coordination to detect potential problems early enough so that corrective action can be planned and initiated before a crisis develops, and at the same time to avoid stifling the initiative of an operating unit or affiliate."[1]

Observation and modification of questions are considerably easier in the domestic business situation than in the international one. Time lags and distance impose formidable communication barriers in international business; special informational machinery is usually required to overcome both the physical and psychological distances which make the control function particularly difficult. This chapter relates coordination and control to organizational structures and identifies specific areas of marketing control. Analysis of the mechanics of the control sequence and methods of control places special emphasis on communication systems for coordination and control of the international marketing effort.

CONTROL AS A MANAGEMENT TOOL

The verb "to control" means to direct, regulate, or manage; controlling, then, is the very essence of management. In oversimplified form,

---

[1] Robert C. King, "Administering an International Computer Systems Function," in *International Management Information Systems* (New York, American Management Association, 1967), p. 26.

business is a process of planning, executing, observing, and modifying or continuing. The decision to modify or continue is based on observations; therefore, all stages of the process are part of the control mechanism. The terms cybernation and feedback loops are familiar in relation to automatic machines. In management, the observation and modification stages of business control are the closing links of the control feedback loop which permit continued planning and more effective execution of plans designed to accomplish the marketer's objectives.

To function effectively as a management tool, the control system must provide information on operations, including distribution, promotion, and every marketing function. It must cover financial situations, including price, volume, cost, and eventually profit information. General background must also be provided, including the state of the market, competition, and political and economic developments.

Information must be not only complete but also timely. One authority has commented that "information flows sequentially today" and observes there may be a significant time lag before data reaches the decision level.[2] Such a situation is most likely to occur when management is highly centralized and when information has to flow through a series of intermediaries. High-speed communications and computerized data handling may be used to reduce time lags, but the question of centralized versus decentralized control systems remains important because of the large amount of subjective decision making necessary in marketing.

A broad aspiration of most managerial control is the maintenance or improvement of the long- or short-term profit level of the international marketing operation. From a marketing standpoint, there are more specific objectives which should also be counted; the company may be more interested in its long-run reputation in overseas markets than in its short-run profit. If marketing is turned over to others (even those employed by the company) without adequate control, short-run objectives will often prevail at the cost of a company's long-run reputation. Such a possibility is particularly relevant in overseas markets where there are so many built-in hazards to the reputation of a foreign firm. Preserving a market may be more important than gaining short-run profits. Adequate control measures help management to accomplish these marketing objectives. The company in international trade, for example, may not expect a short-run profit but may wish to maintain a beachhead position in the market so that it will be in a preferred position for future market expansion. Many foreign markets are large enough for only one competitor, and the existence of one is likely to discourage anyone else from entering this particular area. Therefore, the marketer's goals may be to preclude competition from entering a market. Increased volume alone may be sufficient purpose for staying in a market. Such maintenance of volume may contribute indirect profit by permitting production economies or by offsetting domestic business fluctuations of a seasonal or cyclical nature. To minimize losses, management must be especially control conscious when it is engaging in the overseas business for some reason other than direct short-run profit.

---

[2] John Lutz, "Emerging Trends," in *International Management Information Systems* (New York: American Management Association, 1967), p. 11.

BOX 16–1

Controlling Foreign Operations

It is a fallacy to think of headquarters organizations as control centers rather than as service and coordination centers. The headquarters office can provide vital services for the operating units abroad, in terms of supplies, procurement, executives, technical aid, and managerial systems. They may also perform service functions in providing financing and coordination throughout the international organization for pricing, quality, interchange of parts, engineering design and overall marketing efforts. But because they have an ultimate responsibility to the top management and stockholders for profits, they are lured into the delusion that by "controlling" the operations abroad and by exercising their authority by this "control" they can actually change the behavior of overseas managers and hence increase profits.

This researcher's observation is that the changing of behavior of men located abroad is only slightly influenced by the directives and controls of the home office. Only the individual can change his own behavior. Reports, policies, and controls do not affect it as much as many home office executives assume. Often the only real change which comes about in behavior overseas as a result of home office directives is the reluctant submission due to heavy-handed orders with a recognition of the ultimate need to please those in final authority at home. A reluctant submission does not usually accomplish the effect desired.

Source: W. T. Skinner, *American Industries in Developing Economies* (New York: John Wiley & Sons, Inc., 1968), pp. 186–87. Reprinted with permission.

CENTRALIZATION OF CONTROL

Ultimate responsibility for the success or failure of an international enterprise falls on the chief operating officer of the company. He may delegate responsibility for international operations to the chief international officer, but he expects results. Because of this primary responsibility, home-office management needs to exercise just the right amount of control over affiliated international organizations. Therefore, control functions must be carefully allocated to a level where they can be most appropriately employed. Skinner[3] suggests five possible degrees of involvement:

1. No headquarters control or involvement.
2. General policy involvement in which headquarters helps establish objectives in strategic directions and performs long-term planning.
3. Both the policy role and the short-range planning role, including decisions on specific approaches for achieving goals and direct involvement in the planning of functional activities.
4. Management selection, establishment of systems and procedures,

---

[3] Wickham Skinner, *American Industry in Developing Economies* (New York: John Wiley & Sons, Inc., 1968), p. 188.

and designing of specific procedures for accomplishing goals are included in addition to the elements in 1, 2, and 3 above.
5.   "The home office is deeply and consistently concerned with specific operating decisions—including scheduling, and manpower practices."

It is generally accepted that at a minimum the home office must be responsible for basic policy decisions, major fund allocations, and executive selection.

Not too many years ago, the thrust of international management thinking was toward decentralization of control. Recently, however, the general direction seems to be changing in favor of greater home-office control. This is true partly because communications and information-handling technology have developed to the point where home-office control is more feasible, and partly because full decentralization has not resulted in consistently reliable performance. Behrman suggests that

the tendency toward centralization is based partly on the fact that central headquarters bears the final responsibility, but also because talent is scarce in the field and that skilled manpower is more likely to be available at the home office. Home office personnel have been hired for the problem solving and decision making skills and abilities in the field. Therefore they should be making the major decisions. Further, by being located in the home office the executives have staff support, centralized data, and the opportunity to discuss the problems with superiors or peers in the different operating divisions.[4]

The final argument in favor of centralization of control is that the field manager often has responsibility for only a part of the functions. For example, he may be deprived of authority over prices or product modification or promotion. Given these constraints, he can hardly be held responsible for the total success of the operation. One basic principle of management is that no one should be held accountable for activities over which he has no direct-line responsibility. Control, therefore, tends to centralize to levels where decisions are being made in all of the business areas.

GENERAL CONTROL CONCEPTS

The requisites of a foreign marketing control system are essentially the same as those which pertain to a domestic marketing system, but in almost every instance there are special requirements in the foreign situation which place additional strains and burdens on a control system. Some basic considerations include the following:
1. The control device needs to be reasonable and realistic; international control can seldom be as complete as domestic. A complex or cumbersome control system causes frustration and is likely to be abandoned or ignored.

---

[4] Jack N. Behrman, "Some Patterns in the Rise of Multi-National Enterprise," Research Paper No. 18, University of North Carolina at Chapel Hill, March 1969, pp. 64–65.

2. The cost of communications and the other costs of operating the control system must be commensurate with the benefits derived from this activity.

3. Physical distances, language barriers, lower volume, and other characteristics of the foreign market dictate that the international control system be simpler than a domestic marketing control system. Since the costs of international control are higher and the returns from control are lower, the system must be carefully tailored for the international marketplace.

4. The control system must be fast and sensitive to provide the flexibility needed in rapidly changing heterogeneous marketplaces. A cumbersome control system discourages both the person controlling and those being controlled. The complexity of the international marketplace itself virtually rules out convenience and, by definition, makes the communication and control process more cumbersome.

5. Companies must be prepared to vary their control systems according to the needs of the subordinate companies or affiliates. This is sound theory, but one investigator found that home offices do not treat different countries or different functions very differently. He concludes that "The function or role of headquarters is established more on the amount of control which is possible than on the more logical basis of what kind of control is appropriate."[5] Companies appear to control their subsidiaries in a standardized manner regardless of the type and location of the country in which they are located.

6. The control systems should be simple enough that the control center is not inundated with more data than it can handle. As far as possible, data should be presented so that management is instantly alerted to variations from established plans or standards.

For years foreign countries have required local financial participation in international business; they have also required that local nationals be employed as part of the management team. In recent years, however, a growing emphasis has been placed not only on token local management but on de facto local management. Total control, therefore, can no longer be lodged directly in the foreign or parent firm. Parent-company control is still necessary, but the parent must be certain that his participation is legal.

IMPACT OF ORGANIZATIONAL STRUCTURE ON CONTROL

The organizational structure of the international marketing operation significantly affects the control mechanisms that can be utilized effectively. The organizational form itself may facilitate or hinder control activities. If lines of authority are clear and responsibilities are made specific, the international marketing operation can be more easily controlled than if this is not the case. In a sense it sounds ludicrous to speak of any other circumstance, but it is surprising how often responsibilities in the international organizational structure are not clearly defined.

---

[5] Skinner, op. cit., p. 192.

The basic organizational philosophy of the company will determine whether the control of the marketing function will be centralized or decentralized. Centralized control usually brings a foreign subsidiary or department into closer alignment with domestic operations; on the other hand, decentralized control may lack such closeness but often offers the advantages of flexibility and speed. International Telephone and Telegraph Company combines centralized control and decentralized flexibility through a basic decentralization with a strong follow-up control activity. One I.T.&T. executive comments that his company has a triple check: "We have control and coordination at the local level, the regional level, and finally overall control here in New York."[6] This approach may combine the best of centralized and decentralized control activities.

Certainly the control system must be tailored to and consistent with the parent's organizational form and must be consonant with the objectives of the company; yet, in international marketing, such procedural consistency may be unsuited in the local marketplace. Control systems often compromise consistency for the sake of workability.

AREAS OF CONTROL

The areas of the international marketing operation that should be controlled are primarily those needing control in the domestic marketing situation. The reason for the control, however, and its specific objectives may be quite different from the domestic reasons and relationships. Some of the chief control areas are reviewed briefly in this section.

Overseas marketing costs have a particularly strong tendency to get out of line and require special control emphasis. The reasons are understandable: markets are typically smaller than those in the United States and are more difficult to reach, and transportation and communication costs can easily get out of hand if they are not carefully controlled. The costs of operating foreign branches or subsidiaries are more likely to get out of hand when auditing procedures are inadequate. Even the costs of operating the international division at the home office can be prohibitive if authority and responsibility for budget are not clearly assigned. To facilitate analysis, the international marketing manager may evaluate his control activities from the viewpoint of volume, product, channel of distribution, promotion, manpower, and profit control mechanisms.

Volume Control

Measurement of sales volume is one of the most convenient control mechanisms available. The ease of securing aggregate sales figures makes comparison with forecasts simple and gives management a periodic check of subsidiary progress and of sales by product line. The maintenance of sales volume depends at least partly on the intensity of the marketing efforts, so, in a properly controlled marketing operation,

---

[6] "Organizing for Profit Overseas," *Business Week*, May 23, 1964, p. 120.

the individual responsible for control of the various marketing functions can determine whether promotional expenditures and the amount of sales effort expended are appropriate to the potential returns. The same individual has control of both the kind and the intensity of promotion used. He also should be able to control profit levels through judicious care in all other areas of marketing.

Detailed sales reports provide information on sales: market by market, product by product, and by volume of sales in each gross margin category. They may express sales volume in terms of dollars or units and include breakdowns of sales to subsidiaries or other related companies and may identify governmental or other large-volume purchases in specific terms. Sales reports may be required as frequently as every week or month by local operating divisions and are typically required at least at quarterly intervals by the home office.

Absolute volume information is not sufficient to determine the adequacy of marketing efforts. *Market share* information should also be gathered on a regular basis so that management can have both absolute and relative bases of control.

Price Control

Sometimes middlemen, joint-venture partners, franchises, or even subsidiaries jeopardize a company's market position by charging exceedingly high prices. Volume or gross profit information does not provide adequate guidance; unless headquarters receive regular reports of prices actually being charged or prices at which transactions are made, it is possible to lose volume without any apparent reason. The other side of this question relates to minimizing the possibility of price cutting if it will be damaging to the company's overall profit or market position. Some companies even find themselves in the position of competing with themselves as different subsidiaries bid for choice business. Such price competition may be beneficial to the winning subsidiary but is detrimental to the company profit as a whole. The international executive may also be responsible for preserving price levels by keeping dumped products out of normal markets.

Tariffs add a particular unpleasant note to the attempt to control prices internationally, but, in general, tariffs are rather static and can be worked around. Since each country has different import rates and different methods of tariff code interpretation, it is probable that prices cannot be equalized or controlled for all countries. It is surprising how many firms virtually abdicate control over foreign pricing on the rationalization that such activity is out of the scope of their control. Central management should always retain basic control over the pricing function.

To provide competitive flexibility, management may want to establish price ranges within which its product is to be sold in foreign markets and require that all transactions negotiated at prices above or below this range be reported to the control authority. Such reporting not only has the effect of lessening the number of such sales, but permits decentralization of the pricing function without full loss of control. Regardless of the level of operation and type of middlemen involved, information on prices is needed for home-office control. Even when price authority is decentralized, prices and price policies should be subject to regular review in the home offices.

Product Control

The domestic marketing manager must be certain that his product is suitable for the market and delivered to customers in good condition. Such problems are infinitesimal in a domestic market when compared with the same problems in international marketing, where there are broad variations in the market, the possibility of mishandling in shipping, and the possibility of inferior production in foreign plants. A product or brand image is directly dependent on the customer's experiences with the product and the firm.

The foreign customer is more likely than the domestic to indict all the products of the particular firm if he should have a bad encounter with one. In international markets most customers are accustomed to purchasing from nearby sources and have an initial distrust of big or faraway companies. One study of purchasing patterns in various nations revealed a consistent and overwhelming preference for domestic goods when consumers had the *choice* of similar foreign or domestic products. In other countries, and for certain kinds of products, the opposite is true. In any case, products of the foreign producer are, so to speak, "on trial" at all times—in such cases, indeed, in all cases, product quality control is crucial.

Often, product image is more important than the product itself, and good quality alone is not enough to overcome a poor image. A single company cannot by itself overcome a poor industrywide or nationwide product image. Japan's long-standing reputation for having shoddy, "imitative" products was so firmly entrenched that no single Japanese company could have reversed world opinion. The government, in this case, was sufficiently astute to step in and help develop and police product standards for export products. Gradually the combination of excellent products (in fields such as electric equipment, photographic and optical goods, and motorcycles), plus rigid government standards and inspection of export goods has given Japan a new reputation—but now for high quality.

As we have seen, the domestic marketer cannot always foresee whether his product will be suitable for a foreign country. Indeed, different foreign countries may have varying requirements for the same type of product. Only an effective communication and control system can provide adequate information about product and product-line decisions. If an adequate feedback mechanism is not present, the manager may not be able to identify the cause of purchaser dissatisfaction.

Besides the problem of suitability, there are other hazards pertaining to products which must be controlled. Physical handling of the product when it is shipped long distances over diverse classes of transportation facilities can well lead to damaged goods. Excess damage can be spotted through a well-organized control system. The servicing of the product is also harder to control in a foreign market. Most countries do not have adequate service facilities for many products, and even a company's own pre- and post-sale servicing may not measure up to domestic standards unless there is close supervision and control. When a product is produced by a foreign subsidiary or a licensee or franchisee, the manufacturer runs the risk of losing control of product quality. Here again the risk can be minimized through an adequate control system. Only when the product is closely controlled can management be assured that the product's brand image will be preserved.

Promotional Control

Advertising and personal selling are the primary promotional methods encountered in marketing. Domestic sales force management is subject to a broad range of control systems and mechanisms; in international marketing the same sorts of measures may be applied. A primary question concerning the subject of international promotional activities relates to the location of responsibility. Most personal selling cannot successfully be directed from a home office unless it is on a one country —one salesman basis. The advertising function, on the other hand, may be organized on either a centralized or a decentralized basis; both forms of organization call for significantly different control systems. When advertising is decentralized, the parent company concerns itself largely with questions of advertising costs and results. When it is centralized, the home office is particularly concerned with regular feedback which will help it determine whether it is communicating effectively.

Regardless of the control system employed, management should regularly receive copies of all advertising materials and media being utilized, information on market coverage, and detailed information on expenditures.

Channel Control

Companies must exercise caution in dealing with foreign middlemen; obviously, the primary measure of a middleman's effectiveness will be his volume of purchases from the company. Such information, however, does not provide adequate information about whether the distributor is maintaining reasonable prices or is functioning effectively in the areas of sales and service. Because the middlemen will not or cannot provide objective information about themselves, continuing customer research may be the only method of gaining adequate feedback on such factors as adequacy of sales representation, speed of filling orders, quality of post-sale service, and other distributor functions. If volume and market-share goals are not being reached, the entire distribution setup should be reviewed to determine if it is causing the market problems.

Supervision and control of distribution channels calls for standards that are different from those utilized in domestic trade. A company may find that it has narrow decision latitude in foreign distribution-channel policy and less opportunity to manage and control the distribution channels. Such a simple thing as restricting the number of outlets for particular merchandise may cause managerial trauma. The structure of retailing and wholesaling in many countries does not permit exclusive or restricted distribution. Therefore, a company accustomed to closely controlling a small number of channels may find itself confronted with the need for an entirely different control system in order to supervise a large number of outlets with vastly different characteristics. It is difficult to control the caliber of middlemen employed, because in many cases there are no middlemen who meet normal predetermined standards.

Since exclusive territories or boundaries are hard to control in most foreign countries, there is likely to be some overlapping. Often sales volumes are too low to permit an expensive control mechanism; therefore, unless they are dealing with very few middlemen, most manufacturers are content to exert less control in overseas markets than in domestic. A producer of packaging machinery, for example, discovered quite by accident that its British franchisee was making nearly one third of its quota through sales in another franchisee's territory on the Continent. Through this discovery, the company realized that it had inadequate territorial control and, more importantly, realized that such sales could not have been made if the company had an adequate sales quota control system.

Marketing Manpower Control

In most organizations, particularly industrial marketing firms, manpower is a vital ingredient for the success of a marketing program. Home-office management must always be concerned with at least the top level of marketing management in each country, but, increasingly, companies are taking greater interest in all marketing personnel. Parent companies are viewing manpower development as a home-office function and maintain centralized control over hiring, management development, and compensation. Performance reports are accumulated on a regular basis, and records of managers in different parts of the world are routinely compared as a method of spotting managerial deficiencies. Some companies limit their central or regional supervision to managerial personnel, but others screen applications for sales positions. They retain the final hiring authority to assure that incoming salesmen are qualified to sell the types of products being offered or planned for the future.

Companies using such tight control in marketing manpower have encountered considerable resistance from field managers but maintain the practice because for them it has proven successful in the long run. Such policies may not be unduly restrictive in an era of high-speed data processing and relatively easy person-to-person communications around the world.

Profit Control

Since profit is the ultimate goal of nearly all marketing activity, the ultimate measure of success must be in terms of profit. Profit is a

BOX 16–2

Making a British Giant Jump

Arnold Weinstock, head of Britain's General Electric Co., is a controversial figure. But his blunt tactics are paying off in increased productivity and profits.

Weinstock is building profits with the same techniques he applied earlier. He is closing three underutilized plants, reducing the labor force at several others, streamlining the product line resulting from the merger, and introducing the Weinstock brand of highly decentralized management. Without mincing words, Weinstock has made it perfectly clear to his group managers that he expects them to produce profits—or they, too, will be fired.

Blunt tactics like these have made Weinstock one of the most successful —and controversial—of British businessmen. Often pursuing efficiency to the point of ruthlessness, he was vilified on nationwide television by a GEC worker who likened him to Hitler. Britain's *Sunday Times,* on the other hand, called him "the best manager Britain has produced since the war." With a 1967 loss of $10.8-million on sales of about $625-million, AEI was one of the weakest of Britain's large companies. Though it had a solid reputation for engineering excellence, AEI was saddled with an unwieldy centralized management, a loosely controlled sales force, and large overhead expenses. Says one observer: "AEI had a knack of building £75,000 worth of equipment without stopping to consider whether there was 75 shillings worth of profit." AEI was so loosely organized that eight months after merger Weinstock still doesn't know "exactly what we have."

"There seems to have been no definition of purpose, no conscious decisions."

Basic to the emphasis on making money is Weinstock's highly decentralized management structure. GEC is divided along product lines into more than 50 separate companies, each of which has its own profit-and-loss statement and its own managing director responsible directly to Weinstock and the GEC board of directors. Once the over-all budget is set for the year, each of the managing directors is free to make nearly all the decisions himself.

But they are subject to frequent and rigorous financial checks on their performance and cash balances—what Weinstock calls, "banking with us." The managing directors file a blitz of financial information to GEC headquarters: daily bank balances, weekly profit-and-loss statements, and detailed monthly reports comparing results to the budget and explaining any discrepancy with expected profit.

If Weinstock is dissatisfied with the results, insiders say he follows up in devastating fashion.

In the end, the managing directors must produce or they are sacked. Morton, whose 10 years with the company make him almost the doyen of GEC management, admits: "If you haven't got a stout heart, you'll be quickly demoralized."

Source: *Business Week,* August 24, 1968, pp. 70–71. Reprinted with permission.

measure of managerial effectiveness and of success in building volume, maintaining margins, and controlling costs, but even success in all these functions does not guarantee profit. Indeed, even the very term "profit" is somewhat debatable. One may ask whether profit which is merely maintained on the books and not returned to the parent company can be appropriately called profit. Some companies have never returned profits from their subsidiaries but have reinvested all profits and count their operations most successful. Obviously, any corporation must establish its own methodology for measuring and controlling profits. One of the critical elements in profit management is determination of where the profits will be taken. For this reason, it is most appropriate that ultimate profit control be at the home-office level. In some instances, prudent management virtually dictates that some local activities should not operate at a (visible) profit; the goal of the corporation is generally to maximize worldwide *net* profits. Another question is whether profits are to be minimized in the short or long term; this must be answered through a central management decision. All these factors argue for detailed central profit reporting.

Profit reports can communicate to management the overall health of subsidiary operations and current market conditions. They may also function effectively as trend reports to provide overall management guidance.

In summary, this section has observed that control is a much broader concept than accounting control and that all areas of the marketing operation must be controlled more closely in the overseas operation than in the domestic. Marketers, however, have also discovered that control of most areas of marketing is more difficult and expensive in world markets than in domestic. They also know that each of the control areas mentioned above is closely related to *all* of the others; effective control systems in one area will add little benefit unless the others are covered too. The requirements of close control and its resulting difficulties pose an ever-present dilemma for international marketers.

CONTROL SEQUENCE

A rather definite and logical sequence of action is called for if controls are to be effective in either domestic or international marketing. As this chapter has shown several times, the principles are the same, but the implementation may differ greatly in domestic and overseas markets. Because of these difficulties, it is especially imperative that a logical sequence be employed and utilized in controlling international marketing operations. The steps of the control sequence are as follows: (1) establish objectives; (2) select control method; (3) set standards; (4) determine location of responsibility; (5) establish a communication system; (6) evaluate and review results; (7) initiate corrective action.

As Exhibit 16–1 shows, the seven basic steps are all closely interrelated. It also illustrates that a control system is not static but dynamic and, as such, requires constant reevaluation and periodic modification.

EXHIBIT 16–1

The Control Sequence

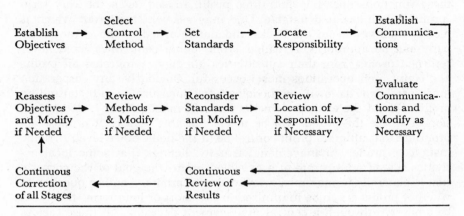

Establish Objectives → Select Control Method → Set Standards → Locate Responsibility → Establish Communications

Reassess Objectives and Modify if Needed → Review Methods & Modify if Needed → Reconsider Standards and Modify if Needed → Review Location of Responsibility if Necessary → Evaluate Communications and Modify as Necessary

Continuous Correction of all Stages ← Continuous Review of Results

Establish Objectives

Newcomers in international marketing are liable to have fuzzy ideas about their precise objectives in entering international competition. Often their objectives seem to be little more than to put in their toes and try the water, all the time being ready to withdraw rapidly if they do not find it to their liking. Such an objective is not completely unacceptable, but it does provide a hazard if substituted for realistic goals and objectives which might be accomplished through adequate planning and a comprehensive control system. Management needs to outline explicitly in advance not only its general objectives but also the specific short- and long-run objectives for the international operation. Unless these are determined, management cannot know what resources are required or what gains are expected. Without knowing objectives, company standards cannot be established, and planned control is impossible.

Companies with a variety of far-flung subordinate organizations often fail to communicate adequately about the firm's objectives and about the goals for specific operating units. Unless statements of objectives are conveyed explicitly they can hardly have relevance to subordinates. Objective statements should identify overall company goals so that everyone concerned knows where the company is going and should provide specific detailed statements of operational objectives to the men directly in charge. Statements may include specific explicit goals such as the attainment of a given market share or specific dollar level of sales or profit or may spell out less tangible goals. Intangibles may be expressed in terms of increasing product visibility, development of channel structure, or improvement of product and company image, etc. It is advantageous to be as concrete as possible in communicating objectives, but inclusion of abstract objectives lends perspective.[7] After the general and operational objectives are established, management should select the basic method or methods of coordination and control most likely to be effective in a given circumstance.

Select Control Method

Direct or indirect controls are the basic alternatives relevant to overseas marketing operations. Methods of direct control include contractual arrangements and ownership participation. Indirect control may rely on communications or competition. The extent and degree of control can vary widely, regardless of the control methods utilized.

Formal contractual arrangements may provide a positive and direct mechanism for controlling overseas operations. Although contracts provide the mechanism, it should be noted that they do not automatically provide the control; specific contract provisions must therefore be provided to permit effective control. Two of the most common control arrangements utilized are quotas and license requirements. Both may require specific performance, but it should be noted that contractual provisions cannot necessarily be enforced. The parent company must realize that it may need to turn to alternative marketing arrangements if contractual requirements are not met. Contractual provisions may rely on elaborate formal administrative mechanism or may depend solely on voluntary compliance.

When a company is able to participate in the administration (or at least policy setting) of its international representatives, a large degree of control is assured. Ownership, even a minority interest, will often offer a substantial opportunity for control through ownership participation in management.

Although not necessarily a control system in itself, a continuing communication system provides the basis for control in international markets. Companies to be controlled have a much greater sense of awareness and responsibility when required to communicate regularly on their progress. Competition is the base for another informal control system. Although it is a backdoor approach, some companies manage to keep their middlemen on the alert by providing or making possible direct competition for the middlemen or by threatening such competition.

Set Standards

Before a control mechanism can work effectively, a set of standards must be adopted by which progress can be measured. Standards are directly based on objectives. They should be expressed as explicitly as possible and need not be limited to financial or cost matters. One kind

---

[7] Some very explicit examples of corporate statements of objectives and standards are found in Earnest C. Miller, *Objective and Standards of Performance in Marketing Management* (New York: American Marketing Association, 1967).

of standard which is needed is a realistic time schedule. Goals may be expressed about time in very general terms—"Gain 5 percent market share in Europe by the end of 1971." Or they may evision accomplishment of intermediate goals—"Have wholesale network in Germany fully developed by May 15." Or they may relate to specific implementation stages—"Deliver basic stock to Berlin wholesaler not later than March 15," or "Initiate consumer newspaper campaign on June 1." Probably the time schedule should include all three kinds of dates. Unless such a schedule is set, months and years may be needlessly dissipated in the establishment of a foreign operation. Certainly the vagaries of international business will require time schedules to be revised periodically; but without such standards it is all too easy to lose track of time requirements entirely.

Standards of achievement for the marketing task may be set concerning profits, sales volume, establishment of channels of distribution, achieving entry into a given foreign market, or some other relevant measure. Achievement standards, like time schedules, provide a yardstick for frequent measurement of accomplishment and can help both domestic and overseas managers to keep their perspective.

Revenue and the expense budgets should both be included in the company's standards for overseas operations. Companies unfamiliar with overseas operations are likely to overlook many unanticipated expense items. They should immediately establish expense budgets so that they can commence to appraise the cost of operation in realistic terms and can make realistic expense plans. Expense budgets typically are understated; but revenue plans, unfortunately, often have a tendency to work the other way. Companies frequently find that, by projecting domestic figures, they have understated expenses and overstated anticipated revenues. Continuing research and analysis of budget and accomplishment standards should be undertaken as early as possible to permit realistic standard setting.

One common mistake in establishing standards for multiunit operations is setting specific standards and objectives at too high a level in the organization. If the home office attempts to set goals which should be established at the European headquarters level, for example, it runs the risk of setting unrealistic goals which are impossible to meet and may create subsequent organizational dislocation. Conversely, standards may be set too low, permitting lax field operations and providing no basis for effective control. Standards must be established at all levels of operation and must be reviewed sequentially by each higher level to determine if they are realistic and consonant with the company's world goals.

Locate Responsibility

The complexities of international organization make it difficult to locate the *ultimate* responsibility for overseas operation, and assignment of responsibility sometimes involves much coordination. Different departments or functional areas of the parent company must be aware of what is going on in other functional areas. Companies organized by product line need greater coordination of efforts in international than in domestic markets. Firms organized for international operations on a national basis need to establish liaison and coordination links among the various nations in which they have trading activities. Many companies utilize different kinds of middlemen for reaching different countries or different market segments. The efforts of these middlemen should also be coordinated by the parent company. Whenever possible, the primary responsibility should be located with one man who can coordinate the efforts of others to permit centralized action and control. In no case should a man be given responsibility which is not in line with the authority delegated to him.

Establish Communication System

A reporting and control system is the company's central nervous system used for accumulating data and dispensing messages calling for action. Informal communication systems are often adequate in domestic marketing, but in international affairs it is imperative that an organized and systematic information system be developed to provide the data necessary for effective central office decision.

Information collection and dispersion are costly activities, so the communication system must be geared to just the right level of reporting. Too much information wastes executive time at both the reporting and receiving levels. Too little fails to give an adequate basis for control. The reporting system must be workable; the task of reporting must not consume so much of the manager's time that he has none left for actual management of his own operation.

Management should remember that language and communication breakdowns occur not only between companies and customers but between managers as well. Both outgoing and ingoing communications must be thoroughly comprehensible to the recipient before they can be effective. Even if the words are understandable to everyone concerned, there may be a loss of communication because the conceptual framework of various managers differs. Such conceptual problems are most likely to occur when dealing with abstractions, such as "good customer relations," or "prompt delivery," so efforts should be made to keep communications in concrete terms.

A key element of the communication's system is an apparatus for collective information. Some basic approaches which may be followed in gathering information include periodic inquiry, automatic collection, examination of company records, and field audits.

Periodic Inquiry. All companies that are active in international trade should make periodic inquiries into their foreign markets. Even companies which have turned over their entire international marketing effort to some other group should make such inquiry for control and evaluation purposes. If the parent company has its own personnel in foreign markets, it very often can secure basic information from those persons. It may also want to use local informants who have no association with the company but who are in a position to evaluate the market or the company's market position independently. In many of the more developed countries, independent marketing researchers or marketing consultants are available to provide such information. The foreign service corps of the government may also be utilized for gathering certain classes of information. Occasionally a company should go directly to the customers in a foreign country to determine their likes and dislikes about the company's products and service.

Automatic Systems.   Routine reports by field sales personnel or the middlemen handling the product can provide needed data. Companies can require reports which include information deemed necessary for efficient home-office control of the foreign operation. Sometimes even customer guarantee cards can provide automatic notification of sales and supply basic market information.

Automatic reporting systems require that reporting forms be standardized and that all information falling into such a system conform to a consistent format which makes possible the use of variance interpretation. Such systems employ the rule of exception and do not call to management's attention routine information, merely reporting that standards are being met. Attention is focused on variance from the standard.

Automatic reporting systems must be controlled; managers tend to seek data that they need only periodically on a continuous basis. Though routine reporting is called automatic, it may still consume time in preparation. Excessive reports add a burden which is hardly needed by the hurried international executive or busy salesman. All reporting systems, automatic or otherwise, require periodic evaluation to determine if they are economical, flexible, accurate, and relevant.

Company Records.   Some companies seem to be interested only in aggregate sales or profit figures from their overseas operations; but for heightened sensitivity to the marketplace, a company should regularly secure detailed information on sales by product and geographic area. If accurate sales information is maintained, such information should be readily available, for access to such data may provide insights into foreign operations.

Field Audits.   One authority suggests that human communication and documentary sources are not enough to assure full understanding of international business and information but that perceptual sources are required as well.[8] The implication is that without being or having been *on location* international managers cannot comprehend some of the situations with which they must deal.

Realistic exposure to the foreign marketplace can be gained through visits to foreign markets by various marketing executives. No other method can provide quite so many insights into a company's foreign problems and opportunities. Visit frequency will be determined by the number and kind of problems encountered, the value and profit potential of the area, the cost of such visits, and the capability of the local

[8] Warren J. Keegan, "Acquisition of Global Business Information," *Columbia Journal of World Business*, Vol. 3, No. 2 (March–April, 1968), pp. 35–41.

managers or representatives. In every case audit trips should be carefully planned in advance and the field auditor should provide himself with an audit checklist prepared in the relative calm of his own office in consultation with other home-office personnel. Only the discipline of such a list will insure adequate field coverage of problem areas.

One note of caution, however, should be sounded about field audits. It is altogether too easy for an inexperienced executive to draw hasty conclusions from a short trip abroad. Field visits must be conducted by personnel who are attuned to the subtleties of culture, geography, and other environmental conditions which may affect the mode of doing business within a given area. Such investigations must also look for the real conditions that prevail and be alert to window dressing applied specifically for the visit. Anyone who has followed the progress of congressional investigating trips abroad can understand the hazards involved.

Communication Breakthroughs. Physical facilities for handling international communications are becoming more sophisticated each year. The last few years have seen the development of international communications systems incorporating leased circuits, radio and teleprinters, Deltex systems (which for the same cost can handle some 20 times as much information as Telex communications), and satellite communication systems, which permit instantaneous transmission via orbiting communication satellites. Such information imputs can be handled directly through computer data handling processes, resulting in direct access to computers from any place in the world and permitting real-time systems of management which allow home-office personnel to participate in or observe operations as they occur. Advances are not limited to such mechanical means of data transmission, however; human communications and facilities have also improved with the advent of direct dial telephoning throughout the world and improved telephone service in nearly every country. (Such direct dialing and improved service, however, tend to cause telephone bills to skyrocket.) Impressive as the technological breakthroughs have become, they are meaningless unless there are parallel conceptual breakthroughs to facilitate the meaningful use of the masses of information now being transmitted internationally.

Evaluate Results and Make Corrections

Evaluation of results and initiation of corrective action to modify defective programs are the final steps of the control sequence. Information which is gathered from the field must be compared with the established operational standards and objectives. If the results are not in proper relationship to the expectations, corrective action must be taken, or the standards and objectives must be modified. In international marketing there is a special likelihood of a significant time lag between the time when corrective action is initiated and when it is completed. Such a time lag is completely understandable in view of the space, cultural difference, and organizational problems involved. Therefore, it is particularly important that evaluation and correction be continuing activi-

BOX 16–3

Government Control

Socialist governments have found that one of their chief problems is maintaining control over the businesses they direct. Problems are sometimes aggravated in a mixed economy such as that of Egypt, where private business and socialized firms exist side by side.

The success of the flourishing general merchandise business of one *Mohamed X* in Cairo agitated government planners, so they established a subsidized store directly across the street from his place of business. The subsidized store purchased all it wanted of goods at reduced government prices, which imposed a distinct threat to the entrepreneur across the street. The private store owner, however, was a student of human nature and quickly made a bargain with the operator of the one-man government store. The former would purchase all of the merchandise from the latter, who could then fulfill his sales quotas and get his sales commission and not be troubled with the problems of keeping the store. Each morning when the government truck delivered the supplies the government-store manager diverted them across the street, collected the day's receipts, and spent his day in leisure.

Officials from the Ministry of Supplies were delighted that the new store had become so successful so quickly. Eventually supervisors made a field investigation and discovered what was happening. Rather than report the situation to their superiors and show up their own possible negligence, they approved the arrangement, and then everyone concerned could continue doing business as usual.

Source: Related by Mohamed Khalil to the authors.

ties. The company should establish, whenever possible, contingency plans in advance and prestructure action patterns which may be employed on short notice to meet unanticipated market conditions.

The control sequence as here discussed has no ending, but rather is an ongoing cycle of establishing, evaluating, reestablishing, and re-evaluating.

SUMMARY AND CONCLUSIONS

In organizations, as in individuals, self-control seems to be at least partly a function of maturity. Many companies that are new to international operations fail to establish even minimal control systems. They reason that the need for flexibility, the complexity of international organization, and the differences in operations from country to country justify neglect of coordination and control systems. Companies that have been most successful in international operations, however, have learned that control systems can be developed to overcome such problems. Controlling of marketing operations is always difficult, and especially in international operations. Such control can be accomplished, however, through analysis of the firm's specific organizational structure as it affects control mechanism and determination of the exact areas in which control is desired. Coupling this information with a basic knowledge of the control sequence should result in an effective program of coordination and control.

The profitability of an international operation depends directly on the relationship between sales volume, the cost of producing the goods, and the cost of marketing or distribution. All four items—profit, volume, production cost, and marketing cost—are subject to control. Production control is beyond the scope of this chapter; but profit, volume, and marketing controls have all been considered. Any effective program for coordinating and controlling world marketing operations requires special attention to the functions of price, promotion, product, and distribution channels.

All marketing areas can be coordinated and controlled through a basic control sequence. The planning stage of the control sequence includes establishing objectives, selecting control methods, setting up standards, and locating responsibility. Ideally, all four of these activities should be undertaken before a firm ever ventures into international marketing operations. Several varieties of information retrieval systems should be utilized to maintain communication during the execution of the marketing plan; then there should be a continual review of results, with subsequent corrections and modifications as required. These are the concepts relevant to coordination and control of international marketing operations.

Although it is impossible to control profit, volume, and marketing functions in the absolute sense, it is in all instances possible to have a system which provides management with the information it needs to utilize effective coordination and control procedures. International marketing poses communication obstacles which are not confronted in the domestic market and which make an adequately planned coordination and control program especially important.

READING

FOREIGN OPERATIONS: A GUIDE FOR TOP MANAGEMENT*

JOHN FAYERWEATHER

Remote Control

Once the foreign operating arrangement is established, the emphasis shifts to the second phase: the management of the arrangement at long distance. There are several key aspects to long-range administration which management should check.

DIVISION OF FUNCTIONS AND RESPONSIBILITIES. It is clearly impossible to run all the daily affairs of a foreign unit from a New York office, though some firms go pretty far in this direction. On the other hand,

---

* Reprinted with permission from the *Harvard Business Review*, Vol. 35, No. 1 (January–February 1957), pp. 133–35.

the parent organization must retain some minimum of control, and there are areas in which the skills of the home office staff and domestic divisions can be valuable aids to the foreign units.

Every case being different, there is no strict formula for dividing up functions and responsibilities. It is important, though, that top managements appreciate the need for working out some kind of middle line. Furthermore, I should say that they ought to work toward the maximum degree of decentralization, imposing only those controls that are absolutely necessary, rather than seeking to maintain tight lines, providing slack only when they must. Unfortunately, many firms do not maintain this attitude. By way of illustration:

One company plans detailed production schedules for each foreign unit from the home office, calls for a variety of cost reports with great frequency, and requires individual parent company approval for such minor expenditures as the purchase of a dictating machine and the addition of an extra clerk. All of this is done, according to the home office, to make the foreign units cost-conscious. I have observed one of these foreign units briefly, and can testify that a degree of cost-consciousness has, indeed, been instilled. But it is also clear that the procedures have significantly dampened the enthusiasm and initiative of the management abroad, and limited its flexibility in meeting local problems and opportunities.

Another company went a long way in the direction of delegation, partly from principle and partly from negligence. It has now reversed the process, because it came to realize that it was not making the full resources of the company in areas like selling techniques available to the foreign units. Furthermore, in some instances the subsidiaries were going off in undesirable directions.

EDUCATION. Top management's approach must inevitably include elements of control and direction, but it must contain a large measure of education as well. The parent company has the responsibility of developing management characteristics in the foreign unit which will lead divisional executives' thinking and decisions along desirable lines. To the extent that these efforts are successful, the need for direction and control will be reduced and the effectiveness of the operation increased. As sound management practices are inculcated, the home office can confidently allow greater initiative and flexibility of movement in the field. Careful attention to this aspect of overseas management will produce permanent effects on the foreign units, rather than the temporary impact of direct controls and supervision.

PERSONAL RELATIONSHIPS. The importance of human relations in any management process is well recognized. In foreign operations, the web of problems that arise in dealing with the human factor is further tangled by such factors as:

Lack of continuous face-to-face contact.

Communication by correspondence—a risky process at best.

Basic cultural and value differences.

I have been so impressed with the significance of this last problem that I have started a major research project to explore it. Many ideas are already emerging from this study; at this stage, I will point out only two aspects which seem to me of crucial importance:

The business structuring of contacts, especially the visits which home office executives make to foreign units, needs careful study. At one extreme is the upsetting visit by the man who flies from unit to unit "solving problems," "straightening things out," and "energizing the local management." At the other extreme is the friendly call by the man who makes a regular swing through the foreign divisions to talk with his associates abroad, to discuss progress, to get ideas, and to make suggestions.

In practice, most international managers fall somewhere between these two poles—and both have their advantages. I feel, however, that too many firms incline toward the first approach and fail to see all the consequences of such action. While they may "get things done" in an immediate sense, possibilities for future communication on basic, long-range programs are cut down by behavior which puts foreign management in a defensive position.

To establish real understanding with people of basically different cultures requires flexibility, maturity, a capacity for respecting other ways of life, a genuine interest in different types of people. And above all it requires genuine personal warmth and emotion. Perhaps the importance of this intangible has something to do with the fact that family and kinship ties play a major role in foreign business circles.

Whatever the reason, the power of personal friendships and respect is mighty in overcoming many organizational and doctrinal differences, and I am inclined to think that this power is no less helpful in surmounting the natural barriers between people of different backgrounds and outlooks. If top executives will send men abroad who have the capacity for personalized management, they will find it far easier to establish smooth and productive working relationships with a variety of people operating at long distances under many different organizational arrangements.

Division Organization

The effective organization of an international division—that is, the body of people who work directly for the parent company, rather than for the foreign units—is becoming an increasingly challenging problem as diversification and mergers expand company product lines and as the extent and variety of foreign operating arrangements grow.

The international division stands between the domestic organization and the foreign units, and bears the responsibility for achieving the firm's objectives—whether they be a high sales volume, quality control, or efficient manufacture. In a typical company, know-how or products for the foreign organization will be supplied by several domestic plants, while other domestic units including the advertising and sales departments have some ties with the overseas operations. At the same time, as I pointed out before, many different kinds of foreign units will be in operation.

The process of liaison between the different home office divisions and the foreign units is clearly a difficult one, and a suitable organizational system is indispensable. Though patterns will differ in each company, there are certain desirable characteristics which hold for any system. If the international division demonstrates an awareness of these common denominators and develops plans to achieve them, top management can have confidence in its program. Here are the three requirements for the international division which impress me as most valuable.

1. *Speed.* In the normal operation of an international business a great many problems arise which must be taken care of quickly. There is an endless series of minor production problems for which the advice of domestic plants is needed; requirements for machinery and parts develop irregularly, and, if foreign inventories are to be kept at a reasonable level, quick delivery from home must be assured; new selling ideas should be passed on quickly to the field organization. All of these situations—and many more which arise in the course of daily business operations—demand systems which involve a minimum of procedural red tape.

2. *Avoidance of Confusion and Conflicts.* If speed were the only consideration, every contact would probably be made directly. A plant manager in India would cable directly to the engineer in Tulsa if he needed help on production problems. A Venezuelan sales manager would place an order directly on the company's New Orleans warehouse if he suddenly ran short of supply. However, the resulting confusion would be appalling, so a compromise obviously has to be worked out.

The great hazard in this process is that the home office personnel will fall prey to the faults which seem to creep into any bureaucracy. All too quickly they become more interested in keeping procedures orderly than in getting things done, and their system of checks and controls becomes important in itself. Top executives are familiar with this process of bogging down in domestic operations; they should be equally aware of this danger in overseas management, where it is increased by the remoteness of the home office from field operations.

3. *Priorities.* Any organization rests on a system of priorities, and the international division is no exception. Managements are constantly faced with choices between two desirable courses of action and must decide which is the better.

The determination of where the regional manager should be located is an example of this problem. A regional manager in the field can be in frequent personal contact with foreign units and thus help them with regular operating problems. A regional manager in the home office, on the other hand, is helpful to the top management in making major decisions or resolving interarea problems.

The choice can only be made by deciding which of these functions is more important to the individual company. If a firm has many new operations in the field, the first arrangement may be of greater value; a well-established organization may find the second one more useful.

Other characteristics are doubtless important to the international division organization, but I believe that these three are the most important in dealing with the type of problems which I outlined at the start of this section.

If an international division is set up to provide a sensible mixture of speed and organizational clarity and with a good sense of priorities, it can be an effective intermediary between the United States and foreign units.

QUESTIONS

1. Define:

Volume control	Field audit
Feedback	Cybernetic

2. What barriers make controlling an international operation more difficult than controlling domestic marketing activities?

3. How do company objectives relate to control systems?

4. "To minimize losses, management must be especially control conscious when it is engaging in the overseas business for some reason other than direct short-run profit." Explain.

5. Discuss the basic requisites of an effective control system.

6. Review the relative advantages of centralized and decentralized systems for controlling international marketing operations.

7. Develop a control system for a marketing program using autonomous foreign franchisees to market a domestic product.

8. Review the control sequence.

9. Explain the importance of "timing" standards and controls.

10. Visit a firm with international sales or marketing activity. Compare their control system with one which you develop for them. Explain the differences.

11. Discuss the difficulties associated with field audits.

CASES—PART IV

WALKERS CORPORATION*
Licensing Foreign Production

Walkers Corporation is a manufacturer of accessory equipment of many years' standing in the machinery, automotive, and aircraft industries. In 1948, Walkers became a subsidiary of the Clorny Co., which is principally an aircraft accessory manufacturer—but each company maintained its original identity and function.

The export activities of the Clorny Co. and Walkers Corporation are similar in that each has an Export Department and an Export Sales Manager who is responsible to the respective Vice President of Sales. Walkers Corporation maintains exclusive distributorship and representation in the major countries of the world for marketing its products. In addition, there are partially-owned and wholly-owned subsidiaries in other countries. There is also a licensee which manufactures various of its products in Japan—Kioto Takka Shimatsu Co., Ltd. (hereafter referred to as "K. T. S.").

One line of products—aviation products—has not been handled by the Export Department until recently. Due to the technical nature of the product, aviation products have been treated as domestic sales in all cases. Overseas sales that were made were through export agents or foreign airline purchasing offices. No foreign representation was permitted due to the extensive military use of these products and the difficulty of exporting items of this nature. Another factor was the relatively limited overseas market for this type of product until recently. However, in late 1966, overseas business began to expand to the point that in mid-1967 the Export Department added a sales representative to the staff to handle these products.

Prior to World War II, Clorny Co., distributed its products to the

---

* Reprinted with permission of the author, Professor Laurence P. Dowd.

Japanese aircraft industry through an agent in Tokyo, K. T. S. In 1956, Clorny reopened business with this firm and subsequently received 25% ownership. K. T. S. management admitted that during hostilities it had borrowed from the design of Clorny products and produced facsimiles during the war, for which it offered reparation by paying royalties on these products and offering 25% stock to Clorny. This was all that was permitted under Japanese law.

Soon after the Clorny-Walkers merger, K. T. S. sent representatives to Walkers to obtain a license to produce certain Walkers' products in Japan. K. T. S. advised that during hostilities it had produced for the Japanese government several versions of Walkers' machinery equipment and offered to pay back royalties. During prevailing negotiations on this matter, K. T. S. management inferred that if they did not obtain the license, K. T. S. would be forced to continue to manufacture regardless of the consequences. Walkers agreed to license K. T. S. for certain of its products to be produced in Japan for the Japanese government and in turn extracted a sizeable royalty fee.

These negotiations, however, did not involve any aircraft products, as K. T. S. was not involved with this type of product during the war. Again in 1965, however, K. T. S. management requested that certain aircraft products be included in the license arrangement. This was refused to K. T. S., who then requested representation of these products in Japan. This was also refused, as Walkers wished to protect its proprietary right to the products and did not consider the Japanese aircraft industry to be of significant scope to warrant introduction of the products in Japan. It was felt that should K. T. S. obtain the license, there would be cheap versions of the products introduced to various countries of the world which would spoil the market for Walkers' products as aviation industries developed around the world. A further consideration was taken of the trade relationships under negotiation between Japan and the Soviet countries at that time.

In the meantime, the United States government and Japanese Self-Defense Agency made arrangements whereby several United States designed aircraft could be produced in Japan for the Japanese Air Force and for the United States military forces in Japan. Some of these aircraft utilized Walkers' aviation products. In most cases, however, the United States government furnished the necessary aircraft accessories for the production of these aircraft in Japan through the Military Grant Aid Program at little cost to the Japanese government. Because of this, Walkers Corporation had no control over the ultimate use of its product.

In late 1966, K. T. S. sent a delegation to Walkers to discuss the matter of representation of aviation products in Japan. The delegation gave a glowing portrayal of the important role which aviation would have in the future economic development of Japan and expressed the wish to have Walkers' products adequately represented in the country. K. T. S. was again refused the right of representing or manufacturing these products, but the possibilities of further negotiations in this matter were not eliminated in the conversations. Soon after this delegation visited Walkers Corporation, the closing out of several small accounts involving airlines and aircraft overhaul stations in Japan was noticed by the Export Department. At the same time, the K. T. S. account became more active for aviation products.

Early in 1967, the Vice President of Sales of Walkers Corporation corresponded with the General Manager of K. T. S. and advised that K. T. S., although not to be considered as a representative for aviation products, could handle inquiries for aviation products which came directly to K. T. S. from Japan, but no discount in price could be accorded K. T. S. for any orders placed with Walkers Corporation. K. T. S. would be dealt with in the same manner as any export customer as far as aviation products were concerned.

Early in 1968, the Japanese government negotiated with the United States government to produce a jet aircraft of United States design in Japan under license. Two hundred and fifty (250) aircraft were involved, and this type of aircraft already in use by United States forces utilized a large number of Walkers' products. K. T. S. representatives immediately came to the United States to negotiate for license to produce several of the accessories on the aircraft. Negotiation with Walkers on this matter was again negative and the matter was dropped.

In late 1968, a representative of K. T. S. involved with the Japanese aircraft industry visited Walkers and stated the case for license production again. He pleaded the case for production or representation of aviation products in Japan exceptionally well and the result of his visit was a memorandum from the Export Sales Manager to Walkers' management as follows:

Subject—Kioto Takka Shimatsu aviation products. . . . The visit of Mr. K. Temma of K. T. S. brings forth a matter which bears consideration. You are no doubt aware that Mr. Temma's mission here was to secure license arrangements for the manufacture of our aviation products in Japan. Some background on this subject is as follows:

1. Both the United States Air Force and the Japanese Self-Defense Agency have used the F86-K aircraft for several years in Japan, with most of the overhaul of aircraft and accessories being performed by Japanese firms.
2. The F86-K has been assembled under license by Nagoya Aircraft Company (Mitsuyama) and accessories were either purchased in Japan or supplied by Greater American Aviation, as is the case with Walkers' products utilized on this aircraft.
3. The Japanese Self-Defense Agency is considering the purchase and licensee production of the Grumman F11-F aircraft in Japan. This aircraft uses Walkers' products also. Approximately 200 F11-F aircraft will be produced in Japan by Mitsuyama at their Nagoya Aircraft Works.
4. The Asama Heavy Industries is producing the Japanese TIF-1 jet aircraft, which utilizes Walkers' products.

There are several things learned from our conversations with Mr. Temma which bear investigation:

1. The Japanese Self-Defense Agency has specified that only Japanese-produced accessories will be utilized on aircraft produced in Japan. The eventual replacement of aircraft accessories not produced internally is specified for aircraft produced under license in Japan.

2. Kioto Takka Shimatsu has been overhauling F86-K accessories, including Walkers' products, for several years for the United States Air Force and the Japanese Self-Defense Agency. It has procured replacement parts from United States government sources.

3. New Town Products is currently negotiating with the Shimizu Company of Osaka to have their products assembled and repaired in Japan to meet current Japanese Ministry requirements. The purpose is to possibly replace all Walkers' equipment now used on aircraft utilized by the Japanese Self-Defense Agency.

4. There are two new aircraft being designed in Japan. K. T. S. has received inquiries concerning the purchase of Walkers' products for these aircraft.

From the foregoing, the following assumptions are submitted:

1. K. T. S. has represented its firm as the exclusive representative and manufacturer of Walkers' products in Japan to the Japanese aircraft industry and to the Japanese Self-Defense Agency. In order to save face, it is now necessary for K. T. S. to secure a license to produce Walkers' aircraft products in Japan.

2. If it is not possible to secure the required license, K. T. S. must then borrow from the design of Walkers' products and produce this equipment outside of a license agreement. With the experience and proprietary information K. T. S. has gained through the overhaul of the F86-K accessories, there is no doubt that this firm is fully capable of performing this task and will do so if not granted the necessary license.

Therefore, it is recommended that we should deal with K. T. S. in the following manner:

1. If the Japanese Self-Defense Agency accepts the Grumman F11-F for production in Japan, we should offer to K. T. S. the exclusive right of representing our products in Japan on a yearly basis only.

2. If the Grumman F11-F program is adopted for Japan, it will involve approximately 600–800 Walkers' accessories on the original equipment. In order for Walkers' products to stay incorporated on this aircraft, it is recommended that we give K. T. S. an agreement to overhaul the Walkers' equipment which is used on the F86-K and the F11-F only, with the understanding that all original products and replacement parts must be purchased directly from Walkers Corporation. This will satisfy in part the Japanese Defense Ministry's restrictions and insure no replacement of Walkers' products by New Town Products' accessories.

3. No license agreement should be granted to K. T. S. for the manufacture of parts or completed units, but only for the overhaul and repair of Walkers' products as used in Japan on the F86-K and the F11-F. Representation of aircraft products should be confined to Japan.

Under the above circumstances Walkers Corporation would be assured of the following:

1. Maintaining proprietary rights to aircraft products design.
2. Control of overhaul and repair techniques.
3. An additional market for aircraft products.
4. Adequate market coverage in Japan.

In summary, it is my feeling that due to current developments in the Japanese aircraft industry there are several approaches to be taken to continue business with aircraft products in Japan.

1. Continue to market aircraft products commercially through Japanese agencies in the United States with limited representation by K. T. S. in Japan, as is currently the practice.
2. Grant K. T. S. exclusive representation of aircraft products in Japan on a yearly basis. Representation by this method would be confined to the Japanese Islands, and Japanese firms which maintain United States procurement offices should be permitted to purchase these products domestically.
3. The representation of Walkers' aircraft products by K. T. S. in Japan and a license to overhaul Walkers' aircraft products utilized on aircraft in use by the Japanese Self-Defense Agency.
4. The license to manufacture products by K. T. S. of those items used on United States designed aircraft utilized by the Japanese Self-Defense Force. This would include also overhaul and representation of aircraft products in Japan by K. T. S.
5. The exclusion of any Japanese firm, including K. T. S. from representing our aircraft products either from the United States or in Japan. This would undoubtedly force the Japanese to manufacture Walkers' products for United States design aircraft in use by the Self-Defense Agency outside of any license agreement.

The Market Research Department estimated the potential business in Japan to be approximately one million dollars annually. With representation or license production in Japan, Walkers could expect to obtain 50% of the market.

In a management discussion pursuant to the Export Sales Manager's memorandum, the Vice President of Sales stated that the Japanese aviation industry did not present enough sales potential for Walkers to get involved with K. T. S. in aircraft products. The Export Sales Manager felt that, if K. T. S. was not granted some concession, they would revert to their wartime tactics of copying designs.

The Engineering Manager was apprehensive of the protection of the proprietary designs and patent rights to the product if manufactured in Japan. However, the Aviation Product Sales Manager felt that, if the product was not adequately represented in Japan, the Japanese government would remove Walkers' products from the existing aircraft and replace them with products available in Japan. This would damage the reputation which the product enjoyed and affect other export sales of this product.

The Market Research Manager and Export Sales Manager insisted that in order to successfully compete in the rapidly expanding aviation markets in other countries the company must expand its efforts through licensing more foreign firms and better representation overseas. However, the Manager of Production felt that the technical liaison required to set up the production of the product would be far too costly and as a result prohibitive. There would have to be a very large market in order to attempt such a venture.

CASE IV-2

SWIFT MOTORS S.A.*

For a number of years the Swift Motor Company of Gary, Indiana, had operated successfully in Latinia, a South American country. At first the company had exported cars on a fully assembled basis; it had then shipped them in semi-knocked-down form. Fully knocked-down was the next stage, and this concluded with the establishment of an assembling plant, a concession to Latinia's progress toward industrial self-sufficiency.

During most of Swift's operations, once these had passed the stage of simple importation of complete vehicles, the company's Latinian subsidiary, Swift Motors S.A., had been managed by a veteran salesman, Henry Charles. Charles, American by birth and upbringing, had quickly adapted to life in Latinia. He learned fluent Spanish, he showed an ability to identify with the Latinian business and government community, and he became, as a Swift headquarters man put it, "More Latinian than the Latinians." Swift's activities were characterized by a lack of difficulty with government offices, by increasing sales to a comfortable market position, and by an overall smoothness.

As a consequence of this, the Swift management in Gary had tended to leave Swift Motors S.A. pretty much alone. The subsidiary earned what the management considered to be an adequate return on invested capital, it financed much expansion from earnings, and Mr. Charles made few demands on Gary or Gary on him. During periodic visits to Nueva Latinia, Latinia's capital, Gary officials were amused by the way Charles had adopted Latinian ways and occasionally teased him about his siesta, his reluctance to talk business at meals, and other habits they found somewhat eccentric.

When Charles retired to live in a country resort some miles from Nueva Latinia, he was succeeded by Peter O'Brien. O'Brien was sent down from Gary since management felt that things in the world of business had changed and that nobody in Swift Motors S.A. was sufficiently in touch with modern management to do the job that the future would require. O'Brien was a young man, a graduate of a school of business and one of a group sometimes known, in imitation of a similar group in a competitive company, as the Whiz Kids. The Whiz Kids were strong figure men, advocates of control through figures, and O'Brien was determined to introduce similar concepts into Swift Motors S.A. He was also known to have remarked that "None of that mañana stuff for me. It might have been good enough for old Henry Charles but I'm going to move that company into tomorrow's world."

Since the habit had been fairly well developed in Gary of leaving Swift Motors S.A. alone, senior management in the Swift head office assumed that things were going well, in the absence of evidence to the contrary. Certainly sales held up, labor difficulties increased only slightly

---

* Copyright © 1960 by the Board of Trustees of the Leland Stanford Junior University. Published herein by express permission.

and were ascribed to the changing tempo of Latinia, and O'Brien appeared to be going well. Abundant returns made their way from Nueva Latinia to Gary.

After O'Brien had been in Latinia for some eighteen months, something happened to disturb the Gary management group. Before Charles retired, he had been working on plans for the establishment of another assembly plant in a city about five hundred miles from Nueva Latinia. Negotiations with the government had dragged on but this, as Charles pointed out, was not surprising. He was confident that his successor would be able to carry the thing through.

O'Brien did try to work out the proposal but reported to Gary that he was not getting the cooperation from government and other quarters that the plan demanded. After all, this was to be a big new plant, automated to the degree possible, carefully designed and a fine addition to Latinia's industrial growth. Yet, he informed his Gary principals, this did not seem to impress Latinian people as it should. Finally, after the eighteen months had passed, he wrote to say that agreement to the proposal had been reached but on such terms and with such conditions that most of the value for Swift had gone.

The Gary management group, disturbed by the result, decided to send a man down to go over the ground with O'Brien and try to find out what had gone wrong and how it could be put right. William Thompson, a man with much overseas experience and with some contacts in Latinia, was chosen and Thompson arrived in Latinia, was met by O'Brien, and started on a round of meetings with government officials.

All were cordial enough but at the end of a week he was no wiser than he had been when he started. There seemed to be no single reason for the difficulties and no way in which they could be gotten around. O'Brien vigorously blamed it on "those stupid Latinians, they just don't know what's good for them. That's true of so many people down here. I had a lot of trouble just introducing decent control machinery in the plant and the offices, and most of the men I know think I'm crazy." Charles, unfortunately, was away on an extended trip and therefore could not help.

One evening, on his return to his hotel, Thompson ran into an old acquaintance, a Latinian whom he had known in several countries and with whom, at one time, he had been friendly. They were still friends, he supposed, but chance had kept them from much contact; nevertheless, they were glad enough to see each other to exchange an *abrazo*[1] and, at Thompson's suggestion, went into the hotel bar for a drink.

Fairly soon the men were back on the same old footing and Thompson found himself telling his friend about his difficulties. "You know," he said, "I can't understand it and neither can O'Brien, and Pete's a pretty smart boy. Top management think the world of him; if he can't put it over, we don't know who can."

There was a moment's silence. Then the other spoke. "William," he slowly remarked, "I don't know if I should tell you this but I think I

---

[1] Literally "embrace," and exchanged by male friends as indicating more cordiality and more intimate friendship than is shown by a handshake.

must. The fault is not with us, with my country, or with your company. Or rather, it is with part of your company. I know a lot about its activities here and I was a good friend of Henry Charles. I know he is unhappy about things but I also know he has determined not to do or say anything which would make it hard for people.

"But he was the reason you have done so well down here, and the reason you are now in difficulty is his successor. Charles knew how to think as we do, to act as we do, and we accepted him as one of us. O'Brien, poor fellow, thinks like an American, and that is his trouble. In eighteen months he has lost you the goodwill that Charles built up for you in twenty years and I don't know how you will get it back. Now, if you will excuse me, I must go, and I apologize for speaking so frankly but I thought somebody should. Good night."

Questions

1. What action should William Thompson take and why?
2. How can he evaluate the truth of the Latinian's statements?
3. How should Swift have protected itself against this possibility?
4. How would you screen a candidate for an overseas position of high responsibility?

CASE IV-3

COMPENSATION FOR OVERSEAS EXECUTIVES
Too Much or Too Little?

Today, serving a hitch overseas for the company is required of almost anyone wanting company advancement. Many problems arise in sending the executive overseas, but one of the most critical is compensation. Some feel that the overseas executive or expatriate is overcompensated; others feel that, considering the sacrifice, he is undercompensated. You be the judge.

Personal Business[1]

On the plus side, a man of 28 to 45 (the usual age range of overseas appointees) generally gets a boost in his career: higher pay, broader responsibilities. Major companies are sending their top-ranking younger men abroad, not employees they want to "bury."

Says a Chase Manhattan Bank executive: "A man is smart to have some overseas time if he really wants to move up the ladder." About 80% of those Chase sends abroad are sent for career development. The same holds for a growing number of big and medium-size international outfits. The usual hitch lasts from two to five years. And the man most

---

[1] Reprinted from the November 30, 1968 issue of *Business Week* by special permission. Copyrighted © 1968 by McGraw-Hill, Inc.

apt to benefit from it is the middle manager. He will probably get control over a whole local operation. That lets him prove his general managerial ability. And, if he is successful, he returns home with higher status. A younger man is smart to go for experience—even without more pay.

A far less attractive deal involves going overseas for an indeterminate period to train a national for a job abroad. This missionary may return home to discover that a former equal has stepped above him. Usually, of course, a man over 50 goes abroad only to fill a high-ranking spot. Some big companies now provide added incentive; they allow foreign service men to retire early (often at 60) with varying retirement benefits.

The big gamble is not so much age and the assignment. It's how well a man's wife and children will adjust to the relocation. There's likely to be at least moderate strain—and there are plenty of cases where relocation has broken up marriages. Even a move to Western Europe can be difficult. "People who have strong family ties back home are poor risks," says a Jersey Standard personnel executive. Some self-examination is a must, say the pros. But too often this is ignored by the man eager to push ahead. Says one old hand in the international field: "If you're just trying to get away from it all, forget about going abroad. Your problems will magnify."

As a rule, you won't get a contract for an overseas hitch (and it's best not to push for one). But there are some things you will want to nail down. You should expect a foreign service premium of 15% to 25% above your base salary. This is what many of the larger outfits are paying. Note that the cost of living abroad can be higher than in the United States. For example, it may cost up to $200 a month more to rent a comparable house in Europe than in the United States. "Making a profit on a tour abroad doesn't work these days," says one pro, "except in a place like Nairobi."

Other Compensation

Moving expenses should be paid, too. This may mean $5,000 to $6,000 (non-taxable) for moving your family to Western Europe. In addition, many companies will pay $800 to $1,000 per child per year for school expenses abroad. Some pay for one round trip a year for a college-age son or daughter studying in the United States. Quite a few companies will even help you in your search for a school and pay exceptional costs such as high tutoring fees in remote areas.

As an example,

a typical United States executive assigned in Brussels might receive in addition to his base salary: (1) a 10%–25% premium; (2) a cost-of-living allowance of several hundred dollars a month; and (3) housing allowance which permits him to live in the best Brussels suburb at about the same cost as a more modest house at home. He drives a European sports car while his wife makes do with the American sedan the company shipped overseas for him. His children attend the best local private schools when they would have gone to public schools at home. His social circle includes some of the top business, professional and government people in the country. His wife is able to visit some of the finest museums, concerts and lectures in the world—if she can find time away from an active social life. And yet they both complain to their friends in the local expatriate community, to local management and to company headquarters that they are being vastly undercompensated, are deeply unhappy, and feel that the company has done them an injustice.[2]

Questions

1. Expatriate executives are overpaid but undercompensated. Discuss.
2. How do you imagine the "typical U.S. expatriate" discussed above would react when he has to come home (U.S.) and lose all his "fringe" benefits?
3. Should international executives be paid a "premium" for accepting a foreign assignment?
4. Discuss other means of getting executives to go overseas without having to do the above. Or would that be impossible considering all the hardships?

CASE IV-4

MOTIVATING JAPANESE SALESMEN
Straight Salary or Commission?

National Office Machines of Dayton, Ohio, manufacturers of cash registers, EDP equipment, adding machines, and other small office equipment, has recently (March, 1968) entered into a joint venture with Nippon Cash Machines of Tokyo, Japan. National Office Machines (N.O.M.) had domestic sales of over _____ million dollars in 1967 and foreign sales of nearly _____ million. Besides the United States, they operate in most of Western Europe, the Mideast and some parts of the Far East. In the past, they have had no significant sales or sales force in Japan although they were represented there by a small trading company until a few years ago. In the United States they are one of the leaders in their field and are considered to have one of the most successful and aggressive sales forces found in this highly competitive industry.

Nippon Cash Machines (N.C.M.) is an old-line cash register manufacturing company organized in 1872. At one time, they were the major manufacturer of cash register equipment in Japan but they have been losing ground since 1950 even though they produce perhaps the best cash register in Japan. Sales in 1967 were _____ yen (360 yen = 1 U.S. dollar), a 15 percent decrease over sales in 1966. The fact that they produce only cash registers is one of their major problems; the merger with N.O.M. will give them much needed breadth in their product offerings. Another hoped-for strength to be gained from the joint venture is

[2] Reprinted from J. Vivian, "Expatriate Executives: Overpaid But Undercompensated," *Columbia Journal of World Business*, November–December, 1967, pp. 61–66. Copyright © 1967 by the Trustees of Columbia University.

to provide them with some of the managerial leadership they so sorely need.

There are 14 Japanese companies which have products that compete with Nippon, plus several foreign giants such as IBM, National Cash Register, and Burroughs of the United States and Sweda Machines of Sweden. Nippon has a small sales force of 21 men, most of whom have been with the company since shortly after World War II and a few from pre-World War II days. These salesmen have been responsible for selling to Japanese trading companies and to a few large purchasers of equipment.

Part of the joint venture agreement was doubling the sales force within a year, with N.O.M. responsible for hiring and training the new salesmen, who must all be young, college-trained Japanese nationals. The agreement also allowed for U.S. personnel in supervisory positions for an indeterminate period of time and retaining the current Nippon sales force.

One of the many sales management problems facing the Nippon/ American Business Machines Corporation (N.A.B.M.C.—the name of the new joint venture) was the sales compensation plan to use, i.e., should they follow the Japanese tradition of straight salary and guaranteed employment until death with no incentive program, or the U.S. method (very successful for N.O.M. in the United States) of commissions and various incentives based on sales performance, with the ultimate threat of being fired if sales quotas continuously go unfilled?

The immediate response to the problem might well be one of using the tried and true U.S. compensation methods, since they have worked so well in the United States and are perhaps the kind of changes needed and expected from the U.S. management. N.O.M. management is convinced that salesmen selling their kinds of products in a competitive market must have strong incentives in order to produce. In fact, N.O.M. had experimented on a limited basis in the United States with straight salary about 10 years ago and it was a "bomb." Unfortunately the problem is considerably more complex than it appears on the surface.

One of the facts to be faced by N.O.M. management is the traditional labor-management relations and employment systems which exist in Japan. The roots of the system go back to Japan's feudal era, when a serf promised a lifetime of service to his lord in exchange for a lifetime of protection. By the start of the country's industrial revolution in the 1880's, an unskilled worker pledged to remain with a company all his useful life if the employer would teach him the new mechanical arts. The tradition of spending a lifetime with a single employer survives today mainly because most workers like it that way. There is little chance of being fired, pay raises are regular, and there is a strict order of job-protecting seniority.

Japanese workers at larger companies still are protected from outright dismissal by union contracts and an industrial tradition that some personnel specialists believe has the force of law. Under this tradition, a worker can be dismissed after an initial trial period only for gross cause, such as theft or some other major infraction. As long as the company remains in business he isn't discharged, or even furloughed, simply because there isn't enough work to be done.

Besides the guarantee of employment for life, the typical Japanese worker receives many fringe benefits from the company. Just how paternalistic the typical Japanese firm can be is illustrated by a statement from the Japanese Ministry of Foreign Affairs which gives the example of "A," a male worker who is employed in a fairly representative company in Tokyo:

> To begin with, A lives in a house provided by his company, and the rent he pays is amazingly low when compared with average city rents. His daily trips between home and factory are paid by the company. A's working hours are from 9 A.M. to 5 P.M. with a break for lunch which he usually takes in the company restaurant at a very cheap price. He often brings back to his wife food, clothing, and other miscellaneous articles that he buys at the company store at a discount ranging from 10% to 30% below city prices. The company store even supplies furniture, refrigerators, and television sets on an installment basis, for which, if necessary, A can obtain a loan from the company almost free of interest.
>
> In case of illness, A is given free medical treatment in the company hospital, and if his indisposition extends over a number of years, the company will continue paying almost his full salary. The company maintains lodges at seaside or mountain resorts, where A can spend the holidays or an occasional weekend with the family at moderate prices. . . . It must also be remembered that when A reaches retirement age (usually 55) he will receive a lump sum retirement allowance or a pension, either of which will assure him a relatively stable living for the rest of his life.[1]

Even though "A" is only an example of a typical employee, a salesman can expect the same treatment. Job security is such an expected part of everyday life that no attempt is made to motivate the Japanese salesman in the same manner as in the United States; as a consequence, selling traditionally has been primarily an order-taking job. Except for the fact that sales work offers some travel, entry to outside executive offices, the opportunity to entertain, and similar side benefits, it provides a young man with little other incentive to surpass his basic quotas and drum up new business. The traditional Japanese bonuses (which normally amount to about two or four months' salary over the year) are no larger for salesmen than any other functional job in the company.

As a key executive in a Mitsui-affiliated engineering firm put it recently: "The typical salesman in Japan isn't required to have any particular talent." In return for meeting sales quotas, most Japanese salesmen draw a modest monthly salary, sweetened about twice a year by bonuses. Manufacturers of industrial products generally pay no commission or other incentives to boost their businesses.

Besides the problem of motivation, a foreign company faces other strange customs when trying to put together and manage a sales force. Class systems and the Japanese distribution system with its penchant for reciprocity put strain on the creative talents of the best sales manag-

---

[1] "Japan's Paternalistic Employment System Is Changing in Face of Tight Labor Market," *The Wall Street Journal*, March 27, 1967, p. 6. Reprinted with permission.

ers, as Simmons, the U.S. bedding manufacturer, was quick to learn. One Simmons' executive explains:

We had no idea of the workings of the class system. Hiring a good man from the lower classes, for instance, could be a disaster. If he called on a client of a higher class, there was a good chance the client would be insulted. There is also a really big difference in language among the classes.[2]

In the field, Simmons found itself stymied by the bewildering realities of Japanese marketing, especially the traditional distribution system which operates on a philosophy of reciprocity that goes beyond mere business to the core of the Japanese character. It's involved with "on," the notion that regards a favor of any kind as a debt that must be repaid. To "wear" another's "on" in business and then turn against him is to lose face, abhorrent to most Japanese. Thus, the owner of large Western-style apartments, hotels, or developments will buy his beds from the supplier to whom he owes a favor, no matter what the competition offers.

In small department and other retail stores, where most items are handled on consignment, the bond with the supplier is even stronger. Consequently, all sales outlets are connected in a complicated web that runs from the largest supplier, with a huge national force, to the smallest local distributor, with a handful of door-to-door salesmen. The system is self-perpetuating and all but impossible to crack from the outside.

However, there is some change in attitude taking place as both workers and companies start discarding traditions for the job mobility common in the United States. Skilled workers are willing to bargain on the strength of their experience in an open labor market in an effort to get higher wages or better job opportunities; in the United States it's called "shopping around." And a few companies are showing willingness to lure workers away from other concerns. A number of companies are also plotting on how to rid themselves of some of the "deadwood" workers accumulated as a result of promotions by strict seniority.

Toyo Rayon Company, Japan's largest producer of synthetic fibers, says it will start reevaluating all its senior employees every five years with the implied threat that those who don't measure up to the company's expectations will have to accept reassignment and possibly demotion; some may even be asked to resign. A chemical engineering and construction firm is planning to ask all its employees over 42 to negotiate a new contract with the company every two years. Pay raises and promotions will go to those the company wants to keep. For those who think they are worth more than the company is willing to pay, the company will offer "retirement" with something less than the $15,000 lump-sum payment that the average Japanese worker receives when he reaches 55.

And a few U.S. companies operating in Japan are also experimenting with incentive plans. Nitta and Company, a belting manufacturer and

---

[2] "Simmons in Japan, No Bed of Roses," *Sales Management,* August 1, 1967, pp. 27–29. Reprinted with permission.

Japanese distributor for Chesterton Packing and Seal Company, was persuaded by Chesterton to set up a travel plan incentive for salesmen who topped their regular sales quotas. Unorthodox as the idea was for Japan, Nitta went along and, the first year, special one-week trips to Far East holiday spots like Hong Kong, Taiwan, Manila, and Macao were inaugurated. Nitta's sales of Chesterton products jumped 212 percent and this year sales are up 60 percent over 1966.

Last April, Nitta took the full step toward an American-style sales program. Under Chesterton's guidance, the company eliminated bonuses and initiated a sales commission plan.

When the first quarterly commission checks were mailed last June, the top salesmen found they had earned an average of $550 per month each, compared to original basic salaries of about $100-a-month.

At first, Nitta's management had resisted any form of incentive program for its personnel, arguing that it would "disrupt" all normal business operations of the company. The virtually instantaneous success of the travel incentives in motivating previously plodding sales performances into an enthusiastic burst of initiative has prompted Nitta to consider installing some form of incentive and/or commission sales plan for its extensive non-Chesterton operations. The company is one of the largest manufacturers of industrial belting in Japan.

IBM also has made a move toward chucking the traditional Japanese sales system (i.e., salary plus bonus but no incentives). For about a year it has been working with a combination which retains the semi-annual bonus while adding commission payments on sales over pre-set quotas.

"It's difficult to apply a straight commission system in selling computers because of the complexities of the product," an IBM-Japan official said. "Our salesmen don't get big commissions because other employees would be jealous." To head off possible ill-feeling, therefore, some non-selling IBM employees receive monetary incentives.

Most Japanese companies seem reluctant to follow IBM's and Nitta's example because they have their doubts about directing older salesmen to go beyond their usual order-taking role. High-pressure tactics are not well accepted here, and sales channels are often pretty well set by custom and long practice (e.g., a manufacturer normally deals with one trading company, which in turn sells only to customers A, B, C, and D). A salesman or trading company, for that matter, is not often encouraged to go after customer Z and get him away from a rival supplier.

Japanese companies also consider non-sales employees a tough problem to handle. With salesmen deprived of the "glamour" status often accorded by many top managements in the United States, even Nitta executives admit they have a ticklish problem in explaining how salesmen—who are considered to be just another key working group in the company with no special status—rate incentive pay and special earning opportunities.[3]

The Japanese market is becoming more competitive and there is real fear on the part of N.O.M. executives that the traditional system just won't work in a competitive market. On the other hand, the proponents of the incentive system agree that the system really has not been tested

[3] "How to Put New Hustle into a Japanese Salesman," *Business Abroad*, November 27, 1967, pp. 33–34. Reprinted with permission.

over long periods or even very adequately, since it has only been applied in a growing market. In other words, was it the incentive system which caused the successes achieved by the companies or was it market growth? Especially is there doubt since other companies following the traditional method of compensation and employee relations have also had sales increases during the same period.

The problem is further complicated for Nippon/American because they will have both new and old salesmen. The young Japanese seem eager to accept the incentive method but older men are hesitant. How do you satisfy both since you must, by agreement, retain all the sales staff? Another very critical problem lies with the nonsales employees; traditionally, all employees on the same level are treated equally whether sales, production, or staff. How do you encourage competitive, aggressive salesmanship in a market unfamiliar to such tactics, and how do you compensate salesmen in such a manner to promote more aggressive selling in the face of tradition-bound practices of paternalistic company behavior?

Questions

1. What should they do—incentives or straight salary? Support your answer.
2. If incentives are out, how do you motivate salesmen and get them to aggressively compete?
3. Design a U.S.-type program for motivation and compensation of salesmen. Point out where difficulties may be encountered with your plan and how the problems are to be overcome.
4. Design a pay system you think would work, satisfying old salesmen, new salesmen, and other employees.
5. Discuss the idea that perhaps the kind of motivation and aggressiveness found in the United States is not necessary in the Japanese market.
6. Develop some principles in motivation which could be applied by an international marketer in other countries.

CASE IV-5

ORGANIZATIONAL AND CONTROL PROBLEMS ABROAD

This case includes three examples of major U.S. companies which encountered ruinous problems in attempting to arrange working relationships with foreign firms. In studying the three examples it is important to try to determine the actual causes behind the problems and to seek common factors for the three examples.

Part A—Snares of Joint Ventures: The Genesco-Interstyle Failure*

A company tempted to enter a joint venture with a well established

---

* Reprinted from the October 4, 1968, issue of *Business Europe*, pp. 317–18, with the permission of the publisher.

manufacturer in order to achieve a substantial foothold in the European market should not overlook the many possible conflicts of interest inherent in this expansion route. Conflicts, which may arise particularly in regard to dividend, export, or sourcing policies, may be all the more acute in the case of 50:50 partnerships—especially if the local partner maintains activities independent of the joint venture that could compete with its operations. Corporate executives who are planning joint ventures (which are particularly attractive for capital-short US firms) should make certain that management control is firmly in their hands. This is the lesson that may be drawn from the recent failure of Genesco-Interstyle, a German-Swiss-US venture created with high hopes eight months ago.

In early 1968, the US clothing giant, Genesco of Nashville, formed a 50:50 joint venture with Interstyle of St. Gall, Switzerland, holding company of Goetz, the German textile group. By the move, Genesco, which already had manufacturing affiliates in Belgium, France, Italy, and the UK, gained a firm foothold in Germany through Interstyle's three German subsidiaries. Interstyle also brought in six firms from other European countries.

Despite great expectations and seeming compatibility, the association between Interstyle and Genesco, at the time renamed Genesco-Interstyle, has been severed.

The basic reasons for the failure are that the Goetz group retained nine textile factories under its own control and that the two partners neglected to fix by contract the limits of competition between the remaining Goetz enterprises and the new joint venture. Hence, Goetz found itself, in numerous instances, to be a partner and a competitor simultaneously. Since vital decisions could not be made if the 50:50 partner disagreed, a deadlock in important planning and policy matters soon developed.

According to some sources, Genesco's dynamic marketing methods met strong resistance from Goetz. It appears that the Goetz family opposed a number of Genesco's measures that may have had a competitive influence on their wholly owned children. Genesco, on the other hand, reports that Goetz made commitments not permissible under its agreement with Genesco, and failed to provide competent management free of conflicts of interest.

As the situation became increasingly untenable, the US firm approached its German associates with the request to buy their entire share in Genesco-Interstyle. Goetz agreed, and the wholly Genesco-owned enterprise has now been renamed Genesco Europa. The price Genesco paid for Goetz's nominal Sfr21 million share (Sfr4.3:$1) has not been disclosed. But despite widespread speculation that it was considerably more than Genesco would have paid had it acquired the entire capital of the Swiss holding company initially, Genesco reports that it purchased the second half of Interstyle at a lower amount than the first half because Goetz had not lived up to its contractual agreements. The Nashville, Tennessee firm now predicts important expansion in each of its Genesco Europa units.

Part B—Hoechst Takeover of Reichhold Chemie Underlines Pitfalls of European Joint Ventures*

Still another horror story underlies the fact that international companies must think twice before succumbing to the insistent siren song of those European governments, banks, or individuals prodding them into setting up joint ventures with local firms.

Joint ventures offer several manifest advantages as a route to investment abroad. In particular, at a time of rampant economic nationalism, joint ventures may help fend off accusations of foreign domination. Also, cash-short companies may find a number of European firms eager to put up capital in new ventures benefiting from advanced foreign knowhow.

But there is the other side of the coin. For a company with worldwide interests, a major disadvantage of joint ventures is the difficulty to integrate them into global operational policy. The partners may bicker endlessly over the disposition of profits, the sourcing of raw materials and components, intercorporate pricing and fees or product strategy. The worst that can happen with a joint venture is to wake up one morning tied up to an unknown, possibly undesirable partner, if the initial partner has decided to sell his shares. This danger is all the greater where the foreign partner has only a minority position in the joint venture.

A few weeks ago, Farbwerke Hoechst offered the local shareholders of Reichhold Chemie AG of Hamburg (RCAG) a price for their stock considerably above the current market value. The offer, calling for an exchange of shares plus an extra cash premium, was made conditional upon a majority of RCAG stockholders turning over their shares to Farbwerke Hoechst. In view of the firm's poor short-term business prospects, the RCAG board advised the shareholders to accept the bid.

Some historical expounding is necessary to understand how Reichhold Chemicals got involved in this situation. Back in 1963, Mr. Reichhold sponsored the creation of Beckacite GmbH, which was later transformed into a joint stock company and rechristened Reichhold Chemie (on which board Mr. Reichhold served as chairman for many years). Following successive capital increases, the shareholding of the Reichhold family in RCAG grew to a reported 35% in 1961. But since then, the multi-million failure of a joint venture (Oleonaphta) between RCAG and Deutsche Erdöl led the Reichhold family to sell a large portion of its RCAG shares. Just before the Hoechst takeover bid, the Reichhold family and relatives in Germany owned a reported 17.5% of the Hamburg company. In the meantime, relations between the US chemical firm and its German affiliate had grown tense, though they were still linked by technical cooperation and licensing agreements, and had a common director.

Two weeks after the RCAG general meeting, during which Hoechst

---

* Reprinted from the July 5, 1967, issue of *Business Europe*, pp. 204–10, with the permission of the publisher.

made its purchase offer, it was unofficially announced that Reichhold Chemicals would make a more generous counterbid. Then it appeared that for the first time in the post-war history of the German chemical industry, two giants would wage a fierce battle for the control of a third firm. And soon after the Hoechst bid became public, the RCAG stock, previously selling at 170% (of par), shot up to 300% (against an offer of 275% a share by Hoechst).

However, Reichhold Chemicals actually never came out with a counterbid, and by the end of June a large majority of RCAG shareholders— about 83%—had accepted the Hoechst offer.

Hoechst's takeover is likely to have far-reaching adverse consequences for Reichhold Chemicals: the German giant has immediately announced that in future RCAG will cooperate closely with another Hoechst subsidiary, Chemische Werke Albert, one of Reichhold Chemicals' toughest competitors in world markets.

Not surprisingly, Reichhold Chemicals has implied that it will cancel its licensing and technical agreements with RCAG, but the fact that Hoechst will not benefit from the US firm's technology is unlikely to prevent it from stepping up its competition against Reichhold Chemicals.

. . . The Hoechst takeover is tantamount to a partial withdrawal of Reichhold Chemicals from Germany, but not on the US firm's own volition.

Part C—Hazards of Investing in Existing Firm: Singer Finds Inherited Ailments Require Costly Remedies*

The recent unhappy experience of the U.S. Singer with its majority-owned German mail-order subsidiary casts once again a sobering light on the dangers of investing abroad via joint venture. Singer's case demonstrates that the risk of a serious financial setback may be even greater if the foreign investor acquires part of an *existing* firm, rather than starting from scratch with a local partner, and if the former owner is allowed to continue running the business.

For Singer, one of the rare manufacturers selling directly to the consumer, the acquisition of a majority interest in a large mail-order house was a natural route to improving distribution of its consumer goods in Germany. Yet the drastic and costly measures that were necessary to turn the joint venture into a profitable operation can serve as a lesson for any would-be investor.

The story began early last year when Singer purchased, for a reported $16 million, a 51% interest in Friedrich Schwab AG, then Germany's third largest mail-order house. The Schwab family retained a 26% participation (enough to block certain basic corporate decisions), and Friedrich Schwab remained chairman of the board. The outstanding 23% of Schwab's equity is widely held by the public.

Schwab's mail-order business is based on a network of over 100,000

---

* Reprinted from the September 29, 1967, issue of *Business Europe*, pp. 305–6, with the permission of the publisher.

part-time sales representatives (mainly housewives, who take orders from their friends) and of some 7,500 retailers, members of the SPAR food chain, who display Schwab catalogs and accept orders. Under its family management, Schwab had concentrated mainly on shoes and textiles, which account for about two thirds of total turnover. Consumer durables ($Dm140$ million) were mostly sold under the manufacturers' brand names.

Within one year after the takeover, Schwab had lost one third of its $Dm52$ million ($Dm4$: US$1) nominal capital, registered a $Dm14.3$ million loss (including a $Dm5.5$ million loss resulting from a severe adjustment of the book value of quasi-worthless items that had been dragged on for years by Mr. Schwab in the inventories), and nearly doubled its bank debts and other liabilities to $Dm100$ million.

Singer attributes this dismal performance primarily to Mr. Schwab's conservative marketing policy and errors of judgment in launching new projects.

To remedy the situation, Singer took a series of measures. . . .

On the personnel side, the US firm replaced Mr. Schwab as board chairman with a top-notch US executive, Mr. Lester Naylor (formerly vice president of Montgomery Ward), retaining the former German chairman only as a consultant (this measure cost Singer some $Dm10$ million in compensation to Mr. Schwab for lost chairman fees). The US firm has also displaced a number of Mr. Schwab's former wartime comrades who had been given executive positions and instructed that all executives use medium-size cars instead of expensive models. Although the firm stresses that no one has been fired, it is the declared policy that from now on, all employees will be used "according to their qualifications."

Besides "cleaning" Schwab's balance sheet, Singer decided to discontinue the former chairman's miscalculated expansion program, which called for setting up old-style department stores in the centers of several towns. Only two of these stores, which operate at a profit, will be maintained—in Berlin and Duisburg. The phasing out of other department store projects cost Singer $Dm6.4$ million, mainly in indemnities for canceling already-signed lease contracts.

Singer will embark upon an expansion program of its own. First, it will set up in the suburbs of large towns a chain of big self-service, multi-line department stores (some 5,000 sq m each) with ample parking space. The construction and operating cost of these stores—a novel type of retail outlet for Germany—is estimated to be only half that of old-fashioned, mid-town department stores. Singer, which intends to pass part of the savings on to the consumer in the form of low "discount" prices, still hopes to make a profit in the first year of operation. The first four stores will be opened in Frankfurt next year. In another move, Schwab will gradually replace brand name goods listed in its catalogs by its own brands.

To finance the new expansion scheme, Schwab will soon float a $Dm24$ million, 10-year convertible bond issue carrying a 7% interest. The formula used for this issue will be a novelty for Germany. The bonds will be registered (bonds are usually issued in bearer form), and bond-holders will be allowed to sell the debentures only with the company's consent. The advantages of this formula, which combines the features of both a public and a private issue, will be twofold: (1) the issue of convertible registered bonds will not require the Ministry of Economics' permission as bearer bonds would; and (2) the company can prevent any undesired trade in its bonds. Initially, Singer will subscribe the whole Schwab bond issue, but other Schwab shareholders will be given an opportunity later to acquire one bond for every two shares.

Questions

1. Identify the chief problem in each example and tell what the three situations have in common.
2. Suggest ways of anticipating or remedying the problems in each example.
3. On a basis of the three examples, what conclusions can be drawn about establishing and controlling joint business arrangements with foreign companies?

V
International Marketing
Management

OUTLINE OF CHAPTER 17

INTRODUCTION

BREADTH AND SCOPE OF INTERNATIONAL MARKETING RESEARCH

THE RESEARCH PROCESS

DEFINING THE PROBLEM AND ESTABLISHING RESEARCH OBJECTIVES

PROBLEMS OF GATHERING SECONDARY DATA

PROBLEMS OF GATHERING PRIMARY DATA
Unwillingness to Respond
Sampling in Field Surveys
Language and Comprehension

PROBLEMS IN ANALYZING AND INTERPRETING RESEARCH INFORMATION

RESPONSIBILITY FOR CONDUCTING MARKETING RESEARCH

SOURCES OF SECONDARY DATA
U.S. Government
International Organizations
Governments of Foreign Countries
Chambers of Commerce
Trade, Business, and Service Organizations

SUMMARY AND CONCLUSIONS

READING
On the Use of Marketing Research in the Emerging Economies, *Journal of Marketing Research*

INTERNATIONAL MARKETING RESEARCH

INTRODUCTION

Tremendous demands for information are created by the intricacies of international operations and the complexity of the environment within which the international marketer must often operate. The preceding chapters have illustrated the variety of questions faced by the foreign marketer in his decision-making task. The responsibility of providing much of the information that an international marketer must have to carry out his marketing plans successfully is assumed by marketing research, "the systematic gathering, recording and analyzing of data about marketing problems toward the end of providing information useful in marketing decision-making."[1] When one is operating in foreign markets, his need for thorough information as a substitute for uninformed opinion is equally as important as it is in domestic marketing.

International marketing research and *marketing research* are synonymous, since the research process is basically the same whether applied in Hoboken, New Jersey, or the principality of Sikkim. Generally, the tools and techniques in foreign and domestic marketing research remain the same, but the environments within which they are applied are divergent, thus creating difficulty. Rather than acquiring new and exotic methods of research, the international marketing researcher must acquire the ability for imaginative and deft application of tried and tested techniques in sometimes totally strange milieus. The mechanical problems of implementing foreign marketing research might vary from country to country, but the overall objectives for foreign and domestic marketing research are basically the same—to answer questions with current, valid information that a marketer can use to design and implement successful marketing programs. Within a foreign environment, the frequently differing emphasis on kinds of information needed, the often limited variety of tools and techniques applicable, and the diffi-

---

[1] R. Still and E. W. Cundiff, *Essentials of Marketing* (Englewood Cliffs, N.J.: Prentice-Hall, Inc., 1966), p. 113.

culty in implementing the research process constitute the challenge facing most marketing researchers.

This chapter deals primarily with the operational problems encountered in gathering information in foreign countries for use by domestic marketers. The emphasis is on those elements of marketing research that usually prove to be especially troublesome in conducting research in an environment other than the United States. In addition, the final section summarizes the sources of secondary information available through the data collection and publication programs of public and private agencies.

BREADTH AND SCOPE OF INTERNATIONAL MARKETING RESEARCH

A basic difference in domestic and foreign market research objectives is the broader scope required for foreign research. Research can be divided into three different types based upon the general information needs. These three types are: (1) general information about the country, area, and/or market; (2) the study of specific information used to solve such problems as advertising, pricing, distribution, and product development in the marketing of specific products; and (3) forecasting future marketing requirements by anticipating social, economic, and consumer trends within specific markets or countries. The domestic market research department is usually responsible for only the second phase, since there are generally other departments responsible for such research activities as business research, economic research, and product development.

In international marketing research, the researcher's activities are frequently much broader than those of a domestic marketer and can involve all types of information essential to conducting business abroad. It would not be unusual to expect a foreign market researcher to provide all the information relevant to the question of a firm entering a new market—political stability of the country, cultural attributes, geographical characteristics, and market characteristics, as well as projections of potential economic growth. In addition, a foreign market research department might also be expected to be a source of information necessary to compensate for a possible lack of empathy within a strange environment, probable language deficiencies, as well as a lack of day-to-day market contact normally maintained in the home market.

One statement of needs of international marketing research is illustrated by the information requirements of the Hoover Company, manufacturers of consumer appliances. Before entering a market, they consider adequate and necessary information to include:

1. *Economy of the Country:* Population; national income and principal sources; income per capita and per family; average wage; retail sales; gross national product; electrical output; value of manufacturing and its relative importance to the economy; value of currency; value of principal imports and exports; climate and topography and their effects.
2. *Industry Data:* Value of electrical-industry imports, production and ex-

ports; value (and units) of appliance-industry imports, production, and exports; percentage of families owning the more common electric appliances; percentage of homes wired for electricity; characteristics of electrical current.

3. *Product Data:* Consumption by year for the past five years for products by type and price range; trends in imports versus local production; percentage of families owning the product; potential customer groups where located, and portion of population they represent; who makes and influences the decision to buy; what persuasive approaches are best calculated to influence prospects to buy; frequency of purchase; seasonal buying patterns.

4. *Competitive Situation:* Companies manufacturing or importing—their number, names, relative strengths, and breadth of product lines; brands offered and approximate share of market accounted for by each. Trends in competitor's share of market; types offered by each brand, and their price ranges; consumer preferences by brand, and type; trend in share of market by principal product types and price range; quality, performance and design of competitive products; appropriateness of design for the market; prevailing trade discounts at wholesale and retail levels. Advertising and other allowances given, if any; price structure at retail level. Do manufacturers establish or recommend retail prices, and are they maintained by law or custom? Is retail discounting practiced? If so, to what degree? Which companies have the best and poorest relations with distribution channels? Why?

5. *Channels of Distribution:* The normal channels used—that is, manufacturer-wholesaler-retailer-consumer, or some combination thereof—and which of them are used by our major competitors; whether door-to-door salesmen are used by manufacturers or retailers. If so, to what extent? The types of wholesalers and retailers who stock the product, and the relative importance of each type; the approximate number of wholesale and retail outlets available in principal markets, including the approximate proportions of large, medium, and small outlets; what selling, promotion, service, and stocking functions are performed by wholesalers and retailers, and what functions (if any) must be supplemented by the manufacturer; what transportation facilities are available for reaching key markets; what warehousing facilities are available.

6. *Competitors' Sales Organizations:* Types of sales force used by major competitors—that is, whether company man or manufacturers' representatives; size and caliber of major competitors' sales forces; function performed by these sales forces at wholesale and/or retail level, and frequency of contact; prevailing amounts and type of compensation—including door-to-door commission structure, if applicable.

7. *Repair and Maintenance Service:* Methods by which product repair and maintenance services are provided by major competitors; degree of satisfaction with service on the part of consumers and trade channels.

8. *Advertising and Promotion:* Type and extent of advertising and promotion used by leading competitors; media available and relative importance of each to potential customers of the product; prevailing rates by type of media.

9. *Credit:* Prevailing credit terms from manufacturer to wholesaler to retailer to consumer; extent of use of consumer credit, and the attitude of retailers and consumers toward its use; government and/or private lending institution restrictions, if any, that apply to consumer credit; general availability of capital for credit purposes.

10. *Sociological Factors:* Is there a general recognition of the benefits of labor-saving home appliances and a desire to own? Is domestic help cheaper than—and considered better than—electric appliances? What is the trend in cost and availability of domestic help? Is home wiring generally adequate for our appliances? What is the extent of plumbing fixtures and hot water for use with washing machines? What effect do decorating and maintenance customs have on our products? For example, what is the extent of rug use as it affects the need for vacuum cleaners? Do people have flooring that can be polished? Are well-polished floors considered socially desirable?[2]

Certainly information of such latitude is necessary for any sound marketing decision; however, for the domestic marketer much of the information is known from years of business experience with a single market. For the marketer in a foreign situation, full, basic information is necessary for every "new" market. Furthermore, a wide variety of related information is collected on a continuous basis.

There are many such checklists of categories of information or "intelligence" necessary for sound international marketing. While they vary in content to some extent, they all typically seem to agree that a system for adequate foreign market information should include those "foreign factors" which can vary from country to country or, quite frequently, from area to area within a country. One marketing research authority indicates that there are at least nine of these "foreign factors" which should always be considered. They are:

1. Competition (U.S., local, and third country)
2. Transportation
3. Electrical characteristics
4. Trade barriers
5. Economic environment
6. Business philosophies
7. Legal systems
8. Social customs
9. Languages[3]

In essence, they can be classified as the foreign-based uncontrollable factors as discussed in Chapter 1; naturally, the marketing problem-oriented information would also be included in any list of the activities and scope of international marketing research.

There is, of course, a basic difference between the kind of information ideally needed and that which is actually collected and/or used. Certainly there are as many firms engaged in foreign marketing who do not make their decisions with the benefit of the information above as there are those who do. Cost, time, and the human element are critical variables. In some firms there is neither appreciation for the need, nor ade-

---

[2] Victor P. Buell, "Planning a Foreign Market Study," *Increasing Profits from Foreign Operations* (New York: International Management Association, Inc., IMA Special Report No. 3, 1957), pp. 44–50.

[3] R. J. Dickensheets, "Basic and Economic Approaches to International Marketing Research," in Henry Gomez (ed.), *Innovation—Key to Marketing Progress* (Proceedings of the American Marketing Association, June 1963), p. 361.

quate time or money for implementation. Generally, as a firm becomes more committed to foreign marketing, the cost of failure increases, and greater emphasis is placed on the research function. Consequently, the international firm or world marketer, i.e., the firm with total commitments to foreign marketing, is most likely to be engaged in the most sophisticated and exhaustive kinds of research activities; whereas the infrequent or part-time exporter is less involved and thus may be less concerned. Even though the part-time or infrequent exporter is less concerned, he still needs this kind of information. Since the need continues to exist, but the extent of involvement is smaller, the degree of importance to the firm diminishes. In addition to the degree of need, the cost of doing the research must always be kept in mind. When the cost of the research versus the risk involved and the probable potential of the market in question are not in balance, then a decision for research may lead to a minimal research commitment. The cost of some types of research can outweigh the practical value of the information gathered and should be evaluated accordingly. Other sources of less costly information are available; for example, many export agencies provide much of the necessary information as part of their services to exporters. In such a case, the type of information may be considered as secondary data and thus a part of the total research effort. Considering the informational needs of the foreign marketer, two questions arise: first, what are the procedures and problems of collecting the necessary information? and, second, who should collect the data? These questions will be answered in their respective order.

THE RESEARCH PROCESS

The quality of information available to a marketer in making his marketing decision can vary from an uninformed opinion to thoroughly researched fact. The purpose of marketing research is to provide the most accurate and reliable data possible within limits imposed by time, cost, and the present state of the arts. The measure of a competent researcher is his ability to utilize the most sophisticated and adequate techniques and methods available within these limits. The final research conducted for any problem is always a compromise, but the final results should be the most accurate and reliable within the conditions just described. Although the variables above will change with each research project and from company to company, a systematic and orderly approach to research should always follow the same pattern. This systematic approach to research or the research process, whether applied in Boulder, Colorado, or Bogota, Colombia, is universally applicable. In an evaluation of properly conducted research, the universality of the research process is evident. Briefly, the research program should include the following steps:

1. Define the research problem and establish research objectives.
2. Determine the sources of information to fulfill the research objectives.

3. Gather the relevant data from secondary and/or primary sources.
4. Analyze, interpret and present the results.

The task of the researcher is to execute each of these steps with maximum objectivity and accuracy within the limitations of cost and time.

Although the steps in a research program are similar for all countries, the problems of implementing each step will vary from country to country because of varying stages of economic development and diverse cultures found in different countries. Subsequent sections will illustrate some of the more common problems which may be encountered, but it must be clearly understood that these problems will not be the same for every country. It is intended to show how foreign marketing research can differ from domestic research and how changes of environment can affect practices taken for granted within a home environment. England or Canada may evidence few differences from the United States, whereas Germany, South Africa, or Mexico may offer a multitude of difficult distinctions. These distinctions become apparent with the first step in the research process—the formulation of the problem.

DEFINING THE PROBLEM AND ESTABLISHING RESEARCH OBJECTIVES

The first step in the research process is to define the research problem and establish specific research objectives. The major difficulty here is translating the business problem into a research problem with a set of specific, researchable objectives.[4] This initial stage of research frequently goes awry because of improper problem definition. Defining the problem is certainly basic, yet a researcher will often embark on the research process with only a vague comprehension of the total problem.

The situation is more acute in foreign marketing research since unfamiliarity with the foreign environment tends to cloud problem definition, thereby complicating the process. This is the result of the researcher either failing to anticipate the influence of the local culture upon the problem or, more critically, failing to isolate the self-reference criterion[5] and thus treating problem definition as if it were in the researcher's home country rather than a foreign environment. Frequently, the student of international marketing reads of some foreign failure resulting from a rather simple error and wonders why the company didn't conduct research. In most cases, further inquiry reveals that research was conducted, but the questions asked were more appropriate for the U.S. market than for the foreign one. Isolating the self-reference criterion can be one of the most critical steps in the problem formulation stage of international marketing research.

Other difficulties in foreign research stem from failure to establish sufficiently broad problem limits to include all the relevant variables.

---

[4] For an interesting discussion of problem formulation, see Chapters 12 and 13 in Richard D. Crisp, *Marketing Research* (New York: McGraw-Hill Book Company, 1957).

[5] See Chapter 4 for discussion of this concept.

Such limits must include a far greater range of factors than necessary for domestic research in order to offset a totally unfamiliar background. Consider for example a U.S. company interested in estimating potential for its 14 to 16 cubic foot refrigerator with freezer compartment for the European market. There, the customary size refrigerator is from 4 to 6 cubic feet, with no freezer. Factors which will affect demand and must be considered in this situation are:

Food shopping habits.
Number of super and/or self-service food stores.
Automobile ownership.
Consumption of frozen foods.
Per capita private consumption expenditures.
Employment of women.
Availability of domestic help.
Availability of consumer credit.
Cost of electricity for residential use.
Dwelling construction and size of new dwellings.
Refrigerator saturation in high-income families.[6]

This list of variables is based on U.S. experience where the most conspicuous growth of demand for large refrigerators occurred with such developments as "ownership of automobiles, growing income, the working housewife, shortage and high cost of domestic help, and the increasing importance of leisure time."[7] Assuming that Europe follows a pattern close to that in the United States, the above factors would be important in estimating potential. Compare this list to those the manufacurer would use in today's U.S. market, and the much broader range of variables necessary in problem definition in foreign research becomes apparent.

Once the problem is adequately defined and research objectives established, the researcher must determine the availability of the information necessary to meet the research objectives. If the data are available, i.e., if they have been collected by some other agency, the researcher should then consult these secondary sources. If no data are available, or the secondary sources are inadequate, it would then be necessary to engage in the collection of primary data.

PROBLEMS OF GATHERING SECONDARY DATA

The breadth of many foreign marketing research studies and the marketer's general lack of familiarity with basic socioeconomic data of a foreign country result in considerable effort being placed on the collection of secondary data in foreign marketing research. In the United States, the government provides comprehensive statistical services for businessmen. Periodic censuses of population, housing, business, and agriculture have been taken, in some cases, for over 100 years. Current estimates of gross national product and other key economic indicators,

---

[6] Dickensheets, op. cit., pp. 359–77.
[7] Ibid., p. 376.

as well as special studies and compendiums of available statistics, are readily available to the researcher. Commercial sources, trade associations, management groups, and state and local governments also provide the researcher with additional sources of detailed market information.

Unfortunately, few foreign countries match the data available in the United States. Data collection in many countries has either been started only recently or never been started at all. Data collection is, however, improving substantially through the voluntary efforts of various interested organizations within countries and such outside organizations as the United Nations and the European Productivity Agency. Surely within the next decade many of the problems presently encountered will have disappeared as a result of greater interest in basic data and better collection methods.

There are generally three critical shortcomings regarding secondary data on foreign markets. First and most critical of the shortcomings concerns the availability of detailed data on specific market areas. Until the United Nations began collecting world economic data, there were little available except as very rough estimates. Even at the present time, detailed data on the numbers of wholesalers, retailers, manufacturers and facilitating services are unavailable for many parts of the world, as, surprisingly enough, are data on population and income. This is true for even the more developed nations. For example, in Japan it is reported that,

> One of the biggest obstacles in the development of marketing research is the fact that statistical data are frequently inconsistent and unreliable with regard to their quality as well as their availability. . . . Such absence of data—and deficiencies in existing data—are especially marked in wholesaling and retailing, even though the Minister of Commerce is attempting to improve this situation by means of a special biannual census and occasionally special surveys.[8]

A second problem relates to the reliability of some of the secondary data that are available. Unfortunately, where there is often an abundance of data, much of it must be screened and carefully selected. In many countries, national pride comes before statistical accuracy; the official statistics are sometimes too optimistic about internal development and progress so that their reliability must be heavily discounted. Many Latin American and Middle and Far Eastern countries are particularly prone to be overly optimistic in reporting relevant economic data about their countries. Furthermore, opinions of a handful of "informed experts" are often reported as fact. Or, as is the case in the E.E.C., tax policies can affect the accuracy of reported data. Production statistics in E.E.C. countries are often inaccurate because these countries have some sort of taxation upon domestic sales. Thus, companies have been known "to shave their production statistics a bit to match the sales reported to the tax authorities. Conversely, foreign trade statistics may

---

[8] Junji Hirata and others, "Marketing Research Practices and Problems in Japan," *Journal of Marketing*, April 1961, pp. 34–37.

International Data: *Caveat emptor*

The statistics used . . . are subject to more than the usual number of caveats and qualifications concerning comparability than are usually attached to economic data. Statistics on income and consumption were drawn from national-accounts data published regularly by the United Nations and the Organization for Economic Cooperation and Development. These data, designed to provide a "comprehensive statistical statement about the economic activity of a country," are compiled from surveys sent to each of the participating countries (118 nations were surveyed by the UN in 1968). However, despite efforts by the UN and the OECD to present the data on a comparable basis, differences among various countries concerning definitions, accounting practices, and recording methods persist. In Germany, for instance, consumer expenditures are estimated largely on the basis of the turnover tax, while in the United Kingdom, tax-receipt data are frequently supplemented by household surveys and production data.

Even if data-gathering techniques in each country were standardized, definitional differences would still remain. These differences are relatively minor except in a few cases; *e.g.,* Germany classifies the purchase of a television set as an expenditure for "recreation and entertainment," while the same expenditure falls into the "furniture, furnishings and household equipment" classification in the United States.

While income and consumption expenditures consist primarily of cash transactions, there are several important exceptions. Both income and expenditures include the monetary value of food, clothing, and shelter received in lieu of wages. Also included are imputed rents on owner-occupied dwellings, in addition to actual rents paid by tenants. Wages and salaries, which make up the largest share of consumer income, include employer contributions to social security systems, private pension plans, life and casualty insurance plans, and family allowance programs. Consumer expenditures include medical services even though the recipient may make only partial payment; if, however, the same services are subsidized wholly by public funds, the transaction is listed as a government rather than a consumer expenditure.

Expenditures, as defined by both the UN and the OECD, include consumption outlays by households (including individuals living alone) and private nonprofit organizations. The latter include churches, schools, hospitals, foundations, fraternal organizations, trade unions and other groups which furnish services to households free of charge or at prices that do not cover costs.

Source: David Bauer, "The Dimensions of Consumer Markets Abroad," The Conference Board Record, June 1970, p. 44. Reprinted with permission.

be blown up slightly, because each country in the E.E.C. grants some form of export subsidy."[9]

A third problem involves the comparability and currency of the avail-

[9] "European Market Research—Hide and Seek," *Sales Management,* February 1, 1969, p. 46.

able data. In the United States, current sources of reliable and valid estimates of socioeconomic factors and business indicators are readily available. In other countries, especially the less developed, data can be many years out of date, as well as having been collected on an infrequent and unpredictable schedule. Naturally, the rapid change in socioeconomic features being experienced in many of these countries makes the problem of currency a critical one. Further, even though many countries are now gathering reliable data, there are no historical series with which to compare the current information.

A related problem is the manner in which data are frequently collected and reported. Too frequently, this is done in categories much too broad to be of specific value. For example, as late as 1964, the German product classification "electronic, mechanical, and manual calculating instruments for adding, subtracting, multiplying, and dividing" lumped computers and abacuses together.[10]

Italians, on the other hand, grouped all conceivable types of electrical welding equipment under one heading, "including spare parts for the above welding electrodes and other welding equipment and accessories." If a company was interested in establishing trend or demand for a single product like spot welders, it would be almost impossible to use the Italian statistical grouping.

A concluding section in this chapter will deal specifically with sources of secondary data on foreign markets. The possibility of the previously mentioned shortcomings, however, should be considered when using any source of information, even though many countries have the same high standards of collection and preparation of data generally found in the United States. Data from any secondary sources from any country (including the United States) must always be checked and interpreted carefully.[11] As a practical matter, the following questions should always be asked in order to judge effectively the reliability of data sources:

1.   Who collected the data? Would there be any reason for purposely misrepresenting the facts?
2.   For what purpose were the data collected?
3.   How were they collected? (methodology)
4.   Are the data internally consistent and logical in light of known data sources or market factors?

In general, the availability and accuracy of recorded secondary data increase as the level of the economic development increases. To be sure, there are many exceptions; India is at a lower level of economic development than many Latin American countries, but it has more accurate and complete development of government-collected data. Fortunately, the governments of more and more countries are realizing the value of extensive and accurate national statistics to facilitate planning for or-

---

[10] "European Market Research—Hide and Seek," op. cit., p. 45.

[11] Victor P. Buell, "What to Study Before Entering the Foreign Market," in W. D. Robbins (ed.), *Successful Marketing at Home and Abroad* (Proceedings of the American Marketing Association, 1958), p. 55.

derly economic growth and are thus placing more effort in the collection of statistical data.[12]

PROBLEMS OF GATHERING PRIMARY DATA

When there are no adequate sources of secondary data, the market researcher must collect primary data. The kinds of problems and weaknesses in foreign primary data collection are different from those in the United States only in degree. The most significant factor in successful primary data collection is the willingness of the respondent to provide the desired information, along with his ability to articulate that which he knows—or, more correctly, the ability of the researcher to get the unwilling respondent to provide correct and truthful information.

In many countries, cultural variations hamper foreign researchers in locating the proper knowledgeable sources of information as well as influencing the general willingness to respond. For instance, in some countries the social structure is such that the husband not only earns the money but dictates exactly how it is to be spent. Since the husband alone controls the spending, it is he and not the housewife who should be questioned to determined preferences and demand for many consumer goods. In such a situation, not only can the researcher fail to identify properly the "correct" source of information, but he might also find varying degrees of unwillingness to answer inquiries that are in any way personal.

Unwillingness to Respond

In many cultures, personal information is inviolably *private* and absolutely not to be discussed with strangers. This attitude may result from cultural influences or it may have more of a practical motivation. Governmental taxes are frequently the motivating factor for privacy when personal possessions and finances are in question. Citizens of many countries do not feel the same legal and moral obligations as Americans to support their governments by actually paying their taxes. Tax evasion is an accepted practice if it can be successfully accomplished, and it can be even a point of pride for the more adept. When such an attitude is found within a country, taxes are rather arbitrarily assessed and anyone asking questions about income or personal possessions is immediately suspected of being a tax agent and is given incomplete or misleading information. In addition, the European businessman has traditionally been much more concerned with competitive secrecy than his U.S. counterpart. In the United States, publicly held corporations are compelled by the SEC to disclose certain operating figures on a periodic basis. In Europe, such information is seldom if ever released and then most reluctantly. In a number of European countries, attempts

---

[12] The reader is referred to Edward L. Brink, "The State of Marketing Intelligence in the United Kingdom," *Proceedings,* American Marketing Association 1965 Fall Conference, pp. 72–78, for further information on the availability of marketing information in the United Kingdom.

BOX 17–2

Phones Golden in Brazil

You're mad at your telephone company because the man was two days late installing your new phone?

Listen to this:

When Guimaraes Rosa, one of Brazil's leading writers, died recently he bequeathed his telephone to his mistress. His two children are challenging the bequest in court.

Then there's the case of Victor Koller. The United States hadn't yet entered World War II when Koller applied for a telephone, on Sept. 15, 1941. Now 65, he received his telephone in July this year—27 years later.

Nasi Felipe, now over 70, received his telephone in time for Christmas last year after a wait of 23 years. "I was just as happy when I got the telephone as I was when my seven grandchildren were born," Felipe said.

Those who don't like to wait and have the money can buy a telephone on the black market. The rate ranges from $600 in Rio de Janeiro to over $1,000 in Sao Paulo.

The problem, if you haven't guessed, is a shortage of telephones in Brazil, and especially in Sao Paulo.

Sao Paulo, with a population of 5,750,000, has just 330,000 telephones, or one for every 17 persons.

New York, by comparison, has one telephone for every two persons.

Although the first telephone was installed in Brazil in 1899, there are less than 1.5 million today. The population of Brazil is 8.7 million.

In 1966 the federal government purchased the Companhia Telefonica Brasileira, which was operated by Canada's Brazilian Light and Traction in the populous states of Sao Paulo, Guanabara, Rio de Janeiro, Minas Gerais and Espirito Santo. The new management decided to solve the problem of finances by having new customers "buy" their telephones in advance.

The 280,000 people then on the waiting list in Sao Paulo were told they'd have to pay about $550 in installments in order to get their telephones, and still have to wait several years for installation. Less than half the people took up the offer.

The stepped-up installation program has not put a damper on the sale of black market telephones. The biggest operator in Sao Paulo is a man with the appropriate name of "Mr. Bell" who advertises in English, Spanish, French, Italian and Portuguese in local newspapers.

The black market dealer acts as a broker, buying and selling telephones. Installation is guaranteed in 90 days following a cash payment. The seller advises the telephone company that he is moving and the telephone is transferred to the home of the buyer.

This, of course, renders telephone directories quite useless.

Source: John Virtue, United Press International, October 1968.

to enlist the cooperation of merchants in setting up a store sample for shelf inventory and sales information ran into very strong resistance that was based primarily on the retailers' suspicions and a tradition of competitive secrecy.[13] The resistance was gradually overcome by the patience of the researcher in his willingness to approach the problem step by step. As the retailer gained increasing confidence in the researcher and realized the value of the data gathered, he agreed to provide more and more necessary information.

In some cultures housewives would never consider being interviewed by a male interviewer or any stranger. French-Canadians, for example, are likely to be reticent, with the result that research findings may "be colored by the fact that the French housewife just plainly does not like to be asked questions. She tends to keep her privacy and that of her family as intact as possible."[14] By the same token, in some countries and societies a man would certainly consider it beneath his dignity to discuss shaving habits or brand preference in personal clothing with anyone; and certainly the researcher would not want to use a female interviewer for this kind of assignment.

The lack of availability of information may be the result of the unwillingness of people to answer questions; equally important is that, in some cases, the respondent may not be able to articulate the desired response. The ability to express attitudes and opinions about any product depends on the respondent's ability to recognize the usefulness and value of such a product. It is difficult for a respondent to formulate ideas concerning needs, attitudes, and opinions about goods, the use of which he may not understand or which have never before been available, or are not in common usage within a community. In fact, it may be impossible for someone who has never owned an electric refrigerator, and has used only iceboxes for generations, to express any accurate feelings or to provide any reasonable information about purchase intentions, likes, or dislikes. Under these circumstances the creative capabilities of the foreign marketing researchers undergoes thorough testing.

Although marketing research may be made more difficult to conduct by cultural differences, it is by no means impossible. In some communities it is necessary to enlist the aid of locally prominent people in order to open otherwise closed doors. In other situations, professional men and local students have been used as interviewers because of their knowledge of the market. In Cuba, prior to the Castro regime, one enterprising firm employed socially prominent women as interviewers as a means of overcoming resistance to surveys. As with most of the problems of collecting primary data, the difficulties are not insurmountable to the researcher who is aware of their existence. The application of the mechanical techniques for researching the respondents, however, poses additional obstacles.

---

[13] "Researching Foreign Markets," National Industrial Conference Board, Inc., Studies in Business Policy No. 75 (New York, 1955), p. 35.

[14] Marcel Pare, "Reticence Attitude Can Explode Research Study," in I. A. Litvak and B. E. Mallen (eds.), *Marketing in Canada* (New York: McGraw-Hill Book Company, 1964), p. 142.

Sampling in Field Surveys

Once the need for collection of primary data has been determined and the problems of collection solved, there are several difficulties encountered in the process of taking samples and conducting field surveys.

The greatest problem stems from the lack of adequate detail of universal characteristics and lists from which to draw meaningful samples. If current and reliable lists are not available, sampling becomes much more complex and generally less reliable. In many countries, telephone directories, cross-index street directories, census tract and block data, and detailed social and economic characteristics of the universe are not available on a current basis, if at all. The researcher then has to estimate characteristics and population parameters, sometimes with little basic data on which to build an accurate estimate. To add to the confusion, in some cities in South America, Mexico, and Asia, street maps are unavailable; and in some large metropolitan areas of the Near East and Asia, streets are not identified and houses are not numbered.

A lack of detailed social and economic information also can hamper the effectiveness of sampling techniques. Without an age breakdown of the universe, for example, the researcher can never be certain he has a representative sample on an age criterion, since there is no basis of comparison with the age breakdown in his sample. Although a lack of detailed information does not prevent the use of sampling in obtaining reliable market information, it does make it more difficult. In place of the probability techniques, many researchers who have found themselves faced with such situations have had to rely upon convenience samples in marketplaces and other public gathering places.

Besides the inadequacy of details on universal characteristics, the effectiveness of the various methods of communications (mail, telephone, and personal interview)[15] in surveys is also limited. In many countries, for example, telephone ownership is extremely low, making telephone surveys virtually worthless unless the survey is intended to cover only the wealthy. Ceylon is a case in point where fewer than 3 percent of the residents have telephones and those who do are typically the wealthy.[16] Inadequate mailing lists and poor postal service also pose problems for the market researcher who wants to use the mail to conduct his research. In Nicaragua, for example, possible delays of weeks in delivery are not unusual and expected returns are lowered considerably because a letter can be mailed only at a post office.[17]

In addition to potentially poor service within countries, there is also the major problem of the time required for delivery and returns when a mail survey is to be conducted from another country. Surface delivery can require three weeks or longer between some points on the globe, and

---

[15] For a very interesting review of the problems of survey research in Brazil, see Leo G. Erickson, "Analyzing Brazilian Consumer Markets," *Business Topics*, Summer 1963, pp. 7–26.

[16] Harper W. Boyd, Jr., and others, "On the Use of Marketing Research in the Emerging Economies," *Journal of Marketing Research*, November 1964, pp. 20–23.

[17] Ibid., pp. 22.

BOX 17–3

Doing Field Research in Brazil

The visitor to Brazil discovers soon that this is a country in which nothing quite works or fits. The hotel stationery is too big for its matching envelope by ⅛ of an inch. Telephone service is such that on one occasion a man in Rio, trying to reach a number six blocks away, is supposed to have given up in despair at last and routed the call via New York, whereupon it came through.

. . . . .

The mail service is fantastically unreliable. Nobody seems to know what postal rates are and mail boxes are few and irregularly empty. On a Copacabana beach, in the heart of metropolitan Rio, we slipped a card into the top of an overstuffed box; we could still see it there three days later.

And telegrams! The American Embassy in Rio cannot establish contact with its own consulate-general in Recife, a city of more than a million people, except by a device equivalent to ham radio. My wife and I sent five telegrams from Brasilia, the new capital, via the national telegraph on a Tuesday morning to friends in Salvador Bahia and in Recife, announcing our impending arrival in these great cities. We reached Salvador on Thursday and Recife the following Monday and beat all five telegrams.

Source: John Gunther, *Inside South America* (New York: Harper & Row, Publishers, 1967), pp. 12 and 6–7. Reprinted with permission.

although airmail reduces this time drastically, it also increases costs considerably.

Although adequate lists and adequate detail on the population may be critically short in some countries, this is not universally true. In those countries where every adult is required to register with various government agencies, there are extremely adequate lists of people, along with ample socioeconomic detail. In many European countries, as well as in Japan, voter lists, police registration lists, and tax records are available to researchers. In Sweden the government publishes a blue book every year listing the incomes of every person over a certain income level. In those areas where there is a paucity of adequate lists, other research tools must be relied upon. Mainly the various convenience sample methods are used.

Language and Comprehension

The most universal problem of survey sampling in foreign countries is the difficulty with language. Differences in idiom and the difficulty of exact translation create problems in obtaining the desired information and in the interpretation of the respondent's answers. The obvious solution of making certain that all questionnaires are prepared or reviewed by someone fluent in the language is frequently overlooked. In one such case, a question concerning washing machines asked a German respondent the number of "washers," i.e., washing machines, which were produced in West Germany for a particular year; the reply reflected the production of the flat metal disc variety instead of washing machines.[18]

Literacy, of course, poses another problem; in some less developed countries with low literacy rates, written questionnaires are completely useless. Within countries, too, the problem of dialects and different languages can make a national questionnaire survey impractical, as is illustrated by India where there are 14 official languages and considerably more unofficial ones. Or as one report on marketing research in Taiwan points out,

. . . student interviewers from the universities are often mainland Chinese who have not learned Taiwanese. While they are able to converse effectively in many sections of the larger cities, they are ineffective in most other areas of Taiwan. . . . In addition to the Taiwanese and Mandarin languages, there are small groups speaking Cantonese Chinese, and about 150,000 mountain dwelling aborigines with their own language. . . . A systematic sampling of the entire population of Taiwan with its diverse languages would require a well-trained multilingual staff of interviewers. Such a staff is extremely difficult to acquire.[19]

In addition, some respondents with a minimum of education may have difficulty in comprehending the meaning of the questions asked. Although answers may be given, they may not be the answers to the questions the researcher has in mind but, rather, answers to the respondent's misinterpretations.

PROBLEMS IN ANALYZING AND INTERPRETING RESEARCH INFORMATION

Once the data have been collected, the final and perhaps most critical step is the analysis and interpretation of the findings in light of the stated marketing problem. Both secondary and primary data collected by the market researcher are subject to the many limitations just discussed. In the final analysis, the researcher must take into consideration these factors and, despite their limitations, produce meaningful guides for management.

The meaning of words, the consumer's attitude toward a product, the interviewer's attitude, or the interview situation can all distort research findings. Just as culture and tradition can influence the willingness to give information, they can also influence the type of information given. In foreign marketing research, accepting information at face value can be a dangerous practice. Newspaper circulation figures, readership and listenership studies, retail outlets figures, and sales volume can all be distorted through local business practice. In the final analysis, to cope

---

[18] Dickensheets, op. cit., p. 371.

[19] Roman R. Andrus, "Marketing Research in a Developing Nation, Taiwan: A Case Example," *University of Washington Business Review*, Spring 1969, p. 43. Reprinted with permission.

BOX 17–4

Industry Statistics?

Considerable confusion arises, for example, when the prescribed product categories overlap: if the Dutch product classifications for the printing industry specify one group comprising "printed matter for advertising purposes" and another comprising "calendars," where should the million-guilder printing job for the Royal Dutch Shell Calendars be reported? One printing company explained, "To balance it off, we reported one way one year and the other way the next."

Source: "European Market Research—Hide and Seek," *Sales Management*, February 1, 1969, p. 46.

with these factors, the foreign market researcher must possess three essential capabilities in order to generate meaningful marketing information.

First, he must possess a high degree of cultural understanding of the market on which he is doing research. In order to analyze, and in some cases, to compensate for research findings, he must understand the customs, viewpoint, semantics, current attitude, and business customs of a society or a subsegment of a society.

Second, the researcher must possess a creative talent in adapting research findings. Unfortunately, the researcher in foreign markets often finds himself "flying by the seat of his pants" and he is sometimes called upon to produce results under the most difficult of circumstances. As summarized in one comprehensive study of research in foreign markets:

Ingenuity and resourcefulness—a willingness to use "catch-as-catch-can" methods to get the facts—are considered prime assets in foreign marketing research. So are patience, a sense of humor, and a willingness to be guided by original research findings, even when they conflict with popular opinion or prior assumptions.[20]

Third, the researcher should be skeptical in handling both primary and secondary data. He might find it necessary to have a newspaper pressrun checked over a period of time to get accurate circulation figures, or he might find it necessary to deflate or inflate reported consumer income in some areas by 25 to 50 percent on the basis of observable socioeconomic characteristics. Frequently, he is the only individual in a business firm capable of making an accurate judgment on the reliability and validity of primary and secondary data sources.

These essential capabilities suggest that the foreign marketing researcher should be either a foreign national or should be advised by someone who can accurately appraise the data collected in light of the local environment, thereby helping to validate secondary as well as primary data.

---

[20] National Industrial Conference Board, *Research in Foreign Markets*, Conference Board Reports, Studies in Business Policy No. 75 (New York, 1955), p. 36.

RESPONSIBILITY FOR CONDUCTING MARKETING RESEARCH

The alternatives available for the selection of the person to conduct the foreign market research are the same as those in domestic operations. Depending upon a company's size and its involvement in foreign marketing, it can rely on either an outside agency foreign-based or a domestic company with a branch within the country in question; it can conduct research using its own facilities; or it can employ a combination of its own research force coupled with the assistance of an outside agency.

Traditionally, the information function has been part of the export manager's job. As both the interest and investment in foreign opportunities increase, the probability of costly errors in foreign business operations increases proportionately, and a more organized and systematic method of providing reliable answers to key questions is required. The results are generally a more formal research effort, with responsibility assigned to either staff or line personnel.

In many companies an executive is specifically assigned the research function in foreign operations. He may select the best way to perform effective research. Such an assignment usually results in the executive working closely with foreign management, staff specialists, and outside research agencies.

In other companies, a separate research department for foreign operations is established, or at a minimum, the assignment of a full-time analyst to this activity is made. For many companies, a separate department is not feasible because of the high costs of operation and the distance from the market being studied. In addition, the diversity in markets would require a large department in order to provide a skilled analyst for every area or region of international business operations. For these reasons, some companies elect the alternative of parceling out specific marketing research tasks as staff assignments. The company electing such a procedure will often employ a marketing statistician for support of such staff assignments.

A trend toward decentralization of the research function is apparent, however. From the point of view of efficiency, it appears that having "your man in Havana" can provide information more rapidly and accurately than a staff research department. The obvious advantage to decentralization of the research function is the fact that control of the research function rests in hands closer to the market. Field personnel, resident managers, and customers generally have an intimate knowledge of the subtleties of the market and an appreciation of the diversity which characterizes most foreign markets. The primary danger in decentralized research management is in ineffective communications with staff-level executives.

Independent research agencies of various types can be used in conjunction with a firm's own research personnel or as a substitute for a formal research staff. Most major U.S. advertising agencies and many research firms have established multiple branch offices around the world. International business consulting and research firms have shown corresponding increases in activity and a broader range of available services. There also has been a healthy growth in foreign-based research and consulting firms. Furthermore, a significant increase has occurred in the activity of international advertising groups and international management associations; newsletters and association bulletins provide for the interchange of ideas between internationally oriented researchers. Some major types of business research organizations are as follows:

1. General business and industrial research organizations.
2. Technical research organizations (specializing in such technical activities as product development research).
3. Advertising research organizations (generally specializing in consumer goods research as related to advertising problems).
4. Consumer research organizations.[21]

Involvement with outside agency support can vary from total reliance on the agency to a situation where it is used selectively for specific problems when competence is needed in unfamiliar countries.

SOURCES OF SECONDARY DATA

For almost any marketing research project, an analysis of available secondary information is a useful and inexpensive first step. In recent years the availability of published information on international markets has increased dramatically. Although there still exist information gaps, particularly for detailed market information, the situation on data availability and reliability has rapidly improved in the 1950s and 1960s.

Data collection and publication programs of public and private sources are being revised with such frequency that a comprehensive list of sources would be impractical for this text. Instead, the principal agencies that collect and publish information useful to the international businessman are presented, with some notations of selected publications.

U.S. Government

The U.S. government actively promotes the expansion of U.S. businesses into international trade. In the process of keeping the U.S. businessman informed of foreign business opportunity, the U.S. government generates a considerable amount of general and specific market data for use by the international market analyst. Although information is available from a number of agencies of the U.S. government, the principal source of information is the Department of Commerce, which makes its services available to the U.S. businessman in a variety of ways. First, information and assistance are available either through personal consultation in Washington, D.C., or through any of the 37 field offices of the Department of Commerce located in key cities in the United States. Second, the Department of Commerce works closely with trade associations, chambers of commerce, and other interested associations in

---

[21] T. L. Jenkins, "The Role of the Independent Research Organization in International Market Research," *Market Research in International Operations*, A.M.A. Management Report No. 53 (New York, 1960), pp. 29–30.

providing information, consultation, and assistance in developing international commerce. Third, the Department publishes a wide range of information which is available to interested persons at nominal cost.

The principal publications of the Department of Commerce relating to international business are as follows:

1. *Trade Lists.* Prepared by the U.S. Foreign Service, trade lists provide for a specific country the names and addresses of foreign companies, classified by commodity and a listing of certain professional groups, institutions, and service organizations. On principal firms the list includes addresses, relative size, type of operation, products handled, and sales territory.

2. *World Trade Directory Reports.* Prepared by the commercial officer at foreign service posts, the *Directory Report* describes the operation of a specific company and lists products handled, U.S. manufacturers from which it buys, size and reputation of the company, its capital and annual capital turnover, and other pertinent facts.

3. *Marketing Handbooks.* Designed to provide specific marketing information relative to certain foreign countries, these handbooks are issued in two series—*The Market for U.S. Products in* (name of country) and *Investment in* (name of country). More than five countries have been covered by the first series, and more are in the planning.

4. *International Commerce* (formerly *Foreign Commerce Weekly*). This is the Department of Commerce's official international magazine. A weekly news magazine, it is an up-to-date source of worldwide business activity covering topics of general interest and new developments in world commerce.

5. *Overseas Business Reports* (formerly *World Trade Information Service*). The *Overseas Business Reports* series, issued in four parts, covers a wide range of marketing information on specific countries or areas which is of interest and value to the market analyst. Each part of this series covers a particular phase of business activity. Part 1—*Economics* includes basic economic and marketing data plus guidelines to business establishment and insurance information of specific countries. Part 2—*Operations Reports* provides information on copyright and trademark protection, property rights, the mechanics of export shipment, export-import regulations, and living costs and conditions. Part 3—*Statistical Reports* deals with figures on U.S. trade with foreign countries, total export and import trade of the United States on a monthly basis, and the foreign trade of the countries of the world. Part 4—*Utilities Abroad* gives information on development of foreign shipping, railways, aviation, highway, and electric power.[22]

It should be recognized that while the Department of Commerce has general responsibility for fostering international commerce, consultation and information are available from a variety of other U.S. agencies. For example, the Department of State, Bureau of the Census, and the Department of Agriculture can provide valuable assistance in the form

---

[22] For additional information, see *Guides for the Newcomer to World Trade* (Washington, D.C.: U.S. Department of Commerce, Bureau of Foreign Commerce, January 1957).

of services and information for the American businessman engaged in international operations.[23]

International Organizations

A number of international organizations, particularly those international and regional organizations formed since World War II, provide information and statistics on international markets. The United Nations publishes a wide range of statistical information dealing with basic economic, social, and business-related data. The *Statistical Yearbook*, an annual publication of the United Nations, provides comprehensive social and economic data for more than 250 countries over the world. Many regional organizations, such as the Organization for Economic Cooperation and Development (OECD), Pan American Union, and the European Economic Community publish information statistics and market studies relating to their respective regions. For example, the OECD publishes *General Statistics* six times each year. This publication includes data on industrial production, population, wholesale and retail indexes, salaries and wages, and finance and economics for member countries.

Governments of Foreign Countries

Most of the industrially developed nations of the world and many of the underdeveloped nations actively promote the collection and dissemination of market information and statistics. Britain, Japan, and a number of other European and Asian countries publish information generally designed to increase the international trade flow and foreign investment in the country of publication. Information about such publications is available from each country's consulate-general.

Chambers of Commerce

In addition to government and organizational publications, many foreign countries maintain chamber of commerce offices in the United States that function as a type of permanent trade mission. These foreign chambers of commerce generally have research libraries available and are knowledgeable regarding further sources of information on specific products or marketing problems. Another source of useful information is the American chamber of commerce operating in a foreign country. There are American chambers in most major trading cities of the world. Often the American Chamber of Commerce in Paris can give more current information and lists of potential business contacts in France than are available from any other source. A listing of chambers of commerce and other government and nongovernment agencies concerned with international trade can be found in *A Directory of Foreign Organizations for Trade and Investment Promotion* published by the

---

[23] For more specific detail, see *Export Marketing for Smaller Firms* (Washington, D.C.: Small Business Administration, May 1963), Appendix 2, pp. 72–82.

U.S. Department of Commerce. The United Chamber of Commerce publication *Foreign Commerce Handbook: Basic Information and a Guide to Sources* is an excellent reference source for foreign trade information. It is divided into four sections. The first section deals with foreign trade services and outlines the functions, activities, and services of the U.S. government, intergovernmental organizations, and private organizations concerned with serving foreign commerce. Devoted to basic data, the second section lists sources of information on specific items of interest to international businessmen. Such items as copyrights, credit information, marine insurance, and advertising abroad are typical subject headings for part two of the handbook. Part three contains an annotated bibliography of up-to-date reference works, books, pamphlets, and periodicals which contain information on many phases of foreign commerce and international operations. Part four of the handbook contains a selected list of organizations, associations, and agencies active in world trade and includes their addresses.

Trade, Business, and Service Organizations

Foreign trade associations are particularly good sources of information on specific products or product lines. For example, *Self-Service 1970* was published by the International Self-Service Organization in three languages. Besides a survey of international self-service operations, it includes a bibliography and membership list. Many of these associations perform special studies or continuing services in collecting comprehensive statistical data for a specific product group or industry. Although some of this information is proprietary in nature and available only to members of the association, it is often available to nonmembers under certain conditions. Membership lists which provide valuable up-to-date lists of potential customers or competitors are often available to anyone requesting such information. A listing of foreign trade associations is often annotated at the end of a specific *Trade List*.

Foreign service industries also supply valuable sources of information for the international businessman. Service companies—such as commercial and investment banks, international advertising agencies, foreign-based research firms, economic research institutes, and foreign carriers, shipping agencies, and freight forwarders—generally regard the furnishing of current, reliable information as part of their service function. The banking industry in foreign countries is particularly useful as a source of information on current local economic situations. The Chase Manhattan Bank in the United States periodically publishes a newsletter on such subjects as the European Common Market. Many foreign banks publish periodic or special review newsletters relating to the local economy, providing a firsthand analysis of the economic situation of specific foreign countries. For example, the Kretiet Bank in Brussels has published *Belgium, Key to the Common Market* and the Banco Nacional Commercio Exterior in Mexico has published *Mexico Facts, Figures, Trends.* These publications are frequently available without charge, although they must generally be translated.

A number of research agencies have developed in the past few years specializing in supplying detailed information on foreign markets. These services are available either on a subscription basis for an entire series or in a specific series relating to an individual foreign country. A listing of commercial and investment banks in foreign countries, as well as a fairly detailed list of special-purpose research institutes, can be found in *The Europa Yearbook*. Advertising and marketing research agencies based in the United States and abroad also publish information on international markets. The U.S. Department of Commerce has published *A Directory of Advertising Agencies and Market Research Organizations,* which lists the addresses of professional market research and advertising agencies around the world.

SUMMARY AND CONCLUSIONS

The market research function has as its basic objective the task of providing management with information for more accurate decision making. This objective is the same for both domestic and international marketing. In foreign marketing research, however, achieving the objective of providing information presents some problems not encountered on the domestic front.

The foreign consumer's attitudes toward providing information to the researcher is culturally conditioned and may require a creative approach to research design. Besides the cultural and managerial constraints about providing information for primary data collection, many foreign markets have adequate or unreliable bases of secondary information.

Several generalizations can be made about the direction and rate of growth of marketing research in foreign marketing. First, there is an increasing awareness and acceptance on the part of both home-based and foreign management of the importance of marketing research's role in decision making. Second, there is a current trend toward the decentralization of the research function in order to put control closer to the area being studied. Third, the most sophisticated American tools and techniques are being adapted to foreign operations with increasing success.

READING

ON THE USE OF MARKETING RESEARCH
IN THE EMERGING ECONOMIES*

HARPER W. BOYD, JR., RONALD E. FRANK, WILLIAM F. MASSY, AND MOSTAFA ZOHEIR

Under what conditions, if any, can the United States export marketing know-how to the world's underdeveloped nations? Certainly this is a timely and important question. Peter Drucker has stated that marketing occupies a critical role in the economic development of these nations;

---

* Reprinted from the *Journal of Marketing Research,* November 1964, pp. 20–23, published by the American Marketing Association.

yet it is typically the most backward part of the economic system and is treated with neglect if not contempt.

Marketing research should be one of the easiest "areas" in marketing to export, if only because it consists of a collection of techniques which, supposedly, can be applied regardless of the state of economic development as contrasted to certain marketing principles and concepts which have been derived from the American scene. One might assume that the emerging nations would eagerly seek to import marketing research know-how because of their obvious need for information about the market in order to effectively plan and control their economic development.

A unique opportunity to assess the extent to which American market research practices have been exported presented itself during the 1963–64 academic year when 40 teachers of marketing from 18 different underdeveloped countries congregated at the International Center for the Advancement of Management Education (ICAME) at the Graduate School of Business, Stanford University, for a year of study. The countries represented were Argentina, Brazil, Ceylon, Chile, Colombia, Ghana, Indonesia, Israel, Mexico, Nicaragua, Peru, Philippines, Republic of China, South Korea, Thailand, United Arab Republic, Yugoslavia, and Turkey.

The comments to follow are based on informal day-to-day contact with the participants, personal interviews and their responses to a self-administered questionnaire.

Despite some evidence to the contrary, there is little to indicate that marketing research has to date been used to any great extent in the emerging countries. And while it is true a rather surprising number of these countries have conducted recent censuses or sample surveys of population, housing, agriculture, wholesaling, and retailing, consumer surveys have not been conducted in any quantities. Indeed, in such countries as Ceylon, Ghana, Yugoslavia, Nicaragua, Thailand, and South Korea, one is hard pressed to find even one such study. Outside of Latin America virtually no organizations comparable to the American Marketing Association exist. Those marketing groups which do exist tend to focus on sales rather than the broader concept we call marketing. Only a few of the underdeveloped countries have publications that print articles on marketing research, and these are typically rather specialized, such as the Brazilian sales magazines, *Vandas + Varejo,* the Korean Trade Promotion Corporation's publication, *Trade Journal Monthly,* and the Taiwan *Economic Monthly.*

Still the picture is not all black. A surprising number of business schools in these countries are installing U.S. type marketing research courses in their curriculum. Especially in South America we find the establishment of firms specializing in marketing research. Advertising agencies, particularly those which are branches of U.S. firms, have been important pioneers in the use of marketing research and through demonstration have forced local companies to follow suit.

It is clear, however, that marketing research will not assume great importance to the economic life of these nations for some time to come. This article will attempt to explain the reasons for this lack of acceptance, as well as discuss the difficulties involved in applying U.S. marketing research practices to these countries.

The Local Environment and Its Effects on the Use of Marketing Research

Perhaps the major obstacle to the use of marketing research in the emerging countries is the attitude toward marketing of business and government administrators. Most such individuals tend to view marketing largely as a mechanistic process involving at best such functions as transportation, storage, and exchange. In point-of-fact the statement is often made that "we have no marketing problems except, of course, in connection with our export marketing efforts."

The economies of the emerging countries can be characterized as production oriented. In addition, most business organizations—whether located in the private or public sector—are concerned primarily with efficient work systems and procedures, high centralization of authority, multiple layers of supervision, and intense specialization. Such an organization is defended—and logically so—on the basis that demand typically exceeds supply. Thus, there is little concern for the market and how its wants and needs affect the decisions of the organization.

Another deterrent to the use of marketing research is the typical industry organization found in the emerging countries. Because of the limited effective demands for any commodity and the *very* scarce resources available, the government follows the policy of deliberately *not* encouraging competition. Thus, many if not most industries are comprised of one or two firms. This policy, coupled with high tariff barriers, produces a situation where little, if any, competition exists within an industry. Under such conditions little check on the activities of management is made, except that which is generated internally—and this is not likely to be important since, as was noted earlier, most of the firms are production oriented and look "inward" rather than "outward." The fact that all but a very few of these countries have laws which prohibit collusion merely further inhibits competition from taking place.

In addition to limited effective demand, most firms are also constrained by the limited availability of managerial talent, thus further taking the edge off competition. This fact, combined with the higher priority given to production resources, leads to a disproportionate shortage of managerial talent in the field of marketing, let alone in market research.

Most companies in the emerging economies are small by U.S. standards, and many are family owned. The desire for survival is inevitably hinged to a perpetuation of the family's control over the enterprise. This means that many companies do not want to expand or change and that their objective is primarily to maintain the status quo. While this attitude is changing gradually, there is little to indicate that the change will generate greater interest in marketing research, if only because of the small size of the firms. It must also be remembered that many firms tend to be speculators because of their economy's inflation.

Few firms do much in the way of advertising or product development. In the case of the latter, products are largely copies of western products and little or no money is spent on R & D. As a consequence there is little need for marketing research, and there will be no such need until more indigenous products are attempted.

Marketing has always been a relatively low-status occupation in many of the emerging nations. Much of this low status was derived because foreigners were so engaged and, further, because much of what was thought to be marketing was, in reality, speculation. For these reasons, as well as others, the field of marketing has not attracted outstanding men with considerable managerial skills. The fact that few firms have a marketing department per se—or even recognize the marketing function in their organization—has acted as a further restraint on the use of research. Certainly marketing personnel have little opportunity to influence the major decisions of the company. Few men with a marketing background ever succeed to a position of high responsibility within the firm. Rather, such positions are more likely to be reserved for engineers or men with financial experience.

What is true of marketing in this regard is particularly true of marketing research. Few people are qualified to undertake marketing research. Usually these individuals are associated with either government bureaus or schools, not with business firms. Unfortunately the gap between academic and corporate life is considerably greater in most of the emerging countries than in the United States. Firms typically do not look upon the academic community as a source of expert advice. Often otherwise qualified academicians feel that work with a business firm is inappropriate, given their role as educators.

A strong point can be made for the use of marketing research by the governments of these countries, especially in new planning work. Conceptually, at least, knowledge about the market place is necessary if proper allocations of scarce resources are to be made. And given the absence of competition and the inability of the market to influence decisions, marketing research should be able to provide meaningful control and reappraisal data. But one has to take into account the nature of the bureaucratic mind. For the most part, civil servants have little desire to make decisions. Indeed, the reward system in these countries is such that one can only "lose" by so doing. Thus, problems are handed "up" for decisions. In addition, there is a great fear of information that might be used against someone. This insecurity is very real, since within most governmental organizations a number of persons are vying for power at the same time. Hence, marketing research is feared because it might be used as a way of pointing up certain deficiencies. If no information is available, one's persuasiveness can be brought to the fore—perhaps with good results.

The above reasons, however briefly described, point clearly to the fact that marketing is not an important subject to most administrators in the underdeveloped countries. As a consequence, few are concerned with obtaining information that could be provided by marketing research. Since most of these reasons are deep seated and tied to basic economic and attitudinal conditions, they are not likely to change quickly.

Technical Application Problems

Marketing research is considerably more difficult to do in the less-developed countries than in the United States. This is especially true in sampling, data collection methods, and field work. Each of these subjects will be discussed briefly from the point of view of application in the emerging countries.

SAMPLING. Probability sampling is not used in most of the countries studied. Except for several countries in Latin America (Argentina, Brazil, Chile, Colombia, and Mexico), most reported small or negligible use of probability sampling. Even where it is used, widespread and severe difficulties are encountered, since maps are rarely up to date—if they indeed exist. Such is even true in the case of the larger cities; and, thus, selection of blocks or equivalent land areas is rendered difficult. As might be expected, block statistics are not available, thereby preventing stratification or the opportunity to draw blocks proportionate to population.

Poor transportation often precludes the use of a dispersed sample, as does the fact that field workers are reluctant or refuse to travel alone (especially women). Then, too, some countries have several different languages. Imagine conducting a nationwide survey in India, which has 14 different "official" languages and, in reality, substantially more!

Sampling within blocks presents all kinds of difficulties since dwelling units are not numbered or otherwise identified. It is often difficult to define a dwelling unit. For example, how does one determine how many families are present in a given structure when, because of the prevalence of extended family, many dwelling units are inhabited by a large number of individuals and several primary family units? It is often difficult to determine who is the "housewife."

The amount of information available upon which to base a sampling plan varies considerably from country to country and city to city. For example, a government agency in the Middle East wanted to find out what socioeconomic groups in a given city were more apt to watch broadcasts from the government-owned television station. Only a map of the city was available. The best information about the geographic distribution of population was the research director's own personal judgment. He divided the city into a large number of areas that he felt were about equal in population. Using probability sampling techniques, he selected fifty of these. In each of the fifty, interviewers were instructed to interview a given number of men and women over sixteen years of age. A second round of interviews was planned in advance, so that if the data for any particular socioeconomic group were too sparse for analysis there would be enough time and funds available to conduct additional interviews.

In contrast, the research director of a Chilean firm concerned with an analysis of certain retailing practices in the major cities of his country not only had a map of each city, but also a virtually complete and recent list of retail outlets classified by type, size, and urban district for each major city in the country. He was, therefore, in an excellent position to employ probability sampling techniques. For the most part, however, fortunate circumstances such as these are relatively rare.

The above difficulties make it relatively easy to rationalize the use of convenience sampling, an often relied-upon technique. Even quota sampling, *i.e.*, nonprobability sampling in which interviewing quotas are established for various kinds of respondents, is not typically possible because of the lack of needed secondary data.

DATA COLLECTION METHODS.   Data collection by telephone and mail surveys is almost impossible in the developing countries, and where such is attempted the biases are likely to be substantial. Few persons in such countries have phones: less than 3 percent in Ceylon, while in Israel the cost is so high (the installation charge is $170 and the monthly service fee is $10) that only the very wealthy can afford them. Then, too, there are different attitudes about the use of a phone. Generally speaking, telephone users, particularly women, are highly suspicious of strangers on the phone. Also, because of their respect (even fear) for the instrument, many men and women will not spend much time in talking on it.

Mail surveys are similarly limited. Since many of the emerging countries have low literacy rates, problems often arise as to what languages and dialects to use, even assuming literacy. Postal service is poor— especially in rural areas. In Nicaragua, for example, it is difficult to conduct a mail questionnaire because one can post letters only at a post office. Then, too, some cultures apparently do not believe in writing answers which will be read by a stranger. In some cases the male head of the family will answer the questionnaire *regardless* of the actual addressee.

RESPONSE ERROR AND THE FIELD FORCE.   The problem of not-at-homes in most of the cities of the underdeveloped countries is not as great as in the U.S. But this is not true in the villages, where in some countries the younger wife's role is at her husband's side in the fields. Under these conditions, the not-at-home rate may reach as high as fifty percent or more. In contrast, in some of the middle eastern countries, where the wife's traditional role requires her presence in the home a high proportion of the time, the rate is much lower.

In many cities and villages, poor lighting, a high crime rate, and the nomadic nature of the population make evening call-backs difficult to conduct and less effective as a technique for dealing with the not-at-home problem.

Refusals to cooperate also probably are considerably higher than in the States. While the cooperation rate varies by country, the general mistrust of strangers tends to produce considerable difficulty in obtaining satisfactory interviews. Thus, for example, Thai and Indonesian women will not talk to strangers, and an Indian woman will not grant an interview unless an acquaintance accompanies the field worker. In many villages in these and other countries, literally no one will cooperate unless the village elders have sanctioned the study. In many cases the permission of the family head is required and frequently he will grant the interview only if he is permitted to answer the questions. Interviews among the well-to-do are difficult because they are protected by servants.

In an effort to gain cooperation, several countries reported the use of samples or premiums; for example, free product samples (the Philippines, Nicaragua, and Yugoslavia), small gifts (United Arab Republic), and free lottery tickets (Indonesia). Appointments are used in some countries to facilitate interviewing the wealthy, while in others college students are used to "get by the servants."

Many respondents refuse to cooperate (either in whole or in part) or distort their answers because they fear the interviewer may be a tax inspector or some other government official. The director of a household budget study for a middle eastern government expected that less than 50 percent of the households contacted would be willing to cooperate due primarily to mistrust of strangers in general and of the government in particular. Many are suspicious because they believe the interviewer to be a house-to-house salesman. One can understand why those interviewers who either are or look like college students obtain relatively high rates of cooperation.

There is a great reluctance among both men and women to discuss certain subjects with strangers. While the degree to which certain topics are taboo varies between countries, there was unanimity in stating that such subjects as sex, personal hygiene, finance, and household expenditures were difficult to discuss. And further, in a number of countries the subject of consumption habits is thought to be taboo.

COMPOSITION OF THE FIELD FORCE. Partly because of their relatively infrequent use, supervisors in these countries are generally poorly trained and controlled.

And it is interesting to note the substantial use of male interviewers in many countries. (While women interviewers are more numerous than male interviewers in Argentina, Israel, and the U.A.R., such is not the case in most of the other countries.) Because women are by tradition quite modest, and because their role is not visualized by the male head of the family as that of a worker outside the family unit, it is difficult to recruit workers. Also, although this situation is changing, the number of educated women is quite small in most of these countries. In at least several countries interviewing is typed as door-to-door selling and, therefore, not considered fit work for women. And as was inferred earlier, women are very frequently not permitted to travel, or to work during evening hours.

How does the use of male interviewers bias cooperation and the responses given to certain questions? It seems clear that a male interviewer has more difficulty in gaining the cooperation of female respondents than would be the case if women interviewers were used. Also, males often would not be able to elicit satisfactory responses to questions dealing with female products and the attitudes of other household members on matters having to do with her role within the family unit.

Concluding Remarks

Marketing research is in an embryonic stage in the vast majority of underdeveloped nations. U.S. techniques would be directly transferrable if the appropriateness of their use did not depend on the state of economic development and information and the cultural mores of the population being studied. Despite these problems, our know-how in this area still provides a valuable mine of information. The problem is that the practices and concepts contained in the mine need to be modified (often substantially) before they are suitable for use in a particular underdeveloped nation.

QUESTIONS

1. Terms—define and show the significance to international marketing:
   International marketing research
   Research process
   Comparability and currency of data
   Overseas business reports
   Trade lists.

2. Discuss the breadth and scope of international marketing research. Why is international marketing research generally broader in scope than domestic marketing research?

3. "The measure of a competent researcher is his ability to utilize the most sophisticated and adequate techniques and methods available within these limits" [of time, cost and the present state of the arts]. Comment.

4. What is the task of the international market researcher? How is it complicated by the foreign environment?

5. Discuss the stages of the research process in relation to the problems encountered. Give examples.

6. Why is the formulation of the research problem difficult in foreign market research?

7. Discuss the problems of gathering secondary data in foreign markets.

8. "In many cultures, personal information is inviolably *private* and absolutely not to be discussed with strangers." Discuss.

9. What are some problems created by language and the ability to comprehend in collecting primary data? How can a foreign market researcher overcome these difficulties?

10. Sampling offers some major problems in market research. Discuss.

11. Select a country. From secondary sources compile the following information for at least a 10-year period prior to the present date:
    Principal imports
    Principal exports
    Gross National Product
    Chief of state

Major cities and population
Principal agricultural crop

12. "The foreign market researcher must possess three essential capabilities in order to generate meaningful marketing information." Discuss.

Reading

1. Discuss the effect of the local environment of an emerging economy upon the use of marketing research.

2. Why is the response error such a problem in emerging nations? How can a market researcher overcome this problem and still get valid results?

OUTLINE OF CHAPTER 18

INTRODUCTION

PRICING POLICY
  Pricing Objectives
  Approaches to International Pricing
  A Sample Policy

COST FACTORS
  Taxes and Tariffs
  Middleman Cost
  Financing and Risk Costs

PRICE ESCALATION
  Sample Effects of Price Escalation
  Strategic Approaches to Price Escalation

MARKET PRICING
  Demand
  Competition
  Dumping

ADMINISTERED PRICING
  Price Setting by Business Groups
    Patent Licensing Agreements
    Cartels
    Combines
    Trade Associations
  Governmental Price Setting
    Establish Margins
    Set Price Floors and Ceilings or Actual Prices
    Restrict Price Changes
    Compete in the Market
    Subsidies
    Government Monopolies and Monopsonies
  International Agreements

INTRACOMPANY PRICING STRATEGY

PRICE QUOTATIONS

SUMMARY AND CONCLUSIONS

READING
  When the Price Is Wrong—by Design, *Columbia Journal of World Business*

PRICING IN INTERNATIONAL MARKETS

INTRODUCTION

Pricing is one of the most mystery-laden variables encountered by the marketing executive in his decision-making process. The subject of price determination has baffled both teachers and students, and the addition of an international parameter certainly does not simplify the pricing process or an understanding of pricing. Nevertheless, the student who has a satisfactory understanding of the economic concepts of price theory and who also has some awareness of the pricing methods of industry does have an adequate basis for comprehending the pricing problems of firms engaged in international business. An executive in a firm with operations in all parts of the world captured the essence of the situation when he commented that

the price factors with which we deal in foreign marketing are not in themselves so new or so different from our operations at home but they are more numerous, more susceptible to change, and more difficult to keep track of. They are, therefore, much more complex to treat on a comprehensive basis.[1]

Whether he is exporting or managing overseas operations, the international marketing manager is ultimately responsible for establishing price policies for his company's international operations. Within the range of prices permitted by the market, by competition, and by various government regulations, he may also be responsible for setting the actual prices for his goods as they are traded in different markets. The marketer will certainly find that operating in different markets brings him many new problems; for example, he may not be able to control prices at the retail or user level as surely as in his home market. He may, in fact, find that he has virtually no control over final prices. Besides all the market variables which must be considered, the market-

---

[1] Herbert J. Seakwood, "Pricing Considerations in the International Market," in *Pricing, the Critical Decision* (New York: American Management Association, Inc., 1961), p. 77.

BOX 18–1

Who Sets Prices?

Pricing problems in international operations are a source of concern to executives with varying and diverse management responsibilities. The international division vice president is concerned with the effect of pricing on divisional profits; the regional manager is concerned with the impact that policies on intercorporate and local market pricing will have in his geographic area; the subsidiary manager tries to operate on a profitable basis within the policy limitations on intercorporate transfer, export, and local market pricing imposed on him. The director of international marketing wants a price that will be competitive in the market place; the controller and the treasurer want prices that will be profitable; and the manufacturing director wants prices that will give longer production runs with evenly distributed plant loads for more efficient operations. The tax manager looks at the implications of pricing policy on the total tax burden to the corporation and tax deferral opportunities; and the lawyer is concerned with pricing policies and practices that may lead to antitrust or restriction of trade violations. Even domestic product managers have an interest in transfer prices to the international division or to overseas units.

Source: *Solving International Pricing Problems* p. 3. Reprinted with the permission of the publisher, Business International Corporation (New York).

ing executive will also find that governmental attitudes vary significantly from country to country. Differing tariffs, costs, attitudes, and methods of price quotation all contribute to confounding the marketing executive.

One economist points out what American marketers know so well: that "the reduction of sale price is only one way to get a product established in a foreign market. Another is to engage in extra cost; to advertise, to establish a distribution system, and to obtain an acceptance of the product in the new market."[2] The role of pricing differs considerably in importance for different types of goods and from market to market. Two basic situations prevail relative to pricing. In one instance the market sets the price rather absolutely and the producer has little control over the level of prices; this is the situation in markets for wheat, raw plastic, standard steel shapes, cement, milk, flour, and other types of standardized or relatively undifferentiated products.

In the second instance the market situation is such that the marketer has genuine alternatives in setting his prices; this condition exists in the typical situation of oligopoly when products are differentiated. This is the case of most manufactured goods being sold in nonregulated markets.

Businessmen from different countries view the strategic role of pricing in different ways. In general, American marketers tend to regard price as an important variable in their marketing decision making. In

---

[2] Charles P. Kindleberger, *International Economics* (4th ed.; Homewood, Ill.: Richard D. Irwin, Inc., 1968), p. 156.

other countries there is a wide range of attitudes toward the importance of pricing. In many countries, managers do not employ pricing as a major competitive element. In his study of the European Common Market for the Marketing Science Institute, Bertil Liander found that "among those manufacturers who have reasonable latitude in setting their prices, there was generally a tendency to disregard pricing as an important element in the marketing strategy."[3] A commentator on the French pricing scene mentions that "one finds the French retailers going to all odds to avoid competition as we know it—particularly price competition. He is likely to join a 'syndicat' to fix prices and many of the rules of doing business."

This chapter will not dwell on the basic economic or strategic concepts underlying pricing behavior, since such subjects are well covered in American economic and marketing literature. It will focus instead on the pricing considerations that are peculiar to, or of particular significance in, the international marketplace.

This chapter first reviews some of the basic policy questions in pricing, because in approaching the pricing process itself, management must be aware of the special cost, market, and competitive factors in foreign markets. Goods traded internationally often incur extra costs and taxes which the marketer cannot control. Since such costs raise the end price of the goods, the process may be called price escalation. Such escalation is considered next, along with some of the strategic approaches to controlling price escalation. Consideration is given to the problems and policies associated with price fixing on business, governmental, and international levels, and mention is made of some of the mechanics of international price quotation. The considerations in this chapter are relevant to all kinds of firms doing business internationally, even though some of the specific items of information are more relevant to one type of organization than to another.

PRICING POLICY

Companies that are actively marketing in a number of different countries find that the number of pricing problems and the number of variables relating to price policy are greatly compounded as compared to those encountered when doing business in one country. Unless the firm has a clearly thought-out, explicitly defined price policy, it will be establishing prices by expediency rather than by design. Pricing activity will be affected by the country in which business is being conducted, the type of product, variations in competitive conditions, and other strategic factors. In any case, it is clear that "the prices for and the terms upon which we sell our American-made products overseas cannot be predicated on domestic criteria alone, for if they are, we shall soon be sadly outmaneuvered and outsold by our competitors abroad."[4]

Who is to set the price? This has become an increasingly important

---

[3] Bertil Liander, *Marketing Development in the European Economic Community* (New York: McGraw-Hill Book Company, 1964), p. 49.

[4] Seakwood, op. cit., p. 73.

question in international marketing. As pricing becomes increasingly complex because of national laws, intracompany competition, and monopsonistic purchasers, there is likely to be less emphasis on market considerations. The ultimate implication is that the marketing executive may end up with inadequate control to permit him to function effectively in international competition. Whether or not group decision making provides the most effective kind of price making, such arrangement is becoming increasingly common in international business. Often marketing, finance, manufacturing, and legal personnel will make pricing decisions after consulting with product managers and regional management. The entire process is likely to be coordinated by the top man in the international division or, in some instances, even the company president. Such large groups are likely to be involved in policy decisions or decisions involving extremely large volumes of business, but it is preferable that day-to-day pricing in local markets be delegated to levels as close to the market as possible.

Pricing Objectives

Two basic choices are available to a company in setting its price policy. It may view pricing as an active instrument for the accomplishment of marketing objectives, or it may consider prices to be a static element in business decisions. If the former viewpoint is adhered to, the company will utilize prices to accomplish certain objectives relative to a target return or profit from overseas operations or for the accomplishment of a target volume of market share. If the second approach is followed, the company will likely be content to sell what it can in overseas markets and look on this as bonus volume. Obviously the second alternative is hardly adequate for enterprises with operations in foreign countries and is more likely to be the viewpoint taken by a firm which exports only and which places a rather low priority on foreign business.

Companies' policies may be framed in terms of control over final prices, or the company may be more interested in the net price received by the business. In the latter case, the producer may not attempt to control the price at which the product is ultimately sold; in the former, price is considered to be an important strategic element of the marketing mix and the company will want to accomplish all possible control over the end price. Firms, however, that follow a price control policy in their domestic business have found that they were unable to control end prices in foreign markets, and therefore have reoriented their thinking to "mill net pricing," e.g., to prices which they receive for their goods when they are shipped from the plant.

Control over prices is a many faceted activity. End prices charged to the consumer must be controlled if the marketer is to reach his desired level of market penetration. Profits and profit margins must be maintained and controlled country by country, product by product, and for every type of transaction. Competition from various elements within a company must be controlled to assure that different divisions or subsidiaries or branches of a company are not undercutting other divisions, branches, or subsidiaries, thus depriving the company as a whole of profits.

Resale price maintenance (R.P.M.) is one of the devices manufacturers use to control the end price charged to consumers. R.P.M. has not been an effective competitive weapon in the United States for a good many years, but until recently it has been a widely used tool in international markets. Currently, however, the whole concept of R.P.M. by manufacturers is functioning in stormy waters. Germany has been a stronghold of such price maintenance, but in recent years its courts have virtually eliminated R.P.M. To use R.P.M. in Germany a manufacturer must have a complete system of price maintenance covering every retailer selling the product, regardless of its sources of supplies. Circumstances vary from country to country, but innumerable difficulties are encountered throughout the world in establishing effective R.P.M., so resale price maintenance as a control tool is effectively denied to most marketers.

One of the complicated areas of pricing policy relates to the objectives sought in intracompany sales, that is, sales between a parent company and a subsidiary, from one subsidiary to another, or from a foreign subsidiary to a parent company. Intracorporate pricing objectives may be related to minimization of tax burdens and duties, repatriation of profits, profit balancing among units and, of course, maximizing profit. The continuing growth and proliferation of marketing activities and organizational arrangements make imperative the establishment of corporate policies and procedures for handling intercompany pricing which can meet these requirements. Intercorporate pricing policy and strategy are discussed later in this chapter.

Approaches to International Pricing

Regardless of whether the orientation is toward control over end prices or over net prices, the company will have a policy relative to the net prices that must be received. Both cost and market considerations are important; the company will not sell goods below cost of production and cannot sell goods at a price which will not be accepted by the market. Firms which are not extremely active in overseas marketing and many firms which produce industrial goods orient their pricing almost solely on a cost basis. Firms which employ pricing as part of the strategic mix, however, will be aware of such alternatives as market segmentation from country to country or market to market, competitive pricing in the marketplace, and other market-oriented pricing factors.

Even firms which orient their price thinking around cost must determine whether they are going to use variable cost pricing or full cost pricing in costing their goods. In variable cost pricing, the firm is concerned only with the marginal or incremental cost of producing the goods that are sold in overseas markets. Such firms regard foreign sales as bonus sales and assume that any return over their variable cost makes a contribution to net profit. These firms may be able to price most competitively in foreign markets; but because they are selling products abroad at lower net prices than they are selling them in the domestic market, they may be subject to charges of dumping. In such case they open themselves to antidumping tariffs or penalties, which takes away their competitive advantage. Companies which follow the full cost pricing philosophy insist that no unit of a similar product is different from any other unit in terms of cost and that each unit bear its full share of the total fixed and variable cost.

In domestic marketing, both variable cost and full cost policies are followed, but there is probably not so much use of variable cost pricing as there is in international marketing. The international firm which uses variable cost pricing is ultimately confronted with the question of whether it regards itself as a marketer exporting from one country into another or as a world marketer. If the firm regards itself as a world marketer, it is more likely to think in terms of full cost pricing for all markets. There is always the question, however, of whether a firm should price below full costs if it will increase profits and if it has no other alternative access to certain markets. These are all questions of policy which must be resolved by the firm.

A Sample Policy

The policy of the Eimco Corporation relative to international pricing is reproduced below. This statement illustrates the complexity of establishing a price policy for a firm which operates differently in various countries and which sells numerous types of products. It also represents an example of a concise, well thought out, general pricing policy for international operations.

A pricing philosophy for this kind of a multiple operation *could* be so complex and sensitive to external situations as to be thoroughly unworkable. Therefore, we chose a rather simple formula which has succeeded for us so far. It was prompted by the fact that many of our customers are themselves engaged in activities around the world and are likely to use our machines in any country.

Where the same product is made and offered for sale by the domestic company and one or more of its subsidiaries, each company is free to compete with the others, although they are substantially geared to market in separate areas. Pricing among our various subsidiaries is generally based on the real costs of each, and there is no attempt to hold to a universal factory price. Our licensees are largely restricted to specific areas where they determine their own pricing policy, which includes the cost of a technical fee or royalty to us.

Eimco maintains its factory list prices in selling its standardized products throughout the world. Except in special circumstances, its dealers may not add a markup of their own but must look to their regularly established discount or commission for their compensation. In other words, regardless of where our machines are made or sold, they will be priced to a customer at the established factory list price of the producing company plus the cost of transportation and related charges.

The pricing of our tailor-made process machinery follows somewhat the same pattern. Prices are primarily geared to the cost of manufacture in the country where they are made and to the usual overheads of that division, plus a markup which is calculated to give a fair and reasonable return.[5]

COST FACTORS

Regardless of the strategic factors involved and the company's orientation to market pricing, every price must be set with cost considerations in mind. At a minimum, prices over a long run must cover costs if a business is to survive. Full costs do not have to be covered in every market. However, as long as company sales as a whole do cover all costs in international marketing, even the determination of the cost of goods sold may occasion much debate. In the case of intracorporate transfers, such transfers may be based solely on direct production costs (variable costs only) or may include profit plus general administrative costs, research and development costs, and other overhead items. In determining producer company overhead, management must be careful not to include factors which would unduly raise prices abroad and thereby reduce sales volume. Sometimes domestic marketing sales and advertising costs are included in the base price of the goods, but because such costs are reincurred in the foreign markets they should not be included in the basic cost determination.

Technically, operations in a given market may contribute profit as long as goods are sold at a price above variable cost, but in reality most companies insist that at least some of the other costs mentioned above be included.

A number of costs which are unique to international marketing or which are exaggerated in international marketing should also be borne in mind by the pricing executive. Some of the major categories considered below are taxes and tariffs; middleman and transportation costs; and financing and risk costs.

Taxes and Tariffs

"Nothing is surer than death and taxes" has a particularly familiar ring in the ears of the international trader because taxes include tariffs, and tariffs are one of the most pervasive features of international trading. Taxes and tariffs affect the ultimate price which the consumer must pay for a good, and in most instances it is the consumer who bears the burden of both. Sometimes, however, the consumer may benefit when manufacturers who are selling goods into foreign countries reduce their net return in order to gain access on a competitive footing to a foreign market. Whether he absorbs them or passes them on, taxes and tariffs are of interest to the international businessman.

A tariff, or duty, is a special form of taxation, and like other forms of tax, it may be levied for the purpose of protecting a market or for raising governmental revenue. A tariff is a fee charged when a good is brought into a country from another country. The level of the tariff is typically

---

[5] Seakwood, op. cit., p. 78.

expressed as the rate of duty and may be levied as specific, ad valorem, or in a combination of these forms. A specific duty is a flat charge per physical unit imported, such as 15 cents per bushel of rye. Ad valorem duties are levied as a percentage of the value of the goods imported, such as 20 percent of the value of imported watches. Combination tariffs include both a specific and an ad valorem charge, such as $1 per camera plus 10 percent of its value. Tariffs and other forms of import tax serve to discriminate against all foreign goods. Fees for import certificates or for other administrative processing can assume such levels that they are in fact import taxes, but such fees, and most other direct taxes, do not discriminate against foreign goods. Many countries, for example, have purchase or excise taxes which apply to various categories of goods, value added or turnover taxes which apply as the product goes through a channel of distribution, and retail sales taxes. Such taxes may increase the end price of the goods rather significantly but, in general, do not discriminate against foreign goods nor detrimentally affect foreign goods.

Indirect taxes, such as income tax, and excise taxes may influence decisions concerning the legal form of operation or the country in which to produce. Generally, however, such taxes are calculated in the basic cost of production of the goods and do not significantly or directly affect the pricing policy of a firm. Such taxes are accounted for in different ways. Under current GATT rules, it is a practice to permit indirect taxes on goods to be rebated at the time of exporting; direct taxes may not be rebated. Some individuals have argued that if the mix of the U.S. taxes were varied to reduce direct taxes and increase indirect taxes, American goods would be more competitive in the world marketplace. One study, however, has indicated that U.S. prices could not be reduced more than 2 percent at the border as the result of such manipulations.[6] In general, then, tariffs are the primary discriminatory tax which must be taken into account in reckoning with foreign competition. All the various taxes, however, must be considered when attempting to establish retail or industrial selling prices.

Middleman Cost

American marketers will generally find that in most other countries channels are longer and middleman margins are larger than is customary in the United States. The diversity of channels used to reach the market and the lack of standardization of the middleman's markups may leave the typical producer in a position of not knowing what his product ultimately sells for.

Channel diversity is difficult to cope with, but the fully integrated marketer operating abroad may also find that he is faced with a large number of unanticipated costs because the marketing and channel of distribution infrastructure is so undeveloped. In addition to the wide

---

[6] Robert Z. Aliber and Herbert Stein, "The Price of U.S. Exports and the Mix of U.S. Direct and Indirect Taxes," *American Economic Review*, September 1964, p. 703.

variations in the cost of international shipping and internal transportation costs, the marketer may incur extra expenses for warehousing and for handling of small shipments, and he may have to bear increased financing costs when dealing with underfinanced middlemen.

Since no convenient source of data on middleman costs is available, the international marketer must rely on experience and marketing research to discover what his middleman cost will be. For example, the Campbell soup company found their middleman and physical distribution costs in the United Kingdom to be some 30 percent higher than in the United States. Among other reasons, extra costs were incurred because soup was purchased in such small quantities—English grocers typically purchase 24-can cases of assorted soups (with each can being hand packed for shipment). In the United States, a typical purchase unit is 48-can cases of one variety, and they are purchased by dozens, hundreds, and carloads. Such small purchases in Europe forced the company to include an extra wholesale level in its channel to facilitate handling of such small orders. Purchase frequency patterns also run up billing and order costs; both wholesalers and retailers purchase two to three times as often as their U.S. counterparts. Sales-call costs become virtually prohibitive. These and other distribution cost factors caused the company to change both its price and price patterns but also forced a complete restructuring of the channel system.

Financing and Risk Costs

The differences in financing international marketing activities contrast with domestic financing essentially in magnitude rather than type. Because of the time lags involved for both the seller and the buyer, international business transactions may tie up capital for considerable lengths of time. Such capital tie-ups increase the cost of financing not only for the seller, but in some instances for the buyer as well. In some countries, for example, when an import certificate is obtained for certain goods the purchaser may have to deposit funds for the purchase of the goods or equipment. In the case of custom-made machine tools or equipment, the funds may be tied up for as long as six months or a year. Such a cost is particularly significant in countries where interest rates are high. In some South American countries, for example, interest rates of 3 percent a month are not unusual. Assuming an interest rate of even 1½ percent, a six-month commitment can, in effect, add 9 percent to the cost of the goods for the ultimate purchaser.[7]

Other than the normal risks encountered in business, some of which may be intensified internationally, inflation and exchange-rate fluctuations constitute significant financial risks which may affect the price of goods, the terms which are offered, the cost of doing business, and even the manufacturer's method of pricing goods and publicizing price changes.

The effects of inflation on cost must be accounted for. In countries

---

[7] See Chapter 14, "Financing International Marketing."

with rapid inflation, selling price should be related not only to the cost of goods sold, but to the cost of replacing the items. Goods are often sold below their cost of replacement plus overhead and sometimes are even sold below replacement cost. In these instances, the company would be better off not to sell the products at all. When payment is likely to be delayed for several months or is worked out on a long-term contract, inflationary change must be figured into the price.

To do business in nations with runaway inflation, such as Brazil, which has experienced inflation at the rates as high as 86 percent per year, companies have learned that they can adjust to the situation by being constantly alert to the rate of change and modifying their prices to match the pace of the inflation. Pharmaceutical manufacturers in Brazil have prices which are fixed by law; yet these manufacturers are faced with wage and material cost increases that cannot be circumvented or absorbed into the production cost. Such companies move as rapidly as possible to secure governmental approval for price increases which will keep pace with inflation.

The problems of exchange-rate fluctuation pose fewer hazards because a number of devices are available for counteraction. Prices, for example, may be quoted in the currency of the home country or in terms of some stable monetary unit, such as the U.S. dollar. When such a contract is unacceptable to the purchaser, the foreign exchange risk may be modified through the process of hedging.[8] Companies with foreign operations have few ways to protect themselves in attempting to repatriate foreign profits; however, the foreign operations are usually in tune with local inflation and exchange rates, so this problem, too, can be minimized.

Innumerable other cost variables could be identified depending on the market, the product, and the situation. The cost, for example, of reaching a market with relatively small potential may be high. Extreme competition in certain world markets can raise the cost or lower the margins available to world businessmen. Even such small things as the payoffs that may be necessary for local officials can introduce unexpected cost to the unwary entrepreneur. In any case, experience in a given marketplace will provide the basis for compensating for cost differences in different markets. With experience, a firm which does its pricing on a cost basis operates in a realm of fairly measurable factors.

PRICE ESCALATION

Businessmen or others traveling abroad are often surprised to find that goods which may be relatively inexpensive in their home country are priced "outrageously" in other countries. Because of the natural tendency to assume that such prices are a result of profiteering, manufacturers often resolve to begin exporting to "crack" these new foreign markets. Excess profits may in fact exist, but more often added costs are the cause of the disproportionate difference in price. What the un-

---

[8] "Hedging" relates to the process of selling or buying foreign currencies in a manner to offset exchange fluctuations.

informed or inexperienced marketer does not understand, however, is the rapid rise of prices which sometimes take place when goods enter foreign markets. Such price increases are here termed price escalation. Specifically the term relates to situations where the ultimate prices are raised by shipping cost, tariffs, longer channels of distribution, larger middlemen margins, and special taxes.

The following sections show how cost and tax variations cause prices to rise differently in various markets under alternative circumstances and offer some possible methods of coping with the specific type of price increases called price escalation.

Sample Effects of Price Escalation

Exhibit 18–1 illustrates some of the possible effects these factors may have on the end price of a consumer item. Because costs and tariffs vary so widely from country to country, a hypothetical but realistic example is used; the student should realize that fluctuations can be wider than those illustrated. For example, tariff rates and international transportation charges are held constant in this example; if they should vary, the end price would vary also.

Exhibit 18–1 assumes that a constant net price is received by the manufacturer; it further assumes that all domestic transportation is absorbed by the various middlemen and reflected in their margins. In the first three foreign examples, it is assumed that the foreign middlemen have the same margins as the domestic middlemen. In some instances foreign middleman margins will be lower, but it is equally probable that foreign middleman margins will be greater (as is assumed at the retail level in the fourth foreign example). In fact, in many instances middlemen will use higher wholesale and retail margins for foreign goods than for similar domestic goods. Such a differential contributes an additional source of price escalation.

Notice that the retail prices for the product range from $1.90 domestically to $2.58 in the most optimistic foreign example (example 1), $3.23 when an importer is involved (example 2) through $3.99 when a cumulative turnover tax of 10 percent is added (example 3) and finally to $4.79 when the channel is longer and the retail margin is greater (example 4). Remember that in all five examples the net price received by the manufacturer is $0.95. The variation in the retail price illustrates the difficulty of price control by manufacturers when they are dealing with overseas retail markets. No matter how much the manufacturer may wish to market his product in a foreign country for a price equivalent to $1.90 U.S., he may find that he has little opportunity for such control. Even assuming the most optimistic conditions of foreign example 1, the producer would need to cut his net by nearly one third to absorb freight plus tariff so that the goods could be priced the same on the foreign and domestic markets.[9]

The National Housewares Manufacturers Association of the United

---

[9] To compute, work backward from the retail price. Retail price minus (retail margin, wholesaler margin, transportation and tariffs) equals manufacturers' net.

EXHIBIT 18–1

Sample Causes and Effects of Price Escalation

	Domestic Example	Foreign Example 1: Assuming the Same Channels with Wholesaler Importing Directly	Foreign Example 2: Foreign Importer and Same Margins and Channels	Foreign Example 3: Same as 2 but with 10% Cumulative Turnover Tax	Foreign Example 4: Long Channels, Larger Retail Margins, no Turnover Tax
Mfg. net	$ .95	$ .95	$ .95	$ .95	$ .95
Transport, c.i.f.	x	.15	.15	.15	.15
Tariff (20%)	x	.19	.19	.19	.19
Importer pays		x	1.29	1.29	1.29
Importer margin when sold to wholesaler (25% on cost)	x	x	.32	.32 + .13 turnover tax % .45	.32
Wholesaler pays landed cost	.95	1.29	1.61	1.74	1.61
Wholesaler margin (33⅓ on cost)	.32	.43	.54	.58 + .17 turnover tax = .75	.54
Local foreign jobber pays	x	x	x	x	2.15
Jobber margin (33⅓ on cost)	x	x	x	x	.72
Retailer pays	1.27	1.72	2.15	2.49	2.87
Retail margin (50% on cost)	.63	.86	1.08	1.25 + .25 turnover tax = 1.50	1.92 (66⅔% on cost)
Retail price	1.90	2.58	3.23	3.99	4.79

NOTE: 1. All figures in $ U.S.
2. x = This cost is not applicable in this example.
3. The exhibit assumes that all domestic transportation is absorbed by the middlemen.
4. Transportation, tariffs, and middleman margins vary from country to country, but for purposes of comparison only a few of the possible variations are shown.

States sponsored a trade mission to Germany, France, Italy, and the United Kingdom. The report of this mission provides numerous examples of price escalation. It was reported that in Italy "a combination electric can opener with a U.S. cost of approximately $5.98 and a retail range of $8.88 to $9.88 was priced in a Milan department store at the equivalent of $24." Tariffs, transportation and other costs causing such price escalation may put foreign manufacturers at a distinct competitive disadvantage. Again, many U.S. appliances in France were reported to be from 20 to 100 percent higher in price than comparable French-produced merchandise. A French automatic toaster, for example, was priced at $15, with a very similar American one priced at $22.

Strategic Approaches to Price Escalation

Although the manufacturer may not be able to control the end price of his goods as closely as he would like, he can employ several strategic approaches designed to counteract the problem of price differentials. Large, well-financed manufacturers may have a number of alternative approaches, but the small firm which is merely engaged in occasional exporting has less flexibility.

A company may attempt to offset tariffs and transportation charges by accepting a lower net price for goods sold in foreign markets. This often is not an acceptable alternative; in the first foreign example in Exhibit 18–1, the manufacturer would have to be willing to accept 67 cents rather than 95 cents a unit to maintain the same retail price in the foreign as in the domestic market. Freight absorption has the same effect and serves essentially the same function as a price reduction in that it lowers the net price received by the producer or exporter.

The type of price reductions mentioned here may be viewed by the importing country as dumping and thus may be subject to being offset by countervailing tariffs which would nullify the intended price advantage.

Tariff differentials can sometimes be at least partially overcome by modifying the product in such a way to bring it into a different rate category or by shipping components and assembling them in the foreign country where they are to be sold. This alternative assumes a fairly well-developed market and is suitable only when assembly costs represent a rather large part of the total product cost or where components can be shipped under substantially lower tariff rates than completed products.

The manufacturer may find that tariff and transportation barriers are so great that he needs to go into overseas production in order to remain competitive in the foreign market. This, of course, is a logical alternative only if the manufacturer is adequately financed, if raw materials and labor are available in the foreign country, and if the market will support such a productive facility.

If the manufacturer can find ways to shorten the channels of distribution or to distribute products directly to customers or consumers, this may keep prices under control. The process of eliminating middlemen is as costly in international markets, however, as it is in domestic markets, and although channels may be shortened, marketing functions are not eliminated and marketing costs may not necessarily be lowered. Many countries have what is called a turnover tax which is levied on goods as they pass through the channel of distribution. Each time a good changes hands, it is taxed. In some countries, such as France, the tax is levied in such a way that it is noncumulative; that is, tax is paid only on the difference (valued added) between a middleman's and selling prices. A good sold by a manufacturer to a wholesaler for $7 would be taxed 70 cents if the tax rate were 10 percent. Thus the cost to the wholesaler must be $7.70. If the wholesaler sold it for $9.50, the tax would amount to 10 percent of the $1.80 margin, so it would be 18 cents, making the wholesaler's selling price $9.68. The "normal" rate of the French value-added tax (T.V.A.) is 20 percent of the sale price, including the T.V.A. itself. It ranges from 6 percent on basic foodstuffs to 25 percent for luxury items. Such items as bread and milk are exempt.[10]

Prior to 1970 all European economic community countries except France had a turnover system of taxation, but all have agreed to go to a T.V.A. system. The new system will employ a higher rate of tax but will tax only the value added at each transfer. In general, such taxes have tended to raise the total tax bill, but the effects are difficult to assess because every country in Europe has a somewhat different taxing system. The T.V.A. tax, incidentally, if often refunded to manufacturers when they export goods, thereby serving, in effect, as a tax subsidy for exports.

In some countries, the turnover tax is cumulative. In such countries the total selling price is taxed each time goods change hands. To follow the previous example, the tax on the sale from the manufacturer to wholesaler would be 70 cents, with the wholesaler costs being $7.70. The wholesaler who marked the price up to $9.50 would have to add 10 percent of that price, 95 cents, making his selling price $10.45. In countries where turnover tax is cumulative, the tax alone provides special incentive for developing short distribution channels. Some nations, however, attempt to lessen such effect on distribution patterns by assessing the tax at different rates. The normal turnover tax rate is about 4 percent, but in certain carefully defined circumstances wholesalers may be taxed at a rate of only 1 percent. In Exhibit 18–1, example 3 assumes a cumulative turnover tax of 10 percent which, in that example, is incurred three times—when the importer sells to the wholesaler, when the wholesaler sells to the retailer, and when the retailer sells to the consumer. The tax in that example totaled 55 cents, or slightly over half of the manufacturer's net price. Shorter channels could have reduced the tax considerably.

MARKET PRICING

Without ignoring the realities of cost, many marketers find that the market constitutes the most satisfactory basis for pricing. Market pric-

---

[10] Information on rates and conditions pertaining to turnover tax is available for many countries in *Information Guide for Those Doing Business in* ———— (country) (New York: Price, Waterhouse and Company), various dates.

ing recognizes the fact that the real value of a product may vary significantly from one country to another, or from one time to another. Considered in the context of demand and supply, the needs of the market and the state of competition are the primary determinants of such price variation.

Demand

Demand conditions set the range of prices which will be paid for goods. On the demand side, the price range is largely a function of the level of need or desire for a product coupled with the customers' ability to pay. In some countries a marketer will have to sell his goods on a narrow margin to remain in the market; in other countries market conditions may permit broad margins.

Logically, demand should be assessed market by market. When establishing prices for goods which are to be sold in many markets, one of the basic questions is whether the prices are to be identical or different in varying countries. Identical or similar prices may be necessary in order to minimize country-to-country arbitrage through companies other than those controlled by the company. If identical or similar prices are to be used, the question becomes which market or markets will be taken into consideration in setting those prices. Typically, prices are established on a basis of demand in the producing country; demand in the consuming countries would probably be much more relevant. For goods with high price sensitivity, prices must be based on a careful interpretation of demand conditions.

Competition

Competition is the other critical element affecting the level of prices in a free marketplace. In any country, competition may be direct or indirect; competition of either type will have a direct effect on price.

Direct competition relates to products similar to one's own but sold by competitors. In the case of direct competition, price may be an important, perhaps the sole, determinant of the source from which products may be purchased. Credit will also play a role in many instances. In the directly competitive situation, prices may be affected more significantly by the level of competitive prices than by the market itself. Direct competition may bring about discounting at all levels in the distribution channel. If margins are high, particularly on simple terms such as replacement parts or supplies, competition may be encouraged to pirate ideas and sell imitation products at substantially reduced prices. In recent years, for example, books originally published and copyrighted in the United States have been reproduced in low-cost areas, such as Hong Kong, in low-quality editions and sold in the United States and other foreign markets at prices as low as one third of the price of the original book. Management must always be alert to the possibility of encouraging such pirating when pricing merchandise.

The chief competitive weapon of some businesses is price cutting; such firms maintain their market position only by selling merchandise at prices below the general market level. In the United Kingdom, the Ilford Company was able to expand its market share of the photographic film market by reducing its prices some 30 percent below those of Kodak, the dominant competitor. Through an ironic twist of fate, the Monopoly Commission recommended that the British Board of Trade require Kodak to reduce its prices because they were out of line. The move was intended to reduce monopoly by lessening Kodak's share of the market. In fact, Ilford was deprived of its price advantage and lost its market share, putting the firm in a precarious financial position and leaving it ripe for a subsequent take-over by a larger company.

Where competition is particularly intense, as may be the case in a country which has suppliers from a half dozen nations feeding products into a limited market, there is a tendency to attempt to limit price competition through various forms of agreement, such as cartels. Various forms of price fixing are considered in a following section. In many markets, and for certain kinds of goods, price competition seems never to have been a significant factor in the marketplace. Some industries view price competition as immoral and seem to view prices as God-given. In many countries discounting is considered to be a predatory practice, even at the retail level. In other countries price bargaining is not only accepted but assumed.

Indirect competition may be of special importance when attempting to sell a product from one culture to another. Indirect competition is encountered when a prospective customer satisfies his need or desire with a completely different variety of product than the one being offered. Industrial equipment makers, for example, often sell their products on a basis of operating cost savings or efficiency. These manufacturers have found that in the developing countries their main competition for laborsaving devices is not other laborsaving devices but labor itself. High capacity earth-moving equipment may have little interest in the Indian market because speed may not be an important factor; if the local contractor finds that it is more economical to move dirt using hand labor and baskets he will follow this alternative.

Indirect competition is also significant for consumer goods. Laborsaving products, such as washing machines and prepared foods, have little appeal for householders who have servants. Even when servants are not available, the householder's pride or prejudice may cause products to be rejected in favor of indirect competitors. Cloth, for example, may compete with ready-made clothing. In some countries it is considered profane for a woman's undergarments to be made by anyone but her. In others, ready-made clothing is considered a mark of poverty.

Companies may find it rather unrewarding to compete directly for a segment of a small market. Emphasis on expanding primary demand and product acceptance may provide significantly greater long-range profits.

In summary, the international marketer must be particularly alert to the variances in types and nature of competition throughout his many markets, and he must not expect the price behavior of either his customers or his competitors to be rationally explicable. He must remember

BOX 18–2

Willy Korf Unsettles the Steel Goliaths

At 39, he has his own steel mini-empire, with headquarters in Kehl, Germany, and with mills and fabricating plants elsewhere in Germany as well as in Nigeria, and the U.S. Yet he is never to be found in the august company of German steel barons, who had a virtual lock on sales before he came along. And there is no love lost between them. Korf says of the German Iron & Steel Federation, with its cartel-like sales organizations made up of such companies as Krupp, Thyssen, and Mannesmann, "They exist to eliminate competition. In the U.S., they would be . . . in jail."

Unlocked Markets. Korf's bitterness is understandable. The steel giants never made it easy for him. Last year they tried to put him out of business when his one-man band of a company, Korf Industrie & Handel, started snatching off 15% to 20% of the German market for reinforcing bar and wire.

Korf first entered the business in the early '50s, when war-torn Germany was strapped for steel. He needed wire mesh for the family building supply company he had taken over on his father's death. Deciding to make his own steel mesh—used in buildings and highways—he started a plant at Kehl, across the Rhine from Strasbourg.

The major companies pounced on him quickly, charging violation of patents. With the case still before the courts, Korf chose to sell. He got $5-million for his plant, but had to promise not to start another steel mesh operation for at least 10 years.

. . . [W]hen the ban expired, in 1965, he returned to the steel business, this time building a rolling mill. Again, the big suppliers proved troublesome.

"I always had difficulties getting steel at all and at the right price," he recalls. "As a steel finisher, you are always competing with the divisions of the big steel. . . ."

When Korf brought his Kehl mini-mill on stream last year, the big companies really put on the pressure. "They wanted to give us a birthday present," he recalls wryly. The present was a 25% cut in the price of reinforcing bar. Korf stormed to the European Coal and Steel community and charged that the big steel makers were gunning for him when they slashed their prices. After discussions, the sales group kicked prices up about 10%.

Spreading Out. Lately, Korf hasn't been bothered much by the cartels, but he is still worried. "We run the risk that through their mergers they will become more dominant, and what they earn they can throw in specific areas—such as concrete reinforcing steel."

Source: *Business Week*, March 29, 1969, p. 68. Reprinted with permission.

that in every case his prices are subject to the whims of the market and the pressures of competition.

Dumping

One of the logical outgrowths of a market pricing policy in international business is that goods are likely to be priced at widely differing prices in various markets. The market and economic logic of such behavior can hardly be disputed, but the practice itself is often considered to be dumping; as such it is likely to be the subject of strong opinion. "Dumping" is defined somewhat differently by various economists. One approach classifies international shipments as dumped if the products are sold below their cost production. The other characterizes dumping as selling goods in a foreign country at prices below the price of the same goods in the home market. Laws may utilize both definitions in order to plug as many loopholes as possible. The *Exporters' Encyclopedia* summarizes the dumping legislation of most countries. Its description of the situation in Norway shows something of the scope of provisions used to make the laws as inclusive as possible. Note especially the provisions for calculating subsidies in determining prices.

Dumping and Countervailing Duty: The law authorizes the imposition of a dumping duty when goods are sold at a price lower than the normal export price or less than the cost in the country of origin increased by a reasonable amount for the cost of sales and profits; and when this is likely to be prejudicial to the economic activity of the country. A countervailing duty may be imposed on foreign goods benefiting from subsidies in production, export, or transport.[11]

In trade talks in Geneva in 1968, new rules were accepted pertaining to dumping. In the case of the United States, these new rules make dumping of products into the United States more acceptable than previously. The chief variation pertains to the definition of the situation in which dumping harms a local producer. The new code, for example, stipulates that imported goods must be *identical* to U.S. goods, whereas the old code indicated that they needed only to be closely related. Furthermore, the new code specifies that protection is granted only to producers who are actually located in the market where the imports are sold. Previously, any producer was protected against dumping anywhere in the nation. Even the consideration on pricing and price differential has been modified; previously, price alone determined whether goods were being dumped, now labor and management efficiency must be examined before it can be specified whether prices of imports are unfair.

Before antidumping laws can be invoked under the new rules, it must be shown not only that prices are lower in the importing country than in the producing country, but also that producers in the importing country are being *directly* harmed by the dumping.

Rigidly interpreted, the concepts of dumping or reverse dumping include any form of price differentiation in different markets. Dumping implies a higher price in the foreign market; reverse dumping indicates a higher price in the domestic market. On the basis of price theory many economists have argued that the whole concept of dumping is fallacious and should be considered merely as differential pricing utilized to meet market demand. As such, it is directly related to price elasticities of demand in the home versus the foreign markets. When the foreign price is lower, they contend, demand is simply more elastic in the foreign

[11] From "Norway," in *Exporters' Encyclopedia*, published annually by Dun & Bradstreet, New York.

market; when it is higher, demand is more elastic in the home market. The company objective in these cases is always to maximize revenue.

To the theoretician, then, the question of dumping simply boils down to whether the world should be considered one free market and whether prices must be established on a full-cost basis or if variable pricing is acceptable. For the businessman and politicians however, the question will continue to be viewed in terms of patriotism and protection of cherished home markets from "cheap foreign goods."

ADMINISTERED PRICING

The terms "administered prices" and "administered pricing" have rather differing connotations. Too, the process of setting prices within a company is often called "price administration." As used in this chapter, all these terms relate to attempts to administer a price for an entire market. Such prices may be arranged through the cooperation of competitors, through national (sometimes also state and local) governments, or by international agreement. The legality of administered pricing arrangements of various kinds differs from country to country and from time to time. It is not unusual for a country to condone price fixing for foreign markets but to condemn it for the domestic market. In the United States, for example, the Webb-Pomerene Export Trade Act of 1918 permits domestic companies to associate for foreign trading, including price fixing. A Webb-Pomerene Export Association (WPEA) is specifically exempted from the Sherman Antitrust Act if it does not attempt to influence domestic competition or the activities of domestic competitors who are not association members. WPEA is important to the some 400 companies which participate in such associations, but exports by WPEA's have never accounted for more than about 6 percent of total U.S. merchandise exports.[12]

In general, the end goal of all administered pricing activities is to reduce the impact of price competition or to eliminate it altogether. Price fixing by business is not generally viewed as an acceptable procedure (at least in the domestic market); but when governments enter the field of price administration, they presume to do it for the general welfare to lessen the effects of "destructive" competition.

When competition becomes destructive depends largely on the country in question. The whole concept of competition is so distasteful to many Orientals that one economist has suggested that "whenever the Japanese allude to competition, they normally assume cut-throat, excessive or unfair competition."[13] To the Japanese, excessive competition is *any* competition in the home market that disturbs the existing balance of trade or gives rise to market disruptions. Few countries apply such rigorous standards in measuring competition as excessive, but no country is in the position of favoring or permitting totally free competition.

---

[12] L. I. Eckstrom, *Licensing in Foreign and Domestic Operations* (3d ed; Essex, Conn.: Foreign Operations Service Inc., 1964), p. 459.

[13] Martin Brofenbrenner, "Excessive Competition in Japanese Business," *Monumenta Nipponica*, Vol. XXI, Nos. 1 and 2, p. 144.

Even economists, the traditional champions of pure competition, increasingly acknowledge that perfect competition is unlikely and agree that some form of "workable" competition must be developed. Hopefully, such competition will regulate prices so they will not usually be so high as to drive consumers from the market nor so low as to eliminate producers. The possibility of such adverse results, however, is what induces businessmen and governments to "rationalize" prices and competition through administered pricing arrangements.

Price Setting by Business Groups

The pervasiveness of price-fixing attempts in business is reflected to some extent by the diversity of the language of administered prices; pricing arrangements are variously called agreements, arrangements, combines, conspiracies, cartels, communities of profit, profit pools, price leadership, customary pricing, or informal interfirm agreements. The arrangements themselves extend from completely informal arrangements in which there is no spoken or acknowledged agreement to highly formalized and structured arrangements, as in the international combine. Even basing-point arrangements are primarily devices for controlling price. In such a system, all prices must be quoted, including freight from certain industrywide designated shipping locations called basing points. For years international oil price quotations assumed that all shipments were made from the Gulf of Mexico; prices were quoted on a Gulf-plus basis which meant the price plus transportation from the Gulf of Mexico regardless of the place from which actually shipped. Many other bulk commodities, such as steel and cement, are also quoted using international basing points. Any type of price-fixing arrangement is adaptable to international business; but of all the forms mentioned above the four which are most directly associated with international marketing are patent licensing, cartels, combines, and trade associations.

Patent Licensing Agreements.   In industries where technological innovation is especially important, patent or process agreements are probably the most common type of international combination. In most countries patent licensing agreements are legally acceptable because what in effect is taking place is that the owner of the patent grants an exclusive license to someone in another country to produce his product. By contractual definition the patent holder can control territorial boundaries and, because of his monopoly, he controls pricing. Often such arrangements go beyond a specific licensing agreement to include a gentlemen's agreement by which the companies involved agree to give their foreign counterparts first rights on their own patents and new developments. Such arrangements can lead to a series of national monopolies which significantly restrict competition and thereby raise product prices. Like so many other agreements related to restricting competition, their legality of patent licensing agreements is difficult to discuss outside the context of a specific situation. The following statement effectively summarizes the present situation on patent licensing:

As to licensing arrangements, it should be recognized, preliminarily, that patents in different countries, although covering the same invention, are entirely separate; the patents of one country confer no legal rights in another country. If an American company owning an invention has both United States and foreign patents thereon, it may grant independent licenses under each patent. A grant of a license under a French patent, for example, would give the licensee no right to sell the patented article in the United States. Conversely, a license under the United States patent would give the licensee no right to sell in France. So long as an American company licenses its foreign patents and depends upon its United States patents for protection from a foreign licensee's competition, it does not run into anti-trust difficulties. Restrictions on United States imports or exports, however, arrived at by agreement and going beyond legitimate patent rights, are not permissible under the anti-trust laws, and such restrictive agreements have been struck down.[14]

Patent licensing arrangements have been an important factor in international marketing in the past and continue to be important despite numerous restrictions.

Cartels. A cartel exists when various companies which are producing similar products associate in order to control markets for the types of goods which they produce. Generally, a cartel pertains to more activities than a patent licensing agreement and endows the participants with greater power. The cartel association may use formal agreements by which they set prices, establish levels of production and sales for the participating companies, allocate market territories, and even redistribute profits. In some instances, the cartel organization itself takes over the entire selling function and sells the goods of all the producers and distributes the profits.

The economic role of cartels is a highly debatable issue, but the attitude of many proponents of cartels is well stated by the Director of Professional Organizations and Disputes of the Belgium Ministry of Economic Affairs:

> It does not appear unjustified to state that most western European industrial circles hold that cartels are to be recommended in many cases for a rational economic organization. It is true that this opinion is not shared in the same way by the public powers and even less by the trade unions. All circles, however, show an inclination to accept the fact that cartels often enable cutthroat competition—which finally turns out to be prejudicial to the community—to be avoided on the export market. It is also frequently accepted that some cartels, because of the resulting co-operation, put industry in a position to promote rationalization and specialization and, consequently, technical progress which finally turns out to the consumers' advantage in the shape of a reduction in costs.[15]

Cartels are often thought of in conjunction with Europe, but U.S. companies have participated in international cartels, and cartels have

---

[14] Wilbur L. Fugate, "Damper or Bellows? Anti-Trust Laws and Foreign Trade," *American Bar Association Journal*, September 1959, p. 747.

[15] Peter M. Raskin, "Belgian Policy in Regard to the Abuse of Economic Power," *Proceedings, International Conference on Control of Restrictive Business Practices* (Illinois: The Free Press of Glencoe, The Graduate School of Business, University of Chicago, 1960), p. 56.

EXHIBIT 18–2

Nationwide Agreements Governing Competition in the Netherlands, 1969

	Total*	Textile Industry	Shoe and Clothing Industry	Chemical Industry	Earthenware, Glass, Limestone, and Ceramics Industry	Food and Luxury Industry	Wholesalers
Total number of agreements	802	28	11	71	60	54	137
Division by Subject Matter							
1. Production	51	6	1	7	5	7	2
a) Rationalization	22	—	—	5	1	2	1
b) Quality control	29	6	1	2	4	5	1
2. Market division							
a) Quotas	157	11	—	31	25	15	31
1. Production	21	1	—	2	5	3	—
2. Sales	120	10	—	25	20	10	22
3. Purchasing	16	—	—	4	—	2	9
b) Territorial division	26	—	—	1	5	3	4
c) Customer division	27	1	—	10	—	1	9
3. Prices							
a) Horizontal	319	18	5	49	19	15	84
1. Minimum prices	155	13	2	25	8	9	34
2. Fixed prices	144	2	—	23	11	5	49
3. Calculation schemes	20	3	3	1	—	1	1
b) Collective vertical price	26	—	—	2	4	6	18
c) Other forms	256	20	4	14	10	12	98
1. Bidding agreements	54	7	3	8	2	—	5
2. Margins and discounts	114	4	—	—	1	6	64
3. Commissions	19	7	1	3	1	1	2
4. Bonuses and rebates	43	2	—	3	4	2	22
5. Miscellaneous	26	—	—	3	2	3	5

4. Price or discount discrimination	20	2	—	—	—	3	9
5. Collective boycotting	106	3	2	9	11	6	90
6. Uniform conditions	252	13	4	36	8	19	96
7. Information exchanges	94	—	—	1	5	1	11
8. Centralized buying and selling	81	1	3	14	17	10	19
a) buying	22	—	2	2	—	5	12
b) selling	59	1	1	12	17	5	7
9. Financial matters	57	1	—	5	4	10	17
a) profit and loss pools	14	1	—	2	—	4	6
b) loans	43	—	—	3	4	6	11
10. Miscellaneous	116	7	2	4	8	5	28

Source: Adapted from Thomas Silbinger, "The Netherlands," in H. M. Blake, Business Regulation in the Common Market Nations (New York: McGraw-Hill Book Company, 1969), pp. 241–43.
*Note: Although only a few selected industries are represented in the table, the total is for all industries.

also included producers from nearly every country at one time or another. Country cartels seem to exhibit a marked tenacity for survival despite attempts to regulate them. Prior to World War I, major international cartels existed in plate glass, electric light bulbs, bottles, steel rails, armaments, aluminum, shipping, and other areas. Many cartels were disbanded during that war but were rebuilt again in the period between the first and second world wars; in fact, even more products were cartelized after the war than before. The first really strong international steel cartel, for example, was not created until 1926. Some of the other products which were cartelized during this period included such minerals as potash, zinc, mercury, copper, tin and nickel, and such processed goods as oil, glue, wood pulp, linoleum, dyestuffs, and natural rubber and steel.

The World War II period also saw a breaking down of traditional cartels, but cartelizers have been active in the period following. World cartels are in current evidence in steel, glass, chemicals, and many other industries. The Netherlands provide an excellent example; in 1950 there were some 450 registered cartels of national scope. Between 1950 and 1956 the number rose to 850. In that same year there were over 1,000 registered cartels of regional or local scope. A national anticartel policy was established in 1956 which has been at least partially successful. Note in Exhibit 18–2 that by 1969 the number of national cartel agreements had been reduced to 802. The table also clearly shows the wide variety of cartel arrangements which can be utilized.

Japan, under the direction of the Supreme Commander of Allied Powers, enacted a rigid antimonopoly law described by a member of Japan's Fair Trade Commission (the enforcing agency) as "in essence, the Sherman Antitrust Act, the Clayton Act, and the Federal Trade Commission Act, all combined into one, a little elaborated, embodying court precedents and theories developed in the United States."[16] The law proved too rigid and was later modified to include provision for, among other things, exemptions for cartels formed to avert "economic crises" and cartels formed for the "rationalization of enterprise." As a result of these exceptions, the commission finds that "validating hundreds of cartel agreements under various 'exemption laws' is another work that is taking more and more of the FTC staff."[17]

The number of court actions involving U.S. companies would indicate that the United States is not completely decartelized at present. Some of the post-World War II landmark cases include such well-known U.S. companies as General Electric, Timken, National Lead, Minnesota Mining, Joseph E. Seagram and Sons, and Webster Electric.[18]

The legality of cartels at present is not clearly delineated. Domestic cartelization is illegal in the United States, and both the European

---

[16] Hirosi Acino (Restrictive Trade Practices Study Team, Japan), op. cit., "Control of Restrictive Trade Practices in Japan," in *Proceedings, International Conference on Control of Restrictive Business Practices*, pp. 91–92.

[17] Ibid., p. 102.

[18] See Commerce Clearing House Trade Regulation reports for additional cases and details on decrees and judgments.

BOX 18-3

Cartel

Westinghouse Electric Corp.'s chances for getting a major stake in France's electrical equipment industry are probably growing dimmer.

This week France's two largest electrical and electronics companies agreed to stop competing. One key element in their cartel-like agreement seems likely to shatter Westinghouse's plans for buying control of a French electrical equipment producer.

Westinghouse has been hoping for some time to buy Société Jeumont-Schneider, France's No. 2 heavy electrical equipment producer, and to build around this a big European manufacturing group.

This would make it tougher for French companies to retain their share of the market. So the French government has been pushing another solution: It wants Jeumont-Schneider to merge with Société Alsthom, a smaller electrical equipment producer.

The new cartel arrangement puts a lot more weight into the government's push for this merger. The cartel deal calls for Compagnie Générale d'Electricité (CGE) to concentrate on electrical equipment and leaves electronics to Thomson-Brandt.

It also will give CGE management control over Société Alsthom—and this makes Alsthom a more attractive merger partner for Jeumont-Schneider.

Source: *Business Week*, June 28, 1969, p. 96. Reprinted with permission.

Common Market and the European Free Trade Association have provisions for controlling cartels. The United States, however, does permit firms to take cartel-like actions in foreign, but not domestic, markets. The European Free Trade Association Treaty has a provision which implies that cartels are not acceptable but provides no specific restriction nor any enforcement mechanism. The European Common Market's Rome Treaty is patterned after the old German cartel laws which technically forbade cartels. In reality the treaty may permit them within the Common Market and generally approves export cartels that don't affect the home country.

Increasingly, it has become apparent that many governments have concluded that they cannot ignore cartels or destroy them completely, so they have chosen to establish ground rules and regulatory agencies which will oversee the cartel-like activities of businesses within their jurisdiction. This has been the explicit goal of Article 85 of the Rome Treaty, which is reproduced below and which shows the level of abstraction that seems to characterize antimonopoly legislations.

ARTICLE 85

1. The following shall be deemed to be incompatible with the Common Market and shall hereby be prohibited; any agreements between enterprises, any decisions by associations of enterprises and any concerted practices which are likely to affect trade between the Member States and which have as their object or result the prevention, restriction or distortion of competition within the Common Market, in particular, those consisting in:

(a)   the direct or indirect fixing of purchase or selling prices or any other trading conditions;

(b)   the limitation or control of production, markets, technical development or investment;

(c)   market-sharing or the sharing of sources of supply;

(d)   the application to parties to transactions of unequal terms in respect of equivalent supplies, thereby placing them at a competitive disadvantage; or

(e)   the subjecting of the conclusion of a contract to the acceptance by a party of additional supplies which, either by their nature or according to commercial usage, have no connection with the subject of such contract.

2. Any agreements or decisions prohibited pursuant to this Article shall be null and void.

3. Nevertheless, the provisions of paragraph 1 may be declared inapplicable in the case of:

—any agreements or classes of agreements between enterprises,

—any decisions or classes of decisions by associations of enterprises, and

—any concerted practices or classes of converted practices which contribute to the improvement of the production or distribution of goods or to the promotion of technical or economic progress while reserving to users an equitable share in the profit resulting therefrom, and which

(a)   neither impose on the enterprises concerned any restrictions not indispensable to the attainment of the above objectives;

(b)   nor enable such enterprises to eliminate competition in respect of a substantial proportion of the goods concerned.

The European Common Market has established a commission for enforcement of Article 85. It also provides what is called a "negative clearance" for contracts which (1) fall under Article 85, (2) are submitted to the commission for regulation, and (3) are determined not to be in violation of Article 85. The U.S. Department of Justice provides a somewhat similar alternative by providing for "Release Letters" pertaining to business plans submitted for review. Besides coping with the various common markets and free trade associations, the international marketer must also consider the antitrust laws of the individual countries. Most of the nations composing the ECM and EFTA have antitrust legislation, as do other countries, including Brazil, Australia, Canada, Spain, and the United States.[19]

Combines.   A combine operates somewhat in the manner of a cartel but provides even stronger control over the marketplace and over producers. Combine agreements are usually drawn more tightly and contain provisions for enforcement which give them great power. Sometimes combine members are fined tens of thousands of dollars for violating their agreements. Often a combine is operated as a single worldwide business with representatives of member companies making up its board of directors. Control over members may be as great as if they were part of a single company. Like cartels and other forms of market agreements, combines are subject to antitrust legislation. Combines do not

---

[19] For greater detail on the international antitrust laws and court interpretations, see Eckstrom, op. cit., chaps. 12 and 13, p. 506 ff.

seem to be a major factor in the affluent world market situation which has prevailed since World War II.

The history of business competition would indicate that as long as there is competition there will also be attempts to avoid competition in as many ways as possible. International marketing is particularly susceptible to price control and market sharing; the firm engaged in the international market must be prepared to cope with this phenomenon.

Trade Associations. The very term "trade association" is so broad as to be almost meaningless. Trade associations may exist primarily as hard, tight cartels or may be merely informal trade organizations having nothing to do with pricing, market share, or levels of production. In many countries, trade associations gather information about prices and transactions within a given industry. Such associations may exert strong or weak control over the actual pricing policies of companies belonging to the association but have the general goal of protecting and maintaining the pricing structure that is most generally acceptable to industry members. In the early 1930s the National Industry Recovery Act gave broad powers to U.S. trade associations for the type of regulation mentioned above. The act was declared unconstitutional, and trade associations in the United States since that time have been enjoined by the antitrust laws from playing a significant role in pricing. In other industrial nations this is not the case: manufacturers' associations frequently represent 90 to 100 percent of an industry. The association is a club which one must join for access to customers and suppliers. It may handle industrywide labor negotiations and is often capable of influencing governmental decisions relating to the industry.

A historic decision involving a trade association in Belgium is summarized below; it illustrates the kind of thinking which is common in Europe relative to trade associations.

When the Cour de Cassation rendered its decision in Gripekoven v. Reglementation Union-Spēpha . . . it made plain that boycottts were permissible against members and non-members alike if the boycott was organized for the defense of the legitimate interests of the members of the association.

Union-Spēpha, the defendant in this civil action, was an association whose members included approximately 600 Belgian and foreign manufacturers of pharmaceutical items as well as the vast majority of Belgian pharmaceutical dealers, wholesalers and retailers. Its main objective was the regulation of prices throughout the trade, including the maintenance of uniform retail prices. Members of the association agreed to refrain from selling to price-cutting retailers and to anyone who sold to such a retailer. The complainant, Gripekoven, a retailer who sold all items at a 10% discount, was boycotted by order of the association. Cut off from the supply of almost all pharmaceuticals, Gripekoven commenced proceedings against Union-Spēpha claiming damages pursuant to article 1382 of the Civil Code. His claim was dismissed in both the first and second instances. In respecting Gripekoven's assertion that as non-members of Union-Spēpha he was entitled to compensation for the loss occasioned by the boycott, the Court stated: "A boycott organized without malicious intent, for the defense of the legitimate interests of the members of an association or of partners to a combination—for example, to prevent sales at prices below the resale prices imposed—is lawful whether aimed at a member of the association or an outsider."[20]

Two kinds of boycotts are identified: The *boycottage-sanction* is directed against a member of an association or a combination by the other members as a penalty for the former's failure to fulfill his obligation to the group. Such a boycott is appropriately regarded as lawful. *Boycottage d'aggression* is directed against an outsider. The lawfulness of a boycott depends exclusively on whether the collective refusal to deal is motivated by "a legitimate interest" of the boycotters rather than simply by a desire to eliminate a competitor.

Governmental Price Setting

Companies doing business in foreign countries will encounter a number of different types of governmental price setting. To control prices, governments may establish margins, set prices and floors or ceilings, restrict price changes, compete in the market, grant subsidies, and act as a purchasing monopsony or selling monopoly.

Establish Margins.   Middlemen may be required to mark up their goods by a government-dictated margin and may not be permitted to deviate significantly from that margin. Even manufacturers may be subject to dictated margins, with the government specifying the amount which a good may be marked up over cost. Both types of margin setting are encountered in Norway, for example, where the government sets maximum ranges but permits some price cutting. Even in the United States, the government sets margins in the regulated public utility field.

Set Price Floors and Ceilings or Actual Prices.   Numerous methods of setting price floors and ceilings are employed in different countries. Some have laws similar to California's much-copied Unfair Practices Act which dictates that goods cannot be sold below their cost plus a government stipulated markup.

Price ceilings imposed by government are not uncommon in the world marketplace. Bread, rice, milk, and other food staples are often subject to price ceilings. Fixed prices in centrally planned economies do not permit the price mechanism to regulate the market; therefore, in the absence of perfect planning, supply and demand are equalized by rationing or the market is characterized by gluts and surpluses. The United States is relatively free of governmental price setting but does regulate prices in the transportation industry and during wartime sets or controls prices in a number of industries.

Restrict Price Changes.   Regardless of the state of economic development of the country they are in, international marketers are likely to find that they cannot change prices without applying for governmental permission or at least giving official notification. In some countries, such as India and Spain, changes in prices of a wide range of products are regulated. The American businessman may chafe at such

---

[20] From *Business Regulation in the Common Market,* by H. M. Blake, pp. 110–13. Copyright 1969, McGraw-Hill Book Company. Used with permission of McGraw-Hill Book Company.

BOX 18–4

Brazil Revises Its Price Control System

Brazil is preparing a major overhaul of its price control system that will affect the fortunes of every company operating in the country. The previous system of fiscal incentives and penalties for companies that kept their price increases within certain general limits is being abandoned, together with its administrative organ CONEP. In its place will be created an Interministerial Council on Prices (CIP), which will develop a new approach based on correlating price increases with variations in costs.

The CIP will have broad authority to supervise and control internal prices at all distribution levels, including prices of goods and services produced by government-controlled entities.

Companies planning to raise their prices will have to obtain prior approval from CIP, if their products are singled out for direct control. The criteria for inclusion of a product in the controlled list include: its importance in the composition of general price indices, or in the cost structure of a given economic sector; the existence of monopolistic or oligopolistic market conditions; or the possibility of erratic behavior in one sector causing repercussions elsewhere.

. . . A primary benefit of the new program will be that producers will know the price at which they may sell goods *before* beginning production; at present CONEP sets prices only on finished goods. . . .

In principle, the grounds for approving or rejecting a proposed price increase will be increases in costs. Obviously, an attempt to examine the cost structures of individual enterprises would inevitably lead to lengthy delays. To enable CIP to issue its rulings within a few days only (compared to two months or longer for CONEP), decisions will apparently be based primarily on a set of "sectorial indices" compiled by the agency. These will take into consideration changes in basic cost factors in different branches of production, services, or commerce.

Source: Reprinted from the March 29, 1968, issue of *Business International,* p. 100, with the permission of the publisher, Business International Corporation (New York).

regulation. President Nixon's direct action against the steel industry price increase in 1970–71, however, served to remind marketers that the U.S. marketplace is not completely free of price change restrictions.

Although not designed primarily to limit freedom in changing prices, tax laws of various nations sometimes affect prices that are charged on final products and tend to restrict price changing. This is particularly true in the case of intercorporate transfers where changeovers from one pricing system to another may bring forth retroactive tax penalties or higher taxes because of excessive profits.

Compete in the Market. Another U.S. example of governmental price control is in the aluminum industry. In the fall of 1965 three companies in the industry raised ingot prices by one-half cent a pound. Within days, the U.S. government announced that it would release two or three hundred thousand tons of aluminum from its strategic stockpile. Shortly afterwards, the companies indicated that they had reevaluated the situ-

BOX 18–5

City Warns Merchants on Price Increases

Store owners found raising prices on essential goods will face stiff fines and possible jail terms, city authorities warned Tuesday.

Stores in the country can raise prices—it was said—to take advantage of the recent minimum wage increase, but the Industry and Commerce Ministry pledged its inspectors will watch stores in major cities to prevent this.

"Industry and Commerce Ministry inspectors are under instructions to fine or jail store owners and middlemen, who may raise prices," a ministry spokesman said.

Industry and Commerce Minister Octaviano Campos Salas told the Mexico City Chamber of Commerce that he would never approve price hikes on essential goods.

Source: *The News* (Mexico City), January 14, 1970.

ation and rolled prices back to their original level. The continuing activity of the U.S. government in wheat and other commodities also has the effect of regulating prices through direct governmental competition.

In countries where the government owns a large share of the productive assets, it goes without saying that the government enterprise competes actively in the market. Some government-owned businesses, such as Italy's ENI, compete not only in the domestic market but in international markets as well.

Subsidies. Governmental subsidies may permit companies to lower the price of their goods in world competition, but they also bring the government into the pricing picture. Subsidies may be direct or indirect. To encourage the development of an industry, a nation may pay a producer of, say, shoes a direct subsidy of 50 cents per pair. That industry may then be able to compete more effectively in the local market against imported shoes because it can sell its goods 50 cents cheaper than it normally would. Or it may be able to compete more effectively in foreign markets because of its subsidy.

Sometimes the subsidy is paid only on exports and is set at a level to make up the difference between the domestic market price and the foreign market price.

An indirect subsidy is created when a nonexported component is subsidized and the component becomes part of an exported product. A tentmaker, for example, may buy canvas that is made from cotton that has a low price because of a subsidy. GATT agreements tend to outlaw direct export subsidies but do not normally apply to indirect subsidies.

Government Monopolies and Monopsonies. Government agencies in socialized countries may act as the sole buyer (monopsony) or the sole seller for certain products at both the domestic and import-export levels. The Soviet Union, for example, handles its international sales through Amtorg, a government trading agency.

Like a private monopolist or monopsonist, the government has price authority when acting in such capacity. Sometimes the government steps into a chaotic market situation and attempts to rationalize it by purchasing and selling the entire output of an industry. The Brazilian government, for example, sponsors the Brazilian Coffee Institute (IBC), a clearinghouse that handles all Brazil's international sales of raw coffee beans. It not only sets domestic prices but also puts Brazilian coffee into a strong market position internationally by monopolizing the world market for Brazilian coffee. Like other monopolies, however, the IBC has learned that falsely inflated prices invite competition. As a result of the monopoly-induced price increases, the coffee market has been so favorable that production was encouraged in French West Africa, Mexico, Guatemala, Indonesia, and other countries which have not historically been important producers. A few decades ago Brazil supplied approximately 80 percent of the world's coffee, but at present it sells less than 40 percent of the coffee in the world marketplace.

Monopsonistic purchasing by the government can be especially troublesome for marketers internationally. They not only have to compete with firms from many countries but also have to play by rules designed by their customers. For example, a company may not be able to vary prices on the open market to meet local situations because some countries have a rule that they will pay only the *lowest price offered to any customer anywhere*. Cutting of margins in any area may require cutting margins on all government sales.

Although nearly all the governmental price controls reviewed above are employed by the U.S. government, the American marketer will be quite impatient with the red tape and pervasive nature of price setting by most foreign governments. Price authority is a cherished prerogative of most U.S. businessmen who hate to surrender such authority when trading internationally.

International Agreements

Governments of producing and consuming countries seem to be playing an ever greater role in the establishment of international prices for certain basic commodities. There is, for example, an international coffee agreement, an international cocoa agreement, and an international sugar agreement. The world price of wheat has long been at least partially determined by negotiations between national governments. The United States is constantly taking part in

. . . conferences, councils, and study groups which are examining proposals for dealing with the problem [of commodity price fluctuation]. All have the basic aim of increasing the export earnings of the underdeveloped countries and most would accomplish this by attempting to keep commodity prices at levels higher than those of the free market. Pressure for international commodity agreements to control prices is growing among other countries.[21]

Despite all the various pressures of business, governmental, and international price agreements, most marketers still have rather wide latitude in their pricing decisions for most products and most markets.

---

[21] "Pressure Grows for Global Price Fixing," *Nation's Business*, May 1963, p. 35.

INTRACOMPANY PRICING STRATEGY

As companies increase the number of worldwide subsidiaries, joint ventures, company-owned distributing systems, and other marketing arrangements, the price charged to different affiliates becomes a pre-eminent question. Transfer prices of goods transferred from operations or sales units in one country to a company's other units elsewhere may be adjusted to achieve a variety of results which enhance the ultimate profit of the company as a whole. Three chief benefits are:

1. Lowering of duty costs, accomplished by shipping goods into high-tariff countries at minimum transfer prices so the duty base and duty will be low.
2. Reduction of income taxes in high-tax countries, achieved by over-pricing goods transferred to units in such countries; thus profits may be eliminated and shifted to low-tax countries. Such profit shifting may also be used for "dressing up" financial statements by increasing reported profits in countries where borrowing and other financing are undertaken.
3. Facilitation of dividend repatriation. When dividend repatriation is curtailed by government policy, invisible income may be taken out in the form of high prices for products or components shipped to units in that country.

The overall objectives of the intracompany pricing system include: (1) maximizing profits for the corporation as a whole, (2) facilitating parent-company control, and (3) offering management at all levels, both in the product divisions and in the international divisions, an adequate basis for maintaining, developing, and receiving credit for their own profitability. Transfer prices that are too low will be unsatisfactory to the product divisions because their overall results will look poor. Prices that are too high make the international operations look bad and limit the effectiveness of foreign managers.

Requisite to an advantageous pricing system is recognition of the complexity of the problem at hand and awareness of the wide variation in local conditions to be taken into account. Pricing policies of the parent company should be such that the international divisions maintain the ultimate market initiative and have the final profit responsibility for their operations. The systems should be simple and comprehensible so that all the participants in the decision and transfer can understand how the prices were established. Finally, the intracorporate pricing system should employ sound accounting techniques and be defensible to the tax authorities of the countries involved. All of these factors argue against a single uniform price or even a uniform pricing system for all international operations.

Four basic arrangements for pricing goods for intracompany transfer are:

1. Sales at the local manufacturing cost plus a standard markup.
2. Sales at the cost of the most efficient producer in the company plus a standard markup.

3. Sales at negotiated prices.
4. Arm's length sales using the same prices as quoted to independent customers.

Of the four, the arm's length transfer is most acceptable to tax authorities and most likely to be acceptable to foreign divisions. Again, however, it should be remembered that the appropriate basis for intracompany transfers depends on the nature of the subsidiaries and market conditions. All cost approaches are difficult to use, because cost is such a difficult element to define. Even within the firm, a company often finds it necessary to use various pricing arrangements for different sales. Sometimes inappropriate pricing policies can completely knock a product out of the market, even though it might contribute significantly to the profitability of the company as a whole.

A *Business International Research Report* gives the following example of an item with a factory cost of $100. The item is transferred to the international division at $120, with additional cost of $10 involved in the export. Assuming competition limits the international selling price to $135, the sale could well be rejected because the $5 profit only brings a 3.7 percent return on sales. The total profit to the corporation however, will be $25, or 18.5 percent *if all* the profit to the corporation were taken into account. Thus what appears to be an unprofitable sale becomes a highly profitable one when viewed from the overall corporate perspective.[22]

PRICE QUOTATIONS

In quoting the price of a good for international sale, a contract may include specific price elements that affect the price, such as those related to credit and sales terms and transportation. In quoting prices for international sale, the parties to the transaction must be certain that the quotation settled on appropriately locates responsibility for the goods during transportation and spells out who is to pay transportation charges and from what point. Three basic types of quotation, each of which has variations, are f.o.b. (free on board—various points), f.a.s. (free alongside), and c.i.f. (cost, insurance, and freight). Price quotation must also indicate whether or not the currency of the buyer or the seller or someone else is being used, and should spell out the credit terms and the type of documentation which is required. Finally, the price quotation and contract should have definitions relating to both quantity and quality. A quantity definition may be necessary, for example, because different countries use different units of measurement. In specifying a ton, for example, the contract should identify it as a metric or an English ton, and as a long or a short ton. Furthermore, there should be complete agreement on the quality standards which are to be used in evaluating the product. The international trader must be careful to review all the terms of the control, because failure to reason

---

[22] *Solving International Pricing Problems,* Business International Research Report (New York: Business International Corporation, 1965), p. 9.

with all these elements may have the effect of modifying prices even though such a change is not intended.

SUMMARY AND CONCLUSIONS

Pricing is one of the most complicated decision areas encountered by the international marketer. Rather than deal with one set of market conditions, one group of competitors, one set of cost factors, and one set of governmental regulations, the international marketer must take all these factors into account, not only for each country in which he operates, but sometimes even for each market within a country. Market prices at the consumer level are much more difficult to control in international than in domestic marketing, but the international marketer must still approach the pricing task on a basis of objectives and policy, leaving enough flexibility for tactical price movements. Pricing in the international marketplace requires a combination of intimate knowledge of market costs and regulations, infinite patience for detail, and a shrewd sense of market strategy.

READING

WHEN THE PRICE IS WRONG—BY DESIGN*

JAMES SHULMAN

Item: Hypothetical country A, revisited by acute payments problems, starts clamping down on dividend remission by local affiliates of large multinational firms. Problem: How to get that income out. Solution: Adjust upward the transfer prices of raw materials and semifinished imports from parent or related firms. Result: The high prices paid by the local affiliate produce a de facto profit repatriation. Corporate goals are satisfied; the restriction is defeated.

Or is it? There may be some question as to what or who has been defeated. But though manipulations of intracorporate transfer prices can hurt the firm and are at times more damaging to corporation–host country relations than they are worth, companies very often have recourse to them. Doing business overseas self-evidently means coping with a whole complex of variables peculiar to the international environment. And coping, the author's research reveals, is scarcely possible without continual adjustment of other than arm's length prices. In fact, transfer prices take first place as the international corporate accommodator. Whether they deserve this pride of place is, in part, the subject of

* Reprinted with permission of Pergamon Press from *Columbia Journal of World Business*, May–June, 1967, pp. 69–76.

Mr. Shulman recently spent a year as Professor of Management at IMEDE, the International Institute of Management in Lausanne, Switzerland, and his research has resulted in the planning of a book on Acquisitions and Mergers in Europe. He has also been Professor of Management at MIT's Sloan School. At present he is the Principal in his own firm of Management Consultants, headquartered in Newton, Massachusetts, which specializes in problems of General Management, Organization and Growth through Acquisition, particularly in large International Firms.

this article, which presents a rough calculus of costs and benefits and then takes a look at the kinds of adjustments management will have to introduce into control systems in order to employ the transfer pricing device effectively and painlessly.

Let us start with some examples of the use of the mechanism to cope with environmental peculiarities, irritations, and snags. Take the matter of taxes. Other things being equal, greater profits will result from shipping goods into low income-tax countries at prices which are lowered in order to raise income in such countries. And if prices of goods shipped from such nations to higher-tax countries are set high, the rate differential may result in maximizing corporate profits in both countries. It is commonly considered that the *bête noire* of taxation is the United States. In fact, however, tax rates in some countries are close to those in the United States (in some cases higher) and the tax-reducing devices available through internal pricing operate between any two countries with different rates of taxation on income. Furthermore, while we seem to think always in terms of differentials in tax rates, statutory differences in computing income subject to taxation also produce real tax differentials. For example, an identical tax rate in two countries may result in widely different real taxes if, say, the methods of allowing depreciation vary substantially, or if the degree of freedom in allocating certain kinds of expenses varies.

High Duties, Low Prices

Transfer prices are also useful in coping with import duties. A change in transfer price may cause a change in the duty, both as to amount and rate. (Given a fixed rate of duty, the higher the value of goods, the higher the import tax. But, in addition, differences in value may subject goods to different rates of duty. For example, a high price may invoke a luxury rate.) Therefore, it adds to a company's profit to send goods at low prices into countries with high rates of duty. It may also be advantageous to ship raw or semiprocessed goods at high prices into countries with low import tax rates. Such considerations affect the source of the end product so long as production processes may be performed on transferred materials equally well, and at no cost differential, in two or more countries with different rates of import taxes.

Adjusting transfer prices for the effects of import or income taxes is a delicate balancing act. For example, the higher the import tax assessed to the importer, the lower the profit remaining as a basis for income taxes. Since there is virtually no coordination of the two revenue-collecting departments in any country, the income-tax collecting branch may be unduly exercised. An added difficulty results from the attempt of the parent to balance the extra cost of duty resulting from a high import price paid by its affiliate against the lower income taxes that the affiliate will be charged with, as well as the potentially higher income taxes that the exporting affiliate may be required to remit.

Another use of transfer prices is in dealing with inflationary tendencies. When goods are shipped into a country suffering from rapidly increasing prices, corporate management must consider to what extent their prices should reflect costs as expressed in the currency of the shipping country or as reflected in that of the recipient nation. Conversely, when goods are shipped out of the latter at highly inflated costs, they may bear no relation to prices prevailing in the country of receipt, and a competitive disadvantage may affect the shipper. Transfer prices may be adjusted to counterbalance the disparate consequences of fluctuating currencies.

We have already touched on how transfer pricing can blunt the effects of controls on dividends remittances (such as exist, for example in Israel and several South American nations). This method serves in other instances of economic restrictions as well. Some governments, in an effort to increase manufacturing activity locally, impose restrictions on the number and kinds of components which may be imported into their country for further processing or assembly into a larger unit. In a study of the automotive industry in Mexico, G. S. Edelberg describes the systematic actions taken by the Mexican government to force United States manufacturers to ship fewer components, thereby causing more parts to be manufactured by local sources of supply.[1] In this case the parent corporation counteracted the restrictive rules of the Mexican government by attaching the mark-up previously connected with forbidden components to permissible imports, thus maintaining its *status quo ante* with respect to total United States income from exported components.

Hedge against Instability

Additional problems arise from unstable governments. When a company operates in a country that regularly changes government, it is in its interest to keep as little cash as possible in that country. The nationalistic feelings which often accompany a revolutionary regime further endanger the assets of foreign businesses and raise the likelihood of expropriation. The fact that a government has been in power for many years is not always a cause for confidence. Cuba and Nigeria are two cases in point: in both comparatively stable governments (one of them of long standing) were overthrown, much to the shock of those managements which were not sensitive to local politics, and were not prepared to deal with the consequences of revolution.

In such environments, low prices on transfers out of the country can facilitate transmittal of excess cash, since exports at low prices tend to reduce cash flowing into such countries. High prices on imports have the same effect. Drastic changes in transfer prices may not go unnoticed in such countries, but a planned policy can be implemented to minimize the risks in unstable areas. Managers who use this device subject themselves to the increased income taxes in the country of export, but at least, they say, what remains after taxes is safe from expropriation and other foreign risks.

[1] G. S. Edelberg, "The Procurement Practices of the Mexican Affiliates of Selected United States Automobile Firms," unpublished doctoral thesis, Harvard Business School, June 1963.

Charging Off the Parent's Costs

A final restriction is that imposed on deductions from local taxable income for expenses incurred and services performed outside the country but for the benefit of the local company. Thus, for example, head office expenses such as administrative and general, R & D, marketing, and other costs may not be charged to the parent's subsidiaries in Venezuela, if the services are performed (as they usually are) elsewhere; while in another country, a firm could not remit royalties. In such cases, costs may be recouped by increases in the transfer prices of the goods shipped to the foreign subsidiary. But if the foreign government suspects the compensating use of transfer prices, local managements will be forced to devote time and effort to justify their actions to government officials.

Careful manipulation of transfer prices can bolster an affiliate's credit status. Many international companies allocate only a fixed sum for investment in a foreign country. For funds required over the fixed sum, such companies borrow money locally. The "voluntary" program initiated by the United States Government in recent years to stem the outflow of dollars and to redress the United States balance of payments has forced United States affiliates to seek further local funds for expansion and other needs. Even though the parent's credit may be pledged to secure loans in such host countries, it still behooves the foreign division to demonstrate earning power so as to satisfy the earnings criteria required by foreign lenders.

The initial operations of a new venture in any country are bound to result in heavy start-up expenses, and to suffer losses before full capacity can be achieved and start-up expenses amortized. Sometimes such losses may continue for a period of years under normal operating circumstances. If goods are shipped into such a foreign division at low prices, start-up losses may be either reduced or eliminated.[2]

Lift for the Balance Sheet

The use of low transfer prices on imports gives the foreign enterprise the appearance of a sounder balance sheet. In some cases foreign lenders may be presented with profitable operating expenses almost from the start, rendering them more willing to advance needed capital to the subsidiary. On the other hand, the effect upon foreign divisional managers may be to foster a false sense of accomplishment in getting a new venture off to a profitable start, while at the same time the exporting company must endure the consequences of shipping goods out at unrealistically low prices.

Transfer prices may be used to strengthen the competitive position of a company, or to control or weaken the competitive position of others in a foreign environment. In the case of extractive industries, where an oligopoly controls worldwide materials supplies, it is possible for such companies to manipulate the price levels at which competitive com-

---

[2] A side effect is the corresponding reduction of income and hence taxes in the shipping division.

panies enter the field for further processing and marketing. In the case of integrated petroleum companies, for example, it seems apparent that producers enjoy substantial profit on the raw product.[3] When competing refiners and refining divisions of the producing company enter the market at this stage, their raw-materials costs have already provided a large measure of profit to the producers (or to the producing division). The small spread remaining in refining, processing and marketing tends to leave the producers in control of final market prices for finished products throughout the world.

Transfer price adjustments also come in handy in dealing with joint-venture partners. Only a few countries (chiefly Japan, Pakistan, and India) insist that foreign-based companies invite local investors to participate in their ventures. Almost without exception, western corporations that wish to operate divisions in those countries share capital participation with nationals. In some instances, participation is confined to a public stock issue; in others, participants may be individuals or corporations with substantial financial investments. For numerous reasons, some companies may desire partnerships in countries of operation, whether or not the host government requires such participation.

Whatever the motivation for the joint-venture setup, parent and local participant, however amicable their overall dealings, must look forward to a certain degree of conflict. It is to the parent's advantage to value goods shipped to joint-venture partnerships at high prices so as to place the lion's share of the profits with the wholly owned shipper. On the other hand, the partners are desirous of low prices, to maximize their own income. D. T. Brash states, in connection with joint ventures in Australia, "the American company has an obvious incentive to charge the maximum price feasible if the subsidiary is jointly owned. Some tendency to charge jointly owned companies more for imports than would be charged to wholly owned companies probably does operate."[4] In such instances, it appears probable that transfer pricing is subject to formal arm's-length bargaining and is not the object of control by central management.

Substitute for the Tax Haven

Finally, the closing of United States tax loopholes has stimulated greater interest in transfer pricing. Until 1962, many United States companies owned subsidiaries in tax-haven countries. As long as these affiliates did not repatriate earnings to the United States, they were not subject to United States income tax. Thus they could accumulate corporate funds for reinvestment in any part of the world, serving in effect

---

[3] The reasons behind this fact are many and complex, and have little relevance to this discussion. For a discussion of petroleum pricing and associated problems see, for example: H. J. Frank, *Crude Oil Prices in the Middle East* (New York: Frederick A. Praeger, Inc., 1965); W. Leeman, *The Price of Middle East Oil* (Ithaca, N.Y.: Cornell University Press, 1962); P. Frankel, *Oil: The Facts of Life* (London, Oxford Press, 1962).

[4] D. T. Brash, "United States Investment in Australian Manufacturing Industry," unpublished doctoral thesis, Australian National University, August 1965.

as bankers to a multinational corporation's worldwide divisions. Since the Revenue Act of 1962 just about wiped out these tax havens, it has been more appealing to use transfer prices as a means of providing needed funds wherever management directs. The last two years of the dollar-saving activity of the United States Government have made this method all the more reasonable for United States companies that prefer not to repatriate and then reexport funds.

Here's the Rub

So much for the advantages of transfer-price manipulation. The list is impressive, but since space is short, by no means exhaustive. There are, however, concomitant disadvantages to the corporation, of both an external and internal nature.

External problems arise when government tax authorities—in both investing and host countries—take exception to corporate efforts to reduce the tax burden, and counterattack. And this is by no means rare. Although international auditing is still relatively new, American government auditors are familiar with corporate tax-minimizing practices and foreign auditors are expanding their awareness of these tactics. Both are taking steps to invalidate the long-standing advantages of corporate tax practitioners. In other words, tax minimization by corporations runs head-on into the tax maximizing of government treasury departments.

Another type of external problem arises when multinational corporations are subject to close scrutiny by labor unions. In Italy, for example, labor unions have the right of access to company books and records in order to audit an employer's ability to raise wages. In Germany and France, labor unions are permitted to place a representative on the corporate board of directors, the only difference being that in France the representative sits without a voice. The results of artificial pricing, then, may be subject to scrutiny by parties with interests opposed to those of the firm.

The form of foreign corporate organization could also cause more public scrutiny than any corporation may be prepared to accept. For example, in Germany, public companies with many stockholders are organized as *Aktien Gesellschaften* (joint-stock companies). Stockholders of this type of corporation are entitled to detailed corporate reports, and under certain conditions may sue a corporation for operating errors. When a corporation has only a few partners, it will at times reorganize as a *Gesellschaft mit beschrankter Haftung* (limited-liability company), whose operating results do not have to be published in as great detail.

Then there is the antitrust headache. The widespread impact of pricing decisions on consumers and on competition is of great interest to the United States Justice Department, which seeks to enforce statutes forbidding price discrimination against users and competitors. We have suggested ways in which transfer prices affect competitive posture. It is not difficult, either, to perceive the consequences of pricing decisions on outside customers of the firms. Internal prices that are established for one or more purposes described above may be very different from prices charged to unrelated customers, and the side effects may be discriminatory to suppliers and users outside the company.

Internal Is More Important

Without seeking to minimize these external difficulties, it can be argued that by far the most serious problems raised by transfer-pricing practices are internal in nature. Whenever management tampers with transfer prices it is adulterating the corporate control-system inputs. Adulterated inputs lead to adulterated outputs. If the control system is to provide meaningful outputs, some adjustments must be made to compensate for the aberrations, resulting from pricing changes.

In one company, when price reductions result from headquarters changes, local budgets are adjusted to compensate for these changes. It would appear, then, that the original agreed transfer prices are guaranteed for control purposes. In most instances, the new price charged to the division will change its local income statement, but records of changes are kept at headquarters for control purposes. In effect, dual sets of books are maintained. One is for local public consumption and tax purposes, while the other is kept for internal measurement and evaluation.

At another firm, headquarters also adjusts for price differentials imposed from above. The international financial officer maintains local income statements and records the adjustments required to compensate the control system. This is also a dual bookkeeping system. The responsible officer admitted that this is a bothersome and expensive operation, but he claimed that it is appropriate under the circumstances and is amply justified by the resultant savings.

Overseas Can't Be Ignored

Of course, this opinion reflects the views of a corporate officer who devises and administers the transfer-pricing systems. Since in the course of his research, the author did not conduct interviews with overseas managers, he cannot report specific personal attitudes or perceived reactions of such individuals. However, it seems that headquarters personnel does attempt to take into account the needs of overseas personnel. And even if they should be disposed to ignore these needs, modern management methods, coupled with today's speedy communication and easy intercontinental travel, make regular interpersonal contacts among management personnel an integral part of corporate life.

While this communication undoubtedly affects headquarters plans and decisions, the author has been able to analyze only the secondary results of the contacts. However, a closer look at overseas reactions and perceptions is obtainable in a somewhat more direct manner. Since it is not uncommon in some firms to practice rotation among foreign divisional personnel, some officials now employed at international headquarters have at one time worked as overseas line managers. The reactions expressed by these individuals, though by no means definitive, may indicate the kinds of interpersonal problems generated by transfer-pricing arrangements.

In the case of a company whose highly directive transfer-pricing system causes a disproportionate share of income to arise overseas, its international managers are sometimes tempted to boast about their "contributions" to corporate profits at periodic meetings of corporate executives. The fact that their profits are in effect allocated rather than earned does not deter their proprietary self-glorification, much to the frustration of domestic managers, not to mention the dismay of headquarters executives.

In all companies whose transfer prices are a function of environmental influences, some method of adjustment is used to give appropriate credit to divisions for their real contribution. The method may be credit-backs, or "dual" sets of books, or some other form of memorandum allowance, or compensation in budgets and profit plans. But regardless of the intent, "some things get lost in the wash," and dissensions result in dysfunctional upsets among all such firms at one time or another. It is a rare manager who waits patiently for a headquarters controller to adjust for profit or costs which are put out of line by headquarters directives. In one company the United Kingdom division was directed to lower its price to a new French subsidiary so as to improve start-up operating results; but a good deal of ill-feeling was generated when headquarters seemed to forget that the resulting poor performance in the United Kingdom was not at all a reflection of local management failure.

"But I'm Subsidizing Him!"

When freedom to purchase and sell outside are sharply limited, divisional managers chafe for two reasons. First, they feel they are being discriminated against by having to overpay to help out a fellow division. Second, they complain because higher internal costs may at times reduce total corporate profit. If headquarters seems too cavalier about corporate profits, local-management frustrations may cause unfortunate attitudes and action in the field. In those companies that present a uniform price to the world, the managers of more efficient plants sometimes complain of having virtually to subsidize less efficient members by reason of their own economies.

These kinds of reactions are sometimes evident in purely domestic operations, but for the most part the far-reaching influence of the multinational environment, when coupled with differences in national temperament and cultural backgrounds, causes complaints of a more serious nature than those that arise in a single country operation.

The establishment and operation of a functional control system to measure, evaluate, and motivate management in purely domestic surroundings is difficult enough by itself. In the case of multinational companies, however, the need for feasible control systems is rendered more urgent by the additional complexities of the larger environment. Many executives emphasize the relatively low degree of confidence placed in foreign managers of his company in the Near East and in Latin America. Other executives emphasize that the risks in international business are larger in number and different in kind than in the domestic environment. Regardless of the risks, however, there is wide recognition among managers that the rewards of the international environment—at least to date—have offered ample incentive to business corporations to expand extensively throughout the world. Nevertheless, any actions that affect the control mechanism are likely to be dangerous to the firm engaged in multinational business. And when adaptations to new conditions cause alterations in an existing system, management must ponder whether it is merely substituting one problem for another.

Accordingly, a successful transfer-pricing method in multinational business is one that does not cause destructive changes in the existing control system. If it threatens to do this, adequate adjustments must be devised to compensate for the changes and keep the system operational.

The Costs of Adulteration

If transfer prices have to be recast in response to changes in cost-of-production inputs, the control system, such as it is, ought not to be changed. If it has been providing useful information in the first place, it will now reflect the new conditions (the causes or inputs) as well as the resultant changes (the effects or outputs). But when a transfer price change is introduced in order to counteract, or take advantage of, circumstances external to the usual routine, then the system will reflect results that are not necessarily the result of the operations it is designed to measure. And if the measurements are wrong, decisions made on the basis of these calculations are also likely to be wrong.

Some Broad Criteria

I consider the three basic requirements of measurement, evaluation, and motivation to be so vital to the promotion of corporate effectiveness that changes in the control system which may react at cross purposes to these requirements should not be tolerated. My recommendation, then, is that the transfer pricing system must be compatible with the operational goals of the control system, and must reinforce its regulatory functions. But when external conditions are of such substance that they either expose the firm to grave threats or make available opportunities for material gains, then the transfer price system may be revamped to facilitate greater return to the firm. The magnitude of threat or gain is of relevance to the proposal, since one should not disturb control systems for every minor circumstance. Under such a practice, systems would soon cease to operate effectively. In each firm, criteria should be established for selection (or elimination) of matters worthy of serious consideration.

Quantitative limits would point up the particular relevance in each case. For example, one might use as measures a relative or absolute profit contribution, or a change in market share. Appropriate measures should be apparent in each case. Qualitative rules also have to be established, although they do not lend themselves to precise measurements. For example, one might consider interpersonal effects among managers (at all levels), reaction of public opinion, or changes in attitude of host or parent governments, to mention just a few. And again, the special conditions in each firm and its environment would dictate the criteria.

In proposing what may be thought of as a flexible approach to transfer pricing in multinational business, the author is at the same time rejecting a simplistic approach to the problems. By this I refer to two extremes of practice. I regard the philosophy which attempts to control too many variables with a single, inadequate principle as too extreme. I also regard a willingness to tinker incessantly with transfer prices to be equally simplistic. Incessant adjustment to the changing world without quantitative or qualitative tests represents too mechanistic and narrow an approach in a highly complex and dynamic world environment.

QUESTIONS

1. Define:

Turnover tax	Administered pricing
Dumping	Agreement
Countervailing duty	Cartel
Full cost	Combine
Subsidy	Monopsony
R.P.M.	C.i.f.
T.V.A.	

2. Why is it so difficult to control consumer prices when selling overseas?

3. Explain the concept of "price escalation" and tell why it can mislead an international marketer.

4. What are the causes of price escalation? Do they differ for exports and goods produced and sold in a foreign country?

5. Why is it seldom feasible for a company to absorb the high cost of international transportation and reduce the net price received?

6. "Regardless of the strategic factors involved and the company's orientation to market pricing, every price must be set with cost considerations in mind." Discuss.

7. "Price fixing by business is not generally viewed as an acceptable procedure (at least in the domestic market); but when governments enter the field of price administration, they presume to do it for the general welfare to lessen the effects of 'destructive' competition." Discuss.

8. Differentiate between cumulative turnover tax and noncumulative turnover tax.

9. Do turnover taxes discriminate against imported goods?

10. Explain specific tariffs, ad valorem tariffs, and combination tariffs.

11. How can an international marketer protect himself from exchange-rate fluctuations?

12. Explain the effects of indirect competition and how it may be overcome.

13. Cartels seem to rise phoenixlike after they have been destroyed. Why are they so appealing to business?

14. Develop a cartel policy for the United States.

15. Discuss the various ways in which governments set prices. Why do they engage in such activities?

16. Discuss the alternative objectives possible in setting prices for intra-company sales.

17. Why are costs so difficult to assess in marketing internationally?

Reading

1. Review the various types of advantages a company may gain by shifting internal transfer prices.

2. What problems do intracompany price manipulations cause?

OUTLINE OF CHAPTER 19

ADVERTISING ABROAD

INTRODUCTION

Perhaps advertising is the side of international marketing with the greatest similarities from country to country throughout the world. Paradoxically, despite its many similarities, it may also be credited with the greatest number of unique problems in international marketing. The basic framework and concepts of international advertising are essentially those that are employed in domestic advertising. Although seldom thought of in this light, advertising may be one of the most important cultural exports the United States has ever developed. World advertising is patterned very much on the American advertising approach and system. American agencies are deeply involved in international advertising, and nearly every large U.S. agency has at least one office or cooperating agency in another country. In many of the more developed countries of the world, a review of the top 10 advertising agencies in a given country would reveal that 3 to 5 of the agencies are either American owned or controlled. Such names as McCann-Erickson and J. Walter Thompson are everyday terms in the advertising vernacular throughout the world.

A review of world advertising activities is somewhat like a review of advertising in the United States. Advertising in underdeveloped countries resembles American advertising at the end of the 19th century. In the more highly developed countries, advertising activities more closely parallel American advertising of recent decades. In one sense, however, this analogy does not hold exactly true. Nearly all countries, regardless of their stage of development, are further advanced (through the importation of American advertising techniques) than was the United States at a similar stage of growth. The quality of international advertising is amazingly high and, in certain kinds of advertising, countries other than the United States are probably preeminent: cinema advertising and poster advertising are major examples of media which are less highly developed in the United States than in other countries.

Advertising is a crucial element in the integrated foreign marketing plan. Advertising trade magazines are full of stories relating the successes and failures of advertising in attempting to cope with vastly different markets. Advertising, as well as every other area of marketing, follows basic principles but requires modification for international markets.

Besides an analysis of the scope and scale of international advertising, this chapter reviews some of the problems and areas of challenge for the international marketer. Basic creative strategy as part of the communication process is a fundamental area of inquiry. Organizational arrangements are reviewed, and special attention is paid to international advertising media.

VOLUME OF WORLD ADVERTISING

Figures developed by the International Advertising Association, the American Association of Advertising Agencies, and *Advertising Age* magazine seem to indicate that advertising expenditures throughout the world are growing at the rate of approximately 5 percent per year. Lawrence Bernard, international editor of an advertising magazine, comments that "the world's important advertising nations—Britain, Germany, Japan, France, and many others—report advertising vigor is keeping pace and is frequently ahead of national economic growth." In the case of Japan, the growth has been little short of phenomenal (see Exhibit 19–1). As Exhibit 19–2 shows, the United States is still ahead

EXHIBIT 19–1

Japan's Advertising Growth

Year	Amount (in billions)	Year	Amount (in billions)
1960	$483	1965	$ 955
1961	586	1966	1,064
1962	676	1967	1,276
1963	828	1968	1,478
1964	969	1970*	2,000

* Estimated.
Source: Dentsu Advertising.

of all other countries in terms of aggregate dollar expenditures for advertising, both as a percentage of gross national product and in dollar expenditures per capita. Because expenditures by countries outside the United States amount to substantially 11 billion, however, it is obvious why the past five years have seen a tremendous growth of interest in international advertising on the part of American agencies.

The magnitude of dollar expenditures for advertising throughout the world can hardly reflect advertising's even greater social impact. Advertising is changing communication customs and habits in nearly all countries. In localities where television and other commercial media are not available, there is a continuing clamor for the development of such media. The development of mass communications broadens the local conceptions of the world and of political affairs and may be of major importance in influei cing and speeding cultural, political, and economic

EXHIBIT 19–2

Leading Nations in Advertising

Country	Advertising Volume ($ billions)		1968 Pop. (millions)	1968 GNP (billions)	Advertising Volume	
	1970*	1968			as % of GNP	Per Capita
United States.........	$20,500	$18,350	200	$830	2.21	$92.0
West Germany.......	2,900	2,152	60	127	1.69	36.0
Great Britain.........	2,100	1,705	56	116	1.47	30.0
Japan...............	2,000	1,478	100	123	1.20	14.0
Canada.............	1,100	902	21	61	1.48	43.0
France.............	1,100	890	50	121	0.73	18.0
Italy...............	650	550	53	71	0.77	10.0
Sweden.............	485	418	8	27	1.55	52.0
Switzerland..........	460	405	6	17	2.38	67.5
Australia.............	455	385	12	28	1.37	32.0
Netherlands..........	420	285	13	24	1.19	22.0
Spain...............	318	276	33	28	0.99	8.0
Mexico.............	315	240	47	26	0.92	5.0

* Estimated by author.
Source: Estimates by authors, and *Advertising Age*.

integration. Many countries which but a few years ago had one or a few magazines now have many. Numerous nations which had no or only one television or radio network have within the past few years developed several. The development of mass advertising media is also important in the development of international markets. In many areas of the world, people have income with which to buy products, but these potential consumers have not been part of the world market because they lacked information about available products.

Although mass communications have improved markedly in the past few years, a UNESCO study indicates that advertisers are still without adequate media alternatives in many parts of the world. The study shows, for example, that some two billion persons residing in 100 countries lack adequate communications facilities. Africa is cited as an example where 19 countries have no daily press, and where newspaper circulation is only 1 per hundred persons as compared to 50 per hundred in the United Kingdom. On the basis of per capita advertising expenditures and of recent growth patterns, it is apparent that nearly all nations can anticipate further advertising expansion.

OVERALL STRATEGY

Creativity and versatility are key concepts in developing the creative strategy for an international advertising campaign. Advertising functions essentially as a communication medium; as such, it must provide the flexibility required to communicate effectively in situations which may change from country to country, from time to time, and from product to product.

BOX 19–1

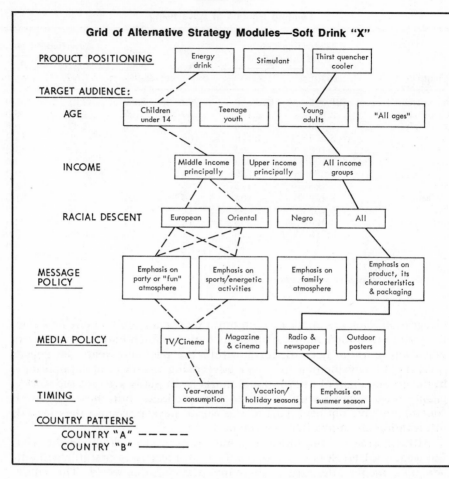

The creative strategy must be firmly grounded in market analysis. Such analysis provides the advertiser with clues as to the homogeneity or degree of segmentation of the market in which he is operating. Once the market is understood, a basic strategy can be formulated. Strategy decisions include considerations related to the use of a single international campaign or a series of individual campaigns tailored to meet market variations. Questions of frequency of advertising, volume of advertising, and media usage also are based on analysis of market information. Company considerations loom large in the market strategy and include such considerations as the level of market penetration desired, the speed of return, the degree of national coverage desired, and the company's competitive position. It is the international advertising manager's job to integrate all of the market and company factors into a coherent advertising strategy.

Two International Ad Approaches

This rather oversimplified grid, says Arthur Stridsberg, outlines advertising alternatives from which the managers in foreign markets can choose local strategy. Centrally-developed materials and strategies in many combinations are available, but international uniformity is maintained. Advantages include flexibility to change strategies on short notice, elimination of erratic results and duplication of effort, less burden on the local manager to handle his advertising, and a generally higher level of creative standards.

Thus, a manager in country "A" might establish that his best potential lies in selling "Brand X" to children under 14 as an energy drink; that purchasing power is vested chiefly in middle income families; and that while the families are mostly oriental, European behavior is admired and emulated strongly. The product would be consumed in connection with activities requiring energy either sports or parties. The children could best be reached via tv and cinema commercials, and while consumption is somewhat higher during summer and vacations, the children could best be reached via advertising beamed to them year-round.

The manager in country "B" might find that, selling the same drink, his greatest potential lies in emphasis on its role as a cooler and thirst quencher for young adults of all income and racial groups, and that its consumption does not depend on strenuous activities or parties. It is drunk at any time, almost any place, putting the advertising emphasis on the product rather than the consumption circumstances. The way the drink is consumed—and heavy consumption during the hot summer period—make radio and newspaper a more effective combination than other media, and obviously the time for greatest campaign weight is mid-year.

Both managers could obtain guidance and probably complete materials for their advertising from central headquarters, in effect two completely different advertising campaigns but not contradictory in their impact. Central control is maintained, but the needs of the local markets are not sacrificed to any attempt at absolute uniformity.

Source: Reprinted with permission from the June 17, 1968, issue of *Advertising Age*, p. 108. Copyright 1968 by Advertising Publications Inc.

One advertising executive suggests six guideposts to international creative strategy. They are as follows: (1) establish a firm policy on the degree of uniformity best suited to the company needs; (2) look for common denominators, not differences; (3) make maximum use of local marketing and creative talents; (4) permit local advertising management to appeal guidepost No. 1 if necessary; (5) do not inhibit creative people; (6) develop a criterion for measuring the creativity and effectiveness of advertising.[1]

Publicity should not be overlooked as an important element of the creative strategy. An advertising budget can often be stretched significantly by the use of well-written, well-placed company and product

---

[1] Norton B. Leo, "Creative Strategy for International Advertising," in N. S. Watson Dunn (ed.), *International Handbook of Advertising* (New York: McGraw-Hill Book Company, Inc., 1964), p. 193.

publicity. Foreign publications, particularly business publications, are often understaffed; when an editor is given a carefully structured press release or other press information there is fairly high probability of its being used.

COMPETITIVE ROLE OF ADVERTISING

The strategic role of advertising in the marketing program varies from time to time, place to place, and company to company. Advertising is but one element of the promotional mix, and promotion is but one element of the marketing mix. The potential cost and accomplishment of advertising must be weighed against the cost and benefits which might be gained by focusing on other elements of the promotional or marketing program.

Advertising can be most effective in a nation with well-developed advertising facilities and a market that responds to this kind of stimulation. Like any other strategic weapon, advertising should be used only when it can economically and effectively contribute to the attainment of a corporate goal. Because a certain type of advertising works in one foreign market does not necessarily mean that it will be effective in another. As shown in this chapter, advertising conditions differ greatly in various markets.

Companies are learning that advertising plays an increasingly important role in maintaining competitive position in foreign markets. Furthermore, the increasing sophistication of the foreign consumer and the presence of competition from *many* countries place great emphasis on the role of advertising. Not too many years ago, American firms had a distinct advantage in that they had extensive experience with mass media advertising. Marketers in most other countries lacked such experience, but today the advertising business itself has grown so extensively that advertisers from all countries (including less developed countries) have picked up American know-how in advertising and have become formidable competitors.

The international marketer must clearly define his advertising objectives and ultimate marketing goals. If the goals are couched in terms of market share, as they often are in the United States, sufficient advertising must be budgeted to provide for achievement of that position. One foreign advertising agency executive has complained that American firms scale their advertising budgets to the size of their sales rather than to the size of the market. He has scored the false economy of American advertisers who think that everything should be cheaper in other countries of the world; the reverse is often true, because foreign markets are harder to reach and have less well-developed media. Adequate coverage may be extremely expensive.

One other interesting sidelight on the competitive aspect of advertising is that in countries where advertising media are inadequate, advertising time and space are not readily available. In these countries, there is even active competition for advertising coverage per se.

CREATIVE CHALLENGES

The growing intensity of international competition coupled with the complexity of marketing multinationality demand that the international advertiser function at the highest level of his creativity. High-level competition comes from an increasing number of sources. In the decades since World War II, advertisers from all around the world have developed their skills and abilities to the point that American firms have lost much of the advantage of having unique advertising skills. Examination of advertisements from different countries reveals a basic similarity, which in turn suggests the growing level of sophistication. To complicate matters even further, the international advertiser must deal with a host of limitations prescribing the boundaries of his creativity. Some of these are company policy, legal, language, cultural, media, production, and cost limitations.

The advertising man must overcome all of these limitations, but he also may have to do a major selling job to convince his company or client that he is going in the right direction. When Qantas, the Australian airline, wanted to sell some used Boeing 707–138B jets in the United States, the advertising agency suggested using a theme that they were "flown only on Sundays by little old pilots from Pasadena" but reportedly had great difficulty selling the ad to people in Australia who had never heard of the little old lady from Pasadena and couldn't get the connection. Ultimately the ad ran and was extremely successful.

Company Policy Limitations

A multinational advertiser helps establish the environment for creativity through its basic advertising policies. Every area of advertising activity needs basic policies. At a minimum, they should cover:

1. Centralized or decentralized authority for the advertising program.
2. Use of single or multiple foreign or domestic agencies.
3. Appropriation and allocation procedures.
4. Copy
5. Media
6. Research

All other areas which are generally covered by policy statements in domestic advertising situations should also be governed by policy statements in foreign operations. One of the most widely debated areas of international advertising policy pertains to the degree of advertising variation which will be used in advertising from country to country. A few years ago the generally accepted view was that advertising had to be customized for each individual country (and in some cases, even regions within a country). Some companies insist that every country is a special problem and should be treated as such. Executives in such companies argue that the only way to achieve adequate and relevant advertising ability is to develop separate campaigns for every country. Such individual treatment seems to be passing out of popularity, largely because of the extreme cost involved in such a program. Although almost no companies argue for completely standardized ads from country to country, most seem to be taking the position that a basic theme should be developed. Erik Elinder, a Swedish advertising executive, comments that

Ladies of London, Oslo, Stockholm, Berlin, Paris, Rome, and Madrid wear exactly the same type of shoe, often manufactured by the same maker or designed by the same designer. Is there any reason why these shoes produced by an international market should not be presented to an international population through an internationally designed advertising that varies from country to country?[2]

The successful Esso "tiger in the tank" campaign was translated and exported intact. Record sales have been rung up because of the slogans *Pack'den Tiger in den Tank* (West Germany), *Stop 'n Tijger in uw Tank* (Netherlands), *Mettez un tigre dans voltre moteur* (France) and *Netti un tigre nel motore* (Italy). In France and Italy "motor" was used because there is no directly translatable word for "tank."

Most companies with long experience in international advertising have found that the question of standardization or modification depends more on the basic existing motivation patterns than on varied geography. Advertising must be related to motivation; if people in different markets buy similar products for significantly different reasons, then obviously the advertising campaigns should be reoriented to these reasons. When the various markets react best to similar stimuli, then it would be unwise to vary the stimulus just for the sake of variation. In most instances, since the purchase motivations are similar for a given product, the majority of companies follow a compromise course. They attempt to maintain the basic elements or basic message and provide only language translation and other minor advertising changes. Even cultural barriers may be transcended if basic purchase motivations are similar. The creator of Maidenform's "Dream" advertisements says they

have been running in every corner of the globe for 15 years with absolutely no change except translation. And yet, when we began this, you never heard such a barrage of protests . . . "We don't show people like that," and "they don't understand your dreams." You wouldn't believe what else we were told. Suffice it to say that the advertisements have run successfully every place after proper translation.[3]

Pepsi-Cola advertises in dozens of countries, yet its policy allows variation in specific detail to suit local market conditions. Certain elements of Pepsi advertising remain constant, whether in Africa, Europe, or South America: the Pepsi-Cola logotype, the basic color combination, the Pepsi crown, and fundamental point-of-purchase units such as illuminated plastic signs, metal tackers, brand signs, etc.

Chesebrough-Pond's largest selling international product is Angel Face pressed powder, which sells in some 30 countries. According to the

---

[2] Erik Elinder at the Fourth Biannual European Conference of the International Advertising Association.

[3] Norman B. Norman, *Problems and Opportunities in Multi-National Advertising* (New York: American Association of Advertising Agencies, April 22, 1965), p. 11.

company's advertising vice president, "We like Chesebrough-Pond's to have a uniform image, to look the same everywhere, and this includes advertising." Despite this policy, the company is not inflexible, and when the pressed powder was introduced in the United States, the initial advertising was educational, promoting a "spillproof" theme. This primary demand emphasis predominated for six or seven years; then a heavier stress was placed on glamour. The earlier primary demand approach was used somewhat later in developing international markets. In summary, contemporary thinking on the subject seems to be that international advertising campaigns should be modified from country to country only when absolutely necessary.

Legal and Tax Considerations

In some countries advertising is more closely regulated than in others, requiring modification of the creative approach from country to country. Laws pertaining to advertising may restrict the amount spent on advertising, the media used, the type of product which may be advertised, the manner in which price may be advertised, the type of copy approach and illustration material which may be used, and other aspects of the advertising program. In Germany, for example, it is against the law to use comparative terminology or even to imply that another product is inferior. A German advertiser cannot say that his soap gets clothes cleaner than does any other soap, because the statement implies that other products do not get clothes as clean as the advertised product. Direct comparison, as between automobile A and automobile B, is strictly forbidden even when brand names are not used. Advertisers live under the threat of immediate lawsuit from competitors if they claim that their brand is best. One German agency executive comments that, "Pharmaceutical advertising is almost impossible; nearly everything is prohibited." Similar restrictions exist in most European countries. In Italy even common words like deodorant and perspiration are banned from television.

Some countries have special taxes which apply to advertising and which might restrict creative freedom in media selection. By way of illustration, until recently the United Kingdom had an 11 percent tax on TV billings, and it has a wide variety of taxes on outdoor advertising. France has an across-the-board advertising service tax of 8.5 percent on commissions and has a number of other special advertising taxes. The tax structure in Austria probably best shows how advertising taxation can distort media choice by changing the cost ratios of various media. In federal states, with the exception of Bergenland and Tyrol, there is a 10 percent ad tax on ad insertions. For posters there is a 10–30 percent tax, according to state and municipality. On radio advertising there is 10 percent tax; however, in Tyrol it is 20 percent, while in Salzburg, Steiermark, Karnten, and Voralbert, there is no tax. There is a uniform tax of 10 percent throughout the country on television. Cinema advertising has a 10 percent tax in Vienna, 20 percent tax in Bergenland, and 30 percent tax in Steiermark. There is no tax in the other federal states.

The Monopolies Commission in England has accused Procter & Gamble and Unilever of creating a monopoly (duopoly?) situation by spending nearly one fourth of their revenues on advertising; incidentally, the companies were also criticized for earning too much. Legislation for new taxes and restrictions on advertising is introduced, and some of it is passed, nearly every year in countries like the United States, Canada, India, and the United Kingdom, which have traditionally imposed minimal restrictions on advertising and free competition. In international advertising, the advertiser will encounter a host of other legal restraints. Most troubles lie, perhaps, in the variations between countries in interpretation of what constitutes acceptable honest advertising. What is completely acceptable in one country may be deemed false and misleading in another.

Language Limitations

Language is one of the chief barriers to effective communication through advertising. The problem involves not only the different languages in different countries or even different languages within one country, but also the subtler problems of linguistic nuance and vernacular.

Incautious handling of language has caused problems for all kinds of companies in nearly every country. Some automotive examples suffice. Chrysler Corp. was nearly laughed out of Spain when it copied the U.S. theme advertising, "Dart is Power." To the Spanish the phrase implied that buyers lack but are seeking sexual vigor. Ford foundered on the linguistic problems of number; in many languages the word company is plural rather than singular, as in English. "Ford Have Something for It" trumpeted one headline in English. American Motors has had its problems too. The advertising manager for Honeywell in Germany wrote of a Rambler ad, "I've been reading the copy over and over again—it does not make sense. Rambler ran into the same trap most U.S. companies run into when they think of using translated U.S. copy. Instead of translating, it needs rewriting in the new language."

Low literacy in many countries seriously impedes communications and calls for greater creativity and use of verbal media. Illiteracy severely limits the size of the market that can be reached through print media. Turkey, for example, has a literacy rate of approximately 25 percent; an advertiser attempting to reach a large segment of the population, then, is forced to utilize radio advertising. Multiple languages within a country or advertising area provide another problem for the advertiser. Even a tiny country like Switzerland has three separate languages. The melting-pot character of the Israeli population accounts for some 50 different languages. A Jerusalem commentator says that even though Hebrew "has become a negotiable instrument of daily speech, this has yet to be converted into advertising idiom."[4]

Language translation encounters innumerable barriers which impede

---

[4] See also the article in Chapter 8 titled "The Language Barrier."

BOX 19–2

Adman's Dilemma in Luxembourg: How to Write Ads in Spoken Tongue?

A former journalist, the thin, thirtyish adman got into the agency field after a friend asked him to write some copy in Luxembourgish. "This was very difficult," said Mr. Binsfeld. "Very difficult, since in Luxembourg we have no written langauge."

"No written language?"

"No. But many claim to write Luxembourgish."

"What do people read?"

"The upper classes read French. The workaday language is German. Everybody, of course, *speaks* Luxembourgish."

By no "written language," it developed, the agency man meant no written grammar. Actually, there is a dialectical form of the language in print, but this varies according to the whims and tastes of the writer.

"If you ask someone to write in Luxembourgish," said Mr. Binsfeld, "he will choose his favorite author or poet and follow that person's particular version of written Luxembourgish. Actually, it is all quite confusing, and the government is currently working on a standardized grammar."

As for advertising, Mr. Binsfeld himself uses a version of Luxembourgish, but only in short chunks and mostly for headlines. "Our people instantly recognize Luxembourgish in a headline, but nobody wants to be tormented by having to read and decipher long pieces of copy in what someone has arbitrarily decided is Luxembourgish," he said. The agency man reached into an attache case and displayed a poster showing a large beer opener and a headline "Hu Der Schons Clausener Am Haus?"

"The headline is Luxembourgish," he said. "But if we were writing an ad in a newspaper, we would use German in the body copy. If we were trying to reach a high-level audience, we would use French in the text."

Source: Reprinted with permission from the November 29, 1965, issue of *Advertising Age.* Copyright 1965 by Advertising Publications Inc.

effective, idiomatic translation and thereby hamper communication. Especially is this situation apparent in advertising materials. Abstractions, terse writing, and word economy all pose problems for translators. Communcation is impeded by the great diversity of cultural heritage and education which exists within many countries and which causes varying interpretations of even single sentences and simple concepts. Some companies have tried to solve the translation problem by hiring foreign translators who live in the United States, but often this is unsatisfactory; both the language and the translator change, so the expatriate in the United States is completely out of touch after a few years. It is not enough to know the language; we must also know the people. Everyday words have different meanings in different cultures. The advertising manager of Ampex commented in an article in *Industrial Marketing* that

In a sense, the translation problem is the most frustrating part of international advertising. For example, we can't do our French translations in Geneva

BOX 19–3

Autos: American's Moment of Truth

After a recent assessment of the nation's social unrest, American Motors officials decided that it was no time to be selling a car called Rebel, as it had been doing. The company's marketing men conducted many expensive consumer-research polls and found a new name for A.M.C.'s intermediate model: Matador, which the studies found meant virility and excitement to consumers. Last week A.M.C. introduced its Matador in Puerto Rico—and ran right into language trouble. Matador, it turns out, is the Spanish word for killer, hardly a good selling point. In an editorial, the daily San Juan *Star* tsk-tsked: "We suggest that the name is an unfortunate choice" for Puerto Rico, which has "an unusually high traffic fatality rate."

Source: *Time*, October 26, 1970.

any more; the French insisted that the patois used by the Genevese was closer to Pawnee or Swahili than the language of their customers. And any day now I expect our man in Marseilles will ask to change our Paris ads for the Marseilles market.

Even pronunciation causes problems; Wm. Wrigley Jr. Co. had trouble selling Spearmint gum in German until it changed the spelling to Speermint. Seeking universally pronounceable brand names, that company selected the brand YUSI for an inexpensive gum to market in low-income countries. Some firms, including the Philips Company of Holland and Volkswagen, are using Esperanto in an attempt to overcome language barriers in international markets. Esperanto is a simplified international language used fairly widely in countries with large numbers of foreign visitors or troops and with obscure or varied local dialects and languages. It is doubtful that such a basic language of which no one is really a master can be expected to render forceful, effective advertising in any but the most elementary applications, but its use shows the desperate need for a simple communication vehicle.

Cultural Diversity

Overcoming the problems of communicating to people in diverse cultures is one of the great creative challenges in advertising. It is axiomatic that in messages moving from one culture to another, communication is more difficult; this is so partly because cultural factors largely determine the ways various phenomena will be perceived. If the perceptual framework is different, perception of the message itself will differ. Robert T. Oliver says in his book *Culture and Communication,*[5]

We've been slow to listen to the lesson of the cultural anthropologist that the very thought—culture—the basic value systems, the fundamental manner of perceiving reality all differ. . . . from culture to culture. As marketers, we

[5] Springfield, Ill.: Charles C. Thomas, Publisher, 1962, p. 155.

have to be concerned not only with differences between cultures but also with subcultures within a given country. We must also be aware that the cultural environments in which we are sending our messages are changing, and changing at an uneven rate.

James Donnelly reminds us that we do not react to the "actual situation that confronts us, but rather to our perception of the situation."[6]

International marketers are becoming accustomed to the problems of adapting from culture to culture. Knowledge of differing symbolism of colors is a basic part of the international marketer's encyclopedia. He knows that white in Europe means pure, but that in Asia it is more associated with death and is the color of the burial garment. Nowadays he is also sophisticated enough to know that color is only a small part of the communication package. Because he understands the symbolism, he has a full choice of using or not using various colors. Presence of black in the West does not automatically connote death; neither does the presence of white in the Eastern countries. A lack of knowledge about cultural diversity has certainly caused marketing failures, but knowledge has also helped avoid cultural failures. General Mills has been on both sides of that situation. When they introduced instant cake mixes in the United States and England, they had the problem of overcoming the housewife's guilt feelings. When they introduced instant cake mixes in Japan, they had a different problem; because cakes are not usually eaten in Japan, a housewife's primary concern there was a fear of failure, so she wanted the cake mix to be as complete as possible. In testing TV commercials featuring the notion that making cake is as easy as making rice, they learned that they were offending the Japanese housewife, who prefers to believe that the preparation of rice requires great skill.[7]

The importance of perceptions was encountered by General Foods executives when they attempted to promote the authentic Italian flavor of a spaghetti sauce marketed in Japan. Advertising executives found that Japanese housewives don't know what authentic Italian sauce is supposed to taste like, so the appeal was meaningless. Existing perceptions which are based on tradition and heritage are often hard to overcome. Marketing researchers in Hong Kong found, for example, that

cheese is almost totally associated with Yeung-Yen (foreigners) and almost totally rejected by Chinese. The concept of cooling and heating of the body is still very important in Chinese thinking—for example, coffee and malted milk are considered heating, while fresh milk is cooling. Brandy is sustaining; whiskey is harmful.[8]

Even marketers in their home country often have to deal with problems of traditional conceptions. French drivers became so accustomed to

---

[6] James H. Donnelly, Jr., "Cross Cultural Communication Theory: Implications for International Advertising," *University of Washington Business Review,* Spring 1969, p. 52.

[7] L. J. Link, "U.S. Food Companies Finding Habits in Japan Not Easy to Change," *Advertising Age,* July 28, 1969, p. 20.

[8] "Researcher Lee Combines Eastern Savvy, Western Know-how for Grant," *Advertising Age,* March 31, 1969.

buying gasoline refined in foreign countries they assumed, when gas began to be refined locally, that the French product was inferior. Heavy promotion was required to overcome this mental set.

As though it were not enough for advertisers to be concerned with differences among nations, they find that subcultures within a country require attention as well. In Hong Kong, for example, 10 different kinds of breakfast eating patterns exist. The youth of a country almost always constitutes a different consuming culture from the older people, and urban dwellers differ significantly from rural dwellers. Besides these differences, there is also the problem of traditions that are changing. In all countries, people of all ages, urban or rural, cling to their own heritage to a certain degree in some areas but are willing to change in other areas of behavior. Not too many years ago, refrigeration was a rarity in Southeast Asia but now nearly a third of all urban homes have mechanical refrigerators. It was unthinkable to try to market coffee in Japan, but in recent years this has become the fashionable drink for younger people and urban dwellers who like to think of themselves as very European and sophisticated. Coffee drinking in Japan was introduced by instant coffee and there is virtually no market for standard varieties. As shown by the examples in this section, cultural diversity requires the advertising man to be constantly alert to cultural variation because it constitutes one of the greatest creative challenges in international business.

Media Limitations

Since advertising media are discussed at length later in this chapter, the limitations on creative strategy imposed by media will not be discussed here. It should be noted, however, that media limitations may diminish the role of advertising in the promotional program and may force marketers to emphasize other elements of the marketing mix.

A marketer's creativity is certainly challenged when he is limited to showing a television commercial 10 times a year with no two exposures closer than 10 days, as is the case in Italy. Creative advertising men in some countries have even developed their own media for overcoming media limitations. In some African countries, advertisers run boats up and down the rivers playing popular music and broadcasting commercials into the bush as they travel.

Production and Cost Limitations

Creativity may be especially important when the budget is small or where there are severe production limitations. Such limitations exist in nearly every advertising medium. Poor quality printing and unavailability of high-grade papers are simple examples. The necessity for low-cost reproduction in small markets poses another problem. In many countries, for example, hand-painted billboards must be used instead of printed sheets because the small number of billboards does not warrant the production of such printed sheets.

The cost of reaching different market segments can become nearly prohibitive in some instances. In Hong Kong, for example, it is imperative that ads be run in both English and Chinese. Even if the market being sought is Chinese, English must be used so Orientals will know the product is not inferior and being advertised only to Asians. To continue the Far Eastern example, advertisers in Bangkok must use English, Chinese, and Thai languages. In Singapore, besides English and Chinese, Malay and Tamil are necessary if the market is to be reached. All of these factors, even translations alone, impose significant cost and production burdens for the advertiser.

ORGANIZATIONAL AND AGENCY ARRANGEMENTS

Almost all large firms use advertising agencies; but whether or not an agency is used, the alternative types of organization are relevant. Under one organizational framework, the parent company maintains central control of the advertising policy and also implements the advertising campaign from a central firm. A second alternative calls for central policy control but local implementation in the countries in question. A third possible organization calls for local policy control and local implementation.

Innumerable variations of these basic patterns have been tried by international advertisers, but basically the question boils down to one of centralization versus decentralization. The chief arguments for centralization relate to the use of high-level talent in managerial skills in the home office, to the economy inherent in running a centralized campaign, and to corporate control. All these arguments relate to managerial *efficiency* but such efficiency in advertising operations may be detrimental to market development and market effectiveness. Such limitations constitute the primary argument for decentralization; proponents of this concept argue that diverse cultures require local expertise, as do the problems of language translation and understanding the media requirements and availabilities in various markets.

Whichever system is utilized, it is probable that the advertiser will employ the services of an advertising agency or agencies.

Agency Arrangements

Four major alternative agency arrangements are available to the international advertiser:

1. He may appoint an agency in his own country to place advertising in foreign countries. Such a method may be most appropriate for the small international marketer.
2. He may seek out his own agency in each country in which he does business. Obviously such a procedure might be time consuming and difficult to control.
3. He might, and most large advertisers do, utilize the services of one of the large international agencies which have branch agencies or affiliates in various countries.
4. He may work through a coordinating agency which deals with in-

dependent agencies in a variety of countries. In this arrangement the coordinating agency provides overall direction, and the independent agencies provide local expertise.

Advertising agencies exist in nearly every commercially significant country in the world. Admittedly, the development of the agency field is somewhat spotty; numerous countries offer only one agency, while others permit only a choice among a few marginal agencies. The problem of having a choice among competent agencies may soon be solved if the world rate of agency formation in recent years is any indicator. However, this solution may be incomplete at present.

Agency Operations

American agencies operating abroad have followed five patterns in developing their international operations. Some of the largest, such as J. Walter Thompson and McCann-Erickson, have set up their own wholly owned agencies. Others, such as Fred Bates and BBDO, have purchased major existing overseas agencies. Still others buy an interest (majority, half, or minority) in foreign agencies, thus gaining the advantages of combining expertise from both agencies. Another system has been used by D'Arcy Advertising, which has joined forces with agencies in other countries to set up third companies which they jointly own. Of all the methods of agency development, the most common has been the development of corresponding agency relationships. These are agencies abroad which handle advertising in that country for American agencies. The commission is usually divided according to some predetermined arrangement. The last arrangement is obviously the easiest, but it provides the least control either for the agency or for the client. Obviously, some major international agencies have used a variety of these devices in building their international networks.

Equally obvious is the fact that, regardless of agency arrangement, there will be great discrepancy in the level and caliber of service provided. The trend in the early 1970s seems to be clearly in the direction of agency mergers, with the probable emergence of a relatively limited number of large multinational conglomerate agencies. Such a trend is fueled partly by the fact that there is a continuing shortage of experienced advertising people in the world and that there is a growing trend toward centralization of creative activities in some 10 or 12 major regional centers.

International billings of U.S. agencies are impressive. Consider the foreign billings of the agencies shown in Exhibit 19–3. Some of the foreign agencies compare favorably with U.S. agencies. Even compared to the $638 million billings of J. Walter Thompson Co. (the world's largest), the following figures seem significant: Dentsu Advertising, $377,000,000; Lintas International, $156,000,000; London Press Exchange, $141,400,000; Hakuhodo Inc., $112,500,000. Foreign agencies of this size certainly have the facilities for handling the world's largest accounts.

EXHIBIT 19-3

Billings of U.S. Advertising Agencies, 1969
(millions of dollars)

Agency	Foreign	Total	Foreign as % of total
J. Walter Thompson Co.	$292	736	40
McCann-Erickson	258	511	51
Young & Rubicam	152	522	29
Ted Bates & Co.	145	375	39
Ogilvy & Mather International	77	230	33
Norman, Craig & Kummel	71	140	50
Leo Burnett Co.	68	356	19
Foote, Cone & Belding	63	266	24
Compton Advertising	60	180	33
Kenyon & Eckhardt	45	140	32

Source: *Advertising Age,* 1970

Compensation arrangements for advertising agencies throughout the world are based on the U.S. system of 15 percent commissions, but agency commission patterns throughout the world are not so consistently uniform as they are in the United States. In some countries, agency commissions vary from medium to medium. France, for example, has commission rates of 15 percent applied to daily and weekly newspapers and radio. Direct mail and transportation advertising have rates up to 20 percent. The technical press and cinema allow 20 percent, and the commissions on outdoor advertising reach 25 percent. Services provided by advertising agencies will be as varied as the commission rates or fees; but in general foreign agencies have not been so prepared to offer "full services" as have American agencies.

Even such a sophisticated business function as advertising may find that it is involved in primitive practices. In some parts of the world, for example, in Mexico, advertisers often pay for their promotion with the product advertised rather than with cash. One correspondent comments that

Almost every newspaper and radio station in Mexico has had to go along with this part of the system known as "intercambio" (interchange). Space and time salesmen, once they have sold a client, are faced with the prospect of peddling the product before they can collect their commissions.[9]

Kickbacks on agency commissions are prevalent in other parts of the world and account in part for the low profitability of international advertising agencies. It has become almost customary in such countries as Mexico, India, and Greece to return to the advertiser half the media commissions. Still another influence on the compensation of advertising agencies is credit. In many of the developing countries, long-term credit

---

[9] Due bills and trade-offs have the same effect and are by no means uncommon in the United States.

is used to attract clients. Venezuela, for example, has a rather highly developed advertising agency system; yet 120 days is the *average* time between the agency's payment to the media and the client's payment. Agencies actually negotiate agency contracts on the basis of the size of the kickback and the duration of the credit extension. Such policies are bound to result in less effective selection and, therefore, less effective advertising effort than in the system where the agency is chosen on its merit only.

The task of selecting and maintaining international advertising agencies cannot be easily overlooked. The comprehensive services of American agencies may be one reason that so many firms seek branch offices of American agencies. In most cases these agencies have U.S. management or U.S. trained management, with a majority of native employees.

ADVERTISING MEDIA

Tactical Considerations

Although nearly every sizable nation has available essentially the same kinds of media, there are a number of specific considerations, problems, and differences encountered from one nation to another. Primary areas to which an advertiser must give special consideration in international advertising include the availability, cost, and coverage of the media. Local variations and lack of market data provide fertile areas for additional attention.

Imagine the ingenuity required of advertising men who confront the following situations:

1. TV commercials are sandwiched together in a string of 10 to 50 commercials within one station break in Brazil.
2. In many countries national coverage requires use of as many as 40 to 50 different media.
3. Specialized media reach sections of the market only. In the Netherlands, there are Catholic, Protestant, Socialist, neutral and other specialized broadcasting systems.
4. In Germany, TV scheduling for an entire year must be arranged by August 30 of the preceding year, and there is no guarantee that commercials intended for summer scheduling will not be run in the middle of winter.

Availability. One of the contrasts of international advertising is that some countries have too few advertising media and others have too many. In some countries some advertising media are forbidden by government edict to accept certain advertising materials. Such restrictions are most predominant in the areas of radio and television broadcasting. In numerous countries there are just too few magazines and newspapers to run all the advertising offered to them. Conversely, some nations segment the market with so many newspapers that the advertiser cannot gain effective coverage at a reasonable cost. Gilberto Sozzani, head of an Italian advertising agency, comments about his country: "One fundamental rule. You cannot buy what you want." An observer of the Dutch advertising scene says, "Demand for time is about five times the amount available."[10] Additional information on availability is found in the section on specific media below.

Cost. Although there is some bickering over the price to be paid for advertising space or time in every country (particularly in the fields of radio and television), most advertising men from the United States are not prepared for the haggling process which goes on in many areas of the world. Media prices are susceptible to negotiation in most countries. Agency space discounts are often split with the client in order to bring down the cost of media. The advertiser may find that his cost of reaching a prospect through advertising is dependent on his agent's bargaining ability. The per contract cost will vary widely from country to country; IMEDE (L'Institut pour L'Etude des Direction de L'Enterprise) researched the cost of reaching a thousand readers in 11 different European countries and discovered a broad range. For example, the mean cost per page per thousand circulation in general magazines ranged from $1.58 in Belgium to $5.91 in Italy. An even broader range was found in women's service magazines, where the page cost range per thousand circulation ranged from $2.51 in Denmark to $10.87 in West Germany. A similar but higher cost range exists in newspapers. See Exhibit 19–5 in specific media section.

A recent five-year study of advertising costs in nine major foreign markets indicated that advertising costs were increasing at a rate of 5 to 7 percent each year, a rate considerably higher than the cost increases in U.S. media. Test marketing in many nations is unnecessarily expensive because of media limitations. Segmentation of the newspaper market, plus the fact that the better educated segment of the market will often subscribe to foreign newspapers or to national editions only, makes local testing difficult. Inevitably, test marketing in foreign markets incurs extreme amounts of wasted circulation.

Coverage. Closely akin to the cost dilemma is the problem of coverage. Two points are particularly important: one pertains to the difficulty of reaching certain sectors of the population with advertising; the other relates to the lack of information on coverage. In many of the world's marketplaces, a broad variety of media must be utilized to reach the majority of the market. In some countries large numbers of separate media have divided markets into uneconomical advertising segments. A large portion of the native population of most countries cannot be reached readily through the medium of advertising.

Verification of circulation or of coverage figures is a difficult task, even when an agency such as the Audit Bureau of Circulation provides guidelines for circulation analysis and verifies the data presented. In the past five years numerous countries have added similar agencies. Even though many countries have organizations like the Audit Bureau of Circulation, this is not necessarily an assurance of accurate circula-

---

[10] "American Industry Must Use European Skills to Operate Effectively Overseas," *Advertising Age*, October 27, 1969, p. 22.

tion and audience data. For example, the president of the Mexican National Advertisers Association charged that newspaper circulation figures are "grossly exaggerated." He suggested that "As a rule agencies divide these figures in two and take the result with a grain of salt."

Radio and television audiences are always difficult to measure, but at least in most countries geographic coverage is known. Not so in Brazil, where privately owned transmitters are under contract to broadcasting stations. When the transcription contracts are shifted from station to station, "a station may advise agencies of its increased audience resulting from a new pact with the owner of a transmitter, while the station that had the old contract does not mention the shift, thus giving rise to a ghost audience."[11]

Private companies gather and disseminate audience and cost data but do not guarantee accuracy. Media rate and date information are available from these subsidiaries of the United States and Canadian Standard Rate and Data Service—British Rate and Data, London; Tarif Media, Paris; Media Daten, Frankfurt. Another private venture, the International Media Guide in New York, provides a worldwide advertising service somewhat similar to the national services mentioned above. The guides provide rates and data on major advertising media for principal countries.

Lack of Market Data. Even in situations where circulation or coverage of an advertising medium can be measured with some accuracy, there is still a question concerning the composition of the market reached. A general and widespread lack of available market data seems to characterize most international markets. At a very minimum, advertisers should have information on income, age, and geographic distribution; but even such basic data seem destined to remain hidden from the objective observer. If adequate market data were available, they would show great variation in the audiences of different periodicals and broadcast media. They would also show the great diversity and variation which exists from country to country. Often even a small nation will have half a dozen or more subcultures within its borders. The advertiser is, therefore, even more confounded in his attempts to select media with which he can communicate easily with an entire market.

Media Patterns

Perhaps the dominant pattern in the arena of world advertising is the proliferation of advertising media. Many countries already have more media than their economy or population can adequately support. Since most countries, however, have been long underdeveloped in terms of commercial mass communication media, the addition of other magazines, newspapers, and radio and television stations will be a boon to many advertisers.

In most countries the introduction of television as an advertising medium greatly distorts traditional media patterns. The pattern of the

---

[11] "Brazil Media Have Reach Problems," *Advertising Age,* November 24, 1969, p. 64.

United States is roughly paralleled in other countries. After the introduction of television, the initial impact is to reduce advertising on radio sharply and cause significant reductions in newspaper and magazine advertising. Within about five years of the introduction of television, there is a gradual shift back toward radio and print media. In most countries, once established, television keeps a strong share of the market. In countries where cinema advertising had been a major medium, television has virtually wiped it out as a contender for advertising dollars.

Exhibit 19–4 illustrates the variety of local media expenditure patterns that are found throughout the world. Variation in dollar expenditures by different kinds of media reflects rather directly the effectiveness of those different media in communicating with local audiences. Note, for example, that in the United States the amount of money expended for advertising in movies is so negligible that it is almost unmeasurable. In Argentina, cinema accounts for almost 3% of all advertising expenditures, and in Austria 20% is spent for cinema advertising. In Israel, adult cinema-goers average almost 30 visits a year and account for some 39 million admissions annually. Analysis of media patterns in Exhibit 19–4 will reveal numerous other such variations.

There are two classes of media on the international advertising scene: national and international media. Every nation has a number of indigenous advertising media. Besides the national media published and distributed in one country, one should also consider the media which are published in one country and consumed in others. In some cases, like the British *Punch,* such international distribution is not particularly intended. Other advertising media are specifically designed for circulation to a wide number of different countries. Such a medium is *Reader's Digest,* which has international editions in different languages and distributes some 10,000,000 copies to nations around the world (besides the 13,000,000 copies circulated in the United States).

Specific Media Information

An attempt to evaluate the specific characteristics of each kind of medium is beyond the scope of this discussion. Furthermore, information provided would probably become quickly outdated because of the rapid changes in the international advertising media field. It may be interesting, however, to examine some of the particularly unique international characteristics of various advertising media. In most instances the major implications of each variation may be discerned from the data presented.

Newspapers. When compared from country to country, the newspaper field evidences great variety. In the more highly developed countries, the newspaper is one of the broadest based mass media. In such countries nearly every household receives a paper daily. The situation is reversed in the developing countries, where illiteracy restricts the coverage to certain classes and certain geographic regions. The literacy barrier results in coverage being spotty and selective rather than intensive.

The newspaper industry is suffering in some countries from lack of

EXHIBIT 19–4

Variety of Local Media Expenditure Patterns
throughout the World

Country	News-paper %	Magazine %	Tele-vision %	Radio %	Direct %	Trans. & Outdoor %	Cinema %
U.S.	29	15	14	6	16	2	—
Canada	37	9	9	9	19	6	—
Europe							
Austria	48	combined	7	11	—	16	20
Belgium	28	15	—	2	16	9	4
Denmark	44	17	—	—	22	3	3
Finland	34	14	2	—	10	4	1
France	55	combined	—	6	13	8	5
West Germany	51	35	9	2	—	4	—
Greece	48	25	—	13	—	—	10
Ireland	71	6	—	4	—	5	3
Netherlands	38	25	—	1	23	5	1
Norway	61	combined	—	—	13	5	3
Portugal	40	combined	10	20	—	25	3
Spain	50	combined	2	32	—	5	11
Sweden	43	19	—	—	23	1	2
Switzerland	45	combined	—	—	10	15	3
U.K.	29	20	19	—	9	7	1
Latin America							
Argentina	34	11	11	21	—	10	3
Brazil	33	12	9	14	21	8	—
Chile	34	5	—	30	—	12	8
Colombia	35	combined	9	26	—	17	4
Netherlands Antilles	42	1	19	21	6	1	1
Curacao							
Peru	32	3	28	18	2	5	4
Mideast & Africa							
Iran	17	7	60	11	—	4	—
Israel	48	6	—	6	12	8	8
Lebanon	31	20	13	—	5	7	12
South Africa	70	20	—	11	—	—	—
Turkey	38	6	—	4	23	21	—
Far East							
Australia	51	12	13	10	3	8	3
Japan	35	6	33	4	4	15	2

Note: The percentages in this table provide only a rough approximation. The base figures are not identical; some include all advertising, and others include only advertising in measured media or national media. When no figure is given, this may mean that information is not available for that medium or it may mean that the percentage figure represented by this medium is less than .5 percent.

Source: Authors' estimates, based in part on *The Advertising Agency Business Around the World,* American Association of Advertising Agencies (New York, 1964–1967).

competition and choking in others because of it. In the United States, there are few cities with more than two major daily newspapers; but in many countries, the opposite situation prevails, and there are so many newspapers that an advertiser must appear in a large number of papers to obtain even partial market coverage. Tiny Lebanon, for example, with a population of only 1.5 million, has 210 daily or weekly newspapers. Only four have a circulation of over 10,000, with the average circulation being 3,500. Imagine the complexity of trying to reach 200,000 households utilizing the newspaper medium in Lebanon. Look also at Turkey where, in addition to the problem of selecting from some 380 newspapers, the advertiser must also concern himself with the political position of the newspapers in which he advertises so that he does not harm his product's reputation through affiliations with an unpopular position. Papers are occasionally closed down by the government, and students are said to have a nasty habit of burning down newspaper offices in Turkey when they feel politically agitated.

Contrast former examples with Japan, which has five national daily newspapers, the largest of which, *Asahi,* alone reaches 85 percent of all politicians and government officials, 81 percent of all businessmen, 44 percent of the nation's college graduates, and nearly 40 percent of the households with incomes in the upper middle range. The problem with *Asahi* is that the complications of producing a Japanese-language newspaper are such that the newspaper is only 16 to 20 pages long, depending on the date of issue. It has been known to turn down over a million dollars a month in advertising revenue. Like everything else in Japan, connections are required in order to buy advertising space.

Newspapers customarily list timeliness and short lead time for advertisements as one of their major advantages, yet here one discovers another contract. In many countries there is a long time lag before an advertisement can be run in a newspaper. In India, for example, paper shortages require that ads be booked up to six months before their desired publication. Similarly, an advertising executive describes the condition in Indonesia: "The situation at the newspapers is almost indescribable. Because of a lack of paper, the bigger newspapers are constantly short of advertising space and this means that you have to bribe the administration every time you want to run an ad. The smaller papers are comparatively too expensive and their circulation too unreliable."

Policy regarding separation between editorial and advertising content in newspapers provides another basis for contrast on the international scene. In some countries, it is possible to buy editorial space for advertising and promotional purposes. One commentator describes the situation as follows: "The news columns are for sale not only to the government but to anyone who has the price. Since there is no indication that the space is paid for, it is impossible to tell exactly how much advertising appears in a given newspaper. The government, along with private industry, helps publishers pay reporters by handing out a monthly stipend to newsmen on a given beat. Both cost (see Exhibit 19–5) and subscriber variations indicate that foreign newspapers cannot be considered as homogeneous advertising entities. The advertiser must exert considerable judgment in spending his international advertising dollars in newspapers.

Magazines. The use of foreign national consumer magazines by international advertisers has been notably low because so many problems are involved. Few magazines have large circulations or provide

EXHIBIT 19–5

Average Full-Page Newspaper Rates and Cost per Thousand

	Average Full Page Rate (incl. tax)	Average Full Page Rate (incl. tax) per 1,000 Circulation		Average Full Page Rate (incl. tax)	Average Full Page Rate (incl. tax) per 1,000 Circulation
WESTERN EUROPE			**OCEANIA**		
Italy	$2,922.00	$24.10	New Guinea	$255.00	$31.81
Greece	1,491.00	23.30	New Zealand	540.00	5.33
France	4,398.00	15.10	Australia	960.00	4.03
Germany (West)	2,655.00	14.03			
Iceland	238.00	13.24	**MIDDLE EAST**		
Norway	779.00	13.23	Kuwait	442.00	29.96
Finland	990.00	12.97	Iran	922.00	26.35
Denmark	949.00	12.61	Lebanon	441.00	22.30
Sweden	1,302.00	10.03	Israel	790.00	10.73
The Netherlands	1,031.00	9.95	Turkey	2,756.00	8.82
Ireland	1,637.00	8.70	U.A.R.	1,958.00	8.24
Belgium	1,055.00	8.53			
Austria	1,036.00	8.33	**LATIN AMERICA**		
Luxembourg	358.00	8.33	Bahamas	427.00	58.22
Switzerland	465.00	7.93	Netherlands Antilles	302.00	29.46
Malta	98.00	6.22	Barbados	528.00	28.55
Portugal	576.00	4.90	Panama	328.00	21.59
United Kingdom	2,889.00	4.16	British Honduras	105.00	21.00
Spain	290.00	3.84	Haiti	120.00	16.41
			Honduras	169.00	14.38
FAR EAST			Nicaragua	308.00	13.80
Thailand	460.00	15.61	Brazil	1,268.00	13.38
Malaysia	737.00	13.73	Guyana	246.00	12.31
Singapore	1,800.00	13.53	West Indies	382.00	11.58
Korea (South)	2,375.00	11.62	Dominican Republic	309.00	9.98
Hong Kong	411.00	10.35	Uruguay	568.00	7.16
Pakistan	653.00	10.29	Venezuela	453.00	6.56
Viet Nam (South)	248.00	10.20	Chile	250.00	6.33
Japan	6,729.00	8.83	Mexico	472.00	6.33
Indonesia	397.00	8.22	Argentina	1,042.00	6.14
Taiwan	933.00	6.99	Ecuador	238.00	5.95
Ceylon	543.00	6.45	Bolivia	250.00	5.55
India	567.00	6.13	Jamaica	361.00	5.47
Philippines	485.00	6.10	Peru	662.00	5.45
			Colombia	456.00	5.45
AFRICA			Costa Rica	122.00	3.50
Uganda	272.00	33.93	Guatemala	167.00	3.38
Zambia	928.00	24.09	El Salvador	151.00	3.03
Ethiopia	239.00	21.72	**UNITED STATES OF**		
Ghana	255.00	21.13	**AMERICA**	2,903.00	7.75
Tunisia	606.00	18.18			
Rhodesia	365.00	11.33			
Kenya	390.00	9.39			
Republic of South Africa	819.00	8.19			
Nigeria	487.00	7.73			

Source: Reprinted from the 1970 issue of *Newspaper International*, published by National Register Publishing Co., Inc., Skokie, Illinois.

dependable circulation figures. Technical magazines are used rather extensively to promote export goods; but as in the case of newspapers, paper shortages cause placement problems. One British agency manager says, "Can you imagine what it feels like to be a media planner here when the largest magazine accepts up to twice as many advertisements as it has space to run them in? Then they decide what advertisements will go in just before going to press by means of a raffle." Local attitudes such as these may be key items favoring the growth of so-called "international media," which attempt to serve many nations.[12]

There is such a shortage of business and technical journals in under-developed nations that in countries like India it is not unusual to find

---

[12] Although all media have a certain "international" coverage, magazines represent the only highly developed medium for advertising.

complicated technical advertising being run in daily newspapers, even though only 1 or 2 percent of the newspaper's readers are likely to be potential customers.

Russia and its satellites have added an interesting planned economy element since they have begun accepting advertising in their magazines and trade magazines. The cost of ads is standardized for all magazines regardless of their circulation. Presumably, therefore, no effort needs to be wasted in attempting to prove circulation. In Russia, for example, all trade magazines charge the equivalent of $222 a page. In Poland, the page price is $160 (U.S.); in Bulgaria, $140; and in Romania, $200. Red China has only three business papers, but they have variable prices ranging from $175 to $275 a page. The Eastern European satellite countries all have advertising agencies and consumer advertising media.

Advertisers who are accustomed to the broad assortment of magazines published in economically advanced countries may have to reassess media strategies involving magazines as they shift their attention from country to country. Lack of periodicals can be particularly critical to a company attempting to sell technical or industrial products. The media void may not only shift media usage but could force the company to change its entire promotion mix and even could affect distribution channels, patterns, and market coverage.

Radio and Television. Possibly because of their inherent entertainment value, radio and television have become major communication media in most nations. As can be seen from Exhibit 19–6 there are some 206 million television receivers in use in the world. The number more than doubled between 1965 and 1970. Few populous areas do not have television broadcasting facilities. In some markets, such as Japan, television has become almost a national obsession and thus finds tremendous audiences for its advertisers. Radio has been relegated to the subordinate position in the media race in countries where television facilities are well developed. In many countries, however, radio is a particularly important and vital advertising medium because it is the only one which can be used to communicate to large segments of the population.

Television and radio play different roles in terms of advertising in various countries. Three patterns seem to predominate: competitive commercial radio, commercial monopolies, and noncommercial broadcasting. Countries with free competitive commercial radio normally encourage competition and have minimal amounts of broadcast regulation. Local or national monopolies are granted by the government in other countries. Individual stations or networks may then accept radio commercials according to rules established by the government. In some countries the commercial monopolies may accept all the advertising they wish; in others, only spot advertising is permissible and programs may not be sponsored. In some countries, live commercials are not permitted. South Africa is organized along the commercial monopoly pattern: it has a nationalized commercial monopoly called Springbok, which encounters commercial competition only from neighboring nations with open commercial broadcasting. Springbok must compete for

EXHIBIT 19–6

Television Ownership in Selected Countries

Country	No. of Receivers (000)	No. of Receivers per 1,000 Population*	Advertising Permitted
Europe			
Austria......................	930	146	Yes
Belgium.....................	1,669	187	No
Bulgaria....................	186		No
Czechoslovakia...............	2,538		No
Finland.....................	864	200	Yes
France......................	7,998	177	Yes
West Germany...............	13,404	251	Yes
East Germany...............	3,385		No
Greece......................	19	−10	No
Hungary....................	1,095		Yes
Ireland.....................	385	145	Yes
Italy........................	7,509	143	Yes
Netherlands..................	2,517	136	Yes
Norway.....................	632	129	No
Poland......................	2,700		Yes
Portugal....................	260	30	Yes
Romania....................	577		No
Spain.......................	2,525	103	Yes
Sweden.....................	2,216	296	No
Switzerland.................	1,666	145	Yes
Turkey.....................	6	−10	No
United Kingdom.............	14,776	285	1 sta. only
U.S.S.R....................	24,135		
Yugoslavia..................	887		Yes
North America			
Canada.....................	5,700		Yes
Cuba.......................	575		No
Dominican Republic...........	85	21	Yes
El Salvador..................	45	16	Yes
Haiti.......................	10	−10	Yes
Mexico.....................	1,860	47	Yes
Puerto Rico..................	400		Yes
United States................	74,800	410	Yes
South America			
Argentina...................	1,705	83	Yes
Brazil......................	3,000	57	Yes
Chile.......................	90	16	No
Colombia....................	380	23	Yes
Ecuador....................	50	12	Yes
Peru.......................	275	24	Yes
Uruguay....................	200	76	Yes
Venezuela..................	650	67	Yes
Asia			
Cambodia...................	20		
China (mainland).............	100		
India.......................	7	−10	No
Indonesia...................	55	−10	No
Iran........................	150	−10	Yes
Iraq.......................	160		

EXHIBIT 19–6 (continued)

Country	No. of Receivers (000)	No. of Receivers per 1,000 Population*	Advertising Permitted
Israel........................	31	16	No
Japan........................	19,625	204	No
Republic of Korea.............	75	−10	Yes
Pakistan.....................	40	−10	No
Philippines...................	190	10	Yes
Saudi Arabia.................	35	−10	No
Thailand....................	210	−10	Yes
Oceania			
Australia....................	2,405	195	No
New Zealand.................	530	213	Yes
Africa			
Algeria......................	50	−10	No
Ghana......................	1	−10	Yes
Kenya......................	14	−10	Yes
Morocco.....................	38	−10	No
Nigeria.....................	52	−10	Yes
Uganda.....................	8	−10	Yes
United Arab Republic..........	475	17	Yes

Note: −10 means fewer than 10 sets per 1,000 population.
Source: United Nations

audience, however, against the government's noncommercial broadcasting network.

In some countries, no commercial radio or television is permitted, but several of the traditional noncommercial countries have changed their policies in recent years. The question of whether television should have commercials is hotly debated in many of the countries which do not have commercial TV. The argument over commercial television in the Netherlands toppled the government and forced the cabinet to resign. As the Prime Minister handed his resignation to the Queen, he said, "I never knew that television was such a difficult business." Some of the countries which have limited commercial television cause availability problems for advertisers. Switzerland, for example, permits only 12 minutes of commercial matter a day, and that is broadcast only between 6:30 and 8:00 A.M. on weekdays; West Germany has three state-operated TV channels, one of which carries no commercials and the others only 30 minutes per day.

Despite the limitations on commercial programming, people in most countries have an opportunity to hear or view commercial radio and television. Entrepreneurs in the radio-television field have discovered that audiences in commercially restricted countries are hungry for commercial television and radio, and have found that marketers are eager to bring their messages into these countries. They have, therefore, developed some ingenious methods of broadcasting into these "closed" countries. Radio Luxembourg, for example, has almost become synonymous with "Radio Europe." It broadcasts commercial materials into Central European countries, including those which preclude private sponsorship. In South Africa, the potential importance of radio as an advertising medium for communicating with the natives has caused some broadcasters in nearby Portuguese East Africa to specialize in beaming commercial broadcasting across the border to South Africa. Denmark and Britain are both "victims" of audience piracy on the high seas. Various private broadcasting interests have outfitted several ships which they anchor in international waters and use as floating transmitters for beaming into these countries commercial messages, along with programs designed to attract large audiences.

Lack of reliable audience data is a major problem in international marketing via radio and television. Measurement of radio and television audiences is always a precarious business, even where techniques are rather highly developed, as in the United States. In most other countries, audience measurement is either unaudited, or auditing associations have no power. The counting of radio or television set ownership has become a basic method of audience measurement, but in many cases such a measure understates the audiences. In many areas receivers are located in public or semipublic areas where large numbers of listeners and viewers who do not own their own receivers may be exposed to the programming and commercial materials. Despite the lack of data on audience, many advertisers use radio and television extensively. They justify their inclusion in the media schedule on the inherent logical element favoring the use of these media or defend its use on a basis of sales results. Despite the problems inherent in the use of radio and TV, and the associated audience-measurements difficulties, these mediums will continue to grow and expand their role in international advertising. Advertisers must be prepared to grow with them in their efforts to reach international consumer markets.

Station proliferation is becoming a problem for international television advertisers just as it is in the United States. Increasing numbers of stations divide the market and require advertisers to be on the air over several stations; thus the cost is increased, while audience coverage is diminished.

Other Media.   The inability of the major media to perform the advertising communication function adequately causes advertisers in different parts of the world to call on lesser media for the solution of particular local problems. As was noted in Exhibit 19–5 above, cinema plays a large advertising role in many countries. In Italy, cinema advertising is so popular that it is difficult to purchase space on reasonably short notice. E. Tal, chairman of the Israel Advertising Association, commented in a discussion of Israeli advertising that "Screen advertising is general and affords ample coverage for local and national advertising." Cinema advertising plays a similar role in other countries.

The dearth of trade and industrial magazines in most countries places great emphasis on direct mail. As is often the case in international marketing, however, even such a basic medium as direct mail is subject to some odd and novel quirks. In Chile, for example, direct mail is virtually eliminated as an effective medium because the sender pays only part of the mailing fee, and his postage does not cover transportation cost. The letter carrier, therefore, collects additional postage for every item he delivers. Obviously, advertisers cannot afford to alienate their customers by forcing them to pay for unsolicited advertisements. In other countries, mail delivery may be unreliable on advertising matter.

Despite the problems of international direct mail, it is an important medium. Industrial advertisers are heavy mail users and rely on catalogs and sales sheets to generate large volumes of international business.

Billboards are regulated in many countries and are subject to some natural limitations. In Switzerland, small signs and posters are permitted in urban areas, but billboards as such are unknown. Billboard spectaculars in urban centers may be particularly good in warm climates where urban residents spend a considerable amount of time in the evening on city streets. Billboards are reputedly also useful in countries with high illiteracy rates because the message can be conveyed pictorially and the illiterate members of the population receive no other print messages.

Another advertising method is found in Haiti, where sound trucks equipped with powerful loudspeakers provide an effective and widespread advertising medium. Private contractors own their equipment and sell advertising space, much as a radio station would. This medium rather effectively combats the problems of illiteracy, lack of radio and television set ownership, and limited print media circulation.

For industrial advertisers one of the most powerful international media is the trade show or trade fair, as it is more commonly called in other countries. Products and product demonstrations almost automatically surmount all communications barriers. At one show alone in Frankfurt, Germany, a few years ago, nearly $3,000,000 worth of goods were sold directly by U.S. exhibitors, with another $20,000,000 in orders anticipated from the Frankfurt Trade Fair. As part of the U.S. Department of Commerce's international promotion activities, the government sponsors trade fair centers in a variety of cities around the world, including London, Frankfurt, Milan, Bangkok, Tokyo, and Stockholm. As evidence of the program's effectiveness, consider that in less than 10 years of operating trade shows, the London center alone has accounted for direct sales of some $200 million, plus over $30 million of sales between shows. Some 8,000 enterprises have participated, over one fourth of which are new to international marketing.

Many nations sponsor trade fairs. A recent government estimate indicated that some $30,000,000 of sales were produced in one year from such foreign-sponsored fairs. In addition to those sponsored by the U.S. and foreign governments, a number of private firms sponsor their own, including a flying fair, using converted jet airliners as exhibition halls, a floating fair, using ships as showrooms, and fairs sponsored by international trade and professional associations.

ADVERTISING AND ECONOMIC DEVELOPMENT

As modern marketing comes to an increasing number of countries in the world, it becomes apparent that advertising is both potentially and actually a force enhancing economic development. Newspapers, magazines, television, and radio have all developed and flourished in large part because of the great sums of money supplied to these media through advertising expenditures. The very existence of such vehicles, the growing economic health of the media, and the freedom from central control which advertising funds make possible greatly enhance communications throughout the world, and effective communication is a basic requirement of economic development.

Most analyses of the economic aspects of advertising concentrate on the contributions of advertising in helping to develop mass markets, which in turn foster mass production and facilitate mass distribution. The old argument about whether advertising creates demand or merely capitalizes on existing demand is superfluous. It suffices to say that there is positive knowledge that advertising does help create mass demand. One way is by introducing new products which are available. Many companies and governments are actively working on the development of low-cost, high-protein, vitamin-enriched foods which will help overpopulated countries fight problems of malnutrition. So far they have found that their greatest success in inducing people to accept these food products is through the use of consumer advertising techniques. It is axiomatic that when consumers are exposed to products which are new and attractive to them, they raise their own personal goals and consumption aspirations and consequently are motivated to work harder to earn the new products they want. David McClellan and other authorities who have studied motivational patterns in underdeveloped countries attribute slow economic development to low levels of personal aspiration and motivation. People who have become apathetic because they are habituated to poverty often can be motivated to increased efforts simply through exposure to a wide variety of desirable goods. Speaking before the Third Asian Advertising Congress in Manila, the Minister of Commerce of the Philippines endorsed advertising as a primary means of raising the standard of living and creating local markets for production capacity now *dormant* in Asian countries.

Once mass markets have been developed, mass production inevitably follows, bringing the consequent economies of large-scale operation. Then advertising enters the picture again to facilitate mass distribution by helping to establish brand names, product preferences, and product information and by performing other consumer-assistance functions. Perhaps the most eloquent testimonial to the economic relevance of advertising is the extensive use of advertising in communist countries, which deny the efficacy of advertising in their economic doctrine but employ it in their distribution systems. GUM, the huge state-owned department store in Moscow, spends some $5, $6, to $7 million each year on advertising and has a staff of some 50 advertising people. Only when mass markets, mass production, and mass distribution are realities will the economic development of most countries be significantly advanced. All are enhanced by advertising and, therefore, it can safely be said that, despite its many shortcomings, advertising does contribute significantly to economic development.

SUMMARY AND CONCLUSIONS

Similarities in advertising from country to country are more apparent than real. Though it is true that the advertising man will be able to adapt his basic skills to any environment, it is equally true that much of his information base will be irrelevant. The international advertiser faces unique legal limitations, language limitations, media limitations, and production limitations. The nature and extent of these limitations varies largely with the stage of economic and marketing development of the countries in which he is doing business. In general, a parallel exists between the stage of economic development and the stage of advertising development; in the more highly developed countries, the advertiser has a wider range of media, production capability, and skilled personnel at his disposal. He still must cope, however, with the problems imposed by cultural, legal, and language variations.

A basic consideration in preparing for international advertising relates to the organizational question of whether to centralize responsibility for international advertising efforts in the parent country or to decentralize and delegate the authority to advertising executives in the various countries in which one is doing business. A somewhat parallel question is whether or not an advertiser should utilize a standard approach and presentation for all countries or should custom advertise for each country in which business is sought. The most logical conclusion seems to be that, when buying motives and company objectives are the same for various countries, the advertising orientation and presentation can be the same. When buying motives and/or company objectives vary from nation to nation, the advertising effort will have to reflect these variations. In any case, variety in media availability, coverage, and effectiveness will have to be taken into consideration in the advertiser's plans. Therefore, even if common appeals are used, they may have to be presented by a radio broadcast in one country; by cinema in another; and by television in still a third.

A skilled advertising practitioner who is sensitive to his environment and alert to new facts about his market possesses the basic equipment for success in international advertising endeavors.

READING

Coordinated Variety Spells Success in Today's International Campaigns*

ALBERT STRIDSBERG

In the past ten years, the approach to international advertising has changed in a subtle but very significant way.

* Reprinted with permission from the June 17, 1968, issue of *Advertising Age*, pp. 104–8. Copyright 1968 by Advertising Publications Inc.

Once upon a time, whether you were a client executive or an agency man, you were concerned with putting together ads for your export markets—or with supervising the advertising done by your associates in other countries. Generally, give or take a few slogans that were international, if *they* did the ads, then the ads were different from country to country. If *you* did the ads, they were probably alike as peas in a pod, except for special cases where some maverick country set up such a howl you did a special one or permitted the local associate to do something of his own as an exception.

The days of the absolutely standardized world campaigns, dominated from central headquarters, inflexible and unadapted to local conditions, and of the fragmented multiple campaigns created locally, with different images, different styles, different strategies and varying qualities of concept and execution are not yet gone. But they are going fast, as the need grows for internationally coordinated advertising.

What do we mean by internationally coordinated advertising? It is advertising, appearing in a number of different countries simultaneously, which develops the maximum uniformity without forcing it to the disadvantage of the advertiser in any local situation.

Such uniformity is increasingly necessary for several reasons:

1. National markets are becoming more similar, although they are not identical in even the most dense geographic areas. This is happening through economic unions, shared communications networks like Eurovision and the satellite systems, the increase in business and recreational travel (which amounts to a constant cultural exchange), and affluence permitting experimentation with other countries' customs and living patterns.

2. New geographic markets are emerging from the straitjackets imposed upon them by national boundaries. These markets, whether related to climate, language, transport routes, or culture, must be handled as unities, no matter where the customs barriers divide them.

3. The younger generation has moved up as an international market of its own, taking differences in language and the other conventional divisive points in its stride and developing a remarkable similarity in worldwide mentality.

4. Multi-national companies are finding an ever-increasing need for centralized coordination and control. This is not because of governmental or economic arrangements such as the Common Market treaties, but because they must manage technology and resources more effectively in the present climate of heightened competition. This can only be done on a supra-national level.

Today, it is unthinkable to find a distributor, licensee, or franchiser for your products in a foreign country, organize to keep him supplied physically with the quantities of product he needs, and leave him to his own devices as to advertising, sales promotion, and merchandising. Nor is it feasible to "go through the motions," as commonly used to be the case, shipping him some mats and some literature with the suggestion that, if he needs anything else, he should write you.

One of the most complex and painful processes going on in international marketing today is the revision of such relationships, many of them long-standing, to bring effective international coordination into play. Almost any company of size finds itself involved in this currently, if they have been operating in foreign markets for any length of time. A friend of mine recently suggested to me that the companies new to international marketing have a decided advantage because, however green they may be, "they don't have to clear up the debris of the past."

Part of the difficulty comes from the revision of organizational structures which generally is required at the same time. Managers who were independent do not appreciate being brought under the authority of others.

But a surprising number of problems seem to come from a failure to grasp how to make coordination work.

One of the biggest soft drink companies in the world presented to its worldwide franchisers a campaign which they were all expected to use. It was developed by a New York advertising agency whose creative team had never been outside the U.S. The campaign was identical in all elements, for all countries. The franchisers set up a hue and cry of protest because it was clear to them that the campaign had been created without any understanding of their problems and, indeed, with considerable misunderstanding of their needs.

At the same time, this soft drink company's two largest competitors, each without knowledge of the other's plans, developed surprisingly similar concepts of their world marketing problems and ways to give their bottlers help on a coordinated basis.

Both competitors started by finding out from the bottlers what they wanted—and why they wanted it. To do this, they used their branch offices and those of their advertising agencies. Many letters had to be written. Young executives spent time talking to shopkeepers and restaurant owners who sold soft drinks. Reports were put together.

As a result, both companies independently concluded that it was not possible to have the same advertising everywhere, worldwide. Instead, certain elements could be developed in common—such as standard trademarks, a standard slogan, and various recommended copy themes.

In Latin America and most of Southeast Asia, American advertising films and American photographs could be used, with careful adaptation of copy and local languages. Europe, however, had to be treated as a completely separate area—where American themes could be used, but American photos, films and creative materials were not suitable. And in the Negro countries of Africa, separate materials were needed, although the key themes could be expressed.

These two companies ended up with effectively coordinated programs. The programs are not simple, but for the improvement in quality and effectiveness of the advertising which they have delivered, they do not cost appreciably more. The local franchisers give credit to the companies and their advertising agencies for helping them improve their competitive positions.

Making coordination work involves a few simple principles—plus a great deal of work. One must:

Ask the people in the foreign markets how they see the problem and what they need, *first*, before starting to develop campaigns.

Supplement the information from within your company with control information from outside sources. An international agency with multiple offices can supply considerable help.

Break the problems reported and the needs stated into their component parts, recognizing the differences but looking for similarities. Do not assume that the similarities will turn up on the basis of common language, or location on the same continent, but hold in mind that it is generally desirable to have reasonable advertising uniformity over large geographic territories.

Organize your strategy alternatives in modules, so that your foreign operations can assemble what they need, sharing the general international approach without having to use identical materials worldwide.

This last concept—modular advertising policies and materials—is often equated with prototype advertising campaigns. Areas in which coordination can produce useful results can be classified into five policy categories:

PRODUCT POSITIONING. While physically the same product, your brand may for various reasons be shooting for a different market or sales pattern in some countries. This may imply differences in packaging, in pricing; possibly even in such elements of formulation as scent or flavor. An example of effective international product policies is the way Unilever positions its detergent and margarine brands in Europe; certain ones are aimed at key segments of housewives which appear uniformly Europe-wide; others are positioned to take advantage of local preferences.

TARGET AUDIENCE. Looking at things internationally, you often note that the best market for your product varies from country to country. To insure coordination and maintain a common approach, despite these differences, it is useful to classify these markets into categories, according to their distinctive characteristics. In this way, it is possible to see which markets can benefit from other countries' experiences, and to make broad overall policy decisions which apply to many countries at a time.

MESSAGE STRATEGY. Here, too, it is possible to work out the alternatives and put together limited or very thoroughgoing packages of materials, centrally planned and often centrally produced, that provide uniformity while meeting the needs of specific markets. As an example, ITT gives its individual operations substantial freedom in the preparation of specific subjects in their advertising campaigns, but has established international criteria standardizing the appearance of its advertising, designed to maintain a family resemblance and to ensure a basic level of effectiveness.

MEDIA STRATEGY. The options vary from country to country, and this is often the excuse for an individual market to go its own way, cutting itself free from central coordination. Systematic inventories of the possibilities, country by country, make it possible to set up policies on how media are to be used to greatest effect, so that the plans of the individual markets interlock and enhance one another.

TIMING. Obviously, launching of brands in new markets has to be coordinated by the central planning group—and with rare exceptions, always is. Less often is the planning for selling seasons, rhythm of special events and merchandising operations coordinated on an international basis. A lot remains to be accomplished in this area.

The grid shown in Box 19–1, p. 716, illustrates how the modular approach could be applied to a soft drink, in terms of its options in various markets. The local manager, identifying his own market's characteristics, can assemble a policy appropriate to his country and obtain from the coordinating group whatever he needs, or be able to explain to them exactly why something special has to be developed. This approach also raises the individual manager's sights, so that he sees not just his own market but how his market fits into worldwide patterns. This promotes better communications and understanding between colleagues.

There is nothing mysterious about this kind of coordination. It takes effort, goodwill, effective communications and practice. It pays off in better advertising and marketing planning, and clearer interchange between top international management and local operations concerning their needs and possibilities.

Whatever the vicissitudes of currencies and economic and political factors, technology is steadily making the world smaller and increasing the requirements of uniformity combined with superior quality in multi-country advertising communications. Very few products and brands can use identical advertising everywhere, but almost any brand has got to work toward uniformity in some of the aspects of its advertising policy. The "coordination" approach recognizes diversity but seeks uniformity within sensible limits, working from the complex to find the simple ideas which are always the basis of really good advertising.

QUESTIONS

1. Define:

Esperanto	Due bill
International media	Pirate radio
Intercambio	

2. "Perhaps advertising is the side of international marketing with the greatest similarities from country to country throughout the world. Paradoxically, despite its many similarities, it may also be credited with the greatest number of unique problems in international marketing." Discuss.

3. Someone once commented that advertising is America's greatest export. Discuss.

4. Select three dissimilar countries from Exhibit 19–2 and explain differences in advertising per capita as best you can.

5. "Advertising is changing communication customs and habits in nearly all countries." Explain.

6. Outline some of the major problems confronting an international advertiser.

7. Defend either side of the proposition that advertising can be standardized for all countries.

8. Review the basic areas of advertising regulation. Are such regulations purely foreign phenomena?

9. How can advertisers overcome the problems of low literacy in their markets?

10. What special media problems confront the international advertiser?

11. Can the magazine cost per thousand differentials from country to country, as reported by IMEDE, be explained?

12. "In many of the world's market places, a broad variety of media must be utilized to reach the majority of the market." Explain.

13. Cinema advertising is unimportant in the U.S. but a major media in such countries as Austria. Why?

14. Identify some of the major differences in media usage patterns from the information in Table 18–2. Explain each variation.

15. "Foreign newspapers obviously cannot be considered as homogeneous advertising entities." Elaborate.

16. Discuss the ethics of pirate radio and TV broadcasting stations.

17. Borrow a foreign magazine from the library. Compare the foreign advertising to that in an American magazine.

OUTLINE OF CHAPTER 20

INTRODUCTION

BASIC STRUCTURAL ALTERNATIVES

Structural Implications

DOMESTIC MIDDLEMEN

Domestic Agent Middlemen

Combination Export Manager

Manufacturer's Export Agent

Broker

Buyer

Selling Group

Norazi Agent

Domestic Merchant Middlemen

Export Merchant and Jobber

Export Buyer and Foreign Importer

Trading Company

Complementary Marketer

MIDDLEMEN IN FOREIGN MARKETS

Agents in Customer Countries

Broker

Manufacturer's Representative

Factor

Managing Agent

Foreign Merchant Middlemen

Distributor

Dealer

Import Jobber

Wholesaler and Retailer

Affiliated Middleman

COMPANY DISTRIBUTION ABROAD

FACILITATING AGENCIES

Communications and Manufacturing Services

Finance, Insurance, and Credit

INTERNATIONAL DISTRIBUTION LOGISTICS

Physical Distribution Middlemen

Carrier

Freight Forwarder

Customs Expediter

Public Warehouse

Travel Agent

SUMMARY AND CONCLUSIONS

READING

How Schick Sharpened Dull Sales Techniques to Cut into German Market, *Business Europe*

THE INTERNATIONAL DISTRIBUTION SYSTEM

INTRODUCTION

In every country, communist or capitalist, and in every market, urban or rural, rich or poor, every consumer and industrial product eventually must go through the actual distribution process. Such a process includes not only the physical handling and distribution of goods but also relates to the passage of ownership and, most importantly from the standpoint of marketing strategy, to the buying and selling negotiations between middlemen, producers, and consumers. These are the concerns of this chapter, in which the types and characteristics of both domestic and foreign middlemen are considered. Further attention is focused on distribution through the company's own marketing apparatus. The facilitating agencies or middlemen that do not become a direct part of the distribution channel are also reviewed, and attention is given to the strategic importance of distribution logistics.

This chapter focuses primarily on the institutions themselves, because without a thorough understanding of these middlemen and agencies, policies leading to the development of an effective distribution system can hardly be established. Chapter 21, which follows, deals with the mechanics of export trade. Finally, Chapter 22 emphasizes policies and strategies pertaining to the channel of distribution and is addressed to the pragmatic questions of distribution channel management.

There is some conceptual overlap of this chapter with Chapter 13, "Dynamics of International Planning and Organization." That material, however, is concerned with intracompany relationships and with basic principles relative to intercompany activities. The present chapter is concerned primarily with the relationship between the company doing business internationally and the middlemen who take responsibility for selling and handling goods traded internationally. Because distribution channels in international business are often directly concerned with the physical handling of goods, basic information pertaining to physical distribution is integrated into the chapter. Such organization is not intended to neglect the importance of physical distribution but rather to illustrate its special importance as it affects international marketing policies.

Although physical distribution may include production, assembly, and importing activities, the chapter is concerned primarily with more basic functions of international exporting and international distribution. Importing is treated only from the viewpoint of international marketers who utilize foreign importers as a channel of distribution for their goods.

Primary consideration is given in this chapter to identification of the basic structural alternatives that are available to firms doing business internationally. It should be noted that the bulk of the discussion pertaining to middlemen applies directly both to consumer and industrial goods. The latter typically employ shorter channels than the former, but the functional alternatives are the same for all types of goods. The actual structures that are available in a given country depend directly on its stage of economic development, but in the more advanced economies all major types of middlemen are represented. In nearly all countries the marketer has a variety of alternative methods of distribution at his disposal.

BASIC STRUCTURAL ALTERNATIVES

The astute marketer who has an adequate understanding of the distribution channels in his own country has an almost automatic basic understanding of the channel types available to him in international activities. There is only a limited number of logical alternate ways in which to distribute a good. The uniqueness of international distribution derives less from the structural alternatives than from the infinite operational and market variables which affect channel operations.

Whatever the country of origin of the goods, a series of alternative channel systems is likely to be employed in building distribution. When export is involved, there is the problem of getting the goods from the producing country to the consuming country. Whether or not export is involved, the marketer must meet the challenge of getting his goods through the channels of distribution into the consumer's hands. Sometimes a producer will use domestic middlemen to handle both the export function and the distribution function. Sometimes he will use a set of domestic middlemen for the export function and a set of foreign middlemen for the distribution function. In each instance the marketer must make the choice whether he is going to handle all distribution himself or turn part or all of it over to various middlemen; often the distribution effort combines the activities of the producer and various middlemen. A manufacturer will use varying distribution methods in different countries, depending on market size, competition, and available distribution structures. A further alternative is to use supplementary systems of distribution, in which the marketer does his own distribution at the same time that he uses various middlemen for similar functions.

Policy and strategy considerations relative to these alternative forms of distribution are considered in Chapter 22, but at this point the key elements in a marketer's distribution decisions should be pointed out. They are: (1) the availability of middlemen, (2) the cost of their services, (3) the functions performed (and the effectiveness with which each is performed), and (4) the extent of control which the manufacturer can exert over the middlemen's activities. Knowledge of the structural alternatives permits the marketing manager to select from available middlemen those who will provide the optimum pattern of function, cost, and control. Company policy may dictate certain basic patterns, and national variations may indicate different solutions to distribution needs for various localities.

The firm has a wide variety of choices in the type and number of middlemen to be used. Exhibit 20–1 shows some of these possible

EXHIBIT 20–1

International Channel-of-Distribution Alternatives

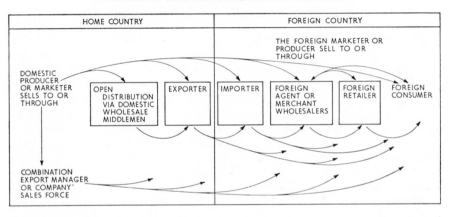

channel-of-distribution alternatives. The lines show those to whom the producer and each of the middlemen may sell. Trace, for example, the path of a product which is sold from the producer to an exporter who in turn sells it to a foreign wholesaler, who sells it to a retailer, who sells it to the consumer. This is but one channel; dozens of alternate patterns are actually followed.

In all instances involving middlemen external to the company, only two basic alternative types of middlemen are available: merchant middlemen, those who take title to the goods and buy and sell on their own account, and agent middlemen, those who directly represent the principal rather than themselves. The latter are compensated on the basis of commissions and fees rather than the resale margins utilized by the merchants. The framework for analysis of both domestic and foreign middlemen hinges on whether the middlemen are agents or merchants. Merchant middlemen, it should be remembered, actually take title to the goods in question, whereas agent middlemen do not.

Three alternative patterns are considered in this chapter: First, employment of middlemen who are physically located in the manufacturer's home country; next, utilization of middlemen who are actually located in the foreign countries in which one desires to sell; and finally, utilization of the company's own personnel as substitutes or supplements to the outside middlemen.

The reader is cautioned that this chapter makes it appear that international channels of distribution are clear-cut, precise, easily defined entities. This is most certainly not the case. It is the exception rather than the rule to find a firm which represents one of the pure types identified here. Many, perhaps most, international middlemen wear several hats and can be clearly identified only in the context of their relationship with a specific firm. One company, for example, engages in both importing and exporting; acts both as an agent and a merchant middleman; operates from offices in the United States, Germany, and Great Britain; provides financial services; and acts as a freight forwarder as well. Indeed, it would be difficult to put this company into an appropriate single pigeonhole; however, it is important to understand the pigeonholes, because one might wish to deal with this firm solely in its capacities as a merchant middleman with offices, salesmen, and storage facilities in Germany. True, many firms do work in a single capacity, but the conglomerate type of middleman described above is a major force in some parts of international business. In Japan, for example, the *zaibatsu* (financial and trading combines) represent a high state of development of the conglomerate international trading company. The four largest trading companies, Mitsui, Mitsubishi Shoji Kaisha, Marubeni-Iida, and C. Itoh & Co., had sales totaling some $20 billion (U.S.) in 1970. These firms are true world traders which deal in imports and exports and handle all kinds of transactions through a vast overseas network of branch offices. Some *zaibatsu* also own manufacturing plants and have tying arrangements with other manufacturing and trading firms. Such firms not only act as import agents and export agents, but they have also played an important role in the history of business in Japan through their financial power and consequent political power. One Japanese newspaper, in fact, has described them as the "prime movers" in the Japanese economy.

It should also be noted that the alternative channels of distribution available to the international marketer directly reflect the stage of economic development of the country in which the marketing is being undertaken. In various articles on the subject, George Wadinambiaratchi has argued, on the basis of his studies of nine countries, that there is a definite correlation between the state of economic development and the level of development of distribution facilities. Specifically, as a country becomes more developed:

1. It tends to reflect more closely the distribution system of the United States.
2. There is a rather clear separation of manufacturing, wholesaling, and retailing.

BOX 20–1

Distribution in Europe

Probably the single most important obstacle to the development of marketing mindedness in companies in Europe is the state of the distribution systems in the various countries. In fact, the final level of distribution, retailing in Europe, has been described as a form of massive underemployment acting as a hedge against future unemployment and as a serious impediment to progress.

Prior political and economic instability in Europe has increased the desire for independence from uncontrollable market factors among persons in, or about to enter, commerce: this helps to explain the existence and even continued proliferation of independent retailers, many of whom seem to have an almost incredible ability to resist change. As their trade is snatched from them by larger and more efficient distribution units, they "make do" on less and less business and their feelings of pride in their independence become more and more intense. Since advertising is expensive, manufacturers find it difficult to use "consumer pull" alone to promote their new products, and are thus often up against the problem of convincing diffident retailers to stock their product with no guarantee of a sales success. A general pattern seems to be that the smaller the retailer is, the less risk he takes. As a result there is a sharp segmentation of newer-concept products in the more progressive stores and more traditional products in the independent, old-line stores.

Source: John Groves & Elizabeth Trotman, "A New Look at European Marketing," *Business Europe,* January 30, 1968, p. 43. Reprinted from the January 30, 1968, issue of *Business Europe,* with the permission of the publisher, Business International S.A. (Geneva).

3. Merchant middlemen such as wholesalers and retailers are more highly developed.
4. The variety, volume of business, and efficiency of middlemen grow.[1]

Structural Implications

Although skeletal structures of international distribution channels vary but little, the international marketer is called upon to have an intimate knowledge of such structures so that he can plan and implement an effective distribution channel policy. Such knowledge may be more thoroughly tested in international business than in domestic because the international marketer may have to use a wide variety of channels to adequately service different markets. A domestic marketer seldom uses more than a few channels.

Furthermore, intimate knowledge of the functions is especially important in international activity because misleading titles can easily fool a marketer who is not able to look beyond mere names. What func-

---

[1] George Wadinambiaratchi, *Business Quarterly,* Winter 1965, pp. 74–82.

| Type of Duties | Agents | | | | |
	CEM	MEA	Broker	Buying Offices	Other Manufacturers
Take title..............	No	No	No	No	No
Take possession..........	Yes	Yes	No	Yes	Yes
Continuing relationship.........	Yes	Yes	No	Yes	Yes
Share of foreign output..............	All	All	Any	Small	All
Degree of control by principal............	Fair	Fair	Nil	Nil	Good
Price authority...........	Advisory	Advisory	Yes (at market level)	Yes (to buy)	Advisory
Represent buyer or seller.................	Seller	Seller	Either	Buyer	Seller
Number of principals......	Few—Many	Few—Many	Many	Small	Few
Arrange shipping.........	Yes	Yes	Not usually	Yes	Yes
Type of goods...........	Manufactured goods and commodities	Staples and commodities	Staples and commodities	Staples and commodities	Complementary to their own lines
Breadth of line...........	Specialty—wide	All types of staples	All types of staples	Retail goods	Narrow
Handle competitive lines..................	No	No	Yes	Yes—utilizes many sources	No
Extent of promotion and selling effort.......	Good	Good	One shot	N.A.	Good
Extends credit to principal..............	Occasionally	Occasionally	Seldom	Seldom	Seldom
Market information......	Fair	Fair	Price and market conditions	For principal not for manufacturer	Good

tions, for example, are performed by the British middlemen called stockists or, for that matter, one who simply calls himself an exporter or importer? One exporter may in fact be an agent middleman, whereas another is a merchant. Only by analyzing functions in skeletal simplicity can one determine the nature of the channels. The reader is again cautioned to bear in mind the great departures from the simple structures described and outlined below and to be equally aware that a thorough understanding of the basic structure provides the only effective way to a comprehensive understanding of more complicated distribution arrangements.

DOMESTIC MIDDLEMEN

Domestic middlemen are located in the same country as the producing firm and provide marketing services from the domestic base. Although they are closer to the manufacturer and may be more convenient to use, domestic middlemen are removed from their markets and may not be able to provide market information or overseas representation as well as foreign middlemen. Domestic middlemen are most likely to be used when the producer is not prepared or able to justify direct overseas

| Intermerchant | Norazi | Merchants | | | | |
		Export Merchant	Export Jobber	Buyers for Export	Importers and Trading Companies	Complementary Marketers
No	No	Yes	Yes	Yes	Yes	Yes
No	Yes	Yes	No	Yes	Yes	Yes
No	No	No	Yes	No	Yes	Yes
Small	Small	Any	Small	Small	Any	Most
Nil	Nil	None	None	None	Nil	Fair
Some	Yes	Yes	Yes	Yes	No	Some
Both at once	Both	Self	Self	Self	Self	Self
Several per transaction	Several per transaction	Many sources	Many sources	Many sources	Many sources	One per product
No	Yes	Yes	Yes	Yes	Yes	Yes
Any	Contraband	Manufactured goods	Bulky and raw materials	All types	Manufactured goods	Complementary to line
	N.A.	Broad	Broad	Broad	Broad	Narrow
Yes	Yes	Yes	Yes	Yes	Yes	No
Nil	Nil	Nil	Nil	Nil	Good	Good
No	No	Occasionally	Seldom	Seldom	Seldom	Seldom
No	No	Nil	Nil	Nil	Fair	Good

contact in many markets. Like the other middlemen, they carry different names; but the classes described in the following sections represent types of operations and services offered. Basic kinds are Domestic agent middlemen and Domestic merchant middlemen.

Exhibit 20–2 summarizes pertinent information pertaining to the major kinds of domestic middlemen operating in foreign markets. No attempt is made to generalize about rates of commission, markup, or pay because so many things influence the compensation. Services offered or demanded, market structure, volume, and product type are some of the key determinants. The data represent the predominant patterns of operations; however, individual middlemen of a given type may vary in their operations.

Domestic Agent Middlemen

One author calls the use of agent middlemen "domestic exporting." Export agents are known by many titles, which can lead to no end of confusion; to compound the confusion, agents may call themselves by one title but function by another or may function in several different agent-middleman capacities. Furthermore, every country has different titles for the middlemen. For example, a broker in Belgium is called a *courtier*, in Germany a *handelsmakler*, in Italy a *mediatore*, in the Netherlands a *makelaar*. Regardless of title, some basic types of domestic agent middlemen may be identified: combination export manager (CEM), manufacturer's export agent (MEA), broker, buyer, selling group, and Norazi agent.

Domestic agent middlemen have the following characteristics in common: they do not take title to the merchandise, they work on a commission basis, and they arrange for sales (at least the initial sale) in the foreign country.

Sometimes domestic agents function almost as a foreign department for a company that wants to conduct international trade with a low capital outlay. The parent company cannot directly control all the activities of such middlemen, but it can establish policy guidelines that usually will be followed by the agents. In many instances, the manufacturer will be able to establish product prices and require that the products be sold at those prices. The manufacturer may undertake his own advertising or may work out some arrangement so that the agent will handle it. In most cases, the manufacturer can require his agent to provide sales records and customer information. In some cases, the agent middleman may even work out of the company office and have a very close working relationship with company marketing officials.

Combination Export Manager.   The combination export manager (CEM) is a particularly important agent middleman for firms with relatively small international volume or for those that do not want to involve their own personnel in the international function. CEM firms range in size from one person to about 100 and handle some 5 percent of the total exports of the United States (which means they handle about 10 percent of the manufactured goods exported). About 1,000 such firms exist, performing the primary function of serving as overseas selling agents for a number of principals and acting as the international marketing department for the firms they represent.

The stock in trade of the CEM is personalized service; typically the firm becomes an integral part of the marketing operations of the client companies. Although he is an agent middleman, the CEM works under the name of his manufacturers, sometimes using letterheads from his principal firms and signing himself as export manager of those firms; the customer seldom knows that he is not dealing directly with the export department of the company. The CEM functions as an effective low-cost independent marketing department with direct responsibility to the parent firm for all policy decisions. In most cases, the parent company designates an executive to serve as a liaison man with the CEM, and the parent company maintains final control over all marketing matters pertaining to its business.

The CEM does not handle lines that are directly competitive but seeks those that will complement one another and permit him some degree of specialization in his marketing efforts. These firms specialize in such products as branded food products, automotive maintenance equipment, machine tools, or fasteners and fastening devices; nearly

BOX 20–2

CEMs Help Increase Sales

Inquiries from potential customers overseas used to pile up on Charles Wade's desk and eventually wind up in the wastebasket. "I never bothered to answer them," says the president of CHD, Inc., a maker of swimming pool equipment. "They were a nuisance, and some were written in a language I couldn't even read."

Today Mr. Wade claims to be the largest exporter of such swimming pool items as filters, lamps and heaters. Foreign letters barely arrive before they are wisked over to Meridian Enterprises, Inc., in nearby Los Angeles. Meridian serves as CHD's foreign sales department and last year sold more than $250,000 of CHD products overseas, 25% of the pool equipment maker's total 1964 sales.

Meridian is one of a rapidly growing breed of concerns, called combination export managers or CEMs, which are carving a niche for themselves in world trade by exporting products made by small companies like CHD.

Source: Frank Morgan, "Little Guys & Trade: Export-Managing Firms Help Small Businesses Gain Markets Abroad," *Wall Street Journal*, September 8, 1965, p. 1. Reprinted with permission.

any area of manufactured goods is likely to constitute a speciality for some CEM. As few as 5 to 10 clients may provide adequate volume for a CEM firm, but some handle as many as 100 different clients.

The CEM firm provides many services for the manufacturer; it may handle all the company's international marketing activities, or some of them may be retained by the company. Advertising, for example, might be integrated and handled by the company's regular advertising agency, but channel-of-distribution arrangements for the same company might be the responsibility of the CEM. In all instances, the main functions of the CEM are contact with foreign customers (sometimes through a CEM's own foreign branches) and negotiations for sales. His specialization in a given field often makes it possible for him to offer a level of service which could not be achieved by the manufacturer himself for many years. The CEM has contact with customers and middlemen in foreign countries and can sometimes provide virtually instant distribution.

The CEM may take full responsibility for promotion of the goods, the cost of which would be paid for by the manufacturer but coordinated by CEM. Credit information is another major function; in some instances the CEM firm not only provides credit information but handles the credit function as well. Physical handling is a direct responsibility of the CEM, who arranges for all shipments and may save his principal considerable sums by consolidating shipments with those of his other principals. The CEM's foreign experience often puts him in a position to provide information and advice in financial, patent, and licensing management matters; he may even take responsibility for setting up subsidiaries or licensees in foreign countries. As part of their information function, some CEM firms undertake basic research in an attempt to determine where there will be active, continuing, stable markets for various types of products. Sometimes the CEM acquires this sort of market information, then seeks out manufacturers of products for which there is a foreign demand and offers its services.

Two of the chief advantages of using CEMs is that a minimum investment is required on the part of the company in order to get into international markets and no company manpower or major expenditure of managerial effort is required. The result, in effect, is an extension of the market for the firm with negligible financial or manpower commitments.

The CEM depends mainly on commissions for his compensation but may also receive a retainer and various other fees. Because the services of CEMs differ so widely, rates of compensation vary too widely to permit generalization. Consider the variety: the CEM may handle a broad group of lines or may specialize in a few products; he may specialize in one country or continent or may provide full international service; he may take full responsibility for all the marketing activities of the firm or may confine himself to sales representation alone. Obviously when the range of the services required is broad, where the CEM is expected to take a significant market or credit risk, or where the volume of sales is small, commission percentages are likely to be higher. In most instances, the commission will range between 10 and 20 percent of the selling price of goods. Usually more than a simple commission arrangement is involved; compensation may include sliding percentage scales, depending on sales volume or size of single sales, some kind of expense-sharing arrangements, and special fees for various services undertaken.

CEMs have traditionally operated only as agent middlemen, but in recent years they have increasingly tended to buy and sell on their own accounts, thus becoming merchant middlemen. Even in this capacity, however, they operate more as agents than as merchants because they usually purchase goods only after they have been sold or after specific markets have been found for them. Sometimes they do go so far, however, as to purchase the merchandise and resell it under their own brand on their own account.

Expansion of corporate international marketing activities has been a mixed blessing for CEMs. Some of the best CEM customer firms have reached operating levels where they can do their own international marketing and therefore no longer need the services of the CEM firm; others have merged or joined forces with companies that have existing international operations. Such problems foster a tendency for CEMs to spread themselves too thinly by handling either too broad a range of products or by attempting to provide representation in too many different countries. This pattern is understandable, because CEMs who are unable to develop clients in a narrow group of related lines tend to reach out to unrelated lines in order to build the sales volume they need to survive. A CEM can seldom afford to make the kind of market investment needed to establish deep distribution for his products, because he must have immediate payout for his sales efforts if he is to survive.

Such a situation does not offer the market advantages gained by a company which can afford to build itself into a market. Carefully selected CEMs can do an excellent job, but the manufacturer must remember the CEM is dependent on sales volume for his compensation and probably will not push the manufacturer's line if he cannot do so profitably in the short run. When he is spread too thinly or when he cannot operate profitably on the volume of business the principal provides, the CEM tends to become merely an order taker and not the desired substitute for a company's international marketing department.

Manufacturer's Export Agent.   The manufacturer's export agent (MEA) is an individual agent middleman or an agent middleman firm providing a selling service for manufacturers. Unlike the CEM, the MEA does not serve as the producer's export department but has a short-term relationship, covers only one or two markets, and operates on a straight commission basis. Thus a manufacturer would be likely to deal with only one CEM, but a manufacturer using MEAs might deal with 6 or 12 or even more. Another principal difference between the MEA and the CEM is that the former does business in his own name rather than in the name of the client. As often as not, the MEA finds that there is a market for a given product in an area in which he operates and seeks out a manufacturer willing to sell through him to that market.

The MEA normally operates strictly as an agent middleman and does no buying or selling on his own account. Within his limited scope of operation, the MEA provides other services similar to those of the CEM; he handles the physical shipment, provides market information, gives credit, and arranges for payment. For an internationally minded firm his chief shortcoming is that he does not provide wide market coverage or a continued market relationship.

Broker.   The term "broker" is a catch-all which is likely to include a variety of different types of middlemen, each of whom performs some agent middleman service or group of services. Most typically, the term is applied to an import-export broker who provides the intermediary function of bringing buyers and sellers together. As such he may represent either the seller or the buyer or both and may receive his commission from either or both. Most brokers operate in the bulky goods of the commodity field and specialize in one or a few commodity types for which they maintain contact with major producers and purchasers throughout the entire world. The broker generally operates on a low percentage margin and does not maintain a continuing relationship with his suppliers or customers.

Some brokers specialize in individual countries rather than commodities. The division of the world into East and West blocs has caused the rise of some import-export firms which specialize in dealing with Soviet Union and Eastern European countries—Satra Corp. in New York, for example, is the largest U.S. concern with such a speciality. Its volume has exceeded $50 million in one year. Clients for such a firm include some of America's giants, which have found attempting to sell to Soviet buyers without such intermediaries too time consuming and frustrating. Obviously the chief advantage such middlemen offer is their specialized knowledge of the trading regulations of the countries they are dealing with.

There exists in Europe a small band of some 20 middleman firms called barter brokers who specialize in arranging international barter transactions for companies in countries with foreign exchange short-ages. Although only a few firms operate in this field, it is an important business. One firm handled transactions in one year totaling over a billion dollars (U.S.). Another has 5,000 worldwide agents and a fleet of 15 freighters to facilitate handling of the exchanged commodities and goods.

The intermerchant is a relative to the barter broker. He is an export broker who arranges trades or triangular trades involving several prin-cipals from different countries who need to overcome soft currency or exchange restrictions. He differs from the barter broker primarily in the fact that he may deal with direct sales transactions in which there is no barter. His speciality is arranging for compensating currency ar-rangements.

Buyer. A variety of agent middlemen may be classified simply as buyers or buyers for export. Their common denominator is their primary function of seeking and purchasing merchandise on request from the principals; as such they do not provide a selling service. In fact, their chief emphasis is on their flexibility and their ability to find merchan-dise from any source, so they do not often become involved in continu-ing relationships with domestic supplies and do not provide a continuing source of representation. The buyer, however, is a good source of sales, and as long as the price, merchandise, and terms are right, he may continue to buy from one firm over a long period of years. Un-fortunately, from a distribution control standpoint, the supplier firm's role is essentially passive.

The resident buyer, the most important form of buyer, specializes in a particular line of goods. Persons familiar with the retail scene will recall that many American retail stores employ a resident buyer firm in New York or London to perform buying functions. The same firms, as well as others which specialize in foreign markets, operate in New York and other major market centers representing retailers and wholesalers from many countries. The resident buyer or resident buying office op-erates on a retainer, fee, or commission basis or on a combination of the three. In a typical operation, he is notified of the type of merchan-dise his client wants and the dollar amount or number of units to be purchased. He then contacts the supplier firms, selects the merchandise, and executes a contract on behalf of his principal. Resident buying of-fices are responsible for a large percentage of the department store merchandise which is directly exported from this country. The buyer takes responsibility for the physical handling and shipment of the goods, as well as paying in cash or providing acceptable paper for the transaction.

A special form of buyer called the export commission house, or com-missionaire, operates in a manner similar to the resident buyer but works only on commission and typically handles a broader range of merchandise than the resident buyer. Most resident buyers maintain a continuing relationship with their clients, but the commissionaire operates on a transaction-by-transaction basis. The commissionaire usually buys and sells in his own name on behalf of the principal; often the seller does not even know the identity of the customer. One should be careful in using the term commissionaire because it is common in Europe to call a broker a *commissionaire*.

Selling Group.   Several types of arrangements have been developed in which various manufacturers or producers cooperate in a joint attempt to sell their merchandise abroad. Such activities may take the form of complementary exporting or of selling to a business combine, such as a Webb-Pomerene export association. Both are considered agency arrangements when the exporting is done on a fee or commission basis.

When business firms have unused marketing capacity or export capacity, they sometimes share their facilities with companies having complementary but noncompeting lines. Such an arrangement is sometimes called piggybacking or complementary exporting. Most piggybacking is accomplished on a merchant middleman basis, but some is accomplished on commission. The benefit to the handling company (sometimes called a mother hen) is that it is able to spread its international cost over greater volume and is sometimes able to broaden its product lines and accomplish more effective communication with the markets. Complementary exporters may provide the full range of marketing services or may limit their activities to such things as packing, shipping, or other physical distribution functions. The subject of piggybacking is covered at length below in the domestic merchant middlemen section of this chapter.

Webb-Pomerene export associations constitute another major form of group exporting. In 1918 the U.S. Congress enacted export trade legislation commonly known as the Webb-Pomerene Act. This law made it possible for American business firms to join forces in export activities without being subject to the Sherman Antitrust Act. Court interpretations over the years have made it clear that Webb-Pomerene associations (WPEA) cannot participate in cartels or other international agreements which would tend to reduce competition in the United States. In recent years WPEAs have been under attack by the Department of Justice, and advocates have been forced to defend them before the Senate Subcommittee on Antitrust and Monopoly. The hearings indicated that the 31 associations existing in the United States account for less than 4 percent of total U.S. exports. Members of the various associations generally agree that there are four major benefits of membership: (1) reduction of export cost, (2) demand expansion through promotion, (3) trade barrier reductions, and (4) improvement of trade terms through bilateral bargaining. In accomplishing the activities above, WPEA associations frequently are in the position of setting prices and standardizing products as well as arranging for disposal of surplus products.

Webb-Pomerene export associations operate in one of four ways. The mode of operation of the association determines its place in the corporate organization. The four alternative basic patterns of operation are as follows:

1. The association limits itself to publicity, advertising, and information dissemination activities.
2. The assocation handles the export procedure for its members but performs only an order-filling function.
3. The association acts as a selling agent for its members. In this instance, the association promotes merchandise, negotiates sales, divides orders among association members, and arranges for shipment.
4. Some associations actually purchase products from their corporate members under terms and proportional allotments agreed on by the membership. The association then acts as a merchant wholesaler and markets the products in foreign countries.

Many organizational variations exist, but in every case the participating corporations are bound by the association agreement. Chief benefits of participation in a Webb-Pomerene export association are that selling and promotional overhead can be spread among the participating members; the association can set prices for overseas shipments; the association can establish private trade practice agreements and uniform contracts; and shipping economies can be affected through consolidating shipping facilities and combined shipments. Note that none of the four methods of operation permit an individual company to modify its share of the export business significantly. The only voice a corporation has is its vote in the trade association meetings. Aggressive firms may, therefore, find that involvement in such an organization restricts them unduly.

A look at some of the associations and their member companies certainly indicates that the Webb-Pomerene associations include some of America's blue-chip companies. Their activities have been primarily in the fields of manufacturing and specialty items; agricultural products; chemicals and raw materials; forest products, pulp and paper; textiles, and motion pictures and television. The largest are:

1. Sulphur Export Corporation (Sulexco): includes Duval Corporation, Freeport Sulphur, Jefferson Lake Sulphur, and Texas Gulf Sulphur.
2. Textile Export Association: 24 members including Burlington Industries, Dan River International, and J. P. Stevens.
3. Potash Export Association: includes Duval Corporation, International Minerals and Chemical Corporation, Potash Corporation of America, Southwest Potash, and Texas Gulf Sulphur Company.
4. Rubber Export Association: includes Firestone, General Tire, B. F. Goodrich, Goodyear, and Uniroyal.

Norazi Agent. A Norazi agent is a typical middleman who specializes in shady or difficult transactions. He deals in contraband materials, such as radioactive products or war materials, and in providing strategic goods to countries that are closed to normal trading channels. The Norazi agent is also likely to be engaged in black market currency operations as well as trade in untaxed liquor, narcotics, and other illicit traffic.

Although he is called an agent, the Norazi does not limit himself to agent-type transactions. In many instances, he becomes a merchant and purchases goods for his own account. When a Norazi perceives the opportunity for an exceptionally large profit he may change from merchant to agent or agent to merchant, whichever is to his advantage. Despite the unsavory trade in which he is engaged, the Norazi agent has a reputation for dealing ethically with his clients. This is mandatory because neither he nor his client works on the basis of written contracts or has recourse to justice through the court system.

Norazi agents exist primarily because tariffs, import taxes, and excise taxes make illegal movements of goods more profitable than legal movements. In Uruguay, for example, the legal cost of a package of U.S. cigarettes is $1.40 (U.S.), but only $.50 on the black market. In that same country the official cost of a Volkswagen made in Brazil to sell for about $3,000 is $6,000 including import duties. Argentina estimates that it loses over $43,000,000 (U.S.) a year in cigarette taxes alone because of smuggling from Uruguay. In Argentina, too, a smuggled Japanese camera can be bought for a little more than half the price of the camera coming through official channels. As a top-ranking LAFTA official commented, "Contrabanding has a major impact on the economies of Latin nations."

The nefarious activities of Norazi agents and others who deal in contraband materials and smuggling have reached such a proportion that a counterforce called Inter-Respol has been organized to combat contrabanding on an international basis. Respol of Chile, for example, recently confiscated $100,000 worth of Japanese radio and television sets which were being flown into Chile from Panama. The Norazi agent is not without his representation in the halls of government, however, and in Bolivia a group called the Union of Minority Businessmen speaks openly in favor of the smuggling trade. It has communicated its story so well that one government official says, "Smuggling is a social and economic necessity since it allows people to buy goods at lower prices."[2]

That most manufacturers do not need or desire the services of Norazi agents is indeed fortunate, because they are difficult to contact and their fees are extremely high. The volume of business transacted by Norazi agents is not known; in fact their obscurity is the chief reason for their inclusion here.

Domestic Merchant Middlemen

Merchant middlemen provide a variety of wholesaling functions, all of which involve purchasing for the merchant's own account and selling in foreign countries; most international merchant middlemen both im-

---

[2] "Where Smuggling Is a Way of Life," *Business Week*, August 15, 1970, pp. 24–25.

port and export. The merchant middleman bears the majority of trading risks for the products he handles, and his profit comes from the gross margin spread. Because the merchant middleman is primarily concerned with sales and profit margins on his merchandise, he can hardly be depended on to represent consistently the best interest of a given manufacturer. Unless he has a franchise on a strong and profitable brand, the middleman seeks goods from any source and is likely to have low brand loyalty; to expect him to do otherwise is unrealistic. Because they actually take title to the goods, such merchant middlemen as wholesalers, distributors, and foreign import houses are less controllable than agent middlemen. In some instances, however, the parent company can retain a fair degree of control over such middlemen if the line is valuable to the middlemen.

To a manufacturer, the key advantages for using domestic merchant middlemen is that they are easy to contact, they minimize credit risk, and they eliminate all merchandise handling outside the United States. Major export middlemen considered in the following section include: export merchants and export jobbers, export buyers and domestic offices of foreign importers, trading companies, and complementary manufacturers.

Export Merchant and Jobber. The export merchant is essentially a domestic wholesaler operating in foreign markets. As such, he operates very much in the fashion of the domestic wholesaler. Specifically, he purchases goods from a large number of manufacturers, ships them to foreign countries, and takes full responsibility for their marketing; sometimes he utilizes his own organization but more commonly he sells through other middlemen. He operates in either consumer or industrial goods; some merchants handle both. The export merchant carries competing lines if it suits his requirements. He has full control over prices and has little loyalty to his suppliers, because only seldom do the goods of one producer account for a significant portion of his sales. Although he has little loyalty to his suppliers, he will continue to handle their products as long as they are profitable for him. Sustained profits often result in long-term relationships between manufacturers and export merchants. Some export merchants will handle nearly any kind of merchandise they can sell, but most tend to specialize in a given field and thereby are able to offer a reasonable amount of foreign market information. The scope of operations varies widely among merchant middlemen; some have extensive staffs and operate in all corners of the world, whereas others may specialize in one or a few countries.

Export jobbers are very similar to domestic drop shippers or desk jobbers; they are in fact, often called export drop shippers. Variations of the export drop shipper include cable merchants and export speculators. Typically these middlemen deal with bulky goods or raw materials. They do not take physical possession of the goods but assume responsibility for arranging transportation. Like the domestic drop shipper, the export jobber represents only himself and typically buys or sells goods only when he has already arranged to complete both sides of the transaction. The export speculator, as his name implies, however, does purchase for his own account whenever he finds an opportunity to buy or sell goods at a particularly favorable price. Obviously, all of these middlemen depend heavily on their knowledge of market conditions. Because they work on a job-lot basis, they do not provide a particularly attractive distribution alternative for most producers.

Export Buyer and Foreign Importer.   The export buyer is a type of export speculator. He is somewhat comparable to an agent buying office in that he buys for customers in other countries, but the export buyer operates on his own account. Generally, he is a bargain hunter, seeking distressed merchandise, overproduction, obsolete products, or other goods which can be bought cheaply and resold in foreign markets.

Domestic offices of importers and trading companies provide a major source of direct distribution for the firm wishing to engage in international business without becoming involved in the actual foreign distribution. Contacts with the import and trading companies can be made in the home country of the manufacturer; the sale is essentially domestic and the middlemen take the responsibility for all credit, shipment, and foreign marketing of the products. The word "importer" has various meanings to different individuals; to some he is an agent middleman, to others he is a merchant middleman; in some instances he imports goods into only one country, in others he operates in many countries. In this discussion, we are considering the importer as a merchant middleman who is operating a buying office in the supplier's country. He may then distribute the goods in one or many different countries. A special form of importer is the trading company. The chief distinction is that an importer may merely purchase the goods and turn them over to some middleman in the country in which they are to be distributed, and that is the end of his responsibility. The trading company, on the other hand, typically has its own well-developed distribution structure within the countries in which it operates.

Trading Company.   Trading companies have a long and honorable history and have been important intermediaries in the development of trade between nations; they have been especially important in recent centuries in trade between developed and undeveloped countries. The earliest trading companies were ventures formed in ancient Greece, Mesopotamia, and Phoenicia some three or four thousand years before the time of Christ; such companies were also active in the days of the Roman Empire.

The chief purposes of the trading companies are, as in the past, the accumulation, transportation, and distribution of goods from many countries. An important element of the early trading company was the spreading of risk among different investors in joint ventures. In concept, the trading company has changed little in thousands of years.

Trading companies were important in the colonial movement and in trade with developing countries. The English Hudson's Bay Company and East India Company were primarily trading vehicles of the 16th, 17th, and 18th centuries. More recently, the United Africa Company (now a subsidiary of Unilever) was formed in 1929 by conglomerating several existing trading companies (including the Royal Niger Company, which was originally licensed by the Crown to *trade and rule* what is today Nigeria). The United Africa Company has a series of department stores and retail grocery stores throughout Africa. It also has a subsidiary, United Africa Motors, with vehicle assembly plants in three countries and automobile agencies throughout the African continent. In addition to its merchandising and manufacturing functions, the company also has consulting companies and a host of other special functions.

The French also were active in building trading companies. Two founded in Africa at the turn of the century are CFAO (Cie Française de l'Afrique Occidentale) and SCOA (Ste. Commerciale de l'Ouest Africain). CFAO operates in 18 African states with sales of some $200,-000,000 (U.S.) in 1970. In addition to a large chain of supermarkets and small country stores, CFAO has a capital goods division, manufacturing facilities, and a brewery. The type of goods hauled indicate something about the state of the consumer market; simple iron utensils such as hoes and pots and pans and other implements account for some three fourths of the company's consumer goods sales. SCOA had sales of around $150 million (U.S.) in 1970 and handles imports of foods, iron utensils, textiles, furniture, capital goods, and motor vehicles. The company also produces Coca-Cola in the Ivory Coast and Senegal. Like the other trading companies, SCOA participates widely in joint ventures with manufacturers and producers of consumer goods.

One other European trading company should be mentioned. That is the East Asiatic Company of Denmark, commonly called "Old East." The company was established in Thailand in 1897 for the production of timber and agricultural products on company-owned plantations. It now also imports and exports a wide range of products in Africa. Old East sells and services automobiles and trucks and deals extensively in raw materials through branches in 35 countries, including 12 in Africa. The East Asiatic Co. had a sales volume in 1970 of some $1 billion (U.S.).

The companies discussed above represent one type of trading company—that located in a developed country which does most of its business in selling manufactured goods to developing countries and buying their raw materials and unprocessed goods. Quite a different pattern is encountered with the Japanese trading companies, which initially were formed about 1700 to facilitate distribution of goods *within* the country. Later they developed into companies which emphasized importing and brought goods into Japan. Their current role is that of merchant importers and exporters with widespread operations throughout the world. Japan has nearly 7,000 trading companies, of which some 300 are engaged in foreign and domestic trade. These 300 firms have some 2,000 branch offices outside of Japan and handle 80 percent of the imports and exports of Japan. Four companies alone handle over $20 billion (U.S.) in trading volume annually. These four are Mitsui and Company, Mitsubishi Shoji Kaisha Ltd., Marubeni-Iida Co., Ltd., and C. Itoh and Co. These companies handle a great majority of all American goods entering Japan and are responsible for marketing the bulk of Japanese goods throughout the world. They perform five major functions: the importing and exporting functions per se, financing, development of joint ventures, technical assistance and advice, and production of goods. The most unique part of the Japanese trading company is its deep involvement in the Japanese distribution system. The omnipresent trading companies virtually control distribution through all levels of channels in Japan; for that matter, trading companies are visible in all aspects of the Japanese economy.

The state trading company which serves as the international business representative of East European countries deserves brief mention. In the Soviet Union, for example, there are some 40 foreign trade organizations which are part of the Ministry of Foreign Trade. Each one has its own organization and is responsible for an exclusive product specialty. One, for example, called Machinoimport, handles welding, mining, oil drilling and refining equipment as well as railroad cars, escalators, electric substations, and pumps and compressors. These foreign trade organizations are represented by government-owned foreign trading companies. In the United States the Soviet trading company is Amtorg Trading Corporation, which technically handles all imports and exports for the Soviet Union. Because the Soviet Union and other East European countries view trade as a matter of foreign policy, it is understandable that its trading companies are tightly controlled on a political level.

The foregoing discussion clearly suggests that the use of merchant importers and trading companies is not only beneficial but imperative in certain circumstances, because sometimes only such trading companies provide adequate coverage, market access, or political acceptability.

Complementary Marketers.   Sometimes companies with marketing facilities or contacts in different countries have excess marketing capacity or feel they could gain by having a broader product line. In such instances the prospect of taking on additional lines for international distribution may be appealing. The generic name for such activities is complementary marketing, but it is commonly called "piggybacking." There are advantages both for the carrier firm and for the supplier firm; many major companies are active in piggybacking. General Electric Company has been distributing merchandise for other suppliers for many years. Its policy has been to accept products that are noncompetitive but complementary and that add to the basic distribution strength of the company itself. Most piggyback arrangements are undertaken when a firm wishes to fill out its product line or keep its distribution channels for seasonal items functioning throughout the year. The motive may be simply to raise volume and make distribution more economical. Singer Sewing Machine Company emphasizes products closely allied to its own. They piggyback fabrics, patterns, notions, and thread. That company, by the way, considers manufacturing or licensing production for its own account as well as piggybacking and takes on piggyback products only when it is the most effective and profitable means of handling the product. Companies may work either on an agency or merchant basis, but by far the greatest volume of piggyback business

EXHIBIT 20–3

Characteristics of Middlemen in Foreign Countries

	Agents			
Type of Duties	*Broker*	*Factor*	*Manufacturer's Representative*	*Import Commission*
Take title..............	No	No	No	No
Take possession.........	No	No	Seldom	Seldom
Continuing relationship...........	No	Sometimes	Often	With buyer, not seller
Share of foreign output..............	Small	Small	All or part for one area	N.A.
Degree of control by principal.............	Low	Low	Fair	None
Price authority..........	Nil	Nil	Nil	Nil
Represent buyer or seller...............	Either	Either	Seller	Buyer
Number of principals....	Many	Many	Few	Many
Arrange shipping........	No	No	No	No
Type of goods..........	Commodity and food	Commodity and food	Manufactured goods	All types manufactured goods
Breadth of line..........	Broad	Broad (often specialized)	Allied lines	Broad
Handle competitive lines.................	Yes	Yes	No	Yes
Extent of promotion and selling effort..........	Nil	Nil	Fair	Nil
Extends credit to principal.............	No	Yes	No	No
Market information.....	Nil	Fair	Good	Nil

is handled on an ownership (merchant) purchase-resale arrangement. Borg Warner, one of the pioneers in this field, has been piggybacking since the 1930s. This firm always buys merchandise at a flat bulk domestic rate from a manufacturing company, then establishes its own selling prices for worldwide distribution.

Primary criteria for selecting new products for piggyback distribution are: (1) Is the product related to the product line, and does it contribute to it? (2) Does the product fit the sales and distribution channel presently employed? (3) Is there an adequate margin to make the undertaking worthwhile? and (4) Will the product find market acceptance and profitable volume? If these requirements are met, piggybacking is likely to be a logical way of increasing volume and profit for both the carrier and the piggybacker.

Other types of cooperative marketing ventures including two or more companies exist, but it is difficult to characterize them under a single heading. In most cases, they work through joint ventures or cost-sharing distribution arrangements. In any piggybacking or cooperative marketing effort, the producer must be certain that he will have sufficient control

| | Merchant | | | |
Comprador	Distributor	Dealer	Import Jobber	Retailer
No	Yes	Yes	Yes	Yes
Yes	Yes	Yes	Yes	Yes
Yes	Yes	Yes	No	Usually not
All one area	All, for certain countries	Assignment area	Small	Very small
Fair	High	High	Low	Nil
Partial	Partial	Partial	Full	Full
Seller	Seller	Seller	Self	Self
Few	Small	Few major	Many	Many
No	No	No	No	No
Manufactured goods	Manufactured goods	Manufactured goods	Manufactured goods	Manufactured consumer
	Narrow to broad	Narrow	Narrow to broad	Narrow to broad
No	No	No	Yes	Yes
Fair	Fair	600	Nil	Nil usually
Sometimes	Sometimes	No	No	No
Good	Fair	600	Nil	Nil

over his product to bring the kind of sales volume and profit required to make the venture worthwhile.

MIDDLEMEN IN FOREIGN MARKETS

Because the manufacturer has little control over most types of domestic export middlemen, and because he can know so little about their foreign operations, the manufacturer may prefer to deal with middlemen in the customer countries. By so doing, he at least gains the advantage of a shorter channel and is able to deal directly with middlemen who are in constant contact with the market.

Such involvement moves the manufacturer closer to the market but involves him more closely with those problems of language, physical distribution, communications, and financing. Foreign middlemen may be agents or merchants; they may be associated with the parent company to varying degrees or may even be temporarily hired for special purposes. Exhibit 20–3 reviews the basic characteristics of leading types of foreign middlemen.

Agents in Customer Countries

Agent middlemen work under a wide variety of names but none take title to the goods with which they deal. Since names are particularly confusing in this field and are not necessarily descriptive, one must investigate the actual functions and activities undertaken by a given type of agent middleman in a foreign country. In general, the range of functions of foreign agents is similar to those of domestic agent middlemen. The major characteristics of various agents are detailed in Exhibit 20–3. Some additional information is noted below.

Broker.   Like the export broker discussed in an earlier section, the broker operating in a foreign country deals largely in commodities and food products. The foreign broker is typically part of a small brokerage firm operating in one country, or in a few contiguous countries. His strength is having good continuing relationships with his customers, and he is able to provide speedy market coverage at a low cost.

One of the greatest difficulties in dealing with a broker is locating one. There are relatively few brokers in most countries, but they account for a large volume of merchandise because of the standard nature of the products and commodities in which they deal. Brokerage relationships may exist for only a single transaction or may continue for a number of years with individual producers.

Manufacturer's Representative.   Manufacturer's representatives may take responsibility for a producer's goods in a given city or market area, in an entire country, or in some cases in several adjacent countries. When responsible for an entire country, the middleman is often called a sole agent; e.g. in Germany, ABC Company is the sole agent for XYZ Company. As in the United States, the well-chosen, well-motivated, well-controlled manufacturer's representative can provide excellent market coverage for the manufacturer in certain circumstances. If a line is valuable to him, he will be highly controllable and if commissions are adequate, he will be motivated to do a good job. The manufacturers' representative is widely used in distribution of industrial goods overseas and is an excellent representative for any type of manufactured consumer goods. As in the United States, the chief problem of using manufacturer's representation worldwide is finding capable men to cover the desired market.

A manufacturer's representative takes no credit, exchange, or market risk but deals strictly as a field sales representative. He does not arrange for shipping or for handling and usually does not take physical possession. Manufacturers who wish the type of control and intensive market coverage which their own sales force would afford but who cannot field such a force may find the manufacturer's representative a satisfactory choice. Foreign manufacturer's representatives have a variety of titles, including sales agent, resident sales agent, exclusive agent, commission agent and indent agent; all provide a selling or negotiating service and normally do not assume any credit or information functions.

Factor.   Because of the importance and complexity of international credit, agents called factors are rapidly growing in significance as international middlemen. The factor performs all of the normal brokerage functions but also finances the sales transactions. He may also take responsibility for financing goods while they are in various stages of manufacture, remanufacture, or assembly. The chief advantage of dealing with the factor is that he relieves the selling company, and usually the buying company, of credit risk. The *del credere* agent is often considered to be a broker but is actually a special type of factor.

Managing Agent. A managing agent conducts his business within a foreign nation under an exclusive contract arrangement with the parent company. The managing agent in some cases invests in the operation and in most instances operates under a contract with the managed company which permits him significant discretion in managing the activities of this firm. Compensation is usually on the basis of cost plus a specified percentage of the profits of the managed company. This type of organizational arrangement is quite popular in some parts of the world, mainly in the Asiatic and African countries.

In Far Eastern countries, the managing agent is likely to be called a comprador; historically he has been particularly important in trade with China. The comprador is essentially a general manager who acts as the representative of a foreign merchant in his operations in a given Oriental country. A comprador is used because of his intimate knowledge of the obscure and enigmatic customs and languages of the importing country. Few of the true general-manager type of compradors are still in operation, but there is a tendency for other kinds of foreign middlemen to expand their functions to accommodate small manufacturers.

Foreign Merchant Middlemen

Merchant middlemen take title and, normally, possession of the goods. Different kinds of merchant middlemen are found in different markets. Although they are known by many titles, merchant middlemen in other countries may be classified in four ways: distributors, dealers, import jobbers, and wholesalers and retailers. The titles imply functions basically the same as those associated with similar merchant middlemen in domestic channels. The advantages and disadvantages of using the merchant middleman in foreign and domestic situations are also similar. The merchant middleman provides time and place utility by purchasing and holding the goods at locations which are relatively convenient to customers; he provides credit service, takes the risk of price fluctuations, and provides varying degrees of sales services. The merchant middleman selects his own selling prices and may have little manufacturer loyalty because he handles large numbers of goods. Since he is likely to neglect merchandise with low margins or slow turnover in favor of more profitable items, it is unwise to place full reliance on the merchant middleman's ability and willingness to promote and sell a product aggressively. As with all middlemen, particularly those working at a distance, effectiveness is directly dependent on the selection of the middleman and on the degree of control the manufacturer is willing and able to exert.

Distributor. A foreign distributor often has exclusive sales rights in a specific country and works in close cooperation with the manufacturer. The distributor has a relatively high degree of dependence on the supplier companies, and arrangements are likely to be on a long-run continuous basis. Often distributor-manufacturer relationships are formalized through franchises or ownership arrangements. Working through distributors permits the manufacturer a reasonable degree of control over prices, promotional effort, inventory, servicing, and other distribution functions. If a line is profitable for a distributor, he can be depended upon to handle it in a manner closely approximating the desires of the manufacturer. Some distributors have their own retail and regional wholesaling operations. Some sell direct to retailers, or they may employ agent middlemen or distribute through independent wholesalers and jobbers.

Dealer. Like other marketing terms, the word "dealer" has many connotations. Generally speaking, anyone who has a continuing relationship with a supplier in buying and selling goods is considered a dealer. More specifically, a dealer is a middleman selling either industrial goods or durable consumer goods direct to the customer; he is the last step in the channel of distribution. The dealer has a continuing, close working relationship with his supplier and has exclusive selling rights for his producer's products within a given geographic area. Finally, he derives a large portion of his sales volume from the products of a single supplier firm. Usually the dealer is an independent merchant middleman, but sometimes the supplier company has an equity in its dealers.

Some of the best examples of dealer-type operations are found in the farm equipment, earth-moving, and automotive industries. In these categories are such companies as Massey Ferguson, with a vast, worldwide network of dealers, Caterpillar Tractor Company, with dealers in every major city of the world, and all of the various automobile companies.

In some instances, a dealer will be responsible for distribution in an entire nation; in others he will be limited to a specific city or market area. Because dealers are generally heavily dependent on their major lines, they can be expected to exert maximum effort in merchandising those lines. Even in these circumstances, of course, the supplier company still must be actively involved in the overseeing and management of dealer activities around the world.

Import Jobber. The import jobber purchases goods directly from the manufacturer. He sells them to wholesalers and retailers and to industrial customers. The import jobber is also known sometimes as an import house or an import merchant. He differs from the distributor mainly in that he does not have exclusive territorial rights. In a given port or country one manufacturer may sell to several import jobbers. The manufacturer has no great hold over the import jobber, who may buy goods on a random or convenience basis unless there is a strong brand preference on which he can capitalize.

Wholesaler and Retailer. Large and small wholesalers and retailers alike engage in direct importing both for their own outlets and for

BOX 20-3

A Wholesaler Is . . . ?

In the consumer field, wholesalers operate in most markets, although with varying degrees of effectiveness. A wholesaler in Malta, for example, is generally also an importer, and sells direct to retailers, so that it is of little use trying to get other wholesalers to handle the product, since they seldom sell to each other. In Belgium, on the other hand, in the grocery trade, the wholesaler is all-important and handles 80% of the food business because of the vast number of retail grocers—17,000 of them. Chinese wholesalers in Malaya are all-powerful, but wholesalers in Holland in the toiletries field are much less important, because most retailers prefer to buy direct from suppliers. Wholesalers on the west coast of Africa are mainly the "mammy traders," who take products into remote areas which strangers, for example, would hardly believe existed.

Source: Henry Deschampsneufs, *Marketing Overseas* (New York: Pergamon Press, Inc., 1967), p. 84.

further redistribution to smaller middlemen. The combination retailer-wholesaler is more important in foreign countries than in the United States; it is not at all uncommon to find most of the larger retailers in any city wholesaling their goods to local shops and dealers.

Wholesale and retail distribution patterns are discussed at length in Chapter 22.

Affiliated Middleman. There is a rapidly growing trend among internationally oriented firms to initiate some type of binding affiliation with overseas middlemen in order to build a stronger bond and provide the manufacturing company with greater control. Two basic devices are franchising and joint ventures; such activities may be conducted at retail, wholesale, or manufacturing levels. More specific information pertaining to these arrangements is presented in Chapter 13.

COMPANY DISTRIBUTION ABROAD

Although the company's own selling force is not usually considered to be part of a channel of distribution per se, it should be, because the foreign marketing arm of the company is sufficiently independent that it often must be dealt with as if it were an independent channel. It also substitutes for or supplements independent channels of distribution. Companies undertake development of their own overseas marketing organizations for two main reasons: (1) to increase volume of sales and (2) to increase control over the distribution system. The two activities should combine to give the company greater profitability and stability. Through the use of its own sales force, the company can closely control advertising and selling efforts, provide good service, and gain useful feedback from field operations. That is the theory; sometimes, instead, the company finds that it loses volume when it gives up established distribution channels and that it encounters intense competition from former distributors and middlemen. It may find that it cannot hire capable manpower to staff the operation and that a high investment is required. Even though it may take two to five years before a new operation reaches the break-even point, many companies have found that establishing their own internal distribution channel has been the only satisfactory way of reaching certain major markets.

Companies that decide to establish their own marketing structures abroad may simply employ salesmen who report directly to the home office or may establish sales branches or subsidiaries abroad. Some companies have utilized the joint-venture plan, participating with other companies or with existing middlemen in the formation of new companies geared specifically to distribution. Companies have also merged with or purchased former middlemen in order to develop their own foreign marketing systems. In some cases even a minority interest in a distributor or wholesaler can assure a manufacturer of continued distribution relationships.

The scale of operations required for a company's own distribution efforts ranges widely. An industrial goods producer may only need one salesman to cover effectively all of the potential customers in a country or in several countries. Twenty or thirty salesmen may be required to call on food retailers in even a small country. The experience of the Tupperware Company in Japan represents the extreme end of the scale. That company developed a selling force of over 20,000 women in less than three years and had its efforts rewarded by reaching a $20,000,000 annual sales volume in that time.

Rather than set up new sales offices or branches, some companies have chosen to utilize their own missionary sales force which, like its domestic counterpart, has the responsibility for making customer contact and sales presentations and for providing follow-up service. The actual physical distribution of the product is handled through an assortment of wholesalers or other middlemen.

FACILITATING AGENCIES

The process of selling and delivering goods calls into play a series of middlemen who are not technically elements of the channel of distribution but who play a distinct role in facilitating basic marketing functions. These middlemen provide various types of service to move and protect the flow of goods in their journey to the consumer. Such middlemen provide services pertaining to communications, management services, financing, and insurance.

Besides those discussed below, there are a number of facilitating agencies which specifically participate in the physical distribution function. They are considered in the next section.

Communications and Management Services

Although we tend to take for granted international mail and telephone service because they are so common, it should not be forgotten that international trade would be impossible to carry out without the services of these and other facilitating communications services using such media as the cablegram, telex message, and facsimile transmission.

International marketing activities, particularly exporting, would be hampered if translation services were not readily available throughout the world. Businesses should select translators who understand the fine subtleties and nuances of both languages involved. Furthermore, effective translation may often require competence and specialization in technical, scientific, or business terminology.

Advertising agencies and marketing research firms may be logically included with the communications middlemen. Advertising agencies, whether domestic, international, or foreign, can significantly enhance or detract from the process of outward communications between the company and its market. The flow of communication from the consumer back to the manufacturer or exporter has benefited greatly from the rapid expansion of international marketing research services in the past decade. Several U.S. research firms, such as A. C. Nielsen and Company and Alfred Politz Research, Inc., have branch offices in various foreign countries, while other agencies participate in voluntary networks of independent marketing research agencies from numerous countries.

The firm entering new markets or new to international marketing may well consider the services of a management or marketing consultant who specializes in international operations and who can provide specific data pertaining to foreign markets. Firms providing special services in international law, accounting, and taxation have greater relevance to the international market than is commonly recognized. Besides providing legal guidance and control data information, such firms also may be in a position to provide management counsel and information of use to international marketers. The U.S.-based accounting firm, Price-Waterhouse and Company, for example, publishes a continuing series called *Information Guide to Doing Business in* _____ (country). Although primarily a reporting service to provide information on the tax laws of individual countries, the service also provides other data valuable to international business.

Finance, Insurance, and Credit

One seldom mentions finance, insurance, and credit institutions in the same breath with marketing channels, but it should be realized that all three have a particular bearing on the international movement of goods. Since ramifications of these services have been explored in another chapter, it will suffice to mention that financing of distribution, even down to the retail level, may be what spells the difference between success and failure in acquiring adequate distribution. The credit which may be so necessary in establishing channels cannot be provided unless there are adequate funds for financing local inventories and providing middlemen with credit. Such credit can be provided more safely through the cooperation of local financial institutions and international credit rating agencies, such as Dun and Bradstreet, Inc., which has a host of international branches and affiliated companies. The U.S. Department of Commerce and the Foreign Credit Interchange Bureau also provide credit data. In Europe and in the Commonwealth there is a special middleman called a confirming house which provides a specialized credit service by standing behind or confirming the credit of buyers in markets. In some countries where the cost of money is high or where there is extreme money market fluctuation or other uncertain credit conditions, international business can scarcely be conducted without the services of a confirming house.

International insurers of various types participate directly in the physical distribution activities of a firm. Rarely do goods travel in international commerce without insurance. Finance resources, carriers, and even governments often require that goods be adequately insured before they can move through international channels.

INTERNATIONAL DISTRIBUTION LOGISTICS

Major cost items in international marketing, which are therefore factors of major concern to management, are the costs of transporting and storing goods—that is, the physical distribution function. In international trade, transportation-related costs can account for 40 percent or more of the selling price of goods.

International logistics is concerned not only with the carriers and the facilitating middlemen who make the international flow of goods possible but also with the managerial aspects of distribution. Further, the concern is not only with moving goods from nation to nation but moving them within the nations to their final destinations as well. International distribution strategy concerns itself with the creation of optimum time and place utilities for the merchandise without incurring excessive money cost or cost in terms of lost opportunities for sales or service.

Management is constantly required to assess the impact of shifting modes of transportation, rapid and frequent variations in transportation costs, and physical requirements; in so doing it must always keep the customer in mind. Boiled down to its simplest terms, international distribution logistics amounts to a battle between cost and convenience and requires a constant balancing of size of shipment, size of inventory, length of storage, time, and customer requirements. Consider the example below.

The sooner the equipment arrives and is installed, the sooner cash starts flowing back to the manufacturer in the form of lease payments. A computer installation which rents for $3,000 a month, has a time-value of $100 a day, reducing transit time by nine days represents an improvement in cash flow of $900. A firm shipping ten computers a week would in effect have $9000 to weigh against the added cost of air freight. Simple principles apply where title actually passes from seller to buyer at time of delivery; whatever the terms of payment, they begin that much sooner and so does the cash flow. Here again the tradeoff is between the value of the improved cash flow and the added cost of air freight, enhanced by minimum packaging expense and set-up time at destination.[3]

---

[3] "What About International Physical Distribution Management?" Japan Airlines, 1969, p. 18.

Modern physical distribution management always considers all movement, storage, and handling cost as part of a logistical system. Management of such a system calls for tradeoffs between the cost and the advantages of all different types of physical handling. Use of the term "zero movement transportation" in place of the term "storage" by logistic specialists characterizes the close relationship of the elements of physical distribution. It is important to note that the channel-of-distribution middlemen (wholesalers, retailers, and any other middlemen who actually take physical possession of the goods) also become part of the physical distribution system for they too are responsible for breaking bulk and creating time and place utilities, and they incur varying shares of the physical distribution cost burden. The actual manipulation of a physical distribution system calls for considerable expertise and may involve a number of the different types of facilitating middlemen discussed in the following section.

Physical Distribution Middlemen

A host of middlemen, besides the actual carriers, facilitate the physical distribution process. These are freight forwarders, packers, public warehouses, customs expediters, and even travel agencies. The strategic employment of such facilitating middlemen gives the international manager considerable latitude in his physical distribution operations. His alternatives essentially relate to time, storage, and movement cost. The astute manager attempts to design his distribution system to gain optimum time and place utility at minimum cost. By shipping on slow carriers, he may tie up his goods for long periods of time but save on direct shipping cost. Effective use of facilities may, for example, utilize low-cost ocean shipping as a basic traveling warehouse or pipeline of goods by staging shipments to arrive as needed, while meeting special requirements through air shipments.

Carrier. International traffic management can have major impact on the profitability of international business operations. The importance goes far beyond exporting because even firms with manufacturing subsidiaries overseas are engaged in transporting parts, equipment, and supplies. The subsidiaries are likely to be engaged in export shipping operations of their own. Three basic types of transportation modes are available—air, ocean, and surface transportation. Freight rates, special charges, and services offered vary widely, not only among the three major transport types, but also from carrier to carrier, time to time, and situation to situation within each class of goods. The international shipper must draw on a vast factual base of information which provides him the raw material for decisions balancing the advantages of speed, low cost, safety, and special handling. The best carrier in one situation may be inappropriate in another.

Ocean shipping predominates in the international transportation picture. The basic reasons behind this are that only about a fourth of the earth's surface is land and the parcels of land are scattered around the globe in such a way that overland transportation is impossible to some markets and is infeasible to others. Fortunately, ocean transportation is

BOX 20–4

Surface Transportation versus Air Transportation
DIRECT COSTS

Packing	Probably you use a standard pack for domestic distribution. Chances are you use additional packing or crating for overseas shipments. Enter in the "Surface Transportation" column the cost of any additional packing needed to assure safe transport of goods overseas by surface.
Insurance	All insurance charges—coverage to the port of embarkation, aboard ship and from discharge port to final destination. (Insurance for air shipment is as much as 90 percent below that for surface shipment.)
Domestic Transport	Truck and/or rail transport costs to shipside at (destination) or airport at (destination).
Storage en Route	Cost of staging or storage en route, including warehousing at dockside.
Brokerage	Use of an export broker or agency is a common practice as a means of avoiding specialized export problems. Enter any applicable brokerage fees—for documentation, messenger service, banking charges, booking and the like.
Embarkation Port Charges	Lighterage and other port charges not covered in the broker's fee.
Transportation Overseas	In the case of surface shipment, this represents freight charges from U.S. port to overseas port only.
Discharge Port Costs	Discharge port dues, brokerage fees and storage at port of destination, if applicable.

Source: "How to Figure Your Real Cost of Distribution Abroad," Pan American Airlines, 1970.

inexpensive. The cost of ocean shipping depends partly on the kind of vessel used. Rates on regular steamship lines are high compared to those on tramp and charter service but offer such offsetting advantages as uniform rates, posted routes and shipping dates, and relatively high-quality service. Ton-mile rates for ocean cargo cost only one tenth to one twentieth as much as rail or truck transportation and cost from one twentieth to one fortieth as much as air transportation (it should be noted, however, that differentials are not quite so extreme because ocean shipping may involve greater mileage, and special packing may increase the tonnage and cost). The ton-mile rate figure can sometimes be misleading, however, for an individual shipper. In some instances, partic-

"HIDDEN" COSTS

Overseas Warehousing	Cost of maintaining overseas inventories. (25% of product cost is the national average for inventory carrying charges.) Include cost of interest on working capital which is tied up in maintaining inventory. Also local taxes on inventory.
Inventory Losses	Losses due to handling, spoilage, obsolescence, theft, and fluctuations in exchange.
Cost of Time in Transit	For as long as goods are tied up in transit—and the working capital they represent is not turning over—the delay in getting to market rolls up a cost. If goods are in transit 30 days by surface—instead of 2 days by air—the impediment to turnover, and the cost, is 15 times as great as it need be. Approximate your "delay of sale" costs due to slow surface transport.
Lost Sales	Loss of profit on sales that were not made due to late arrival of shipment, no C.O.D. or collect service, or the inability to reorder quickly. Also include penalties for delays in filling contracts or meeting delivery deadlines.
Distributor-Customer Dissatisfactions	Effect of large inventories upon profit of distributors and customers—with consequent tying up of capital and risk of markdowns to move obsolete merchandise.
Claims	It's often difficult to arrange *continuous* insurance coverage throughout the many transfers involved in surface shipping . . . , whereas with air shipment, one policy covers your shipment all the way from your door to the destination. Estimate the costs you must bear as a result of not being fully reimbursed for lost or damaged shipment.

ularly where small weights and high value are involved, even the direct cost of shipping by air may be less than that of shipping by ocean cargo, and there are many indirect cost savings.

Rail shipments do not, of course, account for much of the export volume of the United States, but in Europe there is a highly developed network of interconnecting railroad lines which carry sizable amounts of international export goods. Even shipping goods to ports in the United States requires specialized information, however, and export shippers need to be aware of such things as overland common-point-of-rail rates which offer lower rates for export shipments than for similar products shipped for domestic consumption.

Ocean vessels are the workhorses of international trade; airplanes are the glamour girls. Air transportation is fast, convenient, and increasingly competitive in price, but despite the dramatic gains made by air transportation in the last decade, air cargo still amounts to considerably less than 1 percent of the tonnage shipped by ocean vessels. Hardly a midget industry, air cargo accounted for nearly a billion dollars of revenue in 1970. Air transportation use is widespread, and the growth in ton-miles doubles approximately every five to seven years. Each year new products are added to the expanding list of products that are regularly shipped by international air. Electronic and technical products, fashion goods, repair parts, and drugs are shipped largely by air; some of the most famous airline transport products have actually created new market areas—live animals, baby chicks, hatching eggs, and orchids. Air transportation is not limited to small or perishable products, however, and the giant cargo liners with capacities up to 50 tons have carried machinery and equipment weighing up to 10 tons in one container. A decade ago, air transportation was used only as a last resort in emergencies; but according to a recent study, a third of the international shippers now consider air shipping as a "normal" means of distribution. Shippers rate as the chief advantage of air transportation speed and dependability of delivery; but other advantages are the reduced packing costs, minimized damage, savings on warehousing and inventory, and reduced insurance and documentation costs. Emory Air Freight Corporation promotes one-day service from New York to major European cities, two-day service from inland U.S. shippers' points to Europe, and a maximum of three days from any major U.S. city to any major city in the world, including pickups, transportation, clearance of customs, and delivery. When one compares this with the normal shipping lag of 20 to 60 days by ocean transportation or combination ocean and surface, the growth of air transportation is readily understood.

Freight Forwarder. Because of the highly specialized nature of international shipping, very few companies are in a position to effectively handle international shipping without help. Freight forwarders provide more than information and are in fact carriers themselves. In an advertisement defining their role as air forwarders, Emory Air Freight says, "We do not own or operate the planes on which Emory shipments are moved. When we accept a shipment from one of our customers, we do so as a carrier, agreeing to move it safely and swiftly to the consignee and to charge for transportation at our published air freights, but in moving the shipment from origin to destination, we do so as a shipper over whichever airline will get it there most quickly." It sounds simple, and the fact that a forwarder does indeed simplify international shipment may be the reason that some 60 percent of the users surveyed in a Pan-American study use cargo agents or freight forwarders. They offer simplicity, speed, and economy in performing services listed in Exhibit 20–4, which illustrates the amount of detail involved in international movement of goods.

Customs Expediter. As the name implies, a customs expediter is a specialist in preparing paperwork and otherwise facilitating the process-

EXHIBIT 20–4

Activities of Freight Forwarders

1. General operations:

    Act as agents for exporters, importers and government agencies; keep abreast of world-wide developments; render assistance and advice; conduct necessary correspondence; supervise and direct export movements; maintain complete records.

2. U.S. government operations:

    Negotiate export licenses; prepare, coordinate, and clear export declarations; prepare and obtain in-transit entries; apply for B.A.I. certificates; comply with drawback formalities; procure all necessary government permits, priorities, or allotments; represent clients before government bureaus; prepare, file, and follow up transportation tax forms.

3. Inland operations:

    Procure AAR and other embargo permits; route shipments to seaports; trace inland shipments; arrange government bills of lading; arrange in-transit storage.

4. Port operations:

    Arrange storage and delivery to steamer; arrange foreign trade zone storage and manipulation; arrange representation at all U.S. and Canadian ports.

5. Steamship operations:

    Negotiate conference contracts; quote ocean freight rates; issue sailing schedules and ocean freight rates; arrange ocean shipping space; obtain steamer delivery permits; compile dock receipts; compile ocean bills of lading; arrange bill of lading consolidations; check ocean freight rates, shippers' packing lists, ocean freight charges; reconcile any over or undercharges; follow up for onboard bills of lading; arrange through bills of lading to foreign destinations.

6. Consular operations:

    Have knowledge of worldwide customs requirements; convert weights and measurements to metric system; compile consular invoices and certificates of origin; arrange for visa of these consular documents; obtain visaed health or sanitation, food and drug certificates; assist in procurement of import permits; maintain library of foreign customs tariffs.

7. Insurance operations:

    Negotiate open marine policies; obtain and quote marine insurance rates; issue marine insurance binders policies; secure marine insurance cover notes; arrange foreign insurance coverages.

8. Banking operations:

    Complete shippers' invoice by adding charges as required; prepare drafts and documents for presentation; issue banking instructions; negotiate against letters of credit; arrange foreign collection and discounts; assist in buying and selling foreign exchange; follow up foreign collections and remit proceeds to clients.

9. Documentary operations:

    Dispose of ocean documents to shippers, consignee, and others at interest.

10. Accessorial operations:

    Present and collect claims against carriers, insurance companies, other parties at interest; arrange cable, telegraph, or mail clearances, and messenger service as required; arrange for recoopering, export boxing, weighing, inspection, and sampling.

11. Financial operations:

    Advance charges for railroad freight, storage or demurrage, lighterage ocean freight; advance consular fees; pay insurance premiums; render invoices for disbursements and service charges.

Source: This summary represents a highly abridged version of a list of services prepared by the Customs Brokers and Forwarders Association of America, Inc.

BOX 20–5

Dutch Warehousing

Under the flexible Dutch warehousing system, unpacking, repacking, sorting, and light processing operations are allowed in bonded warehouses, and the goods must not lose their identity in the latter operation—i.e., the warehouse may not be turned into a factory. Companies that wish to carry out extensive assembling or processing operations for reexport may instead import goods duty-free under temporary admission certificates. One US company, Parker Hannifin, of Cleveland, is reaping the benefits of both the entrepôt and the temporary admission systems in a single location. Since 1960, the US firm, through its Dutch subsidiary, Parker Hannifin NV, has been operating its own private bonded warehouse at the Schiphol airport for the distribution of hydraulic and pneumatic systems and seals. The warehouse is divided into two sections by a wall. In one section, a normal entrepôt under customs supervision, only inspection and packaging operations can be carried out. In the factory section of the warehouse, which is not under direct customs supervision, goods admitted under temporary admission certificates can be manipulated, assembled, or processed in any manner without restriction. Repairs are also made on goods either damaged in transit or returned by customers. The company reports that this setup works well and has resulted in transport cost savings and in shortened order-processing and delivery times.

Source: Reprinted from "How Two Companies Store, Process Goods under Flexible Dutch Warehouse System," *Business Europe,* December 8, 1967, p. 387, with the permission of the publisher, Business International S.A. (Geneva).

ing of goods through customs. These middlemen may be called customs brokers or custom house brokers. They are typically licensed by the countries in which they are located, and their offices are usually at or near customs houses. The broker may actually physically handle the merchandise and display it for customs officials. He may observe the examination of goods; he calculates the customs fees independently of the customs agent, will argue classifications and rates, and performs other services necessary to clear the goods through customs at a minimum cost. Often the customs expediter is connected with a freight forwarding firm which combines the functions of forwarding and customs brokerage.

Public Warehouse.   Years ago when an international trader needed to store goods in various markets, he had to rely on middlemen in his channels of distribution, provide his own storage space, or make complicated arrangements for housing in various locations. With the growth of international trade, however, several firms specializing in international public warehousing have initiated services in Europe. Functioning much as do domestic public warehouses, they not only store the goods but also break bulk, deliver, invoice and provide other distribution services.

In some countries, such as the Netherlands, private and public warehouses offer custom-free facilities and serve, in a sense, as free ports. In that country there are three types of public warehouses: *public bonded warehouses,* in which goods can be moved and replaced, handled and reshipped without incurring duties unless they are shipped into the country itself; *private warehouses,* owned by companies themselves, which provide the same types of services; and *factory bonded warehouses,* where raw materials and semifinished goods can be processed or assembled into finished products.

As international public warehouse facilities become available in more markets, they will provide a valuable service in bridging the gap between the characteristically small inventories carried by foreign middlemen and the inventories needed to service reorders rapidly.

Travel Agent. All international businessmen tend to think of transportation as being primarily related to goods. Most internationally active companies, however, also find that there is a continuous parade of executives and specialists from country to country. Travel agencies which specialize in international service have the kind of knowledge which makes international travel as convenient and inexpensive as possible. Besides saving time and money for the international businessman, the expert travel agent can provide many types of useful information, such as the proper way to handle samples and catalog materials for trouble-free customs clearance. Because the major part of their fees is paid by the passenger carriers, such middlemen can be employed with little expense. The return in convenience is great.

SUMMARY AND CONCLUSIONS

From the foregoing discussion, it is evident that the international marketer has a broad range of alternatives, both in channels of distribution and in physical distribution. In the hands of a creative, knowledgeable marketer, the alternatives provide the opportunity to develop an economical, efficient, high-volume international distribution system. To the uninitiated, however, the variety may be simply overwhelming.

Careful analysis of the functions performed suggests more similarity than difference between international and domestic distribution systems; in both cases there are the three primary alternatives of using agent middlemen, merchant middlemen, or a company's own sales and distribution system. In many instances, all three types of middlemen will be employed on the international scene, and channel structure may vary from nation to nation or from continent to continent. The neophyte company in international marketing can gain strength from the knowledge that information and advice are available relative to the structuring of international distribution systems and that many well-developed and capable middleman firms exist for the international distribution of goods. Within the past decades, international middlemen have become more numerous, more reliable, more sophisticated, and more readily available to marketers in all countries. Such growth and development offer a wider range of possibilities than ever in entering foreign markets, but the international businessman should remember that it is also easier for his competitors.

This chapter has emphasized the structure and institutions of international distribution. The next chapter is concerned with the mechanics of export trade, and Chapter 22 deals with patterns of distribution and the development and implementation of international distribution strategy.

READING

HOW SCHICK SHARPENED DULL SALES TECHNIQUES TO CUT INTO GERMAN MARKET*

The successful German experience of Schick Safety Razor has recently proven that one practical way of making a new and costly sales network pay off rapidly is to sell the products of other manufacturers on a commission basis. Known as piggybacking in American business terminology, the system of sharing a sales team with other manufacturers may appeal not only to firms that have one or a few product lines but also to companies whose many product lines cannot be sold through a single distribution network.

By opting for piggybacking as a method of selling its products in Germany, a highly competitive market with many regions, after two unsuccessful attempts at cracking that market, the California company has been able to:

Establish a large distribution network that covers all parts of Germany;

Cover a portion of the high fixed costs of its sales organization with the sales commissions received from its partners; and

Increase rapidly its share of the market.

For companies that use another firm's sales network to launch a product in a new market, piggybacking helps cut distribution costs to a minimum. In fact, these firms need only pay sales commissions to their partners and bear the cost of advertising. But there is one caveat: Such companies will not have much control over the degree to which their partners' salesmen push their products.

Before adopting the piggybacking technique, Schick used the conventional method of employing an independent distributor. It soon became clear that, although the distributor was aggressive and well established, his sales staff was too small to call regularly on all cosmetics retailers in Germany.

Unhappy with the results, Schick canceled its contract with the dealer and entrusted distribution of its products to the German sales subsidiary of Sweden's Barnängens Tekniska Fabrikers, a chemicals and light metals company that manufactures, among other products, the Vademecum line of toiletries. One of Schick's reasons for choosing Barnän-

---

* Reprinted from the September 6, 1968, issue of *Business Europe*, with the permission of the publisher, Business International S.A. (Geneva).

gens was that the Swedish firm markets its articles through food stores as well as through specialized cosmetics shops. At first, Schick's German sales rose substantially, but the situation suddenly soured when Barnängens launched a flower preservative that proved to be a best seller. Barnängens salesmen concentrated their efforts on this new product, for which orders were easy to land, rather than on the harder-to-sell Schick toiletries.

Having again failed to penetrate the German market satisfactorily, Schick set up its own sales subsidiary and hired as manager a former executive of its major competitor, Gillette. Schick then faced the basic choice of either:

1. Keeping initial costs at a minimum by recruiting a small sales force and later expanding it; or

2. Hiring a large staff and launching a major sales effort immediately—a riskier but more promising long term solution.

Choosing the second alternative, Schick hired some 50 salaried salesmen. The company estimated that this sales force would be large enough to visit all retailers once every two months, if it marketed no more than three product lines.

But Schick soon realized that, in view of the heavy sales expenses involved, it might be five years before its German subsidiary could turn a profit. Fortunately, American Cyanamid was then seeking an independent distributor for its Breck hair cosmetics. Although Cyanamid had its own sales organization in Germany to market pharmaceutical products, its salesmen were concentrating on pharmacies and physicians, rather than on cosmetic shops. In early 1968, Schick and Cyanamid found a solution to their distribution problems by signing a piggybacking agreement under which Schick became exclusive agent for Breck products in Germany (see box for details of the contract).

During the initial phase of the partnership, Breck products are being market-tested in the Hesse province only, but they are soon to be sold throughout Germany. Cyanamid, which under the contract bears the advertising expenses, is spending all sales proceeds minus commissions on advertising.

Pleased with the experiment with Cyanamid, Schick has recently taken a further step in piggybacking. Last week, the razor firm signed a contract with Associated Products (AP) of New York under which Schick will handle German distribution of the cosmetic articles manufactured in AP's Lyons plant.

Schick's sales figures are an eloquent testimonial to the merits of piggybacking. In one year, the razor company's share of the German market has grown from 3% to 7%, a growth that might not have been achieved with a small sales force.

Schick-Cyanamid Piggyback Setup

The Schick-Cyanamid contract provides that Schick sell Breck cosmetics in its own name but for the account of Cyanamid—i.e. the products remain Cyanamid property until they are sold. Schick agrees not to sell its own similar products or similar products of a third company. Should any question arise concerning "similarity" of a new product, Cyanamid must be consulted before a marketing decision is made.

The contract stipulates that Schick receive a higher commission during the launching period. (As a rule, German agents' commissions in the field of cosmetics are about 25% of sales, as their high fixed costs range between 10% and 16%.) Cyanamid is authorized to check Schick's accounts with an independent auditor and to withdraw Breck cosmetics from the market if sales are disappointing. Should Schick be taken over by a third company, Cyanamid has the right to cancel the contract immediately.

QUESTIONS

1. Define:

   Distribution structure   CEM
   Distribution channel   Factor
   Facilitating agency   Confirming house
   Zaibatsu   Barter broker

2. "Many, perhaps most, international middlemen wear several hats and can be clearly identified only in the context of their relationship with a specific firm." Discuss.

3. To what extent, and in what ways, do the functions of domestic middlemen differ from their foreign counterparts?

4. Why is the CEM sometimes called an independent export department?

5. Differentiate between a wholesaler and a distributor.

6. Can facilitating agencies be called a part of the channel of distribution? Explain.

7. "Ocean vessels are the workhorses of international trade; airplanes are the glamour girls." Discuss.

8. Explain the role of the freight forwarder in international business. Does he have a domestic counterpart?

9. Discuss how physical distribution relates to channel policy and how they affect one another.

10. Why should a company owned sales organization be considered part of the channel structure?

11. Explain how and why distribution channels are affected as they are when the stage of development of an economy improves.

12. In what circumstances is the use of a CEM logical?

13. Predict whether the Norazi agent is likely to grow or decline in importance.

14. Discuss the possible antitrust ramification of WPEAs.

15. In what circumstances are trading companies likely to be used?

Reading

1. How did Cyanamid protect itself against poor performance? What else might it have done?

2. Both companies benefited; is it probable that the addition of other lines will be advantageous to Schick also?

OUTLINE OF CHAPTER 21

INTRODUCTION

REGULATIONS AND RESTRICTIONS OF EXPORTING

U.S. Export Restrictions
  Types of Licenses
  Country Classification
  Commodity Control List

Import Restrictions
  Tariffs
  Exchange Permits
  Quotas
  Import Licenses
  Other Restrictions

Free-Trade Zones

EXPORT DOCUMENTS

PACKING AND MARKING

FOREIGN COMMERCIAL PAYMENTS

Letters of Credit

Bills of Exchange

Cash in Advance

Open Accounts

SUMMARY AND CONCLUSIONS

READING

  Guidelines in Exporting for the Small Company, *Business View-points*

EXPORT TRADE MECHANICS

INTRODUCTION

A large majority of American companies actively engaged in foreign marketing manufacture products in the United States and export them to foreign customers. Although some of these companies maintain elaborate marketing departments abroad that are responsible for the sale of their products, others maintain no foreign sales staff but rely exclusively upon export middlemen to market their products in the foreign country. These middlemen are, in essence, their customers for these products. Increasingly common are companies engaged in manufacturing activities in several countries, a situation which involves them in exporting from all these countries, instead of the traditional situation of exporting from the home country to foreign destinations. In any of these cases, or any variation thereof, the foreign marketer who manufactures goods in one nation to be exported to another is faced with specific requirements when moving goods between countries. In addition to the general marketing activities required of marketing executives, the exporter must handle those requirements peculiar to the export trade which are not necessarily encounted in domestic marketing.

Whether a foreign marketer maintains marketing control over his product until it reaches its intended consumer or sells to an intermediary early in the distribution process, his marketing program should remain basically the same. He must study his target market, design his product, set his prices, plan his promotional program, and select his distribution channels in view of market requirements and the various uncontrollable environmental elements (see Chapter 1). Essential requirements unique to export marketing that must be considered relate to required documents: the means of payment, the requirements of tariff systems, and other impediments to the free flow of goods between independent sovereigns. Sometimes the mechanics are considered to be the essence of foreign marketing; but, although their importance should not be minimized, they should not be looked upon as comprising the major task of foreign marketing. These mechanics of export marketing are the special concern of this chapter.

REGULATIONS AND RESTRICTIONS OF EXPORTING

All countries impose some form of regulation and restriction on the exportation and importation of goods; such restrictions are placed on the movement of goods in foreign markets for many reasons. The country from which goods are being exported may design their regulations for reasons of conservation of scarce goods for home consumption and/or the control of strategic goods to enemies, actual or potential. In the importing country, regulations may be imposed for the protection of health, the conservation of foreign exchange, economic reprisals against actual or potential enemies, protection for home industry, and/or as a source of revenue in the form of tariffs. To comply with these regulations, the exporter may have to acquire licenses or permits from his own country as well as ascertain that his potential customer has the necessary permits for the importation of his goods.

U.S. Export Restrictions

No formal or special license to engage in an export business is required. For many kinds of goods, however, shipment outside the United States is regulated and thus permission (or a license) is required before they can be exported. Most items that require special permission or license for exportation are under the control of the Department of Commerce. The exceptions to this are as follows:

1. Arms, ammunition, and other implements of war are licensed by the U.S. Department of State.
2. Atomic energy material is licensed by the U.S. Atomic Energy Commission.
3. Gold and U.S. coins containing silver are licensed by the U.S. Department of the Treasury.
4. Narcotic drugs are licensed by the U.S. Department of Justice.
5. Natural gas and electric energy are licensed by the U.S. Federal Power Commission.
6. Fissionable materials and facilities for manufacturing such materials are licensed by the Atomic Energy Commission.
7. Tobacco plants and seeds are licensed by the Department of Agriculture.
8. Vessels are licensed under the United States Maritime Commission.[1]

Unless an exporter's products fall into one of the exceptions above, he must look to the Department of Commerce to determine whether a specific license to export the product is required. The export licensing controls administered by the Department of Commerce apply to: (1) exports of commodities and technical data for the United States, (2) reexports of U.S.-origin commodities and technical data from a foreign destination to another foreign destination, (3) U.S.-origin parts and components used in foreign countries to manufacture foreign products

---

[1] *A Summary of U.S. Export Control Regulations* (Washington, D.C.: U.S. Department of Commerce, June 1, 1969), p. 1.

BOX 21–1

New York Exporter Sentenced and Fined for Illegal Shipment

An electronics exporter of New York, N.Y., was sentenced by U.S. District Court Judge Edmund L. Palmieri to four months in jail and fined $2500 on Jan. 13.

The sentence and fine were imposed as a result of the company's owner having knowingly and willfully exported $6,709.60 worth of U.S.-origin oscilloscopes on Feb. 12, 1963, without first having obtained the requisite validated export licenses or other authorization required by law.

On Nov. 8, 1968, the company's owner had entered a plea of guilty to having effected such an exportation. Since May 1, 1964, the owner and his firm, have been denied all participation in any manner in the export trade of the United States for the duration of export controls.

The Department of Commerce denial order had contained a provision that, after two years from the effective date of the denial, the owner could seek to be placed upon a probationary status. However, both the owner and his firm remain denied to date.

Source: *International Commerce*, January 27, 1969, p. 25.

for export; and (4) in some instances, the foreign-produced direct product of U.S.-origin technical data.

All regulations imposed by the Department of Commerce are published in the *Comprehensive Export Schedule* which is periodically revised and supplemented by the *Current Export Bulletin*. The respective departments of bureaus should be contacted for the latest control regulations, since the specific products controlled vary from time to time.

Types of Licenses. There are two general types of licenses for exporting from the United States: a general license and a validated license.

A general license is a privilege permitting exportation within limits without requiring that an application be filed or that a license document be issued.

A validated license is a document authorizing exportation within the specific limitations it sets forth; it is issued only upon formal application.[2]

Application must be made in accordance with procedures set forth in the *Comprehensive Export Schedule*. Most commodities can be exported from the United States to free-world countries under a general license, but a validated license is required when exporting strategic goods and when exporting to unfriendly countries. Two points—the country of destination and the type of commodity to be exported—determine which type of license is needed for exportation requiring authorization by the Department of Commerce.

Country Classification. All the countries of the world, except Canada, are classified into seven groups designated by the symbols S, T, W, X, Y, Z, and V. The countries included in each group are as follows:

---

[2] Morgan Guaranty Trust Company, *Export and Import Procedures* (New York, September 1965), pp. 32–33.

S—Southern Rhodesia.

T—All countries of the Eastern Hemisphere, except Cuba.

W—Poland (including Danzig) and Romania.

Y—Albania, Bulgaria, Czechoslovakia, East Germany (Soviet Zone of Germany in East Berlin), Estonia, Hungary, Latvia, Lithuania, Outer Mongolia, and the U.S.S.R.

Z—Communist China, North Korea, Communist controlled area of Vietnam, and Cuba.

V—All other countries except Canada.[3]

The most stringent license requirements are set for Group Z, with validated licenses being required on almost all commodities considered for export to these countries. At present, in fact, there is a complete embargo on all commercial shipments to Communist China, North Korea, North Vietnam, and Cuba and a near total embargo on trade to Southern Rhodesia. Note: Country classifications can be changed rapidly however; e.g. Communist China in 1971.

Commodity Control List. In the United States commodities are classified according to their availability for export. The movement into foreign countries of goods that are considered scarce or strategic in nature is either prohibited altogether or restricted with regard to quantity. All commodities under the export control of the Department of Commerce are listed in the *Commodity Control List* of the *Comprehensive Export Schedule.* By consulting this list, an exporter can determine whether or not a validated or general license is required for shipment of a particular commodity to a specific country. If a validated license is required for the exportation of a commodity to a particular country, the exporter must acquire this license before export shipment will be allowed. For shipments not requiring a validated license, the exporter must indicate in the "Shipper's Export Declaration" a specific notation as to what kind of general license is applicable. The types of general licenses can be obtained from the *Comprehensive Export Schedule.*

Import Restrictions

In any analysis of the feasibility of exporting to a foreign country, it is necessary to examine not only the restrictions placed by the home country on exportation but also the import restrictions and regulations of the foreign country. Although the responsibility of import restrictions would generally rest with the importer, they are an important consideration to the exporter in terms of the feasibility of conducting business with a particular foreign customer.

Import tariffs imposed by the foreign country are probably the major impediment to trade with another country, although there are many other types of restrictions. *Business International* groups 30 basic barriers to exporting into three categories: regulatory devices, discriminatory devices, and arbitrary devices.

---

[3] *A Summary of U.S. Export Control Regulations,* op., cit., p. 3.

The most important regulatory devices used to restrict imports other than tariffs are considered by *Business International* to be:

1. Import licensing.
2. Quotas and other quantitative restrictions.
3. Currency restrictions on payments for imports.
4. Allocation of exchange at unfavorable rates.
5. Devaluations.
6. Prohibitive prior imports deposits.
7. Prohibition of collection-basis sales and insistence on cash letters of credit.
8. Arbitrarily short periods in which to apply for import licenses.
9. Delays resulting from pressure on overworked officials.
10. Delays resulting from competitors' influence on susceptible officials.[4]

Of these trade restrictions, the most frequently encountered are tariffs, exchange permits, quotas, and import licenses.

Tariffs. Tariffs are the taxes or customs duties levied against goods imported from another country. All countries have tariffs for the purpose of raising revenue or protecting home industries from the competition of foreign-produced goods. Tariff rates are based on value or quantity, or a combination of both. In the United States, for example, the types of custom duties used are classified as: (1) ad valorem duties, based on a percentage of the determined value of the imported goods; (2) specific duties, a stipulated amount per unit weight or some other measure of quantity; and (3) a compound duty which combines both specific and ad valorem taxes upon a particular item, i.e., a tax per pound plus a percentage of value (ad valorem). Published tariff schedules for every country are available to the exporter on a current basis, since tariffs are subject to frequent change.

Exchange Permits. Especially important to the exporter are the exchange restrictions placed on the flow of currency by some foreign countries. In order to conserve scarce foreign exchange and alleviate balance of payment difficulties, many countries impose restrictions on the amount of their currency they will exchange for the currency of another country. In effect, they ration the amount of currency available to pay for imports.

Exchange controls may be applied in general to all commodities, or, as is frequently the case, a country may employ a system of multiple exchange rates based on the type of import. Essential products might have a very favorable exchange rate, whereas nonessentials or luxuries would have a less favorable rate of exchange. In some cases, no exchange permits at all would be issued for certain classes of commodities. In countries that utilize exchange controls, the typical procedure is for the importer to apply to the control agency of his country for an import permit; if the control agency approves the request, an import license is issued. Then, through the proper governmental agency of his country,

---

[4] "48 Management Checklists for Foreign Operations," *Business International*, January, 1964, p. 8. Reprinted with permission.

he can use this import license to have his local currency exchanged for the currency of the seller.

The above procedure, however, does not work when currency is in short supply, even though exchange permits have been issued. In a recent transaction between the government of Colombia and Kaiser Industries, there was a scarcity of U.S. currency to exchange for the 1,000 jeeps Colombia wanted to purchase. The problem was solved through a series of exchanges, however. Colombia did have a surplus of coffee which Kaiser accepted and traded in Europe for sugar, then the sugar for pig iron, and finally, the pig iron for U.S. dollars. This rather complicated but effective transaction has become increasingly more frequent. In fact, a new international marketing middleman, sometimes called the intermerchant, has evolved[5] as a result of these switch or triangular trades in which several principals from different countries are involved.

Since exchange procedures can be very complicated, the exporter should seek the advice of his bank or some other informed source when questions of foreign exchange arise.

Quotas.   Countries may also impose limitations on the quantity of certain goods imported during a specific period. These quotas may be applied to imports from specific countries or from all foreign sources in general. The United States, for example, has specific quotas for the importation of some products, such as sugar, wheat, cotton, tobacco, and rice; in the case of some of these items, there are limitations on the amount imported from specific countries as well.

Quotas are set for a variety of reasons, the most important ones being to protect domestic industry and to conserve foreign exchange. Some importing countries also set quotas to insure an equitable distribution of a major market among friendly countries.

Import Licenses.   As a means of regulating the flow of exchange and the quantity of particular commodities imported, countries often require import licenses. The requirement of licenses for the importation of goods may be a means of maintaining control in administering exchange controls, quotas, and tariffs, or it may be used similarly for quotas in limiting the quantity of goods imported into the country. The fundamental difference between quotas and import licenses when used to control the quantity of a commodity brought into a country is the greater flexibility of the import license. Quotas are generally set for a certain period of time, but licensing can limit quantities on an individual basis from day to day.

Other Restrictions.   Many other kinds of restrictions are also imposed on imports, such as regulations affecting the importation of harmful products, drugs and medicine, and amoral products and literature. Products must also comply with all government standards set for health, sanitation, packaging, and labeling.

For example, in the Netherlands, all imported hens' and ducks' eggs

---

[5] See Exhibit 20–2, Chapter 20.

must be marked in indelible ink with the country of origin;[6] in Spain, imported condensed milk must be labeled to show its fat content when less than 8 percent fat is involved;[7] and in Mexico, all animals imported from the United States must be accompanied by a sanitary certificate issued by an approved veterinary inspector and a visa secured from a Mexican consulate.[8] Failure to comply with these regulations can result in severe fines and penalties. Since requirements vary with each country, regulations for all countries must be consulted individually. *Overseas Business Reports,* issued periodically by the Department of Commerce, provides the foreign marketer with the most recent foreign trade regulations of each country as well as the U.S. regulations regarding each country.

Free-Trade Zones

In order to facilitate international trade and lessen the difficulties caused by various import restrictions, some countries have established free ports and/or trade zones. There are more than 100 of these zones in operation in 40 countries. A free port or trade zone can receive shipments of goods for importation to be stored or processed in some manner without paying the required import duties until they leave the free zone area. Thus exporters can ship in large quantities to such free ports as Hong Kong, Beirut, or Barcelona for storage and processing and then supply other areas with smaller quantities as demand arises. By making use of free ports, an exporter foregoes the actual payment of import duties until the goods are shipped into a duty area.

In the United States, free trade zones are located in seven principal areas: New York, New Orleans, San Francisco, Seattle, Toledo, Honolulu, and Mayaquez, Puerto Rico. Goods subject to U.S. custom duties can be landed in these areas for storage or such processing as repackaging, cleaning, and grading before being brought into the United States or reexported to some other country. In either case, U.S. import duties are not payable unless the goods actually leave the free-trade zone for further commercial transaction in the United States; if they leave the free-trade zone for another country, U.S. import duties never have to be paid.

Through the use of free-trade zones, the importer can avoid paying duties on goods while they are being stored or processed in some manner. In those cases where goods are imported into the United States to be combined with American-made goods and reexported, the importer or exporter can avoid payment of U.S. import duties on the foreign portion and the subsequent application for a "drawback," i.e., a request

---

[6] "Foreign Trade Regulations of the Netherlands," *Overseas Business Reports* (Washington, D.C.: U.S. Department of Commerce, March 1964), p. 2.

[7] "Foreign Trade Regulations of Spain," *Overseas Business Reports* (Washington, D.C.: U.S. Department of Commerce, May 1964), p. 1.

[8] "Foreign Trade Regulations of Mexico," *Overseas Business Reports* (Washington, D.C.: U.S. Department of Commerce, March 1964), p. 4.

for a refund from the government of 99 percent of the duties paid on imports which are later reexported.

Bonded warehouses, regulated by the government, are similar to free-trade zones and allow for the postponement of federal duties and levies while goods are properly stored within them. Free-trade zones, however, are generally larger areas 'where companies can maintain processing facilities, while bonded warehouses are used primarily for storage. An example of the activity in the free-trade zone located in New York shows that in one year 520 commodities from 66 countries received many different kinds of processing which included such activities as "assembling, repacking, and marking watch movements and cases; repacking and marking silverware; sampling, grading, repacking ores, hides and tobacco; repacking, recoopering, and bungfilling liquors; and curing, cleaning, and packaging Brazil nuts."[9] A free-trade zone is in essence an enclave and not considered a part of the country to which it is contiguous as far as import regulations are concerned. If an item leaves a free-trade zone area for distribution and is imported into the country where the free-trade zone is located, all duties and regulations for imports are imposed.

Information about free-trade zones, free ports and similar customs-privileged facilities abroad may be obtained from the Transportation and Insurance Division, O.C.F.P., Bureau of International Commerce.[10]

EXPORT DOCUMENTS

Various documents are necessary for every export shipment, to satisfy government regulations controlling exportation and to meet the requirements for international commercial payment transactions. The most frequently required documents are the export declaration, the consular invoice or certificate of origin, the bill of lading, the commercial invoice, and the insurance certificate. In addition, such documents as import licenses, export licenses, packing lists, and inspection certificates for agricultural products are often necessary.

The preparation of these documents can be handled as a routine procedure, but their importance should not be minimized. Incomplete or improperly prepared documents lead to delays in shipment, and in some countries, penalties, fines, or even confiscation of the goods can result from errors made in some of these documents. Export documents are the end result of requirements imposed by the exporting government, of requirements set by commercial procedures established in foreign trade, and, in some cases, of the supporting import documents required by the foreign government. Principal export documents are:

1. *Export Declaration*. In order to maintain a statistical measure of the quantity of goods shipped abroad and to provide a means to deter-

---

[9] Paul V. Horn and Henry Gomez, *International Trade* (Englewood Cliffs, N.J.: Prentice-Hall, Inc., 1959), p. 128.

[10] "Introductory Guide to Exporting," (Washington, D.C.: U.S. Department of Commerce, April 1969), p. 32.

BOX 21–2

French Firm Loses U.S. Export Rights

The French firm Procida (Produits Chimiques Industriels et Agricoles S.A.), manufacturer of agricultural chemicals with offices in the Puteaux, a suburb of Paris, and factories in Marseilles and Beaucaire, has been denied U.S. export privileges for five months and placed on probation for the balance of three years for violating U.S. export control regulations.

According to the U.S. Commerce Department's Bureau of International Commerce (BIC), Procida early in 1967 obtained from an agency of the Cuban government an order for 300 tons of an insecticide containing primarily chlordane. To formulate this product Procida ordered 190 tons of chlordane from a U.S. supplier.

Before any of the material was shipped to Procida one of its employees knowingly misinformed the U.S. supplier that the finished product was for use in France and West Africa. The invoices for the material from the U.S. supplier to Procida carried notices prohibiting its distribution to certain destinations, including Cuba. The company mixed the chlordane with other ingredients to formulate the insecticide which it shipped to Cuba.

BIC found that it was not company policy to ship U.S. goods to Cuba in violation of the U.S. restriction and that this was an isolated instance carried out by responsible employees without the knowledge of high-level officials of the company.

The U.S. export regulations provide that without authorization from the Department of Commerce, no party may trade in commodities or technical data exported from the United States with a party he knows has been restricted from dealing in U.S. exports.

Source: *International Commerce*, July 21, 1969, p. 12.

mine whether regulations are being met, most countries require shipments abroad to be accompanied by an export declaration. Usually such a declaration, which is presented at the port of exit, includes the names and addresses of the principals involved, the destination of the goods, a full description of the goods, and their declared value. When manufacturers are exporting from the United States, the United States Customs and the United States Department of Commerce require an export declaration for all shipments. If specific licenses are required to ship a particular commodity, the export license must be presented with the declaration for proper certification. In this way, the export declaration document serves as the principal means of control for those goods whose exportation is in some manner regulated by agencies of the U.S. government.

2. *Consular Invoice or Certificate of Origin.* Not all countries require consular invoices, but those that do are typically very exacting in the manner in which the invoices are prepared. Proper forms must be obtained from the country's consulate and returned with two to eight copies in the language of the country along with copies of other required

documents, such as the import license, commercial invoice, and bill of lading, before certification is granted. The consular invoice probably involves the most red tape and is the most exacting to complete. Preparation of the document should be handled with extreme care because fines are levied for any errors uncovered. Since the procedure in most countries is to share the fine with whomever detects it, few errors go undetected.

3. *Bill of Lading.* The most important document required to establish legal ownership and facilitate financial transactions is the bill of lading. It serves the following purposes: (1) as a receipt from the carrier for shipment, (2) as a contract for shipment between the carrier and shipper, and (3) as a certificate of ownership, or title to the goods. Bills of lading are issued in the form of straight bills, which are nonnegotiable and are delivered directly to a consignee, or order bills, which are negotiable instruments. Bills of lading are frequently referred to as being either clean or foul. A clean bill of lading means that the items presented to the carrier for shipment were properly packaged and clear of apparent damage when received; a foul bill of lading means that the shipment was received in damaged condition, and this fact is noted on the bill of lading.

4. *Commercial Invoice.* Every international transaction requires a commercial invoice, i.e., a bill or statement for the goods sold. This document often serves several purposes in that some countries require a copy for customs clearance, and it is also one of the financial documents required in international commercial payments.

5. *Insurance Policy or Certificate.* The risks of shipment due to political or economic unrest in some countries, and the possibility of damage from the sea and weather, make it absolutely necessary to have adequate insurance covering loss resulting from damage, war, or riots. Typically, the method of payment or terms of sale require insurance on the goods, so that few export shipments are uninsured. The insurance policy or certificate of insurance is considered a key document in export trade.

Export or import licenses are additional documents among many frequently required in export trade. In those cases where import licenses are required by the country of entry, a copy of the license or the license number is usually required in order to obtain a consular invoice. Whenever a commodity requires an export license, it must be obtained before an export declaration will be properly certified. Sanitary and health inspection certificates attesting to the absence of disease and pests may also be required for certain agricultural products before a country will allow the goods to enter its borders. Packing lists with correct weights are also required in some cases.

PACKING AND MARKING

Special requirements of packing and marking must be considered as one of the mechanics of export trade for those shipments destined to be transported over water, subject to excessive handling, and/or destined to parts of the world with extreme climate. Packing which is adequate for domestic shipments often falls short when the goods are subject to the conditions mentioned above. Protection against rough handling, moisture, temperature extremes, and pilferage may require heavy crating which increases total cost for packing as well as freight rates because of increased weight and size. Since some countries determine import duties on gross weight, packing can add a significant amount to import fees. In order to avoid the extremes of too much or too little packing, the marketer should consult export brokers, export freight forwarders, or other specialists.

All countries have some regulations on marking goods and containers being imported. These regulations should be strictly adhered to, since noncompliance can result in severe penalties.[11] The exporter should be especially careful that all marking on the container conforms exactly to the data on the export documents, because discrepancies are often interpreted by custom officials as an attempt to defraud. A basic source of information for American exporters is the Department of Commerce series of pamphlets entitled *Preparing Shipment to* (country)[12] which detail the necessary export documents as well as outlining pertinent U.S. and foreign government regulations regarding such matters as labeling, marking, packing, and customs procedures.

FOREIGN COMMERCIAL PAYMENTS[13]

The sale of goods in other countries is further complicated by additional risks encountered when dealing with foreign customers. There are risks resulting from inadequate credit reports on customers, problems of currency exchange controls, distance, different legal systems, and the cost and difficulty of collecting delinquent accounts which require different emphasis on payment systems utilized. In U.S. domestic trade, the typical payment procedure for established customers is an open account, i.e., the goods are delivered and the customer is billed on an end-of-the-month basis. In fact, with the exception of certain industries, most business is conducted on an open account basis. The most frequently used term of payment in foreign commercial transactions for both export and import sales is by letter of credit, followed closely in importance by commercial dollar drafts or bills of exchange drawn by the seller on the buyer. Of rather insignificant importance are open accounts and cash payment in advance. Open accounts are reserved for well-established customers, and cash in advance is required of only the poorest credit risks. Because of the time typically required for shipment of goods from one country to another, advance payment of cash is an unusually costly burden for a potential customer. For this reason, cash places a

---

[11] See Chapter 8 for additional legal details.

[12] *Preparing Shipment to* (country) series, available for 88 countries from U.S. Department of Commerce, Operations Reports, Superintendent of Documents, U.S. Government Printing Office, Washington, D.C.

[13] This section draws heavily from *Export and Import Procedures,* op. cit.

seller at a definite disadvantage competitively unless, of course, all sellers require cash.

Terms of a sale are typically arranged between the buyer and seller at the time of the sale. The type of merchandise, the amount of money involved, business custom, the credit rating of the buyer, the country of the buyer, whether the buyer is a new or old customer, are all items to be considered in establishing the terms of sale. The basic types of payment arrangements discussed in this section are (1) letters of credit, (2) bills of exchange or dollar drafts, (3) cash, and (4) open accounts.

Letters of Credit

A large part of all American exports is handled on the basis of export letters of credit which are opened in favor of the seller by the buyer.

Letters of credit shift the credit risk of the buyer to the bank issuing the letter of credit. When a letter of credit is employed, the seller can ordinarily draw a draft against the bank issuing the credit and receive dollars with the presentation of the proper shipping documents. Except for cash in advance, letters of credit afford the greatest degree of protection for the seller.

The procedure when using a letter of credit generally begins at the completion of the contract when the buyer goes to his local bank and arranges for the issuance of a letter of credit; the buyer's bank then notifies its correspondent bank in the seller's country that the letter has been issued. When the seller meets the requirements of the letter of credit, he can draw a draft against the credit (in effect the bank issuing the letter) for payment of the goods. The precise conditions of the letter of credit are set out within it and generally require the presentation of certain documents with the draft before the correspondent bank will honor the draft. The usual documents required are (1) the commercial invoice, (2) the consular invoice (when requested), (3) a clean bill of lading, and (4) an insurance policy or certificate. Upon presentation of the proper documents and a draft, the correspondent bank will then honor the draft under the terms of the letter of credit.

The main advantage of the letter of credit in the eyes of the seller is the shifting of risk to a third party. Payment is guaranteed by one or more banks.

Since all letters of credit, by their nature, must be very exact in terms and considerations, it is important for the exporter to check the terms of the letter of credit carefully to be certain that all the necessary documents have been acquired and properly completed. One of the larger American banks dealing in international financial payments lists the following as being the most frequent discrepancies found in documents, causing delay in honoring drafts or letters of credit:

1. Letter of credit has expired or time for shipment has expired.
2. Invoice or draft exceeds amount of letter of credit.
3. Charges included in invoice are not authorized in letter of credit.
4. Insurance coverage is not complete either as to amount or as to risks covered.

5. Insurance document is not endorsed.
6. Insurance document is not countersigned.
7. Date of insurance certificate is later than date on bill of lading.
8. Bill of lading is not "clean"—that is, it bears notations that qualify the good order and condition of the merchandise, or its packing.
9. Bills of lading do not indicate "on board," or the "on board" endorsement of bills of lading or changes in bills of lading are not signed by the carrier or its agent, or initiated by the party who signed the bills of lading.
10. Bills of lading are made out to "order" (shipper's order, blank endorsed), whereas the credit stipulates "straight" (direct to consignee) bills of lading or vice versa ("order" bills of lading to some countries are prohibited and heavy penalties or additional duties are assessed for failure to ship on a "straight" bill of lading).
11. Bills of lading are not endorsed.
12. Bills of lading do not indicate "freight prepaid" as stipulated in letter of credit.
13. Bills of lading are not marked "freight prepaid" when freight charges are included in invoice.
14. Description, marks, and numbers of merchandise do not appear the same on all documents presented, or as called for in letters of credit.
15. Not all the documents required under letter of credit are presented.
16. Documents are "stale dated."
17. Invoice states "used," "second hand," or "rebuilt" merchandise or machinery for which specific authorization is not incorporated in the terms of letter of credit.
18. Invoice does not set forth terms of shipment as stipulated in letter of credit, such as C&F, CIF, FOB, FAS, etc.
19. Invoice is not signed as required by letter of credit.
20. Drawings are not proportionate to price or quantity shown in letter of credit.[14]

Bills of Exchange

Another important form of international commercial payment is handled through the use of sight or time drafts drawn by sellers on foreign buyers. In letters of credit, the credit of one or more banks is involved; but, in the use of bills of exchange (or dollar drafts), the seller assumes all risks until the actual dollars are received. The typical procedure followed is for the seller to draw a draft on the buyer and present it with the necessary documents to his bank for collection. The documents required are principally the same as those required for letters of credit. Upon receipt of the draft, the U.S. bank forwards the draft with the necessary documents to a correspondent bank in the buyer's country; then the buyer is presented with the draft for his acceptance and immediate or later payment. With his acceptance of the draft, the buyer receives the properly endorsed bill of lading, which he uses to acquire the goods from the carrier.

Bills of exchange or dollar drafts generally have one of three time periods—at sight, arrival, or time. A sight draft requires that acceptance

---

[14] *Export and Import Procedures*, op. cit., pp. 15–16.

and payment be made upon presentation of the draft and often before arrival of the goods. An arrival draft requires that payment be made upon arrival of the goods. Unlike the other two kinds, a date draft has an exact date for payment and in no way is affected by the movement of the goods. There may be time designations placed on the sight and arrival drafts which stipulate a fixed number of days after acceptance when the obligation must be paid. Usually this period is from 30 to 120 days, thus providing one means of extending credit to the foreign buyer.

Dollar drafts have advantages for the seller because he can generally discount an accepted draft with his bank and, therefore, get a part of the money before payment is actually made. Banks, however, usually discount drafts only with recourse, i.e., if the draft is not honored by the buyer, the bank returns it to the seller for payment. An accepted draft is also much sounder evidence in case of default and necessary litigation than an open account would be.

Cash in Advance

The volume of business handled on a cash-in-advance basis is not very large. Cash places unpopular burdens on the customer and is typically used only when credit is doubtful, when exchange restrictions within the country of destination are such that the return of funds from abroad may be delayed for an unreasonable period, or when the American exporter for any other reason may be unwilling to sell on credit terms.[15]

Although payment in advance is infrequently employed, partial payment (from 25 to 50 percent) in advance is not unusual when the character of the merchandise is such that incompletion of the contract may result in heavy loss. For example, complicated machinery or equipment manufactured to specification or special design would necessitate advance payment which would be, in fact, a nonrefundable deposit.

Open Accounts

Sales on open accounts are not generally made in foreign trade except to customers of long standing with excellent credit reputation, or when sales are made to a subsidiary or branch of the exporter. Open accounts obviously leave the seller in a position where most of the problems of international commercial finance work to his disadvantage. It is generally recommended that sales on open account should not be made when it is the practice of the trade to use some other method, when special merchandise is ordered, when shipping is hazardous, when the country of the importer imposes difficult exchange restrictions, or when political unrest requires additional caution.[16]

---

[15] *Export and Import Procedures,* op. cit., p. 30.

[16] It is suggested that the reader refer to Chapter 20 for a discussion of the credit guarantees available to the foreign marketer.

SUMMARY AND CONCLUSIONS

An awareness of the mechanics of export trade is indispensable to the foreign marketer who engages in exporting goods from one country to another; these mechanics, however, should not be considered the essence of foreign marketing since they are only one aspect which must be incorporated in a total marketing plan. Although most marketing techniques are open to interpretation and creative application, the mechanics of exporting are very exact; there is little room for interpretation or improvisation with the requirements of export licenses, quotas, tariffs, export documents, packing, and marking, and the various uses of commercial payments.

The very nature of the regulations and restrictions surrounding importing and exporting can lead to frequent and rapid change. In handling the mechanics of export trade successfully, the manufacturer must keep abreast of all foreign and domestic changes in requirements and regulations pertaining to the product involved.

READING

GUIDELINES IN EXPORTING FOR THE SMALL COMPANY*

JOHN E. WALSH, JR.

The importance of world trade and the deep involvement of most large and many middle sized American companies have provided an impetus for the smaller companies, (i.e., those employing less than 500 employees) to export their goods and services. Total world trade in 1966 was in excess of $300 billion annually, with the leading country in exports and imports being the United States. American firms exported $29.3 billion worth of goods and services, and imported more than $25.5 billion. Approximately 7,000 of our 300,000 manufacturing firms have conducted business in more than 100 foreign countries. Although yearly totals may fluctuate, no changes are expected in the long-run trend of increased growth in international marketing, because of the interdependence of the economies of many of the nations of the world.

Why Smaller Companies Should Export

Many executives of smaller companies will raise the question: Why should my company export? In many instances, their firms are using most of their production capacity for the United States market. If expansion is desired, why not expand at home where there is greater familiarity with the markets, the competition, and the types of problems that must be solved?

There are several reasons why the smaller company should take a

* Reprinted from *Business Viewpoints*, pp. 75–81, Graduate School of Business Administration, Washington University (St. Louis), 1968.

serious look at selling in foreign markets. President Kennedy provided with brevity and lucidity one answer to the question of "why export?" in an Executive Order in 1961 on the ceremony of the President's "E" award:

I call on both management and labor to exert their utmost efforts toward producing and selling in the world market. . . . Here is the next great frontier we must cross. . . . The United States must in the best traditions of American competitiveness and ingenuity, push forward with the development and sale of goods in all markets of the world. . . . An increased level of exports is absolutely essential for a healthy situation in our international balance of payments. Such a healthy situation in turn will enable us to carry out international responsibilities for preservation of freedom. . . . More exports will mean a stronger America; a more prosperous America; and greater assurance of a free world.

It should be recognized that exporting does not necessarily mean selling to countries in distant parts of the world. There are companies in Massachusetts that are closer to Canadian markets than they are to the Midwest. There are companies in the Midwest closer to Mexico than they are to California. As a matter of fact, both Canada and Mexico are major importers of American products. Canada actually is our best customer having imported over $6 billion worth of goods last year, and Mexico imported over $1 billion.

Many American companies have found that there is money to be made overseas. They have recognized opportunities in countries of the world where the economy is growing at a faster rate than the United States, while at the same time the degree of competition is considerably less. They have recognized opportunities in countries where markets have opened recently for their type of product, or where trade restrictions have been relaxed. They have recognized opportunities in foreign countries receiving assistance from the Agency for International Development (AID) under the Buy America Act. And they have recognized opportunities of exporting to foreign affiliates of United States firms.

How One Small Company Sold Its Product in a Foreign Country

Assuming that the reasons cited for exporting are accepted as valid and evoke interest, the next question requiring an answer is, "How does a small company sell its product in a foreign country?" A case example, which appears in *Business International,* and which depicted how a small company producing electronic air purifiers with sales of approximately $3 million a year got a running start in the European market without a major investment, will serve in part as an answer.

Until 1961 all export sales of this company were handled by a major United States international appliance maker. But in 1962 the small company decided to handle its own export activities. The first decision of the firm brought about its modest budget which introduced to the three most promising European countries only seven of its many models.

The countries that were selected were: France, the United Kingdom, and West Germany.

The company's products were unknown in these countries, and the company lacked the necessary capital for a mass advertising campaign. To make up this deficiency, a sales office was established in Frankfurt, Germany, with one United States salesman and a local clerical staff to coordinate all European sales. The company then took the following four steps:

1.   The products were first introduced at the Trade Fair of Frankfurt, the Lyon Fair, and the United States Trade Center in London. During the exhibitions, the company selected a distributor in each of the three countries who was selling complementary and noncompetitive lines. The United Kingdom distributor had warehousing facilities which the company used. In West Germany, however, the company set up a private warehouse to service both the German and French distributors. This efficient and economical move enabled the company to accomplish its warehousing objectives at the lowest cost possible.

2.   With the help of J. Walter Thompson in Paris, the company entered into a wide publicity campaign that was far less expensive than advertising. For example, the firm installed its air purifiers in the automobile of Sterling Moss, the popular racing driver, and in the famous submarine at the Lausanne Exposition; these and similar promotional approaches gave the company wide publicity throughout the Continent.

3.   The next gambit was to sell to mail order houses such as Harold's in the United Kingdom and Kueller in West Germany. The mail order houses then proceeded to promote the company's products at no charge to the company through regular mail order catalogues and special mailings.

4.   Finally, the company launched its own selected mailing campaign to various medical and professional organizations. It also sent mailings to chain stores, discount houses, retail buying groups, voluntary chains, wholesaler buying groups, and others.

All of these steps were supervised and coordinated by the salesman in Frankfurt, who spent three weeks a month traveling and visiting with executives having major accounts.

There were weaknesses in the company's campaign. Distributors tended, as one might expect, to give priority servicing to their previously established main product lines. As a result, servicing for the company's lines was slow.

Yet, despite this limitation and financial problems, the company was able to triple its sales within one year. Using a similar strategy, the company expanded operations to include Austria, Switzerland, Belgium, and Italy.

Export Strategies of Two Small Companies

Is this illustration typical of the successful export strategy of smaller firms? Let us review the export strategies of two small companies in the St. Louis area. The Sunnen Company and Marsh Stencil Company have been highly successful in selling in world markets; their export strategies can be compared with the company previously cited. Certain basic procedures were common to all three companies, but each company exhibited different strategies based on the product, the type of export organization, the country and the nature of the markets, funds available, and the like.

The companies were similar in that each manufactured quality products which met the highest standards of design and performance at a competitive price in the United States. All concentrated on product development. All gathered data on countries which offered sales opportunities, and countries where the currency was convertible to United States dollars. Within the countries selected, all attempted to locate markets which offered the greatest sales potential. All sold through distributors who were selected after extensive investigation through correspondence, personal visits, or both. All exhibited their products in International Trade Fairs. All made personal visits to overseas distributors to follow up on sales activities. Finally, all gave their wholehearted effort to the foreign operations.

The companies in the St. Louis area differed in the following manner. Organizations and methods of advertising varied. The Sunnen Company, a manufacturer of precision honing machines, contracted with an export agent on a commission basis, who reported directly to the president and who was responsible for the entire export operation. The Marsh Stencil Company of Belleville, Illinois, employed an export manager, who reported directly to the president. The Sunnen Company advertised extensively in foreign language editions of American magazines and international trade publications. Marsh Stencil Company used case histories and photographs of the successful utilization of their equipment in foreign plants and offices. There were other ways these two companies differed; but in the main, their basic products and strategies, like the electronics company, were fundamentally sound for the export market.

Materials and Services Available to the Small Company

Let us turn now to the numerous materials and services available that can be of substantial value to the small firm desiring to export. As an initial step, a firm should diligently review pertinent publications of the United States Department of Commerce, its Bureau of International Commerce, and the Small Business Administration. Reading the weekly publication, *Business International,* which has a wide assortment of articles pertinent to exporting, is also suggested. For a detailed explanation of the mechanics of exporting, "Adventures in Exporting" by Audrey Marsh King and Walton C. Marsh, is quite helpful. In addition, the materials and services of the large commercial banks, and most of the standard texts and periodicals published by major publishing companies, will provide the kind of information needed to appraise opportunities for exporting and for keeping up-to-date once a market has been established.

The Need for Attention to Detail

Yet, studying these materials and using the services, good as they are, will not assure the small firm of success. Ultimate success requires utmost attention to minute detail and perhaps some luck. Exporting requires working in a more complex environment with considerably less information and constantly changing pressures and conditions. Constant vigilance is absolutely necessary. A firm can never accept information without first checking and rechecking the source, and then checking on other possible sources for the same or complementary information.

As a case in point, what country ranks as our closest competitor in exporting? A review of United Nations statistics discloses it is the Republic of West Germany. While our exports are listed as being almost $7 billion greater than West Germany, these figures require deeper appraisal, because exports include agricultural products, military aid, and sales tied to foreign aid. A better comparison of exports to the United States and West Germany would be to consider primarily chemicals, machinery, transportation equipment, and miscellaneous manufactured goods. Comparative figures are not available for 1964 or 1965. But our exports in these categories in 1963 were less than $12 billion, and West Germany was slightly under $10 billion. These figures stress the importance of West Germany as an exporting nation.

No exporting firm can expect success by only superficially performed operations. Executives must know thoroughly the market and non-market environment of each country where they plan to sell. They must know their distributors and agents almost as well as their own sales force. They must know what their competitors are doing. They must have constant feedback on conditions that can affect product sales.

Germans, like most Europeans, recognized and concentrated on the export market long before the United States. Consequently, most German executives knew, as anyone who takes exporting seriously should know, that to succeed in a foreign country a company must prepare for a sustained effort.

Skills and Persons Necessary for Successful Exporting

A very successful businesman, who will be nameless here, once remarked at a luncheon given in his honor that he attributed his success to his ability to have at his disposal a good lawyer and a good accountant to consult with on important business decisions. If he would continue this practice and would not enlarge his group of associates and advisors in connection with exporting, it is probable that he would quickly find himself in a quagmire looking for a rope. Not that accountants and lawyers are unimportant in the export scene, because indeed they are extremely important. But exporting requires additional skills and people who have these skills. For the small company it requires a good foreign distributor or agent familiar with the market environment, who has one or more persons in his organization highly proficient in English. Further, it requires contact with one or more persons familiar with the non-market environment, the history values, and norms of the people of the countries where sales are anticipated. Such persons might include an anthropologist, a professor of business administration, a trader, or a missionary; the person or persons may or may not be a native of the country. It should be noted that the commercial officers of the United States embassies were not mentioned above, simply because these officials seldom work in one country more than three years which is often insufficient time for them to acquire the type of knowledge needed on the non-market environment.

Since the contributions of the accountant in setting cost targets for the export market, or the lawyer in reviewing distributorship agreements, contracts, purchase agreements, and laws of the country involved are generally understood, their importance will not be discussed further. But it is appropriate to discuss in more detail the foreign distributor or agent and persons familiar with the non-market environment.

The Foreign Distributor or Agent

It is fundamental that the distributor or agent's integrity and financial responsibility, if not beyond reproach, will at least be free from excessive stain or pollution. Also, he should have the right sales coverage, physical facilities, experience, and the like. But these conditions would be required in selecting a distributor or agent in the United States. The unique and also the essential ingredient in selecting a foreign distributor or agent is that he, or one or more of his employees, have a masterly command of spoken and written English.

A distributor or agent represents a critical position in the channel of communications from manufacturer to consumer. Generally, the distributor receives correspondence from the exporter in English and returns correspondence in English, while communicating with customers in the language of the country. Because of the greater probability of communications distortion brought about notably by distance, type of communication, language translation, and environment, it is imperative that the distributor clearly understand the meaning intended. But this understanding requires, as a prerequisite, excellent facility with English. If a distributor understands 90% of the words in a written or oral communication, comprehension of the meaning transmitted can vary from 100% comprehension to complete confusion. It is not unusual to find communications interpreted diametrically opposite their intended meaning.

A Mistake to Be Avoided

One of the critical mistakes made by some American companies in foreign countries has been the inability of American executives to understand the non-market environment, and not to seek advice from persons who do. Failure to understand the non-market environment is excusable, since such understanding is not acquired quickly or easily.

But failure to seek advice and guidance from persons who know the values, norms, and sentiments of the people of a foreign country in order to understand the non-market environment is quite inexcusable and potentially dangerous. Yet, last year a large corporation in the Midwest began selling its products in an East Asian country. A professor at a nearby university who had recently returned from the Asian country, after conducting extensive research of accounting systems in the country, offered his assistance to the executive of international operations in the large corporation. No mention was made of a fee. Still, the executive refused the professor's advice with the statement, "We will let our people learn for themselves when they go out to the country." And no doubt they will, but might not the learning experience be a costly one?

Executives of a smaller firm may not be able to learn through experience alone. But they can utilize and benefit from the experience of individuals and from the experience of other American companies, large, medium, and small. They should even use the facilities of the large companies where feasible, since the "piggy-back" system initiated by the Department of Commerce has made this possible. This system permits small firms to use the channels of distribution of the large firms, assuming the large firm consents, when the products of the two companies are either complementary, or at least not competitive.

Before quitting this paper, it must be said that, in the writer's view, only the most important guidelines have been discussed. It scarcely needs statement to mention there are many more. It is now possible to sum up the material that has been presented.

Summary

This paper has attempted to provide the reader with several sources of materials and services, case examples of small firms which have profited by exporting, and brief insights for formulating an overall export strategy. Although all of these suggestions will hardly be acceptable in their entirety to executives of specific smaller firms, basic approaches to exporting should not differ radically. With the rising standard of living in many countries of the world and the subsequent emergence of more sophisticated buyers, it seems apparent there will be an ever increasing need for the kinds of goods and services that our smaller firms can produce. Exporting, despite many obstacles, offers a great opportunity to the small American firm which has a perceptive, imaginative, and energetic management.

QUESTIONS

1. Define and show the significance to international marketing of the following terms:

Commodity control list	Ad valorem duty
General license	Intermerchant
Commodity classifications	Foul bill of lading
Validated license	Letter of credit
Exchange permits	Clean bill of lading
Duty	

2. Explain the reasoning behind the various regulations and restrictions imposed on the exportation and importation of goods.

3. Define the two types of licenses required for exporting goods from the United States.

4. What determines the type of license needed for exportation? Discuss.

5. Discuss the most frequently encountered trade restrictions.

6. What is the purpose of an import license? Discuss.

7. Explain free-trade zones and illustrate how they may be used by an exporter. By an importer. How do free-trade zones differ from bonded warehouses?

8. Explain each of the following export documents:
   a) Bill of lading
   b) Counselor invoice or certificate of origin
   c) Commercial invoice
   d) Insurance certificate

9. What are the differences between straight bill of lading and order bill of lading? What are the differences between clean bill of lading and foul bill of lading?

10. Discuss the basic types of payment arrangements. Under what conditions would each be likely to be used?

11. Illustrate the typical procedure followed when using a letter of credit.

12. Describe the procedure followed by the seller when using a dollar draft.

13. Select a food product, a manufactured industrial product, and a consumer good. Assume you are an exporter shipping to the following countries. Determine what kind of license would be required in shipment of these goods from the United States to each country. Also discuss the type of foreign commercial permit which would be best.

East Germany	Cuba
Canada	Communist China
France	Japan
Mexico	

14. Discuss the different ways in which a free-trade zone would be of value to an exporter in shipping:
   a) Agricultural raw materials
   b) Manufactured industrial products
   c) Unassembled electrical appliances

OUTLINE OF CHAPTER 22

INTRODUCTION

DEVELOPING CHANNEL POLICIES AND STRATEGIES

Policy

Strategic Goals
Cost
Control
Coverage
Character
Continuity

ADAPTING TO DISTRIBUTION PATTERNS

General Patterns
Social Acceptance
Middleman Services
Line Breadth
Cost and Margins
Channel Length

Wholesale Patterns
Power and Competition
Services and Efficiency

Retail Patterns
Size Patterns
Change
Self-Service
Discounting
Co-ops, Chains, and Groups
Resistance to Change

BUILDING INTERNATIONAL CHANNELS

Tactical Decisions

Operational Challenges
Finding Middlemen
Selection
Coming to Terms

Solving Distribution Problems
Nonexistent Channels
Blocked Channels
Stocking and Servicing

Motivating Middlemen

CHANNEL CONTROL

SUMMARY AND CONCLUSIONS

READING
Planning for Distribution, *Marketing Insights.*

INTERNATIONAL DISTRIBUTION PATTERNS AND STRATEGY

INTRODUCTION

Chapter 20 considered at length the various types of domestic and foreign middlemen who participate in the channels of distribution in international business. Such a treatment is of necessity static and descriptive; it cannot convey the tremendous complexity of the international distribution process. It is the task of this chapter to deal with the dynamics of international distribution strategy and the substrategies which result from the overall plan.

Every country, indeed in some countries every market area, presents the international marketer with unique distribution patterns and problems. For each market a separate solution may be required, but the first step in developing a channel program is to develop an overall strategy for marketing and distribution. At this point, basic decisions are called for relative to the degree of commitment to achieving distribution in a given country and the amount of control which the company wants to exert over its worldwide distribution. The overall strategy provides a framework for analysis of distribution patterns in the different countries in which goods are to be marketed. Retail and wholesale patterns and the general distribution pattern for both urban and rural market sectors need to be considered.

Based on this analysis, the actual channel plan can be developed, and the process of building the channel or modifying existing channel relationships can be undertaken. Once the channels have been developed and are being employed, the channel commander retains the responsibility for motivating all the middlemen in the channels of distribution and extracting peak performance from them. In addition, he is responsible for maintaining control over the channels of distribution to assure maximum volume, adequate market coverage, appropriate servicing, and proper selling prices; his decisions affect the results and all of the distribution costs which, in turn, make the marketing enterprise profitable or unprofitable for the producing company. These are the primary considerations of this chapter on international distribution strategy.

DEVELOPING CHANNEL POLICIES AND STRATEGIES

A host of policy and strategy questions confronts the international marketing manager. The policy problem areas are not in themselves very different from the problem areas encountered in domestic distribution, but the answers may differ because of different market patterns and channel alternatives.

Despite market-by-market variations, the company should establish basic policy lines from which it will not deviate until the change has been given full consideration. Policies must, however, be broad and flexible enough to permit geographic variation in the marketing strategies and tactics which are employed and must permit changes over time. The firm operating in several countries cannot content itself with one set of solutions; there must be a solution for each separate marketplace. Take, for example, the case of exclusive agents or exclusive distributors. In countries like Japan or Belgium channel structures are such that a single middleman can often accommodate national distribution. Unfortunately, however, there is a tendency for some businessmen to think of Africa as a similar entity, but Africa is neither small nor homogeneous. It is a conglomeration of over 30 independent nations, none of which has really adequate distribution facilities. There is no one middleman, not even one type of middleman, who can adequately cover this continent three times the size of the United States.

Policy

As marketing structures develop in the years to come, manufacturers will be able to have greater latitude in their policy decisions, but at present answers to policy questions rest largely in terms of the (possibly unsatisfactory) alternatives that are available. Questions of control, size of margins, length of channels, terms of sale, and even channel ownership will be decided more on an environmental than a preferential basis. Because of the difficulty of laying down precise operating policies, the international marketer may find that he must couch his policies in terms of return on investment, sales volume, long-run potential, and other general guidelines; he must acknowledge that the lesser problems must be solved on the strategic level. However, unless it relishes the prospect of becoming bogged down in a morass of conflict and confusion, the company must establish basic policies to direct its international marketing efforts. Such policies should explicitly detail the extent of commitment, in terms of money and manpower, which the company is willing to make in developing international distribution for its goods. All policies, of course, need to keep the profit goals of the company in a foremost position. Within those general guidelines, specific marketing goals for the international operation must be established. Such goals may be expressed in terms of volume, market share, and margin requirements. More specifically, the company's policy may delineate the relationship between long- and short-term goals of the company and may specify the company's levels of involvement in the distribution system and the extent of its ownership of middlemen.

Regardless of the nature of the policies, the company must provide adequate flexibility for meeting local conditions and leave opportunity for the marketing strategist to ply his skills. Companies which have forgotten the basic lessons of flexibility and adaptability or which have lost sight of the primary policy objectives have not generally fared well in the international marketplace. Frigidaire and Whirlpool, two major U.S. producers of electrical appliances, were routed from the French refrigerator market after years of market involvement when aggressive Italian competitors moved in. German companies did no better against the intensive competition in either France or in their own country. Marketers were hampered by corporate policy restrictions requiring them to refuse to supply discount and mail-order firms; the companies feared retaliation by their dealers who were extremely conscious of the retail price maintenance policies of the companies. Because they tried to hold the line, the German companies lost 20 percent of the German refrigerator market within two years to Italians who were marketing through the mail-order and discount channels. In the dynamic situation of world marketing, policies must not only be flexible and adaptable, they must also be susceptible to review on relatively short notice.

Strategic Goals

While the overall marketing strategy of the firm must embody the company's goals of healthy profits in both the short and the long run, the channel strategy itself may be considered to have five very specific strategic goals. These may be characterized as the five Cs of channel strategy—cost, control, coverage, character, and continuity.

Cost. Two kinds of cost are encountered in developing and maintaining distribution channels; the capital or investment cost of developing the channel and the continuing cost of maintaining it. The latter may be in the form of direct expenditure for the maintenance of the company's selling force or it may be in the form of the margins, markup, or commission of various middlemen who handle the goods. Realistically viewed, marketing costs (the bulk of which is channel cost) must be considered to be the entire difference between the factory price of the goods and the price the customer ultimately pays for the merchandise. The cost of middlemen activities is hard to allocate specifically because it includes so many different components. How, for example, does one divide the 20 percent which a wholesaler may charge for distributing hardware? Separate parts of the efforts of the wholesaler are involved in transporting and storing the goods, in breaking bulk, in handling the paperwork, in handling credit, and in local advertising, sales representation, and negotiations. The marketing decision maker may have a difficult time predicting what his costs will be for performing these various functions. Many companies which thought that they could perform distribution miracles at low cost have been forced to rethink or restructure their channels of distribution when their cost-saving dreams were not realized.

The entire distribution strategy is based on balancing the desirable goals of minimizing distribution costs and maximizing the advantages of the other four Cs. Despite the old truism that you can eliminate middlemen but you can't eliminate their functions or cost, creative marketing does permit channel cost to be reduced in many circumstances. Various marketers have found, in fact, that they can reduce cost by using shorter channels. The Majestic Group, Mexico's largest producer of radio and television sets, has built a $36 million per year sales volume on its ability to sell goods at a low price because it eliminated middlemen, established its own wholesalers, and kept margins low.[1] Conversely, many firms (particularly U.S. firms) that are accustomed to using their own sales force in large-volume domestic markets have found that they must lengthen channels of distribution to keep costs in line in foreign markets.

Control.   One major reason that companies involve themselves deeply in the distribution of their own goods is that they wish to be in a better position to control their marketing destinies. It is generally conceded that the company's own sales force permits maximum control even though it may impose additional cost burdens. Each type of channel arrangement, indeed each specific middleman, has a different level of susceptibility to control. It is well known that as channels of distribution grow longer, the ability of the parent company to control these channels, which means to control price, volume, promotion methods, and type of outlets, is diminished. Some companies have given up any semblance of an attempt to control the end destiny of their products and are satisfied merely to place the goods in the hands of some middleman who in turn passes them into other hands for international distribution. Such a company can hardly know where its product is going, what volume of sales can be expected, or the future of the international portion of its business.

Coverage.   The third major goal of the international channel-of-distribution strategy is to achieve full market coverage. More specifically this means (1) gaining the optimum volume of sales obtainable in the markets in which the company is operating, (2) securing a reasonable market share, and (3) attaining satisfactory market penetration. Coverage may be assessed on a geographic basis or may be measured by other kinds of market segments. A company's desire for adequate market coverage may cause it to change its distribution system from country to country or time to time. Sometimes when products are being introduced to new markets, use of local middlemen permits rapid market coverage at a satisfactory level because the middlemen already possess the subchannels or customer contacts necessary to assure distribution. At some later time a company may decide to develop its own distribution system in order to gain more intensive coverage of the market through aggressive representation.

Coverage also includes the concept of full representation for all of the lines a company wishes to sell within a given market. Sometimes

---

[1] "Latins Turn North to One of Their Own," *Business Week*, March 21, 1970, p. 49.

middlemen will take on the more lucrative parts of a line but will either neglect or refuse to handle other products which the manufacturer wants to emphasize. Without full-line coverage, a manufacturer can be seriously crippled in his attempts to build profitable distribution.

Coverage is not easy to develop in highly competitive areas or in sparse markets. Imagine the plight of the marketing manager who complained to the authors that in every country his one or two manufacturer's representatives are in competition with from six to twelve well-trained, aggressive, company salesmen employed by his leading competitor. Because the competitor has a broader line and has been established in worldwide operations for many years, his marketing costs are probably lower than the modest commission paid to the manufacturer's representatives. What a difficult way to attempt to build market coverage in foreign markets!

Sometimes companies have to exercise considerable ingenuity to break into small or undeveloped markets without incurring excessive costs. Three dairy product companies in France, for example, joined forces to create a sales subsidiary to handle their products in other European countries. Fromageries Bel produces packaged cheeses, Fromageries Ch. Gervais produces cream cheeses, and *Danone* produces yogurt; the three formed a company called Gerdabel. Each of the parent companies handles its own advertising and promotion, but the channel relationships and physical distribution are handled by Gerdabel. The broadened lines make it possible to have a strongly controlled sales force in markets that would not support such efforts for individual companies. Creative channel strategies such as this are imperative if adequate coverage is to be gained in many worldwide markets.

Character. The channel-of-distribution system selected must fit the character of both the company and the markets in which it is doing business. Sometimes fitting the two characters is impossible, so companies have given up markets rather than compromise on company standards. In other instances, company standards have been adhered to and local channel characteristics ignored, with resulting distribution disasters.

The channel commander must be aware that channel patterns do change; he cannot assume that once he has developed a channel that fits the character of both the company and the market he can stop worrying. Great Britain, for example, may epitomize the emphasis on distribution through speciality-type middlemen. Distributors, wholesalers, and retailers, in fact all middlemen, have tended to work within narrow product speciality areas but within the past few years there has been a rapid trend toward broader lines, conglomerate merchandising, and mass marketing. The firm that neglects the growth of self-service, scrambled merchandising, or discounting may find that it has lost large segments of its market because its channels no longer reflect the character of the market.

Continuity. Channels of distribution often pose longevity problems. Most agent middlemen firms tend to be small institutions or one- or two-man firms. When one individual retires or moves out of a line of business, the company may find that it has lost its distribution in an area. Wholesalers and especially retailers are not noted for their long continuity in business, either. Even more of a problem is that most middlemen have little loyalty to their vendors. They handle brands in good times when the line is making substantial amounts of money but will quickly reject such products within a season or a year if they fail to produce during that period. Distributors and dealers are probably the most loyal types of middlemen, but even with them, manufacturers must attempt to build brand loyalty downstream in a channel lest middlemen shift allegiance to other companies who tempt them with larger margins, better promotional allowances, or other types of inducements.

If a channel is to perform consistently well, it must have continuity. That reason alone has caused some companies to develop their own company-controlled distribution organizations. One American company operating in a highly competitive field with major competitors producing in Germany, England, and the Netherlands lost middlemen accounting for nearly 50 percent of its volume in Latin America within one year. The chief cause of the loss was more readily discovered than remedied. Two of the major competitors had simultaneously hit on methods of squeezing the U.S. firm out of the market. One, which marketed a broad product line, forced distributors to drop the U.S. company's narrow line if they wished to continue as distributors of the broader line. The other company purchased an interest in several large distributors which had previously carried the U.S. company's products. Much to its chagrin, the U.S. company found that within a year it had lost over one quarter of its foreign distribution system. Continuity is important.

In building the overall channel-of-distribution strategy, the five Cs of channels must be matched, balanced, and harmonized with one another to build an economical, effective, distribution organization. This must be accomplished within the long-range channel-of-distribution policies of the company, which in turn must fit the firm's overall marketing program. Building channels, as any international marketer will testify, is one of the most difficult tasks in international business.

ADAPTING TO DISTRIBUTION PATTERNS

It is important for the international marketer to have a general awareness of the patterns of distribution with which he is confronted in the world marketplace. Nearly every international trading firm is *forced* by the structure of the market to use at least some middlemen in the distribution arrangement. It is all too easy to conclude that because the structural arrangements of foreign and domestic distribution seem alike, foreign channels are the same as domestic channels of the same name or they are similar to one another. Such thinking is most misleading. Only if one understands the varied intricacies of actual distribution patterns can he appreciate the complexity of the distribution task. Hopefully, the material in the following sections will dispel any such false notions and at least convey a sense of the variation in world distribution patterns.

General Patterns

Generalizing about the internal distribution channel patterns of various countries throughout the world is almost as difficult as generalizing about behavior patterns of people throughout the world. Because individual men and women have certain characteristics in common with all the other men and women in the world, there is a basic similarity among all men; yet no one would say that behavior patterns of people throughout the world are anything but dissimilar. There are certain patterns of similarity among distribution channels, and if one understands the basic distribution alternatives in the United States or any other highly developed country, he has a skeletal understanding of the alternatives available or potentially available in the other countries. Even though a specific type of middleman described in a textbook is clearly differentiated from the other types of middlemen, the segmentation is less valid in reality. Certainly there are middlemen who represent the specific classifications; in general, however, most middlemen undertake activities reflecting the characteristics of several different kinds of middlemen. This conglomerate middleman pattern prevails in *all* countries, regardless of their level of market development. A title may not be particularly descriptive when applied to a given individual because he may operate in a manner quite dissimilar from that implied by his title.

Despite the similarities in middlemen which may exist from country to country, we cannot assume that marketing channels and methods are the same throughout the world. Marketing methods at the wholesale and retail levels that are taken for granted in the United States are rare in many countries. One pattern which seems to recur in studying country after country is that middlemen in most countries are predominantly either very large or very small. The middle-sized wholesalers and retailers seen in the United States are unable to survive at either the wholesale or retail level in many economies. This phenomenon is particularly striking to the American student because middle-sized middlemen are relatively abundant in the United States.

In the following sections, some generalizations relating to both wholesalers and retailers are given first, followed by discussion of patterns unique to wholesaling or retailing.

Social Acceptance. The social status of tradesmen or middlemen reflects to some extent the level of productivity of the nation. In underdeveloped countries where the emphasis is directed to production, wholesalers and retailers are generally considered to be unproductive. Understandably, countries like England, which have long depended on trade for their prosperity, give the middleman a considerably higher place in the economy than countries like India and Africa, where traders are considered to take their profit by impoverishing both producers and consumers without adding any utility to the products. These attitudes create some rather strange paradoxes, as in the case of Japan, which now depends so heavily on trading, but where attitudes of many can be traced back to its pretrading period. In Africa, middlemen are so scorned that most make their basic living from some other profession and trade on the side. The irony here is that many of the traders are lawyers, doctors, and other members of the educated elite. Because of the caste system, there is little part-time trading in India; but despite their lack of social acceptance, members of the trading caste are occupying increasingly important positions in the political and economic life of India.

In some parts of the world, there is such a repugnance toward trading that it is left to foreigners. One student of African marketing comments that "in general the typical African has an antagonistic attitude towards tradesmen; not so much for import-export and wholesale firms, whom he does not contact directly, but towards the thousands of small wholesale and retail businesses which serve him." West African firms are owned by Levantines, while in East Africa the tradesmen are of Arabic, Pakistani, or Indian origins. Much of the large-scale wholesaling and retailing is in the hands of Europeans. The Chinese have played a similar role in the Philippines, but the prosperity which their shrewd trading has generated has resulted in considerable animosity and jealousy among the native Filipinos. This in turn has resulted in government restrictions which gradually will close off new trading opportunities to the Chinese.

In considering these foreign evidences of strong negative attitudes toward middlemen, we should remember that even in the United States a good many people continue to be skeptical about the value added by retailers and wholesalers. Acceptance of middlemen has grown along with the country's industrial development, so one should not be too hasty in contrasting social attitudes toward middlemen in other countries. Acceptance of tradesmen may be somewhat related to an economy's stage of development and the extent of its dependence on trade for prosperity.

Middleman Services.   At both the retail and wholesale levels, there is an extreme diversity from country to country in tradesmen's attitudes toward the services of the middleman. In Egypt, for example, there is virtually no consumer orientation; the primary purpose of the simple trading system is to handle the physical distribution of available goods. Even time and place utilities are treated as minor services in Turkey; a group of writers has characterized marketing transactions in that country as "hunting expeditions." Describing the process, they say

the customers search among the retail stores; the retailers shop continuously among the wholesalers; the wholesalers go from manufacturer to manufacturer. The objectives of these hunts are good quality, cheaper prices, and more services such as credit and delivery. To the extent that this latter description is valid, the activities in the marketing channel work backward, and the doors to marketing offices swing inward to customers far more than they swing outward as company salesmen depart.[2]

India provides quite a different example of middleman service. Because there are so many tradesmen in India, margins are low and there

---

[2] Mehmet Oluc, Nezih Neyzi, Emre Gonensoy, and Ernest J. Enright, "Wholesaling in Turkey," in Robert Bartels, *Comparative Marketing* (Homewood, Ill.: Richard D. Irwin, Inc., 1963), p. 90.

is a continuing battle for customer preference; therefore, both wholesalers and retailers seek ways to offer extra services which will make their goods particularly attractive to customers.

All dimensions of distribution have been greatly affected by the influence of American marketing methods and the world trend toward the internationalization of business. In Israel, most small retail establishments have traditionally closed for several hours during the noon period. In this and other countries with similar customs, the advent of self-service stores which are open throughout the day (and some into the evening hours) is causing shopkeepers to rethink their policies on hours.[3] The high rate of industrialization in Japan has caused a curtailment of many traditional retail services because wages have escalated so rapidly. Milk delivery in that country, for example, began shifting to alternate-day distribution in the early 1970s. Self-service shopping, which evolved in the United States over a period of some 30 years, has literally exploded with success when introduced in most industrialized countries. In Japan, the number of self-service stores went from zero to 4,000 in less than 10 years and continues to grow at the rate of 500 to 700 new stores per year. The growth has been such that some 20 percent of the grocery sales in Japan were being handled by self-service stores only 15 years after the first one opened. And that, remember, is in an extremely tradition-oriented country.

Line Breadth. Each nation seems to have its own distinct patterns relative to the breadth of line carried by wholesalers and retailers. The distribution system of some countries seems to be characterized by middlemen who carry or can get everything. In other countries, such as Egypt, every middleman seems to be a specialist dealing only in extremely narrow lines. In the United States, specialization appears to increase with firm size. In other countries there is an inverse relationship.

Governmental regulations in some countries limit the breadth of line which can be carried by middlemen. Norway has rather specific licensing requirements for middlemen, and in Italy there is municipal discretion over the lines to be handled. In the city of Milan a dairy store may sell boiled eggs or boiled rice with oil but may not sell boiled eggs with butter or boiled rice with tomato sauce. (Contrast this backward practice with the more modern outlook in some states in the United States, where for years grocery stores have been able to sell warm, but not cold, beer.) In selling a wide variety of products in many countries, Procter & Gamble has encountered a host of restrictions which require continuous adaptation on its part. In Italy, for example, stores need a license for every product category they sell; therefore, some sell only soaps and others sell only detergents. Imagine the effect on distribution costs when specific merchandising ordinances vary considerably from city to city. The common end result has been a general stifling of progress in the

---

[3] Eugene D. Jaffe, "Growth and Performance of Self-Service Food Shops in Israel: A Study of the Adoption of an American Marketing Innovation in a Developing Country," *University of Washington Business Review,* Summer 1968, pp. 60–66.

distributive trades, discouragement of more advanced merchandising techniques, and the granting of a premium to inefficient practices.

Cost and Margins.   Cost levels and middleman margins vary widely from country to country, depending partly on the level of competition, the services offered, the efficiencies or inefficiencies of scale, and the geographic and turnover factors related to market size, purchasing power, tradition, and other basic determinants. Contrasting instances have been cited. In Italy, the political potency of the myriad small middlemen has kept direct competition to a minimum and costs high. In India competition in large cities is so great that costs are low and margins thin; but in the rural areas lack of capital has permitted the few traders who do have it to gain monopolies with the consequent raising of prices and margins. Dr. Theodore Kreps commented at the conclusion of a tour in which he analyzed distribution in Middle Eastern countries that the middlemen seem to have no concept of turnover but try rather to make their entire fortune, as he put it, "in one transaction."[4]

In many instances the middlemen should not be condemned for picking what seem to be excessively large margins. Both wholesale and retail margins may have to cover much activity. Goods may have to be moved under primitive conditions; communications often are difficult; credit is questionable; customers are sparsely scattered; and much time may be involved in finding appropriate goods. In most developing countries manufacturers do not bear much of the marketing burden but shift directly to the channel of distribution such functions as credit, storage, shipping, market development, and even research. Even the high cost of money in many countries contributes to the middleman's need for a high margin.

Channel Length.   Some correlation may be found in the stage of economic development and the length of marketing channels. In every country, of course, channels are likely to be shorter for industrial goods and for high-priced consumer goods than for low-priced products. In general, there is an inverse relationship between channel length and the size of the purchase, but there are exceptions: in Japan most channels are complex and diverse; three or more wholesale links are not at all unusual. Even a large department store may purchase men's socks daily in quantities of three or four pairs from a neighborhood wholesaler rather than purchasing direct from the manufacturer or a large wholesaler.

Combination wholesaler-retailers or semiwholesalers exist in many countries, adding one or two links to the length of the distribution chain. Probably one could safely generalize that channels in the United States and in Russia are shorter than in most countries. In the United States length is shortened by efficiencies of scale and in Russia channels are shortened by administrative edict, but this shortening often results in distribution inefficiencies because goods may not be available when or where needed.

With the internationalization of business, merchandising ideas and

---

[4] Letter to the authors.

systems are being picked up and transferred from one country to another with almost alarming speed. One of the results of this kind of intelligence interchange is that channels throughout the world appear to be growing somewhat shorter. Information, of course, is not the only cause of such modification; also considered must be the influence of increasing competition which may cause manufacturers to sell direct when they cannot utilize other channels. Growing affluence among the world's consumers means that the consumer or family buying unit is buying in larger quantities, is less dependent on the credit of small middlemen, and, therefore, is likely to buy from a middleman higher up in the channel. (Remember in most countries large retailers operate also as wholesalers, and there may be several levels of wholesaler-retailers from whom the consumer may choose.) The automobile has been a factor in causing channel shortening because supermarkets, discount houses, and self-service stores all depend on large numbers of customers being able to reach them conveniently. These retailers in turn become large-scale customers and are likely to deal directly with manufacturers or distributors, cutting out several layers of wholesalers in some countries.

The astute observer of the marketing scene can trace some of the channel length differences back to the underlying factors causing such variation. One can make such an analysis if he has knowledge of differences in factors such as aggregate market potential, population and income distribution patterns, shopping habits, product preference, dealer inventory, supply sources, etc. Consideration of these elements helps explain many of the apparent differences, can help the marketer in his planning, and may show the way to channel innovation.

Wholesale Patterns

A wholesaler is a middleman who sells to retailers or industrial users. His chief fields are negotiating, buying, selling, and storing. He may also offer a host of other services. A study of the wholesaling sector of an economy may provide some important clues to the stage of a nation's economic development. Many of the general channel patterns mentioned earlier pertain to wholesaling, and characteristics of wholesalers per se are discussed below.

Power and Competition. The dichotomized structure of wholesaling, with a cluster of extremely large middlemen at one end of a scale and a mass of small middlemen at the other end, provides the basis for an interesting study in contrasts. Large-small patterns seem to simplify wholesaling in most countries. In Malaya, for example, fewer than a dozen (European) merchant houses handle over half of the import trade, while hundreds of local trading companies handle the balance. In Israel there are some 1,500 wholesalers, most of whom are small. Contrast these with Hamashbir Hamerkazi, giant Israeli wholesaler who handles all kinds of products and has full or partial ownership in 12 major industrial firms; this one company reportedly handles approximately one fifth of all the wholesaling volume of Israel. Such giant wholesalers are major factors in the political and competitive life of their countries. Their power is derived from their financial, wholesaling, and manufacturing interest in the country.

There appears to be a worldwide trend toward more vertical integration from the wholesale or retail level back to manufacturing. Such a development, of course, is of great concern to the marketer who has been dependent on wholesalers to handle his product, because in many cases he finds that the channel is blocked not by a competing manufacturer but by the wholesaler handling his own custom-manufactured

EXHIBIT 22–1

Wholesale Patterns in 16 Countries

Country	Population (000,000)	No. of Wholesalers	No. of Wholesale Employees	Population per Wholesale Establishment
United States............	203	311,464	3,519,000	650
Canada.................	21	30,855	255,200	680
Switzerland.............	6	11,010	11,900	555
Norway.................	4	10,065	76,400	390
West Germany...........	60	112,748	1,006,000	535
Belgium.................	10	36,179	157,300	268
United Kingdom.........	55	35,358	737,000	1156
Israel..................	3	2,524	20,000	1090
Italy...................	53	81,033	377,000	650
Japan..................	101	287,000	3,072,000	351
Greece.................	9	20,600	60,900	428
Argentina..............	24	36,978	236,800	667
Turkey.................	34	20,104	73,100	1665
Brazil..................	88	18,264	143,000	4870
Taiwan.................	14	10,057	57,100	1390
Ghana.................	8	3,525	32,100	2240

Note: All figures in U.S. dollars.
Sources: *U.N. Statistical Yearbook 1969* and various national censuses.

products. Some wholesalers handle a manufacturer's product until they build a sufficient volume in that type of product to undertake manufacturing; then the original supplier is displaced. In India, outside companies may have a hard time gaining distribution because the large wholesalers have such an entrenched position that by providing "the package of financial and marketing services (they are) able to obtain monopsonistic power."[5] Monopsony exists when one buyer can exert control over the market because the many sellers have no satisfactory alternate outlet. Japan's *zaibatsu* (trading and financial combines) finance subwholesalers, retailers, and manufacturers as well, making completely integrated distribution arrangements centering around the strongest middlemen. In short, the marketer who must compete with such companies has many barriers to overcome.

[5] Leon V. Hirsch, "Wholesaling in India," in *Comparative Marketing*, op. cit., p. 144.

Another trend in the wholesale market which tends to concentrate distribution power in the hands of relatively small numbers of wholesalers is the trend toward development of voluntary chains sponsored by wholesalers. In the United Kingdom an A. C. Nielsen study has indicated that some 75 percent of all grocery purchases by retailers goes through chains that represent only a little more than 1,000 of the 3,000 wholesale buying points in that country. The same study predicts that some 85 percent of the market will be served by 800 to 900 chain middlemen within a few years. In Norway a government study showed that nearly three fourths of the total sales of soft goods wholesalers were handled by one third of those firms, nearly all of which had set up voluntary chains with retailers. The two thirds of the firms handling a minority of the business were not associated with voluntary retail chains.

The financial power of large wholesalers affects the geographic distribution patterns they undertake. In Japan, Israel, and Australia, for example, nearly all major wholesalers operate on a nationwide basis. This is in sharp contrast to countries like Italy, Turkey, and Egypt where government regulations, scattered markets, and poor transportation facilities have created an opposite situation; there are few national wholesalers so the marketer must contact many, many middlemen to secure distribution. These are some of the patterns of power and competition with which the foreign marketer must cope in dealing with the international marketplace.

Services and Efficiency. Services and efficiency of wholesalers vary widely from country to country.

A wholesaler is never considered to be a strong, hard-selling middleman, but in some countries wholesalers and even distributors barely perform the minimal selling functions. A U.S. Department of Commerce overseas business report on Iran, for example, comments that "Even the largest distributors ordinarily employ no sales force, limiting their sales efforts to the placing of samples of their products on consignment in as many retail houses as possible." Although it does hold true for most countries, even the oft-repeated complaint that wholesalers do an inadequate job of selling merchandise does have exceptions. In some countries where there are strong national distributors, as in Japan, one finds a fairly high level of selling; in fact, wholesalers in some such countries utilize the power of their position in pressure selling. The intense competition in India, on the other hand, also encourages aggressive selling. It is interesting, and perhaps somewhat ironic, that in such socialistic states as Yugoslavia wholesalers have entirely taken over the selling function from manufacturers.

Manufacturers in many free countries are also so production-oriented that they do not want to concern themselves with distribution. The introduction of the marketing concept and the consequent emphasis by manufacturers on marketing may be one of the really revolutionary effects to come out of increasing U.S. involvement in world trade.

Services other than selling offered by wholesalers vary widely from country to country. Credit is one of the major services that seems to be offered throughout the world, but even such basic things as adequate

BOX 22–1

Chinese Credit Mao's Power of Thinking to Sales Success

By William L. Ryan
AP Special Correspondent

Chou Hsin-li is a district manager of the "Shanghai Municipal Fruit & Sundry Goods Co." He is a crashing success.

He is a success because he sold ripe watermelons on a glutted market. He did this by applying Mao Tze-tung's thinking "On Contradiction."

"On Contradiction" was written about Communist tactics in war, but Chou Hsin-li has found one can apply it to watermelons.

Chou wrote about this in an article entitled "Let us talk about the philosophy of selling watermelons in the big cities." It appeared in Liberation Army Daily—leading voice of a current Chinese Communist party purge —and other papers. People in high places are being purged because they do not sufficiently value Mao's thinking.

. . . [One summer,] the Municipal Fruit & Sundry Goods Co. was inundated by watermelons and the staff felt "overwhelmed and simply hopeless." Watermelons rotted.

. . . [The next summer,] Chou Hsin-li sent his staff to investigate. It was awed by the prospect of a 50 per cent rise in ripe summertime watermelons.

Mao had written that "there is nothing that does not contain contradictions."

Well, says Chou, you "make a careful analysis of the contradictions." You conclude that "the problem is in contradiction between the heavy rush of supplies in a limited period and the use of the sales force. This exposure of contradictions helped the staff to see the size and nature of the problems to be tackled."

Mao had said one must "concentrate on a superior force to destroy the enemy forces one by one."

Watermelons were the superior force. The manager enlisted hundreds of his staff to concentrate on watermelons, forgetting the "sundry goods." They gave it the old Chinese hard sell. When he saw the watermelons selling, reported manager Chou, "It made me cry."

"It made me realize deeply that the reason for our success in selling watermelons was completely attributed to the invincible might of Mao Tze-tung's thinking," said Chou.

Prospects are for more ripe watermelons this summer than ever before.

Says manager Chou: "We organize the masses of cadres to expose fully the contradiction involved in the sale of watermelons and set up a program for studying Mao Tze-tung's works for those workers who are frightened at the thought of having too many watermelons to sell."

Source: Reprinted with permission of The Associated Press.

---

inventories do not characterize most of the world's wholesaling. The high cost of money in most countries keeps middleman inventories low, so that the customer is likely to be faced with long reorder periods.

The wholesaler's efficiency varies with his size, financial ability, market density, communications facilities, and a host of other things. Perhaps two contrasting statements can summarize the extremes of feeling pertaining to wholesaler efficiency.

These facts clearly illustrate the basic nature of Italian wholesaling: a family business with little volume and relatively small net profits, which in most instances serves as a drag upon, rather than a boon to, marketing efficiency.[6]

Compare this to the statement,

The Netherlands is a small, densely populated country with a highly organized transportation system. Still, the wholesale trade appears to be fairly important. This is explained by the fact that it provides for lower distribution costs.[7]

Retail Patterns

Retailing shows even greater diversity in its structure than does wholesaling. In some countries, such as Italy and Morocco, retailing is composed largely of speciality houses carrying narrow lines. In other countries, such as Finland, most retailers carry a rather general line of merchandise. Retail size is represented at one end by Japan's giant Mitsukoshi Ltd., which reportedly enjoys the patronage of more than 100,000 customers every day. The other extreme is represented in the market of Ibadan, Nigeria, which has some 3,000 one- or two-man stalls and not many more customers.

Exhibit 22–2 contrasts retail patterns in the United States and 15 other countries. The number of persons per retail store and the sales volume per store are over three times greater in some countries than in others. Imagine how much wider the spread would be if other less developed countries of the world were considered. Imagine, too, the impact of such variation on wholesale structure and channel policy.

Size Patterns. Retailing in every country is a study of extremes providing the contrasts of huge stores with retailers of infinitesimally small size. This dichotomous big-small pattern is similar to that which predominates in the wholesaling field. Exhibit 22–2 dramatically illustrates some of the basic retailing relationships for European countries. Effective interpretation requires analysis of per capita consumption expenditures, average total sales per retail store, and number of customers per retail store. The statistics alone do not tell the whole story, though. As an authority comments,

One would assume logically that as population density increases, retail units would become more efficient—each unit serving the greater number of people now within walking distance and driving distance. However, it has been demonstrated in Europe that instead of the efficiency per unit increasing, the number of units increases disproportionately as the population density goes up, with the result that large European cities frequently have more marginal retail units than the sparsely settled country areas.[8]

---

[6] Pietro Gennaro, in Bartels, *Comparative Marketing,* op. cit., p. 42.

[7] A. F. Haccou, "Wholesaling in the Netherlands," in *Comparative Marketing,* op. cit., p. 56.

[8] Albert Stridsberg, "Great Differences within European Common Market Can Trap U.S. Manufacturers, Expert Warns," *Advertising Age,* January 30, 1961, p. 77.

EXHIBIT 22–2

Retail Patterns in 16 Countries

Country	Population (000,000)	GNP per Capita	Private Sector Consumption Factors	Consumption per Capita
United States.........	203	$4,303	x.61	$2,625
Canada...............	21	3,182	x.61	1,941
Switzerland...........	6	2,801	x.58	1,625
Norway..............	4	2,362	x.64	1,512
West Germany........	60	2,206	x.56	1,235
Belgium..............	10	2,154	x.63	1,357
United Kingdom......	55	1,862	x.64	1,192
Israel................	3	1,472	x.67	986
Italy................	53	1,418	x.64	908
Japan................	101	1,404	x.52	730
Greece...............	9	858	x.70	600
Argentina............	24	724	x.69	499
Turkey...............	34	346	x.72	249
Brazil...............	88	322	x.75	241
Taiwan..............	14	300	x.60	180
Ghana...............	8	283	x.73	207

Note: All figures in U.S. dollars.
Sources: *UN Statistical Yearbook 1969* and various national censuses.

He concludes that the small retailer can hardly survive his small stock, his lack of capital, merchandising information, selling and marketing training, and time, or his slow inventory turnover. The retail structure and the problems it engenders cause real difficulties to the international marketing firm selling consumer goods. Large dominant middlemen are approachable, but they only represent a small proportion of any country's sales. There is no adequate channel of distribution by which to make an effective marketing presentation to the small retailers who, in the aggregate, handle the great volume of sales. These problems are not unique to one area, but tend to permeate the distribution structure of nearly every country.

Change. Retailing around the world has been in a state of active ferment for the past few years. The rate of change appears to be directly correlated to the stage and speed of economic development in the countries concerned, but even the least developed countries are experiencing dramatic changes. Self-service retailing has grown at a nearly overwhelming rate throughout the world. Supermarkets of one variety or another are blossoming in developed and underdeveloped countries alike. Discount houses have taken increasing shares of the market in countries where such activity is legally permissible. Automatic vending and mail-order trends are being set around the world, and in both fields the United States has been eclipsed by fast-moving businessmen in other countries. It is generally conceded that in Western Europe the automatic vending of food and general merchandise is ahead of the United States, and their equipment is superior. The mail-order business of Sears and

No. of Retailers	No. of Retail Employees	No. of Customers per Store	Average Sales (000) per Store	Average Sales per Employee
1,415,000	8,626,000	143	$375	$ 61,550
153,620	255,200	135	262	50,948
37,994	11,900	162	264	45,108
35,208	76,400	109	164	46,850
428,134	1,006,000	142	174	41,215
170,109	157,300	56	77	44,717
504,412	737,000	111	131	25,780
4,556	20,000	593	594	131,456
818,983	377,000	64	58	31,162
1,375,000	3,072,000	74	54	29,238
104,700	60,900	84	50	30,726
370,559	236,800	64	32	15,136
134,163	73,100	250	62	36,857
325,177	143,000	271	68	31,685
114,260	57,100	122	22	10,421
127,274	32,100	66	11	6,515

Wards in the United States has been declining as a portion of their overall sales, but this type of business has been booming elsewhere. In the United States mail order accounts for about 1 percent of all retail sales, but in the United Kingdom the figure is now closer to 5 percent. Germany has had a similar growth in mail order, and in both countries sales of certain items such as shoes, household textiles, and small electrical appliances by mail order account for 10 to 20 percent of sales.

Widespread automobile ownership has encouraged the growth of shopping centers in many countries. In Germany, for example, a group of Canadians has backed a huge shopping center, Main-Taunus Zentrum, at a major highway intersection six miles from downtown Frankfurt. Some 65,000 motorists jammed the center's huge parking lots on opening day, and the shops were reportedly doing better than planned three months after the opening. Analysis of other trade patterns in Europe indicates a similar aggressiveness. The food industry is marked by highly developed voluntary chains, multiple chain stores, consumer co-ops, supermarkets, and mail-order houses.

Self-Service. Started in the United States in 1930, self-service had only a few early imitators in other parts of the world. Sweden and Germany, for example, opened self-service stores in 1938. Since the end of World War II, however, self-service has been a major element in world retailing. The table below shows the growth of supermarkets and self-service units. Because of the larger unit size their share of sales has grown even more rapidly.

Britain provides a good example of the growth of self-service. As

BOX 22–2

The World's Newest Mass Market

The differences in physical setting, social patterns, and buying habits give a unique character to consumer marketing in Japan. Their influence on retailing and wholesaling patterns is both conspicuous and critical.

With a population about half as large as ours, and with personal incomes less than one-fourth as large, Japan boasts more than 650,000 retail food stores, as against some 300,000 in the United States. Comparable patterns prevail in other industries. Honda's motorcycles, for instance, move through 30,000 outlets (compare Harley-Davidson's 800-odd U.S. dealerships!), and Citizen watches are sold through about 25,000 retailers, more than Bulova and Benrus combined in the U.S.

In all, it is estimated that Japan has about 1,300,000 retail stores. They average less than $15,000 in annual sales, nation-wide. Three out of four have no more than one employee besides the owner. Most Japanese "supermarkets" have less than 600 square feet of floor space (the U.S. average approximates 20,000), and the more typical retail shop is about the size of a clerk's cubicle in an American office. During the day, to gain floor space, displays are set out on the sidewalk; at night, the tiny aisles are crammed with these displays, and the storekeeper closes the door on a jampacked shop. Such a shop, obviously, will order not by the case or carload but by the package, bottle or pound, and its inventory will be limited to what it has on display. . . . The majority of Tokyo's present supermarkets are capitalized at less than $15,000 (versus a typical $500,000 in the United States); most are one-store operations housed in one-story wooden buildings; and only one in ten provides parking space for its customers. In Tokyo and Osaka, by far the most modern cities in Japan, supermarkets account for barely 3 percent of retail sales.

Source: J. C. Abegglen and R. D. Norby, "The World's Newest Mass Market," *The McKinsey Quarterly*, Winter 1965, p. 44.

late as 1955 nearly all food retailing was done in small independent shops, but by 1963 there were nearly 400 supermarkets and by 1970 supermarket chains had begun to dominate the scene. Tesco, for example, has over 350 supermarkets; Fine Fair has over 450. Even Safeway stores from the United States have over 30. The effect on a manufacturer's marketing policy has been little short of revolutionary. Just a few years ago, a company selling in the food field had to have literally hundreds of salesmen, but now many companies have cut back their sales force to only the small number required to deal with wholesalers and with the chains. The small grocers are never visited by these salesmen and must now seek out merchandise themselves through wholesalers. Some companies such as the British firm Beechams have developed different sales forces to deal with the different types of outlets: one force for grocery chains, one for large supermarkets, one for wholesalers, and one for the small retailers.

EXHIBIT 22-3

Retailing Patterns in Europe

	Self-Service Stores				Supermarkets			
	1958	1962	1967	1970	1961	1964	1967	1970
Germany..................	3,183	30,680	72,241	110,000	250	719	1,500	2,300
United Kingdom..........	3,000	9,212	18,320	32,000	74	438	753	1,400
France..................	603	2,691	12,593	20,000	49	323	700	1,000
Sweden..................	3,515	6,000	8,360	10,000	2	337	744	1,000
Netherlands..............	668	2,779	6,119	10,500	7	96	203	300
Denmark.................	465	1,592	4,328	6,500	—	277	462	600
Switzerland..............	1,148	2,163	4,272	6,700	42	105	172	240
Norway..................	1,288	1,650	2,777	4,200	—	—	—	100
Italy....................	33	344	2,185	3,800	18	141	287	400
Finland..................	60	625	2,179	3,400	—	—	—	60
Spain...................	3	506	2,150	3,500	—	—	—	40
Belgium.................	155	573	1,679	3,000	20	107	188	250

Source: Based on studies by the Comité Belge de la Distribution.

BOX 22–3

"Way Back in 1965"—Self-Service and Supermarkets

The first of the GEM Super-Centres in Britain, which opened a year ago at West Bridgford, Nottingham, is just beginning to break even with sales at £1 million a year. Mr. Jim Kalal, managing director of the American firm's British subsidiary, admitted that GEM had been too optimistic and their objective of five to ten stores a year was some way off. "From the outset," he said, "not sufficient account was taken of the innate conservative outlook, the ingrained prejudices of the trading community in this country, and the attitudes never encountered in all our operations in the US."

Discounting. The advent of national brands (and international brands) and heavy advertising to develop consumer awareness and brand preference has helped discounting become a major factor in most affluent nations. The strong antitrust provisions of the various common markets and free-trade areas (especially the European Common Market) and the general rejection of retail price maintenance laws in countries such as the United States, Germany, Britain, and Japan have speeded up the trend to discount merchandising.

Germany provides a good case study of rapid growth in the field of discounting. In 1953 the first discount houses were opened. By 1957 there were still only 27, but by 1963 there were over 300 and by 1970 well over 1,000. Even the numbers do not tell the story, however, for until the late 1960s nearly all of the discount stores were fairly small and offered a limited assortment of goods. But as chains such as Gebrüder Albrecht KG, which has over 270 *aldi* shops, grew, there was also a tendency to broaden the assortment of merchandise. The new discount firms called *verbraucher märkte* (consumer markets) are large self-service department stores with the same wide range of merchandise as department stores. By 1970 some 100 of these markets were making a substantial impact on the German retailing scene. Another interesting development is that mass merchandising has started a trend to the use of one price policy in markets where the retailers traditionally priced merchandise according to what they thought the customer could pay.

Co-ops, Chains, and Groups. Integration of buying activities has been a dominant pattern in European retailing for many years. Consumer cooperatives have had minimal success in the United States, but are tremendously important in most European countries. In Switzerland, co-ops account for one fifth of the retail food stores and over one fourth of retail food sales. The Union of Swiss Cooperative Societies (U.S.K.) and the Federation of Migros Co-operatives (Migros) account for nearly 10 percent of Switzerland's total (not only food) retail sales. Each of the two leading co-ops boasts memberships exceeding one third of the households in Switzerland. Despite the presence of these giants, however, two thirds of the retail business of Switzerland is carried out by small independent stores. In Germany the Co-operative Wholesale Society has established a central organization to start and operate self-service discount department stores. In one of the projects they have developed a shopping center at Porz between Cologne and Bonn which will include a huge supermarket, a nonfood superstore, and a cafeteria all set in one co-op shopping center. Leased-space co-op department stores are popular in Scandinavia. In some ways these resemble the old farmers' markets where dozens of independent merchants lease space in a single building or department store. Small businesses are conducted in each space, with overall coordination in advertising, personnel training, and display.

Resistance to Change. Such developments as consolidation of middlemen, larger store size, self-service, and discounting have not gone unnoticed by small merchants; distribution is enmeshed in a battle between politically powerful independent retailers and wholesalers and economically powerful chain discount and department stores. In many cases it is the manufacturer who gets caught in the middle of this battle. If he avoids the large-volume retailers, they turn to other sources, and he has lost a portion of the market. If he moves to the large-volume outlets, he is likely to be scorned by his former small-scale middlemen and lose that market segment.

In some countries, such as Italy, small but numerous independent merchants seem to be waging an effective delaying battle against discounting. In that country someone wishing to open a new retail outlet must obtain a license from the municipal board in the city where he plans to do business. Usually that board is composed of well-entrenched local tradesmen who, needless to say, hardly welcome tough new competition. In a several-year period some 200 applicants seeking to establish supermarkets in Milan were able to secure only 10 new licenses. In Belgium national legislation does not permit new department stores to be opened in towns of less than 50,000, and in that country any store that employs as few as five persons is considered to be a department store. In some countries, potential businessmen are forced to become members of trade associations or pass irrelevant or difficult examinations before being allowed to open new stores. In Norway and Sweden potential entrepreneurs must serve a long apprenticeship in the business before they are able even to be considered for licensing. Licenses are frequently so severely restricted that new ones are issued only when some other retailer has gone out of business. As in the United States, much of the discriminatory legislation aimed at large-scale retailers was passed in the 1930s, but unlike the United States, most of the legislation and discriminatory taxes are still in effect. It appears in many cases that governments have placed a premium on retailing inefficiency in order to support politically powerful merchants. Taxes are consistently a favorite restrictive tool of the small retailer and penalize the discounter or self-service store. Even health and sanitary regulations are called into play in order to restrict large-scale retailing. Milk in Switzerland, for example, may not be sold with other

BOX 22–4

French Distribution

There are in France other elements that hamper the movement toward concentration and slow it down. We have already mentioned the market stalls and the itinerant retailers. Many French people have a feeling of attachment for these markets; they like their prices, their atmosphere, and they often like the quality of the goods they sell.

Another limiting factor consists in the difficulties of motor traffic which means that the consumer tends to stay in his own district and make use of the services provided by his own neighborhood shopkeeper (especially for food). The shop is near at hand, whereas the big stores, which are still not very numerous, are sometimes hard to get to by car. The very consumption habits of French people as far as meals are concerned (for example, a considerable consumption of liquids and especially of wine, involving the transportation from the shop and back again of many glass bottles that are very heavy) are a contributory factor for shopping near one's home, whatever the size of the nearby shop and sometimes whatever the prices it charges.

Source: Michel David, "Developments in the Structure of Distribution in France," *Journal of Retailing*, Summer 1965, p. 44. Reprinted with permission.

---

merchandise; supermarkets, therefore, cannot handle this product, so small dairy product retailers flourish.

Nationalism has been a major force limiting the introduction of mass merchandising techniques by foreign firms. Unilever, for example, found that consumers in Turkey were chafing under the exorbitant prices charged by monopolistic local tradesmen, so it purchased a fleet of van-type trucks and introduced mobile supermarkets to the countryside. The reaction was swift and certain; local merchants found their monopolies evaporating, contacted the government, and within a matter of months, Unilever was out of the Turkish retailing picture. Through a joint venture, Safeway attempted to introduce a series of supermarkets in Japan, but as soon as plans were announced, nationalistic groups seized on this as a major "cause." The resulting furor caused parliamentary debate on the subject, and Safeway discreetly withdrew. Argentinian terrorists planted phosphorus bombs in all 17 of IBEC's (International Basic Economy Corporation) supermarkets when Governor Nelson Rockefeller visited Buenos Aires on a goodwill tour. Seven markets were destroyed, and six were severely damaged. It is ironic that IBEC's minimax stores were selected because IBEC had been founded by Rockefeller in an effort to show how "U.S. business can improve the lot of people in underdeveloped lands and still make a profit."[9] IBEC had opened Argentina's first supermarkets in 1962 but

---

[9] "Hard Times Hit a Rockefeller Enterprise," *Business Week*, July 26, 1969, p. 60.

BOX 22–5

Puerto Rican Arsonists Plague U.S. Concerns Operating on Island
By Kenneth G. Slocum

The crowds drifting through the big Bargain Town discount store here aren't all shoppers these days. That burly fellow idly browsing through a rack of suits is very likely a plainclothes detective, and the "customer" at the sporting goods counter is a fellow policeman.

Their job: To keep the store from being burned out by terrorists who have planted fire bombs in Bargain Town stores and some 70 other business establishments on this tropical isle in the past 11 months. . . .

The ownership by remote U.S. companies apparently is what makes the stores prime targets of the arsonists. Puerto Rican officials and U.S. Government investigators blame the bombings on a small, radical and possibly Castro-inspired political element that seeks independence for Puerto Rico, now a commonwealth voluntarily affiliated with the United States.

"The Yankee Invader." The goal of the terrorists seems to be to scare off present and potential U.S. investors and thus weaken Puerto Rico's substantial ties with mainland business. A letter sent to the local press, purportedly by the terrorist group itself, promised to "continue dealing bigger and bigger blows to the Yankee invader and his imperialist financial investments until they leave our country. . . ."

"Almost all of the bombings have been directed at big U.S. stores which hurt the little Puerto Rican merchant," says one economist. "It's the same kind of resentment you find in a small American town when a big chain puts the Mom and Pop stores out of business."

Source: *Wall Street Journal,* September 11, 1968, pp. 1 and 13. Reprinted with permission.

had been losing ground to some aggressive large-scale discount and supermarket operations which had developed in recent years.

Opposition to retail innovation prevails everywhere, yet in the face of all the restrictions and hindrances, self-service, discount merchandising, and large-scale chains continue to emerge because they offer the consumer a broad range of quality branded products at advantageous prices. Ultimately the consumer does prevail.

BUILDING INTERNATIONAL CHANNELS

The actual process of building channels for international distribution is seldom easy and is sometimes virtually impossible. Many companies have been stopped in their efforts to develop international markets by their inability to construct a satisfactory system of channels. Some of the largest mistakes in international business have occurred when marketers failed to differentiate between channel theory and channel reality. Several manufacturing or processing plants built in emergent nations with development funds have actually been abandoned (in one case after the expenditure of some $10,000,000) when it was discovered that producing the goods was not enough—they had to be distributed too. Contrast that with the three years of intensive channel development undertaken by International Mineral and Chemical Co. before it opened its fertilizer plant in India. Though the product has a very unfavorable bulk to value ratio, the company shipped fertilizer to India from the United States during the development period so the developing sales force would gain experience and market entry. The company conducted nearly 1,200 field demonstrations to illustrate results for farmers throughout the country before locally produced products were even available.

If the channel-building process is to function smoothly, it must be based solidly on preplanning, incorporating the master channel policy decisions and general strategies discussed earlier in this chapter and supplemented by a series of tactical decisions pertaining to the particular country or market in question. Once these decisions have been made, the marketer is in a position to meet the operational challenges and problems inherent in finding and selecting individual middlemen who will best represent the company and in making working arrangements with those middlemen in order to secure distribution.

Tactical Decisions

Differing circumstances impose a series of local, tactical policy decisions in each market. A company which is deeply committed to international operations, for example, may have a relatively low level of commitment in a particular specific market and want to maintain low investment in building channels in that market. Such considerations may be dependent on whether the company is merely testing the market or has entered it on a permanent basis. Proctor & Gamble in Italy was up against well-established Unilever and entrenched Colgate when it tried to enter that country. Therefore it was reluctant to make a full-scale investment in plant and distribution until it had established basic market acceptance. It subcontracted manufacturing to a local company that had been producing for Colgate and arranged for an aggressive selling agent to handle the marketing of its product. The intent was to shift to its own sales force when the brand had received market acceptance, but the selling agent did such an outstanding job that he was retained long after the economics of the situation would have permitted development of the company's own sales force. Because Proctor & Gamble characteristically relies heavily on its own sales force, this example illustrates an opportune tactical departure from normal company procedures relative to the use of internal versus external channels.

Channel length and multiple channel questions must be also answered at the local level. In one country a short channel may provide excellent results, whereas another market virtually demands longer channels. Similarly, a company may prefer a nice clean channel arrangement utilizing only one major type of distribution, but in order to achieve coverage it may have to use all of the available channels. Furthermore, it may be impossible for a company to maintain parallel channels in different markets. A decision made in New York to use the same types of channels in different countries may look very logical on paper but may not work at all in different markets; a company therefore may find itself using its own sales force in one country, manufacturers' agent channels in another country, and merchant wholesale channels in still another.

The level of selectivity employed in distribution must also be established tactically. It may be nice to think in terms of exclusive dealers or a highly selective distribution network, but if such a system fails to cover certain markets adequately or does not produce the requisite sales volume, it may be necessary to seek a more intensive type of distribution system. Only when companies learn that operating management decisions of the variety mentioned here are best made at the local level will international channels operate with optimum efficiency.

Operational Challenges

Despite the rather chaotic condition of international distribution channels, international marketers can follow a logical procedure in developing channels of distribution. After general policy guides are established, marketers need to develop general criteria for the selection of specific middlemen. Construction of the middleman network offers unique challenges and problems in every market. Basically the process includes the steps of seeking out or finding potential middlemen, selecting those who fit the company's requirements, and establishing working relationships with them.

In international marketing where titles and functions bear little correlation, where grandiose names may denote one man, part-time operations, and where one vies with competitors from every country in the world for the favor of middlemen, the channel-building process is hardly routine. Obviously, the more middlemen required, the larger the job of channel building. It also, therefore, follows that the closer the company wants to get to the consumer in its channel contact the larger the sales force that will be required. If a company is content with finding an exclusive importer or selling agent for a given country, channel building may not be too difficult, but if he goes down to the level of the subwholesaler or the retailer and attempts to function at that level, he is taking on a tremendous task and must have an internal staff and sales force capable of such an effort.

Finding Middlemen. The search for prospective middlemen should be undertaken only after a study of the market in which one expects to do business and only after the determination of criteria which may be used for evaluation of middlemen serving that market. Whenever possible, the company's broad general policy guidelines should be followed, but often expediency will (and should) override policy.

Most companies develop a checklist of the criteria they employ in selecting overseas middlemen. The list will differ according to the type of middlemen being chosen and the nature of their relationship with the company. Basically, such lists are built around four major subject areas: productivity or volume, financial strength, managerial stability and capability, and nature and reputation of the business. Emphasis is usually placed on either the actual or potential productivity of the middleman. Questions for determining productivity include: What is the company's sales volume? Does it have an adequate sales and sales service organization? Does it have good salesmen? and How has it performed for other manufacturers? Questions about financial and business acumen are asked to determine whether the company will be able to pay its bills and whether it is likely to continue to do business in the future. Those pertaining to reputation help the company to discern something about the nature of the prospective middleman's customers and operations.

Setting policies and making checklists is easy; the difficult job is implementation. The major problems will be discovering middlemen who are available to handle one's merchandise and locating information to aid in selection and choice of specific middlemen. Firms seeking overseas representation should compile for screening a list of the middlemen who might logically be utilized. A variety of sources of existing names is available.

1. The U.S. Department of Commerce *Trade List* and *World Trade Directory Reports* provide valuable information. The department also will conduct trade contact surveys through U.S. commercial offices located in the countries in question. Such surveys are specifically undertaken for an individual client at a relatively low cost.
2. Commercially published directories, such as *Trade Directories of the World* and a *Guide to Foreign Business Directories,* provide additional names.
3. Foreign consulates may have lists or sources of lists of middlemen in their countries.
4. Chamber of commerce groups located abroad, such as the American Chamber of Commerce in Spain, may provide useful contacts. Members of such chambers are typically American businessmen living in the foreign country; as such, they are familiar with the marketing structures and requirements of both the home and foreign countries.
5. An especially valuable source for many companies is contact with other manufacturers producing similar but noncompetitive goods. Field experience with their own middlemen provides accurate information which they may be willing to share.
6. Other sources include middlemen associations, business publications, management consultants, and carriers. Airlines particularly have been actively engaged in providing overseas business assistance in recent years.

Selection. Finding prospective middlemen is less of a problem than discovering which of them can perform adequately. Most prospects will be hampered by low volume or low potential volume, many will be underfinanced, and some just can't be trusted. In many cases when the manufacturer is not particularly well known abroad, the reputation of the middleman becomes the reputation of the manufacturer, so poor choice at this juncture can be devastating.

The criteria mentioned above for locating middlemen can also be used for the selection of the most promising middlemen. The screening and selection process itself may utilize the following sequence:

First, the firm or marketer should send a letter in a foreign language to each of the prospective middlemen discovered in the search process. The letter should include product information and distributor requirement and should request a reply from interested firms. Second, a follow-up letter can be utilized to procure more specific information concerning the lines handled, the territory covered, size of firm, number of salesmen, and other background information. Third, those contacted firms that offer most promise should be asked for references from other clients. Their customers should also be contacted, and a credit check through either private agencies such as Dun and Bradstreet or the Foreign Credit Interchange of the National Association of Credit Managers or through government agencies is beneficial. Finally, if possible, the businessman may find it a good investment to conduct a personal checkup on the most promising firms. One instance of the value of such a visit is cited as follows:

One American businessman who visited a potential representative in Latin America discovered a small office lined with hundreds of catalogues from firms throughout the world. This "agent," is was found, sat in his office and waited for customers to come in and request products. When a customer arrived, the agent went to his catalogues to see if the product could be found. Needless to say, his "line" included everything from soup to nuts.[10]

Coming to Terms. Once a potential middleman has been found and evaluated, there is still the task of detailing the arrangements with that middleman. So far the company has been in a buying position; now it must shift into a selling and negotiation position so that it can convince the middleman to handle the goods and accept a distribution agreement that is workable for the company. Mechanical and legal elements of a distributor agreement are highlighted in Exhibit 22–4, an excellent checklist produced by *Business International* as a general guide. There is no general guide, however, to the mode of negotiation which will be most effective in consummating agreements with foreign middlemen. At this point, success will depend on a good product and company reputation, a skilled negotiator or salesman, and an intimate knowledge of the market, the middleman, and the environment within which he works.

Solving Distribution Problems

The variety of problems encountered in international marketing is only slightly greater than the variety encountered domestically. The real difficulty relates to the intensity of the problems and the complexity of

---

[10] "Export Marketing for Smaller Firms," *Small Business Administration* (May, 1963), p. 63.

EXHIBIT 22–4

Elements of a Distributor Agreement*

I. BASIC COMPONENTS

1. Parties to the agreement.
2. Statement that contract supersedes all previous agreements.
3. Fixing the duration (perhaps after a 3–6 months' trial agreement).
4. Territory: (a) exclusive; (b) non-exclusive; (c) sole; or (d) manufacturer's right to sell direct at reduced or no commission to local government and old customers.
5. Products covered.
6. Expression of intent to comply with government regulations.
7. Clause limiting sales forbidden by US Export Act.

II. MANUFACTURER'S RIGHTS

1. Arbitration: (a) if possible in manufacturer's country; (b) if not, before International Arbitration Association; (c) define rules to be applied (e.g., in selecting arbitration panel); or (d) make sure award will be binding in distributor's country.
2. Jurisdiction should be that of manufacturer's country (e.g., complete the signing at home).
3. Termination conditions (e.g., manufacturer need not indemnify if contract is cancelled after due notice).
4. Clarification of tax liabilities.
5. Payment and discount terms.
6. Conditions for delivery of goods.
7. Non-liability for late delivery beyond manufacturer's reasonable control.
8. Limitation on manufacturer's responsibility to provide information.
9. Waiver of manufacturer's responsibility to keep lines manufactured outside the US (e.g., by licensees) outside of covered territory.
10. Right to change prices, terms, and conditions at any time.
11. Right of manufacturer or his agent to visit territory and inspect books.
12. Right to re-purchase stock.
13. Option to refuse or alter distributor's orders.
14. Training of distributor personnel in US subject to: (a) practicability; (b) costs to be paid by the distributor; (c) waiver of manufacturer's responsibility for US immigration approval.

III. DISTRIBUTOR'S LIMITATIONS AND DUTIES

1. No disclosure of confidential information.
2. Limitation of distributor's right to assign contract.
3. Limitation on distributor's position as legal agent of manufacturer.
4. Penalty clause for late payment.
5. Limitation on right to handle competing lines.
6. Placing responsibility for obtaining customs clearance.
7. Distributor to publicize his designation as authorized representative in defined area.
8. Requirement to remove all signs or evidence identifying him with manufacturer if relationship ends.
9. Acknowledgment by distributor of manufacturer's ownership of trademark, trade names, patents.
10. Information to be supplied by distributor: (a) sales reports; (b) names of active prospects; (c) government regulations dealing with imports; (d) competitive products and competitors' activities; (e) price at which goods are sold; or (f) complete data on other lines carried on request.
11. Information to be supplied by distributor on purchasers.
12. Accounting methods to be used by distributor.
13. Requirement to display products appropriately.
14. Duties concerning advertising and promotion.
15. Limitation on distributor's right to grant unapproved warranties, make excessive claims.
16. Clarification of responsibility arising from claims and warranties.
17. Responsibility of distributor to provide repair and other services.
18. Responsibility to maintain suitable place of business.
19. Responsibility to supply all prospective customers.
20. Requirement that certain sales approaches and literature be approved by manufacturer.
21. Prohibition of manufacture or alteration of products.
22. Requirement to maintain adequate stock, spare parts.
23. Requirement that inventory be surrendered in event of a dispute, which is pending in court.

* While it is presumably applicable to agreements between firms in different countries, laws of the other party's country should, of course, be checked; some laws subjecting various elements of distributor contracts to overriding considerations of the public interest.

their solutions. A few of the more troublesome distribution problems are reviewed below.

Nonexistent Channels. One of the first things companies discover about international channel-of-distribution patterns is that in most countries it is nearly impossible to gain adequate market coverage through a simple channel of distribution. In many instances appropriate channels just do not exist; in others, parts of a channel system are available but other parts may be lacking. Several distinct distribution channels often must be established to reach different segments of a market; channels that are suitable for distribution in urban areas seldom provide adequate rural coverage. Companies may have to depart from their customary channel patterns to gain distribution. For example, Proctor & Gamble, which is so well known for its mass merchandising in the United States and which has been a mass merchandising pioneer in Europe, sells soap and its other products by door-to-door salesmen in the Philippines, Iran, and other developing countries. It is interesting to note that, in earlier stages of economic development, the same company began operations by selling door-to-door in the United States.

Blocked Channels. As mentioned in the preceding section, an appropriate middleman may not exist in a given market; a more usual situation encountered by the international marketer is when there is a channel in existence but he is blocked from using it. Blockage may exist because competitors have already established their lines in the various channels, because trade associations or cartels have closed up certain channels, or because customary marketing patterns preclude market acceptance of still other middlemen. Finally, a major type of blockage is political.

Competition for the few available middlemen in most of the world marketplaces creates extreme difficulties for the marketer seeking an outlet for his product. Such blockages are not rare in the United States but they are intensified when the number of middlemen available is smaller and the number of potential suppliers is larger than in this country. Many companies are forced to suffer through spotty distribution for extended periods of time because they simply cannot gain entry through existing channels and cannot afford to establish new ones. One manufacturer found that he was completely prevented from entering European markets because every middleman who logically could handle his product was either financially tied to a competitor or had long-term relationships or commitments to competitors.

Sometimes competition has been so intense for distribution that businessmen have established trade associations, cartels, or other regulatory groups to divide the market and eliminate new competition. General Tire Co. was finally forced out of Europe because the tire cartel would not tolerate its presence and used duress to render its channels of distribution ineffective. Europe's potash cartel has agreements with governments of Germany, France, and Spain prohibiting potash importing into these countries without the written permission of all the producers. A marketing director commented to the authors, "It's all very simple. All we have to do is convince the producers that they need one more competitor in an already crowded market."

Associations of middlemen sometimes restrict the number of distribution alternatives available to a producer. Druggists in many countries, for example, have inhibited distribution of a wide range of goods through any retail outlets but drugstores. The drugstores, in turn, have been supplied by a relatively small number of wholesalers who already have long-established relationships with their suppliers. Thus, through a combination of competition and association, a producer may be completely kept out of the market.

Government has been a major nonmarket force in blocking channels, particularly to foreign interlopers. Japan is notorious for its activities to protect local business. Safeway Stores tried to enter the Japanese market in the late sixties but were thoroughly stopped in their attempt by traditional middlemen who feared the competition. The Japan Soft Drink Bottlers Association staged an anti Coca-Cola campaign in which they charged unfair marketing tactics. Then when the Coca-Cola Company applied to introduce Fresca, the association put so much pressure on various Japanese ministries that the company withdrew the application. When it achieved "too much success," General Foods' Japanese subsidiary was required to cut down its promotional efforts and limit sales of curry products; it had earlier had the same experience with instant coffee. Japan is by no means the only country to use strong political measures to limit competition in distribution. Unilever established grocery stores in vans which traveled throughout Turkey. The truck stores were welcomed by Turkish villagers who had been virtual captives of local monopolies, but the local tradesmen were quick to induce the government to pass an edict eliminating the traveling stores.

Blocked channels can be opened up in many instances. Sometimes the company hoping to enter a market can buy equity in middlemen and assure itself of market entry. United Fruit Company, for example, found that the only way in which it could adequately gain satisfactory distribution in Europe was to purchase distributors. A blocked company may simply "buy distribution" by offering extremely wide margins, contract bonuses, or other forms of cash settlement to middlemen who take on their line. In some instances when distribution through normal channels is not available, companies may seek completely different types of channels; such changes in the past have been responsible for causing virtual distribution revolutions when the new channel caught on with the public.

Companies may also be forced to build their own channels. This is usually the most expensive method of gaining entry, but it may be the only method. When a company has its own distribution, it is assured that someone else will not be able to buy it out. Smith, Kline and French, marketer of Contac, was not willing to simply drop its cold remedy into the long, chaotic, and overcompetitive channels used by cold remedies in Japan for fear that the product would be lost in the seven- to nine-level distribution pattern prevailing in the Japanese proprietary medicine market. The company built a short, compact marketing system using 33 pharmaceutical wholesaler middlemen, compared to 200 to 400 used by their competitors. All were prohibited from engaging in secondary wholesaling (to other wholesalers) and sold only to 18,000 selected retailers who signed a resale price maintenance contract and agreed not to sell to other retailers or wholesalers. The Japanese press attempted to make an issue of the skipping of traditional channels; one headline read "Foreign Company Attacks Domestic Pharmaceutical Industry with Guerrilla Tactics." Product superiority and the market's receptiveness in this case insured the success of the Smith, Kline and French channel restructuring attempts. The kinds of political blockage discussed above are often the most absolute and most difficult to cope with and can sometimes be overcome only through political means per se.

Stocking and Servicing. The high cost of credit, danger of loss through inflation, lack of capital, and other concerns cause foreign middlemen in many countries to carry inadequate inventories, causing out-of-stock conditions and loss of sales to competitors. Physical distribution lags intensify this problem, so that in many cases the manufacturer must provide local warehousing or extend long credit, to encourage middlemen to carry large inventories. The physical distribution problem can be overcome through the use of air transportation; but considerable ingenuity, assistance and, perhaps, pressure are required to induce middlemen in most countries to carry adequate or even minimal inventories.

The services required or desired by manufacturers may be quite dissimilar from those the middlemen are willing or able to furnish. Since middlemen are unable to extend adequate credit to their customers, the selling company itself may have to take on the credit burden. In most nations middlemen are notoriously disinterested in promoting or selling individual items of merchandise; the manufacturer, then, must provide adequate inducement to the middlemen or undertake much of the promotion and selling effort himself.

Motivating Middlemen

Once middlemen are selected, a promotional program must be instituted to maintain high-level interest in the manufacturer's products. A relatively larger proportion of the advertising budget must be devoted to channel communications than in the United States, because there are so many small middlemen who must be contacted. Consumer advertising is of no avail unless the goods are actually available. Furthermore, few companies operating in international business have the strong brand image which they have in their own country. Even giants whose products are taken for granted in their home country may have little brand following in countries where they have been operating for years. Retailers and wholesalers in most countries are only minimally brand conscious, and yet they control to a large degree the success or failure of the products in their countries.

In large part the level of distribution and the importance of the individual middleman to the company will determine the nature of the activities undertaken to keep the middleman on his toes. On all levels, there is a clear correlation between the middleman's motivation and his sales volume. The hundreds of motivational techniques that can be employed to maintain middleman interest and support for the product may be grouped into five major categories: financial rewards, psychological rewards, communications, company support, and corporate rapport.

Obviously, financial rewards must be adequate if middlemen of any variety are to continue to carry, much less promote, a company's product. Margins or commissions must be set to meet the needs of the middlemen and may vary according to the volume of sales which can be produced and the level of services offered. Without a combination of adequate margin and adequate volume, middlemen cannot afford to pay very much attention to any product.

Being human, middlemen and their salesmen also need psychological rewards and recognition for the job they are doing. For most businessmen throughout the world, a trip to the United States or to the parent company's home or regional office is a great honor. The American company has been pictured as the business with all the answers, so foreign associates are likely to be particularly flattered if it seeks his advice. Publicity in company media and local newspapers also builds esteem and involvement among foreign middlemen.

In all instances the company should maintain a continuing flow of communication in the form of letters, newsletters, and periodicals to all its middlemen. The more personal these are, the better. One factor that was partly responsible for the success of Smith, Kline and French in building their own channels, as mentioned above, was that they established a monthly periodical specifically published for the 1,200 wholesale salesmen dealing in their product.

The company can support its middlemen by offering advantageous credit terms, adequate product information, technical assistance, and product service. Such support helps build the distributor's confidence in his product and in his own ability to produce results.

Finally, considerable attention should be paid to the establishment of close rapport between the company and its middlemen. The positive methods noted above can be supplemented by making certain that conflicts that arise are handled skillfully and diplomatically. The American image abroad does not particularly aid in the establishment of this rapport, because American firms are considered brutal, cutthroat, and impersonal, but that image can be overcome if the people representing the company make special efforts in this direction. It should be borne in mind that in all of the world, business is a personal and vital thing to the people involved.

CHANNEL CONTROL

The extreme length of channels typically utilized in international distribution makes control of middlemen particularly difficult. Some companies have solved this problem by establishing their own distribution systems; others issue franchises or exclusive distributorships in an effort to maintain control at least through the first stages of the channels. Until the various world markets are more highly developed, most international marketers cannot expect to exert a high degree of control over their international distribution operations. Nevertheless, the fact that control is difficult does not mean that the company should not attempt to control its distribution. There is every reason to believe that companies that succeed in their attempt to control distribution channels are most likely to be the successful international marketers. Commenting on the importance of channel control, an American manufacturer commented that "The first to have a controlled system of outlets will be *the one* in Europe. That is the reason for Singer's success. You have to have your own outlets with trained people you can control."[11] Indeed, the desire for control is a major reason why companies initiate their own distribution systems in domestic as well as in international business.

Two types of basic control are called for in international business; control over the system and control over middlemen. The first relates to control over the distribution channel *system* per se. This implies overall controls of the entire system to be certain that it is operating within the range of cost and market coverage objectives discussed earlier in this chapter. The specifics of distribution must also be controlled because pricing margins, transshipping and other specific elements all affect the overall system. Some manufacturers who have lost control, for example, have discovered that in certain instances they are competing at a disadvantage with their own product in foreign markets. This comes about when domestic wholesalers or middlemen dump goods into a foreign country in order to get rid of obsolete merchandise or to build up sales volume. Such action may directly conflict with exclusive arrangements made with distributors in other countries and may undermine the entire distribution system by harming relationships between the manufacturer and his channels.

The second type of control is at the middleman level. When possible the parent company should know (and to a certain degree control) the activities of the middlemen in respect to their volume of sales, market coverage, services offered, prices, advertising, payment of bills, and even profit. All levels of the distribution system cannot be controlled to the same degree or by the same methods, but quotas, reports, and personal visits by company representatives can all be beneficial in controlling middleman activities at any level of the channel.

The ultimate step in controlling the middleman whose performance is inadequate or destructive to the company's well-being is to separate him from the company. In the United States such an act is usually simple regardless of the type of middleman—agent, merchant, or employee, one simply fires him. It is not that easy in other parts of the world; the middleman typically has some legal protection which makes

---

[11] Vern Terpstra, *American Marketing in the Common Market* (New York: Frederick A. Praeger Inc., 1967), p. 98.

it difficult to terminate relationships with him. In Norway, for example, a manufacturer can hardly change agents unless he has evidence of negligence on the part of the agent he seeks to replace. Even if he does dismiss the agent he is likely to have to repay him for his investment in establishing customer contacts and creating goodwill. A 1969 court decision confirmed the customary practice of giving the dismissed agent indemnity equal to one year's commissions. Such restrictions may destroy a company's marketing plans and may make distribution difficult for firms which have merged. In one recent case, two Norwegian firms selling cranes merged, and the surviving firm maintained a dual distribution system through two competitive firms rather than pay the large indemnity required to eliminate one of them. In some countries an agent cannot be dismissed without going through an arbitration board to determine whether the relationship should be ended. Some companies make all contracts with middlemen for only one year, but in a few instances even termination under these contracts has been contested. In all countries, of course, premature termination of a contract may make a company liable for a breach of contract and for payment of damages. Competent legal advice is a mandatory prerequisite to writing contracts with middlemen in any country.

Complex as the problems of international distribution are, they are not impossible to overcome. Although the distribution patterns are inefficient, the markets still may be virgin and offer international businessmen adequate reward for their efforts. Even though it does not reduce the magnitude of the problems involved, the international marketer may take comfort from the fact that his competitors are laboring under similar handicaps.

SUMMARY AND CONCLUSIONS

An ineffective distribution system can invalidate the most carefully developed marketing program. The international marketer must be thoroughly familiar with the various alternate methods of organizing for international distribution. Distribution decisions hinge on middlemen availability, cost, controllability, functions performed, and effectiveness. If the company plan calls for the use of middlemen external to the company's own sales organization, management may choose to use domestic middlemen who serve overseas markets or may elect foreign middlemen. In either case, the further alternative of using agent or merchant middlemen is available. Finally, specific kinds of middlemen must be chosen and specific middlemen must be selected and induced to handle the company's product or line.

International marketers must cope with a wide range of problems and need to be cognizant of the wide variation in distribution systems from market to market. Physical distribution of goods takes on a completely new dimension when entering international markets. The marketer must be prepared to cope with high transportation costs, slow movement, complex packing and documentation requirements, and with the unwillingness of middlemen to carry adequate stocks of merchandise.

International distribution facilities have developed rapidly in recent years to accommodate the increasing flow of goods and the development of new markets. As markets and economies grow and develop, the marketing system inevitably grows and develops along with them. Since developing nations are quick to capitalize on the marketing knowledge of the highly industrialized economies, the next few years will see an even greater growth in international channels of distribution which will provide manufacturers more ready access to world markets.

READING

PLANNING FOR DISTRIBUTION*

A. N. ROGER

Assumptions—instead of conclusions based on collected facts—are as dangerous in the setting of distribution policies as they are in most areas of marketing.

Take the example of the pet food manufacturer who could assume, quite logically, that the best channel of distribution for his products would be through pet shops. What a shock he would get after a short while! His business would languish and quickly fail—simply because he was concentrating his efforts on the wrong channels of distribution.

Research shows that 80% of all United Kingdom pet food sales are located in grocery outlets, and he would be covering only a very small percentage of the available market.

So, clearly the first priority in distribution planning is to establish basic data under three broad headings—sources of purchase; organization of the trade; and long-term trends.

1. Sources of purchase

How a product (or similar competitive products, if this is a new entrant to the market) is purchased by the consumer can be established through consumer research employing either an *ad hoc* study on the product class, or purchasing regular consumer audit data covering the product class. This will establish *who* buys the product, *how much* they buy, *how frequently* and *where*.

2. Organization of the trade

Clearly the retail trade is our most likely main source of business, and so we need to establish how it is organized in our market. Its size, its make-up, the relative values of various sectors, and above all, the number of viable distributive points available to us.

The Board of Trade's Census of Distribution provides the information

---

* Reprinted from the April 13, 1970, issue of *Marketing Insights*, pp. 10–13. Copyright 1970 by Crain Communications, Inc., Chicago, Ill.

EXHIBIT 1

Retail Shop Distribution (United Kingdom)

	Number of Outlets	Percentage Total Outlets
Grocers	122,000	26.2
Dairies	4,500	4.0
Butchers	38,000	6.6
Fish/poultry	5,600	0.7
Greengrocery	27,000	2.8
Bread & flour	18,000	2.6
Off-licenses	11,000	2.0
Confectionary, tobacco, newsagents	63,000	9.5
Clothing & footwear	93,000	15.3
Household goods	74,000	11.6
Other non-food	57,000	8.9
General stores	3,000	9.8

Source: BOT Census 1966

we are seeking (Exhibit 1). It shows that there are over 500,000 retail shops in the United Kingdom.

We now need to determine which of the various types are likely to be the most effective sellers of our products. Our previous research gave us a clue, although it was not a quantitative assessment. If we want this, and I believe it is a vital part of the basic data, we have to buy retail audit data showing how much of our commodity—in this instance biscuits—is sold by each of the types of retailers covered by the audits.

The next stage is to establish whether any sub-sectors of the broader types of retailer assume much greater significance or require different treatment from everyone else. This is an important factor in determining the distribution service to be provided. In the case of biscuits it will be

EXHIBIT 2

The U.K. Grocery Scene

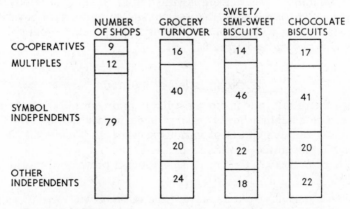

Source: A. C. Nielsen

found (see Exhibit 2) that multiples account for just under half of total biscuit sales through grocers, and obviously merit special consideration.

3. Long-term trends

We now need to know how this pattern will develop. You may think this is being over-conscientious, but the examples shown in Exhibit 3 show quite clearly how the consumer's source of purchase can shift dramatically in just a few years. A manufacturer who fails to spot such trends quickly enough can find himself in real trouble.

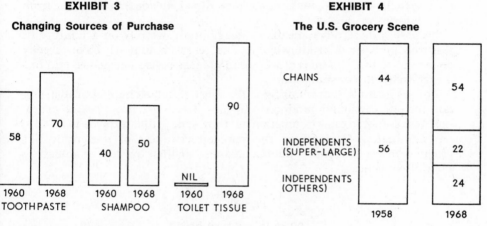

EXHIBIT 3

Changing Sources of Purchase

EXHIBIT 4

The U.S. Grocery Scene

Note: Percent through grocers

Equally important is the trend that enables one to forecast what is likely to happen to the retail trade at large. As Exhibit 4 shows, there has been a marked swing to the multiple chains and a consequent decline in importance of independent grocers.

If we study these trends in conjunction with the pattern of retailing development in our own market over the last five years, we come up with the possible prediction shown in Exhibit 5.

This demonstrates the continuing concentration of food retailing power amongst multiple grocers, and suggests an almost total collapse of the smaller independent grocer.

Our research to date seems to point to a distribution policy which concentrates on the retail trade. Before accepting that unequivocally as our major area of effort, it is as well to check out alternative and as yet untried methods of distribution:

We could decide to sell our products to an agency and let them be responsible for the final distribution; we could go into the direct mail business selling our products direct to the consumer through the post; indulge in another form of direct consumer selling through the door-to-

EXHIBIT 5

EXHIBIT 5

Food Retailing Trends—A Projection for 1966–77

	1966	*1972*	*1977*
Supermarkets.............	2,500	5,500	7,500
Self-service................	20,500	21,500	22,500
Counter service...........	99,000	63,000	50,000
Total grocery.............	122,000	90,000	80,000
Other food................	103,000	72,000	55,000
Grand total...............	225,000	162,000	135,000

door system; or, at a pinch, encourage direct customer collection from our factories or depots.

To assess these other means of distribution, we rely on a mixture of research and personal knowledge. The research that we have already done tells us that the market we are in is mass consumer goods, and has a very frequent consumption.

So we conclude that retailing is the most suitable channel of distribution for our particular products and have to choose the *types* of operation best suited to our circumstances. In practice, this resolves itself into an examination in depth of the pure effectiveness of presenting our products to the consuming public, balanced against the cost of achieving such effectiveness.

EXHIBIT 6

Top 20 U.K. Biscuit Sellers

	Shop	*Sterling*
Group A		
McVitie Chocolate Homewheat............	83	92
McVitie Digestive........................	85	93
McVitie Jaffa Cakes.....................	79	88
McVitie Rich Tea........................	74	88
McVitie Ginger Nuts.....................	76	82
McVitie Royal Scot.....................	68	82
Group B		
Rowntrees Kit-Kat......................	92	93
Jacobs Cream Crackers..................	88	90
Cadbury Chocolate Fingers..............	46	74
Nabisco Ritz...........................	69	88
Crawfords Tuc..........................	84	93
Macdonalds Penguin....................	74	88
Group C		
Crawfords Rover........................	52	69
Macfarlanes Vienna.....................	58	74
Crawfords..............................		
Tartan Shortbread......................	60	80
PF Shortcake..........................	42	64
PF Family Assorted.....................	43	66
Grey Dunn Blue Riband.................	48	60
Macdonalds Bandit......................	42	64
HP Butter Osborne.....................	40	65

Again research can help in making this assessment. In most markets one can usually find manufacturers using most of the alternatives open to one, so all one has to do is to establish the *effectiveness* of their various policies.

Exhibit 6 shows the level of retail distribution achieved for a selection of the United Kingdom's best selling biscuits. The brands in Group A are those marketed by McVitie's which rely solely on direct retail delivery. Those in Group B are marketed by other elements of United Biscuits or by their main competitors, who use direct retail delivery combined with wholesale and central drops.

Those in Group C rely to a very large extent on wholesale and central delivery and only have a very limited amount of direct retail callage.

The non-McVitie products achieving high levels of distribution with a combined retail/wholesale operation are supported by a heavy weight of direct advertising support (Exhibit 7).

EXHIBIT 7

Advertising Expenditure

Biscuit brand	Annual Average (£'000s)
Kit Kat	470
Penguin	120
Tuc	250
Ritz	175
Cadbury's Chocolate Fingers	140
Jacobs Cream Crackers	130

Source: Legion.

This seems to suggest that one is really faced with two basic alternatives if one wants to achieve a saturated level of distribution: Direct retail coverage exclusively, as operated by McVitie's; or a combination of direct/wholesale coverage, *plus* heavy direct advertising investment. Both methods are likely to be expensive!

Exhibit 8 shows a typical comparison of costs for exclusive direct delivery, mixed wholesale and direct delivery including and excluding advertising support, and predominantly wholesale delivery. Clearly one has to pay a premium for exclusive direct delivery over mixed wholesale and direct delivery in its various forms, but this form of distribution is most likely to be considerably cheaper than heavy direct advertising if one has more than a few major lines to sell.

The determining factor is whether the extra sales generated by saturation-type availability will more than offset the extra costs. But before arriving at this decision point, it is necessary to examine the needs of the different types of retail organization. In some it is sufficient for a manufacturer to get his products over the threshold; in others such an approach is courting disaster.

With today's emphasis increasingly on self-service, not only must the product be available in the store, but it must be seen by the consumer and prominently displayed. This gives another yardstick against which

EXHIBIT 8

Comparison of Distribution Costs

	100% Direct	Part Direct/ Central (including advertising)	Part Direct/ Central (excluding advertising)	Mainly Central
Salesmen..................	72	58	58	15
Sales management.............	14	11	11	4
Cars, expenses, etc.............	62	50	50	13
Order administration...........	55	36	36	20
Trade discount............	98	125	125	160
Distribution................	115	94	94	53
Advertising (3 brands)...............	—	—	50	50
Total cost factor...................	416	374	424	315
Index.....................	100	90	102	83

to measure the viable distribution alternatives. Central delivery into a multiple chain warehouse is very economical but it relies entirely on the branch managers to order the products and the store staff to put them on the shelf or build off-shelf displays.

Relying on a wholesaler for distribution means that your products will not even get into the stores unless the wholesaler's salesman actually sells them to his customers. This wholesaler may be handling some 3,000 lines, and none of them are going to get a great deal of selling time from his salesmen.

There is a danger of failing even to get your products over the storekeeper's threshold unless you are prepared to create such a demand (by advertising) that storekeepers actually ask for them from the wholesalers.

With direct representative coverage, however, you can guarantee that your products get into the store.

Before deciding on the expensive coverage, we have to examine certain other factors that exist in the market place: Since the job to be done in self-service and counter service stores is very different, perhaps there is some justification in having different policies for these two groups of outlets.

In United Biscuits, we are unanimous in believing that the only way to sell our products effectively in self-service stores is through direct representative coverage. In the counter services area, however, we have a different situation: One division supports total representative coverage, and the other is quite prepared to rely on the wholesale trade to get its distribution. Both have been proved very effective.

What then is the reason for this dichotomy? The division that believes in servicing the counter service stores through direct retail coverage only has a very streamlined production operation.

To maintain this form of production and the massive savings that result, we must have the maximum possible volume from each individual product line. This justifies us in using the most effective methods of presenting our product to the consumer and the cost of doing so is not the paramount consideration.

The other division has a number of high quality specialist products which require multi-processing and therefore do not lend themselves as well to automated production systems. These products also have a considerable amount of individuality and as such are ideal subjects for consumer advertising.

That's the situation at the moment. But one needs to look ahead in formulating distribution policies. The growing importance of the symbol group and cash and carry movements, for instance, could well induce manufacturers who previously indulged in direct delivery to the bottom end of the retail trade to leave coverage of this sector to these two wholesale factors.

The facts, as far as biscuits are concerned, still point to an exclusive direct retail coverage operation which means that there are a total of 225,000 potential calls for us to make. We have to decide whether we are going to treat all outlets alike—in terms of coverage and frequency of visit:

COVERAGE—TIMING.   We decided earlier that self-service and counter service stores call for different types of service; now we must decide how much time we intend our salesmen to spend in each case. This should be based on the potential turnover of the outlets concerned as that will ultimately determine the profitability to us of that call.

Operational research can be used to determine the type of job required in each outlet and the time necessary to complete that job satisfactorily. Much depends on the type of product and length of the product list being sold, but a typical set of timings is as follows:

```
Supermarkets........................................ 75 min.
Self-service stores (over 1,000 sq. ft.)................ 40 min.
Small selfservice and large and medium counter service.... 20 min.
Small counter service, non-grocers, non-retailers......... 15 min.
```

COVERAGE—FREQUENCY.   How do we distinguish between stores needing a weekly service and those which only require servicing once every two months? Again business done is our major yardstick, but other factors like the amount of storage space available and the extent of in-store servicing work required should also be considered.

As a general rule, supermarkets and the larger self-service stores will probably require a weekly call; other self-service stores and some of the larger counter service units, a fortnightly call; and the remainder of outlets will be serviced monthly or bi-monthly.

Application of the timing and frequency factors to the retail outlet data collected will determine the number of salesmen required. But it says nothing about the types of men.

We believe that the job and the man required for selling to the supermarket and larger self-service store is very different from the job and man required to service the counter service and non-grocery sector of the food trade. To accommodate these differences, a two-tier sales force structure is suggested with the better, more highly paid man, whose forte is selling and negotiation in a businesslike way, working on the self-service/supermarket outlets.

The management controlling the salesmen should be similarly split into two groups—the "specialist" manager on the one hand, who handles the supermarket salesmen, and the "general" manager on the other, who controls the "run of the mill" salesmen. The span of their control of these two types of managers differs in accordance with their various duties.

EXHIBIT 9

Sales Force Organization—Divisional Structure

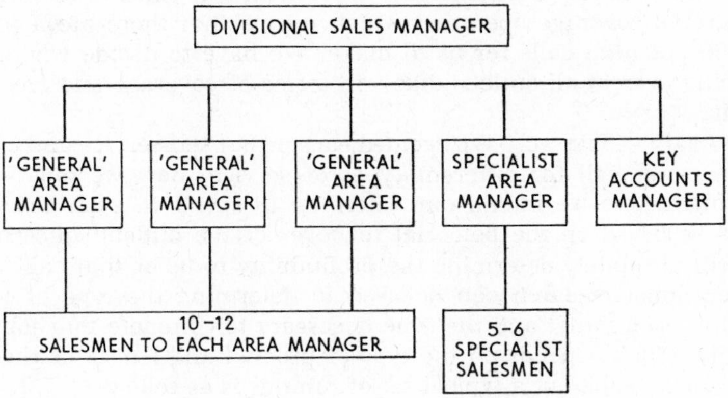

The "specialist" will control five or six salesmen, while the "general" man will probably handle 10–12 men. At second line level there should be an echelon of managers who will control both the "specialist" and "general" managers and have overall responsibility for the total sales operation in their assigned geographic areas. The span of control here should be five or six managers, and again the organizational structure should be designed to meet the needs of the trade being serviced.

A typical divisional structure within United Biscuits is shown in Exhibit 9. With this structure we are able to *implement* our agreed distribution policy *effectively* and, within the special situation obtaining in our business, economically.

Having established a policy and set up the necessary structure to implement it, the manufacturer must now set up and maintain the necessary controls to ensure that the policy is being implemented as originally envisaged. As before, research has a key role to play.

The first thing the manufacturer will want to know is whether his policy is working. Retail audits will show how many of the available outlets in any retailer type are stocking the product on a regular basis, how many normally stock it but are out of stock at the time of the audit, and how many do not stock it at all.

This is a measurement of the organization's effectiveness at getting the product over the threshold of the retail store, but it does not reveal how much on-shelf exposure a manufacturer's products are getting, both in isolation and compared with competition, or how much off-shelf display support.

These are two vital pieces of information for the sophisticated manufacturer to establish, if he is to measure the effectiveness of his selected distribution policy thoroughly.

Retail audit research also enables us to assess the effectiveness of promotional and advertising activity. Say, for example, there was a distribution weakness on a specific brand and a special form of promotion had been devised to improve it. Retail audits would measure the distribution position before and after the promotion.

The question of measurement against pre-determined criteria is important. Any distribution policy has its breakeven point, and specific criteria should be established beforehand, based on the overall cost of implementing the accepted policy.

In this connection, retail audit research enables you to compare your performance with that of your competitors. If you find that they are being just as successful with a much cheaper operation, then obviously some re-thinking of your own distribution policies is needed!

Another area where control is vital is in the checking of basic trends in the market. The service provided by the A. C. Nielsen Co. in their booklet "The Researcher" can be of considerable assistance in these broader areas.

No policy is sacrosanct and it must be constantly reviewed in the light of changing conditions.

In these circumstances a new assessment of the revised facts is essential and alterations must be made to the policy to enable its effectiveness to be maintained within the bounds of the cost limits set.

The tremendous use made of basic research in determining, implementing and controlling distribution policies is apparent.

QUESTIONS

1. Review the key variables which affect the marketer's choice of distribution channels.

2. Account, as best you can, for the differences in channel patterns which might be encountered in a highly developed country and an underdeveloped country.

3. Identify some of the underlying factors affecting channel-of-distribution patterns. Explain the role of each.

4. "Acceptance of tradesmen may be somewhat related to an economy's stage of economic development and the extent of its dependence on trade for prosperity." Discuss.

5. Explain why middleman margins vary so much from country to country.

6. Review the implications of the variations in sales volume and number of customers shown in Exhibit 22–2.

7. One of the first things companies discover about international channel-of-distribution patterns is that in most countries it is nearly impossible to gain adequate market coverage through a simple channel-of-distribution plan. Discuss.

8. Relate capital availability to channel of distribution structure.

9. Discuss the various methods of overcoming blocked channels.

10. Review the five C's of channel strategy and show their interrelationships.

11. What strategy might be employed to distribute goods effectively in the dichotomous small-large middleman pattern which characterizes merchant middlemen in most countries?

12. Explain the wide variation and erratic pattern in population per wholesaler in Exhibit 22–1.

Reading

1. Mr. Roger seems to imply that advertising costs and distribution costs are interchangeable and can be traded off. Is such a conclusion defensible?

2. Under what circumstances is "direct delivery" most likely to be appropriate in dealing with the retail grocery market?

3. What differences might one expect in U.K. and U.S. grocery distribution practices?

CASES—PART V

CASE V–1

MARKETING BABY FOODS IN JAPAN: A PRELIMINARY REPORT

As assistant to the vice president of marketing for American Baby Foods, you have been given the task of preparing a preliminary report on Japan as a possible market for one of the company's product lines.

The American Baby Food Company, located in Camden, New Jersey, is a well-established manufacturer of a wide line of baby products. Its motto "Babies are our business . . . our only business," aptly describes the parameters of the firm's activities. The product line is divided into food and nonfood items for the baby. Nonfood items include rubber pants, bibs, bottles, nipples, toys, and other accessory items. The food items are cereals, fruits and vegetables, and strained meat products which meet the dietary requirements for babies 2 to 18 months old. The products are widely used in the United States and Canada and compete to a moderate degree in Europe with the products of Kraft, Heinz, Carnation, and Gerber.

The product to be considered for marketing in Japan is the line of instant dry cereals which need only water or milk added to make them ready for eating. They can be used as the only food or as a supplement to other foods in a baby's diet until the infant is on a full, varied diet of table food at about 18 months. The cereals come in 1-ounce, 8-ounce, and 16-ounce packages. The 8-ounce size contains about two weeks' supply of cereal. American Baby Foods produces oatmeal, barley, rice, mixed cereal, and high protein cereals, which will all be considered for marketing in Japan.

As is usually the case, the vice president of marketing wants the report yesterday. What he really wants to know is if there is reason to spend additional money to prepare a complete market analysis on Japan. Since this is a "hurry up" job, about all you can be expected to do is the following:

1. Make a rough estimate of market demand.
2. Outline the major marketing problems that will face American Baby Foods in successfully marketing the cereal.
3. Suggest steps that might be taken to overcome the problems.
4. Suggest to research the additional information necessary before a thorough market analysis and report can be made.

About all the information that research could dig up on such short notice is reproduced below. While there are some real holes in the data, there should be enough to make a preliminary report. Remember, one of your main tasks is to advise research on what other data you will need.

Population Facts

In 1966, the total population of Japan was approximately 100 million persons. Exhibit 1 shows 1965 population figures for the major urban areas of Japan.

EXHIBIT 1

	Population (millions)	Percent of Total Population
Tokyo	10.9	11
Osaka	6.7	6
Hokkaido	5.2	5
Aichi	4.8	4.8
Kanagawa	4.4	4.6

The birth rate for 1965, according to the Ministry of Welfare, was 18.5 per 1,000 people. A steady but slow increase was predicted for the future. Exhibit 2 shows the number of live births in the major urban areas of Japan for 1965.

EXHIBIT 2

Perfecture	Live Births
Tokyo	187,436
Kanagawa	69,773
Toyama	16,060
Ichikawa	16,273
Fukui	12,821
Yamanashi	13,068
Nagano	31,579
Gifu	30,629
Shizuoka	50,993
Aichi	85,652
Mie	25,726
Shiga	13,853
Kyoto	32,711
Osaka	116,930
Hyogo	70,229
Total	752,733

Diet[1]

By tradition, a Japanese starts his day with a bowl of mashed soybean soup, pickled horseradish, and seaweed. The rest of the day, he's apt to eat a few bits of raw octopus or dried squid accompanied by gobs of the inevitable Asian staple—rice.

Now, as the Japanese grow in affluence and sophistication, such picturesque eating habits are changing. And as they do so, more and more U.S. and European food-processing companies are moving into Japan to take advantage of it. Among the American companies that have already established beachheads in Japan are Kellogg (cornflakes), H. J. Heinz (catsup), Del Monte Corp. (tomato juice), General Mills (cake mixes), Libby, McNeil & Libby (canned peaches), Corn Products (Knorr packaged soups), General Foods (Maxwell House instant coffee), Coca-Cola, Pepsi-Cola, and Canada Dry. Switzerland's food giant, Nestlé, has scored big in Japan with its Nescafé instant coffee. Waiting to get a food-processing stake in Japan right now are Beatrice Foods Company and Swift & Company.

Says an executive of one of the biggest U.S. food companies: "Japan should be one of the two fastest-growing food markets in the world this year." (The other is Mexico.) Beyond this, the Japanese are improving their diet as a matter of pride. They are a small people by U.S. standards, and they want to become bigger. It's humiliating when a Japanese basketball team is matched against an American basketball team.

Year by year, the Japanese diet is improving. They now eat less rice and more animal and vegetable protein. But their Ministry of Health and Welfare points out that the 2,200 calories a day the typical Japanese gets is still below the Westerner's 3,000 calories, and it urges a more substantial and varied diet.

"We have become aware of the value of nutrition and a balanced diet," says Tomi Egami, who runs Japan's biggest cooking school.

Japanese babies normally are fed milk only until the age of four months, at which time they are given supplemental soft foods prepared in the mother's kitchen. These soft foods are often a mashed mixture of rice, liver, spinach, or other highly nutritional foods saved from the adults' meal. As in many foreign countries, a mortar and pestle are used to grind the food for the babies and small children.

Market Characteristics[2]

There are headaches at the processing level. Many Japanese industries are fragmented, but food is the most fragmented of all—there are almost 100,000 companies engaged in food processing in Japan. Japan has more than 5,000 makers of soy sauce and more than 500 flour milling concerns. U.S. companies would like to spend much more on advertising and promotion but are limited by the Japanese govern-

---

[1] "Can Stew Supplant Sukiyaki?" Reprinted from the April 6, 1968 issue of *Business Week* by special permission, pp. 58–60. Copyrighted © 1968 by McGraw-Hill, Inc.

[2] Ibid.

ment in the amount of money that can be pumped in by the foreign parent. Japanese companies are under no such restrictions, and in some cases a large manufacturer has almost a monopoly position in a market. Even so, Western food companies are pushing to get into Japan in several ways, and each has its limitations and advantages. Some companies, such as Campbell Soup Co., do a fair business in Japan through exports. But it's tough to turn a profit this way, because of high freight costs and Japanese import duties that range from 15 to 50 percent. A few companies have tried licensing. Kellogg set up a subsidiary to provide technical and sales assistance to Ajinomoto Co., Japan's top maker of seasonings, which produces several varieties of Kellogg dry cereals. And Gerber Products Company licenses its baby food processes and labels to a Japanese group. But here again, profit potential is limited.

U.S. companies that would like to set up their own processing plants in Japan run into tough restrictions against letting foreigners control Japanese industry. Last year (1968), Japan's Ministry of International Trade and Industry relaxed restrictions a bit, allowing foreign companies to get a controlling interest in certain industries. But the food business categories included in the liberalization were few: beer (no outsider could hope to compete against the three big Japanese breweries), monosodium glutamate (Ajinomoto has an impregnable position), and ice (nobody is interested in making ice in Japan).

To be sure, a few of the more successful Western food operations are subsidiaries owned 100 percent outside Japan. Among them are Nestlé, Coca-Cola, and General Foods. But these were established years back when it was possible to set up subsidiaries capitalized in yen, not dollars; neither the capital nor profits could be repatriated. Such 100 percent ownership deals can't be made now.

Most companies have sought out Japanese partners with which to form joint ventures. Through such ventures, Heinz is linked with Nichiro Fisheries; Corn Products with Ajinomoto; Unilever (the British-Dutch giant) with Hohnen Oil Co.; General Mills with Morinaga Confectionery; Libby with Mitsubishi Shoji Kaisha; and Del Monte with Mitsui & Company and Kikkoman Shoyu Company.

Among new moves, Beatrice Foods' Hawaiian subsidiary has asked for Japanese government authorization to enter into joint ventures with two Japanese companies, and Swift & Company is nearing agreement with Nippon Ham Company and Mitsubishi Shoji Kaisha for a joint venture to raise and process broiler chickens. National Dairy Products is studying a deal to have its Kraft brand cheese made in Japan, and Corn Products and Ajinomoto last month introduced a new line of mayonnaise in Japan.

Company Experiences[3]

Most Western companies' efforts to cash in on changing Japanese diets haven't proved very profitable. As well as differences in tastes and

---

[3] Ibid.

other problems, they are confronted with an excruciating array of restrictions imposed by the Japanese government on foreign companies doing business there.

As a result, U.S. food companies have only a very small share of the more than $20 billion that the Japanese spend annually for food and drink (although sales of American agricultural products to Japan—wheat, soybeans, etc.—run to more than $750 million a year).

But food companies are persisting because of the obvious attractions of the Japanese market. Japan is big—over 100 million population—and it's growing more Western in its tastes. More important, its fast economic growth rate in recent years has brought more disposable income for food. This year, Japan's gross national product is expected to rise 7.6 percent to $133 billion (behind only the U.S. and the Soviet Union). Per capita income is expected to top the $1,000 mark, but companies have had mixed results trying to sell processed foods in Japan.

Nichiro-Heinz, established in 1961, had by last year piled up deficits totaling almost $2 million. Corn Products has done well with packaged dry soups. General Foods' Maxwell House is battling to hold its estimated 10 percent of the instant coffee market. (Nestlé, which spent heavily in creating a brand image at a time when the instant coffee idea was new to Japan, has 70 percent.) Among European companies, Unilever has run up sizable losses in its venture with Hohnen Oil Company. Heinz and Unilever ran into serious difficulties with their Japanese partners and have since been allowed to boost their equity to over 50 percent.

In addition, the American food companies have found plenty of other problems. For instance, the Japanese government, to protect domestic manufacturers, restricts foreign companies to producing limited lines of products and imposes ceilings on volume. Foods often have to be adapted to the Japanese palate, which may be getting away from traditional dishes, but still hasn't accepted Western tastes exactly. Heinz's spaghetti sauce has to be blander than the U.S. product. Corn Products' mayonnaise isn't as sweet as the American. Largely because of the underdevelopment of Japan's milk industry, Kellogg's dry cereals generally are eaten right out of the box as a confection.

Indeed, Japan's limited agriculture poses problems in getting raw materials for foods. Heinz, Del Monte, and Libby all are obligated to use domestic tomatoes in their catsup, but can only get small quantities. Corn Products' concern over making mayonnaise is how to get a steady supply of fresh eggs.

Food Imports

Japan is not self-sufficient in food production, and her ability to feed herself has declined since the end of World War II. In 1964, Japan was required to import over 20 percent of all food products consumed, and this trend is likely to continue as the population increases and the land suitable for food production diminishes. As an example, in 1964, over

500,000 metric tons of rice were imported, which was nearly twice that imported in 1963.

Distribution System

In 1962, Japan had 1.74 million retail and wholesale outlets which employed 6.67 million people. Over 85 percent of the retail outlets were individually or small-family owned and only 5 percent of the retailers had more than $30,000 (U.S. dollars) in sales. There were 230,000 wholesalers, which amounted to one wholesaler for every six retail units.

Wholesaling in Japan is a major economic factor in distribution. A large percentage of all consumer goods go through three or more wholesalers between manufacturer and ultimate consumer, with two middlemen being the minimum.

CASE V–2

OLYMPIA SHOES*

In October 1958, after one year's manufacturing experience, the Olympia Gymnastic Shoes Company found itself entirely at a loss to plan the next year's production.

This was not due to any lack of planning effort on the part of the owners, the Eisenstein brothers. Joseph Eisenstein had immigrated to Israel in 1957 from Poland, where he had been the owner of a gym shoe factory. With him he brought, first of all, the "know-how" of years of production and management; and in addition he had succeeded in bringing from Poland a considerable part of his equipment, in the form of electrical molding dies and sewing machines. Joseph was well known in his profession. Even in Israel he had many acquaintances in the shoe industry who still remembered the good name he had made for his products.

The second brother, Abraham, was already living in Tel Aviv, where he was a building contractor by profession. As the building trade was in a recession, the two brothers had decided to set up a shoe factory together, Joseph contributing his know-how and Abraham his savings. And so, Joseph Eisenstein went out to study the lay of the land, and Abraham to construct the factory building.

The production of gym shoes is based on a simple process: The raw material—natural rubber—is mixed with other chemical ingredients and rolled. The upper part of the shoe is cut out of cloth and sewn together on machines. Through a vulcanization process the rubber sole is permanently affixed to the shoe by electrical molding dies.

Joseph Eisenstein concluded his initial survey in March 1957. He had learned that competition on the market would be pretty stiff. There were two or three small factories in Israel, but the main producer here was Hamegaper, who covered some 80% of the local demand in gym

---

* "Copyright The Hebrew University of Jerusalem.

shoes. In view of the various sales channels open to him, as against those available exclusively to Hamegaper (such as Hamashbir[1]), he decided to start with production of children's shoes only for one year, so as to enable him to acquire the "feel" of the market.

These shoes he decided to turn out in two designs: the usual flat gymnastic shoe (from now on called flat), and a high gym-boot, looking very much like a basketball shoe (from now on called high) but produced by the same process as the flat one, unlike the real basketball shoe, which is usually made by hand. Mr. Eisenstein expected his shoe to stand up well against competition, and even to sell at a much lower price.

In order to break into the market he decided to price his flat shoes at 15% and his high shoes at 25–30% below the prevailing market prices. First cost calculations—utilizing a narrow profit margin and

EXHIBIT 1

Age	Number of Children
7	38,500
8	49,000
9	42,000
10	28,000
11	28,000
12	31,000
13	31,500
14	31,500
15	35,000
16	35,000

taking into consideration the equipment he had brought with him and the low overhead in their factory—indicated that such a price policy would be feasible.

Having reached these major decisions, Mr. Eisenstein started market research, as he was accustomed to in Europe.

He first turned to the Shop Owners' Association, with which he already had contact. There was not much they could tell him about the gym shoe market, but they confirmed his prices and the models he showed them, and promised to help him regarding information and distribution. They could not give him any statistical information. Nor could he get the information he wanted at the Manufacturers' Association. Here, as well as at the Ministry of Commerce and Industry, they referred him to the statistical section of the Ministry of Interior.

Mr. Eisenstein assumed as his starting date December 1957, with full production in January 1958, and based his calculations on children between the age of 7 and 16. There were about 350,000 in Israel, split into boys and girls evenly. Exhibit 1 gives the numbers of children (round figures).

---

[1] Hamegaper is a so-called "Histadruth" factory, i.e., a factory owned and managed by the General Federation of Israel Workers. As such, it naturally becomes the foremost supply of other Histadruth businesses, such as the Hamashbir retail store chain.

After interviewing nineteen shop owners, Mr. Eisenstein figured out the approximate sales of the previous year, 1956 (Exhibit 2). He also figured out what the division of colours had been.

Talking with these shop owners, some of whom he had known before and some to whom he was introduced by friends, Mr. Eisenstein came

EXHIBIT 2

	Sizes to 33 (French)	Sizes from 34
Flat gym shoes	90%	80%
High gym shoes	10%	20%

to the conclusion that it should be possible for him to penetrate 30% of the urban market and 5% of the rural market—an average of 20% of the over-all Israeli market. The conditions would be: prices of flat shoes lower by 15% and of high shoes lower by 25–30% than other makes available, with quality at least as good. Because of the particularly cheap price of the high shoe he expected that his sales would be biased in its direction and accordingly drew up a general sales forecast (Exhibit 3).

EXHIBIT 3

	Up to Size 33	34 and Larger
Flat	75%	67%
High	25%	33%

Assuming that every child in Israel needs a new pair of shoes a year, Joseph Eisenstein calculated his share out of a sales forecast for the year 1958 (Exhibit 4). He then prepared a production schedule, based on his previous experience in Poland (Exhibit 5).

Based again on his policy of prices lower by 15%–30%, he prepared a pricelist (price to consumer, including purchase tax) (Exhibit 6).

EXHIBIT 4

Age	Size (French)	Flat	High	Total Pairs
7	29	5,900	1,800	7,700
8	30–31	7,500	2,500	10,000
9	32	6,400	2,100	8,500
10	33–34	4,100	1,400	5,500
11	34–35	3,700	1,800	5,500
12	36–37	4,300	2,200	6,500
13	37–38	4,300	2,200	6,500
14	38–40	4,300	2,200	6,500
15	39–42	4,700	2,300	7,000
16	39–43	4,700	2,300	7,000
Grand Total		49,900	20,800	70,000

EXHIBIT 5

Months	%	Pairs
	Production Schedule 1958 (Flat and High)	
January–February............	14	9,800
March–April.................	16	11,350
May–June...................	20	14,100
July–August................	20	14,100
September–October...........	16	11,350
November–December..........	14	9,800
	100%	70,500

The Eisenstein brothers registered their firm as Olympia Gymnastic Shoes, and started production in October 1957. The factory reached full output in January 1958.

Within a short time they concluded that their production schedule was well founded: Olympia Shoes were of good quality, of good design, and cheaper than other shoes on the market. As early as March, parents and children were already demanding Olympias, and there was no accumulation of stocks in the stores. Sometimes clients even had to wait up to ten days for their orders.

At the same time the efficiency of the factory rose with increased production in March–April. At the end of May the Eisensteins concluded their first quarter:

1. Sales forecast found correct, generally.
2. Estimate of sales penetration of flat shoes (20% of over-all market) was also correct, and could even be raised by another 5%.
3. The high shoes have not yet established themselves completely, but deviations from estimates are negligible.
4. Conclusion: Continue to produce according to original schedule. "Our position is ideal, as long as no stock is accumulating, and production is just keeping up with sales!"

EXHIBIT 6

	Size	Price (IL)	Market Price (IL)
Gym shoes, flat, white..........	29–34	3.000	3.500
	35–39	3.200	3.750
	40–43	3.400	4.000
Gym shoes, flat, coloured......	29–34	3.400	4.000
	35–39	3.600	4.250
	40–43	3.800	4.500
Gym shoes, high, all colours.....	29–34	4.100	5.400
	35–39	4.450	5.900
	40–43	4.800	6.400

A few days after the schools closed for summer vacation at the end of July pressure started. Urgent orders for flat shoes came pouring in. As orders grew bigger, until they reached batches of hundreds, Mr. Eisenstein was forced to tell the shoe stores: "Sorry, you'll have to wait two or three weeks."

Pressure built up. "If I cannot get your shoes now," one client told him, "I won't need them any more. I'll sell Hamegaper. The kids go to camps, and they won't wait, but will pay higher prices."

The Eisensteins stepped up production. The plant worked overtime and took on additional workers. In August they raised production by 50% above schedule (15% of annual production, instead of 10%).

And then a strange thing happened. After the storm, sales dropped. Two thousand eight hundred pairs of flat shoes remained in stock. Sales of high shoes continued as expected.

In September they returned to their original schedule, laid off their temporary workers and discontinued overtime. But sales still dropped off (they were now 10% less than forecast) and some 400 additional pairs accumulated in the store.

The Eisenstein brothers were puzzled and dubious about following their production schedule in the coming months.

The final blow to the production schedule came at the beginning of October when schools re-opened. Again the unforeseen happened: this time orders came pouring in for high shoes. Joseph Eisenstein very efficiently channelled production towards a larger share of high shoes, and by the end of the month the output of the two styles was divided about 50:50. But demands for high shoes still rose, and orders came pouring in from all over the country.

In late October the two brothers sat down with a chart showing the

EXHIBIT 7

Comparison Between Production Estimates and Actual Production

Month	Flat Shoes		High Shoes		Total Shoes		
	Production Plan	Realized Production	Production Plan	Realized Production	Production Plan	Realized Production	Sales Forecast for Total Market
January	3,500	3,450	1,400	1,350	4,900	4,800	24,000
February	3,500	3,480	1,400	1,450	4,900	4,930	25,000
March	4,000	4,000	1,700	1,700	5,700	5,700	28,000
April	4,000	3,950	1,700	1,700	5,700	5,650	28,000
May	5,000	5,000	2,000	2,100	7,000	7,100	35,000
June	5,000	5,000	2,000	2,100	7,000	7,100	35,000
July	5,000	4,900	2,000	2,100	7,000	7,000	35,000
August	5,000	7,450	2,000	2,000	7,000	9,450	35,000
September	4,000	4,000	1,700	1,650	5,700	5,650	28,000
October	4,000	2,900	1,700	2,800	5,700	5,700	28,000
November	3,500		1,400		4,900		25,000
December	3,500		1,400		4,900		24,000
Total	50,000		20,400		70,400		350,000

original production plan as compared to the realized production figures (Exhibit 7) in order to set up a production plan for the following month. There was nothing stable any more to go on. Sales forecasts were completely out of line and workers were nervous, since the routine was changed daily.

"What kind of country is this?" groaned Joseph, "I do not know any more what to do: go over to high-shoe production? Or is this only another seasonal occurrence?"

Brother Abraham did not help much: "This is worse than in the building trade. Look at the sales graphs! I don't know a thing about shoes. What shall we do?"

CASE V–3

PACKAGING FOR THE PHILIPPINE MARKET*

The executives of the Pawtucket Polish Company differed in their reactions to suggestions made by a consultant with respect to package design for their product in the Philippines. An afternoon meeting was scheduled for full evaluation of the consultant's report.

The Pawtucket Polish Company was a medium-sized, family-held corporation which was founded in 1873 and which currently produced a wide line of liquid and paste polishes and waxes for furniture, floors of all types and cars. The chief executives of the company, sons and grandsons of the founder, held the majority of the stock. They had decided that the greatest potential for expansion of sales lay in overseas markets.

After investigating various possibilities, Pawtucket had decided to initiate foreign operations by producing in the Philippines a single product. The product selected was Pawtucket Blue Dot, a liquid floor wax which did not require buffing and was sold in the United States to home and institutional or industrial users.[1] The only change in formula would be the addition of an insecticide. All ingredients would be available locally. The remaining questions concerned the supply of glass and metal containers for use in the Philippines and which, if any, changes should be made in the design of the package. These questions were referred to a consultant who submitted the following report.

A Package for Pawtucket Polish in the Philippines

I. INTRODUCTION. In merchandising products for overseas areas there are two extreme attitudes possible. The first was expressed by Mr. J. J. Soughan—of Pepsi-Cola International Ltd. at the 1967 meeting of

---

* This case, Packaging for the Philippine Market, FT 879, was prepared as the basis for class discussion in the Harvard University Graduate School of Business Administration rather than to illustrate either effective or ineffective administration. Copyright © 1960 by the President and Fellows of Harvard College. Used by specific permission.

[1] Blue Dot normally sold at retail in the U.S. at 98¢ a pint, $1.65 a quart, $2.98 a half gallon, $4.40 a gallon and $26.00 for 15 gallons.

International Advertisers. "Each day as thousands of people pass street corners they look up and see a sign—the sign they see in Paris, France or in Paris, Kentucky, in Lima, Peru or in Lima, Ohio, is the same sign. Yes, the product is the same all over the world. The ingredients, the bottle, the color combinations are identical, the type is reproduced in the same manner, the size is constant from country to country."

On the other hand at the same meeting Mr. Robert Otto of Otto Co., Inc. said, "The problem is one of adapting—in marketing abroad just a few of the handicaps to be overcome are: suitability of the package, translation of the package copy, determination of package size in relation to local purchasing power."

Pawtucket Polish in the Philippines could exactly reproduce its United States package in the Pepsi-Cola philosophy; however this paper will attempt to show why it should not, and what kind of package it should use.

A. Limitations of the Product.   We intend to produce a liquid wax polish for home and industry in Manila. In the United States such polish is sold in either glass or tin containers. However, in the Philippines the wax might eventually find its way onto hundreds of islands, conveyed there by costal trading ships varying in size and stability from LST types to small outboards. Once outside Manila the wax will be borne over primitive roads, often on trucks with antiquated springs. For these reasons the glass container would present a serious breakage problem and we can confine our study to the tin can.

B. Supply of Cans.   Cans may be obtained in Manila from the Philippine Tin Lithography Co. or the Oriental Tin Can and Metal Sheet Mfg. Co., Quezon City. In its advertisement in the 1967 Industrial Philippines Yearbook, the latter company shows a wide range of conventional tin cans, including the elongated rectangular can with capped pouring spout most often associated with liquid wax products. In addition the firm advertises its color lithography. In order to obtain a maximum amount of our supplies in the Philippines, thereby boosting our Social Productivity Rating with the Central Bank, it seems advantageous to use these locally-produced wax cans.

C. The Buyer.   Our first target area is Manila, a market of about 2 million persons. In previous reports we have estimated that there are at least 100,000 households of upper or upper middle class status as judged from the Philippine census of professional persons, income distribution, ownership of telephones and number of servants employed in Manila. These households are our primary market. It is safe to assume that buying polish in these homes is done by servants among the more affluent or by the housewife in other groups. Because few Filipinos shop by car, according to our consultants, the quantity purchased each trip must be easily carried.

Our industrial sales on the other hand will be purchased by purchasing agents of large firms or janitors of smaller firms and will be in larger more cost-saving quantities.

Accordingly we should market at least two types of containers, a one-quart size for the home and a gallon-size for the larger purchaser.

D. The Retailer. The Philippine census indicates 15,000 retail stores in Manila. The typical store is the sari-sari or general store of which there are 7,000. Another 1,500 are classified as "grocery stores" and 2,000 as general merchandise stores. Most of these stores are small mama-papa type stores, run by families, the average number of hired employees being between two or three. No stores of supermarket type are yet in Manila.

Of the 15,000 stores, 10,400 are owned by Filipinos. Yet these Filipino stores have only 30% of the total assets and 43% of the total gross sales in the city. Almost all of the remaining 57% of sales is accounted for by the Chinese merchants who continue to dominate retail trade despite legal measures designed to keep them out of public market places. In the rest of the Philippines the same condition holds, with the Filipinos controlling only 50% of total assets and accounting for only 43% of gross sales.

E. Conclusions. For our consumer wax we desire a package which will appeal to the Filipino servant or housewife, and be such that the Chinese merchant will give it some amount of display space in a small store crowded with all types of goods. Because the customer does not serve himself and goods are typically in shelves behind a counter in the sari-sari store, it is important that the product name be legible at a distance of some 6–8 feet, the distance from consumer to package.

II. COMPANY IMAGE. The Philippine Chamber of Industries in its 1957 Yearbook states:

A deplorable fact that has long characterized our country and made it practically a sterile ground for the growth of local industries is the appalling apathy of our people towards Philippine-made products. There is no need to belabor the fact that we generally consider foreign-made goods superior to our own although there are local products which can compare favorably with imported articles in point of quality as well as in price.

In spite of the intensive campaign of the National Economic Protectionism Association (NEPA), Filipino consumers continue to patronize imported goods forgetting and neglecting our own to the detriment of our local manufacturers.

This quotation indicates two lessons. First there is a preference for non-Filipino goods. Secondly that an intensive drive to Filipinize manufacture and eliminate the preference is under way. For these reasons a policy of moderation seems in order. Pawtucket should stress its American aspects, but also in its packaging make clear its local manufacture. Thus Pawtucket can try to avoid being just another Manila wax maker on the one hand, or just another alien producer on the other.

III. THE PACKAGE ITSELF. The consumer package will be one quart in size, a round-cornered oblong in shape with a pouring spout as indicated.

A. Name. Since the name "Pawtucket" is long, cacophonous, has no associative value and will not have Pepsi-Cola's advantage of wide-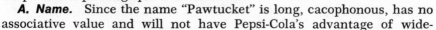

spread advertising, it seems undesirable to use it as a trademark on the can. In addition it should be kept in mind that the Philippines as a whole has a high illiteracy rate, close to 40%, and if we are eventually to expand beyond Manila we should have a brief, easily recognized name which can be associated with a picture or symbol. As a glance through Philippine advertising pages will show, the use of a product name closely connected with a symbol is quite common.

B. Wording.   The problem of language is not as acute in the Philippines as in the rest of Asia, since over 40% of the Filipinos speak English. Among the higher classes of Manila this percentage is much higher, closer to 95%, as indicated by our Philippine consultant. For this reason we intend to devote the front of our package entirely to English.

Nevertheless as we move out from Manila we will come in contact with the 40% of the Filipinos whose tongue is Tagalog. In addition a small but wealthy aristocracy of 2% are Spanish speaking. For these reasons we intend to devote part of the back of the can to Tagalog and Spanish, using the most common dialect of Tagalog, Bisoyan. A small identifying line of Chinese at the bottom rear of the can will help goodwill with the Chinese merchants without antagonizing the Filipinos by excessive prominence.

C. Color.   In choosing colors for our package we should try to avoid any associations which might cause resentment or psychological barriers to our product.

Religion.   Eighty-three percent of the Filipinos are Roman Catholics, so it would be well to look into the significance of color in that religion. The liturgical colors of the Church are five: white, red, green, violet, and black.

White: symbolizes innocence and is used on feasts of the Lord, the Virgin Mary, Confessors, and children's funerals.

Red: symbolizes fire and blood and is used on the feast of Pentecost, of the Apostles and of Martyrs.

Green: symbolizes hope and is used on the Sundays of Epiphany and after Pentecost.

Violet: signifies penance and mortification and is used during Lent and other seasons of sorrow.

Black: used on Good Friday and for funerals.

Gold: May be substituted for other colors in times of special rejoicing.

About 5% of the Filipinos are Moslems who hold the color green as a holy color. In addition exports from the Philippines might run into this problem.

Among our Chinese merchants, white is considered a color of mourning, so its excessive use should be avoided.

Forms of orange, particularly saffron, are used by Buddhist Monks and are used as sacred spots in the foreheads of Hindu pundits. These associations are widely known in Asia.

Of course red is the international color of Communism and the Filipinos are particularly aware of this since the Huk rebellions.

National. The Philippine national colors are red, white, blue and yellow, the national flag being as shown.

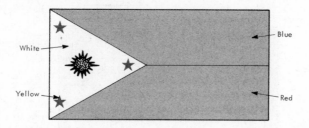

Aesthetics. Walter Sargant[2] who studied the preferences of various peoples for color says:

A preference for blue over other colours seems to be fairly universal, while except for the Orient, few prefer yellow unless they have given special study to the colour. Yellow is a hue which gains in charm as we study its qualities and use it in combination with other colours.

EXHIBIT 1

Proposed Can for the Philippines
Front View—⅔ Actual Size

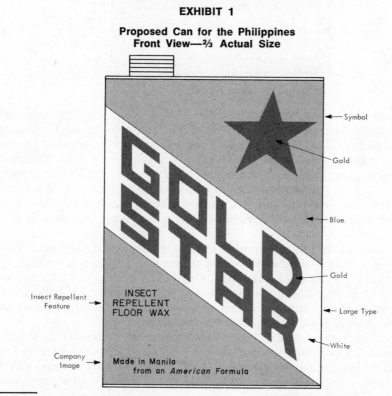

---

[2] See R. F. Wilson, *Colour and Light at Work* (London: Seven Oaks Press, 1953)

EXHIBIT 2

Rear View of Can

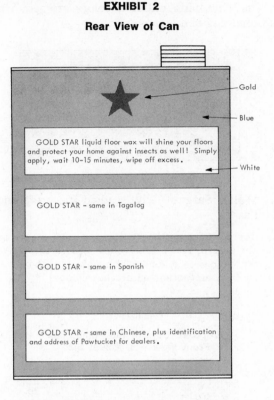

Since blue is aesthetically pleasing and a color which is politically and religiously relatively neutral, it seems desirable to use blue as the predominant color in our package. The color yellow is popular in Asia, as ascertained by Sargant's studies; it is prominent in the Philippine flag, and gives associative values of sunlight and brilliance properly identified with our product. It is a complement to blue and is a logical choice for our second color. Except for a small amount of white background it will be most economical and simple to limit ourselves to these two colors.

Because of the high illiteracy previously mentioned, and the desirability of having a simple easily recognized symbol for our product and advertising I recommend the star. Using this symbol we can call our polish "Gold Star Wax." The star is a symbol of universal honor, is on the flag of the Philippines (although not an obvious adaptation) and can be identified with the sparkle of our floor wax.

The illustrations in Exhibits 1–3, although not an artist's final proof, are intended to show the kind of package I consider best suited to Pawtucket in the Philippines for customer wax. Industrial cans will be similar in color and symbol, but larger, and contain directions more suited to large-scale waxing.

EXHIBIT 3

Side Views of Can

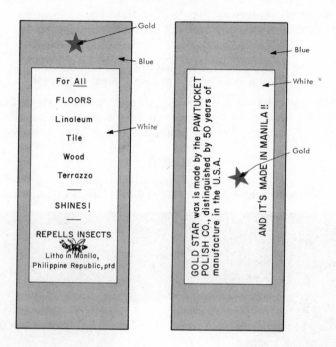

CASE V-4

ARBEITSGEMEINSCHAFT DEUTSCHE TIEFKÜHLKETTE, E.V. (B)*

As a result of the eight advertising agency presentations during the fall of 1957, the Arbeitsgemeinschaft Deutsche Tiefkühlkette, E.V. (German Frozen Food Association), under the direction of Mr. E. Rudolphi, retained J. Walter Thompson, GmbH, of Frankfurt, Germany to carry out the association's advertising and promotion campaign.

The campaign itself was visualized in three stages:

Stage 1: Up to about 15,000 retail freezer cabinets in Western Germany—chances for sale very limited—only very scattered retail outlets—little financial means—great need for information.

Stage 2: Up to about 30,000 cabinets—chances for sales increasing—distribution system better organized—more money available for advertising—increased information.

Stage 3: Frozen foods known everywhere—frozen foods in great de-

---

* Copyright 1970 by l'Institut pour l'Etude des Méthodes de Direction de l'Entreprise (IMEDE), Lausanne, Switzerland. Reprinted by permission.

mand—distribution system completed—even more money available—quality label for frozen foods to be introduced.

As of the end of 1959 the first stage had been completed and the second was well underway. Up to that time the association had taken the steps described in the following section.

Steps Taken by the German Frozen Food Association between the Fall of 1957 and the End of 1959

A. DEVELOPMENT OF AN IMAGE.   One of the first steps that the association took was to design and introduce a common emblem to symbolize all frozen foods. Exhibit 1 gives a rough idea of the appearance

EXHIBIT 1

Illustration of the Emblem Designed to Create a Common Image for Frozen Foods in the Minds of German Consumers

of the emblem. This emblem was used in all advertising and promotional activity conducted by the association. It served as a focal point toward which the consumer's attention was directed. It was hoped that the use of this emblem would help to develop a common image in the minds of all consumers and thus help to make frozen foods more widely known. The emblem could be used without restriction by all members. It could, for example, be displayed in shop windows, on retail freezer cabinets, on vans, etc. There was, however, one exception: no firm was permitted to put it on a package. This exception was made with the thought in mind that the association might want to use the emblem later as a kind of seal of approval or quality guarantee.

B. Test Market. In order to study and assess the best advertising possibilities, a rather large portion of available funds were concentrated in a test market run in Munster, Germany, in March, 1959. During this test the association ran heavy local advertising in all types of media, conducted in-store promotions, ran a contest, and held classes for local housewives. As a result of the campaign, frozen food sales in Munster jumped 35% and continued to climb even after the test was completed. To obtain more precise information on advertising possibilities, housewives in the test city were interviewed after the test was over. Exhibit 2 gives a summary of the results of these interviews along with a comparison with the results obtained in the market survey which had been conducted earlier in the whole of Western Germany.

EXHIBIT 2

The German Consumer's Knowledge of Frozen Foods
Comparison of the Results of Two Surveys

	October 1958 Western Germany	April 1959 Test Market One City—Munster
Detailed knowledge	7%	19%
Sketchy knowledge	22	34
Rather vague	31	29
No knowledge	2	10
False ideas	4	4
Never heard about it	34	4

Exhibit 3 shows the success of various advertising methods used in the test city of Munster.

EXHIBIT 3

	Percentage of Interviewees
Saw deepfreeze cabinets in retail stores	44%
Saw advertising materials in retail stores	39
Read press articles	38
Saw advertisements in the newspapers	29
Recommend by retailers	21
Heard through relatives or friends about it	20
Saw advertisements in cinema	9
In a contest	3
Saw television advertisement	2
At housewives' meetings, lectures, cooking demonstrations	1

C. Education. On the theory that the best way to educate housewives concerning frozen foods would be to first educate key people in the distributive trade and then let them "spread the word," the association conducted a series of one-week courses for employees of wholesalers and processors. These courses were primarily technically oriented and attempted to teach the proper methods of using, handling, and storing frozen foods. Twenty-five men were in each course. The cost of the course, 150 marks per man, including room and board, was paid by the man's employer. By the end of 1959, six courses had been held with a total of about 250 participants. Since there were about 250 major wholesalers and 40 frozen food processors in Western Germany, it was estimated that at least another six sessions would be needed before the courses would have covered someone from each of these firms. The next session was scheduled to be held in May, 1960.

Also in line with the overall education program, the association was, in late 1959, in the process of preparing a series of educational slides and accompanying sound tapes. It was planned that these slide programs would be made available to wholesalers for a nominal sum of about 100 D. marks a piece to cover production costs, and that wholesalers would make use of them in conducting classes for retailers.

D. PROMOTIONAL MATERIALS. The association designed and printed a variety of display materials for advertising frozen foods in retail stores. These materials were distributed to retail stores through the normal marketing channels, i.e., the association made the materials available to manufacturers and wholesalers who, in turn, distributed them to retailers. One-third of the cost of these materials was borne by the association and two-thirds was borne by wholesalers and retailers. In 1958, approximately 98,000 D. marks of in-store display materials were produced, of which the association paid 32,000 D. marks.

E. PUBLICITY WORK. Publicity work, which prior to 1958 had been conducted only on a sporadic basis, was thereafter conducted on a fixed plan. Under this plan the association's central office in Bremerhaven began periodically to provide publicity material for various public information agencies. One of the features of this program was a regular cooking recipe service which reached housewives through newspapers and magazines. Also in line with this publicity program, the association had tried to bring frozen foods into the public spotlight by attempting to get various well-known people to begin using them. For example, Chancellor Konrad Adenauer was given a freezer full of frozen foods on his birthday and local opinion leaders were invited to frozen food dinners.

F. CITY-BY-CITY PROMOTIONS. In an attempt to promote frozen foods on a regional basis, the association was, in late 1959, just beginning a program of city-by-city promotions. The first had been held in Braunschweig, a city of 250,000, during one week of November, 1959. In this promotion, classes, conducted by a specialist, were held for retailers, and a contest with prizes was held for consumers. In the contest, consumers were given entry blanks at their grocers and asked to answer a series of simple questions about frozen foods. Then the entries of all consumers who answered the questions correctly were put in one container and the winners were determined by a drawing held at the end of the week. The primary prizes were two home freezers, two refrigerators, and one kitchen range, all donated by appliance manufacturers. Twenty thousand consumers filled out entries. Cost of the whole promotion (5,000 D. marks) was covered by assessing each wholesaler in the city 30 marks for each retail freezer which he serviced. The next city-wide promotion was scheduled to be held in Bielefeld during late January, 1960.

Mr. Rudolphi's Evaluation of the Work of the Association

Summing up concerning the overall efforts of the association, Mr. Rudolphi made the following comments in December, 1959:

Considering our rather limited means, we did not expect to achieve an overwhelming success with our joint advertising and promotion campaign. But it can now be said that a certain success was achieved. Trade and industry are, in any case, quite satisfied with the results. Concerning the future, I feel that we have just about reached the point where cooperative advertising and promotional activities must begin to be replaced by company-sponsored brand advertising. The association will, of course, probably continue to sponsor its city-by-city promotions and its program of providing frozen food education for wholesalers and retailers. Gradually, however, we will begin to turn our attention more and more to the problem of establishing and maintaining high standards of quality throughout the industry. Along this line, we are presently preparing a code of industry standards which we hope will be ready to be presented to our members for adoption at the association's next annual meeting in May or June, 1960. If it is adopted, there is a good chance that we will get into the business of laboratory testing, inspecting, and issuing an association seal of approval to those firms which measure up to association standards.

CASE V–5

ACME ELECTRIC COMPANY*

In March 1957, the management of Cia, Acme Electric, S.A., was considering what to do about Casa Diaz, one of the Acme's dealers. Casa Diaz sold more Acme products than other dealers in Mexico City, but the selling practices employed by Mr. Diaz were the source of considerable concern and difficulty to the Acme management.

Cia, Acme Electric, S.A.

Cia, Acme Electric, S.A., assembled and sold Acme radios and television sets in Mexico. The ownership of the company was divided between the Acme Electric Company (60%) and top executives in the local management (40%). Acme products were distributed throughout the Mexican nation. In the southern half of Mexico, including the Federal District, Acme distributed directly to retail dealers. This area included 66% of the Mexican population. The rest of the country was handled by wholesale distributors located in the major cities.

---

* This case, Acme Electric Company, FT 864, was prepared by Professor John Fayerweather, then of Harvard University Graduate School of Business Administration, as the basis for class discussion rather than to illustrate either effective or ineffective administration. Copyright © 1957 by the President and Fellows of Harvard College. Used by specific permission.

The company had grown rapidly in the post-World War II period, especially during the 1950's after the introduction of television in Mexico. In 1955, sales had doubled over 1954, and in 1956 they had increased another 50%. This expansion was based upon the high quality of Acme products developed in the United States and a strong sales promotion program in Mexico. The Acme name stood as high in consumer acceptance as any product in its field in Mexico.

Acme's promotion activities included an extensive advertising program on which Acme spent about 5% of sales. Part of this budget was contributed to a cooperative advertising fund for the benefit of the dealers and distributors. In the area outside of its own wholesale distribution system, the company contributed 2½% of sales which was matched by 2½% by the distributors and 5% by the dealers. In its own wholesale area, the company made both the manufacturer's and distributor's contributions, or a total of 5%. These funds were used for newspaper advertisements and other promotion efforts by the dealers themselves. Some dealers used the full allowance of the cooperative system, while others never used it despite frequent urging by Acme. The rest of the advertising budget was spent on company-sponsored advertising, including a daily 15-minute television program, two half-hour variety programs on the radio each week and extensive display advertising.

Casa Diaz

Casa Diaz was owned by Mr. Alfonso Diaz who, until 1952, had been a free-lance salesman. He had made direct sales to the employees of various large companies. He handled such varied products as watches, dresses and refrigerators which he purchased direct from wholesaling concerns. Acme had sold him a few radios during this period and had extended a small amount of credit to him. He was evidently an extremely effective and energetic salesman and had built himself up from virtually nothing to a significant volume of business.

In 1953, Mr. Diaz established his own store under the name of Casa Diaz. The store was located on the periphery of the central business district of Mexico City. It was a very simple establishment of a type common to small commercial enterprises in Mexico City. The store front was about 20 feet wide and the interior extended back about 50 feet in a single room. There were no windows or doors, the store being closed by a steel shutter which extended completely across the front and was pulled down at night. The store was furnished very simply and was crowded with new and used television sets, radios, and refrigerators.

The sales area of Casa Diaz extended throughout the Federal District. Mr. Diaz provided financing for his customers at approximately the same terms as other dealers (usually about 20% down with 20 months to pay the balance and 1% interest per month on the total initial unpaid balance). He also provided delivery, usually by means of a motorcycle equipped with a flat sidecar.

When he set up his business, Mr. Diaz became an authorized Acme dealer. In this position, he was obligated to provide service on Acme products which he had sold, to make no misrepresentations in his advertising, and to conform to the retail prices recommended by Acme. For the first few months, he conformed to these obligations relatively well and his sales of Acme products grew rapidly as a result of his own hard work and effective sales techniques.

As 1954 progressed, Acme began to have difficulties with Mr. Diaz. He began to cut prices radically and in effect became a discount house, selling at the normal wholesale price. His advertisements became very extreme and often misleading in that they promised things to customers which were not then made available, and he failed to provide service. The latter situation was particularly embarrassing to Acme. Acme itself provided a written warranty covering tubes and parts for 90 days, and the picture tube of television sets for one year. The dealer was expected to provide for other service costs to assure initial satisfactory operation of television sets, and he could, if he chose, provide additional service.

Casa Diaz made a practice of promising customers one year of service as part of their sales presentation; however, when customers had difficulties, they found that Casa Diaz would not in fact furnish this service. Since the dealer did not provide an actual written contract, the customer had no claim. In some cases, however, they went directly to Acme, which felt obliged to provide the necessary service to protect the company's good name.

In general, it was apparent that Mr. Diaz was following a policy of getting customers into his store in any way he could and selling them products without particular concern for the ethics of his sales arguments. Acme felt that these practices were very detrimental to the reputation of the company. Furthermore, other dealers were complaining about the practices of Casa Diaz. The Acme management on several occasions asked Mr. Diaz to change his practices. He would, after each of these talks, make some changes in the direction desired by the company, but then his methods would rapidly return to the previous practices. By the end of 1954, Acme had come to the conclusion that he was incorrigible and therefore despite the loss of sales involved, they terminated the dealer agreement.

Mr. Diaz then obtained a dealership from Presto Radio Company, another major United States firm. He handled their line of radio and television for about 6 months, following approximately the same practices that he had employed with Acme. Apparently these practices did not sit well with Presto because at the end of 6 months, they terminated the dealership and printed a large advertisement in all of the Mexico City newspapers announcing that he was no longer their dealer.

Throughout this period, Casa Diaz also had handled the products of a few companies which would be classed as minor brands and which were not supported by extensive advertising. Apparently he felt the need to have at least one major brand product in his store, and at the end of 1955, he applied to Acme to be reinstated as a dealer. At that time, he expressed his complete willingness to conform to the company's desires and swore that he would not return to the practices which had previously resulted in terminating the Acme dealership. He also agreed to allow the Acme advertising department to check all advertisements which he would place to assure that he would not say anything misleading. The Acme management agreed to give him a try, and for a couple of months the agreement worked out very satisfactorily. In fact, he was a better customer than most dealers in that he paid cash rather than requiring any credit. He rapidly became the company's biggest dealer. Within a few months, however, he began to revert to his earlier selling practices. He cut prices to 31% below normal retail price. His advertisements became misleading and were not checked with the Acme advertising department, and he failed again to provide service. Acme was having to provide service for a half dozen to a dozen Diaz customers every month.

At the beginning of 1957, the situation became quite serious. The major Acme dealers in Mexico City held a meeting to discuss possible action in the face of the extreme competition presented by Casa Diaz. They did not reach an agreement resulting in a united front against Acme, but the company heard about the meeting a short while later, and during February 1957, 3 important dealers refused to buy further Acme products until Casa Diaz was either dropped as a dealer or forced to change its practices. From time to time during this period, the Acme management called Mr. Diaz in and told him that he would have to change his methods. These conversations resulted again in slight modifications, but no basic change in his selling approach. The management therefore came to the conclusion that further words were useless and that if anything were to be done, drastic action would be necessary.

The management was reluctant to drop Casa Diaz because at that time the store was accounting for approximately 15% of the company's sales in the Federal District, with purchases from Acme running at an annual rate of 6,000,000 pesos. Furthermore, there was a possibility of some further repercussions if he was dropped. When this action was threatened in February, Mr. Diaz had asserted that he would take his case to the Ministry of Economy. The Acme management was aware that it had no legal right to dictate the prices at which its customers resold. Though it was an accepted practice to use exclusive dealerships in Mexico, theoretically a company was obliged to sell to anyone who wished to buy its products at its quoted prices. The company was confident that it would be perfectly within its rights to cut off a dealer who failed to provide service as was the case with Casa Diaz. However, they were not anxious to become embroiled in extended arguments with the government.

On the other hand, it was clear that further difficulties with the other dealers could be expected if nothing were done. The radio and television business in Mexico City was becoming increasingly competitive. Most of the dealers were providing some form of extra incentives for customers in an effort to improve their position. One dealer, for example, sold at list price but allowed customers 12 months to pay without any interest. Another dealer in mid-March 1957 announced that it would cut the interest rate on financing from 1% a month to ½ of 1% per month. No other dealers, however, had gone to the extremes of Casa Diaz.

In addition to the possibility of dropping Casa Diaz, the Acme management was considering a change in its basic discount policy. Currently, the company was selling to dealers at a standard 31% discount below list price, plus 5% for cash, with an additional graduated discount schedule on annual sales volume as shown in Exhibit 1.

EXHIBIT 1

$$
\begin{array}{ll}
200,000-\ 400,000 \text{ pesos} \dotsb & 1\% \\
400,000-\ 600,000 \text{ pesos} \dotsb & 2 \\
600,000-\ 800,000 \text{ pesos} \dotsb & 4 \\
800,000-1,200,000 \text{ pesos} \dotsb & 6 \\
\text{over } 1,200,000 \text{ pesos} \dotsb & 8
\end{array}
$$

In addition to Casa Diaz, two other dealers reached the highest discount. Under consideration was a new discount structure for volume which is shown in Exhibit 2, along with the number of dealers in the Federal District and outside of it which would have qualified for each category on the basis of sales in 1956.

EXHIBIT 2
Proposed Volume Discount Structure and Dealer Distribution by Volume

Annual Volume (pesos)	Proposed Discount	Number of Dealers	
		Federal District	Outside Federal District
40,000– 100,000	1%	3	0
100,000– 200,000	2	2	0
200,000– 400,000	3	8	6
400,000– 600,000	4	11	9
600,000–1,000,000	5	41	31
over 1,000,000	6	68	100

The dealers in the top four categories were designated as Class A dealers, and they accounted in total for about 90% of the company's business. These were quite substantial stores with large showrooms and usually show windows and adequate parts and service departments. The next group was classed as Class B dealers. Typically, they were small shops of the open to the street, steel shutter type, which handled a few radios, record players, and small television sets. They accounted for about 7% of the company's sales. The final group was called Class C dealers. They were either smaller hole-in-the-wall shops or in some cases parts and repair shops which handled a few new radios or television sets.

CASE V–6

LEVI STRAUSS & CO., PART K*
Export Sales, 1963[1]

The General Problem

By the spring of 1963 Levi Strauss & Co., a San Francisco clothing manufacturer, was well established in the export business with sales reaching into most parts of the world.[2] Although export sales accounted for a relatively small percentage of the company's dollar volume, this percentage was based on a total that was both substantial and expanding. Thus, export sales represented an appreciable absolute dollar volume with—in view of the company management—considerable growth potential. In September 1962 the company was given the "E-for-Export" award by the United States Department of Commerce for its outstanding contribution to the export expansion drive. In addition, because its Levi's blue jeans were among the most wanted items sought by foreign buyers, Levi Strauss & Co. was one of the few firms selected to have a permanent exhibit of its products on display at the new Dulles Airport in Washington, D.C. The problem confronting management, therefore, was no longer how to enter foreign markets but rather how to allocate long-run expansion resources between domestic and export business and among the alternative foreign markets themselves and how to employ the allocated resources to the best advantage within each market.

The International Division

In the spring of 1963 export sales were being handled through an International Division with the head of the division referred to as the International Director. This person was directly responsible to the president of the company and was located in the company's home office in San Francisco. He had a staff of one assistant, a secretary, and a clerk in the home office and since January 1963, a resident manager for Europe based in Brussels. The company also had a bonded warehouse in Antwerp under the control of the International Director and, in turn,

---

* Reprinted by permission of Richard H. Holton, University of California, Berkeley.

[1] Data and at times management opinions and decisions have been altered in preparing this case in order to protect confidential information and/or to focus the case problem along a particular line.

[2] Levi's overall, the company's rugged, tight-fitting blue jean, is the most important garment manufactured by Levi Strauss & Co. It has been the mainstay of the company since the company's founding in 1850. In 1928 Western wear—including stockman pants and Western shirts—became the first of several additions to the company's assortment. The introduction of Western wear was followed with wool shirts in 1949, casual wear—including pants, slacks, shorts, and coordinated jackets—in 1952, double-knee jeans in 1954, and matched work sets of pants and shirts in 1956. In 1953 part of the Western wear line was separated out into a more style-promoted line called ladies' California Ranch Pants—including pants and shorts for women and girls. In 1962 colored cotton twill jeans were taken out of the Levi's line to form a separate product group called the White Levi's line. Thus, by 1963 Levi Strauss & Co. was producing and marketing eight lines of clothing.

of his European resident manager. This warehouse stocked all fast-moving items and could make delivery to any European point within two to three days.

Europe accounted for a large share of the 1962 export volume with the principal markets being France, Western Germany, and Great Britain. The Far East, primarily Japan, was also an important market. It, plus Africa, Australia, and Latin America, made up most of the remaining export volume. Foreign sales were largely from the Levi's line and the new White Levi's line. The latter line was formally set up in late 1962 and included selected colors of cotton twill jeans using the Levi's jean pattern. These garments with their unique cut and the traditional images of the American West and the American teenager associated with that cut, enjoyed a ready market among the teenagers of most countries. Other lines such as the casual line were also exported; however, these lines met more market resistance. Close substitutes manufactured domestically were frequently available. Furthermore, these garments carried no cherished image for any major market segments such as did the Levi's jean for the teenagers.

In Europe and the Far East, sales were typically handled through distributors, equivalent to domestic jobbers, who were fully responsible for local warehousing and reselling to retailers. These distributors were billed directly for all merchandise shipped. Levi Strauss & Co. exercised no direct control over distributor selection of retail accounts or credit policies; however, it did strongly recommend its own domestic policies of dealing primarily with department stores and independent retailers and of striving for a stable, uniform resale price among retail accounts. Promotional expenditures were on a 50–50 basis; thus, here Levi Strauss & Co. required home office approval of distributor plans and procedures although their proposals were typically accepted with little modification. Distributors could, and frequently did, handle related lines such as Western boots and/or hats, but they could not sell competing clothing items. Pricing to the distributors was on the basis of a common price schedule for all distributors regardless of their country. This, of course, resulted in widely varying retail prices from country to country owing to variations in import restrictions as well as in local market conditions.

Distributors were now limited to no more than one per country, with some cases of several small countries—e.g., Belgium, Luxembourg, and The Netherlands—being combined under one distributorship. Initially more than one distributor had been taken on in some of the larger countries; however, enough interdistributor squabbles resulting almost inevitably in price cutting and hard feelings had arisen from such arrangements that they had been discontinued.

In Africa and Australia sales were made through agents located within the various countries. These agents carried no inventory. Shipments were typically made direct to the retail accounts with the agent being responsible for any extension of credit. Most of the Central and South American countries had restrictions against importing goods that were also manufactured locally. Thus, sales to these countries were generally closed off; however, some of the Levi Strauss & Co. merchandise sold to domestic exporters did find its way into the Central and South American markets. Furthermore, merchants in the U.S. border towns did a thriving business with Mexican nationals shopping on the U.S. side.

Trademark Violations

The desire of foreign teenagers to emulate both the American West and American teenagers, and the strong association between the cut of the Levi's jean and the foreigner's images of the American West and the American teenager, tempted foreign manufacturers to duplicate the traditional Levi Strauss & Co. pattern and construction. Some even tried to offset the prestige of owning an authentic pair of Levi's jeans by copying the Levi's pocket tab and the leather back-patch that served as brand symbols for the Levi Strauss & Co. garment. While most countries had laws dealing with pirating brand names and trademarks, these regulations were often vague and the enforcement lax, particularly when the complaints originated from foreigners. Furthermore, in some countries violators were allowed to continue their activities until final disposition of the case was made by the courts. Skillful legal maneuvering could often delay such final disposition not just for months but for years.

The Italian market was a prime example of where copying was both skillfully and extensively done and where legal action was particularly difficult to achieve. A similar problem—though minor in comparison because it primarily evolved around only one producer—had existed in France but had in time been fairly satisfactorily solved through legal channels. Australian sales, on the other hand, were faced with competition from AMCO Clothing Co. Pty. Ltd., which manufactured and sold blue jeans in Australia under the name, "Levi's^R." Although these garments were not cut to the Levi's jean pattern and did not copy the Levi's pocket tab and leather back-patch, the use of the same trade name as that used by Levi Strauss & Co. made clear-cut brand differentiation at the consumer level extremely difficult. Levi Strauss & Co. had repeatedly charged AMCO Clothing Co. Pty. Ltd. with trademark infringement. Thus far, however, the Australian courts had taken no action against AMCO Clothing Co. Pty. Ltd.

The Question of Foreign Production

From a long-run point of view three major decision areas now confronted the management of Levi Strauss & Co. in the company's international operations. The first of the three areas involved the question of whether the company should move into foreign production and, if so, in which markets and under what type of arrangement, i.e., outright ownership and operation, some type of joint venture, or a licensing agreement. The International Director made several observations relevant to this decision area. First, two of the company's major competitors in the domestic market—Lee and Blue Bell—already had pilot plants operating in Belgium. Second, although technological change was on the move in the clothing industry, scale economies in quality clothing production were still slight so that when distribution costs and service were taken into account, relatively small plants could be justified. Such plants gave greater flexibility in that capital could be committed in relatively small chunks and in a more or less experimental manner. Also scattered small units gave the investor better protection against political instability, tariffs, duties, etc. and better adaptability to local consumer tastes and preferences. Third, trade restrictions between individual foreign countries were often far less than those existing between these countries and the United States, e.g., trade between the United States and members of the Common Market or, in the case of Central and South America, trade between the members of the Latin American Free Trade Association, i.e., Lafta, compared to trade between United States and members of Lafta. As noted earlier many of the Central and South American countries barred foreign-made goods that competed directly with domestically manufactured items. These barriers, however, had been collectively negotiated away among the Lafta members so that most goods produced by a plant located in one Lafta country could readily enter another Lafta market. Fourth, the type and quality of denim insisted upon by Levi Strauss & Co. for its Levi's jean was not available within the individual foreign markets. Furthermore, production scale economies at the textile mill level would generally dictate that the denim be purchased from United States mills even though the garments were manufactured overseas. And fifth, the "Made in U.S.A." label had both positive and negative merchandising considerations that had to be evaluated individually for each product, company, and country.

The Question of Appropriate Channel

The second major decision area was concerned with the channel of distribution. Should Levi Strauss & Co. build its long-run foreign sales program around independent distributors, or should such distributors be viewed as transitory stepping stones in the path of market development with the long-run foreign distribution system being similar to the company's domestic system—i.e., company salesmen contacting retail accounts directly? Some company personnel maintained that considerations of control and sales effectiveness would eventually bring about direct selling to retailers in the primary foreign markets. These individuals countered comments about the value of being represented by an accepted and established local firm that not only had knowledge of the market but also had a cultural feel for its behavior by pointing out that local foreign nationals would still do the selling to retailers but they would do it as Levi Strauss & Co. employees rather than as employees of independent distributors. The International Director noted that if the direct channel elements within the company should prevail, extreme care would need to be taken in initiating the changeover in order to avoid alienating distributors and their retail accounts in those markets where changeover was contemplated and to prevent demoralizing the retained distributors.

The Question of Long-Run Demand

Contingent to dealing with the first two long-run decision areas was a third major area, that of making a general appraisal of the export demand. As already indicated, the current strong export demand primarily rested on the desire of foreign teenagers to identify with the American West and American teenagers and on the image of the Levi's jean as the traditional garment of American Westerners and American teenagers.[3] Was such a demand stable from a long-run perspective, and if not, what were the prospects for stablizing it? Export sales may merely be riding a fad that might be largely wiped out by a rise of anti-Americanism or might die simply because the next generation of foreign teenagers did not follow in the footsteps of their predecessors. The more optimistic members of the management team noted that Westernism had persisted for some time among American youth and furthermore that with skillfull merchandising the American Western and American teenager images of the Levi's jean could be exploited in gaining market entry and then gradually be replaced with the more stable image of the company's blue jean as a rugged garment of top quality construction capable of standing up under extremely heavy wear. The latter image also had merit in that it could be tied to—and therefore in time identified with—local living patterns. Furthermore, once established, the quality image had possibilities for positive transference to other non-Western lines, such as matched work sets and casual wear, thereby facilitating the entry of these lines into foreign markets. In short, the optimists foresaw a stable long-run demand for blue jeans in the export market. They did not maintain that native substitutes such as lederhosen would disappear but rather that blue jeans were now being purchased by an increasingly wide segment within most of the foreign markets, that once tried the basic utility and serviceability of the garment would assure a high rate of repeat purchasing, and that Levi Strauss & Co. could successfully differentiate the Levi's jean from com-

---

[3] The September, 1961, issue of *The Western Horseman*, for example, made the following observation on France:

> American horse operas being shown on the television networks of France have caused a boom in the western wear business. Clubs called "Les Amis de Far West" are being formed throughout France and members dress in authentic cowboy garb for their regular meetings. Sales of Levi's also reflect this trend of "going western" by both teenage and adult Frenchmen alike.
>
> In Paris, Levi's blue jeans have a new and fashionable home which has become a gathering place for devotees of this new culture of the west. "Establissements Frankel," French distributor for Levi Strauss & Co., San Francisco, has opened an expanded and modern headquarters at 39 Rue Notre Dame de Nazareth for cowboy garb. In addition to Levi's jeans, "Establissements Frankel" also stocks Levi's casual sports clothing. Sales gains over the past couple of years indicate a high acceptance of the American-made lines in the traditional style center of the world.

petitive offerings and secure and maintain sufficient brand loyalty to support foreign production.

The more pessimistic members granted that the above market penetration procedure had worked well in the domestic market as the company expanded from regional sales into a nationwide market. They, however, pointed out that American Western and the American teenager living patterns were of foreign source to those making up the export market and as such, the images based on these patterns were likely to be much more fragile than similar images held in the domestic market. Furthermore, they noted that differences in the cultural orientation of the foreign markets gave little validity to projecting the company's domestic success in building a quality image to the export market or, for that matter, to projecting experience accumulated in any one foreign market to another foreign market. Given, in addition, the basic instability of the export market—i.e., the instability both of the internal political affairs of many foreign governments and of international relationships, including trade regulations such as tariffs, duties, exchange rates, and privileges and special taxes on foreign capital, the more pessimistic management personnel felt it would be prudent to go slow in foreign expansion until these markets had proven themselves over time. Meanwhile, they noted, the potential of these markets could continue to be tapped successfully along the current lines without any major commitment of company personnel or capital to foreign locations.

Questions

1. Should Levi Strauss & Co. go into foreign production of its garments?
2. Assuming that top management has decided in favor of foreign production, what production arrangements would you propose them? Defend your recommendations through a comparative evaluation of the other reasonable alternatives.
3. Should Levi Strauss & Co. eventually set up its own sales force to sell direct to retailers within the major foreign markets? If yes, what timetable and pattern of action should the company follow to bring this about?

CASE V–7

MILLER LABORATORIES, INCORPORATED: BARRIA CASE (A)*[1]

Miller Laboratories, Incorporated is a large ethical drug firm with headquarters in Los Angeles, California. The firm manufactures for both *human* and *veterinary* markets, and concentrates mainly on biologicals (such things as: serums, vaccines, intravenous solutions, plasma, and blood fractions) and pharmaceutical specialties. It does

---

* Reprinted by permission of Richard H. Holton, University of California, Berkeley.

[1] The events in this case are reported substantially as they occurred. The name of the firm has been disguised.

business in fifty-eight countries in addition to the United States. In eight of these countries Miller has no representatives; the company merely accepts and fills whatever unsolicited orders it receives from these markets. In the other fifty countries, appointed representatives actively promote sales. To help finance its rapid expansion abroad, Miller has incorporated its foreign sales subsidiary, Miller International Laboratories Corporation, in Panama to take advantage of that country's tax laws. All Miller's sales abroad are made by MILC, which buys from the parent company at very low prices so that the profits on the foreign sales accrue to MILC in Panama rather than to the parent company in the United States. Panama does not tax these profits, whereas the United States corporate profits tax of 52 percent would, of course, apply if the profits were earned by or remitted back to the parent company.

Because of the nature of its products and a number of other factors involved in its business, Miller has always used distributors to handle sales in foreign countries. Matters of volume, capital investment, etc. have thus far made it unwise for the firm to establish its own branches abroad, although it does have a few jointly owned or wholly owned affiliated companies.

Drug distribution requires a double sales effort. The usual sales force is required to service the wholesale drug houses and the retailers. In addition, another group of salesmen, called a "detail" force, is required to contact the doctors, who must be introduced to the products and convinced of their value before they will prescribe their use. In foreign countries some drug distributors perform both of these functions. Others rely on their principals to do the detailing while they restrict their own activities to the servicing of wholesalers and retailers.

Miller usually has better sales results when doing the detailing job itself. But because of capital and administrative limitations imposed by rapid expansion, it presently prefers to select a distributor who handles both sales and detailing. However, in some cases it has taken over detailing when there was no suitable alternative. It uses one or more distributors per country depending upon the size and the geographic dispersion of the market, and it performs partial or complete manufacturing operations within certain countries because of legal or economic considerations.

Recently, Miller has found some advantages in establishing affiliated companies in foreign countries. In these cases, it has tried outright ownership, majority control, equal participation with nationals, minority participation, and licensing, depending on the specifics of the situation.

Mr. Willard W. Wyman is a travelling representative for Miller whose responsibility is the selection and evaluation of the various distributors in his section of South America. Company executives have found that the usual forecasting procedures they use in the United States for determining market potential and market share will not work at all in foreign countries because the situation is usually changing much too rapidly to use historical data, and because current statistics are either not available or prohibitively expensive to collect. Therefore, they selected Mr. Wyman for his ability in evaluating performance and for his experience in judging market potential. Recent observations by Mr. Wyman have led Miller executives to believe that their distributor of veterinary products in Barria, a medium-sized South American country, is selling far less than the market potential for Miller veterinary products in his country, although he does seem to be doing a fair job with some of the lines he handles for other firms.

Barria is primarily an agricultural and raw materials producing nation. It is divided by natural barriers into three areas, each of which supports both farming and animal husbandry. As world markets for its products fluctuate, Barria is periodically faced with shortages of foreign exchange and has in the past imposed certain import restrictions and exchange controls for short periods of time. In her recent history she has never restricted the importation of drugs, and it does not seem likely that she will do so in the next five to ten years. The government is stable and its officials are freely elected by the people. Barria has a good, well-established body of law, protects private property rights, and the political climate is considered a safe one for foreign investments.

Mr. Wyman reports that the country's three areas have unequal potential for Miller's veterinary medicines. He rates them at an annual volume of approximately $250,000, $100,000, and $50,000 respectively. This $400,000 volume is about one-half of the total market. He feels that the areas will require four, two, and one detail men respectively. Miller's total volume in Barria at present is only about $100,000 annually. These figures are all in terms of MICL's suggested list prices, i.e., the prices at which the local distributor should sell the products.

The present distributor seems unwilling to hire detail men to handle Miller products exclusively, even though it would mean a further reduction in the net prices which he pays to Miller. He doubts the accuracy of Mr. Wyman's estimates of market potential because he has been in business for a number of years and has never seen such large volumes for any of his lines. Mr. Wyman has usually been reasonably correct in his estimates in other countries, although in one case he appears to have been over-enthusiastic by about fifty percent, and in one other case actual volume exceeded his predictions by about twenty percent. The distributor feels that the existing volume has resulted entirely because of the efforts of his multiproduct detail force and that he has a rightful vested interest in any further sales of Miller products in Barria. He has a good reputation among his customers, and if he were actively to oppose changes in Miller's distribution channel, he could probably cause a considerable amount of difficulty, loss of goodwill, and finally a lowering of the estimated market potentials. Mr. Wyman and other home office executives are not certain what his reaction would be. MILC executives feel that he would not cause any substantial difficulty.

Mr. Wyman feels that there is another distributor in Barria who would do a better job and who seems eager to gain Miller representation. The MILC management favors a change to this new distributor.

The home office executives are divided into two groups. One feels that a jointly owned venture with the new distributor would be best, and the other feels that the selection of three small distributors, one in each of the three areas, would be preferable. Inquiries about the legal status of joint ownership have been submitted through consular channels to the Barrian government, but no reply has as yet been received.

There is no sentiment favoring the establishment of a Miller branch to handle distribution because, if the present distributor makes trouble, it will be easier for a Barrian national to handle it and, in addition, the experiences of two other large drug firms in having their property seized in Cuba has made Miller wary of 100 percent ownership under all but the most stable and time-honored governments.

MILLER LABORATORIES, INCORPORATED: BARRIA CASE (B)

Supplementary Statement on Competition, Pricing, Advertising

Drug distributors abroad customarily handle a number of noncompeting lines for several different manufacturers. However, on occasion, they handle competing lines, one of a "first" quality, the other of a lesser quality. Miller prefers the first arrangement, but has in certain cases, used the second if there were no acceptable alternative.

Miller studies the foreign market, then sells to the distributor at a price designed to leave him a 50 percent mark-up over landed cost. It then does some advertising in the various national trade publications, but does not pay for any distributor advertising. If the distributor does not perform detailing, the price to him is adjusted to provide a 30 percent mark-up over cost.

Miller's competition in Barria comes mainly from two firms which were established in the market before Miller got a foothold. Neither has had a very aggressive sales program in the past. However, Miller expects both to begin more active efforts very soon.

MILLER LABORATORIES, INCORPORATED: BARRIA CASE (C)

Supplementary Statement on Continuing Present Distributor or Changing to New Distributor

Miller has decided to make one last effort to maintain the existing relationship. The home office executives believe that changeover costs should be avoided if at all possible. They also feel that, if new arrangements have to be made, Miller should be able to say that it has done all it could do to continue working with the old distributor, in case he decides to try to ruin the Miller name or to impede the effectiveness of the new distribution network.

Mr. Wyman will try offering to have Miller do the detailing, but the old distributor is expected to say that he is unwilling to accept the lower margin available under that arrangement. Mr. Wyman will show an impressive collection of figures on what is happening in other countries, and try once more to convince the distributor to hire detail men who will handle Miller products exclusively. He will paint a very bright potential profits picture, and he will hint that other arrangements will have to be made, but nothing is expected to change the distributor's mind. The distributor believes that anybody who makes an added investment in promoting the Miller line is simply not going to realize enough additional returns to make it worthwhile. He argues that Mr. Wyman's figures on potential are leaving the attitudes of the farmers out of the picture, that he understands those attitudes well, and that the farmers will not easily be convinced of the value of additional expenditures for drugs.

Therefore, Mr. Wyman has assembled all available information on the new distributor. He has discovered that the new man has a net worth of $90,000, but that about half of that amount is tied up in a building in which the firm's offices are located. About two-thirds of the space is rented out to other firms. He carries five lines, one of which will have to be dropped, thus releasing about $7,500 in working capital. The owner indicates a willingness to borrow $30,000 on his building, which Mr. Wyman has determined he could do. This means a total free capital of $37,500 available for operations with Miller products. Mr. Wyman knows that this will support a volume of about $200,000 (at suggested list prices) annually. The new distributor indicates that he will hire detail men immediately if he is given the line and that Mr. Wyman can have them for two weeks for training.

There are some other facts concerning the new distributor which are of importance. He received an MBA from a large university in the United States and worked for a progressive wholesale drug firm in Los Angeles for about three years. He has just recently returned to Barria and has taken the reins of the family's business. He is aggressive and anxious to expand his operations. On the day before Mr. Wyman left Barria for the home office conferences, he recognized a representative of one of Miller's competitors coming out of the new distributor's building. Mr. Wyman then checked with some friends and quickly became convinced that the competitor is considering some sort of connection with this very same distributor. However, he feels sure that its investigations are not yet complete, and that if Miller moves quickly, it can get the new man if it wants him.

At present, sales in Barria make a contribution to overhead and profit for MILC of about $35,000 per year.

MILLER LABORATORIES, INCORPORATED: BARRIA CASE (D)

Supplementary Statement on the Use of Three Separate Distributors

Mr. Wyman had not anticipated the suggestion that three distributors be named, and before he returned for the home office conferences, he had not fully investigated the possible firms in each area which might be considered as distributors. Although the decision might be postponed while Mr. Wyman returns to Barria to investigate the three-distributor alternative more thoroughly, Wyman is certain that if the decision is delayed very long, one of Miller's competitors, a smaller but aggressive and rapidly growing firm, will sign up the prospective new distributor.

Mr. Wyman knows of possible distributors in the two regions in addition to that in which the present one and the prospective alternative distributor are located. The two most likely candidate firms he knows to be well-established, which in Barria usually means that they either have good cash resources or good credit connections, or both. They are both competent enough (although the management in both cases is older than in the prospective alternative single distributor) but both would probably require considerable initial help from Mr. Wyman. He estimates that altogether they would probably take his full time for at least four months. There is no one else presently available on the Miller staff to do this job, and Mr. Wyman's other duties would have to be neglected. These two distributors would probably be willing to drop any line now competing with Miller's, but this is not known with any degree of certainty.

MILLER LABORATORIES, INCORPORATED: BARRIA CASE (E)

Supplementary Statement on Direct Investment

Replies from the Barrian government have satisfied the Miller legal staff that a joint operation in Barria would be safe and acceptable from a legal viewpoint.

Miller's current return on investment for its total operations is about 8–10 percent before taxes.

Mr. Wyman has learned from the prospective distributor that his balance sheet (verified by the distributor's bank) is as follows (amounts are rounded to the nearest $1,000):

ASSETS		LIABILITIES AND OWNER'S EQUITY	
Cash......................	$ 7,000	Accounts payable..........	$ 21,000
Accounts receivable...........	24,000	Note payable..............	9,000
Inventory...................	51,000	Other current payables.....	4,000
Buildings, land and other			
fixed assets................	42,000	Net worth.................	90,000
	$124,000		$124,000

The condensed P and L statement for the latest year is as follows:

Net sales.....................		$173,000
Cost of goods sold.............		102,000
Gross profits...........		$ 71,000
Salesmen's expense............	$34,000	
Advertising..................	3,000	
Admin. expenses..............	19,000*	56,000
Net profit..............		$ 15,000

*Includes $10,000 owner's salary.

CASE V–8

SURPRISING DANGERS CAN ARISE AS NATIONAL MARKETS ARE BLENDED INTO REGIONS*

A fully integrated regional market for all or part of Europe is an ideal few people will quarrel with today, but the long and sometimes torturous

*Reprinted from *Business Europe*, August 23, 1967, pp. 265–66, with permission of the publisher, Business International S.A. (Geneva).

process of breaking down old nationalistic barriers between countries can cause unexpected and startling problems for international companies operating throughout Europe. A fascinating case in point is that of Philips Nederland NV, the giant electrical manufacturer, which woke up one morning this month to discover that in the large Dutch department store, Vroom & Dreesmann, the prices of a number of its goods were being undercut by as much as 30% by the products of *its own German subsidiary*, and the parent was helpless to stop this competition.

The key elements in this bizarre situation:

First, Philips has many factories located throughout Europe that are manufacturing the same products. Thus, from a supply standpoint its facilities (German and Dutch in this case) are potential competitors.

Secondly, when resale price maintenance (RPM) was abolished in the Netherlands in 1964, Philips was reduced to setting "recommended" or "fair" prices. Retailers could undersell these, but Philips insisted that the retailers should neither refer to the suggested prices nor advertise that the goods were being sold beneath those prices. If these conditions were not met, Philips would cancel its contracts with the retailers and refuse them further supplies, which is legal under Dutch antitrust law.

Thirdly, the EEC Commission's antitrust ruling, that companies must not seek to prevent independent distributors or wholesalers from exporting (or reexporting) goods freely to other EEC countries, left Philips' German subsidiary with no authority to obstruct the export of its goods even into the parent's territory.

Fourthly and finally, the Philips German operation is aided by several factors tending to reduce substantially German wholesalers' prices: bigger turnover, keener competition, lower production costs, lower interest rates on loans, and a big 7% German Government export subsidy. This last factor makes it possible for a Philips vacuum cleaner to be imported from the Netherlands by a German wholesaler and reexported to the Netherlands, where it is sold competitively.

To round out the picture, this price war between Dutch and German manufactured goods of the same company is conditioned by a couple of moderating elements. First of all, the big department store may be unable to obtain the full range of models of the goods on which prices are cut—principally vacuum cleaners, TV sets, radios, electric razors, and tape recorders. Philips Germany makes, for example, only a limited range of TV models that conceivably would be insufficient to enable Vroom & Dreesmann to compete in the long run with Dutch Philips dealers normally carrying a much wider range of models. It is also doubtful that the department store can give the 100% maintenance and repair service supplied by regular dealers and insisted on by Philips.

Normal trade relations are, however, being continued between Philips Nederland and Vroom & Dreesmann on goods other than those whose prices were cut. Further, there are indications—since Philips must face this kind of competition from abroad in other big stores—that the company would quietly restore a full line of supplies to Vroom & Dreesmann if future announcements of lower prices did not mention price comparisons or the fact that the prices were indeed lower.

At the present time, the two sides appear to be in a wait-and-see standoff, each sitting tight until the other makes a move.

Questions

1. Should Philips continue its "business as usual" attitude concerning other products being sold to Vroom-Dreesmann?
2. What action should Philips take to break the standoff?
3. How can future incidents such as this be avoided?

CASE V–9

WHY SWISS, UK FIRMS MUST ABANDON GERMAN MANUFACTURING*

The German fiascoes of two EFTA-based confectionery firms, followed by far-reaching reappraisals of their marketing and manufacturing strategies in that country, provide a lesson for all consumer goods companies attempting to enter a hotly competitive market with a relatively small investment. Both firms—the UK's Cadbury Bros. and Switzerland's Kambly—have been forced to shut down their manufacturing operations but have managed to maintain their presence in Germany, thanks to licensing agreements with competitors.

The Firms' Rise and Fall

To establish itself in Germany, Cadbury purchased in 1961 a medium-sized chocolate manufacturer, Hanseaten-Schokoladewerke of Bremen, and subsequently set up a completely new marketing subsidiary, Cadbury-Fry, also in Bremen. A new chocolate factory was opened in 1963 and further expanded in 1966, when the manufacturing subsidiary's capital was raised from $Dm5$ to $Dm12.6$ million ($Dm4:\$1$). This month, to its competitors' surprise, the UK firm announced that it would soon close its German plant. Some insiders believe that Cadbury had never gotten out of the red in Germany, although sales had progressively risen to an estimated $Dm20$ million annually.

When it searched for a manufacturing base behind EEC's high tariff walls, the smaller Kambly company also chose Germany, but it followed a less expensive investment route from Cadbury. In 1965, this family-owned firm created Kambly GmbH in Untermünstertal for the manufacture of fine biscuits, but actual production was taking place in a manufacturing line specially established on the premises of an Untermünstertal chocolate manufacturer, Gubor, which was also acting as distributor for Kambly products. Initially, Kambly's biscuits met such success with German housewives that workers at the Untermünstertal plant had to work two shifts. But at the end of 1967, Kambly decided to close down its German manufacturing line.

---

* Reprinted from *Business Europe*, June 21, 1968, p. 195, with permission of the publisher, Business International S.A. (Geneva).

Reasons for the Firms' Failures

Both companies place the main blame for their fiascoes on the German antitrust authorities' decision to abolish resale price maintenance (RPM) for chocolate in 1964. Actually, RPM's elimination hurt Kambly only indirectly; the real victim was its partner, Gubor, but the latter's debacle disorganized Kambly's German operations. Cadbury, however, was hit hard by the authorities' move. Supermarkets, discount houses, and chain stores started using chocolate bars as loss leaders to attract customers. As a result, retail prices for chocolate plummeted downward by as much as 50%. The big retail organizations, which had rapidly become the largest sellers of chocolate, were then in a position to talk manufacturers into granting them high rebates on factory prices. A subsequent rise in cocoa prices, which Cadbury had to absorb, ate further into the firm's meager profit margin. Competitors also noted that Cadbury committed a significant offense when designing its merchandising policy for the German market. The firm decided to market its best-selling chocolate line in brick form instead of in the flat bars usually manufactured in Germany. German consumers prefer to buy chocolate in bar form because they believe that they are getting more chocolate for the same price.

As for Kambly, its entry into the German biscuit market, where competition from both local and US firms is intense, appeared to have been ill timed, as it coincided with the beginning of the German recession.

Without underestimating the importance of the above external factors in the firm's failure, it is likely that Cadbury seriously miscalculated the strength of its future competitors—e.g. Nestlé, Suchard, Storck, and Sprengel—when it decided to enter the German market through the purchase of a small firm. To cut costs and remain competitive in the oversized German chocolate industry, which consistently operates below capacity, such firms as Sprengel and Storck have made considerable investment in automated equipment. Cadbury tried to save its position by signing cooperation agreements with other firms, but it failed to find suitable partners. (Kambly, a family-owned firm, never had the resources to make a sizable investment.)

The Firms' New German Structures

Cadbury has signed licensing agreements with two local competitors. Storck, which has acquired the exclusive right to use Cadbury's name in Germany, will manufacture part of Cadbury's product line; this German firm has also bought part of the UK company's equipment. Several other Cadbury specialties will be produced under license by XOX Biskuitfabrik of Kleve (a Dutch-owned firm), which will also lease special equipment from Cadbury.

Kambly has used a different, probably less profitable approach. The Swiss firm has sold the installations of its German subsidiary and has licensed the manufacture of its products to Bahlsens, Europe's largest biscuit producer. Kambly specialties are sold under Bahlsens' own trademark, but mention is made on the packaging that the biscuits are made under Kambly license and according to the original old Swiss recipe.

Questions

1. What dangers of an R.P.M. system are highlighted in this case?
2. Was pricing Kambly's real problem or were other marketing problems even more important?
3. How could Cadbury have handled the supermarket price-cutting problem?
4. Could the situations in the case have been avoided?

CASE V–10

GOODYEAR INTERNATIONAL*

How do you do it? How do you fit your advertising to the individual needs of separate markets and still keep some continuity? How do you tiptoe between two pitfalls—rigid sameness around the world on one side; spotty, uncoordinated performance on the other?

Goodyear's answer is a simple one in essence, but the application of this answer has involved several years of hard work and turned the company's advertising executives into globe-trotters. It is called "prototype advertising."

The Goodyear International Corp., which directs the destinies of Goodyear companies outside the United States, handles a wide variety of products ranging from shoe materials to chemicals and industrial items. It makes and markets some 2,200 different types of tires, its chief product. The program has an estimated budget of around $3,500,000, with local companies spending more than 90 percent of this sum and Akron headquarters the remainder—mainly by plugging the holes in the international media. Passenger tire advertising gets 30 percent of the budget, truck tires 40 percent; the remainder goes for other rubber products.

A Critical Appraisal

Some eight to ten years ago, the Goodyear subsidiaries handled their advertising almost entirely on an autonomous and local option basis, each one shaping its campaigns to fit local requirements. Copies of these advertisements were sent to GIC in Akron.

"As a result," said director of advertisement, Dean Peebles, "This brought home a very forceful realization that there was practically no continuity of effort and the various subsidiary companies were not pulling together in a common effort."

In order to achieve conformity, Goodyear made an effort toward strict

* Based on articles entitled "Goodyear Gets Global Look," by Alan Dodd, Jr., reprinted from *Printer's Ink,* May 13, 1966, p. 56, copyright 1966 by Decker Communications, Inc., 501 Madison Ave., New York, N.Y. 10022, and "Goodyear International Adopts Prototype Ad Method," by Lawrence Bernard, reprinted with permission from the August 24, 1964, issue of *Advertising Age.* Copyright 1964 by Advertising Publications, Inc.

home office control and total standardization. But, aside from the obvious problems of the language translation, market differences spelled doom for a one-ad policy.

The firm took initial steps to bring a degree of order to this diversity. Corporate requirements were established governing the size, shape, color and placement of the firm's famed diamond logo, the Goodyear Wingfoot and the Wingfoot signature. In addition, more elements illustrating features common to all Goodyear tires were required to appear in all advertising.

Next, Goodyear tried a system of advertising drop-ins of ad elements to plug particular features which the head office felt should be given worldwide exposure. This method brought the Goodyear diamond back into focus around the world but failed to have much impact in other ways, and errors in the drop-ins' sizes, shape and styles were common.

Advertising executives plunged into an exhaustive analysis of the worldwide advertising picture and the extensive reshaping of doctrine. Their final conclusion: They would try to guide the advertising from Akron through the use of "prototype" campaigns. These would be based on representative markets around the world. This meant that the "prototype" campaigns would point the way toward more effective efforts through example.

"In this instance," said their agency's account executive, "we knew that the tires are a fairly low interest item everywhere and that most people regard buying them as a chore. Our idea, therefore, was to put them into an exciting and colorful context. The three things a customer wants in a tire are road-holding qualities, durability and safety."

The entire "prototype" TV film package includes four commercials, product demonstration sequence, six minutes of working footage, scripts for 60-second and suggested 20-second versions and a brochure for print advertising, showing available still photos and suggested layouts. In markets around the world, the subsidiaries then blend these basic ingredients. A sound track is added and shots are deleted, inserted or edited. In the end, what emerges is a local commercial geared to a worldwide theme.

Up to this point, overseas reaction to the "prototype" program has varied mainly because it has been handled by advertising managers of many different nationalities. "I can say in general," Peebles reported, "that the overall attitude was much more cooperative than I probably estimated in advance. This is primarily because we took the presentation to the people and sold them on the idea and helped them work with it rather than just mailing it to them with cold instructions.

"On the minus side," Peebles continued, "there were a couple of men who . . . felt bound to use the prototypes without change or bound to challenge the campaign as not fitting their markets."

Questions

1. Identify the mistakes Goodyear International Corp. made in the past and tell how they could have been avoided.

2. What problems exist in the new approach and what should Goodyear International Corp. do now to minimize future problems?

3. Do you agree with the statement that buyers in all countries regard tires as a low-interest item and consider buying them a chore?

4. Do you agree that the three things a customer wants in a tire are road-holding qualities, durability, and safety? Would there be regional variations?

CASE V–11

ADVERTISING ON A PRIVATE STATION*

Cyprus Station's Ads in Hebrew May
Goad Israel to Air TV Commercials

JERUSALEM, *May 20*—Israel's infant television station here may be catapulted toward broadcasting faster than anticipated, now that the word has been received from Cyprus of plans for inaugurating commercial programming in Hebrew which could be received by practically all sets in Israel.

The reception of Hebrew commercials from Cyprus channels, it is believed, might provide the kinds of impetus to commercial TV in Israel that the reception of Arab programming by Israeli viewers gave for the introduction of the medium itself into Israel eight months ago.

As for the "offshore commercials" from Cyprus, Israeli agency men point out that there could be some difficulty about the transfer of foreign currency to pay for time on the foreign channel, but they explain that Cyprus imports many goods and services from Israel which could be used as payment for broadcasting time.

With the growing popularity of TV in Israel and its ability to reach people with only a limited reading knowledge of Hebrew, it is felt that there would be a sellout of broadcasts from Cyprus very quickly. Many large advertisers here have indicated their interest in TV advertising in some form.

Questions

1. Should a U.S. advertiser in Israel use the Cyprus channels even if it is boycotted by the Israel government?

2. What steps would an advertiser on the pirate station take to be certain that there will not be retaliation from Israel?

---

* Reprinted with permission from the May 26, 1969, issue of *Advertising Age*. Copyright 1969 by Crain Communications Inc.

Bibliography

BIBLIOGRAPHY

General

BODDEWYN, J. *Comparative Management and Marketing.* Glenview, Ill.: Scott, Foresman & Co., 1969.

BROWN, COURTNEY. *World Business: Promise & Problem.* New York: Free Press, 1970.

CARSON, DAVID. *International Marketing and Comparative Systems Approach.* New York: Wiley, 1967.

DOWD, LAWRENCE P. *Principles of World Business,* rev. ed. Boston: Allyn & Bacon, Inc., 1964.

DYER, JOHN M. *Guidelines to Operating in Latin America.* Miami, Fla.: Academy of the Arts and Sciences of the Americas, 1970.

FAYERWEATHER, JOHN. *International Marketing,* 2d ed. Englewood Cliffs, N.J.: Prentice-Hall, 1970.

KINDLEBERGER, CHARLES P. *American Business Abroad.* New Haven, Conn.: Yale University Press, 1969.

KOLDE, ENDELL J. *International Business Enterprise.* Englewood Cliffs, N.Y. Prentice-Hall, 1968.

KRAMER, RONALD L. *International Marketing,* 3d ed. Cincinnati: South-Western Publishing Co., 1970.

LEIGHTON, DAVID S. *International Marketing.* New York: McGraw-Hill, 1966.

MARTYN, HOWIE. *Multinational Business Management.* Lexington, Mass.: Heath Lexington Books, 1970.

MAZZE, EDWARD M. International Marketing Administration. San Francisco, Calif.: Chandler, 1967.

MIRACLE, GORDON E., and ALBAUM, GERALD. *International Marketing Management.* Homewood, Ill.: R. D. Irwin, 1970.

PATTY, ROBERT, and VANDENBERG, HARVEY. *Readings in Global Marketing.* New York: Appleton, Century, Crofts, 1969.

PETERSON, RICHARD D. *Bibliography on Comparative* (International) *Management.* Seattle: Graduate School of Business Administration, University of Washington, 1969.

SOMMERS, M. S., and KERNAN, J. B. (eds.). *Comparative Marketing Systems.* New York: Appleton, Century, Crofts, 1968.

THOMAS, MICHAEL J. (ed.). *International Marketing Management.* Boston: Houghton-Mifflin, 1969.

ZEFF, STEPHEN A. (ed.). *Business Schools and the Challenge of International Business.* New Orleans, La.: Graduate School of Business Administration, Tulane University, 1968.

903

Chapter 1

HALL, RICHARD W. *Putting Down Roots.* New York: Celanese Corporation/ Vantage Press, 1969.

HELLMAN, RAINIER. *The Challenge to U.S. Dominance of the International Corporation.* Cambridge, England: University Press, 1970.

OGRAM, ERNEST W. *The Emerging Pattern of the Multinational Corporation.* Atlanta: Bureau of Business & Economic Research, School of Business Administration, Georgia State College, 1965.

WILSON, CHARLES. *The History of UNILEVER.* New York: Praeger, 1968.

Chapter 2

BEARD, MIRIAM. *A History of Business.* Volumes I and II. Ann Arbor: University of Michigan Press, 1962.

BURSK, EDWARD C., CLARK, DONALD T., and HIDY, RALPH W. *The World of Business.* Volumes I–IV. New York: Simon and Schuster, 1962.

KINDLEBERGER, CHARLES P. (ed.). *The International Corporation.* Cambridge, Mass.: MIT Press, 1970.

ROLFE, SIDNEY E. and DAMM, WALTER. *The Multinational Corporation and the World Economy.* New York: Praeger, 1970.

THE ATLANTIC INSTITUTE. *The Technology Gap; U.S. and Europe.* New York: Praeger, 1970.

WILKINS, MIRA. *The Emergence of the Multinational Enterprise.* Cambridge, Mass.: Harvard University Press, 1970.

Chapter 3

BALASSA, BELA. *Trade Liberalization Among Industrial Countries.* New York: McGraw-Hill, 1967.

BARDHAN, PRANAB K. *Economic Growth, Development & Foreign Trade.* New York: Wiley, 1970.

FULDA, CARL H. and SCHWARTZ, WARREN F. *Regulation of International Trade and Investment.* Mineola, N.Y.: The Foundation Press, 1970.

KINDLEBERGER, C. P. *International Economics,* 4th ed. Homewood, Ill.: R. D. Irwin, 1968.

————. *The Politics of International Economics and the Economics of International Politics.* New York: Basic Books, 1970.

KRAUS, W. and MATHIS, F. J. (eds.). *International Economics and Business.* Boston, Mass.: Houghton-Mifflin, 1968.

MARCUS, EDWARD and MARCUS, M. R. *International Trade and Finance.* New York: Pitman, 1965.

METZGER, STANLEY D. *Trade Agreements and the Kennedy Round.* Fairfax, Va.: Coiner, 1964.

STALCY, CHARLES E. *International Economics.* Englewood Cliffs, N.J.: Prentice-Hall, 1970.

WASSERMAN, MAX. *Modern International Economics.* Cambridge, Mass.: Schenkman, 1970.

Chapter 4

BARKER, B. and BARKER, E. G. *European Social Class.* New York: Macmillan, 1965.

BEALS, RALPH L. and HOIJER, HARRY. *An Introduction to Anthropology.* New York: Macmillan, 1953.

BENEDICT, RUTH. *Patterns of Culture.* New York: The New American Library, 1934.

BOHANNAN, PAUL and DALTON, GEORGE (eds.). *Markets in Africa.* Evanston, Ill.: Northwestern University Press, 1962.

CLEVELAND, HARLAN. *The Overseas American.* New York: McGraw-Hill, 1960.

FARMER, RICHARD N. and RICHMOND, BARRY M. *International Business and Operational Theory.* Homewood, Ill.: R. D. Irwin, 1966.

KUST, MATTHEW J. *Foreign Enterprise in India.* Chapel Hill: University of North Carolina Press, 1964.

MCCREARY, EDWARD A. *The Americanization of Europe.* New York: Doubleday, 1964.

SERVAN-SCHREIBER, J. J. *The American Challenge.* New York: Atheneum, 1968.

Chapter 5

BEHRMAN, JACK N. *National Interests and the Multinational Enterprise.* Englewood Cliffs, N.J.: Prentice-Hall, 1970.

GODFREY, DAVE and WATKINS, MELL (eds.). *Gorden to Watkins to You.* Toronto, Canada: New Press, 1970.

LITVAK, ISAIAH A. and MAULE, CHRISTOPHER (eds.). *Foreign Investment: The Experience of Host Countries.* New York: Praeger, 1970.

NEHRT, LEE CHARLES. *Political Climate for a Foreign Investment.* New York: Praeger, 1970.

Chapter 6

BAVISH, N. H. and VERHULST, MICHAEL. *Management Sciences in the Emerging Countries.* New York: Macmillan, 1965.

BELSHAW, CYRIL S. *Traditional Exchange and Modern Markets,* p. 149. Englewood Cliffs, N.J.: Prentice-Hall, 1965.

CROCKET, JEAN. *Consumer Expenditures and Incomes in Greece.* New York: International Publications Service, 1967.

HIGGINS, BENJAMIN. *Economic Development.* New York: Norton, 1959.

MOYER, REED (ed.). *Markets and Marketing in Developing Economies.* Homewood, Ill.: R. D. Irwin, 1968.

SKINNER, WICKHAM. *American Industry in Developing Economies.* New York: Wiley, 1968.

Chapter 7

BOESCH, HANS. *A Geography of World Economy.* Princeton, N.J.: Von Nostrand, 1964.

HAGHSMITH, RICHARD M. and NORTHAM, RAY M. *World Economic Activities and Geographic Analysis.* New York: Harcourt, Brace, Jovanovich, 1971.

HOFFMAN, L. A. *Economic Geography.* New York: The Ronald Press, 1965.

JAMES, PRESTON E. *Introduction to Latin America.* New York: Odyssey, 1964.

KENDALL, HENRY M., GLENDINNING, ROBERT M. and MACFADDEN, CLIFFORD H.

Introduction to Geography, 4th ed. New York: Harcourt, Brace, Jovanovich, 1971.

WOYTINSKY, W. S. and WOYTINSKY, E. S. *World Commerce and Governments: Trends and Outlooks.* New York: The Twentieth Century Fund, 1955.

Chapter 8

LILLICH, RICHARD B. *The Protection of Foreign Investment.* Syracuse, N.Y.: Syracuse University Press, 1965.

MUHAMMAD, V. A. SEYID. *The Legal Framework of World Trade.* New York: Praeger, 1958.

MUSGRAVE, PEGGY B. *United States Taxation of Foreign Investment Income.* Cambridge, Mass.: Law School of Harvard University, 1969.

U.S. TRADEMARK ASSOCIATION. *Trademarks in the Marketplace.* New York: 1965.

———. *Trademark Management—A Guide for Businessmen.* New York: 1960.

Chapter 9

BROMBERGER, SERGE and BROMBERGER, MARY. *Jean Monnet and the United States of Europe.* New York: Coward, 1969.

COOPER, RICHARD N. *The Economics of Interdependence.* New York: McGraw-Hill, 1968.

ELLIS, H. B. *The Common Market.* Cleveland: World, 1965.

"The European Communities Today and Tomorrow," *Business International.* Geneva, 1969.

HAY, PETER. *Federalism and Supranational Organizations.* Urbana: University of Illinois Press, 1966.

KOHLER, HEINZ. *Economic Integration in the Soviet Bloc.* Englewood Cliffs, N.J.: Prentice-Hall, 1965.

KRAUSE, LAWRENCE B. *European Economic Integration and the United States.* Washington, D.C.: Brookings, 1968.

LIANDER, BERTIL. *Marketing Development in the European Economic Community.* New York: McGraw-Hill, 1964.

SAMPSON, ANTHONY. *Anatomy of Europe.* New York: Harper & Row, 1969.

TERPSTRA, VERN. *American Marketing in the Common Market.* New York: Praeger, 1967.

Chapter 10

COOK, DON. *Floodtide in Europe.* New York: Putnam, 1965.

HOLLANDER, STANLEY C. *Multinational Retailing.* East Lansing: Michigan State University Press, 1970.

A Survey of Europe. New York: Reader's Digest, 1970.

Chapter 11

ALEXANDER, RALPH S., CROSS, JAMES S. and HILL, RICHARD M. *Industrial Marketing.* Homewood, Ill.: R. D. Irwin, 1967.

DODGE, ROBERT H. *Industrial Marketing.* New York: McGraw-Hill, 1970.

Chapter 12

BODDEWYN, JAY (ed.). *Comparative Management: Teaching, Training and Research.* New York: New York University, 1970.

CHILD, SARAH. *Poverty & Affluence: An Introduction to the International Relations of Rich and Poor Economies.* New York: Schocken, 1970.

CLEVELAND, HARLAN and MANGONE, GERARD J. *The Art of Overseasmanship.* Syracuse, N.Y.: Syracuse University Press, 1960.

HECK, HAROLD J. *International Business Environment.* New York: AMA, 1968.

KILBY, P. *Entrepreneurship & Economic Development.* New York: Free Press, 1970.

McCLELLAND, DAVID C. *The Achieving Society.* New York: Van Nostrand, 1961.

———. *Motivating Economic Achievement.* New York: Free Press, 1969.

WEINER, M. and MEHRABIAN, A. *Language Within Language.* New York: Appleton, Century, Crofts, 1968.

Chapter 13

BOLLON, ROBERT J. (ed.). *Joint Ventures and Japan.* Rutland, Vt.: Tuttle, 1967.

CHAMBERLAIN, NEILL W. *Enterprise and Environment; The Firm in Time and Place.* New York: McGraw-Hill, 1968.

KILBY, P. *Entrepreneurship and Economic Development.* New York: Free Press, 1970.

KINDLEBERGER, CHARLES P. *International Firm: A Symposium.* Cambridge, Mass.: MIT Press, 1970.

POLLZIEN, G. M. and BRONFEN, G. B. *International Licensing Agreements.* Indianapolis: Bobbs, Merrill, 1965.

STERNER, G. A. and CANNON, W. *Multinational Corporate Planning.* New York: Macmillan, 1966.

STIEGLITZ, HAROLD. *Organization Structures of International Companies.* New York: NICB, 1965.

TOMLINSON, J. W. *Joint Venture Process in International Business.* Cambridge, Mass.: MIT Press, 1970.

Chapter 14

BAKER, JAMES C. *The International Finance Corporation.* New York: Praeger, 1968.

COOPER, RICHARD N. *International Finance.* Baltimore, Md.: Penguin, 1969.

DUNNING, J. H. *Studies in International Investment.* New York: Humanities Press, 1970.

HICKMAN, JOHN H. (ed.). *Financing East-West Business Transactions.* New York: AMA, 1968.

HIRSCH, FRED. *Money International.* New York: Doubleday, 1969.

MIKESELL, RAYMOND F. *Financing World Trade.* New York: Crowell, 1969.

MUNDELL, R. A. and SWOBODA, A. K. (eds.). *Monetary Problems of The International Economy.* Chicago: University of Chicago Press, 1969.

WARD, RICHARD J. *International Finance.* Englewood Cliffs, N.J.: Prentice-Hall, 1965.

WASSERMAN, MAX J., HULTMAN, C. W. and ZSOLDOS, L. *International Finance.* New York: Simmons-Boardman, 1963.

WHITMAN, MARINA VON NEUMAN. *Government Risk-Sharing in Foreign Investment.* Princeton, N.J.: Princeton University, 1965.
ZENOFF, D. and ZWICK, J. *International Financial Management.* Englewood Cliffs, N.J.: Prentice-Hall, 1969.

Chapter 15

CHORAFAS, D. N. *Developing the International Executive.* New York: Macmillan, 1967.
FARMER, RICHARD N. *International Management.* Belmont, Calif.: Dickenson, 1968.
FORTUNE MAGAZINE EDITORS. *Businessmen Around the Globe.* Englewood Cliffs, N.J.: Prentice-Hall, 1967.
HYMAN, STANLEY. *Management and World Development.* New York: Pitman, 1967.
VERNON, RAYMOND. *Manager in the International Economy.* Englewood Cliffs, N.J.: Prentice-Hall, 1968.

Chapter 16

FAYERWEATHER, JOHN. *International Business Management.* New York: McGraw-Hill, 1969.
SALERA, VIRGIL. *Multinational Business.* Boston, Mass.: Houghton-Mifflin, 1969.

Chapter 17

ALSEGG, ROBERT J. *Researching the European Markets.* New York: AMA, 1969.
AMERICAN MANAGEMENT ASSOCIATION. *International Directory of Marketing Research Houses and Services.* Chicago, 1969.
————. *Market Research in International Operations.* (Management Report No. 53). New York, 1960.

Chapter 18

KRAVIS, IRVING B., et al. *Measuring International Price Competitiveness.* New York: Columbia University Press, 1965.
WALLIS, W. A. *Restrictive Business Practices.* New York: Free Press, 1960.

Chapter 19

AMERICAN ASSOCIATION OF ADVERTISING AGENCIES. *Advertising Agency Business Around the World.* New York: 1967.
Advertising Conditions and Regulations. Basel: Verlag fuer Recht und Gesellschaft, 1965.
BUZZI, GIANCARLO. *Advertising: Its Cultural and Political Effects.* Minneapolis: University of Minnesota Press, 1968.
DeFLEUR, MELVIN L. *Theories of Mass Communications.* New York: McKay, 1970.
DUNN, S. WATSON. *International Handbook of Advertising.* New York: McGraw-Hill, 1964.

FISCHER, H. D. and MERRILL, J. (eds.). *International Communication: Media, Channels, Functions.* New York: Hastings, 1970.

MEXICAN CHAPTER INTERNATIONAL ADVERTISING ASSOCIATION. *Advertising in Mexico.* 1970.

MIRACLE, GORDON. *Management of International Advertising.* Ann Arbor: University of Michigan Press, 1966.

NETTL, J. P. and ROBERTSON, R. *International Systems and the Modernization of Societies: The Formation of National Goals and Attitudes.* New York: Basic Books, 1968.

SIMON, JULIAN L. *Issues in the Economics of Advertising.* Urbana: University of Illinois Press, 1970.

WEIDMANN, KURT. *Ad One: The International Survey of Advertisements.* New York: Praeger, 1966.

Chapter 20

BARTELS, ROBERT. *Comparative Marketing.* Homewood, Ill.: R. D. Irwin, 1963.

HALL, MARGARET, et al. *Distribution in Great Britain & North America.* New York: Oxford University Press, 1961.

HODDER, P. W. and UKWA, U. I. *Markets in West Africa.* New York: Africana, 1969.

PRYBYLA, JAN S. *Comparative Economic Systems.* New York: Appleton, Century, Crofts, 1969.

The Role of Freight Forwarder in Developing Countries. Geneva: International Trade Center, 1970.

Chapter 21

COFFEY, CHASE C. *The International Marketing Export Guide.* New York: Carlton, 1968.

How to Get Started in Exporting: A $243 Billion Market. New York: Crowell, 1970.

International Physical Distribution. Proceedings of a Conference Held by the School of Business and Technology. Corvallis: Oregon State University, 1968.

NEILLANDS, ROBIN and DESCHAMPSNEUFS. *Exporting.* London: Pan Books Ltd., 1969.

Chapter 22

KAPOOR, ASHOK. *International Business Negotiations: A Study in India.* New York: New York University Press, 1970.

RYANS, J. K. and BAKER, J. C. *World Marketing.* New York: Wiley, 1967.

Index

INDEX

This book has been set in 9 point Primer (with Century Bold) and 8 point Primer, leaded 2 points. Part numbers and titles and chapter numbers and titles are in Helvetica and Helvetica Medium. The size of the type page is 27 by 46⅓ picas.